SOCIOLOGY

IAN ROBERTSON

SOCIOLOGY

SECOND EDITION

WORTH PUBLISHERS, INC.

Sociology, Second Edition

Copyright © 1977, 1981 by Worth Publishers, Inc.

All rights reserved

Printed in the United States of America

Library of Congress Catalog Card Number: 80-54232

ISBN: 0-87901-134-3

Third Printing, June 1982

Editor: Peter Deane

Production: George Touloumes

Picture Editor: June Lundborg

Design: Malcolm Grear Designers

Typography: New England Typographic Service, Inc.

Printing and Binding: Rand McNally & Company

Cover: *La Place, Clichy* (detail), Louis Anquetin

Wadsworth Atheneum, Hartford, Connecticut

The Ella Gallup Sumner and Mary Catlin Sumner Collection

Worth Publishers, Inc.

444 Park Avenue South

New York, New York 10016

Preface

Like its predecessor, this edition of *Sociology* rests on two basic premises. The first is that sociology is both a humanistic art and a rigorous science; in fact, much of its excitement arises from the insights offered by this unique blend of two intellectual traditions. The second premise is that sociology can be, and should be, a profoundly liberating discipline. By challenging conventional wisdoms and by dissolving the myths about social reality, the discipline provides an acute awareness of the human authorship of, and responsibility for, both the social world and much of our personal experience and identity. Sociology thus offers that crucial sense of options and choice that is essential to human freedom.

The original impetus to write this book grew out of several years' experience as a teacher and professional writer in radically different societies in North America, Europe, and Africa. I count the book successful to the extent that it conveys to the reader the fascination and sheer pleasure that I draw from sociology myself.

Changes in This Edition

The present edition of the text represents a thorough revision of its predecessor, but not a radical one; in other words, although I have made innumerable additions, modifications, updatings, and other changes throughout, the essential character of the book is unaltered.

In general, the coverage of the field reflects the same goal that I had for the first edition, when I decided at the outset not to write a slender "core" text covering a few selected topics. The problem with such an approach, of course, is that one person's core may be another's apple—or vice versa—with the result that some instructors are left without text discussion of material they consider essential. Instead, I have again tried to give a broad and thorough coverage of the main fields of the discipline, while keeping the text sufficiently flexible to be adapted to the needs of individual instructors. The book thus provides full coverage of the "traditional" material in the introductory sociology course. It seems to me important, however, that the text should do much more: it should also convey a strong sense of the "cutting edge" of the discipline, of the vital issues and trends in contemporary sociology. For this reason, I have once more included much material that is unusual or even unique in an introductory book. In particular, I have written substantial new sections on ethnomethodology and on the sociology of sport, of age stratification, and of health. I have also greatly expanded the material on several other topics, including social movements, the life cycle, dying and death, interest groups, modernization, and America's rapidly growing Hispanic population. As before, a full chapter is devoted to the sociology of science, a subject of particular interest, perhaps, to those science majors who may take only one sociology course. There is also an entire chapter on the micro order, in which various interactionist approaches are applied to the ordinary routines of everyday life. A chapter is devoted, too, to the sociology of sexual behavior, a subject of high student interest and one admirably suited to illustrate the interplay of biological, social, and cultural factors in the shaping of human behavior. I have also included new discussions of many other fields of current interest, such as rape, the Jonestown mass suicide, unemployment (especially as it affects graduates), new religious sects, school busing, "credentialism" and the declining standards in education, ecological and energy concerns, sociobiology, and alternatives to traditional marriage. In some chapters, in fact, I have added a current-trends section that summarizes new or anticipated developments. As before, I have taken care throughout the book to avoid sexist language, with its unintended yet inevitable implication that it is only men who do, and act, and create the social world.

Organization

I have again divided the book into five units. Unit I provides an introduction to sociology and to the methods of sociological research. Unit II deals with the individual, culture, and society, and focuses on the influence of social and cultural forces on personal experience and social behavior. The chapters in this unit cover culture, society, socialization, social interaction, social groups, deviance, and sexual behavior. Unit III discusses various forms of social inequality, and emphasizes the role of ideology as well as coercion and tradition in the maintenance of inequalities. The first chapter in the unit deals with the general problem of social stratification and introduces the basic concepts that apply throughout the unit; the second deals with inequalities of social class; the third, with inequalities of race and ethnicity; and the fourth, with inequalities of gender and of age. Unit IV discusses several important social institutions: the family, education, religion, science, the economic order, and the political order. Finally, Unit V focuses on some issues of social change; it contains chapters on population and health, urbanization and urban life, collective behavior and social movements, and on the general problem of social change and modernization.

I have taken great care, however, to structure the book in such a way that instructors can, if they wish, omit some chapters and present others in a different order. Nearly all instructors will want to cover the first five chapters, in which the most important terms and concepts of the discipline are introduced. (Chapter 2, on methods, could be omitted, but devoting some lecture time to research methods would then be advisable.) The sequence of the remaining chapters can then be freely rearranged to suit the convenience of the individual instructor, and there are ample cross-references to the five basic chapters and to relevant topics in other chapters to facilitate any alternative sequence.

Features

I have included a number of distinctive features that are intended to enhance the book's effectiveness as a teaching and learning tool.

Cross-cultural material. While this book is not intended as an exercise in comparative sociology, I have started from the assumption—a surprisingly unusual one—that sociology is something more than the study of American society. Throughout the text there are occasional references to other cultures and to the historical past. This material is intended to serve two purposes. The first is to enliven the text, for the ways of life of other peoples—particularly in so-called primitive societies—are inherently fascinating. The second purpose, more serious, is to undermine ethnocentric attitudes by highlighting, through comparison, distinctive aspects of American society that might otherwise pass unnoticed or be taken for granted.

Theory. A basic sociology text should not, in my view, be a heavily theoretical one. But conversely, a sound introduction to sociological theory should be an essential feature of the introductory course, and we fail both the discipline and our students if we do not provide it. The treatment of theory in this book is shaped by two convictions. The first is that theory can be presented in a clear, concise, interesting, and understandable manner, and that its practical value can be readily appreciated by the student. The second conviction is that theory must not, as happens all too often, be briefly introduced in the first chapter and then hastily buried: this tactic can only confirm the student's worst suspicions that theory is an irrelevant luxury.

I have again taken a fairly eclectic approach to sociological theory and have utilized all three of the main perspectives in the contemporary discipline: functionalist theory (primarily for issues of social order and stability), conflict theory (primarily for issues of social tension and change), and interactionist theories (primarily for "micro" issues). Above all, I have carried these perspectives throughout the book—not by applying them mechanically to everything, but by introducing particular theoretical perspectives where they will genuinely enhance understanding of a specific problem. Where the perspectives complement one another, as they often do, this is made clear; where they seem contradictory, the problem is discussed, and, if possible, resolved. I have drawn extensively, of course, on the ideas of contemporary sociologists; but in keeping with the continuing resurgence of interest in classical thinkers, I have given due emphasis to such writers as Marx, Durkheim, and Weber.

Readings. I have added a number of readings from original sources at appropriate places in the text. These readings have been chosen for their interest and relevance, and are designed to give the student a deeper, more first-hand experience of sociological writing and research.

Pedagogical aids. Several features of the book are designed to aid the learning process. Each chapter begins with a brief overview of its major topics and closes with a numbered, point-by-point summary of the contents. All important terms are italicized and defined where they first appear, and unfamiliar terms are illustrated by an example. These terms are also listed (with the number of the page on which they are defined) for end-of-chapter review. Throughout the book there are occasional "boxes" containing short and relevant items of interest. The illustrations in the previous edition were a particularly well-received feature of the text, and I have spent countless hours poring over photographs, cartoons, fine art, and other graphic materials in order to further enhance this aspect of the book. The present edition is more abundantly illustrated, and employs more color, than its predecessor; but, as before, I have carefully selected the illustrative material for pedagogical rather than purely decorative reasons, and have provided unusually full captions that reinforce and amplify the text discussion. Numerous tables and charts, up-to-date and easy to read, are used to aid the student's understanding of concepts and sociological data. Each chapter also contains an annotated list of suggestions for further reading.

Glossary. The book contains an extensive glossary—virtually a mini-dictionary—of over three hundred important sociological terms. The glossary can be used both for ready reference and for reviewing purposes.

Library research techniques. I have included a brief appendix on techniques of library research. This appendix is intended as a handy guide to library facilities; it offers many suggestions for tracking down sources and information and should prove useful to students working on term papers or research projects.

Supplementary Materials

A new *Study Guide* is available to help students in both their understanding and their reviewing of the course. The guide, prepared by Carla B. Howery (The University of Wisconsin, Milwaukee) and Alfred A. Clarke, Jr. (Western New England College), includes learning objectives, chapter summaries, multiple-choice questions, application exercises, and case studies.

The text is further complemented by a comprehensive *Instructor's Manual,* extensively revised by Donald P. Irish (Hamline University) and Carla B. Howery. Also available are a *Test Bank,* revised by M. Jay Crowe (University of Colorado, Denver) and consisting of nearly a thousand class-tested multiple-choice questions (many of them computer-validated), and an accompanying *Computerized Test-Generation System.* The text has also served as the basis for a series of video lectures, prepared for open-circuit broadcast and cable television by the Dallas County Community College District. (The series is supplemented by a study guide and faculty manual.)

In addition, I have prepared an anthology of readings in applied sociology, *The Social World.* Organized in the same sequence as the text, it should provide a useful accompaniment to it.

Thanks

Many people have helped in the preparation of this book, including the hundreds of users—both professors and students—whom I have talked to personally or with whom I've corresponded about the text. I am especially grateful to a number of my colleagues who evaluated various parts of the published first edition or of the manuscript for the second edition for accuracy, coverage, readability, currency, and teachability. The book owes a great deal to the many constructive criticisms and suggestions they offered. The reviewers were:

Stephen Beach, Avila College
Ivar Berg, Vanderbilt University
Randall Collins, University of Virginia
Peter Dodge, University of New Hampshire
Arthur Greil, Alfred University
Phillip S. Hughes, Rutgers University
Donald P. Irish, Hamline University
Dennis R. McGrath, Community College of Philadelphia
Keith Melville, President's Commission for a National Agenda for the Eighties
James D. Orcutt, Florida State University
Anthony M. Orum, University of Texas, Austin
Vincent N. Parrillo, The William Paterson College of New Jersey
Chad Richardson, Pan American University
Howard Robboy, Trenton State College
Barrie W. Robinson, University of Alberta
Edwin Rosenberg, Western Washington University
Daniel Rossides, Bowdoin College
Pepper Schwartz, University of Washington
Donna L. Scott, Portland State University
Guy E. Swanson, University of California, Berkeley
Shirley Weitz, The New School
Joan Weston, Dallas County Community College
John Wilson, Duke University

I must record a special word of thanks to Donald Irish, who read the entire manuscript of both editions; the book has benefited enormously from his cogent criticism and humane wisdom. A number of students from different colleges and universities also critiqued the manuscript from the student viewpoint or helped with the research for the book, and I am especially grateful to Robert L. Cohen, Sunil Sen Gupta, Christopher Philips, and Kevin Williams.

Of course, I have not always agreed with the reviewers (nor have they always agreed with one another!) and the responsibility for the final manuscript is entirely my own.

Finally, I have been fortunate to continue my association with Worth Publishers, a young and vigorous company with a well-deserved reputation for its commitment to quality at every stage of the publishing process. For the effort they put into this book, my sincere thanks go to the staff of Worth, and particularly to Linda Baron Davis, editorial manager, to Peter Deane, the editor, and to George Touloumes, production manager, for their remarkable skills, talent, and dedication.

February, 1981

IAN ROBERTSON

Contents

The Author

Ian Robertson spent most of his early years in South Africa, where he obtained a B.A. degree in Political Science at the University of Natal. As president of the multiracial National Union of South African Students he organized several campaigns against that country's apartheid laws, until he was arbitrarily "banned" by Prime Minister Vorster. After leaving South Africa, he studied at Oxford, Cambridge, and Harvard universities, supporting himself through scholarships and writing. During this period his articles on various social topics appeared in such publications as the *Times* and *Guardian* in England and the *New Republic* and *Nation* in the United States.

Ian Robertson trained as a teacher at Oxford, where he was awarded a Diploma in Education in English and Latin. At Cambridge he took a First-Class Honors degree and M.A. in sociology and was elected Senior Scholar in Sociology at King's College. At Harvard he was awarded both a master's degree and a doctorate in the sociology of education. Dr. Robertson has a wide teaching experience: he has taught basic curriculum to retarded children in England, high school social studies in Massachusetts, sociology of education to Harvard graduates, and sociology to Cambridge undergraduates. He is currently devoting himself to his writing and research.

In addition to various articles, Dr. Robertson has edited *Readings in Sociology: Contemporary Perspectives* (Harper & Row, 1976), *Race and Politics in South Africa* (Transaction Books, 1978), and *The Social World* (Worth, 1981). The second edition of his successful *Social Problems* text was published by Random House in 1980.

UNIT 1 *Introduction to Sociology*

Like any subject that deals with people, sociology is inherently fascinating. This introductory unit explains what sociology is, as well as what sociologists do and how they go about their work. In reading it you will discover sociology's distinctive perspective on human society and social behavior.

The first chapter offers you a general overview of the discipline, presenting sociologists as "strangers" in the familiar landscape of their own society: in other words, as people who look afresh at the world others take for granted. The chapter explains the "sociological imagination"—the vivid awareness you will gain of the close link between personal experience and wider social forces. It also discusses the scientific nature of sociology, the relationship of sociology to other social sciences, the history of the discipline, and the major theoretical approaches that sociologists use to make sense of their subject matter.

The second chapter discusses the methods sociologists use to investigate the social world. Sociological research is essentially a form of detective work, in which the sociologist tries to find out what is happening in society and why. The value of the sociologist's conclusions is obviously influenced by the accuracy and reliability of the methods that are used to collect and analyze the evidence. The chapter therefore examines the problems of tracing cause and effect in social behavior, the unique difficulties sociologists face in their research, and the methods they use to uncover the facts about social life.

CHAPTER **1**   *Sociology: A New Look at a Familiar World*

Alone among living creatures, human beings are fully self-aware—capable of inquiring and reflecting about themselves. Throughout history, our ancestors pondered human nature as it is revealed in the social life of our species. Why do human beings form families and why do they worship gods? Why is the way of life of one group so different from that of another? What makes some people break social rules while others obey them? Why are some people rich when others are poor? What makes one group go to war with another? What might a human being who had not been raised in the company of other people be like? What holds societies together, and why do all societies constantly change over time?

Until quite recently the answers to these and similar questions came from intuition, from speculation, and from the dead weight of myth, superstition, and traditional "folk wisdom" handed down from the past. Only in the course of the last century or so has a new method been applied to the study of human society and social behavior: the method of science, which provides answers drawn from facts collected by systematic research.

This new mode of inquiry has produced the lively but still-infant discipline of sociology. *Sociology is the scientific study of human society and social behavior.* Its subject matter is huge, complex, and varied, and the knowledge produced by sociological research remains imperfect in many ways. Yet, in the brief time that the discipline has been in existence, it has taught us a great deal about ourselves that we could never have learned by relying on speculation alone. We have learned to conceive of human beings and social life in an entirely new way—a way you will find sometimes disconcerting, yet often fascinating.

3

Sociology as a Perspective

The world does not consist of a reality that everyone sees in exactly the same way. A house may seem to be simply a house, but different people will look at and interpret it quite differently. An architect, a real estate broker, a prospective burglar, an artist, and a demolition expert, for instance, would each view the house from a distinctive perspective, and would see quite different things as a result. In the same way, sociology offers a particular perspective on society and social behavior, a viewpoint quite unlike that of, say, the poet, the philosopher, the theologian, the lawyer, or the police officer.

The sociological perspective invites us to look at our familiar surroundings as though for the first time. It allows us to get a fresh view of a world we have always taken for granted, to examine our own social landscape with the same curiosity and fascination that we might bring to an exotic, alien culture. As Peter Berger (1963) has observed, sociology is nothing less than a special form of consciousness. It encourages us to focus on features of our social environment we have never noticed before and to interpret them in a new and richer light.

Sociology also gives us a window on the wider world that lies beyond our immediate experience, leading us into areas of society we might otherwise have ignored or misunderstood. Ordinarily, our own view of the world is shaped by our personal experience of it. However, sociology can take us into the worlds of the rich and the powerful, the poor and the weak, the worlds of slum dwellers, addicts, cult members, and criminals. Because these people have different social experiences, they have quite different definitions of social reality. Sociology enables us to appreciate viewpoints other than our own, to understand how these viewpoints came into being, and in the process, to better understand ourselves, our attitudes, and our own lives.

The Basic Insight

Sociology starts from the premise that we are basically social animals—not just from force of habit but because we could not otherwise survive. We live out our brief lives, for better or worse, in a society that existed long before we were born and will exist long after we are gone. We are all born into human groups and derive our identities, hopes,

Figure 1.1 To an outsider, the behavior of this New Guinea tribesman may seem bizarre, but in the context of his own society, the ritual in which he is taking part is perfectly understandable. Legend has it that the members of the tribe once hid from their enemies in a riverbed. When they emerged, covered with white mud, their enemies mistook them for ghosts and fled. The ritual commemorates this event—and, like any other ritual, it also does much more. Although the participants may not be aware of it, they are also reaffirming loyalty to their group and its traditions, and thereby enhancing the unity of their tribe. Sociology invites us to examine with fresh insights the behavior we have always taken for granted in our own society—for example, the rituals of Thanksgiving Day, Christmas, or the Fourth of July.

fears, troubles, and satisfactions from them. The basic insight of sociology is this: *human behavior is largely shaped by the groups to which people belong and by the social interaction that takes place within those groups.* We are what we are and we behave the way we do because we happen to live in particular societies at particular points in space and time. If you had been born, say, a modern Chinese peasant, or an African pygmy, or an ancient Greek, or a feudal aristocrat, your personality, your options in life, and your social experience would be utterly different. This fact seems obvious enough, but it is easily overlooked. People everywhere tend to take their social world for granted, accepting their society and its customs as unquestioningly as they do the physical world that also surrounds them. But the sociological perspective enables us to see society not as something to be taken for granted as "natural" but as a temporary social product, created by human beings and therefore capable of being changed by them as well.

The main focus of sociology is the group, not the individual. Studies of particular individuals are useful to sociologists, but the sociologist is mainly interested in *social interaction*—the ways in which people act toward, respond to, and influence one another. All social behavior, from shaking hands to murder, and all social institutions, from religion to the family, are ultimately the product of social interaction. The group, then, provides the sociologist's main frame of reference—whether the group being studied is as small as a gang or a rock band, as large as an ethnic community or a city, or as vast as a modern industrial society.

The Sociological Imagination

This emphasis on the group always leads back to the individual, however, for by understanding society, we more fully understand ourselves. C. Wright Mills (1959) described the perspective of the discipline as "the sociological imagination"—a vivid awareness of the relationship between private experience and the wider society. People usually see the world through their limited experience in a small orbit of family, relatives, friends, and fellow workers. This viewpoint places blinders on their view of the wider society. But it does more than that. Paradoxically, it also narrows their view of their own personal worlds, for those worlds are shaped by broader social forces that can easily pass unrecognized.

The sociological imagination allows us to escape from this cramped personal vision—to stand apart mentally from our own place in society and to see with a new clarity the link between private and social events. When a society

Strangers in a Familiar World

Anthropologists use the term "culture shock" to describe the impact of a totally new culture upon a newcomer. In an extreme instance such shock will be experienced by the Western explorer who is told, halfway through dinner, that he is eating the nice old lady he had been chatting with the previous day. Most explorers no longer encounter cannibalism in their travels today. However, the first encounters with polygamy or with puberty rites or even with the way some nations drive their automobiles can be quite a shock to an American visitor. With the shock may go not only disapproval or disgust but a sense of excitement that things can *really* be that different from what they are at home. To some extent, at least, this is the excitement of any first travel abroad. The experience of sociological discovery could be described as "culture shock" minus geographical displacement. In other words, the sociologist travels at home—with shocking results. He is unlikely to find that he is eating a nice old lady for dinner. But the discovery, for instance, that his own church has considerable money invested in the missile industry or that a few blocks from his home there are people who engage in cultic orgies may not be drastically different in emotional impact. Yet we would not want to imply that sociological discoveries are always or even usually outrageous to moral sentiment. Not at all. What they have in common with exploration in distant lands, however, is the sudden illumination of new and unsuspected facets of human existence in society.

People who like to avoid shocking discoveries, who prefer to believe that society is just what they were taught in Sunday School, who like the safety of the rules and the maxims of what Alfred Schutz has called the "world-taken-for-granted," should stay away from sociology. People who feel no temptation before closed doors, who have no curiosity about human beings, who are content to admire scenery without wondering about the people who live in those houses on the other side of that river, should probably also stay away from sociology. They will find it unpleasant or, at any rate, unrewarding. People who are interested in human beings only if they can change, convert or reform them should also be warned, for they will find sociology much less useful than they hoped. And people whose interest is mainly in their own conceptual constructions will do just as well to turn to the study of little white mice. Sociology will be satisfying, in the long run, only to those who can think of nothing more entrancing than to watch and to understand things human.

Source: Peter L. Berger, *Invitation to Sociology* (Garden City, N.Y.: Doubleday & Company, Inc., Anchor Books, 1963).

Figure 1.2 *The "sociological imagination" enables us to trace the links between individual experience and social forces. The options and life-styles of these people, from the upper class in Europe, from a pygmy tribe in the Congo rain forest, and the Chinese countryside, are very different. People's lives are shaped by historical and social forces over which they have little personal control.*

becomes industrialized, rural peasants become urban workers, whether they like it or not. When a nation goes to war, spouses are widowed and children grow up as orphans, for reasons that are beyond their personal power to control. When an economy sags, workers are thrown out of their jobs, no matter how efficiently they have performed them. The sociological imagination permits us to trace the intricate connection between the patterns and events of our own lives and the patterns and events of our society. As Mills expressed it,

> the sociological imagination enables us to grasp history and biography and the relationship between the two within society. That is its task and its promise.... It is by means of the sociological imagination that men now hope to grasp what is happening to themselves as minute points of the intersection of biography and history within society.

What Is Science?

Science refers to the logical, systematic methods by which knowledge is obtained and to the actual body of knowledge produced by these methods. The sciences are usually divided into two main branches: the *natural sciences,* which study physical and biological phenomena, and the *social sciences,* which study various aspects of human behavior. There are important differences between the two branches, but both have the same commitment to the scientific method.

All science, natural and social, assumes that there is some underlying order in the universe. Events, whether they involve molecules or human beings, are not haphazard. They follow a pattern that is sufficiently regular for *generalizations* to be made about them. It is possible to generalize, for example, that hydrogen and oxygen will always form water if they are combined at an appropriate temperature. Similarly, it is possible to generalize that all human societies will create some system of marriage and family. Generalizations are crucial to science because they place isolated, seemingly meaningless events in patterns we can understand. It then becomes possible to analyze relationships of cause and effect and thus to *explain* why something happens and to *predict* that it will happen again under the same conditions in the future.

Science relies for its generalizations, explanations, and predictions on careful, systematic analysis of verifiable evidence—that is, evidence that can be checked by others and will always yield the same results. Nonscientific, "common-sense" explanations, on the other hand, are based on *belief.* The ancient Romans, for example, believed that the sun is drawn across the skies each day by a god in a chariot, although none of them had actually seen this happen. Scientists have since observed, of course, that the apparent movement of the sun is caused by the daily rotations of the earth, an observation any competent scientist can verify by using the same methods. In short, the scientific approach gives a more reliable interpretation of reality than common-sense assumptions.

This does not mean that common sense cannot provide accurate explanations and predictions; it can, and often does. However, the problem is that without using the methods of science, there is no way to tell whether common sense is correct. For centuries common sense told

people that the world is the center of the universe and that the earth is flat. Using scientific methods, Copernicus found that the world is simply one planet among others; and the investigations of Columbus and other geographers proved that the earth is round. In making their factual investigations, these men and others like them risked their reputations and sometimes even their lives, for their findings contradicted important social beliefs of the time. But their challenge to ideas held dear by their societies tells us something else about science: there are no areas so sacred that science cannot explore them. Any question that can be answered by the scientific method is, in principle, an appropriate subject for scientific inquiry—even if the investigation and the findings outrage powerful interests or undermine cherished values. Yet science is not arrogant: it recognizes no ultimate, final truths. The body of scientific knowledge at any particular moment represents nothing more than the most logical interpretations of the existing data. It is always possible that new facts will come to light or that the available data will be reinterpreted in a new way, shattering the existing assumptions. Science therefore takes nothing for granted: everything is always open for further testing, reinterpretation, correction, and even refutation. That is why scientists, and especially sociologists, are so often "the destroyers of myths" (Elias, 1978). And sometimes the myths they destroy are their own.

Sociology as a Science

On the whole, social life does not consist of a series of random events: under most conditions, society and its processes are ordered and patterned. Consequently, sociology is able to employ the same general methods of investigation that all sciences do, and to use its findings to make reasonably reliable generalizations. Like natural scientists, sociologists construct theories, collect and analyze data, conduct experiments and make observations, keep careful records, and try to arrive at precise and accurate conclusions.

The Scientific Status of Sociology

Like the other social sciences, however, sociology is relatively less advanced as a discipline than most of the natural sciences. There are two reasons for this. First, the scientific method has been used to study social behavior only in recent times, whereas the scientific method has been applied to the natural world for centuries. Second, the study of human behavior presents many problems that natural scientists do not have to confront. Sociologists are dealing with people—in other words, with subjects who are conscious, self-aware, and capable of changing their behavior when they choose to. Unlike rocks or molecules, people may be uncooperative. They may behave in unforeseen ways for private reasons of their own. They may radically change their behavior when they know they are being studied. They cannot in good conscience be made the subject of experiments that affront their dignity or infringe on their basic human rights. And their behavior usually has extremely complex causes that may be difficult to pinpoint. (We shall explore these problems more fully in Chapter 2 when we discuss how sociologists go about their research.)

Although both natural and social scientists recognize that it may be impossible to prove there are "universal laws" that apply to any thing or event in all circumstances, the natural sciences can generally offer more precise explanations and predictions than can sociologists. But sociology is still young. Its research methods are constantly being improved, and we can expect that they will achieve greater precision in the future.

Sociology, then, is not less "scientific" than biochemistry or astronomy: it simply faces greater problems of generalization, explanation, and prediction. Yet the suspicion persists in some quarters that sociology is not "really" a science. In part this is because the popular image of the scientist is often that of someone working in a laboratory in a white coat, something sociologists rarely do. But the origin of the suspicion probably lies deeper. Few people are experts in molecular biology or planetary motions, but all of us can consider ourselves experts on society, because everyone has years of experience of social living. Sociologists, it is suggested, merely state the obvious in complicated language, telling us virtually nothing common sense has not told us already.

It is true that the language of sociology is sometimes a little strange to the beginner. The sociologist uses a specialized vocabulary and often employs everyday words, such as "status," "role," and "culture," in precise but unfamiliar ways. Sociologists use this vocabulary for the same reason that all scientists must: unless terms have an agreed-upon,

definite meaning, communication will be ambiguous and confusing, and findings will be difficult to verify. We do not expect a chemist to say, "I took some white crystals, mixed in a bit of black powder, chucked in some yellow stuff, threw in a match, and blew the place up." Unless the chemist tells us he or she was using potassium chlorate, carbon, and sulfur in specific quantities under particular conditions, the information is useless.

Similarly, it is not enough for a sociologist to say, "I showed this violent movie to some kids, and afterward they started acting much rougher than before." We need to know what is meant by "violent": what sort of violence, in what context, involving what kind of people? We need to know about the "kids": how old, which sex, what background? We need to know what is meant by "rougher than before": what is "roughness," how is it measured, how rough were they, in what ways, under what circumstances, for how long afterward, and toward whom? Only when the experiment is described with precision does it have any value as science, for it can then be repeated by other scientists to check the original findings. The need for precision means that, as a general rule, sociological writing will not have you chewing your fingernails in suspense or guffawing out of your armchair at an author's wit and humor—but you will find many sociological articles and books that are absorbing to read.

Sociology and Common Sense

But does sociology merely state the obvious by reporting what common sense tells us anyway? Here are some widely held common-sense views about society and social behavior. As you read through them, you might like to check them off as true or false.

1. Human beings have a natural instinct to mate with the opposite sex. (T/F)

2. Lower-class youths are more likely to commit crimes than middle-class youths. (T/F)

3. On average, high-income people in the United States pay a greater proportion of their income in taxes than low-income people. (T/F)

4. Revolutions are more likely to occur when conditions remain very bad than when previously bad conditions are rapidly improving. (T/F)

5. Exposure to pornography makes people more likely to commit sex crimes. (T/F)

6. The amount of money spent on a school's equipment and facilities has a strong effect on the academic success of its pupils. (T/F)

7. A substantial proportion of people on welfare could work if they really wanted to. (T/F)

8. One thing that is found in every society is romantic love. (T/F)

9. People who are regular Christian churchgoers are less likely to be prejudiced against other races than people who do not attend church. (T/F)

10. The best way to get an accurate assessment of public opinion is to poll as many people as possible. (T/F)

11. The income gap between blacks and whites has narrowed in recent years. (T/F)

12. The income gap between male and female workers has narrowed in recent years. (T/F)

13. Husbands are more likely to kill their wives in family fights than wives are to kill their husbands. (T/F)

14. The number of federal government civilian employees has grown sharply over the past two decades. (T/F)

15. For religious reasons, most American Catholics oppose birth control and are less likely than Protestants to enter interfaith marriages or to be divorced. (T/F)

All of the above assumptions may seem to be in accord with common sense, but sociological research has shown that every single one of them is false.

1. Human beings do not have an instinct to mate with the opposite sex. Our sexual preferences are entirely learned (Chapter 9); in fact, if an instinct is defined as an inherited complex behavior pattern, human beings do not have any instincts at all (Chapters 3 and 5).

2. Lower-class youths are not more likely than middle-class youths to commit crimes. Middle-class youths are at least as likely to engage in delinquent acts, but they are less likely to be arrested, and therefore do not show up as frequently in court statistics (Chapter 8).

3. High-income people pay roughly the same propor-

tion of their income in direct and indirect taxes as low-income people do. The reasons are that the rich can use many tax loopholes and that sales and other indirect taxes take a relatively larger percentage of a poor person's earnings (Chapter 11).

4. Revolutions are actually more likely to occur when conditions have been bad but are rapidly improving. When conditions are bad and stay bad, people take their misfortune for granted, but when conditions suddenly improve, people develop higher aspirations and become easily frustrated (Chapter 19).

5. Studies of sex offenders show that they are actually less likely than nonoffenders to have been exposed to pornography. Far from encouraging sex crimes, pornography seems to provide some people with an alternative outlet (Chapter 9).

6. The amount of money spent on a school's facilities seems to have little influence on pupil achievement. Performance is primarily related to family and social-class background (Chapter 15).

7. Less than 2 percent of the people on welfare are adult males who have been out of work for several months. Nearly all are children, old people, handicapped people, or mothers who are obliged to stay at home to look after their families and have no other source of income (Chapter 11).

8. Romantic love may seem a part of "human nature" to us, but in many societies it is unknown and in many others is regarded as ridiculous or tragic (Chapter 14).

9. Regular churchgoers are generally not less racially prejudiced than nonchurchgoers; in fact, they tend to be more prejudiced (Chapter 16).

10. The number of people involved in an opinion poll is largely irrelevant. What matters is that the sample should be fully representative of the population whose opinion is wanted. A properly chosen sample of two or three thousand Americans can give a highly accurate test of national opinion; a poorly chosen sample of 3 million, or even 30 million, could be hopelessly off target (Chapter 2).

11. Despite civil rights and other legislation, the income gap between blacks and whites has actually widened in recent years: black workers are generally less skilled than white workers, and less skilled workers suffer more in times of recession (Chapter 12).

12. The income gap between male and female workers has also widened rather than narrowed: women hold few high-paying positions, and the average working white woman earns less than the average working black man (Chapter 13).

13. Husbands and wives are equally likely to kill one another: although husbands are usually stronger, wives are more likely to resort to lethal weapons.

14. The number of federal civilian officials has remained almost constant for twenty years, although the number of state and local-government employees has risen significantly (Chapter 19).

15. More than 80 percent of American Catholics favor birth control; Catholics are more likely than Protestants to enter interfaith marriages; and Catholics have a higher divorce rate than Protestants (Chapter 16).

Of course, common-sense views are not always so relentlessly contradicted by sociological research. Indeed, intuition and common sense in sociology are a rich source of insights. But they can provide only hunches. The hunch must be tested by the methods of science.

The Social Sciences

We have already referred to the social sciences, a related group of disciplines that study various aspects of human behavior. The social sciences are sociology, economics, psychology, political science, and anthropology. Of course, human behavior does not fit neatly into compartments, and in practice the boundaries between the social sciences are vague and constantly shifting. Each of the disciplines has different historical origins, and the distinctions among them have since been preserved largely as a matter of convenience. Nobody could possibly be an expert in all of them, and the fragmentation of the social sciences permits specialization. But social scientists realize how much the concerns of the various disciplines overlap, and they freely "invade" each other's territory whenever it seems useful.

Economics

Economics studies the production, distribution, and consumption of goods and services. Economists examine, for example, how prices are determined or what effects taxes will have. Economics is in many ways the most advanced of the social sciences. Its subject matter is often more easily measured than that of the other disciplines, and economists have developed sophisticated mathematical tools for their explanations and predictions. But the economy is also a part of society: goods and services do not produce, distribute, and consume themselves. These social aspects of economic life are the subject of the sociology of economics.

Psychology

Psychology studies human mental processes, such as emotion, memory, perception, and intelligence. This discipline, more than any other social science, focuses on the individual. Partly because it has its roots in natural sciences such as biology, it also relies more heavily on laboratory and clinical experiments. Psychology shares one major field of interest with sociology: *social psychology,* the study of how personality and behavior are influenced by the social context. Social psychology is a genuine hybrid discipline. In many colleges and universities, in fact, it is as likely to be taught in sociology as in psychology departments.

Political Science

Political science has traditionally focused on two main areas: political philosophy and actual forms of government, with special emphasis on how the two are related. In recent years, however, the discipline has been strongly influenced by political sociology, which analyzes political behavior and studies the social interaction involved in the process of government. Political scientists are now asking more "sociological" questions, such as why people vote the way they do, why some people are more likely to take part in politics than others, or what happens "behind the scenes" in the informal manipulation of power. Sociological research, too, is increasingly used in shaping government policies. The interests of political scientists and political sociologists have been gradually converging and now often overlap.

Anthropology

Anthropology is sociology's sister discipline. It differs from sociology mainly in that it usually focuses on entire, small-scale, "primitive" societies, whereas sociology concentrates more on group processes within large modern industrial societies. Anthropology has several branches: archaeology, which deals with the remains of extinct civilizations; linguistics, which deals with certain aspects of language; physical anthropology, which uses fossil and other evidence to trace human evolution; and *cultural anthropology*, which studies the ways of life of other peoples. A study made by a cultural anthropologist is called an *ethnography*, and sociologists often find ethnographic evidence useful when they want to compare modern societies with other societies that have very different ways of life. In fact, now that small-scale, traditional societies are rapidly becoming extinct, many cultural anthropologists are studying groups in modern industrial societies. Sociologists and cultural anthropologists draw freely on one another's work.

In this book we shall make use of findings from the other social sciences whenever this is helpful for the understanding of social behavior. We shall place particular emphasis on information from social psychology and cultural anthropology. The research of social psychologists often throws light on the ways in which the social environment influences behavior, and the ethnographies of cultural anthropologists enable us to highlight aspects of our own society by comparing our practices with those of other peoples.

The Development of Sociology

Before the mid-1800s the study of society was the domain of social philosophers, thinkers who were often less concerned about what society actually *is* like than what they thought it *ought* to be like. Yet in a relatively short period this entire emphasis was reversed.

The Origins

When sociology began to emerge in the middle of the nineteenth century, it was in the context of the sweeping changes the Industrial Revolution brought to Europe. No social changes in history had been as widespread or as far-reaching, and this transformation—which is still taking place in the less developed nations of the world—cried for analysis and explanation.

Industrialization threw into turmoil societies that had been relatively stable for centuries. New industries and

Figure 1.3 Sociology emerged as a separate discipline during the early stages of the Industrial Revolution, when traditional societies were suddenly thrust into an era of rapid social change and unprecedented social problems. Sociology was born out of the attempt to understand the transformations that seemed to threaten the stability of European society.

technologies changed the face of the social and physical environment. Peasants left rural areas and flocked to the towns, where they worked as industrial laborers under appalling conditions. Cities grew at an unprecedented rate, providing an anonymous environment in which the customs and values of the small, tight-knit traditional community could scarcely survive. Social problems became rampant in the teeming cities. The ancient view that the social order was preordained by God began to collapse. A rising middle class, spurred by the examples of the French and American revolutions, clamored for democracy, and aristocracies and monarchies crumbled and fell. Religion began to lose its force as an unquestioned source of moral authority. For the first time in history, rapid social change became the norm rather than an abnormal state of affairs, and people could no longer expect that their children's lives would be much the same as their own. The direction of change was unclear, and the stability of the social order seemed threatened. An understanding of what was happening was urgently needed.

Two other factors also encouraged the development of sociology. One was the example of the natural sciences—if their methods could make so much sense of the physical world, could they not be applied successfully to the social world as well? The second factor was the exposure of Europe to the radically different societies their colonial empires had engulfed. Information about the widely contrasting social practices of these distant peoples raised fresh questions about society in general. Why, for instance, were some societies apparently more advanced than others, and what lessons could the European countries learn from comparisons of various societies?

Early Sociologists

The title "founder of sociology" usually goes to Auguste Comte (1789-1857), a French thinker who first coined the term "sociology" and who argued, in 1838, that the methods of science should be applied to the study of society. Comte established two specific problems for sociological investigation, social statics and social dynamics. *Social statics* refers to the problem of order and stability—how and why do societies hold together and endure? *Social dynamics* refers to the problem of social change—what makes societies change and what determines the nature and direction of the changes? Comte was so confident that the scientific method would unlock the secrets of society that he came to regard sociologists as a "priesthood of humanity," experts who would not only explain social events but would also guide society in the direction of greater progress. Although later sociologists have generally had more modest ambitions, they have continued to wrestle with the problems of social order and change.

Figure 1.4 Auguste Comte

Herbert Spencer

Another important nineteenth-century figure was Herbert Spencer (1820–1903), who took up the problems of social statics and dynamics and believed he had found the answer. Spencer compared human societies to living organisms. The parts of an animal, such as the lungs and the heart, are interdependent and contribute to the survival of the total organism. Similarly, Spencer argued, the various parts of society, such as the state and the economy, are also interdependent and work to ensure the stability and survival of the entire system. This theory took care of the problem of statics. To explain dynamics, Spencer pushed his analogy even further. Applying Darwin's theory of evolution to human societies, he argued that they gradually evolve from the forms found in the "primitive" societies of the world to the more complex forms found in the industrializing societies of his own time. Spencer believed that evolution meant progress, and he strongly opposed attempts at social reform on the grounds that they might interfere with a natural evolutionary process. Spencer's ideas seem rather strange today, but they remain influential in a very modified form. Many sociologists still see society as a more or less harmonious system whose various parts contribute to overall stability. Many also believe there has been a general

Figure 1.5 Herbert Spencer

Figure 1.6 Karl Marx

tendency for societies to move from the simple to the complex, although they do not necessarily equate this "evolution" with "progress" toward something better.

Karl Marx

The third and most important of the nineteenth-century social thinkers was Karl Marx (1818–1883). Marx was born in Germany, but after being expelled from various countries for his revolutionary activities, he eventually settled in England. An erratic genius, he wrote brilliantly on subjects as broad and diverse as philosophy, economics, political science, and history. He did not think of himself as a sociologist, but his work is so rich in sociological insights that he is now regarded as one of the most profound and original sociological thinkers. His influence has been immense. Millions of people accept his theories with almost religious fervor, and modern socialist and communist movements owe their inspiration directly to him. It is important to realize, however, that Marxism is not the same as communism. Marx would probably be dismayed at many of the practices of communist movements, and he cannot be held responsible for policies pursued in his name decades after his death.

To Marx, the task of the social scientist was not merely to describe the world: it was to change it. Whereas Spencer saw social harmony and the inevitability of progress, Marx saw social conflict and the inevitability of revolution. The key to history, he believed, is *class conflict*—the bitter struggle between those who own the means of producing wealth and those who do not, a contest that would end only with the overthrow of the ruling exploiters and the establishment of a free, humane, classless society. Marx placed special emphasis on the economic base of society. He argued that the character of virtually all other social arrangements is shaped by the way goods are produced and by the relationships that exist between those who work to produce them and those who live off the production of others. Modern sociologists, including many who reject other aspects of Marx's theories, generally recognize the fundamental influence of the economy on other areas of society.

Emile Durkheim

The French sociologist Emile Durkheim (1858–1917) has strongly influenced the discipline. Durkheim dealt with the problem of social order; he argued that societies are held together by the shared beliefs and values of their members,

Figure 1.7 Emile Durkheim

Figure 1.8 Max Weber

especially as these are expressed in religious doctrine and ritual. Like Spencer, he wanted to establish how the various parts of society contribute to the maintenance of the whole. His method was to ask what *function* a given element has in maintaining social order—an approach that has been very influential in modern American sociology. Durkheim also made the first real breakthrough in sociological research with his painstaking statistical study of suicide in various population groups. He was able to show that suicide rates vary consistently from one group to another, proving that the act of suicide is influenced by social forces and is not simply the individual matter that it might appear to be.

Max Weber

The German sociologist Max Weber (1864–1920), a contemporary of Durkheim, has perhaps had a stronger influence on Western sociology than any other single individual. He was a man of prodigious learning whose sociological investigations covered such diverse fields as politics, law, economics, music, cities, and the major world religions. Throughout his adult life Weber felt a great tension between his role as a scholar, dispassionately observing society, and his desire to influence events through political leadership. This tension may have contributed to a severe mental breakdown that incapacitated him for several years of his academic career. Weber remains an enigmatic and somewhat melancholy figure in sociological history. He viewed the direction of social change in industrial societies with distaste, feeling that the world was being "disenchanted" by bureaucracy, by the cold rationality of petty experts who knew no value other than efficiency.

Much of Weber's work can be seen as "a debate with the ghost of Karl Marx." Although he deeply admired much of Marx's work, Weber took issue with him on several points. He regarded trends toward greater social equality as inevitable, but he did not particularly welcome them, because he foresaw that such moves would involve an increase in the power of the state over the individual. Weber did not believe that social change could always be directly traced to changes in the economy, as Marx had implied. He suggested that other factors, such as religious ideas, could also play an independent role. Perhaps most important, Weber believed that sociologists should be *value-free* in their work; that is, that their personal convictions or biases should never creep into their research or conclusions. His stance in this respect was quite unlike that of Marx.

Modern Developments

The major development of sociology in this century has taken place in the United States, where the discipline has sunk roots far deeper than in any other country. Lester Ward (1841–1913) repeated Comte's call for social progress guided by sociological knowledge, and under his influence the discipline rapidly became committed to social reform. William Graham Sumner (1840–1910) studied the minute aspects of daily life found in the ordinary customs of the people. Under the influence of these men, American sociologists lost most of their interest in the larger problems of social order and social change and concentrated instead on the study of smaller and more specific problems.

Until about 1940 the University of Chicago's sociology department dominated the discipline in the United States. Sociologists such as George Herbert Mead developed the new discipline of social psychology, and others such as Robert E. Park and Ernest Burgess turned their attention to social problems and the lives of criminals, drug addicts, prostitutes, and juvenile delinquents. Many of the "Chicago School" sociologists were Protestant ministers or the sons of Protestant ministers, and under their leadership sociology became strongly identified with social reform.

From the forties until the early sixties, the center of attention shifted from Chicago to such universities as Harvard, Columbia, Michigan, and Wisconsin, and from reform to the much more neutral field of developing theories. Talcott Parsons influenced a generation of American sociologists, such as Kingsley Davis and Robert Merton, with his abstract models of society as a fairly stable, harmonious system of parts with interrelated functions. Other sociologists concentrated on perfecting research methods and statistical techniques, and the earlier activist strain in the discipline was almost lost. C. Wright Mills, a vociferous critic of this trend, seemed to be crying in the wilderness. The social turmoil of the sixties, however, encouraged a revival of the activist tradition in American sociology. During that decade, a survey found that over 70 percent of sociologists felt that part of their role was to be a critic of society and acknowledged that their work was not always value-free (Gouldner and Sprehe, 1965).

Figure 1.9 George Herbert Mead

Figure 1.10 Talcott Parsons

Figure 1.11 Robert Merton

Figure 1.12 C. Wright Mills

The sociology of the seventies and early eighties is not dominated by any single concern; its interests are more diverse than ever, and range from such old problems as inequality to such new ones as the social impact of energy shortages. Still, the question of whether the sociologist should be detached and value-free or activist and committed remains controversial. Some sociologists take the view that the science should be "ethically neutral," that it should attempt only to understand social processes and add to the sum of scientific knowledge. Others argue that sociological knowledge should be used to criticize and reform existing social arrangements.

Theoretical Perspectives

A crucial element in sociology, as in all science, is theory. A *theory* is a statement that organizes a set of concepts in a meaningful way by explaining the relationship among them. If the theory is valid, it will correctly predict that identical relationships will occur in the future if the conditions are identical. Although it is sometimes thought that "the facts speak for themselves," they do nothing of the kind. Facts are silent. They have no meaning until we give meaning to them, and that meaning is given by theory.

We are often prone to poke fun at "theorists" and to regard more highly the "practical" person. But theory and practice cannot be separated; virtually every practical decision you make and every practical opinion you hold has some theory behind it. A person may reject the views of prison reformers as being mere "theory" and prefer the "practical" approach that criminals should be severely punished in order to discourage crime. But in actuality this practical approach implies several theories—the theory that people always rationally choose whether or not to commit a crime, the theory that people try to avoid punishment, the theory that the most severe punishments make the best deterrents to crime. Even the most practical gadgets of everyday life, from can openers to automobiles, could not be constructed or used without some theory of how they operate. Theory is not an intellectual luxury practiced only by academics in their ivory towers.

Theory makes the facts of social life comprehensible. It places seemingly meaningless events in a general framework that enables us to determine cause and effect, to explain, and to predict. Sociological theories vary greatly in their scope and sophistication. Some attempt to explain only a small aspect of reality (such as why some people become heroin addicts). Others are more sweeping and confront large-scale, societal problems (such as those of social order and social change). The leading figures in the early development of sociology, including Spencer, Marx, Durkheim, and Weber, offered grand theories of the latter type. Later sociologists, with the notable exception of Talcott Parsons, have generally felt that such attempts involve biting off more than one can chew and have concentrated instead on narrower theories aimed at explaining specific, limited social issues.

Despite this preference for more limited theories, most sociologists are guided in their work by major *theoretical perspectives*—broad assumptions about society and social behavior that provide a point of view for the study of specific problems. There are three of these general perspectives in modern sociology, and you will meet them repeatedly throughout this book. They are the functionalist, the conflict, and the interactionist perspectives. We shall look at each in turn.

The Functionalist Perspective

The *functionalist perspective* draws its original inspiration from the work of Herbert Spencer and Emile Durkheim. As we have seen, Spencer compared societies to living organisms. Any organism has a *structure*—that is, it consists of a number of interrelated parts, such as a head, limbs, a heart, and so on, that play a *function* in the life of the total organism. In the same way, Spencer argued, a society has a structure. Its interrelated parts are the family, religion, the military, and so on. Ideally, each of these components also has a function that contributes to the overall stability of the social system. Modern structural-functionalism (usually called functionalism) does not press the analogy between a society and an organism. But it does retain the same general idea of society as a system of interrelated parts. Functionalism in modern American sociology is associated particularly with the work of Talcott Parsons (1951) and Robert Merton (1968).

The Social System

Functionalist theory implies that society tends to be an organized, stable, well-integrated system, in which most members agree on basic values. Under normal conditions, all the elements in the social system—such as the schools, the family, or the state—tend to "fit together," with each element helping to maintain overall stability. The family, for example, *functions* to regulate sexual behavior, to transmit social values to children, and to take care of young and aged people who could not otherwise survive.

Figure 1.13 The functionalist perspective focuses on the functions, or consequences, that a given element has in society. Economic activity, for example, functions to provide the goods and services on which society depends for its existence. It also gives people roles in life, enabling them to earn a living and to draw a sense of identity from the work they do. These functions contribute to the stability of the social system as a whole.

In the functionalist view, a society has an underlying tendency to be in equilibrium, or balance. Social change is therefore likely to be disruptive unless it takes place relatively slowly, because changes in one part of the system usually provoke changes elsewhere in the system. If the economy, for example, requires an increasing number of highly trained workers, the government will pour more money into education, and the schools and colleges will produce more graduates. But if the economy expands (or contracts) so rapidly that the other elements in the social system cannot "catch up," disequilibrium will result. In times of very rapid economic growth, the educational system may be unable to provide qualified personnel quickly enough to fill the new jobs; during a recession, on the other hand, the system may continue to produce graduates even though there are not enough jobs for them.

Functions and Dysfunctions

How does one determine what the functions of a given element in the social system are? Essentially, sociologists ask what its *consequences* are—not what its *purposes* are believed to be. They do this because a component can have functions other than those that were intended. Robert Merton (1968) distinguishes between *manifest functions*—those that are obvious and intended—and *latent functions*—those that are unrecognized and unintended. The schools, for example, have the manifest function of teaching literacy and other skills that are essential if a modern industrial society is to survive. But they also have latent functions that are not intended or generally recognized. For example, they keep children in an industrial society occupied until they are old enough to work. In the same way, the welfare system has the manifest function of preventing the poor from starving, but it also has the latent function of averting the civil disorder that might result if millions of people had no source of income.

Merton also points out that not all features of the social system are functional at all times: on occasion some element may actually disrupt the social equilibrium and therefore be *dysfunctional*. The high birth rate in the less developed countries of the world, for example, is dysfunctional for those societies because their economies cannot support their ever increasing population. Sometimes a component of the social system can be functional in one respect and dysfunctional in another. American industry, for example, has the manifest function of providing the goods on which our way of life depends, but it also has the latent function of polluting the environment and is therefore dysfunctional in this sense. The full implications of any element in the social system therefore have to be carefully explored.

The functionalist perspective, then, is obviously useful in explaining why some elements in a society exist and persist, but it also has some disadvantages. An important criticism of the functionalist view is that it tends in practice to be inherently conservative. Because their main emphasis is on social order and stability, functionalists risk the temptation of dismissing disruptive changes as dysfunctional, even if those changes are necessary, inevitable, and beneficial in the long run.

The Conflict Perspective

The *conflict perspective* in modern sociology derives its inspiration from the work of Karl Marx, who saw the struggle between social classes as the "engine" of history and the main source of change. Although the conflict perspective has dominated Western European sociology ever since, it was largely neglected in American sociology until the sixties. The social and political turmoil of that decade was more readily analyzed through the conflict perspective than through the functionalist. Conflict theory has been popular among American sociologists since that time.

Modern conflict theory, which is associated with such sociologists as C. Wright Mills (1956) and Lewis Coser (1956), does not simply focus, as Marx did, on class conflict; it sees conflict among many groups and interests as a fact of life in any society. These conflicts may involve, for example, the old versus the young, producers versus consumers, urbanites versus suburbanites, or one racial or ethnic group versus another.

Conflict and Change

Conflict theorists assume that societies are in a constant state of change, in which conflict is a permanent feature. "Conflict" does not necessarily mean outright violence; it includes tension, hostility, competition, and disagreement over goals and values. This conflict is not an occasional event that disrupts the generally smooth workings of society: it is a continuing and inevitable part of social life. The things that people desire—such as power, wealth, and prestige—are always scarce, and the demand for them exceeds the supply. Those who gain control of these resources are able to protect their own interests at other people's expense. Conflict theorists regard the functionalists' vision of a general consensus on values as pure fiction: what actually happens, they argue, is that the powerful coerce the rest of the population into compliance and conformity. In other words, social order is maintained, not by popular agreement, but rather by force or the implied threat of force.

Conflict theorists do not see social conflict as a necessarily destructive force, although they admit that it may sometimes have that effect. They argue that conflict can often have positive results. It binds groups together as they pursue their own interests, and the conflict among competing groups focuses attention on social problems and leads to beneficial changes that might otherwise not have occurred. In this way, social movements—such as those for civil rights or women's liberation—become an important source of change. The changes caused by social conflict prevent society from stagnating.

Who Benefits?

The conflict perspective, then, leads the sociologist to inquire into whose interests are involved and who benefits or suffers from existing arrangements. In analyzing social inequality, for example, conflict theorists argue that it exists not because it is functional for society as a whole but because some people have been able to achieve political and economic power and have managed to pass on these advantages to their descendants. In the same way, conflict theorists would not see environmental pollution as a "latent dysfunction" of industrialism. Instead, they would point to the fact that powerful corporate interests make their profits from manufacturing processes that pollute the environment. To take another case, tobacco, an addictive drug that has been conclusively linked to lung cancer, is freely marketed in the United States, but the use of marijuana, which on present evidence does not seem to be as physically harmful, is generally illegal. Why? A conflict analysis would point out that wealthy and influential interests benefit by manufacturing, advertising, and selling tobacco. Marijuana, on the other hand, is used chiefly by the young and the powerless. However, as marijuana spreads to more influential groups in society, and as large corporations become interested in marketing the drug themselves, pressures to decriminalize its use are likely to increase. Social change, in this area as in others, is influenced by the shifting relationships and interests of groups competing for their own advantage.

Figure 1.14 The conflict perspective focuses on tensions, disagreements, and competition in society. Conflict is assumed to be a permanent and inevitable aspect of social life and an important source of change. Conflict over nuclear energy, for example, may lead to significant changes in American energy policies in the future.

A modern society contains a wide spectrum of opinions, occupations, life-styles, and social groups. On any social issue there are some people who stand to gain and some who stand to lose. Social processes cannot be fully understood without referring to this conflict of interest, a conflict whose outcome always favors the stronger party. To understand many features of our own society, then, we must pay particular attention to the values and interests of those who exercise power—primarily people who are white, middle-aged, Protestant, wealthy, male, and of Anglo-Saxon background.

The conflict perspective has the advantage of highlighting aspects of society that the functionalist perspective, with its emphasis on consensus and stability, tends to ignore. But this fact also suggests an important criticism of the conflict perspective. By focusing so narrowly on issues of competition and change, it fails to come to grips with the more orderly, stable, and less controversial dimensions of social reality.

The Interactionist Perspective

The *interactionist perspective* in sociology was strongly influenced by Max Weber, who emphasized the importance of understanding the social world from the viewpoint of the individuals who act within it. Later developments in interactionist theory have been strongly influenced by social psychology and by the work of early leaders in the Chicago School, particularly George Herbert Mead. The important difference between this perspective and the two we have considered is that it does not focus on such large structures as the state, the economy, or social classes. Instead, it is concerned primarily with the everyday social interaction that takes place as people go about their lives.

Interaction: The Basis of Social Life

The main reason interactionist theorists are wary of the emphasis other sociologists place on the major components of society is that concepts such as "the economy" or "the state" are, after all, abstractions; they cannot exist or act by themselves. It is people that exist and act, and it is only through their social behavior that society can come into being at all. Society is ultimately created, maintained, and changed by the social interaction of its members.

The interactionist perspective is a broad one, containing a number of loosely linked approaches. Erving Goffman (1959), for example, takes a "dramaturgical" approach to social interaction. In other words, he sees social life as a form of theater, in which people play different parts and "stage-manage" their lives and the impressions they create on others. George Homans (1974) takes an "exchange" approach. He focuses on the way people control one an-

Figure 1.15 The interactionist perspective focuses on social behavior in everyday life. It tries to understand how people create and interpret the situations they experience, and it emphasizes how countless instances of social interaction produce the larger structures of society—government, the economy, and other institutions.

other's behavior by exchanging various forms of rewards and punishments for approved or disapproved behavior. Harold Garfinkel (1967) adopts what he calls an "eth-nomethodological" approach. This formidable term simply implies an attempt to scrape below the surface of social behavior to find out how people create and share their understandings of social life, and how they base their actions on those understandings. The most widely used approach is that of "symbolic interaction" (Mead, 1934; Blumer, 1969), and this is the one we shall emphasize here and elsewhere in this book.

Symbolic Interaction

A *symbol* is something that can meaningfully represent something else—signs, gestures, shared rules, and, most important, written and spoken language are examples of symbols. *Symbolic interaction* is the interaction that takes place between people through symbols. Much of this interaction takes place on a face-to-face basis, but it can also occur in other forms: symbolic interaction is taking place between you and the author as you read this sentence, and it occurs whenever you obey (or disobey) a traffic signal or a no-trespassing notice. The essential point is that people do not respond to the world directly: they place a social meaning on it and respond to that meaning. The words of this book, the red light of a traffic signal, a wolf whistle in the street, have no meaning in themselves. Rather, people learn to attach symbolic meaning to these things, and they order their lives on the basis of these meanings. We live in a symbolic as well as in a physical world, and our social life involves a constant process of interpreting the meanings of our own acts and those of others.

The interactionist perspective, then, leads the sociologist to inquire into people's interpretations of, and responses to, their interaction with others. Sociologists using this perspective usually focus on the specific, detailed aspects of personal everyday life. By what process, for example, does someone become a prostitute? Why is it that strangers in elevators so scrupulously avoid eye contact with each other, staring anywhere—at their shoes, at the ceiling, at the nearest wall—rather than directly into another passenger's face? How does someone learn to experience marijuana smoking as pleasurable? What unspoken tactics are used by a male doctor and a female patient to minimize embarrassment during a pelvic examination? What processes are involved in group decision-making? What happens if you stand "too" close to someone during a conversation, and why?

The interactionist perspective provides a fascinating insight into the mechanics of everyday life, and it has the advantage of revealing fundamental social processes that other perspectives easily overlook. But the perspective is open to the important criticism that it neglects larger social institutions and societal processes of stability and change—institutions and processes which, after all, have powerful effects on social interaction and on our personal experience.

An Evaluation

Since each of these perspectives starts from different assumptions, and each leads the investigator to ask different questions, each viewpoint is likely to produce different types of conclusions. In many respects the theories seem quite contradictory. But this does not mean that one of them is "better" than the others, or even that they are always incompatible. The reason is that each perspective focuses on a different aspect of reality: functionalism, primarily on social order and stability; conflict theory, primarily on social tension and change; and interactionism, primarily on the ordinary experiences of everyday life. Each of the perspectives has a part to play in the analysis of society. In fact, there is nothing unusual in a scientist's using apparently incompatible theories to study the same subject. Physicists find it useful to regard light sometimes as a continuous wave and sometimes as a series of particles, and they gain a better understanding of the nature of light as a result.

Thus all three perspectives could be applied, for example, to the study of education. A functionalist approach would emphasize the functions that the schools play in maintaining the social system as a whole. It would point out how education provides the young with skills they need in later life, how it sorts and selects people for different kinds of jobs, how it transmits cultural values from one generation to the next, and even how it keeps millions of adolescents off the streets. A conflict approach would emphasize that education is believed to be an important avenue to social and financial success in life. It would point out how social-class background affects a pupil's academic achievement, how more resources are channeled to the schools of the

Figure 1.16 People's views of the world are largely shaped by their own experience of it. Their age, race, sex, nationality, social class, and personal histories all affect their values, attitudes, and interpretations of reality. These two groups of Americans, each from different walks of life, probably interpret many social issues in different ways.

wealthy than to those of the poor, and how educational credentials are used by different individuals and groups jockeying for competitive advantage. An interactionist approach would emphasize the daily activities within the school. It would point to the forms of interaction between teachers and pupils, the influence of the student peer group over its individual members, or the ways in which the school rules are broken or followed. None of these approaches gives answers that are any more "true" than the others, and taken together they provide a broader and deeper understanding of the entire institution of education.

Some sociologists, of course, do argue that one or another of the perspectives gives an understanding generally superior to the others, and they systematically try to apply their chosen perspective to all or most problems. No such approach is adopted here—not just because the author does not accept that any one perspective is always the most useful, but because it would be a disservice to the introductory student to offer only one viewpoint.

In this book, then, you will regularly encounter all three perspectives. The interactionist perspective will be used particularly in the discussion of "micro" (small-scale) processes; the functionalist and conflict perspectives, in the discussion of "macro" (large-scale) processes. Sometimes the perspectives will contradict each other. When this happens, we shall evaluate their respective merits. At other times they will complement each other, giving a fuller and richer understanding of the subject.

The Problem of Objectivity

We have seen that people in different walks of life may interpret the same phenomenon—whether it is a house, a riot, a president's conduct in office, or an energy shortage—in very different ways. In other words, people tend to see the world from a *subjective* viewpoint, one based on their own opinions, attitudes, and experiences. We have also seen that sociologists themselves can adopt varying perspectives on the same problem and can come to different and even contrasting conclusions as a result. This fact raises a very important issue. Is an *objective* understanding of society possible? In other words, is there any way of interpreting the facts about the social world so that personal judgments are eliminated?

If the world consisted simply of some self-evident reality that everyone perceived in exactly the same way, there might be no disagreement among observers. But the truth of the matter is that what we see in the world is not determined by what exists "out there." It is shaped by what our past experience has prepared us to see and by what we consciously or unconsciously want to see. Knowledge and belief about the world do not exist in a vacuum; they are social products whose content depends on the context in which they are produced. A black in an urban ghetto will see American race relations in one way; a Ku Klux Klan member, in another way; a white liberal college student, in yet another. Each is inclined to perceive facts selectively and to interpret them in particular ways.

The same is inevitably true of social scientists, whose outlook on the world is also influenced by their background, training, and prior experiences. Most American social scientists are well educated, urban, white, middle-class, and male, and they naturally tend to interpret reality differently from people who do not share these characteristics. Their background and interests, for example, make them overwhelmingly liberal in political orientation: as Figure 1.17 shows, social scientists are more liberal than scholars in other disciplines. Among social scientists, so-

ciologists are the most liberal of all, with more than 70 percent describing themselves as "liberal" or "very liberal" (Lipset and Ladd, 1972). Inevitably, then, sociologists, like anyone else, will be guilty of some measure of *bias*—the tendency, often unconscious, to interpret facts in ways that are influenced by subjective values and attitudes. This problem occurs in all sciences, but it becomes particularly acute in the social sciences, whose subject matter often involves issues of deep human and moral concern. How can the problem be resolved?

The first step is to recognize that subjectivity and objectivity are not two neat and separate categories; they are really matters of degree. By exercising scrupulous caution the sociologist can attempt to be as objective as possible. This caution involves a deliberate effort to be conscious of one's own biases so that they can be kept out of the process of research and interpretation. The ethical code of the discipline requires that sociologists be intellectually honest—that they attempt to be aware of their own values and not allow these values to distort their work; that they relentlessly hunt down the relevant facts and not ignore those that are inconvenient for their pet theories; that they not manipulate data to prove a point; and that they not use research to suppress or misuse knowledge. Moreover, the

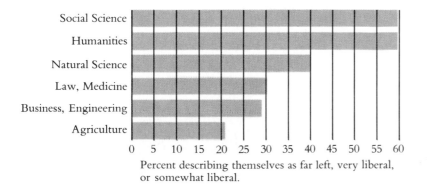

LIBERALISM OF FACULTY MEMBERS BY ACADEMIC FIELD

Percent describing themselves as far left, very liberal, or somewhat liberal.

Source: Everet C. Ladd, Jr., and Seymour M. Lipset, "The 1977 Survey of the American Professoriate," in *Public Opinion,* May/June 1978, p. 37.

Figure 1.17 American social scientists are more liberal in their political outlook than scholars in other fields. These data are drawn from an extensive survey of college faculty in 1977.

sociological community does not have to rely entirely on the integrity of the individual to ensure that objectivity is strived for. When research is published, it becomes available for the critical scrutiny of the entire community. Other sociologists can assess the findings and attempt to verify them by repeating the research to see if it yields the same results. This procedure provides an extremely effective check against gross distortions.

Total objectivity is probably impossible to achieve in any science, since some bias is always unconscious. But a self-conscious effort to be as objective as possible will produce vastly less biased results than not making this attempt. And if objectivity is defined as thought sufficiently disciplined to minimize the distortions caused by personal bias, then it is certainly possible. The pursuit of objectivity does not necessarily mean that sociologists should not express personal opinions, or *value judgments*. It means that these judgments should be clearly labeled as such and that they should not intrude into the actual process of research and interpretation. It would be perfectly legitimate, therefore, for a sociologist to give as objective an account as possible of a social problem, and then to add a subjective judgment—provided that the judgment was presented as a matter of personal opinion.

Summary

1. Sociology is the scientific study of human society; it differs from other modes of understanding the social world in that it relies on systematic observation of verifiable facts.

2. Sociology provides a unique perspective on society, enabling us to see the intimate relationships between social forces and individual experience.

3. Science refers to the logical, systematic methods by which reliable knowledge of the universe is obtained and also to the actual knowledge produced by these methods. Science assumes order in the universe, and it attempts to establish generalizations that can be used for the purposes of explanation and prediction.

4. The subject matter of sociology poses many problems the natural sciences do not face, but sociology nonetheless has the same commitment to the scientific method. Socio-

logical explanations are therefore more reliable than those based only on common sense.

5. The social sciences are a related group of disciplines that study various aspects of human behavior. The main social sciences are sociology, economics, psychology, political science, and anthropology.

6. Sociology emerged in the middle of the nineteenth century, in the context of the changes caused by the Industrial Revolution.

7. Early sociologists, such as Comte, Spencer, Marx, Weber, and Durkheim, concentrated on problems of social order and social change. The subsequent development of sociology, which has taken place largely in the United States, has focused primarily on more restricted theories and studies and on the refinement of research techniques. Particularly since the sixties, there has been controversy over whether sociologists should be value-free or socially committed.

8. There are three major theoretical perspectives in modern sociology. The functionalist perspective focuses primarily on processes of order and stability; the conflict perspective, on processes of competition and change; the interactionist perspective, on processes of everyday social behavior. These three perspectives are not necessarily incompatible.

9. Complete objectivity is particularly difficult to achieve in the social sciences. By rigorously excluding personal biases and by submitting research findings to the criticism of the sociological community, however, sociologists can guard against subjective distortions and can reach a high degree of objectivity.

Important Terms

sociology (3)
social interaction (5)
science (7)
social sciences (7)
social psychology (10)
cultural
  anthropology (11)

ethnography (11)
social static (order) (12)
social dynamics
  (change) (12)
value-free (14)
theory (16)

theoretical
 perspective (17)
functionalist
 perspective (17)
structure (17)
function (17)
manifest function (18)
latent function (18)
dysfunction (18)
conflict perspective (18)

interactionist perspective
 (20)
symbol (21)
symbolic interaction (21)
objectivity (22)
subjectivity (22)
bias (23)
value judgment (24)

Suggested Readings

ABRAHAMSON, MARK. *Functionalism.* Englewood Cliffs, N.J.: Prentice-Hall, 1978.

A succinct introduction to functionalist theory, with a consideration of some criticisms of the perspective.

BART, PAULINE, and LINDA FRANKEL. *The Student Sociologist's Handbook.* Morristown, N.J.: General Learning Press, 1976.

A useful and comprehensive guide to sociological literature and sources of information.

BERGER, PETER L. *Invitation to Sociology.* Garden City, N.Y.: Doubleday, 1963.

A brief and elegantly written introduction to the field. Berger provides an absorbing account of the distinctive "sociological perspective."

COLLINS, RANDALL, and MICHAEL MAKOWSKY. *The Discovery of Society.* Random House, 1978.

A short and readable account of the history of sociology.

CHAMBLISS, WILLIAM J. (ed.). *Sociological Readings in the Conflict Perspective.* Reading, Mass.: Addison-Wesley, 1973.

A selection of short articles that analyze various social phenomena from the conflict perspective.

MILLS, C. WRIGHT. *The Sociological Imagination.* New York: Oxford University Press, 1967.

Written from a conflict perspective, this book has become a classic introduction to sociology. Mills elaborates on the intimate connection between private experience and social context.

ROBBOY, HOWARD, SIDNEY L. GREENBLAT, and CANDACE CLARK (eds.). *Social Interaction: Introductory Readings in Sociology.* New York: St. Martin's Press, 1979.

A collection of interesting articles on a wide range of social topics. The book provides an excellent sampling of research conducted from an interactionist perspective.

SHOSTAK, ARTHUR B. (ed.). *Our Sociological Eye: Personal Essays on Society and Culture.* Port Washington, N.Y.: Alfred Publishing, 1977.

An anthology of first-person essays, in which sociologists apply the insights of their discipline to a variety of personal experiences.

Reading

Invitation to Sociology   *Peter L. Berger*

In this reading, Berger describes the inherent fascination of sociology and invites the newcomer to this "very special kind of passion." It should be noted that Berger was writing at a time when an unconscious sexism was reflected in the general usage of the language—hence, the sociologist was assumed to be "he," and "his" subject matter, "men." Berger's "invitation" nevertheless deservedly has remained a classic portrait of the discipline's appeal.

The sociologist . . . is a person intensively, endlessly, shamelessly interested in the doings of men. His natural habitat is all the human gathering places of the world, wherever men come together. The sociologist may be interested in many other things. But his consuming interest remains in the world of men, their institutions, their history, their passions. And since he is interested in men, nothing that men do can be altogether tedious for him. He will naturally be interested in the events that engage men's ultimate beliefs, their moments of tragedy and grandeur and ecstasy. But he will also be fascinated by the commonplace, the everyday. He will know reverence, but this reverence will not prevent him from wanting to see and to understand. He may sometimes feel revulsion or contempt. But this also will not deter him from wanting to have his questions answered. The sociologist, in his quest for understanding, moves through the world of men without respect for the usual lines of demarcation. Nobility and degradation, power and obscurity, intelligence and folly—these are equally *interesting* to him, however unequal they may be in his personal values or tastes. Thus his questions may lead him to all possible levels of society, the best and the least known places, the most respected and the most despised. And, if he is a good sociologist, he will find himself in all these places because his own questions have so taken possession of him that he has little choice but to seek for answers.

It would be possible to say the same things in a lower key. We could say that the sociologist, but for the grace of his academic title, is the man who must listen to gossip despite himself, who is tempted to look through keyholes, to read other people's mail, to open closed cabinets. Before some otherwise unoccupied psychologist sets out now to construct an aptitude test for sociologists on the basis of sublimated voyeurism, let us quickly say that we are speaking merely by way of analogy. . . . What interests us is the curiosity that grips any sociologist in front of a closed door behind which there are human voices. If he is a good sociologist, he will want to open that door, to understand these voices. Behind each closed door he will anticipate some new facet of human life not yet perceived and understood.

The sociologist will occupy himself with matters that others regard as too sacred or as too distasteful for dispassionate investigation. He will find rewarding the company of priests or of prostitutes, depending not on his personal preferences but on the questions he happens to be asking at the moment. He will also concern himself with matters that others may find much too boring. He will be interested in the human interaction that goes with warfare or with great intellectual discoveries, but also in the relations between people employed in a restaurant or between a group of little girls playing with their dolls. His main focus of attention is not the ultimate significance of what men do, but the action in itself, as another example of the infinite richness of human conduct. . . .

In these journeys through the world of men the sociologist will inevitably encounter other professional Peeping Toms. Sometimes these will resent his presence, feeling that he is poaching on their preserves. In some places the sociologist will meet up with the economist, in others with the political scientist, in yet others with the psychologist or the ethnologist. Yet chances are that the questions that have brought him to these same places are different from the ones that propelled his fellow-trespassers. The sociologist's questions always remain essentially the same: "What are people doing with each other here?" "What are their relationships to each other?" "How are these relationships organized in institutions?" "What are the collective ideas that move men and institutions?" In trying to answer these questions in specific instances, the sociologist will, of course, have to deal with economic or political matters, but he will do so in a way rather different from that of the economist or the political scientist. The scene that he contemplates is the same human scene that these other scientists concern themselves with. But the sociologist's angle of vision is different. When this is understood, it becomes clear that it makes little sense to try to stake out a special enclave within which the sociologist will carry on business in his own right.... Any intellectual activity derives excitement from the moment it becomes a trail of discovery. In some fields of learning this is the discovery of worlds previously unthought and unthinkable. This is the excitement of the astronomer or of the nuclear physicist on the antipodal boundaries of the realities that man is capable of conceiving. But it can also be the excitement of bacteriology or geology. In a different way it can be the excitement of the linguist discovering new realms of human expression or of the anthropologist exploring human customs in faraway countries. In such discovery, when undertaken with passion, a widening of awareness, sometimes a veritable transformation of consciousness, occurs. The universe turns out to be much more wonderful than one had ever dreamed. The excitement of sociology is usually of a different sort. Sometimes, it is true, the sociologist penetrates into worlds that had previously been quite unknown to him— for instance, the world of crime, or the world of some bizarre religious sect, or the world fashioned by the exclusive concerns of some group such as medical specialists or military leaders or advertising executives. However, much of the time the sociologist moves in sectors of experience that are familiar to him and to most people in his society. He investigates communities, institutions and activities that one can read about every day in the newspapers. Yet there is another excitement of discovery beckoning in his investigations. It is not the excitement of coming upon the totally unfamiliar, but rather the excitement of finding the familiar becoming transformed in its meaning. The fascination of sociology lies in the fact that its perspective makes us see in a new light the very world in which we have lived all our lives. This also constitutes a transformation of consciousness. Moreover, this transformation is more relevant existentially than that of many other intellectual disciplines, because it is more difficult to segregate in some special compartment of the mind. The astronomer does not live in the remote galaxies, and the nuclear physicist can, outside his laboratory, eat and laugh and marry and vote without thinking about the insides of the atom. The geologist looks at rocks only at appropriate times, and the linguist speaks English with his wife. The sociologist lives in society, on the job and off it. His own life, inevitably, is part of his subject matter. Men being what they are, sociologists too manage to segregate their professional insights from their everyday affairs. But it is a rather difficult feat to perform in good faith.

The sociologist moves in the common world of men, close to what most of them would call real. The categories he employs in his analyses are only refinements of the categories by which other men live— power, class, status, race, ethnicity. As a result, there is a deceptive simplicity and obviousness about some sociological investigations. One reads them, nods at the familiar scene, remarks that one has heard all this before and don't people have better things to do than to waste their time on truisms—until one is suddenly brought up against an insight that radically questions everything one had previously assumed about this familiar scene. This is the point at which one begins to sense the excitement of sociology.... It can be said that the first wisdom of sociology is this— things are not what they seem. This too is a deceptively simple statement. It ceases to be simple after a while. Social reality turns out to have many layers of meaning. The discovery of each new layer changes the perception of the whole.... To be sure, sociology is an individual pastime in the sense that it interests some men and bores others. Some like to observe human beings, others to experiment with mice. The world is big enough to hold all kinds and there is no logical priority for one interest as against another. But the word "pastime" is weak in describing what we mean. Sociology is more like a passion. The sociological perspective is more like a demon that possesses one, that drives one compellingly, again and again, to the questions that are its own. An introduction to sociology is, therefore, an invitation to a very special kind of passion.

Source: Peter L. Berger, *Invitation to Sociology* (Garden City, N.Y.: Doubleday & Company, Inc., Anchor Books, 1963).

Chapter 2

Doing Sociology: The Methods of Research

Sociological research is inherently interesting and exciting: it offers the stimulation and challenge of going as a "stranger" into the familiar world, often to find one's assumptions shattered by the facts that one discovers. Research in sociology is really a form of detective work—it poses the same early puzzles and suspicions, the same moments of routine sifting through the evidence and inspired guessing, the same disappointments over false leads and facts that do not fit and, perhaps, the same triumph when the pieces finally fall into place and an answer emerges. Research in sociology is where the real action takes place. It is in the field, far more than in the lecture room, that the sociologist comes to grips with the subject.

There are two sides to the sociological enterprise: theory ✓ and research. Both are essential, and each thrives on the other. Facts without theory are utterly meaningless, for they lack a framework in which they can be understood. Theories without facts are unproved speculations of little use to anybody, because there is no way to tell whether they are correct. Theory and research are thus parts of a constant cycle. A theory inspires research that can be used to verify or disprove it, and the findings of research are used to confirm, reject, or modify the theory, or even to provide the basis of new theories. The process recurs endlessly, and the accumulation of sociological knowledge is the result.

Guesswork, intuition, and common sense all have an important part to play in sociological research, but on their own they cannot produce reliable evidence: that requires a reliable research methodology. *A methodology is a system of rules, principles, and procedures that guides scientific investigation.* The sociologist is interested in discovering what happens in the social world and why it happens. Research methodology provides guidelines for collecting evidence about what takes place, for explaining why it takes place, and for doing so in such a way that the findings can be checked by other researchers.

The methods of sociology can be applied only to questions that can be answered by reference to observable, verifiable facts. The sociologist cannot tell us if God exists, because there is no way to test theories on the subject. But the sociologist can tell us what percentage of Americans claim to believe in God, or what reasons they have for believing in God, because these facts can be established by using appropriate research methods.

The Logic of Cause and Effect

To explain any aspect of society or social behavior, the sociologist must understand relationships of cause and effect. One basic assumption of science is that all events have causes—whether the event is a ball rolling down a hill, an atomic bomb exploding, a nation going to war, an electorate choosing a Republican over a Democrat, or a student passing an examination. A second basic assumption is that under the same circumstances, the same cause will repeatedly produce the same effect. If we did not make these assumptions, the world would be utterly unpredictable and

therefore unintelligible to us. The problem facing the sociologist is to sort out cause from effect and to determine which of several possible causes, or which combination of causes, is producing a particular effect.

Variables

Like all scientists, the sociologist analyzes cause and effect in terms of the influence of variables on one another. A *variable* is simply a characteristic that can change or differ—across time, across space, or from one individual or group to another. Differences in age, sex, race, and social class are variables. So are the rates of homicide, divorce, and narcotics addiction. So are differences in intelligence, nationality, income, and a sense of humor. Causation occurs when one variable, such as quantity of alcohol consumed, influences another variable, such as the likelihood of traffic accidents. A theory simply attempts to generalize about the influence of one variable on another: "Drunken driving contributes to traffic accidents." "Wealthy voters tend to support the Republican party." "Malnutrition causes children to perform poorly in schoolwork." All these statements serve to link variables in a cause-and-effect relationship.

Figure 2.1 There are many similarities between a courtroom and scientific procedures. In fact, both emerged in the seventeenth century, when people realized that more rigorous methods of establishing the facts were necessary. Each is concerned with objectivity: scientists must try to exclude biases from their work; judges and jurors must disqualify themselves from trials in which they are biased. Both courts and science assume that ordinary observation is fallible; they therefore have rules about what is admissible as evidence (in each case, for example, hearsay is not acceptable). In each instance careful records are kept—in the case of courts, for possible use by a superior court in the event of an appeal; in the case of science, for possible use by other scientists who wish to check the results. Both assume that their results can be replicated: scientists assume that an identical study will yield identical results with different researchers; courts assume that the same evidence would yield the same verdict with different juries.

The variable that causes the effect is called the *independent variable*, and the variable that it influences is called the *dependent variable*. Degree of drunkenness is one independent variable (though not necessarily the only one) that can produce the dependent variable of a traffic accident. Extent of wealth is an independent variable (though, again, not necessarily the only one) that can influence people to vote Republican. The same variable can, of course, be independent in one context and dependent in another. The amount of alcohol consumed is an independent variable where the quality of driving depends on it; it is a dependent variable where the extent of drunkenness depends on the amount consumed.

A *generalization* is a statement about the recurrent relationships among particular variables. A generalization applies to the whole category of variables that is being considered, not to any specific case within it. Thus, medical scientists can tell us the characteristics of the people most likely to suffer a heart attack at some time in their lives, but they cannot tell us precisely which individuals will be affected. In the same way, a sociologist can tell us about the general characteristics of the marriages most likely to end in divorce, but cannot predict the fate of specific marriages. All generalizations in science are statements of *probability*—not certainty—for the entire category of variables under consideration.

Correlations

Determining cause and effect, then, involves tracing the effect of variables upon one another. But how does the sociologist find out if a relationship exists between variables?

The basic method is to establish whether there is a *correlation* between the variables—that is, whether they are associated together in a regular, recurrent fashion. By analyzing the statistics, the sociologist can easily establish whether there is a correlation between malnutrition and poor school performance or between drunken driving and traffic accidents. In both cases, the evidence shows conclusively that the correlation is very high. This seems to prove the case. But does it?

Logically, no. The fact that two variables correlate highly does not prove that one caused the other, or even that they are related in any way at all. The following example should make this clear. In North America there is a high correlation between the sale of ice cream and the incidence of rape. The more ice cream that is sold, the more likely it is that rapes will occur. If a high correlation between these two variables were sufficient to prove a causal connection, we would have to conclude that eating ice cream causes rape or, alternatively, that rape causes people to eat huge amounts of ice cream. Clearly, neither of these theories is acceptable: they fail to link the facts in a meaningful way. But what explains the correlation? A moment's thought suggests the answer, in the form of a third variable that influences the other two: the heat of summer. People eat more ice cream when it is hot than when it is cold. Rapes are far more likely to occur in the summer than in the winter, partly because people are more likely to venture out of their homes at night and partly because the nature of rape is such that the act is not easily performed outdoors in freezing weather. The rape–ice cream correlation exists, but it is *spurious*. In other words, it is merely coincidental and does not imply any causal relationship whatever. Spurious correlations present a constant trap for the careless researcher.

Controls

How, then, can we determine whether a correlation between two variables is a causal one? To find out, sociologists must apply *controls*—ways of excluding the possibility that some other factors might be influencing the relationship that interests them. It might be, for example, that most people who drive when they are drunk do their drunken driving after dark and that poor visibility, not alcohol consumption, is the prime cause of the accidents. The sociologist has to control this variable by comparing the accident rates of both drunken and sober drivers during daylight and at night. If the drunken drivers are still proportionately more likely to become involved in traffic accidents under both driving conditions, the possibility that visibility is an influencing variable is eliminated. Similarly, it might be that children who are malnourished typically do not have a father in the home and therefore lack paternal encouragement in their academic work. Again, the sociologist has to control for this possibility by comparing the school performance of both well-nourished and malnourished children with and without a father in the home.

Basic Statistical Terms

Although some sociological research uses sophisticated mathematics, introductory students will be able to find their way through most sociological writing by relying on a few basic statistical concepts. The concepts you will encounter most frequently are those of averages and correlations.

Averages. The word "average" is often used loosely in ordinary conversation. There are actually three different ways of calculating averages, or *central tendencies,* and each method can produce a different figure from the same data.

Suppose a researcher has studied nine individuals and finds that their annual incomes are

$3000	$3800	$9000
$3000	$6500	$9000
$3500	$9000	$150,000

For some purposes it may be sufficient to present all this information in the form given above, but it is often more useful to provide a single figure that reveals the central tendency of all the numbers involved.

The *mode* is the number that appears most often in the data. In our example the mode is $9000. Although it is sometimes useful for the researcher to show which figure recurs most frequently, the mode has the disadvantage of not giving any idea of the range of the data as a whole.

The *mean* is the figure obtained by dividing the total of all the figures by the number of individual cases involved. In this case the total is $196,800; divided by nine, it gives a mean figure of $21,866.66. The mean has the advantage of taking account of all the data, but it can give misleading results. In our example, the central tendency is distorted by the presence of one extreme figure, $150,000, which hides the fact that all the other individuals

earn $9000 a year or less. (The mean is the measure of central tendency that we usually call the "average" in ordinary speech.)

The *median* is the number that falls midway in a range of numbers; in our example, it would be $6500. If the number of cases were an even rather than an odd number—say, ten instead of nine—the median would be the mean ("average") of the two numbers in the middle, namely the fifth and sixth items. The median is sometimes useful because it does not allow extreme cases, such as the income of $150,000, to distort the central tendency. Sociologists often present an average in more than one form, particularly when a single measure might give a misleading impression.

Correlations. A correlation expresses the strength of a relationship between two variables; it is usually expressed as a number called a *correlation coefficient.* When two variables have absolutely no consistent relationship to one another (as in the case of volcanic eruptions in Japan and the birth rate in Dallas), the correlation coefficient is zero. When one variable is always associated with the other (as in the case of the moon's gravitational pull and the oceans' tides), there is a perfect *positive* correlation, expressed as a correlation coefficient of 1.0. Weak positive correlations of around 0.2 or 0.3 are not very significant, but stronger correlations of around 0.6 and above indicate an increasingly significant relationship between the variables. When the presence of one variable is always associated with the absence of the other (as in the case of snowstorms and sunbathers), there is a perfect *negative* correlation, and the correlation coefficient is −1.0.

A high correlation coefficient may suggest a causal relationship between the variables involved, but it is always possible that the correlation is coincidental or is produced by a third variable that influences the other two. Correlations therefore have to be interpreted with great care.

Only when the sociologist has controlled for the other possibilities—often a difficult task, because some possibilities are not immediately obvious and may be overlooked—can it be said with confidence that a causal connection exists between the variables. In the cases of our drunken drivers and malnourished children, a high correlation still exists when other possible independent variables have been eliminated. Have we now proved conclusively that malnutrition causes poor school performance and that drunken driving causes traffic accidents?

Not necessarily. The fact that variable A has a causal connection with variable B does not necessarily mean that A causes B. Until we probe deeper, we can conclude with equal justification that B causes A. In other words, the fact that a causal relationship exists between two variables does not tell us which is the independent and which is the dependent variable. That remains to be established, by one or both of two methods.

The first method is to make a logical, realistic assessment about which of the two possibilities is more likely. Either drunken driving causes traffic accidents, or traffic accidents cause some drivers to immediately become drunk. Either malnutrition causes poor school performance, or poor school performance causes malnutrition. In each case the latter relationship is logically impossible—ridiculous, in fact—and we can dismiss it, leaving the former as the only remaining possibility. In most instances, simple logic will tell us which variable influences which.

Sometimes, however, this kind of analysis does not yield such an obvious answer. We may find, for example, that there is a high correlation between drug abuse and dropping out of college. We may be able to eliminate the possibility that some third variable, such as low grades, has produced the other two and that the relationship between drug abuse and dropping out of college is causal, not spurious. But which causes which? One person's hunch might be that dropping out makes people more likely to abuse drugs; another person's hunch might be that drug abuse makes people more likely to drop out. Both conclusions seem reasonable. To determine which is the independent (causal) variable and which is the dependent (resulting) variable, a second logical approach is needed—one that considers the variable of *time*. An event that causes another event must always precede it. If students drop out first and use drugs afterward, then dropping out is the independent variable; if they abuse drugs first and then drop out, drug abuse is the independent variable. We can also use this method to validate further our conclusions about malnourished children and drunken drivers, by asking which came first—the malnutrition or poor school performance, the drunkenness or the accidents?

Misinterpretation of cause-and-effect relationships between variables is a major source of sloppy thinking, not only in everyday common-sense understandings of the world but sometimes also in scientific writings. An association between variables must be studied carefully before valid conclusions about a cause-and-effect relationship can be drawn.

Difficulties in Sociological Research

As we noted in Chapter 1, the sociologist's subject matter presents some research problems of a kind that natural scientists rarely have to deal with. The sociologist's subjects are not inanimate objects or unreflecting animals. They are people who are self-aware, who have complex individual personalities, and who are capable of choosing their own courses of action for both rational and irrational reasons. The fact that the sociologist is studying human beings poses five major problems to research methodology.

1 *The mere act of investigating social behavior may alter the very behavior that is being investigated.* When people know they are being studied, they may not behave as they normally would. Suppose, for example, that a sociologist who was studying family interaction patterns visited your home. Would your family behave in exactly the same way as usual? The presence, personality, and actions of the observer can affect the behavior under investigation. Sometimes the problem is compounded when the subjects know or guess (correctly or incorrectly) what the sociologist is trying to find out: they may try to "help" by consciously or unconsciously behaving in ways they feel will conform to the researcher's expectations.

2 *People—unlike bacteria or hydrogen atoms—have emotions, motives, and other highly individual personality characteristics.* They may give false information deliberately, to put themselves in a better light, or unintentionally, because they misinterpret a question or do not understand the reasons for their own behavior or attitudes. They may also behave in unpredictable ways for a variety of peculiar reasons of their own, something inanimate objects do not do. As a result, sociological explanations and predictions are often less precise than those of the natural sciences.

3 *The origins of social behavior are almost always extremely complex, involving many social, psychological, historical, and other factors.* It is usually much more difficult for the sociologist than for the natural scientist to sort out cause and effect because so many more variables tend to be involved. It is relatively easy to establish why water boils or what the effect of pressure is on the volume of a gas. It is much more difficult to establish why people fall in love, or why they fall in love with the people that they do.

Figure 2.2 Running stark naked through a public place, or "streaking," was an international but short-lived fad of the early seventies. Study of the behavior offers an example of some of the difficulties faced by social scientists in their research. (1) By observing, photographing, or interviewing a streaker, the researcher might alter the very behavior that is being studied. (2) The streaker's behavior, unlike that of a virus or a molecule, is highly personal and unpredictable; it is difficult to know when, where, or how the behavior might occur. (3) The reasons for the emergence and disappearance of the fad are very complex and hard to untangle. (4) Streaking is essentially spontaneous and is therefore difficult to study under controlled conditions. (5) The researcher might have a personal attitude toward streaking—perhaps of amusement, perhaps of disgust—and this may hamper objective analysis. Natural scientists rarely face problems like these.

4 *It is not permissible, for ethical reasons, to perform certain kinds of experiments on human beings.* The natural scientist has no moral qualms about experimenting with rays of light and often few qualms about experimenting with animals. But the dignity and privacy of human beings must be respected. We cannot deliberately raise boys as girls to see what effect the experience would have on their later sex-role adjustment, however interesting and valuable the findings might be. Nor can we arrange to have parents ill-treat their children so that we can trace the effects on personality, no matter how useful the results might be to social workers or psychiatrists. Ethical considerations place severe limitations on the methods the sociologist can use.

5 *The sociologist, unlike the natural scientist, is part of the very subject he or she is studying.* It is therefore much more difficult to maintain a detached attitude. The geologist may be interested in establishing the composition of a particular rock sample but is unlikely to be emotionally involved in the findings. The sociologist, who may be studying such issues as race relations or poverty, can become passionately involved in the outcome of the research. The researcher may identify strongly with the problems and experiences of the subjects, and there is a risk that the process of investigation and interpretation will be distorted as a result.

All sociologists recognize these problems, but not all are agreed on how to deal with them. Some focus on refining statistical and similar techniques, modeling their methodology as closely as possible after the example of the natural sciences. They aim to make sociology as exact a science as possible. Others protest that excessive dependence on these methods produces mounds of figures but very little understanding. Instead, these sociologists often rely on their own subjective descriptions and interpretations of behavior, even when these may be difficult for others to verify. Debate between the more zealous advocates of each approach has at times become heated. Advocates of a strongly interpretative approach have referred to sociologists relying on computers and statistical techniques as "number crunchers" or "the IBM mafia," while advocates of the latter approach have dismissed the descriptive writings of the other camp as "pop sociology" or a "sociology of pot smokers." Most sociologists, however, probably accept the viewpoint expressed by Max Weber many decades ago. Weber believed that sociology must model itself as far as possible on the natural sciences but that its subject matter, being so different, sometimes also calls for an interpretative, subjective approach.

Subjective interpretation—which Weber called *Verstehen,* or empathetic understanding—is in no sense a substitute for the scientific method. Wherever possible, the conclusions drawn from subjective interpretation must be verified scientifically. Weber himself used *Verstehen* when he was trying to prove a causal link between the beliefs of early Puritans and the development of capitalism. The Puritans, he argued, felt that they were predestined to either heaven or damnation. They could not know what their actual fate would be, but they all had the duty of working for the greater glory of God. In their anxiety to find out if they were to be saved or not, they took signs of success in work as an indication of God's favor, and so worked all the harder. But their Puritan ethic forbade them to spend the resulting income on luxurious living, so they simply reinvested it. By accumulating and reinvesting wealth—instead of immediately spending it, as others were prone to do—they unwittingly created modern capitalism. This argument seems plausible, but there is no way to prove it scientifically because we cannot know whether the Puritans really did experience this "salvation panic." Weber's method was to place himself in the Puritans' shoes in order to understand their feelings and motives. By combining his subjective interpretations of Puritan psychology with a rigorous analysis of the development of capitalism, he enhanced the richness (but not necessarily the validity) of his study.

Figure 2.3 *In attempting to establish a link between the "Protestant ethic" and the development of capitalism, Max Weber tried to gain a subjective understanding of the psychology of the early European merchants and other entrepreneurs. The resulting insights enriched Weber's work, but (as he himself emphasized) subjective interpretations alone are no substitute for scientific analysis. Such interpretations do have a place in sociology, but they must be tested where possible against verifiable facts.*

Basic Research Methods

At the heart of the research process are the actual procedures sociologists use to collect their facts. One or more of four basic methods can be used: the experiment, the survey, the observational study, and the use of existing sources of information. Each of these has its advantages and its drawbacks, and the success of a research project depends largely on the researcher's choice of an appropriate method.

Experiments

The experimental method provides a reliable way of studying the relationship between two variables under carefully controlled conditions. Experiments can be conducted either in the laboratory or in the field. In a *laboratory experiment* the subjects and any necessary materials are brought into an artificial environment that can be carefully regulated by the researcher. A *field experiment* takes place outside the laboratory under somewhat less artificial conditions, perhaps in a prison, hospital, or factory. The laboratory experiment is more appropriate when the researcher wants to control the situation in minute detail, whereas the field experiment is more suitable when the researcher wants to minimize the possibility that people will change their behavior in the laboratory setting.

The Experimental Method

In the typical experiment, an independent variable is introduced into a carefully designed situation and its influence on a dependent variable is recorded. Let's say the researcher decides to run an experiment on the effects that classroom integration has on white students' attitudes about blacks. The researcher must first measure the white students' attitudes, then introduce black students into the class, and then, after a suitable period, measure the white students' attitudes again to find out if any change has taken place. But this procedure is not enough to establish a causal link between the two variables. Any changes in the students' attitudes might have been caused by coincidental factors—racial disturbances in the neighborhood, perhaps, or a mass-media campaign against racism that happened to take place while the experiment was in progress.

The researcher therefore has to control the situation in such a way that other possible influences can be discounted. The standard method of doing this would be to divide the white students into two groups whose members are similar in all relevant respects. Both groups are then tested on their racial attitudes, but only one group, the *experimental group*, is exposed to classroom integration. The other group, the *control group*, is subjected to all the experiences of the experimental group except integration. Finally, both groups are again tested on their racial attitudes. Any difference between the groups is assumed to be the result of the independent variable.

The "Hawthorne Effect"

One of the best-known experiments in sociology was conducted before World War II at the Hawthorne plant of Western Electric (Roethlisberger and Dickson, 1939). The management was eager to improve productivity and wanted to know what kind of incentives would encourage the workers to increase output. The researcher who inves-

tigated the problem, Elton Mayo, separated a group of women from the other workers and systematically varied lighting, coffee breaks, lunch hours, methods of payment, and so on. At first, Mayo and his associates were delighted: each new change increased levels of productivity. But when the researchers found that productivity rose no matter which variables were involved, they became suspicious. When the workers were finally returned to their original conditions, their productivity rose yet again! Something was seriously wrong with the researchers' theoretical assumptions. Whatever had caused the changes in the dependent variable—productivity—it was not the independent variables the experimenters had introduced, and from this point of view the experiment was a failure. But the reasons for the experiment's failure have taught sociologists a great deal. Production rose, it seems, because the women enjoyed all the attention they were getting: they became a tight-knit, cooperative group, they knew what effects the sociologists were trying to produce, and they did their best to please. This phenomenon—the contamination of the experiment by the subjects' assumptions about what the sociologist is trying to prove—is still known as the *Hawthorne effect*.

The experimental method is useful because it allows the researcher to investigate specific topics that often cannot be systematically examined under everyday conditions, where so many other influences might conceal or distort the processes involved. The method has some disadvantages, however. It can be used only for narrowly defined issues. People may behave very differently in the artificial experimental situation than they would in the world beyond. And experimenters may sometimes unwittingly produce the effect they are looking for.

Surveys

Surveys are frequently used in sociological research, either simply for the purpose of getting facts (such as the political opinions of college students) or for finding out about the relationship between facts (such as how sex, parental opinions, or social class influences students' political views).

The total group of people whose attitudes or behavior the sociologist is interested in is called the *population*. It may consist of all students in college, all mothers with children under the age of five, all twins in the state of Nevada, or the entire nation. In some cases it is possible to survey the entire population, but time and expense make this procedure impractical unless the population is a small one. In most cases it is necessary to survey a *sample,* a small number of individuals drawn from the larger population. This sample must accurately represent the population in question. If it does not, then any conclusions are valid only for the actual people who were surveyed—the *respondents*—and cannot be applied to the entire population from which the sample was drawn. (The same is true, incidentally, of experiments: the findings of an experiment cannot be generalized to a larger population unless the subjects are representative of the population concerned.)

In 1936, the popular magazine *Literary Digest* conducted an opinion poll to predict the outcome of that year's presidential election. Millions of names were selected from telephone directories and automobile registration lists, and 2 million responses were obtained. The results pointed to a landslide victory for the Republican candidate, Alfred E. Landon, who had a lead of nearly 15 percentage points over his Democratic opponent. If you have never heard of Alfred E. Landon, you need not be unduly concerned by your ignorance. He was beaten by Franklin D. Roosevelt in every state except Maine and Vermont and disappeared into the footnotes of the history texts. The correct outcome of the election was predicted, however, by a young man named George Gallup, who used a much smaller sample for his purposes. The *Literary Digest* became a national laughingstock and soon went out of business, while the Gallup poll has become a regular feature of the American scene.

Why was Gallup's poll so much more reliable than the *Literary Digest*'s, even though it used a much smaller sample? The answer, of course, is that Gallup's sample was more representative than the *Literary Digest*'s. During the Depression years only middle- and upper-class people could afford telephones and automobiles, and these people tended to be Republican. As a result, lower- and working-class people, who were overwhelmingly Democratic, were largely excluded from the sample. In effect, the poll was a survey of how a predominantly Republican sample intended to vote, and so it produced a wildly inaccurate prediction for the nation as a whole. Gallup was able to predict the result more accurately because his sample faithfully represented the proportions of Democrats and Republicans in the electorate.

Figure 2.4 Harry S Truman holds aloft a copy of the Chicago Daily Tribune *on the night of his victory over Thomas E. Dewey in the 1948 presidential election. The paper had gone to press before the results were announced, relying for its unfortunate headline on earlier opinion polls. In this case the polls were inaccurate primarily because polling stopped too soon before the election. In the closing stages of the campaign the great majority of the "undecideds" swung to Truman, but this trend went undetected. Modern opinion polls continue until the final days of a presidential election campaign.*

Random Samples

Whether a sample is representative has very little to do with its size. A representative sample of two or three thousand Americans can be used to predict the outcome of a presidential election to within 2 percentage points of the actual result; as we have just seen, an unrepresentative sample of several million can be hopelessly off target. The standard method of ensuring that the sample is representative is to make a *random* selection of subjects from the population concerned—that is, to make the selection in such a way that every member of the population has the same chance of being selected. The simplest way to select a random sample is perhaps to pull names out of a hat, but sociologists can use more sophisticated techniques for drawing random samples from large populations.

One method is to systematically take, say, every tenth or thirty-ninth person from the population. This must be done with care: if you were surveying your college's student population, for example, you could not obtain a random sample by asking every tenth person who walked up the library steps. All you would get would be a random sample of students who use the library and who happened to be using it at the time you made your survey. To make your sample representative you would have to draw it from a complete listing of all students. A second method of obtaining a random sample is to assign a number to each member of the population and then to select the sample by using random numbers produced by a computer. This method is the most reliable because it eliminates most sources of human error. Sometimes it is useful to divide the population into various categories—perhaps according to age, race, sex, or any other variable that one's theory suggests might be relevant—and then to draw a random sample from each category. This technique, known as *stratified random sampling,* ensures that the categories will be represented in the sample in precisely the same proportion as they occur in the population. Stratified random sampling guarantees, for example, that if people in a very high income bracket constitute 1 percent of the population, they will constitute 1 percent of the sample. The slight margin of error in ordinary random sampling may produce a sample containing virtually no people in this category, and the results of the survey may be slightly biased as a result.

Questionnaires and Interviews

A survey may use questionnaires, interviews, or a combination of the two. If the questionnaire is self-administered without an interview, the respondents are asked to complete it and often to return it by themselves. If the interview technique is used, the researcher asks the questions directly. In a structured interview the researcher has a checklist of questions and asks them in exactly the same form and exactly the same order with each respondent. The respondent is asked to choose among several predetermined answers, such as "yes/no/don't know" or "very likely/likely/unlikely/very unlikely." The structured interview is very inflexible, but it enables the researcher to make careful tabulations and comparisons of the answers. If other information about the respondents is included, such as income, geographical location, or age, all these variables can be fed

into a computer, and correlations between them can be extracted in a few seconds. By using statistical controls on the data, the researcher can often establish causal links between the different variables in the survey. The unstructured interview is much more flexible and "open-ended." The researcher puts more general questions to the respondents, allows them to answer freely, and follows up on their comments. This approach allows the researcher to get insights that a structured interview may overlook, but it has some disadvantages. The answers are often extremely difficult to compare: if people are asked, for example, "Do you intend to vote at the next election?" they will give such answers as "Maybe," "I might if I feel like it," "Depends on who's running," "I suppose so," "I haven't decided yet," and so on. The interviewer also has to be on guard against influencing the respondents' answers by such subtle signals as choice of words, tone of voice, and facial expressions.

To be useful, survey questions must be put in straightforward, unemotional language and must be phrased so that all respondents will understand them in the same way. The question "Are you religious?" is almost useless because it will be interpreted in various ways by different people; it is necessary to ask more specific questions about church attendance, belief in God, and so on. Questions should be stated in a neutral manner: one that begins "Do you agree that...?" will draw a higher proportion of affirmative responses than one that begins "Do you think that...?" Double-barreled questions, such as "Do you think that marijuana and heroin should be legalized?" inevitably produce confusion because people may have different opinions about the two drugs. The word "not" should be avoided if possible: if the researcher asks "Do you think the United States should not get militarily involved in the Middle East?" many people will read over the word "not" and misunderstand the question.

The survey is an indispensable source of information about social characteristics and the relationships among them. It is particularly useful for tracing changes in these characteristics over time, for questionnaires or interviews can be repeated at suitable intervals. The method has its disadvantages, however. People will sometimes express opinions on subjects they know nothing whatever about. (Even if people are asked to express opinions on a nonexistent law—say, the "Hodge Act"—a large minority will declare themselves for or against it!) In addition, many peo-

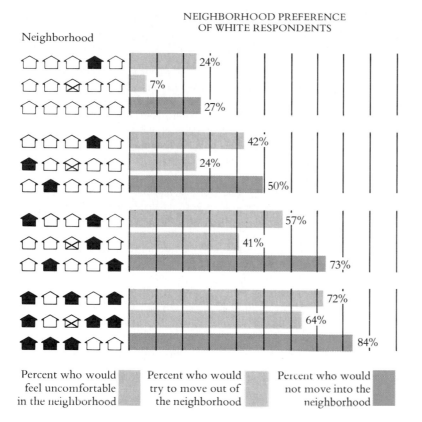

NEIGHBORHOOD PREFERENCE
OF WHITE RESPONDENTS

Neighborhood

Percent who would
feel uncomfortable
in the neighborhood

Percent who would
try to move out of
the neighborhood

Percent who would
not move into the
neighborhood

Source: Institute for Social Research *Newsletter*, University of Michigan, Summer 1979, pp. 3–5.

Figure 2.5 The results of a survey are strongly influenced by the precise wording of the questions. If white Americans are simply asked whether they would object to a black neighbor, most say they would not. But if they are asked more specific questions, a rather different picture emerges. In this survey, respondents were shown diagrams representing neighborhoods with different racial mixes (black houses and white houses). The house in the center of the neighborhood was designated "your house." The responses clearly show that whites become less willing to live in an area as the percentage of black residents increases; indeed, a quarter of whites are uncomfortable in a neighborhood where merely one home in fifteen is occupied by a black family.

ple—often more than half—fail to return self-administered questionnaires. An unsatisfactory response rate introduces bias into the sample because those who do return questionnaires may be different in important respects from those who do not—in particular, they are more likely to have strong views on the subject being surveyed. To complicate matters, at least 10 percent of American adults are not sufficiently literate to complete a questionnaire. Respondents may also give false information, particularly in face-to-face interviews. People may deny their racist views, for example, because they know these views are not "respectable." Finally, surveys rarely permit in-depth study of social behavior, and they can be expensive.

Observational Studies

Observational studies usually involve an intensive examination of a particular group, event, or social process. The researcher does not attempt to influence what happens in any way but aims instead at an accurate description and analysis of what takes place. The analysis usually traces cause-and-effect relationships, but some sociologists are content merely to give a precise account of their observations. This information often provides rich insights into social behavior and for that reason alone adds to the sum of sociological knowledge; moreover, it can be used by other researchers for other purposes.

How to Read a Table

Sociologists make considerable use of statistical tables, both as a source of data and as a way of presenting the results of their own research. You will be able to grasp the information in a table quickly if you follow a systematic procedure. Here are the main steps you should follow (using the accompanying table as a model).

1. *Read the title.* The title should tell you exactly what information the table contains. Our table tells about the willingness of Americans to vote for a female president.
2. *Look for headnotes.* Immediately below the title you will sometimes find a headnote. The headnote may give information about how the data were collected, how they are presented, or why they are presented in a particular way. In this case, the headnote tells us the exact form of the question that was asked.
3. *Examine the source.* At the bottom of a table you will find a statement of the source of the data. The source helps you to judge the reliability of the information and tells you where to find the original data if you want to check the statistics further. In the example the source is a reliable one, the Gallup poll.
4. *Read the labels.* There are two kinds of labels in a table, the column headings at the top and the headings along the left-hand side. You must make sure that you understand the labels, and you will have to keep both column and side headings in mind as you read the table. In our table the column headings represent na-

tional, female, and male opinions, while the side headings indicate the years in which the surveys were made.
5. *Find out what units are used.* The statistics in a table may be presented in hundreds, thousands, percentages, rates per 1000, rates per 100,000, and so on. Sometimes this information is not contained in the headnote but appears instead in the column or side headings. In our table, the overall column head indicates that figures are presented as percentages.
6. *Make comparisons.* Compare the data in the table, both horizontally and vertically, and notice any differences, similarities, or trends in the statistics. If you read our table horizontally, you will be able to compare the percentage of the nation willing to vote for a female president with the percentages of women and men willing to do so. If you read the table vertically, you will be able to compare opinions in any category from one year to another.
7. *Draw conclusions.* Finally, draw conclusions about the data and consider any questions that the statistics raise. You will notice, for example, that willingness to vote for a woman president has increased dramatically between 1937, when a minority of both men and women were favorable, and 1978, when an overwhelming majority of both sexes would vote for a woman. You will also note that in earlier years the idea of a woman president drew comparatively more support from women, but that in later years more men than women favored it, and you may want to investigate this further.

Table 2.1   WILLINGNESS OF AMERICANS TO VOTE FOR A WOMAN PRESIDENT

Question: If your party nominated a woman for president would you vote for her if she were qualified for the job?

	Would Vote for Woman President (in percent)		
	National	Women	Men
1937	34	41	27
1949	50	53	47
1955	54	59	49
1963	57	53	61
1976	76	74	78
1978	80	81	80

Source: Gallup poll.

Like the experiment, an observational study can be conducted in the laboratory or in the field. In a laboratory observation, for example, the sociologist might bring a group of subjects together and present them with a problem in order to observe the processes by which leaders emerge and decisions are made. The researcher may choose to tape-record the interaction and to watch and film it through a two-way mirror rather than risk influencing the course of events by joining the group and taking notes on the spot. In the field observation the sociologist studies something that is happening or has happened without attempting to structure the conditions of observation. Most observational studies take place in the field.

Case Studies

The most common form of field observation is the *case study*—a complete and detailed record of an event, group, or social process. Some case studies deal with events that have already taken place. The sociologist reconstructs these events through extensive interviews with the participants and by referring to other sources of data, ranging from police records to newspaper files. This method is often used for the analysis of infrequent, temporary events such as riots. Other case studies are conducted at the time the action is taking place. These "eyewitness" studies are an exceptionally rich source of sociological information and insights.

The sociologist in a case study may choose to be either a detached or a participant observer. The *detached observer* remains as aloof as possible, and the subjects may not know they are being studied. Observing from a distance may obscure the view, however. Many sociologists therefore prefer to become *participant observers,* taking part in all the activities of the people they are studying. Sometimes the participant observer makes it clear to the subjects at the outset that he or she is a sociologist; at other times the sociologist pretends to be an ordinary member of the group. The latter approach has the advantage that people will behave in more typical ways if they do not know they are being observed, and it also enables the sociologist to gain access to groups—such as some religious sects—that would not normally allow themselves to be studied. Concealing one's identity can raise serious ethical problems, however, because the sociologist is using deceit to observe the details of people's lives.

The case-study tradition in American sociology is full and varied. An influential early study was that of Robert and Helen Lynd (1929), who participated fully in the life

Figure 2.6 Sociology deals with people, and therefore with human hopes and passions, fears and frailties. Under these circumstances it is often difficult for researchers to be objective, especially when they are working with people at close hand. A sociologist who made a participant observer's study of the arrival and settlement of Cuban refugees, for example, might become deeply emotionally involved in their lives.

of the small town of Muncie, Indiana. Their case study provided fascinating details about the daily life of this community and has inspired a long series of similar studies. William Whyte (1943) became a participant observer in an Italian slum neighborhood of an American city. Sociologists had previously assumed that such a slum community would not be highly organized. Whyte showed that it was, although not along the lines dictated by middle-class values. Leon Festinger and his associates (1956) penetrated a cult whose members believed that the earth was doomed to imminent destruction but that a select few would be saved by aliens in a flying saucer. He eventually found himself on a hilltop awaiting the event with members of the cult, and he detailed their reactions when the prophecy failed. Erving Goffman (1961) spent many months as an observer in a mental hospital (he worked in the hospital as an aide). His account of how the organization of an asylum systematically depersonalizes the patients and may even aggravate their problems has been influential. Ned Polsky (1964) spent long periods as a participant observer with poolroom hustlers, noting how they "set up" their victims and analyzing their code of ethics. Elliot Liebow (1967), a white man, joined a group of apparently aimless black men who "hung out" on street corners. He was eventually able to win the confidence of the group and

to provide a detailed account of its members' lives. John Lofland (1966) participated in a religious cult—the "Moonies"—at a time when it had only a handful of converts, and he was later (1977) able to use the knowledge from his case study to analyze the reasons for the cult's subsequent rapid growth.

Observational studies of this kind place a heavy obligation on the sociologist. The identities of informants must be protected, especially when their behavior is disreputable. Systematic notes must be kept each day while memory is fresh. The observer must be careful not to influence the behavior he or she is studying. Gaining access to the group and winning the trust of its members can be extremely difficult, especially if the backgrounds of the sociologist and the subjects are dissimilar. The assumption behind participant observation is that some things can be fully understood only by intimate experience of them, but the method relies heavily on the skills and subjective interpretations of the observer.

Observational studies have the advantage that they come to grips with real-life situations, thereby offering insights that years of experimenting and surveying might overlook. They have the disadvantage, however, of sacrificing scientific precision to some extent. The observer may misinterpret events, may unwittingly ignore things that are

Figure 2.7 Infrequent, spontaneous events, such as riots, usually have to be studied after they have taken place. It would be almost impossible to make an objective analysis on the spot, even if a trained researcher happened to be there at the time. Such events can often be reconstructed and analyzed through a retrospective case study.

relevant and focus on things that are trivial, and may become so emotionally involved with the lives of the subjects that objectivity suffers. Another disadvantage is that the findings of a single observational study cannot be generalized to all apparently similar cases. The phenomenon that has been studied may have been exceptional in unknown but important ways, so findings in one case cannot be uncritically applied to what seem on the surface to be parallel situations.

Existing Sources

Sometimes the sociologist does not have to generate new information through experiments, surveys, or observational studies. The relevant data may already exist and merely have to be collected and analyzed. A great deal of useful information is available in published or unpublished form, whether it consists of the statistics issued by government agencies, newsreels, diaries, letters, court records, works of art and literature, or the research findings of other social scientists.

One of the most important sources of information for the American sociologist is the population census report published every ten years by the U.S. Bureau of the Census and supplemented annually with a wealth of information on subjects ranging from birth and death rates to details of income, sex ratios, and urbanization trends. Other government departments issue statistical data every year on subjects as diverse as education, trade, health, transport, and military spending. Similar material for Canadian society is issued by Statistics Canada, a government agency that collects important social, economic, and other data.

Another important source of existing information is the accumulated body of sociological research. Information from this source can be collected and reinterpreted; findings of previously isolated reports can be related to one another in new and revealing ways; the data that one sociologist collected to answer one question can often be used by another sociologist to answer a different question.

Durkheim's Study of Suicide

Emile Durkheim's classic study of suicide, first published in 1897, remains an outstanding example of the use of existing sources. Durkheim wanted to find out why people commit suicide, and he suspected that explanations focusing on the psychology of the individual were inadequate. Experiments on suicide were obviously out of the question. Case studies of past suicides would be of little use, because they could not provide reliable generalizations about all suicides. Survey methods were hardly appropriate, because one cannot survey dead people. But statistics on suicide were readily available, and Durkheim chose to analyze them.

Durkheim was able to dismiss some theories of suicide—such as the possibility that suicidal tendencies are inherited—by applying statistical controls to the data and eliminating these variables. He was left with an interesting and suggestive pattern: the incidence of suicide varied from one social group to another and did so in a consistent manner over the years. Protestants were more likely to commit suicide than Catholics; people in large cities were more likely to commit suicide than people in small communities; people living alone were more likely to commit suicide than people living in families. Durkheim isolated one independent variable that lay behind these differences: the extent to which the individual was integrated into a social bond with others. People with fragile ties to their community are more likely to take their own lives than people who have stronger ties.

Durkheim then considered a form of suicide that is more typical of traditional societies: the suicide that takes place because it is expected by the community. In ancient Rome or traditional Japan, for example, a suicide was regarded as a highly honorable act under some circumstances. In traditional Indian society, a widow was sometimes expected to throw herself on her husband's funeral pyre and was considered a dutiful wife if she did so. In these cases it is not the weakness but the strength of the individual's ties to the community that accounts for the suicide. People in these societies may actually take their own lives in response to social expectations they themselves share, whereas in our society they may take their lives because they do not share social expectations with anybody.

Durkheim was thus able to show that suicide—surely the most individual act anyone is capable of—can be fully understood only in its social context, particularly in terms of the presence or absence of shared social expectations that influence individual behavior. To understand why a specific person commits suicide, of course, we must look at that person's personality and the pressures to which he or she has been subjected. To understand why suicide rates are

Figure 2.8 Suicide is a highly individual act, yet the motives for a suicide can be fully understood only by reference to the social context in which it occurs. The Vietnamese Buddhist monk is publicly burning himself to death as a form of political protest; his act is one of principled self-sacrifice for a moral cause. The young American leaping to his death probably has very different reasons, stemming from loneliness, despair, and a lack of close and meaningful bonds with other people.

higher for some groups than for others, however, we have to look at the larger social forces that predispose individuals to suicide. Durkheim's insight—that individual behavior can be fully understood only by referring to the social environment—has become the basis of the modern sociological perspective. And his careful, systematic use of the evidence he gleaned from existing sources helped to establish sociology as something more than inspired speculation: it proved that the young discipline was a science.

A Research Model

Suppose you wanted to conduct some sociological research. Exactly how would you go about it? Most research in sociology follows the same basic, step-by-step procedure. The one outlined here is merely an ideal model, and not all sociologists stick to it in every detail, but it does provide the guidelines for most research projects.

① *Define the problem.* The first step is to choose a topic for research. The general area will usually be one in which the sociologist takes a personal interest. The specific topic can be chosen for a variety of reasons: perhaps because it raises issues of fundamental sociological importance, perhaps because it has suddenly become a focus of controversy, perhaps because research funds have become available to investigate it.

② *Review the literature.* The existing sociological research bearing on the problem must be tracked down and reviewed. Knowledge of the relevant literature is essential. It provides background information, suggests theoretical approaches, indicates which areas of the topic have already been covered and which have not, and saves the sociologist the labor and embarrassment of unwittingly duplicating research that has already been done.

③ *Formulate a hypothesis.* The research problem must be stated in such a way that it can actually be tested. This is achieved by formulating a *hypothesis,* a tentative statement that predicts a relationship between variables. The hypothesis must be stated in clearly defined terms that the researcher can operate with effectively; these terms are called *operational definitions.* The hypothesis might be "Exposure to antiracist propaganda reduces racist attitudes in the subjects." Each of these terms must then be given an operational definition: "exposure" might be an intense ten-minute session repeated once a week for three weeks; "antiracist propaganda" might consist of a film with a particular content; "racist attitudes" might be measured by a specific test; "subjects" might be volunteer sociology students or a random sample of American housewives. Different researchers may produce different operational definitions of the same terms, which is one reason why investigations of what seems to be the same subject may produce varying conclusions.

④ *Choose a research design.* The sociologist must now select one or more means of gathering data—a survey, an experiment, an observational study, the use of existing sources, or a combination of these. The advantages and disadvantages of each method must be carefully weighed because the *research design*—the actual plan for the collection and analysis of the data—is the crux of the research process.

5. *Collect the data.* The conclusions will be no better than the data on which they are based, so the researcher

A RESEARCH MODEL

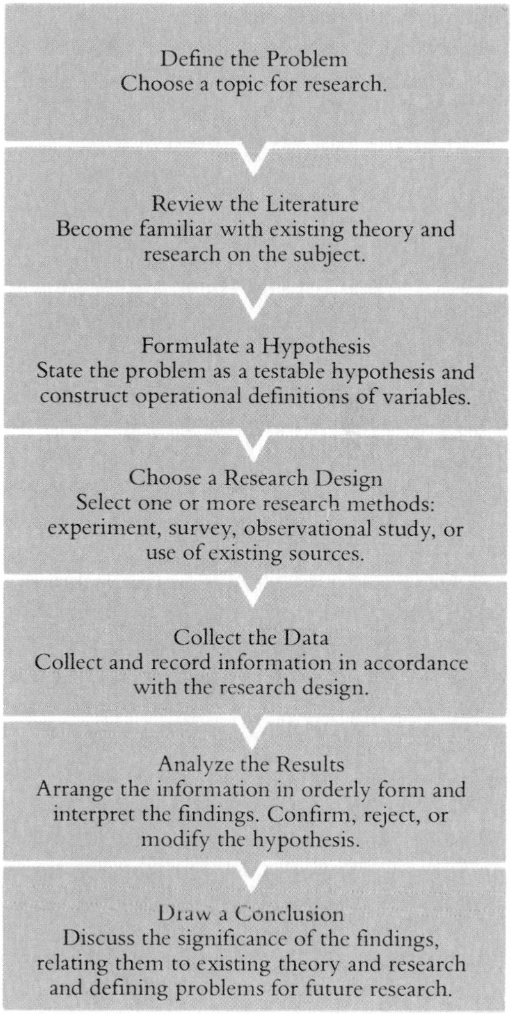

Define the Problem
Choose a topic for research.

Review the Literature
Become familiar with existing theory and research on the subject.

Formulate a Hypothesis
State the problem as a testable hypothesis and construct operational definitions of variables.

Choose a Research Design
Select one or more research methods: experiment, survey, observational study, or use of existing sources.

Collect the Data
Collect and record information in accordance with the research design.

Analyze the Results
Arrange the information in orderly form and interpret the findings. Confirm, reject, or modify the hypothesis.

Draw a Conclusion
Discuss the significance of the findings, relating them to existing theory and research and defining problems for future research.

Figure 2.9 This chart shows the seven basic steps that a researcher might follow in any sociological research project.

must take great care in collecting and recording information. As we have seen, each research method has its limitations, and the researcher must scrupulously take them into account at all times.

6. *Analyze the results.* When all the data are in, the sociologist can begin to classify the facts, clarifying trends and relationships and tabulating the information in such a way that it can be accurately analyzed and interpreted. This task also requires scrupulous attention, for a given set of facts can often be interpreted in several different ways, and the researcher has to evaluate each of these possibilities with as much objectivity as possible. The theory, as expressed in the hypothesis, can now be confirmed, rejected, or modified.

7. *Draw a conclusion.* Assuming that all has gone as planned, the sociologist can now draw up a succinct report of the project, tracing the steps already mentioned and concluding with a discussion of the findings. The report will relate the conclusions to the existing body of theory and research, suggesting where current assumptions should be modified to take account of the new evidence. The report may also identify unanswered questions that seem to call for further research, and the sociologist may suggest new hypotheses that others can explore. If the research makes a significant contribution to sociological knowledge, it may be published, probably in the form of an article in a scholarly journal. It then becomes the common property of the scientific community, whose members can attempt to *replicate* the study—that is, repeat it to verify the findings—if they wish to do so.

Being an ideal, this model does not reveal the messiness that often accompanies the actual process of research. It tells us nothing, for instance, about the sheer frustrations, the inspired guesses, or the pure luck involved in research. Then, too, some researchers hardly use the model at all; they are more interested in describing social behavior and leaving it at that. Some researchers start with a vaguely defined hypothesis but continually modify it and their operational definitions as they go along. Sometimes the data disprove the hypothesis the researcher had in mind at the beginning but seem to prove some other hypothesis he or she had not thought of. The researcher may then try to fit the facts to the new hypothesis. The final report, however, should make clear what happened and why.

Ethical Issues

Sociological research sometimes runs into serious ethical problems. One of two types of dilemmas is usually involved. The first concerns the use to which the sociologist's work is put. Sociological research on propaganda techniques, for example, might be used by advertisers to sell worthless goods, or research on political movements could be used by people who are interested in suppressing those movements. Such possibilities may also raise questions about the relationship between the researcher and those who fund the research, particularly when the funders specify the topic. The second kind of dilemma concerns the sociologist's intrusions into people's private lives, especially when the subjects are engaged in deviant or illegal behavior. Sociologists who do not declare their professional identities to their subjects may be gathering information under false pretenses, and a violation of trust may be involved. An example of each type of problem will illustrate the issues.

Project Camelot

The U.S. military has long been a major source of funds for scientific research at universities and elsewhere. These funds have been used to support the research projects of natural scientists, often for the purpose of refining military technology and weaponry. In 1964, however, the army made a major attempt to recruit social scientists for research on Project Camelot.

The objective of this project was "to devise procedures for assessing the potential for internal war within national societies" and "to identify . . . those actions which a government might take to relieve conditions which are assessed as giving rise to a potential for internal war." Moreover, it was intended that "the geographical orientation of the research will be toward Latin American countries." In plain English, the army wanted to know how to predict and avoid revolutions in Latin America. The results of the research, then, could be used to interfere in the domestic affairs of other nations. Several million dollars were made available for the project, and many social scientists agreed to participate in it.

The project was aborted within a year. News of the research and the source of its funds was leaked in Chile,

Figure 2.10 The horror of revolutionary war in Latin America may seem far removed from the world of the sociologist in the United States—but many American social scientists became deeply involved in Project Camelot, a Pentagon attempt to learn more about revolutions in order that they might be prevented.

where it caused an immediate furor. The U.S. ambassador complained to the federal government, and both Congress and the State Department applied pressure to have the project canceled. The military backed down, and Project Camelot was abandoned. But the affair contributed to a persistent wariness in other countries about the motives of American social scientists. American sociologists conducting research abroad still encounter the suspicion that they are working for the CIA or some other branch of the U.S. government.

Why did the social scientists allow themselves to become involved in the project? Irving Louis Horowitz (1967) found that they did not regard themselves as "spies," nor were they interested in maintaining antidemocratic regimes in Latin America. They described themselves as "reformers" whose insights into the real causes of revolutions—poverty and oppression—might "educate" the army. None of them actually believed, however, that the military would take their recommendations seriously. They had been presented with an opportunity to do major research with almost unlimited funds, and they simply overlooked some of the ethical issues involved.

Sociological research is not self-supporting. It depends on the grants of public and private institutions, and the line between accepting a grant from them and working for them is a thin one. Sociologists have to be aware that their research may be put to questionable uses, including some they may not be able to foresee.

"Tearoom Trade"

In 1970, Laud Humphreys published *Tearoom Trade*, an observational study of homosexual acts that took place between strangers in certain men's rest rooms that were used almost exclusively for sexual encounters ("tearooms"). Only a tiny minority of people with homosexual inclinations participate in this highly impersonal form of sexual activity, and Humphreys was interested in finding out more about the special characteristics of those who do. Because the participants wanted to avoid any involvement with juveniles or the police, one person always served as a lookout. By taking this role, Humphreys was able to observe hundreds of sexual encounters without his identity as an outsider becoming known.

To get further information, Humphreys noted the automobile registration numbers of the participants and traced their addresses. After waiting a year to ensure that he would not be recognized, he visited their homes under the guise of a survey researcher looking for information on a quite different topic. He was thus able to obtain a great deal more information about them—including, for example, the surprising fact that the majority of them were married and living with their wives. Humphreys's ingenious study won the C. Wright Mills award of the Society for the Study of Social Problems for outstanding research, but it was strongly criticized by some sociologists and by editorial writers in the press.

One charge was that Humphreys was a "snooper," delving into a subject unworthy of professional study. This is a criticism few sociologists would accept. All sociologists are in some sense "snoopers," and research cannot be excluded simply because some people find its subject matter distasteful. A second criticism was that Humphreys had endangered his subjects by recording details of their illegal acts and by keeping lists of their names and addresses. If the material had fallen into the wrong hands, blackmail, extortion, or arrest could have followed. Humphreys replied that he had kept his list of names secure in a bank deposit box, that he once allowed himself to be arrested rather than disclose his identity to the police, that he eventually destroyed his data, and that he took every precaution to conceal the identities of the participants in his report. Humphreys's attitude seems to have been a responsible one, but the fact remains that other researchers would not necessarily have been as careful. The third and most serious criticism was that Humphreys had used systematic deception, both to observe the sexual encounters and later to gain entry to the subjects' homes. In the second edition of his book (1975), Humphreys acknowledges the force of this criticism and agrees that he should have identified himself as a researcher, even at the cost of sacrificing some sources of information. His dilemma highlights a problem that keeps recurring in sociological research: the distinction between legitimate investigation and unjustified intrusion is often difficult to make. In many marginal cases there are no clear guidelines for ethical conduct, and the sociologist may have to make a personal decision on the issue.

Summary

1. Research methodology refers to the system of rules, principles, and procedures that regulates scientific investigation. Reliable research findings can be produced only by the use of a reliable research method.

2. All events have causes, and the task of science is to trace these causes in the form of the influence of variables upon one another. Generalizations are statements of probability about relationships between particular variables and can be used for the purposes of explanation and prediction.

3. Cause and effect can be traced by establishing correlations between variables. It is necessary, however, to apply controls to analysis—ways of excluding the possibility that some variable other than the one being studied is influencing the relationship under investigation. Logical analysis is also necessary to establish that a relationship is causal, not spurious.

4. Sociological research presents several difficulties that derive from the nature of the subject matter: the act of investigating behavior may change the behavior; people may behave in unpredictable ways; the origins of social behavior are extremely complex; certain kinds of experiments cannot be performed on human beings; and the sociologist's personal involvement with the subjects can introduce bias.

5. Some of these problems can be resolved by combining a rigorous scientific methodology with subjective interpretation, which Weber called *Verstehen*. Subjective interpretation on its own, however, is no substitute for the scientific method.

6. There are four basic methods of sociological research. The experiment is useful for narrowly defined issues in which independent variables can be introduced into controlled situations. The survey is useful for obtaining facts about a population, but the sample must be random if it is to be representative. Observational studies, particularly case studies, are useful for in-depth analyses of social processes but rely heavily on the skills of the researcher. Existing sources can often be used to establish new relationships between facts.

7. An ideal research model consists of the following basic steps: defining the problem, reviewing the literature, formulating a hypothesis, choosing a research design, collecting the necessary data, analyzing the results, and drawing a conclusion.

8. Sociological research poses important ethical problems, notably those involving the use to which research is put and those involving intrusion on the privacy of others. Project Camelot and *Tearoom Trade* illustrate problems of each type.

Important Terms

methodology (29)

variable (30)

independent variable (31)

dependent variable (31)

generalization (31)

correlation (31)

spurious correlation (31)

controls (31)

Verstehen (35)

experiment (35)

experimental group (36)

control group (36)

Hawthorne effect (36)

survey (36)

population (36)

sample (36)

respondent (37)

random sample (37)

stratified random
   sample (38)

case study (41)

detached observation (41)

participant
   observation (41)

hypothesis (45)

operational
   definition (45)

research design (45)

replication (46)

Suggested Readings

BABBIE, EARL R. *The Practice of Social Research.* 2nd ed. Belmont, Calif.: Wadsworth, 1979.

An excellent text, providing a clear and comprehensive coverage of social science research methods.

DIENER, EDWARD, and RICH CRANDALL. *Ethics in Social and Behavioral Research.* Chicago: University of Chicago Press, 1978.

A good introduction to ethical issues in research on human subjects, the book includes actual examples of the ethical dilemmas researchers have faced.

GLAZER, MYRON. *The Research Adventure.* New York: Random House, 1972.

An interesting account of several sociological research projects. Each example is chosen to illustrate the challenges and problems the researchers had to overcome.

HAMMOND, PHILIP E. (ed.). *Sociologists at Work.* New York: Basic Books, 1964.

A collection of firsthand essays by sociologists on how they conducted their own research projects.

HUFF, DARRELL, and IRVING GEIS. *How to Lie with Statistics.* New York: Norton, 1954.

A short and readable volume on the use and abuse of statistics. The writers alert the reader to the many ways statistics can be misleadingly presented or interpreted.

SANDERS, WILLIAM B. (ed.). *The Sociologist as Detective: An Introduction to Research Methods.* New York: Praeger, 1974.

A useful anthology of articles about sociological research. In his introduction and overviews, the editor draws interesting parallels between the work of social researchers and detectives.

UNIT 2 *The Individual, Culture, and Society*

The theme of this unit is the dynamic interrelationship among individuals, their society, and its culture. The personality and social behavior of individuals are deeply influenced by the culture and society in which they happen to live, while culture and society are themselves produced and maintained by the interaction of countless individuals.

The first chapter in the unit discusses culture—that is, the total way of life of a society. The second focuses on society itself, showing how every society has a social structure that helps it to "work" in a fairly smooth and predictable way. We then explore socialization, the process through which the human animal becomes a fully social being by learning the culture of his or her society. Then we take a close-up view of social interaction, showing how sociological analysis can throw fascinating light on the taken-for-granted reality of our everyday lives. The following chapter discusses social groups, both small and large, and the ways in which groups can influence the behavior of their members. The next chapter turns to the problem of deviance—that is, behavior that violates the cultural expectations of a society. Finally, we discuss human sexuality as a specific example of the complex process by which individual, culture, and society interact in the shaping of human behavior and social life.

CHAPTER 3 *Culture*

Human beings, unlike other animals, are not born with rigid, complex, behavior patterns that enable them to survive in specific habitats. Instead, they must learn and invent ways of adapting to many different environments, ranging from arctic snows to desert wastelands and teeming cities. These learned ways of life, which are modified and passed on from one generation to the next, are what sociologists call "culture." An understanding of culture is basic to the understanding of human social life.

In ordinary speech, the word "culture" is often used to refer to sophisticated tastes in art, literature, or music. The sociological use of the term is much wider, for it includes the entire way of life of a society. In this sense, everyone who participates in society is "cultured." To the sociologist, *culture consists of all the shared products of human society*. These products are of two basic kinds, material and nonmaterial. *Material culture* consists of all the artifacts, or physical objects, human beings create and give meaning to—wheels, clothing, schools, factories, cities, books, spacecraft, totem poles. *Nonmaterial culture* consists of more abstract creations—languages, ideas, beliefs, rules, customs, myths, skills, family patterns, political systems.

It is possible, at least conceptually, to distinguish "culture" from "society." Culture consists of the shared *products* of society; society consists of the interacting *people* who share a culture. But the two are closely interrelated. A society could not exist without culture. A culture cannot exist without a society to maintain it (except, perhaps, in the form of archaeological ruins and historical records). Society and culture are closely linked, and because the English language does not have a word meaning "culture-and-society," sociologists often use either word interchangeably to refer to the complex whole. In this chapter,

53

Figure 3.1 *Modern Egyptians enact a cultural ritual by praying in the direction of Mecca, and in doing so, they turn their backs on the idols of ancient Egypt. Culture and society are interwoven, and neither can exist without the other—although cultural artifacts may outlast the society that created them.*

however, we shall try as far as possible to keep the two concepts distinct and shall use the term "culture" in its more specific sense.

The anthropologist Clifford Geertz (1968) observes that noncultured human beings "do not in fact exist, never have existed, and most important, could not in the nature of the case exist." Without culture, neither individual human beings nor human society could survive. To understand why this is so, we must examine the unique characteristics of our own species.

The Human Species: What Kind of Animal?

"What a piece of work is man!" exclaims Hamlet in Shakespeare's play. "How noble in reason! How infinite in faculty! In form, how moving, how express and admirable! In action, how like an angel! In apprehension, how like a god! The beauty of the world! The paragon of animals! And yet . . . What is this quintessence of dust?"

What are we? Hamlet's question is probably as old as the unique human capacity for self-awareness, a capacity that extends back tens and perhaps hundreds of thousands of years into prehistory. There is no simple answer to the question, for we are a remarkable and extraordinarily complex species—the most intelligent, resourceful, and adaptable that has ever existed on the planet. In the Western world until very recently we tended to regard ourselves as completely apart from the rest of nature—as beings created in the very image of God, a little lower than the angels but far removed from the rest of the animal world. Today we have a better understanding of our place in nature. We know that we are related by ancient common ancestry to apes and eagles, sharks and lizards, that we are social animals whose bodily form and behavioral potentials have been shaped by millions of years of evolution in changing environments.

Modern science cannot give a comprehensive answer to Hamlet's question. But we do know infinitely more about the human species than we did even a few years ago, and we have learned that many traditional ideas about "human nature," some of them still very popular, are hopelessly naive and misguided. This book is about a particular animal, *Homo sapiens,* about the societies this animal forms, and about social behavior within those societies. Before we proceed to the study of culture and society, then, we must try to establish exactly what kind of creature we are talking about and which of its characteristics make it unique.

The Evolutionary Background

In 1859, Charles Darwin published *On the Origin of Species,* a book that has dramatically and permanently altered the human self-concept. With careful argument and a mass of detailed evidence, Darwin showed that all life forms are shaped by an endless process of physical evolution. Far from being created in the literal image of God, we are a recent product of an evolutionary process that can be traced back to the very beginnings of life on earth more than 3 billion years ago.

How does this process of evolution work—how do living organisms adapt to their environment from one generation to the next? The sociologist Herbert Spencer expressed the essence of the process in his phrase "the survival of the fittest." All species tend to produce far more offspring than their environment can support, and a high proportion fall victim to starvation, predators, disease, and other perils. But there is great physical variation among the individuals in any species: some are swifter, some more resistant to disease, some equipped with better eyesight, some better camouflaged. Those that have any advantage in the struggle for survival are more likely to live longer and to breed, and they therefore tend to pass on their characteristics to the next generation. Nature thus "selects" the fittest members of each species to survive and reproduce, a process Darwin called "natural selection." In time, the characteristics that are selected tend to spread throughout the entire species.

Tracing the evolution of the human species is no easy task. We have to rely for the most part on fossil evidence, and this evidence is often scanty. As a result, there are gaps of millions of years in our knowledge of our own origins. Peering into our ancestral past is like peering into a landscape shrouded in mist. The mist parts periodically to reveal the dim outlines of creatures like us yet not like us, but gradually growing more recognizably human with the passage of time.

We do know, however, that we are a member of the primate order, a group of related species that emerged relatively late in evolutionary time. The planet earth is about 4.7 billion years old. The first living organisms emerged approximately 3 billion years ago. The earliest land animals, amphibian creatures, appeared about 400 million years ago and eventually evolved into reptiles. Mammals, which evolved from reptiles about 180 million years ago, are a recent but very successful evolutionary development, primarily because they are more intelligent and adaptable than other life forms. They have an exceptional capacity to learn from experience, and in the higher mammals learning becomes progressively more important

in the determination of behavior. This development reaches its climax in human beings. Our almost total reliance on learned behavior is the single most important characteristic distinguishing us from other creatures.

The first primates emerged about 70 million years ago, and our own line diverged from that of our closest relatives, the great apes (the chimpanzee, gorilla, and orangutan), between 8 and 14 million years ago. The first distinctly human species appears in the fossil record well over 2 million years ago. What was the physical and behavioral heritage of our ancestor?

The higher primates share a number of common characteristics, all of which give us clues to our own evolutionary background. First, they tend to be very *sociable:* they live in groups with a high degree of affection and interaction among members. Second, they have high *intelligence,* with brains that are exceptionally heavy in relation to body weight. This is especially true of human beings, whose brains have evolved to an unparalleled complexity. Third, primates have *sensitive hands.* In other mammals the hands have become highly specialized: the horse has a hoof, the porpoise a flipper, the bat a wing. Other animals can only paw or nuzzle at objects, but primates can use their hands as instruments for lifting, gripping, and manipulating things. In the higher primates the thumb can be placed opposite the forefinger to give a firm, precision grip. The importance of this single characteristic cannot be overestimated: try writing, sewing, or using any tool efficiently without opposing the thumb to the forefinger! Fourth, primates are extremely *vocal;* they are among the noisiest of all species and constantly call and chatter to one another. In human beings this characteristic has developed into the capacity for language. Fifth, primates have a potential for *upright posture.* Many primate species are capable of walking on their hind legs, although they do so only rarely and for short distances. In human beings, however, bipedal (two-footed) standing and walking have become normal.

In the course of their evolution, our ancestors developed two additional characteristics. The first, found in few other animals, is the potential for *year-round mating.* Human beings do not have a breeding season, a fact that encourages mates to form stable, permanent bonds. The second, found to a much greater extent in human beings than in any other animal, is the *long period of dependence* of the human infant on adults. This lengthy dependence encourages a

*Figure 3.2 Our three closest relatives: the chim-
panzee, the gorilla, and the orangutan. For some
14 million years, our own line has evolved sepa-
rately from that of the great apes, and we have become very unlike them in several important ways.
Apart from obvious physical differences (such as
our virtual hairlessness and habitual upright posture), we have very much larger brains. As a result, we are capable of abstract thought and language, and our behavior is shaped by learning
rather than by "instinct."*

division of labor between adult females and males.
Throughout most of history, females have tended to take
responsibility for domestic and child-rearing activities, and
males have concentrated on other activities, such as hunting
and defense. The dependency period also provides the
young human being with the opportunity to learn the
cultural knowledge necessary for survival as an adult.

By about 50,000 years ago the modern human form of
Homo sapiens was achieved. The long evolutionary process
made us what we are: an almost hairless, bipedal, tool-
using, talking, family-forming, self-aware, highly intelligent social animal. Our physical form bears the evidence of
our ancestral heritage, and not always in ways convenient
to us. Our upright posture has been achieved at the cost of a
contortion of the spine into a somewhat **S**-shaped column,
making us liable to that frequent human complaint,
lower-back pain. Our pelvis and rib cage no longer provide
much support for the stomach, leaving us susceptible to
hernias and other ruptures. Finally, bipedalism has narrowed the pelvis, bringing the legs closer together. Because
our big-brained infants have a very large head in relation
to body size, this last change has made giving birth more
difficult for the woman than for the female of any other
species.

The Significance of Culture

These physical adaptations and the behavioral flexibility
offered by our huge brains have made us the most creative
species in the planet's history. *Homo sapiens* has spread to
every continent, sometimes driving other animal species to
extinction in the process. It has become the most widely
dispersed species on the planet, occupying mountains and
valleys, deserts and jungles, shorelines and tundra, yet
always finding some specialized means of living in these
widely differing environments. The total weight of all
living members of the species far exceeds that of any other
animal, and the human population is now growing so
rapidly that it will double within the next thirty-five years.

What accounts for the unprecedented success of our species? The answer, in a word, is culture. We create culture, but culture in turn creates us. We are consequently no longer the helpless victims of the environment. We make our own social environment, inventing and sharing the rules and patterns of behavior that shape our lives, and we use our learned knowledge to modify the natural environment as well. Our shared culture is what makes social life possible. Without a culture transmitted from the past, each new generation would have to solve the most elementary problems of human existence over again. It would be obliged to devise a family system, to invent a language, to discover fire, to create the wheel, and so on.

Clearly, the contents of culture cannot be genetically transmitted. There is no gene that tells us to dance the polka, to drive on the right, to believe in a particular god, to get married, or to build houses. Everything in culture is learned. Culture is thus a substitute for "instinct" as a means of responding to the environment, and it provides a vastly superior way of doing so. The emergence of a species that depends for its survival on a learned culture is perhaps the greatest breakthrough in evolutionary history.

Culture frees us from reliance on the slow, random, accidental process of physical evolution by offering us a new, purposive, efficient means of adapting to changing conditions. If we waited for natural selection to enable us to live at the North Pole, to fly to the moon, or to live under the sea, we would wait forever. But cultural inventions enable us to be insulated from the cold of the arctic, to travel in outer space, and to live in submarines—all without any recourse to physical evolution. Unlike other animals, we can self-consciously adapt to our environments and can adapt environments to meet our own needs.

"Human Nature"

A recent Harris poll found that a substantial majority of Americans agree with the statement "Human nature being what it is, there will always be wars and conflict." This finding indicates the persistence of popular but utterly misguided views about our species. The problem with such ideas about "human nature" is that they are deeply colored by the cultural beliefs of the societies in which they are found. In the industrialized countries of the world, partic-

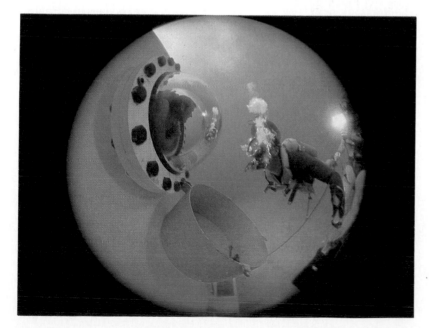

Figure 3.3 The significance of culture is that it enables us to invent and learn ways of adapting to our environments and changing situations. All other animals must rely on the slow and accidental process of biological evolution to adapt them to the environment, but human beings can adapt quickly to radically different environments.

ularly in the West, we tend to think of people as being "naturally" self-seeking, selfish, competitive, and even aggressive. But this kind of behavior is virtually unknown among many of the "primitive" peoples of the world, such as the Arapesh of New Guinea, the pygmies of the Ituri forest in central Africa, the Shoshone of the western United States, or the Lepchas of Sikkim in the Himalayas. Many societies never fight wars at all, and there is even one group, the Tasaday of the Philippines, that apparently does not even have words in its language to express enmity or hatred. These people presumably have a very different conception of "human nature" (Montagu, 1978).

Then what, exactly, is human nature? The question has been argued for thousands of years, and the debate is by no means over. In fact, it has recently become especially heated as a result of the appearance of *sociobiology,* a scientific discipline that tries to use biological principles to explain the behavior of all social animals, including human beings. In the past, biologists and others who study animal behav-

ior have usually restricted their observations to nonhuman species, but in his groundbreaking survey of sociobiology, the insect specialist Edward Wilson (1975) laid claim to human behavior as well. Social sciences such as sociology, psychology, and anthropology, he announced, would eventually be absorbed by the new discipline, because their subject matter could be better explained in terms of inborn, genetic programming. In the ensuing debate, Wilson has won the support of some biologists (although they disagree among themselves on how strong the genetic influence on human behavior is supposed to be), but, not surprisingly, he has found few allies among social scientists (Barash, 1977; Sahlins, 1977; E. Wilson, 1978; Gregory, Silvers, and Sutch, 1978; van den Berghe, 1978; Caplan, 1978; D. Freedman, 1979; Quadagno, 1979).

The quality of the debate has suffered, perhaps, from the fact that most social scientists lack the benefit of expert knowledge of genetics, while Wilson and other sociobiologists appear innocent of many basic findings of social sci-

Figure 3.4 The Tasaday, a recently discovered "stone age" tribe in the Philippines, apparently do not have words in their language to express enmity or hatred. Competition, acquisitiveness, aggression, and greed are all unknown among these gentle people. The existence of societies like the Tasaday challenges Western assumptions about "human nature."

ence research. Each camp approaches human behavior from a very different perspective. Sociobiologists, used to seeing genetically programmed behavior (such as mating rituals) in other species, are quick to assume that apparently similar behavior in human beings (such as courtship rituals) has the same origins; social scientists, whose training and experience make them sensitive to the flexibility and cultural diversity of human behavior, are apt to downplay any genetic influences. To social scientists (and to many biologists), analogies between human beings and other animal species are fundamentally faulty: one is no more justified in explaining human behavior in terms of the genetic principles that govern the behavior of, say, a sheep, than one is justified in explaining a sheep's behavior in terms of the social and psychological principles that govern human behavior. Human beings differ from other animals precisely in that their capacity for cultural learning frees them from dependence on the rigid genetic programming on which other species rely. Indeed, there is even a biological basis for this unique human feature: our huge cerebral cortex, the part of the brain that is responsible for higher mental functions such as abstract thought. The cerebral cortex is entirely absent in most animals, and even in the species that have it, such as the other primates, it is relatively undeveloped. All sheep, all swans, all shrimps behave in much the same way because their behavior closely follows a genetic blueprint. Human individuals and human cultures display such a bewildering variety of behavior because they are *not* prisoners of their genes.

The work of the sociobiologists is provocative, but thus far their attempt to apply sociobiological principles to people must be counted a failure: they have yet to prove that a single example of human social behavior is under the control of a specific gene or genes, and their theories on the subject consist exclusively of speculative analogies of dubious logic. This does not mean, of course, that there are no genetic influences on our behavior: there certainly are, but it seems that they supply the possibilities and the limits, rather than the specific content, of our actions.

"Human nature," if there is such a thing at all, is highly flexible. Our behavior is a product of an interaction between our basic biological heritage and the learning experiences of the particular culture in which we happen to live. For example, we have the biological capacity to speak, but which language we use and how we use it depend on our environment. We have the biological capacity to laugh, to cry, to blush, to become angry, but the circumstances under which we might do any of these things are learned. Nature provides us with legs, but we are not obliged to use them only for walking. We can use them to kick footballs, or to kick other people, or to ride bicycles, or to do a war dance, or to sit cross-legged while contemplating.

Most modern psychologists agree that human beings do not have any "instincts." An instinct is a *complex* pattern of behavior that is genetically determined, such as nest building in birds or termites. Any instincts we once had have been lost in the course of our evolution. The idea that we do not have instincts is difficult for some people to accept, because it seems to run counter to "common sense." One reason for the difficulty is that the word "instinct" is often used very loosely in ordinary speech. People talk about "instinctively" stepping on the brake or "instinctively" mistrusting someone, when these actions and attitudes are, in fact, culturally learned. Another reason is that much of our learned behavior is so taken for granted that it becomes "second nature" to us. The behavior seems so "natural" that we lose the awareness that it is learned, not inherited.

We do have some genetically determined types of behavior, of course, but these are *simple reflexes*—starting at an unexpected loud noise, throwing out our arms when we lose our balance, pulling back our hand when it touches a hot surface. We also have a few inborn, basic *drives*—needs for self-preservation, for food and drink, for sex, and perhaps for the company of other people. But the way we actually satisfy these drives is learned through cultural experience. We all periodically experience hunger, but we have to learn what can be eaten and what may be eaten. Human beings are not genetically programmed to eat specific kinds of food: we have to learn through experience that some things are edible and some are inedible. We also have to learn that some edible foods may not be eaten. Roaches, pigs, dogs, snails, cows, crabs, butterflies, and human beings are all edible and nutritious. Each of these animals is regarded as "food" in some societies, while in others it would be unthinkable to eat them. Similarly, we experience drives for sexual satisfaction, but the form this satisfaction takes is learned. Some people learn to derive satisfaction from the opposite sex, some from the same sex, some from both, some from inanimate objects, some from other species, and some from one or more of various other possibilities. Most people, of course, learn to satisfy their drives in the way their culture tells them to. But we are not programmed to satisfy them in any particular way. If we were, we would all fulfill our drives in a rigid, identical manner. In fact, unlike all other species, we can even override our drives completely. We can ignore the drive for self-preservation by committing suicide or by risking our lives for others. Protesters can go on hunger strikes, even if it means starvation. Priests and others can suppress the sex drive and live out their lives in celibacy.

Within very broad limits, "human nature" is what we make of it, and what we make of it depends largely on the culture in which we happen to live. One of the most liberating aspects of the sociological perspective is that it strips away myths about our social behavior, showing that what seems "natural" or "instinctive" is usually nothing more than a cultural product of human society.

Norms

When Captain Cook asked the chiefs in Tahiti why they always ate apart and alone, they replied, "Because it is right" (Linton, 1945). If we ask Americans why they eat with knives and forks, or why their men wear pants instead of skirts, or why they may be married to only one person at a time, we are likely to get similar and very uninformative answers: "Because it's right." "Because that's the way it's done." "Because it's the custom." Or even "I don't know."

The reason for these and countless other patterns of social behavior is that they are controlled by social *norms*— shared rules or guidelines which prescribe the behavior that is appropriate in a given situation. Norms define how people "ought" to behave under particular circumstances in a particular society. We conform to norms so readily that we are hardly aware they exist. In fact, we are much more likely to notice departures from norms than conformity to them. You would not be surprised if a stranger tried to shake hands when you were introduced, but you might be a little startled if he or she bowed, curtsied, started to stroke you, or kissed you on both cheeks. Yet each of these other forms of greeting is appropriate in other parts of the world. When we visit another society whose norms are different, we quickly become aware that things we do *this* way, they do *that* way.

Some norms apply to every member of society. In the United States, for example, nobody is permitted to marry more than one person at the same time. Other norms apply to some people but not to others. There is a very strong norm in American society against the taking of human life, but this norm does not apply to police officers in shootouts, soldiers in combat, or innocent people acting in self-defense against armed attackers. Other norms are even more specific and prescribe the appropriate behavior for people in particular situations, such as college students in lecture rooms, salespeople in a store, or marijuana smokers rolling and sharing a joint.

Folkways and Mores

Norms ensure that social life proceeds smoothly, for they give us guidelines for our own behavior and reliable expectations for the behavior of others. This function of norms is so important that there is always strong social pressure on people to conform. But although most of us conform to most norms most of the time, all of us tend to violate some norms occasionally. In the case of certain norms, the folkways, a fair amount of nonconformity may be tolerated, but in the case of certain other norms, the mores, very little leeway is permitted (Sumner, 1906).

Folkways

Folkways are the ordinary usages and conventions of everyday life; they are, quite literally, the "ways of the folk." Conformity to folkways is expected but not absolutely insisted upon. We expect people to keep their lawns mowed, to refrain from picking their nose in public, to turn up on time for appointments, and to wear a matching pair of shoes. Those who do not conform to these and similar folkways are considered peculiar and eccentric, particularly if they consistently violate a number of folkways. But they are not considered immoral or depraved, nor are they treated as criminals.

Mores

Mores (pronounced "mor-ays") are much stronger norms. People attach a moral significance to them and treat violations of them much more seriously. (The word "mores" was a Latin term for the ancient Romans' most respected and even sacred customs.) A man who walks down a street wearing nothing on the upper half of his body is violating a folkway; a man who walks down the street wearing nothing on the lower half of his body is violating one of our most important mores, the requirement that people cover their genitals and buttocks in public. Theft, drug abuse, murder, rape, desecration of the national flag, or contemptuous use of religious symbols all bring a strong social reaction. People believe their mores are crucial for the maintenance of a decent and orderly society, and the offender may be strongly criticized, punched, imprisoned, committed to a mental asylum, or even executed. Some violations of mores are made almost unthinkable by *taboos*—powerful social beliefs that the acts concerned are utterly loathsome. In the United States, for example, there is a strong taboo against eating human flesh, a taboo so effective that most of our states do not even have laws prohibiting the practice.

Not all norms can be neatly categorized as either folkways or mores. In practice, norms fall at various points on a continuum, depending on how seriously they are taken by society. There is also a constant shift in the importance attached to some norms. The fashion of short hair for men was apparently regarded by many Americans as one of our mores for most of this century. Youths who grew their hair long in the early 1960s were sometimes insulted, attacked, and even shot at. Since the early 1970s, however, long hair on young males has almost become a folkway. In many parts of the country a youth with a crewcut might draw curious glances, at least from his own age group.

Some norms, particularly mores, are encoded in law. A *law* is simply a rule that has been formally enacted by a political authority and is backed by the power of the state. The law usually codifies important norms that already exist, but sometimes political authorities attempt to introduce new norms by enacting appropriate laws. Civil rights legislation in the United States, for example, was aimed at destroying some traditional norms of race relations and replacing them with new ones. Attempts to introduce new norms in this way are not always successful, as the American attempt to legislate the prohibition of liquor in the 1920s proved. Laws that run counter to cultural norms, particularly in the area of personal morality, are often ineffectual and tend to fall into disuse. For example, many of our drug laws and laws prohibiting sports and entertainments on Sundays are now widely disregarded.

Social Control

Every society must have a system of *social control*, a set of means of ensuring that its members generally behave in expected and approved ways. Some of this social control over the individual can be exercised by others, either formally through such agencies as the police and government inspectors or informally through the reactions of other people in the course of everyday life. All norms, whether they are codified in law or not, are supported by *sanctions*, rewards for conformity and punishments for nonconformity. The positive sanctions may range from an approving nod to a ceremony of public acclaim; the negative sanctions may range from mild disapproval to imprisonment or even execution. Only a tiny fraction of social behavior can be policed by formal agencies of control, and most sanctions are applied informally. If you help your neighbors and are polite to them, you will be rewarded with smiles and popularity. If you use "bad" language in the wrong company or offer your left hand rather than your right when someone wants to shake hands with you, you will receive raised eyebrows, glares, stares, or comments designed to make you uncomfortable and more likely to conform to social expectations in the future.

Most social control, however, does not have to be exercised through the direct influence of others. We do it ourselves, internally. In the process of growing up in society we unconsciously *internalize* the norms of our culture, making conformity to them a part of our personality and following social expectations without question. Like the chiefs on Tahiti and like people all over the world, we think and act in ways that are to a great extent shaped by the society we live in, though we are seldom aware of this fact. For the most part, we behave the way we do because "That's the way it's done."

Values

The norms of a society are ultimately an expression of its *values*—socially shared ideas about what is good, right, and desirable. The difference between values and norms is that values are abstract, general concepts, whereas norms are behavioral rules or guidelines for people in particular kinds of situations.

Figure 3.5 Social norms reflect social values. The American norm requiring that marijuana be shared reflects the high value placed on intimacy and solidarity in those nonconformist groups in which marijuana use first arose. A tobacco cigarette, in contrast, is rarely shared in the same way, because cigarette smoking does not have the same cultural origins and is generally regarded as an individual affair. A tobacco smoker may, however, offer other cigarettes from the pack to those present, a folkway that expresses the value we place on small acts of generosity.

The Importance of Values

The values of a society are important because they influence the content of its norms. If a society values education highly, its norms will make provision for mass schooling. If it values a large population, its norms will encourage big families. If it values monogamy, its norms will not permit people to marry more than one partner at a time. In principle at least, all norms can be traced to a basic social value. The norms that prescribe the routines of office work and assembly-line production, for example, reflect the high value we place on efficiency. The norms that require a student to be more polite and formal to a professor than to other students express the value our society places on respect for authority and learning. The norms that insisted on short hair for men reflected the high value placed on men's "masculinity" in American culture; until it became fashionable, long hair was regarded as "effeminate."

Although all norms express social values, many norms persist long after the conditions that gave rise to them have been forgotten. The folkway that requires a male to walk on the side nearest the street when accompanying a female, for example, dates back to a time when the sidewalk was regularly splashed with mud as horses trotted along the unpaved streets. The norm simply reflected the high value placed on chivalry in the male and dependence in the female. The folkway that requires us to shake hands, especially when greeting a stranger, seems to have originated long ago in the desire to show that no weapon was concealed in the right hand. Our folkway of showering a bride and groom with rice or confetti as they emerge from the wedding ceremony may seem rather meaningless, but it actually stems from the practice in earlier ages of showering newlyweds with nuts, fruits, and seeds as symbols of fertility.

American Values

Unlike norms, whose existence can easily be observed in everyday behavior, values are often more difficult to identify. The values of a society have to be inferred from its norms, so any analysis of social values relies heavily on the interpretations of the observer.

One of the most influential attempts to identify the major values of American society is that of Robin Williams

(1970), who detects a number of basic "value orientations" that are expressed in the norms that guide our behavior. These include achievement and success, activity and work, humanitarianism, efficiency and practicality, progress, material comfort, equality, freedom, conformity, science and rationality, nationalism and patriotism, democracy, individualism, and the superiority of one racial or ethnic group over another.

It is obvious that some of these values are not entirely consistent with one another. Many of them, too, are changing or are accepted by some Americans but rejected by others. It is also clear that Williams's list does not exhaust all the possibilities. Other writers have identified rather different sets of values. James Henslin (1975), for example, includes several items on Williams's list but adds others, such as education, religiosity, male supremacy, romantic love, monogamy, and heterosexuality. Although these and other analyses may be overlapping and imprecise, they give us useful insights into our culture and thus into the norms that guide our social behavior.

Cultural Variation

The culture of every society is unique, containing combinations of norms and values that are found nowhere else. Americans eat oysters but not snails. The French eat snails but not locusts. The Zulus eat locusts but not fish. The Jews eat fish but not pork. The Hindus eat pork but not beef. The Russians eat beef but not snakes. The Chinese eat snakes but not people. The Jalé of New Guinea find people delicious. We spend our lives accumulating private possessions; the BaMbuti of the Congo forests spend their lives sharing their goods; the Kwakiutl of the Pacific Northwest periodically gave them away or even destroyed them at great ceremonies. Our norms have traditionally valued premarital chastity; the norms of the Mentawei of Indonesia require women to become pregnant before they can be considered eligible for marriage; the norms of the Keraki of New Guinea require premarital homosexuality in every male. Women in traditional Arab societies must cover the entire body and even the face; American women may expose their faces but must keep their breasts and the entire pelvic region concealed; women in many parts of Africa may expose their breasts and buttocks but not the genital region; women in Tierra del Fuego may not expose their backs; and Tasaday women in the Philippines proceed about their daily lives stark naked. The range of cultural variation is so immense that probably no specific norm appears in every human society. How can we account for this variation?

The Functionalist Approach

One way of analyzing the components of culture is to look for the *functions* they play in maintaining the social order as a whole. Functionalist theorists regard society and culture as a system of interdependent parts. They argue that no one cultural element can be understood in isolation from the social and cultural whole. To explain a particular cultural trait, therefore, one has to establish its functions in making the entire system "work." The functionalist approach has long been popular in studies of other cultures (for example, Radcliffe-Brown, 1935, 1952; Malinowski, 1926) and has been influential in American sociology during much of this century (for example, Parsons, 1951; Merton, 1968).

In traditional Eskimo society, hospitality to a traveler was highly valued. A host was obliged to do everything possible to make a traveler comfortable, even if he found the man personally offensive. There was even a norm requiring a host to offer his wife to a guest for the night. This culture trait of obligatory hospitality is an unusual one, entirely unknown in urban, industrial societies. But it was highly functional in Eskimo culture. Travel through snows and arctic blizzards would be utterly impossible unless the traveler could rely on the certainty of food, warmth, and rest at the next settlement, and the host in turn could expect the same hospitality when he traveled. Without this norm, communication and trade among various groups might have been too hazardous to undertake. A similar norm does not exist in the United States today, where it would make no sense. We have other arrangements, such as restaurants and motels, to serve the same function, and the need for shelter from the environment is not so pressing.

The Cheyenne Indians periodically gathered for a sundance ceremony. Why? The activity brought no obvious rewards and seemed only to distract the various bands from the more mundane activities of making a living in their own areas. A functionalist analysis again suggests the rea-

Figure 3.6 Many of the variations among cultures can be explained in ecological terms. The way of life of the Eskimos of the Arctic Circle differs radically from that of these New Guinea villagers, for each people faces very different environmental pressures. The clothing of the Eskimo, for example, reflects the need for protection against the intense cold. In the tropical climate of New Guinea, where elaborate clothing would be a hindrance, more emphasis is given to body ornaments.

son. The sun dance gave the entire tribe an opportunity to gather together for a common purpose, to reestablish social bonds, and to confirm their sense that they were not simply a scattering of isolated bands but rather a tribe united by similar cultural practices. In the same way, the high value Americans place on competition and success can be explained in terms of its function in maintaining the capitalist system on which American economic life is believed to depend.

Functionalist theory can thus help us to understand why a particular culture trait is present in one society but not in others. It sometimes has the disadvantage, however, of focusing on how things "fit together" at a particular moment in cultural history and thus neglecting the process of cultural change. Changes—the introduction of a new religion, for example—may throw other parts of the cultural system into some disorder, and there is always a temptation to see these changes as "dysfunctions," as irritants to the system rather than as useful adaptations to changing conditions.

The Ecological Approach

A second approach has recently become increasingly popular, particularly among anthropologists studying other cultures (for example, Harris, 1975, 1977, 1979; Bennett, 1976; Hardesty, 1977). These writers attempt to explain a great deal of the variation in human cultures by taking an *ecological* approach—that is, by analyzing cultural elements in the context of the total environment in which the society exists. Culture, as we have seen, is a means of adapting to the environment, and a people's cultural practices are necessarily linked to the pressures and opportunities of the environment in which they live.

The culture of the Bedouin Arabs offers an obvious example of this kind of adaptation because their harsh desert environment sets such severe limits on their cultural options. They live in a region so arid that farming is impossible: accordingly, they cannot form permanent settlements or live in houses. Instead, they are nomads, spending a large part of the year wandering from one oasis to another, always moving on when the water dries up. Their shelter necessarily consists of tents, the only form of housing that can be easily transported. They have herds of camels, not pigs or moose, because camels are the only animals in the region that can withstand long periods without water. Their material possessions are neither many, large, nor heavy, for they must be regularly packed, moved for tens or hundreds of miles, and then unpacked again. The Bedouin have evolved norms about the conservation of water, and unlike North Americans they are not offended if people do not wash for days or weeks on end. They place a high value on the ability to navigate the almost featureless desert. Their religion does not include gods of the sea or spirits of the jungle; instead, like many pastoral peoples, they conceive of a god who is like a shepherd to his human flock. When they think of paradise, they imagine a place of cool shade, pleasing fountains, and an abundance of fresh fruits—the things that they lack in this world. In short, almost every important element of their culture can be traced to the influence of the environment in which the Bedouins live (Vidal, 1976).

The relationship of other cultural practices to the total environment is not always as obvious, but the ecological approach has been used to explain several otherwise puzzling practices. Marvin Harris (1974), for example, applies this perspective to the apparently irrational veneration Indians have for cows. Although only one Indian in fifty has an adequate diet, the Hindu religion forbids the slaughter of cows. As a result, over 100 million cows roam freely through the countryside and cities of India, snarling traffic and defecating in public places. Western observers (and

some Indians in the more industrialized parts of the country) are apt to regard most of these cows as "useless." They are scrawny animals, yielding little milk and apparently contributing nothing of value to Indian life.

Harris points out, however, that the cows are vital to the Indian economy. A large part of the population lives on small farms that require at least one pair of oxen for plowing. These farm families live on the brink of starvation and cannot afford tractors. They must use oxen, and their oxen are, quite obviously, produced by cows. Widespread cow slaughter would worsen the already critical shortage of draft animals, making the existing farms too unproductive and driving as many as 150 million people into the severely crowded cities. Moreover, the cows provide India annually with some 700 million tons of manure. About half is used as fertilizer by farmers who could not possibly afford chemical substitutes. The remainder serves as cooking fuel, a vital resource in a country that has little oil or coal and an acute shortage of wood. And when the cows finally die, they are eaten, not by Hindus, but by outcastes who are not bound by the Hindu religion and who are generally even poorer and hungrier than the rest of the population. The hides of the animals are then used in India's huge leatherworking industry. The cows themselves do not compete with human beings for food. Unlike American cattle, which are often fed grain, they scavenge what they can from roadsides and other unproductive land.

Figure 3.7 Cows are highly valued in India—so much so that they roam the streets unmolested, even though many of the people around them are on the brink of starvation. This veneration of the cow seems inexplicable—yet it is a fundamental assumption of sociology that all human behavior, no matter how puzzling it may seem at first, can be rationally explained.

In short, the sacred cow is an important element in the entire Indian ecology. As Harris observes, the Indians would probably rather eat their cows than starve, but they would surely starve if they did.

Different societies, of course, may adopt different solutions to similar functional requirements or ecological problems. Many societies face the problem that their environment does not offer enough food to maintain a growing population. The Eskimo solved the problem by deliberately leaving a proportion of female infants and many aged, unproductive people out in the snow to die. The Yanamamö of Brazil control their population by killing or deliberately starving female infants and by practicing incessant and bloody fighting among males. The Keraki of New Guinea limit population increase by requiring males to engage in exclusively homosexual relations for several years after puberty. Americans restrict population growth by valuing relatively small families, by permitting abortion, and by using such cultural artifacts as birth-control pills. In Bangladesh and many overpopulated developing nations, the cultural response is not nearly as effective. Little attempt is made to limit population growth, with the result that in the first few years of life, as many as half of the children die from diseases related to malnutrition.

It must also be recognized that not all cultural elements can be readily explained in functional or ecological terms. Some practices may diffuse from one culture to another as a result of invasion, migration, or trading, and these alien elements may be adopted as long as they are not dysfunctional or counterecological in the long run. Cultural elements may also persist for decades or centuries after the conditions that gave rise to them have vanished. Culture always tends to be conservative, and traditions may be followed long after their origins are forgotten and the need for them has disappeared.

Cultural Universals

Are there any *cultural universals* in the midst of this variety—practices found in every culture? The answer is that there are a fairly large number of general cultural universals, but there do not seem to be any specific ones. Every culture, for example, has norms prohibiting murder, but different cultures have different ideas about which homicides constitute murder and which do not. We would

consider human sacrifice murder, but the Aztecs did not. Vietnamese peasants no doubt considered the systematic bombing of their communities as murder, but many Americans did not. We would consider the slaughter of an inoffensive stranger as murder, but there are still some small, isolated societies in which the norms permit any outsider to be killed on the spot.

Cultural universals derive from the common problems the environment poses for our species. The weather is often too hot or too cold for comfort, and clothing and housing arrangements must be made to adapt us to the climate. Children need care and attention, and some cultural provision must be made for this requirement. People become sick, and attempts must be made to cure them. Individuals must be distinguished from one another, and so they are given names. Life is often hard and death awaits us all, and people everywhere invent myths and maintain religious beliefs to explain the human predicament.

The anthropologist George Murdock (1945) compiled a lengthy list of general traits found in every culture, including the following: athletic sports, bodily adornment, cooking, cooperative labor, courtship, dancing, dream interpretation, family, feasting, folklore, food taboos, funeral ceremonies, games, gift-giving, incest taboos, laws, medicine, music, myths, numerals, personal names, property rights, religion, sexual restrictions, toilet training, toolmaking, and weather-making efforts. But these are only general traits; their specific content varies from one culture to another.

Ethnocentrism

Cultures may vary, but most human beings spend their entire lives within the culture in which they were born. Knowing little about other ways of life, they see their own norms and values as inevitable rather than optional. As one anthropologist (Linton, 1936) observed:

> It has been said that the last thing which a dweller in the deep sea would discover would be water. He would become conscious of its existence only if some accident brought him to the surface and introduced him to air. Man, throughout most of his history, has been only vaguely aware of the existence of culture. . . . The ability to see the culture of one's own society as a whole . . . calls for a degree of objectivity which is rarely if ever achieved.

Figure 3.8 The norms and values of a culture cannot be arbitrarily judged by those of another culture. From the viewpoint of American culture, the traditional Middle Eastern practice of hiding the entire female body from view seems silly; from the point of view of these Arab women, the American practice of exposing so much of the female body to public view would be shameful and obscene. Neither viewpoint is objectively "right," for each practice can be fully understood only in its own context. In fact, before we smile too quickly at how easily other peoples are shocked at the sight of scantily clad women, we might consider the likely reaction if the American women went in their bikinis to a church, a corporate office, or a college lecture.

For this reason, people in every society are to some extent guilty of *ethnocentrism*—the tendency to judge other cultures by the standards of one's own. People everywhere are apt to take it for granted that their morality, their marriage forms, their clothing styles, or their conceptions of beauty are right, proper, and the best of all possible alternatives. Here are some examples of ethnocentric thinking. Our women put rings through their ears and cosmetics on their faces because it enhances their beauty; their women put bones through their noses and scars on their faces because, in their pitiful ignorance, they don't realize how ugly it makes them. We won't eat cats or worms because that would be cruel or disgusting; they won't eat beef or drink milk because of some silly food taboo. We cover our private parts because we are decorous and civilized; they walk around naked because they are ignorant and shameless. Our brave troops achieve glorious victories over the enemy; their fanatical hordes perpetrate bloody massacres on us. Our sexual practices are moral and decent; theirs are primitive or perverse. Our religion is the one true faith; theirs is heathen superstition.

Ethnocentrism is particularly strong in isolated societies that have little contact with other cultures. But even in modern industrial societies, where citizens have the advantages of formal education, mass communication, and international travel, such attitudes still prevail. As Linton observes, one reason for the persistence of ethnocentrism is that it is almost impossible to view one's own culture objectively; but another reason is that ethnocentrism can be functional to a society. It provides faith and confidence in one's own tradition, discourages penetration by outsiders, and thus ensures the solidarity and unity of the group. But under some conditions ethnocentrism can have many undesirable effects. It can encourage racism, it can cause hostility and conflict between groups, and it can make a people unwilling to recognize the need for changes in their own culture.

Ethnocentrism also poses a severe problem for social scientists analyzing other cultures, because they may bring to the task unconscious and often unfounded assumptions about other people and their practices. Even trained observers experience "culture shock" when confronted with cultures radically unlike their own. Napoleon Chagnon, an anthropologist who studied the Yanamamö of Brazil, was aghast when he first met his subjects. They stank to him (though not, of course, to themselves), the heads of the men were covered with scars from their incessant fighting, and they were under the influence of a local psychedelic drug—one of whose effects was to produce strings of green mucous that hung from their noses and were rarely wiped away. Chagnon (1967) recalls:

> I am not ashamed to admit . . . that had there been a diplomatic way out, I would have ended my fieldwork there and then. I did not look forward to the next day when I would be left alone with the Indians: I did not speak a word of their language, and they were decidedly different from what I had imagined them to be. The whole situation was depressing, and I wondered why I had ever decided to switch from civil engineering to anthropology in the first place.

Yet Chagnon was eventually able, after living among the Yanamamö for many months, to adjust to their culture and to develop a sympathetic understanding of their way of life.

Cultural Relativism

The ability to achieve a full understanding of another culture depends largely on one's willingness to adopt the position of *cultural relativism,* the recognition that one culture cannot be arbitrarily judged by the standards of another. We are quick to complain when foreign critics—the Russians, for example—judge us in terms of their own values, for we feel that such a judgment distorts the reality of our culture and society. We have to be equally on guard against using our own standards to judge other cultures.

It is probably never possible to be entirely free of bias in favor of one's own culture. However hard we try, the sneaking feeling is likely to persist that our standards *are* better. Yet we must recognize that judgments about good and bad, moral and immoral, depend very much on who is doing the judging; there is no universal standard to appeal to. People everywhere may *feel* that their own standards are superior, but there is no logical way they can *prove* it. An inability to adopt the position of cultural relativism is simply another example of ethnocentrism, and the problem with ethnocentrism is that it works both ways. We are shocked at the traditional Eskimo practice of leaving the aged to perish in the snow, but the Japanese are appalled at our practice of excluding aged parents from the family and leaving them to die in old-age homes. We are shocked at the Yanamamö practice of infanticide, but the San ("Bushmen") of the Kalahari could not begin to comprehend how we can permit poverty and malnutrition in our own society when we have so much surplus wealth.

Cultural relativism does not mean we can never pass judgment on the practices of another society. No responsible social scientist, for example, could fail to condemn the mass murders perpetrated by the Nazis. What cultural relativism means is that the practices of another society—including Nazi Germany—can be fully understood only in terms of its own norms and values. For the practical purpose of understanding human behavior it is vital that observers try, as far as possible, to remove the blinders of their own culture when they are looking at another.

Cultural Integration

A culture does not consist of a random collection of different elements. The skills, customs, values, beliefs, practices, and other characteristics of a culture tend to complement one another—to be *integrated* into a complex whole. If a culture is to survive, it must be integrated to a considerable extent, although in practice some cultures are more integrated than others.

In traditional, preindustrial societies, culture is usually highly integrated. These societies tend to be relatively small, and people share similar values. Culture is generally homogeneous, and the rate of cultural change is often very slow. In modern industrial societies, on the other hand, the various elements are not as well integrated. Industrial societies are often large and contain diverse groups with different ways of life. Culture is relatively heterogeneous, and there is often considerable dispute over values. Social and cultural change occur rapidly and unevenly, with the result that different components of the culture are constantly having to adjust to changes elsewhere in the system.

The fact that cultures tend to be integrated is often not apparent until changes occur in one part, throwing other parts into disorganization or generating widespread resistance to change. This was the fate of the culture of the Plains Indians (see Figure 3.9).

Figure 3.9 The entire culture of the Plains Indians centered around the buffalo. Their religion focused on the buffalo hunt, and the prestige of individual males was linked to their skills and courage as hunters. The carcass of the buffalo provided most of the items in the Indians' material culture—hides, tendons, bones, and membranes were all put to use for various purposes, including clothing and shelter. The Indians' nomadic way of life was based on the need to follow the migrations of the animals on which they depended for a living. When white settlers used their superior technology to systematically slaughter the buffalo, the culture of the Plains Indians disintegrated and their societies collapsed. When the Indians were settled on reservations and given cattle to raise, they sometimes turned the animals loose and hunted them like buffalo: there was nothing in their culture that prepared them to tend and milk cows.

Real Culture and Ideal Culture

One common source of strain in a culture is the discrepancy that sometimes exists between ideal culture, as expressed in the values and norms a people claim to believe in, and real culture, as expressed in their actual practices. In the United States, for example, we claim to believe in equality, yet our society contains people who are millionaires and people who are impoverished. We place a high value on honesty, yet citizens who would never dream of shoplifting or picking pockets routinely evade payment of part of their taxes if they can get away with it. There is often a considerable gap between our ideal norms and our real norms: we have a traditional norm, for example, that sexual intercourse should take place only in the context of marriage, but the statistical data on premarital and extramarital intercourse show that this norm is violated by the great majority of Americans at one time or another.

A society is often able to overlook the contradictions between real and ideal culture. As devout Buddhists, fishermen in Burma are forbidden to kill anything, including fish. Yet they must fish to live. How do they overcome the contradiction? What happens is that the fish are first caught and then "are merely put on the bank to dry after their long soaking in the river, and if they are foolish or ill-judged enough to die while undergoing the process, it is their own fault" (Lowie, 1940). In a similar way, Americans claim to value forthrightness and fair play, yet often tolerate highly questionable commercial and advertising practices on the grounds that "business is business." Sometimes, however, the strains between real and ideal culture become so great that changes must be made to integrate the two more closely. The strains between the American value of equality and the reality of racial discrimination became so great that a civil war and widespread disturbances took place before the society was brought into a state of greater, but by no means complete, cultural integration.

Subcultures and Countercultures

A second source of strain in a culture arises from the existence of groups that do not participate fully in the dominant culture of the society. These groups are especially common in large, heterogeneous modern industrial societies, in which there are many cultural differences between members of different regional, religious, occupational, and other communites (Yinger, 1960, 1977; Westhues, 1972).

Subcultures

A *subculture* shares in the overall culture of the society but also has its own distinctive values, norms, and life-style. In North America, for example, there are subcultures of the young, of the rich and the poor, of different racial and ethnic groups, and of different regions. Smaller subcultures exist in the military, in prisons, on college campuses, among drug addicts, or among street-corner gangs. People in each of these subcultures tend to be ethnocentric in relation to other subcultures, for membership in a subculture colors one's view of reality. A member of a wealthy, "jet-set" subculture doubtless has a different perspective on American social reality than someone from a subculture of Hell's Angels or Chicano migrant laborers. If the differences between subcultures are sufficiently great, the results may be *value conflict,* deep disagreements over goals and ideals.

It is important that sociologists—and sociology students —should adopt a position of cultural relativism toward subcultures as well as toward other cultures. It is all too easy for sociologists—most of whom are white and middle class—to adopt ethnocentric attitudes toward subcultures within American society, arbitrarily judging other groups by the standards of the dominant culture. The practices of any subculture, whether it is made up of ghetto blacks, poor whites, heroin addicts, or the very rich, can be fully understood only by reference to its own norms and values.

Countercultures

A *counterculture* is a subculture that is fundamentally at odds with the dominant culture: it consciously rejects some of the most important norms of the wider society and is usually proud of it. The youth movement of the sixties is a good modern example of a counterculture; its "dropout" hippie wing and its "activist" political wing together challenged a whole range of treasured American norms and values, including those centered on success, hard work, material comfort, conformity, scientific rationality, white superiority, and sexual restrictiveness (Roszak, 1969; Wuthnow, 1976). A large counterculture inevitably generates strain and value conflict in society, as the turmoil of the sixties showed. In this particular case, a measure of cultural integration was finally achieved partly because some countercultural values and norms were incorporated by the mainstream culture and many others were abandoned by the young (Kunen, 1973).

Language

One of the most important of all human characteristics is our capacity to communicate with one another through language. Although apes can be taught to construct "sentences" by using hand signs or by manipulating physical objects (Mounin, 1976; Hill, 1978), only human beings have spoken language. Language is a form of communication that differs radically from the kinds used by other species. Other animals can communicate with sounds, gestures, touch, and chemical emissions, but the meanings of these signals is fixed, and their use is limited to the immediate situation. With the exception of the artificial "languages" that gorillas and chimpanzees have been taught to use, the signals in animal communication are genetically predetermined and are merely automatic responses to given conditions. These signals can be used to warn of danger, to indicate the presence of food, to claim territory, or to express fear, aggression, and sexual arousal—but little else. They cannot be combined in new ways to produce different or more complex information. A monkey can signal "food!" but not "bananas, tomorrow!"

Language, on the other hand, does not consist of fixed signals: it consists of learned symbols. A *symbol* is simply something that meaningfully represents something else. Gestures, facial expressions, drawings, and numbers are all symbols, but the most useful and flexible symbols are spoken or written words. Words are arbitrary symbols for objects and concepts, and every human language consists of hundreds of thousands of words whose meaning is socially agreed upon. These words can be combined according to grammatical rules to express any idea of which the human mind is capable.

The Importance of Language

Language is the keystone of culture. Without it, culture could not exist. Culture, by definition, is shared, and complex patterns of thought, emotion, knowledge, and belief could not be passed from individual to individual or generation to generation without the medium of the spoken word. When an animal dies, everything it has learned from experience perishes with it. But language gives human beings a history—access to the accumulated knowledge and experience of the generations that have gone before.

Helen Keller: The Importance of Language

Although we usually think of our sight as our most important sense, people who are born deaf are more often disadvantaged than people who are born blind: for example, they are more likely to be intellectually retarded. The reason is that deafness makes it difficult for them to learn language, and thus cuts them off from the symbolic world of other human beings. The achievements of Helen Keller, who was left blind and deaf by a serious disease in infancy, are therefore all the more remarkable. Although she was unable to see or hear the world around her, she was able, at the age of seven, to learn the use of spoken language. Language gave her an intelligent understanding of an environment that until then had been almost meaningless to her. She was later able to write books, and even to conduct orchestras by responding to the vibrations of the musical instruments. The following passage, taken from Helen Keller's moving biography, is an account of how she first discovered language.

The most important day I remember in all my life is the one on which my teacher, Anne Mansfield Sullivan, came to me. I am filled with wonder when I consider the immeasurable contrast between the two lives which it connects. It was the third of March, 1887, three months before I was seven years old.

The morning after my teacher came she led me into her room and gave me a doll. The little blind children at the Perkins Institution had sent it and Laura Bridgman had dressed it; but I did not know this until afterward. When I had played with it a little while Miss Sullivan slowly spelled into my hand the word "d-o-l-l." I was at once interested in this finger play and tried to imitate it. When I finally succeeded in making the letters correctly I was flushed with childish pleasure and pride. Running downstairs to my mother I held up my hand and made the letters for doll. I did not know that I was spelling a word or even that words existed; I was simply making my fingers go in monkey-like imitation. In the days that followed I learned to spell in this uncomprehending way a great many words, among them *pin, hat, cup,* and a few verbs like *sit, stand,* and *walk.* But my teacher had been with me several weeks before I understood that everything has a name.

One day, while I was playing with my new doll, Miss Sullivan put my big rag doll into my lap also, spelled "d-o-l-l" and tried to make me understand that "d-o-l-l" applied to both. Earlier in the day we had had a tussle over the word "m-u-g" and "w-a-t-e-r." Miss Sullivan had tried to impress it upon me that "m-u-g" is *mug* and that "w-a-t-e-r" is *water,* but I persisted in confounding the two. In despair she had dropped the subject for the time, only to renew it at the first opportunity. I became impatient with her repeated attempts and, seizing the new doll, I dashed it upon the floor. I was keenly delighted when I felt the fragments of the broken doll at my feet. Neither sorrow nor regret followed my passionate outburst. I had not loved the doll. In the still, dark world in which I lived there was no strong sentiment or tenderness. I felt my teacher sweep the fragments to one side of the hearth, and I had a sense of satisfaction that the cause of my discomfort was removed. She brought me my hat, and I knew I was going out into the warm sunshine. This thought, if a wordless sensation may be called a thought, made me hop and skip with pleasure.

We walked down the path to the well-house, attracted by the fragrance of the honeysuckle with which it was covered. Someone was drawing water and my teacher placed my hand under the spout. As the cool stream gushed over one hand she spelled into the other the word *water,* first slowly, then rapidly. I stood still, my whole attention fixed upon the motions of her fingers. Suddenly I felt a misty consciousness as of something forgotten—a thrill of returning thought; and somehow the mystery of language was revealed to me. I knew then that "w-a-t-e-r" meant the wonderful cool something that was flowing over my hand. That living word awakened my soul, gave it light, hope, joy, set it free! There were barriers still, it is true, but barriers that could in time be swept away.

I left the well-house eager to learn. Everything had a name, and each name gave birth to a new thought. As we returned to the house every object I touched seemed to quiver with life. That was because I saw everything with a strange, new sight that had come to me. On entering the door I remembered the doll I had broken. I felt my way to the hearth and picked up the pieces. I tried vainly to put them together. Then my eyes filled with tears; for I realized what I had done, and for the first time I felt repentance and sorrow.

I learned a great many new words that day. I do not remember what they all were; but I do know that *mother, father, sister, teacher,* were among them—words that were to make the world blossom for me, "like Aaron's rod, with flowers." It would have been difficult to find a happier child than I was as I lay in my crib at the close of that eventful day and lived over the joys it had brought me, and for the first time longed for a new day to come.

Source: Helen Keller, *The Story of My Life* (New York: Doubleday, 1903).

Through language we are introduced to the collective experience of our society.

Equally important, language enables us to give meaning to the world. Events in themselves have no meaning; we impose meaning on them by interpreting the evidence of our senses. Without language, all but the most rudimentary forms of thought are impossible. With language, we can apply reason to the world. We can think logically from premises to conclusions: we can categorize; we can order our experience; we can contemplate the past and the future, the abstract and the hypothetical; we can formulate and utter ideas that are entirely new. Nearly all that we learn in human culture is learned through language in the course of social interaction with others. It is through language that we become cultured and thus fully human.

Linguistic Relativity

Shortly after World War II, George Orwell published a futuristic novel, *1984,* about a totalitarian dictatorship in which every aspect of social behavior was strictly controlled. The rulers of the state had even deliberately constructed a new language, Newspeak, whose vocabulary and grammar made it impossible for people to think certain thoughts:

The word *free* still existed in Newspeak, but it could only be used in such statements as "This dog is free from lice" or "This field is free from weeds." It could not be used in the old sense of "politically free," or "intellectually free," since political and intellectual freedom no longer existed as concepts, and were therefore of necessity nameless. . . . Countless other words such as *honor, justice, morality, internationalism, democracy, science,* and *religion* had simply ceased to exist. A few blanket words covered them, and, in covering them, abolished them. All words grouping themselves around the concepts of liberty and equality, for instance, were contained in the single word *crimethink,* while all words grouping themselves around the concepts of objectivity and rationalism were contained in the single word *oldthink.* [Orwell, 1949]

Is it possible for the language we speak to structure our reality in this way? For many centuries it has been generally accepted that all languages reflect reality in the same basic way and that words and concepts can be freely and accurately translated from one language to another. But in the course of this century some social scientists have raised the intriguing possibility that this assumption is unfounded. Studies of many of the thousands of languages in the world have revealed that they often interpret the same phenomena quite differently, and several writers have suggested that languages do not so much mirror reality as structure it.

Figure 3.10

"Tell me, Sara, why does your young man keep calling your mother 'man'?"

Drawing by Wm Hamilton; © 1971 The New Yorker Magazine, Inc.

The Linguistic-Relativity Hypothesis

The *linguistic-relativity hypothesis* holds that speakers of a particular language must necessarily interpret the world through the unique grammatical forms and categories their language supplies. This hypothesis was strongly propounded by two American linguists, Edward Sapir and his student Benjamin Whorf, and is sometimes known as the Sapir-Whorf hypothesis. Sapir (1929) argued forcefully that "the worlds in which different societies live are distinct worlds, not merely the same world with different labels attached."

In what ways do languages "slice up" and organize the world differently? The most common differences are in vocabulary: some languages have words for objects and concepts for which other languages have no words at all. The Aztecs, for example, had only one word for snow, frost, ice, and cold, and presumably tended to see these as essentially the same phenomenon. We have only one word for snow; the Eskimo have no general word for snow at all, but have over twenty words for different kinds of snow—snow on the ground, snow falling, snow drifting, and so on. Their language forces them to perceive these distinctions, while our language predisposes us to ignore them. The Koya of South India do not distinguish among snow, fog, and dew, but their language forces them to make distinctions among seven types of bamboo—distinctions that are important to them but that we would be unlikely to notice.

Even the color spectrum is dissected in different ways by different languages. The human eye can make between 7 and 10 million different color discriminations, but all languages recognize only a handful of different colors. Most European languages recognize black, white, and six basic colors—red, orange, yellow, green, blue, and purple. Many languages, however, recognize only two colors: the Jalé of New Guinea, for example, divide the spectrum into the colors *hui* and *ziza,* representing the warm and cold colors of the spectrum, respectively. Other cultures, such as the Arawak of Surinam, the Toda of India, and the Baganda of Uganda, recognize only three colors (Berlin and Kay, 1969). All these peoples see the same color spectrum, but they divide it up in different ways.

Other distinctions exist in the grammatical usages of different languages. Many European and other languages require a speaker to indicate the relative social statuses of the speaker and the person spoken to. In French, for example, the word *tu* is used for "you" by someone addressing a social equal or inferior, but the word *vous* is used to signify formality and respect. These languages thus oblige speakers to determine the nature of their relationships as soon as they begin to talk to one another, a requirement that English speakers can avoid. The language of the Navajo Indians contains no real equivalent to our active verbs; in Navajo thought people do not so much act on the world as participate passively in actions that are taking place. This linguistic feature is perhaps related to the extremely passive nature of the Navajo people. Even more startling to us is the language of the Hopi Indians, which does not recognize the categories of time and space that we do. The Hopi language lacks the equivalent of past, present, and future tenses, and organizes the universe instead into categories of "manifest" (everything that is or has been accessible to the physical senses) and "manifesting" (everything that is not physically accessible to the senses). If this concept is difficult to understand, it is because our language is poorly equipped to express it, just as the Hopi language has difficulty expressing our concepts of time and space.

Evaluation

The linguistic-relativity hypothesis does not imply that speakers of different languages are *incapable* of expressing the same ideas or seeing the world in the same way, although Sapir and Whorf did take this position in some of their earlier writings. All normal human beings are biologically capable of similar perceptions and reasoning (Lévi-Strauss, 1966). What the hypothesis does mean is that the language we speak *predisposes* us to make particular interpretations of reality. We need only consider the likely attitudes of a white child who is taught to call blacks "niggers" or of a black child who is taught to call whites "honkies" to see the truth of this statement. Another contemporary example may remind us of the peculiar use to which the word "free" was put in the society described in Orwell's *1984.* Americans commonly use the phrase "the free world" to refer to all noncommunist societies. In reality, most of the societies in the "free world" are anything but free in the sense that we understand the word in our own country. The "free world" has at various times included dictatorships or brutal regimes in Spain, Greece, Iran, Zaire, Uganda, Brazil, Chile, South Korea, South Africa, Haiti, and many other countries. But the phrase predisposes us to gloss over these uncomfortable facts and to adopt what is really a simplistic and often distorted view of international politics. Language and culture, then, are in constant interaction: culture influences the structure and use of language, and language influences cultural interpretations of reality.

Cultural Change

No culture is ever static. But although all cultures change, they do so in different ways and at different rates. Under most conditions, cultural change is fairly slow: culture tends to be inherently conservative, especially in its nonmaterial aspects, for people are reluctant to give up old values, customs, and beliefs in favor of new ones. When changes do occur in one area of a culture, they are usually accompanied, sooner or later, by changes elsewhere. If this were not the case, cultures would inevitably become poorly integrated over time. Some of the most important changes involve the ways in which a society earns its living and exploits the environment. Economic activity is so basic to human life that all other cultural elements have to adapt to it.

Three different processes can lead to cultural change: discovery, invention, and diffusion. *Discovery* is the perception of an aspect of reality that already exists—the hallucinogenic properties of peyote, the social structure of a termite colony, the functions of the heart, the cultural practices of another society. *Invention* is the combination or new use of existing knowledge to produce something that did not exist before—the compass, the United Nations, the atomic bomb, rock music. All inventions are based on previous discoveries and inventions. *Diffusion* is the spread of cultural elements from one culture to another and is probably the source of most cultural change. As implied by "The One Hundred Percent American," the reading at the end of this chapter, countless cultural elements we consider distinctively our own are in fact derived from other cultures and often have histories of many hundreds or even thousands of years.

Inventions, discoveries, and diffused cultural traits become part of a culture only if they are accepted and shared by the society in question. People are quicker to recognize the usefulness of new material artifacts than of new norms

Figure 3.11 A great deal of cultural change takes place through diffusion of cultural traits from one society to another. When the British colonized the west African country of Nigeria at the beginning of this century, they introduced, among other cultural traits, the Christian religion and western European rituals of Christmas. To this day, black Santas are to be found in Nigerian stores during the Christmas period, although their beards and heavy robes are hardly suited to the hot climate. The Western version of Santa is also, of course, the result of cultural diffusion—in this case, of the combination of Christian tradition with that of pagan Europeans, who used to celebrate a great feast in midwinter, presided over by a figure appearing much like the modern Santa.

and values. For this reason, innovations such as the wheel or the can opener are more readily accepted into a culture than new ideas or religions. Moreover, an innovation must be compatible with the basic values of the culture and must "fit" into its total environment. The wearing of skirts by men remains unacceptable in the United States, and automobiles cannot be successfully introduced into a society that lacks roads, gas stations, traffic regulations, or mechanics.

Are We Prisoners of Culture?

Through its profound effects on our behavior, values, attitudes, and personalities, the culture into which we are born influences our sense of who we are and what our goals in life should be. As the anthropologist Clyde Kluckhohn (1962) has pointed out, "Culture regulates our lives at every turn; from the moment we are born until we die there is, whether we are conscious of it or not, constant pressure on us to conform to certain types of behavior." But where does this leave human freedom? Are we simply the prisoners of our cultures?

The answer is no. Culture makes us, but we also make culture. As Karl Marx declared:

> Men make their own history, but they do not make it just as they please; they do not make it under circumstances chosen by themselves, but under circumstances directly encountered, given, and transmitted from the past. [1969, originally published 1852]

Culture sets certain limitations on our options and behavior, but it cannot control us completely. If it did, there would be no cultural change, for we would all conform rigidly to existing norms and values. Culture provides general guidelines for behavior, but in specific situations people act in ways that often require individual ingenuity, interpretation, and choice. There are times when human beings must be creative, imaginative, and ready to improvise. The broad limits within which they do these things are determined by culture, but their specific acts often break with tradition and generate change. As individuals, few of us have the opportunity to modify culture; collectively, we do it all the time. Culture is created, sustained, and changed by the acts of human beings, and that is the measure of our freedom.

Summary

1. Culture consists of all the shared products of human society, both material and nonmaterial. Culture and society are closely related and cannot exist independent of one another.

2. Human beings are the most advanced of the primates. Our distinctive characteristics include sociability, high intelligence, sensitive hands, language, upright posture, potential for year-round mating, and lengthy infant dependence on adults. Culture provides a superior mode of adaptation to the environment. It enables us to adapt quickly to changed conditions, or even to change the environment to meet our needs.

3. Human nature is extremely flexible and is the product of an interaction between biological potentials and cultural learning.

4. Norms are shared rules or guidelines that prescribe appropriate behavior. Violations of folkways are more readily tolerated than violations of mores. Some acts are prohibited by taboos and some by laws. Norms are an important element in the system of social control through which a society ensures that its members behave in approved ways. Norms are formally or informally enforced through positive or negative sanctions.

5. Values are shared ideas about what is good or desirable. Norms express social values, although the origin of the norms may be forgotten. The United States has a unique set of important values, some of them contradictory and some of them shared by certain subcultures but not by others.

6. Cultures vary widely and each is unique. Cultural variation can be explained in terms of the functions that particular elements serve in maintaining the social system, and in terms of their ecological significance as an adaptation to the total environment. Cultural traits may also result from diffusion from one culture to another.

7. There are a number of general cultural universals, but no specific practices are found in every society. We tend to be ethnocentric toward other cultures, judging them in terms of our own standards. It is important that a social scientist adopt a position of cultural relativism and attempt to understand other cultures and subcultures in their own terms.

8. Cultures, particularly in preindustrial societies, tend to be integrated. Changes in one area of culture often provoke changes in other areas. One source of cultural strain is the gap between real and ideal culture. Another is value conflict between the dominant culture and subcultures or countercultures.

9. Language is fundamental to society and culture; it permits the transmission of culture and the interpretation of reality. Different languages interpret reality in different ways. The linguistic-relativity hypothesis holds that different languages predispose speakers to interpret reality in different ways.

10. Cultural change is inevitable, although its rate is variable. It stems mainly from discovery, invention, and diffusion. Changes tend to be accepted into a culture only if they are compatible with existing norms and values. Changes in material culture are usually more readily accepted than changes in nonmaterial culture.

11. We are not the prisoners of culture. Culture shapes us, but collectively we, in turn, shape and change the culture we pass on from generation to generation.

Important Terms

culture (53)

material culture (53)

nonmaterial culture (53)

sociobiology (58)

norms (60)

folkways (60)

mores (60)

taboos (61)

law (61)

social control (61)

sanctions (61)

internalize (61)

values (61)

functionalist approach (63)

ecological approach (64)

cultural universals (66)

ethnocentrism (67)

cultural relativism (68)

cultural integration (68)

subculture (70)

counterculture (70)

symbol (70)

linguistic relativity (73)

discovery (74)

invention (74)

diffusion (74)

Suggested Readings

AHRENS, W., and SUSAN P. MONTAGUE (eds.). *The American Dimension: Cultural Myths and Social Realities.* Port Washington, N.Y.: Alfred, 1976.

A fascinating collection of articles about various aspects of American culture, ranging from soap operas to bagels.

CAPLAN, ARTHUR L. (ed.). *The Sociobiology Debate.* New York: Harper & Row, 1978.

A useful collection of articles about sociobiology. The book provides a good introduction to this controversial and important topic.

DENISOFF, R. SERGE. *Solid Gold: The Popular Record Industry.* New Brunswick, N.J.: Transaction Books, 1975.

An interesting sociological analysis of a significant aspect of American popular culture.

HARRIS, MARVIN. *Cannibals and Kings: The Origins of Cultures.* New York: Random House, 1977.

An entertaining and provocative application of the ecological perspective to a variety of peculiar and apparently inexplicable cultural practices.

ROSZAK, THEODORE. *The Making of a Counter Culture.* Garden City, N.Y.: Doubleday, 1969.

A sociologist's analysis of the youth culture of the sixties. The optimism of the book now seems a little dated, but it remains an interesting analysis of the value conflict between culture and counterculture.

SLATER, PHILIP. *The Pursuit of Loneliness.* Rev. ed. Boston: Beacon Press, 1976.

A penetrating critique of American culture, which Slater believes is so contradictory in some respects that it is at the breaking point.

SPRADLEY, JAMES P., and DAVID W. MCCURDY. *Conformity and Conflict: Readings in Cultural Anthropology.* Boston: Little, Brown, 1977.

An interesting collection of articles that view aspects of various cultures from an anthropological perspective.

WILLIAMS, ROBIN. *American Society: A Sociological Interpretation.* New York: Random House, 1970.

A useful text that examines American society and culture. It contains an influential analysis of American norms and values and their impact on social life.

Reading

The One Hundred Percent American *Ralph Linton*

This classic essay pointedly demonstrates that many cultural traits that we consider distinctively American have in fact diffused from other cultures and often have histories of thousands of years.

There can be no question about the average American's Americanism or his desire to preserve this precious heritage at all costs. Nevertheless, some insidious foreign ideas have already wormed their way into his civilization without his realizing what was going on. Thus dawn finds the unsuspecting patriot garbed in pajamas, a garment of East Indian origin; and lying in a bed built on a pattern which originated in either Persia or Asia Minor. He is muffled to the ears in un-American materials; cotton, first domesticated in India; linen, domesticated in the Near East; wool from an animal native to Asia Minor; or silk whose uses were first discovered by the Chinese. All these substances have been transformed into cloth by a method invented in Southwestern Asia. If the weather is cold enough he may even be sleeping under an eiderdown quilt invented in Scandinavia.

On awakening he glances at the clock, a medieval European invention, uses one potent Latin word in abbreviated form, rises in haste, and goes to the bathroom. Here, if he stops to think about it, he must feel himself in the presence of a great American institution; he will have heard stories of both the quality and frequency of foreign plumbing and will know that in no other country does the average man perform his ablutions in the midst of such splendor. But the invidious foreign influence pursues him even here. Glass was invented by the ancient Egyptians, the use of glazed tiles for floors and walls in the Near East, porcelain in China, and the art of enameling on metal by Mediterranean artisans of the Bronze Age. Even his bathtub and toilet are but slightly modified copies of Roman originals. The only purely American contribution to the ensemble is the steam radiator.

In this bathroom the American washes with soap invented by the ancient Gauls. Next he cleans his teeth, a subversive European practice which did not invade America until the latter part of the eighteenth century. He then shaves, a masochistic rite first developed by the heathen priests of ancient Egypt and Sumer. The process is made less of a penance by the fact that his razor is of steel, an iron-carbon alloy discovered in either India or Turkestan. Lastly, he dries himself on a Turkish towel.

Returning to the bedroom, the unconscious victim of un-American practices removes his clothes from a chair, invented in the Near East, and proceeds to dress. He puts on close-fitting tailored garments whose form derives from the skin clothing of the ancient nomads of the Asiatic steppes and fastens them with buttons whose prototypes appeared in Europe at the close of the Stone Age. This costume is appropriate enough for outdoor exercise in a cold climate, but is quite unsuited to American summers, steam-heated houses, and Pullmans. Nevertheless, foreign ideas and habits hold the unfortunate man in thrall even when common sense tells him that the authentically American costume of gee string and moccasins would be far more comfortable. He puts on his feet stiff coverings made from hide prepared by a process invented in ancient Egypt and cut to a pattern which can be traced back to ancient Greece, and makes sure they are properly polished, also a Greek idea. Lastly, he ties about his neck a strip of bright-colored cloth which is a vestigial survival of the shoulder shawls worn by seventeenth-century Croats. He gives himself a final appraisal in the mirror, an old Mediterranean invention, and goes downstairs. . . .

He places upon his head a molded piece of felt, invented by the nomads of Eastern Asia, and if it looks like rain, puts on outer shoes of rubber, discovered by the ancient Mexicans, and takes an umbrella, invented in India. He then sprints for his train—the train, not the sprinting, being an English invention. At the station he pauses for a moment to buy a newspaper, paying for it with coins invented in ancient Lydia. Once on board he settles back to inhale the fumes of a cigarette invented in Mexico, or a cigar invented in Brazil. Meanwhile, he reads the news of the day, imprinted in characters invented by the ancient Semites by a process invented in Germany upon a material invented in China. As he scans the latest editorial pointing out the dire results to our institutions of accepting foreign ideas, he will not fail to thank a Hebrew God in an Indo-European language that he is a one hundred percent (decimal system invented by the Greeks) American (from Americus Vespucci, Italian geographer).

Source: Ralph Linton, *The American Mercury,* 40 (April 1937), pp. 427–429.

CHAPTER **4**   *Society*

Human beings are social animals. The quality we call "humanity" can be achieved only through social living, for there is no such thing as a person whose behavior and personality have not developed within some human society. We take social living so much for granted that we sometimes fail to recognize the immense influence society has over us. But in the complex interaction between the individual and society, the latter is usually the dominant partner. Society exists long before we are born into it, and it exists long after we are gone. Society gives content, direction, and meaning to our lives, and we, in turn, in countless ways, reshape the society that we leave to the next generation.

We are not social animals just because we happen to find social living convenient. Without society we could not survive. No infant could reach maturity without the care and protection of other people, and no adult could remain alive without using the vast store of information about the world that has been learned and passed on through society. Almost everything that we do is social in some sense—learned from others, done with others, directed toward others. Some very rare individuals try to escape from society, yet even they carry with them into their isolation the techniques, the ideas, and the identities they have learned from others. Hermits in their caves live with society in their memories.

What exactly is a society? Several conditions must be met before people can be said to be living in one. First, they must occupy a common territory. Second, they must not only share this territory but must also interact with one another. Third, they must to some extent have a common culture and a shared sense of membership in and commitment to the same group. We may say, then, that *a society is a group of interacting individuals sharing the same territory and participating in a common culture.* A society is not necessarily the same as a nation-state, although in the modern world the two are often identical. Many nation-states include smaller societies within their own borders. Most of the countries of South America, for example, contain societies of indigenous Indian peoples who have not been integrated into the larger society.

Many nonhuman animals are also social—such as ants, herrings, geese, and elephants. But nonhuman societies depend for their survival and functioning primarily on unlearned ("instinctive") patterns of behavior. As a result, different societies of any one species, be they termites or zebras, are virtually identical. Their societies may vary somewhat in size, but there is little or no difference in the social behavior of their members from one society to another. When you have seen one nest of a particular termite species, you have for most purposes seen all the nests of that species.

Human societies, however, are astonishingly diverse. The organization and characteristics of each human society are not based on the rigid dictates of its members' "instincts." They are created by human beings themselves and are learned and modified by each new generation. Consequently, although all human beings are members of the same biological species, every human society is different—so different that a person suddenly transplanted from, say, the United States to a jungle tribe of Brazil (or vice versa) would have very little idea of how to behave appropriately. Each society therefore presents a fresh and exciting challenge to the sociologist's understanding.

In this chapter we shall look at two main topics. First, we shall examine the social structure that underlies all human societies. Second, we shall consider some basic types of societies, showing how and why they differ from one another. In particular, we shall examine the radical differences between modern industrial societies and the traditional, preindustrial societies that they are rapidly replacing all over the world.

Social Structure

All complex things, from bacteria to planets, have a structure—that is, they consist of parts that are related to one another in an organized way. The structure of a building,

for example, consists of a floor, walls, a roof, an entrance, and probably such fittings as windows and utility lines. All buildings have much the same basic structure, although the character of any particular building—such as a cottage, a warehouse, a shack, or a multistory office tower—depends on the precise nature of its parts and their relationship to one another.

Sociologists sometimes find it helpful to use the metaphor of "structure" when they describe or analyze human societies. A society is not just a chaotic collection of randomly interacting people who happen to occupy the same area. Despite the human capacity for flexible and creative action, there is an underlying regularity, or pattern, to social behavior in any society. To sociologists, therefore, *social structure* refers to the organized relationships among the basic components in a social system. These basic components provide the framework for all human societies, although the precise character of the components and the relationships among them vary from one society to another. The most important components of social structure are statuses, roles, groups, and institutions. These concepts are of fundamental importance in sociology, and you will encounter them throughout this book.

Statuses

A society consists ultimately of individuals. Each of these persons occupies one or more socially defined positions in the society—woman, carpenter, teacher, son, old person, and so on. Such a position is called a *status*. A person's status determines where that individual "fits" in society and how he or she should relate to other people. The status of daughter, for example, determines the occupant's relationships with other members of the family; the status of corporation president determines the occupant's relationships with employees, shareholders, other corporation presidents, or tax collectors. Naturally, a person can have several statuses simultaneously, but one of them, usually an occupational status, tends to be the most important, and sociologists sometimes refer to it as the person's "master status."

The word "status" can be used either to refer simply to one of the many socially defined positions in a society, or to refer to the fact that some positions rank higher or lower than others. In most societies there is considerable inequality among different statuses. The person who has the status of Supreme Court justice, for example, enjoys more wealth, power, and prestige than the person who has the status of janitor. People of roughly equivalent status in an unequal society form a *class:* they enjoy greater access to the society's wealth and other resources than do those with lower statuses, and they have less access than do those with higher statuses. It is usually clear from the context whether sociologists are using the word "status" simply to refer to a position in society in general or to refer to a position of social rank.

We have little control over some of our statuses. Whether you are young or old, male or female, or black or white, for example, there is nothing you can do about it. Such a status is said to be *ascribed,* or arbitrarily given to us by society. But we have a certain amount of control over other statuses. At least partly through your own efforts you can get married, become a college graduate, a convict, or a member of a different religion. Such status is said to be earned, or *achieved.*

Roles

Every status in society carries with it a set of expected behavior patterns, obligations, and privileges—in other words, a *role.* The sociological concept of role is taken directly from the theater; it refers to the part or parts you play in society. The distinction between status and role is a simple one: you *occupy* a status, but you *play* a role (Linton, 1936). Status and role are thus two sides of the same coin.

The presidency of the United States, for example, is a status. Attached to this status is a presidential role, defined by social norms prescribing how the occupier of the status should behave. The status of president is a fixed position in society, but the role is more flexible, for there is considerable variation in how occupants of the status actually play it. In practice a single status may involve a number of roles. The status of college professor, for example, involves one role as teacher, one role as colleague to other professors, one role as researcher, and perhaps other roles, such as student adviser or writer of scholarly articles. A cluster of roles attached to a single status is sometimes called a "role set."

The roles people play in life depend on the status they happen to be occupying at any given time. If you are talking to your professor as a student, both of you will

Figure 4.1 There are two kinds of social status— those that are ascribed *to the individual on grounds over which he or she has no control, and those that are* achieved *by the individual through personal effort. The status of Queen of Great Britain is an ascribed one: Elizabeth II has the status because she was next in line of succession to her father, the late king. The status of prime minister of Great Britain is an achieved one: Margaret Thatcher has the status because she was elected to the leadership of her party and won a general election. Both women, of course, have other statuses as well—for example, each has the ascribed status of middle-aged woman and each has the achieved status of wife.*

STATUS AND ROLES

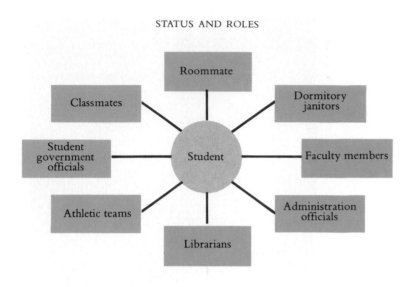

Figure 4.2 The status of student carries with it a number of different roles, some of which are illustrated here. As a student, you will adopt somewhat different roles in your interaction with people who have other statuses and are playing other roles. They will also interact with you in accordance with your student status and with the particular role you present to them. The status of student is only one of your statuses, although it is probably your most important status, or master status, at present. You also have other statuses—such as male or female, black or white, son or daughter—and each of these has different roles attached to it. The complex of roles that are carried by your particular status form a role set.

behave very differently than you would if, for example, you were sitting on a jury together and playing the roles of jurors. If in later years you return to visit the campus as a wealthy alumnus, your role relationship to your old professor will be changed again.

We play many different roles during the course of each day. The content of our role behavior is determined primarily by *role expectations,* the generally accepted social norms that define how a role ought to be played. Our actual role behavior is called *role performance.* How people react to one another often depends on whether role performance conforms to role expectations. If someone playing the role of physician asks you to undress, you will comply; if the same person asks you to undress when playing the role of host at dinner, you will probably respond quite differently.

The fact that people may have several different statuses, each with several different roles attached, can obviously cause problems when role expectations conflict. Sometimes contradictory expectations are built into a single role. A factory supervisor, for example, is expected to maintain good relations with the workers but is also expected to enforce regulations that the workers may resent. The result may be *role strain,* a situation in which a person for some

reason cannot meet role expectations. Another problem arises when a person plays two or more roles whose requirements are difficult to reconcile. For example, police officers sometimes find themselves in a situation in which they ought to arrest their own children: in such circumstances, the role expectations of a parent and of a police officer can be at odds with one another. When two or more of a person's roles clash in this way, a situation of *role conflict* exists. But although role expectations may sometimes cause strains and conflicts in role performances, they do for the most part ensure the smooth and predictable course of social interaction. Roles enable us to structure our own behavior along socially expected lines. We can anticipate the behavior of others in most situations, and we can fashion our own actions accordingly.

Groups

Most social behavior takes place within and among groups that are constantly being formed and re-formed. A *group* consists of people interacting together in an orderly way on the basis of shared expectations about each other's behavior. Put another way, a group is a number of persons whose statuses and roles are interrelated. A group therefore differs from a mere aggregate of people who just happen to be temporarily in the same place at the same time, such as pedestrians in a busy street.

Because human beings are essentially cooperative social animals, groups are a vital part of social structure. The distinctive characteristics of any society depend largely on the nature and activities of the groups that it contains.

Groups can be classified into two main types, primary and secondary. A *primary group* consists of a small number of people who interact over a relatively long period on an intimate, face-to-face basis. The members know one another personally and interact in an informal manner. Examples of this kind of group are families, cliques of friends and peers, and small communities. These groups are important building blocks of social structure; in fact, the social organization of some small-scale, traditional societies rests almost entirely on kinship groups.

A *secondary group,* in contrast, consists of a number of people who interact on a fairly temporary, anonymous, and impersonal basis. The members either do not know one another personally, or, at best, know one another only in terms of particular formal roles rather than as whole people. Secondary groups are usually established to serve specific purposes, and people are generally less emotionally committed to them than they are to their primary groups. Examples of secondary groups are formal organizations such as General Motors, political parties, or government bureaucracies. These large organizations are not found in the simplest of human societies, but they are increasingly important in large modern societies. (Both primary and secondary groups are discussed in more detail in Chapter 7, "Social Groups.")

Institutions

Every society must meet certain basic social needs if it is to survive and provide a satisfying life for its members. For example, children must be raised and cared for; the cultural knowledge of one generation must be passed on to the next; important social values must be shared and upheld; social order must be maintained; goods and services must be produced. Over time, the members of each society create patterns of thought and action that provide an appropriate solution for these recurrent challenges. These patterns of behavior are what sociologists call institutions.

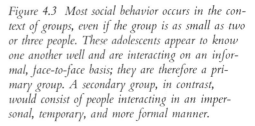

Figure 4.3 Most social behavior occurs in the context of groups, even if the group is as small as two or three people. These adolescents appear to know one another well and are interacting on an informal, face-to-face basis; they are therefore a primary group. A secondary group, in contrast, would consist of people interacting in an impersonal, temporary, and more formal manner.

An *institution* is a stable cluster of values, norms, statuses, roles, and groups that develops around a basic social need. (Figure 4.4 lists major institutions of modern societies, with examples of each of these elements.) Thus, the family institution provides for the care of children. The educational institution transmits cultural knowledge to the young. The religious institution provides a set of shared values and the rituals that reaffirm them. The political institution allocates power and maintains order. The economic institution provides goods and services. These major institutions, too, contain smaller units within themselves: for example, baseball is a pattern of behavior within the overarching institution of sport; the hospital is part of the overall medical institution; the prison system is an aspect of the legal institution; and so on.

MAJOR SOCIAL INSTITUTIONS

Institution	Social Need	Some Values	Some Norms	Some Statuses/ Roles	Some Groups
Family.	Regulate sexual behavior; provide care for children.	Marital fidelity.	Have only one spouse.	Husband; grandmother.	Kinship group.
Education.	Transmit cultural knowledge to the young.	Intellectual curiosity.	Attend school.	Teacher; student.	High school clique; college seminar.
Religion.	Share and reaffirm community values and solidarity.	Belief in God.	Attend regular worship.	Rabbi; cardinal.	Synod; congregation.
Science.	Investigate social and natural world.	Unbiased search for truth.	Conduct research.	Physicist; anthropologist.	Research team; science society.
Political system.	Distribute power; maintain order.	Freedom.	Vote by secret ballot.	Senator; lobbyist.	Legislature; political party.
Economic system.	Produce and distribute goods and services.	Free enterprise.	Maximize profits.	Accountant; vendor.	Corporate board; labor union.
Medical system.	Take care of the sick.	Good health.	Save life if possible.	Physician; patient.	Hospital staff; ward of patients.
Military.	Aggress or defend against enemies of the state.	Discipline.	Follow orders.	General; marine.	Platoon; army division.
Legal system.	Maintain social control.	Fair trial.	Inform suspects of their rights.	Judge; lawyer.	Jury; cell mates.
Sport.	Recreation, exercise.	Winning.	Play by the rules.	Umpire; coach.	Baseball team; fan club.

Figure 4.4 All institutions have arisen over time as people develop social responses to the particular needs of their society. Each institution is a stable cluster of values, norms, statuses, roles, and participating groups, and it provides an established pattern of thought and action that offers a solution to the recurrent problems and demands of social living. This table lists the major institutions of modern society, with examples of each of the elements involved.

One important characteristic of institutions is that they are inherently conservative. Patterns of social behavior become institutionalized, or securely established, only when they have been reinforced by custom and tradition to the point where they are accepted almost without question. People tend to resent and resist any attack on the institutions they know. (Imagine, for example, the likely response in North America to a serious attempt to abolish the family, to end compulsory schooling, to replace existing churches with new cults, or to apply communist principles to the economy.) This resistance to change is often functional, for it can ensure social stability; but in times of social conflict or rapid change, a slow response may be dysfunctional if the old forms have become outmoded, ineffectual, or even oppressive.

A second characteristic of institutions is that they tend to be closely linked within the social structure. As we noted in Chapter 3 ("Culture"), the various aspects of a culture tend on the whole to fit together; if they do not, cultural strain and even cultural disintegration result. In the same way, the components of social structure must be fairly well integrated if too much structural strain is to be avoided and the threat of social disintegration averted. For this reason, a society's major institutions tend to uphold similar values and norms, to reflect compatible goals and priorities, and to benefit or penalize the same groups and interests. Because all the institutions share common features, any one of them can yield insights into the others and can serve to some extent as a microcosm of the larger society.

A third characteristic of institutions is that when they do change, they rarely do so in isolation: significant modifications in any major institution are likely to be accompanied or followed by changes in others. This is especially true of changes in the economy, for the way people make their living has multiple effects on almost everything else they do. Thus, if a society were to change from a basic subsistence strategy of rural farming to one of urban manufacturing, many other institutional adjustments would be needed to maintain social integration.

An Illustration: Sport

Many of the principles of social structure that we have discussed can be illustrated by the example of *sport*—that is, competitive physical activity guided by established rules. Like other institutions, sport provides in some respects a microcosm of the entire society. By understanding crucial aspects of sport—the kinds of games that are popular, the social groups that participate, the statuses and roles of those involved, the distribution of power and wealth within the institution, the linkages of sport with other institutions, and the values sport represents—we can learn much about American society as a whole. We can also, incidentally, see what is distinctive about the sociological approach to a familiar aspect of social life.

Sport in American Society

In American society, sport is an important institution directly affecting the lives of the majority of the population who are either participants in, or spectators of, various sports. Three out of four Americans report that they discuss sport frequently. National television networks devote an average of twenty-four hours a week to sports coverage, and an event like the Superbowl may attract as many as

Figure 4.5 In many respects sport, like any other institution, provides a microcosm of the society in which it exists. For example, ice hockey, which developed in Canada, has become a competitive, professionalized, spectator sport—features that assume a competitive society with a highly developed division of labor and large urban concentrations of people with a fair amount of leisure time. Such a sport could not, and did not, exist in this form in the significantly different Canadian society of a hundred years ago.

100 million viewers. The sports section of newspapers is typically longer than even the sections on politics and economics, and is by far the most popular part of the paper; in fact, it is the only section that millions of Americans ever read. More than 2 million high school and college students participate in organized sports, and tens of millions of Americans attend football, baseball, and basketball games. Clearly, sport is not a trivial aspect of American life. Indeed, in recent years it has been the subject of extensive sociological study (H. Edwards, 1973; Talamini and Page, 1973; Ball and Loy, 1975; Coakley, 1978; Eitzen and Sage, 1978; Loy et. al, 1978; Leonard, 1980).

Like any other institution, sport serves various social functions. It provides organized leisure activities in a society that has a good deal of leisure time; it offers opportunities for physical exercise; it provides, through its famous athletes, role models whose success, skills, and determination are held up for emulation; it acts, perhaps, as a safety valve for spectators and participants, allowing them to express aggressive energies in a generally harmless way; and, as we shall see, it serves to reinforce many of the basic values of the society (H. Edwards, 1973; Coakley, 1978; Eitzen and Sage, 1978).

The kinds of sporting activities that have been popular over the last century or so tell us a good deal about the changes in American society during that period. Before about 1870, the favorite sports of Americans included such activities as footracing, boat racing, cockfighting, hunting, and fishing: the large-scale organized spectator sports of today were almost unknown. The change in popular taste parallels the transformation of American society from a predominantly rural, farming nation to an urban, industrialized one. This fundamental change in the economic institution had many implications for sport. As standards of living rose, a wider participation in sports became possible; and as the work week became shorter, more leisure time was made available for sports activities. Then, too, the advent of electric light stimulated the development of such indoor sports as volleyball and basketball. The growth of cities provided the concentrated populations necessary to support huge stadiums. Radio and then television brought spectator sports into homes across the nation. Innovations in land and air transportation made it possible for teams and fans to travel easily and frequently to interregional and even international competitions. These changes have had many effects on American sport. Whereas sport was once informal and participant-oriented, it has become highly organized and generally spectator-oriented. Control of sport, which was once in the hands of small, primary groups of players, has passed to large, secondary groups such as the American Athletic Union, the U.S. Olympic Committee, or the National Collegiate Athletic Association. Most significant, a new role emerged, that of the full-time professional athlete who specializes not only in a single sport but also in a single status (pitcher, quarterback). To the professional, sport tends to become work rather than play.

Spectator sport is now much more than just a form of public entertainment: it is big business. The teams of the four major professional sports—baseball, basketball, football, and hockey—are corporate organizations, similar in most respects to other business organizations. The fundamentally commercial nature of these sports is revealed by the way the teams buy, sell, and trade players, as though athletes were economic commodities. In many other countries these practices are relatively uncommon: more typical is a mutual loyalty between hometown fans and players that makes the idea of selling one's own athletes or importing outsiders distasteful. The American attitude, however, seems to be that if you cannot win with the team you have, you should buy a better one. For its part, American business is the major sponsor of organized sports: many sports could not exist in their present form without revenue from advertising and television coverage. The relationship between sports and business is mutually rewarding: a minute of TV Superbowl advertising costs a quarter of a million dollars; the sales of sporting goods alone total over $30 billion a year.

But who benefits from the immense wealth generated by the sporting industry? The answer here—as elsewhere in the society—is that the wealth is unequally shared, with a disproportionate amount going to a handful of high-status individuals such as the owners of franchises and other business leaders whose industries benefit from links with the sporting enterprise. Few of the athletes themselves grow rich, a fact that is perhaps obscured by the publicity surrounding the huge earnings of the tiny minority who do. The full-time players in the four major team sports are, in fact, well paid, but their total number is less than 2500. In addition, most of those who do achieve financial success enjoy it for only a brief period—the median career of a professional football player, for instance, lasts less than five years—and a sharp drop in earnings and social status usually follows. (Beyond the major sports, in tennis, horse racing, boxing, and the like, only a handful of athletes are able to make a good living from their profession.) Nevertheless, millions of Little Leaguers and other juvenile athletes are encouraged to aspire to become professionals in their sport, a status they have a less-than-1-percent chance of attaining (Blitz, 1973; Rosenberg, 1979; Eitzen and Sage, 1979). Clearly, the idea that sport is a good avenue to social and economic success is simply part of the "rags to riches" mythology that pervades American society.

Sport and American Values

One reason Americans view sport so favorably is that it embodies some highly regarded values: perseverance, discipline, hard work, competition, success. These same values are found in other American institutions—in the political system, for example, which relies on the competition of ideas, interests, and candidates, or in the educational system, which prizes diligence, conformity to rules, and competition among students for high grades. Perhaps most important, the principles of free enterprise that underlie the economy assume that the way to success is to work one's way up by competing with others.

The presence of organized sport at every level of the educational system is often justified by reference to these values: it is widely believed that participation in sports "builds character" by introducing the young to discipline and competition. Sport therefore becomes a major concern of the schools, as evidenced by the space devoted to it in school newspapers and yearbooks, by the public display of trophies, and by the time and money devoted to coaching and training, to bands and cheerleaders, and to interschool sports. In high schools, the prestige of males among their peer group is influenced more by their athletic prowess than by their scholarly achievements—although the latter, rather than the former, are supposed to be the goal of education (J. Coleman, 1965; Eitzen, 1976). Actually, however, the idea that participation in sports develops traits of character finds little support in the research on the subject (Ogilvie and Tutko, 1971). Rather, it seems that those who already display the necessary character traits are more likely to become athletes. And since athletics produces not only

skilled players and victors but also incompetents and losers, it is even possible that failure in school sports may leave some students with diminished feelings of self-worth.

The use of sports to uphold norms and values is even more apparent when a team represents a community, region, or especially a nation. As the surrounding nationalistic pageantry of flags and anthems suggests, international competitions are far more than a test of athletic skills. Citizens are apt to feel that the reputation and prestige of their nation depends on the performance of its athletes, almost as it would if they were warriors representing the country in a battle. A classic example of this phenomenon occurred when the Olympics were held in Germany in 1936. The Nazis used the games for blatantly political purposes, hoping the success of their athletes would prove their racial and cultural superiority to the world—an ambition that was largely wrecked when a black American, Jesse Owens, easily defeated his blond, blue-eyed, "Aryan" competitors. In the modern world, the Soviet Union and its East European satellites are particularly inclined to equate victory in international sports with superiority in

Figure 4.6

"Oh sure, enormous wealth has been fun; Marian and the kids have been a joy; and success has been stimulating—but do you know that, deep down, nothing yet has given me the kick catching that winning pass in the Harvard game did?"

world politics, and they devote immense resources to identifying, subsidizing, and training promising athletes. The boycott of the 1980 Moscow Olympics by the United States and many of its allies caused great concern to the Soviet Union, which had intended to use the event as an international showcase for the Soviet system.

Winning is so highly valued in American sports that the result of an athletic contest seems to have become more important than the process of actually participating in it. A century ago it might have been said, "It matters not who won or lost, but how you played the game"; today, a more appropriate slogan would be Vince Lombardi's dictum, "Winning isn't everything; it's the only thing." This emphasis on victory extends throughout the institution, and is a familiar feature of that uniquely American system, intercollegiate sports. Although interschool sports were originally organized by students for their own pleasure, they are now run along business lines by college administrators and professional coaches. Students and alumni tend to regard victory in sports as an index of a college's prestige, and a winning team is considered a superb advertisement for a college, serving to attract students, alumni contributions, and grants from state legislatures. For this reason the schools compete vigorously for promising athletes, often offering athletic scholarships to people who are not really "scholars" in the traditional sense of the word (and frequently causing role conflict for those recipients who try to meet the rival demands of both their academic and sporting roles). So intense does the competition for new recruits become that there is a good deal of cheating, usually in the form of attracting athletes by offering them disguised financial benefits that exceed the legal scholarship limit (Durso, 1975; Denlinger and Shapiro, 1975; Benagh, 1976; Luschen, 1976). Recently, however, several major American universities were found to have falsified high school transcripts and credited athletes with courses they never took, all in an attempt to make them eligible to enter and remain in school (Underwood, 1980).

The idea that victory is the only possible purpose of competition is so deeply embedded in American culture—and, indeed, in that of most modern industrial societies—that it is difficult for us to imagine any alternative. Yet there are many societies where sports have a quite different objective. The Tangu people of New Guinea play a game in which each of two teams throws a spinning top at a cluster of stakes that have been driven into the ground. The object of the game is not to have one team win by hitting the most stakes; instead, it is to have each team hit exactly the same number of stakes, at which point the game ends. The Tangu, who place great emphasis on equality in their sharing of food and in other interpersonal relationships, have created a game that reflects their cultural values (Burridge, 1957). The Gahuku people of New Guinea use sport as a harmless substitute for combat between hostile groups. When one group has a grievance against another, a team representing the offending group enters a contest with one score in its favor. The object of the game is for the team representing the aggrieved group to even the score. Once a tie has been achieved, the game is over and the grievance has been satisfactorily redressed (Read, 1965). In the traditional society of the Zuñi of northern New Mexico, rivalry was viewed as socially destructive. A person who constantly won footraces would be disqualified from future competition: the Zuñi preferred a game that gave the participants fairly equal chances, and felt that an outstanding athlete spoiled the fun for everybody else (Benedict, 1961). In modern China, too, there is little interest in the outcome of sporting events. Schools do not keep trophies or records of the success or failure of their teams, and athletes regard the result of a game as merely incidental to other aspects of sport—the development of skill and technique, the forming of friendships, the refinement of teamwork, the display of physical prowess (W. Johnson, 1973). In short, societies that are interested in sharing and cooperation tend to prefer to play sports in a noncompetitive way; those that are interested in individual achievement and success tend to prefer more competitive sports (Stipes, 1973). Indeed, the popularity in America of such aggressive sports as hockey, football, boxing, and car racing is probably linked to the comparatively high level of aggression in American life as a whole (as evidenced, for example, by the fact that the United States has by far the highest homicide rate in the industrialized world).

Class, Race, Sex, and Sport

A person's class, race, and sex status influence his or her chances to play a role in a variety of American institutions. In the political institution, for example, the wealthy are heavily overrepresented in Congress (millionaires comprise

SEGREGATION BY POSITION IN PROFESSIONAL BASEBALL AND FOOTBALL

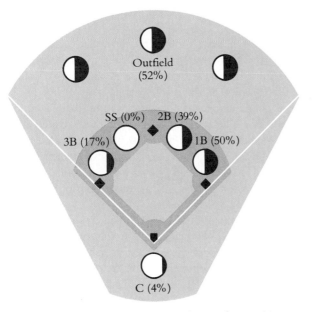

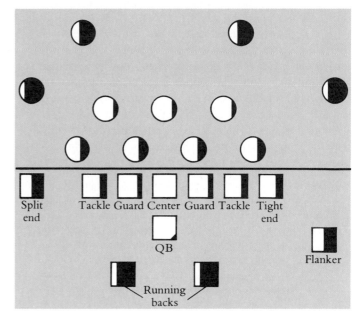

Percentage of black players in regular starting positions
in the 1974 major league baseball season

Percentage of players in starting offensive and defensive positions in
the 1974–75 football season

Source: Jay J. Coakley, *Sport in Society: Issues and Controversies* (St. Louis: Mosby), 1978, pp. 284, 287.

Figure 4.7 These illustrations show the percentage of black players in various positions in baseball and football in the mid-seventies. Blacks are un-derrepresented in the central positions, a feature that still persists today.

less than 1 percent of the population but over a fifth of the senators), whereas blacks and women are strikingly un-derrepresented (blacks comprise about 11.7 percent of the population, but there are no black senators; women comprise over 50 percent of the population, but only 2 of the 100 senators are female). It is hardly surprising that the situation in sport parallels that in other institutions.

Social class strongly affects the individual's preference for particular sports, whether as a participant or as a spectator. Only the upper classes, for example, can take part in such expensive sports as yachting and polo. Both the upper and the middle classes may be able to afford tennis, golf, skiing, or scuba diving. The lower classes, however, may be able to participate only in such sports as bowling, pool, baseball, basketball, boxing, or wrestling. These class biases toward particular sports tend to be passed on from one generation to the next. A child whose parents belong to a country club is likely to develop an interest in golf, tennis, or swimming, and to develop the necessary skills. A child who grows up in an inner city slum is more likely to turn to basketball, a game that needs little more in the way of facilities than a strip of asphalt and a backboard and hoop. Members of different social classes also tend to have different tastes as spectators: people of higher social status are more likely to view college sports or such genteel games as golf and tennis; people of lower status gravitate toward games that offer more daring, strength, and even violence, such as motocross racing and demolition derbies (Loy, 1969; Axthelm, 1970; Luschen, 1969; Gruneau, 1975).

It is popularly believed that unlike other institutions in the United States, sport is color-blind: since winning is so important, gifted nonwhite athletes are supposedly able to get ahead solely on the basis of their talent. In addition, the high proportion of blacks in the major professional sports of baseball, football, and basketball has led to the widely held view that sport provides unique opportunities for talented ghetto youngsters to reach the heights of celebrity and fortune. As one writer in *Sports Illustrated* expressed it:

> Sport is a way out of the despair of the slums, a route to social prestige among one's peers and sometimes a way to quick wealth. Few other roads to fame and financial reward have been open to the young black.... Every male black child, however he might be discouraged from a career with a Wall Street brokerage firm, knows he has a sporting chance in baseball, boxing, basketball, or track.... The black youngster has something real to aspire to ... [Quoted in Coakley, 1978]

Unhappily, the facts contradict both of these beliefs on a number of counts (Olsen, 1968; Rosenblatt, 1967; Edwards, 1969, 1973; Loy and McElvogue, 1970; Yetman and Eitzen, 1971).

To begin with, blacks are virtually absent from most forms of sport except football, baseball, basketball, and boxing. There are virtually no black figure skaters, race-car drivers, polo players, or skiers. High black participation in the few sports where they are well represented is a relatively recent phenomenon, dating in most sports from the late fifties and sixties, a time when the civil rights movement was beginning to achieve similar changes in other institutions.

Second, despite the notion that sport represents the fast lane out of the ghetto, the fact is that sport offers a very minimal career opportunity for young blacks. Although much is made of the success of famous individual players, the number of blacks who make their living out of sport is tiny. There are only about 900 full-time professional black athletes in the three major team sports; if we add to these the professional black athletes from all other sports plus coaches, trainers, and others, it is doubtful if more than 1500 blacks earn a living from sport (Coakley, 1978). If young blacks were urged to aspire to a career in any other national industry that could offer only about 1500 mostly temporary jobs, the idea would seem absurd. It is a tribute to the power of the myth that it persists in the face of these facts.

Third, and perhaps most significant, blacks have to be better players than whites to be selected for major professional teams. Studies of major league baseball between 1953 and 1975 show that the mean batting average for blacks was 20 points above that for whites, and there is ample evidence that blacks must outperform their white counterparts if they are to get into and remain in professional baseball (Rosenblatt 1967; Yetman and Eitzen, 1977; Scully, 1974). The case is the same for professional basketball (Johnson and Marple, 1973) and professional football (Brower, 1973).

Fourth, blacks are virtually excluded from certain statuses within teams—essentially, from the central positions that offer the most opportunity for leadership and the most responsibility for the outcome of the game. In major league baseball during the seventies, for example, 96 percent of the catchers and 100 percent of the shortstops were white or Hispanic, whereas 52 percent of those holding outfield positions were black. Likewise in professional football, 100 percent of the centers and 96 percent of the quarterbacks were white, but 42 percent of the noncentral positions were black (Dougherty, 1976). Thus even the allocation of statuses within the teams parallels that in the society beyond.

Fifth, sport offers virtually no career opportunities for blacks in any role other than that of athlete. Coaches, managers, umpires, officials, administrators, sportscasters, and owners are almost all white. Even when it comes to promoting commercial products, the players used are disproportionately white.

It remains true, however, that blacks are disproportionately represented in professional baseball (over 20 percent of the players), football (over 40 percent), and basketball (over 60 percent). Why is this so? A frequent explanation is that blacks have some inborn, genetic traits that make them especially talented at these sports. This is an ironic reversal of the argument that was used earlier in the century to justify their exclusion from professional sport; namely, that they are genetically incapable of playing games that require so much sophistication. In its way, the new argument is unconsciously racist, for it tends to deny black athletes the same credit for individual hard work and perseverance that would be accorded to white players, and instead attributes their skills to group physiology. This fact is more apparent if we consider that similar arguments are not used to account for the special skills that other groups display in particular sports. Nobody proposes genetic factors, for example, to explain why East Germany has produced so many excellent swimmers, why Canadians do well at hockey, why Japanese-Americans are disproportionately represented in judo—or, for that matter, why the British are hopeless at baseball while white Americans are equally inept at cricket. In each case, it is easy to see that cultural factors, not genetic ones, are at work. Even a comparison of black American athletes with black African athletes yields the same impression: the Africans are superb at long-distance running, but poor at events under 1500 meters; black Americans do well at sprints and jumps, but poorly in long-distance events.

What cultural factors explain the black predominance in some American sports? The opportunity structure of American society suggests why many black children look to sport as a career in the first place: it is one of the few fields in which a relatively large number of blacks have achieved publicly recognized success, and one of the few that offers successful, highly visible role models for the ambitious young black. White children correctly perceive that they have an array of career opportunities other than sport, so they are less apt to give sport the same single-minded dedication that many black children do. It is likely, then, that a higher proportion of blacks than of whites see sport as a potential career, and that they work harder to achieve entry. As to why they choose baseball, football, and basketball, the answer is obvious enough: the facilities for these games are freely available at public expense in the school or neighborhood. Naturally, then, black athletes will excel at these sports and not at skiing, skating, or golfing, where facilities and coaching are not available to them (H. Edwards, 1969, 1973; J. Phillips, 1976).

Like blacks, women have been, and to a great extent still are, denied entry to many athletic roles: sport has long been an almost exclusively male preserve, and the few women who participated in the past were apt to be regarded as unwelcome intruders. In this respect, sport once again paralleled such other American institutions as religion, the economy, politics, law, the military, and science, in which women were also refused access to high statuses. The reason for the exclusion of women from sport is a cultural one, namely, that the traditional role expectations for women seemed fundamentally at odds with role expectations for athletes. As we shall see in Chapter 13 ("Inequalities of Gender and Age"), there are many non-Western societies

Figure 4.8 Women, though long denied equal opportunities in the area of sport, are now taking an increasingly active—and successful—part in the institution. Increased female participation in athletics parallels the changes that are occurring in all other institutions, especially the economy—and provides further evidence of the tendency for changes in one institution to be accompanied by adjustments in the others.

in which heavy physical labor is considered a woman's job, not a man's. But for centuries in Western culture, there has been a basic assumption that women are biologically limited in their physical abilities, that they are in need of male protection and are incapable of vigorous, competitive activity. In North America it is widely felt that the more dominant and active a man is, the more "masculine" he is; the more passive and delicate a women, the more "feminine" she is. As a result, the combined role expectations of a feminine woman and a competitive athlete have raised the prospect of severe role conflicts, and a woman who wanted an athletic pastime, let alone a career, put her femininity at severe risk. The institution of sport thus served to reinforce the role expectations of the larger society. The men were the active doers on the field; the women, the cutely dressed cheerleaders giving emotional support to their menfolk—a suitable preparation for the later roles of each (Hoepner, 1974; Gerber et al., 1974; Eitzen and Sage, 1978).

In recent years sex roles have changed significantly, primarily because unprecedented numbers of women have entered economic life and have demanded equality with men, at first in the workplace and then in other areas of life. Thanks to the efforts of the women's movement, court decisions, and legislation, women are now increasingly active in sport. Title IX of the 1972 Education Amendments provided that sex cannot serve as grounds for exclusion from participation in any educational program or activity that receives federal assistance, and this measure is having a profound impact on schools and colleges. Athletic scholarships for women, once unheard of, are becoming common; administrators who once apportioned as little as 1 percent of their sports budget to women's sports are now giving both sexes equal financial consideration; and female athletes are for the first time enjoying adequate coaching and other facilities, instead of being relegated to ancient gyms that the men had abandoned. By 1980, more than a third of high school and college athletes were women, and the proportion continues to grow. Although the opportunities and rewards for female athletes still do not bear comparison with those for males, women are participating in a variety of sports. In 1970, virtually no teen-aged girls played soccer; by 1980, 1 million did so. In the same ten-year period, the number of female tennis players increased from 3 million to 11 million and the number of golfers from half a million to 5 million. Female joggers, almost nonexistent in 1970, represented a third of all joggers ten years later

(Wood, 1980). Women are also becoming successful jockeys, race-car drivers, javelin throwers, high jumpers, long-distance runners and swimmers, gymnasts, and basketball players.

What truth is there, then, in the traditional view that women are unsuited to take part in certain sports? Certainly there does seem to be little possibility that men and women will be able to compete on equal terms in all sports. On average, men are stronger, faster, and heavier than women, and are at a particular advantage in activities that require superior upper-body strength or short-term endurance. But although this means that a female football team would almost certainly be defeated by a male football team, there is no more reason to think females cannot successfully compete among themselves in such a sport than there is to think that lightweight boxers lack skills or talent because they are likely to be defeated by heavyweight boxers.

In other sports there is scope for direct competition and female victory; this applies particularly to events that do not require great muscle power, such as riflery, precision parachuting, and equestrian sports. In many track and swimming events, too, women may be able to compete successfully with men: women runners and swimmers are today breaking records set by men a few years ago, and the gap between male and female records in these fields is narrowing so rapidly that it may shrink to insignificance. In other events that require long-term physical endurance, trained women may prove superior, for they are able to convert body fat to energy for longer periods than most men. This is especially true in long-distance swimming, which is becoming a predominantly female sport, and in marathons of fifty miles or more. In all these sports there is no physical reason why women cannot participate: they have no greater risk of injury than men, and can avoid damage to vulnerable parts of the body in the same way that men do, through the use of protective clothing and rules of fair play. Nevertheless, on the playing field as elsewhere in life, women are often still valued for their decorative aspects rather than their individual talent. For example, sportswriters would never dream of raving about the physical charms of a male athlete, yet are quick to include descriptions of the shape, size, hair style, and eye color of female athletes. One *Sports Illustrated* writer, for example, describes a female golfer in the following, somewhat unathletic, terms:

A cool, braided California blond named Laura Baugh made quite a splash...her perfectly tanned, well-formed legs swinging jauntily. The hair on her tapered arms was bleached absolutely white against a milk-chocolate tan. Her platinum hair was pulled smartly back in a Viking-maiden braid. [Quoted in Eitzen and Sage, 1978]

One key cultural factor determines which sports women are now freely accepted in and which they are not: men, who still control sport, want female athletes to appear "ladylike." It is therefore acceptable for women to take part in sports involving the display of grace and beauty, such as figure skating, tennis, swimming, or skiing, and in non-contact sports such as basketball, baseball, and track. It is unacceptable, however, for women to take part in any sport in which they have physical confrontation with an opponent, or in which they become too unkempt, exhausted, and sweaty. Football, wrestling, ice hockey, and boxing therefore remain among the male preserves, for it is not so much talent as the individual's ascribed status (male or female) that determines access to an achieved status (such as skater or wrestler) (Metheny, 1977).

Our analysis of a single American institution and the statuses, roles, and groups within it has illuminated many other aspects of the society—its social changes and other institutions, its values and myths, its intergroup relations and inequalities. We shall explore many such aspects of this specific society in more detail later, but we must first turn to a consideration of human societies in general.

Types of Societies

If we compressed the entire history of life on the planet into a single year, the first modern human being would not appear until December 31 at about 11:53 P.M., and the first civilizations would have emerged only about a minute before the end of the year. Yet our cultural achievements in the brief time that we have occupied the planet have been remarkable. Some 15,000 years ago our ancestors were practicing religious rituals and painting superb pictures on the walls of their caves. Around 11,000 years ago, some human groups began to domesticate animals and plants, thereby freeing themselves from total dependence on the food that they could hunt and gather. About 6000 years ago people began to live in cities, to specialize in different forms of labor, to divide into social classes, and to create

distinct political and economic institutions. Within a few thousand years empires were created, linking previously isolated groups and bringing millions of people under centralized rule. Advanced agricultural technologies improved the productivity of the land, resulting in growing populations and the emergence of large nation-states. A mere 250 years ago the Industrial Revolution began, thrusting us into the modern world of factories and computers, jet aircraft and nuclear reactors, instantaneous global communications and terrifying military technologies.

Although thousands of different human societies have existed since the beginning of human history, they can be classified into a limited number of basic types according to the technologies they have used to exploit the natural environment. In general, there has been a historical trend of *sociocultural evolution,* the tendency for societies' social structures and cultures to grow more complex over time (Steward, 1955; L. White, 1959; Sahlins and Service, 1960; Parsons, 1966; Fried, 1967; Lenski and Lenski, 1978). This process has some similarities with biological evolution. Like an organism, a society has to adapt to its environment in order to exploit food resources. Different societies have used different subsistence strategies, and those societies that have found more productive strategies have tended to grow larger and more complex, often enjoying their success at the expense of societies using more primitive technologies. This process of sociocultural evolution is not in any sense a "law" applicable to all societies: it represents only a general trend that has been observed in the historical and archaeological evidence. Some societies have evolved further and faster than others; some have become "stuck" at a particular level; some have disintegrated and disappeared; and all have changed in ways that are unique to themselves. In general, however, societies can be classified according to their basic reliance on one of five subsistence strategies: hunting and gathering, pastoralism, horticulture, agriculture, or industrialism, with social structure growing increasingly complex at each succeeding level.

As we noted in the previous chapter, the *ecological* approach views human society in the context of its total environment. By applying this approach to the types of societies that appear in the course of sociocultural evolution, we can account for many of the differences in their social structure and culture (Lenski, 1966; Vayda, 1969; Cohen, 1974; Bennett, 1976; Hardesty, 1977; Boulding, 1978; M. Harris, 1979).

Hunting and Gathering Societies

For almost all of the time that human beings have existed, they have relied on hunting wild animals and gathering wild vegetation for their survival. All societies used this subsistence strategy until only a few thousand years ago, and even today there are still a handful of isolated peoples, such as the Aranda of the central Australian desert, who retain this way of life.

Hunting and gathering societies tend to consist of very small, scattered groups. The reason is simple: the environment cannot support a large concentration of people who rely on whatever food they can find or catch from one day to the next. Hunting and gathering peoples therefore live in small primary groups that rarely exceed forty members.

Figure 4.9 The Aranda aborigines of the Australian desert are one of the few hunting and gathering peoples that have survived into the modern world. They live in small nomadic groups based mainly on kinship. Accustomed to our own affluent life-style, we are inclined to regard their life as one of constant hardship. But the Aranda feel very few "needs," and they are able to satisfy them with only a few hours' work each day. Their way of life is doomed, however, for their society is being absorbed by the industrial society of modern Australia.

Even so, each group may require several hundred square miles of territory to support itself, so contact between groups is brief and infrequent. The groups are based on kinship, with most members being related by ancestry or marriage. In fact, the family is almost the only distinct institution in these societies. It fulfills many of the functions that are met by more specialized institutions in other societies, such as economic production, the education of the young, and the protection of the group. Political institutions are absent: statuses in these societies are essentially equal, and although there is sometimes a part-time headman with very limited authority, most decisions are made through group discussion.

Hunting and gathering peoples are constantly on the move because they must leave an area as soon as they have exhausted its food resources. As a result, possessions would be a hindrance to them, so they own very few goods. No individual can acquire wealth, because there is no wealth to be acquired. People who do find a substantial food resource are expected to share it with the whole community. Warfare is extremely uncommon among hunting and gathering peoples, partly because they have so little in the way of material goods to fight about. Yet, contrary to popular belief, the life of hunting and gathering peoples is not usually one of constant hardship on the brink of starvation. Their needs are simple and easily satisfied, and they spend less time working for their living than the average inhabitants of any other type of society. They are among the most leisured people on earth (Lee, 1968, 1979; Sahlins, 1972).

There are very few statuses in these societies except for those based on sex, age, or kinship. The roles performed by men and women, by the young and the old, and by various kin are somewhat different, but there are no other specialized roles. Most people do much the same things most of the time, and as a result of their common life experiences they share almost identical values. Their religion almost never includes a belief in a powerful god or gods who are active in human affairs; instead, they tend to see the world as populated by unseen spirits that must be taken account of, but not necessarily worshiped.

The use of hunting and gathering as a subsistence strategy thus has a very strong influence on social structure and culture. The social structure of these societies is necessarily very simple, and their cultures cannot become elaborate and diversified.

Figure 4.10 Pastoralists in Afghanistan prepare to leave their temporary winter encampment. They take their herds from one place to another in search of grazing and water, using the camels for transport, milk, and meat. Surplus camels are sold or traded for other items the people need. Not all pastoralists are nomadic, however; those that live in areas that can support continuous grazing are able to form small, settled communities.

Pastoral Societies

Between ten and twelve thousand years ago, some hunting and gathering groups began to develop pastoralism, a subsistence strategy based on the domestication of herds of animals. This strategy has been adopted by many peoples living in deserts or other regions that are not suited to the cultivation of plants, but which contain animals—such as goats or sheep—that can be readily tamed and used as a food source. Many pastoral societies still exist in the modern world, particularly in Africa and in the Middle and Near East.

Pastoralism is a much more reliable and productive strategy than hunting and gathering. Not only is a steady food supply assured, but the size of the herds can be increased over time through careful animal husbandry. An important result is that societies can grow much larger, perhaps to include hundreds or even thousands of people. Equally significant, the greater productivity of pastoralism permits the accumulation of a surplus of livestock and food. Through such means as trade, this surplus can be converted into other forms of wealth—which can be used, in turn, to acquire power. For the first time some individuals can become more powerful than others and pass on their status to their descendants. Patterns of chieftainship begin to appear, as these powerful and wealthy families are able to secure their positions.

Pastoralists are usually nomadic because they must con-stantly take their herds to new grazing grounds. As a result, their material possessions are few in number but are more elaborate than those of hunting and gathering peoples because they can be carried by animals. Cultural artifacts in these societies therefore consist of items that are easily transportable—tents, woven carpets, simple utensils, jewelry, and so on. Their nomadic way of life often brings pastoralists into contact with other groups. One consequence is the development of systematic trading; a second is that disputes over grazing rights frequently lead to warfare. Slavery, unknown in hunting and gathering societies, makes its appearance as captives in war are put to work for their conquerors.

Pastoral peoples tend to develop a belief that is found in very few religions: they commonly believe in a god or gods who take an active interest in human affairs and look after the people who worship them. This belief seems to have been suggested by the pastoralists' experience of the relationship between themselves and their flocks (Lenski and Lenski, 1978). The few modern religions based on this view of the relationship between human beings and a god—Judaism and its offshoots, Christianity and Islam—originated among pastoral peoples.

The subsistence strategy of pastoral societies thus provides distinctive social and cultural opportunities and limitations. Populations become larger, political and economic institutions begin to develop, and both social structure and culture become more complex.

Horticultural Societies

Horticultural societies also first appeared between ten and twelve thousand years ago, when some hunters and gatherers began to deliberately sow, tend, and harvest edible vegetation. Horticulturalists are essentially gardeners cultivating domesticated plants by hand with hoes or digging sticks. Unlike pastoralists, they live a relatively settled life, although they must periodically move their gardens or villages short distances. Their subsistence strategy is typically based on a "slash and burn" technology, in which they clear areas of land, burn the vegetation they have cut down, raise crops for two or three years until the soil is exhausted, and then repeat the process elsewhere. Horticulture is really an alternative to pastoralism, and the choice of one strategy or the other depends primarily on environmental factors. Horticulture is much more likely to be adopted if the soil and climate favor crop cultivation. Many horticultural societies still exist in Africa, Asia, South America, and Australasia.

Like pastoralism, horticulture is much more efficient than hunting and gathering because it provides an assured, expandable food supply and the possibility of a surplus. Again, this surplus allows some wealthy individuals and families to become more powerful than others, and political institutions emerge in the form of hereditary chieftainships. The existence of a surplus also means that some people can do work other than food production, so specialized new statuses and roles appear, such as those of shaman, trader, or craft worker.

The emergence of some of humanity's grimmer endeavors is closely associated with horticulture. Warfare, for example, is extremely common in horticultural societies, partly because it is often more convenient to steal one's neighbors' goods than to produce one's own. The rare practices of cannibalism, headhunting, and human sacrifice are found almost exclusively in a few of the more aggressive horticultural societies. Cannibalism usually involves eating one's slain enemies as an act of ritual revenge. The successful hunting of heads is taken as evidence of the courage and skill of the warrior. The emergence of human sacrifice coincides with the tendency of advanced horticultural peoples to believe in capricious gods who must be worshiped and appeased, a development that is probably associated with their own experience of chieftainship and social inequality (Swanson, 1960).

Because they live in relatively permanent settlements, horticulturalists can create more elaborate cultural artifacts than can hunters and gatherers or pastoralists. They can produce, for example, houses, thrones, or large stone sculptures. In the more advanced horticultural societies, political and economic institutions become well developed as conquest and trade link various villages together. The settled way of life and relatively large populations of these societies thus permit more complex social structures and cultures.

Figure 4.11 Lacking draft animals, horticulturalists have to tend their gardens by hand, a laborious process that limits the productivity of the land. Because the soil may quickly become exhausted, many horticultural peoples must either leave some of their gardens fallow every two or three years or find new areas for cultivation. These horticultural people in the Amazon jungle are using a "slash and burn" technology; they cut down the vegetation, burn it, grow crops until the land is exhausted, and then repeat the process elsewhere. Horticulture permits relatively settled communities, and it can also generate enough food to support fairly large populations in the same area.

Agricultural Societies

About 6000 years ago the plow was invented and the agricultural revolution was under way. The use of the plow greatly improves the productivity of the land; it brings to the surface nutrients that have sunk out of reach of the roots of plants, and it returns weeds to the soil to act as fertilizers. The same land can be cultivated almost continuously, and fully permanent settlements become possible. The use of animal power to pull the plow makes one agriculturalist far more productive than several horticulturalists. As a result, food output is greatly increased and a substantial surplus can be produced.

The potential size of agricultural societies is much greater than that of horticultural or pastoral communities; it can run to several million people. A fairly large part of this population does not have to work the land and can engage instead in highly specialized, full-time roles (such as that of blacksmith or barber), most of which are conveniently performed among concentrations of other people. Cities appear for the first time, consisting essentially of people who directly or indirectly trade their specialized skills for the agricultural products of those who still work the land. The society itself often consists of several such cities and their hinterlands, loosely welded together by periodic shows of force by those in central authority.

As political institutions become much more elaborate, power is concentrated in the hands of a single individual, and a hereditary monarchy tends to emerge. The power of the monarch is usually absolute, literally involving the power of life and death over his or her subjects. In the more advanced agricultural societies an elaborate court and government bureaucracy is established, and the state emerges for the first time as a separate social institution. Distinct social classes also make their appearance in virtually all agricultural societies. The wealth of these societies is almost always very unequally shared, with a small landowning minority enjoying the surplus produced by the working majority; one example of this pattern was the old feudal system of Europe. Religion also becomes a separate social institution, with full-time officials and frequently with considerable political influence. The religions of agricultural societies often include a belief in a "family" of gods, one of whom, the "high god," is regarded as more powerful than other lesser gods. This belief probably stems from peoples' experience of different levels of political authority, ranging from local rulers to the absolute monarch. A distinct economic institution also develops; trade becomes more elaborate, and money is used as a medium of exchange. The need for accurate records of crop harvests, taxation, and government transactions provides a powerful incentive for the development of writing, and some system

Figure 4.12 Agriculture can be a highly productive subsistence strategy. Agriculturalists, like these Asian peasants, cultivate the soil with plows instead of hoes and digging sticks. Nutrients are thus returned to the surface of the soil, and the land can be continuously cultivated year after year. The high productivity of agriculture frees a large part of the population from the need to toil on the land, permitting them to engage in other specialized roles.

of writing is found in virtually all advanced agricultural societies.

Agricultural societies tend to be almost constantly at war and sometimes engage in systematic empire-building. These conditions demand an effective military organization, and permanent armies appear for the first time. The need for efficient transport and communications in these large societies leads to the development of roads and navies, and previously isolated communities are brought into contact with one another. The relative wealth of agricultural societies and their settled way of life permit resources to be invested in new cultural artifacts—paintings and statues, public buildings and monuments, palaces and stadiums.

A society relying on agriculture as a subsistence strategy thus has a far more complex social structure and culture than any of the less evolved types of societies. The number of statuses and roles multiplies, population size increases, cities appear, new institutions emerge, social classes arise, political and economic inequality becomes built into the social structure, and culture becomes much more diversified.

Industrial Societies

The industrial mode of production originated in England about 250 years ago and proved so immensely successful that it has since spread all over the world, absorbing, transforming, or destroying all other types of society in the process.

Industrialism is based on the application of scientific knowledge to the technology of production, enabling new energy sources to be harnessed and permitting machines to do the work that was previously done by people or animals. It is a highly efficient subsistence strategy, for it allows a relatively small proportion of the population to feed the majority. Because inventions and discoveries build upon one another, the rate of technological innovation in industrial societies is swift. New technologies—such as the steam engine, the internal combustion engine, electrical power, or atomic energy—tend to stimulate changes in the economy and other institutions. Unlike other societies, therefore, industrial societies are in a continual state of rapid social change.

Figure 4.13 Industrial societies rely on an advanced technology and mechanized production for their subsistence. This strategy is so efficient and produces so much wealth that industrialism is rapidly becoming the dominant mode of production all over the world. Despite its many advantages, however, industrialization poses a range of new problems to human society: pollution, resource depletion, overpopulation, and a rapid rate of social change that causes continuing social disorganization.

Figure 4.14 Industrialism has radically changed the way of life of human societies. By freeing the bulk of the population from work on the land, it has permitted the growth of densely populated cities in which daily life is utterly different from that in preindustrial villages. These two pictures—of a village in a horticultural society of the South Pacific and of a single street in Manhattan—give some idea of the sweeping transformation that has taken place.

Industrial societies may be very large, with populations running into tens or hundreds of millions. They are also highly urbanized; in all the advanced industrial societies a majority of the population lives in or around cities, where most jobs are located. The population growth rate rises sharply in the early stages of industrialism as new medical technologies and improved living standards extend life expectancy, but population size tends to stabilize in the later stages of industrialism as birth control becomes popular. The division of labor becomes highly complex as tens of thousands of new, specialized jobs are created. More and more statuses are achieved rather than ascribed: a person may be born into the circumstances of a lord or peasant but can actively achieve such new statuses as teacher, politician, or auto mechanic.

Family and kinship become progressively less important in the social structure. The family loses many of its earlier functions. It is no longer a unit of economic production, nor does it have the main responsibility for the education of the young. Kinship ties are weakened, and people live with their immediate family but apart from more distant kin. The influence of the religious institution also shrinks. People no longer share similar life experiences and consequently hold many different and competing values and beliefs. Inevitably, traditional religion loses its hold as an unquestioned source of moral authority. Science, however, emerges as a new and important social institution, for technological innovation depends on the growth and refinement of scientific knowledge. Similarly, education becomes a distinct institution. An industrial society requires mass literacy, and for the first time formal education becomes compulsory for the many rather than a luxury for the few.

In the early stages of industrialism there is usually a yawning gap between the incomes of the rich and the poor as the rural peasantry is transformed into an urban work force, often under the most wretched conditions. The general trend in industrial societies, however, is toward a steady reduction in social inequalities, although there are some notable exceptions (Lenski, 1966). Hereditary monarchies pass away and tend to be replaced by more democratic institutions. The influence of the state increases markedly as government becomes involved in such diverse areas as education, welfare, and the regulation of economic activity. Although preparedness for warfare may reach new heights of intensity, actual outbreaks of war are relatively infrequent. One study of preindustrial European societies found that, over periods of several centuries, they were at war, on the average, almost every second year (Sorokin, 1937). In contrast, most of the industrial societies of modern Europe have been at war only twice in the course of this century, and some have not been at war at all. Warfare can be ruinous for an advanced industrial society, largely because it involves such devastating weaponry and economic dislocation. Indeed, the major industrial societies might not survive a nuclear war.

Secondary groups multiply throughout industrial societies—corporations, political parties, government bureaucracies, and special-purpose organizations and associations of every kind. More and more social life takes place in secondary rather than primary groups; consequently a good

THE GREAT TRANSFORMATION

	Preindustrial Society	Industrial Society
Social structure	Relatively simple: few statuses and roles; few developed institutions other than the family.	Complex: many statuses and roles; many highly developed institutions, such as education, science, etc.
Statuses	Mostly ascribed.	Some ascribed, but many achieved.
Social groups	Mostly primary (personal, intimate).	Mostly secondary (impersonal, anonymous).
Community size	Typically small (villages).	Typically large (cities).
Division of labor	Relatively little, except on grounds of age and sex.	A great deal: occupations are highly specialized.
Social control	Mostly informal, relying on spontaneous community reaction.	Often formal, relying on laws, police, and courts.
Values	Tradition-oriented, religious.	Future-oriented, secular.
Culture	Homogeneous: most people share similar norms and values; few subcultures.	Heterogeneous: many subcultures holding different norms and values.
Technology	Primitive, based mainly on human and animal muscle power.	Advanced, based mainly on machines and energy in the form of electricity, etc.
Social change	Slow.	Rapid.

Figure 4.15 The most significant change in the history of sociocultural evolution is that between traditional, preindustrial societies and modern industrial ones. This table lists some of the typical differences between each type of society.

deal of social interaction is anonymous and impersonal. The range of new life-styles and values creates a much more heterogeneous culture than that found in other types of societies. The overall characteristics of industrial societies tend to be broadly similar, however, partly as a result of the effects of global mass communication and partly because industrialism imposes the same basic requirements on social structure and culture everywhere.

Industrial society is rapidly becoming the dominant form in the modern world. Its triumph is due to its unprecedented effectiveness in exploiting the natural environment, but this success has caused a variety of problems. Industrial societies have to contend with pollution, shortages of energy and other scarce resources, population problems, the destruction of traditional communities, the disruption of kinship systems, mass anonymity, and a breakneck rate of social change that constantly threatens to disorganize the existing social structure.

Industrial and Preindustrial Societies: A Comparison

The sharpest break in the course of sociocultural evolution occurs between the various preindustrial societies on the one hand and modern industrial society on the other. The changes involved are profound, and a major task of sociology has been to identify their nature.

In 1887, for example, the German sociologist Ferdinand Tönnies distinguished between the *Gemeinschaft*, or "community," and the *Gesellschaft*, or "association." The former type of society, he argued, is characterized by intimate, face-to-face contact, strong feelings of social solidarity, and a commitment to tradition. The latter is marked by impersonal contacts, individualism rather than group loyalty, and a slackening of traditional ties and values. In 1893 the French sociologist Emile Durkheim distinguished between societies based on *mechanical solidarity* and those based on *organic solidarity:* the former are held together by the fact that their members perform much the same roles and therefore share similar values; the latter are held together by the fact that their members play highly specialized roles and are therefore dependent on one another. More recently, in 1941, the American anthropologist Robert Redfield

distinguished between the small *folk society*, which is bound by tradition and intimate personal links, and the large-scale *urban society*, marked by impersonal relationships and a pluralism of values. All these writers were trying to describe essentially the same phenomenon: the differences between what in this book we shall call "traditional," or "preindustrial," societies, and "modern," or "industrial," ones.

Some of the basic differences between preindustrial and industrial societies are summarized in Figure 4.15. The changes wrought by this great transformation are entirely new in the history of the human species, and industrial societies are still in the difficult process of adjusting to them. In this book we shall be dealing primarily with the most technologically advanced industrial society in the world, the United States. But from time to time we shall refer to preindustrial and other industrial societies—both to give some sense of the immense and often fascinating variety of human social behavior and to offer, through comparison, a greater awareness of the distinctive features of your own society.

Summary

1. Human beings are social animals, by habit and by necessity. A society is a group of interacting individuals occupying the same territory and sharing a common culture.

2. Social processes are generally patterned and predictable. The basic components of a social system tend to be linked in an organized relationship, termed social structure.

3. A status is a socially defined position in society. Some statuses rank higher or lower than others; people of roughly equivalent status form a class. Ascribed statuses are arbitrarily assigned by society; achieved statuses are earned.

4. A role is a part played by the occupant of a given status. Social norms prescribe how particular roles should be played. Role performance, however, may differ from role expectations. Role strain occurs when a person has difficulty in meeting role expectations; role conflict occurs when two or more of a person's roles impose conflicting demands.

5. A group consists of a number of people interacting on the basis of shared expectations. A primary group is small and intimate; a secondary group is more anonymous. Groups are important building blocks of social structure.

6. Institutions are stable clusters of norms, values, statuses, roles, and groups that develop around basic needs of society. They tend to be conservative, to be closely interrelated within social structure, and to adjust to significant changes in other institutions.

7. Sport is a significant American institution, providing in some respects a microcosm of the society; in particular, it reflects important social values and has patterns of class, race, and sex participation that are similar to those of other institutions.

8. Societies can be classified according to their basic subsistence strategies. There has been a general trend of sociocultural evolution from small and simple societies to large and complex ones. The main types of societies are hunting and gathering societies, pastoral societies, horticultural societies, agricultural societies, and industrial societies. Culture and social structure grow more complex at each stage.

9. Industrial societies are radically unlike preindustrial societies. They experience a rapid rate of social change, and virtually all aspects of culture and social structure are transformed by the modernization process that accompanies industrialization. Sociologists are still attempting to grasp the full significance of these changes.

Important Terms

society (79–80)
social structure (80)
status (80)
class (81)
ascribed status (81)
achieved status (81)
role (81)
role expectation (82)
role performance (82)
role strain (82)
role conflict (82)
group (82)
primary group (83)
secondary group (83)
institution (83)

sport (85)
sociocultural evolution (93)
hunting and gathering society (94)
pastoral society (95)
horticultural society (96)
agricultural society (97)
industrial society (98)
Gemeinschaft/Gesellschaft (101)
mechanical solidarity/organic solidarity (101)
folk society/urban society (101)

Suggested Readings

AHRENS, W., and SUSAN P. MONTAGUE (eds.). *The American Dimension.* Port Washington, N.Y.: Alfred.

A collection of interesting articles on various aspects of American culture and society. Many of the contributions are both insightful and amusing.

EITZEN, D. STANLEY, and GEORGE H. SAGE. *Sociology of American Sport.* Dubuque, Iowa: Wm. C. Brown, 1978.

A readable and up-to-date overview of the sociology of sport, a rapidly growing subfield of the discipline.

HOROWITZ, IRVING L. (ed.). *Society.*

A useful sociological journal containing readable articles on a variety of topics, including many current problems of American society. The journal can be used to supplement texts and other course materials with commentary and analysis on social issues.

LENSKI, GERHARD, and JEAN LENSKI. *Human Societies.* 3rd ed. New York: McGraw-Hill, 1978.

This book examines societies from the perspective of sociocultural evolution and traces the changes that take place in social structure in the course of the process.

NISBET, ROBERT. *The Social Bond.* New York: Knopf, 1970.

This book addresses the problem of order and cohesion in society. It includes a careful analysis of the various components of social structure, showing how the "social bond" derives from the relationships among them.

PLOG, FRED, and DANIEL G. BATES. *Cultural Anthropology.* 2nd ed. New York: Knopf, 1979.

A concise account of human societies from an anthropological perspective. The book includes sections on hunting and gathering, pastoral, horticultural, agricultural, and industrial societies.

SKOLNICK, JEROME H., and ELLIOTT CURIE. *Crisis in American Institutions.* 4th ed. Boston: Little, Brown, 1979.

A collection of readings on modern American social problems. The book systematically relates these problems to strains and failures in American institutions and stresses the conflicts of interest involved in many of the problems.

TURNBULL, COLIN. *The Mountain People.* New York: Simon and Schuster, 1972.

An absorbing and disconcerting study of the Ik of Uganda. Formerly a hunting and gathering people, they were forced by their government to become settled horticulturalists. The result—aggravated by a long drought—was cultural and social disintegration.

Reading

Status and Role in a Mock Prison *Philip Zimbardo*

Philip Zimbardo, a social psychologist, set up a mock "prison" in which students played the roles of prisoners and guards. The results were frightening. Zimbardo's report shows how the roles that we play deeply influence our social behavior.

In an attempt to understand just what it means psychologically to be a prisoner or a prison guard, Craig Haney, Curt Banks, Dave Jaffe and I created our own prison. We carefully screened over 70 volunteers who answered an ad in a Palo Alto city newspaper and ended up with about two dozen young men who were selected to be part of this study. They were mature, emotionally stable, normal, intelligent college students from middle-class homes throughout the United States and Canada. They appeared to represent the cream of the crop of this generation. None had any criminal record and all were relatively homogeneous on many dimensions initially.

Half were arbitrarily designated as prisoners by a flip of a coin, the others as guards. These were the roles they were to play in our simulated prison. The guards were made aware of the potential seriousness and danger of the situation and their own vulnerability. They made up their own formal rules for maintaining law, order and respect, and were generally free to improvise new ones during their eight-hour, three-man shifts. The prisoners were unexpectedly picked up at their homes by a city policeman in a squad car, searched, handcuffed, fingerprinted, booked at the Palo Alto station house and taken blindfolded to our jail. There they were stripped, deloused, put into a uniform, given a number and put into a cell

with two other prisoners where they expected to live for the next two weeks. The pay was good ($15 a day) and their motivation was to make money.

At the end of only six days we had to close down our mock prison because what we saw was frightening. It was no longer apparent to most of the subjects (or to us) where reality ended and their roles began. The majority had indeed become prisoners or guards, no longer able to clearly differentiate between role playing and self. There were dramatic changes in virtually every aspect of their behavior, thinking and feeling. In less than a week the experience of imprisonment undid (temporarily) a lifetime of learning; human values were suspended, self-concepts were challenged and the ugliest, most base, pathological side of human nature surfaced. We were horrified because we saw some boys (guards) treat others as if they were despicable animals, taking pleasure in cruelty, while other boys (prisoners) became servile, dehumanized robots who thought only of escape, of their own individual survival and of their mounting hatred for the guards.

We had to release three prisoners in the first four days because they had such acute situational traumatic reactions as hysterical crying, confusion in thinking and severe depression. Others begged to be paroled, and all but three were willing to forfeit all the money they had earned if they could be paroled. By then (the fifth day) they had been so programmed to think of themselves as prisoners that when their request for parole was denied, they returned docilely to their cells. Now, had they been thinking as college students acting in an oppressive experiment, they

would have quit once they no longer wanted the $15 a day we used as our only incentive. However, the reality was not quitting an experiment but "being paroled by the parole board from the Stanford County Jail." By the last days, the earlier solidarity among the prisoners (systematically broken by the guards) dissolved into "each man for himself." Finally, when one of their fellows was put in solitary confinement (a small closet) for refusing to eat, the prisoners were given a choice by one of the guards: give up their blankets and the incorrigible prisoner would be let out, or keep their blankets and he would be kept in all night. They voted to keep their blankets and to abandon their brother.

About a third of the guards became tyrannical in their arbitrary use of power, in enjoying their control over other people. They were corrupted by the power of their roles and became quite inventive in their techniques of breaking the spirit of the prisoners and making them feel they were worthless. Some of the guards merely did their jobs as tough but fair correctional officers, and several were good guards from the prisoners' point of view since they did them small favors and were friendly. However, no good guard ever interfered with a command by any of the bad guards; they never intervened on the side of the prisoners, they never told the others to ease off because it was only an experiment, and they never even came to me as prison superintendent or experimenter in charge to complain. . . . By the end of the week the experiment had become a reality.

Source: Philip G. Zimbardo, "Pathology of Imprisonment," *Society,* 9 (April 1972), pp. 4–8.

Socialization

At birth the human infant is a helpless organism. The newborn knows nothing, and cannot survive for more than a few hours without the help of other people. Unlike those of other animals, the infant's later patterns of behavior will have to be learned. Somehow this biological being must be transformed into a fully human being, a person able to participate effectively in society. That transformation is achieved through the complex process of socialization.

Socialization is the process of social interaction through which people acquire personality and learn the way of life of their society. It is the essential link between the individual and society—a link so vital that neither individual nor society could survive without it. Socialization enables the individual to learn the norms, values, language, skills, beliefs, and other patterns of thought and action that are essential for social living. And socialization enables the society to reproduce itself socially as well as biologically, thus ensuring its continuity from generation to generation.

One of the most important outcomes of socialization is individual personality. In ordinary speech we use the word "personality" rather loosely to refer to a person's character or temperament, but the sociological use of the term is both more broad and more precise. *Personality* refers to the fairly stable patterns of thought, feeling, and action that are typical of an individual. Personality thus includes three main elements: the *cognitive* component of thought, belief, perception, memory, and other intellectual capacities; the *emotional* component of love, hate, envy, sympathy, anger, pride, and other feelings; and the *behavioral* component of skills, aptitudes, competence, and other abilities. Nobody is born a great mathematician, the life of the party, or a skillful carpenter. People may be born with the potential to become any of these, but what they actually become is primarily the product of their unique experiences.

Figure 5.1 The content of the socialization process varies from one culture to another. These young people from Iran, Mali, and the Philippines jungle all learn very different ways of life. Within each society, there are typical personality patterns that differ from those in other societies.

Social interaction takes place according to the norms and values of the culture in question. The content of socialization therefore differs greatly from one society to another, and the personality types that are most admired and imitated vary among cultures. Attempts to pinpoint differences in "national character" have met with only limited success, however. One difficulty is that social psychologists do not have sufficiently sophisticated means of measuring personality, especially in a way that would be valid cross-culturally. Another difficulty is that ideas of what other people are like are often influenced by an ethnocentric attitude toward their society. During World War II, for example, Americans viewed Japanese as cruel and treacherous, but now that they are our allies, we regard them as civilized and industrious.

Nonetheless, it is clear that there are characteristic personality traits in every society—patterns that result from a common experience of socialization in a unique culture.

Within every society, however, each person is different, and these differences are also largely the product of socialization. We are born and live not only in a society but also in a specific part of it, and we are therefore influenced by the particular subcultures of our family, friends, class, race, religion, and region. Distinctive new experiences in these contexts are continually blended with old ones, so every person's biography and personality are unique. The socialization process thus helps to explain both the general *similarities* in personality and social behavior within a society and the many *differences* that exist between one person and another.

Socialization is a lifelong process, for we continually encounter new or changing conditions and must learn to adjust to them. The most important socialization, however, occurs during infancy and childhood, when the basic foundations of later personality are laid. For this reason we shall concentrate primarily on early socialization.

"Nature" and "Nurture"

From the middle of the last century until relatively recently, social scientists debated the issue of whether our personalities and social behavior are the product of heredity ("nature") or of learning ("nurture"). The debate led nowhere and is now recognized as one of the most futile controversies in the history of social science.

The "nature" viewpoint was dominant in the late nineteenth and early twentieth centuries. Charles Darwin's book *On the Origin of Species,* published in 1859, had shown us to be simply one animal species among all others. The behavior of other animals was obviously largely or wholly determined by inherited factors, and it seemed to follow that the same should be true of human beings. A few theorists, such as Karl Marx, emphatically rejected this view, but their arguments were for the most part ignored. Some sociologists applied a simple-minded Darwinism to human society, arguing that classes, nations, or races were superior or inferior to one another because of their inherited qualities. A number of psychologists began to compile endless lists of supposed human "instincts." Warfare was attributed to an "aggressive" instinct, society to a "herding" instinct, capitalism to an "acquisitive" instinct, and so on. The problem with this enterprise was that it soon got out of hand. One researcher reviewed the existing literature and found that over 10,000 supposed instincts had already been "discovered" by various authors (Bernard, 1924). To make matters worse, evidence mounted to show that behavior that social scientists in Western cultures had declared "instinctive" in the human species often did not appear at all or was reversed in other cultures. The situation was becoming ludicrous, and the old concept of "instinct" went out of fashion. Most contemporary psychologists do not regard the word as meaningful and refuse to use it in discussing human behavior.

Throughout most of this century, the "nurture" viewpoint held sway. At the turn of the century Ivan Pavlov, a Russian physiologist, noticed that dogs salivate not only at the sight of food but also at exposure to anything they have associated with feeding, such as their dish or even the ringing of a bell. If dogs could learn by association, would not human beings have an even greater capacity to do so? Pavlov's theories were taken up by the American psychologist John B. Watson, who argued that human behavior and personality are completely flexible and can be molded in any direction. Watson triumphantly taught an infant to call his milk bottle "mama" by offering him a bottle whenever he uttered the word. He capped his performance by teaching a little boy named Albert to fear white rabbits by frightening the boy with a loud noise whenever the rabbit was presented. In a widely quoted statement Watson (1924) declared:

> Give me a dozen healthy infants, well-formed, and my own specified world to bring them up in, and I'll guarantee to take any one at random and train him to become any type of specialist I might select—doctor, lawyer, artist, merchant-chief and, yes, even beggar, and thief, regardless of his talents, penchants, tendencies, abilities, vocations, and race of his ancestors.

Although some psychologists still seem to accept this view, most regard it as hopelessly naive. The current consensus is that the "nature versus nurture" debate was a pointless one, for it opposed two factors that are closely interrelated and cannot be separated. We are the product not of either heredity or learning but rather of a complex interaction between the two.

We can readily see that this is the case with some of our physical features. Height and weight are partly determined by heredity. But people born with genes for tallness or fatness may not actually become tall or fat. If they are underfed, they will be shorter and thinner than they might otherwise have been. The same appears to be true of many aspects of personality. So far scientists have not found any genes that can be shown to influence personality, but it is suspected that some genetic influence might exist. Even from the moment of birth some infants are active, some passive; some are irritable, some easily pleased. Many aspects of personality, such as intelligence and artistic abilities, appear to be partly influenced by hereditary factors. But these factors provide only a basic potential. People learn to develop and satisfy their potentials in a social setting, and it is primarily their social experience that will determine whether they realize or fall short of these potentials. A placid baby, if systematically ill-treated, can become an irritable and neurotic adult; a person born with a capacity for high intelligence, if raised in a stultifying environment, can become an adult dullard. Biology may set the broad outlines and limits of our potential, but the use to which

Figure 5.2 There is overwhelming evidence that infants need to develop a warm, intimate relationship with at least one other person (not necessarily the mother). If such a relationship is not formed in early childhood, severe damage to later personality is likely to result.

that potential is put is determined by the environment in which we live. The key to understanding the interaction of "nature" and "nurture" is the process of socialization, where biology and culture meet and blend.

Effects of Childhood Isolation

For many centuries people have wondered what human beings would be like if they were raised in isolation from human society. Some speculated that such children would be mere brutes, revealing the essence of our real "human nature." Others felt that they would be perfect beings, perhaps speaking the language of Adam and Eve in the Garden of Eden. Today there are obvious ethical considerations that make any experiment involving the deliberate isolation of children impossible, but earlier ages were not always under such moral inhibitions. In the thirteenth century the emperor Frederick II conducted just such an experiment, recorded by a medieval historian in these terms:

His . . . folly was that he wanted to find out what kind of speech and what manner of speech children would have when they grew up, if they spoke to no one beforehand. So he bade foster mothers and nurses to suckle the children, to bathe and wash them, but in no way to prattle with them or to speak to them, for he wanted to learn whether they would speak the Hebrew language, which was the oldest, or Greek, or Latin, or Arabic, or perhaps the language of their parents, of whom they had been born. But he laboured in vain, because the children all died. For they could not live without the petting and joyful faces and loving words of their foster mothers. [Quoted in Ross and McLaughlin, 1949]

The unhappy fate of the children comes as no surprise to modern social scientists, for it has been proved beyond doubt that children need more than mere physical care if they are to survive and prosper. They need close emotional attachments with at least one other person; without this bond, socialization is impaired, and irreversible damage may be done to the personality. Evidence for this view comes from four main sources: reports of so-called feral (untamed) children who were allegedly raised by wild animals; studies of children who were deliberately reared in isolation by their own families; studies of children in institutions; and experiments that study the effects of isolation on other primates.

"Feral" Children

The evidence relating to "feral" children is highly dramatic but also highly unreliable. Many societies have myths about children being raised by animals. The Romans, for example, believed that the founders of Rome, Romulus and Remus, had been raised by a wolf. In the late nineteenth and early twentieth centuries, however, a few cases of the discovery of children whose behavior seemed more like that of animals than human beings were reported from India, France, and elsewhere (Singh and Zingg, 1942; Malson, 1972; H. Lane, 1976; McLean, 1978; Shattuck, 1980). In every case the children could not speak, reacted with fear or hostility toward other human beings, slouched or walked on all fours, and tore ravenously at their food. Attempts to socialize the children are said to have met with little success, and all died at a young age.

There are two difficulties with these reports. The first is that the subjects were never systematically examined by trained investigators, and the second is that we know nothing about the history of the children before they were discovered. It seems highly improbable that they had been raised by wild animals. It is far more likely that they had been abandoned by their own parents shortly before they were discovered by other people. It is also possible that the children were already mentally disturbed, autistic, or had been raised in some form of isolation before being abandoned (Bettelheim, 1959).

Children Raised in Isolation

Much more convincing evidence comes from studies of children who were deliberately raised in isolation by their own families. Two such instances, both occurring in the United States, have been reported by Kingsley Davis (1940, 1947, 1948).

The first child, Anna, was discovered at the age of six. She had been born illegitimate, and her grandfather had insisted that she be hidden from the world in an attic room. Anna received a bare minimum of physical care and atten-

tion and had virtually no opportunities for social interaction. When she was found she could not talk, walk, keep herself clean, or feed herself; she was totally apathetic, expressionless, and indifferent to human beings. In fact, those who worked with her believed at first that she was deaf and possibly blind as well. Davis (1948) comments: "Here, then, was a human organism which had missed nearly six years of socialization. Her condition shows how little her purely biological resources, when acting alone, could contribute to making her a complete person."

Attempts to socialize Anna had only limited success. The girl died four-and-a-half years later, but in that time she was able to learn some words and phrases, although she could never speak sentences. She also learned to use building blocks, to string beads, to wash her hands and brush her teeth, to follow directions, and to treat a doll with affection. She learned to walk but could run only clumsily. By the time of her death at almost eleven she had reached the level of socialization of a child of two or three.

The second child, Isabelle, was discovered about the same time as Anna and was approximately the same age, six-and-a-half. She too was an illegitimate child, and her grandfather had kept her and her mother—a deaf-mute—in a dark room most of the time. Isabelle had the advantage, over Anna, of social interaction with her mother, but she had no chance to develop speech; the two communicated with gestures. When Isabelle was discovered, her behavior toward other people, especially men, was "almost that of a wild animal." At first it was thought that she was deaf, for she did not appear to hear the sounds around her, and her only speech was a strange croaking sound. The specialists who worked with her pronounced her feebleminded and did not expect that she could ever be taught to speak.

Unlike Anna, however, Isabelle had the training of a skilled team of doctors and psychologists. After a slow start, she suddenly spurted through the stages of learning that are usually characteristic of the first six years of childhood, taking every stage in the usual order but at much greater speed than normal. By the time she was eight-and-a-half years old she had reached an apparently normal level of intellectual development and was able to attend school with other children. Her greater success seems to be related to the skills of her trainers, the fact that her mother was present during her isolation, and the fact that, unlike Anna, she was able to gain the use of language.

Institutionalized Children

The socialization of children who are raised in orphanages and similar institutions differs from that of other children in one very important respect. Institutionalized children rarely have the chance to develop close emotional ties with specific adults, for although the children may interact with a large number of staff members, the attendants simply do not have the time to devote much personal attention to any one individual. The standard of nutrition and other physical care in institutions is sometimes good and comparable to that in private homes, but relationships between child and adult are usually minimal.

In 1945, the psychologist René Spitz published an influential article on the effects that these conditions have on children's personalities. Spitz compared some infants who were being raised by their own mothers with infants of the same age who had been placed in the care of an orphanage. The infants living with their mothers had plenty of opportunity for close social interaction, but those in the institution received only routine care at mealtimes and when their clothing or bedding was changed. Spitz found that the infants in the orphanage were physically, socially, and emotionally retarded compared with the other infants—a difference, moreover, that increased steadily as the children grew older.

Spitz's report was followed by a large number of studies on the effects of institutionalization on infants and children, most of which have arrived at similar conclusions (Bowlby, 1969; Rutter, 1974). William Goldfarb (1945), for example, compared forty children who had been placed in foster homes soon after birth with forty children who had spent the first two years of life in institutions before being transferred to foster homes. He found that the institutionalized children suffered a number of personality defects that persisted even after they had left the institutions. They had lower IQ scores, seemed more aggressive and distractible, showed less initiative, and were more emotionally cold. Many other studies have reported similar depressing effects on physical, cognitive, emotional, and social development, and have confirmed that such disabilities suffered in early childhood tend to persist or even to grow worse in later years (for example, Provence and Lipton, 1962; Yarrow, 1963; Dennis, 1960; Dennis and Najarian, 1957).

Monkeys Raised in Isolation

Harry Harlow and his associates at the University of Wisconsin have conducted a series of important experiments on the effects of isolation on rhesus monkeys (Harlow, 1958, 1965; Harlow and Harlow, 1962; Harlow and Zimmerman, 1959). Harlow's work has shown that even in monkeys, social behavior is learned, not inherited. The monkeys

Figure 5.3 In his experiments with monkeys raised in isolation, Harry Harlow has found that the animals prefer a soft, cuddly "mother" substitute to a "mother" that feeds them but is made of wire. The young monkeys clung to this cuddly "mother" for much of the time, especially if they were frightened. The wire "mother" was used only as a source of food. Harlow's study shows that the young monkeys placed greater priority on intimate physical contact than on food.

raised in isolation in his labs behave in a way similar to that of human psychotics. They are fearful of or hostile to other monkeys, make no attempt to interact with them, and are generally withdrawn and apathetic. Monkeys reared in isolation do not know how to mate with other monkeys and usually cannot be taught how to do so. If female monkeys who have been isolated since birth are artificially impregnated, they become unloving and abusive mothers, making little or no attempt to take care of their offspring. In one experiment Harlow provided isolated monkey infants with two substitute mothers—one made of wire and containing a feeding bottle and one covered with soft cloth but without a bottle. The infant monkeys preferred the soft, cuddly "mother" to the one that fed them. This wretched substitute for affection seemed more important to them even than food.

Like all animal studies, Harlow's experiments must be treated with caution when inferences are made for human behavior. After all, we are not monkeys. His studies show, however, that without socialization, monkeys cannot develop normal social, sexual, emotional, or maternal behavior. Since we know that human beings rely much more heavily on learning than monkeys do, it seems fair to conclude that the same would be true of us.

The evidence from these varied sources, then, points overwhelmingly in the same direction: without socialization, we are almost devoid of personality and are utterly unable to face even the simplest challenges of life. Lacking the "instincts" that guide the behavior of other animals, we can become social and thus fully human only by learning through interaction with other people. Let us now examine more closely that learning process and its consequences for human development.

Theories of Learning

Learning refers to a change in an individual's thought, emotion, or action that results from previous experience. All animals have some capacity for learning, an ability that is very limited in the lower animals but highly developed in mammals and especially in human beings. But exactly how do human beings learn? Two general theories have been proposed: the behaviorist and the developmental.

The Behaviorist Approach

The behaviorist school in psychology is founded on the work of Ivan Pavlov and John B. Watson, and it has found favor with American psychologists throughout most of this century. Behaviorism arose as a reaction to the early theories of "instinct" that focused on invisible processes in the mind. Advocates of the new school argued that the concept of "mind" is merely an abstraction that cannot be scientifically studied; one person's guess about what goes on inside "the mind" is as good as another's. Learning theory, they argued, could be scientific only if it focused on something that could be observed and analyzed, namely, actual behavior—hence the term *behaviorism*.

The essence of the behaviorist approach is that all learning takes place as a result of *conditioning* through rewards and punishments. If an animal is repeatedly rewarded for a particular response—such as getting food every time it presses a lever—the response will recur. If the animal is repeatedly punished for making a particular response—such as getting an electric shock every time it presses the lever—the response will not recur. This pattern of rewards or punishments is called *reinforcement*, and learning occurs through *association* once the animal makes the link between the behavior and its effects.

By using these techniques, behaviorists have produced impressive displays of learning in laboratory animals; pigeons have been taught to play table tennis, and rats have learned to make their way through highly complicated obstacle courses to get food. Behaviorist psychologists, most notably B. F. Skinner (1971), have argued that virtually all human learning can be explained in terms of conditioning. Skinner has even advocated a utopian society based on behaviorist principles. Under the appropriate learning conditions, he argues, human behavior could be regulated in such a way that a perfect society would result. Skinner does not confront the problem, however, of precisely who would decide what kind of behavior the rest of us would be conditioned into performing.

Other psychologists in the behaviorist tradition have modified the approach. They point out that some learning does not result from any obvious rewards. In traveling from one location to another, for example, we learn details of our surroundings en route, even though we are not rewarded for doing so. They also argue that a good deal of behavior seems to be learned as a result of imitation of other human models, especially if the models are seen to be rewarded. Children, for example, may imitate their parents or even TV or comic-book characters. This modified approach is called *social learning,* a theory that relies on behaviorist principles but recognizes that some learning occurs incidentally or through imitation, even in the absence of punishments or rewards (Bandura and Walters, 193; Bandura, 1977).

The Developmental Approach

The developmental school in modern psychology is a broad one, loosely linked by a belief that conditioning alone cannot adequately account for human learning. Unlike the behaviorists, the developmentalists are not disturbed by the concept of "mind." They place great emphasis on the individual's internal *interpretation* of situations rather than on such external factors as punishments and rewards. Learning, they argue, is a matter of the continual development of the mind through different *stages;* more advanced forms of learning are possible only when the basis has been laid in the mind by earlier experiences and personal interpretations. The leading exponent of the school was the Swiss philosopher and psychologist Jean Piaget (1950, 1954, 1969). Piaget pointed out, for example, that a child of three simply cannot learn about the concept of speed. Children at this age will say that a car traveling in front of another is going faster, even if the one behind is rapidly catching up. The minds of very young children are not capable of understanding speed as a relationship between time and distance, and no amount of rewards and punishments can make them understand it.

In the same way, the American linguist Noam Chomsky (1957, 1968, 1971) argues that the behaviorist approach cannot explain how children learn language. Most of the sentences we speak are novel ones that have never been spoken by anyone before. If children had to learn how to construct sentences by a process of association, it would take them forever. What actually happens, Chomsky argues, is that children of a certain age are able to interpret basic rules of grammar. Once they understand these, they can construct original sentences that any other speaker of the language can understand. Similarly, the American psychologist Lawrence Kohlberg (1966) has ar-

gued that children do not learn sex roles primarily by being rewarded for the "appropriate" masculine or feminine behavior. Although this conditioning is important, the crucial part of the process comes when the children understand sex differences and define themselves as male or female. Once they have come to think of themselves as boys or girls, rewards or punishments are powerless to affect that basic judgment.

The difference between the two approaches, then, lies mainly in the importance they attach to the inner workings of the individual's mind. The behaviorists tend to see people as essentially passive, with their behavior the outcome of conditioning by the environment. The developmentalists acknowledge that a good deal of learning occurs in this way but insist that people are essentially active—judging, interpreting, defining, and personally creating their behavior. The developmental approach, which is winning increasing acceptance among modern social scientists, is more humanist, for it places greater emphasis on free will and choice.

The Emergence of the Self

At the core of personality lies the *self*—the individual's conscious experience of a distinct, personal identity that is separate from all other people and things. Unlike other animals, we are fully self-conscious, capable of thinking as subjects about ourselves as objects. You can be "proud of yourself" or "ashamed of yourself"; you can "love yourself," "change yourself," or "lose control of yourself"; and you can even "talk to yourself."

The concept of "self" is perhaps a rather vague one. But we certainly experience it as real; all of us have some fairly definite notion of who and what we are. Our sense of self seems to consist primarily of the various roles that we play and the various qualities of character that we believe we possess. If people are asked to write down as fast as possible twenty answers to the question "Who am I?" the initial answers are usually roles—student, female, Catholic, black, brother, and so on. The subsequent answers are usually character traits—generous, friendly, honest, humorous, hard-working, and the like (Kuhn and McPartland, 1954). But whatever our sense of self consists of, where does it come from? The answer is that it is a social product,

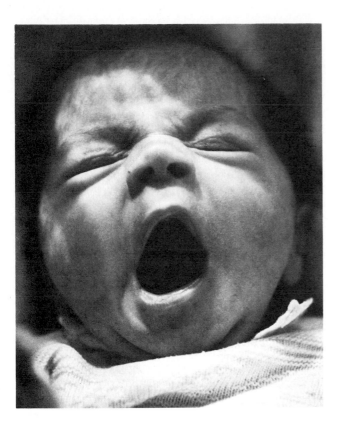

Figure 5.4 At birth, the human infant has no sense of self, no awareness of an identity separate from those of everyone else. The self emerges slowly in the course of socialization, and an awareness of self is essential for effective social interaction. Once children are aware that they have selves, they can appreciate that other people also have selves. By taking the role and viewpoint of other people, they can predict how other people are likely to respond to their own behavior.

created and modified throughout life by interaction with other people.

At the time of birth we have no sense of self, no awareness of having a separate identity. The infant does not show any recognition of other people as distinct beings until around six months of age and does not begin to use words such as "I," "me," and "mine" until at least the age of two.

Only in the years that follow do young children gradually come to realize that other people also have distinct selves, with needs and outlooks that are different from their own. And only then can the child fully appreciate that his or her own self is an identity separate from all others.

How does the self emerge in childhood and how is it continually modified throughout the life cycle? This question has been of great interest to sociologists, psychologists, and social psychologists. Three major theories have been proposed: by Sigmund Freud, Charles Horton Cooley, and George Herbert Mead. Although the details of the theories are different, each emphasizes that concepts of the self are learned through social interaction.

Freud's Theory

Sigmund Freud (1856–1939) was one of the founders of modern psychology. He is regarded as one of the most profound and original thinkers of the past century, and various versions of his theories are still influential. Freud's major insight into personality was that the motives for much if not most human behavior are *unconscious:* we are very often unaware of the real reasons for our actions. Freud believed that early childhood experiences, though often lost to conscious memory in later years, are of fundamental importance for later development of the personality. The unconscious motives that guide a good deal of human behavior, he argued, can sometimes be detected through analysis of dreams, slips of the tongue, and prolonged, probing interviews with a trained expert—an approach that he called *psychoanalysis.*

Freud believed that the relationship between the individual and society is essentially one of conflict. He argued that people are born with basic drives, especially for sex and aggression, and that social order would be impossible unless these drives were controlled. Society therefore imposes its will on the individual, suppressing and channeling the drives into socially acceptable outlets—but often doing so in ways that lead to later neuroses, or personality disturbances. Freud placed particular importance on the social control of the sex drive. He believed this drive is present even in young infants and that it leads to constant tension between the individual and society.

Personality, Freud proposed, can be divided into three basic, interacting parts. The *id* is the reservoir of drives present in the individual at birth and throughout life; it is entirely unconscious and demands continual, instantaneous satisfaction. The self of the very young child consists almost entirely of the id, but the child soon learns through interaction with others that the id cannot always be satisfied and must often be repressed. Accordingly, there emerges the *ego*—the conscious part of the self that rationally tries to balance the demands of the social environment and the urges of the id. The child learns about the demands of society from other people, particularly from parents, and finally internalizes these demands into the personality in the form of the *superego,* which is roughly equivalent to the person's conscience. The superego is thus an internal version of the moral authority of the society, and it works through feelings of shame and pride to influence the decisions of the ego.

The ego, or conscious self, thus has two tasks. The first is to reconcile the demands for self-gratification that come from the id with the demands for socially acceptable behavior that come from the superego. The second task is to mediate between the personality as a whole and the social environment. If the conscious self achieves a harmonious balance within the personality, and between the entire personality and society, the individual is well adjusted; if the ego fails in this task, personality and self-concept may be severely impaired.

Of course, Freud did not argue that the brain is physically divided into these three categories. He merely proposed his theory as a useful way of understanding the development of the self. Some psychologists still find his model useful; others do not. But Freud did make valuable contributions. He stressed that personality is a product of the interaction between the human organism and the social forces that surround it, and he emphasized the crucial influence of early childhood socialization on later conscious and unconscious motives and behavior.

Cooley's Theory

Charles Horton Cooley (1864–1929) was an American economist turned social psychologist. Like Freud, Cooley (1902) maintained that the self is essentially a social product, but he believed that it emerges through a very different process. His theory relies far more heavily on sociological insights.

The central concept in Cooley's theory is the *looking-glass self.* The "looking glass" is society, which provides a mirror in which we can observe the reactions of others to our own behavior. Our concept of ourselves is derived from this reflection. It is only through seeing the attitudes of others that we can learn whether we are attractive or ugly, popular or unpopular, respectable or disreputable. By observing the responses of others—or by imagining what their response would be like to some behavior we are contemplating—we are able to evaluate ourselves and our actions. If the image that we see or imagine in the social mirror is favorable, our self-concept is enhanced and our behavior is likely to be repeated. If the image is unfavorable, our self-concept is diminished and our behavior is likely to change.

Of course, people may misjudge the way others see them. We do not get a direct impression of the reactions of others, but must infer their meaning. All of us are guilty of misinterpretations at times, and some people habitually misjudge the opinion of others and have unrealistically high or low self-concepts as a result. But whether our reading of the image in the "looking glass" is accurate or not, it is through this interpretation that we learn our identity. There can be no self without society, no "I" without a corresponding "they" to provide our self-image.

Like Freud, Cooley believed that the self-concepts formed in childhood are more stable and lasting than those formed later in life and therefore are more crucial in personality development. He emphasized, however, that the process of self-evaluation continues throughout life whenever a person enters a new social situation. Unlike Freud, Cooley did not accept the idea that individual and society are in eternal conflict. He saw them as inseparable: society cannot exist without interacting individuals, and the individual self is an impossibility without social interaction.

Mead's Theory

George Herbert Mead (1863–1931) is one of the most important figures in American social science. A philosopher and social psychologist, Mead was by all accounts a fascinating lecturer, yet he never wrote a book—his attempts to commit his ideas to paper led him to agonies of frustration. His students and colleagues, however, compiled and published his work from lecture notes and other sources.

Mead (1934) elaborated on Cooley's ideas by introducing the concept of *symbolic interaction,* the interaction between people that takes place through symbols such as gestures, facial expressions, and, above all, language. Language is socially learned and is essential for all but the most simple forms of thought. In this sense the mind—through which we interpret our own behavior and that of others—is a social product.

Mead pointed out that a vital outcome of socialization is the ability to anticipate what others expect of us and to shape our own behavior accordingly. This capacity, he argued, is achieved by *role-taking*—pretending to take, or actually taking, the roles of other people, so that one can see oneself from their viewpoints. In early childhood children are able to internalize the expectations only of the *particular other,* that is, specific other people such as parents. But as they grow older they learn to internalize the expectations of the *generalized other,* the attitudes and viewpoint of society as a whole. This internalized general concept of social expectations provides the basis for self-evaluation and hence for self-concept.

Mead illustrated this idea by showing how children progress from mere play to organized games. Very young children typically *play* at taking the roles of specific other people: they walk about in their parents' shoes, pretend to be an adult and scold a doll, or play "house," "doctors and nurses," and so on. In this play the children are merely pretending to take the roles of specific other people, but in doing so they learn to see the world from a perspective that is not their own. Later, the children take part in organized *games*—preludes to the "game" of life—in which their roles are real and in which they must simultaneously take account of the roles and perspectives of all the participants. A baseball pitcher, for example, must be aware not only of his or her own role requirements but also of the roles and likely responses of every other player—and of the symbolic system of rules that guides the conduct of the game. Very young children cannot play organized games, for they do not understand the rules, cannot take the role of other players, and thus cannot anticipate how others will respond to their own actions.

Mead pointed out, however, that socialization is never perfect or complete. He distinguished between what he called the "I" (the spontaneous, self-interested, impulsive, unsocialized self) and the "me" (the socialized self that is conscious of social norms, values, and expectations). Although Mead did not regard the individual and society as being in conflict, he felt that the "I" was never completely under the control of the "me." The socialized self is usually dominant, but we all have the capacity to break social rules and violate the expectations of others.

Cognitive Development

Mead emphasized that the mind is a social product; and, indeed, one of the most important achievements of socialization is the development of *cognitive* abilities—intellectual capacities such as perceiving, remembering, reasoning, calculating, believing. Our knowledge of this process is based largely on the work of Jean Piaget. Born in 1896, he published his first scientific papers in his early teens and maintained a prodigous and highly influential output of books and articles until his death in 1980. Like all developmental theorists, Piaget (1950, 1954, 1969) emphasized the internal processes of the mind as it matures through interaction with the social environment. He saw us as actively trying to make sense of the world rather than being passively conditioned by it.

Piaget's many experiments with children showed that human beings gradually pass through a series of different *stages* of cognitive development, with the attainment of new cognitive skills at each stage requiring successful completion of the previous stage. Piaget outlined four basic stages of cognitive development, each of them characterized by the particular kind of "operations," or intellectual processes, that a person at that stage can perform.

The Sensorimotor Stage

In the sensorimotor stage, which lasts from birth until about the age of two, the intelligence of children is expressed only through sensory and physical contact with the environment. Lacking language, infants cannot "think" about the world. In fact, until the age of four months or so, infants cannot even differentiate themselves from their environment. They are thus unaware of the results of their acts; they do not realize, for example, that their own movements cause a rattle to make a sound. Similarly, children under the age of eight months do not understand that objects have a permanent existence: if a toy is removed from their vision, or if a parent leaves the room, they react as though the toy or parent has ceased to exist. By the end of the sensorimotor stage, however, a child will look for a missing object with persistence. This is a considerable achievement, for it shows that the child now sees the world as a stable environment, not simply a shifting chaos.

The Preoperational Stage

This stage, on which Piaget focused most of his attention, lasts from around the age of two to seven. Piaget called the stage "preoperational" because during this period children are unable to do many simple intellectual operations, largely because they have no real understanding of such concepts as speed, weight, number, quality, or causality. Particularly during the early years of this stage, for example, children invariably assume that the larger of two objects must be the heavier. (They will typically state that a pound of feathers weighs more than a pound of lead.) Although they may be able to count, they do not really understand the concept of number. They assert that a long row of beads contains more beads than a shorter row, even if the short row is more densely packed with a greater number of beads. They have a limited understanding of cause and effect—often believing, for example, that trees waving in the wind are actually making the wind. They attribute life to inanimate objects, such as the sun and moon, and may believe that a table is "hurt" when it is bumped.

Children in the preoperational stage are also highly *egocentric:* they see the world entirely from their own perspective because they are unable to take the roles of others. If a young boy is asked "How many brothers do you have?" he may correctly answer "One." But if he is asked "How many brothers does your brother have?" he is likely to answer "None," because he cannot see himself from his brother's point of view. Similarly, if young children are asked to draw an object as it appears to them from their own location in the room, they can do so. But if they are asked to draw the same object from the point of view of someone situated elsewhere in the room, they will draw it exactly as before, being incapable of taking another person's perspective.

Figure 5.5 Children at the preoperational stage have great difficulty in realizing that the quantity of water does not change in volume when it is poured from one container to another of a different shape. If water is poured before the children's eyes from a tall, thin bottle into a short, wide flask, they insist that there is now less water than before. Children at this stage judge the volume of the water only by the height of the water level and cannot understand that its volume remains constant no matter what the shape of the container is.

The Concrete Operational Stage

In this stage, which lasts from about the age of seven to twelve, the thinking of children is still tied to the concrete world. They think mainly in terms of real situations, not abstract or purely hypothetical ones. If children of this age are asked to talk about abstract concepts, such as death or the afterlife, they have great difficulty in doing so without referring to concrete events or images, such as the death of a pet or the physical appearance of God and heaven.

Children at this stage, however, are able to handle the concrete world with much the same cognitive skill as an adult. They can perform the various operations related to weight, speed, number, or quantity that were not possible in the previous stage. They can also understand cause and effect, can take the roles of others and appreciate their perspectives, and can participate effectively in games and other organized social relationships.

The Formal Operational Stage

In this stage, which begins at the onset of adolescence, people are able to achieve formal, abstract thought. They can think in terms of theories and hypotheses and can manipulate concepts, such as those of mathematics or morality, that are not tied to the immediate environment. They are able to use general rules to solve whole classes of problems, and they can reason logically from premises to conclusions with a sophistication that would not be possible in earlier stages. They can think about abstract personal goals and even utopian social conditions, a capacity that is often expressed in adolescent idealism.

Piaget believed that the *process* of cognitive development is universal in all societies: people everywhere advance through the same stages in the same order. But the *content* is culturally variable. If one's culture believes that the earth is flat or that cause and effect are related to magic and witchcraft, then it is through these concepts that one will interpret the world. Moreover, not everyone reaches the final stage; many adults never get beyond concrete operational thought and have great difficulty in understanding abstract concepts. This is particularly true of people who have little exposure to formal thinking in their social environment. As Piaget commented, "Social life is necessary if the individual is to become conscious of his own mind." Without the necessary socialization, the mind will not develop beyond a certain stage.

Agencies of Socialization

The socialization process involves many different influences that affect the individual throughout life. The most important of these influences are *agencies of socialization,* institutions or other structured situations in which socialization takes place. Four agencies of socialization—the family, the school, the peer group, and the mass media—are especially important in modern societies, for they affect almost everyone in a powerful and lasting way.

The Family

The family is without doubt the most significant single agency of socialization in all societies. One reason for the importance of the family is that it has the main responsibility for socializing children in the crucial early years of life. The family is where children establish their first close emotional ties, learn language, and begin to internalize cultural norms and values. To young children the family is all-encompassing. They have little social experience beyond its boundaries and therefore lack any basis for comparing and evaluating what is learned from family members. A great deal of the socialization that takes place in the family is deliberate, but much of it is quite unconscious. The patterns of social interaction within the family, for example, may provide unintended models for the later behavior and personality traits of the children when they grow to adulthood.

A second reason for the importance of the family is that it has a specific location in the social structure. From the moment of birth, therefore, children have an ascribed status in a subculture of race, class, ethnicity, religion, and region—all of which may strongly influence the nature of later social interaction and socialization. For example, the values and expectations that children learn depend very much on the social class of their parents (Kohn, 1963, 1977). To appreciate the significance of family background for socialization and personality, we need only consider the likely differences between the experiences of, say, a child born into a poor family of fundamentalist Baptists living in rural Alabama and a child born into a wealthy professional family of Episcopalians living in the exclusive suburbs of Los Angeles.

The School

The school is an agency formally charged by society with the task of socializing the young in particular skills and values. We usually think of the school as being mainly concerned with teaching skills and knowledge, and this is certainly one of its major functions. But the schools in every society also engage in outright indoctrination in values. We may find this fact more readily apparent in societies other than our own—until we consider the content of civics classes or the daily ritual of the Pledge of Allegiance. The school socializes not only through its formal academic curriculum but also through the "hidden curriculum" implicit in the content of school activities, ranging from regimented classroom schedules to organized sports. Children learn that they must be neat and punctual. They learn to sit still, keep quiet, wait their turn, and not be distracted from their work. They learn that they should respect and obey without question the commands of those who have social authority over them.

In the school, the young come for the first time under the direct supervision of people who are not relatives. The children learn to obey other people not because they offer love and protection but because a social system requires uniform adherence to rules. The individual child is no longer considered somebody special; he or she is now one of a crowd, subject to the same regulations and expectations that everyone else is subject to. Personal behavior and academic achievements or failures become part of a permanent official record, and the children learn to evaluate themselves by the same standards that others apply to them. Participation in the life of the school also lessens the children's dependence on the family and creates new links to the wider society beyond.

The Peer Group

As children grow older they spend more and more time in the company of their *peers*—equals of roughly the same age, background, and interests. As the influence of the peer group increases, that of the parents diminishes. In the United States young people of school-going age spend on average twice as much time with peers as with parents, and most of them prefer to spend their time this way (Bronfenbrenner, 1970).

Figure 5.6 The peer group is an important agency of socialization throughout life, but it is particularly influential during late childhood and adolescence. Young people at this age are establishing relatively settled identities, a process that may involve a reaction against earlier patterns learned in the family and at school. The peer group provides new norms and values for its members and offers them the opportunity to interact with others as equals.

Membership in a peer group places children for the first time in a context where most socialization is carried out without any deliberate design. They are able at last to choose their own companions and friends and to interact with other people on a basis of equality. Unlike the family or school, the peer group is entirely centered on its own concerns and interests. Its members can explore relationships and topics that are tabooed in the family and the school, and they can thus learn to break away from the influence of these two agencies and establish separate (and often disapproved) roles and identities. In modern industrial societies, the generations are often highly compartmentalized, with the youthful peer group claiming the primary loyalty of its members and often demanding that they reject the values and authority of parents and teachers. The influence of the peer group climaxes in adolescence, when young people are apt to form a distinctive subculture with its own tastes, leisure activities, dress, jargon, symbols, values, and heroes. By rewarding members for conformity to peer-group norms and by criticizing or ostracizing them for nonconformity, the group exerts a very strong influence on their social behavior and personality.

The Mass Media

The mass media are the various forms of communication that reach a large audience without any personal contact between the senders and the receivers of the messages: newspapers, magazines, books, television, radio, movies, and records. Although they are unquestionably a powerful socializing influence, the precise impact of the media is difficult to gauge. The most influential medium is probably television. There is a TV set in 95 percent of American homes, and the average American between the ages of three and sixteen spends more time in front of the TV set than in school.

The media provide instant coverage of social events and social changes, ranging from news and opinions to fads and fashions. They offer role models and glimpses of life-styles that people might otherwise never have access to. Through the media, children can learn about courtroom lawyers, cowboys, police detectives, or even such improbable characters as Batman and Darth Vader. (The fact that many of these images are not very realistic does not necessarily lessen their influence.) Through media advertising, too, the young learn about their future roles as consumers in the marketplace, and about the high value the society places on youth, success, beauty, and materialism. Changing social norms and values are quickly reflected in the media and may be readily adopted by people who might not otherwise be exposed to them. The rapid spread of new trends in youth culture, for example, depends heavily on such media as popular records, television, FM radio, youth-oriented magazines, and movies.

Other Agencies

The individual may be influenced by many other agencies of socialization—religious groups, Boy Scouts and Girl Scouts, youth organizations, and, later in life, by such agencies as the military, corporations or other employment settings, and by voluntary associations such as clubs, political movements, and retirement homes. It is obvious that the influences of the various agencies are not always complementary and can often be in outright conflict. The church, for example, may hold quite different values from the military; the peer group, quite different values from the school. It is also obvious that people do not always learn what they are supposed to learn. The socialization process may fail in certain respects, and people may come to behave in ways that were never anticipated or intended. Personality and behavior are never entirely stable; they change under the influence of socialization experiences throughout the life cycle.

Socialization over the Life Cycle

Socialization continues from the moment of birth throughout maturity and old age until death. The more complex the social structure of a society and the more rapid the pace of its social change, the more intensive and varied is the ongoing socialization process.

Types of Socialization

The socialization that we experience in the course of a lifetime may be one or more of five different kinds: primary socialization, anticipatory socialization, developmental socialization, reverse socialization, and resocialization.

Primary Socialization

This is the basic socialization that takes place in the early years of life. It focuses on the teaching of language and other cognitive skills, the internalization of cultural norms and values, the establishment of emotional ties, and the appreciation of others' roles and perspectives.

Anticipatory Socialization

This kind of learning is directed toward a person's future roles rather than those that the person has at the time of learning. When children play at "house," they are involved in anticipatory socialization for their future roles as parents. Much of the socialization in the school anticipates the pupils' roles in their occupational careers. Training programs in business, industry, or the armed forces have similar intent.

Developmental Socialization

This kind of learning is based on the achievements of primary socialization. It builds on already acquired skills and knowledge as the adult progresses through situations—such as marriage or different jobs—that require new expectations, obligations, and roles. New learning is added to and blended with old in a relatively smooth and continuous process of development.

Reverse Socialization

This kind of learning occurs when the younger generation transmits cultural knowledge to its elders (Falkman and Irish, 1974). In traditional societies, reverse socialization is uncommon, but it happens quite frequently in heterogeneous modern societies. Immigrant families provide an obvious example: the younger members attend school, rapidly learn the new language, and interpret the surrounding culture to their parents. In times of rapid social change, too, much of the elders' knowledge may become obsolete, and the young may have more relevant information about some aspects of the world, ranging from rock music to the "new math" and the effects of illicit drugs. Adult society may even be influenced by the content of youth culture, as happened in the United States during the sixties.

Resocialization

This kind of learning involves a sharp break with the past and the internalization of radically different norms and values. It frequently takes place in a context where people have been partly or wholly isolated from their previous background. Resocialization occurs, for example, in conversion to a different religion, in the experience of an anthropologist who lives among an alien people, or in "brainwashing" situations in which the victim's personality is systematically stripped away and rebuilt. It also occurs within a *total institution*—a place of residence where the inmates are confined for a set period of their lives, where they are cut off from the rest of society, and where they are under the almost absolute control of a hierarchy of officials (Goffman, 1961). Examples of a total institution are an army boot camp, a naval vessel, a prison, a mental asylum, and a traditional boarding school. In each case the inmates experience an abrupt break from their former existence; they surrender control over much of their lives to an ad-

Figure 5.7 Military trainees are subjected to systematic resocialization, a form of socialization that involves an abrupt break with earlier experiences. Resocialization often takes place in the context of "total institutions," such as army camps, traditional boarding schools, prisons, and mental asylums. In these institutions the inmates are strictly segregated from the rest of society, placed in uniforms and treated alike, and are made subject to the almost absolute authority of the officials in charge.

THE LIFE CYCLE

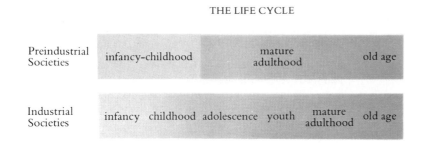

Figure 5.8 The stages of the life cycle are influenced by social as well as biological factors. Preindustrial societies generally did not recognize separate stages of infancy, childhood, and adolescence. Childhood was not recognized in Europe until after the Middle Ages, and adolescence has been recognized in industrial societies only in this century. More recently, an additional, optional stage, that of youth, has appeared in the life cycle of advanced industrial societies.

ministrative staff; they are to some extent depersonalized by having to wear uniforms and obey rigid rules; and they are under great pressure to conform to the values and regulations of their new environment.

The Life Cycle

The human life cycle seems at first sight to be purely a matter of biology. But the sequence of birth, childhood, maturity, old age, and death is also a social one, for its length, stages, challenges, and opportunities depend very much on the society in which one lives. Life expectancy, for example, is strongly influenced by social as well as biological factors. In North America, people are not considered old until they are in their sixties or seventies; among the malnourished Ik of Uganda, old age sets in by the late twenties. In modern industrial societies, we associate the idea of death with the aged, but in traditional, preindustrial societies more people died in childhood than in old age. Thanks to such social factors as modern medicine, improved nutrition, and higher standards of sanitation, infectious diseases such as smallpox, diptheria, and cholera no longer kill more than half of all children before the age of ten. For the first time in history, most people can now expect to grow old.

Every society imposes its own conception of a life cycle upon the physical process of growing up and growing old. Consequently, the human life span is arbitrarily sliced up into a series of stages, each offering distinctive rights and responsibilities to the relevant age group. The number, length, and content of these stages vary from one society to another. But if a society is to survive at all, it must successfully socialize its members into accepting and effectively performing their changing roles at each stage in the sequence from early childhood until death.

Childhood

Childhood seems a "natural" part of the life cycle to us, yet the very concept of childhood is a comparatively recent one: preindustrial societies typically did not recognize it as a separate stage of life. Instead, the young passed directly from a prolonged infancy into their adult roles. In the Europe of the Middle Ages, for example, children dressed like adults, took part in the same games, did the same work, and were even portrayed in paintings as "little adults," with small bodies but mature faces (Aries, 1962; Gilles, 1974; de Mause, 1974). There was no separate way of life reserved for childhood, with the distinctive songs, toys, privileges, and activities that we take for granted today. In these preindustrial societies, people began to play adult economic and social roles as soon as they were physically able to do so, and children of five or six would work in the fields as long as any adult. Child labor was not considered a scandal; that would have required a concept of childhood and of children's rights. Even in early industrial societies, children continued to perform adult economic roles: in the United States in 1900, a quarter of the boys aged ten to fourteen were in the labor force. Countries that are now in the early stages of industrialization still have only a limited concept of childhood and continue to make use of child labor. In 1979 the International Labor Organization reported that tens of millions of children between the ages of five and thirteen work full time, even in factories and coal mines, in such countries as Morocco, India, and Colombia.

The Nightmare of Childhood in Ages Past

For most people in our society, infants and children are small people to whom we should try to offer aid and comfort whenever possible. This attitude is new. A search of historical sources shows that until the last century children were instead offered beatings and whippings, with instruments usually associated with torture chambers. In fact, the history of childhood is a nightmare from which we have only recently begun to awaken.

. . .

Virtually every child-rearing tract from antiquity to the 18th century recommended the beating of children. We found no examples from this period in which a child wasn't beaten, and hundreds of instances of not only beating, but battering, beginning in infancy.

One 19th-century German schoolmaster who kept score reported administering 911,527 strokes with a stick, 124,000 lashes with a whip, 136,715 slaps with his hand and 1,115,800 boxes on the ear. The beatings described in most historical sources began at an early age, continued regularly throughout childhood, and were severe enough to cause bruising and bloodying.

. . .

The baby was tied up tightly in swaddling bands for its first year, supposedly to prevent it from tearing off its ears, breaking its legs, touching its genitals or crawling around like an animal. Traditional swaddling, as one American doctor described it, "consists in entirely depriving the child of the use of its limbs by enveloping them in an endless bandage, so as to not unaptly resemble billets of wood, and by which the skin is sometimes excoriated, the flesh compressed, almost to gangrene . . ."

Swaddled infants were not only more convenient to care for, since they withdrew into themselves in sleep most of the day, but they were also more easily laid for hours behind hot ovens, hung on pegs on the wall, and, wrote one doctor, "left, like a parcel, in every convenient corner." In addition, they were often thrown around like a ball for amusement. In 16th-century France, a brother of Henri IV, while being tossed from one window to another, was dropped and killed.

. . .

Although there were many exceptions to the general pattern, the average child of parents with some wealth spent his earliest years in the home of a wet nurse, returned home at age three or four to the care of other servants, and was sent out to service, apprenticeship, or school by age seven, so that the amount of time parents of means actually spent raising their children was mini-mal. . . . Of 21,000 children born in Paris in 1780, 17,000 were sent into the country to be wet-nursed, 3,000 were placed in nursery homes, 700 were wet-nursed at home and only 700 were nursed by their own mothers. Even those mothers who kept their infants at home often did not breastfeed them, giving them pap (water and grain) instead.

. . .

Children were always felt to be on the verge of turning into actual demons, or at least to be easily susceptible to "the power of the Devil." To keep their small devils cowed, adults regularly terrorized them with a vast army of ghostlike figures, from the Lamia and Striga of the ancients, who ate children raw, to the witches of Medieval times, who would steal bad children away and suck their blood. One 19th-century tract described in simplified language the tortures God had in store for children in Hell: "The little child is in this red-hot oven. Hear how it screams to come out . . ."

. . .

Another method that parents used to terrorize their children employed corpses. A common moral lesson involved taking children to visit the gibbet, where they were forced to inspect rotting corpses hanging there as an example of what happens to bad children when they grow up. Whole classes were taken out of school to witness hangings, and parents would often whip their children afterwards to make them remember what they had seen.

. . .

In antiquity infanticide was so common that every river, dung-heap and cesspool used to be littered with dead infants. Polybius blamed the depopulation of Greece on the killing of legitimate children, even by wealthy parents. Ratios of boys to girls in census figures ran four to one, since it was rare for more than one girl in a family to be spared. Christians were considered odd for their opposition to infanticide, although even that opposition was mild, with few penalties. Large-scale infanticide of legitimate babies continued well into Medieval times, with boy-girl ratios in rich as well as poor families often still running two to one. As late as 1527, one priest admitted that "the latrines resound with the cries of children who have been plunged into them."

Source: Lloyd DeMause, "Our Forebears Made Childhood a Nightmare," *Psychology Today,* April 1975.

Figure 5.9 Most traditional, preindustrial societies lacked a clear concept of childhood as a separate stage of life. There was no distinct sphere of childhood games and other activities; the young were expected to participate instead in most adult activities. Preindustrial Western art reflects this attitude: even as late as 1751, when this picture was painted, children were portrayed as "little adults" with serious, mature faces and none of the innocence or "cuteness" that we might look for in children today.

Advanced industrial societies, on the other hand, tend to be very child-centered. Children are socialized quite differently: they have distinctive forms of dress and have their own separate spheres of activity, ranging from children's TV and games to kindergartens and elementary schools. They are exempted from playing any economic roles—in fact, the law forbids it—and have minimal social responsibilities. Adults tend to romanticize childhood as a period of carefree innocence, and they take pains to protect children from premature knowledge of such taboo subjects as death and sex. Parents typically derive great gratification from their children, and indulgently devote their resources to ensuring the optimum development of their offspring during what are regarded as the crucial formative years.

Adolescence

In simple, preindustrial societies there were, in effect, only two main stages of life, immaturity and adulthood. In such societies the change from one status to another was usually a clear and abrupt one, often marked by initiation cere-monies involving great pain or feats of endurance. As soon as these rituals were completed, however, the young person became an adult, with the same rights and responsibilities as other mature members of the community.

In the course of their development, modern industrial societies have added a new stage to the life cycle: instead of passing directly from prolonged infancy or childhood to adulthood, we go through adolescence, a period roughly coinciding with the teen-age years. Like childhood, adolescence is a social invention; in fact, the word came into use only at the beginning of this century. This new stage was introduced into the life cycle as a consequence of extended education.

In preindustrial and early industrial societies, most teen-agers were full-time workers, and many were married. But industrial societies required a work force whose members could at least read and write, and they needed a substantial number of professionals with highly sophisticated skills. Prolonged education therefore became necessary, but this inevitably entailed changes in the statuses and roles of those who remained in school. The result was a

Figure 5.10 In many preindustrial societies the transition from childhood to adulthood is very abrupt. This transition usually takes place at puberty and is often marked by a social ceremony, the puberty rite. These aboriginal boys in Australia are undergoing a painful circumcision ceremony, after which they will be able to take their place as adult members of the society. Traces of initiation ceremonies that mark changes in a young person's status are still found in modern societies—for example, the Jewish bar mitzvah, the high school graduation ceremony, the "hazing" ordeals that college freshmen must sometimes face, and the "sweet sixteen" birthday party.

large and unprecedented category of people who were physically and sexually mature, yet denied such adult responsibilities as full-time employment and marriage. At the turn of the century less than 7 percent of Americans completed high school, compared with over 80 percent today—a significant and rapid change which, not surprisingly, has had disruptive effects on the traditional life cycle.

Because it is a relatively new stage of the life cycle in a rapidly changing society, adolescence is an ambiguous and often confusing period, marked by vaguely defined rights and responsibilities. The American socialization process equips people poorly for the challenges of adolescence, for teen-agers are constantly confronted with contradictory demands and pressures. The media, for example, extol the virtues of sexual satisfaction and the value of material goods, but adolescents are usually forbidden full access to either, even though they have the physical maturity to achieve both. Having more freedom than children but less than adults, adolescents are constantly tempted to question or test the authority of parents and teachers. Segregated from other age groups in high schools, they tend to form their own subculture, with norms, values, and attitudes that may differ significantly from those of adult society, sometimes to such a degree that a "generation gap" results. Adolescence is therefore often experienced as a time of emotional turmoil and confused identity.

In the more advanced industrial societies a high proportion of high school graduates continue on to college and even graduate school, further delaying their acceptance of full adult responsibilities. Kenneth Kenniston (1970) suggests that yet another stage is now being introduced into the life cycle, that of "youth." This stage is an optional one that runs from about eighteen to thirty and contains students and other young people who for one reason or another do not immediately "settle down" into the usual defining characteristics of mature adulthood—a steady job, marriage, and a family.

Mature Adulthood

Sometime around the mid-twenties the individual enters mature adulthood. At this stage most primary socialization is completed, and the individual has developed a core identity that is henceforth unlikely to be radically modified (except under such extreme conditions as resocialization in a prison, mental hospital, or religious cult). For the most part, socialization is now of the developmental kind, building on the fairly stable foundations of prior experience, although frequently there is also some anticipatory socialization for roles that are yet to come—senior executive, grandparent, retiree, and so on.

Most people marry in their twenties or early thirties, establishing a home and a family. Their task becomes that of developing a life-style that will give them satisfaction in the years ahead, at the same time maintaining a warm relationship with one another and their offspring. In a rapidly changing modern society these tasks are far harder, perhaps, than they would have been in a traditional, preindustrial society, for the future is more uncertain. The only real certainty, in fact, is that social change will render a good deal of prior socialization outmoded and irrelevant in meeting new challenges that constantly arise. A few short decades ago, for example, the roles of husband and wife were fairly rigid: the husband worked and was the economic mainstay of the family; the wife stayed home and raised the children. This pattern is now the exception rather than the rule. Today, more than 40 percent of the nation's labor force is female, and a majority of these working women have children under the age of eighteen. Yet neither partner was socialized for this change in traditional roles.

The forties and fifties are a period of consolidation, in which the pattern of the individual's existence becomes settled and predictable. There is no more time now for illusion: root changes in personal, social, and economic life grow more unlikely, and what people have become is what, more or less, they will continue to be. Men and women both face the inevitable physical and psychological signs of aging: physical prowess and beauty fade, and an awareness grows that one's life is more than half over. It is now recognized that this period can sometimes include a "midlife crisis," marked by increased rates of depression, alcoholism, divorce, and suicide. Men in particular must face the fact that if they have not "made it" in their chosen field by now, they probably never will. At the same time, women socialized to regard their beauty and their children as their main sources of identity are often dismayed as they increasingly lose both. Now without maternal responsibilities, and perhaps feeling that she has in some sense wasted

a part of her life, a wife may strike out for a fresh career, a new independence, only to find this causes more problems with a husband whose self-confidence is faltering. Yet the "crisis" is by no means inevitable, and, even if it occurs, it can usually be overcome. For the many people who have successfully negotiated the life cycle up to this point, these years are among the most comfortable and satisfying of their lives (Levinson, 1979; Gould, 1975; Haan and Day, 1974; Rubin, 1979).

Old Age

Perhaps the greatest failure of the American socialization process is its inability to equip people adequately to face old age (and later, death). Preindustrial societies were generally oriented toward the old rather than the young: the aged were respected for their wisdom and held an honored place in the family and the community. They had many roles to fill—familial, social, religious, and even economic, for they typically worked until advanced old age. In modern industrial societies the situation is quite different. The knowledge of the elderly is obsolete, their authority is negligible, and they are frequently unwanted by their children: often, the best they can do is attempt not to be a "burden." There are virtually no useful roles for the aged: they generally retire at or around age sixty-five, and are left with little or no part to play in social or economic life. Retirement, in fact, can have a devastating effect, for it can be much more than a change from work to leisure: it often signifies an abrupt transition from a clearly defined and meaningful role to an ambiguous and almost meaningless one, from independence and material comfort to dependence and material hardship.

In time, too, the burden of the years affects everyone: signs such as baldness, wrinkling, and stiffness in the limbs all announce the gradual degeneration of the body that comes with advanced age. Of course, different people age physically at very different rates; but ill-health becomes steadily more common until more than three-quarters of those aged sixty-five or over suffer from some chronic health condition. Yet the infirmity of some of the aged can have social as well as physical causes: in a sense, all we offer the very old is a sick role, that of an infirm person who has outlived any real usefulness to society, and it is not surprising that some of the elderly live up to the expectations that

Figure 5.11 The elderly had an honored and respected role in traditional societies, and typically spent their last years living with their children and grandchildren. In the modern United States, however, the old are often segregated from the rest of society, typically by being placed in old-age homes or geriatric institutions. More than two-thirds of all deaths now take place in hospitals and geriatric institutions.

society may have of them. Some of the aged, of course, are able to enjoy their retirement to the full, and to review a life with its share of satisfaction and fulfillment. But in a society that worships youth and gives power, wealth, and prestige to the middle-aged, old age is apt to become a tragedy. (The problems of the aged are discussed in more detail in Chapter 13, "Inequalities of Gender and Age.")

Death

Socialization for death is almost nonexistent in the United States. In preindustrial societies deaths usually took place at home in the context of the family, and young people grew up with a close understanding of the experience. In modern America, however, death is very much a taboo subject; we speak of it in hushed tones and use such euphemisms as "passed away." As children we fear the subject; as adults we avoid it—particularly when we are in the presence of someone who is dying.

The reason for this distinctively modern taboo seems to be that death, almost alone of natural processes, remains beyond the control of our advanced technology. Although modern medicine has extended life expectancy (the length of life the average newborn will enjoy), it has had little, if any, effect on our life span (the maximum length of life possible in the species). The final point of the life cycle—the annihilation of the self, the ultimate confrontation with the unknown—mocks our claim to human mastery of the world, and we therefore try to deny the mystery and power of death by excluding it from our discussions and thoughts.

We also effectively exclude the dying from the ongoing life of the community. We have sanitized death and removed it as far as possible from everyday experience by ensuring that most people die in nursing homes, hospitals, and similar formal organizations that care for the sick and aged. The dying thus face their end in a bureaucratic environment, surrounded by other ill persons and a professional staff, rather than in the intimacy of their homes with their loved ones. Often, in fact, there is a conspiracy of professionals and relatives to hide the fact of death from the dying person. Recent research into the sociology of death and dying, however, has produced an impressive and growing body of evidence to suggest that people die far more happily—even contentedly—if death is openly discussed with them beforehand (Glaser and Strauss, 1965, 1968; Kübler-Ross, 1969, 1972, 1975; Green and Irish, 1971; Brim et al., 1970; Marshall, 1975; Lofland, 1978; Pattison, 1979).

Our understanding of death and dying has been greatly increased by the pioneering work of Elisabeth Kübler-Ross, who conducted extensive interviews with dying people in the 1960s. She identified five stages through which a terminally ill person typically proceeds after learning the truth. The first is *denial,* usually expressed in disbelief—"It can't be happening to me." The second stage is *anger*—"Why me?" The third stage is *bargaining*—an implicit agreement to go willingly if God or fate will just allow the dying person to live a little longer, perhaps until some significant event such as a family birthday or wedding. The fourth stage is *depression,* a state of deep anxiety over the loss of self and the loss to one's family. The final stage is *acceptance,* in which the dying person approaches death with true peace of mind. Some of the most healthy and accepting attitudes toward death, in fact, are found in old-age homes and other places where the elderly live together and have been able to frankly discuss their dying with others (Marshall, 1974; Rosenfield, 1978). As the findings of sociological research into death and dying become more widely known, socialization for death is likely to become more effective: in recent years, for example, courses on the subject have appeared at high schools and colleges and have attracted large enrollments. (The process of dying in a modern hospital is discussed in more detail in Chapter 6, "Social Interaction in Everyday Life.")

Socialization and Free Will

If our behavior and personalities depend so much on the content of our individual socialization, what becomes of human free will? Do we have any choice over our personal behavior, or is it all shaped for us by our past experiences?

Dennis Wrong (1961) has drawn attention to what he calls the "oversocialized conception" of human beings—the view that we are little more than the predictable products of a harmonious socialization into the social order. Wrong points out that people often feel coerced by society into doing things they do not want to do, a clear indication that socialization is less than perfect. Socialization, he argues, can never completely wipe out any basic personality traits with which we are born. Our innate drives for food, sex, and security are not as easily channeled as some people might like to think, nor are our socially acquired desires for power, wealth, or prestige.

Wrong also points out that the experiences of past socialization are not simply added together; they are blended in unique ways by each person. Everyone faces the problem that different socializing influences contradict one another. Parents may tell us one thing, friends something else, the media something else again. And the different roles that a person plays may also be in conflict. As a student, you should stay home and work on your term paper; as a member of your peer group, you should go to a party. The individual is pushed this way and that and constantly has to make personal judgments and decisions in new and unanticipated situations. Our personal histories may strongly influence our choices of action, of course. That is why courts are often willing to take an offender's past background into account before passing sentence, particularly when dealing with juveniles. But in practice the courts, like the rest of society, always insist at some point that people (unless they are mentally disordered) are capable of deciding on alternative courses of action and of "reforming" their personalities. We hold people responsible for their behavior precisely because they *can* exercise choice over what they do. Our socialization experiences are not necessarily imposed on us; sometimes we actually choose them.

For whatever reasons, everyone violates social norms at some time or another, often in novel and sometimes socially disapproved ways. Hearing a "different drummer," we do not keep pace with our companions—or, in Mead's more sociological terms, the unsocialized "I" is never completely subservient to the socialized "me." Within very broad limits, we are free to fabricate our selves and our behavior as we wish—particularly if we understand the social process through which we became what we are.

Summary

1. Socialization is the lifelong process of social interaction through which people acquire personality and learn the way of life of their society. The process is essential for the survival of both individual and society. People in the same culture tend to be similar in some general respects, but their unique experiences make them different.

2. The "nature versus nurture" debate is now recognized as a pointless one. Human personality and social behavior are the outcome of an interaction between biological potentials and cultural learning.

3. Evidence concerning children reared in isolation, children reared in institutions, and monkeys reared in isolation indicates that intimate social interaction is essential if later personal development is not to be severely impaired.

4. There are two main theories of learning. Behaviorist theory regards learning as the outcome of conditioning through punishments and rewards, although some social-learning theorists point out that learning can take place incidentally or through imitation. Developmental theorists acknowledge that a great deal of learning takes place in this way but believe that learning can be fully explained only as the outcome of personal interpretations of reality as the mind matures through different stages.

5. The emergence of the self is crucial for the development of personality. Freud argued that the self is composed of three parts, the id, ego, and superego. Cooley argued that the self emerges through the "looking glass" supplied by the reactions of other people. Mead emphasized symbolic interaction, particularly through language, and the development of the ability to take the role of others.

6. According to Piaget, cognitive or intellectual abilities develop through four basic stages: the sensorimotor stage, the preoperational stage, the concrete operational stage, and the formal operational stage.

7. In the United States and most industrial societies, there are four main agencies of socialization: the family, the school, the peer group, and the mass media. Other agencies also socialize the individual throughout life.

8. There are five possible types of socialization in the life cycle: primary socialization, anticipatory socialization, developmental socialization, reverse socialization, and resocialization. The content and stages of the life cycle are influenced by social as well as biological factors. American socialization often fails to equip people adequately for certain stages of the life cycle, particularly adolescence, old age, and dying. In industrial societies, the life cycle now includes infancy and childhood, adolescence, youth (optionally), mature adulthood, old age, and death.

9. There is a danger of accepting an "oversocialized conception" of human beings. Socialization is never fully successful. We still retain a measure of free will and are responsible for our acts.

Important Terms

socialization (105)
personality (105)
learning (111)
behaviorism (111)
conditioning (111)
social learning (112)
developmental
  approach (112)
self (112)
psychoanalysis (113)
id (113–114)
ego (114)
superego (114)
looking-glass self (114)
symbolic interaction
  (115)
role-taking (115)

particular other (115)
generalized other (115)
cognitive
  development (115)
agencies of
  socialization (117)
primary
  socialization (120)
anticipatory
  socialization (120)
developmental
  socialization (120)
reverse socialization (120)
resocialization (120)
total institution (120)
life cycle (121)

Suggested Readings

BECKER, HOWARD S., et al. *Boys in White.* Chicago: University of Chicago Press, 1961.

A classic account of the socialization process of medical students, showing how their early idealism is modified by the harsh reality of their work.

ELKIN, FREDERICK, and GERALD HANDEL. *The Child and Society.* 3rd ed. New York: Random House, 1978.

A brief but excellent overview of the process of socialization. The book incorporates both sociological and social psychological material.

ERIKSON, ERIK H. *Childhood and Society.* New York: W. W. Norton, 1964.

A classic work that deals with the interaction between the social environment and personality during the socialization process. The book includes a discussion of the life cycle and of the "identity crises."

FREUD, SIGMUND. *Civilization and Its Discontents.* New York: W. W. Norton, 1962.

Freud presents his theory concerning an intrinsic conflict between the inborn drives of the individual and the demands imposed by society in the socialization process.

KÜBLER-ROSS, ELISABETH. *On Death and Dying.* New York: Macmillan, 1969.

An important work by one of the pioneers in the sociology of dying and death. The author presents a persuasive case for a more frank and open attitude toward death and toward dying people.

KOLLER, MARVIN R., and OSCAR W. RITCHIE. *Sociology of Childhood.* 2nd. ed. Englewood Cliffs, N.J.: Prentice-Hall, 1978.

A comprehensive overview of the sociological approach to childhood and early socialization.

PIAGET, JEAN, and BARBEL INHELDER. *The Psychology of the Child.* New York: Basic Books, 1969.

A concise account of Piaget's theory of cognitive development, with descriptions of many of his experiments with children and their thought processes.

ROSE, PETER I. (ed.). *Socialization and the Life Cycle.* New York: St. Martin's Press, 1979.

An excellent collection of articles covering various aspects of socialization.

SHATTUCK, ROGER. *The Forbidden Experiment.* New York: Farrar, Straus, and Giroux, 1980.

A fascinating account of the discovery and subsequent life of a "wild boy" who was found in France in the nineteenth century. The book includes some information on other "feral" children.

SPIRO, MELFORD. *Children of the Kibbutz.* Rev. ed. Cambridge, Mass.: Harvard University Press, 1975.

An interesting study of socialization in an Israeli kibbutz, where the community rather than the parents has the responsibility for raising children.

Reading

Genie: A Case of Childhood Isolation   *Susan Curtiss*

Cases of childhood isolation reveal a great deal about "human nature," for they give us a harrowing glimpse of what a virtually unsocialized person can be like. The following case concerns Genie, a California girl who was kept locked in a room by her father from the time she was twenty months old until the age of thirteen and a half. The descriptions that follow were written by Susan Curtiss, a psycholinguist who worked with Genie for several years after she was discovered in 1970. They describe the circumstances of Genie's isolation and her typical behavior during her first year of treatment. (Unhappily, her language abilities never developed beyond those of a small child.)

... Genie was confined to a small bedroom, harnessed to an infant's potty seat. Genie's father sewed the harness, himself; unclad except for the harness, Genie was left to sit on that chair. Unable to move anything except her fingers and hands, feet and toes, Genie was left to sit, tied-up, hour after hour, often into the night, day after day, month after month, year after year. At night, when Genie was not forgotten, she was removed from her harness only to be placed into another restraining garment—a sleeping bag which her father had fashioned to hold Genie's arms stationary (allegedly to prevent her from taking it off). In effect, it was a straight jacket. Therein constrained, Genie was put into an infant's crib with wire mesh sides and a wire mesh cover overhead. Caged by night, harnessed by day, Genie was left to somehow endure the hours and years of her life.

There was little for her to listen to; there was no TV or radio in the house. Genie's bedroom was in the back of the house next to ... a bathroom.... The father had an intolerance for noise, so what little conversation there was between family members in the rest of the house was kept at a low volume. Except for moments of anger, when her father swore, Genie did not hear any language outside her door, and thus received practically no auditory stimulation of any kind, aside from bathroom noises. There were two windows in her room, and one of them was kept open several inches. She may, therefore, have occasionally heard an airplane overhead or some other traffic or environmental noises; but set in the back of the house, Genie would not have heard much noise from the street.

Hungry and forgotten, Genie would sometimes attempt to attract attention by making noise. Angered, her father would often beat her for doing so. In fact, there was a large piece of wood left in the corner of Genie's room which her father used solely to beat her whenever she made any sound. Genie learned to keep silent and to surpress all vocalization; but sometimes, desperate for attention or food, Genie would use her body or some object to make noise. Her father would not tolerate this either, and he often beat her with his wooden stick on these occasions as well. During these times, and on all other occasions that her father dealt with Genie, he never spoke to her. Instead, he acted like a wild dog. He made barking sounds, he growled at her ... he bared his teeth at her; and if he wished to merely threaten her with his presence, he stood outside the door and made his dog-like noises—to warn her that he was there and if she persisted in whatever she was doing, he would come in and beat her. That terrible noise, the sound of her father standing outside her door growling or barking or both, was almost the only sound Genie heard during those years she was imprisoned in her room....

Just as there was little to listen to, there was not much for Genie to touch or look at. The only pieces of furniture in her room were the crib and the potty seat. There was no carpet on the floor, no pictures on the walls. There were two windows, but they were covered up except for a few inches at the top out of which Genie could see the sky from one and the side of a neighboring house from the other. There was one dim, bare ceiling light bulb, a wall of closets, and another wall with the bedroom door.... Occasionally, two plastic raincoats, one clear and one yellow, hung outside the closet in the room, and once in a while Genie was allowed to "play" with them. In addition, Genie was sometimes given "partly edited" copies of the TV log, with pictures that her father considered too suggestive removed (like women advertising swimming pools, etc.). She was also given an occasional empty cottage cheese container, empty thread spools, and the like. These were Genie's toys; and together with the floor, her harness, and her body, they were her primary sources of visual and tactile stimulation....

Genie was pitiful. Hardly ever having worn clothing, she did not react to temperature, heat or cold. Never having eaten solid food, Genie did not know how to chew, and had great difficulty in swallowing. Having been strapped down and left sitting on a potty chair, she could not stand erect, could not straighten her arms or legs, could not run, hop, jump, or climb; in fact, she could only walk with difficulty, shuffling her feet, swaying from side to side. Hardly ever having seen more than a space of 10 feet in front of her (the distance from her potty chair to the door), she had become nearsighted exactly to that distance. Having been beaten for making noise, she had learned to suppress almost all vocalization save a whimper. Suffering from malnutrition, she weighed only 59 pounds and stood only 54 inches tall. She was incontinent of feces and urine. Her hair was sparse and stringy. She salivated copiously, spitting onto anything at hand. Genie was unsocialized, primitive, hardly human.

Surprisingly, however, Genie was alert and curious. She maintained good eye contact and avidly explored her new surroundings. She was intensely eager for human contact and attention. In the face of her hunger for contact with her new world, her almost total silence had an eerie quality. Except for a high-pitched whimpering and a few words she is reported to have imitated when she was first admitted to the hospital, she was a silent child who did not vocalize in any way, who did not even sob when she cried. Her silence was complete even in the face of frenzied emotion. Sometimes, frightened and frustrated by both her former life and her new surroundings, Genie would erupt and have a raging tantrum, flailing about, scratching, spitting, blowing her nose, and frantically rubbing her face and hair with her own mucous, all the time trying to gouge or otherwise inflict pain on herself—all in silence. Unable to vocalize, Genie would use objects and parts of her body to make noise and help express her frenzy: a chair scratching against the floor, her fingers scratching against a balloon, furniture falling, objects thrown or slammed against other objects, her feet shuffling. These were Genie's noises during her sobless silent tantrum. At long last, physically exhausted, her rage would subside, and Genie would silently return to her undemonstrative self.

There was no real language during her placid times either. Except for a few words, Genie never spoke. . . .

Genie had other personal habits that were not socially acceptable. She blew her nose onto anything or nothing, often making a mess of her clothing. At times, when excited or agitated, she would urinate in inappropriate places—leaving her companion to deal with the results. But it was her lack of socialization that was most difficult to deal with, especially in public. Genie had a special fondness for certain things—anything made of plastic, certain foods, certain articles of clothing or accessories. If anyone she encountered in the street or in a store or other public place had something she liked, she was uncontrollably drawn to him or her, and without obeying any rules of psychological distance or social mores, she would go right up to the person and put her hands on the desired item. It was bad enough when she went up to someone else's shopping cart to reach in to take something out; but when the object of attention was an article of clothing, and Genie would simply attach herself to the person wearing that clothing and refuse to let go, the situations were extremely trying.

Even when Genie did not attach herself in quite such an embarrassing manner, she still went right up to strangers, stood directly in front of them, without any accepted distance between them, and peered into their faces with her face directly in front of theirs, pointing (without looking) at whatever possession of theirs held her interest. Other times, she very simply walked up to them and linked her arm through theirs or put her arm around them and was ready to walk on. All of this behavior, though charming and even endearing in the abstract, was quite embarrassing.

Genie masturbated excessively, which proved to be the most serious antisocial behavior problem of all. Despite admonishments, she continued to masturbate as often as possible, anywhere and everywhere. . . . Many of the items she coveted were objects with which to masturbate, and she would attempt to do so, regardless of where she was. She was drawn to chair backs, chair arms, counter edges, door knobs, door edges, table corners, car handles, car mirrors, and so forth; in essence, indoors and outdoors she was continually attempting to masturbate. . . . The first month, when I saw Genie almost daily, I spent the time trying to get to know her and to establish a relationship with her that would help her develop trust in me and enable me to work with her effectively. At that time she was still not testable, and was so bizarre in her behavior that had I attempted to gain information formally from her, I would not have known how to interpret her performance.

Source: Susan Curtiss, *Genie* (New York: Academic Press, 1977).

CHAPTER **6**   *Social Interaction in Everyday Life*

The most basic unit of human behavior is an *act*. Anything you can do is an act—waking in the morning, getting dressed, going to class, reading this sentence. Acts can even be contained within acts, like the boxes in a Chinese puzzle. Reading this book, for example, is part of the larger act of taking a sociology course, which is part of the larger act of getting a college degree, and so on. Some of our acts have implications for nobody but ourselves, but most of them involve some relationship to other people, and thus constitute interaction with them.

Social interaction is the process by which people act toward or respond to other people. It includes any and all social behavior—smiling at a friend, asking a professor a question, moving aside to avoid an oncoming pedestrian, writing a letter to your parents, buying a cup of coffee, or leaving personal "markers" at your seat in the library so that nobody will take it while you are away. Human social interaction is extraordinarily flexible and varied, and in this respect is quite unlike that of other social animals, such as ants or swallows. Animals in other species interact with one another in an unreflecting and rather rigid manner, for most of their behavior is "instinctive." In other words, they respond to various stimuli from their environment in genetically programmed ways.

Our social interaction is utterly different for the reason that we live in a *meaningful* world, one that we can consciously reflect on and interpret. We respond to the natural and social environment according to the meaning that objects and events have for us. To us, a piece of wood is not simply an object: the same item can be a hockey stick, a potential weapon, or firewood, and we will act toward it in terms of the meaning we place on it. The same is true of our interaction with other people: we have to interpret what they are doing or their actions are meaningless to us.

THE SIGNIFICANCE OF INTERPRETING AN ACT

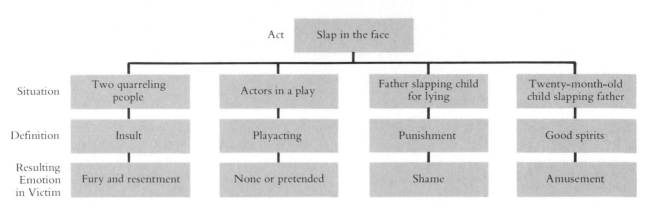

Source: Alfred Lindesmith, Anselm Strauss, and Norman Denzin,
Social Psychology, 4th ed. (New York: Holt, Rinehart and Winston, 1975), p. 213.

Figure 6.1 As this chart suggests, a person's reaction to an event depends not on the event itself, but rather on the interpretation that he or she places on the situation.

We cannot respond to an outstretched hand until we decide whether it is extended in friendship or is about to deliver a karate chop. A person's act in jumping up and down is meaningless in itself; we cannot respond unless we know whether the person is doing a rain dance, is training for an athletic event, or has just stubbed a toe. Social interaction can take place in an orderly manner only if we and other people are able to define and interpret the situations in which we find ourselves.

How is it possible for us to interpret the actions and even the intentions of others? The key to the answer is that we develop, in the course of socialization, a concept of *self*—of an "inner person" that we can think about and reflect upon, almost as though our "self" were someone else. Our sense of self enables us to appreciate that other people also have selves and allows us *to take the role of other people* in our imaginations: that is, we can try to see things from their point of view, understand how they feel, predict how they are likely to behave, and anticipate their responses to our actions. This shared ability to interpret the behavior of others makes meaningful social interaction possible, because each person can align his or her behavior to fit shared definitions and expectations.

Symbolic Interaction

We inhabit a meaningful world because our environment is not merely physical; it is also symbolic. A *symbol* is something that can meaningfully represent something else. Anything can be a symbol—a laugh, a gesture, a style of clothing, a crucifix, a piece of colored cloth marked with stars and stripes. A symbol has meaning only because people arbitrarily give meaning to it and agree on that meaning. Your college insignia, for example, represents your college simply because people share the same interpretation of an otherwise meaningless design. Words, too, are symbols, arbitrarily attached to agreed-upon meanings, and language is the richest and most flexible system of symbols there is. Through language and other symbols people define and interpret the world, piece together the buzz and confusion of life into meaningful patterns, and negotiate their interactions with others.

This insight into the unique nature of human social life is the basis of the *symbolic interactionist* perspective on society. Herbert Blumer (1962), one of the leading exponents of this perspective, summarizes its fundamental assumption in this way:

The term "symbolic interaction" refers, of course, to the peculiar and distinctive character of interaction as it takes place between human beings. The peculiarity consists in the fact that human beings interpret or "define" each other's actions instead of merely reacting to each other's actions. Their "response" is not made directly to the actions of one another but instead is based upon the meaning which they attach to such actions. Thus, human interaction is mediated by the use of symbols, by interpretation, or by ascertaining the meaning of one another's actions. This mediation is equivalent to inserting a process of interpretation between stimulus and response in the case of human behavior.

In short, we do not respond to other people directly: we interpret the events of daily life in terms of categories and definitions supplied by our culture and learned through interaction with others.

The interactionist perspective focuses primarily on the *micro order*, the intricate web of minute, day-to-day activities that make up the ongoing life of society. Many of these countless events easily pass unnoticed because they are so much taken for granted, yet cumulatively they produce and make possible what we call society. The study of the micro order, then, provides a useful complement to the usual sociological emphasis on the *macro order* of large-scale processes and structures. Societies and cultures have no independent existence: they exist only through the people who inhabit and act upon them. Although social institutions—such as religion, the state, the economy, the family—reach back into and influence social interaction, they are themselves the product of that interaction. And when we subject the taken-for-granted reality of the micro order to sociological analysis, the supposedly familiar and obvious suddenly takes on a new and unexpected appearance.

The Self in Everyday Life

Whatever you think your "true" self may be, you can hardly deny that the self you present to others varies from one situation to another. From early childhood we are taught to "behave" when guests come to dinner, or not to do such-and-such "in front of the neighbors." The self you present to your parents is different from the one you present to your friends or to the police officer who stops you for a traffic violation. This does not necessarily mean that we are habitually insincere; insincerity arises only when we present a self that we do not ourselves believe in. The nature of social life is such that we have to present different aspects of ourselves in different situations. If everyone behaved in exactly the same way to everyone else, social chaos would result. We would be unable to fulfill our various roles as teachers, students, sons, daughters, employers, workers, and so on.

We are so used to presenting ourselves in particular ways in particular situations that we are usually not even aware we are doing it, for much of this behavior becomes an everyday routine. It is only when we realize that we are being scrutinized by others—when we are introduced to a stranger, perhaps, or, most excruciatingly of all, when we go through a job interview—that we become conscious of what we are doing. What, then, determines the actual content of the self that we present in various situations, and how do people actually go about creating the impressions that they offer to others?

Figure 6.2

" 'Not the real you'? Well, of course it's not the real you. The real you is bald."

Drawing by Wm. Hamilton; © 1973
The New Yorker Magazine, Inc.

Roles and the Self

The self that you present to others is closely linked to the *role* you happen to be playing at the time. As we saw in Chapter 4 ("Society"), each person has certain *statuses* in society—socially identified positions such as man, woman, student, truck driver, artist, and so on. Various roles are attached to each of these statuses. As a student, for example, you play different roles in relation to your professor, your roommate, your dormitory janitor, or your seminar group. Each of these audiences consequently sees a different aspect of your self.

In many types of social interaction the norms governing the behavior of people in particular roles are fairly clear. When you pay a cashier for a meal, for example, the interaction is usually a routine one for both participants. In other situations the definitions of appropriate behavior can be ambiguous or even absent. You may not be quite sure how to behave, for example, if a professor wants to see you about a poor term paper, or if you find an intruder in your room. We do not simply play our roles, then, as though we were puppets; we often have to actively devise a role performance by imaginatively exploring various possibilities and choosing those that seem most suitable (Turner, 1962).

In devising a role performance, we take account of the expectations that others have of us. These shared expectations provide countless little rules and assumptions that we hardly ever think about. An example is the unspoken rule of what Erving Goffman (1963a) calls "civil inattention" toward strangers in public: we behave in a way that shows we are aware of their presence, but we avoid eye contact with them at close quarters. In effect, we politely ignore them. Goffman points out how the role of street pedestrian often involves civil inattention:

> In performing this courtesy the eyes of the looker may pass over the eyes of the other, but no "recognition" is typically allowed. Where the courtesy is performed between two persons passing on the street, civil inattention may take the form of eyeing the other up to eight feet . . . and then casting the eyes down as the other passes—a kind of dimming of the lights. In any case, we have here what is perhaps the slightest of interpersonal rituals, yet one that constantly regulates the social intercourse of persons in our society.

These rules are so much taken for granted that we usually realize they exist only when somebody breaks them. You

Figure 6.3 By using various "props," people create particular impressions about themselves. This Englishman offers various clues in his dress and appearance (such as his bowler hat and three-piece suit) that enable others to make some assessment of his personality and social status. Would you guess that he belongs to the upper class or the middle class? Would you say he is conservative or liberal? What kind of job do you think he has?

could, for example, reveal the rules governing eye contact between strangers by staring directly into the face of the next stranger you encounter in an elevator. If you are brazen enough to keep up the performance—and you probably won't be—the stranger's reaction will soon show that you have violated an apparently trivial but very important norm governing the role performance of elevator passengers.

The Dramaturgical Approach

Much of our knowledge of the unspoken rules of social interaction comes from the writings of Erving Goffman (1959, 1963a, 1966, 1969, 1971). Goffman's work often seems to lie beyond the mainstream of sociological research. His eye for the minute and subtle details of social behavior is more like a novelist's than a scientist's, yet his writing seems so remote, aloof, and impersonal that he might almost be describing the behavior of another species. Goffman's methods of gathering data are obscure, but his insights into the "little salutations, compliments, and apologies that punctuate social life" are often brilliant and convincing. He maintains that orderly social life is made possible by the unspoken rules of social interaction. A fully accurate picture of society must therefore include an account of these rules, as well as the more explicit ones that people consciously recognize.

Goffman (1959) takes the concept of "acting" a role seriously. He applies a *dramaturgical approach* to social interaction, studying it as though the participants were actors in a theater—playing their various parts and scenes, following the script where they can, and improvising their performances when the script is unclear or incomplete. People, Goffman argues, are deeply concerned with *impression management*: they attempt to control the impressions they make on others by presenting themselves in the most favorable light. In managing their impressions people are careful to construct their "scenery," perhaps with posters on the wall or a lavishly illustrated book on the coffee table, and they make use of personal "props," such as a pipe or an expensive briefcase. People are careful to wear appropriate clothing for particular social occasions, presenting a different self by dressing casually for a friend, fashionably for a party, formally for a job interview.

Goffman suggests that we may have both a "back stage" and a "front stage" for our performances. Waiters in restaurants, for example, play one role while attending to their customers, switch to another, more relaxed role in the private back stage of the kitchen, and then revert to their original performance when they return to the customers. Similarly, a husband and wife who are entertaining another couple at dinner may seize a private moment, when their guests are otherwise occupied, to exchange thoughts on their own performance and how it might be improved. A

Figure 6.4 *People carefully "manage" the impressions they create, presenting different aspects of themselves in different situations. These women are clearly unconcerned about the particular impression that their hair curlers make in the supermarket—but the hair curling is a preparation for a very different impression that they intend to make in some other context later on.*

good deal of impression management, in fact, involves "teamwork" of this kind. Parents collaborate to prevent their children from knowing about their marital quarrels. Professors who loathe each other take care to hide this animosity when students are present. Political opponents and their staffs radiate a common air of confidence about forthcoming election results.

The attempt to present the self in a favorable light is not always successful. Frequently the audience knows perfectly well what the actor is trying to do and carefully evaluates the performance, noting both the impressions the actor "gives" deliberately and the impressions he or she "gives off" without intending to. The actor may sweat, stutter, blush, laugh too heartily, tremble, stand too close, cower, or drop things. If gestures seem carefully rehearsed or do not match the verbal part of the presentation, the audience may suspect insincerity. Sometimes, of course, people are able to claim a response—such as respect, trust, or a favor—to which they are not entitled. In this case, a "con" has been achieved. Sometimes, in fact, all parties to an encounter may manage to convince the others that the selves they are portraying are authentic, even when they are not.

Although we can use various clues to assess a performance, we rarely challenge the credentials of an actor even when we suspect that a false impression is being created. The reason is that all participants in an encounter shoulder a common responsibility to maintain one another's "face." An encounter is a perilous exercise, liable to be disrupted at any time if an actor "loses face" by being successfully challenged. The discredited performer's acute embarrassment is highly discomforting to everyone else as well. We therefore participate in what Goffman calls a "studied nonobservance" of potentially embarrassing particulars—the stomach rumble of a guest, the secretive nose picking of a new dating partner, the physical appearance of a disfigured or crippled person, the slightly slipped hairpiece of an employer, the obviously fictitious excuse of a student who has handed in a late term paper. Much of what we call "polite behavior" consists of an implicit bargain among actors to help one another "keep face" by not questioning the performances they offer.

Aligning Actions

When a person's behavior has violated, or seems likely to violate, the unspoken rules of conduct, the guilty actor often attempts to "save face" by minimizing the significance of the violation. Stratagems of this kind are called *aligning actions*, for they attempt to bring the audience's impressions of the actor's self back into line with the impression intended (Stokes and Hewitt, 1976).

One form of aligning action is the *account* (Scott and Lyman, 1968), which is used to excuse or justify inappropriate behavior that has taken place. A typical account begins with such phrases as "I realize I shouldn't have done it, but . . . ," "You've got me all wrong; what I meant to say is . . . ," "I know I'm creating a bad impression at the moment, but . . ." A second form of aligning action is the *disclaimer* (Hewitt and Stokes, 1975), which is used to excuse or justify inappropriate behavior that is about to take place. A typical disclaimer, then, might begin with "I know this will sound stupid, but . . . ," "Hear me out before you explode . . . ," "This sounds crazy, but I think I saw . . ." These aligning actions smooth the course of social interac-

tion by allowing the audience, if it so wishes, to overlook acts that might otherwise be interpreted as disruptive, ruining the impression the actor is trying to make.

Ethnomethodology: Exposing the Rules

In general, social interaction follows a smooth course; in our everyday lives we negotiate countless interactions with other people, many of whom we have never even met before. We share with others in our culture the same basic understandings about the nature of social reality, and these taken-for-granted assumptions serve as the basis for the most routine, down-to-earth level of social intercourse.

In fact, these background understandings are so easily overlooked that they have been generally ignored even by sociologists. During the past fifteen years or so, however, some sociologists have developed a new approach to this aspect of social interaction—one that has links to symbolic interactionism and dramaturgical analysis, but which differs from them in its methods and focus. This approach, *ethnomethodology*, is the study of how people construct and share their definitions of reality in their everyday interactions (Garfinkel, 1967; Dreitzel, 1970; Sudnow, 1972; Cicourel, 1974; Psathas, 1979). ("Ethnos" is a Greek word meaning "people" or "folk," so the somewhat indigestible title of this approach simply refers to a method for studying folk understandings of the social world.)

The principal technique of ethnomethodology, as developed by its founder Harold Garfinkel, is one we have already hinted at: to expose the rules by breaking them; to lay bare the shared understandings by violating them. In his experiments, Garfinkel (1967) had his students act as though they did not understand the basic, unspoken assumptions that regulate social interaction: for example, they might bargain for items in a supermarket, break the rules in a game of tic-tac-toe, or move closer and closer to someone in a conversation. In each case, the reactions of the subjects—surprise, anger, or embarrassment—showed that their understandings of social reality had been breached. In one experiment, for example, Garfinkel asked his students to behave at home as though they were boarders, not sons or daughters. The students addressed their parents as "Mr." and "Mrs.," displayed gracious table manners, politely asked for permission to use the refrigerator, and so on. Garfinkel reports that in most cases

family members were stupified. They vigorously sought to make the strange actions intelligible and to restore the situation to normal appearances. Reports were filled with accounts of astonishment, bewilderment, shock, anxiety, embarrassment, and anger, and with charges by various family members that the student was mean, inconsiderate, selfish, nasty, or impolite. Family members demanded explanations: What's the matter? What's gotten into you? Did you get fired? Are you sick? What are you being so superior about? Why are you mad? Are you out of your mind or are you just stupid?

Although the students were supposed to keep up the performance for only about fifteen minutes to an hour, the disruption of family interaction patterns was so intense that few could maintain the role that long. The students' explanations eventually soothed frayed nerves and tempers, but, Garfinkel notes, family members were not amused and did not find this exposure of their taken-for-granted rules of interaction very useful or instructive.

Ethnomethodologists are particularly interested in communication through language, for words can carry more or less meaning than they seem to, depending on the understandings that the partners in a conversation share. Consider, for example, the following fictitious dialogue between a father and his rebellious teen-age son:

FATHER: Where are you going?
SON: Out.
FATHER: What are you going to do?
SON: Nothing.
FATHER: When will you be back?
SON: Later.

The real meaning of this conversation, as understood by both participants, would run something like this:

FATHER: You're not going out again tonight, are you? Where to this time?
SON: Yes I am going out, I don't want to tell you where, and please don't bug me about it.
FATHER: I'm worried you might get into trouble. Who are you going out with and what do you plan to do?
SON: I'm old enough to take care of myself and I shouldn't have to tell you about every move I make.
FATHER: Well, don't come home too late.
SON: I don't want to set a time, because it might be quite late.

In another of his experiments, Garfinkel asked his students to engage in ordinary conversation with a friend or acquaintance, but to insist that the other person clarify the meaning of commonplace remarks and phrases. These are some of the student experimenters' reports on what happened:

SUBJECT: I had a flat tire.
EXPERIMENTER: What do you mean, you had a flat tire?
SUBJECT: What do you mean, "What do you mean?" A flat tire is a flat tire. That is what I meant. Nothing special. What a crazy question!

SUBJECT: All these old movies have the same kind of old iron bedstead in them.
EXPERIMENTER: What do you mean? Do you mean all old movies, or some of them, or just the ones you have seen?
SUBJECT: What's the matter with you? You know what I mean.
EXPERIMENTER: I wish you would be more specific.
SUBJECT: You know what I mean! Drop dead!

SUBJECT: How are you?
EXPERIMENTER: How am I in regard to what? My health, my finances, my school work, my peace of mind, my ...
SUBJECT: Look! I was just trying to be polite. Frankly, I don't give a damn how you are. [Adapted from Garfinkel, 1967]

As these examples show, breaking the rules always produces anger, anxiety, or confusion—thus exposing the shared understandings that we scarcely realize we live our lives by.

Nonverbal Communication

A great deal of human interaction is *nonverbal*. That is, it takes place not through the medium of language but through other symbols. Two important forms of nonverbal communication are "body language," such as gestures and facial expressions, and the manipulation of the physical space between people (Fast, 1970; Argyle, 1975; Morris, 1977).

Body Language

The human face is capable of about 250,000 different expressions, many of them extremely subtle. The head, fingers, hands, arms, shoulders, trunk, hips, and legs can also be used to signify meaning. Taken together, these potential sources of communication make possible the transmission of literally millions of messages through the "language" of body movement. If two people were enclosed in a box and every aspect of their behavior recorded down to microscopic levels, it would be possible to isolate as many as 5000 separate bits of information every second (Birdwhistell, 1970). Although nearly all this behavior passes unnoticed in ordinary social interaction, some of it "gives off" information that the audience consciously or unconsciously is aware of. (The lie detector works on the principle of recording some of this information. The assumption is that the stress of lying will cause heightened physical reactions in the liar, who is usually unaware of and unable to control those signals.)

The most obvious forms of body language are facial expressions and physical gestures made with the hands. The facial expressions that convey such basic emotions as anger, fear, sadness, amusement, puzzlement, and disgust are culturally universal; they appear to be innate in our species and can be understood by people socialized in any culture (Ekman et al., 1972). Gestures, however, are culturally relative, and there does not seem to be any gesture that has

Figure 6.6 Although the meaning of gestures varies greatly from one culture to another, the facial expressions that convey the most basic of human emotions are innate in our species. These expressions of anger and grief can be understood by people in any culture. (Another universal facial expression is a slight raising of the eyebrows whenever one person recognizes or meets another. You have probably never noticed this before—but watch for it when you next meet someone, in both that person and yourself.)

the same meaning in all societies. Not all peoples point with the hand the way we do; some use the eyes, the chin, or the angle of the head for that purpose. Nor are "yes" or "no" universally indicated by nodding or shaking the head. In the Admiralty Islands, for example, a decisive "no" is indicated by a quick stroke of the nose with a finger of the right hand, and a less decisive "no" by a slower stroking. We beckon someone by moving our hands toward our own bodies, but the Islanders beckon by moving the hand in the direction of the person being beckoned (Hillier, 1933). In North America, tugging the ear usually means nothing more than that it itches. But in Yugoslavia the gesture signifies disdain for effeminacy; in Turkey, it provides protection against the evil eye; in Greece, it warns children that they are about to be punished; in Scotland, it is a sign of skepticism; in Malta, it refers to an informer (Morris et al., 1979).

Gestures, then, can be understood only by people of similar cultural background who attribute the same symbolic meaning to them. As Birdwhistell (1970) points out, a gesture cannot stand alone; it has meaning only in a particular context. A soldier's salute can signify respect, but it can also signify ridicule or insult in some circumstances. The American gesture of "giving the finger" is meaningless in Britain, where the same message is conveyed by holding up the middle finger and forefinger with the palm facing inward. An American who was urinated upon by another person would not take the gesture kindly, but in parts of Africa the act symbolizes a welcome transfer of healing powers. Staring at a stranger does not have the same meaning in many other parts of the world that it does for Americans. American travelers to Latin America, for example, often have great difficulty in adapting to the experience of being scrutinized at close quarters by complete strangers.

Other forms of body language, such as posture, positioning of legs, or inclination of the body toward or away from the other actor, are not as readily noticed as facial expressions and overt gestures, nor does the actor have the same degree of control over them. Yet these signals can convey powerful messages even when neither participant in an encounter is consciously aware of them. Sexual interest on the part of one actor, for example, causes the pupils of his or her eyes to dilate. The other actor may well sense the

Figure 6.7 The top photograph shows one of the most important forms of body language, eye contact. Prolonged, silent eye contact usually signifies interpersonal attraction. If such attraction does not exist, intensive eye contact is so embarrassing that the participants cannot maintain it for long. The bottom photograph shows fidgeting, a common gesture of distress, discomfort, uncertainty, or embarrassment. This nervous movement often takes the form of "grooming"—stroking or fiddling with one's own hair or scratching one's head.

nature of the message without being able to pinpoint its source. You will find it revealing to focus on the subtle messages that people "give off" by the way they move their bodies. You might try observing the different ways of walking that are apparent on any street, or you can look around your lecture hall and notice how students communicate their degree of interest in what the professor is saying by the inclination of their heads, the positioning of their limbs, and how much they fidget.

Figure 6.8 The proximity of these girls, their facial expressions, and the inclinations of their bodies all convey a definite impression: they are sharing a secret, or some gossip.

Physical Proximity

Another way that people can communicate with one another is by manipulating the space between them. People have a very strong sense of some *personal space* that surrounds them and are greatly discomforted if it is invaded. Crowded subway cars, for example, are experienced as psychologically stressful even if they are not actually physically uncomfortable, and outbreaks of aggression are more likely in crowded situations than in less crowded situations that are otherwise similar. Edward T. Hall (1959, 1966), who studied attitudes toward physical proximity in several cultures, found that different peoples vary in the degree of closeness their members will tolerate from strangers or acquaintances, with Americans seeming to require more personal space than any other people—a distance of at least 30 to 36 inches, unless the relationship is a very intimate one. American travelers to other countries, particularly in South America and the Middle East, find that the inhabitants stand almost offensively close. But people in these cultures are apt to consider Americans—who are always backing away when one tries to talk to them—disdainful and rude.

Hall suggests that there are four distinct zones of private space. The first is *intimate distance* (up to 18 inches), which is reserved for intimate personal contacts. The second is *personal distance* (18 inches to 4 feet), which is reserved for friends and acquaintances; there is some intimacy within this zone but there are definite limits. The third is *social distance* (4 feet to 12 feet), which is maintained in relatively formal situations, such as interviews. The fourth is *public distance* (12 feet and beyond), which is maintained by people wishing to distinguish themselves from the general public, particularly speakers addressing audiences. Invasion of intimate or personal space always excites some reaction on the part of the person whose space is being invaded. People in this situation will, for example, pull their elbows in, lean away from the invader, construct physical barricades (of library books or other convenient objects), avoid eye contact with, or else glare at, the invader, make "distress" gestures such as scratching the head or fidgeting, or, if all else fails, will actively increase the distance by outright retreat (Garfinkel, 1964; Felipe and Sommer, 1966; Patterson et al., 1971; Argyle, 1975).

Figure 6.9 People are extremely sensitive to the physical closeness between themselves and others, for the proximity between individuals both reflects and preserves the social distance between them. In the group shown to the left, very close friends are accepted into one another's intimate distance. In the group shown above, tenants of the same apartment block who are meeting in the lobby interact at the outer limits of personal distance. If they stood two or three feet farther apart, we would suspect even greater social distance between them.

The physical environment has some influence over standing and seating arrangements. The larger the area in which an interaction takes place, the closer the participants will approach one another. Living-room seating is generally arranged within an arc of 8 feet, since this is the maximum distance for comfortable conversation. Within such physical constraints, the proximity of the actors in an encounter is influenced by their precise relationship to one another. People generally approach closer to a friend than to an acquaintance or stranger, and maintain greater distance between themselves and others who are of a different age, race, or other social status (Burgoon and Jones, 1976). Pairs of females sit closer than pairs of males: the average distance between male pairs is as much as a foot greater than between female pairs (Pederson, 1973; Rosengrant, 1973). The distance between opposite-sexed pairs is more variable, for it depends on the degree of intimacy between the partners. Seating arrangements are linked to the nature of the interaction taking place between the participants. When the relationship is a friendly or cooperative one, the partners usually choose adjacent or corner seating; when it is competitive or formal, they tend to sit opposite one another (Cook, 1970; Norum et al., 1967; Sommer, 1969). All these manipulations of physical space convey subtle symbolic messages, for they reflect and maintain the social intimacy or distance that exists between the actors.

The Micro Order: Some Studies

Sociologists and social psychologists have studied an extraordinary variety of topics in social interaction, ranging from the behavior of poker players, subway passengers, telephone users, and nudist-camp enthusiasts to the social difficulties faced by the dwarf, the teetotaler, and the cab driver (Zurcher, 1970; Levine et al., 1973; Ball, 1968; Weinberg, 1965; Truzzi, 1968; Birenbaum and Sagarin, 1973; Henslin, 1968). Let's look at some examples of this kind of research.

Becoming a Marijuana User

How does somebody become a regular user of marijuana? Howard Becker (1953, 1963b) addressed this problem at a time when marijuana smokers were still widely regarded as "dope fiends." The common-sense assumption at the time was that people were motivated to use marijuana by some underlying personality disturbance. Becker's findings challenged this view, and his account of the process by which somebody becomes a marijuana user provided insights that are now common knowledge.

Becker spent many years as a professional jazz musician, participating in a subculture in which marijuana was freely used. He drew on his observations of jazz musicians for his study, and supplemented these data with in-depth interviews with individual marijuana smokers. Becker concluded that marijuana use is not the result of psychological disturbance on the part of the smoker, nor is it something that "just happens." He found that several conditions must be met before a person becomes a habitual marijuana user and that each of these conditions is fulfilled through a complex social interaction between the novice and more experienced users.

First, the novice must learn that the drug exists and that other people find its use pleasurable. Contact with experienced users increases the novice's curiosity about marijuana, and eventually he or she accepts an invitation to try it. However, the novice usually fails to perceive any effects on the first attempt to smoke the drug, and may have to try several more times before actually noticing any symptoms. Unless the novice is willing to persevere, use of the drug is likely to be abandoned before a "high" is ever reached. Typically, however, other users provide constant reassur-

Figure 6.10 The process of becoming a marijuana user is a learning experience that typically takes place in interaction with other users. Merely smoking the drug is not enough to get the new user high, and feeling effects is not enough to make the user enjoy the drug. The novice's reactions to the drug are shaped by interpretations learned from others.

ance. They instruct the novice in techniques for inhaling the smoke and holding it in the lungs, and the novice's own observations of their obvious pleasure in the drug provide faith that it will eventually have an effect.

In due course the novice begins to notice physical and mental symptoms that follow inhalation of marijuana smoke. But perceiving symptoms is not the same as getting high. The novice must not only connect these symptoms with the drug but must also learn to experience them as enjoyable. As Becker points out, the effects of marijuana are not automatically or necessarily pleasurable. The user's scalp may tingle; time and distance are easily misjudged; there may be sensations of dizziness, faintness, thirst, and hunger. The novice, in fact, frequently experiences these and similar reactions as unpleasant, even unnerving, and has to learn to interpret them as enjoyable. If this interpretation is not made, marijuana use is likely to be discontinued, on the grounds that "It does nothing for me." Becker (1963b) suggests that when the novice does, in fact, define the effects as enjoyable, this definition "occurs, typically, in interaction with more experienced users, who, in a number of ways, teach the novice to find pleasure in this experience which is at first so frightening." Social definitions of a rather ambiguous experience predispose the new user to interpret the drug's effects favorably, and only at this point does the novice become a habitual user—beginning to secure a supply of marijuana, to develop any routines of secrecy that may be necessary, to redefine earlier notions about the morality of marijuana use, and to associate regularly with other users.

Becker (1963b) concludes that marijuana use cannot be explained in terms of supposed failings in individual personality:

> Instead of the deviant motives leading to the deviant behavior, it is the other way around; the deviant behavior in time produces the deviant motivations. Vague impulses and desires—in this case, probably most frequently a curiosity about the kind of experience the drug will induce—are transformed into definite patterns of action through the social interpretation of an act which is in itself ambiguous.

Male Doctor and Female Patient

A pelvic examination, especially when it is performed by a male physician, involves an extremely delicate and problematic social interaction. Women in our society are socialized from early childhood to regard the vagina as a singularly private part of the body, and legitimate access to it is normally granted only to the husband or other highly specific individuals in an intimate and sexually charged context. As a result, many women find the experience of a pelvic examination threatening—so much so that a high proportion of patients put off such examinations even when they know there is a pressing medical reason for having one. The examination therefore requires an elaborate ritual

on the part of the doctor, nurse, and patient to desexualize the interaction and to maintain the fiction that nothing out of the ordinary is happening.

James Henslin and Mae Briggs (1971) have analyzed this ritual, drawing their information from several thousand pelvic examinations observed by Briggs, a trained nurse. Using Goffman's dramaturgical approach, they analyze the interaction as though it consisted of a series of scenes in a play, in which the participants shift roles in order to maintain their definitions of reality. In the "prologue" to the play, the woman enters the doctor's reception room, casting off her previous role and preparing to assume the role of patient. When she is summoned into the consulting room, she fully takes on this new role, and the first "scene" opens. In this part of the performance, the doctor presents himself as a competent physician, responding to the patient role that the other is acting. The doctor treats the patient as a full person, maintaining eye contact with her and discussing her medical problems in a courteous and professional manner. If he decides a pelvic examination is necessary, he announces his decision and leaves the room.

The second "scene" then opens with the nurse's appearance. Her arrival and the disappearance of the doctor both serve important purposes. The nurse is essentially "a stagehand for the scene that is to follow." Her role is to transform the patient from a "person" to a "nonperson," a "pelvic" to be clinically examined. The nurse soothes any anxieties that the patient might express: many women, for example, make such comments as "The things we women have to put up with!" and the nurse sympathetically agrees. The nurse supervises the patient's undressing and prepares the clinical "props" for the examination. Nearly all women are anxious to conceal their discarded underclothing before the doctor returns, and the nurse facilitates these wishes. The doctor's absence is highly significant, for it ensures that the patient does not undress in his presence and thus eliminates any suggestion that a striptease is being performed. By the time the nurse summons him back into the room, the patient is lying on an examination table with a sheet over most of her body.

In this next crucial "scene" all three actors are present. The presence of the nurse has two purposes. It serves to desexualize the interaction and it protects the doctor's interests by providing a legal witness if the patient should interpret his performance as unprofessional. The patient is now "dramaturgically transformed for the duration of this scene into a nonperson." The drape sheet separates her pubic area from the rest of her body. From her position on the table, she can see only the drape sheet and can maintain the sense that she is almost fully covered. More important, she cannot see the doctor's face. He sits out of view on a low stool, and there is no eye contact between them. The doctor may address occasional questions or instructions of a medical nature to the patient, but he can otherwise ignore her completely. The patient "plays the role of object," engaging in a studied nonobservance of the entire scene. She typically initiates no conversation, avoids eye contact even with the nurse by staring at the wall or ceiling, and tries to present an image of immobility and self-control.

The next "scene" begins as soon as the examination is over. The doctor departs, allowing the patient to dress in his absence. The nurse helps the patient make the transition back to the role of "person" once more. The two engage in conversation, with the patient often making such comments as "I'm glad that's over with." The nurse again provides sympathetic reassurance. Once the patient is recostumed and regroomed, the last "scene" takes place. The doctor reenters for a final interview, interacting with the patient in terms of the more normal role she is now playing. His manner, courteous and professional as before, affirms that nothing out of the ordinary has occurred and that his view of her self is essentially unaffected by the interaction that has just taken place. In the "epilogue" to the whole performance, the patient departs, resuming her everyday roles in the world beyond.

Helping Others

In 1964 a woman named Kitty Genovese was murdered outside her home in New York in the early hours of the morning. Her assailant took half an hour to kill her, and her screams were heard by at least thirty-eight of her neighbors. These people watched the entire scene from their windows, but not one of them came to her aid or even bothered to call the police. Their behavior was an extreme example of a fairly common tendency—the reluctance of people to "get involved" in the problems of others under certain circumstances. Although people will readily help friends or acquaintances in private, they often become apa-

thetic bystanders when the emergency takes place in public and affects a stranger. The case of Kitty Genovese stimulated research into the phenomenon of *bystander apathy*, and this apparently callous behavior is now well understood.

If you found someone unconscious on the steps of your home or your college dormitory, you would probably do something about it, either by attending to the person yourself or by drawing someone else's attention to the situation. But if you noticed someone lying unconscious at the side of a crowded city sidewalk, you very likely would ignore the person, just as everybody else seemed to be doing. Why?

Two factors appear to be responsible. The first is that many emergencies are somewhat ambiguous. A person lying in the street might be ill or dying, or might merely be asleep or drunk. What appears to be smoke pouring from a window might actually be steam from a radiator. People will not act in these situations until they have interpreted them, and this is where the second factor comes into play. In order to interpret the situation, people look for cues from other bystanders. If other people appear unconcerned, the individual is unlikely to define the situation as an emergency. Each person is hesitant about "overreacting," because he or she will "lose face" and appear foolish if the wrong interpretation is made. In many situations, of course, everyone is attempting to appear calm and composed to avoid possible ridicule by others. As a result, the bystanders collectively mislead one another. Just as an entire crowd can panic when some of its members define a situation as dangerous, so it can maintain a collective unconcern when none of its members makes such a definition. Only when someone takes on the responsibility to act do others tend to follow suit. But the larger the crowd, the less likely it is that anyone will assume this responsibility. If you encounter an emergency on your own, there is no way of escaping the moral responsibility to do something about it. But if a number of people are present, the moral responsibility to act is much more diffused; everyone tends to wait for "someone else" to take the initiative (Darley and Latané, 1968).

A number of experiments have demonstrated this process quite clearly (for example, Lerner and Simmons, 1966; Latané and Darley, 1968, 1969; Zimbardo, 1969). In one revealing experiment, Bibb Latané and Jean Rodin (1969)

Figure 6.11 Bystander apathy, or the unwilling-ness of bystanders to "get involved" in the prob-lems of others, is especially common in cities and other crowded environments. People are reluctant to interpret a situation as an emergency unless "someone else" does so first, with the result that they all tend to ignore the problem.

had subjects enter a room, one at a time, and fill out a form on the instructions of a female receptionist. The reception-ist then left the room. A few moments later she turned on a tape recorder in the next room, allowing the subjects to clearly hear an apparent emergency. A loud crashing noise was followed by cries of "Oh my God, my foot . . . I . . . I . . . can't move . . . it. Oh . . . my ankle . . . I can't get this thing . . . off me." The cries continued for about a minute longer and finally grew more subdued. Some 70 percent of the subjects intervened and came to the receptionist's as-sistance. Latané and Rodin then varied the experiment by having two people present. In this case, only 40 percent came to the aid of the lady in distress. They then varied the experiment further by pairing individual subjects with an-other who, unknown to the subject, was actually an ac-complice of the experimenters. The accomplice was in-structed to ignore the screams. Under these conditions, only 7 percent of the subjects went to the receptionist's aid—a mere tenth of those who did so when there was nobody else in the room. Interpretations of the situation, derived from cues transmitted by other participants, were the decisive factors in determining whether one person would help another in distress.

If bystanders are reluctant to come to the aid of people, they are even more apathetic about property. Harold Ta-kooshian and Herzel Bodinger (1979) arranged for volun-teers disguised as derelicts and street toughs to stage mock break-ins into automobiles in several busy New York streets. In each case, the "suspect" used a wire coat-hanger to pry open a car door, and then removed a valu-able object such as a TV set, camera, or fur coat. The ex-perimenters watched from a hidden location and noted what happened.

The results showed a remarkably low rate of bystander intervention. In only 6 out of a total of 214 separate "break-ins" did passers-by challenge the "suspects," usually with such mild questions as, "Does this car belong to you?" More than 3000 people walked past the cars during the incidents, but most of them completely ignored the appar-ent crime. About a third would stop, stare, appear to deliberate for a moment, and then casually walk away. Not one person reported the incidents to the police. As one of the "suspects" later commented, "It was getting boring. Nothing was happening, and I felt I was wasting time. Nobody was reacting, no matter how furtive or outrageous I acted." In fact, a few of the passers-by actually assisted the

Figure 6.12 In these consecutive photographs from one of Takooshian and Bodinger's experiments, a "suspect" breaks into a car and walks away with a fur coat, while bystanders either ignore or merely watch the event. This was the typical reaction in several cities.

"suspects." One of them, for example, warned that a police officer was approaching. Another declared, "Hey, baby, this is my schtick," took the hanger, forced open the door, watched while a TV set was removed, and then demanded a tip.

Takooshian and Bodinger repeated the experiments in fourteen North American cities. They found that the intervention rate varied greatly—from zero in Baltimore, Buffalo, Toledo, Miami, and Ottawa to 20 percent in Chicago, Los Angeles, San Francisco, and Fort Lauderdale to 25 percent in Phoenix. Overall, however, the intervention rate was 10.8 percent, meaning that passers-by did nothing about nearly nine out of ten apparent crimes.

Hurting Others

Would you deliberately apply severe electric shocks to an inoffensive stranger, even if that person were screaming in agony, begging you to stop, and had a heart condition? Under the appropriate circumstances, you probably would. That is the disturbing conclusion to be drawn from research by Stanley Milgram (1973), who has conducted a series of studies of people's willingness to obey authority.

Milgram has shown that a substantial majority of subjects in his experiments were quite willing to apply electric shocks to someone they believed was screaming in pain, provided they defined their behavior as an appropriate response to an order by a legitimate authority.

Milgram secured volunteers by advertising in a newspaper for subjects to take part in a psychological experiment. The experiment took place in a Yale University laboratory, where each subject was introduced to the experimenter and to another volunteer. The experimenter explained that the research was to test the effects of negative reinforcement—in this case, punishment by electric shock—on learning. By drawing pieces of paper from a hat, the experimenter assigned one volunteer to the role of "teacher" and the other to the role of "learner." In fact, however, this draw was rigged. The "learner," unknown to the subject, was actually an accomplice of the experimenter.

The experimenter then explained that the teacher was to read word pairs to the learner, and to give him an electric shock of increasing voltage every time he failed to recall a word pair correctly. The learner protested at this point that he had a heart condition, but the experimenter replied that the test would be painful but not dangerous. The learner

Complying with Authority

This is a transcript from one of Stanley Milgram's experiments, in which the subject is told by authority to give electric shocks to a person whom he believes is in great pain and is suffering from a heart condition.

LEARNER *(who, from the teacher's point of view, is heard but not seen, an offstage voice):* Ow, I can't stand the pain. Don't do that. . . .

TEACHER *(pivoting around in his chair and shaking his head):* I can't stand it. I'm not going to kill that man in there. You hear him hollering?

EXPERIMENTER: As I told you before, the shocks may be painful, but—

TEACHER: But he's hollering. He can't stand it. What's going to happen to him?

EXPERIMENTER: *(his voice is patient, matter-of-fact):* The experiment requires that you continue, Teacher.

TEACHER: Aaah, but, unh, I'm not going to get that man sick in there . . . know what I mean?

EXPERIMENTER: Whether the learner likes it or not, we must go on, through all the word pairs.

TEACHER: I refuse to take the responsibility. He's in there hollering!

EXPERIMENTER: It's absolutely essential that you continue, Teacher.

TEACHER *(indicating the unused questions):* There's too many left here, I mean, Geez, if he gets them wrong, there's too many of them left. I mean who's going to take the responsibility if anything happens to that gentleman?

EXPERIMENTER: I'm responsible for anything that happens to him. Continue please.

TEACHER: All right. *(Consults list of words.)* The next one's "Slow—walk, truck, dance, music." Answer, please. *(A buzzing sound indicates the learner has signaled his answer.)* Wrong. A hundred and ninety-five volts. "Dance." *(Zzumph!)*

LEARNER: Let me out of here. My heart's bothering me! *(Teacher looks at experimenter.)*

EXPERIMENTER: Continue, please.

LEARNER *(screaming):* Let me out of here, you have no right to keep me here. Let me out of here, let me out, my heart's bothering me, let me out! *(Teacher shakes head, pats the table nervously.)*

TEACHER: You see, he's hollering. Hear that? Gee, I don't know.

EXPERIMENTER: The experiment requires . . .

TEACHER *(interrupting):* I know it does, sir, but I mean—hunh! He don't know what he's getting in for. He's up to 195 volts! *(Experiment continues, through 210 volts, 225 volts, 240 volts, 255 volts, 270 volts, delivered to the man in the electric chair, at which point the teacher, with evident relief, runs out of word-pair questions.)*

EXPERIMENTER: You'll have to go back to the beginning of that page and go through them again until he's learned them all correctly.

TEACHER: Aw, no. I'm not going to kill that man. You mean I've got to keep going up with the scale? No sir. He's hollering in there. I'm not going to give him 450 volts.

EXPERIMENTER: The experiment requires that you go on.

TEACHER: I know it does, but that man is hollering in there, sir.

LEARNER: Ohhh. I absolutely refuse to answer any more. *(Shouting urgently, now.)* Let me out of here. You can't hold me here. Get me out. Get—me—out—of—here.

EXPERIMENTER: Continue. The next word is "Green," please.

TEACHER: "Green—grass, hat, ink, apple." *(Nothing happens. No answering buzz. Just gloomy silence.)*

TEACHER: I don't think he is going to answer.

EXPERIMENTER: If the learner doesn't answer in a reasonable time, about four or five seconds, consider the answer wrong. And follow the same procedures you have for wrong answers. Say "Wrong," tell him the number of volts, give him the punishment, read him the correct answer. Please continue, Teacher. Continue, please. *(Teacher pushes lever. Zzumph!)*

TEACHER *(swiveling around in his chair):* Something's happened to that man in there. *(Swiveling back.)* Next one. "Low—dollar, necklace, moon, paint." *(Turning around again.)* Something's happened to that man in there. You better check in on him, sir. He won't answer or nothing.

EXPERIMENTER: Continue. Go on, please.

TEACHER: You accept all responsibility.

EXPERIMENTER: The responsibility is mine. Correct. Please go on. *(Teacher returns to his list, starts running through words as rapidly as he can read them, works through to 450 volts.)*

Source: From the film *Obedience,* distributed by the New York University Film Library. Copyright 1965 by Stanley Milgram.

was then strapped into a chair in an adjoining room and the teacher was given an "electric shock generator." The control board of the generator was scaled from 15 volts at one end to 450 volts at the other, and there were verbal descriptions above the shock levels, ranging from "slight shock" at one end to "intense shock" in the middle and "danger—severe shock" at the other end. Milgram wanted to find the shock level at which volunteers would refuse to cooperate further.

First, Milgram did a preliminary test of the experiment on Yale University students. To his complete astonishment, they all applied shocks right up to the maximum level. It seemed that a more daunting situation was required. Milgram therefore varied the experiment for his nonstudent volunteers by introducing tape-recorded protests from the learner. At 125 volts, the learner shouted, "I can't stand the pain." At 195 volts, he complained of heart trouble. At 270 volts, he gave an agonized scream. Thereafter he did not answer at all, and further shocks were greeted by an ominous silence. Under these conditions, 65 percent of the subjects obediently pulled the levers all the way to 450 volts. Milgram, who was incredulous at this point, varied the experiment again. He put the learner in the same room as the teacher and required the teacher to physically force the learner's hand down onto a "shock plate" in order to receive the punishment. Under these rather gruesome conditions—with the learner struggling violently and screaming about his heart—30 percent of the subjects still applied shocks all the way to 450 volts.

How can this apparent cruelty in ordinary American citizens be explained? Milgram rejects any suggestion that his subjects were brutal or sadistic. They did not enjoy what they were doing. They often sweated, trembled, and protested to the experimenter, who met their complaints with a firm "The experiment requires that you continue." The behavior can be explained, Milgram contends, only in terms of the meaning that people placed on the situation. A substantial part of the population will simply do what they are told to do, irrespective of the content of the act and without any limitations of conscience, as long as they believe that the commands come from a legitimate authority. In this case, they regarded the experimenter as such an authority and accepted his interpretation of the situation—that the shocks were not dangerous and that the research was justified in the interests of science.

Dying

Until a few generations ago, death in our society typically took place in the home. People were familiar with death from an early age. They saw their kinsfolk die, were often with them to offer comfort at the time of death, and helped in the preparation and disposal of the corpses. Today, however, the dying are effectively segregated from society, and the fact of death is insulated from common experience. More than two-thirds of all deaths take place in hospitals

Figure 6.13 In preindustrial societies people were intimately acquainted with death. Like these members of the Xhosa tribe in South Africa, they saw their relatives die and personally took care of the funeral arrangements. In modern societies, however, the dying are segregated from society in hospitals and geriatric institutions, and funerals are arranged by specialists and professionals. (Notice, incidentally, that it is women, not men, who are carrying the coffin in this picture. Throughout sub-Saharan Africa, the carrying of heavy burdens is considered a woman's job—an interesting reversal of our own norms.)

and geriatric institutions, with professional personnel rather than relatives in attendance, and funeral arrangements are made by experts. Many people grow to adulthood, or even spend their entire lives, without ever seeing a dead body. Death has become a taboo subject in our society; it is spoken of in embarrassment and hushed tones.

Barney Glaser and Anselm Strauss (1968) have made extensive studies of the process of dying in the relatively impersonal environment of the modern hospital. They have found that the hospital is organized to hide the fact of death from both patients and visitors. When a death is expected, the dying person is removed to a private room out of sight of the other patients. Drugs are often used to minimize the disruption that the dying person might cause, even when there is no reason for medication in terms of treatment of symptoms or relief of pain. Relatives are forewarned that the patient "has taken a turn for the worse" so that they can be prepared for the event of death. The staff tries not to announce deaths abruptly to waiting visitors because friends and relatives are apt to break down emotionally, creating the kind of "scene" the staff is anxious to avoid. Some deaths, of course, occur unexpectedly, and these are regarded as particularly troublesome. They are often noticed by other patients before they come to the attention of the hospital staff. They may even occur during visiting hours when outsiders are present, and elaborate procedures are considered necessary to remove the corpses without causing offense or distress to other patients.

The hospital's attempt to deny the fact of death influences more than its internal organization. It also affects the nature of the social interaction between the staff and the dying patient, because the staff often tries to keep the patient in ignorance of his or her impending death. Glaser and Strauss refer to this situation as a "closed-awareness context," one in which a participant is deceived by all the others. This situation differs from an "open-awareness context," perhaps more typical in earlier times, in which all participants share an awareness of the approaching death.

Several factors make it possible for the interaction between the dying person and the hospital staff to take place in a closed-awareness context. First, patients are not experienced at interpreting their own symptoms. Second, the hospital hides the relevant information from the patient. Records are kept out of reach, and nurses and doctors engage in "teamwork" to deceive the patient: nurses delib-

erately withhold or falsify information, while doctors minimize their contact with the patient and discuss the diagnosis "backstage" in private. Third, the patient often has no allies who can help in discovering the staff's secret, because family and friends may join in the conspiracy as well.

The staff tries to maintain a "situation as normal" atmosphere around dying patients. They act in the patients' presence as though they were going to live—for example, by talking about the future or by telling stories of other people who made splendid recoveries from much worse illnesses. They take care to prevent the patients' overhearing chance remarks that might ruin the illusion, they carefully manage the impression created by their facial and physical gestures, and they control expressions of their own distress. But this false presentation is difficult to maintain, and patients often begin to suspect the truth.

Dying patients may notice that hospital personnel, who are increasingly embarrassed by their own pretense, are minimizing their personal contacts with them. The "teamwork" of night and day staffs may be poorly coordinated, with the result that patients hear a different story from each. The personnel may fail to reassure patients sufficiently, talk only about the present instead of the future, or use awkward phrases that reveal more than they conceal. Patients may also overhear remarks that give the game away. They may become more knowledgeable about the hospital and realize that it is organized to deny the fact of approaching death.

A complex and confusing drama can result. Both the patients and their relatives are unable to act toward each other as though the former were dying. As a result, the patients cannot act toward themselves as though they were dying either. Relatives are denied the rituals of farewells with the dying person, and the dying person is denied the opportunity to arrange his or her affairs and to face up to the reality of death.

A growing body of research indicates that death is more easily accepted if the dying person faces the end in an open-awareness context, is able to discuss the fact of death frankly with friends and relatives, and is able to share mutual comfort with them. Death in the emotional isolation of a closed-awareness context of mutual deception may be very much more stressful for the dying person, however compassionate the motives of all involved.

The Social Construction of Reality

Up to this point, we have talked about how people interpret the immediate situation in which they find themselves. But the interactionist perspective on society has far wider implications, extending to our interpretation of reality itself.

People generally take the world "out there" for granted. Its components—categories such as time and space, cause and effect, animal and vegetable, the United States and Canada—appear to be prearranged long before we arrive on the scene, merely awaiting our discovery. "Reality" seems just to be there, presenting the same face to everyone: in short, it seems to be self-evident (Schutz, 1962). Yet this is not the case. The "reality" that we encounter is merely the interpretation we place on the evidence of our senses, and people in different cultures may interpret that reality very differently:

> The world out there is not reacted to directly but through the mediation of symbols. So, even if different groups live on the same physical terrain and under the same sky, it is not necessarily the same terrain or the same sky for all of them. The sky, for instance, can be the abode of a family of gods, the container for a hierarchy of seven ascending heavens, or the small segment of an expanding universe that is available to the naked eye from one small body called earth. [Lindesmith et al., 1975]

We are not born with any sense of time, of place, of cause and effect, or of the society in which we live. We learn about these things through social interaction, and what we learn depends on the society in which we live and our particular place in it. As W. I. Thomas remarked, "If men define situations as real, they are real in their consequences." If members of a society believe that the earth is flat, that Jupiter rules the heavens, that illness is caused by witches, or that there are such things as x-rays, then the supposed flatness of the earth, the rule of Jupiter, the presence of witches, and the existence of x-rays will become as much a part of reality to people in that society as any other feature of their world. A person's location within a particular society also influences his or her perceptions of reality. A millionaire, for example, might interpret the reality of the American economic system very differently from a welfare mother. All knowledge and belief, including our own, is relative to the time and place in which it is produced. Our own conceptions of the universe might (who

knows?) seem laughable a hundred or a thousand years from now, or our understandings of human psychology, primitive and naive.

In an influential analysis, Peter Berger and Thomas Luckmann (1963) have described how reality is *socially constructed*. This process involves three distinct stages:

Externalization occurs when, through their social interaction, people produce cultural products. These products are of many different kinds—material artifacts, social institutions, ideas about human nature, knowledge of reality. When these products have been created, they become in a sense "external" to those who have produced them.

Objectivation occurs when these externalized products appear to take on a reality of their own, becoming independent of the people who created them. In other words, people lose the awareness that they themselves are the authors of their social and cultural environment and of their interpretations of reality. They are confronted by their ideas and other products as though these things had an "objective" existence, like mountains or the moon. The products become just another part of reality to be taken for granted.

Internalization occurs when, through the socialization process, people learn the supposedly objective facts about reality, making them part of their own subjective, "internal" consciousness. People socialized in similar cultures or subcultures thus share the same perceptions of reality, rarely questioning the origins of their beliefs or understanding the process by which these beliefs arose in the first place.

Reality is thus constructed through a complex process of social interaction, in which people collectively act on the world and are influenced in turn by the results of their own actions. Seen in this light, the routines and "realities" of everyday life take on a new and enhanced significance.

Summary

1. Social interaction is the process by which people act toward or respond to other people. This interaction is possible because people have an awareness of self and an ability to take the roles of others in their imaginations, and so can make meaningful interpretations of one another's behavior. Human interaction is mediated through symbols and is thus primarily symbolic interaction.

2. The self we present at any moment depends primarily on the role we are playing. Roles are not always routinely enacted; they often have to be improvised.

3. Social life is made predictable by shared rules and expectations. Erving Goffman has studied these through a dramaturgical approach that focuses on unspoken social assumptions, on the way people manage the impressions they create, and on the way these impressions are interpreted by others. Aligning actions are used by social actors to readjust potentially disruptive interactions.

4. Ethnomethodology is the study of how people construct and share their definitions of reality. These taken-for-granted definitions can be revealed by breaking the unspoken rules of social interaction.

5. A great deal of human communication is nonverbal. Some of this communication is through body language, which includes facial expressions and physical gestures, many of them unconscious and unintended. Information can also be communicated through the manipulation of physical space between the actors, which reflects and maintains the social intimacy or distance between them.

6. Studies of the micro order provide insights into situations that are beyond the reach of functionalist or conflict analyses. The processes of becoming a marijuana user, maintaining definitions of reality in the course of a vaginal examination, helping others, hurting others, and dying in a hospital all involve social interpretations of potentially problematic situations. These interpretations are created through social interaction among the participants.

7. Reality is socially constructed. People do not perceive a reality "out there" directly; they create shared interpretations of reality. This process has three stages: externalization, objectivation, and internalization.

Important Terms

social interaction (133)
self (134)
role-taking (134)
symbol (134)
symbolic interaction (134)
micro order (135)
dramaturgical approach (137)
impression management (137)
aligning actions (138)
ethnomethodology (138)
nonverbal communication (140)
personal space (142)
bystander apathy (146)
social construction of reality (152)
externalization (152)
objectivation (152)
internalization (152)

Suggested Readings

BERGER, PETER L., and THOMAS LUCKMANN. *The Social Construction of Reality.* New York: Doubleday, 1963.

An influential analysis of the way in which interpretations of reality are created and sustained through social interaction.

BIRENBAUM, ARNOLD, and EDWARD SAGARIN (eds.). *People in Places.* New York: Praeger, 1973.

A lively collection of articles, many of them influenced by Goffman's work, that detail research on social interaction in various situations.

GOFFMAN, ERVING. *Behavior in Public Places.* New York: Free Press, 1963.

A shrewd and acute description and analysis of social behavior in public settings. Goffman illuminates many aspects of interactive behavior that we normally take for granted or do not notice.

GOFFMAN, ERVING. *The Presentation of Self in Everyday Life.* New York: Doubleday, 1959.

The classic statement of Goffman's dramaturgical perspective on social interaction.

HEWITT, JOHN P. *Self and Society: A Symbolic Interactionist Social Psychology.* 2nd ed. Boston: Allyn and Bacon, 1979.

A good introduction to social psychology for the student who wants to explore the discipline from a sociological perspective.

MELTZER, BERNARD, et al. *Symbolic Interactionism: Genesis, Varieties, and Criticism.* Boston: Routledge and Kegan Paul, 1975.

A short introduction to symbolic interactionism, dramaturgical analysis, and ethnomethodology.

MORRIS, DESMOND. *Manwatching: A Field Guide to Human Behavior.* New York: Abrams, 1977.

An interesting and well-illustrated introduction to "body language," written in an entertaining style.

NASH, JEFFREY E., and JAMES P. SPRADLEY. *Sociology: A Descriptive Approach.* Chicago: Rand McNally, 1976.

An anthology of articles on various aspects of the micro order. The topics cover a very wide range and the articles use many different perspectives.

CHAPTER 7 *Social Groups*

"No man is an island," wrote the poet John Donne several centuries ago. He was drawing attention to one of the most distinctive of all human characteristics: the fact that we are social animals whose behavior and personalities are shaped by the groups to which we belong. Throughout life, most of our daily activities are performed in the company of others. Whether our purpose is working, raising a family, learning, worshiping, or simply relaxing, we usually pursue it in groups, even if the group is as small as two or three people. Our need for human contacts is not merely a practical one; it is a deep psychological need as well. If people are deprived of the company of others for prolonged periods, mental breakdown is the usual result. Even the Geneva Convention, an international agreement that regulates the treatment of prisoners of war, recognizes this need. It regards solitary confinement for more than thirty days as a cruel and barbarous form of torture.

In its strictest sense, *a group is a collection of people interacting together in an orderly way on the basis of shared expectations about each other's behavior.* As a result of this interaction, members feel a common sense of "belonging." They distinguish members from nonmembers and expect certain kinds of behavior from one another that they would not necessarily expect from outsiders. A group differs from an *aggregate*, a collection of people who happen to be in the same place at the same time, such as the passengers in a bus or a crowd in a street. The members of an aggregate do not interact to any significant extent and do not feel any shared sense of belonging. A group also differs from a *category*, a number of people who may never have met one another but who share similar characteristics, such as age, race, or sex. Although sociologists sometimes use the word "group" loosely to refer to aggregates and categories, in this chapter we shall use the term only in its stricter sense.

The essence of a group is that its members interact with one another. As a result of this interaction, a group develops an internal structure. Every group has its own boundaries, norms, values, and interrelated statuses and roles, such as those of leader, follower, joker, or scapegoat. In some groups this structure is rigid and explicit: members may hold official positions, and values and norms may be embodied in written objectives and rules. In other groups the structure may be much more flexible: values and norms may be vague and shifting, and statuses and roles may be subject to negotiation and change.

People form groups for a purpose, generally one that the members cannot achieve satisfactorily through individual effort. The purpose of a group may be an explicit one, such as raising money for charity or waging war against an enemy, or it may be less clearly defined, such as having a good time. The fact that the members of a group share common goals means that they tend to be generally similar to one another in ways that are relevant to the group's purpose. If the goals of the group are political, the members tend to share similar political opinions. If the goals are leisure activities, the members tend to be of similar age, social class, and race, and have common leisure interests. The more the members interact within the group, the more they are influenced by its norms and values and the more similar they are likely to become.

Primary and Secondary Groups

There are two basic types of social groups: primary and secondary.

A *primary group* consists of a small number of people who interact in direct, intimate, and personal ways. The relationships among the members have emotional depth, and the group tends to endure over time. Primary groups are always small because large numbers of people cannot interact in a highly personal, face-to-face manner. Large groups therefore tend to break down into smaller, more intimate cliques. Typical primary groups include the family, the gang, or a college peer group.

A *secondary group* consists of a number of people who have few, if any, emotional ties with one another. The members come together for some specific, practical purpose, such as making a committee decision or attending a convention. There is limited face-to-face contact, and members relate to one another only in terms of specific roles, such as chairperson, supervisor, and employee. Secondary groups can be either small or large. Any newly formed small group is a secondary group at first, although it may become a primary group if its members come to know one another well and begin to interact on a more intimate basis. A college seminar group, for example, may start out as a secondary group, but after a while it may become a primary group, or smaller primary groups may develop within it. All large groups, however, are secondary groups. These groups, which are often called *associations,* include organizations such as business corporations, large factories, gov-

Figure 7.1 A primary group contains a small number of people who interact in direct and intimate ways, usually over a long period of time. In preindustrial societies virtually all social life took place in the context of primary groups. This small fishing community in Ghana is a primary group. Its members know one another well and interact together as full persons, not in terms of specific roles.

Figure 7.2 A secondary group contains a number of people who have few emotional ties to one another. They usually meet together for some practical purpose, and they interact with one another in terms of specific roles rather than as full persons. Secondary groups, such as these employees in a large modern organization, are characteristic of modern industrial societies.

ernment departments, political parties, and religious movements. Large secondary groups always contain smaller primary groups within them. Colleges and army camps, for example, are secondary groups, but they may contain hundreds of primary groups.

In traditional, preindustrial societies almost all social life took place in the context of primary groups, such as the kinship network or the small village. In modern industrial societies, dense urban populations and the growth and spread of large associations have made social life much more anonymous. Many of our daily interactions involve secondary relationships with people we encounter in limited and specific roles and may never meet again. As we saw in Chapter 4 ("Society"), the growth of secondary groups and the multiplication of secondary relationships is one of the outstanding features of modern societies.

Small Groups

A *small group* is one that contains sufficiently few members for the participants to relate to one another as individuals. Whether a small group is primary or secondary depends on the nature of the relationships among its members. A gathering of old friends is a primary group; a number of

previously unacquainted people trapped in an elevator for half an hour is a small secondary group.

Half a century ago the German sociologist Georg Simmel suggested that the interaction within small groups would prove to be an important subject for sociological research. His suggestion was largely neglected until after World War II, when Robert Bales and his associates began an influential series of studies of small-group processes (Bales, 1950, 1970; Homans, 1950; J. Davis, 1969; Hare et al., 1965; Hollander, 1964; T. Mills, 1967). Most of these studies took place in a laboratory setting, in which groups of volunteers were given some task to work on while researchers observed the interaction that took place. Although there is some question whether it is valid to apply the findings of these studies to "real life" situations, this research has illuminated many aspects of small-group interaction (Hare, 1976; S. Wilson, 1978; McGrath, 1978).

The Importance of Size

The single most important feature of small groups is probably their size, for this characteristic determines the kinds of interaction that can take place among the members. The smaller the group is, the more personal and intense the interaction can become.

Figure 7.3 The size of a group has a strong in-fluence on the kind of interaction that can take place within it. When a group contains less than about seven members, the interaction can be direct and personal. Beyond that point relationships tend to become more formal, and a leader usually has to regulate the interaction among the members. Larger groups, like the cocktail party, tend to break down into smaller and more intimate groups.

The smallest possible group, a *dyad*, contains two people. A dyad differs from all other groups in that its members have to take account of one another. If one member ignores the conversation of the other or begins daydreaming, the interaction is disrupted, and if one member withdraws from the group, it simply ceases to exist. If a third member is added, to form a *triad*, the situation changes significantly. Any one member can ignore the conversation of the others without destroying the interaction in the group. Two members can form a coalition against one, so any member can become subject to group pressure. As more members are added, the nature of the interaction continues to change. People can take sides in discussions, and more than one coalition can be formed. In a group of up to about seven people, all the members can take part in the same conversation, but beyond that point it becomes progressively more likely that smaller groups will form, with several conversations taking place at the same time.

If the group becomes larger than about ten or twelve people, it is virtually impossible for them to take part in the same conversation unless one member assumes the role of leader and regulates the interaction so that everyone has a chance to contribute. In groups of this size, the style of conversation changes because people can no longer talk to each other as individuals. They cannot tailor their speech to meet the expectations of specific people, so they tend to talk in a more formal way. Members no longer "talk" to the group: they "address" it, with a grammar and vocabulary unlike that used in ordinary conversation. The interaction is now markedly different from that in our original dyad.

Sudden changes in group size tend to be disruptive, particularly if there is a rapid increase in the number of new members. This disruption is partly caused by the fact that interaction grows more difficult as the group becomes larger, but another factor is that members often resist the assimilation of newcomers. The presence of new members threatens the norms of interaction the group has already developed, and old members are uncomfortable until new norms have evolved (Berelson and Steiner, 1964).

Leadership

One element is always present in groups, even in those that try to avoid it: leadership. A *leader* is someone who, by virtue of certain personality characteristics, is consistently able to influence the behavior of others. Groups always have leaders, even if the leaders do not hold formal positions of authority.

Research has indicated that there are two distinct types of leadership in small groups (Bales, 1953; Slater, 1955). *Instrumental leadership* is the kind necessary to organize the group in pursuit of its goals. An instrumental leader proposes courses of action and influences the members to follow them. *Expressive leadership* is the kind necessary to create harmony and solidarity among the members. An expressive leader is concerned about keeping morale high and minimizing conflicts. The expressive leader is well liked by the group. When a newly formed group is asked to choose a leader, it usually gives both roles to the same person, because individuals who are well liked also tend to dominate group activities. Leaders generally do not fill both roles for long, however, because people who direct group activities tend to lose popularity. In one experiment

on small groups, Philip Slater (1955) found that most members gave top rating to the same person for both expressive and instrumental leadership at the first meeting, but by the end of the fourth meeting, only 8 percent of the members still considered the leader likable. The original leader may retain the instrumental role, but another group member emerges to assume the expressive role.

Do leaders have distinctive characteristics that are not shared by their followers? While there are certainly no hard and fast rules, it seems that leaders are likely to be taller than the average group member, to be judged better-looking than other members, to have a higher IQ, and to be more sociable, talkative, determined, and self-confident. In addition, leaders also tend to be more liberal in outlook, even in conservative groups (Berelson and Steiner, 1964; Stouffer, 1955; Stogdill, 1974). Style of leadership may be one of three basic kinds: *authoritarian,* in which the leader simply gives orders; *democratic,* in which the leader attempts to win a consensus on a course of action; and *laissez-faire,* in which a leader is easygoing and makes little attempt to direct or organize the group. In the United States, at least, democratic leaders seem to be most effective in holding small groups together and seeing that they accomplish their tasks. Authoritarian leaders are much less effective, because the work of the group becomes bogged down in internal conflicts. Laissez-faire leaders are usually ineffectual, for the group lacks directives and tackles problems in a very haphazard way (White and Lippitt, 1960). This does not mean, however, that democratic leadership is the most effective in all situations. Research on American subjects, who have been socialized to react negatively to authoritarian leaders, cannot be generalized to cultures in which authoritarian leadership is expected and in which there is no experience of democratic decision making.

One cannot talk of "good" or "bad" leaders without specifying the conditions in which the leader is operating. A person who is ineffectual in one situation may be highly effective in another (Fiedler, 1969). An authoritarian leader, for example, is more effective in emergency situations, where speed and efficiency outweigh other considerations. For this reason, leadership in armies, police forces, and hospital emergency rooms is typically authoritarian. Democratic leaders are more effective in situations where group members are concerned about individual rights or where there is disagreement over goals.

Figure 7.4

*"All in favor of putting everything on
the back burner, say 'Aye.'"*

Drawing by Stevenson; © 1977
The New Yorker Magazine, Inc.

Group Decision Making

There is a general assumption in our society that when it comes to making decisions, two heads, or preferably several heads, are better than one. We have great faith in democratic decision making, believing that group decisions are likely to be wiser than decisions made by individuals acting alone. How valid is this belief?

The answer depends to some extent on the problem that has to be solved. In "determinate tasks"—problems that have only one correct solution, such as a crossword puzzle—group effort increases the chances of finding the answer. As a matter of simple probability, a group is more likely to come up with the correct solution than a single person is. If the problem is a complex one, involving specialized knowledge, the efficiency of the group is far superior to that of the individual, because group members can contribute a broader range of expertise and skills. The situation is rather different for "indeterminate tasks"—problems that have no necessarily correct solution, such as selecting one of several applicants for a job or deciding on how to handle an aircraft hijacking. In such cases different groups may arrive at very different decisions, probably because each group is influenced by the opinions of partic-

ular dominant members. Sometimes group decisions for solving indeterminate problems seem better than those of individuals, but sometimes they seem worse.

It is often thought that groups are less likely than individuals to make bold and imaginative decisions. As Roger Brown (1965) comments, "the academic committees on which one has served . . . do not leave one breathless with their daring." There is considerable evidence, however, that committees do sometimes make more risky decisions than individuals. J. A. Stoner (1961) asked individual subjects to come to tentative decisions on hypothetical problems, and he then combined the subjects into groups to consider these problems. He found a strong tendency toward what he called the "risky shift," a change to a decision for a more daring course of action. More recent research has shown that the risky shift is by no means universal; some groups are more cautious than their individual members would be. Research on the problem is continuing, to account both for the risky shift and for the fact that it occurs in some groups but not in others. One plausible hypothesis for the risky shift is that in group decisions, responsibility is diffused among the members. No individual anticipates feeling personally guilty if the decision turns out to be the wrong one (Kogan and Wallach, 1964).

Irving Janis (1972; Janis and Mann, 1977) has pointed out that in some cases of group decision making, individual loyalty to the group prevents members from raising controversial and uncomfortable questions. The members become so concerned with maintaining group harmony and consensus, particularly when a difficult moral problem is involved, that they withhold their reservations and criticisms. The result is what Janis calls "groupthink," a decision-making process in which members ignore information and alternatives that do not fit with the group's original assumptions. As an example of groupthink Janis cites the decision of President Kennedy and his top advisers to launch the ill-fated Bay of Pigs invasion of Cuba in 1961. This decision, which produced a military and diplomatic fiasco, was based on strategic assumptions that were almost ludicrous. Several members of the decision-making group had strong private objections to the plan, yet the decision to launch the invasion was unanimous. Janis quotes one of the participants as commenting afterward: "Our meeting was taking place in an atmosphere of assumed consensus. Had one senior adviser opposed the venture, I believe Kennedy would have canceled it. Not one spoke up." (The ancient Persians seem to have been aware of the groupthink phenomenon. The historian Herodotus tells us that whenever they made an important decision in a sober, rational frame of mind, they always reconsidered the matter later while thoroughly drunk.)

Most group decision making on controversial issues, however, does involve debate and even antagonisms among the participants. The process of decision making in small groups generally proceeds through a sequence of stages. The first stage is that of collecting information; the members orient themselves to the problem by analyzing the facts. The second stage is that of evaluating the information; at this point members express opinions and react to the opinions of others. The third stage is that of reaching a decision. Emotional tensions may rise at this stage as coalitions form and an emerging majority imposes its view on the minority. The fourth stage occurs once the decision is made; it involves a general effort to restore harmony in the group. The members react more positively to one another, and there may be a certain amount of joking and frivolity. In this way the continuing solidarity of the group is assured (Bales and Strodtbeck, 1951).

Group Conformity

The pressure to conform to social expectations is strong in every aspect of life, but it seems to be particularly powerful in the intense atmosphere of a small group (Festinger et al., 1956). One of the most dramatic examples of this tendency comes from some classic experiments by Solomon Asch (1955), who found that people are willing to disavow the evidence of their own senses if other members of the group interpret reality differently.

Asch assembled groups consisting of between seven and nine college students in what was described as a test of visual discrimination. However, in each group only one of the students was actually a subject in the experiment: the others were secret accomplices of the experimenter. In a series of eighteen trials Asch displayed pairs of cards like those shown in Figure 7.6. One card contained a single line, which was to serve as a standard. The other card contained three lines, one the same length as the standard, and the other two of significantly different lengths from the standard and from each other. The members of the group were asked one by one to state aloud which of the lines matched the standard.

Figure 7.5 Group decision-making processes have been studied extensively by sociologists. One surprising finding has been that groups are often willing to make much more risky decisions than any of their individual members would. Another finding is that individual members sometimes suppress criticisms of controversial proposals as a result of their loyalty to the group.

When the first pair of cards was presented, the group gave a unanimous judgment. The same thing happened on the second trial. In twelve of the remaining sixteen trials, however, all of Asch's accomplices agreed on what was clearly an incorrect answer. How did the real subject of the experiment react to this uncomfortable situation? In about a third of the cases, the subject yielded to the majority and conformed to its decision. In separate experiments with a control group consisting only of genuine subjects, Asch found that people made mistakes less than 1 percent of the time. Subsequent interviews with those who yielded to the majority revealed that only a few of them had, in fact, perceived the majority choice as correct. Although these few subjects actually disbelieved the evidence of their own senses, most of the yielders admitted that they thought they had judged the length of the lines correctly but did not want to be the "odd one out" by giving the right answer. The experiment vividly shows a group's power to induce conformity.

Ingroups and Outgroups

Every group must have some boundaries, for there would otherwise be no way of distinguishing between members and nonmembers. Sometimes these boundaries are formal and clearly defined, with access to the group available to "members only" on the basis of predetermined criteria. In such cases the boundary may be maintained by symbols, such as badges, membership cards, or even secret signs. A police department, a family, or a labor union has no difficulty in maintaining boundaries, because the criteria for membership are formally defined. In other cases the boundaries are not nearly as clear. A high school or college peer group, for example, has no specific criteria for membership, and the boundary between actual members and hangers-on may be very blurred.

All groups, however, tend to maintain their boundaries by developing a strong sense of the distinction between the "we" of the group and the "they" who are outside it. Members tend to regard their own group, the *ingroup*, as being somehow special, whereas any *outgroup* to which other people belong is regarded as less worthy and may even be viewed with hostility. A common way of maintaining boundaries between groups, in fact, is through some form of conflict between them. The presence of a common enemy (real or imaginary) draws members together and increases the solidarity and cohesion of the group (Coser, 1956).

An experiment by Muzafer Sherif (1956) illustrates how ingroup loyalties can help to maintain group boundaries and solidarity. Sherif's subjects were eleven-year-old American boys, all from stable, white, middle-class, Protestant backgrounds. None of them knew each other before the experiment began. Sherif took his subjects for an ex-

Figure 7.6 These are the lines presented to subjects in one trial in Asch's experiment. Asch asked the subjects to state which of the comparison lines appeared to be the same length as the standard line. Control subjects (who made the judgment without any group pressure) chose the correct line over 99 percent of the time, but experimental subjects who were under group pressure to choose the wrong line did so in nearly a third of the cases.

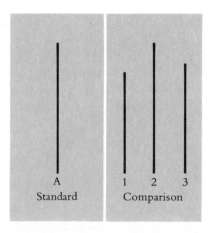

STANDARD AND COMPARISON
LINES IN THE
ASCH EXPERIMENT

A
Standard

1   2   3
Comparison

Source: Adapted from Solomon Asch, "Effects of Group Pressure upon the Modification and Distortion of Judgments," in H. Proshansky and B. Seidenberg (eds.), *Basic Studies in Social Psychology* (New York: Holt, Rinehart and Winston, 1965), pp. 393-401.

tended stay at a summer camp, where they soon began to form friendship cliques. Once these groups had been formed, Sherif randomly divided the boys into two main groups and lodged them in separate cabins some distance apart. In doing so, he disrupted the cliques that had already formed, but the boys soon began to develop strong loyalties to their new groups. Next, Sherif pitted the two groups against each other in various competitive activities. The result was increasingly intense antagonism and hostility between the groups, including between those members on either side who had earlier been in the same friendship cliques. Finally, Sherif created some emergency situations, such as a disruption of the water supply, that required both groups to cooperate as a team. Within a short period, members of the two groups began to interact as a single group, their old hostilities forgotten. Sherif's experiment shows clearly how feelings of group loyalty contribute to the maintenance of group boundaries, how the presence of conflict between the groups heightens these loyalties, and how ingroup feelings lessen and disappear once the members of both groups are obliged to unite in pursuit of common goals.

Reference Groups

There is one kind of group to which people may feel they "belong" even if they are not actually members. This is the *reference group,* a group to which people refer when making evaluations of themselves and their behavior.

We constantly evaluate ourselves—our behavior, our appearance, our values, our ambitions, our life-styles, and so on. In making these evaluations, we always refer to the standards of some group. The group may be one of which we are a member, such as the family or the peer group. But it may also be one we do not actually belong to. People may judge themselves, for example, by the standards of a community they previously lived in or of a community they hope to join in the future. A sociology student who hopes eventually to take a graduate degree may evaluate his or her progress in terms of the standards of graduate students rather than those of an undergraduate peer group. A medical student may refer to the standards of physicians rather than those of fellow students.

Our evaluations of ourselves are strongly influenced by the reference groups we choose: if you get a B in an examination and compare yourself with A students, your self-evaluation will be very different than it would be if you were to compare yourself with C students. Reference groups are therefore an important element in the socialization process, for they can shape individual behavior and personality just as powerfully as any other group to which a person feels loyalty.

The influence of reference groups on individual behavior and attitudes is illustrated by a long-term study by Theodore Newcomb (1958) at Bennington College, a liberal women's college in New England. Most of the students, Newcomb found, came from conservative families, and the values they brought with them conflicted with those they met in the college. The longer the students stayed at the college, the more liberal most of them became, although a minority retained their earlier conservative outlook. Those who became liberal appeared to use their new peers or the faculty as a reference group; those who remained conservative continued to refer to the values and standards of their families. Adoption of a new reference group or loyalty to an old one correlated closely with the political opinions of the students.

Formal Organizations

Until a century or so ago, nearly all social life took place within the context of small primary groups—the family, the church congregation, the schoolhouse, the farm or shop, and the village community. Today the social landscape is dominated by large, impersonal organizations that influence our lives from the moment of birth. Some of these organizations are *voluntary,* in the sense that people may freely join them or withdraw from them. Examples include religious movements, political parties, and professional associations. Some are *coercive,* in the sense that people are forced to join them—for example, prisons or elementary schools. Other organizations are *utilitarian,* in the sense that people enter them for practical reasons: they join business enterprises, for example, in order to earn a living (Etzioni, 1975). But whichever organizations we belong to and whatever our reasons for joining them, we spend a substantial part of our lives within these large, impersonal groups.

ORGANIZATIONAL CHART OF A PUBLISHING COMPANY

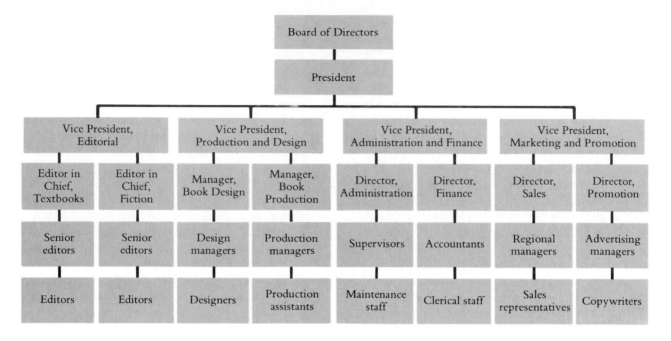

Figure 7.7 This diagram is a typical organizational chart, setting out the formal chains of command and communication within a formal organization, a hypothetical publishing company. Similar charts, some of them extremely complex, can be drawn for any formal organization.

Secondary associations of this type are generally *formal organizations,* large social groups that are deliberately and rationally designed to achieve specific objectives. Unlike primary groups, which are informal, these organizations have a carefully designed structure that coordinates the activities of the members in the interests of the organization's goals. For example, formal organizations typically include a number of official statuses, such as those of president, secretary, and treasurer. Rights and responsibilities within the organization are attached primarily to the office a person occupies, not to the person as an individual. It is possible to draw a chart of any formal organization, showing the relationship of the various official positions to one another, without any reference to the actual individuals involved. (See Figure 7.7.)

Most people seem to have an ambiguous attitude toward formal organizations. On the one hand, our affluence and our very way of life are clearly dependent on the existence of organizations such as corporations, colleges, government departments, and large factories. On the other hand, the size, impersonality, and power of formal organizations are often seen as dehumanizing and threatening. Formal organizations, in fact, have been held responsible for much of the feeling of alienation that is said to characterize modern industrial society (Roszak, 1969). As Amitai Etzioni (1964) points out,

> without well-run organizations our standard of living, our level of culture, and our democratic way of life could not be maintained. Thus, to a degree, *organizational rationality* and human happiness go hand in hand. But a point is reached where happiness and efficiency cease to support each other. . . . Here we face a true dilemma.

Bureaucracy

The larger and more complex a formal organization becomes, the greater is the need for a chain of command to coordinate the activities of its members. This need is fulfilled by a *bureaucracy,* a hierarchical authority structure that operates under explicit rules and procedures. Understanding bureaucracy is the key to the analysis of formal organizations.

The word "bureaucracy" usually carries negative connotations in everyday speech. It brings to mind images of "red tape," forms in triplicate, lost files, incorrect bills, unanswered letters, counter clerks blinded by petty regulations, "runarounds," and "buck-passing." Yet although "bureaucracy" often seems synonymous with "inefficiency" from the point of view of the individual, the bureaucratic form has thrived for the simple reason that it is, for most purposes, highly efficient. It is the most effective means ever devised of making a large organization work. Sociologists therefore use the word in a neutral sense, without the overtones it generally has in ordinary usage.

This does not mean, however, that sociologists refrain from passing judgment on the bureaucratic form. In fact, there is a deep current of distaste for bureaucracy running through Western sociology, right back to such early thinkers as Karl Marx and Max Weber. Marx (1843) loathed bureaucracy, which he saw as an "excrescence" on society. Weber, whose writings have provided the foundation for almost all later research on bureaucracy, declared in 1909:

> The passion for bureaucracy is enough to drive one to despair.... The great question is ... not how we can promote and hasten it, but what we can oppose to this machinery in order to keep a portion of mankind free from this parcelling out of the soul, from this supreme mastery of the bureaucratic way of life.

Despite his misgivings about bureaucracy, however, it was Weber who first systematically analyzed the system and demonstrated its efficiency.

Weber's Analysis

To Max Weber (1922), the master trend in the modern world was the process he called *rationalization.* By this concept he meant the way in which traditional, spontaneous, rule-of-thumb methods of social organization are replaced by abstract, explicit, carefully calculated rules and procedures. This gradual rationalization process can be seen in nearly every aspect of modern social life. In education, the tutor with a small circle of students is replaced by the vast modern college campus, with lectures supplied on videotape and multiple-choice examinations graded by computer. The traditional market of small stalls is succeeded by the modern supermarket. The "justice" meted out by a village headman evolves into an intricate system of laws and courtroom procedures. Individual craft workers disappear, to be replaced by laborers on the assembly line. Varied forms of architecture give way, in country after country, to the familiar oblong office building. In each case, the result of the rationalization process is a marked increase in efficiency, but this efficiency is achieved at a cost. The world, Weber felt, was becoming dull, drab, and "disenchanted," its mystery and beauty subverted by the new value of technical rationality. Weber believed bureaucracy was an especially threatening form of rationalization. Unlike other forms, which involve the manipulation of physical objects (such as machinery) or of procedures (such as the legal system), bureaucracy involves the calculated organization and subordination of *human beings* in the interests of impersonal, technical goals. As a result, Weber felt, people were becoming imprisoned in an "iron cage" of their own making.

Weber analyzed bureaucracy in terms of what he called an ideal type. An *ideal type* is simply an abstract description, constructed by the sociologist from observations of a number of real cases in order to reveal their essential features. (For example, an ideal type of an American college might refer to such features as the statuses of college administrators, professors, and students; to such activities as teaching, learning, and research; and to other characteristics such as fraternities, sororities, honor societies, and so on. The result would be an abstract description of a "typical" American college. For some purposes—explaining American education to a foreigner, for instance—this ideal type might be more useful than a description of a particular college.) Weber's ideal type of bureaucracy therefore shows us the essential characteristics of the bureaucratic form, although any individual bureaucracy will not necessarily conform to this description in every way.

Figure 7.8 A characteristic feature of bureaucracies is the anonymous, impersonal nature of the relationships between officials and outsiders. This painting, Government Bureau, *by the American artist George Tooker, captures the formality that prevails in these interactions.*

According to Weber, a bureaucracy has the following typical features:

1. There is a clear-cut division of labor among the various officials. Each member of the organization has a specialized job to do and concentrates on this specific task.

2. There is a hierarchy of authority within the organization. This hierarchy takes the shape of a pyramid, with greater authority for the few at the top and less for the many at the bottom. The scope of an individual's authority is clearly defined; each official takes orders from the officials immediately above and takes responsibility for those immediately below.

3. An elaborate system of rules and regulations (mostly in written form) governs the day-to-day functioning of the bureaucracy. Decisions are based on these rules and on established precedents.

4. Officials treat people as "cases," not as individuals. The members of the organization remain impersonal in their contacts with the public. They also adopt a detached attitude to other members of the organization, interacting with them in terms of their official roles. Personal feelings are thus excluded from official business and do not enter into or distort the decision-making process.

5. A bureaucracy includes a specialized administrative staff of managers, secretaries, recordkeepers, and others. Their sole function is to keep the organization as a whole running smoothly.

6. Employees usually anticipate a career with the organization. Candidates for positions in the hierarchy are appointed on the basis of seniority or merit, or some combination of the two—not on the grounds of favoritism, family connections, or other criteria that are irrelevant to organizational efficiency.

Weber argued that such an organization would be highly efficient at coordinating the activities of its members and achieving specific objectives. As an ideal type, his analysis has stood the test of time. Later researchers have found it necessary to make one major modification, however, to take account of the informal, primary relationships that exist in all bureaucracies.

The Informal Structure of Bureaucracy

The formal structure of a bureaucracy is easily determined by a glance at its organizational chart, which will show the lines of authority along which communications flow from one official to another, usually in writing. In practice, however, no bureaucracy ever works strictly by the book. People get to know one another as individuals, not simply as officials. They establish primary relationships with one another, they bend and break the rules, they develop informal procedures for handling problems, and they take shortcuts through the hierarchy whenever they can (Blau, 1963; Blau and Meyer, 1971; R. Hall, 1972a, 1972b; Perrow, 1979; Lehman and Etzioni, 1980).

The existence of these informal networks was estab-

lished in the course of research carried out between 1927 and 1932 at the Hawthorne plant of the Western Electric Company. Industrial sociologists were trying to discover incentives that would encourage the employees to work harder. In a classic study of fourteen men who wired telephone switchboards, the researchers found that output was determined, not by the official rules or even by financial incentives, but rather by informal norms within the group itself. The men worked rapidly in the mornings, but eased off in the afternoons. To make their work more interesting and varied they often traded tasks, although this practice was against the regulations. The workers had strong informal norms against working too hard; anyone who attempted to do so was called a "rate buster." They also had norms against working too slowly; anyone who appeared to slack off was called a "chiseler." They had an informal norm, too, against telling a superior about the failings of any individual; anyone who did so was considered a "squealer." The output of the workers was determined by an informal, unspoken agreement on what they felt was reasonable—not by what the management, for all its rational and careful calculations, believed they could or should do (Roethlisberger and Dickson, 1939).

More recent research has confirmed that the formal structure of a bureaucracy always breeds informal relationships and practices. Employees establish their own norms about how long a "lunch hour" should be. They swap tasks to make their work more interesting and take over one another's duties when someone wants unofficial time off. They develop norms about the type and amount of company property they can "take home" for private use. Because information travels slowly through official channels and because some decisions at the executive level are deliberately concealed from subordinates, an informal channel of communication develops—the "grapevine." People who, in terms of the organizational chart, ought not to be in possession of important information often gain access to it.

Lower-status members of the hierarchy (such as secretaries in corporations or nurses in hospitals) often have a good deal of influence over higher-status officials. The underlings cannot exercise this influence too blatantly, however, and so develop subtle means of ensuring that their superiors still consider themselves fully in charge. In the following late-night telephone conversation between a

Figure 7.9 The bureaucratic form is efficient because it relies on highly rationalized procedures. Officials do not, for example, retain information in their heads or in the form of jottings on odd scraps of paper. All information is carefully coded in a uniform manner and filed away so that it is readily accessible.

nurse and a doctor on hospital call, for example, both try to preserve the illusion that it is he, not she, who is making a medical diagnosis and recommendation:

DOCTOR: This is Dr. Jones.
[An open and direct communication.]
NURSE: Dr. Jones, this is Miss Smith on 2W—Mrs. Brown, who learned today of her father's death, is unable to fall asleep.
[This message has two levels. Openly, it describes a set of circumstances, a woman who is unable to sleep and who that morning received word of her father's death. Less openly, but just as directly, it is a diagnostic and recommendation statement; i.e., Mrs. Brown is unable to sleep because of her grief, and she should be given a sedative. Dr. Jones, accepting the diagnostic statement and replying to the recommendation statement, answers.]
DOCTOR: What sleeping medication has been helpful to Mrs. Brown in the past?
[Dr. Jones, not knowing the patient, is asking for a recommendation from the nurse, who does know the patient, about what sleeping medication should be prescribed. Note, however, his question does not appear to be asking her for a recommendation. Miss Smith replies.]
NURSE: Pentobarbital mg 100 was quite effective night before last.

[A disguised recommendation statement. Dr. Jones replies with a note of authority in his voice.]
DOCTOR: Pentobarbital mg 100 before bedtime as needed for sleep; got it?
[Miss Smith ends the conversation with the tone of a grateful supplicant.]
NURSE: Yes, I have, and thank you very much doctor.
[Quoted in L. Stein, 1977]

In fact, the formal structure of the organization provides only a general framework in which people play out, often in highly personal ways, their bureaucratic roles. Without its participants the organization has no real existence: it is merely an abstraction. It is people who create, operate, change, and *are* the organization. For this reason, some sociologists have stressed that a bureaucracy is a "negotiated reality" (Day and Day, 1977; Blankenship, 1977). In other words, the organization derives its existence and character from the process of social interaction through which the members continuously create and re-create it. In the course of this interaction, informal patterns emerge that may bear little relationship to the formal hierarchy.

Members of a bureaucracy are never treated entirely in terms of the offices they hold. One person may be known as an incompetent whose advice should never be taken; another as an "old-timer," with valuable knowledge of rules and precedents and how to bend them; another as a "crown prince" marked out for future promotion and worth cultivating in the meanwhile. Following the tortuous route of the official channels is no less irritating to members of a bureaucracy than it is to outsiders, and they quickly learn to short-circuit the process by informal contact with friendly officials elsewhere in the hierarchy. Government bureaucrats may bend the rules to help someone who has gained their sympathy, or they may subtly obstruct a case involving a member of the public who has been rude or offensive.

Dysfunctions of Bureaucracy

Although Weber did not make it explicit, his view of bureaucracy was essentially a *functionalist* one. He analyzed bureaucracy as a functional response to a problem in social organization, showing how the various elements in bureaucratic structure promote the survival, efficiency, and goals of the organization as a whole. Weber did not elaborate on the *dysfunctions* of bureaucracy, although he was certainly aware of them.

Other sociologists have subsequently identified a number of dysfunctions that are built into the bureaucratic form and may hinder its efficiency. The most obvious of these dysfunctions is occasional inefficiency—a failing which, paradoxically, is an inevitable by-product of the overall efficiency of the system. Bureaucracies are efficient because their rules are designed for typical cases and problems. Officials can handle these cases quickly and effectively by applying uniform rules and procedures. Yet this means that the bureaucracy is ill equipped to handle unusual cases—the taxpayer whose file has been lost; the illiterate who cannot complete the necessary forms; the American citizen who was born in Romania sixty years ago, wants a passport, but cannot produce or trace the necessary birth certificate. When an unprecedented case arises that does not fit the rules, the bureaucracy is stumped. The problem may then circulate from desk to desk for weeks, months, or even years, before it finally reaches someone who is authorized and willing to make a decision on the problem.

Blind adherence to existing rules and procedures may result in what Thorstein Veblen caustically termed "trained incapacity"—the inability to make any new, imaginative response because of previous bureaucratic training. An example of trained incapacity was the typical reaction of college bureaucracies to student disturbances in the sixties and early seventies. Faced with this unanticipated situation, college administrators fell back on the only procedures they knew. They set up committees and commissioned reports, as administrators typically do when they are presented with a problem that might involve changes in

Figure 7.10 Formal organizations are never quite as formal in practice as they may be in theory. People do not rigidly perform the routines that have been planned for them, and informal networks and relationships develop within the organizational structure. By helping to cut bureaucratic "red tape," these relationships probably facilitate rather than hinder the work of the organization.

ILLINOIS DEPARTMENT OF LABOR
BUREAU OF EMPLOYMENT SECURITY

MEMORANDUM

To: David Gassman, Statistician

From: Benjamin Greenstein, Chief
         Research and Statistics

Subject: Hazardous Use of Coffee Pot

The afternoon of April 29, while Mr. Arthur Haverly was on vacation, an electric coffee pot was plugged in his office and left unattended. It spread noxious fumes through the office and scorched a table belonging to the State.

You admitted that you plugged in that coffee pot and that you did it, although Mr. Haverly had told you that I had requested that it should not be done due to previous adverse experience. When I asked you why you plugged in that coffee pot, although I had requested that it should not be done, you stated that you did not take it that seriously.

I may note also that Mr. Haverly informed me the previous day that he had not authorized you to connect the coffee pot in his office.

The following facts, therefore, emerge:

1. You had used your supervisor's office for cooking coffee without his authorization.

2. You did so, although you knew that I had requested that it should not be done.

3. You had left the coffee pot unattended. For that matter, there may have been a conflict between performing agency work and attending to the coffee pot.

4. You created a fire hazard for your fellow workers and subjected them to noxious fumes.

5. When I asked you why you plugged in the coffee pot in spite of my request to the contrary, you stated that you did not take it seriously. This is a rejection of supervision.

6. Your disregard of my authority has resulted in discomfort to your fellow workers and damage to State property.

7. On April 30, the day following the above actions and conversation, at 8:25 in the morning, I noted that you had again plugged in the coffee pot. When I pointed out that you were aware that I had asked you not to plug it in, you replied that it is not 8:30 yet. I then told you that I am in charge of the section, even though it is not 8:30 yet.

What should be done with respect to your actions, as specified above, is under consideration. In the meantime, you are emphatically requested not to repeat the hazard you created by plugging in the coffee pot.

Source: The Washington Monthly, 1974, reprinted in Rafael Steinberg, *Man and the Organization* (New York: Time-Life Books, 1975), p. 115.

Figure 7.11 This memo reveals several features that distinguish formal organizations from more informal groups. (1) The communication is in writing. Composing, dictating, typing, and transmitting it may have taken hours of official time. (2) The people involved are relating to each other in their official roles, as "Chief, Research and Statistics" and "Statistician." (3) The superior official is deeply concerned that the appropriate hierarchical relationship between the two members of the organization should be observed. (4) The junior official has attempted to disobey the senior official by bending the rules. (5) An excessive amount of effort has been put into resolving an issue that would be regarded as trivial in a less formal group, where it would be handled with a few spoken words. The goals of the organization have become temporarily forgotten while energies are devoted to this internal problem.

established routines. This response was frequently interpreted by the students as nothing more than a stalling device or an attempt to "coopt" their leaders into the campus bureaucracy, and it merely served to increase campus tensions. Organizations, then, face a perennial problem: that of balancing their own need for stability and predictability with the requirement that they respond effectively to—or even anticipate—constant change in the social environment outside.

Another dysfunction of a bureaucracy is that the running of a large organization generates problems that may be entirely unconnected to its original purpose, and day-to-day behavior becomes centered on handling them. Members of the organization, whose livelihoods depend on its continued existence, may become more concerned with preserving the organization and their own prospects within it than with attaining its intended goals (Selznick, 1943). There is often pressure to keep an organization going long after its purpose has been served—either by finding new work to do or by claiming there is still work to be done. The National Foundation for Infantile Paralysis, for example, was established to combat polio. The discovery of the Salk vaccine virtually eliminated polio within a few years, but the organization did not disband. It looked for new goals and now combats arthritis and other ills (Sills, 1957). Government agencies are particularly notorious for finding a new reason for existence once their original purpose has either been achieved or abandoned.

The formal communications system of bureaucracies also has its dysfunctions. In theory, communications flow upward and downward through appropriate channels. In practice, communications flow almost entirely downward and are often distorted at the middle levels during the process. Those at the top of the hierarchy are unlikely to be aware of the problems or feelings of those at the bottom. Because the structure of a bureaucracy is essentially authoritarian, officials at lower levels may conceal defects, mistakes, and inefficiencies from superiors.

The authoritarian structure generates further problems. A bureaucracy is by nature a hierarchy of unequals. The level of an official's status may be indicated by such things as a convenient parking space, the presence of a secretary, the type of carpeting in the office, and the size of the desk and the amount of paper on it (the less paper and the bigger the desk, the higher the official). There is conse-

Figure 7.12

"That may be your point of view down there, Hodgins. It's not our point of view up here."

Drawing by Ed Fisher; © 1976
The New Yorker Magazine, Inc.

quently always a tendency for an "us against them" attitude to develop at different levels in the hierarchy, causing all the problems that the presence of ingroup-versus-outgroup conflicts can create. Victor Thompson (1961) writes of the "bureaupathology" of large organizations. He found that bureaucracies are characterized by tensions, anxieties, and frustrations largely caused by the authoritarian hierarchy.

Robert Merton (1968) has suggested another dysfunction of bureaucracy—its effects on the personalities of the bureaucrats. Merton argues that rigid routines and pressures for conformity may stifle individual creativity and imagination. In extreme cases, he claims, the bureaucrat focuses obsessively on means rather than ends, ritually following rules and procedures without any concern for the goals they were designed to serve. The title of William Whyte's book *The Organization Man* (1956), which presented a roughly similar picture, has entered popular speech

"Parkinson's Law" and the "Peter Principle"

Bureaucracies have been the subject of many satirical criticisms. The two best-known onslaughts are expressed in "Parkinson's Law" and the "Peter Principle."

Parkinson's Law is named after the writer who proposed it, C. Northcote Parkinson. The law is a simple one: In any bureaucracy, "work expands to fill the time available for its completion." The natural tendency of any formal organization, Parkinson points out, is to grow. Officials have to appear busy, and therefore they create tasks for themselves. In due course they have so much work to do that they need assistants. When an official has an assistant, however, the burden of work on the official actually increases, because he or she now has to supervise the subordinate. Much of the subordinate's time is taken up in turn with submitting reports to the superior official. As work continues to expand, more assistants and officials are added, some of whom are responsible solely for supervising others or handling the flow of communications between the multiplying personnel. An immense amount of time and effort is then spent on form filling, memo writing, and file keeping and on checking the form filing, memo writing, and file keeping of others. Parkinson argues that virtually all of this activity is unnecessary.

The Peter Principle is named after its discoverer, Lawrence Peter. This principle, too, is a simple one: "In any hierarchy every employee tends to rise to his level of incompetence." Peter points out that officials who are competent at their jobs tend to be promoted. If they are competent at their new jobs, they are promoted again. This process continues until they finally reach a job that is beyond their abilities—and there they stay. The result is expressed in "Peter's corollary": "In time, every post tends to be occupied by an employee who is incompetent to carry out its duties." Bureaucracies are able to function, Peter suggests, only because at any given time there are enough officials who have not yet reached their level of incompetence and are capable of performing their jobs efficiently.

Sources: C. Northcote Parkinson, *Parkinson's Law* (Boston: Houghton Mifflin, 1957); Lawrence J. Peter and Raymond Hull, *The Peter Principle* (New York: William Morrow, 1969).

---

to describe people so involved in an organization that other areas of their personal experience are distorted and impoverished. Merton's argument is controversial, however, as more recent research shows that workers in bureaucracies tend to be fairly open-minded, self-directed, and willing to accept change (Kohn, 1971, 1978). The current stereotype of the bureaucrat may yet prove to be based on myth. Perhaps the real danger that large-scale bureaucratization poses to the human spirit is a different one: an insidious and alienating loss of freedom. Peter Blau and Richard Scott (1962) comment:

> The most pervasive feature that distinguishes contemporary life is that it is dominated by large, complex, and formal organizations. Our ability to organize thousands and even millions of men in order to accomplish large-scale tasks—be they economic, political, or military—is one of our greatest strengths. The possibility that free men become mere cogs in the bureaucratic machines we set up for this purpose is one of the greatest threats to our liberty.

The Problem of Oligarchy

The relationship between human freedom and bureaucracy is a complex one, for it involves much more than the subordination of individuals to the needs of organizations. Bureaucracy tends to result in *oligarchy*, or rule by the few—in this case, by officials at the top of the hierarchy. In a society dominated by large formal organizations, therefore, there is a danger that social, political, and economic power will become concentrated in the hands of those who hold high positions in the most influential formal organizations.

This issue was first raised in 1911 by Robert Michels, a sociologist and friend of Max Weber. Michels was a dedicated socialist at the time and was dismayed to find that the new socialist parties of Europe, despite their democratic structure and provisions for mass participation in decision making, seemed to be dominated by their leaders just as much as the traditional conservative parties were. Michels came to the conclusion that the problem lay in the very nature of large organizations. "Who says organization," he stated, "says oligarchy." According to his "iron law of oligarchy," democracy and large-scale organizations are incompatible.

Any large organization, Michels pointed out, is faced with administrative problems that can be solved only by creating a bureaucracy. A bureaucracy, in turn, must be hierarchically organized, because the many decisions that have to be made every day cannot be made by large numbers of people. The effective functioning of an organization therefore requires the concentration of power in the hands of a few people.

This situation is aggravated by certain characteristics of both the leaders and the members. People achieve leadership positions precisely because they have unusual political skills; they are adept at getting their way and persuading others. Once they hold high office, their power and prestige are further increased. They have access to knowledge and facilities that are not available to the rank-and-file members of the organization, and they can control the information that flows down the channels of communication. The leaders are strongly motivated to maintain their own position and to persuade the organization of the rightness of their views, and they use all their skills and opportunities to do so. They also tend to promote junior officials who share their opinions, with the result that the oligarchy becomes a self-perpetuating one.

The members, on the other hand, tend to admire the leaders, whose prestige is enhanced by their office as well as by their personal qualities. Unlike the leaders, the members may have only a part-time commitment to the organization and are prepared to allow the leaders to exercise their own judgment on most matters. Less sophisticated and informed than their superiors, the rank and file look to the leaders for policy directives. The very nature of large-scale organization, Michels concluded, makes oligarchy inevitable. And the socialist ideal of human equality is therefore merely a dream of utopia: "The socialists might triumph, but not socialism, which would perish in the moment of its adherents' triumph." Michels became progressively disillusioned. While teaching in Italy later in his life, he became for a time an ardent supporter of the Fascist party and an admirer of Mussolini.

Michel's argument is a persuasive one, but it should not be accepted uncritically. Although he was correct in his

Figure 7.13 Many areas of society are now dominated by large bureaucracies, and the bureaucracies themselves tend to be dominated by oligarchies of high-ranking officials. The individual is thus separated from control over the decision-making processes that affect so many aspects of private and public life.

view that power in organizations tends to be concentrated among the top officeholders, he neglected certain checks on the power of the leadership. In many organizations, from corporations to political parties, there are usually two or more competing groups. If the dominant group gets too far out of line with rank-and-file opinion, it risks being displaced by another group, as happened to the Democratic party establishment in 1976 when an almost unknown outsider, Jimmy Carter, won the Democratic presidential nomination. Similarly, it is often possible for the mass membership to defect if the leadership no longer reflects its will, as millions of Republicans did when the party convention nominated Barry Goldwater for president in 1964. Successful challenges to the power of the oligarchy have been recorded in a variety of other bureaucratic organizations as well, ranging from labor unions to the military (Lipset et al., 1956; Zald and Berger, 1978). Michels also overlooked another vital aspect of organizations: whether they are oligarchic or not, they are often the best means of achieving a given goal. Many of the democratic advances of the last century have resulted, directly or indirectly, from the efforts of large-scale organizations.

The relationship between bureaucracy and freedom is a paradoxical one. Human freedom in a modern industrial society is dependent on bureaucracy, yet bureaucracy tends to undermine human freedom. Max Weber pointed out that the trend toward greater liberty requires bureaucratization of social institutions. We cannot have impartial justice if decisions are handed down in an arbitrary way on the basis of whim or favoritism: there must be a rational system of laws and a judicial bureaucracy to ensure that everyone is treated in the same way. We cannot have free elections without a representative list of voters, but then we need a formal bureaucracy to register voters and keep the lists up to date. We cannot prevent some people from infringing on the liberties of others unless there are formal organizations, ranging from police forces to federal regulatory agencies, to protect those liberties. In short, the preservation of liberty requires impartial rules and procedures and formal organizations to apply them.

Yet bureaucracy may undermine as well as protect human freedom. The reason is that bureaucracy separates individuals from control over the decisions that affect their lives. Government departments, for example, are theoretically responsible to the electorate, but this responsibility is almost entirely fictional. It often happens, in fact, that the electorate—and even Congress—do not know what these bureaucracies are doing. Government departments are now so large and complex that they often cannot be supervised effectively. In the mid-seventies, congressional investigations following the Watergate scandal revealed that over the preceding years, government agencies such as the CIA and the FBI had been guilty of thousands of crimes, ranging from burglaries of the homes of members of legitimate opposition groups to the experimental administration of LSD to unsuspecting subjects. It also emerged that for a period of at least fifteen years, the United States had been involved in attempts to assassinate the heads of state of several foreign countries through plots that included the use of Mafia "hit men." Very few of the elected representatives of the American people had any idea that these policies were being pursued.

Our democratic theories have their roots in the small-scale world of the eighteenth century. The thinkers and revolutionaries who created those theories could not anticipate the growth and spread of vast, formal organizations. Despite the democratization of other areas of life, formal organizations have further separated us from control over major social, political, and economic decisions. In this respect, as in many others, the radical changes that have taken place in the group basis of social life present a range of new problems.

The Future of Formal Organizations

How are formal organizations likely to develop in the future? A fairly safe prediction would be that they will tend to grow bigger and more complex. Governmental bureaucracies will grow simply because the demands we make on government, and the range of public services we require, are also growing. Corporate organizations will grow because large organizations appear to be profitable—although it is entirely possible that there is some optimal limit beyond which their growth will become dysfunctional, leading to difficulties in supervision and coordination, inefficiencies, and reduced profits.

Figure 7.14

"Mr. Bradshaw, today is my retirement day, and I want you to know that I've saved every single memo you've ever sent me."

Drawing by Stan Hunt; © 1970
The New Yorker Magazine, Inc.

Some writers have predicted that bureaucracies will tend to become less centralized, perhaps through being reorganized into self-contained, more temporary units. Alvin Toffler (1970) argues that the traditional, impersonal organization is not capable of meeting the challenges of modern society. Temporary or rapidly changing conditions demand a more fluid organization—what Toffler calls an "ad-hocracy," a special-purpose unit that is dissolved when its task is done. Warren Bennis (1966, 1970) suggests that future organizations will contain "task forces" to deal with specific problems. Organizational charts would then consist of a series of project groups rather than traditional hierarchies. This prospect is perhaps more tempting than persuasive. Although organizations may have to modify their structures to deal with new problems, many of their traditional concerns will remain, and their traditional structures are likely to remain as well.

One potentially significant trend is the increasing reliance of formal organizations on professional advice—from economists, physicists, sociologists, and other highly trained experts. These professionals do not readily fit into the hierarchical structure of the bureaucracy. Their knowledge and expertise are individual properties, attaching to them as people rather than to their offices. These professionals require the freedom to innovate, experiment, and take risks, and they expect their work to be judged by others in their own reference group—not by a bureaucrat who has no knowledge of their field of expertise. For this reason, there is often tension between, say, administrators and physicians in a hospital or between administrators and faculty in a college. As formal organizations come to rely more and more on highly advanced technologies and expert advice, there is likely to be some change in the traditional hierarchical relationships (Benson, 1973; Blankenship, 1977).

The growing resistance of the young to the impersonality and authoritarianism of formal organizations may also provoke changes in organizational structure and relationships. Weber held forth the hope that an excess of rationalization would cause a reaction in favor of greater informality and spontaneity, and the values of the sixties "counterculture" can be seen as just such a reaction to the rationalization of American institutions. The humanistic trends that have been present in America since the brief flowering of that "counterculture" have had a subtle but lasting effect on American culture, and formal organizations have not been immune to this influence.

In fact, the period since the late sixties has seen the spread of a nonbureaucratic kind of organization, the collective. Typically, collectivist groups consist largely of volunteers or part-time workers who administer community projects such as free schools, alternative newspapers, medical or legal-aid clinics, and art centers. As Joyce Rothschild-Whitt (1979) points out, the collectivist form of organization differs sharply from the bureaucratic one in several key respects. For example, individual members of the collective are encouraged to contribute a variety of talents, since there is little division of labor; authority arises from the consensus of the collective as a whole, not from a hierarchy of officials; individual initiative is valued more highly than rigid adherence to a set of rules; members of the collective treat the public as individual people, not as a series of impersonal "cases"; and the status of members within the group depends more on their personal qualities than on any official titles they might have. The continued existence of collectives alerts us to the fact that bureaucracy is not the only possible kind of organization—although it seems that bureaucracy is more efficient where large-scale, complex tasks must be attempted. Finally, we shall have to confront the problem that formal organizations pose for democratic values. A challenge in the future will be to develop better means of social control over bureaucracy and thus to ensure that we shall not be dominated by the organizations we have established for our own convenience.

Summary

1. Human beings are social animals who spend much of their time in groups. Groups are distinguished from aggregates and categories by the fact that their members interact.

2. Primary groups consist of a small number of people who interact on an intimate basis. Secondary groups may be large or small, but their members interact without any emotional commitment to one another.

3. Extensive research has been devoted to small-group interaction. The size of groups is an important factor in determining the kind of interaction that can take place. Leadership in groups may be instrumental or expressive. Democratic leaders are more effective than authoritarian or laissez-faire leaders, at least in American laboratory experiments. Groups are more effective than individuals at solving determinate problems. Group performance on indeterminate problems varies. There is sometimes a tendency toward a "risky shift" and sometimes toward "groupthink." Most group decisions proceed through a regular sequence of stages. As Asch's experiments reveal, there is strong pressure for conformity in groups.

4. Members of groups tend to regard their group as an "ingroup" and other groups as "outgroups." Conflict and tension between groups heighten feelings of group solidarity and loyalty, as Sherif's experiment shows.

5. Reference groups are those to which an individual refers when making self-evaluations. One need not be a member of a reference group in order to identify with it.

6. Large secondary groups, or associations, generally take the form of formal organizations. These social groups dominate modern life.

7. Formal organizations are coordinated through bureaucracies. Weber saw bureaucracy as a form of rationalization, and by constructing an ideal type, analyzed the way they operate. His analysis has since been modified to take account of the informal structure that exists in all bureaucracies. Although bureaucracies are highly efficient, they have many dysfunctions as well, particularly when faced with unprecedented or unfamiliar situations.

8. Bureaucracies tend to be oligarchic, a feature that Michels argued was incompatible with democracy. Although bureaucracies are necessary for a mass democracy, they also undermine liberty by separating people from the decision-making processes that affect their lives.

9. Although some modifications are likely in formal organizations in the future, they are an indispensable social tool. The increasingly bureaucratic nature of social institutions continues to present many problems, however.

Important Terms

group (155)   association (156)

aggregate (155)   small group (157)

category (155)   dyad (158)

primary group (156)   triad (158)

secondary group (156)   leader (159)

instrumental leadership (159)

expressive leadership (159)

ingroup (162)

outgroup (162)

reference group (163)

formal organization (164)

bureaucracy (165)

rationalization (165)

ideal type (165)

oligarchy (172)

Suggested Readings

BLAU, PETER, and MARSHALL W. MEYER. *Bureaucracy in Modern Society*. 2nd ed. New York: Random House, 1971.

Blau, one of the foremost sociologists in the field, offers a brief but comprehensive analysis of the functions, dysfunctions, workings, and social implications of bureaucracies.

ETZIONI, AMITAI (ed.). *A Sociological Reader on Complex Organizations*. New York: Holt, Rinehart and Winston, 1969.

A useful collection of articles on formal organizations; the selection includes excerpts from Weber's work as well as contributions from modern sociologists.

JANIS, IRVING L., and LEON MANN. *Decision Making*. New York: Free Press, 1977.

An excellent overview of theory and research on the question of how groups arrive at their decisions.

MICHELS, ROBERT. *Political Parties*. New York: Free Press, 1967.

Although this book was first published more than half a century ago, it remains a readable and relevant analysis of the relationship between democracy and oligarchic organizations.

OLMSTED, MICHAEL S., and A. PAUL HARE. *The Small Group*. 2nd ed. New York: Random House, 1978.

A brief and readable summary of the main findings of social science research on small groups.

PARKINSON, C. NORTHCOTE. *Parkinson's Law*. Boston: Houghton Mifflin, 1957.

A satirical account of the inefficiencies of large organizations. The book includes a presentation of "Parkinson's Law," which states that in any organization, work expands to fill the amount of time available for its completion.

PERROW, CHARLES. *Complex Organizations*. 2nd ed. Glenview, Ill.: Scott, Foresman, 1979.

An important initial discussion of formal organizations and their implications for modern society.

CHAPTER **8**   *Deviance*

In the preceding chapters we have emphasized the basically orderly nature of society. Most people conform to most norms most of the time, and social life therefore takes on a fairly regular and predictable pattern. Yet this picture is incomplete. We need only look at the world around us to see that social norms are often violated as well as adhered to. People rob, rape, and defraud others. They wear peculiar clothing, shoot heroin, and take part in riots. They embrace alien religions, become mentally disordered, and commit bigamy. A full picture of society, therefore, must include deviance from social norms as well as conformity to them.

What exactly is deviance? One sociologist put the question "Who is deviant?" to people from various backgrounds and obtained more than two hundred and fifty different answers. Predictably, the range of responses included alcoholics, drug addicts, homosexuals, radicals, prostitutes, and criminals. But it also included liars, women, Democrats, reckless drivers, atheists, young folks, card players, bearded men, straights, prudes, the president, divorcees, modern people, artists, pacifists, know-it-all professors, and smart-aleck students (Simons, 1969). College students confront the problem more succinctly: the deviance course in sociology departments is often known as "nuts, sluts, and 'preverts.'"

This list certainly tells us something about deviants and deviance: obviously, the words refer to people and acts that other people strongly disapprove of. But it hardly provides us with a definition that could help us decide who is a deviant and who is not. A review of the sociological literature on the topic would reveal that sociologists also find the concept a slippery one to pin down. Howard Becker

179

(1963b) tries to resolve the issue by defining deviance as "behavior that people so label." Kai Erikson (1966) tells us that deviance is behavior that people feel "something ought to be done about." Some sociologists restrict the concept to behaviors, such as prostitution or robbery, that people seem to engage in by choice. Others extend it to characteristics over which people have no control: Fred Davis (1961), for example, includes blacks and cripples in the category of deviants, and Erving Goffman (1963b) includes lepers and the badly scarred.

Strictly speaking, deviance is any behavior that does not conform to social norms. But this definition is not very helpful because many norms are not regarded as particularly important, and varying degrees of deviance from them are tolerated or even ignored. The social reaction you get if you turn up late for appointments, don't eat three meals a day, or occasionally wear mismatched socks is very different from the reaction you get if you mug an old lady in the streets, participate in orgies, or announce that you are Napoleon.

Minor deviations from norms, or deviations from norms that nobody bothers much about, have few if any social consequences and are not of particular sociological interest. The sociology of deviance is primarily concerned with violations that are considered offensive by a large number of people. The one characteristic shared by those who are widely regarded as deviant is *stigma*—the mark of social disgrace that sets the deviant apart from those who consider themselves "normal." Erving Goffman (1963b) has perceptively remarked that the stigmatized person has a "spoiled identity" as a result of negative evaluations by others. For our purposes, then, *deviance refers to behavior or characteristics that violate significant social norms and expectations and are negatively valued by large numbers of people as a result.* This definition brings us closer to an understanding of deviance, and three additional points will clarify the concept further.

First, social deviance should not be confused with statistical rarity. To jog for a mile before breakfast is to be statistically unusual, and to run for the U.S. Senate even more so, but people who do these things are not socially deviant for that reason. In addition, although most forms of deviance are practiced by a minority of people, it occasionally happens that a majority of the population deviates from a significant norm. Since no society can survive for long if most of its members violate important norms, the usual result is that the norm itself is modified or abandoned. For example, American society has always had a norm prohibiting premarital sex, but for many years a majority of Americans have deviated from this norm. As a

Figure 8.1 Behavior that may be regarded as deviant in one culture may be conformist and highly valued in another. The first of these pictures shows a member of the Maori of New Zealand, a people who used tattoos and incisions to create elaborate facial patterns; the second shows a devotee of an Indian religious sect whose members insert knives and hooks through fleshy parts of the body in rituals intended to prove their faith. People who acted in these ways in American culture would be regarded as strange, or even mad.

result, the norm has been losing its force—so much so that it is questionable if it can still be considered a norm at all in its traditional form.

The second point is that society cannot be divided neatly into the sheep and the goats, the "normals" who conform and the "deviants" who do not. Although a majority of people usually conform to any specific norm that is important to society, most people have violated one or more important norms at some time in their lives. If we were to subtract from "normal" society all the people who have engaged in prohibited sexual acts, all the people who have ever stolen something, all the people who have suffered a mental disorder, and all the people who have used illegal drugs—to mention just a few out of hundreds of possibilities—we would have very few "normal" people left. Most people, however, escape discovery of their deviant behavior, are not stigmatized, and generally do not even regard themselves as deviant at all.

The third point is that deviance is relative. No act is inherently deviant. It becomes deviant only when it is socially defined as such, and definitions vary greatly from time to time, place to place, and group to group. The heretic of one age may be the saint of the next; the "freedom fighter" of one group may be a "terrorist" to another; conservative views in one society may seem dangerously radical in a different society. Who and what are defined as deviant depend on who is doing the defining and who has the power to make the definition stick.

It is even possible for the same act to be differently interpreted depending on the precise context in which it takes place. If you talk to God in a synagogue or church, your behavior is regarded as perfectly normal; if you talk to God in a bus or a restaurant, of if God talks back to you, you are considered mentally disordered. It is quite acceptable for you to "do nothing" at home, but our society demands that you be "doing something" in public. If you stand around a street corner long enough, you will probably be arrested for loitering. The police are entitled to ask you what you are doing, and "nothing" is not an acceptable answer. An act may also draw different reactions depending on the social status of the person concerned. If a lower-class male exposes himself in a park, he will probably be charged with public indecency. If a corporation president does the same, he has an excellent chance of being referred to a psychiatrist for treatment of a "nervous breakdown."

Deviance and Social Control

Under most conditions, social behavior is remarkably orderly and predictable. You can generally rely on your sociology professor to show up for class, and you can expect that he or she will talk mostly about sociology and not something else. You can take it on faith that banks will be open during working hours, not closed because the tellers became bored and decided to throw a private party. And you can be almost certain that your neighbors will wear much the same clothes tomorrow as they did yesterday, and will not appear on the streets half naked or painted with blue dye. In short, people generally fulfill their roles in accordance with social expectations. In doing so they make social order, and therefore society, possible.

As we noted in Chapter 3 ("Culture"), social order can exist only if there is an effective system of *social control*—that is, a set of means of ensuring that people generally behave in expected and approved ways. Social control starts with the socialization process, which ideally ensures that everyone internalizes and follows the norms of the society. On the whole, socialization is highly successful: people conform to social norms most of the time through sheer habit, and rarely question why they act as they do. In general, human beings abide by the rules—not just when the rules seem sound and useful, but even when they are petty, arrogant, outdated, contradictory, or oppressive. Nevertheless, socialization is always to some extent imperfect and incomplete. People may be born with different potentials; they are exposed to different socializing influences; they interpret these influences in different ways; and they are often faced with novel situations in which they must improvise new behavior on their own.

To the extent that socialization cannot guarantee sufficient conformity, further means of social control are necessary. Society has to enforce its norms through *sanctions*—that is, rewards for conformity and punishments for deviance. Both types of sanction can be applied either formally, in a patterned and organized way, or informally, through the spontaneous reactions of other people. A *formal positive sanction*, for example, might be the presentation of a medal or graduation certificate; a *formal negative sanction* might be imprisonment or execution. An *informal positive sanction* might be a pat on the back or a congratulatory handshake; an *informal negative sanction* might be a shouted

Figure 8.2 The seventeenth-century Puritans of Salem, Massachusetts, created deviants where they did not exist, in the form of witches. Shown here is an old woman being arrested and charged with witchcraft; by the time the Puritans' witch hunt ended, several women had been executed. In persecuting "witches," the Puritans reaffirmed their own solidarity as a community and enhanced their sense of righteousness. A witch hunt of a different sort occurred in the United States during the 1950s, when the late Senator Joe McCarthy made indiscriminate charges that "reds" were infesting various areas of the national life, ranging from the movie industry to the State Department. Congress set up a Committee on Un-American Activities, which tried to track down these alleged communist sympathizers. These were the early days of the "cold war" with the Soviet Union, and the search for deviants closer to home provided a focus for national solidarity against communism. Although he recklessly smeared the reputations of hundreds of people, McCarthy could never substantiate his claims. When he finally began to attack even the U.S. Army, public revulsion led his colleagues in the Senate to formally censure him, and this search for "un-American" deviants came to an end.

insult or simply avoidance of the offender. The award of positive sanctions indicates that social control is working effectively and that people are fulfilling the expectations others have of them. But the use of negative sanctions implies that social control has failed and deviance has occurred.

Paradoxically, however, the presence of deviance can actually contribute to the effectiveness of social control. Emile Durkheim (1964a, originally published 1893) strongly argued that a limited amount of deviance is *functional* for society. The reason is that the existence of deviants is necessary to define the boundaries of permissible behavior. When society stigmatizes thieves or prostitutes, it does more than punish them. It also reaffirms the existing norms and implicitly warns other people what their fate will be if they stray from the rules. The public example of the stigmatized deviant provides evidence that social control has failed, but it also tends to restrain others from deviating and thus strengthens the norms. In applying sanctions to deviants, moreover, other people are made conscious of their own conformity, and so feel solidarity as the normal "us" against the deviant "them."

Durkheim felt that this function of deviance is so important that if there were no deviants, they might have to be invented. And, in fact, there is evidence that many groups do precisely that. In highly conformist societies such as China, periodic purges take place against political deviants whose ideological differences with the "party line" are minimal. The early American Puritans invented deviants in the form of witches and reaffirmed their own moral purity in the process (K. Erikson, 1966). In the 1950s the United States was seized with an almost hysterical crusade against supposed "communists," led by the late Senator Joe McCarthy. The senator brandished "lists" of nonexistent "reds," indiscriminately accused his critics of communist sympathies, and ruined many reputations.

Deviance thus arises from the very nature of society and the necessity for social order. Without rules there can be no rule breakers; but where there are rules, there will always be people tempted to break them. The individual deviant may be abnormal, but deviance itself is intrinsic to social living.

Theories of Deviance

The extent and the content of deviant behavior vary a great deal from one society to another and among different groups within a society, a fact that requires explanation. Psychologists have investigated the personal characteristics of individual deviants, explaining their behavior in terms of a weak ego, an inability to take the role of other people, a failure to identify with parental authority, a process of social learning, a reaction to frustration, and so on. These explanations may well provide an adequate account of why particular people adopt the deviant practices that they do. But the sociological problem is not to explain why a particular person becomes deviant: it is to understand why deviance arises at all, why it follows specific patterns, and why some acts rather than others are defined as deviant in the first place. Four main theories have been offered.

Biological Theories

Early approaches to deviance started from the assumption that there was something basically "wrong" with the deviant. The distinction between deviant and normal behavior was regarded as absolute and self-evident, and the failure of some people to follow social rules was explained in terms of sin, wickedness, degeneracy, or "moral insanity." The problem of why some people should be more prone to these vices than others was addressed by the Italian criminologist Cesare Lombroso (1911), whose research convinced him that he had found the answer: criminal behavior was inborn.

By using a number of crude tests to measure the physical characteristics of prison inmates, Lombroso identified certain features typically found in the criminal population. Among these characteristics, he announced, were shifty eyes, receding hairlines, red hair, strong jaws, wispy beards, and the like. Lombroso came to the conclusion that criminals are a form of evolutionary throwback to a more primitive human type. The criminal, it seemed, was a

> being who reproduces in his person the ferocious instincts of primitive humanity and the inferior animals. Thus were explained [the characteristics] found in criminals, savages, and apes: insensitivity to pain, extremely acute sight, tattooing, excessive idleness, love of orgies, the irresistible craving for evil for its own sake, the desire not only to extinguish life in the victim, but to mutilate the corpse, tear its flesh, and drink its blood.

Lombroso's work attracted a number of admirers, none of whom noticed the fatal flaw in the criminologist's methodology. He had neglected to measure noncriminals as well, and therefore had not proved that his list of telltale features appeared more frequently in criminals than in the general population. A British physician, Charles Goring (1913), corrected this oversight and disposed of Lombroso's theory by showing that the physical characteristics of criminals did not differ in any detectable way from those of ordinary citizens.

Biological theories of criminal deviance have reappeared periodically since Lombroso's time. The psychologist William Sheldon (1940) attempted to classify people in terms of three basic body types: the *endomorph,* who is soft and round; the *mesomorph,* who is muscular and agile; and the *ectomorph,* who is skinny and delicate. After investigating a small number of juvenile delinquents in Boston, Sheldon (1949) concluded that mesomorphs were disproportionately represented in his sample. Sheldon Glueck and Eleanor Glueck (1956) used Sheldon's classification to compare 500 juvenile delinquents with a carefully matched sample of 500 nondelinquents. They also found that meso-

SHELDON'S BODY TYPES

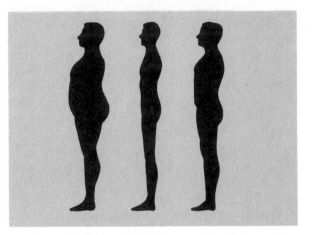

Figure 8.3 William Sheldon identified three basic body types: the soft and round, the skinny and delicate, and the muscular and agile. Sheldon's research convinced him that the muscular and agile type was more prone to criminal behavior, but this conclusion has since been called into question.

morphs predominated in the delinquent sample, although all three body types were present in both groups. The Gluecks concluded that body type, together with other personal characteristics and experiences, might predispose certain people toward crime. This finding has to be interpreted very carefully, because it is easy to overlook the interaction that takes place between biological and social factors in the shaping of behavior. People react to others in subtle ways on the basis of their physical appearance, and these responses in turn influence the behavior of the individuals concerned. The delicate youth, for example, is not likely to be selected by his peers for a gang fight, nor the stout youth for a burglary that might involve climbing a drainpipe or a headlong flight from the police. The muscular and agile youth is presumably more likely to become involved in the adventurous and high-spirited behavior that may be defined as delinquency, but this hardly means that his body type is a *cause* of his criminal tendencies.

Interest in biological factors was revived more recently when it was discovered that some violent criminals have a chromosome disorder. Normal males have an XY chromosome makeup, but these criminals had an extra chromosome, giving them the combination XYY. Subsequent studies indicated that XYY criminals are not more violent than other criminals, but that they do appear more often in criminal than in noncriminal groups (Owen, 1972). The great majority of XYY males have never been convicted of a crime, however, and appear to lead normal lives. Research on the issue is continuing, but it seems unlikely that the extra chromosome is a cause of criminal behavior. XYY individuals often have low intelligence and are unusually tall; they may therefore suffer social stigma and restricted job opportunities, and may react by turning to crime (I. Taylor et al., 1973).

Although biological factors may be relevant to very specific kinds of deviance—particular forms of mental disorder, for example—they are of little use in the explanation of deviance in general. As we have pointed out, every society defines deviance differently, and a highly deviant act in one society may be a conforming and virtuous one in another. Inborn characteristics cannot provide a comprehensive explanation of culturally relative forms of behavior (Jeffery, 1979).

Anomie Theory

The concept of *anomie* was introduced to modern sociology by Emile Durkheim (1964, originally published 1893) to describe the confused condition that exists in both individuals and society when social norms are weak, absent, or conflicting. A society with a high level of anomie risks disintegration, for its members no longer share common goals and values. Individuals in a state of anomie lack guidelines for behavior, for they feel little sense of social discipline over their personal desires and acts. Robert Merton (1938, 1968) has modified this concept and applied it to deviant behavior.

Merton writes from a *functionalist* perspective and regards deviance as the outcome of an imbalance in the social system. To Merton, anomie is the situation that arises when there is a discrepancy between socially approved goals and the availability of socially approved means of achieving them. If a society places a high value on the goal of affluent living for all but denies people equal access to socially approved ways of getting rich, it invites theft, fraud, and similar crimes. As Merton (1968) explains:

> It is only when a system of cultural values extols, virtually above all else, certain *common* success goals for the *population at large,* while the social structure rigorously restricts or completely closes access to approved modes of reaching these goals *for a considerable part of the same population,* that deviant behavior ensues on a large scale.

In small, traditional communities the goals offered to the general population are usually matched to the opportunities for achieving them. But in large modern societies, many people may lack access to the approved means of achieving valued goals. Americans are readily socialized into the belief that one has to "make it" in the world or be a "failure." But they are not always as easily socialized into accepting socially approved ways of "making it" as being the only possible ways of achieving success.

People who accept the goal of success but find the approved avenues blocked may fall into a state of anomie and seek success by disapproved methods. As Merton puts it, "in this setting, a cardinal American virtue, 'ambition,' becomes a cardinal American vice, 'deviant behavior.'" The strength of Merton's approach is that it locates the source of deviance squarely within the culture and social structure, not in the failings of individual deviants. Society itself—through discrepancies between its approved goals and its approved methods of reaching them—exerts a definite pressure on some people to deviate rather than conform.

Merton suggests that people may respond to this situation in one of five different ways, depending on their acceptance or rejection of the goals or the means (see Figure 8.4).

Conformity occurs when people accept both the approved goals and the approved means. Conformists want to achieve such goals as success and materialism. They work hard, save money, and generally use approved means of seeking the goals—even if they are unsuccessful.

Innovation occurs when people accept the approved goals but resort to disapproved means. This is the most common form of deviance: it occurs, for example, when a student wants to pass a test but resorts to cheating; when a candidate wants to win an election but uses "dirty tricks" to discredit an opponent; when a man wants sexual satisfaction but turns to a prostitute.

MERTON'S TYPOLOGY OF DEVIANCE

Modes of Adapting	Accepts Culturally Approved Goals	Accepts Culturally Approved Means
Conformist	yes	yes
Innovator	yes	no
Ritualist	no	yes
Retreatist	no	no
Rebel	no (creates new goals)	no (creates new means)

Source: Adapted from Robert K. Merton, *Social Theory and Social Structure* (New York: Free Press, 1968), p. 194.

Figure 8.4 According to Merton's theory, people will conform or deviate depending on their acceptance or rejection of culturally approved means and/or culturally approved goals. This table illustrates the various outcomes that are possible.

Ritualism occurs when people abandon the goals as irrelevant to their lives but still accept and compulsively enact the means. The classic example is the bureaucrat who becomes obsessed with petty rules and procedures, losing sight of the objectives that the rules were designed to achieve. Ritualism is the mildest form of deviance, and except in extreme cases is not usually regarded as such.

Retreatism occurs when people abandon both the approved goals and the approved means of achieving them. The retreatist is the "double failure" in the eyes of society—the vagrant, the chronic narcotics addict, the "skid-row bum," or anyone else who has lost commitment to both the goals and the means that society values.

Rebellion occurs when people reject both the approved goals and means and then substitute new, disapproved ones instead. The rebel, for example, may reject the goal of personal wealth and the means of capital accumulation as the way to achieve it, turning instead to the goal of social equality achieved through revolution.

Applications

Anomie theory has been usefully applied to several forms of deviance, particularly that of delinquent juvenile gangs. Albert Cohen (1955) points out that gangs are generally composed of lower-class boys who, lacking the social and educational background that would enable them to achieve success via the approved channels that are open to middle-class youth, try to gain the respect of their peers through "hell-raising" and other forms of behavior that conform to gang norms. Richard Cloward and Lloyd Ohlin (1960), also applying anomie theory to delinquent gangs, suggest that there are three types of delinquent subcultures. The *criminal* type is organized for material gain through theft, robbery, and the like; the *conflict* type is concerned with territorial defense and gang warfare; and the *retreatist* type emphasizes less visible activities, such as drug and alcohol abuse, as its source of "kicks." In each case, the gang provides people who cannot achieve a "respectable" status with the opportunity for other forms of achievement, even if these are disapproved by the wider society.

Evaluation

Merton's theory of deviance is an elegant, thoughtful, and influential one. It not only has the virtue of locating the cause of deviance in society, not the deviants themselves, but it also provides a plausible explanation of why people commit certain deviant acts, particularly crimes involving property. It is less useful, however, for explaining other forms of deviance, such as homosexuality, exhibitionism, or marijuana use. And because Merton shares the implicit functionalist assumption that there is a general consensus of values in society, he largely ignores the process by which some people are defined as deviant by others—a process that often involves a conflict of values between those who have the power to apply these definitions and those who do not.

Cultural-Transmission Theory

Earlier in this century Clifford Shaw and Henry McKay (1929) found that high crime rates had persisted in the same Chicago neighborhoods for twenty years, even though these areas had changed in other ways as different ethnic groups had come and gone. How could this finding be explained? The answer, they felt, was that if deviant behavior already exists as a cultural pattern in some group or community, it will tend to be transmitted to newcomers and the young. New arrivals in a high-crime neighborhood, Shaw and McKay reasoned, were learning deviant behavior in social interaction with the residents.

A sociologist who was influenced by Shaw and McKay, Edwin Sutherland, produced a theory to explain exactly how this *cultural transmission* of deviance takes place. According to Sutherland (1939), deviant behavior is learned through a process of *differential association*. This concept is really a sophisticated version of the old "bad companions" formula ("He was such a good boy until he fell in with that lot"). Just as people will tend to be conformist if their socialization emphasizes a respect for the prevailing norms, so they will tend to become deviant if their socialization encourages a contempt for these norms. As Sutherland put it, "A person becomes delinquent because of an excess of definitions favorable to violation of the law over definitions unfavorable to violation of the law."

Sutherland begins with the assumption that criminal behavior, like all social behavior, is learned from other people. Nobody is exposed exclusively to conformists or deviants, and several factors determine which influences will be the stronger. The first is the *intensity* of contacts with others; a person is more likely to be influenced by deviant friends or family members than by more distant acquaintances who are deviant. Another is the *age* at which the contacts take place; influences in childhood and adolescence are more powerful than those occurring later in life. Another is the ratio of contacts with deviants to contacts with conformists.

In short, nobody is born with the knowledge, the techniques, or the justifications that are available to the deviant. Like any other elements of culture, these things must be transmitted from one person or group to another.

Applications

An interesting implication of cultural-transmission theory is that deviance will tend to be more common when a society contains a number of distinctive subcultures (Wirth, 1931; Sellin, 1938; Sorokin, 1941; Cohen, 1955; Nisbet, 1953). When a culture is homogeneous, as is usually the case in small, traditional communities, the inhabitants share the same norms and values and have little difficulty in passing them on to succeeding generations. They rarely rely on formal methods of social control, such as laws, police, courts, or prisons; people are kept "in line" by the overwhelming force of public opinion. Under these conditions deviance—particularly crime—is rare. A large and heterogeneous modern society, on the other hand, may contain a range of subcultures based on such characteristics as race, ethnicity, religion, age, or economic status. People may feel a greater loyalty to their own subculture than to the common culture, even though their subcultural norms may be defined as deviant by the society as a whole.

Walter Miller (1958) uses this insight in his analysis of gang delinquency, arguing that mere acceptance of certain lower-class norms and values can put juveniles in trouble with the law. Miller identifies several "focal concerns" of lower-class culture: *toughness,* an emphasis on physical strength; *smartness,* the capacity to be "street wise" and hold one's own in the world; *excitement,* in the form of "kicks" intended to relieve the routine of a life in which one never "gets ahead"; *autonomy,* the wish to be free of external controls and authority; and *fate,* the sense that what happens to a person is less a matter of personal responsibility than of luck or fortune. The gang, Miller argues, offers an environment in which these values can be expressed. It provides security, stability, and support for juveniles who have internalized the norms of their own community rather than the predominantly middle-class norms of the culture beyond. Simply by accepting the values of their own subculture, lower-class juveniles may become delinquent in the eyes of the wider society.

Evaluation

Cultural-transmission theory has the merit of drawing attention to the fact that deviant behavior is learned. People do not find out how to shoot heroin or forge checks in total isolation. But it is possible to learn deviant behavior without any actual contact with deviants, a fact that differential-association theory does not adequately explain. Many forms of deviant behavior are learned through contact with ideas, not people. A check forger or heroin shooter need not have had personal instruction in how to perform the acts, and a child molester almost certainly will not have learned the behavior directly from others. Moreover, the theory does not explain why some people who have frequent contacts with deviants—as lawyers do with criminals—may resist becoming deviant themselves. Nor does it take account of the fact that some forms of deviant behavior are actually learned in contact with conforming citizens. One can learn the techniques of embezzlement, for example, by taking a course in bookkeeping (Sagarin, 1975). Some sociologists have extended Sutherland's theory

Figure 8.5 *Cultural-transmission theory implies that people raised in a particular subculture may become deviant simply through learning the values and norms of their own subculture. Living in a slum environment, these boys learn patterns of behavior that are readily defined as deviant by the mainstream culture.*

in a way that helps to deal with these difficulties. They argue that deviant behavior is acquired through a process of social learning. As we noted in Chapter 5 ("Socialization"), social-learning theory holds that behavior is shaped partly by rewards and punishments, and partly by imitation of others or even by incidental contact with ideas (Burgess and Akers, 1966; Akers, 1977; Akers et al., 1979). Even with this modification, however, an important criticism still remains: cultural-transmission theory explains only how deviance is learned, not how it arose in the culture or why it was defined as deviance in the first place.

Labeling Theory

A newer theory confronts some of the problems that earlier explanations ignored or were unable to resolve. This approach emphasizes the relativity of deviance: a person or act becomes deviant only when the *label* of "deviance" has been successfully applied by other people. Labeling theorists argue that the process by which people are labeled as deviants, not their acts, should be the focus of sociological attention. The theory draws heavily on the insights of the *interactionist* perspective for its understanding of the label-

Figure 8.6 Labeling theorists place special emphasis on the fact that deviance is never an absolute matter; it all depends on the viewpoint of the people making the definition. These women are clearly reacting negatively to the young man (note, incidentally, the "body language" of their elbows as well as their faces), but his own peer group would not respond in this way.

ing process, and in recent years it has used the *conflict* perspective to explain why some people and acts rather than others are labeled as deviant at all.

Early labeling theorists, notably Edwin Lemert (1951, 1967) and Howard Becker (1963b), point out that virtually everyone behaves in a deviant manner at some time or another. Most of this behavior is temporary, exploratory, trivial, or easily concealed, and falls into the category of *primary deviance.* The primary deviant may be a wealthy man who misrepresents his income to the tax collector, an overburdened mother who sometimes becomes hysterical, an adolescent who occasionally has homosexual relations with a friend, or a youth who tries an illicit drug "to see what it's like." This behavior may pass unnoticed, and the individuals concerned do not regard themselves as deviants and are not regarded as such by others. But if these acts are discovered and made public by significant other people—friends, parents, employers, school principals, or even the police and the courts—the situation changes radically. The offender is confronted by the evidence, often in a situation that Harold Garfinkel (1956) calls a "degradation ceremony." In this "ceremony" the person is accused of the deviant act, lectured to and perhaps punished, and forced to acknowledge the moral superiority of the accusers. Most important, the person is now labeled by others as a deviant—as a "nut," "whore," "queer," "weirdo," "crook," "dope addict." Other people begin to respond to the offender in terms of this label. As a result, the offender consciously or unconsciously accepts the label, develops a new self-concept, and begins to behave accordingly. The behavior now takes the form of *secondary deviance.* The label proves prophetic, and the deviance becomes habitual.

Once people have been labeled as deviants, their biographies are significantly altered. "Normal" people apply stigma to the deviants, often forcing them into the company of other deviants. The result is that the sanctions have the effect of reinforcing the very behavior they were intended to eliminate. The deviants live up to the labels, frequently because they have no options, and are thrust into a *deviant career.* Deviance then becomes their master status, and much of their behavior is interpreted by others in the light of this single characteristic, however irrelevant it may actually be to ordinary day-to-day interactions (Goffman, 1963b). This interpretation may even be applied retrospectively, and often incorrectly, to the individual's past behavior. The earlier friendliness of the person who is now labeled a homosexual is reinterpreted as a sexual advance; the business proposition once made by the person who is now known to be an ex-convict is reinterpreted as an attempt at fraud; the mild tantrum by the person who is now known to have been a mental patient is reinterpreted as a sign of underlying instability.

Applications

Why are certain people and acts rather than others labeled as deviant? Several sociologists have argued that the answer is to be found in the conflict of values and interests between those who have the power to label and those who are powerless to reject the label (for example, Liazos, 1972; Lemert, 1974; Chambliss and Mankoff, 1976). As Edwin Schur (1965) points out, people with high social, economic, and political resources have a high ability to resist charges of deviance; a high ability to resist sanctions such as arrest, conviction, and imprisonment; and a high ability to impose the actual rules that define deviance. Conversely, those with lesser resources have a lower ability to achieve these things. Alexander Liazos (1972) notes that the label of deviance is rarely applied to the politician who starts a war or the corporate executive whose decisions lead to environmental pollution. These acts have far more serious social consequences than those of the person who steals

bicycles or never washes, but the latter offenders, not the former, attract the stigma of deviance. Similarly, begging n the streets is considered deviant, but living in idleness off inherited wealth is not. These and similar inconsistent judgments can be explained only by the fact that the prevailing interpretations of reality in any society are those of the people who hold social, political, and economic power; they are able to impose absolute definitions on what is really a relative matter.

Jock Young (1971) uses a similar argument to explain the social reaction to different forms of drug use. The National Commission on Marijuana and Drug Abuse (1973) reported that alcohol abuse "is without question the most serious drug problem in the country today." Between 5 million and 9 million Americans are alcoholics, and about a third of the crimes recorded each year by the FBI are alcohol-related. Yet the commission found that only 7 percent of American adults consider alcohol abuse a problem, and less than 40 percent even regard alcohol as a "drug" at all. Tobacco is causally linked to lung cancer, emphysema, and heart disease. It is also highly habit-forming: of those who smoke more than one cigarette in adolescence, 70 percent continue smoking for the next forty years (Russell, 1971). Yet both these drugs are accepted in the most respected circles and are manufactured, advertised, and distributed by large and legitimate corporations.

Figure 8.7 Labeling theorists argue that definitions of who and what are deviant can be fully understood only in terms of the power relationships among different or competing groups. Powerful groups are able to use social-control agencies to enforce their own definitions and to uphold their own interests. Less powerful groups, however, cannot successfully apply the label of deviance to those with superior power.

SUBSTANCES REGARDED AS DRUGS

	Adults (Percent)	Youth (Percent)
Heroin	95	96
Cocaine	88	86
Barbiturates	83	91
Marijuana	80	80
Amphetamines	79	86
Alcohol	39	34
Tobacco	27	16
No opinion	1	1

Source: *Drug Abuse in America: Problem in Perspective, Second Report of the National Commission on Marijuana and Drug Abuse* (Washington, D.C.: U.S. Government Printing Office, 1973), p. 10.

Figure 8.8 *Public attitudes toward drugs bear very little relationship to the properties of the drugs themselves. The main killer drugs in the United States are alcohol and tobacco, yet a large majority of American adults and youth do not regard them as drugs at all. In contrast, the only substance on this list that is neither addictive nor potentially lethal—marijuana—is regarded as a drug by 80 percent of adults and young people.*

Marijuana use, on the other hand, is generally illegal, and hundreds of thousands of young people are arrested each year for smoking or possessing it. Although it is possible that research will disclose some adverse effects of marijuana, there is currently a general agreement among experts that it is not as harmful to health as alcohol or tobacco.

How can these different attitudes toward various forms of drug use be explained? For one thing, of course, alcohol and tobacco use is already entrenched in the culture, but Young suggests that the real explanation lies deeper. The social reaction to drug use, he argues, has little or nothing to do with the pharmacological characteristics of the drug in question: it has to do with the social characteristics of the people who use it. Marijuana use was associated in the past with such "disreputable" groups as blacks, jazz musicians, "hippies," and the rebellious young. Society identifies the drug with the people who use it, and if the people are disapproved, so is the drug.

Evaluation

Labeling theory has the important advantage that it can explain why only certain people and acts are considered deviant. Yet the theory runs into several objections. One is that empirical research has shown that in many cases, labeling is not an important influence on deviant behavior (Gove, 1980). For example, some habitual shoplifters or users of pornography might never have been discovered and labeled, yet many still behave in a consistently deviant way. However, this objection overlooks the possibility that some people may become secondary deviants by labeling *themselves* in terms of how they think others would see them. Another objection to the theory is that it ignores the fact that labeling may actually jolt the offender out of deviance altogether. In other words, a "degradation ceremony" may reform the deviant rather than reinforce the deviance (Mankoff, 1971). Another problem with labeling theory is that it tends to encourage an indiscriminate sympathy for the "underdog" as the helpless victim of definitions arbitrarily imposed by the powerful. But not all inmates of a prison or an asylum are there simply because somebody chose to label them, although labeling was certainly part of the process that put them there. Some deviant acts are so socially disruptive that society must impose severe sanctions if social order is to be maintained, and the extreme relativism of labeling theory sometimes obscures this fact.

Each of these theories, then, has some part to play in the explanation of deviance. Let's turn now to an examination of crime, one of the most widespread forms of deviance in contemporary American society.

Crime

A *crime* is an act that has been formally prohibited by a political authority, usually through the enactment of a law. An act is likely to be defined as a crime under the following two conditions: first, it must be considered too socially disruptive to be permitted; second, the act must be difficult to control through informal sanctions alone. By defining certain acts as crimes, political authorities ensure that the social reaction to them takes place in an orderly and predictable form. The law is thus used to specify the nature of the crime, to indicate which categories of persons are prohibited from performing the act, and to organize the use of formal negative sanctions against the offender.

Although many forms of deviance are defined as crimes, not all crimes are regarded as forms of deviance. Some crimes, such as jaywalking, are committed so frequently and ignored by social-control agencies so often that the offender is not stigmatized, even in the rare cases where an arrest does take place. Other acts are crimes only in a technical sense, in that the laws against them have fallen into disuse but are still on the books. A majority of Americans could doubtless be imprisoned if existing laws governing nonmarital sexual behavior or Sunday sport and entertainment were actually enforced. But as the American experiment with the prohibition of alcohol so conclusively demonstrated, any law that does not enjoy sufficient public support tends to become unenforceable and is eventually repealed or forgotten.

Like all forms of deviance, crime is a relative matter. In Singapore it is illegal for males to have long hair; in medieval Iceland it was illegal to write verses of more than a certain length about another person; in the Soviet Union it is illegal to form a new political party; in South Africa it is illegal to consume alcohol with a member of another race without a government permit. Although certain acts, such as murder, are regarded as criminal in all societies, each society defines these crimes in different ways. What may be murder in one society is regarded as a justifiable and even praiseworthy act in another. People in every society tend to regard the difference between criminal and noncriminal behavior as absolute and beyond question, but these distinctions are based entirely on the cultural assumptions of the time and place in question.

Types of Crime

The main types of crime in the United States can be conveniently classified into four principal categories: crimes of violence, crimes against property, crimes without victims, and white-collar crime.

Crimes of Violence

Crimes of violence are the ones that Americans fear the most. The cry for "law and order" rarely refers to senators who accept illegal campaign donations or middle-class homeowners who defraud insurance companies by making inflated claims; it refers to those offenses that put the victim at risk of bodily injury and even death. FBI statistics for 1979 show that, on average, a violent crime reportedly occurred in the United States every 27 seconds: a murder every 24 minutes, a forcible rape every 7 minutes, a robbery every 68 seconds, and an aggravated assault every 51 seconds. Violent crime represents only a miniscule proportion of crime as a whole, but this is small consolation to those who are its victims. In 1979, 5 out of every 100 Americans suffered a crime of violence, and 1 in every 10,000 was murdered. Moreover, the rate of violent crime is rising fairly rapidly: during the 1970s, it increased by 47.3 percent.

The fear of violent crime is heightened by anxiety about being attacked by a complete stranger, but in fact most people who are murdered, and a high proportion of those who are assaulted or raped, are already acquainted with the attacker. Murders and assaults are particularly likely to arise in the course of family arguments and romantic entanglements. The United States is an extremely violent country in which the general availability of guns and other

Figure 8.9 The homicide rate in the United States is without parallel in any other modern industrial society. One reason appears to be the ready availability of handguns, the weapons used in most murders.

weapons contributes to a homicide rate without parallel in other modern industrial societies. In 1979, over 10,000 people were murdered by handguns alone. A single city such as Detroit, Chicago, Houston, or Los Angeles records more murders in a single year than does the whole of England, where even the police do not carry guns.

Crimes Against Property

Crimes against property are those offenses in which the criminal steals or damages something that belongs to someone else. These crimes are far more common than those involving violence: on average, one occurs every 3 seconds, and in 1979, some 49 Americans in every 1000 were victims. The main forms of this offense are burglary (one every 10 seconds), larceny-theft (one every 5 seconds), motor-vehicle theft (one every 29 seconds), and arson. The FBI has only recently begun to keep detailed statistics on arson, but it is clear that the crime has become almost epidemic. Nearly 70,000 cases were reported in 1979, but since arson is often difficult to prove, the total number is undoubtedly much higher. Although vandalism and revenge often are behind this crime, insurance fraud is probably the most important factor.

Like the rate for violent crime, the property-crime rate increased markedly in the seventies—by 37.7 percent. Part of the increase in crime is more apparent than real, for it merely reflects greatly improved procedures for collecting and reporting the data. Of the real increase, much—but by no means all—was the result of a growth in the proportion of the population between the ages of sixteen and twenty-five. People in this category are arrested for 57 percent of the main violent and property crimes, so any increase or decrease in the number of persons in this age group relative to the entire population will affect the crime rate. The rest of the increase, however, does seem to reflect more extensive criminal activity in the population as a whole. The precise reason for this trend is not known, but the fact that hundreds of thousands of narcotics addicts must find large sums of money to support their daily habits must be a significant factor.

Crimes Without Victims

There is an entire category of offenses from which nobody suffers directly, except perhaps the offenders themselves. These are the victimless crimes, such as gambling, prosti-tution, vagrancy, illicit drug use, prohibited sexual acts between consenting adults, and the like (Schur, 1965). These acts are defined as crimes primarily because powerful social groups regard them as morally repugnant and have ensured that they are made illegal. The United States invests immense resources in its attempts to control victimless crime; well over a third of all arrests each year involve offenses of this kind. In 1979 there were over 1.1 million arrests for public drunkenness and about 37,000 for vagrancy, 55,000 for gambling, 89,000 for prostitution, 84,000 for curfew violations and loitering, and 558,000 for drug offenses—including over 391,000 arrests involving marijuana.

Victimless crime is notoriously difficult to control. One reason, of course, is that there is no aggrieved victim to bring a charge, or to give evidence, against the offender. Another reason is that the offenders often regard the laws, not themselves, as immoral: although they may be law-abiding in other respects, they feel no guilt at committing an offense such as smoking marijuana. The fact that such acts are illegal presents two additional problems. First, it stimulates the activities of organized crime, which, ever since Prohibition, has depended for its existence on supplying illegal goods and services, such as narcotics and gambling, to others who are willing to pay for them. Second, the prosecution of these petty offenders consumes an enormous amount of police effort and clogs the jails and the courts, at a time when the system can scarcely cope with more serious offenders.

White-Collar Crime

The phrase "white-collar crime" was first used by Edwin Sutherland (1940) to refer to offenses "committed by a person of respectability and high status in the course of his occupation." Sutherland documented the existence of this form of crime by investigating seventy large and respected corporations and establishing that they had accumulated a total of 890 criminal convictions. Behind these offenses of false advertising, copyright infringement, swindling, stock manipulation, price fixing, and so on, were highly respectable citizens. Many sociologists now extend the concept of white-collar crime to refer to all the crimes typically committed by high-status people, such as tax evasion, corruption of public officials, embezzlement, and fraud (Geis and Meier, 1977; Johnson and Douglas, 1978). White-collar

Figure 8.10

"In examining our books, Mr. Mathews promises to use generally accepted accounting principles, if you know what I mean."

Drawing by Wm. Hamilton; © 1972
The New Yorker Magazine, Inc.

crime is generally regarded with more tolerance than most other forms of crime, yet its economic impact is often greater. The President's Commission on Law Enforcement and the Administration of Justice (1967) compared the annual cost of four major categories of white-collar crime (embezzlement, forgery, tax evasion, and fraud) with the annual cost of four major categories of other crime (auto theft, robbery, burglary, and larceny) and found that the total cost of the white-collar crime was almost three times that of the other crimes. Since most white-collar crime probably goes either undetected or unreported, the total cost is doubtless much greater than these figures indicate.

The fact that this form of crime is so prevalent, even at the highest levels of society, raises serious doubts about traditional notions of criminals and crime. It has often been thought, for example, that "poverty breeds crime" by giving low-status people an incentive to steal and rob. There is doubtless much truth in this view, but it also seems that greed can breed crime in high-status people. In fact, there is not the slightest evidence that criminal behavior is any more common at the lower level of society than at any other. It seems, rather, that people of different statuses have different opportunities to commit various crimes. The criminal poor are hardly in a position to embezzle trust funds or manipulate the price of stocks, so they resort to high-risk, low-yield crimes such as larceny and burglary. The criminal nonpoor have no need to hold up gas stations or snatch purses, so they resort to low-risk, high-yield crimes such as tax evasion and computer fraud.

Who Are the Criminals?

At first sight it seems easy enough to establish who the criminals are: we need only look at the statistics published each year by the FBI in its *Uniform Crime Reports*. The 1979 report tells us that 40 percent of all persons arrested were under twenty-one, that males were five times more likely than females to be arrested, that persons arrested were much more likely to live in large cities than in small towns or rural areas, and that they were disproportionately likely to be black—in fact, blacks constituted 11.6 percent of the total population, but 24.7 percent of all arrestees.

The problem is that official crime statistics are highly suspect, largely because a great deal of crime is not reported at all, even if it is detected. Indeed, surveys indicate that the actual crime rate is probably two or three times as high as the official statistics indicate. The problem is compounded by the fact that the FBI reports statistics for only twenty-nine categories of crime and concentrates on eight offenses: murder, rape, robbery, aggravated assault, burglary, larceny, auto theft, and arson. White-collar crimes such as tax evasion, price-fixing, environmental pollution, bribery, and embezzlement are hardly mentioned in the reports. The inclusion of statistics on these crimes might substantially alter our picture of the "typical" criminal, who would become significantly whiter, older, more suburban, and more "respectable."

Most significant, the crime statistics exclude the largest group of criminals—those who escape detection. And the disconcerting fact is that this category includes virtually all of us. This does not mean, of course, that there are not important differences between people who are habitually law-abiding and people who are habitually criminal, or between people who commit minor crimes and people who commit serious ones. But a large number of self-report studies in which people were asked to give anonymous details of any crimes they have committed indicate that close to 100 percent of Americans have committed some kind of offense (Doleschal and Klapmuts, 1973). One study of New York residents, for example, found that 91 percent admitted that, as adults, they had broken at least one law for which they could have been fined or imprisoned (Wallerstein and Wylie, 1947). A national survey of youths between the ages of thirteen and sixteen found that 86 percent admitted delinquent acts, although only 4 percent had criminal records; studies of high school populations have uncovered thousands of violations by students with no police records; and in one study, over 90 percent of illegal acts reported by juveniles had gone undetected by the police (Empey and Erickson, 1966; Dentler and Monroe, 1961; Gold, 1970). These studies have a disturbing implication for our traditional distinctions between criminal and law-abiding citizens. The "typical" criminal is not the typical criminal at all but rather the one who typically gets arrested, prosecuted, and convicted. The tiny proportion of offenders who actually suffer formal negative sanctions for their acts are the product of a long process of social selection.

Selecting the Criminal

There are several stages in the process of selecting the criminal. Only a proportion of crimes are detected, only a proportion of those detected are reported to the police, only a proportion of those reported lead to an arrest, only a proportion of arrests lead to prosecution, only a proportion of prosecutions lead to conviction, and only a proportion of convictions lead to imprisonment. The evidence is overwhelming that the chances of going from one stage to the next depend largely on the social status of the offender (Chiricos and Waldo, 1975; Lizotte, 1978; Reiman, 1979; Hazel et al., 1980).

The crimes that go either undetected or unreported are predominantly petty crimes against property and "white-collar" offenses such as inflated insurance claims or tax evasion. When a crime is actually detected, the social status of the offender, all other things being equal, appears to be the determinant of whether an arrest and prosecution will follow. This tendency is especially apparent in the treatment of juvenile offenders. The great majority of juveniles in the arrest statistics are lower-class males, but this does not mean they commit most juvenile crimes—only that they are more likely to be arrested. Self-report studies of juveniles have found either little or no relationship between the incidence of delinquent acts and the social class of the offenders, or else have found that middle-class juveniles are actually more likely to commit crimes, including thefts and assaults (Doleschal and Klapmuts, 1973; Dentler and Monroe, 1961; Short and Nye, 1957; Gold, 1970; Hirschi, 1969; Williams and Gold, 1972; Voss, 1966; Tittle et al., 1978). Studies have also shown that contrary to the earlier assumptions of sociologists, juvenile crimes are more likely to be committed by people acting alone rather than in gangs (M. L. Erickson, 1971, 1973; Hindelang, 1971a). As David Matza (1964) points out, the distinction between delinquents and nondelinquents is a tenuous one at best; many young people are in a state of "drift" between basically conformist behavior and occasional misbehavior.

Why, then, are lower-class youths more likely to be selected for arrest? Two researchers, Irvin Piliavan and Scott Briar (1964), spent nine months riding in police cars of the juvenile bureau of a West Coast police department. They found that more than 90 percent of the incidents that came to police attention were very minor. In these cases the police were reluctant to take official action unless they felt that the offender had a basically "bad character." In making this assessment the police were guided by such cues as race, dress, and demeanor. Of those who were polite, contrite, and cooperative, less than 5 percent were arrested; but of those who were defiant, nonchalant, and uncooperative, fully two-thirds were arrested. William Chambliss (1973) studied two teen-age gangs in the same town, a lower-class gang he called the "Roughnecks" and a middle-class gang he called the "Saints." The Saints committed far more delinquent acts than the Roughnecks, but the Roughnecks were defined by the community as delinquents and were constantly in trouble. (His analysis appears in the reading at the end of this chapter, "The Saints and the Roughnecks.")

This pattern of selective perception and labeling appears to be fairly typical. Two separate incidents occurring at the same time in adjoining California neighborhoods illustrate this tendency further. In the first incident a group of high school seniors went on a rampage, committing crimes of arson, rape, auto theft, assault, and breaking and entering. In the second incident a nine-year-old boy stole a nickel from a schoolmate. But the high school seniors were from wealthy white families, and after a conference between community leaders and the police, they were simply returned to their parents for private discipline. The child who stole the nickel was from a black ghetto, and spent six weeks in a detention center awaiting a hearing of his case (Mitford, 1973). Another example of differential treatment is provided by an experiment conducted in Los Angeles by Frances Heussenstamm (1971). At the time, members of the Black Panther party were complaining that the police were bombarding them with traffic citations, a charge the police denied. Heussenstamm recruited twenty university students to attach "Black Panther Party" stickers to their cars. All the students had exemplary driving records and had received no citations in the previous year. In addition, they were instructed to drive with the utmost care, and their vehicles were thoroughly checked to make sure they were not defective. Within seventeen days the students had received a total of thirty-three traffic citations, and in several cases their cars were searched as well. The experiment came to an end at this point because a fund to pay fines had been exhausted.

The process of selecting the criminal continues when the offender appears in court. Although every accused person has the right to counsel, to pretrial bail, to a jury trial, and to appeal to higher courts, the system does not work this way in practice. Many people cannot afford bail and may spend weeks or months awaiting trial. Moreover, people who are not released on bail before a trial are likely to receive heavier sentences for the same offense than people who are freed. Actual courtroom procedure rarely follows the stylized confrontations seen in TV dramas. Over 90 percent of the people who appear in lower courts plead guilty and are sentenced on the spot. One reason is that the poor, unlike the rich, cannot afford their own lawyers. They have to rely on overworked court-appointed lawyers, who frequently urge them to plead guilty. Those who demand a jury trial and are eventually convicted tend to receive a more severe sentence than those who plead guilty. In effect, they are punished for wasting the court's time (Rosett and Cressey, 1976; Weinreb, 1977).

In comparison with their counterparts in other countries, American judges have exceptional discretion in determining the severity of the sentence, and there is strong evidence that the race and social class of the offender influence judicial decisions (Seymour, 1973; D. A. Bell, 1973).

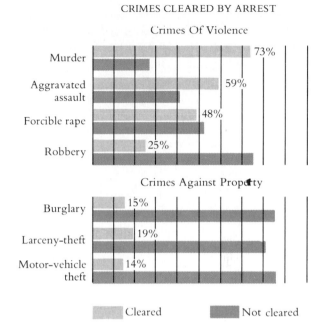

Source: *Crime in the United States: Uniform Crime Reports* (Washington, D.C.: U.S. Government Printing Office, 1979), p. 178.

Figure 8.11 On the whole, the police are not very successful at solving crimes: of all the serious offenses shown in this chart, only homicide results in an arrest in a majority of cases. The arrest rate for other crimes, such as white-collar offenses, is very much lower. Moreover, not all those arrested are actually prosecuted. The process of selecting the criminal continues in the courts, where some defendants are acquitted and others are found guilty of lesser crimes. Of those convicted, only a minority are eventually imprisoned.

In one experiment, three dozen judges were given fact sheets on hypothetical cases and asked to determine an appropriate sentence. The sheets contained the following basic information:

"Joe Cut," 27, pleads guilty to battery. He slashed his common-law wife on the arms with a switchblade. His record showed convictions for disturbing the peace, drunkenness, and hit-and-run driving. He told a probation officer that he acted in self-defense after his wife attacked him with a broom handle. The prosecutor recommended not more than five days in jail or a $100 fine.

On half of the fact sheets, however, "Joe Cut" was described as white and on the other half as black. The judges who thought he was white gave him sentences of three to ten days, while those who thought he was black gave him sentences of five to thirty days (D. Jackson, 1974).

Judges also tend to take the social status of a convicted criminal into account before passing sentence, frequently reasoning that a higher-status offender has "already suffered" through damage to reputation and perhaps loss of employment (Oelsner, 1972). Although most convicted car thieves go to prison for three years, business executives accused of white-collar crimes involving much larger stakes are more likely to be fined or to receive very short sentences. An outstanding example of differential treatment of offenders was provided by the trials that followed the Watergate and related scandals in the seventies. Vice-President Agnew pleaded "no contest" to a charge of tax evasion and received a fine, without even having to face the more serious charge that the money on which he had not paid taxes was obtained through bribery and extortion. High-status offenders in the Watergate cases generally received fines or light sentences, but low-status offenders—such as burglars who followed their superiors' instructions—were still in prison years later.

Prisons

Prisons are a relatively recent innovation. Until two centuries ago, convicts were more likely to be executed, tortured, deported, or exposed to public ridicule in the stocks. The original idea behind the prison was that it would provide the convict with the opportunity for solitary repentance and thus for rehabilitation, but this goal has

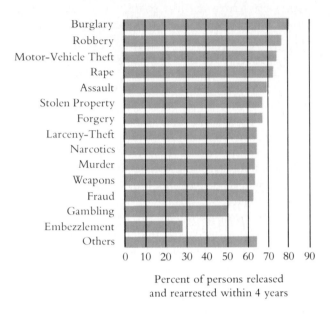

PERCENT REPEATERS BY TYPE OF CRIME

Percent of persons released
and rearrested within 4 years

Source: Crime in the United States: Uniform Crime Reports (Washington, D.C.: U.S. Government Printing Office, 1975), p. 45.

Figure 8.12 A substantial proportion of convicted offenders repeat their crime within a few years of conviction. The existing system of treating offenders is clearly failing in what most Americans, according to opinion polls, consider its main task to be: the reform of criminals.

certainly not been achieved in practice. Imprisonment is now regarded as having several distinct functions: *punishment* for the crime, *deterrence* for others who might be tempted to commit the crime themselves, *incapacitation* of the offenders by removing them from society, and *rehabilitation* by helping them develop the attitudes and skills that will enable them to take up a law-abiding life on release. A recent Harris poll showed that nearly 80 percent of the American public believes that rehabilitation should be the main aim of the prison system, but it is painfully clear that this goal is not being adequately addressed. Although the United States spends more than $1 billion a year on penal institutions, only five cents in each dollar is spent on rehabilitation. A 1975 FBI study found that 74 percent of offenders released after serving their prison time were rearrested within four years. Since other released prisoners presumably also returned to crime but were not arrested, the actual rate of crime among released convicts is probably even greater.

About 1.3 million offenders are held each day in the nation's 5000 local and county jails and 400 state and federal prisons. About half of these inmates have not been convicted of any crime, and of these, four out of five are eligible for bail but cannot raise the cash. Because its custodial function takes priority over all other goals, a prison is organized as what Erving Goffman (1961) calls a *total institution.* As we noted in Chapter 5 ("Socialization"), such institutions, which include army camps, traditional boarding schools, and mental asylums, are places of residence where the inmates are confined for an entire period of their lives. The inmates share a similar situation, are cut off from the rest of society, and are under the absolute control of the administrative authorities. Entry into a total institution is a transition in which people give up their former, self-determining roles and assume the roles of inmates. The new entrants are identified, examined, and coded and are stripped of their personal possessions and issued uniforms. There is an absolute division between the administrators and the residents; the latter surrender all personal control of their lives and are deprived of liberty, heterosexual outlets, and personal autonomy. Goffman argues forcefully that the very nature of a total institution aggravates the existing problems of the inmates, and in the long run can leave them incapable of assuming normal social responsibilities.

Advocates of prison reform also point to the effects of the differential association with other criminals that the prison environment guarantees. A Harris poll taken in the early seventies revealed that nearly two-thirds of American adults believe that "jails are the real breeders of crime," a view that probably has considerable validity. Prison inmates can scarcely fail to learn about new possibilities and techniques for crime. Separated from the rest of society and thrown into the company of criminals, they encounter "an excess of definitions favorable to violation of the law" and

Figure 8.13 Despite occasional and isolated reforms, the treatment of prisoners is not very different from what it was many decades ago. The prison is still a "total institution," in which criminals are thrown together under conditions of regimentation, overcrowding, boredom, tension, and even fear. These conditions seem more appropriate to outright revenge than to the prisons' supposed goal of rehabilitation.

may become predisposed toward further crime, not rehabilitation. The argument that radical reform of the corrections system is desirable does not imply, of course, that society should be "soft" on all criminals: some may be so dangerous and unreformable that imprisonment is the only alternative. James Q. Wilson (1975), for example, offers the interesting argument that society should stop wasting its energies on the counterproductive practice of imprisoning petty offenders, for whom other forms of correction might be more appropriate, and should concentrate instead on incapacitating dangerous and persistent offenders by locking them up for very long periods if necessary.

The Social Effects of Deviance

Deviance has a number of social consequences, some of which are dysfunctional and some of which are functional to society.

Dysfunctions of Deviance

The most obvious dysfunction of deviance is that widespread violation of significant social norms can disrupt social order by making social life unpredictable and causing tensions and conflict between conformist and deviant elements. This is true for small groups as well as the larger society. The idle worker can clog the flow of the assembly line, the psychotic can disrupt the family, the embezzler can threaten the commercial enterprise.

A second dysfunction of widespread deviance is that it diverts resources into efforts at social control when those resources could more usefully be directed elsewhere. Crime control in the United States is a case in point. The society would benefit considerably if the resources devoted to controlling this form of deviance could be channeled instead to more productive uses.

A third dysfunction of deviance is that it undermines trust. Social relationships are based on the assumption that people will behave according to accepted norms of conduct: that they will not break contracts, not exploit friendships, not molest children left in their care, not rob strangers they meet in the street. Widespread deviance undermines this trust and generates anxiety in everyone, conformists and deviants alike.

A fourth dysfunction of deviance is that if it goes unpunished in some people, it undermines other people's will to conform. The example of the stigmatized deviant is a powerful incentive to others to abide by the rules, and if deviants are seen to "get away with it," other people may be tempted to do the same. Many forms of deviance are pleasurable and profitable for the individual but disruptive for society, and unless deviance is closely controlled, it can spread, with sometimes dangerous consequences.

Functions of Deviance

The most important function of deviance is probably the one identified by Durkheim: the existence of deviance helps to clarify social norms and indicate the limits of social tolerance. It might be said that if there were no deviants, there could be no conformists; there can be no "we" without a corresponding "they."

The second function of deviance is implied by the first. By collectively reacting against deviants and deviance, conforming members of society reaffirm their norms and values and are thus made aware of their group solidarity. Provided it is kept within reasonable limits, deviance has the function, then, of maintaining the integration and cohesion of society.

A third function of deviance is that it serves as a safety valve for social discontent; people can violate the rules rather than attack the rules themselves. Resorting to prostitution, for example, allows men to find sexual satisfaction outside marriage without directly endangering the marriage system. If prostitution did not exist, extramarital sexual relations would be more likely to involve emotional attachments that would threaten the entire institution of marriage. Deviance can thus function to take the strain off the social order by preventing an excessive accumulation of discontent (Cohen, 1959).

A fourth function of deviance is that it may signal some defect in social organization. In certain circumstances norms are violated through *institutionalized evasion*—large-scale, patterned deviance involving many or most people in society. The institutionalized evasion that accompanied Prohibition or "blue laws" forbidding Sunday entertainment are useful examples; they showed that existing legislation was simply unenforceable. Other forms of deviance—such as excessive rates of alcoholism in some social

Figure 8.14 The most important function of deviance, perhaps, is that its presence indicates the boundaries of permissible behavior. When society punishes deviants, both the rules and the penalties for breaking them are made explicit to everyone, so the norms of conformity are reinforced. This was the main reason, in fact, why executions and other formal negative sanctions were so often performed in public in the past: the entire community could express solidarity against the offender. This picture shows early New England deviants in the stocks, where they had to endure the censure and taunts of the populace.

Deviance is not intrinsically "good" or "bad." It can be socially useful or threatening, depending on the circumstances. Nor is it a rare or temporary phenomenon that suddenly afflicts a society. It is an inevitable—and sometimes constructive—product of social living.

group or truancy from a particular school—also provide a signal that something is amiss (Cohen, 1959; Coser, 1962).

A final function of deviance is that it is often a source of social change: what is deviant today may be conformist tomorrow. Any person or group that sets out to change existing norms risks stigmatization for deviance, but these changes may be necessary and may not come about effectively or quickly unless people are prepared to take this risk. A contemporary example is offered by the women's liberation movement. In its initial stages, its leaders were ridiculed, scorned, and accused of lesbianism or sexual frustration, but the "deviant" roles and attitudes they espoused have become almost "conformist." Indeed, in some social groups today, it is the woman who adheres to traditional sex roles who is likely to be regarded as somewhat deviant.

Summary

1. Deviance refers to socially disapproved violations of important norms and expectations; deviants share the characteristic of stigma. Deviance is a relative matter, because the determination of who is deviant depends on who makes the definition.

2. Deviance signals a failure of social control. Social control is applied through the socialization process and through sanctions, which may be formal or informal, positive or negative. Some measure of deviance, however, reinforces social control by demonstrating the consequences of deviance to the rest of society.

3. Biological theories attempt to explain deviance in terms of inherited characteristics. Lombroso proposed that criminal tendencies are inherited. Sheldon proposed that they are linked to body type. Recent research suggests that some specific deviant tendencies, such as certain forms of mental disorder, may have hormonal or chromosomal origins, but no general category of deviance has been linked to inherited characteristics.

4. Anomie theory, as propounded by Merton, explains deviance as the result of a discrepancy between socially approved goals and access to socially approved means of achieving them. Individual reaction to this situation may take the form of conformity, innovation, ritualism, retreatism, or rebellion. This theory has been usefully applied to juvenile gangs.

5. Cultural-transmission theory, especially as expressed in the concept of differential association, regards deviant behavior as learned through intensive and regular contacts with other deviants. In a culturally heterogeneous society, people's acceptance of subcultural values may make them deviant in the eyes of the wider society.

6. Labeling theory explains deviance as a process through which some people successfully label others as deviant. People who engage in primary deviance may become habitual, secondary deviants after being labeled. Labeling often involves a conflict of values and interests; the socially powerful are able to label others as deviant in accordance with their own values.

7. The main types of crime in the United States may be classified as crimes of violence, crimes against property, crimes without victims, and white-collar crimes.

8. The selection of criminals involves a long process in which higher-status offenders are disproportionately more likely to escape sanctions. Only a small minority of offenders are ultimately imprisoned. Prisons are total institutions, and their nature is such that they are ineffective at rehabilitation.

9. Deviance has several dysfunctions: it disrupts social order, diverts social resources, undermines trust, and, if deviants go unpunished, undermines the will of others to conform. Deviance also has several functions: it clarifies social norms, maintains social integration among conformists, serves as a "safety valve" for discontent, signals defeats in social organization, and is a source of social change.

Important Terms

deviance (180)

stigma (180)

social control (181)

sanctions (181)

positive sanctions (181)

negative sanctions (181)

formal sanctions (181)

informal sanctions (181)

anomie (184)

conformity (185)

innovation (185)

ritualism (185)

retreatism (185)

rebellion (185)

cultural transmission (186)

differential association (186)

labeling (188)

primary deviance (188)

secondary deviance (188)

deviant career (188)

crime (190)

total institution (197)

Suggested Readings

BECKER, HOWARD S. *Outsiders.* New York: Free Press, 1963.

A highly influential book in which Becker outlines the labeling theory of deviance and applies the theory to various "outsiders," such as marijuana smokers.

CLINARD, MARSHALL B., and ROBERT F. MEIER. *Sociology of Deviant Behavior.* 5th ed. New York: Holt, Rinehart and Winston, 1979.

A comprehensive text on the sociology of deviance. The book is recommended for the student who wants to study the subject in detail.

ERIKSON, KAI T. *Wayward Puritans.* New York: Wiley, 1966.

A study of the early Puritans in Massachusetts. Erikson shows that the Puritans created deviants where none really existed and thus affirmed their own normality and solidarity.

MITFORD, JESSICA. *Kind and Usual Punishment.* New York: Knopf, 1973.

A critical look at the American criminal justice system. The book is interestingly written and contains many illustrations of failures in the system.

SCARPITTI, FRANK R., and SUSAN K. DATESMAN (eds.). *Drugs and Youth Culture.* Beverly Hills, Calif.: Sage, 1980.

A useful collection of articles on a significant form of deviance in contemporary America, the use of illicit drugs by young people.

SILBERMAN, CHARLES E. *Criminal Violence, Criminal Justice.* New York: Random House, 1978.

An important and readable discussion of crime in the United States, with particular emphasis on violent crime and its relationship to race and poverty.

SYKES, GRESHAM M. *Criminology.* New York: Harcourt Brace Jovanovitch, 1978.

An excellent introductory text on criminology, offering a lucid and thorough overview of the field.

SZASZ, THOMAS. *The Manufacture of Madness.* New York: Harper & Row, 1970.

A highly controversial book, in which Szasz argues forcefully that the label "mental illness" is often used by society as a means of social control over certain types of deviants.

WILSON, JAMES Q. *Thinking About Crime.* New York: Basic Books, 1975.

A provocative and well-argued analysis of crime and deterrence; the author urges a more pragmatic and tougher approach to criminals.

Reading

The Saints and the Roughnecks   *William J. Chambliss*

Two youth gangs in a small community were equally delinquent. Yet one gang was perceived by the community as nothing more than a group of high-spirited youths having a good time, while the other was perceived as delinquent. Chambliss uses labeling theory to explain why.

Eight promising young men—children of good, stable, white upper-middle-class families, active in school affairs, good pre-college students—were some of the most delinquent boys at Hanibal High School. The Saints were constantly occupied with truancy, drinking, wild driving, petty theft and vandalism. Yet not one was officially arrested for any misdeed during the two years I observed them.

This record was particularly surprising in light of my observations during the same two years of another gang of Hanibal High School students, six lower-class white boys known as the Roughnecks. The Roughnecks were constantly in trouble with police and community even though their rate of delinquency was about equal with that of the Saints. What was the cause of this disparity?

By midnight on Fridays and Saturdays the Saints were usually thoroughly high, and one or two of them were often so drunk they had to be carried to the cars. Then the boys drove around town, calling obscenities to women and girls; occasionally trying (unsuccessfully so far as I could tell) to pick girls up; and driving recklessly through red lights and at high speeds with their lights out. Occasionally they played "chicken."

Searching for "fair game" for a prank was the boys' principal activity after they left the tavern. The boys would drive alongside a foot patrolman and ask direc-

tions to some street. If the policeman leaned on the car in the course of answering the question, the driver would speed away, causing him to lose his balance. The Saints were careful to play this prank only in an area where they were not going to spend much time and where they could quickly disappear around a corner to avoid having their license plate number taken.

Construction sites and road repair areas were the special province of the Saints' mischief. A soon-to-be-repaired hole in the road inevitably invited the Saints to remove lanterns and wooden barricades and put them in the car, leaving the hole unprotected. The boys would find a safe vantage point and wait for an unsuspecting motorist to drive into the hole. Often, though not always, the boys would go up to the motorist and commiserate with him about the dreadful way the city protected its citizenry.

Leaving the scene of the open hole and the motorist, the boys would then go searching for an appropriate place to erect the stolen barricade. An "appropriate place" was often a spot on a highway near a curve in the road where the barricade would not be seen by an oncoming motorist. The boys would wait to watch an unsuspecting motorist attempt to stop and (usually) crash into the wooden barricade. With saintly bearing the boys might offer help.

Abandoned houses, especially if they were located in out-of-the-way places, were fair game for destruction and spontaneous vandalism. The boys would break windows, remove furniture to the yard and tear it apart, urinate on the walls and scrawl obscenities inside.

The Saints were highly successful in

school. The average grade for the group was "B," with two of the boys having close to a straight "A" average. Almost all of the boys were popular and many of them held offices in the school. One of the boys was vice-president of the student body one year. Six of the boys played on athletic teams.

At the end of their senior year, the student body selected ten seniors for special recognition as the "school wheels"; four of the ten were Saints. Teachers and school officials saw no problem with any of these boys and anticipated that they would all "make something of themselves."

How the boys managed to maintain this impression is surprising in view of their actual behavior while in school. Their technique for covering truancy was so successful that teachers did not even realize that the boys were absent from school much of the time. Occasionally, of course, the system would backfire and then the boy was on his own. A boy who was caught would be most contrite, would plead guilty and ask for mercy. He inevitably got the mercy he sought.

The local police saw the Saints as good boys who were among the leaders of the youth in the community. Rarely, the boys might be stopped in town for speeding or for running a stop sign. When this happened the boys were always polite, contrite and pled for mercy. As in school, they received the mercy they asked for. None ever received a ticket or was taken into the precinct by the local police.

Hanibal townspeople never perceived the Saints' high level of delinquency. The Saints were good boys who just went in for an occasional prank. After all, they were well dressed, well mannered and had nice cars. The Roughnecks were a different story. Although the two gangs of boys were the same age, and both groups engaged in an equal amount of wild-oat sowing, everyone agreed that the not-so-well-dressed, not-so-well-mannered, not-so-rich boys were heading for trouble.

The fighting activities of the group were fairly readily and accurately perceived by almost everyone. At least once a month, the boys would get into some sort of fight, although most fights were scraps between members of the group or involved only one member of the group and some peripheral hanger-on.

More serious than fighting, had the community been aware of it, was theft. Although almost everyone was aware that the boys occasionally stole things, they did not realize the extent of the activity. Petty stealing was a frequent event for the Roughnecks. Sometimes they stole as a group and coordinated their efforts; other times they stole in pairs. Rarely did they steal alone.

The thefts ranged from very small things like paperback books, comics and ballpoint pens to expensive items like watches. The nature of the thefts varied from time to time. The gang would go through a period of systematically shoplifting items from automobiles or school lockers. Types of thievery varied with the whim of the gang. Some forms of thievery were more profitable than others, but all thefts were for profit, not just thrills.

Roughnecks siphoned gasoline from cars as often as they had access to an automobile, which was not very often. Unlike the Saints, who owned their own cars, the Roughnecks would have to borrow their parents' cars, an event which oc-

curred only eight or nine times a year. The boys claimed to have stolen cars for joy rides from time to time.

There was a high level of mutual distrust and dislike between the Roughnecks and the police. The boys felt very strongly that the police were unfair and corrupt. Some evidence existed that the boys were correct in their perception.

The main source of the boys' dislike for the police undoubtedly stemmed from the fact that the police would sporadically harass the group. From the standpoint of the boys, these acts of occasional enforcement of the law were whimsical and uncalled for. It made no sense to them, for example, that the police would come to the corner occasionally and threaten them with arrest for loitering when the night before the boys had been out siphoning gasoline from cars and the police had been nowhere in sight. To the boys, the police were stupid on the one hand, for not being where they should have been and catching the boys in a serious offense, and unfair on the other hand, for trumping up "loitering" charges against them.

Over the period that the group was under observation, each member was arrested at least once. Several of the boys were arrested a number of times and spent at least one night in jail. While most were never taken to court, two of the boys were sentenced to six months' incarceration in boys' schools.

The Roughnecks' behavior in school was not particularly disruptive. During school hours they did not all hang around together, but tended instead to spend most of their time with one or two other members of the gang who were their special buddies. Although every member of

the gang attempted to avoid school as much as possible, they were not particularly successful and most of them attended school with surprising regularity. They considered school a burden—something to be gotten through with a minimum of conflict.

Teachers saw the boys the way the general community did, as heading for trouble, as being uninterested in making something of themselves. Some were also seen as being incapable of meeting the academic standards of the school. Most of the teachers expressed concern for this group of boys and were willing to pass them despite poor performance, in the belief that failing them would only aggravate the problem.

Why did the community, the school and the police react to the Saints as though they were good, upstanding, nondelinquent youths with bright futures but to the Roughnecks as though they were tough, young criminals who were headed for trouble? Why did the Roughnecks and the Saints in fact have quite different careers after high school—careers which, by and large, lived up to the expectations of the community?

Differential treatment of the two gangs resulted in part because one gang was infinitely more visible than the other. This differential visibility was a direct function of the economic standing of the families. The Saints had access to automobiles and were able to remove themselves from the sight of the community. In as routine a decision as to where to go to have a milkshake after school, the Saints stayed away from the mainstream of community life. Lacking transportation, the Roughnecks could not make it to the edge of town. The center of town was the only practical place for them to meet since their homes were scattered throughout the town and any noncentral meeting place put an undue hardship on some members. Through necessity the Roughnecks congregated in a crowded area where everyone in the community passed frequently, including teachers and law enforcement officers. They could easily see the Roughnecks hanging around the drugstore.

On their escapades the Saints were also relatively invisible, since they left Hanibal and travelled to Big City. Here, too, they were mobile, roaming the city, rarely going to the same area twice.

To the notion of visibility must be added the difference in the responses of group members to outside intervention with their activities. If one of the Saints was confronted with an accusing policeman, even if he felt he was truly innocent of a wrongdoing, his demeanor was apologetic and penitent. A Roughneck's attitude was almost the polar opposite. When confronted with a threatening adult authority, even one who tried to be pleasant, the Roughneck's hostility and disdain were clearly observable. Sometimes he might attempt to put up a veneer of respect, but it was thin and was not accepted as sincere by the authority.

In the eyes of the police and school officials, a boy who drinks in an alley and stands intoxicated on the street corner is committing a more serious offense than is a boy who drinks to inebriation in a nightclub or a tavern and drives around afterwards in a car. Similarly, a boy who steals a wallet from a store will be viewed as having committed a more serious offense than a boy who steals a lantern from a construction site.

Visibility, demeanor and bias are surface variables which explain the day-to-day operations of the police. Why do these surface variables operate as they do? Why did the police choose to disregard the Saints' delinquencies while breathing down the backs of the Roughnecks?

The answer lies in the class structure of American society and the control of legal institutions by those at the top of the class structure. Obviously, no representative of the upper class drew up the operational chart for the police which led them to look in the ghettoes and on street corners—which led them to see the demeanor of lower-class youth as troublesome and that of upper-middle-class youth as tolerable. Rather, the procedures simply developed from experience—experience with irate and influential upper-middle-class parents insisting that their son's vandalism was simply a prank and his drunkenness only a momentary "sowing of wild oats"—experience with cooperative or indifferent, powerless, lower-class parents who acquiesced to the laws' definition of their son's behavior.

The community responded to the Roughnecks as boys in trouble, and the boys agreed with that perception. Their pattern of deviancy was reinforced, and breaking away from it became increasingly unlikely. Once the boys acquired an image of themselves as deviants, they selected new friends who affirmed that self-image. As that self-conception became more firmly entrenched, they also became willing to try new and more extreme deviances. With their growing alienation came freer expression of disrespect and hostility for representatives of the legitimate society. This disrespect increased the community's negativism, perpetuating the entire process of commitment to deviance. Lack of a commitment to deviance works the same way.

Selective perception and labeling—finding, processing and punishing some kinds of criminality and not others—means that visible, poor, nonmobile, outspoken, undiplomatic "tough" kids will be noticed, whether their actions are seriously delinquent or not. Other kids, who have established a reputation for being bright (even though underachieving), disciplined and involved in respectable activities, who are mobile and monied, will be invisible when they deviate from sanctioned activities. They'll sow their wild oats—perhaps even wider and thicker than their lower-class cohorts—but they won't be noticed. When it's time to leave adolescence most will follow the expected path, settling into the ways of the middle class, remembering fondly the delinquent but unnoticed fling of their youth. The Roughnecks and others like them may turn around, too. It is more likely that their noticeable deviance will have been so reinforced by police and community that their lives will be effectively channelled into careers consistent with their adolescent background.

Source: William J. Chambliss, "The Saints and the Roughnecks," *Society* (November 1973), pp. 24–31.

CHAPTER 9   *Sexuality and Society*

For centuries, the societies of the Western world have shrouded sexuality in myth, taboo, and ignorance. Even sociologists, supposedly dedicated to studying social behavior regardless of the prejudices and obstacles in the way, did not accept human sexuality as a legitimate field of research until after World War II. Yet the fact remains that every society contains two sexes, a feature that obviously has important and far-reaching implications for personal behavior and social life.

Sexuality is a significant ingredient of individual personality. Our self-concepts are strongly influenced by our feelings about our own sexuality—feelings that may range from competence or incompetence to guilt or moral self-righteousness. Much of our leisure time is occupied with sexual acts, thoughts, feelings, or even fears. Even in situations that are not defined as sexual—the street, the workplace, the college dining hall—undertones and overtones of sexuality are often present. Interpersonal communications and relationships are often rich in various forms of sexual expression, ranging from overt acts to the most subtle glances, gestures, and other signals.

Sexual relationships have an even greater importance in the broader societal context, especially when they are institutionalized in the form of marriage. The sexual bond between husband and wife is the basis of the marital arrangement, and marriage, in turn, is the basis of the family. The family is the fundamental institution in the social structure of all societies. It has the responsibility for, among other things, legitimate birth, primary socialization, the allocation of many ascribed statuses to its members, and the transmission of property and other rights from generation to generation. It is small wonder, then, that every society carefully regulates the sexual behavior of its members, channeling their biological potentials into outlets that are socially regarded as natural and moral.

Figure 9.1 Sexuality is an important element in both personal and social life. As this picture suggests, sexual thoughts and feelings are present even in everyday situations that are not usually defined as sexual, including public places.

The public discussion of sexuality in the Western world dates primarily from the work of Sigmund Freud (1856–1939), who shocked many of his contemporaries when he claimed that sexual impulses are present in human beings from the time of birth and are a crucial factor in adult personality. Other sex researchers, such as Havelock Ellis (1859–1939), amassed a great deal of information on sexual behavior, but much of it was based on hearsay and inaccurate personal impressions. These early researchers were continually harassed by critics who regarded the mere investigation of the subject as immoral. The breakthrough in sex research came in 1948, when Alfred Kinsey published a massive volume on the sexual behavior of American men, followed in 1953 by a companion volume on American women. Kinsey's surveys, which were sociological in method and presentation, became best sellers and encouraged the development of a sociology of sex.

The sociological perspective on human sexuality may at first seem to run counter to common sense and everyday experience. The sex drive appears to be essentially biological in its character and mode of expression. It involves the use of specific bodily organs and is linked to the biological process of maturation. To most people nothing seems more natural, or even more "instinctive," than that they should mate in a particular way with a member of the opposite sex. But this popular view is simply wrong, for unlike the sexual behavior of most other animals, our sexual responses are not dictated by genes. *Human sexual behavior and feelings are learned through the socialization process and generally conform to the prevailing norms of the society concerned.* We talk, think, and learn about sex. We place complex meanings on physical acts and personal emotions, and we do so according to specific cultural norms and values. Ideas about what is sexually appropriate or inappropriate, moral or immoral, erotic or offensive, are purely social in origin. Even people who deviate from the prevailing norms of their culture tend to do so in predictable, patterned ways that are typical of each society.

Some aspects of human sexuality are still imperfectly researched, partly because continuing social inhibitions have hindered the accumulation of the necessary information. Nevertheless, there is now sufficient scientific knowledge about sexual attitudes and behavior, in our own society and in many others, to provide an intelligent understanding of the subject. In this chapter we shall first examine the nature of human sexuality, especially as it is revealed in the widely varying practices of different societies. Then we shall review what is known about contemporary sexual values and behavior in North America. Finally, we shall apply the sociological perspective to four specific topics: the incest taboo, rape, homosexuality, and prostitution.

The Nature of Human Sexuality

Researchers in several disciplines now recognize that human sexual behavior is highly flexible and that we can learn to attach our erotic desires to almost anything— human beings, animals, inanimate objects such as shoes or underwear, or even the experience of pain and humiliation. Kingsley Davis (1971), one of the first sociologists to study sexual behavior, states flatly that "like other forms of behavior, sexual activity must be learned. Without socialization, human beings would not even know how to copulate." John Gagnon and William Simon (1973), two prominent sociologists of sex, observe that "the very experience of sexual excitement that seems to originate from hidden internal sources is in fact a learned process and it is only our insistence on the myths of naturalness that hides these social components from us." Alfred Kinsey (1953), a zoologist, wrote, "It is not so difficult to explain why a human animal does a particular thing sexually. It is more difficult to explain why each and every individual is not involved in every type of activity." Similar views have been expressed by psychologists, anthropologists, and medical scientists (for example, J.C. Coleman, 1976; Ford and Beach, 1951; Money and Ehrhardt, 1972). The same principle seems to apply to some higher primates as well. Harry Harlow's experiments with rhesus monkeys (discussed in Chapter 5, "Socialization") have shown that if monkeys are raised in isolation, they do not know how to mate in later life, and it is extremely difficult, especially in the case of the males, to teach them how to do so.

The human sex drive can usefully be compared to the hunger drive. We all have an innate tendency to feel hungry periodically, but we have to learn through the socialization process what we may eat and what we may not eat, although different societies teach rather different lessons in this regard. By taking various objects into its mouth, the infant soon learns which are edible and which are not. But the growing child also learns through interaction with other people that some items, although edible, are taboo and may not be eaten. Unlike the inhabitants of some societies, the well-socialized American who encounters a dog, rat, or spider does not for one moment consider the creature as "food": we have what seems to be an "instinctive," but is in fact a learned, aversion to the idea. The way we learn norms of sexual conduct is similar. We start with a basic, undirected drive and learn through the socialization process to recognize some stimuli as nonsexual, some as sexual and appropriate, and some as potentially sexual but taboo. The fact that our sex drive is so flexible is, of course, the reason every society goes to such lengths to regulate it. If we all behaved "instinctively" in a rigid and predictable manner, there would be no need for the guidelines supplied by powerful norms and taboos, and they would not exist.

Sexual Behavior in Other Cultures

The sexual practices approved by different societies vary greatly, but two general norms are universal. First, in no society may people mate at random. Every society has an *incest taboo,* a powerful prohibition against sexual contact between certain categories of relatives. Second, every society insists on at least some conformity to a norm of genital, heterosexual intercourse within the context of marriage. Without this norm there might be so much nonmarital or nonreproductive sexual activity that both the family and the society's capacity to reproduce itself would be undermined.

The most comprehensive study of cross-cultural variations in sexual behavior is that of Clellan Ford and Frank Beach (1951), who analyzed data from the United States and from 190 traditional, preindustrial societies. The data for these small-scale societies were drawn from the ethnographic reports of anthropologists, and the societies themselves were selected to provide as diverse a cultural and geographical sample as possible. The following data are from Ford and Beach unless otherwise indicated.

Conceptions of Beauty

A great deal is known about conceptions of female beauty in other cultures, but there is little information on the standards by which other peoples judge the attractiveness of men. The main reason, it seems, is that most societies have more specific ideas about female than about male beauty, for men are much more likely to be valued for characteristics other than physical appearance.

The most obvious fact about notions of female attractiveness is that there are few if any universal standards.

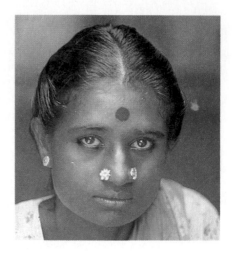

Figure 9.2 Conceptions of beauty and sexual attractiveness are culturally learned; in fact, what may be attractive in one culture may seem repulsive in another. Pictured here are a man from the Amazon jungle, a woman from Japan, a man from East Africa, a woman from India, a woman from Panama, a man from Chad, and an American beauty queen.

Some peoples regard the shape and color of the eyes as the main determinant of beauty; others are more concerned about the formation of the mouth, nose, or ears. In some societies small, slim women are admired, but there is a strong cross-cultural tendency for men to prefer fat women; in some African societies the sexy woman is one who is positively obese. The Thonga of eastern Africa admire a woman who is tall and powerful; the Tongans of Polynesia are more concerned that a woman's ankles be small. The Masai of eastern Africa prefer women with small breasts, whereas the Apache prefer women with very large breasts. In many tropical societies women do not cover their breasts, but this does not mean that the men are in a constant state of erotic frenzy. The breasts are simply not considered a sexual stimulus at all, and attention may focus instead on the legs, buttocks, back, or elsewhere. In Western cultures, notions of beauty have changed over time: the ideal female forms in the work of Reubens, Rembrandt, or Raphael are, to modern eyes, distinctly plump.

Restrictiveness and Permissiveness

Most societies in the Ford and Beach sample were more permissive than restrictive in their attitudes toward sexual behavior. Only ten of the societies wholly disapproved of both premarital and extramarital intercourse. Like the United States, these restrictive societies practice a public conspiracy to keep sexual knowledge from young children,

but some of them carry their prohibitions even further. Among the Arapaho Indians, for example, the sexes were strictly segregated from childhood and could not play together; in later adolescence they could meet only in the presence of chaperones. Among the Gilbertese Islanders of the Pacific a girl who was seduced could be put to death with her seducer, and among the Vedda of Ceylon a man seen merely talking to an unmarried woman could be killed by her relatives.

These attitudes contrast sharply with those of more permissive societies. Well over a third of the societies in the sample allow some form of what we would call adultery. The Siriono of Bolivia permit a man to have sexual relations with his wife's sisters and with his brothers' wives and their sisters. Among the Toda of southern India married men and women are free to form sexual liaisons with others; their language contains no word for adultery. Among many peoples, such as the Lesu of the Pacific, sexual knowledge is fully available to young children, and the parents openly copulate in front of them. The Trukese of the Carolines encourage sexual experimentation by children, and little huts are constructed outside the main compound for this purpose. The Lepcha of the Himalayas believe that young girls will not mature without the benefit of sexual intercourse, and Trobriand Island parents give their children sexual instruction at a very early age, enabling them to begin full intercourse at the age of six to eight for girls and ten to twelve for boys.

Heterosexual Behavior

There is very wide cross-cultural variation in the norms governing adult *heterosexual behavior.* Even the position that the partners adopt in sexual intercourse differs from one society to another. The usual position in most Western societies is for the couple to lie face to face with the male on top; Kinsey found that 70 percent of American couples had never tried any other position. In the South Sea Islands incredulous women laughingly called this approach the "missionary position," for it had been quite unknown to them until they had sexual intercourse with visiting missionaries. In a survey of the evidence from 131 other societies, the anthropologist Clyde Kluckhohn (1948) found that the "missionary position" was customary or preferred in only 17 cases. Other peoples conduct intercourse from the side, from the rear, with the female on top, with the male kneeling over the female, and in other positions.

The context and content of heterosexual intercourse is also highly variable. Some peoples regard full nakedness as desirable or obligatory; others, as quite improper or even dangerous. The Hopi Indians insist that intercourse take place indoors; the Witoto of South America insist that it take place outside. The Masai of eastern Africa believe that intercourse in the daytime can be fatal; the Chenchu of India believe that intercourse at night can lead to the birth of a blind child. Some people insist on privacy; others are indifferent to the presence of observers. Some, such as the

Trobriand Islanders, believe that women are sexually insatiable and expect them to take the initiative; others, such as the Chiricahua Indians, expect that a woman will remain completely passive. Kissing is unknown in some societies; the Siriono consider it a particulary disgusting act. Foreplay before intercourse is unknown among the Lepcha but may occupy several hours among the Ponapeans of the Pacific. Kinsey (1948) found that the great majority of American males reached orgasm within two minutes of starting intercourse, but the Marquesan men of the Pacific habitually perform for several hours. Even the frequency of intercourse is related to cultural norms. The Keraki of New Guinea are reported to average once a week; Americans, two or three times a week; the Aranda of Australia, three to five times a day; and the Chagga of eastern Africa are alleged to manage ten episodes in a single night. Some peoples have learned to experience violence during intercourse as erotically exciting. The Siriono find pleasure in poking their fingers into each others' eyes; Choroti women in South America spit in their partners' faces; Ponapean men tug out tufts of their mates' hair; and Apinaye women in the Brazilian jungle are reported to bite off pieces of their lovers' eyebrows, noisily spitting them aside to enhance the erotic effect.

Figure 9.3

"What's new on the sexual front? Are our chaps still on top?"

Homosexual Behavior

Attitudes toward *homosexual behavior* vary widely. In a minority of the societies in the Ford and Beach sample homosexual behavior is thoroughly disapproved of; some peoples react only with ridicule, but others, such as the Rwala Bedouins, consider the death penalty an appropriate response. In about two-thirds of the societies, however, homosexuality is tolerated, approved, or even required—either for some members of the community all the time, or for all males in the community for some of the time. Male homosexuality is almost everywhere more common and more likely to be accepted than female homosexuality. All societies that permit very extensive homosexual practices also expect those involved to be heterosexual or bisexual at some point in the life cycle.

Some societies, such as the Lango of eastern Africa, the Koniag of Alaska, and the Tanala of Madagascar, allow marriages between men. In a few societies, particularly in Siberia and among some Indian peoples of North and South America, there was a clearly defined homosexual role that had specific social duties attached to it, often those of the tribal shaman. Clyde Kluckhohn (1948) found that male homosexuality was accepted by 120 American Indian peoples and rejected by 54; in many of the former groups the homosexual had high social status. In some societies, such as the Aranda of Australia, the Siwans of northern Africa, and the Keraki of New Guinea, every male is required to engage in exclusively homosexual behavior during adolescence but is expected to be bisexual after marriage. Among the Keraki, for example, the initiation ceremony for adolescent males requires them to take the passive role in anal intercourse for a full year; thereafter they spend the remainder of their youth initiating younger boys in like manner. (The social function of this behavior seems to be to prevent illegitimate births by diverting adolescent sexual energies away from heterosexual intercourse—a goal that other societies try to achieve by means ranging from strict dating practices to the use of contraceptives.) The ethnographic literature appears to record only two societies in which homosexuality is actually preferred to heterosexuality, although both these societies have also institutionalized heterosexual marriage. The Etero, a New Guinea tribe, place a taboo on heterosexual intercourse for 295 days a year, while the neighboring Marindanim people are so strongly homosexual that they sometimes have to resort to kidnapping children from surrounding tribes in order to maintain their population size (Van Baal, 1966; Kelly, 1977; Kottak, 1978).

Evaluation

This cross-cultural evidence can be misleading in one respect, for it deals only with the sexual practices of small, preliterate societies. No comparable study of modern industrial societies has been made, but it seems likely that sexual behavior in these societies, like most other aspects of their cultures, is subject to much less variation. Since the majority of the world's population lives in industrialized or industrializing societies, it seems safe to conclude that the sexual practices of most people in the world no longer differ radically from our own. The evidence from these preindustrial societies is very valuable, however, for it shows how the interplay between biological potentials and cultural norms produces the extraordinary diversity of human sexual conduct.

The conclusion from the cross-cultural data may be disconcerting to some, but it is inescapable. If you were an Alorese mother in Indonesia, you would habitually masturbate your infants to pacify them. If you were a Siwan male in northern Africa, you would engage freely in both heterosexual and homosexual intercourse, and you might lend your son to other men for sexual purposes. If you were a male Copper Eskimo, you might have intercourse with live or dead animals. If you were a Chewa parent in central Africa, you would encourage your preadolescent daughter to have intercourse in the belief that she would otherwise be infertile when she grew up. If you were a Kwoma male in New Guinea, you would have learned to regard sex as so forbidding that you would never touch your own genitals, even when urinating. If you were an adolescent girl in traditional Mohave society, you would expect your first heterosexual intercourse to involve anal penetration. You would do these things with the full knowledge and approval of your community, and if your personal tastes ran counter to the prevailing norms, you might be considered distinctly odd—even wicked. Being no less ethnocentric than peoples in other societies, you would also regard American sexual attitudes and practices as most peculiar, to say the least.

Sexual Behavior in America

The most striking feature of sexuality in America is the tension between a tradition of highly restrictive standards, on the one hand, and a climate that values individuality and personal freedom, on the other. Restrictive patterns of sexual behavior have long been regarded as the cornerstone of public and private morality, yet the pleasures of sexual gratification are constantly extolled, implicitly and explicitly, especially through the mass media. Not surprisingly, the attempt to maintain the standards of earlier generations is largely unsuccessful. As a result, there is a discrepancy between the sexuality portrayed in the *ideal culture* of norms and values and the sexuality actually practiced in the *real culture* of everyday life.

Traditional Values

The traditional sexual values of American society, and of Western society in general, have their roots in a particular interpretation of ancient Judeo-Christian morality. Sexual activity can have two basic purposes: reproduction and pleasure. The Western tradition has strongly emphasized the former and has taken a generally negative attitude toward the latter: sex was morally acceptable only if the partners were married and only if their primary purpose was reproduction (Boswell, 1980).

The tradition that the main purpose of sex is to produce children comes from the Old Testament, which urges the faithful to "be fruitful and multiply," censures those who "waste" their seed, and imposes severe penalties for nonreproductive sexual acts. Sexuality itself, however, was not regarded as sinful, and the Old Testament permitted premarital and extramarital sex under certain circumstances. (The commandment forbidding adultery refers only to adultery with someone else's spouse; a married man with an infertile wife could have intercourse with unmarried women, particularly household servants, if the intent was to produce children.) The emphasis on premarital virginity and the blanket prohibition on sex outside marriage comes from the New Testament—not from the teachings of Jesus, who had little to say about sex, but from those of Saint Paul, who recommended total abstention from sex. Saint Paul believed that celibacy was preferable even to marriage and tolerated marriage only on the grounds that it was

"better to marry than to burn." This view was strongly endorsed by such theologians as Saint Augustine and is the source of the Catholic Church's requirement of celibacy in its priests. By the early Middle Ages sex was virtually equated with sin; the doctrines of the medieval Church "were based, quite simply, upon the conviction that the sexual act was to be avoided like the plague, except for the bare minimum necessary to keep the race in existence. Even when performed for this purpose it remained a regrettable necessity. Those who could were exhorted to avoid it entirely" (G. Taylor, 1970). The Church even tried to limit the number of days on which a married couple could have sex. Intercourse on Sundays, Wednesdays, and eventually Fridays was forbidden, with the result that sexual activity was prohibited for the equivalent of about five months of the year.

Subsequent centuries were marked by alternating periods of restrictiveness and relative permissiveness, with particularly restrictive attitudes occurring among the early Puritans and among the Victorians of the past century (Bullough and Bullough, 1977). Prudery reached its climax with the middle-class Victorians, who were unable to refer to anything remotely sexual except in the most discreet terms. Sweat became "perspiration" and then "glow"; legs became "limbs"; underwear became "unmentionables"; chicken breast became "white meat"; prostitutes became "fallen women"; pregnancy became "an interesting condition." Women were careful to cover even their ankles from the gaze of men, and some zealots actually covered the legs of their furniture from the public view. Masturbation was

Figure 9.4 Traditional Western attitudes toward sexuality derive from a particular interpretation of Judeo-Christian morality. The Genesis tale of the sin of Adam and Eve and their subsequent expulsion from the Garden of Eden, depicted in this painting by the Italian artist Masaccio, has strong sexual overtones; forever after, the human species was sinful, and nakedness was shameful. Under the influence of Saint Paul, the medieval Church took a strongly negative attitude toward any sexual activity that was not aimed at reproduction; sexual activity for pleasure alone was considered immoral. Traces of this attitude still persist today.

regarded as a dreadful vice that caused such maladies as deafness, blindness, heart disease, epilepsy, hair on the palms, and insanity. Some lunatic asylums even had separate wards for inmates who were believed to be victims of this "self-abuse."

To the concern for reproduction and the sense of the erotic as sinful, one further ingredient was added in medieval times: the *double standard* of conduct for men and women. The tradition of chivalry and courtly love in the Middle Ages emphasized the purity and chastity of women, while acknowledging and tolerating the baser desires of men. Sex came to be seen as woman's noble duty and man's brutal pleasure. Women were expected to remain virtuous and innocent, while men, although formally expected to do the same, were in reality allowed much greater freedom. The notion of the inherent purity of women led to a widely accepted myth that (with the possible exception of prostitutes) they were essentially sexless. William Acton, a nineteenth-century expert on marriage, wrote that "the belief that women have a sexual appetite is a vile aspersion"; a surgeon-general of the United States stated that "nine-tenths of the time decent women feel not the slightest pleasure in intercourse"; and an eminent gynecologist felt that "sexual desire in a woman is pathological" (Hunt, 1959). The double standard has persisted until the present, particularly in the working class of the Western world. Premarital intercourse is frequently seen as a matter of surrender by the female and conquest by the male, with the woman's status being cheapened in the process and the man gaining status and respect among his peers.

These traditional values remain powerful in America today. Sex is still often regarded as somehow dirty and unmentionable, and practices that do not potentially lead to reproduction are widely considered perverted. Despite the introduction of sex-education programs into some schools, a conspiracy of silence may still prevent the young from obtaining accurate and objective information about sex. Parents, if they discuss the subject with their offspring at all, often do so with embarrassment, and most information is acquired from the peer group. Whatever else these attitudes achieve, they certainly contribute to many problems of sexual adjustment in later life. The young are often brought up to view sex as a forbidden and taboo subject, but as adults they are expected to unlearn these prohibitions without difficulty. This transition is not always smoothly

Figure 9.5   Although the general tendency throughout western European history has been toward a strongly negative view of sexuality, there have been occasional periods and occasional groups (particularly in the eleventh and twelfth centuries) in which more permissive attitudes have prevailed—as this illustration from a medieval manuscript suggests.

achieved. Frigidity in women is generally the result of earlier attitudes that sex is dirty and frightening, and impotence in men often stems from feelings of anxiousness and guilt (Cooper, 1969; Masters and Johnson, 1970, 1975).

The United States still attempts to control the private sexual behavior of consenting adults by law. About half of the states have laws against extramarital intercourse. Pros-

Figure 9.6 Considerable value conflict still exists in the United States over sexual standards and attitudes. Opinion polls and other research indicate that these different values are related to age, with older people generally adhering to more conservative standards and young people becoming increasingly permissive in their attitudes and behavior.

titution is illegal in every state except Nevada, where local counties can decide for themselves whether they will permit it. In addition, most states have "sodomy" laws, directed at what are often referred to as "crimes against nature." Oral-genital and anal-genital contacts, even between husband and wife, are illegal in over thirty states, with penalties of up to twenty years' imprisonment. Homosexual acts were illegal in all states until the late sixties, and they still carry severe penalities in most states. Until a few years ago Connecticut banned the use or sale of contraceptives, and Indiana has a law against encouraging anyone under twenty-one to masturbate. Some states regard any position for intercourse other than the "missionary position" as a crime against nature. Until the forties, half the states of the Union prohibited interracial sexual relations, another interesting example of how temporary norms are confused with absolute morality. Most of these laws have fallen into disuse, but prosecutions under some of

them are by no means unknown. These laws have few parallels in the modern world; Canada and the Western European nations have generally abandoned similar legislation, in some cases as long as a century ago. Indeed, the few other countries that still actively try to police private sexual behavior fall almost exclusively into two categories—communist-ruled states like the Soviet Union and Cuba, and fundamentalist Muslim nations like Iran and Saudi Arabia. In 1976, however, the U.S. Supreme Court upheld the rights of states to make laws regulating the private sexual behavior of consenting adults.

Contemporary Practices

Research into the sexual practices of Americans is very limited and often unreliable. The greatest obstacle to obtaining fuller knowledge is the difficulty of surveying a representative, random sample of the population. It is easy enough to use standard survey methods to discover how Americans will vote or which brand of soap they use, but it is much more difficult for researchers to inquire in depth into the sex lives of complete strangers. Understandably, many of those sampled will refuse to answer such questions. Since these people may differ in unknown but perhaps significant ways from those who are willing to answer, the results of the survey may be biased. No sex researchers have yet been able to overcome this problem as far as the general population is concerned, although there are many useful studies of specific groups—prostitutes, "swingers," homosexuals, transvestites, and so on. Even these studies, however, run into the difficulty that people may not tell the truth when asked for details of their sexual practices.

The first major research into the sexual behavior of Americans was that of Alfred Kinsey, who despite considerable harassment was able to obtain full histories of the sex lives of more than 16,000 Americans. Kinsey relied on two main sources: individual volunteers and specific groups of people, ranging from prison populations to sports clubs, which he persuaded to take part in his research. By trying to select people and groups from every walk of white American life, he attempted to put together a fairly representative cross-section of the white American population. His study was not statistically perfect by any means, but it remains the most ambitious and reliable sex survey ever undertaken. Other attempts at a national survey have been made since, but most are methodologically much less satis-factory. *Playboy* magazine, for example, commissioned a random survey, reported by Morton Hunt (1974). But the actual survey did not reach a random sample of the popu-lation: it left out "strongly deviant" individuals, and, worse, some 80 percent of those surveyed refused to coop-erate. *Psychology Today* magazine also asked its readers to return a detailed questionnaire, whose results were reported by Robert Athanasiou and his colleagues (1972). The findings, however, are presumably representative only of those readers of the magazine who responded. The same is true of *Cosmopolitan*'s 1980 readers' poll, despite the fact that 106,000 women participated in the survey. In a survey aimed only at young people, Robert Sorensen (1973) tried to get information from a random sample of teen-agers aged thirteen to nineteen. But the parents of 40 percent of the sample would not let their children take part and about 20 percent of those who were allowed to cooperate refused to do so, with the result that Sorensen's findings may also be biased in some way. Melvin Zelnick and John Kantner (1977, 1978), however, had a high rate of success in their interviews with national samples of teen-age women aged fifteen to nineteen, and their work seems to give a reliable picture of sexual behavior in this restricted part of the population.

Despite these difficulties, all the evidence points over-whelmingly in the same direction. There is a glaring gap between the moral norms specifying how Americans ought to behave and the statistical norms revealing how they actually do behave. Nowhere is this more evident than in Kinsey's volumes, *Sexual Behavior in the Human Male* (1948) and *Sexual Behavior in the Human Female* (1953), which stunned American society with revelations of wide-spread deviation from moral norms.

Kinsey found, for example, that 85 percent of all men had experienced premarital intercourse. Nearly 70 percent of the men had visited a prostitute. One man in six had as much homosexual as heterosexual experience. Over 90 percent of the men had masturbated, and nearly 60 percent had engaged in heterosexual oral-genital contacts. Half the married men had committed adultery, and a further 25 percent favored the idea of doing so. About 8 percent of the men had engaged in sexual contacts with animals, and among some rural populations the proportion rose as high as 50 percent. In accordance with the double standard, 40 percent of the men wanted their spouses to be virgins at the time of marriage. Nearly half the women had experienced premarital intercourse, although in the great majority of cases their only partner had been their prospective husband. A quarter of the married women had committed adultery, 28 percent had had homosexual experience or desires, nearly 60 percent had masturbated, nearly 60 percent had engaged in heterosexual oral-genital contacts, and nearly 4 percent had taken part in sexual activities with animals. On this evidence, Kinsey concluded that "a call for a cleanup of sex offenders in the community is in effect a proposal that 5 percent of the population should support the other 95 percent in penal institutions."

Recent studies all confirm that sexual behavior in the United States is much more permissive than the moral norms would suggest. Morton Hunt's study, for example, found that 95 percent of the males and 85 percent of the females under the age of twenty-four had experienced premarital intercourse. He also found that only a quarter of his sample considered anal intercourse "wrong" and that nearly a quarter of married couples under the age of thirty-five have used the technique. Robert Sorensen's survey of teen-agers found that by the age of nineteen, 59 percent of the boys and 45 percent of the girls had experi-enced intercourse; 13 percent of the sample had done so by the age of twelve or younger. Melvin Zelnick and his associates (1979) found that two-thirds of American teen-age women have had intercourse by the time they are nineteen, by which age a quarter of them have become pregnant—in nearly all cases, premaritally.

These findings, together with such highly publicized phenomena as readily obtained abortions, nudity in the movies, gay liberation, and the availability of pornography, appear to indicate that there has been a sexual revolution. But appearances can be deceptive, and closer examination of the evidence suggests that the revolution is primarily one of attitudes, not behavior. The real sexual revolution began, largely unnoticed, much earlier in the century—certainly before World War II. Developments since that time have simply been a continuation of the trend that sociologists believe was rather abruptly established then. Social norms and values are now finally catching up with social behavior; what was previously concealed and private is now becom-ing open and public. The trend toward greater permissive-ness is a long-term one, propelled by a complex of factors.

Figure 9.7 A couple dancing the Charleston in the 1920s. The real sexual revolution began during this era, but because people still professed values that they did not practice, it passed largely unnoticed. The sexual "revolution" of recent decades is primarily a revolution of attitudes and values, not behavior.

Another obvious change is in the amount and availability of pornography in the United States: more than 85 percent of adult men and 70 percent of adult women have been exposed to it. Most regular users of pornography are male, middle-aged, white, middle class, and married, and well over a quarter of the adult male population has frequent experience of pornographic material. Although there is some concern that pornography may stimulate sex crimes, the reverse appears to be the case. Pornography may actually serve as an outlet for people who might otherwise find satisfaction in less acceptable ways: indeed, studies of sex offenders have consistently shown that they have had less experience of pornography than nonoffenders. After considering a mass of research evidence, the President's Commission on Obscenity and Pornography (1970) concluded that "there is no evidence that exposure to pornography operates as a cause of misconduct in either youths or adults." The commission specifically rejected the view that the material has "a detrimental effect upon moral character, sexual orientation, or attitudes" of young people.

The most important change in recent years appears to be a redefinition of sexual morality. Right and wrong in matters sexual are now being judged less and less in terms of the absolute rules handed down by earlier generations. Instead, it seems that judgments about sexual morality are increasingly based on the attitude that any behavior is acceptable as long as it involves mutual respect, is experienced as pleasant, and does not do any physical or psychological harm to those involved.

The Incest Taboo

The problem of the incest taboo offers a useful example of how sociological analysis can explain an otherwise puzzling practice. Every known society has had an incest taboo that prohibits sexual relations between specific categories of relatives. The taboo almost always applies to relations between parent and child and between brother and sister, and it always applies to other classes of relatives as well, although different societies have different rules in this regard.

The exceptions to the parent–child and brother–sister rule are few and far between. Brother and sister were expected to marry in the royal families of ancient Egypt, Hawaii, and Peru, probably to prevent defilement of the

The most important of these are the development of birth-control techniques, which permit a separation of the reproductive and the pleasurable aspects of intercourse, and the general erosion of traditions in all industrial societies.

The changes that have taken place in recent years are probably fewer than are generally realized. One that is quite evident, however, is the rapid decline of the double standard. Although premarital sexual intercourse and even promiscuity are still more acceptable in men than in women, the stigma that previously attached to such behavior is disappearing. Norms of female chastity make little sense from a functional point of view when contraception enables women to be sexually active with the kind of freedom that was previously reserved for men.

royal lineage by commoners. The Thonga of West Africa permit a father to have ritual intercourse with his daughter before he goes on a lion hunt; the Azande of central Africa expect their highest chiefs to marry their daughters; and the mothers of Burundi are expected to cure impotence in their adult sons by having intercourse with them. There is also evidence that brother-sister and parent–child marriages were occasionally practiced among the general population at certain periods in ancient Egypt and Iran, perhaps as a means of keeping property within the family (Ford and Beach, 1951; Murdock, 1949; La Barre, 1954; Albert, 1963; Middleton, 1962). The general cross-cultural rule, however, is that people regard intercourse with certain close relatives as utterly immoral and even unthinkable. Why?

A ready response might be that the taboo is instinctive, because we certainly experience our reaction to the idea of incest as though it were an "instinct." But this view is clearly wrong, for several reasons. First, no other animal observes an incest taboo, and it is highly unlikely that we, who rely less than any other species on inherited behavior, would have evolved an instinct that all other animals lack. Second, if the attitude to incest were instinctive, there would be no need for the taboo—yet every society finds it necessary to have the taboo and laws to prevent the behavior. As social workers and others have long known, incest—usually father-daughter, but sometimes brother-sister—is a fairly common crime, although it is rarely reported (Justice and Justice, 1979.) Third, definitions of incest vary from one society to another. In some societies it is incestuous to marry any cousin; in other societies all cousins may intermarry. In some societies it is incestuous to marry the child of one's father's brother or one's mother's sister, but it is obligatory to marry the child of one's father's sister or one's mother's brother, even though all these cousins are equally closely related. The Mundugumor of New Guinea recognize blood relationships in such a complex way that three-quarters of all women in the society are ineligible as sex partners for any given man, and seven women out of eight are ineligible as wives. It would be a very strange instinct indeed that turned up in such different guises in different societies, scrupulously observing local and national boundaries in the process.

A second likely response might be that the incest taboo exists to prevent the physical and mental degeneration that comes from inbreeding. This explanation sounds plausible,

but for several reasons it is also incorrect. First, inbreeding does not necessarily produce degeneration: it merely intensifies certain traits, good or bad, that are already present in the related partners. Brother-sister marriages in Egypt and among the Inca resulted in no degeneration over as many as fourteen generations; indeed, the beautiful and intelligent Cleopatra was the product of such a union. Agricultural scientists now use selective inbreeding, in fact, to produce healthier stock. Second, any ill effects of inbreeding usually take place too slowly and too haphazardly to be noticeable over a few generations. People living in simple, traditional societies would not be likely to link cause and effect, especially when other explanations, such as illness or witchcraft, are more readily available. Third, some peoples apparently failed to recognize that pregnancy is the result of intercourse: the Trobriand Islanders, for example, denied that intercourse leads to conception, and other peoples attribute pregnancy to the work of their dead ancestors. Yet these societies have some of the most complex incest taboos ever recorded.

Then why the taboo? There are three main reasons, and they are social, not biological. The first is that early human beings—living primarily in small kinship groups of hunters and gatherers—needed to protect themselves by forming alliances with other groups. By forcing their children to marry into families outside their own, each group widened its social links and provided itself with allies in time of conflict and help in time of famine or other hazards. These groups, it has been said, faced the alternatives of marrying out or dying out. Marriage in most traditional societies is a bond between groups, not individuals. That is why marriages are arranged by the parents, often when their offspring are still children and sometimes even before they are born (White, 1969). The same principle was applied for centuries in European diplomacy: allegiances among entire societies were formed by arranged marriages between members of their respective royal families.

The second reason for the incest taboo is that the family itself could not function without it. As Kingsley Davis (1948) points out:

> The confusion of statuses would be phenomenal. The incestuous child of a father-daughter union, for example, would be a brother of his own mother, i.e. the son of his own sister; a stepson of his own grandmother; possibly a brother of his own uncle; and certainly a grandson of his own father.

The third reason is that without an incest taboo, sexual rivalry between family members would disrupt the normal roles and attitudes of the various relatives. The father, for example, might experience role conflict as both the disciplinarian and the lover of his daughter; the mother might be jealous of both. Faced with constant conflict and tension, the family institution might simply disintegrate.

Of course, neither traditional nor modern societies consciously appreciate the reasons for the taboo. They and we simply accept it as natural and moral.

Rape

Rape is a terrifying, brutal, and sometimes life-threatening crime, one that often leaves deep, long-term psychological scars. It is estimated that there are 280,000 incidents of rape in the United States each year, only a fourth of which are brought to the attention of the police. The reason that rape is so underreported is that most victims, in addition to being traumatized by the crime itself, are unwilling to relive the experience by submitting to police interrogation, medical examination, and court proceedings. The fear of this crime touches virtually all women, instilling in them a wariness of male strangers and an apprehension about walking alone at night or being in deserted places.

Although many people still regard rape as an expression of unrestrained, impulsive sexual desire, the sociological and psychological research of recent years has proven this view to be a myth. Rape is a crime of violence, not of passion; it is a ritual of power and humiliation which, although socially regarded as intolerable, has its origins in approved patterns of interaction between the sexes (Brownmiller, 1975; Chappell et al., 1977).

The Social Context

The social relations of the sexes are marked by two features relevant to rape: the domination of women by men, and the tendency of men to view women as actual or potential sexual property—that is, as sex objects. A classic example of this tendency is the barrage of whistles, catcalls, and obscene suggestions that often assails a young woman walking past a group of male construction workers. Since the likelihood that the woman will respond favorably to this kind of attention is approximately zero, the behavior clearly serves

Figure 9.8 When a man and a woman pass close together, they almost always turn as they do in this picture—the man toward the woman, the woman away from the man. This subtle form of body language reflects the different roles that men and women commonly play in their interaction with one another: the man as aggressor and pursuer, the woman as nonaggressive and pursued. (You might wish to observe some bottleneck in human traffic for a while, and see this body language being enacted over and over again.)

some other purposes. What it actually does is to allow the men to bolster their own egos, to demonstrate their "masculinity" to their peers, and to reassert their view that the role of women is to gratify men.

In fact, this view of women is quite prevalent in the workplace, where the sexual harassment of women is a common and serious problem. In the office or factory, as elsewhere in society, men have a virtual monopoly of power and influence. All too often, they take advantage of

Men Talking About Women

In casual conversations among themselves, men reveal a great deal about their attitudes toward women. The following comments about women, sexuality, and rape were made in a tavern frequented by blue-collar workers, and were recorded by E. E. LeMasters, a sociologist who was a participant observer there.

It is difficult, if not impossible, to talk with men at The Oasis about the opposite sex without feeling that they view women with suspicion and distrust....

One man said: "The trouble with American women is they don't know their place. I was in Japan after World War II and by God those women know who is boss. You tell one of them babes to jump and all they ask is, 'how high?' But an American woman will say, 'why?'"

. . .

"What in the hell are they complaining about?" one man asked. "My wife has an automatic washer in the kitchen, a dryer, a dishwasher, a garbage disposal, a car of her own—hell, I even bought her a portable TV so she can watch the goddamn soap operas right in the kitchen. What more can she want?"

. . .

The expression "making love" is not used by the men at The Oasis when referring to sexual intercourse. They have a colorful assortment of terms which do refer to this behavior but none of them include the word "love." One can only conclude that for these men ... sex is a physical need, and sexual satisfaction refers to physical relief, not psychological fulfillment.

. . .

[The men at The Oasis feel] that a man *has* to have regular sex to remain healthy, whereas this is not necessary for women. This means that a man is justified in taking sex where he can find it if his wife (or his girl friend) is not providing sexual relief.

This belief in the sexual needs of men versus those of women leads to a justification of adultery on the part of husbands while this right is denied wives. In other words, a woman who seeks extramarital sexual partners is a "slut," whereas a man who engages in the same behavior is "starved" for sexual relief by his wife.

. . .

These men have an ambivalent attitude toward rape. While they do not approve of males using force to obtain sexual favors from a female, at the same time they believe that many forcible rape charges are fictitious—that the woman "had it coming to her."

"By God," one man said, "if I were on a jury the woman would have to prove her case. A lot of women lead a man on until he can't control himself and then they yell *rape*. Bullshit, I say."

Another man said: "Did you ever try to screw a woman that didn't want to screw? It ain't easy, I can tell you. They can put up a hell of a fight. Take my word for it.

"Of course," he added, "if a man uses a knife or gun that's a different story. Then the sonofabitch deserves a good stretch in the state prison."

. . .

The men at The Oasis are also skeptical about statutory rape. Many of them feel that the age of consent for girls is too high—eighteen in this particular state.

"They should tatoo their birth date right on the girl's belly at birth," a plumber said. "Then a man would know whether they're old enough or not."

Source: E. E. LeMasters, *Blue-Collar Aristocrats* (Madison, Wis. The University of Wisconsin Press, 1975).

---

this superior status to indulge in uninvited and unwanted sexual advances, ranging from ogling, leering, squeezing, pinching, bottom-patting and the like to making outright propositions accompanied by the implied or explicit threat of dismissal if these advances are refused. The norms of this kind of interaction require comparatively little self-control by the men; instead, it is the women who are expected to manage the situation. Many men, it seems, have convinced themselves that any normal woman will welcome and be

flattered by sexual attention in any form; women, for their part, have been socialized to receive these advances as gracefully as possible, regardless of their own personal feelings. The myth has it that they enjoy the attention, that they find it easy to deal with, and that this kind of behavior is trivial in any case. But surveys show the reverse to be true: almost unanimously, women declare that sexual advances in the workplace make them feel powerless, trapped, defeated, nervous, intimidated, or demeaned. (This finding

Figure 9.9 Members of the women's movement protest rape in a march past downtown pornographic theaters. The efforts of the movement are leading to many changes in public policies toward rape. For example, female police officers are being trained to deal with women reporting rape; telephone hotlines are being set up for victims who need help and counseling, and some courts are refusing to allow defense lawyers to besmirch the reputation of the victims.

really should come as no surprise. Imagine how young male workers would feel if the situation were reversed—if middle-aged female executives with the power to hire and fire pinched their buttocks and pestered them for dates.) These are some comments from women who have been sexually harassed by their male superiors at work:

> That job was really important to me. I'd poured my life into it. But this guy refused to believe that I really didn't want to date him. He just kept after me and kept after me. Finally I had to quit. I'd poured all my hopes and ambitions into a career in that field and it was years before I could try again.

> I'd been trying to get a job as a filmmaker for years. It's practically an all male field, nobody would even look at my work. Finally I got an offer on the condition that I go away with this guy for the weekend. What amazed and frightened me was that I actually considered doing it! I wanted the job so badly. I said no, but I couldn't take it anymore. I gave up.

> It didn't matter that I was there for six months and that he knew I had only taken the job on the condition that I be promoted at the first opening. If I wasn't going to sleep with him, I wasn't going to get my promotion. It made me feel powerless and dehumanized. I can't tell you how it affected me. [Cited in Evans, 1978]

These norms of sexual harassment have a wider social significance. In all cases, the male's message is the same: your responsibility is to satisfy me, you are not my equal, don't compete, your real value is your body (Evans, 1978; Chapman and Gates, 1978; Farley, 1978).

The Nature of Rape

Rape is an extreme manifestation of approved activities in which one segment of society dominates another, socially and sexually. That it is not an act of sudden impulse is evidenced by the fact that the majority of these crimes are planned in advance, with the rapist carefully selecting a time, place, and victim for the attack. Nor is rape the result of any lack of alternative sexual outlets: many rapists are married, many have other sexual partners, and most could easily afford the services of a prostitute. In fact, lust seems to have remarkably little to do with rape: a high proportion of rapists are completely impotent, and many more become sexually aroused only when they have sufficiently terrified and debased their victim through verbal and physical abuse. This victim's report is fairly typical:

> He hit me in the face and knocked me on the floor. He pulled off my robe and nightgown and I screamed and he threatened

to kill me. He stuffed the nightgown in my mouth and tied the rest around my throat and the gown strangled me. He tied my hands behind my back and he pressed my neck so hard I passed out. Then he asked me if I needed air and I nodded and he let it loose a bit but still kept it in my mouth. He tied my legs up to the tie on my hands ... then he got my butcher knife from the kitchen and ran the point all over my body. [Quoted in Shram, 1978]

All the evidence indicates that the sexual aspect of rape is of secondary importance. The primary object is to humiliate, degrade, and subjugate the woman, and thus to bolster the aggressor's feelings of power, superiority, and masculinity. The man who rapes is an insecure bully who lacks any better means of asserting his manhood (Amir, 1971; Brownmiller, 1975; Russell, 1975; Gage and Schurr, 1976; Walker and Brodsky, 1976).

The effects of rape can be devastating for the victim, involving physical and emotional damage and the disruption of personal, social, familial, and sexual life. If the victim reports the attack to the police, the emotional trauma may be reexperienced months or years later in a courtroom, where the intimate details of the rape are dissected before an audience of strangers. Typically, defense lawers try to shift the burden of guilt from the accused to the victim. They may try to show that the woman is "loose," implying that if she has consented to any man before, she must have been willing on this occasion also. Or, utilizing the myth that women somehow enjoy being raped, they may claim that the victim consciously or subconsciously encouraged the assault. They may even argue that she was provocatively dressed and was therefore at fault (another example of the way in which responsibility for the control of male advances is shifted to the female). One woman, whose attacker slashed her face and neck to make her stop screaming, recalls her courtroom interrogation:

My trial did not come until eighteen months after I'd been raped. All this time the guy had been out on only twenty-five hundred dollars bail, and he had raped and shot a woman in Evanston and had immediately gotten out on bail again. In the meantime they kept using every delay tactic in the world. The defense attorney, who is now a civil court judge, was famous for his delaying tactics....

. . .

It was the ugliest experience I've ever had. It was equal to the rape, because it was humiliating to have the jurors and everybody else watching. They were all men, except one woman.... There were two guys on the jury, and one of them was giggling.

The prosecutor led me through the direct examination and I told what happened. And then it came to the cross-examination. It was terrifying. [The defense attorney] more or less implied that I was a whore and I had gotten in a fight with my pimp or my john or something like that. It was implied that I was a whore because I ... was unemployed in Chicago at the time it happened. I had to go through my whole finances and everything. And he just kept implying that I was a hooker.

I don't think the whore thing was going over too well. So then he tried to make it appear that I'd been raped by someone else, even the super of the apartment building. He asked me, "Do you know the super?" And I said yes. And he said, "And *he* certainly knows you." My answer should have been, "Yes, I spoke to him over the phone one day because the stove was broken." It's very frustrating. It's yes or no or I don't remember. You can't explain anything. You seem to always say it in a way that doesn't sound good for you. He even tried to imply that maybe the rapist was the guy next door who called the police. That guy was all of five foot three and he had a Prince Valiant blond hair-do and I do not think he was interested in women at all.

So the next thing he tried was "Okay, so maybe it happened, but she deserved it." The question was, "When he had you on the bed, you didn't scream?" "No," says I, "because ..." "Judge," he says, "would you please direct the witness to answer yes or no." So it was, "No, I didn't scream." The reason I didn't scream was because I'd already been screaming and he had a knife at my throat. But you can't explain that. "Well," the defense attorney said, "why didn't you get out of the apartment? Were both of your legs broken or something?" So in the end, it was my fault that it happened to me anyway.

I was on the witness stand for two days and it was the most vicious attack I've ever been through. It was just so incredibly ugly, you wouldn't believe it.

The trial kept going on. The defendant never got on the stand. I was at work the next week and the D.A. called and told me it was a hung jury. And I just started crying ... [Quoted in Barkas, 1978]

Such a line of defense would never be attempted in cases involving other offenses; it is unique to the crime of rape. Even this aspect of the act and its aftermath can be fully understood only in terms of the overall patterns of sexual interaction in the society (Hilberman, 1976; Holmstrom and Burgess, 1976).

Homosexuality

Homosexuality, much more evident now that the gay liberation movement has encouraged its adherents to "come out" and openly declare their preference, is one of the most stigmatized forms of sexual variance in American society. The ancient Greeks, in the cradle of Western civilization, regarded male homosexual love as a higher value than heterosexual love and institutionalized a system of sexual and spiritual relationships between boys and older men. Since then, however, Western attitudes toward homosexuality have generally been negative. Homosexuality was tolerated for a few periods in the Roman Empire and the Middle Ages, usually at times when emperors, kings, and popes themselves had homosexual tastes, but homosexuals have generally been persecuted until modern times. The persecution reached its climax in Nazi Germany, when hundreds of thousands of suspected homosexuals were sent to the gas chambers along with Jews and political dissidents.

Why has homosexuality prompted this negative reaction? The reason lies yet again in the Western moral tradition that tolerates sexual acts only if they occur within marriage and can lead to reproduction. Homosexual acts are pursued for their own sake and are necessarily nonreproductive; and if homosexuality serves as an exclusive outlet for individuals, it is impossible to reconcile it with the central institutions of marriage and the family. Until the global population explosion of the present century, widespread exclusive homosexuality would have been highly *dysfunctional.* Preindustrial societies had a very high death rate, especially among children, and a society that did not encourage high birth rates might risk extinction. In a world faced with a crisis of overpopulation, however, homosexuality is no longer dysfunctional in this respect: it may even be functional. The growing tolerance of homosexuality (and of abortion, contraception, masturbation, and nonreproductive forms of heterosexual activity) is probably related to this fact.

Incidence of Homosexuality

How common is homosexuality in the United States? The answer to this question is not easily arrived at, for it depends in part on the definition of homosexuality. Americans, unlike many other peoples, tend to see homosexuality and heterosexuality as "either/or" categories. This view is incorrect, however, for many people fall on a continuum

KINSEY HOMOSEXUAL RATING SCALE

Figure 9.10 Alfred Kinsey's research established that homosexuality and heterosexuality are not mutually exclusive categories. Elements of both are found in most people in varying degrees. Kinsey's seven-point scale provides a way of measuring the balance in particular individuals. The scale runs from one extreme of exclusively heterosexual acts or feelings through to the other extreme of exclusively homosexual acts or feelings.

Source: Adapted from Alfred C. Kinsey et al., *Sexual Behavior in the Human Male* (Philadelphia: W. B. Saunders, 1948), p. 638.

between the two. Any attempt to divide the population into two distinct categories must fail because of the countless ambiguous cases that arise—people whose desires are heterosexual but whose behavior is homosexual, people who have homosexual histories but whose current behavior is heterosexual, people who alternate between both forms of behavior, and so on.

No findings of the Kinsey studies caused a greater furor than his data on homosexuality, which indicated that only 50 percent of the male population could be considered exclusively heterosexual in terms of both their sexual acts and their feelings since puberty. Kinsey found that 37 percent of males had experienced at least one homosexual contact to the point of orgasm and that a further 13 percent had experienced homosexual desires but had not acted on them. Some 18 percent of the men had as much homosexual as heterosexual experience, and 8 percent had engaged in exclusively homosexual relationships for at least three years since adolescence. The proportion of lifelong exclusive homosexuals, however, was much smaller: 4 percent. The incidence of homosexuality in women was significantly lower; 13 percent had experienced homosexual contacts, a further 15 percent had experienced homosexual desires but had not acted on them, and only about 2 percent of the female population was exclusively homosexual. The lower incidence of female homosexuality is probably related to the great emphasis in female socialization on conformity and on the expectation of motherhood. Kinsey (1948) concluded that

> the world is not divided into sheep and goats.... Only the human mind invents categories and tries to force facts into separated pigeon holes. The living world is a continuum in each and every one of its aspects. The sooner we learn this concerning human sexual behavior the sooner we will reach a sound understanding of the realities of sex.

Kinsey accordingly constructed a seven-point rating scale, with exclusive homosexuality at one end and exclusive heterosexuality at the other (see Figure 9.10).

How accurate are Kinsey's figures? Kinsey himself reported that he was "totally unprepared" for his findings, but when he rechecked them by twelve different methods, he found much the same pattern emerging in group after group in his survey. Subsequent studies seem to support Kinsey's figures, but they have serious methodological limitations. The *Psychology Today* survey found precisely the same figures as Kinsey's—37 percent of the sample had experience of homosexual acts and 4 percent were exclusively homosexual throughout their lives—but the sample was so unlike Kinsey's that this finding is probably coincidental. The *Playboy* study is also of little help. Morton Hunt admits that it specifically omitted "many, if not most" of the "committed homosexuals," but he believes that the Kinsey figures are a little high. Even a conservative estimate, however, indicates that over 20 million Americans are exclusively or substantially homosexual (American Psychological Association *Monitor*, 1974), a minority about as large as that of American blacks and one that also suffers much prejudice and discrimination.

The Gay Community

Homosexuality has been such a forbidden topic in America that until a quarter of a century ago, no newspaper would dare print the mere word "homosexual." In the absence of informed discussion of the subject, homosexuality has been surrounded by myths, many of which are still widely believed. The sociological research of recent years has made a more objective picture possible, at least in the case of males; female homosexuality, or lesbianism, is still inadequately researched.

It is not true that homosexuals are typically "effeminate" in the case of men and "masculine" in the case of women. The great majority are indistinguishable in manner and appearance from heterosexuals, and there is no evidence to suggest that "effeminacy" and "masculinity" are any more common in homosexual than in heterosexual men and women. Nor is it true that homosexuals typically suffer from gender confusion, believing they are, or wishing they were, members of the opposite sex. This myth stems from a confusion between homosexuality and *transvestism*, the wearing of the clothing of the opposite sex. A transvestite is sexually aroused by cross-dressing in this way, but the evidence available suggests that most transvestites are heterosexual married men (Buckner, 1970; Newton, 1972).

Another myth has it that homosexuals typically assume a "passive" or an "active" role in their sexual relationships; in fact, most alternate between the two. The preferences of the small minority who do prefer a particular role cannot be inferred from their physical appearance, any more than

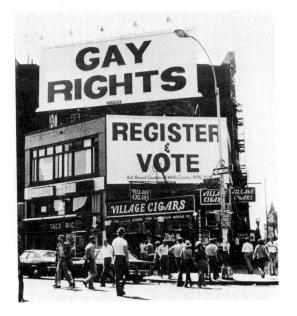

Figure 9.11 Gay communities, like the one in Greenwich Village, New York, are to be found in most large cities. These communities not only provide a full range of social and commercial facilities; they also offer a set of subcultural norms and values that validate the gay life-style and enable the members to maintain positive self-concepts.

any specific sexual preferences of heterosexuals can be inferred from their appearance (Hooker, 1965). It is also not true that homosexuals pose a particular menace to the young; child molestation by heterosexuals is proportionately much more frequent. Nor is it true that homosexuals as a group have disturbed or even characteristic personality patterns; except for their sexual orientation they are psychologically indistinguishable from heterosexuals (Hooker, 1957; Thompson et al., 1971; Bell and Weinberg, 1978). And it is not true that homosexuals fail to form stable sexual relationships. Although male homosexuals tend to be more promiscuous than heterosexuals, the great majority form long-lasting, affectionate partnerships with others; and lesbians seem to maintain even more stable relationships than heterosexual couples do (Weinberg and Williams, 1974; Masters and Johnson, 1979; Martin and Lyon, 1972; Wysor, 1974; Tanner, 1978; Ettmore, 1980).

Some homosexuals attempt throughout their lives to "pass" as heterosexuals, but a growing number participate in the homosexual community that is centered in urban America. Most large cities contain definable areas that are occupied primarily by homosexuals and in which shops, restaurants, hotels, churches, beaches, or other amenities cater almost exclusively to the homosexual community—primarily to gay males, but increasingly to lesbian women as well (Wolf, 1979). Membership in this community provides entrance to a subculture in which people who have identified themselves as homosexual can be resocialized by learning new roles, norms, and values. The climate of the community neutralizes earlier conceptions of homosexuality as perverted, sinful, and abnormal and enables gay people to build positive self-concepts (Hooker, 1962; Humphreys, 1972; Warren, 1974; Harry and de Vall, 1978; Delph, 1978). A central institution in the community is the gay bar, of which there are dozens or even hundreds in large cities. The bar provides opportunities for social interaction, for the exchange of information, for the making of sexual contacts, and above all for the sense that one belongs to a worthwhile and accepting group. As one homosexual recalls:

> I was resigned to the fact that I was a foul, dirty person, but I wasn't actually calling myself a homosexual yet. . . . The time I really caught myself coming out is the time I walked into this bar and saw a whole crowd of groovy, groovy guys. And I said to myself, there was this realization, that not all gay men are dirty old men or idiots, silly queens, but there are some just normal looking and acting people, as far as I could see. I saw gay society and I said, "Wow, I'm home." [Quoted in Dank, 1971]

Learning Sexual Orientation

How do people learn their eventual sexual orientation—and, more specifically, why do some people become homosexual in the face of so much social discouragement? Several theories have been offered.

Biological Factors

Some people, including some homosexuals, assume that homosexuals are simply "born that way." But since we know that even heterosexuals are not "born that way," this explanation seems unlikely. Many attempts have been made to find genetic or hormonal factors that might predispose individuals toward homosexuality, but there is no plausible evidence that homosexual tendencies are inherited or caused by hormones (D. Rosenthal, 1970; Tourney et al., 1975; Marmor, 1979). Since homosexuals have a low rate of reproduction, any inherited causes would have eventually been bred out of a population. Moreover, biological factors cannot explain the different extent of homosexuality in different societies at different times, or the changes that may take place during the lifetime of an individual. Homosexuality, like other sexual behavior, is learned.

Early Experiences

A common popular view is that homosexuality is caused by early childhood experiences, particularly seduction. But while this may be true in some specific instances, it cannot provide a comprehensive explanation. The great majority of American preadolescents and a substantial proportion of adolescents have had some homosexual experience, but only a small minority of them become exclusive homosexuals. Other people who have never had any homosexual experience in their entire lives may still privately define themselves as homosexual (Dank, 1971). Conversely, the great majority of people who are predominantly homosexual have experienced heterosexual intercourse earlier in their lives—but with no apparent effect on their later sexual orientation.

Family Environment

Psychoanalysts have attempted to isolate factors in the family background of homosexuals, usually in the belief that homosexuality is a form of mental disorder or "sickness" resulting from pathological family interactions. The leading proponent of this theory is Irving Bieber (1962), whose investigations led him to believe that homosexual males typically had domineering, possessive mothers and ineffectual or hostile fathers. Bieber's study was widely acclaimed when it was published but has since been criticized as a shoddy piece of research. His sample consisted entirely of patients under psychiatric care and was thus no more representative of the general homosexual population than a group of similar heterosexuals would be of the general heterosexual population. A study of heterosexuals under psychiatric care would doubtless reveal problems in

their family background, but these could hardly be taken as an explanation for their heterosexuality! Other studies (for example, Hooker, 1969) have found no consistent personality differences between homosexuals and heterosexuals. This fact is now accepted by the American Psychiatric Association, which in 1973 removed homosexuality from its list of mental disorders, offering this "sick" community an instant cure. Although family background may predispose some individuals toward homosexuality, this theory is yet to be proved.

Social Learning

Another view comes from psychologists who offer what is essentially a behaviorist or social-learning account of homosexuality. The orientation, they argue, is learned through rewards and punishments. A person who finds a homosexual experience pleasurable may repeat the experience, find it pleasurable again, and have the orientation further reinforced. Particularly if heterosexual contacts are simultaneously experienced as unpleasant or threatening, a homosexual identity may result. This approach is helpful, but it still has two major defects. First, why should some specific rewards overcome the many punishing responses that the homosexual receives from the total social environment? The balance of rewards and punishments in society heavily favors a heterosexual orientation, and it is difficult to see how specific rewards in a limited context would counter this powerful social experience. Second, some homosexuals clearly do not find their orientation rewarding. They may wish to abandon their homosexual life-style but seem unable to do so. It is difficult to see how their sexual preference can be fully explained in terms of the punishments and rewards it offers them.

Self-Definition

A more recent approach to the problem avoids many of these difficulties. It sees homosexual identity as the result of a self-definition that people may impose on themselves. This definition can be made consciously or unconsciously, voluntarily or involuntarily, but it is made in accordance with the prevailing beliefs of the culture concerned (Sagarin, 1973, 1975; Blumstein and Schwartz, 1974). In this view, both heterosexual and homosexual behavior are learned through a similar process. People who experience heterosexual acts or desires achieve a sense that they are heterosexual and define themselves accordingly. Believing that heterosexuality and homosexuality are mutually exclusive, they also define themselves as not homosexual. A similar process applies to people who become homosexual. As a result of early homosexual experiences or desires, they come to think of themselves as homosexual. They become trapped within this self-definition and—irrespective of social rewards and punishments—cannot escape from it. If they are labeled as homosexuals by others, the self-definition is further reinforced. As Sagarin (1973) suggests,

> it might be useful to start from the premise that . . . there is no such thing as a *homosexual,* for such a concept is . . . an artificially created entity that has no basis in reality. What exists are people with erotic desires for their own sex, or who engage in sexual activities with same-sex others, or both. The desires constitute feeling, the acts constitute doing, but neither is being. . . . However, people become entrapped in a false consciousness of identifying themselves as *being* homosexuals. They believe that they discover what they are. . . . Learning their "identity" they become involved in it, boxed into their own biographies. . . . There is no road back because they believe there is none.

Cultural beliefs determine the self-definition that the individual makes. It is quite possible to engage in homosexual acts without defining oneself as or becoming homosexual, provided one's culture or subculture offers this option. In many contemporary Arab societies, for example, people would tend to regard their homosexual desires and acts as evidence not of homosexuality but of potential bisexuality, because the category of bisexuality is recognized and accepted in these cultures. Among American male prison communities, in which homosexuality is very common, the dominant partner in a sexual encounter is defined as heterosexual (even though he achieves sexual gratification from his homosexual acts) and the submissive partner is defined as homosexual (even if he is unwilling and even if he is raped). The participants in the acts learn to accept these definitions (Kirkham, 1971; A. Davis, 1968; Lockwood, 1979). Similarly, many homosexual prostitutes define and think of themselves as fully heterosexual, because their subculture permits them to believe that they are "just doing it for the money" (Reiss, 1961; Humphreys, 1971). In general, exclusive homosexuality is found only in societies that define heterosexuality and homosexuality as mutually exclusive. In societies that offer bisexuality as a cul-

tural option, people with homosexual tendencies are more likely to define themselves and to be defined by others as bisexual and to behave accordingly (Duberman, 1974). The precise content of the homosexual, heterosexual, bisexual, or any other sexual role, and the process by which people come to assume it, can be understood only in terms of the prevailing cultural definitions.

Prostitution

Prostitution is the relatively indiscriminate exchange of sexual favors for economic gain. Not all exchanges of sex for gain are prostitution: the person who "marries for money," the kept mistress, the actress who sleeps with film directors en route to stardom, or the wife who "holds out" on her husband until he parts with his paycheck are not prostitutes. What distinguishes the prostitute is a willingness to perform sexual services for virtually anyone in return for some gain. In theory, four forms of prostitution are possible: women for men, men for men, women for women, and men for women. In practice the last two types are very rare indeed. Male homosexual prostitution is common in large cities, but by far the greatest number of prostitutes are women offering their services to men.

In some preindustrial societies the prostitute enjoyed high social status. In ancient Greece high-class prostitutes, the *hetairae,* were welcomed in literary and political circles. They appeared in public with leading statesmen, and their portraits and statues adorned public buildings. In many ancient societies of the Middle and Far East, prostitution assumed a sacred form and was practiced in the temples. In some societies, such as ancient Cyprus, all women were expected to prostitute themselves in a temple at least once in their lives as a religious ritual. Sacred prostitution even occurred among the early Hebrews, although the Old Testament later forbade the practice. But the occupation of prostitute since early Christian times has been anything but a respected one. Although she may consort on the most intimate terms with politicians and bank presidents, judges and bishops, the prostitute's status is very low.

The reason can again be traced to the Judeo-Christian moral tradition. Men engage in prostitution for pleasure alone, and neither they nor the prostitute have any intention that the relationship should lead to reproduction. By

Figure 9.12 Prostitution has often been called "the world's oldest profession." These prostitutes and their rather elegant surroundings were painted by the Italian artist Carpaccio in the sixteenth century. Despite numerous attempts to stamp out the profession, prostitution has continued to thrive.

definition, prostitution can take place only outside the context of marriage. In further violation of social norms, the prostitute in Western cultures offers her services for money in a society that regards love as a prerequisite for legitimate sex. And to make matters worse still, she flouts the double standard with her promiscuity.

Types of Prostitution

The main types of female prostitute today are the streetwalker, the housegirl, and the call girl; there are also various types of male prostitute (Greenwald, 1958, 1970; Benjamin and Masters, 1964; Winick and Kinsie, 1971; Laner, 1974; Heyl, 1977).

The Streetwalker

The streetwalker has the lowest status and earnings of all prostitutes. She solicits clients in public places, usually in the street or the lobbies of hotels. Some streetwalkers, including teen-age runaways, are newcomers to the occupation, but many are older prostitutes who can no longer compete at the higher levels of the market. Because the streetwalker is the most visible of all prostitutes, she attracts the most public criticism and attention from the police.

The Housegirl

The housegirl works and sometimes lives in a brothel, an organized house of prostitution. Before World War II most prostitution took place in brothels, often in notorious "red light" districts of large cities. Some of the houses of prostitution in Chicago, Galveston, and New Orleans won international fame for the elegance and splendor of their decor. The brothels were usually run by a "madame," often a retired prostitute, who organized the house and took a percentage of the housegirls' earnings. These brothels are largely a thing of the past; they have been replaced by houses of prostitution disguised as "massage parlors" or "clubs."

The Call Girl

The call girl has the highest status and earnings in the occupation; she is generally more attractive and better educated than the other types of prostitute, and her competition is partly responsible for the decline of the brothel. She may work on her own from a hotel room or apartment, or she may be part of a call-girl network disguised as an "escort agency." In either case, she makes her contacts through personal introductions. Many call girls see their occupation as a potential avenue to higher social status as the mistress or perhaps ultimately the wife of a wealthy man.

Figure 9.13 The traditional brothel has almost disappeared from American society. Instead, commercial sex now often takes the form of organized call-girl networks, "escort agencies," or "massage parlors." Advertisements like these are printed in sex-oriented magazines in all large American cities.

The Male Prostitute

Male prostitution is more common than is generally realized in the United States, partly because youths "hanging out" on a street corner do not attract the same attention as young women, and partly because many local laws are directed only at female prostitution. The lowest status in the profession is that of the "street hustler," generally a teen-ager. The "bar hustler" is often slightly older and solicits clients in certain gay bars. Most of these hustlers regard their activities as a temporary means of earning money, and many consider themselves basically heterosexual. The "houseboy" works in, but rarely lives in, a male house of prostitution, of which there are a few in some large cities. The "call boy" has the highest status and earnings in the profession. A male prostitute may hope to become a "kept boy," the homosexual equivalent of a mistress, under the guise of being a wealthy man's "secretary," "chauffeur," or "nephew."

Prostitution as an Occupation

Recruitment into the role of prostitute is rarely the result of an abrupt decision. People tend to drift into the role and to serve a period of apprenticeship before finally defining themselves as prostitutes and relying on the occupation as a major or sole source of income (Bryant, 1965; N. Davis, 1971). Most prostitutes come from lower-class or lower-middle-class backgrounds. They often have histories of considerable promiscuity in early adolescence and are frequently alienated from their families, especially their fathers.

Drift into prostitution may begin when a woman accepts a casual offer from a man, or when she meets another prostitute or a pimp. A pimp is a man who organizes female prostitution and lives off the proceeds. He introduces women to their new role and thereafter serves as lover, business manager, and protector. He arranges contacts, pays court fines and bail, and safeguards the prostitute's territory against competitors. Housegirls, call girls, and male prostitutes have little need of pimps, but a high proportion of streetwalkers have arrangements with them. They generally take pride in the life-style they provide for the pimp, since his affluence provides evidence of their occupational success. The relationship between prostitute and pimp is a curious one. It involves a reversal of the usual sex-role expectations, for the female partner or partners are more promiscuous than the male and serve as breadwinners for him.

The new entrant to the occupation is resocialized by pimps and other prostitutes. She learns various techniques—how to solicit in public, how to recognize plain-clothes police officers, how to handle difficult customers, and how to service her clients and get rid of them as soon as possible. She also acquires a new set of values that alienate her further from her previous life. She learns to hold "respectable" women in contempt, to view her clients as mere exploiters, to regard society as hypocritical, and to justify her own activities as socially valuable. Despite the stigma attached to the occupation and the fact that it is inherently a dead-end job—the prostitute's only real asset is her transient youth and beauty—prostitutes seem to be reasonably satisfied with their work. One study found that although only one-fifth of prostitutes would advise other women to take up this career, two-thirds of them expressed no regret about their choice of occupation (Pomerory, 1965).

Reasons for Prostitution

Why does prostitution exist, despite the stigma that attaches to the institution? The reason is that both men and women have found sound reasons for entering into the relationship. From the point of view of the prostitute, the occupation offers far higher earnings, even after the pimp has taken his share, than would be available in a "straight" job. Nor is the work particularly difficult. It can be much less tedious or time-consuming than many alternative occupations, such as those of waitress, keypunch operator, or assembly-line worker. There is always the possibility, too, of meeting and forming relationships with high-status men whom the prostitute would normally never encounter.

From the point of view of the prostitute's client, prostitution offers a convenient opportunity for sexual contacts that might otherwise be unavailable or difficult to arrange. The prostitute's services often cost less than the price of entertaining a woman for an evening in the hope of seducing her. Relationships with a prostitute involve no complications, obligations, or emotional entanglements. Men who are away from home may find the prostitute a convenient substitute for their wives, and men whose sexual preferences are somewhat unusual may find that prostitutes will cater to tastes that their wives would not. And for the old and the physically unattractive, prostitution may offer the only means by which a man can enjoy sex with a young and attractive woman. As Kingsley Davis (1932) points out, prostitution is functional. Many men, it seems, desire a variety of sexual outlets. Prostitution meets this need without undermining the family system in the way that more affectionate extramarital relationships would.

Can Prostitution Be Eliminated?

For centuries prostitution has survived every effort to eradicate it. Consequently, many countries have legalized prostitution, justifying their action on several grounds. First, prostitution is a victimless crime. There is no aggrieved party to complain to the police or to give court evidence, so convictions are difficult to obtain—unless the police resort to the morally questionable tactic of posing as

Figure 9.14 American prostitutes attending a "Hookers' Convention" in San Francisco. In 1974 prostitutes formed a new organization called COYOTE ("call off your old tired ethics"), which is now working for reform of the nation's vice laws.

potential clients in order to make arrests. Second, prostitution involves a private act by consenting adults, and many people feel that what happens in private beds is no business of the state. Third, when prostitution is legalized, it may be taken out of the hands of organized crime, becoming just another commercial enterprise. Fourth, legalized prostitution can be publicly regulated: for example, prostitutes can be licensed, taxed, and periodically checked for venereal disease. Fifth, police attention can be focused on public nuisances associated with prostitution (such as blackmail, theft, and blatant soliciting) rather than on the thankless task of trying to suppress the institution itself. The idea that prostitution should be legalized is strongly resisted in the United States, however, mainly on the grounds that this would legitimate the practice, encourage more use of prostitutes' services, and so undermine public morality.

As Kingsley Davis (1932, 1976a) points out, however, prostitution cannot be eliminated in a sexually restrictive society, for it arises in response to those very restrictions. In the more permissive societies in the Ford and Beach cross-cultural sample, prostitution is extremely rare, for the reason that people have considerable opportunity for legitimate outlets beyond marriage. As Davis points out, prostitution could be completely eliminated only in a society that was totally permissive and in which sexual relations were freely available to all. Such a society could never exist, for total sexual freedom would imply a breakdown of the family system. The more restrictive a society is, the greater the pressure for prostitution to provide outlets for those who are not married or who find that exclusive sexual relationships with their spouses are unsatisfactory.

There is also an economic reason why prostitution cannot be eliminated. Police crackdowns might temporarily reduce the number of prostitutes, but the demand for their services would remain constant. The result would be an immediate increase in the fees for prostitution, which in turn would attract more women into the profession—including some who would not otherwise have considered it (Benjamin and Masters, 1964).

The sociological perspective on prostitution, as on all other forms of human sexual expression, offers a more acute insight into this aspect of social behavior—and with that understanding, perhaps, comes a more tolerant attitude to the varied ways of men and women in our own society and elsewhere.

Summary

1. Sexuality is an important element in social life. Human sexual behavior is not innate, but is learned through the socialization process. The subject has been poorly researched until recently.

2. Human sexuality is extremely flexible; for this reason, every society makes strong efforts to regulate it in culturally approved ways.

3. There are considerable variations in sexual practices in other societies, particularly preindustrial societies. Societies vary in their conception of beauty, their permissiveness or restrictiveness, their norms of heterosexual conduct, and their attitudes toward homosexuality. This variation reveals the interplay of biological potentials and cultural learning.

4. Sexual behavior in the United States is marked by a contrast between real and ideal norms and values. Traditional values emphasize sex as legitimate only in the context of marriage and only if its primary purpose is reproduction, but they tolerate a double standard of behavior for males and females. The work of Kinsey and others indicates that these norms and values are extensively violated. Recent permissive trends appear to signal changes in attitudes more than in practices.

5. Some form of incest taboo is universal. The taboo is not instinctive, nor does it exist to prevent any ill effects of inbreeding. It exists to encourage alliances between groups through marriage, to prevent confusion of statuses in the family, and to prevent sexual jealousies between family members.

6. Rape is a crime of violence, not of passion. Men tend to dominate women and to view them as sex objects, often subjecting them to sexual harassment in the workplace and elsewhere. Rape is an extreme manifestation of such established patterns of behavior, in which the aggressor bolsters his feelings of power and masculinity by abusing and humiliating the victim.

7. Homosexuality has long been stigmatized In Western societies. Homosexual and bisexual behavior is, however, fairly common. Many traditional beliefs about homosexuality are inaccurate. Homosexual life, particularly in urban centers, focuses on a defined homosexual community. Sev-

eral theories of causation have been offered: biological factors, early experiences, family environment, social learning, and self-definition in terms of cultural beliefs.

8. The practice of prostitution violates several traditional values and is stigmatized in the United States, although it was approved of in some ancient societies. The main types of prostitute are the streetwalker, the housegirl, the call girl, and the male prostitute. Entry into the occupation is usually a matter of drift, often involving contact with a pimp. Prostitution offers certain advantages for both prostitutes and their clients and is functional in relieving potential strains on the family system. It cannot be eliminated in a sexually restrictive society, since it arises in response to those restrictions.

Important Terms

incest taboo (207)

heterosexual
  behavior (209)

homosexual
  behavior (210)

ideal culture (211)

real culture (211)

double standard (213)

prostitution (226)

Suggested Readings

BULLOUGH, VERN L. *Sexual Variance in Society and History.* New York: Wiley, 1976.

An interesting historical and cross-cultural survey of human sexual practices.

DE LORA, JOANN S., and CAROL A. B. WARREN (eds.). *Understanding Sexual Interaction.* Boston: Houghton Mifflin, 1977.

A collection of articles on human sexuality, with a strong emphasis from interactionist sociology.

FORD, CLELLAN S., and FRANK A. BEACH. *Patterns of Sexual Behavior.* New York: Harper & Row, 1951.

An important study of sexual behavior in other cultures and in other species. The authors use this material to draw basic conclusions about human sexuality.

GAGNON, JOHN, and WILLIAM SIMON. *Sexual Conduct.* Chicago: Aldine, 1973.

A sociological interpretation of human sexual behavior from a social-learning perspective.

HENSLIN, JAMES M., and EDWARD SAGARIN (eds.). *The Sociology of Sex: An Introductory Reader.* 2nd ed. New York: Schocken, 1978.

A collection of articles on various aspects of the sociology of sex. The book provides a useful overview of research in this field.

HUMPHREYS, LAUD. *Out of the Closets.* Englewood Cliffs, N.J.: Prentice-Hall, 1972.

A sociological account of the gay liberation movement. Humphreys includes descriptive material on the American homosexual community.

HYDE, JANET SHIBLEY. *Understanding Human Sexuality.* New York: McGraw-Hill, 1979.

A readable and up-to-date college text that provides a good overview of human sexuality. The book integrates material from several disciplines.

WINICK, CHARLES, and PAUL M. KINSIE. *The Lively Commerce: Prostitution in the United States.* Chicago: Aldine, 1971.

A useful sociological analysis of prostitution, containing both historical and modern data on the institution and those who participate in it.

UNIT 3   *Social Inequality*

Social inequality exists when some people have a greater share of power, wealth, or prestige than others. Such inequality is as old as society itself, and throughout history it has been a constant source of tension, conflict, violence, injustice, and oppression. In most societies, social inequality is built into the social structure in such a way that it is passed down from generation to generation. When this happens, whole categories of a population are denied a fair share of their society's resources virtually from the moment of birth.

The first chapter in this unit deals with the general problem of social stratification, or the ranking of a population into unequal "strata." The second chapter takes up the issue of social class, focusing on the United States, a country that is formally committed to human equality but in which there are severe inequalities among different segments of the population. The third chapter discusses race and ethnicity, dealing with the hostility and inequality that are often present between peoples who are physically or culturally different from one another. The last chapter discusses inequalities of gender and of age, showing how traditional roles have ensured the dominance of men over women, and how social change has made the once-respected elderly a disadvantaged group. Throughout the unit, it is stressed that these social inequalities are rarely maintained primarily through force. Instead, they are sustained by the power of ideas. Members of both the dominant and the subordinate group are inclined to accept unquestioningly the ideologies, or sets of ideas, that justify the inequalities and make them seem "natural" and even moral.

Social Stratification

All societies differentiate among their members, treating people who have certain characteristics differently from those who do not. Every society, for example, distinguishes between the old and the young and between males and females. In addition, a society may also treat its members differently on a variety of other grounds, such as religion, skin color, physical strength, or educational achievement. The usual result of this differentiation is social inequality.

Social inequality exists when people's access to social rewards (such as money, influence, or respect) is determined by their personal or group characteristics. Such inequality is universal: in all societies known to us, large or small, modern or extinct, there have been distinct differences in the statuses of the individual members. When a society values males over females, the rich over the poor, Christians over Moslems, or whites over blacks, people who have the preferred characteristic enjoy a higher status than those who do not, and have a superior access to whatever rewards the society offers; those with the lower status are deprived of these advantages.

In a very few simple, preindustrial societies, social inequality (other than that based on age and sex) is restricted to differences in the status of specific *individuals*. One person may have higher status than others, for example, because of some personal quality such as wisdom, hunting skill, or beauty. In all other societies, however, entire *categories* of people have higher or lower status than other categories. This inequality is built into the social structure and passed down from generation to generation. Like the layers of rock that we can see in the cliffs of the Grand Canyon, people in these societies are grouped into "strata," so the society as a whole is said to be stratified. *Social stratification*

Figure 10.1 In a stratified society the population is divided into categories of people who enjoy different social rewards. People in the different strata have varying incomes, life-styles, power, and prestige. The worlds of these upper-middle-class and lower-class Americans contrast in many respects. The members of each group, too, will tend to transmit their statuses to their children, so the inequalities will be passed on from generation to generation.

is the structured inequality of entire categories of people, who have different access to social rewards as a result of their status in the social hierarchy. Individuals within a particular stratum share similar *life chances*, or probabilities of benefiting from the opportunities that their society offers. They generally view others within their stratum as equals, those in any higher stratum as in some way superior, and those in any lower stratum as in some way inferior.

Throughout history, social stratification has been a source of tensions, revolutions, and social change. It has generated bloody conflict between slave and master, peasant and noble, worker and capitalist, poor and rich. Ever since Karl Marx brought the issue of social stratification to the forefront of political debate with his *Communist Manifesto* in 1848, these tensions have assumed global importance. Today the nuclear powers of East and West are divided mainly by their different views on how wealth should be distributed in society. If these powers ever came into open conflict, much of the human life on the planet might be wiped out within minutes.

Social stratification is a central concern of sociology, and not only because it can lead to conflict and change. Sociologists have found that almost every aspect of our lives is linked to our status in the social hierarchy: our scores on IQ tests, our educational achievements, the size of our families, our standards of nutrition and health care, the likelihood that we will be imprisoned or committed to a mental institution, our tastes in literature and art, and even the probability of our keeping the lights on during sexual intercourse.

Stratification Systems

Systems of stratification vary a great deal from one society to another. There are obvious differences, for example, between the structured social inequality of the modern United States and that of feudal Europe—with its lords, clergy, and peasants—or ancient Rome—with its aristocrats, common people, and slaves. Sociologists have developed a few basic concepts that help in analyzing stratification systems and the differences among them.

Caste and Class

A stratification system may be either closed or open. In a *closed system,* the boundaries between the strata are very clearly drawn, and there is no way for people to change their statuses. A person's position in the hierarchy is determined at birth, perhaps on such grounds as skin color or ancestry, and the status is a lifelong one. In an *open system,* on the other hand, the boundaries between the strata are more flexible. People can sometimes change their statuses through their own efforts or failings—for example, by making money or losing it, or by marrying someone of a different status.

Caste Systems

A system of the closed type is called a *caste* system. Since a person's social status in such a system is determined entirely by birth, it is, obviously, always the same as one's parents'. A common feature of caste systems is that they are *endogamous:* people may marry only within their own group. Endogamy helps to keep up the boundaries between the strata, for it prevents the confusions that would arise if a person were born to parents of different castes. Individual status in a caste society is *ascribed,* since it is attached to people on grounds over which they have no control.

Caste systems existed in several ancient societies, but they are uncommon in the modern world. However, one of the caste systems that has survived into the 1980s is South Africa's, which is based on color. Every inhabitant of the country is officially classified as a member of one of four racial groups—white, mixed race, Asiatic, or black. These groups are ranked in a hierarchy, with the whites having the most rewards and the blacks the least. Strict segregation is maintained: each group has its own residential neighborhoods, hospitals, schools, colleges, and other facilities. Income is directly linked to color: a white teacher, for example, earns more than a black teacher of identical qualifications and experience. Marriage or sexual contact between the races is taboo and illegal, and many other forms of interracial contact are forbidden by law or custom (H. Adam, 1972; Robertson and Whitten, 1978). The racial segregation system in the United States was fairly similar, particularly in the South before the abolition of slavery: status was ascribed on the grounds of color, and intermarriage between the strata was outlawed.

Class Systems

A system of the open type is called a *class* system. The boundaries between its strata are more blurred than are those in a caste system, and because an individual's status usually depends on the economic position of the family breadwinner, it is possible for people to become members of a social class other than that of their parents. In addition, there are no formal restrictions against marriages between people of different classes. Status in a class society, then, is at least partly *achieved,* for it depends to some extent on characteristics over which the individual has some control.

Class systems are found in almost all agricultural and industrial societies. In agricultural societies, such as those that existed in feudal Europe and that are still found in some of the least developed nations of the world, there are usually two main classes: a very wealthy class of landowners and a very poor class of peasants. In industrial societies, on the other hand, there are usually three main classes: an elite upper class, a fairly large middle class of professionals and skilled white-collar workers, and a large working class of less skilled workers. (The socialist societies of the world claim to have virtually abolished classes, but this is a view-

Figure 10.2 Racial segregation in the American South was a form of caste stratification. As in all caste systems, the upper stratum was deeply concerned about "ritual pollution" through certain forms of contact between the strata.

Figure 10.3 Social stratification in medieval Europe eventually took the form of the "estate" system, a type that had some caste and some class characteristics. The society was ruled by a hereditary monarch, but some power was shared among three "estates"—the nobility, the Church, and the commons (knights and wealthy townsfolk). The peasantry had virtually no power at all. Although social status was generally ascribed, some mobility was possible: a knight, for example, might be made an earl. (Traces of these ancient patterns still exist in some European countries. Great Britain still has a hereditary monarch and a parliament consisting of a House of Lords—which includes Anglican bishops—and a House of Commons; but the latter now has unchallenged power.)

point that most American sociologists would reject, for reasons we shall discuss shortly.)

In practice, stratification systems do not fall neatly into either category. There is usually a small amount of achieved status in caste societies, for a few people may move from one caste to another (for example, by being expelled from one group and forced to join another lower in the hierarchy). And there is always a great deal of ascribed status in class societies, for in even the most open systems some people are trapped in a particular class because of characteristics, such as skin color or the poverty of their parents, over which they have no control. Stratification in virtually all modern societies, however, is basically of the open, class type, so we shall concentrate mainly on these systems.

Social Mobility

Movement from one social status to another is called *social mobility*. The more social mobility there is in a society, the more open its stratification system is.

Types of Social Mobility

Social mobility can take several forms. *Horizontal mobility* involves a change from one status to another that is roughly equivalent—say, from that of a plumber to that of a carpenter. *Vertical mobility* involves a change from one status to another that is higher or lower—for example, from plumber to corporation president, or vice versa. *Intragenerational mobility* involves a change in status (horizontal or vertical) during an individual's career, while *intergenerational mobility* involves a change (horizontal or vertical) in the status of family members from one generation to the next. Sociologists are especially interested in vertical intergenerational mobility, which occurs, for example, when a plumber's child becomes a corporation president or vice versa. The amount of this intergenerational mobility in a society is of great significance, for it tells us to what extent inequalities are built into the society. If there is very little intergenerational mobility, people's life chances are for the most part being determined at the moment of birth. If there is a good deal of mobility from one generation to the next, people are clearly able to achieve new statuses through their own efforts, regardless of the circumstances of their birth.

Determinants of Mobility

The extent of social mobility in a society is determined by two factors: the number of statuses that are available, and the ease with which people can move from one status to another.

The more statuses there are, the greater the chances for people to achieve mobility. As we noted in Chapter 4 ("Society"), preindustrial societies have far fewer statuses than industrial societies; consequently, they have little social mobility. In feudal Europe, for example, most people were peasants, and the number of high-status positions (such as lord or bishop) was very limited. Since there were so few high statuses for people of low status to move into, there could be virtually no upward mobility. In fact, there was a steady downward mobility of children from high-status families: only one child—the eldest son—could inherit the family land and title, so all the other children had to settle for a lesser status than their father had enjoyed, perhaps by joining the army or the church.

Industrial societies, on the other hand, contain an array of different statuses. They therefore offer a good deal of social mobility, although its form is influenced by economic conditions. In times of recession, for example, the proportion of high-status positions decreases while that of lower-status positions increases. This results in a general downward trend in mobility as people lose their jobs and are unable to find employment of the kind that their family background and education have prepared them to expect. In a rapidly expanding economy, on the other hand, the demand for workers to fill new high-status positions causes a general upward trend in social mobility. The long-term tendency in industrial societies has been toward an increase in the proportion of upper-status positions, leading to the growth of a large middle class whose members had origins in the lower strata (Lipset and Bendix, 1959; Wilensky, 1978).

The second factor affecting social mobility is the ease with which people can become mobile. As we have already seen, the more a society's statuses are ascribed, the less mobility there is likely to be. For example, preindustrial societies—in addition to having few statuses in the first place—had legal and traditional restrictions that made it almost impossible for a person of low status to become a member of the upper class: once a peasant, always a peasant.

On the other hand, in industrial societies, which place high value on individual merit, the rate of mobility is much greater. Nevertheless, some categories of people in industrial societies still suffer from the effects of ascribed status. In the United States the rate of social mobility for most racial minorities is lower than that for whites, and the mobility of women is lower than that of men (although women can compensate by marrying socially mobile men).

Criteria of Class Membership

What is your social class? You may hesitate over the answer, and you may find that other people would not agree about your precise social position. The problem is that in a class system, the boundaries between the strata are so blurred that many people may have no very clear idea of precisely where they fit.

Marx's Analysis

An analysis of the problem can usefully begin with the work of Karl Marx (1967, originally published 1867–1895). Although social class was the main focus of Marx's writings, he never dealt with the issue systematically. The unfinished third volume of his book *Capital* breaks off, in fact, at precisely the point where he seems to have intended to present his ideas on the subject in rigorous detail. The general principles of his theory have to be extracted from a lifetime's work of voluminous, diffuse, and sometimes contradictory writings.

Marx defined a class as all those people who share a common relationship to the means of economic production. Those who own and control the means of production—slaveholders, feudal landowners, or the owners of property such as factories and capital—are the dominant class. Those who work for them—slaves, peasants, or industrial laborers—are the subordinate class. The relationship between the classes is one not only of inequality but also of exploitation, because the dominant class takes unfair advantage of the subordinate one. The workers produce more wealth in the form of goods and services than is necessary to meet their basic needs. In other words, they produce *surplus wealth*. But they do not have the use of this surplus. Instead, those who own the means of production are able to seize it as "profit" for their own use. This, in Marx's view, is the essence of exploitation and the main source of conflict between the classes that has occurred throughout history.

Marx linked this analysis to the idea that the economic base of society influences the general character of all other aspects of culture and social structure, such as law, religion, education, and government. The dominant class is able to control all these institutions and to ensure that they serve its own interests. The laws therefore protect the rich, not the poor. The established religion supports the social order as it is, not as it might be. Education teaches the virtues of the existing system, not its vices. Government upholds the status quo rather than undermines it.

The Marxist definition of class has been a very influential one. Many sociologists still find it convenient to regard as a class any category of people who have a similar degree of control over, and access to, basic economic resources. Yet Marx's definition can be misleading in many marginal cases. This is particularly true in advanced industrial societies, which have changed a great deal since Marx's time. When Marx wrote, industry was owned and controlled primarily by individual capitalists, but this is no longer the case. Most industry is now run by large corporations, which are owned by thousands or even hundreds of thousands of stockholders but are controlled by salaried managers. As a result, the *ownership* and the *control* of the means of production have been largely separated (Berle and Means, 1933; Burnham, 1941). Indeed, it seems that a "new class" of executives, technicians, scientists, and other professionals has arisen—a class of well-educated experts who use their knowledge to gain high social status and the rewards that come with it. But because these people who control the means of production do not own it, Marx's definition does not help very much in determining their social class (Gouldner, 1979; Bruce-Biggs, 1979).

Other cases also present problems. What is the social class of a dropout, who does not own or control the means of production but does not work either? What is the social class of an impoverished member of the European aristocracy, who enjoys high social prestige because of ancestry rather than any relationship to the means of production? What is the class of a wealthy black surgeon who suffers racial prejudice and discrimination almost every day of his or her life? In Cambridge, Massachusetts, police officers are paid more than assistant professors at Harvard University in the same city. How do we assess their relative social statuses when the police officers have more income but considerably less prestige and influence than the professors?

The Marxist analysis does not handle these ambiguous cases very satisfactorily.

Weber's Analysis

The German sociologist Max Weber (1946) offered an influential analysis that confronts these problems. Weber's approach is a multidimensional one. He breaks the single concept of class down into three distinct but related elements, which we may translate as political status, or *power*, economic status, or *wealth*, and social status, or *prestige*. Clearly, a person may be politically powerful but have little wealth (like Ralph Nader), or may be very wealthy but have no prestige (like a Mafia boss), or may have prestige but not wealth (like an impoverished aristocrat). The multidimensional approach enables us to take account of many inconsistencies that the Marxist approach overlooks. Instead of trying to decide whether a Cambridge police officer is of a higher or lower class than a Harvard assistant professor, we can rank both of them on all three dimensions. In this case the police officer would have superior economic status, whereas the professor would have superior political and social status.

Power, wealth, and prestige can thus be independent of each other. In practice, however, they are usually closely associated. The reason is that any one can often be "converted" into any of the others. This is particularly true of wealth, which can readily be used to acquire power or prestige. The prestige ratings given by the public to various occupations have been studied by sociologists since 1927 through opinion polls in industrialized societies. These ratings have been very consistent over the years, both within the United States and Canada and among the various countries that have been studied (Inkeles and Rossi, 1956; Hodge, Siegel, and Rossi, 1964; Hodge, Treiman, and Rossi, 1966; Armer, 1968; Pineo and Porter, 1967; Blishen and McRoberts, 1976; Treiman, 1977).

As Figure 10.4 suggests, prestige is closely linked to the income of workers in different occupations, and the holders of political power tend to be ranked highly. There are a few exceptions, however. Professionals who earn relatively low incomes, such as ministers and teachers, seem to draw their prestige from their professional identity and educational achievements rather than their income. Slightly stigmatized workers, such as funeral undertakers and nightclub singers, have a lower prestige than their incomes would

PRESTIGE RATINGS OF OCCUPATIONS IN THE UNITED STATES

Occupation	Score	Occupation	Score
U.S. Supreme Court justice	94	Trained machinist	75
Physician	93	Farm owner and operator	74
Nuclear physicist	92	Undertaker	74
Scientist	92	City welfare worker	74
Government scientist	91	Newspaper columnist	73
State governor	91	Policeman	72
Cabinet member	90	Reporter on a daily newspaper	71
College professor	90	Bookkeeper	70
U.S. representative in Congress	90	Radio announcer	70
Chemist	89	Insurance agent	69
U.S. diplomat	89	Tenant farmer	69
Lawyer	89	Local official of a labor union	67
Architect	88	Manager of small city store	67
County judge	88	Mail carrier	66
Dentist	88	Railroad conductor	66
Mayor of a large city	87	Traveling wholesale salesmen	66
Member of a corporation's board of directors	87	Plumber	65
Minister	87	Barber	63
Psychologist	87	Machine operator in factory	63
Airline pilot	86	Owner-operator of a lunch stand	63
Civil engineer	86	Playground director	63
Head of a department in a state government	86	Corporal in the regular army	62
		Garage mechanic	62
Priest	86	Truck driver	59
Banker	85	Fisherman with own boat	58
Biologist	85	Clerk in a store	56
Sociologist	83	Milk route man	56
Captain in the regular army	82	Streetcar motorman	56
Accountant for large business	81	Lumberjack	55
Public school teacher	81	Restaurant cook	55
Building contractor	80	Singer in a nightclub	54
Owner of a factory that employs about 100 people	80	Filling-station attendant	51
		Coal miner	50
Artist who paints pictures that are exhibited in galleries	78	Dock worker	50
		Night watchman	50
Author of novels	78	Railroad section hand	50
Economist	78	Restaurant waiter	49
Musician in a symphony orchestra	78	Taxi driver	49
		Bartender	48
Official of an international labor union	77	Farmhand	48
		Janitor	48
County agricultural agent	76	Clothes presser in a laundry	45
Electrician	76	Soda fountain clerk	44
Railroad engineer	76	Sharecropper	42
Owner-operator of a printing shop	75	Garbage collector	39
		Street sweeper	36
		Shoe shiner	34

Figure 10.4 This table shows the prestige ratings given by Americans to various occupations. The most prestigious jobs appear to be those that yield high income, offer political power, or require specialized knowledge.

Source: Robert W. Hodge et al., "Occupational Prestige in the United States, 1925–1963," *American Journal of Sociology*, 70 (November, 1964), pp. 286–302.

predict. Despite these minor discrepancies, the overall trend is clear.

Recognizing this close connection among wealth, power, and prestige, many sociologists assess people's social positions in terms of their overall *socioeconomic status* (SES). This concept takes into account a complex of factors, such as years of education, income, type of occupation, and sometimes place of residence. An SES rating thus includes the dimensions of power and prestige as well as that of wealth. (We shall discuss the difficulties of determining social-class membership more fully in the next chapter, when we consider the American class system in detail.)

Stratified Societies: Three Examples

Our discussion up to this point has been mostly theoretical. To examine stratification in practice, we can look at it in three very contrasting modern societies: India, in which there is still a caste system; Great Britain, which is perhaps the most class-conscious of the advanced industrial societies; and the Soviet Union, a society that claims to have abolished classes altogether.

India: A Caste Society

The Indian caste system has been a fundamental feature of Indian life for over 2500 years. Although the system was officially abolished by the Indian government in 1949, it is still an important element in the social life of the country, especially in rural areas that are comparatively unaffected by modernization.

In theory there are four main castes, or *varnas,* which were originally based on racial or ethnic differences in the Indian population. The highest *varna* is that of the *Brahmins,* or priests and scholars; next are the *Kshatriyas,* or nobles and warriors; below them are the *Vaishyas,* or merchants and skilled artisans; and finally there are *Shudras,* or common laborers. Beyond the actual castes are the *Harijans,* or outcastes. The outcastes are often called "untouchables" because merely to touch an outcaste, or even to be touched by an outcaste's shadow, is a form of ritual pollution for members of the higher *varnas.* The rules concerning ritual pollution and the ritual purification that must follow it are highly elaborate. In some regions a *Shudra*'s or *Harijan*'s mere glance at a cooking pot is sufficient to defile the food,

and the passage of a low-caste person over a bridge may pollute the entire stream beneath. In some areas untouchables are not allowed in the villages during the early morning and late afternoon hours, because their bodies would cast such long shadows at these times that they would be a ritual danger to others. Some low-caste groups are not only untouchable but also unseeable. There is one group of washerwomen who for this reason must work only at night.

In practice these four Indian castes actually consist of thousands of subcastes, or *jati.* The *jati* are sometimes confined to local areas, but membership in some of them is spread across India. Many *jati* contain only a handful of members; others contain millions. A *jati* is often linked to a particular occupation—scavenging, silkworm-raising, or even snake charming—and all its members are expected to do the same work. Individuals cannot change their statuses, since status is determined at birth by the caste of one's parents. Intermarriage between castes is taboo, and intermarriage between members of different *jati* is strongly disapproved of and rarely takes place.

The Indian caste system is closely interwined with the Hindu religion, which is explicitly concerned with maintaining the stratified social order. Adherence to the rules of behavior of each of the *varnas* and *jati* is vital, for according to Hindu doctrine, each person is reincarnated again and again through a series of lifetimes, and one's status in the next lifetime depends on how well one observes the required behavior in this one. Failure to live up to the obligations of the stratification system may result in reincarnation as a member of a lower *varna,* or perhaps as an outcaste, or even as an animal. The Hindu religion is both an expression of the caste system and the basic mechanism for maintaining it.

The Indian caste system is breaking down fairly rapidly in urban areas, where the difficulty of determining another person's caste in a crowded and anonymous environment makes it impossible to observe the complicated rules of ritual distance or to avoid constant ritual pollution. Industrialism has caused many changes in the urban occupational structure, and it is no longer considered a sacred obligation to do the work traditionally done by members of one's *jati.* Industrial development has also caused a good deal of social mobility, both upward and downward, and there are now many poor *Brahmins,* many rich *Shudras,* and even wealthy outcastes. In the rural areas, however, a highly rigid and closed system still dominates the lives of millions of Indians (Hutton, 1963; Zinkin, 1962; Berreman, 1973; Robertson, 1976; Srinivas et al., 1978; Singh, 1976; Leonard, 1978).

Great Britain: A Class Society

Modern British society is stratified along the lines of class. The number of classes in a class system and the exact boundaries between the classes are always a matter of some debate. Most observers would probably agree, however, that the country has a very small upper class consisting mostly of families that have been wealthy for some generations; a small upper middle class consisting of professionals and other more recently wealthy people; a fairly large lower middle class containing skilled white-collar workers; and a large working class containing somewhat more than half of the total population.

Unlike most other European societies, Great Britain survived the transition from feudalism to industrialism without a revolution. The monarchy was never abolished, and an intricate system of prestige awards—knighthoods, peerages, earldoms—survives intact. The parliamentary system still reflects feudal arrangements. There are two legislative assemblies, the elected House of Commons and the largely hereditary House of Lords. Although the power of the monarch and of the House of Lords has been whittled away to insignificance, rituals of pomp still surround these aspects of British life. The mere presence of people entitled to put "Sir," "Lady," or "Lord" before their names obviously heightens differences between the upper class and the bulk of the population, and people in Great Britain are acutely aware that theirs is a class society.

Despite the efforts of post–World War II leftist governments, wealth remains very unequally distributed in British society. Tax laws have been very effective in reducing differences in income. In recent years incomes over $35,000 have been taxed at rates as high as 86 percent, and tax loopholes are almost nonexistent. Yet there are still glaring disparities between the rich and the poor because most wealth is acquired not through salaried income but through inheritance. A 1976 Royal Commission reported that the richest 1 percent of the population owned 25 percent of the nation's wealth, the richest 5 percent owned nearly 50 percent, and the richest 10 percent owned over 60

Figure 10.5 This woman is a member of the outcaste category of Indian society. The social status of the outcastes is so low that they are not even included in the caste system. Members of higher strata may consider it a form of ritual pollution even to be touched by the shadow of an outcaste—and in some cases, even to be looked at by such a person.

Figure 10.6 *Modern British society is marked by very noticeable class divisions. Despite attempts by successive socialist governments to redistribute the wealth of the society, there is still an affluent upper class that lives mainly off inherited wealth and capital investments. Members of this tiny class dominate most British institutions.*

percent. These inequalities are being gradually reduced through heavy inheritance taxes, but the process is a slow one because it must await the deaths of the rich.

Apart from the inheritance of wealth, the principal mechanism for maintaining the class system is education. Approximately 5 percent of the nation's children attend what are called "public" schools but are not. They are private, with very high fees, and most of them are single-sex boarding schools. Children of the upper classes share a common experience in these schools and benefit from their superior academic facilities. Attendance at these schools confers great advantages later in life. No less than eighteen former pupils of the most prestigious private school, Eton, have become prime ministers, and as recently as the sixties, half of the members of the cabinet came from this one school alone (Gathorne-Hardy, 1978). The pattern is repeated at the college level. Two universities, Oxford and Cambridge, enjoy far greater prestige than the others, and about half of their entrants come from the private schools. Graduates of Oxford and Cambridge are very disproportionately represented at the upper levels of British society and dominate politics, law, the church, the media, corporations, and the civil service (Halsey et al., 1980). The

country's elite maintains its contacts through exclusive men's clubs and forms what is known in Great Britain as "the establishment" or "the magic circle."

Class differences in life-styles and behavior are far more evident in Great Britain than in the United States. The single most important indicator of social class, however, is accent. There are distinct differences among the accents of the upper, middle, and lower classes, and there are minute variations of accent within these classes. Any inhabitant of Great Britain can pinpoint the social status of another the moment that person utters a sentence, and this indicator overrides any others that might be inconsistent with it, such as style of dress. The observant American tourist will notice that the British tend to respond to one another quite differently on the basis of accent. A salesperson, for example, will call someone with an upper-class accent "sir" or "madam," but may address a person with a lower-class accent as "dear," "love," or "mate."

Social mobility in Great Britain compares unfavorably with that in the United States and in several other industrialized societies (Treiman and Terrell, 1972; Lipset and Bendix, 1959; Goldthorpe, 1980). One study found that a person of manual-worker origins has a better chance of reaching the elite in the United States than does a person of middle-class origins in Great Britain (Fox and Miller, 1965b). Although the country's depressed economy has heightened class tensions in recent years, many members of the lower classes remain deferential toward the middle and upper classes. More than a quarter of manual workers, in fact, identify themselves as middle class, and about a third of the working-class voters consistently support the predominantly middle- and upper-class Conservative party.

The Soviet Union: A Classless Society?

The government of the Soviet Union has abolished private ownership of the means of producing and distributing wealth and claims to be working toward the creation of a totally egalitarian, communist society. Although the Soviet Union is often described as "communist" in the West, there is actually no society that regards itself as communist. The Soviet Union claims only to have reached the intermediate stage of socialism, in which classes have been formally abolished but strong centralized government is still needed to guide the transition to the future society.

There is no doubt that the Soviet Union does not have a dominant, profit-making class such as those found in all capitalist societies. Large amounts of wealth cannot be inherited, special privileges such as private education cannot be bought for the next generation, and the amassing of private profit is illegal. In fact, "profiteering" is punishable in some instances by the death sentence. But whether the Soviet Union has successfully abolished classes is a matter of some debate (Parkin, 1971; Lane, 1978; Hough, 1977). In the Soviet Union, as in all other East European socialist societies, there appears to be a "new class" of administrators and other educated experts. About 16 million people (9 percent of the adult population) are members of the Communist party, and of these, about 1 million form a bureaucratic elite. The incomes of these officials are several times the earnings of ordinary people. The elite enjoy many advantages denied to the masses, such as better housing, luxurious vacation facilities, and the use of free automobiles. They also have privileges that would be considered intolerable in the West: for example, they have the exclusive right to use special shops that are stocked with luxury consumer goods unavailable to the ordinary people, and many city streets have special traffic lanes that can be used only by high officials (Djilas, 1957; Matthews, 1979).

Figure 10.7 These Russian women are relaxing after the ordeal of a day spent shopping. Because the Soviet Union invests such a large part of its resources in heavy industry and its defense budget, there is a chronic shortage of consumer items of every kind. These women, who take string bags on all their shopping trips so that they can carry home whatever suitable merchandise becomes available, may have to wait in line for hours to make a single purchase. High government and Communist party officials, however, have access to special stores that are stocked with a variety of consumer goods, many of which are imported from the West.

The small elite of officials who rule the Soviet Union has only a fictional responsibility to the general population. It is significantly more powerful than any comparable elite in the West, for two reasons. First, it has both political and economic power concentrated in its hands, whereas in capitalist societies power is more diffuse. Second, the Soviet elite does not have to face periodic free elections, and its policies are not subject to public criticism. (In the national election of 1979, voter turnout was claimed to be 99.99 percent—but there was only one candidate for each position.)

There is little doubt that power, wealth, and prestige are very unequally distributed in Soviet society, and that occupational status is often passed down from one generation to the next (Lipset, 1973; Dobson, 1977). Whether the elite actually constitutes a class is perhaps a matter of definition. If we define a class in terms of its control over basic national resources, then the Soviet elite is clearly a class, and a very powerful one. If, however, we specify that the ruling class must use its control of resources primarily for its own benefit, as is the case in all other stratified societies, then the elite cannot be considered a class. The Soviet system certainly differs from all other stratification systems in that there is no "leisure class" that lives off accumulated wealth, and, perhaps more significantly, people cannot inherit large sums of wealth from their parents. There also seems to be more social mobility and less of a gap between the strata in the Soviet Union than we find in Western capitalist societies. The issue of whether the Soviet Union is a class society is still unsettled, and it remains to be seen whether that country—or any other society with a different interpretation of communism, such as China—can arrive at an unambiguously classless society.

Maintaining Stratification: The Role of Ideology

How do stratification systems survive? At first sight, it seems highly unlikely that any of them would last for very long, because in every case a small minority enjoys unequal access to scarce resources and thus deprives the majority of a fair share in what the society produces. Yet stratification systems do persist, and some of the most rigid and inegalitarian—such as the European feudal system and the Indian caste system—last for many centuries. How are these systems maintained?

Any successful system requires some kind of legitimacy. If the bulk of the people do not regard it as *legitimate*—that is, as valid and justified—the system is inherently unstable and will inevitably collapse. The ruling elite can apply force to try to maintain inequality, but in fact most stratification systems survive without much use of force. The reason is simple. The inequality is usually taken for granted and regarded as "natural" by all concerned. The legitimacy of the system rests on its habitual, unthinking acceptance by the people—the subordinate as well as the dominant strata.

A political system is legitimated by an *ideology*—that is, a set of beliefs that explains and justifies a given social system. It was Karl Marx who explored the role of ideologies in legitimating social stratification, and his views are now widely accepted, even by sociologists who reject some of his other theories. Marx's argument was simple. The dominant ideology in any society is always the ideology of the ruling class, and it always justifies that class's economic interests. Of course, other ideologies may exist in a society, but none of them can ever become dominant or widely accepted unless the class that holds it, and whose own interests it justifies, becomes the controlling class. In a society controlled by capitalists, therefore, the dominant ideology will be capitalism, not socialism. In a society controlled by socialists, the dominant ideology will be socialism, not capitalism. In a society controlled by slaveholders, the dominant ideology will justify slavery, not the emancipation of slaves.

It is obvious why members of the controlling group might regard the dominant ideology as "natural," but what about the members of the subordinate group? Their acceptance of the legitimacy of the system is a phenomenon Marx called *false consciousness*—a subjective understanding that does not accord with the objective facts of one's situation. The oppressed class fails to realize that the life chances of its individual members are linked to their common circumstances as an exploited group. Instead, they attribute their low status to fate, luck, the will of God, or other factors beyond their control. Only if members of the subordinate stratum gain a *class consciousness*—an objective

Figure 10.8 There have been many riots by black South Africans since the mid-seventies, most of them led by schoolchildren. Although a large segment of the older generation of South African blacks have opposed the rioting, young blacks appear to have developed a general awareness of oppression. In Marxist terms, part of the older generation still accepts the legitimacy of the South African caste system, but the younger generation has developed a class consciousness. Inevitably, white minority rule has been challenged, and outright conflict between the dominant and subordinate racial castes has resulted.

awareness of their common exploitation by the dominant stratum—do they begin to question the legitimacy of the system. They then develop a new ideology, one that justifies their own interests and consequently seems revolutionary to the dominant class. According to Marx, *class conflict* will then follow.

An ideology is a complex belief system. It may include religious, political, economic, and other elements. The advanced feudal system, for example, was legitimated by the political and religious doctrine of the divine right of kings, which held that the monarch derives authority directly from God. When the king delegated some of this authority to the nobles, it followed logically that the peasants were under a divine imperative to obey them also. The peasants seem, on the whole, to have accepted this doctrine as unquestioningly as their masters did. The feudal system was

eventually overthrown when a class of urban capitalists emerged, armed with an ideology of political democracy and economic freedom. In much the same way, the ideology of European colonialism provided a justification for the acts of the colonists. They saw themselves not as exploiters of raw materials and others' labor but as bearers of the "white man's burden," the noble but demanding task of bringing Christian civilization to "inferior" peoples. The subject peoples seem to have accepted the colonists' view, and their acceptance of the legitimacy of the colonial system made it easier for tiny European minorities to dominate vast populations until a new nationalist ideology emerged in the colonies after World War II. The Indian caste system is yet another example. It is legitimated primarily by religion and has been accepted almost without question by all castes, even outcastes, for thousands of years.

BELIEFS ABOUT CHANCES TO GET AHEAD BY INCOME GROUP

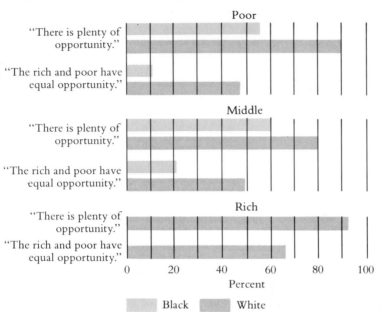

Figure 10.9 Lower-class white Americans are almost as convinced as upper-class Americans that there is "plenty of opportunity" in the United States and that the rich and the poor have equal opportunity—a belief that sociological research has shown to be entirely incorrect. Black Americans, however, seem to have a more realistic assessment of the opportunities available to members of different classes.

Source: Joan H. Rytina et al., "Income and Stratification Ideology: Beliefs about the American Opportunity Structure," *American Journal of Sociology*, 75 (January 1970), p. 708.

Like the inequalities of feudal, colonial, or Indian societies, stratification in America is also legitimated by an ideology that tends to be accepted unquestioningly by the dominant and subordinate classes alike. In the American ideology, inequality is justified as a means of providing incentives and rewarding achievement. The class system is thus legitimated by the belief (though not the fact) that people have an equal opportunity to improve their status. Everyone is supposed to have the same chance to get rich by working hard. Those who do not get rich (that is, most of us, and especially those who started out from a low-status family) therefore have only bad luck or themselves to blame: the well-socialized American who becomes a "failure" in the class system does not blame the system itself (Huber and Form, 1973; Robertson, 1976).

Theories of Stratification

Why are almost all societies stratified? Sociologists have tended to take one of two distinct positions on this question. The *functionalist* perspective, adopted mainly by theorists influenced by Talcott Parsons (1937, 1940), sees stratification as an inevitable and even necessary feature of society. The *conflict* perspective, taken by theorists under the direct or indirect influence of Karl Marx, sees stratification as avoidable, unnecessary, and the source of most human injustice. More recently, Gerhard Lenski (1966) has offered a third perspective, an *evolutionary* approach that combines elements of the other two and explains why some types of societies are more stratified than others. We shall examine each of these approaches in turn.

The Functionalist Approach

Functionalist theory assumes that elements in culture and social structure have effects, or functions, that contribute to the stability and survival of society as a whole. Functionalists therefore argue that if stratification is universal, it must have some useful function in maintaining societies. The classic statement of this position is that of Kingsley Davis and Wilbert Moore (1945), who contend that some form of stratification is a social necessity. They emphasize, however, that they are merely trying to explain this situation, not to justify it.

Davis and Moore point out that some social roles require scarce talents or prolonged training. Not everyone can be a surgeon, a nuclear physicist, or a military strategist. If a society is to function effectively, it must find some way of attracting to these roles the people who have the talents and skills to play them. The roles that require scarce talents or lengthy training usually involve stress, considerable sacrifice, and heavy responsibilities. These important roles must therefore offer wealth, power, prestige, or some combination of the three to provide incentive for individuals to take them on. Thus a society that values senators above garbage collectors will give higher status and rewards to senators; one that values social scientists above carpenters will give higher status and rewards to social scientists; one that values warriors more than priests will give higher status and rewards to warriors. This unequal distribution of social rewards is functional for society because roles that demand scarce talents are played by the most able individuals. Social stratification, however, is the inevitable result.

This analysis was popular among American sociologists for many years. perhaps because it fitted so well with American cultural values about individual achievement. Some critics have argued, however, that the functionalist argument contains serious flaws (Tumin, 1953, 1955, 1963; Buckley, 1958; Wrong, 1959).

The principal criticism of the theory is that it seems to lose touch with reality in several respects. Stratification systems simply do not work in practice the way Davis and Moore have them working in theory. Some people whose roles have no apparent value to society, such as the jet-setting inheritors of family fortunes, are often highly rewarded. Some people whose roles are of limited value, such as film stars, may earn very much more than people whose roles are very important, such as the president of the United States. Above all, many people have low rewards because their social status is ascribed: blacks in the United States, outcastes in India, and so on. Others have high rewards for the same reason: wealthy aristocrats in Great Britain, whites in South Africa.

The functionalist argument is at its weakest in all cases where social status is inherited rather than achieved. This is the situation in all caste societies, and to a large extent it is the situation in all class societies. Even in the most open class systems, the rate of intergenerational mobility is very low (Lipset and Bendix, 1959). In general, social stratification does not function to ensure that the ablest people train for and fill the most important roles. It functions to ensure that most people stay where they are. It is true that some people in some stratified societies can gain high status through personal efforts. But these people, like the poor, then pass their status on to their descendants. Inequality thus spreads with the passage of time, until the stratification system bears little resemblance to its original form, whether that form was functional or not.

Davis and Moore overlook the *dysfunctions* of stratification for society. In practice, social stratification ensures that people do not have equal access to social roles, so it hinders rather than encourages the allocation of roles on merit. All stratification systems offer entire categories of people different life chances because of the circumstances of their birth, and therefore stratification does not make the best use of the talents of the population. And if the lower stratum comes to believe that the system is unjust, social conflict will result. In such cases stratification does not help to maintain the social system. It can, and frequently does, lead to the disruption of the entire social order through violent revolution.

The Conflict Approach

Conflict theorists reject the functionalist view of society as a balanced system whose various features contribute to overall social stability. Instead, they regard conflict over social values and group interests as intrinsic to any society. The conflict approach to stratification has always found favor with European sociologists, perhaps because their societies have a long history of class conflict and still have more noticeable class hostilities than those found in America.

Marx's view—that history is essentially the story of class conflict between the exploiters and the exploited—sees social stratification as created and maintained by one group in order to protect and enhance its economic interests. Stratification exists only because the rich and powerful are determined to preserve their advantages. Marx viewed class conflict as the key to historical change: every ruling class is eventually overthrown by the subordinate class, which then becomes the new ruling class. This process repeats itself until the final confrontation between workers and capitalists in industrial society. Writing in England at a time when workers were subjected to appalling conditions in the factories, Marx predicted that the capitalists would grow fewer and stronger as a result of their endless competition, that the middle class would disappear into the working class, and that the growing poverty of the workers would spark a successful revolution. The workers would then create a new socialist society in which the means of producing and distributing wealth would be publicly owned. Socialism would lead ultimately to a communist society, in which inequality, alienation, conflict, and human misery would be things of the past.

Marx's theories have tended to be neglected by American sociologists for most of this century. One reason is that Marx has been associated, rather unfairly, with the corruption of his ideas by the Soviet Union and other societies of Eastern Europe. Another reason is that his predictions about the future of industrial capitalism were hopelessly wrong. He did not foresee that individual capitalists would be largely replaced by corporations. He did not anticipate that the wealth of industrialism would create a much larger middle class or that the poor would be better off, both relatively and absolutely, than they were in his own time. He was even wrong in predicting that successful socialist revolutions would take place in highly industrialized societies. Without exception, these uprisings have taken place in such countries as Russia, China, and Cuba when they were advanced agricultural societies. Very few Western sociologists accept Marx's view that historical forces will lead us inevitably to a classless society.

Despite the flaws in Marx's theory, there has recently been a great renewal of interest in his work. Sociologists now appreciate that Marx's failure as a prophet does not necessarily invalidate his basic insight: that conflict over scarce resources leads to the creation of caste and class systems and that in every case the interests of the dominant class are served by the ideology and the power of the state. The implication of the conflict perspective is clear. Stratification is not a functional necessity at all—although it is certainly convenient for those who benefit by it.

The Evolutionary Approach

The debate between conflict and functionalist theorists became at times very heated, especially during the sixties. Several writers have pointed out, however, that the two perspectives are not necessarily incompatible (for example, Dahrendorf, 1958; Van den Berghe, 1963). The most promising attempt at a synthesis of the two positions is that of Gerhard Lenski (1966), who emphasizes both conflict and functionalist elements in the evolution of stratification systems. Essentially, he argues that the basic resources a society needs in order to survive are allocated in the way the functionalists claim they are—that is, to match scarce talents with important roles. But Lenski maintains that a society's surplus resources—those not needed for survival—are distributed through conflict among competing groups.

Lenski starts with the idea that people generally find it more rewarding to fulfill their own wants and ambitions than those of others. He accepts that this tendency may be regrettable and that it may be possible to socialize human beings so that they do not behave in this way, but he points out that it remains an almost universal feature of social life. Since the demand for most of the things that people want exceeds the supply, there will in all societies inevitably be some conflict over the distribution of these rewards. And because people are unequally equipped for the competitive struggle, social inequalities will also inevitably result. Sometimes these inequalities will be functional for society, but most societies are much more stratified than they need to be, and forms of stratification will tend to persist long after they have ceased to be useful.

Lenski then traces the evolution of social stratification, showing how the form it takes is related to the society's means of economic production. In *hunting and gathering* societies there is no stratification. Populations are small and intimate, and the members are essentially equal. There is no surplus wealth, so there is no opportunity for some people to become wealthier than others, let alone to pass their status on to their descendants. In *horticultural* and *pastoral*

Figure 10.10 Lenski's evolutionary approach shows how the nature of stratification varies from one type of society to another. In ancient Egypt, an agricultural society, there was a vast gap between the upper class and the peasants. Tens of thousands of the lower class toiled for years simply to create enormous burial monuments for their rulers. In modern Egypt such inequalities would be inconceivable, as they would be in any industrializing or industrialized society.

societies a surplus product is possible, and chieftainships emerge when powerful families gain control over the surplus. These societies are usually not stratified, however, because inequalities exist only among specific individuals or families, and there are no distinct castes or classes. But with the development of advanced horticulture into agriculture, the picture changes radically. In *agricultural* societies people can produce a considerable surplus, and a dominant elite makes claim to this wealth. The society becomes divided into strata according to their access to wealth and other rewards. Power becomes concentrated in the hands of an hereditary aristocracy headed by a monarch, who typically has almost absolute control over the subjects.

These rigid divisions are undermined, however, when a society shifts to *industrialism*. This form of production requires a skilled and mobile labor force, and its efficiency is impaired if people are prevented from using their talents to the full. In the early stages of industrialism there is a vast gap between the rich and the poor, as a rural peasantry is transformed into an urban work force—a situation that still prevails in the less industrialized nations of the world. In the more advanced industrial societies, however, the rate of social mobility increases as a variety of new jobs is created.

The lower class shrinks in size, and the middle class expands rapidly because the entire society shares, however unequally, the great wealth that industrialism produces. Governments become more democratic, and new social inventions such as public welfare and progressive income taxes limit excessive inequalities in wealth.

Lenski's theory is not a rigid one, and he accepts that there may be some exceptions to the general trend he outlines. He also notes that independent factors, such as external threats or the role of particular leaders, may have an impact on the way stratification systems evolve. In general, however, he believes that the long-term trend in all industrial societies will be toward less social inequality. His theory explains why inequalities are often more extreme than could ever be functional: once stratification is built into a society, privileged groups use their advantages to gain even more advantages. While Lenski acknowledges the importance of conflict in stratification systems, he does not reduce all explanations to this one factor alone. He allows that some inequalities may be unavoidable and even useful.

Whichever view one accepts, one must recognize that social stratification cannot simply be taken for granted.

THREE VIEWS OF STRATIFICATION: A COMPARISON

The Functionalist View	The Conflict View	The Evolutionary View
(1) Stratification is necessary and inevitable.	(1) Stratification is not necessary or inevitable.	(1) Some stratification may be necessary and inevitable, but much is not.
(2) Social needs shape the stratification system.	(2) The interests of the powerful shape the stratification system.	(2) The society's subsistence strategy shapes the stratification system.
(3) Stratification arises from the need to match scarce talents with the roles that demand them.	(3) Stratification arises from group conquest, competition, and conflict.	(3) Stratification arises partly from the need to reward scarce talent, partly from competition and conflict.
(4) Stratification is an expression of shared social values.	(4) Stratification is an expression of the values of powerful groups.	(4) Stratification rests on some consensus in values, but it primarily expresses the values of the powerful.
(5) Tasks and rewards are fairly allocated.	(5) Tasks and rewards are unfairly allocated.	(5) Some tasks and rewards are fairly allocated, but many are not.
(6) Stratification facilitates the optimal functioning of society.	(6) Stratification impedes the optimal functioning of society.	(6) Some stratification facilitates the optimal functioning of society; too much impedes it.

Figure 10.11 This table compares and contrasts the essential ingredients of the functionalist, conflict, and evolutionary views of stratification.

Castes and classes are socially constructed in society after society by countless men and women. Since social stratification is socially created, it must, in principle, be socially modifiable as well—provided only that people are conscious of their own ability to change the systems they have built.

In this chapter we have considered the general principles of social stratification. In the next chapter we apply these principles to a specific stratification system, social class in America.

Summary

1. All societies differentiate among their members. This differentiation leads to social inequality, which in most societies becomes built into the social structure, resulting in social stratification. Under social stratification, entire categories of a population have different life chances.

2. Stratification systems may be closed or open. In closed systems the boundaries between strata are fixed, and status is ascribed and lifelong. In open systems the boundaries are flexible, and new statuses can be achieved. Closed systems take the form of castes; open systems, of classes.

3. Change from one status to another is called social mobility. Mobility may be horizontal or vertical, and may be intragenerational and intergenerational. The extent of mobility in a society depends on the number of statuses that are available and the ease with which people can move from one status to another.

4. It is often difficult to determine an individual's status in a class society. Marx argued that economic factors are decisive; those who own and control the means of production are the dominant class; those who do not, and are exploited, are the subordinate class. Weber broke the concept of class into three related dimensions: power, wealth, and prestige. In practice, these three variables correlate strongly.

5. India is a caste society, in which the different *varnas* and *jatis* are endogamous and have different access to valued resources. The system has been maintained in the past by the Hindu religion, but it is tending to break down. Great Britain is a class society in which wealth is unequally shared and in which a small elite enjoys disproportionate power

and prestige. Education is an important factor in maintaining the system. The Soviet Union claims to have virtually abolished classes, but in fact there are many disparities in power, wealth, and prestige between the bureaucratic elite and the rest of the population. It is doubtful whether the Soviet Union has really abolished classes.

6. An ideology is a belief system that explains and justifies, or legitimates, some situation. Stratification systems are legitimated by ideologies that are usually accepted by both dominant and subordinate groups. If the subordinate group rejects the ideology, class conflict will follow.

7. Functionalists argue that stratification is functional because it matches important roles with scarce talents. In practice, however, stratification prevents the allocation of roles on merit. Conflict theorists argue that stratification arises because it serves the economic interests of some groups in society; the privileged group maintains the system and transmits its advantages to the next generation. Lenski's evolutionary theory shows how the nature of stratification is influenced by the complexity of a society and its mode of economic production; his theory combines elements of both functionalist and conflict theories.

Important Terms

social inequality (235)

social stratification (235)

life chances (236)

closed system (237)

open system (237)

caste (237)

endogamy (237)

ascribed status (237)

class (237)

achieved status (237)

social mobility (238)

horizontal mobility (238)

vertical mobility (238)

intragenerational mobility (238)

intergenerational mobility (238)

surplus wealth (239)

power (240)

wealth (240)

prestige (240)

socioeconomic status (242)

legitimacy (246)

ideology (246)

false consciousness (246)

class consciousness (246)

class conflict (247)

Suggested Readings

ADAM, BARRY B. *The Survival of Domination: Inferiorization and Everyday Life.* New York: Elsevier, 1978.

An interesting analysis of the way dominant groups in modern society use ideologies to convince subordinate groups that they are indeed inferior and that the inequality is therefore justified.

BENDIX, REINHARD, and SEYMOUR MARTIN LIPSET (eds.). *Class, Status and Power.* New York: Free Press, 1966.

An important and comprehensive collection of articles on social stratification. The selections include many classic contributions to the field and cover virtually all the major issues raised by social stratification.

BOTTOMORE, T. B. *Classes in Modern Society.* New York: Pantheon, 1965.

An excellent and clearly written short introduction to the class systems of modern industrial societies, including Great Britain, the United States, and the Soviet Union.

HOLLANDER, PAUL. *Soviet and American Society: A Comparison.* Chicago: University of Chicago Press, 1978.

A detailed sociological analysis of the world's two foremost powers and of their rival political and economic systems.

HUTTON, J. H. *Caste in India: Its Nature, Functions, and Origins.* New York: Oxford University Press, 1963.

This book is the classic analysis of the Indian class system. Hutton shows how the caste system evolved and how it is closely intertwined with Hindu religion. The book includes interesting information about the rituals surrounding the caste system.

LENSKI, GERHARD. *Power and Privilege: A Theory of Social Stratification.* New York: McGraw-Hill, 1966.

Lenski outlines his original and influential theory of stratification. The book contains much fascinating detail about social inequalities in preindustrial as well as industrial societies.

MARX, KARL. *Selected Writings in Sociology and Social Philosophy.* Tom Bottomore and Maximilian Rubel (eds.). Baltimore, Md.: Penguin, 1964.

An excellent selection from Marx's writings on a variety of subjects, including social inequality, economic exploitation, and class conflict. The book is recommended as an accessible introduction to Marx's thought.

MATRAS, JUDAH. *Social Inequality, Stratification, and Mobility.* Englewood Cliffs, N.J.: Prentice-Hall, 1975.

A detailed and comprehensive text that summarizes research and theories on social stratification and mobility. The book includes material on the United States but also contains a good deal of comparative data.

CHAPTER 11 · *Inequalities of Social Class*

In the previous chapter we considered some general principles of social stratification. In this chapter we shall focus on the social-class system of the United States, which, despite some unique features, is broadly similar to that of the other advanced industrial nations of the West, particularly Canada (Porter, 1965; Clement, 1975).

The founders of the United States declared in ringing tones that "all men are created equal," and this value has been a central one in American culture ever since. Yet slavery was practiced in the United States for nearly a century after the Declaration of Independence, and legal discrimination against blacks persisted until the 1960s. For decades after the new republic had been founded, the vote was restricted to adult white males who owned property; women were not permitted to vote until early in the twentieth century. Despite its professed belief in equality, the United States now contains over 570,000 millionaires while about 24 million people live below the official poverty line.

The reality of American life, then, has fallen far short of the ideal. In practice, the value of equality has always been contradicted by other values, such as those emphasizing white supremacy, male superiority, the desirability of youthfulness, and economic competition. As a result, the modern United States is a very unequal society. We shall reserve our discussion of inequalities associated with race, sex, and age until later chapters, focusing here on the economic inequalities that make the United States a class society.

Social Inequality in the United States

As we saw in Chapter 10 ("Social Stratification"), all forms of inequality involve an unequal distribution of wealth,

255

power, or prestige. The evidence shows that all three, particularly wealth and power, are very unequally distributed in American society.

Wealth

It seems to be generally true that the distribution of wealth (such as capital and other property) and income (such as salaries and wages) becomes steadily more equal as a society becomes more industrialized (Lenski, 1966; Cutright, 1967; Wilensky, 1978). There is general agreement among researchers, however, that the United States is an exception to this trend (Rossides, 1976). There has been little or no equalization of wealth or income in the United States for at least the last quarter century. Moreover, the economic inequalities that exist between the rich and the poor are enormous.

The bulk of the nation's wealth (assets) is owned by a small minority of the population. As Figure 11.1 shows, the poorest fifth of Americans owns only 0.2 percent of the national wealth and the next poorest fifth owns only 2.1 percent. The richest fifth, however, owns 76.0 percent of

the national wealth. To put this another way, while the richest fifth owns more than three-quarters of the nation's wealth, the poorest fifth owns only one five-hundredth of it. More than half of the country's wealth, in fact, is owned by one-twentieth of the population. Information on the distribution of wealth in the United States in the past is rather sketchy, but the available data show little change since the early nineteenth century (Lampman, 1962; Gallman, 1969).

We have rather better information on the distribution of income (earnings) during this century. There was a small decline in differences in the earnings of families during the early thirties and forties (Kuznets, 1953), but there has been virtually no redistribution of income since that time (H. P. Miller, 1972; Glenn, 1974). As Figure 11.3 shows, there is a huge gap between the incomes of the very rich and the very poor. The bottom fifth of American families receives only 5.2 percent of the income, while the highest fifth receives 41.5 percent. These shares have hardly changed at all since the end of World War II.

Despite these marked disparities in wealth and income, the rising standard of living in the United States has

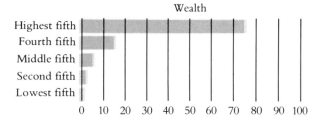

THE DISTRIBUTION OF WEALTH IN THE UNITED STATES: FIFTHS OF CONSUMER UNITS RANKED BY WEALTH

Source: Executive Office of the President, Office of Management and the Budget, *Social Indicators, 1973* (Washington, D.C.: U.S. Government Printing Office, 1973), Chart 5/15.

Figure 11.1   Wealth—that is, assets such as property and other capital—is very unequally distributed in the United States. As this chart shows, the richest fifth of consumer units (families and single individuals) owns more than three-quarters of the wealth of American society.

Figure 11.2

"How little we really own, Tom, when you consider all there is to own."

Drawing by Wm. Hamilton; © 1976
The New Yorker Magazine, Inc.

brought benefits to virtually the entire society. Even allowing for inflation, the median income of Americans has more than doubled over the last quarter century. The poor are probably better off in absolute terms than they were earlier in the century, even if their relative earnings have changed little. The proportion of the nation that is living in poverty has declined from about 27 percent in the late forties to about 12 percent today.

We know much less about the very rich than about the very poor, a fact that probably reflects the ability of the wealthy to keep inquisitive sociologists at arm's length. We do know, however, that the rich consist mainly of two overlapping elements: those living largely on inherited capital investments and those holding high executive positions in major corporations. The private ownership of stock is highly concentrated among a few wealthy individuals and families. The wealth of a handful of these families is colossal: about 155 of them are worth $100 million each, and about 60, between $100 million and $500 million each. The top 1 percent of individuals and families own more than half the total market value of all privately owned stock and receive nearly half the total dividend income from stocks (Blume et al., 1974). According to a 1979 report by the Internal Revenue Service, there are 1769 American families with annual incomes of over $1 million; most of this money is unearned income from stock and other investments. In a 1980 survey of over a thousand chief executives of the nation's largest corporations, *U. S. News and World Report* found that they enjoyed a median annual salary of over $300,000, about fifteen times greater than the median family income for the nation as a whole. Nine of them, in fact, were paid more than a million dollars a year. Wealth, incidentally, is certainly no disadvantage to those individuals who seek political power: in 1980, at least 31 senators were worth half a million dollars and at least 20 more of them were worth over $1 million.

The evidence, then, points to a very unequal distribution of the country's economic rewards. As a result of these inequalities, the life chances of those in the upper strata of society are very different from the chances of those in the lower strata. To give but one example, the United States, despite its great affluence, ranks fifteenth among the nations of the world in the prevention of infant mortality. The great majority of the nation's preventable childhood deaths occur among the impoverished (Gortmaker, 1979).

PERCENTAGE SHARE OF TOTAL INCOME RECEIVED BY EACH FIFTH AND TOP 5 PERCENT OF FAMILIES, 1958 TO 1978

| Year | Percent Distribution of Aggregate Income | | | | | |
	Lowest Fifth	Second Fifth	Middle Fifth	Fourth Fifth	Highest Fifth	Top 5 Percent
1958	5.0	12.5	18.0	23.9	40.6	15.4
1960	4.8	12.2	17.8	24.0	41.3	15.9
1962	5.0	12.1	17.6	24.0	41.3	15.7
1964	5.1	12.0	17.7	24.0	41.2	15.9
1966	5.6	12.4	17.8	23.8	40.5	15.6
1968	5.6	12.4	17.7	23.7	40.5	15.6
1970	5.4	12.2	17.6	23.8	40.9	15.6
1972	5.4	11.9	17.5	23.9	41.4	15.9
1974	5.4	12.0	17.6	24.1	41.0	15.3
1976	5.4	11.8	17.6	24.1	41.1	15.6
1978	5.2	11.6	17.5	24.1	41.5	15.6

Source: U.S. Bureau of the Census.

Figure 11.3 The distribution of income—salaries, wages, and similar earnings—has remained virtually unchanged since the end of World War II. The richest fifth of American families has consistently received over 40 percent of the total income during this period, while the poorest fifth has consistently received around 5 percent.

Power

Like wealth, power is very unequally shared in the United States. The extension of voting rights to the poor, to women, and to blacks seems at first sight to represent a steady broadening of the power base to include different groups in society. Progress in this area, however, has been offset by the growth of vast federal bureaucracies and powerful corporate interests. As a result, power has become concentrated more and more at the upper levels of the executive branch of government and the corporate economy.

Figure 11.4

"Tom Willoughby, meet Howard Sylvester—one of us."

Drawing by Bernard Schoenbaum; © 1977
The New Yorker Magazine, Inc.

Sociologists have tended to take one of two basic views of the distribution of power. Some, such as C. Wright Mills (1956), argue that American society is dominated by a *power elite* consisting of high officials in government and corporations. This elite operates informally and makes most of the important decisions that affect political and economic life. These decisions are usually made "behind the scenes," and even Congress often has little influence over them. Other sociologists, such as David Riesman (1961), argue that the power structure is more *pluralistic*. In this view, a variety of powerful interest groups struggle for advantage but counterbalance one another in the long run. Different groups compete over various issues, and often attempt to win public support to further their own interests. We do not yet have enough information to prove or disprove either of these views, but it is significant that the ordinary voter does not figure at all in the power-elite model and is a marginal element in the pluralistic model. Even in the arena of local politics, power is unequally shared. Over the decades, sociological studies of some thirty-three American communities have shown that power at this level is always exercised either by a small elite or by powerful interest groups (Walton, 1966). A recurrent complaint in American life over the last fifteen years or so—heard from all parts of the political spectrum—is that the ordinary citizen is powerless to influence major decisions.

Those with political power in the United States tend to be white, middle-aged, male, Protestant, and, perhaps most significant, wealthy. Several studies (for example, Domhoff, 1967, 1971, 1978, 1980; Anderson, 1974; Allen, 1974; Dye, 1976; G. Moore, 1979; Useem, 1978, 1979) have shown that there is a tight-knit "establishment," or "governing class," of people with these characteristics, and that this group has a strong informal influence on policy decisions, particularly in economic and foreign affairs. It is also clear that powerful interests have a privileged and sometimes improper influence over the decision-making process. Investigations following the Watergate scandals uncovered many cases of bribes and payoffs to public officials by commercial interests, including dozens of the most powerful corporations in the United States. These payments were intended to bring about policy decisions favorable to the corporations concerned. (The power structure of the United States is discussed in more detail in Chapter 19, "The Political Order.")

An outstanding example of the successful use of behind-the-scenes influence can be found in the tax laws, which contain numerous loopholes that were inserted under pressure from powerful interests. In theory, the tax system is progressive; that is, it should take away a progressively greater proportion of earnings as income rises. In fact, however, the tax laws place as heavy a burden on the poor as on the rich, because the wealthy are able to exploit a wide range of loopholes. The result is that the wealthy—those earning over $50,000—pay much the same proportion of their income in direct and indirect tax as those earning only a few thousand dollars a year. Philip Stern (1973) claims that loopholes have turned the American tax system into "Uncle Sam's welfare program for the rich." Every year, many super-rich Americans pay little or nothing in taxes. In 1976, for example, nearly 250 people with incomes above $200,000, and 5 with incomes above $1 million, did not contribute a cent in income tax—quite legally. (Perhaps the most outstanding example of this tax avoidance was provided in the sixties by the late John Paul Getty. In a year when he enjoyed a daily income of $300,000 and would otherwise have paid a tax of no less than $70 million, he used loopholes so effectively that his tax bill was only a few thousand dollars.) Many tax deductions, of course, are socially and economically useful and justifiable. They provide, for example, incentives for investment and for gifts to charity. Some deductions, however, are widely used by powerful and wealthy individuals and corporations to avoid paying their share of the nation's taxes.

Prestige

A person's social prestige seems to be determined mainly by his or her job. Occupations are valued largely in terms of the incomes associated with them, although other factors can also be relevant—particularly the amount of education a given occupation requires and the degree of control over others it provides (Reiss et al., 1961). As Figure 10.4 in Chapter 10 ("Social Stratification"), p. 241, suggests, the holders of political power also tend to have high prestige.

Unlike power and wealth, which do not seem to be becoming more equally shared, the symbols of prestige have become available to an increasing number of Americans. The main reason is the radical change in the nature of jobs over the course of this century. In 1900 nearly 40 percent of the labor force were farm workers and less than 20 percent held white-collar jobs. At the beginning of the 1980s, however, less than 5 percent of the labor force worked on farms, and white-collar workers were the largest single occupational category. Blue-collar workers, the largest category in the mid-fifties, now constitute less than a third of all workers. The increase in the proportion of high-prestige jobs has allowed a much greater number of Americans to enjoy these statuses and the life-styles that go with them.

The American Class System

It is inevitable that there will be some inequalities in any human group, if only because its various members will have different talents, skills, looks, personalities, physical strength, and so on. Inequality becomes a major sociological concern when it is *structured* into society. When this happens, entire categories of the population have unequal access to wealth, power, and prestige, and these inequalities are passed on from one generation to the next. This kind of inequality is deeply entrenched in American society in the form of the class system. But how many classes are there in the United States, and what are the characteristics of the different classes?

Problems of Analysis

Social classes do not exist "out there," any more than inches, gallons, or kilograms do. The concept of class, like the concept of an inch, is something people impose on reality. What exists "out there" is social inequality, but various observers may draw the precise boundaries of class in quite different ways. Just as we could create many ways of measuring off the length of a piece of wood, so we can create many ways of categorizing a population into classes.

A sociologist can use three methods to analyze the class structure of a society. The first is the *reputational method*, in which the researcher asks people what class they believe other people belong to. The second is the *subjective method*, in which the researcher asks people what class they believe they themselves belong to. The third is the *objective method*, in which the researcher fits people into an arbitrary number of classes on the basis of some fixed standard, such as annual income. All three methods have been used in the United States, and they have given a generally similar picture of the class system. The precise details vary, however, depending not only on which method is used but also on the wording of the questions and the kind of community in which the respondents live.

The Reputational Method

One of the most influential studies using the reputational method was made by W. Lloyd Warner and Paul Lunt (1941) in the small Massachusetts town of Newburyport. Warner and Lunt conducted in-depth interviews with many residents of this community, which had a population of about 17,000 at the time. In these interviews, they tried to find out how many classes the residents saw in their community and why they believed that specific people belonged to one class rather than another. It was soon clear that this small town was anything but classless. Respondents continually described other people as "old aristocracy," "the folks with the money," "snobs trying to push up," "nobodies," "society," "poor folk but decent," or "poor whites." Using these and other cues, Warner and Lunt divided the community into six social classes: an upper, a middle, and a lower, each containing an internal upper and lower level.

The reputational method is useful in small communities where the residents know one another. In these cases it can provide fascinating insights into people's conceptions of the class system. The method has two main disadvantages, however. First, it is difficult or even impossible to apply it to a large community where people do not know many others well, or to an entire society. Second, the method depends heavily on the personal interpretations of the observer. By analyzing their data differently, Warner and Lunt might have been able to find, say, four or ten classes.

The Subjective Method

The subjective method, in which people are asked to locate themselves in the class system, has been used in several studies—usually at the national rather than local level.

In the late forties a *Fortune* poll found that 80 percent of the respondents claimed to be middle class. The magazine took this finding as evidence that the United States was a truly middle-class society. Richard Centers (1949) objected to this conclusion. He pointed out that the poll had offered the respondents only three choices: "upper class," "middle class," or "lower class." Using a national random sample, Centers added a fourth choice, "working class." Approximately half of his respondents placed themselves in this category—a finding that suggested that the United States was primarily a working-class society. The *Fortune* poll had not shown that the United States was a middle-class society; it had simply reflected the fact that Americans have a distaste for the term "lower class." Low-income people will proudly identify themselves as "working class" but will call themselves "middle class" rather than "lower class" if only these two options are given.

The proportion of Americans identifying themselves as working class has shrunk since Centers did his research. In a 1978 New York Times–CBS News survey, 35 percent of a national sample described themselves as "middle class," and 34 percent as "working class." Some 6 percent declared that they belonged to some "other class"—and 25 percent asserted that they did not belong to any class at all. This change presumably reflects alterations in the class structure and in attitudes toward class since the earlier survey.

The subjective method has the advantage that it can be applied to a large population by polling a random sample. But the method also has its disadvantages. First, the results are influenced by the form of the question that is asked. Second, many people may rank themselves higher than their incomes and life-styles seem to justify.

The Objective Method

This method carries a misleading label, for it implies that the approach is more "scientific" and unbiased than the others. In fact, however, it is a purely arbitrary way of analyzing a class system. The sociologist first sets a standard for determining class membership and then divides the population into a number of classes on this basis.

The objective method was pioneered by Lloyd Warner (1949) in his analysis of the class system of a small community. He constructed an "index of status characteristics," based at first on six main indicators: occupation, type of house, area of residence, source of income, amount of income, and amount of education. All these factors, however, were found to correlate fairly strongly. August Hollingshead (1949) also applied the objective method in his study of Morris, Illinois. Using the criteria of place of residence, occupation, and level of education, he divided the families in the community into five classes. Later investigators have often found it sufficient to use the income of the family breadwinner as the main or even the sole criterion of class membership.

The objective method has the advantage that it gives clear-cut results and usually requires no painstaking collection of data. The relevant statistics are readily available from the Bureau of the Census and other agencies and merely have to be interpreted. The main disadvantage of the method is that it is so arbitrary. Different sociologists may use different criteria for determining class membership and may divide the same population into very different class categories. The method also ignores the beliefs that the people themselves have about the class system. There is some debate about whether a sociologist can validly classify people as, say, "working class" when those people are convinced that they belong to another class.

The Social Classes

What, then, is the structure of the American class system? Most sociologists would probably accept, at least in general outline, the picture drawn by Daniel Rossides (1976). He suggests that there is an upper class consisting of about 1 to 3 percent of the population, an upper middle class of 10 to 15 percent, a lower middle class of 30 to 35 percent, a working class of 40 to 45 percent, and a lower class of 20 to

THE AMERICAN CLASS SYSTEM IN THE TWENTIETH CENTURY: AN ESTIMATE

Class (and Percentage of Population)	Income	Property	Occupation	Education	Personal and Family Life	Education of Children
Upper class (1–3%)	Very high income	Great wealth, old wealth	Corporate heads, high civil and military officials	Liberal arts education at elite schools	Stable family life Autonomous personality	College education by right for both sexes
Upper-middle class (10–15%)	High income	Accumulation of property through savings	Managers, professionals, high-level executives	Graduate training	Better physical and mental health	Educational system biased in their favor
Lower-middle class (30–35%)	Modest income	Some savings	Small business people and farmers, semiprofessionals, sales and clerical workers	Some college High school	Longer life expectancy	Greater chance of college than working-class children
Working class (40–45%)	Low income	Some savings	Skilled labor Unskilled labor	Some high school Grade school	Unstable family life Conformist personality	Educational system biased against them Tendency toward vocational programs
Lower class (20–25%)	Poverty income (destitution)	No savings	Highest unemployment	Illiteracy	Poorer physical and mental health Lower life expectancy	Little interest in education, high dropout rates

Source: Adapted from Daniel W. Rossides, *The American Class System* (Boston: Houghton Mifflin, 1976), p. 26.

Figure 11.5 An illustration of the general outlines of the American class system and the characteristic of each class. There is always disagreement on where the boundaries between the strata fall in any class system, but this broad outline would be accepted by most American sociologists. It was constructed from a variety of sources, including government statistics, sociological studies of various communities and of the national population, and interpretative works.

25 percent (see Figure 11.5). A number of other researchers (for example, Coleman and Neugarten, 1971) have come to fairly similar conclusions. We shall now take a look at the characteristics of these classes in more detail. The portraits presented here are, of course, broad generalizations; there are many individual exceptions to the overall class patterns.

The Upper Class

The *upper class* is a very small one, yet its members own at least a quarter of the nation's wealth, and they are disproportionately represented at the highest levels of political and economic power. This class consists of two main elements. The *upper upper class* consists of the old aristocracy of birth and wealth. To be fully respectable in America, money, like wine, must age a little. One can become a member of the upper upper class only by being born into it.

Figure 11.6 This photograph of two successive presidents of the United States illustrates a distinction between the upper upper and the lower upper class. President Kennedy, with a pained expression, is apparently restraining then Vice-President Johnson from behaving in what Kennedy seems to regard as a vulgar way. Kennedy was a member of the upper upper class: he was born to great wealth and the attendant "social graces." Johnson entered the upper class through his own efforts. Throughout his career Johnson was suspicious and resentful of the "Eastern Establishment," which, he felt, looked down on him because of his origins.

The names of people in this class are familiar ones: the Chryslers, Rockefellers, Fords, Roosevelts, Kennedys, Astors, Vanderbilts. The founding ancestors of many of the present clans were never accepted into the upper upper class because their origins were too humble and their wealth was too recently acquired. Only a generation ago Mrs. David Lion Gardiner, the "empress" of the aristocratic Gardiner family of New York, forbade her grandson to play with the Rockefeller grandchildren on the grounds that "no Gardiner will ever play with the grandchild of a gangster" (Lundberg, 1968). Similarly, the author once heard a dowager of an ancient Boston lineage refer to the newly wealthy Kennedy family, at a time when one of them had become president of the United States, as "those low street-Irish." The members of the upper upper class tend to know one another personally, to attend the same schools, to visit the same resorts, and to intermarry. Their names are included in the *Social Register* or the *Blue Book*—volumes that self-consciously imitate *Debrett's Peerage*, a listing of the British aristocracy.

The *lower upper class* are those who have become very wealthy more recently. They may actually have more money, better houses, and larger automobiles than the upper uppers, but they lack the right "breeding" to win full acceptance into the very highest social circles.

The distinctions between the two upper classes are not generally recognized by the rest of society, and they are of little importance outside the elite circles themselves. As we have seen, the upper class as a whole has great power and prestige, and such influence on both domestic and foreign policy that it affects the lives not only of other classes but also of other nations throughout the world (Domhoff, 1971).

The Middle Class

The *middle class* lacks the cohesion of the upper class but has a distinctive life-style: in fact, the values of the middle class form the dominant morality of the United States. Middle-class attitudes and tastes are respected and endorsed by politicians, media, advertisers, and schools. This class also contains two fairly distinct elements.

The *upper middle class* consists primarily of high-income business and professional families. Like the upper class, this group contains a disproportionate number of people from white, Protestant, Anglo-Saxon backgrounds. Members of

Figure 11.7 The upper middle and lower middle classes differ primarily in the life-styles that their different incomes make possible. While both classes enjoy a comfortable standard of living, the higher occupational status of the upper middle class offers its members more options, influence, and prestige, and permits them to pursue a more affluent way of life.

the upper middle class are highly "respectable," but they are not "society." They tend to live in comfortable suburban homes, to enjoy a stable family life, and to have a high sense of civic duty. They are very active in political life and dominate community organizations. They are concerned with personal career advancement and have high aspirations for their children, who are expected to receive a college education as a matter of course.

The *lower middle class* share most of the values of the upper middle class, but they lack the educational or economic advantages that would let them enjoy the same life-style. This class consists of people whose diverse jobs do not involve manual labor. It includes small-business operators and sales representatives, teachers and nurses, police officers, and middle-management personnel. The lower middle class is very concerned about "proper" behavior, about decency and the value of hard work. Members of this class, who, in fact, usually have to work hard to achieve and retain what they have, are often politically and economically conservative.

The Lower Class

The *lower class* consists essentially of those whose jobs and educational levels prevent them from enjoying the status and life-style of that "typical" American family portrayed in schoolbooks and the media. Racial and ethnic minority groups are disproportionately represented in this class. The lower class can also be divided into two strata.

The upper lower, or *working class*, consists primarily of blue-collar workers—small tradespeople, service personnel, and semiskilled workers of various kinds. Their jobs typically involve manual labor and have little public prestige. Although certain of these workers earn incomes that are higher than those of some members of the middle class, their jobs typically lack the "fringe benefits" of pensions, insurance, sick leave, paid vacations, and job safety. Most members of the working class have modest incomes, and few of them are able to save money. The members of this class cannot afford to live in desirable residential areas but take great pride in being "respectable," a self-image they

Figure 11.8 The upper lower, or working, class consists primarily of blue-collar workers who earn a modest income from their semiskilled jobs. Members of this class place great value on respectability and the virtues of hard work. The lower lower class (usually just termed the lower class) consists primarily of the "disreputable poor." Members of this class tend to be habitually unemployed or underemployed, and are often stigmatized by people in higher strata.

derive largely from the sense that they work hard—at "real" work done with the hands. They are sharply aware of the differences between themselves and the stratum below, against which they often feel antagonistic, especially when they believe that their taxes are being used to support alleged welfare chiselers.

The *lower lower class* (usually simply called the "lower class" to distinguish it from the working class) consists of the "disreputable poor." This class includes the permanently unemployed, the homeless, the illiterate, the chronic "skid-row" alcoholic, and the impoverished aged. They are virtually worthless on the labor market and so are virtually worthless in terms of power and prestige as well. Members

of this class are poorly regarded by other Americans. Their supposed laziness, promiscuity, and reliance on public handouts are contrasted with the "morality" of the middle class. They tend to lack a common consciousness, to be alienated from, and cynical about, society, and to be fatalistic about their own chances in life.

Since a person's class status depends primarily on the income of the family breadwinner—usually the father—it is easy to see why class distinctions tend to be handed down from generation to generation. As William Goode (1964) comments, "The family is the keystone of the stratification system, the social mechanism by which it is maintained."

The social class of the family strongly influences the opportunities of the children. A child in a high-status family, for example, has a good opportunity to acquire the values, attitudes, personal contacts, education, and skills that make for success in American life. A child from a low-status family is raised in an atmosphere of poverty, interacts only with low-status peers, and lacks the career ambitions and opportunities that children in other classes take for granted. As a result, most people are likely to remain for a lifetime in their class of origin.

Correlates of Class Membership

One of the many reasons social class is important is that class membership correlates with a variety of other aspects of social life.

Political Behavior

The higher a person's social class, the more likely he or she is to take an interest in political affairs, to register as a voter, and to vote. Party affiliation also correlates with social class. People higher in the social hierarchy are more likely to be Republican; people lower in the hierarchy are more likely to be Democrats. The working class is liberal on many economic issues that affect its own interest, but on most other issues it is more conservative than the other classes. Tolerance in attitudes toward issues of civil liberty tends to increase as social class rises (Alford and Friedland, 1975; Wolfinger and Rosenstone, 1980; Nunn et al., 1978; Hyman and Wright, 1979).

Marital Stability

Divorce is more common at the lower social levels, perhaps because unemployment and economic problems generate friction between partners (Goode, 1965). Traditional sex roles are most entrenched in the lower class, and there is evidence that marital relations at this level are relatively lacking in warmth (Komarovsky, 1962; Rubin, 1976). Female-headed families are found predominantly in the lower class, particularly in the black community.

Religious Affiliation

There is a strong correlation, at least among whites, between Protestantism and high status—perhaps because Protestants were the first to establish themselves in the United States and to gain wealth and political power.

Within the Protestant churches there is a fairly close correlation between income and membership in a particular denomination. The upper classes prefer denominations that offer quiet and restrained services, while the lower classes are disproportionately represented in revivalist and fundamentalist sects. The most prestigious Protestant denomination appears to be Episcopalian, followed in rough order by the Congregational, Presbyterian, Methodist, Lutheran, and Baptist denominations (Gockel, 1969; Lauer, 1975; Nelsen, 1976; Newport, 1979).

Educational Achievement

Social-class membership has a strong influence on IQ and on educational achievement: the higher the social class of the parents, the more likely it is that their children will have high IQs and high educational achievement. Since the well-educated usually get the best jobs, existing inequalities tend to be reinforced by education (Sewell and Hauser, 1975; Griffin and Alexander, 1978; Jencks et al., 1979). This discrepancy in achievement is not necessarily related to differences in intellectual ability. Less than 10 percent of students with high incomes and high abilities fail to enter college, but about 25 percent of low-income students with comparable abilities do not manage to get to college (Jencks et al., 1972).

Health

In almost all industrialized countries except the United States, health care is regarded as a social service and is therefore available either free or for a low sum. These countries take it for granted that the quality of one's medical attention should depend on how sick one is, not on how wealthy one is. In the United States people have to pay for their health care themselves, either directly or through some form of health insurance. However, about 24 million Americans are not covered by health insurance of any kind, and fear of possible expenses often makes these people reluctant to seek early treatment of medical problems or even causes them to leave some problems unattended. Rich people are very much healthier than poor people. The incidence of most diseases, including diabetes, heart disease, and cancer, is significantly higher in the lower social classes. The higher one's social status, the longer one is likely to live (Fuchs, 1974; Krause, 1977; Kosa and Zola, 1978; Luft, 1978).

Mental Disorder

The incidence of mental disorder, and the treatment received, are closely linked to social class (Dohrenwend, 1970; Fried, 1975; Kessler and Cleary, 1980). One study (Hollingshead and Redlich, 1958) found that hospitalization for schizophrenia was eleven times more common for lower-class than for upper-class persons. The upper-class patients were more likely to be treated with psychotherapy and to be hospitalized for only brief periods. Lower-class patients were more likely to be treated with drugs and electric-shock therapy and to be hospitalized for long periods. Another study in Manhattan (Srole et al., 1962) found that nearly one person in every two in the lowest class was psychologically impaired, although only 1 percent of these people were receiving treatment.

Social Participation

The middle and upper classes participate extensively in community activities and organizations—charities, parent-teacher associations, women's groups, civic associations, and the like. (In this context, the upper class tends to play high-prestige roles, such as that of honorary president, and the middle-class members are more likely to take on routine roles.) In the working and lower class, on the other hand, social relationships are more inclined to center around family, kin, and neighbors (Komarovsky, 1962; Bott, 1971).

Values and Attitudes

Middle- and upper-class people feel a relatively strong sense of control over, and responsibility for, their lives. They are generally prepared to defer immediate gratification in the hope of greater future rewards. Although their values and attitudes set the general moral standards of the whole society, they are somewhat more tolerant of ambiguity in sexual behavior, religion, and other areas than are members of the working and lower classes. Members of the working and lower classes are less likely to defer gratification, and the working class is inclined to be particularly intolerant of unconventional behavior and attitudes. People in the lowest class tend to have a strongly fatalistic attitude toward life. They often see their chances as being determined primarily by luck and other forces beyond their personal control.

Child-Rearing Practices

Middle- and upper-class child-rearing practices are chiefly concerned with teaching principles of behavior and helping children to decide for themselves how to act in accordance with these principles. Working- and lower-class practices tend to focus on teaching children to obey the rules and stay out of trouble. Middle- and upper-class training often uses withdrawal of love as a control device, which may cause anxieties and guilt in children. Working- and lower-class training is more disciplinarian and may involve more physical punishment (M. L. Kohn, 1969, 1977; Walters and Stinnett, 1971). These child-rearing practices inevitably color the later personalities of people in different classes.

Criminal Justice

A large number of self-report studies have concluded that almost every American has committed some kind of crim-

Figure 11.9

"My family was very poor, and I never finished school. But in this great land of ours you don't have to be defeated by such things, even though I was."

Drawing by Handelsmen; © 1979
The New Yorker Magazine, Inc.

inal offense (Doleschal and Klapmuts, 1973). However, lower-class people are more likely to be arrested for criminal offenses, denied bail, found guilty, and given long sentences than are members of other classes. This does not necessarily mean that lower-class people commit more crimes; it means that they are more likely to be caught and less likely to have access to "equal justice." In addition, typical lower-class crimes, such as robbery, larceny, auto theft, and burglary, are regarded as much more serious than typical middle- or upper-class crimes, such as embezzlement, forgery, tax evasion, and fraud.

Social Mobility in the United States

Abraham Lincoln was born in a log cabin but made it to the White House. Andrew Carnegie, John D. Rockefeller, and J. P. Morgan started life in poverty but became millionaires. These tales are such a treasured part of our folklore that it is easy to overlook the countless would-be millionaires or presidents who remained in poverty or obscurity despite their ambitions and efforts.

In European societies, with their long feudal histories and obvious social divisions, people tend to regard their class systems as rigid. They recognize that *social mobility*, or movement from one status to another, is no easy matter. In the United States, with its deep commitment to the ideal of human equality, the belief that one can get ahead with hard work is a central part of the national ethic. What are the facts?

Research on social mobility since the twenties has shown that the American dream of ambition and hard work as the key to success rarely becomes a reality. In one early study, Pitirim Sorokin (1927) found that most men started their occupational careers at about the same level as their father's and that only a very few made significant advances thereafter. In their study of Muncie, Indiana, Robert and Helen Lynd (1929) found that whatever an ordinary worker's chances of becoming a foreman might be in theory, in practice they were minimal. Ely Chinoy (1955) drew similar conclusions from his study of auto workers. Seymour Martin Lipset and Reinhard Bendix (1959) studied the backgrounds of business executives born between 1770 and 1920 and found that some 70 percent of them had come from the upper class, 20 percent from the

middle class, and only 10 percent from the working class. Joseph Kahl (1961) found that only 18 percent of the executive elite in the early fifties came from working-class origins. Another study of professional people in the sixties found that some 40 percent of them were the offspring of professional fathers—nearly five times as many as would be expected in a perfectly open system (Jackson and Crockett, 1964).

The most detailed work on social mobility in the United States was conducted by Peter Blau and Otis Dudley Duncan (1967), who collected data from 20,000 men. By analyzing information on the educational and occupational background of the fathers and of the sons, they were able to show that 37 percent of the men in white-collar jobs had a father who held a blue-collar job. Blau and Duncan also established that a person's own level of education has more influence on social mobility than does the father's occupation or education. A person's educational achievement is related to the social background of the family, of course, but Blau and Duncan found that a well-educated son of a working-class father has much the same chance of upward mobility as the poorly educated son of a middle-class father.

These findings do not mean that there is very little social mobility in the United States. In fact, there is a great deal. But most of this mobility involves relatively minor changes of status, not great leaps from lowly origins to lofty positions. The general pattern in American society is one of moderate upward mobility from one generation to the next.

Blau and Duncan suggest three reasons for this trend. First, the American economy has been expanding steadily throughout this century. As the proportion of white-collar occupations has increased, people from working-class origins have inevitably filled the new middle-class jobs. Second, the higher classes have lower birth rates than the lower classes. The higher classes thus fail to supply the personnel needed to fill new high-status jobs, so people lower down in the social hierarchy are able to move upward. Third, immigration of unskilled workers from other parts of the world and from rural areas within the United States has tended to push existing urban groups into higher occupational statuses. Social rather than individual factors thus account for much of the social mobility in the United States.

Figure 11.10 Despite the American ideology of equality of opportunity, social status tends to be transmitted from generation to generation, and the rate of social mobility between the classes is rather low. A family's class background has a profound effect on the attitudes, motivations, educational achievement, prospects for inheriting wealth, and social opportunities of its children. Do these two young people—one from the upper class and one from the lower class—really have equal opportunity to "make it" in American society?

What makes one person more likely than another to achieve a higher status? A number of factors have been identified, several of them being characteristics over which individuals have little or no control. They include willingness to postpone marriage, willingness to defer immediate gratification in favor of long-term goals, residence in an urban rather than a rural area, high IQ, level of education, racial or ethnic background, childhood nutrition, physical appearance (especially among women), random factors such as chance introductions to future employers or partners, and, of course, class of origin (Blau and Duncan, 1967; Lipset and Bendix, 1959; J. S. Coleman, 1966; Porter, 1968; Hauser and Featherman, 1978; Jencks et al., 1979).

How does intergenerational mobility in the United States compare with that in other industrialized societies? In a classic study of this question, Seymour Martin Lipset and Reinhard Bendix (1959) compared rates of mobility from blue- to white-collar occupations in several industrial societies. They concluded that there was little difference among them. In the United States the mobility rate from blue- to white-collar occupations was about 34 percent, compared with 32 percent in Sweden, 31 percent in Great Britain, 29 percent in France, and 25 percent in West Germany and Japan. In this regard, at least, the United States does not seem to be a land of especially great opportunity.

There is one respect, however, in which mobility in the United States is higher than that in other industrial societies. Working-class Americans have a significantly greater chance of entering the professional elite than do members of the working class in other societies (S. M. Miller, 1960; Fox and Miller, 1965; Blau and Duncan, 1967). About 10 percent of Americans of working-class origins enter the professional elite, compared with about 7 percent in Japan and the Netherlands, less than 3 percent in Great Britain, less than 2 percent in Denmark, West Germany, and France, and less than 1 percent in Italy. Even so, a working-class American's chances of mobility into the highest strata of society are small.

There is only very limited truth, then, to the belief that this is a country of equal opportunity. The fact is that most people remain at or near the level of the families into which they were born and that many of the factors that determine social mobility are beyond personal control.

Poverty in the United States

The term "poverty," as used by the federal government, applies to those individuals whose incomes are considered inadequate to meet basic needs for food, clothing, and shelter. In real terms, poverty means the deaths of thousands of infants every year, malnutrition in hundreds of thousands of American children, and aged people eating dog food in order to survive. It means illiteracy and ignorance, disease and misery, and the stunting of human lives and potential. Most Americans are so accustomed to affluence that they may find it hard to believe that one American in ten lives in poverty.

Defining Poverty

How do we determine if someone is "poor"? There are two basic ways of defining poverty: in terms of *absolute deprivation*, the lack of basic necessities; or in terms of *relative deprivation*, the inability to maintain the living standards customary in the society.

Absolute Deprivation

This concept refers to a situation in which people cannot afford the basic standards of health care, nourishment, housing, and clothing (Kolko, 1962). This is the definition of poverty that is most often used in the United States. Analysts simply determine an annual income below which an individual or family will be deprived of the basic necessities of life. There is naturally some debate about exactly what this level is, but as established by the Social Security Administration, the official poverty line for a nonfarm family of four in 1979 was $7410. (In contrast, the Labor Department determined in that year that the average family of four would need $11,546 to maintain a "lower level" living standard; and the median family income for the nation as a whole was $19,937.) This level is determined by calculating the cost of adequate nutrition under "emergency or temporary conditions," and then trebling that figure to cover other necessities, such as clothing, housing, heating, and medical care. Adjustments are made for differences in family size, place of residence, and other factors. Rural families, for example, are expected to live on a lower income because housing is less expensive and they can grow some of their own food.

Relative Deprivation

This concept refers to a situation in which people may be able to afford basic necessities but are unable to maintain the standard of living considered normal in the society. In some ways this definition is a more realistic one. For example, electricity may not be an absolute necessity in the home—most people in the world get by without it—but it is thought to be a necessity, not a luxury, in our society. It would be hard not to regard an American family living without electricity as impoverished, even if the family's income were somewhat above the poverty line. Under this definition of poverty, the poor are arbitrarily defined as some proportion of the lowest income earners in society, often the bottom fifth or tenth. Their poverty is then measured, not in terms of how their incomes compare with the poverty line, but rather in terms of how their incomes compare with those of the rest of society. This approach assumes that poverty cannot be eliminated as long as significant economic inequalities persist.

Who Are the Poor?

As we might expect, poverty in the United States is not randomly distributed. It is concentrated in specific groups and areas (Bureau of the Census, 1978a).

Fatherless families. More than half of the families that live in poverty have a female householder, with no husband present—a proportion of the poor that has doubled over the past two decades. Some 37 percent of families headed by females are impoverished, compared with 6 percent headed by males.

Children. More than 10 million children live in poverty, over half of them in fatherless homes. In fact, children under the age of eighteen constitute 40 percent of the poor. The great majority of them rely almost entirely on welfare payments for their basic needs.

Minorities. About two-thirds of the poor are white, but minority groups are disproportionately likely to suffer poverty: about a third of Indian families, a quarter of Chicano families, and nearly a third of black families live in poverty. In contrast, less than one white in ten is poor.

The aged. People aged sixty-five or over represent about 13 percent of the poor. Many others survive on pensions

Figure 11.11 These people are living in what some social scientists regard as a "culture of poverty." Oscar Lewis, for example, maintains that the poor remain poor because of the attitudes and values they learn from their impoverished families and communities. Other social scientists are critical of this approach. They charge that it involves "blaming the victim" for poverty, rather than blaming the society that permits poverty to exist.

that lift them just above the poverty line, so nearly half of the aged live in poverty or conditions bordering on it.

The regional poor. Poor people are concentrated in certain areas of the country, notably decaying central-city neighborhoods and pockets of rural poverty. About 38 percent of the poor live in the central cities and about 40 percent in depressed rural regions—both areas where employment prospects are dim.

The Causes of Poverty

Poverty has no single cause. It is produced by a number of interrelated factors.

Economic Factors

Poverty is usually associated with a lack of jobs. The high unemployment rates found in specific geographic areas and specific sectors of the economy are usually the result of structural changes in economic life. Small farmers and agricultural laborers, for example, have been steadily displaced over the past few decades by mechanized agriculture, and they can no longer earn a decent living on the land. Automation in many industries has displaced unskilled workers, but these workers lack the training that would enable them to compete for jobs in industries using advanced technologies. Many workers are trapped in the less skilled service industries—as shoe shiners, domestic cleaners, dishwashers, or parking-lot attendants. The poor, if they are able to find employment at all, are concentrated in those jobs that offer only low wages and little security.

Discrimination

Given the prevailing patterns of discrimination in other aspects of social and economic life, it is hardly surprising that poverty is found disproportionately among minority-group members and among families headed by women. Nonwhites generally earn less than whites, even when they have similar qualifications, and women generally earn less than men. Nonwhite women suffer from double discrimination on grounds of both race and sex, and more than half the black families headed by women are in poverty. However, although it is a factor, discrimination in employment practices may not be the primary cause of their economic plight. The origins lie deeper, in the many subtle influences that prevent both women and minorities from acquiring the education, training, and attitudes that are necessary for success in a competitive society.

Cultural Factors

Poverty tends to be transmitted from one generation to the next. This fact has alerted investigators to the possibility that the cultural values of the poor may make it even more difficult for them to enter the mainstream economy. Oscar Lewis (1966, 1968), an anthropologist, has argued that a distinctive *culture of poverty* exists among poor groups in capitalist societies all over the world. According to Lewis, the poor have a strong sense of fatalism, helplessness, and inferiority. They are oriented to the present and do not plan for the future. They have a narrow outlook and do not see their problems in a broader social context. They also make little use of, and are hostile to, major social institutions. A person growing up in such a culture and internalizing its norms will be ill equipped to participate in the larger society. This general argument was widely accepted during the short-lived "War on Poverty" of the sixties. Immense efforts were devoted to changing the culture of the poor, primarily through education, but these efforts had little apparent impact on the problem. Although most sociologists would accept that the poor do have some distinctive cultural norms, many argue that this culture is mainly a result rather than a cause of poverty. Middle-class values and interests may have little relevance to an impoverished person, and it would not be surprising if they were replaced by ones more immediately useful. Cultural factors no doubt contribute to the persistence of poverty, but their precise influence is still a matter of debate. It seems important, however, that cultural factors not be used to "blame the victim"—that is, to focus on the supposed faults of the poor rather than on the social forces that create poverty in the first place (Ryan, 1976).

Political Factors

Poverty exists in America because the society is unequal, and there are overwhelming political pressures to keep it that way. Any attempt to redistribute wealth and income will inevitably be opposed by powerful interests. Some people can be relatively rich only if others are relatively poor, and since power is concentrated in the hands of the rich, public policies will continue to reflect their interests.

As Herbert Gans (1973) has pointed out, poverty is actually functional from the point of view of the nonpoor. It ensures that "dirty" work gets done. If there were no poor people to scrub floors and empty bedpans, these jobs would have to be rewarded with high incomes before anyone would touch them. Poverty creates jobs for many of the nonpoor, such as police officers, welfare workers, pawnbrokers, and government bureaucrats. Poverty makes life easier for the rich by providing them with cooks, gardeners, and other workers to perform basic chores while the rich themselves enjoy more pleasurable activities. Poverty provides a market for inferior goods and services, from day-old bread and spoiling produce to shoddily made clothing and the advice of incompetent physicians and lawyers. Poverty legitimizes the values of the middle class, because the fate of the poor seems to confirm the desirability of the qualities they are supposed to lack—the virtues of thrift, honesty, monogamy, and a taste for hard work. Poverty also provides a group that can be made to absorb the costs of change. For example, the poor bear the brunt of unemployment caused by automation, and it is their homes, not those of the wealthy, that are demolished when a route has to be found for a new highway. It is not that there is a deliberate, conscious "conspiracy" of the wealthy to keep the poor in poverty. It is just that poverty is an inevitable outcome of the American economic system, which the poor are politically powerless to change.

Attitudes Toward Poverty

It has been calculated that the United States could eliminate absolute poverty by spending $16.7 billion per year to raise all impoverished families above the poverty line (Bureau of the Census, 1978a). This sum is less than 2 percent of our gross national product. It represents less than a fifth of our annual expenditure on defense, or a little more than we spend each year on tobacco. The United States could wipe out poverty easily by placing an income floor under those who cannot earn enough to stay above the poverty line, instead of deliberately keeping welfare payments to a minimum. The reason for not adopting a guaranteed-income policy lies in a peculiar American myth: that the poor are poor because they are idle and prefer not to work. This attitude was clearly expressed by former President Nixon (1971):

I advocate a system that will encourage people to take work, and that means whatever work is available. If a job puts bread on the table, if it gives you the satisfaction of providing for your children and lets you look everyone else in the eye, I don't think that it is menial. . . . Low income workers feel somehow that certain kinds of work are demeaning—scrubbing floors, emptying bedpans. . . . It is not enjoyable work, but . . . there is as much dignity in that as there is in any work to be done in this country, including my own.

This attitude implies that the poor should not be pampered with welfare because it destroys their incentive to work. Such a view is very widely held. A 1972 Harris poll found that nearly nine out of ten Americans favored the idea of "making people on welfare go to work," and a Gallup poll in the same year found that more than half of the population regards the poor as responsible for their own poverty. A 1978 New York Times–CBS News poll found that 54 percent of the population believed that "most people who receive welfare could get along without it if they tried."

These attitudes bear virtually no relationship to reality. A quarter of the poor are actually engaged in full-time employment but simply do not earn enough to bring their incomes up to the poverty line. What about those on welfare, the supposed freeloaders who choose not to work? An analysis revealed the following about their composition:

children under fourteen	34.4 percent
elderly, sixty-five and over	18.2 percent
ill and disabled	4.7 percent
in school, fourteen and over	6.6 percent
	63.9 percent

In other words, nearly 64 percent of the poor on welfare were incapable of working anyway. Of the remaining 36.1 percent, 23.8 percent worked and 12.3 percent did not. Of this 12.3 percent who could have worked, 10.9 percent were female, the vast majority of whom were at home caring for small children. Thus only 1.4 percent of all those on welfare were able-bodied unemployed males, many of them lacking skills and many of them living in areas of high unemployment (Department of Health, Education, and Welfare, 1972; Mears, 1977). Other unfounded beliefs about welfare recipients abound: that they are mostly black (actually, over two-thirds are white); that welfare families have large numbers of children (in fact, the majority have only one or two children); that most welfare children are illegitimate (more than 70 percent are legitimate); that people stay on welfare indefinitely (more than half the families on welfare have received it for less than twenty-one months); and that most welfare recipients prefer to receive a "handout" than to work (a belief that could be held only by those who have never attempted to live on or raise a family on an income that, in most states, falls below the poverty line).

Why do these curious myths about the poor persist? As we saw in Chapter 10 ("Social Stratification"), social inequality is always legitimated, or made to seem fair and acceptable, by an ideology, or belief system, that justifies the social arrangements in question. The American class system is legitimated by the belief that everyone has the same chance to get ahead, and that inequality provides the necessary incentives and rewards for individual effort. If those who are successful can claim personal credit for their achievements, it therefore follows that those who fail must be blamed for their failures. For this reason, the poor are held in low regard (whatever the reason for their poverty), and the rich in high regard (even if they have inherited their wealth). To acknowledge that success or failure is largely the outcome of social forces rather than individual effort would be to undermine the legitimacy of the entire system, for its basic unfairness would then be exposed (Huber and Form, 1973; Rainwater, 1974; Feagin, 1975; Grønbjerg et al., 1978).

The reluctance to support the poor is reflected in the deep public concern about welfare fraud. Although fraudulent welfare claims are very rare—less than 1 percent of all cases—every welfare application is investigated for possible cheating. In contrast, only one tax return in fifty is investigated, even though the extent of cheating and the sums involved are very much greater. According to IRS estimates, about 10 percent of income taxes go uncollected because people deliberately misreport, or fail to report, their earnings: in 1980 the IRS figured the concealed income of Americans to be at least $100 billion and possibly as much as $139 billion. This sum would have yielded taxes of at least $18 billion—more than enough to totally eradicate poverty from the United States by bringing the income of everyone above the poverty line. But although losses through tax fraud must be compensated for by adding an

BELIEFS ABOUT PERSONAL ATTRIBUTES AS A CAUSE OF INCOME

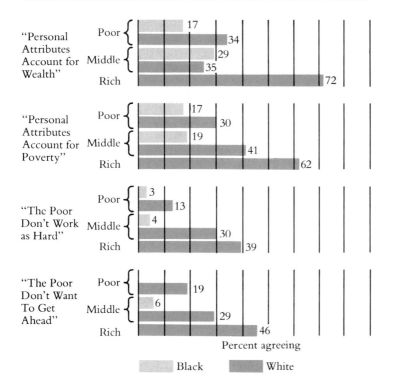

Figure 11.12 Can poverty and wealth be explained in terms of personal attributes? Americans have very different opinions on this question, but their opinions are related to their own social status and race-group membership. Significantly, nearly a third of poor whites believe that poverty can be explained in terms of personal characteristics, a fact that suggests they share the common American belief that they are responsible for their own plight. But blacks, perhaps because they have a greater class consciousness, are much less inclined to share this view. Although nearly half of the rich whites believe that "the poor don't want to get ahead," none of the poor blacks hold this view.

Source: Adapted from Joan H. Rytina et al., "Income and Stratification Ideology," *American Journal of Sociology,* 75 (January 1970), p. 713.

average of 10 percent to the tax bill of those who pay in full, Congress and the powerful interest groups that affect tax policy have remained largely indifferent to this massive evasion. The IRS has found that for each additional dollar it spends on investigation of tax returns and tax fraud, it collects between four and twelve times as much additional revenue, but Congress has persistently refused to allocate money for this purpose. The reason always given is that increased investigation would intrude too much into people's private lives—a valid argument, perhaps, but one that has rarely been applied to intrusion into the private lives of poor people on welfare. (Welfare investigators sometimes

try to gather information by spying on recipients and by questioning their friends, neighbors, and relatives. Until the courts ended the practice, investigators freely entered recipients' homes, prying around for evidence of alternative sources of income—such as the presence of a man's clothing in the home of a woman claiming to live alone.) And while a minor case of welfare fraud—for example, a mother drawing two or three checks under different names—is likely to be portrayed in local newspapers as a scandal, massive tax evasion is regarded as almost insignificant. Nearly all cases of evasion detected by the IRS are quietly settled out of court. Despite the huge amounts of money involved, the IRS indicted less than 2000 people for tax fraud in 1978. Of these, about 400 cases went to trial, about 240 led to convictions, and about 120 led to a prison sentence (Schultz, 1980; Cowan, 1980).

One further little-known fact deserves mention: we pay out far more in welfare to the nonpoor than to the poor. This fact is seldom recognized because these massive government handouts are not called "welfare." As Dale Tussing (1974) points out:

> Two welfare systems exist simultaneously in this country. One is explicit, poorly funded, stigmatized and stigmatizing, and is directed at the poor. The other, practically unknown, is implicit, literally invisible, is nonstigmatized and nonstigmatizing, and provides vast but nonacknowledged benefits for the nonpoor. Our welfare systems do not distribute benefits on the basis of need. Rather, they distribute benefits on the basis of legitimacy. Poor people are viewed as less legitimate than nonpoor people.

Housing provides one example of these "welfare" payments to the nonpoor. If you cannot afford to buy a home, you have to rent one. But you would not expect the federal government to help you pay your landlord, and it is highly unlikely that Congress would ever vote funds to subsidize the ordinary citizen's rent. However, if you can afford to buy a home, the federal government immediately comes to your aid: it allows you to deduct the cost of your property taxes and your mortgage interest from your taxable income. In effect, this is a "rent supplement" to homeowners—one that costs the government over $5 billion a year, more than four times the amount spent on all housing projects and programs for the poor. The larger and more expensive a home is, the more this tax deduction is worth to the homeowner. This pattern applies to virtually all of the many tax deductions that are available: a 1979 U.S. Treasury report found that the 5.3 percent of the nation's taxpayers who earn over $30,000 received some 66 percent of the total tax breaks, while the 52 percent that earned under $10,000 received only 12 percent of the breaks. In his analysis of the tax deductions obtained by people with annual incomes of over $1 million, Philip Stern (1972) found that these super-rich Americans saved, on average, a handsome $720,000 a year. It makes little difference whether this income is called "tax relief" or "welfare," because the effect is the same: the wealthy have more money to spend, the U.S. Treasury is $2.2 billion poorer,

and others must pay higher taxes to make up the difference. As conflict theory would predict, the system benefits the "haves" rather than the "have nots."

Poverty is only one sign of social inequality in America. Like all other forms of social inequality, it is built into the very structure of society and legitimized by a set of beliefs that justify its existence. In the next two chapters we shall see the same processes at work in the inequalities of race and ethnicity, gender, and age.

Summary

1. Although equality is a core value in American culture, the United States is a very unequal society. It is stratified along lines of social class.

2. Wealth and income are very unequally distributed in the United States, and there has been little change in the distribution of these rewards since the end of World War II. Power is also unequally distributed. Ordinary citizens have little influence over political decisions, but there is debate as to whether power is exercised by an elite or by powerful interest groups that struggle for advantage on specific issues. Prestige, however, has become available to an increasing number of Americans, largely because of the increase in the proportion of white-collar jobs.

3. The structure of the class system has been analyzed by the reputational method (asking people where they think others fit), the subjective method (asking people where they think they themselves fit), and the objective method (establishing criteria for class membership and dividing the population into preselected classes). Each method has its advantages and disadvantages, but all give a generally similar picture of the class system.

4. Most sociologists view the American class system as containing six strata: the upper upper class, the lower upper class, the upper middle class, the lower middle class, the upper lower (working) class, and the lower lower class. Each class has distinctive characteristics and life-styles that are related to the economic inequalities among the classes.

5. Class membership correlates with a variety of other aspects of life, including political behavior, marital stability, religious affiliation, educational achievement, health, life expectancy, mental disorder, social participation, values and attitudes, child-rearing practices, and criminal justice.

6. Research on social mobility indicates that there is a fair amount of intergenerational mobility in the United States, but most of it involves minor changes in status and results from the increase in the proportion of white-collar jobs. Opportunities for social mobility are not significantly greater in the United States than in other industrial societies, except that working-class people have a rather better chance of reaching the professional elite. Most people, however, remain at or near the status of their parents.

7. One American in ten is officially regarded as poor. Poverty may be defined in terms of absolute deprivation (lack of basic necessities) or relative deprivation (inability to maintain customary living standards). Poverty is concentrated in depressed areas, among minority groups, among fatherless families, and among the very old and the very young. There are a number of causes of poverty, including economic factors, discrimination, political factors, and, possibly, the culture of the poor itself. Americans are inclined to blame the poor for their poverty, an attitude that is not justified by the facts. Indeed, the nonpoor receive more "relief" from the federal government than the poor do.

Important Terms

wealth (256)	objective method (259)
power (257)	social mobility (267)
power-elite model (258)	poverty (269)
pluralistic model (258)	absolute deprivation (269)
prestige (259)	relative deprivation (269)
reputational method (259)	culture of poverty (271)
subjective method (259)	

Suggested Readings

DOMHOFF, G. WILLIAM (ed.). *Power Structure Research.* Beverly Hills, Calif.: Sage, 1980.

A collection of articles that offers a good overview of sociological work on this topic; the evidence presented strongly suggests that power is concentrated in the hands of an elite or elites.

DYE, THOMAS R. *Who's Running America?* Englewood Cliffs, N.J.: Prentice-Hall, 1976.

An analysis of the American governing circles, showing how wealth is translated into power, influence, and prestige.

FEAGIN, JOE. *Subordinating the Poor.* Englewood Cliffs, N.J.: Prentice-Hall, 1975.

An illuminating analysis of American beliefs about poor people and the welfare system.

GOULDNER, ALVIN W. *The Future of Intellectuals and the Rise of the New Class.* New York: Seabury Press, 1979.

A provocative book in which the author asserts that there is a new class of "brain workers"—highly educated technocrats and administrators—in modern industrial society.

JENCKS, CHRISTOPHER, et al. *Who Gets Ahead? The Determinants of Economic Success in America.* New York: Basic Books, 1979.

An important analysis of the available data on social mobility in the United States. Jencks emphasizes the importance of family background and of such apparently random events as being "in the right place at the right time" to take advantage of opportunities for employment or promotion.

LIPSET, SEYMOUR MARTIN, and REINHARD BENDIX. *Social Mobility in Industrial Society.* Berkeley, Calif.: University of California Press, 1959.

A classic study of social mobility in the United States and several other industrial societies. Despite many methodological problems, Lipset and Bendix were able to compare mobility rates in these societies and to establish that there was little variation among them.

PORTER, JOHN. *The Vertical Mosaic: An Analysis of Social Class and Power in Canada.* Toronto: University of Toronto Press, 1965.

A useful analysis of the class system of Canada, which has many similarities to—and a few significant differences from—the system in the United States.

RAINWATER, LEE, and RICHARD COLEMAN. *Social Standing in America.* New York: Basic Books, 1978.

A good portrait of the class system in the modern United States. The book incorporates the results of extensive sociological research on the subject.

ROSSIDES, DANIEL W. *The American Class System.* Boston: Houghton Mifflin, 1976.

A very thorough and sophisticated text on social stratification in the United States. The book is strongly recommended to the student who wants to pursue the subject in some depth.

Reading

Blaming the Victim   *William Ryan*

Americans frequently blame the poor for their poverty, the uneducated for their lack of education, the unemployed for their reliance on welfare. This practice, Ryan argues, is part of a deep-rooted tendency to blame the victim for failings that are actually caused, in many cases, by social forces over which the victim has no control.

Twenty years ago, Zero Mostel used to do a sketch in which he impersonated a Dixiecrat Senator conducting an investigation of the origins of World War II. At the climax of the sketch, the Senator boomed out, in an excruciating mixture of triumph and suspicion, "What was Pearl Harbor *doing* in the Pacific?" This is an extreme example of Blaming the Victim.

Twenty years ago, we could laugh at Zero Mostel's caricature. In recent years, however, the same process has been going on every day in the arena of social problems, public health, anti-poverty programs, and social welfare. A philosopher might analyze this process and prove that, technically, it is comic. But it is hardly ever funny.

Consider . . . the miseducated child in the slum school. He is blamed for his own miseducation. He is said to contain within himself the causes of his inability to read and write well. The shorthand phrase is "cultural deprivation," which, to those in the know, conveys what they allege to be inside information: that the poor child carries a scanty pack of cultural baggage as he enters school. He doesn't know about books and magazines and newspapers, they say. (No books in the home: the mother fails to subscribe to *Reader's Digest*.) They say that if he talks at all—an unlikely event since slum parents don't talk to their children—he certainly doesn't talk correctly. . . . If you can manage to get him to sit in a chair, they say, he squirms and looks out the window. (Impulse-ridden, these kids, motoric rather than verbal.) In a word he is "disadvantaged" and "socially deprived," they say, and this, of course, accounts for his failure (*his* failure, they say) to learn much in school.

Note the similarity to the logic of Zero Mostel's Dixiecrat Senator. What is the culturally deprived child *doing* in the school? What is wrong with the victim? In pursuing this logic, no one remembers to ask questions about the collapsing buildings and torn textbooks, the frightened, insensitive teachers, the six additional desks in the room, the blustering, frightened principals, the relentless segregation, the callous administrator, the irrelevant curriculum, the bigoted or cowardly members of the school board, the insulting history book, the stingy taxpayers, the fairy-tale readers, or the self-serving faculty of the local teachers' college. We are encouraged to confine our attention to the child and to dwell on all his alleged defects. Cultural deprivation becomes an omnibus explanation for the educational disaster area known as the inner-city school. This is Blaming the Victim.

The generic process of Blaming the Victim is applied to almost every American problem. The miserable health care of the poor is explained away on the grounds that the victim has poor motivation and lacks health information. The problems of slum housing are traced to the characteristics of tenants who are labeled as "Southern rural migrants" not yet "acculturated" to life in the big city. The "multiproblem" poor, it is claimed, suffer the psychological effects of impoverishment, the "culture of poverty," and the deviant value system of the lower classes; consequently, though unwittingly, they cause their own troubles. From such a viewpoint, the obvious fact that poverty is primarily an absence of money is easily overlooked or set aside. . . . Every important social problem—crime, mental illness, civil disorder, unemployment—has been analyzed within the framework of the victim-blaming ideology.

I have been listening to the victim-blamers and pondering their thought processes for a number of years. That process is often very subtle. Victim-blaming is cloaked in kindness and concern. . . . In this way, the new ideology is very different from the open prejudice and reactionary tactics of the old days. Its adherents include sympathetic social scientists with social consciences in good working order, and liberal politicians with a genuine commitment to reform.

Blaming the Victim is, of course, quite different from old-fashioned conservative ideologies. The latter simply dismissed victims as inferior, genetically defective, or morally unfit; the emphasis is on the intrinsic, even hereditary, defect. The former shifts its emphasis to the environmental causation. The old-fashioned conservative could hold firmly to the belief that the oppressed and the victimized were born that way—"that way" being defective or inadequate in character or ability. The new ideology attributes defect and inadequacy to the malignant nature of poverty, injustice, slum life, and racial difficulties. . . . But the stigma, the defect, the fatal difference—though derived in the past from environmental forces—is still located *within* the victim, inside his skin.... It is a brilliant ideology for justifying a perverse form of social action designed to change, not society, as one might expect, but rather society's victim.

We must particularly ask, "To whom are social problems a problem?" And usually, if truth were to be told, we would have to admit that we mean they are a problem to those of us who are outside the boundaries of what we have defined as the problem. Negroes are a problem to racist whites, welfare is a problem to stingy taxpayers, delinquency is a problem to nervous property owners.

Now, if this is the quality of our assumptions about social problems, we are led unerringly to certain beliefs about the causes of these problems. We cannot comfortably believe that *we* are the cause of that which is problematic to us; therefore, we are almost compelled to believe that *they*—the problematic ones—are the cause....

Blaming the Victim ... is central in the mainstream of contemporary American social thought, and its ideas pervade our most crucial assumptions so thoroughly that they are hardly noticed. Moreover, the fruits of this ideology appear to be fraught with altruism and humanitarianism, so it is hard to believe that it has principally functioned to block social change.

A major pharmaceutical manufacturer, as an act of humanitarian concern, has distributed copies of a large poster warning "Lead Paint Can Kill!" The poster, featuring a photograph of the face of a charming little girl, goes on to explain that if children *eat* lead paint, it can poison them, they can develop serious symptoms, suffer permanent brain damage, even die. The health department of a major American city has put out a coloring book that provides the same information. While the poster urges parents to prevent their children from eating paint, the coloring book is more vivid. It labels as neglectful and thoughtless the mother who does not keep her infant under constant surveillance to keep it from eating paint chips.

Now, no one would argue against the idea that it is important to spread knowledge about the danger of eating paint in order that parents might act to forestall their children from doing so. But to campaign against lead paint *only* in these terms is destructive and misleading and, in a sense, an effective way to support and agree with slum landlords—who define the problem of lead poisoning in precisely these terms....

It is not accurate to say that lead poisoning results from the actions of individual neglectful mothers. Rather, lead poisoning is a social phenomenon supported by a number of social mechanisms, one of the most tragic by-products of the systematic toleration of slum housing. In New Haven, which has the highest reported rate of lead poisoning in the country, several small children have died and many others have incurred irreparable brain damage as a result of eating peeling paint. In several cases, when the landlord failed to make repairs, poisonings have occurred time and again through a succession of tenancies. And the major reason for the landlord's neglect of this problem was that the city agency responsible for enforcing the house code did nothing to make him correct this dangerous condition.

The cause of the poisoning is the lead in the paint on the walls of the apartment in which the children live. The presence of the lead is illegal. To use lead paint in a residence is illegal; to permit lead paint to be exposed in a residence is illegal. It is not only illegal, it is potentially criminal since the housing code does provide for criminal penalties. The general problem of lead poisoning, then, is more accurately analyzed as the result of a systematic program of lawbreaking by one interest group in the community, with the toleration and encouragement of the public authority charged with enforcing that law. To ignore these continued and repeated law violations, to ignore the fact that the supposed law enforcer actually cooperates in lawbreaking, and then to load a burden of guilt on the mother of a dead or dangerously ill child is an egregious distortion of reality. And to do so under the guise of public-spirited and humanitarian service to the community is intolerable.

But this is how Blaming the Victim works. The righteous humanitarian concern displayed by the drug company, with its poster, and the health department, with its coloring book, is a genuine concern, and this is a typical feature of Blaming the Victim. Also typical is the swerving away from the central target that requires systematic change and, instead, focusing in on the individual affected. The ultimate effect is always to distract attention from the basic causes and to leave the primary social injustice untouched. And, most telling, the proposed remedy for the problem is, of course, to work on the victim himself.

Source: William Ryan, *Blaming the Victim* (New York: Pantheon, 1971), pp. 3–24.

CHAPTER **12**   *Inequalities of Race and Ethnicity*

One of the most fascinating aspects of our species is the extraordinary physical and cultural diversity of its members. Yet this diversity is often a source of conflict and inequality, because human relationships are all too often conducted on the basis of the differences rather than the similarities between groups.

As we saw in Chapter 10 ("Social Stratification"), all societies differentiate among their members, and these distinctions are usually translated into social inequalities. One common way of differentiating among people is to distinguish them on the basis of their physical characteristics or cultural traits. As a result of these social distinctions, the groups in question come to regard themselves, and to be regarded and treated by others, as "different." *Race and ethnic relations are the patterns of interaction among groups whose members share distinctive physical characteristics or cultural traits.* Those people who share similar physical characteristics are socially defined as a "race," and those who share similar cultural traits are socially defined as an "ethnic group."

Throughout history, relationships among racial and ethnic groups have been marked by prejudice, antagonism, warfare, and social inequality. Even in the course of the past decade, hundreds of thousands of people were slaughtered, and millions more subjected to cruelty and injustice, for no apparent reason other than their membership in some despised group. In the United States, a country formally committed to human equality, the physical and cultural differences among various groups still have a strong influence on their members' social status.

279

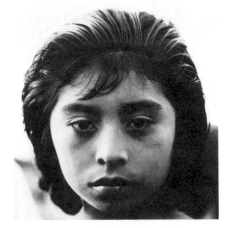

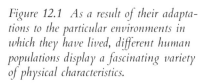

Figure 12.1 As a result of their adaptations to the particular environments in which they have lived, different human populations display a fascinating variety of physical characteristics.

The Concepts of Race and Ethnicity

The term "race" refers to the genetically transmitted physical characteristics of different human groups, and the term "ethnicity" refers to culturally acquired differences. Both words are often misused in ordinary speech, and we must examine their meaning more closely.

Race

As a biological concept, the word "race" is almost meaningless. There are over 4 billion people in the world, and they display a wide variety of skin colors, hair textures, limb-to-trunk ratios, and other characteristics, such as distinctive nose, lip, and eyelid forms (see Figure 12.1). Although the human animal can be traced back for well over 2 million years, the racial differences that we see today are of comparatively recent origin—50,000 years at the most.

These physical differences have resulted from the adaptations that human groups have made to the environments in which they lived. For example, populations in tropical and subtropical areas tend to have dark skin, which protects them against harmful rays from the sun. Populations in high altitudes tend to have large lung capacity, which makes breathing easier for them. Populations in very cold climates tend to have relatively short limbs, which enable them to conserve body heat. So far as is known, these evolutionary differences affect only physical characteristics. There is no convincing evidence that different groups inherit psychological characteristics, whether these be general traits such as intelligence or more specific ones such as artistic ability.

Confronted with this vast range of physical types, anthropologists have tried for decades to create some kind of conceptual order by dividing the human species into races and subraces. The number of races that is discovered, however, depends very much on the particular anthropologist who is doing the discovering: estimates range from three races to well over a hundred. The reason for the confusion is that there is no such thing as a "pure" race. Different population groups have been interbreeding for tens of thousands of years, and a continuum of human types has resulted. Categories of "race" are a creation of the observer, not of nature.

The classification that has won broadest acceptance in the past divides the human species into three major categories: the Caucasoids, with fair skin and straight or wavy hair; the Mongoloids, with yellowish skin and a distinctive fold around the eyes; and the Negroids, with dark skin and woolly hair. However, there are many people who cannot be neatly fitted into this classification. The Indians of Asia have Caucasoid features but dark skin. The Ainu of Japan have Mongoloid facial features but Caucasoid hair and skin color. The aborigines of Australia have dark skin, but their wavy hair is often blond. The San of Africa have coppery skin, woolly hair, and Mongoloid facial features. There are also many millions of people, such as those of Indonesia, whose ancestry is so mixed that they cannot possibly be fitted into one of the main categories. Many, if not most, anthropologists have now abandoned the attempt to classify the human species into races and consider the term "race" to have no scientific meaning at all (Banton and Harwood, 1975; Montagu, 1975; Kuper, 1975).

The physical differences between human groups, then, are simply a biological fact. As such, they are of no particular concern to the sociologist. The intense sociological interest in race derives from its significance as a *social* fact, because people attach meanings to the physical differences, real or imagined, between human groups. If people believe that a certain group forms a biological unity, they will act on the basis of that belief. The members of the group will tend to develop a common loyalty and to intermarry with one another, and members of other groups will regard them as "different." From the sociological point of view, then, a *race* is a large number of people who, for social or geographical reasons, have interbred over a long period of time; as a result, they have developed identifiable physical characteristics and regard themselves, and are regarded by others, as a biological unity.

Whether social beliefs about race have any biological basis is of little relevance. It is people's beliefs about race rather than the facts about race that influence race relations, for better or worse. Many people, for example, consider the Jews a race. In biological terms, this view is nonsense. Jews have always interbred to some extent with their host populations, and many Jewish people are blond and blue-eyed in Sweden, small and swarthy in eastern Europe, black in Ethiopia, or Mongoloid in China. Even in Nazi Germany, which attached such great importance to the distinctions between Jews and non-Jews, Jewish citizens were obliged to wear yellow stars so that their persecutors could distinguish them from the rest of the population. Yet when any group is arbitrarily defined as a race, as Jews were in Nazi Germany, important social consequences may follow.

Ethnicity

Whereas race refers only to physical characteristics, the concept of ethnicity refers to cultural features. These features may include language, religion, national origin, dietary practices, a sense of common historical heritage, or any other distinctive cultural trait. Many groups, such as blacks or American Indians, are both racially and ethnically distinct. Such groups are regarded as doubly "different." In other cases, ethnic groups cannot be distinguished from the rest of the population by their physical characteristics. German- and Polish-Americans, for example, are physically indistinguishable, but members of the two groups may form distinct subcultures based on their different ethnic backgrounds.

From the sociological viewpoint, then, an *ethnic group* is a large number of people who, as a result of their shared cultural traits and high level of mutual interaction, come to regard themselves, and to be regarded, as a cultural unity.

Unlike racial differences, ethnic differences are culturally learned and not genetically inherited—a point that seems obvious enough, until we remember how often the supposed "intelligence," "industriousness," "warlikeness," "inscrutability," "laziness," or other characteristic of some group is assumed to be an inborn trait of its members. But no ethnic group has any inborn cultural traits; it acquires them from its environment. The Japanese of Japan and Americans of Japanese ancestry share the same genetic heritage, yet they display very different cultural norms and values.

Minority Groups

The simple, preindustrial societies of the past were usually small and homogeneous. Within these societies everyone spoke the same language, shared the same values, worshiped the same gods, and had very similar physical characteristics.

In the modern world, however, many societies are large and heterogeneous. As a result of colonial settlements, missionary work, migrations, and the flight of refugees from famine, poverty, and persecution, these societies frequently contain minorities whose physical appearance and cultural practices are unlike those of the dominant group. In such

Figure 12.2 An Italian mother and her children arriving in the United States at the turn of the century. As a result of massive immigration during the latter part of the nineteenth and the early twentieth centuries, the United States contains several ethnic minorities. Each new wave of immigrants from Europe encountered prejudice and discrimination on arrival; this was particularly true of Catholic groups and groups from southern and eastern Europe.

cases, the dominant group often differentiates between its own members and the minority. It treats minority-group members in an unequal way, typically by denying them equal access to the power, wealth, and prestige that its own members enjoy.

The concept of a *minority group* is an important one in sociology, and sociologists use it in a very specific sense. There are many numerical minorities in American society—such as people of Scottish extraction, blue-eyed people, or auto mechanics—but these are not regarded as minority groups. The term is used only in the sense in which it was first defined by Louis Wirth (1945):

> We may define a minority as a group of people who, because of their physical or cultural characteristics, are singled out from the others in the society in which they live for differential and unequal treatment and who therefore regard themselves as objects of collective discrimination.

This concept of a minority group has since been further refined, and sociologists now regard a part of the population as a minority group if it has the following distinguishing features (Wagley and Harris, 1964; Williams, 1964; Vander Zanden, 1972):

1. *The members of a minority group suffer various disadvantages at the hands of another group.* This situation not only represents the denial of equal access to power, wealth, and prestige to the minority; it is also an important source of the dominant group's advantage. The dominant group exploits the minority, keeping its members in low-status positions and draining off their labor and resources. And the members of the minority group are not merely exploited: they are the victims of prejudice, discrimination, abuse, humiliation, and deeply held social beliefs that they are somehow "inferior."

2. *A minority is identified by group characteristics that are socially visible.* The characteristics and boundaries of a minority group are socially defined on arbitrary grounds. All people sharing some visible or noticeable characteristic, such as skin color, religion, or language, are lumped together into a single category. No matter what characteristic is used to make this differentiation, it is believed to be of great social importance. Individual characteristics of a minority-group member are regarded as less significant than the supposed characteristics of the group to which the individual belongs.

3. *A minority is a self-conscious group with a strong sense of "oneness."* Members of a minority, such as Jews, American blacks, or Palestinians, tend to feel a strong affinity with one another. Their "consciousness of kind," or sense of common identity, is often so strong that differences within the group become submerged in a common loyalty to "the people." The minority group's shared experience of suffering heightens these feelings; in fact, the more its members are persecuted, the more intense their group solidarity is likely to become.

4. *People usually do not become members of a minority group voluntarily; they are born into it.* The sense of common identity usually comes from an awareness of common ancestry and traditions. It is often difficult for a member of a minority group to leave the group, for the reason that the dominant group regards anyone with minority-group ancestry as a permanent member of that minority. In the United States, for example, a person with one black parent—or even with one black grandparent—is still regarded as black rather than white.

5. *By choice or necessity, members of a minority group generally marry within the group.* This practice (called endogamy) may be encouraged by the dominant group, by the minority group, or by both. Members of the dominant group are typically reluctant to marry members of the stigmatized minority group, and the minority group's consciousness of kind predisposes its members to look for marital partners within the group. As a result, minority status within a society tends to be passed on from generation to generation.

There is one aspect of the sociological use of the term "minority group" that may seem rather peculiar at first: a minority group can sometimes be a numerical majority. Minority-group status is not a matter of numbers; it is determined by the presence of the distinguishing features outlined above. In practice, of course, it is very rare for a numerical majority to be a minority group in their own society, but examples of this situation do exist. In the African country of Burundi, the small Tutsi tribe dominates the large Hutu tribe, and in South Africa the small white population dominates the much larger black population. Some sociologists have also argued that women in the United States can be regarded as a minority group, although they slightly outnumber men.

Patterns of Race and Ethnic Relations

Race and ethnic relations may follow many different patterns, ranging from harmonious coexistence to outright conflict. George Simpson and Milton Yinger (1972) have identified six basic patterns of intergroup hostility or cooperation. Their list covers virtually all the possible patterns of race and ethnic relations, and each pattern exists or has existed in some part of the world.

1. *Assimilation.* In some cases a minority group is simply eliminated by being assimilated into the dominant group. This process may involve cultural assimilation, racial assimilation, or both. Cultural assimilation occurs when the minority group abandons its distinctive cultural traits and adopts those of the dominant culture; racial assimilation occurs when the physical differences between the groups disappear as a result of interbreeding. Brazil is probably the best contemporary example of a country following a policy of assimilation. With the exception of some isolated Indian groups, the various racial and ethnic groups within the society interbreed fairly freely. Portugal attempted a policy of assimilation in the African colonies that it ruled until the mid-1970s. The Portuguese even created a special status, *assimilado,* for those Africans or people of mixed race who were considered sufficiently Portuguese in color or culture to share the privileges of the dominant group.

2. *Pluralism.* Some minorities do not want to lose their group identity; their members have a strong consciousness of, and pride in, their heritage, and are loyal to their own group. The dominant group in the society may also be willing to permit or even to encourage cultural variation within the broader confines of national unity. Tanzania, for example, is a pluralistic society that respects the cultural distinctions among its African, Asian, European, and Middle Eastern peoples. In Switzerland four ethnic groups, speaking German, French, Italian, and Romanche, retain their sense of group identity while living together amicably in the society as a whole.

3. *Legal protection of minorities.* In some societies, significant sections of the dominant group may have hostile attitudes toward minority groups. In such cases the government may find it necessary to introduce legal measures to protect the interests and rights of the minorities. In Great Britain, for example, the Race Relations Act of 1965 makes it illegal to discriminate on racial grounds in employment or housing. It is also a criminal offense to publish

Figure 12.3 Population transfer—often involving the expulsion of the unwanted group—is a drastic but not uncommon phenomenon in race and ethnic relations. One recent example was Vietnam's expulsion of hundreds of thousands of ethnic Chinese, many of whom were forced to buy the right to flee the country on old fishing boats and other vessels, many of which were not seaworthy. Thousands died when the overloaded boats capsized, and many more sailed from port to port, only to be repeatedly refused landing permission. The United States and Canada were among the few countries to accept these "boat people" in significant numbers.

or even to utter publicly any sentiments that might encourage hostility between racial and ethnic groups in the population.

4. *Population transfer.* In some situations of intense hostility between groups, the problem is "solved" by removing the minority from the scene altogether. This policy was adopted, for example, by the former president of Uganda, Idi Amin, who simply ordered Asian residents to leave the country in which they had lived for generations. In a few cases, population transfer may involve outright partition of a territory. Hostility between Hindus and Muslims in India was so intense that the entire subcontinent was divided between them in such a way that a new Muslim state, Pakistan, was created. There are signs that Cyprus is becoming permanently divided into Greek and Turkish territories, and Lebanon into Muslim and Christian territories. Voluntary and forced population transfers have been taking place in both countries.

5. *Continued subjugation.* In some cases the dominant group has every intention of maintaining its privilege over the minority group indefinitely. It may be fully willing to use force to achieve this objective, and it may even physically segregate the members of the various groups. Historically, continued subjugation has been a very common

policy. In the eighteenth and nineteenth centuries, for example, the European powers implicitly assumed that their domination over the subject peoples of their colonies was to be a permanent state of affairs. The climate of world opinion is now such that few countries dare to openly endorse a policy of continued subjugation, but the pattern does persist in some cases. The outstanding example is South Africa, where, under the policy of *apartheid*, the white minority proposes to keep its power over the black majority forever, and has made clear its willingness to use all necessary force to achieve this goal. Less overt policies of continued subjugation are found in several Latin American countries, where dominant Hispanic groups continue to oppress the indigenous Indian minorities.

6. *Extermination.* The extermination of entire populations, or *genocide,* has been attempted and even achieved in several parts of the world. The methods of genocide include systematic slaughter by force of arms and the deliberate spreading of infectious diseases, particularly smallpox, to peoples who have no natural immunity to them. Dutch settlers in South Africa entirely exterminated the Hottentots and came close to exterminating the San, who at one point in South African history were actually classified as "vermin." British settlers on the island of Tasmania wiped out the local population, whom they hunted for sport and

Figure 12.4 The Nazis attempted the systematic genocide of the Jewish population of Germany and of several countries that they occupied in World War II. This scene is from the concentration camp at Dachau, one of several centers where up to 6 million Jews were murdered.

even for dog food. There is strong evidence that economic interests in Brazil, with the connivance of the Brazilian government, have slaughtered the Indian occupants of land that is wanted for agricultural development. Between 1933 and 1945 several million Jews were murdered in Germany. A more recent example of attempted genocide occurred in the African state of Burundi in 1972, when the dominant Tutsi tribe massacred nearly 100,000 members of the Hutu tribe.

These patterns are not necessarily mutually exclusive, and a society can adopt more than one of them at the same time. It is interesting to note that at some point in their history the United States and Canada have made use of every single one of these six strategies. Immigrant groups, particularly those from Scandinavia and other parts of northern Europe, have been *assimilated* into the mainstream of North American life. There is a strong trend toward *pluralism* at present, with different groups, such as blacks in the United States and the French in Canada, asserting pride in their own cultural traditions. *Legal protection of minorities* has been entrenched in law in both countries. *Population transfer* was used extensively against the Indians of North America, who were often forced to leave their traditional territories and to settle on remote reserves. The United States and Canada both practiced *continued subjugation* of their minorities, with the most extreme example being that of slavery in the Southern states. *Extermination* was used against American Indians in both countries, and several tribes were in fact hounded out of existence.

Racism

Some racial and ethnic groups, then, are able to live together in conditions of equality and mutual respect, but others are in a state of constant inequality and conflict. Clearly, there is no inherent reason why different groups should be hostile to one another. Poor relations among racial and ethnic groups have social causes. But what are these causes? How and why do racial and ethnic inequalities and antagonisms develop?

The Nature of Racism

As we saw in Chapter 3 ("Culture"), most human groups tend to be *ethnocentric;* that is, they unquestioningly use their own values and way of life to judge other groups. Not surprisingly, they frequently find the other groups deficient in some respects. To most people, it is self-evident that

Figure 12.5 Like many modern societies, Canada includes racial and ethnic minorities, most notably its Indian and French populations. French Canadians, who form a majority in the province of Quebec, have long complained of prejudice and discrimination on the part of the English-speaking majority in the country as a whole. In recent years the national government has given legal protection to the French language and the rights of French Canadians, apparently in time to defuse a strong separatist movement in Quebec. Yet the status of French Canadians (and of other minorities such as the Eskimos) remains a source of controversy and even tension.

their own norms, religion, attitudes, values, and cultural practices are right and proper, while those of other groups are peculiar, bizarre, or even immoral. A certain amount of ethnocentrism is almost inevitable in any racial or ethnic group. In fact, it may even be *functional* for the group's survival. Ethnocentric attitudes ensure the solidarity and cohesion of the group that holds them, providing its members with faith and confidence in their own cultural tradition. Such attitudes also discourage outsiders from penetrating the group.

The difficulty is, of course, that ethnocentric attitudes that are functional for the group that has them may be highly *dysfunctional* for other groups. Under certain conditions, ethnocentric attitudes can take an extreme and aggressive form and can be used to justify racial or ethnic oppression. This is the phenomenon of *racism*, in which a group that is seen as inferior or different is exploited and oppressed by a dominant group (Nash, 1962; Blauner, 1972; Noel, 1972; W. Wilson, 1972). Racism is not an inevitable result of contact between different groups. It is perfectly possible to identify with one's own group and take pride in its heritage while respecting the culture and traditions of other groups. Ethnocentrism develops into racism only under certain conditions, and a major task of sociology has been to specify what those conditions are.

The Causes of Racism

The most useful approach to the problem of racism is to view it from the perspective of *conflict* theory. Seen in these terms, racism is the outcome of a competition between different groups for scarce resources. For racism to develop, three basic conditions must usually be met (Noel, 1968; Vander Zanden, 1972):

1. There must be two or more social groups, identifiable by their visible physical characteristics or cultural practices. Unless people are aware of differences between the groups and are able to identify people as belonging to one group rather than another, racism cannot develop.

2. There must be competition between the groups for valued resources, such as power, land, or jobs. In this situation, members of one group will be inclined to secure their own interests by denying members of other groups full access to these resources.

3. The groups must be unequal in power, enabling one of them to make good its claim over scarce resources at the expense of the other group or groups. At this stage inequalities become structured into the society.

From this point on, events follow a fairly predictable course. The more the groups compete, the more negatively

Figure 12.6 From the conflict perspective, problems of race and ethnic relations are primarily about access to resources such as housing and jobs, and have little to do with skin color or such ethnic features as language or religion. The Miami riots of 1980 involved not only hostility between blacks and English-speaking whites, but also between blacks and Hispanics. Members of both minorities seemed to view one another as competitors for whatever resources were available, and therefore as potential enemies.

they view one another. The dominant group develops racist views about the supposed inferiority of the minority group or groups to justify its continued supremacy. Attempts by the minority group to assert its own interests are likely to be regarded as threatening by the dominant group, and further oppression may follow.

From the conflict perspective, economic inequalities underlie racism. The disputes between groups are not so much about actual racial or ethnic distinctions as about the use of supposed distinctions to preserve an unequal society. Racism may even arise when competition is expected at some point in the future: white settlers in North America quickly developed racist attitudes toward the native population, whom they saw as potential competitors for possession of land and other resources. And because social attitudes, like any other part of culture, tend to be inherently conservative, racism may live on long after the conditions that gave rise to it have disappeared. Negative conceptions about the American Indians, for example, persisted for many decades after they were finally defeated and their lands seized. In short, racism may develop rapidly, but slowly disappear.

The European colonial period offers a good case study of the relationship between racism and economic interests.

There was very little racism in the European powers before they started building their respective colonial empires. In fact, occasional visitors from exotic foreign lands were often treated with honor and sometimes with awe. Under the colonial system, however, a few European nations seized control of almost half of the land area and population of the world, and developed a strong economic interest in oppressing the colonial peoples. The colonists relied on the indigenous populations for cheap labor and on their countries as a source of raw materials and as a market for manufactured goods. This era of colonial expansion was marked by an intense race consciousness among European peoples.

The European powers, particularly those that practiced slavery, risked a severe moral dilemma. Their treatment of colonial peoples was clearly incompatible with their avowed Christian beliefs. Since no Christian could legitimately make a slave of another human being, an obvious justification presented itself: to classify the colonial peoples as subhuman. In the 1840s one of the early anthropologists, James Pritchard, found it necessary to devote considerable effort to the question of whether "primitive" peoples were truly human:

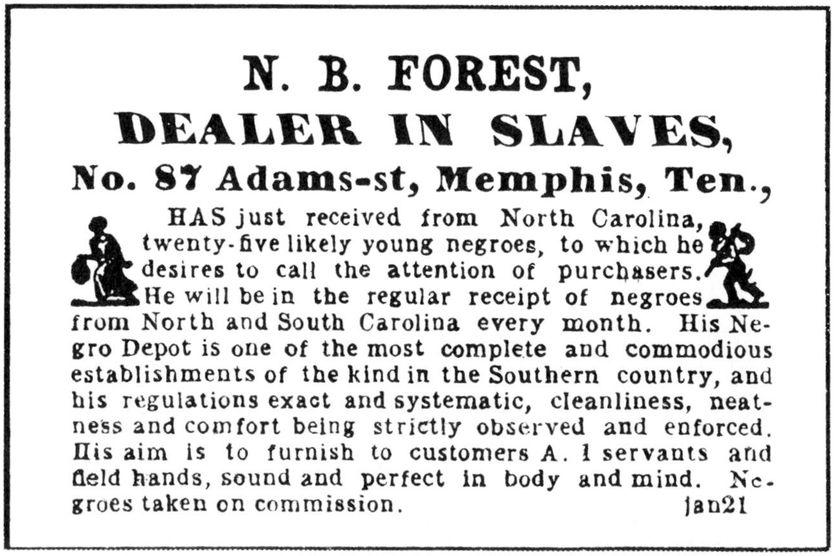

N. B. FOREST,
DEALER IN SLAVES,
No. 87 Adams-st, Memphis, Ten.,

HAS just received from North Carolina, twenty-five likely young negroes, to which he desires to call the attention of purchasers. He will be in the regular receipt of negroes from North and South Carolina every month. His Negro Depot is one of the most complete and commodious establishments of the kind in the Southern country, and his regulations exact and systematic, cleanliness, neatness and comfort being strictly observed and enforced. His aim is to furnish to customers A. 1 servants and field hands, sound and perfect in body and mind. Negroes taken on commission.   jan21

Figure 12.7 As this advertisement from a slave dealer suggests, slaves were regarded as less than human: the advertiser might as well have been talking about livestock. This racist attitude helped to lessen any moral qualms about the institution of slavery. It would have been much more difficult to make slaves of other people if their full humanity were recognized.

If the Negro and Australian are not our fellow creatures and of one family with ourselves, but beings of an inferior order, and if our duties toward them were not contemplated . . . in any of the positive commands on which the morality of the Christian world is founded, our relations with these tribes will appear to be not very different from those which might be imagined to subsist between us and a race of orangutans. [Quoted in Lienhardt, 1966]

Darwin's theory of evolution was also used by those who wanted to prove the subhuman status of nonwhite peoples. Some argued that the colonial peoples were at a lower point on the evolutionary ladder than whites; others that they were products of a completely separate process of evolution and were thus half animal.

These attitudes became deeply embedded in western European culture and were transported by white settlers to North America, where many traces of them remain to this day. Racist beliefs provided a convenient justification for slavery in the South and for the slaughter and dispossession of American Indians. Blacks were considered suitable for slavery "by nature," and the destruction of Indian societies by a "superior" white civilization was seen as a matter of "manifest destiny."

The racism of the Western powers was notable for its international scale and systematic theoretical justification by theologians and scientists alike. But racism is by no means restricted to Western whites. It is found throughout the world, invariably in situations of economic competition between different groups. Kenya, as well as Uganda, for example, has expelled tens of thousands of its Asian residents. In both societies, the Asian minorities had an economic status far superior to that of the indigenous Africans, who took over the Asians' jobs and businesses after they had left. Similarly, many of the conflicts between blacks and Arabs in sub-Saharan Africa are related to the struggle for scarce resources as the desert steadily spreads into drought-stricken lands that were once fertile.

Intergroup conflicts generally do not subside until economic inequalities are overcome, as the history of American race relations suggests. The strong prejudices that existed against Japanese, Chinese, Irish, Italian, and other immigrants have gradually lessened as these groups have gained entry to the middle class. Prejudice is still greatest against those groups, such as blacks or Hispanic-Americans, who

remain impoverished. There is strong evidence that the greater prejudice against minority groups in America is found among low-status whites who feel most threatened by the economic progress and competition of the minorities (Selznick and Steinberg, 1969; Cohen and Hodges, 1963). The evidence from other countries has also shown a consistent pattern of racial intolerance among low-status members of the dominant group (Lipset, 1959a).

The Ideology of Racism

A dominant group always tries to legitimate its interests by means of an *ideology*, or set of beliefs, that explains and justifies the existing social system (see Chapter 10, "Social Stratification"). The ideology of racism serves to legitimate the social inequalities between the groups by making them seem "natural," or "right." If one can believe that "slaves are happy," or that American Indians are so subhuman that "the only good Indian is a dead Indian," then slavery and slaughter become more acceptable policies.

The ideology of racism does not only justify the existing inequalities; it also reinforces them by the social process of the *self-fulfilling prophecy* (Merton, 1968). One of the founders of American sociology, W. I. Thomas, first expressed this idea in a simple but profound statement that has since become famous as the "Thomas theorem": "If men define situations as real, they are real in their consequences." Thus, to cite an example given by Merton, if people wrongly believe that a bank will go bankrupt, they will rush to withdraw their money—with the result that the bank *will* go bankrupt. The self-fulfilling prophecy is a false definition of a situation, but the definition leads to behavior that makes the prediction come true.

In the field of race and ethnic relations, the self-fulfilling prophecy works as follows. The racist ideology of the dominant group defines the minority as inferior. Because the members of the minority group are considered inferior, they are believed to be unsuited for high-status jobs, advanced education, or responsible positions in society. Accordingly, they are not given access to these opportunities. Consequently, they hold low-status jobs, are poorly educated, and fill few responsible positions in society. This situation is then cited to "prove" that the minority group is inferior, and the racist ideology is confirmed.

It often happens, too, that an oppressed group accepts the ideology that justifies its oppression. There is little doubt, for example, that colonial peoples accepted the colonizers' view of their inferiority, at least until the surge of nationalism in these countries after World War II. In such cases the minority is in a state of what Marx called *false consciousness,* a subjective understanding of one's situation that does not accord with the objective facts.

White racist theory reached its most extreme forms during the course of this century in the rantings of Adolf Hitler (1948), a short, dark man who believed that the tall, blond "Aryan" race was infinitely superior to all others and had to maintain its purity:

> All the human culture, all the results of art, science, and technology that we see before us today, are almost exclusively the product of the Aryan.... He is the Prometheus of mankind from whose singing brow the divine spark of genius has sprung at all times.... It is no accident that the first cultures arose in places where the Aryan, in his encounters with lower peoples, subjugated them, and bent them to his will.... History has shown with terrible clarity that each time Aryan blood has become mixed with inferior peoples the result has been the end of the culture-sustaining race.

This view neglected several uncomfortable facts. First, there is no such thing as a "pure" race, and certainly no such thing as an "Aryan" race. Second, complex civilizations existed thousands of years ago in India, Egypt, Mesopotamia, and China at a time when northern Europeans had still to invent the alphabet, the wheel, the plow, and the city. Third, it is a matter of scientific fact that interbreeding between different human populations is likely (as is the case with other plant and animal species) to produce offspring that are healthier than either parental stock (Simpson and Yinger, 1972). Nevertheless, Hitler's theories fired Germany with a sense of national identity—and led to gas chambers and concentration camps, to the murder of up to 6 million Jews, and to a global war. As a result, racist ideology was made utterly disreputable, and few people or governments today, whatever their private attitudes, dare to openly endorse a racist attitude. It is worth noting, however, that the United States fought Hitler with a racially segregated army and that German prisoners of war ate in canteens in which black American soldiers were refused service.

Prejudice and Discrimination

Prejudice and discrimination are found in any situation of hostility and inequality between racial and ethnic groups. The two terms are often used interchangeably in ordinary speech, but in fact they refer to two different, though related, phenomena. *Prejudice* is a "prejudged" *attitude* toward members of another group. These people are regarded with hostility simply because they belong to a particular group, and they are assumed to have the undesirable qualities that are attributed to the group as a whole. *Discrimination,* on the other hand, refers to *action* against people on the grounds of their group membership—particularly the refusal to grant members of another group the opportunities that would be granted to similarly qualified members of one's own group.

In a classic study conducted in the thirties, Richard LaPiere showed the importance of distinguishing between the two concepts. He traveled around the United States with a Chinese couple, stopping at over 250 restaurants and hotels on the way. In only one case were they refused service—that is, discriminated against. Six months later, LaPiere wrote to each of the establishments he had visited and asked if they were willing to serve "members of the Chinese race." Over 90 percent of the replies indicated that Chinese would not be welcome—that is, there was prejudice against them. Clearly, prejudice was not necessarily translated into discrimination. There is also the possibility that many of those who replied to LaPiere were not even prejudiced against Chinese, but thought it would be good for business to pretend that they were. LaPiere's study is one of many examples of sociological research that reveals the discrepancy between what people say and what they do (Deutscher, 1973).

Robert Merton (1949) has proposed a prejudice-discrimination typology containing four different types of persons and their characteristic responses. The model may not neatly accommodate a particular individual, but it does cover all the possibilities.

The *unprejudiced nondiscriminator* accepts the formal values of American democracy and adheres to the ideal of equality in both theory and practice. Such a person is not prejudiced and does not discriminate against others on racial or ethnic grounds.

Racism

**IN THE SUPERIOR COURT OF THE STATE OF CALIFORNIA
IN AND FOR THE COUNTY OF SANTA CLARA JUVENILE DIVISION**

HONORABLE GERALD S. CHARGIN, Judge
In the Matter of PAUL PETE CASILLAS, JR., a minor.

STATEMENTS OF THE COURT

San Jose, California   September 2, 1969   10:25 a.m.

APPEARANCES

For the Minor: FRED LUCERO, ESQ. Deputy Public Defender
For the Probation Department: WILLIAM TAPOGNA, ESQ. Court Probation Officer

The Court: There is some indication that you more or less didn't think that it was against the law or was improper. Haven't you had any moral training? Have you and your family gone to church?

The Minor: Yes, sir.

The Court: Don't you know that things like this are terribly wrong? This is one of the worst crimes that a person can commit. I just get so disgusted that I just figure what is the use? You are just an animal. You are lower than an animal. Even animals don't do that. You are pretty low.

I don't know why your parents haven't been able to teach you anything or train you. Mexican people, after 13 years of age, it's perfectly all right to go out and act like an animal. It's not even right to do that to a stranger, let alone a member of your own family. I don't have much hope for you. You will probably end up in State's Prison before you are 25, and that's where you belong, any how. There is nothing much you can do.

I think you haven't any moral principles. You won't acquire anything. Your parents won't teach you what is right or wrong and won't watch out.

Apparently, your sister is pregnant; is that right?

The Minor's Father, Mr. Casillas: Yes.

The Court: It's a fine situation. How old is she?

The Minor's Mother, Mrs. Casillas: Fifteen.

The Court: Well, probably she will have a half a dozen children and three or four marriages before she is 18.

The County will have to take care of you. You are no particular good to anybody. We ought to send you out of the country—send you back to Mexico. You belong in prison for the rest of your life for doing things of this kind. You ought to commit suicide. That's what I think of people of this kind. You are lower than animals and haven't the right to live in organized society—just miserable, lousy, rotten people.

There is nothing we can do with you. You expect the County to take care of you. Maybe Hitler was right. The animals in our society probably ought to be destroyed because they have no right to live among human beings. If you refuse to act like a human being, then, you don't belong among the society of human beings.

Mr. Lucero: Your Honor, I don't think I can sit here and listen to that sort of thing.

The Court: You are going to have to listen to it because I consider this a very vulgar, rotten human being.

Mr. Lucero: The Court is indicting the whole Mexican group.

The Court: When they are 10 or 12 years of age, going out and having intercourse with anybody without any moral training—they don't even understand the Ten Commandments. That's all. Apparently, they don't want to.

So if you want to act like that, the County has a system of taking care of them. They don't care about that. They have no personal self-respect.

Mr. Lucero: The Court ought to look at this youngster and deal with this youngster's case.

The Court: All right. That's what I am going to do. The family should be able to control this boy and the young girl.

Mr. Lucero: What appalls me is that the Court is saying that Hitler was right in genocide.

The Court: What are we going to do with the mad dogs of our society? Either we have to kill them or send them to an institution or place them out of the hands of good people because that's the theory—one of the theories of punishment is if they get to the position that they want to act like mad dogs, then, we have to separate them from our society.

Well, I will go along with the recommendation. You will learn in time or else you will have to pay for the penalty with the law because the law grinds slowly but exceedingly well. If you are going to be a law violator—you have to make up your mind whether you are going to observe the law or not. If you can't observe the law, then, you have to be put away.

Figure 12.8 *Racial prejudice is still very common in the United States, although it has lost its "respectability." These pictures show some extreme examples: a ceremony of the Ku Klux Klan; a demonstration by young supporters of the American Nazi party, and a protest by white residents of Chicago against open housing.*

The *unprejudiced discriminator* has no personal prejudices, but may discriminate when it is convenient to do so. For example, an employer may have no personal hostility toward members of another group, but may not hire them for fear of offending customers.

The *prejudiced nondiscriminator* is a "timid bigot" who is prejudiced against other groups but who, because of legal or social pressures, is reluctant to translate attitudes into action.

The *prejudiced discriminator* does not genuinely believe in the values of freedom or equality (at least as far as minority groups are concerned) and discriminates on the basis of prejudiced attitudes. Such a person may, however, attempt to hide his or her prejudice by using other justifications for discriminatory acts. For example, the prejudiced discriminator may refuse to rent a room to a minority-group member on the grounds that "it's already been taken," or may inflate the rent to discourage minority-group applicants.

The Social Psychology of Prejudice

A major focus of the work of social psychologists, particularly in the decade after World War II, has been the psychology of prejudice. How and why do people become prejudiced, and what are the characteristic features of prejudiced thought?

Stereotypes

Prejudiced thought always involves the use of a rigid mental image that summarizes whatever is believed to be typical about a group. This kind of image is called a *stereotype*.

Like ethnocentrism, stereotyped thinking is an almost unavoidable feature of social life. The ability to form general categories is essential if we are to make sense of the world. The use of these categories allows us to respond to the general rather than the particular and thus to simplify greatly the complexity of our surroundings. You probably have your own stereotype of what an Australian aborigine or an Eskimo is like. The essence of prejudiced thinking, however, is that the stereotype is not checked against reality. It is not modified by experiences that contradict the rigid image. If a prejudiced person finds that an individual

member of a group does not conform to the stereotype for the group as a whole, this evidence is simply taken as "the exception that proves the rule" and not as grounds for questioning the original belief. Robert Merton (1968) shows how the same behavior can be interpreted differently to fit an existing stereotype:

> Did Lincoln work far into the night? This testifies that he was industrious, resolute, perseverant, and eager to realize his capacities to the full. Do the out-group Jews or Japanese keep the same hours? This only bears witness to their sweatshop mentality, their ruthless undercutting of American standards, their unfair competitive practices. Is the in-group hero frugal, thrifty, and sparing? Then the out-group villain is stingy, miserly, and penny-pinching. All honor is due to the in-group Abe for his having been smart, shrewd, and intelligent, and, by the same token, all contempt is owing the out-group Abes for their being sharp, cunning, crafty, and too clever by far.

The "Authoritarian Personality"

Do some people have personality patterns that make them more prone to prejudice than others? In the late forties, Theodore Adorno and his associates (1950) tried to answer this question.

Adorno tested his subjects on three different dimensions: an F (fascism), and E (ethnocentrism), and an A-S (anti-Semitism) scale. His method was to present the subjects with a series of reactionary, ethnocentric, and anti-Semitic statements. The subjects then indicated their degree of agreement or disagreement with each statement. The significant finding was that people who scored high on any one of the scales also tended to score high on the others. In other words, those who were prejudiced against Jews were also likely to be prejudiced against blacks and other minorities, to favor strong, authoritarian leadership, and to have a very ethnocentric view of their own customs and values.

Adorno concluded that some people have a distinct set of personality traits that together make up what he called the *authoritarian personality*. People who have this personality pattern are intolerant, insecure, highly conformist, submissive to superiors, and bullying to inferiors. They tend to have anti-intellectual and antiscientific attitudes; they are disturbed by any ambiguity in sexual or religious matters; and they see the world in very rigid and stereotyped terms. The authoritarian personality, Adorno claimed, is primarily a product of a family environment in which the parents were cold, aloof, disciplinarian, and themselves bigoted.

Adorno's work has since inspired over a thousand pieces of research and critical articles. Some writers have pointed out that Adorno's methodology was weak in certain respects; others that he neglected the possibility of an authoritarian personality among radicals as well as conservatives; others that his concept is too general and sweeping in its scope. Some critics have suggested that a third variable—such as lack of exposure to different values and norms—is responsible for both authoritarianism and prejudice (Selznick and Steinberg, 1969). Despite these and other criticisms, however, it is now generally accepted that some people are psychologically more prone to prejudiced thinking than others.

One interesting finding of Adorno's research was how irrational and inconsistent prejudiced thought is. In one of their measures of anti-Semitism, the researchers deliberately inserted pairs of mutually contradictory statements. One series of pairs, for example, dealt with the alleged "seclusiveness" and the alleged "inclusiveness" of Jews. Here are two such pairs:

Much resentment against Jews stems from their tending to keep apart and exclude gentiles from Jewish social life.

The Jews should not pry too much into Christian activities and organizations nor seek so much recognition and prestige from Christians.

and

Jews tend to remain a foreign element in American society, to preserve their old social standards and resist the American way of life.

Jews go too far in hiding their Jewishness, especially such extremes as changing their names, straightening their noses, and imitating Christian manners and customs.

The researchers found that nearly three-quarters of those who were prejudiced against Jews for being too seclusive were also prejudiced against them for being too intrusive. Similarly, those who disliked them for being too capitalistic and for controlling business also disliked them for being too communistic and subversive of the capitalist system. Those who disliked Jews for begging and scrounging also disliked them for giving money to charity as a means of gaining

prestige, and so on. Clearly, prejudiced people are not concerned about genuine group characteristics; they simply believe any negative statement that feeds their existing attitude.

A fascinating study by Eugene Hartley (1946) throws further light on this phenomenon. Hartley gave his subjects a list of thirty-five racial and ethnic minorities and asked them to select their reactions to these groups from a wide range of options. Again, people who were prejudiced against one minority group tended to be prejudiced against others. Nearly three-quarters of those who disliked Jews and blacks also disliked such people as the Wallonians, the Pireneans, and the Danireans. Some of the subjects even recommended that members of the latter three groups be expelled from the United States. As it happens, however, the Wallonians, the Pireneans, and the Danireans do not exist and never have. Their names were concocted by Hartley to see if people who were prejudiced against existing groups would also be prejudiced against groups they could never have met or even heard of. His study suggests that prejudice is often learned not through contact with the groups against whom prejudice is directed, but, rather, through contact with other prejudiced people.

Scapegoating

A psychological mechanism that has been identified in some situations of racial or ethnic antagonism is *scapegoating*, or placing the blame for one's troubles on some individual or group incapable of offering resistance. Scapegoating typically occurs when the members of one group feel threatened but are unable to retaliate against the real source of the threat. Therefore they vent their frustrations on some weak and despised group. Low-status whites, for example, may resent their low social and economic status, but they cannot strike at the source of the problem—the employer or "the system." Instead, they direct their hostility at minority-group members whom they believe to be competing for jobs at the same level. The outstanding example of a scapegoated group were, again, the Jews of Nazi Germany, who were conveniently blamed for Germany's economic troubles after World War I. Scapegoating another group also has the psychological function of enhancing the self-image of the group that does the scapegoating, for it proves that they are superior to someone at least.

Figure 12.9 Chinese immigrants to the western United States often served as scapegoats for the frustrations of low-status whites, who saw them as competitors for jobs. This engraving shows an anti-Chinese riot in Denver, Colorado, in 1880.

Projection

Another psychological element present in many situations of racist interaction is *projection,* which occurs when people attribute to others the characteristics they are unwilling to recognize in themselves. The myth of the insatiable sexual appetite of the black male, especially as directed toward white women, has its origins in projection. Lillian Smith (1949) explains:

> Because [the slaveowners] were Puritan, they succeeded in developing a frigidity in their white women that precluded the possibility of mutual satisfaction. Lonely and baffled . . . they could not resist the vigor and kindliness and gaiety of these slaves. And succumbing to desire, they mated with these dark women whom they had dehumanized in their minds. . . . The race-sex-sin spiral had begun. The more trails the white man made to the back-yard cabins, the higher he raised his white wife on her pedestal when he returned to the big house. The higher the pedestal, the less he enjoyed her whom he had put there, for statues are after all only nice things to look at. More and more numerous became the little trails of escape . . . and more and more intricately they began to weave in and out of southern life. Guilt, shame, fear, lust spiralled after each other. Then a time came . . . when white man's suspicion of white woman began to pull the spiral higher and higher. It was of course inevitable for him to suspect her of the sins he had committed so pleasantly and often. *What if,* he whispered, and the words were never finished. . . . White man . . . in jealous panic began to project his own sins on to the Negro male.

The lynchings of black men in the South, often on the merest suspicion of their desire for white women, can be fully understood only when seen as a result of the projection of the white man's own lusts onto his black victim.

Forms of Discrimination

Discrimination occurs when the dominant group regards itself as entitled to social advantages and uses its power to secure them at the expense of minority groups. These advantages may be of many different kinds. The dominant group may, for example, reserve positions of political power for itself; it may establish a claim over desirable residential areas; it may demand the exclusive use of certain recreational facilities and schools; it may claim a right to high-status jobs. In extreme cases, it may even enforce the physical segregation of the minority group from the rest of society.

Discrimination takes two basic forms: *de jure*, or legal, discrimination encoded in laws; and *de facto*, or informal, discrimination entrenched in social customs. *De jure* discrimination was applied in all the colonies established by the European powers, where the laws reserved certain rights and privileges for the dominant group. Similar laws existed in many parts of the United States until the 1960s, when they were gradually repealed or struck down by the Supreme Court. *De facto* discrimination is always present in any situation in which a dominant group maintains advantages over a minority. Unlike *de jure* discrimination, which can be eliminated by law, *de facto* discrimination is very difficult to eradicate. Those who hoped that the repeal of discriminatory laws in the United States would be the end of discrimination have been sorely disappointed.

De facto discrimination has persisted in the United States because it has become deeply embedded in our customs and other institutional arrangements. This *institutionalized discrimination* pervades many areas of society. For example, informal barriers to residential integration have resulted in a pattern of urban racial segregation, which in turn tends to produce segregation in schools and other facilities. Similarly, there is a strong tendency toward discrimination in

hiring practices, one that leads to blacks' having much higher unemployment rates and consistently less earnings than similarly qualified whites. Blacks are underrepresented in all high-status positions in society—for example, in Congress, in the judiciary, and at the upper levels of military and corporate power. Only one means has so far been found to directly combat institutionalized discrimination—"affirmative action" programs, under which colleges and public and private employees may be required to give preference in admissions, hiring, or promotions to members of racial minorities (and to women) until the minority in question is fairly represented in the college or workplace. These programs are highly controversial, for the obvious reason that what is "affirmative action" to one group is "reverse discrimination" to another.

Race and Ethnic Relations in the United States

The Declaration of Independence, signed on July 4, 1776, proclaimed to the world:

> We hold these truths to be self-evident, that all men are created equal, that they are endowed by their Creator with certain inalienable rights, that among these are life, liberty, and the pursuit of happiness.

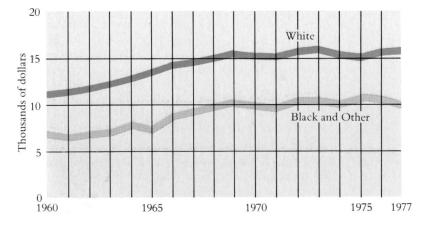

MEDIAN ANNUAL MONEY INCOME OF FAMILIES, BY RACE: IN CONSTANT (1977) DOLLARS

Figure 12.10 This chart gives some indication of the nature and extent of institutionalized discrimination in the United States. Although blacks have made economic gains in recent years, their earnings relative to those of whites have changed hardly at all. In a situation of truly equal opportunity, there would be no discrepancy between the average earnings of different population groups.

Thomas Jefferson, who wrote these words of stirring idealism, was a slaveholder, and so were many of the men who appended their signatures to the document.

As the Swedish sociologist Gunnar Myrdal pointed out in 1944 in his classic study of American race relations, *An American Dilemma*, there has always been a deep tension between the expressed ideals on which the United States was founded and the actual treatment that minorities have received at the hands of the dominant group. This tension, Myrdal predicted, would ultimately have to be resolved, but the nation is still a long way from a final resolution. American society remains a substantially racist one, in which inequalities of power, wealth, and prestige tend to follow the lines of racial and ethnic divisions.

Unlike most societies, the United States is primarily a nation of relatively recent immigrants; the forebears of most Americans came here as explorers, adventurers, colonizers, refugees, deported criminals, or captive slaves. It is a cherished American belief that the society has served as a "melting pot" for these diverse peoples. The essence of this credo was captured in *The Melting Pot*, a popular Broadway success of 1908 (Zangwill, 1933):

> America is God's crucible, the great Melting Pot, where all the races of Europe are melting and re-forming! Here you stand, good folk, think I, when I see them at Ellis Island, here you stand in your fifty groups, with your fifty languages and histories, and your fifty blood hatreds and rivalries. But you won't long be like that, brothers, for these are the fires of God you've come to ... Germans, and Frenchmen, Irishmen and Englishmen, Jews and Russians—into the Crucible with you all! God is making the American.

The truth, however, is very different. The first settlers on our shores came mostly from "Anglo-Saxon" northern Europe, and they quickly gained control of political and economic power. To a considerable extent, their descendants have managed to keep this power ever since, and their cultural values have become the dominant ones of the entire nation (Graham and Gurr, 1969). Successive waves of immigrants have often had to struggle long and hard to be assimilated into the American mainstream, and many have failed. Those who were racially or ethnically akin to the dominant "WASP" (white, Anglo-Saxon Protestant) group, such as the Scandinavians and Germans, were accepted fairly readily. Those who were racially akin but

ethnically different, such as the Catholic Irish and Poles, faced much more prejudice and discrimination. Those who were both racially and ethnically dissimilar to the dominant group, such as blacks and Hispanic-Americans, have been systematically excluded by formal and informal barriers from equal participation in American society (Feagin, 1978; Schaefer, 1979; Parrillo, 1980).

We shall now look at the background and the contemporary situation of some of these minority groups: blacks, Indians, Hispanics, Asians, and "white ethnics."

Blacks

Black Americans are the largest minority group in the United States; they number over 25.6 million and represent about 11.7 percent of the population. Their history in the United States has been one of sustained oppression and discrimination.

The first Africans were brought in shackles to North America in 1619, and within a few decades the demand for their labor had created a massive slave trade that ultimately transported some 400,000 captives to these shores. Contrary to common belief, the slaves were not seized by whites on the West African coast. They were captured by other blacks from the slave-owning kingdoms of the interior and sold to white traders at the coastal ports. The slaves were then chained wrist to wrist and ankle to ankle for a two-month sea voyage, during which they were often packed so tightly that they could not even sit up. To prevent the risk of mutiny and suicide among the captives, they were frequently kept in this position for days or weeks on end, lying in their own blood and excrement (Elkins, 1963; Cheek, 1970). Many of the slaves tried to starve themselves to death and were force-fed through metal funnels that were jammed into their mouths. (For years an intense economic debate raged between two groups of slave traders: the "tight packers," who held that profits would be greater if as many slaves as possible were crammed aboard, and the "loose packers," who argued that crowded conditions caused so many deaths that, all things considered, it was better to allow the captives a little more space.) On arrival in the United States the slaves were sold at public auction and set to work, mostly on plantations. The original culture of these African people had little relevance in this new

situation, and their old traditions, language, and religion soon fell into disuse and eventually disappeared. (One cultural feature that did survive in modified form, however, was the rhythm of West African traditional music. Transformed over the generations into blues, jazz, soul, rhythm and blues, and ultimately rock music, it has become a major contribution to contemporary American and world culture.)

At first, the slaveholders justified slavery, not by racist attitudes, but rather by their frankly admitted need for cheap labor in the cotton and tobacco fields. In time, however, the practice of slavery led to the creation of a racist ideology that justified the continued subjugation of the slaves by depicting blacks as subhuman: they were said to be innately irresponsible, promiscuous, stupid, lazy—and happy with their subordinate status. The experience of slavery set the stage for all the subsequent interaction between black and white in the United States.

The Northern states began to outlaw slavery in 1780, but it persisted in the South until it was ended by the Civil War and legislation that followed Lincoln's emancipation of slaves in 1863. During the period of Reconstruction, which lasted for just over a decade after Lincoln's declara-

tion, there was a concerted attempt to ensure that the newly freed slaves would indeed enjoy equality. However, white political dominance was subsequently reasserted by depriving the blacks of the vote and by the use of such terror tactics as lynching. Segregation remained the norm, and was gradually encoded into law. Throughout the country, including supposedly liberal metropolitan areas of the North, segregation in hotels, restaurants, and other public facilities was common. In 1954, however, the Supreme Court ruled in the historic *Brown* v. *Board of Education* case that segregated schools were inherently unequal and ordered nationwide school desegregation "with all deliberate speed." From that time on, the courts and the federal government began to dismantle the system of racial segregation and discrimination. Yet progress toward greater equality was painfully slow until the emergence of a powerful civil rights movement and a series of violent and costly riots in Northern cities during the sixties. As conflict theory would suggest, this heightened tension between the competing groups generated rapid changes. In particular, the principles of racial equality and desegregation were enshrined in the law of the land through a series of civil rights acts.

Figure 12.11 Some stages in the changing relationship of the white and black groups in the United States: a slave auction in the 1860s; a lynching during the 1930s; institutionalized discrimination in the 1950s; a civil rights march in the 1960s; members of the black power movement of the early 1970s; and a presidential candidate seeking black support in 1980.

One of the most important outcomes of the racial turmoil of the sixties was a change in both black goals and black self-image. From the early days of slavery onward, many blacks and their white liberal sympathizers had hoped for an integrated society—in effect, one in which blacks would be accepted into the WASP middle-class culture. The rise of the black power movement, with its emphasis on black pride and the validity of black culture, marked an important change of direction. The self-image of blacks was radically revised, and the black community showed signs of unprecedented self-confidence. As a result, many blacks began to demand a plural society, rather than assimilation into the dominant culture—a demand that has had profound effects on the way many other minorities have come to view themselves as well.

The social and economic changes since the sixties, on the other hand, have been far less extensive than many people assume. The most significant changes have probably been in the field of education, where the gap between blacks and whites has been narrowing rapidly. In 1979 the average black person had 11.9 years of education, compared with 12.5 years for whites; 31.5 percent of black high school graduates went to college, compared with 32.2 percent of white graduates; and blacks, with 11.7 percent of the total population, represented 10 percent of the nation's college enrollment—more than double the figure in the mid-sixties. In most other respects, however, black gains have been less impressive. Residential neighborhoods still remain substantially segregated in virtually every part of the country. Although nearly 5000 blacks hold local elective offices, there has been little progress at higher levels of the political system: in 1980 only 3 percent of members of Congress were black, and there was no black senator and no black state governor. More important, blacks are actually losing ground in the economy relative to whites. In 1969, black median income was 60 percent that of whites; ten years later, in 1979, it had shrunk to 57 percent of white income. Only 13.4 percent of black families earn more than $25,000 a year, compared with 29.5 percent of white families. Unemployment rates for blacks are typically double those of whites; in 1980, black unemployment averaged 13.5 percent, and in some urban areas the rate for black teenagers was over 50 percent. Even among college graduates the unemployment rate for blacks was high—27.2 percent, compared to 22.3 percent for white high school dropouts.

Institutionalized discrimination against blacks still pervades the United States—perhaps more so in the North (where more than half of all blacks now live, primarily in urban ghettos) than in the South, which in some respects has adjusted more readily to the changing relationships of black and white. Unhappily, many whites fail to recognize the persistence of this discrimination: believing that the civil rights acts and such measures as affirmative-action programs have brought great—or even unfair—benefits to minorities, they overlook the stark facts contained in the statistics on unemployment, average income, childhood mortality, life expectancy, and the like. Opinion polls have consistently shown that members of the two groups have vastly different perceptions of black progress. For example, a 1978 New York Times–CBS News poll found that two-thirds of the whites felt there had been "a lot of progress" in getting rid of discrimination, but more than half the blacks felt there had not been "much real change"; nearly half the blacks felt that black people missed out on jobs and promotions because of discrimination, but less than a fifth of the whites felt this to be true.

It is certainly the case that, for the first time, a significant minority of blacks—perhaps a quarter to a third—has achieved middle-class status. But the great majority of blacks have been left behind, and many of them form a permanent "underclass" of impoverished people who have little hope that their lives will ever improve (W. Wilson, 1978). People from this category, it seems, were prominent in the riots that shook Miami and other Southern cities in 1980. Unless a radical improvement in the economic conditions of this ghetto underclass takes place, there is every likelihood of recurrent urban violence throughout the present decade and even beyond.

Hispanic-Americans

The Spanish-speaking population of the United States contains at least 13 million people, and probably considerably more. The exact size of this category is not known because a significant proportion of Hispanics are illegal immigrants who avoid contact with public officials and who do not complete census forms. As a Spanish-speaking, Catholic, and generally poor people in an English-speaking, predominantly Protestant, and generally affluent society, the Hispanic population shares certain common characteristics. Yet these shared features should not obscure the fact that there is considerable diversity among the various Hispanic groups. The largest group are the Chicanos, or Mexican-Americans (about 7.2 million); the next largest, the Puerto Ricans (about 1.8 million); and the third largest, the Cubans (about 900,000). In addition, there are approximately 2.4 million other Spanish-speaking residents from various nations of Central and South America. The Hispanic population is growing very rapidly indeed—partly because it contains a disproportionate number of people in the early childbearing years, partly because of a cultural reluctance to practice birth-control, and partly because there is a constant flow of new immigrants, legal and illegal, from Mexico and elsewhere. Many population experts believe that the Hispanic population will become larger than the black population sometime during this decade, making Hispanics the nation's largest minority group. This fact has not been lost on some black Americans, who realize that they may have to compete with Hispanics for whatever benefits the larger society bestows on its minorities; indeed, conflict between blacks and Cubans was a disturbing feature of the 1980 riots in Miami.

The Chicano population is concentrated in five states—Texas, New Mexico, Colorado, Arizona, and California. Many of its members have come as legal or illegal immigrants from Mexico; others are descendants of people who have occupied these territories for over four centuries, and who were involuntarily made residents of the United States in 1848 when Mexico ceded parts of the Southwest to its victorious neighbor after the Mexican-American War. Unlike other racial and ethnic minorities, Chicanos have been able to maintain intimate ties with their country of origin because of its proximity. One effect of this circumstance is that their problems as a minority have been aggravated by a tacit assumption that they are not "really" Americans at all, but rather, Mexicans who can go home if they are not satisfied.

Migrant workers from Mexico have always been viewed as a convenient source of labor for the United States, and they have been encouraged or discouraged from crossing the border according to how great the need for their services has been from time to time. In the earlier part of this century, Chicanos were imported in large numbers to help build the railroads and industries of the Southwest; during the Great Depression, when jobs were scarce, half a million

Figure 12.12 This scene is all too common on the U.S.-Mexican border, where hundreds of thousands of Chicanos are apprehended each year as they attempt to do what tens of millions of other people have done over the decades—to come to the United States in search of a better way of life. The difference is, of course, that most immigrants in the past were wanted, and entered legally; many workers from Mexico, however, must either enter illegally or not at all.

Chicanos were deported to Mexico (often illegally, since some had been born in the United States and were citizens); between the forties and the early sixties, Chicano workers were again in demand and were systematically imported; since then, there have been active campaigns to restrict the number of immigrants and to deport any illegal aliens among them. Illegal immigration is now a virtual torrent: immigration officials catch over 800,000 would-be immigrants each year, but for each one that is intercepted, at least four cross the border undetected. There is little prospect that this flow of immigrants will cease, or even decline: Mexico has an unemployment rate of well over 30 percent and the country is so poor (despite its growing oil revenues) that a fifth of the population earns less than $100 a year. Moreover, there is a continuing demand in the Southwest for the services of illegal aliens, who are willing to do jobs that "Anglos" will not touch, for wages that are often far below the national minimum wage.

Although Chicanos have traditionally worked as migrant farm laborers, the mechanization of agriculture has steadily driven them into urban areas, where over 80 percent now live in barrios, or ghettos. The average family income in 1979 was around $10,000, and about a fifth of Chicanos live below the poverty line. A fifth of the population has received less than five years of schooling, and, in fact, low educational achievement and a poor command of English are continuing barriers against better job opportunities for many Chicanos. The time-honored use of the schools to "Anglicize" and assimilate minority children has resulted in a backlash of resentment among Chicanos. As a result, they have successfully demanded Spanish or bilingual education for their children—a step that will undoubtedly enhance pride in Chicano culture, but which may do little to improve the command of English that is so necessary for social mobility in an English-speaking country.

Like other minority groups, the Chicanos are rapidly becoming more militant. The Chicano leader Cesar Chavez has successfully organized migrant farm workers, and this example has been followed in other areas as well. Chicanos are clearly becoming more reluctant to be assimilated into the mainstream culture, and they are increasingly aware of the political muscle that their numbers will give them in the future (Stoddard, 1974; Moore and Pachon, 1976; Hernandez et al., 1976; Lindsey, 1979; Acuña, 1980).

The Puerto Ricans are a people of mixed Spanish, Indian, and Negroid origins. The Island of Puerto Rico has

Figure 12.13 The Puerto Ricans are sometimes described as the "people of the islands"—the islands being their Caribbean home and Manhattan. In climate, economy, and life-style, the two islands could hardly be more different, yet most adult Puerto Ricans have experienced living in both. The scene of this photo is Manhattan.

been an American possession since the Spanish-American War, and Puerto Ricans have been United States citizens since 1917. Many of them have immigrated to the continental United States in search of better jobs, with more than half of them settling in New York City. Living primarily in ghetto areas, they are one of the most impoverished groups in the nation: almost 40 percent of Puerto Rican families live below the poverty line. Perhaps because of these poor economic conditions, they have done something that no other immigrant group has done before: in almost every year since 1972, Puerto Ricans have returned home in greater numbers than they have immigrated (Steiner, 1974; Wagenheim, 1975; Stockton, 1978).

The Cuban population differs significantly from the other major Hispanic groups. After the Cuban revolution in 1959, nearly 500,000 Cubans fled the Castro regime and came to live in the United States, where most have now settled permanently. Unlike Chicano and Puerto Rican migrants, however, the bulk of these Cuban refugees were middle-class people, usually well-educated and often with skills and experience in the professions, business, and allied fields. These Cubans adapted remarkably quickly to their new environment, and their average income is much closer to the national average than to the income of other Hispanic immigrant groups. Miami, where the bulk of the Cubans settled, has been transformed from a fading resort town to a thriving commercial center largely through Cuban enterprise. In 1980, however, there was a second wave of Cuban immigration when over 110,000 "boat people" sought refuge in the United States. On the whole, this group lacks the qualifications and background of the earlier migrants, and it is unlikely that they will achieve the same degree of success in as short a time. The overall characteristics of the Cuban population, however, do underline the diversity that exists among the various Hispanic groups.

American Indians

Few groups in the United States have been as cruelly treated or as absurdly stereotyped as the original inhabitants of the country. When the first settlers arrived from Europe, there were at least 1.5 million native Americans, but by 1850 their numbers had been reduced to a mere 250,000. There are now around 1 million Indians, about a third of whom are in urban areas, with the remainder living on or near 267 reservations. The Indians comprise over 500 highly diverse tribal groups, and about fifty of their original languages are still in use.

When the first white settlers arrived on the northeast coast, the native inhabitants befriended them. But the two groups were soon in open conflict as the settlers, armed with a superior military technology, started their relentless drive westward. On any objective analysis of the facts, the invading whites were morally in the wrong in their dispossession of the Indians, but since American history has been written primarily by whites, a grossly distorted picture of the events has been handed down to us. The ethnocentrism of the standard historical accounts is remarkable: the whites are described as "pioneers," not "invaders"; the native peoples' defense of their way of life and economic assets is "treacherous," not "courageous"; the military successes of the whites are "victories," but those of the Indians are "massacres."

The policy toward the native Americans was frequently one of outright genocide. As early as 1755 the following proclamation was issued in Boston against the Penobscot Indians:

> At the desire of the House of Representatives ... I do hereby require his majesty's subjects of the Province to embrace all opportunities of pursuing, captivating, killing and destroying all and every of the aforesaid Indians.... The General Court of this Province have voted that a bounty ... be granted: For the capture of every male Penobscot Indian above the age of twelve and brought to Boston, fifty pounds. For every scalp of a male Indian above the age aforesaid, brought in as evidence of their being killed as aforesaid, forty pounds.... For every scalp of such female Indian or male Indian under the age of twelve years that shall be killed and brought in as evidence of their being killed as aforesaid, twenty pounds. [Quoted in Paine, 1897]

It is a curious fact of history that settlers who were willing to pay large sums for the scalp of a murdered child under the age of twelve were able to successfully portray the Indians as savages and themselves as entirely righteous. (The practice of scalping, in fact, originated among the settlers, not the native Americans.) Yet this stereotype, much reinforced during the present century by Western movies, has persisted almost unchallenged until very recently.

Figure 12.14 The Battle of Wounded Knee marked the end of the Indians' military resistance to the white settlers who took their land and disrupted their way of life. Yet even today there are disputes over Indian lands, which in many cases have become valuable assets because of their water rights and rich mineral deposits. The Indian woman pictured here is prepared to protect her ancestral land against industry efforts to open it up for the strip mining of coal.

The westward advance of the whites shattered the cultures of the Indian peoples. The federal government broke treaty after treaty, and entire tribes were hounded from one area to another as new waves of settlers arrived and coveted the land the Indians had been promised. Four thousand Cherokee, for example, died when they were forced to walk a thousand miles in mid-winter along a "trail of tears" from Carolina and Georgia to Oklahoma. After 1871 all the Indians were made "wards" of the federal government—a legal status usually given to people, such as minors and imbeciles, who must have a guardian because they are incompetent to fulfill normal adult responsibilities. Not until 1924 were the descendants of the original inhabitants of the land granted the right of citizenship in it.

The current social and economic position of the Indians is probably worse than that of any other minority group in the United States. The average Indian has only eight years of schooling. Unemployment generally ranges between 45 and 55 percent, but reaches 80 percent in some areas and seasons. Almost half of employed Indians who live on the reservations work in some capacity for government agencies. About a third of the Indian population lives below the poverty line, and many, if not most, reservation dwellings

are substandard: thousands of people are living in unheated log houses, tarpaper shacks, old tents, caves, and even abandoned automobile bodies. The life expectancy of the average Indian is ten years below that of the nation as a whole. The suicide rate is double the national average, and the alcoholism rate is at least five times as high.

Inspired by the success of the civil rights and black power movements, Indians have become increasingly militant in their demands for equality. A "red power" movement has arisen, intertribal organizations have been formed, and the American Indian Movement (AIM) has campaigned vigorously on behalf of Indian interests. One of the most significant of the steps the Indians have taken has been to demand that lands illegally seized from them in the past be returned. More than a hundred such legal claims, involving millions of acres in states from New England to the Southwest, are pending, and in several cases the courts have granted tribes large cash awards in compensation for the loss of their territories. Like black Americans, many Indians are now demanding not assimilation but respect for their own culture, and with it the right to self-determination on their reservations (Bahr et al., 1972; Josephy, 1971; American Indian Policy Review Commission, 1976).

Asian-Americans

Asian-Americans are, with some exceptions, the only racial minority that has approached any real degree of equality with the whites, although they are still often regarded as intruders into American life. About 1 percent of Americans are of Asian origin. The largest groups are the Chinese and the Japanese, but there are also significant numbers of Filipinos, Hawaiians, Koreans, and Vietnamese (one effect of American military involvement in Southeast Asia is that over 300,000 refugees from the area have settled in the United States). Asian-Americans are currently concentrated in two states, California and Hawaii.

Over 300,000 Chinese settled in the United States between 1850 and 1880, most of them imported to California as laborers in the mining industry and in railroad construction. Their presence aroused violent anti-Chinese feeling, especially among low-status whites who feared job competition from them. Frequent anti-Chinese riots took place. There were a number of lynchings of Chinese in California and even a wholesale massacre of Chinese in Wyoming in 1885. Fears of the "yellow peril" led Congress to pass the discriminatory Chinese Exclusion Act of 1882 that restricted the number of Chinese immigrants, and the entry of Chinese laborers to the United States was totally prohibited between the turn of the century and World War II. The Chinese have remained largely isolated from the mainstream of American life ever since, a fact that is reflected in their exceptionally high poverty rate. Living in their own very closed and densely populated communities, they remain largely inconspicuous to other Americans, who seem to value them primarily for their cuisine (Li, 1976; Lyman, 1974).

Japanese began to immigrate to the United States somewhat later than the Chinese, and most of them settled in the Pacific states. During World War II the entire Japanese-American population of the West Coast, including tens of thousands of second-generation United States citizens, was interned in "security camps" (actually, concentration camps, complete with barbed wire and gun turrets) in the Western deserts and the Rocky Mountains. Many of them suffered economic ruin as a result. The reasoning behind this drastic infringement of civil liberties was that the Japanese-Americans might be disloyal to the United States, but the racist implications of the step can be

Figure 12.15 The entire Japanese population of the West Coast (including American-born citizens) was interned in "relocation centers" during World War II—a remarkable and unparalleled violation of civil rights. This photograph shows Japanese residents at one of these guarded camps as they salute the American flag. Not a single Japanese-American was ever found guilty of any disloyalty to the United States before or during the war.

Figure 12.16 Chinese-Americans have tended to remain isolated from the American mainstream—partly as a result of discrimination, but also partly through a desire to preserve their language and cultural heritage. In recent years, however, they have begun, like other minority groups, to demand fairer access to jobs and other resources.

gauged by the fact that no discriminatory action was taken against Italian- and German-Americans at the time. Today, however, the Japanese have been relatively well assimilated into American society. Although some prejudice against them persists, they have the highest per capita income and educational achievements of any racial minority and are the only one that does not live mainly in neighborhood ghettos (Daniels, 1972; Kiefer, 1974; Kitano, 1976; Wilson and Hosokawa, 1980).

White Ethnics

One of the least expected events in American intergroup relations of the past decade or so has been the resurgence of group consciousness among the "white ethnics," or Americans of Polish, Italian, Greek, Irish, and Slavic origins (Greeley, 1974). This development, it seems, is the indirect result of the militancy among other minority groups, and, in turn, it has lent new impetus to the society's growing acceptance of pluralism as a desirable goal.

When the various ethnic groups from Ireland and various countries in southern and eastern Europe first came to the United States, they encountered a degree of hostility that is difficult to comprehend today. Anti-Catholic riots occurred again and again in the cities where the new immigrants settled; Italians were lynched by mobs in several states; Irish laborers—if employers would hire them at all—were offered lower wages than blacks. In a fairly typical example of this prejudice, one editorial writer commented in 1886:

> These people are not Americans, but the very scum and offal of Europe . . . long-haired, wild-eyed, bad-smelling, atheistic—reckless foreign wretches, who never did an honest hour's work in their lives. . . . Crush such snakes . . . before they have time to bite. [Quoted in Parrillo, 1980]

The response of many of these European ethnics was to try as far as possible to be assimilated into the mainstream culture; frequently, for example, they Anglicized their last names, and they often insisted that their children speak only English, even in the home. Middle- and upper-class ethnics have since been readily absorbed into WASP society, but working-class ethnics, particularly in large cities, have tended to live in close-knit communities and to retain some traditional loyalties. They have also felt resentful of the dominant WASP culture, whose members appear to have much easier access to social, political, and economic opportunity.

This resentment increased significantly in the sixties, perhaps because many working-class ethnics believed that the WASP-dominated political authorities were giving preferential treatment to blacks over other minorities. In this view, the emergence of the new ethnic consciousness is, in effect, a backlash reaction to the presumed success of blacks in extorting benefits from the policy makers, rather than waiting for their turn to rise in the social hierarchy, as other groups before them had done (Novak, 1971; Rose, 1974; Kricus, 1976; Patterson, 1977; Hill, 1977). There may be some truth to this picture, but there is growing evidence that the stereotype of the white ethnics as a somewhat bigoted and primarily working-class group has little basis in reality. White Catholics, in fact, have the same number of years of education as the national average, and their average income slightly exceeds that of the nation as a whole. (Most of the progress achieved by white ethnics, however, has been made by the groups that originated in western Europe and have been in the United States the longest—the Irish and the Italians.) There is also no evidence that the white ethnics are more prejudiced against racial minorities than are other whites (Greeley, 1976, 1977). In any event, loyalties to the old ethnic traditions remain powerful, even among the youngest generation whose members have had minimal contact with the culture of their forebears. More important, ethnic identity is now perceived as something respectable, as a potential source of group pride and strength.

The Future of American Race and Ethnic Relations

There is some indication that American intergroup relations are improving, but the process still has a long way to go. Opinion polls of white Americans show a steady trend in the direction of greater tolerance and less prejudice. In 1942, only 35 percent of whites would not have objected to a black neighbor, but by 1978 fully 65 percent declared they would "not mind at all" if a black lived next door. Harris polls show that the number of whites who feel that blacks are "inferior" dropped from 31 percent in 1963 to 15 percent in 1978 and the number of whites who think blacks are moving "too fast" fell from 71 percent in 1966 to 37 percent in 1978. On the other hand, these polls show that as recently as 1978 only 35 percent of whites favored "full integration" of the races, with a further 42 percent favoring "integration in some areas." In addition, whereas an overwhelming majority of blacks believe that they are discriminated against in many important institutional areas, most

Figure 12.17 This anti-immigrant cartoon was published almost a century ago, and is typical of the prejudiced and often vicious attitude that many established inhabitants had toward new immigrants from Poland, Ireland, Russia, Italy, Germany, and elsewhere. Today, descendants of these immigrant groups are sometimes found decrying the arrival of Cambodians, Mexicans, Haitians, Cubans, and other new immigrants, and using exactly the same arguments to do so: that there are not enough jobs, that the immigrants are a burden on society, and so on. Yet, in time, the United States may have a Vietnamese-American president or Cuban-American secretary of state, just as it produced an Irish-American president and a Polish-American secretary of state—something the cartoonist and many of his contemporaries would never have believed possible.

whites do not share this view. For example, 72 percent of blacks felt there was discrimination in the way they were "treated as human beings," but only 40 percent of whites held this opinion; 72 percent of blacks felt they were not "getting full equality," but only 40 percent of whites agreed; 61 percent of blacks thought there was "discrimination in wages paid," but only 22 percent of whites believed this to be the case. These data suggest that there is considerable scope for increased hostility between the dominant and the minority groups in the United States if the rate of progress toward equality slows down.

The future pattern of race relations in the United States is difficult to predict because there is no consensus on what the nation's goals should be. Many Americans no longer criticize the society for its failure to provide a "melting pot" for the assimilation of the various groups. Instead, they would prefer a pluralist society in which the groups interact on the basis of mutual equality and respect.

According to Milton Gordon (1961, 1977) there are three main options that are open to the United States in race relations: Anglo-conformity, melting pot, and cultural pluralism.

Anglo-conformity assumes that it is desirable to maintain modified English institutions, language, and culture as the dominant standard in American life. In practice, "assimilation" in the United States has always meant Anglo-conformity.

Melting pot is a rather different concept, involving a totally new blend, culturally and biologically, of all the racial and ethnic groups in the United States. In practice, the melting pot has been of limited significance in the American experience.

Cultural pluralism assumes a series of distinct but coexisting groups, each preserving its own tradition and culture, but each loyal to broader national unity. In practice, there has always been a high degree of cultural pluralism in the United States, but this pluralism has been marked by severe inequalities among the various racial and ethnic groups.

Current indications are that, for the foreseeable future at least, American race and ethnic relations will be conducted primarily within a pluralist framework—although the melting pot may well be the society's ultimate destiny. Pursuit of cultural pluralism may be a dangerous course, for it presumes some degree of ethnocentrism on the part of the participating groups, and it can provide a workable solution only if it is based on equality, respect, and interdependence. But if we can achieve that, we may finally, after three centuries, resolve our "American dilemma."

Summary

1. Race and ethnic relations are the patterns of interaction among groups whose members share distinctive physical characteristics or cultural traits. People who have similar physical characteristics are socially defined as a race; people who share similar cultural characteristics are socially defined as an ethnic group.

2. A minority group is one that is differentiated from the rest of the population and treated unequally. Minorities (a) suffer social disadvantages, (b) are socially visible, (c) have a consciousness of kind, (d) consist mainly of people born into the group, and (e) generally marry within the group.

3. Six possible patterns of race and ethnic relations are assimilation, pluralism, legal protection of minorities, population transfer, continued subjugation, and extermination. All have been attempted in North America.

4. Racism refers to a situation in which one group is regarded as inferior to and dominated by another. From the conflict perspective, racial or ethnic inequality arises as a result of competition among different social groups for scarce and valued resources. Intergroup tensions tend to decline as competition subsides. The domination of one group by another is justified by an ideology of racism, which defines the situation as just and the minority group as unfit for equal status.

5. Prejudice refers to negative attitudes toward members of other groups; discrimination refers to negative actions against them. Prejudice is not necessarily translated into discrimination. Several psychological processes are involved in prejudiced thinking: stereotypes, authoritarian personality patterns, scapegoating, and projection. Discrimination may be both *de jure* (encoded in law) and *de facto* (entrenched in custom). Institutionalized discrimination may pervade many areas of life and is very difficult to eradicate.

6. The United States has never been a "melting pot" for all its peoples; those racially or ethnically unlike the dominant

group have been excluded to some extent from equal participation in American society. Important minorities in the modern United States are blacks, Hispanics, Indians, Asians, and white ethnics. All have suffered in various ways and in various degrees from prejudice and discrimination.

7. There are signs that American race and ethnic relations are improving, but considerable hostility and resentment still remain. The most likely trend for the foreseeable future is one of cultural pluralism, in which different groups preserve their own traditions and culture.

Important Terms

race (281)

ethnic group (282)

minority group (283)

genocide (285)

ethnocentrism (286)

racism (287)

ideology (289)

self-fulfilling
  prophecy (289)

false consciousness (290)

prejudice (290)

discrimination (290)

stereotype (293)

authoritarian
  personality (293)

scapegoating (294)

projection (295)

de jure
  discrimination (296)

de facto
  discrimination (296)

institutionalized
  discrimination (296)

Suggested Readings

BROWN, DEE. *Bury My Heart at Wounded Knee.* New York: Bantam, 1972.

An account of the early relationships between white settlers and native Americans, told from the point of view of the latter. The book is a useful corrective to the usual treatments of this era of American history.

GREELEY, ANDREW M. *The American Catholic: A Social Portrait.* New York: Basic Books, 1977.

An interesting analysis of information, from surveys and other sources, about the Catholic population of the United States.

HERNANDEZ, CAROL A., et al. (eds.). *Chicanos: Social and Psychological Perspectives.* 2nd ed. St. Louis: Mosby, 1976.

A good selection of articles dealing with various aspects of Chicano life and culture in the United States.

JACOBS, JANE. *The Question of Separatism: Quebec and the Struggle for Sovereignty.* New York: Random House, 1980.

An interesting analysis of relationships between English- and French-speaking Canadians.

JONES, JAMES M. *Prejudice and Racism.* Reading, Mass.: Addison-Wesley, 1972.

A comprehensive and useful summary of social-science knowledge about racial prejudice.

KITANO, HARRY L. *Japanese Americans: The Evolution of a Subculture.* 2nd ed. Englewood Cliffs, N.J.: Prentice-Hall, 1976.

A good overview of the history and problems of Americans of Japanese origin.

LYMAN, STANFORD M. *Chinese Americans.* New York: Random House, 1974.

An excellent historical and sociological survey of one of America's Asian minorities.

PARRILLO, VINCENT J. *Strangers to These Shores: Race and Ethnic Relations in the United States.* Boston: Houghton Mifflin, 1980.

An excellent survey of the relationships among the various groups that have made the United States their home. The book includes both sociological and psychological material on prejudice, discrimination, and intergroup relations.

PINKEY, ALPHONSO. *Black Americans.* 2nd ed. Englewood Cliffs, N.J.: Prentice-Hall, 1975.

A good survey of the history and contemporary situation of the black American population.

SCHAEFER, RICHARD T. *Racial and Ethnic Groups.* Boston: Little, Brown, 1979.

A comprehensive and readable survey of race and ethnic relations in the United States. The book includes separate discussions on each of the minority groups.

SKLARE, MICHAEL (ed.). *The Jew in American Society.* New York: Behrman House, 1974.

A good collection of articles about various aspects of the American Jewish community.

WILSON, WILLIAM J. *The Declining Significance of Race: Blacks and Changing American Institutions.* Chicago: University of Chicago Press, 1978.

Wilson presents a controversial argument: that differences of social class are becoming more significant than differences of race in their effect on the status of black Americans.

CHAPTER **13**   *Inequalities of Gender and Age*

In the preceding three chapters we have seen how various human societies use an extraordinary range of criteria to differentiate among their members—criteria that include class, caste, religion, race, language, and a host of other features. Yet only two such criteria are used in all societies: sex and age. Differentiation on these grounds is universal, for they represent ascribed characteristics that inevitably arise from the human condition: our species contains two sexes, and we all grow older from the time of birth to the moment of death.

Every society categorizes its members on the basis of their sex, treating men and women in different ways and expecting different patterns of behavior from them. Likewise, all societies distinguish among people on the grounds of age, treating members of various age groups in dissimilar ways and requiring them to play different roles. These distinctions do not necessarily imply that one sex or one age group must have greater access to social rewards than does the other sex or another age group, but in practice social differentiation is always translated into social inequality.

In every society known to us, certain rights and opportunities have been denied to women on the basis of social assumptions about the different talents and potentials of the sexes. Throughout history, the inferior status of women has been seen as a self-evident fact of nature, supported by beliefs shared by both men and women and passed on from generation to generation as part of culture. Similarly, the rights and responsibilities granted to people of different ages also vary significantly in all societies, although here the patterns of inequality are not so rigid. In traditional societies, the old usually have the greatest access to such rewards as power, wealth, or prestige; modern societies, on the other hand, are dominated by the middle-aged, with the old

311

taking on many of the characteristics of an oppressed minority. In this chapter we shall examine inequalities between men and women and between different age groups, using the same general principles of stratification that we have already applied to other forms of structured social inequality.

Gender and Society

In societies all over the world, the first question parents ask at the birth of a child is always the same: "Is it a boy or a girl?" The urgency of the question reveals the great importance that all human societies attach to the distinctions between men and women.

This division of the human species into the categories of "male" and "female" is based on a biological fact, *sex*. All societies, however, elaborate this biological fact into secondary, nonbiological differences—that is, into notions of gender, or "masculinity" and "femininity." *Gender refers to social conceptions about what personality traits and behavior are appropriate for members of each sex.* In other words, the concept applies not to biological characteristics but to purely social ones, such as differences in hair styles, clothing patterns, occupational roles, and other culturally approved activities and traits. In every society, however, people tend to assume that their own version of masculinity and femininity is as much a part of "human nature" as the biological distinctions between males and females.

Every social status has one or more roles, or expected patterns of behavior, attached to it. A person who occupies the status of male or female is therefore expected to play certain roles whose content is specified by cultural norms. *Sex roles* are the learned patterns of gender behavior expected in any society. Because the social status of males is superior to that of females, sex roles both reflect and reinforce a pattern of male dominance and female subordination.

It is precisely this situation that is now under such strong attack in many modern societies, particularly in North America and Western Europe. The structured inequality of the sexes, so long taken for granted, is now being vigorously challenged. What was once regarded as an unalterable fact of life is now seen by millions of people to be nothing more than a cultural product of human society. Although women still occupy a subordinate status in nearly every area of society, there is a growing consensus that this situation is irrational and unjust.

Figure 13.1 The women's liberation movement has strongly challenged traditional American sex roles. Although a feminist movement existed earlier in the century, it lost most of its impetus after women gained the vote. The new women's movement has renewed earlier calls for sexual equality. Largely as a result of these efforts, sex discrimination is now regarded as a major social problem.

How Different Are the Sexes?

Just how different are the sexes? Any attempt to change traditional roles must confront the question of whether there are any inborn behavioral differences between men and women and, if so, how important these differences are. Are sex roles completely flexible, as some people suggest, or are there some natural, genetically determined boundaries beyond which change is impossible?

To answer this question, sociologists have drawn on evidence from three other disciplines: biology, which tells us about the physical differences between men and women and their possible effects on behavior; psychology, which tells us about the nature and origins of any personality differences between the sexes; and anthropology, which tells us about variations in sex roles among the many cultures of the world.

Biological Evidence

Men and women differ from one another anatomically, genetically, and hormonally.

The *anatomical* differences are those in the physical structure and appearance of the sexes. The most important of these distinctions are in the reproductive systems. As John Moncy (1980) puts it, "In the final analysis, the irreducible difference between the sexes is that men impregnate, and women menstruate, gestate, and lactate." In other words, it is women who become pregnant and suckle children, a biological responsibility that places periodic restrictions on their social and economic activity. Men, in contrast, are never subject to restrictions of this kind. There are also other anatomical dissimilarities in such characteristics as height, weight, amount of body hair, distribution of body fat, and musculature. These distinctions are socially important, both because they make it easy for others to recognize an individual's sex and because they make men more physically powerful than women, at least in short-term feats of exertion. Their greater strength gives men the potential to dominate women by force, a fact that helps to explain why there has never been a society in which women have had political status superior to that of men.

The *genetic* differences between the sexes are based on the makeup of their sex chromosomes. Females have two similar sex chromosomes (XX), while males have two dissimilar chromosomes (XY). Scientists do not yet know whether this feature has any direct effect on the personalities of the sexes. It does, however, have important biological effects. Except in the area of short-term feats of physical strength, the male's lack of a second X chromosome makes him in many respects the weaker sex. Male infants are more likely than females to be stillborn or malformed. Over thirty hereditary disorders, such as hemophilia and webbing of the toes, are found only in men. Throughout the life cycle, the death rate for men is higher than it is for women. Although in the United States about 106 males are born for every 100 females, the ratio of the sexes is equal by the time a generation has reached its mid-twenties, and among people over sixty-five there are only 85 males for every 100 females. Women are more resistant than men to most diseases and seem to have a greater tolerance for pain and malnutrition (Yorburg, 1974; Weitz, 1977).

The effects, if any, of *hormonal* differences have not yet been determined. A hormone is a chemical substance that is secreted by glands in the body, and it is known that hormones can influence both physical development and certain forms of behavior. Both sexes have "male" as well as "female" hormones, but the proportion of male hormones is greater in men and that of female hormones is greater in women. Experiments with some animals have shown that artificially increased levels of male hormones can heighten aggressiveness and sex drive, even in females. This evidence cannot be uncritically applied to human beings, however, for the increase in brain size during the course of our evolution has been accompanied by a corresponding decrease in the influence of hormones and other inborn factors on our behavior. The present consensus among natural and social scientists is that hormonal differences probably do have some influence on the behavior of men and women but that this influence is a minor one (Teitelbaum, 1976; Weitz, 1977).

Psychological Evidence

The typical personality patterns of adult men and women are clearly dissimilar in many ways. But are these differences inborn or learned? In the case of adults, this question cannot be answered, since it is impossible to untangle the effects of biological and social influences on personality. For this reason, psychologists have focused much of their research on very young infants. Babies have had very little exposure to learning situations, and the earlier sex-linked differences in behavior appear, the more likely it is that they are the result of inborn factors.

Many studies of young infants have found sex-linked personality differences early in life. Even in the cradle, for example, male babies are more active than females; female babies smile more readily and are more sensitive to warmth and touch than males. These are only general tendencies, however. Many male babies show traits that are more typical of female babies, and vice versa (Maccoby and Jacklin, 1974). These and other findings seem at first sight to indicate some inborn personality differences between the sexes, but the case is not proved. It remains possible that even these early variations are learned. From the time children are born, the parents treat them in subtly different ways according to their sex: girl babies are cooed over; boy babies are bounced on the knee. Parents handle infant girls more affectionately and tenderly and are more tolerant of restlessness and aggression in boys. In addition, adults are more likely to interpret signs of distress in a female baby as fear, but to perceive the same behavior in male babies as anger, and to respond accordingly. The infants may therefore learn to behave differently even in the first few weeks of life (Sears et al., 1957; Parke, 1979; Condry and Condry, 1976).

Some of the most important research on sex-linked behavior concerns children who for some reason have been raised as a member of the opposite sex. (This situation may arise when mentally disturbed parents raise a boy as a girl or vice versa; or when genital deformities result in a baby's being mistakenly assigned to the wrong sex; or when, on the recommendation of psychiatrists, a boy who lacks a penis is raised as a transsexual female.) If a child is biologically a boy but is raised as a girl, what happens? If gender were determined by biological factors, it should be impossible to socialize a child into the "wrong" sex role. But research by John Money and his associates (Green and Money, 1969; Money and Ehrhardt, 1972; Money, 1977; Green, 1975) indicates that people can easily be raised as a member of the opposite sex. In such cases, in fact, children beyond the age of about three or four strongly resist attempts to change their "false" gender and have great difficulty making the adjustment, in exactly the same way as a girl or boy raised in the "right" role would do. Money

concludes that the human species is "psychosexually neuter at birth" and that gender is independent of biological sex.

The present consensus among psychologists is that there may be some predispositions toward minor variations in the behavior of the sexes at birth but that these differences can easily be overriden by cultural learning. It is also worth noting that the differences so far discovered in the early years of life are insignificant and certainly provide no justification for the elaborate sex-role distinctions found in human societies all over the world (Diamond, 1965, 1977; Beach, 1965, 1977; Maccoby and Jacklin, 1974; Friedman et al., 1974; Teitelbaum, 1976; Weitz, 1977; Kagan, 1977; Unger, 1980).

Cross-Cultural Evidence

If anatomy were destiny and if gender were largely determined by inborn differences, we would expect the roles of men and women to be much the same in all cultures. On the other hand, if sex roles vary a great deal from one culture to another, then their content must be much more flexible than has usually been assumed in the past.

Anthropologists have reported a number of societies whose gender characteristics are very unlike our own. The classic study in this field was done by Margaret Mead (1935) among three New Guinea tribes. In one tribe, the Arapesh, Mead found that both sexes conformed to a personality type that we would consider feminine. Both males and females were gentle, passive, and emotionally warm. Aggression, competitiveness, and possessiveness were strongly discouraged in both sexes. Men and women were believed to have identical sexual appetites, and both were responsible for child care. In contrast, the neighboring Mundugumor tribe were a cannibalistic, headhunting people who expected both men and women to be violent and aggressive. The Mundugumor women showed little trace of what we sometimes call the "maternal instinct." They dreaded pregnancy, disliked nursing their children, and were especially hostile toward their daughters. Both sexes conformed to a personality type that we would consider masculine. The third tribe, the Tchambuli, differed from the other two in that there were strong differences in their sex roles. But these roles were the reverse of those that we would consider "normal." The women were domineering and energetic, wore no ornaments, and were the major economic providers. The men, on the other hand, were artistic, gossipy, expressive, and nurturant toward children. Mead concluded that gender traits of masculinity and femininity have no necessary connection to biological sex. Since then, anthropologists have studied several other societies in which there are minimal differences in sex roles or in which the roles that we consider "normal" tend to be reversed (Barry et al., 1957; D'Andrade, 1966).

These cases, however, are exceptional, and the overall cross-cultural evidence points to a very strong pattern of male dominance. Despite mythical tales of societies ruled by Amazons or other warrior females, there is no record of any society in which men were not politically dominant, even if they allowed women greater authority in some domestic matters. The general cross-cultural tendency has been for men to have more domineering personalities than women and for women to be more passive and nurturant than men. These personality characteristics do not develop "naturally," however; in every culture, children are systematically socialized into acceptance of the prevailing sex roles (Barry et al., 1957; Friedl, 1975).

In all societies there is some division of labor between men and women. Child-rearing and home maintenance are usually considered a woman's task, while hunting and fighting are always reserved for the man. Men generally take on tasks that require vigorous physical activity or travel away from the home, such as hunting or herding. Women, on the other hand, are responsible for tasks that require less concentrated physical effort and can be performed close to home. Beyond these basic patterns, however, there is great cross-cultural variation in the kind of labor that is considered appropriate for men and women (see Figure 13.3).

Interestingly, the Western view that women are exceptionally delicate is a rather unusual one and does not fit the general cross-cultural trend. Whereas there have been many laws in the United States restricting the amount of weight a woman may carry at work, the bearing of heavy burdens is considered a woman's job in most traditional societies. In most of sub-Saharan Africa, for example, heavy agricultural labor is almost always considered women's work, and in the rural areas of these regions husbands typically travel on horseback while their wife or wives proceed on foot, carrying firewood, produce, or other baggage on their heads. In many traditional societies, too, a

Figure 13.2 Many of our contemporary attitudes toward gender are rooted in the medieval tradition of chivalry. The cultural norms of upper-class European society at that time emphasized the delicacy and frailty of women and the boldness and strength of men.

man is fully entitled to beat his wife if she displeases him; in our culture, such behavior, though far from uncommon, is considered deviant and brutish. The Western conception of the female as a delicate creature arose among the upper classes in twelfth-century Europe and has persisted in various forms ever since. Traces of this medieval chivalry are still to be found, for example, in the male practice of giving up seats to, opening doors for, and concealing coarse language from, females.

THE DIVISION OF LABOR BY SEX: A CROSS-CULTURAL COMPARISON

Number of Societies in Which Activity Is Performed by:

Activity	Men Always	Men Usually	Either Sex Equally	Women Usually	Women Always
Pursuing sea mammals	34	1	0	0	0
Hunting	166	13	0	0	0
Trapping small animals	128	13	4	1	2
Herding	38	8	4	0	5
Fishing	98	34	19	3	4
Clearing land for agriculture	73	22	17	5	13
Dairy operations	17	4	3	1	13
Preparing and planting soil	31	23	33	20	37
Erecting and dismantling shelter	14	2	5	6	22
Tending fowl and small animals	21	4	8	1	39
Tending and harvesting crops	10	15	35	39	44
Gathering shellfish	9	4	8	7	35
Making and tending fires	18	6	25	22	62
Bearing burdens	12	6	35	20	57
Preparing drinks and narcotics	20	1	13	8	57
Gathering fruits, berries, nuts	12	3	15	13	63
Gathering fuel	22	1	10	19	89
Preserving meat and fish	8	2	10	14	74
Gathering herbs, roots, seeds	8	1	11	7	74
Cooking	5	1	9	28	158
Carrying water	7	0	5	7	119
Grinding grain	2	4	5	13	114

Source: Adapted from George P. Murdock, "Comparative Data on the Division of Labor by Sex," *Social Forces* 15 (May 1935), pp. 551–553.

Figure 13.3 There is great cross-cultural variation in the tasks that are considered appropriate for men and women. In many cases, in fact, the division of labor is quite unlike our own. The general tendency, however, is for men to be responsible for tasks involving strenuous effort or travel, and for women to be responsible for tasks that can be performed near the home. The data in this table come from a survey of 224 traditional preindustrial societies.

Sex roles in the other modern industrialized societies of the world are much the same as in the United States, except that the ideal male is typically less aggressive than his American counterpart, and the ideal female is typically much more submissive. Some countries, notably the socialist societies of Eastern Europe and Asia, have made a formal attempt to equalize the statuses of men and women, usually by entrenching sexual equality in the constitution. In practice, however, sex roles in these societies are not very different from our own. In the Soviet Union, women are encouraged to take up independent careers, and they have made inroads into many professions previously dominated by men. About three-quarters of Soviet physicians are women, but their entry into the profession has been ac-

companied by a decline in the status of doctors, who earn less than two-thirds of the salaries of skilled nonprofessionals. High social status is still very much a male preserve: there are virtually no women at the upper levels of politics, law, the military, industry, or science—but women are still responsible for housework (Lapidus, 1978).

The general conclusion from the cross-cultural evidence, then, is that although male dominance is the norm, sex roles, like any other learned behavior, are highly flexible. We have only to look at the recent history of our own culture, in fact, to see that this is the case. It is not so very long ago that a due concern with wigs, perfumes, and silk stockings was a characteristic of every self-respecting upper-class male in Western culture.

A Functionalist View

It is clear from our survey of the evidence that anatomy is not destiny. Human beings can be socialized into a very wide range of sex roles with their accompanying gender characteristics. It is equally evident, however, that most societies have adopted a fairly consistent pattern in their sex roles. Why?

The answer seems to lie in the fact that originally it was highly functional in traditional, preindustrial societies for men and women to play very different roles. A society is more efficient if tasks and responsibilities are allocated to particular people, and if the members are socialized to fill specific roles. This division of labor need not necessarily be along sex lines, but sexual differences do offer an obvious and convenient means of achieving it.

The human infant is helpless for a longer period after birth than any other animal, and it has to be looked after. It is convenient if the mother, who bears and suckles the child and who may soon become pregnant with another, stays home and takes care of it. Since she is staying at home, domestic duties tend to fall on her as well. Likewise, it is convenient if the male, who is physically more powerful and who is not periodically pregnant or suckling children, takes on such tasks as hunting, defending the family against enemies or predators, and taking herds to distant pastures.

Because the female is largely dependent on the male for protection and food and because the male is physically capable of enforcing his will on the female, he inevitably becomes the dominant partner in this relationship. As a result of his dominance, his activities and personality patterns become more highly regarded and rewarded. Over time, these arrangements become deeply structured into the society and are passed down from generation to generation. Men accept their role as "natural," and women submit not because they are coerced by the men but because submission has become the custom. The social origins of gender differences are lost to human consciousness, and the roles of men and women are regarded instead as being inextricably linked to biological sex.

Are these traditional sex roles still functional in a modern industrial society? Two functionalist theorists, Talcott Parsons and Robert Bales (1954), argued that they are. Parsons and Bales claim that a modern family needs two

Figure 13.4 These photographs from a rural area in the African country of Chad show a typical sex-based division of labor: men tend the herds away from the home; women do domestic chores.

Functionalist theorists have tried to explain this pattern on the grounds that the family is more efficient if the sexes play different roles and are socialized into contrasting gender characteristics.

adults who will specialize in particular roles. The "instrumental" role, which is usually taken by the father, focuses on relationships between the family and the outside world. The father, for example, is responsible for earning the income that supports the family. The "expressive" role, which is usually taken by the mother, focuses on relationships within the family. The mother is thus responsible for providing the love and support that is needed to hold the family together. The male's instrumental role requires that he be dominant and competent; the female's expressive role requires that she be passive and nurturant. The family unit functions more effectively than it would if gender differences were not so sharply defined.

A Conflict View

The theory of Parsons and Bales has been much criticized, mainly on the grounds that it seems to be an example of functionalism defending the status quo. Critics have argued that the traditional sex roles may have been functional in a preindustrial society, but make very little sense in a diversified modern society, where the daily activities of men and women are far removed from these primitive origins. In addition, functionalist theory says nothing about the strains that the traditional roles place on women who want to play an "instrumental" role in society or on men who would prefer to play an "expressive" role. It also says nothing about the *dysfunctions* to society of preventing half of the population from participating fully in economic life.

A functionalist analysis can explain how sex-role inequalities arose, but a conflict analysis may offer a better explanation of why they persist. Helen Hacker (1951) argues that women can be regarded as a minority group in society, in much the same way as racial or other minorities that suffer from discrimination. She draws a number of convincing comparisons between the situation of women and the situation of blacks in American society, showing that both groups are at a disadvantage as a result of an ascribed status based on the arbitrary grounds of sex or race (see Figure 13.5). The parallel is not an exact one, however, because women, unlike blacks, are found in equal proportion to the dominant group in every social class—for the simple reason that their economic status is linked to that of their husbands or fathers. The stratification of men and

women therefore takes an unusual form. Women are found at all positions in the class hierarchy, but at any one of them they have inferior status to men who are at the same position.

Randall Collins (1971a, 1974) argues that sexual inequalities, like any other structured social inequality, are based on a conflict of interests between the dominant and subordinate group. Sexual inequalities prevent the lower-status group from making the best use of its talents and thereby provide greater opportunities for the higher-status group to do so. Men can enjoy superior status only if women have inferior status, and the existing sex-role patterns allow them to maintain their political, social, and economic privileges. This does not mean, of course, that there is a deliberate, conscious conspiracy by men to maintain the prevailing inequalities. It simply means that the dominant group benefits from the existing arrangements and has little motivation to change them. Since the cultural arrangements of any society always reflect the interests of the dominant group, sex roles continue to reinforce the pattern of male dominance.

The underlying source of sexual inequality, in the view of conflict theorists, is the economic inequality between men and women. As we noted in Chapter 10 ("Social Stratification"), wealth is a prime source of social status; moreover, it can readily be converted into power and prestige as well. It follows that if men make a greater economic contribution to the family and the society than women, then men are likely to have superior social status in both. Conversely, if the economic contribution of women increases relative to that of men, then the inequalities between the sexes should diminish. And, in fact, the cross-cultural evidence lends strong support to this analysis. In *hunting and gathering* societies meat is highly prized, and men tend to do the hunting, though with infrequent success: they may hunt with their primitive weapons for days on end and catch nothing. The women, on the other hand, do the gathering of fruits, vegetables, insects, and other items, and so provide the bulk of the society's food. In these societies, there is remarkably little sexual inequality. In *horticultural* and *pastoral* societies, on the other hand, men make a greater economic contribution: it is they who are usually responsible for clearing the land or tending the herds, and this fact is reflected in the greater sexual inequality that is always a feature of these societies. In *agri-*

THE SOCIAL STATUS OF BLACKS AND WOMEN: A COMPARISON

	Blacks	Women
Social Status	Ascribed on grounds of race.	Ascribed on grounds of sex.
Social Visibility	High—based on skin color and other physical characteristics.	High—based on anatomy and other physical characteristics.
Supposed Attributes	Inferior intelligence, smaller brain, scarcity of geniuses. More free in instinctual gratifications, more emotional, "primitive" and childlike. Imagined sexual prowess is envied.	Inferior intelligence, smaller brain, scarcity of geniuses. Irresponsible, inconsistent, emotionally unstable, lacking strong will. Seen as sexual "temptresses."
Common Stereotype	"Inferior."	"Weaker."
Justifications of Status	"All right in their place." Myth of the contented black—happy in a subordinate role.	"Woman's place is in the home." Myth of the contented woman—happy in a subordinate role.
Attitudes to Superior Group	Deferential manner. Concealment of real feelings. Outwit "white folks." Careful study of points at which dominant group is susceptible to influence. Fake show of ignorance.	Flattering manner. "Feminine wiles." Outwit "menfolk." Careful study of points at which dominant group is susceptible to influence. Fake appearance of helplessness.
Discrimination	Limitations on education—should fit "place" in society. Confined to traditional jobs—barred from supervisory positions. Their competition feared. No family examples for new aspirations. Deprived of political importance. Social and professional segregation. Unwelcome in facilities used by dominant group—hotels, swimming pools, etc.	Limitations on education—should fit "place" in society. Confined to traditional jobs—barred from supervisory positions. Their competition feared. No family examples for new aspirations. Deprived of political importance. Social and professional segregation. Unwelcome in facilities used by dominant group—clubs, bars, etc.
Similar Problems	Roles not clearly defined, but in flux as a result of social change. Conflict between achieved and ascribed status.	Roles not clearly defined, but in flux as a result of social change. Conflict between achieved and ascribed status.

Source: Adapted from Helen Hacker, "Women as a Minority Group," *Social Forces*, 30 (October, 1951), pp. 60–69.

Figure 13.5 This table shows a number of striking similarities between the social status of blacks in relation to whites and women in relation to men. In fact, the general features listed here are fairly typical of those found in any situation of structured social inequality. (You might try to extend this table to cover other such situations, involving, say, Anglos and Chicanos, white settlers and Indians, straights and gays, colonizers and colonized, or the middle-aged and the old.)

cultural societies, men produce an even greater proportion of the society's wealth, for they are typically responsible for heavy agriculture, craft work, military plundering, and the other mainstays of the economy. In these societies, inequalities between men and women become extreme. This situation persists in early *industrial* societies, in which the bulk of the labor force is male and in which the few women who do work are paid very low wages. Entirely dependent on men for their livelihoods, the women in these societies are hardly in a position to assert their equality. But in the more advanced industrial nations, the picture begins to change. Women play an increasing role in the labor force, and as they do so, they gradually gain more and more

COMPOSITION OF THE LABOR FORCE,
PERCENTAGE BY SEX

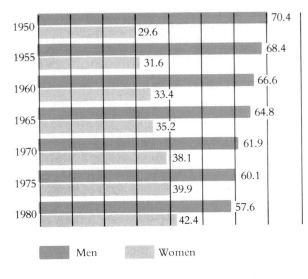

	Men	Women
1950	70.4	29.6
1955	68.4	31.6
1960	66.6	33.4
1965	64.8	35.2
1970	61.9	38.1
1975	60.1	39.9
1980	57.6	42.4

Men   Women

Source: Bureau of the Census, 1980.

Figure 13.6 Particularly since World War II, women have played an increasing part in the American economy, and they have achieved more equality with men in the process. Conflict theorists emphasize that economic inequality underlies the social inequality of men and women, and predict that the status of women will continue to improve only if they play a greater part in the economy.

equality with men (Martin and Voorhies, 1975; Schlegel, 1977; Nielsen, 1978). In 1940, for example, only 27.4 percent of the American labor force was female; by 1980 the proportion had risen to 42.4 percent. During this period, the sexes have grown steadily more equal; and as women come to play an even greater part in the economic life of the nation, full sexual equality will become a reality.

Conflict and functionalist theories are not as contradictory on this issue as they might initially seem to be. Many conflict theorists accept that sex inequalities may have arisen because they were functional, even if they are functional no longer. Many functionalist theorists would also accept that traditional sex roles are becoming dysfunctional in the modern world. More important, both agree on one point: existing gender characteristics are primarily social in origin, not biological.

Sexism

As we saw in our earlier discussion of economic and racial inequalities, the domination of one group by another is always justified by an *ideology*, a set of beliefs that legitimates social arrangements and makes them seem natural and morally acceptable. Just as the Indian caste system is legitimated by Hindu religion or as racial discrimination is legitimated by racism, so the inequality of the sexes is justified by an ideology that is generally accepted by the dominant and the subordinate groups alike. This is the ideology of *sexism*.

Sexist ideology is based on the view that gender characteristics and the superiority of men over women are rooted in the natural order. This belief has been ingrained in cultural traditions for thousands of years. Even our language, like many others, reflects male dominance. Whenever we talk about people in general, the language predisposes us to talk only of men: for example, we usually speak of "man" and "mankind" when we really mean human beings and humanity. The English language does not even have a pronoun to cover cases of "he or she," and so we generally use "he" when referring to someone whose sex is not specified. (Such linguistic usage is actually reasonably easy to avoid; no such sexist language is used by the author in this book.)

Like most ideologies that justify social inequality of various kinds, the ideology of sexism is to some extent endorsed by religion. Even the image of God in Western culture is male. According to the Genesis story, God made man in His own image, with woman as a subsequent and secondary act of creation. There is, in fact, an antifeminist bias in the Judeo-Christian religious tradition. The ancient Israelites were a strongly patriarchal people, and even today a male orthodox Jew is expected to say this prayer every morning:

> Blessed art thou, oh Lord our God, King of the Universe, that I was not born a gentile. Blessed art thou, oh Lord our God, King of the Universe, that I was not born a slave. Blessed art thou, oh Lord our God, King of the Universe, that I was not born a woman.

This bias was transmitted to Christianity. Jesus himself seems to have been remarkably free from the patriarchal attitudes of his time, but Christianity as we know it today has been strongly influenced by the later teachings of Saint Paul, who explicitly saw the inferior role of women as part of a divinely ordained natural order.

> A man ... is the image of God and reflects God's glory; but woman is the reflection of man's glory. For man did not come from woman; no, woman came from man; and man was not created for the sake of woman, but woman was created for the sake of man. [I Corinthians 11:7–9]

And elsewhere in the New Testament we find:

> Wives should regard their husbands as they regard the Lord, since as Christ is head of the church and serves the whole body, so is a husband the head of his wife; and as the Church submits to Christ, so should wives submit to their husbands, in everything. [Ephesians 5:22–23]

Even today many Christian churches and denominations reserve their priesthoods or equivalent positions for men.

In America and elsewhere sexist attitudes still persist in a strong consensus about the different qualities and abilities of men and women. Unfounded beliefs about "masculinity" and "femininity" are uncritically accepted by millions of people of both sexes and are incorporated into their self-concepts, shaping the way they relate to one another and go about their private lives (Gornick and Moran, 1971; Klein, 1975; Rothman, 1978).

As our previous discussions of economic and of racial and ethnic inequalities revealed, the subordinate group tends to accept the dominant group's legitimating ideology because it sees the existing arrangements as "natural" and does not question them. Marx called this kind of attitude *false consciousness,* a subjective understanding of one's situation that does not accord with the objective facts. Only when the subordinate group loses this false consciousness does it challenge the existing system and demand that changes be made. This is precisely what has been happening since the early sixties. By using "consciousness-raising" techniques and other methods, the women's movement has tried to make women aware that they are unjustly discriminated against.

Figure 13.7

"Sexism! *For heaven's sake, Nancy, I'm not even over* racism *yet.*"

Copyright Wm. Hamilton.

What Do You Want to Be When You Grow Up?

Preschoolers' ideas about adult occupations are already ossified stereotypes. I often tell the story of a friend who took a childrearing leave of absence from her job as a newspaper reporter. One day, when her three-year-old, Sarah, expressed interest in a TV story about a crime reporter, my friend decided to explain her own career: "Before you were born, I used to have a job like that," the mother said, building to a simple but exciting description of journalism. "I went to fires or to the police station and the stories I wrote were printed in the newspaper with my name on them."

After listening attentively, Sarah asked, "Mommy, when you had this job before I was born, did you used to be a man?"

Obviously, the child had not yet developed the concept of gender constancy; but what necessitated the magical thinking that turned her mother into a man was Sarah's inability to associate the exciting job of a newspaper reporter with the female sex.

Seventy Wisconsin children, ages three to five, had much the same problem. When asked "What do you want to be when you grow up?" the boys mentioned fourteen occupations: fireman, policeman, father/husband, older person, digger, dentist, astronaut, cowboy, truck-driver, engineer, baseball player, doctor, Superman, and the Six-Million-Dollar Man. Girls named eleven categories: mother/sister, nurse, ballerina, older person, dentist, teacher, babysitter, baton-twirler, iceskater, princess, and cowgirl.

Next, the children were polled on their more realistic expectations: "What do you think you *really* will be?" they were asked. The girls altered their choices toward even more traditional roles—changing from ballerina, nurse, and dentist, to mother—while the boys changed to *more* active, adventurous futures—for instance, from husband to fireman.

Taking into account the narrow range of occupations familiar to nursery-school children, it still seems pitiful to have had job options closed to you before you are three or four years old.

Pittsburgh children of the same ages were asked "What do you want to be when you grow up?" followed by "If you were a boy (girl), what would you be when you grow up?" For the first question, most chose stereotyped careers: policeman, sports star, cowboy, and one "aspiring spy" for the boys; nursing and the like for the girls. To the second—what they would be if they were the "opposite" sex—the children answered with stereotyped other-sex occupations as well. But their *reactions* to that second question were striking. The boys were shocked at the very *idea* of being a girl. Most had never thought of it before, some refused to think about it, and one "put his hands to his head and sighed. 'Oh if I were a girl I'd have to grow up to be nothing.' "

The girls, on the other hand, obviously had thought about the question a great deal. Most had an answer ready. "Several girls mentioned that this other-sex occupational ambition was their *true* ambition, but one that could not be realized because of their sex." More poignantly, the gender barrier had become so formidable that it even blocked out fantasies and dreams. "Thus, one blond moppet confided that what she really wanted to do when she grew up was to fly like a bird. 'But I'll never do it,' she sighed, 'because I'm not a boy.' "

Source: Letty Cottin Pogrebin, *Growing Up Free* (New York: McGraw-Hill, 1980).

Although the movement has scored major successes, it is clear that many women remain in a state of false consciousness and continue to accept the system that puts them at a disadvantage. There is considerable evidence that women have tended to internalize the rigid social image, or *stereotype,* of themselves as inferior and incompetent. More than two decades of research has shown that as girls grow up, they come to value boys more and themselves less (McKee and Sherriffs, 1956; Bennet and Cohen, 1959; Horner, 1968, 1969; Mendelsohn and Dobie, 1970; Watson and Mednick, 1970; Pogrebin, 1980). In one study of this type, for example, some female college students were divided into two groups and given identical sets of scholarly articles. In the sets given to one group, however, the author was identified as "John T. MacKay" and in those given to the other group, as "Joan T. MacKay." When the students were asked to rate the articles for their value, persuasiveness, profundity, writing style, and general competence, they overwhelmingly preferred the articles by "John." This was true even of articles in traditionally "female" fields, such as dietetics (Goldberg, 1968). Another study using the same method found that female students had similar attitudes toward the work of "male" and "female" artists (Pheterson et al., 1971). More recently, a 1980 Roper poll questioned women on whether they would have more confidence in a male or a female in various professions. It found that 26 percent of women would have more confidence in a male doctor in an emergency; 26 percent would have more confidence in a male mayor; 27 percent, more confidence in a male lawyer; and 48 percent, more confidence in a male pilot.

Similarly, research on the attitudes of housewives showed that many of them believed that housework should be their main source of fulfillment, even if they did not find the work very satisfying. One housewife interviewed by Ann Oakley (1974) commented, "I like housework. I'm quite domesticated really. I've always been brought up to be domesticated—to do the housework and dust and wash up and cook—so it's a natural instinct really." Asked whether she was satisfied or dissatisfied with her life as a housewife, another woman responded, "Satisfied, I suppose. I suppose I have to be. What's the point in being the other way when you know you've got to be satisfied?" And another woman who was asked about her attitude toward a reversal of sex roles in the home replied:

> Oh, that's ridiculous—it's up to the woman to look after the kids and do all the housework. It wouldn't be my idea of a man. I think a man should go out to work and a woman should look after the house. I don't agree with men doing housework—I don't think it's a man's job.... I certainly wouldn't like to see my husband cleaning a room up. I don't think its mannish for a man to stay at home. I like a man to be a man.

A fairly large number of women, then, still do not wish to see much change in the existing sex roles. Although a 1980 Roper poll found that only 9 percent of females believe there are more advantages in being a woman than a man (compared with 43 percent who believe there are more advantages in being a man), over a third of the women polled either opposed efforts to improve their status or were undecided on the issue (See Figure 13.8). Around the turn of the decade, too, proposals to guarantee the equal rights of men and women were defeated at the polls in several states, partly through the opposition of women voters. Attitudes such as these reveal how deeply sexist ideology is engrained in the culture and in the consciousness of the subordinate group.

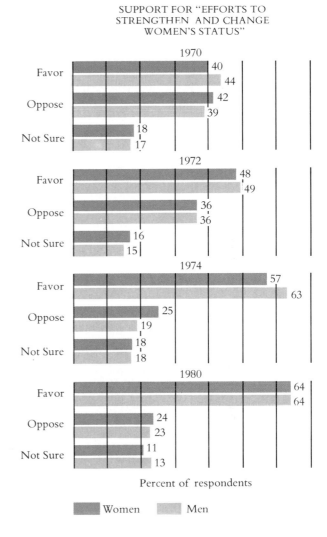

Source: Roper poll, 1980.

Figure 13.8 As this chart shows, women have been slow to support proposals to improve their status; until 1980, in fact, more men than women favored such reforms. Like many subordinate groups, women were at first so accustomed to their roles that they were reluctant to demand or even support measures that would give them greater equality with the dominant group.

Sex Roles in America

American sex roles are far more flexible than those found in most other societies. There are still many traditional norms, however, that structure the experience of men and women and provide the basic options within which they live out their lives. An increasing amount of deviance from these norms is permitted, but if the deviance is too great, it usually leads to a strong negative reaction. The woman who is too "masculine," and more particularly, the man who is too "effeminate," in manner, dress, or interests still invite ridicule. The strength of the reaction to deviance from the norms is a good indication of the strength of the norms themselves. Clearly defined sex roles still exist, and they are reflected in the temperament, attitudes, interests, clothing, family responsibilities, and economic activities of men and women.

Figure 13.9 There is a strong tendency in the United States, as in many other societies, to value women as "sex objects" rather than as people with individual personalities. Promotions like the above have been criticized by the women's movement on the grounds that they encourage these attitudes.

Sex and Personality

Despite the changes of recent years, there still appears to be some consensus about the personality traits that are most desirable for each of the sexes, and it is possible to outline these characteristics, at least in a generalized way.

The American woman is still widely expected to be conformist, passive, affectionate, sensitive, and dependent. She is not supposed to be too assertive, ambitious, or interested in sports, politics, and economics. She should not take the initiative in sexual relationships but instead should entrap the male by shrewd psychological manipulation. She is expected to be deeply concerned about her physical appearance, and her life should revolve primarily around the home. The self-image of a woman comes essentially not from achievement in the outside world but rather from a satisfactory fulfillment of a nurturant role for her children and a supportive role for her husband.

The American man, on the other hand, is still widely expected to be self-reliant, competent, independent, and in certain circumstances aggressive. He should keep his emotions under fairly strict control and is expected to have firm opinions on public affairs. In his relationships with the opposite sex he is supposed to take the initiative, and he is often more interested in sexual gratification than romantic involvement. He may give some authority in the home to his wife, but on major domestic issues, such as relocating to a different region, his decision is final. His self-image comes mainly from his achievements in the outside world, and his work is a major focus of his life. He has a moral duty to be the family breadwinner, and his self-image may be severely undermined if his wife takes that role, or even if she earns more than he does.

These portraits, of course, represent only the traditional ideal types. Millions of American men and women totally reject them, and millions more deviate from them in significant ways. There are also important subcultural variations from these patterns along lines of both race and class. Generally speaking, the lower a person's social class, the more likely he or she is to conform to the traditional stereotypes. Working-class men have a greater need to maintain an image of toughness, and working-class women are inclined to be more passive and emotional than their middle-class counterparts (Yorburg, 1974). The reason is probably that poorer and less educated people have less freedom and effective choice in their lives, and so are slower to challenge established patterns. Hispanic-Americans, too, tend to conform more closely to established sex-role patterns, partly because they tend to be relatively conservative in matters relating to sexuality and family life, and partly because a certain degree of "machismo" is still entrenched in their culture. Black Americans, on the other hand, are the least male-dominated of the racial and ethnic groups in the United States, and a disproportionate number of family breadwinners in the black community are female. Black women also tend to be more aggressive than white women, irrespective of social class. Black men, too, are often more emotionally expressive in their relations with one another and with women than are white men (Centers et al., 1971; Scanzioni, 1971). But despite these variations, the traditional patterns generally provide the standard against which all others are measured.

Sex and the Division of Labor

Sex is a major determinant of occupational statuses in the United States. In general, the jobs that are informally reserved for women are those that do not compete with but rather aid the work of men: secretaries, sales clerks, airline attendants, nurses, social workers, telephone operators. Women represent only 35 percent of writers, artists, and entertainers, 34 percent of college teachers, 30 percent of accountants, 10 percent of physicians, and 3 percent of engineers. On the other hand, they account for 71 percent of teachers (mostly in elementary schools), 80 percent of librarians, 87 percent of cashiers, 97 percent of nurses and child-care workers, and, not very surprisingly, 99 percent of secretaries (Bureau of the Census, 1980). Although women are often thought to be innately suited for roles of this kind, their supposed talents are very selectively interpreted. Women's deft fingers are presumed to equip them admirably for sewing, but not so well for surgery; their intuitive understanding makes them good mothers, but not such good psychiatrists; their nurturant skills suit them as nurses, but less well as doctors.

Although the average American woman spends only 3 percent of her entire life in the reproductive functions of pregnancy and suckling children, it is still sometimes felt that the woman's place should be the home. Employers

Figure 13.10

"*Very pleased to meet you. What does your husband do?*"

Copyright Wm. Hamilton

may be reluctant to promote single women lest they get married and become housewives, and they may hesitate to promote married women lest they become pregnant and stay home to bring up their children. To make matters worse, the self-fulfilling prophecy that a female child will not enter a professional career has its effect. Socialized to believe that they are better suited for domesticities, women are much less motivated than men to spend extra years in education, so they end up, in fact, poorly equipped to compete at the upper levels of the labor market. Indeed, the overall unemployment rate for women seeking work is generally about a third higher than that for men.

In almost every major field of public and professional life, men hold the dominant positions. In 1980 women held only two seats in the U.S. Senate, only one seat in the cabinet, and only one state governorship. Every chairmanship and presidency of major corporations and almost every presidency of major universities was held by a man. Women represent only 18 percent of our scientists—and only 9 percent of our lawyers and judges, although over 42 percent of the total work force is female. Even today, women receive only one of every four medical degrees, one of every three law degrees, and one of every six degrees in engineering (Bureau of the Census, 1980).

Figure 13.11 The people in every culture are inclined to take their own gender characteristics for granted as part of "human nature." It would be distinctly abnormal for an American man to wear a skirt, but in traditional cultures the practice of women wearing pants and men wearing skirts is as common as the reverse arrangement. Traces of this pattern are to be found in the Scottish male custom of wearing kilts, which is still practiced in the military and in rural regions.

The median income of women is lower than that of men, even for people holding similar qualifications in the same occupations. The average earnings of women are less than three-fifths those of men, a share that reflects a steady widening of the income gap: in 1955 the average female worker earned 63.9 percent of the income of the average male worker; in 1970, 59.4 percent; and in 1979, 59.0 percent. Discrimination by employers is not the only or even the main reason for this discrepancy. The underlying cause is the institutionalized sexism of our society, which makes it unlikely that women will be trained or motivated for occupational achievement. The lingering cultural emphasis on the male as breadwinner and the female as homemaker still has implications throughout social and economic life.

Socialization into Sex Roles

As we have already seen, sex roles are learned in the course of the socialization process. The basic gender characteristics expected of the sexes are learned in the family environment very early in life, and are then reinforced in the schools, in peer groups, in the mass media, and in many other specific agencies, ranging from sports teams to workplaces.

The Family

From the time that children are born, their parents treat them differently on the basis of their sex. Little boys are dressed in blue, little girls in pink. Girls are treated protectively, boys are given more freedom. Girls are valued for their docile and pleasing behavior and are not required to be achieving or competitive; charm and attractiveness receive more approval than intelligence. This kind of treatment is likely to produce timid, conformist personalities. Boys, on the other hand, are given much more rigorous sex-role training. The little girl may be allowed some tomboyish behavior, but the little boy cannot be allowed to be a sissy. Parents usually view any "effeminate" behavior or interests with great alarm, and if these tendencies persist, they may be seen as a sign of psychological disturbance. The boy is constantly expected to prove his masculinity, particularly by performing well at sports. He is taught to "act like a man"—in other words, to suppress his emotions and particularly his tears. As Ruth Hartley (1970) points out, the requirement that the boy avoid anything "sissy" can breed a hostility toward femininity that may later develop into a contempt for the opposite sex.

As a result of this training, children learn their sex roles quickly and effectively. In fact, they are certain of the existence of two sexes and of their own identification with one of them long before they are aware of the biological basis for these distinctions (Thompson, 1975). By the age of three, nearly all children know whether they are male or female, and by the age of four, they have very definite, even exaggerated, ideas of what masculinity and femininity should involve. In their playacting, children permit all kinds of changes of plot and switching of roles—except sex roles. For example, a boy playing "doctor" might freely agree to switch roles with another boy playing "patient"—but it is highly unlikely that he would switch roles with a girl playing "nurse" (Garvey, 1977).

The psychological process by which children learn their sex roles is a complex one, but it contains three main elements. The first is *conditioning* through rewards and punishments, usually in the form of parental approval or disapproval. The child who behaves in the "right" way is encouraged, but the boy who plays with dolls or the girl who plays with mud is strongly discouraged. The parents also deliberately arrange conditioning experiences—for example, by giving children sex-related toys. The second element is *imitation.* Young children tend to imitate older children and adults and are inclined to imitate those whom they regard as most like themselves. Young children thus use other people of the same sex as models for their own behavior. The third and perhaps the most important element is *self-definition.* Through social interaction with others, children learn to categorize the people around them into two sexes and to define themselves as belonging to one sex rather than the other. They then use this self-definition to select their future interests and to construct their personalities and social roles (Kohlberg, 1966). (This is why children who have been assigned to the wrong sex at birth have such difficulty in identifying with the correct sex after the age of about three or four. The boy who has been raised as a girl "knows" that he is not a boy and naturally resists attempts to make him into one.)

Figure 13.12 Children learn their gender identities early in the family environment. Parents reward behavior that is regarded as sex-appropriate and discourage behavior that is not. By giving the children sex-related objects, for example, they encourage them to make the "right" sex-role identification. Once the children have identified themselves as members of a particular sex, they use this self-definition as a basis for selecting their later interests and activities.

The Schools

The schools reinforce traditional gender stereotypes in many ways. Perhaps the most obvious is the manner in which many curricular and extracurricular activities—academic courses, hobbies, sports, and so on—tend to be segregated by sex. Girls are channeled into the cooking class, boys into the mechanics class; girls play softball, boys play hardball. The pressures for conformity are, as usual, stronger for the boy. Today, a girl could probably gain entry to the printing workshop without too much difficulty, but the boy who wants to take sewing classes faces the likelihood of discouragement from his teachers and ridicule from his peers. The girl who aspires to "masculine" pursuits is behaving in a way that is at least understandable to others, for she is seeking a status that is acknowledged to be superior, if inappropriate. But the boy who has "effeminate" interests is likely to be seen as behaving incomprehensibly, for he is deliberately seeking an inferior status.

Because the boy is supposedly destined to be the family breadwinner, his education is considered more important than that of the girl, and the school tends to be much more concerned with his academic success and the chances of his going on to college. Counselors are likely to make greater efforts to persuade boys to undertake further education; there is a lingering belief that a woman's advanced education will be "wasted" if she gets married and stays at home. Girls gain little prestige from being bright, and although they are on average better achievers than boys in school, far fewer of them go on to college and fewer still to graduate school. Lacking the confidence that they will be good at science or at other subjects that might lead to a professional career, they may be more likely to concentrate on courses that will prepare them for domestic duties or for such supportive or nurturant jobs as secretary or elementary school teacher.

The schoolbooks of the kind that most of today's college students were brought up on also encouraged acceptance of the traditional gender characteristics. When sociologists first began to study this literature in the early seventies, they found that, from preschool onward, it presented sex-typed images of how children and adults should behave. In a study of picture books that had been awarded prizes for "excellence" by the American Library Association, Lenore Weitzman and her associates (1972) found that male characters outnumbered females in a ratio of eleven to one, and in the case of animals with obvious sex identities the ratio was even higher: ninety-five to one. Throughout the books, boys took part in adventurous and varied activities; girls were more likely to be helping their mothers in the kitchen or taking care not to soil their clothes at play. In another study of school textbooks, Marjorie U'Ren (1971) found that only 15 percent of the illustrations that featured people included women. As she points out, "We tend to forget the simple fact that the female sex is half the human species, that women are not merely a ladies' auxiliary to the human species." These and similar studies have alerted educators and authors to the inherent sexism of much of the reading material that is presented to schoolchildren. Many new publications try (not always successfully) to present more realistic portraits of the social world, but the accumulated children's literature of the past—which includes many ever popular "classics"—will continue to offer stereotyped gender characteristics to the young for the forseeable future.

The Mass Media

The mass media—films, books, magazines, comics, television, radio, and records—are a powerful agency for socialization. In all forms of mass media, from television soap operas to the lyrics of popular tunes, there is a strong emphasis on traditional gender stereotypes (Goffman, 1976; Tuchman et al., 1978; Williams et al., 1981).

Perhaps the most insidious of these media presentations is the image of women in advertising. Women are typically portrayed either as sex objects, in an attempt to market various products to men, or as domesticated housewives, in order to market home-maintenance products to women. Market research has shown that one of the most effective ways for advertisers to reach a male audience is to associate their product, however remotely, with a seductive or smiling female. The sexuality of women is thus exploited by having buxom models stroking new automobiles, cradling bottles of whiskey, or being sent into raptures by the odor of a particular pipe tobacco. Advertising directed at women, on the other hand, shows females delighted beyond measure at the discovery of a new canned soup, or thrilled into ecstasy by the blinding whiteness of their wash. As Lucy Komisar (1971) comments:

Figure 13.13

*"I married Momma because her towels were soft and fluffy
and her dishes were bright and clean."*

Reproduced by special permission of *Playboy* Magazine;
copyright 1975 by Playboy.

Advertising... legitimizes the ideal, stereotyped roles of
woman as a temptress, wife, mother, and sex object, and
portrays women as less intelligent and more dependent than
men. It makes women believe that their chief role is to please
men and that their fulfillment will be as wives, mothers, and
homemakers. It makes women feel unfeminine if they are not
pretty enough and guilty if they do not spend most of their
time in desperate attempts to imitate gourmet cooks.... It
makes women believe that their own lives, talents, and interests ought to be secondary to the needs of their husbands.

What is remarkable about advertising is how little its
gender stereotypes have changed over the past decade or so.
Although some advertisements patronizingly try to capi-
talize on the growing independence of women (for example, by suggesting that the "liberated" modern woman
should buy a bottle of sherry and boldly invite a man to her
home to share it), most still portray females as simple-
minded creatures, bickering endlessly over which tooth-
paste or fabric softener is better. (To fully appreciate the
implications of these stereotypes, try mentally substituting
men for the women on the screen the next time you watch
TV advertisements, and note how utterly demeaning the
portrayals would be.)

The Costs and Consequences of Sexism

Traditional sex roles are maintained at a heavy social,
economic, and psychological cost. They deny the full use of
the talents of half of our population, and they require an
adherence to norms of conduct that are increasingly irrelevant in modern society.

One of the most obvious consequences of sexism is the
limitation it places on the career options of women, to their
great economic loss. It is no accident that women earn less
than similarly qualified men or that more than a third of
the families living in poverty in the United States today
rely on a female breadwinner. But the nation suffers too by
artificially restricting the economic contribution of part of
the population. To be fully efficient, a modern industrial
economy must allow social mobility on the grounds of
merit, not restrict it on the grounds of an irrational,
ascribed status such as race, caste, or sex.

Equally important, however, are the psychological costs
to women. One of the major features that distinguishes us
from all other animals is our creative capacity, our ability
to act on and shape the environment. Yet this fundamental
human experience is largely restricted to men. Women
frequently experience it only second hand, through their
supportive role of the men who act, and do, and shape the
world. To the extent that this happens, the core of women's
experience becomes passive rather than active; they tend to
be objects, not subjects, in the social environment.

Conformity to established gender characteristics cuts
women off from many educational, political, cultural, and
economic opportunities, leaving them to spend a lifetime
impersonating an absurd notion of a feminine ideal—the
Playboy beauty and perfect housewife. If they accept these
stereotypes, they must surrender all possibility of fully exploring their talents. If they reject them, they risk severe
role conflicts and the accusation that they are unfeminine.
Because the female self-concept depends so much on physical appearance and a motherhood role, the process of aging
is one that many women face with distaste and even shame.
Growing old is not such a trial for a man. He may still hope
to attract young women when he is in his forties and fifties,
and his job provides a continuing source of identity that is
denied to the mother when her children mature and leave
home. American women may find the last two-thirds of

He Is Playing Masculine. She Is Playing Feminine

He is playing masculine because she is playing feminine. She is playing feminine because he is playing masculine.

He is playing the kind of man that she thinks the kind of woman she is playing ought to admire. She is playing the kind of woman that he thinks the kind of man he is playing ought to desire.

If he were not playing masculine, he might well be more feminine than she is—except when she is playing very feminine. If she were not playing feminine, she might well be more masculine than he is—except when he is playing very masculine.

So he plays harder. And she plays . . . softer.

He wants to make sure that she could never be more masculine than he. She wants to make sure that he could never be more feminine than she. He therefore seeks to destroy the femininity in himself. She therefore seeks to destroy the masculinity in herself.

She is supposed to admire him for the masculinity in him that she fears in herself. He is supposed to desire her for the femininity in her that he despises in himself.

He desires her for her femininity which is his femininity, but which he can never lay claim to. She admires him for his masculinity which is her masculinity, but which she can never lay claim to. Since he may only love his own femininity in her, he envies her her femininity. Since she may only love her own masculinity in him, she envies him his masculinity.

The envy poisons their love.

He, coveting her unattainable femininity, decides to punish her. She, coveting his unattainable masculinity, decides to punish him. He denigrates her femininity—which he is supposed to desire and which he really envies—and becomes more aggressively masculine. She feigns disgust at his masculinity—which she is supposed to admire and which she really envies—and becomes more fastidiously feminine. He is becoming less and less what he wants to be. She is becoming less and less what she wants to be. But now he is more manly than ever, and she is more womanly than ever.

Her femininity, growing more dependently supine, becomes contemptible. His masculinity, growing more oppressively domineering, becomes intolerable. At last she loathes what she has helped his masculinity to become. At last he loathes what he has helped her femininity to become.

So far, it has all been symmetrical. But we have left one thing out.

The world belongs to what his masculinity has become.

The reward for what his masculinity has become is power. The reward for what her femininity has become is only the security which his power can bestow upon her. If he were to yield to what her femininity has become, he would be yielding to contemptible incompetence. If she were to acquire what his masculinity has become, she would participate in intolerable coerciveness.

She is stifling under the triviality of her femininity. The world is groaning beneath the terrors of his masculinity.

He is playing masculine. She is playing feminine.

How do we call off the game?

Source: Betty and Theodore Roszak (eds.), *Masculine and Feminine* (New York: Harper & Row, 1970).

---

their lives something of an ordeal as their youth and their children are slowly lost to them.

These psychological costs to women have received a great deal of attention in recent years, but the strains placed on men have been neglected. In fact, however, the role traditionally played by men is a very stressful and demanding one, and there is no shortage of hard data to bear this out. Men are five times more likely than women to commit suicide. They are three times more likely to suffer from severe mental disorders. They are disproportionately likely to suffer from all stress-related illnesses, such as ulcers, asthma, hypertension, and heart disease. They are six times more likely than women to become alcoholics, and the overwhelming majority of narcotics addicts are male. Men are far more frequently involved in acts of violence: they are arrested eight times as often for murder as women and are also arrested for 88 percent of violent crimes.

The various requirements of the traditional male role also frequently result in a costly emotional insensitivity. Men find it embarrassing to reveal signs of anxiety or distress, and they cannot show too much affection for other men. Because their masculine image is defined by the rejection of anything that smacks of femininity, they often develop a low regard for women and are unprepared for the emotional closeness that is increasingly expected of a lover or husband. Their frequent assumption that women are in some ways inferior makes truly meaningful relationships with women difficult for them, for such relationships cannot be conducted on a basis of inequality. In their relationships with women, many American men feel obliged to adopt a "cowboy" role as the strong, silent, 100 percent American he-man and are virtually incapable of showing tenderness to the opposite sex. Others adopt a "playboy" role, treating females as commodities and avoiding personal involvement with them; the emphasis is on "playing it cool" and on sexually manipulating women (Balswick and Peck, 1971). In many cases, the male's nurturant potential as a husband and father is undermined by his continual need to strive, compete, and achieve.

Sex Roles in the Future

American sex roles are changing very rapidly. This change is inevitable, for it is the product of many powerful social forces. As the family loses more of its traditional functions to other institutions, the motherhood role is becoming less rewarding. As the economy becomes more diversified, the old sex-based division of labor is being steadily undermined. The trend toward sexual permissiveness is freeing women from the ancient double standard of sexual morality. The increasingly higher levels of female educational achievement are encouraging greater freedom of choice for women and greater motivation to exercise that choice. The male role as sole breadwinner is being rapidly eroded, and with it the male's dominance in the family and in other areas of society. The mood of the times is against artificial restrictions on equality of opportunity, and we are probably more sensitive to charges of discrimination than at any other time in our history. Many states now have laws guaranteeing equal rights for men and women, and an Equal Rights Amendment to the U.S. Constitution awaits ratification. Much of the tension that surrounds our sex-role patterns is caused by the lag in the adjustment of gender characteristics to these other social changes.

There remain some barriers to change. One difficulty will obviously be the necessity for the male population to modify its roles and attitudes to fit the changing circumstances. Like the members of any privileged group, men may be reluctant to surrender their superior status. At present, many men seem to find their role obligations rather confused. At a trivial level, they wonder whether they should open a door for a woman. Some women still expect it, but others might be insulted. At a more serious level, men are now finding their sexual obligations more difficult to define. The burden for a successful sexual relationship has shifted from women to men within the last few years, and college psychiatrists now report far fewer women concerned about frigidity and far more men concerned about impotence.

Another barrier to change will be the attitudes of women themselves. Many women are still dedicated to their traditional roles and do not regard themselves as the victims of the system at all: they "enjoy being feminine" or being "treated like ladies." As we have already noted, this kind of attitude is common in disadvantaged groups all over the world and throughout history, and the first task of any new liberation movement is always to alert the consciousness of its own group. Black power had first to convince the black community that "black is beautiful"; gay liberation had first to convince the homosexual community that "gay is good"; similarly, women's liberation has had to raise the consciousness of women.

What will the final shape of our sex roles be? Sexual equality does not necessarily mean gender similarity or a "unisex" society. It does not necessarily mean that women will gradually adopt the characteristics of men or that the two existing genders will converge on some happy medium. The most probable pattern is one in which many alternative life-styles and roles will be acceptable for both men and women. American society is individualistic and highly open to change and experimentation, and it is likely that men and women will explore a wide variety of possible roles. True liberation from the restrictions of gender would mean that all possible options would be open and equally acceptable for both sexes. A person's individual human qualities, rather than his or her biological sex, would be the primary measure of personal worth and achievement (Chafetz, 1978; Giele, 1978; Richmond-Abbott, 1979).

Finally, it is worth noting that the changes that have taken place and will take place result, in a sense, from the application of the sociological perspective to inequalities of gender. What was once regarded as an unalterable part of the natural order is now recognized as a social creation, and therefore as something that we can refashion in accordance with present and future values.

Figure 13.14 In most traditional societies, the aged have an honored and respected place in the community, and old men typically have the greatest economic power and political authority. Decisions are often made by a council of elders or some similar body of older men, like this one in Senegal.

Age and Society

As we saw in Chapter 5 ("Socialization"), the human life cycle is as much a social as a biological process. The average person's life expectancy, for example, is strongly influenced by such social factors as the presence (or absence) of competent medical care, good nutrition, adequate sanitation, environmental pollution, warfare, or widespread access to such potentially injurious or lethal instruments as handguns and automobiles. A person born in the United States today can expect to live, on average, for seventy-four years, but a person born in the social setting of the United States of 1900 could expect to live, on average, for only forty-seven years.

The content of the life cycle, too, is affected by social factors, for each society imposes its own culturally defined "stages" (such as adolescence or old age) on the continuous process of human aging. Furthermore, all societies distribute different rights and responsibilities to individuals on the basis of their ascribed status as members of a particular age category. In the United States, for example, a person aged eight must attend school, but a person of eighty need not do so; a person of seventy can become president or can collect a Social Security retirement pension, but a person of twenty-five is not entitled to do either; a person of eighteen can be required to fight in a war, but a person of seventeen cannot.

There are obvious similarities between the way societies distribute roles according to sex and the way they do so on the basis of age. But whereas all societies throughout history have given greater access to valued roles and other social rewards to men than to women, there has been no such clear-cut distribution of rewards among various age categories. As a general rule, however, preindustrial societies granted the greatest power and prestige to the old; industrial societies, on the other hand, accord the most valued rewards to the middle-aged and offer the old virtually no roles at all (Cowgill, 1974; O'Donnell, 1974; Palmore and Manton, 1974; Kalish, 1975; Fischer, 1978; Kett, 1979; Atchley, 1980).

In most preindustrial societies, the aged were, in fact, so respected that younger people sometimes looked forward to old age. The old were the repository of the community's folklore, knowledge, experience, and wisdom, and other members of society looked to them for guidance. In these preliterate societies there was no other source of information about the past, and much of that information was relevant to the daily life and recurrent problems of the community. How long might a drought last? Were there distant kinfolk in a community elsewhere? How could a certain sickness be cured? What weapons and tactics could best defeat an enemy? It is hardly surprising, then, that in most preindustrial societies power was vested in older people: often, in fact, a "council of the elders" or some similar body regulated the affairs of the community. Ownership of wealth, too, was linked to age, for the primary source of wealth in most preindustrial societies was land, which was typically held by the oldest male in the family until it passed, on his death, to his eldest son. The elderly also dominated the family. The large *extended family*, consisting of many relatives living in close proximity, was the norm, and it was typically headed by the oldest male. And because nearly all preindustrial societies were relatively unproductive and needed every hand they could get for labor in the fields, the aged played an active economic role until they were too infirm to work any longer. Of course, there were exceptions to this picture. A few preindustrial societies sometimes treated the aged harshly: the Eskimo occasionally left them out in the snow to die, and even today the malnourished Ik of Uganda allow old people to starve to death. But these are highly unusual cases, arising only in societies that exist under conditions of such extreme hardship that they cannot support those who cannot provide for themselves.

In industrial societies, on the other hand, the status of the aged is very different. In these highly technological and rapidly changing societies, the store of relevant knowledge constantly alters and expands. Access to most of this knowledge comes through formal education, yet the schools are centered almost exclusively on the young and make virtually no provision for the aged. The accumulated experience of the old is no longer respected, and their wisdom is rarely sought after; rather, their knowledge is regarded as outmoded. Grandchildren may know more (or believe they know more) about the modern world than their grandparents. The economic status of the aged also changes markedly. Ownership of land becomes a less significant source of wealth in an industrial society as new sources of wealth are created; and the main beneficiaries of this change are middle-aged, high-ranking executives and other professionals. To make matters worse, the old are deprived of any meaningful economic role (and therefore of the political and social influence that economic power implies). Industrial societies are highly productive, and a recurrent problem they face is not a shortage of labor but,

Figure 13.15 The status of the aged is generally low in industrial societies. In such countries, power passes to the middle-aged, and the characteristics of the young, not the old, are the most desired.

rather, a surplus: in other words, they have to deal with persistent unemployment and underemployment. Partly in response to this problem, industrial societies exclude two age categories from the competition for jobs: the young and the old. A new social invention, compulsory schooling, keeps the very young out of the work force, and another new invention, compulsory retirement, ensures that the old must give up their jobs. But whereas the young can look forward, in due course, to entering a career, the old are permanently relegated to positions of little importance and thus become, in many ways, expendable. The role of old people in the family also changes: instead of heading the family, the aged are increasingly isolated from it, for the extended family gives way, in virtually all industrialized societies, to the *nuclear family*—a unit consisting of a married couple and their dependent children, living apart from other relatives. Indeed, the urbanization process that always accompanies industrialization often results in residential segregation for the elderly, whether they live in decaying, inner-city neighborhoods or in affluent retirement communities. Moreover, the elderly may even become stigmatized rather than honored, partly because of the increasing association between old age and that still-taboo subject in modern society, death. In preindustrial societies, death regularly occurred throughout the life cycle, and particularly in early childhood; today, it is primarily a phenomenon of old age.

A Functionalist View

The radical alteration in the rights and responsibilities of different age categories clearly results from the variety of changes that take place as a society shifts from a preindustrial to an industrial mode of production. But the unequal status of the elderly is not an inevitable outcome of this situation: in other words, the rest of society could still find other ways of keeping old people actively involved in useful roles if there were good reason to do so. Some functionalist theorists have tried to explain the situation of the aged by suggesting that their "disengagement" from society is to everyone's benefit, including that of the old.

The principal statement of this view is that of Elaine Cumming and William Henry (1961), who are strongly influenced by the general functionalist assumption that society is a balanced system in which various elements function smoothly to maintain overall stability. The status of the elderly, they argue, is the result of a mutual process of disengagement, in which society gradually withdraws roles from the old, while the old gradually surrender their roles to other, younger, members of society. Cumming and Henry point out that since all people will eventually die, a society must, if it is to outlive its individual members, arrange an orderly transition from the aged to those who are younger. As people grow older, the probability that they will soon die increases; hence, society phases out those

Figure 13.16 Some functionalists have argued that the diminished status of the aged is a result of a mutual "disengagement," in which society withdraws roles from the old while the old voluntarily surrender them. This theory has been much criticized on the grounds that the "disengagement" process is one-sided: the old are deprived of meaningful social roles whether they want to give them up or not.

individuals whose future contributions are problematic. For their part, people slowly relinquish their roles as they grow older, for they want to conserve their energies and devote more of their time to themselves. Social norms evolve to provide the guidelines for this disengagement process: for example, it becomes the standard practice to retire at about sixty-five, and the event is often marked by some ceremony (such as the gift of a gold watch) that signals the changed status of the individual. The net result is, supposedly, a decreased interaction between the aging person and the surrounding society, to the mutual satisfaction of both.

This theory has been much criticized in recent years, primarily because empirical research has failed to lend it much support. There is little question that society withdraws roles from the aged, but, equally, there is little doubt that the elderly are generally reluctant to give up these roles. As Robert Atchley (1977) comments after a review of this research, "Disengagement is not what most older people want. It is, however, what older people get."

A Conflict View

In the conflict view, the situation of the elderly in modern society results not from any mutually acceptable "disengagement" but rather from discrimination against the aged. In other words, the relationship between the elderly and other age categories arises from a form of social stratification, little different in principle or practice from other kinds of structured social inequality, such as those based on differences in wealth, race, ethnicity, or sex. The aged, in fact, can be considered a minority group in society. Like other disadvantaged minorities, they are subject to job discrimination, unequal opportunity, disproportionately high rates of poverty, prejudice based on inaccurate stereotypes, high rates of victimization by criminals, general isolation from the mainstream of society, and, all too often, low self-esteem (Riley et al., 1972; Streib, 1965; Pratt, 1976).

Conflict theorists argue that the various age groups in society are not merely social categories; they are also strata that are ranked in a hierarchy of power, prestige, and wealth, and are in constant competition for scarce social resources. Younger workers, for example, have a strong interest in the compulsory retirement of older workers: if the latter were to remain at their jobs several more years

into the life cycle, fewer openings and promotions would be available for their juniors. Similarly, different strata have different interests in the allocation of society's public spending: the young, for example, are apt to think that cheaper and better college education is a top social priority; the middle-aged are more likely than the young to be concerned that property taxes should not increase; the aged have a vested interest in better Social Security or Medicaid benefits.

In the competition for scarce and valued resources, the more powerful strata are able to secure a disproportionate share for themselves, and any change in the relative power of the age strata is therefore likely to be reflected in changing patterns of age inequality. In the conflict view, the declining status of the aged in industrial societies results from the widespread social changes that have enabled the middle-aged to wrest control of social resources from their elders. Any improvement in the situation of the aged would have to come about through a change in the power relationships of the strata. For example, if the proportion of the population that is old increases, or if the aged organize powerful social movements to press their case, they might effectively challenge the structured inequality between themselves and the other strata.

Ageism

As we have seen, the dominant stratum in any unequal society uses an *ideology* to justify its position. Employing the analogy of racism and sexism, sociologists have coined the word *ageism* to refer to the set of beliefs that is used to legitimate the systematic discrimination against old people. The ideology of ageism, in fact, is remarkably similar to the ideologies that justify inequalities of race and gender. For example, the subordinate status of the old, like that of women or racial minorities, has been assumed to be rooted in biological characteristics: specifically, it is held that the mental or physical abilities of the aged are so diminished that they are unable to play a full role in society and may therefore be excluded from significant participation. Similarly, the ideology of ageism takes no account of individual differences, and instead treats all old people as though age were their single most important characteristic. And, like sexism or racism, the ageist ideology ignores the fact that

OLD PEOPLE'S PERCEPTIONS OF THEMSELVES COMPARED WITH PUBLIC
PERCEPTIONS OF "MOST PEOPLE OVER 65"

Characteristics of People over 65	Self-Perceptions of People 65 and over (Percent)	Public Perceptions of "Most People over 65" (Percent)	Net Difference
Very friendly and warm	72	74	+ 2
Very wise from experience	69	64	− 5
Very bright and alert	68	29	−39
Very open-minded and adaptable	63	21	−42
Very good at getting things done	55	35	−20
Very physically active	48	41	− 7
Very sexually active	11	5	− 6
How People over 65 Spend "a Lot of Time"			
Socializing with friends	47	52	+ 5
Gardening or raising plants	39	45	+ 6
Reading	36	43	+ 7
Watching television	36	67	+31
Sitting and thinking	31	62	+31
Caring for younger or older members of the family	27	23	+ 4
Sleeping	16	39	+23
Just doing nothing	15	35	+20
Working part time or full time	10	5	− 5
Doing volunteer work	8	15	+ 7

Source: Adapted from National Council on the Aging, "The Myth and Reality of Aging in America," Washington, D.C. (mimeographed), 1975, pp. 53, 59.

Figure 13.17 As this table shows, there are some marked discrepancies between old people's perceptions of themselves and the view that younger people have of them.

many of the differences between the strata are caused by social factors—including differences that result from discrimination and unequal opportunity (Palmore and Manton, 1973; Butler, 1975).

An important feature of ageism, as with racism and sexism, is its reliance on negative stereotypes about the minority concerned. For example, it is widely believed that the old are not such productive workers as the young (actually, they have better job-attendance and productivity records); that many or most of them are infirm (more than 80 percent of the population over sixty-five are fully capable of getting around on their own); that a high proportion of the aged are senile (less than 10 percent of the aged under seventy-five display symptoms of senility); or that

many of the elderly are confined to nursing homes or old-age homes (only 5 percent of those over sixty-five are in this situation). In addition, there are a variety of beliefs about the typical personalities of the aged—that they are cranky, forgetful, sexless (if they are interested in sex, they are likely to be regarded as "dirty old men" or "dirty old women"), highly conservative, and the like—beliefs that either ignore the vast differences among old people (for, after all, individuals grow more different, not more similar, as they age), or have no basis in fact whatever. But no matter how inaccurate the public stereotype of the aged may be, it provides an implicit justification for excluding them from significant roles in the economy, the family, and other areas of society.

The Problems of the Aged

Like other minorities in the United States, the aged—usually defined as those aged sixty-five or over—face a number of characteristic problems. As Robert Butler (1975) comments, the tragedy of aging is not that we grow old, but that the process has been made painful, humiliating, and isolating: "At best, the living old are treated as though they were already half dead . . . In America, childhood is romanticized, youth is idolized, middle age does the work, wields the power and pays the bills, and old age . . . is a period of quiet despair, deprivation, desolation . . ."

Health

Advancing age inevitably brings with it a series of health problems, for the human body gradually degenerates with the passage of the years. Of course, the rate at which people appear to age varies a great deal, and people of seventy or eighty may be healthier, and even seem younger, than people twenty years their junior. Nonetheless, more than three-quarters of those over the age of sixty-five suffer from some chronic health problem, and although the aged represent only 11 percent of the total population, they fill a third of all hospital beds and use a quarter of the drugs prescribed each year. The most common ailments suffered by the aged include arthritis, diabetes, glaucoma, cancer, heart disease, and senility—diseases that can usually be treated, but not cured. Senility is perhaps the most notorious disability of the aged as far as the rest of the population is concerned, but the disease (which is caused by the loss of brain cells and affects various mental functions, particularly short-term memory and concentration) is rare among people under seventy-five; only thereafter does it become more common. Many aged people are labeled as senile, however, when they are really suffering from depression, from the side effects of medication, or from undiagnosed respiratory or cardiovascular problems that impede the flow of blood and oxygen to the brain.

The high incidence of poor health among the aged is compounded by two factors. First, the aged have much higher medical expenses than the nonaged—six times greater than the expenses of young adults, and three times greater than those of the middle-aged. The old often face these expenses at a time when they have lost their job-related medical insurance as a result of retirement. Al-

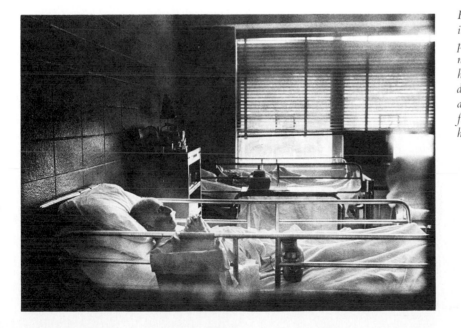

Figure 13.18 As people grow older, they become increasingly likely to suffer from chronic health problems—diseases that can often be treated, but not cured. A few generations ago, the aged would have been cared for by the family until the time of death; today, they are more likely to face illness and death in a hospital or nursing home, isolated from their kin except, perhaps, during visiting hours.

though it is widely supposed that Medicaid and Medicare cover most of the medical bills of old people, this is far from the case; these programs assume only about 45 percent of the financial burden, and their coverage specifically excludes drugs prescribed outside hospitals as well as items that the old are disproportionately likely to need, such as hearing aids and eyeglasses. The second factor is the general lack of interest that the American medical profession has in the problems of the elderly. Physicians are usually more interested in acute diseases among the young and the middle-aged—diseases that offer the rewarding possibility of successful treatment and even dramatic cure. There is far less interest in treating conditions that will almost always grow worse, in patients who will inevitably die within a few years. Joseph Freeman (1971) found that over half the medical schools in the United States did not offer a single course in the medical problems of the aged—a striking statistic, given the fact that more than one hospital patient in three is over sixty-five.

Social Isolation

A common source of depression among the elderly is loneliness. Lacking the secure place in the family and the active role in the economy that old people in earlier generations had, many of the aged lapse into social isolation. A quarter of the elderly, in fact, live alone. Most of these old people are women: because females live longer than males, there are 140 aged women for every 100 aged men, and two-thirds of women aged seventy-five or over are widowed. Those who live alone are usually the poorest of the elderly, and they frequently live in decaying inner-city neighborhoods where the fear of street crime may make them afraid to leave their homes or to answer their doorbells. Even those who do not live alone may experience feelings of isolation and uselessness: their advice is not wanted by their mature children; their skills are not wanted by the economy; and even their presence at social events may be unwanted by members of other age strata. It is not surprising if apathy, alcoholism, boredom, and frustration result. Indeed, one of the few roles we offer the aged is the sick role—the pattern of behavior expected of someone who is ill. People generally conform to the expectations others have of them, and if the elderly are expected to become frail, isolated, and inward-looking, that is, in fact, what they will tend to become. And as we noted in Chapter 2 ("Doing Sociology: The Methods of Research"), suicide in modern societies is especially common among people who have few meaningful links with their community. One of the greatest tragedies of old age is the high rate of suicide (particularly among men) at this point of the life cycle—a rate significantly higher than at any other stage.

Figure 13.19 This elderly woman is telling her young audience about her childhood experiences with a pioneering family in Colorado around the turn of the century. But opportunities for such contact between the aged and the young are brief and infrequent: our society is simply not structured to facilitate them.

Figure 13.20 In most preindustrial societies, the elderly—like this man in the Middle East and this woman in Asia—work until advanced old age. There is no concept of "retirement" in these societies, for every extra worker is needed and valued. Industrial societies, in contrast, arbitrarily exclude most of the aged from the work force.

Mandatory Retirement

American society no longer permits discrimination in employment on the grounds of race or sex, yet like most industrialized societies, the United States has a legal mandatory retirement age for nearly all workers. Thus an entire age category may be forced from the labor market on the basis of supposed group characteristics and without any reference to the skills and talents of the individual. The age was sixty-five years until 1978, when Congress raised it to seventy years. Most workers still retire at sixty-five, however, partly because Social Security and other benefits remain tied to that age, and partly because many people are only too willing to retire as soon as possible.

A substantial minority, however, do not want to retire, and they point to the practice of mandatory retirement as an example of intolerable discrimination, especially since there is no evidence to suggest that people of sixty-five or seventy are incapable of working. Although only 20 percent of men over sixty-five worked full-time in 1980, 70 percent of the men in this category were in the labor force in 1900, and it is obviously absurd to suppose that people are competent at their jobs until the day before their sixty-fifth birthday and incompetent immediately thereafter. There are two reasons for mandatory retirement, and they have little to do with the physical or mental capacities of people of that age. The first reason, as we have already noted, is that mandatory retirement, combined with a system of Social Security pensions, permits surplus labor to be drawn off from the work force, thus opening up opportunities for younger workers. The second reason is that mandatory retirement is an administrative convenience for the large formal organizations—usually government agencies and corporations—that now employ 80 percent of American workers. In time, aging will make everyone unfit to hold a job, and large organizations therefore face the problem of how to phase out unproductive older workers. The fair but cumbersome way of achieving this goal would be to periodically review the performance of each employee; the unfair but less cumbersome method is to retire everybody at an arbitrary age. And arbitrary it is: the original retirement age of sixty-five was chosen, not on the basis of medical, psychological, sociological, or other scientific evidence, but on the personal whim of one man in 1889. Germany introduced the first social-security laws in that year, and the chancellor, Bismarck, in his entirely subjective wisdom, selected sixty-five as the age at which benefits could be drawn. American legislation simply followed the German precedent.

Low Income

Although most workers look forward to retirement, many are reluctant to give up their occupations: opinion polls show that about a third of retired people would prefer to work if suitable jobs were available. One reason is their fear that permanent unemployment will bring a loss of social identity; people who have been active all their lives may dread having "nothing to do." But the most common reason for the desire to continue working is an economic one, for retirement typically brings a sharp drop in income. Although most of the aged own their homes, few have any significant savings or other assets, and only a minority have pensions from private employers. For 80 percent of retired Americans, Social Security is their only source of income. And Social Security pensions hardly guarantee an affluent life-style, although the retired have been better off since 1972, when Congress determined that future increases in their pensions would be linked to increases in the cost of living. At the beginning of the last decade, 25 percent of the

aged lived in poverty; today, less than 14 percent do so. Many more, however, live just above the poverty line, and the number of old people who live in conditions of real affluence is small.

Again, the economic problems of the aged are compounded by factors that affect them specifically. One, already mentioned, is the high cost of medical care, which can easily wipe out aged people's savings and consume most of their income. Another is that old people find it very difficult to get loans or credit. Their homes, too, tend to be older and more in need of repair than those of the rest of the population. Their fuel bills are often higher, for they feel the cold more than younger people do. Those who live alone must often buy food and other supplies in small quantities, so they cannot take advantage of the savings available for those who can buy the larger, "economy" sizes. The aged are especially likely to be victimized by criminals, ranging from muggers to swindlers. And, of course, they have no access to the means that society recommends for everyone else who pleads poverty—a job.

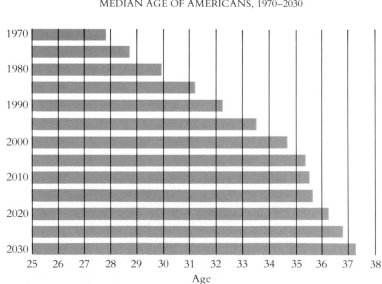

MEDIAN AGE OF AMERICANS, 1970–2030

Figure 13.21 The median age of the American population is steadily rising, making the United States one of the "oldest" peoples in the world. Over the next few decades this trend will have profound effects on the society, for it will become oriented more toward the aged than toward the young.

Source: Bureau of the Census.

The Graying of America

The United States is in the midst of a profound change in population structure, a change that will make Americans a significantly older people. At the time of the first U.S. census in 1790, half the people in the country were 16 or younger. But by 1900, the median age had risen to 22.9; by 1970, to 27.9; and by 1980, to 30. The median age is expected to reach 35 by the year 2000 and may go as high as 37 by the year 2030. At present there are about 25 million aged Americans, representing 11 percent of the population. By 2030 their number will have grown to 55 million, or 18 percent of the population.

The reasons for this dramatic increase in the proportion of the elderly lie in changes in the American birth rate over the past few decades. For several years after World War II there was a "baby boom": birth rates rose sharply, resulting in a "bulge" in the society's population structure (see Figure 13.21). During the 1950s and 1960s the baby-boom generation flooded the schools and colleges, necessitating vast expansion of educational facilities and creating a youth culture that had a significant impact on the society. Throughout the 1970s this stratum crowded the job market, adding to unemployment and forcing many college graduates to take jobs below their level of qualification. Today, as this generation settles down and marries, it is placing a squeeze on the housing market, pushing up the costs of rent and home ownership. During the 1980s and 1990s, there will be a middle-aged bulge in the population structure. And finally, when the baby-boom generation retires early in the next century, American society will be largely oriented toward the elderly. Moreover, two further factors will reinforce this "graying" process. One is the "baby bust" that began in the mid-1970s: birth rates have declined during the past few years to unprecedented lows, meaning that there will be even fewer younger people in the decade or two ahead. The other is the gradual increase in life expectancy, which means that more people are living for longer than ever before. (All these aspects of population change are discussed in detail in Chapter 20, "Population and Health.")

The graying of America will bring about a variety of changes, some of which are already apparent. To begin with, elementary schools and even high schools all over the nation are closing their doors, and teachers are being thrown out of work. Changes in population structure are being reflected in marketing trends as well: for example, Gerber baby foods now sells life insurance; Levi's jeans are now designed with more generous proportions for a market that is steadily tending toward middle-age spread; models in TV advertisements appear to be somewhat older than they were a few years ago, for they must appeal, in large measure, to an audience that is entering its thirties.

Other changes are clearly in the offing. Educational facilities will have to offer more courses in continuing education for older people, or they may have so few students that they will not survive. The medical problems of the aged will become a major growth area in medicine, for American physicians, despite their lack of enthusiasm for this field in the past, are likely to specialize where the greatest market is. Nursing homes, funeral homes, and crematoriums will proliferate. And in all likelihood, the aged will achieve a more respected status in society.

There are currently many signs that this process has begun. The elderly are already organizing themselves into an effective political lobby, represented by such organizations as the American Association of Retired Persons and such movements as the Grey Panthers. Their campaigns have already had some positive effects: as we have seen, the age of mandatory retirement has been increased, Social Security pensions have been linked to the cost of living, Medicaid has been designed to cover certain medical expenses of the aged, but not of the nonaged. Gradually, older people are staking their claim to a greater share of the society's resources. The possible implications of this trend—which include a potential for fresh conflict among the age strata—are most clearly seen in the Social Security system, under which pensions for those who are retired are paid for by those who are working. In 1945 there were thirty-five workers to one Social Security recipient; by 1955 the ratio was seven to one; by 1980, three to one. Within the foreseeable future there may be two workers supporting every retiree, and the burden may be heavier still if the retired people of the future are able to secure more generous pensions—and if they live longer (Sheppard and Rix, 1978; Ehrbar, 1980; Jorgensen, 1980). In 1980, programs for the elderly consumed nearly 25 percent of the federal budget, but projections show that this share could rise to 63 percent by the year 2025 (Storey and Hendricks, 1980). Forty years or so from now, sociology textbook chapters on age stratification may be lamenting the domination of the young by the old. But for the present, it is the status of the old as the unequal, isolated, and often unwanted members of society that is of prime sociological concern.

Important Terms

sex (male/female) (312)

gender (masculine/ feminine) (312)

sex roles (312)

ideology (320)

sexism (320)

false consciousness (321)

stereotype (322)

extended family (333)

nuclear family (334)

ageism (335)

Summary

1. All societies treat their members unequally according to ascribed statuses of sex and age. These structured social inequalities are specific forms of the general phenomenon of social stratification.

2. Sex refers to the biological distinctions between men and women; gender refers to culturally learned notions of masculinity and femininity. Sex roles are the learned patterns of gender behavior expected in any society.

3. The biological differences between the sexes are anatomical, genetic, and hormonal. Apart from reproductive functions, these differences have few inevitable implications for sex roles. Some minor psychological differences exist in young infants, although even these may be learned. The general cross-cultural trend is toward male dominance and female subordination, although many cultures are unlike our own in certain respects.

4. Sociologists generally accept that sex roles are social, not biological, in origin. In the functionalist view, sex-role differences were useful in traditional societies, and some theorists argue that this is still the case. In the conflict view, traditional sex roles reflect a conflict of interest between men and women, and will change as women gain more economic power.

5. Sexism, like other ideologies, is a belief system that upholds the social arrangements in question. Both men and women are inclined to regard sexual inequalities as being rooted in biology. Members of the subordinate stratum are in a state of false consciousness in this respect.

6. There are still distinct sex-role differences in the United States, expressed in personality traits and in the division of labor. Men are expected to have more dominant personalities and to play the more important economic roles.

7. Several agencies of socialization systematically ensure that the sexes learn gender characteristics. The most important of these agencies are the family, the schools, and the mass media; each reinforces the existing patterns.

8. Sexism has important costs and consequences. Traditional sex roles prevent part of the population from playing an effective part in the economy and have undesirable social and psychological effects on both men and women.

9. American sex roles are changing rapidly and are likely to offer both men and women a wider range of acceptable options.

10. The life cycle is a social as well as a biological process; all societies define stages of life and assign different rights and responsibilities to people in various age categories. In general, preindustrial societies gave high status to the aged; industrial societies give them low status.

11. In the functionalist view, the status of the elderly results from a process of mutual disengagement, by which society withdraws roles from them and they relinquish roles voluntarily. In the conflict view, the status of the elderly results from competition among different age strata for valued social rewards.

12. Ageism is the ideology that justifies the unequal treatment of old people; it assumes that they are physically or mentally incapable of participating fully in society and that their exclusion from many roles is therefore justified.

13. Some problems of the aged are health, social isolation, mandatory retirement, and low income.

14. America is "graying" as a result of changes in population structure; gradually, the society will become oriented toward the aged rather than the young.

Suggested Readings

ATCHLEY, ROBERT C. *The Social Forces in Later Life.* 3rd ed. Belmont, Calif.: Wadsworth, 1980.

An excellent introduction to social gerontology, the study of the social aspects of aging.

BUTLER, ROBERT N. *Why Survive? Being Old in America.* New York: Harper and Row, 1975.

A good survey of the plight of the elderly in America. The book is recommended as a well-written overview of the issue.

HESS, RUTH B. (ed.). *Growing Old in America.* 2nd ed. New Brunswick, N.J.: Transaction Books, 1980.

An up-to-date selection of sociological articles on various aspects of aging in contemporary America.

KANTER, ROSABETH MOSS. *Men and Women of the Corporation.* New York: Basic Books, 1977.

An important study of career patterns and social interactions of men and women within a large corporation.

PETRAS, JOHN W. *Sex: Male/Gender: Masculine.* Port Washington, N.Y.: Alfred Publishing Co., 1975.

A very useful anthology of articles on men, masculinity, and the male sex role. The selection includes material on male liberation and likely trends in "masculinity."

RUBIN, LILLIAN. *Women of a Certain Age: The Midlife Search for Self.* New York: Harper and Row, 1979.

A sensitive study of an important subject: the reactions of women to a "midlife crisis" in a social environment that devalues both women and the old.

WEITZ, SHIRLEY. *Sex Roles: Biological, Psychological, and Social Foundations.* New York: Oxford University Press, 1977.

A useful survey of the facts about sex roles and gender characteristics. The book incorporates material from several relevant disciplines to give an integrated view of the topic.

Reading

On Raising a Boy as a Girl *John Money and Patricia Tucker*

Some of the most interesting research on sex and gender comes from studies of children who, as a result of genital deformity, the actions of mentally disturbed parents, or some other misfortune, are raised as members of the opposite sex. In this reading, leading researchers in the field describe a case in which a male infant was brought up to have a feminine gender. This is only one of several such cases, all of which have indicated that biological sex need have little or no influence on gender.

Dramatic proof that the gender identity option is open at birth for normal infants and that social forces can intervene decisively at least up to a year and a half after birth comes from a few unusual cases such as one that occurred more than ten years ago.

A young farm couple took their sturdy, normal, identical twin boys to a physician in a nearby hospital to be circumcised when the boys were seven months old. The physician elected to use an electric cauterizing needle instead of a scalpel to remove the foreskin of the twin who chanced to be brought into the operating room first. When this baby's foreskin didn't give on the first try, or on the second, the doctor stepped up the current. On the third try, the surge of heat from the electricity literally cooked the baby's penis. Unable to heal, the penis dried up, and in a few days sloughed off completely, like the stub of an umbilical cord.

When the parents saw what had happened they were stunned, and as soon as the baby could leave the hospital they took him home. They had no idea of where to turn for help, and they were so numbed by the catastrophe that they could hardly talk about it, even with each other. Eventually they recovered themselves enough to make inquiries, but the problem was beyond the experience of their local doctors. Finally they took the baby to a famous medical center, but even there no help was forthcoming. They went back home without hope, their slender finances drained and they themselves almost paralyzed by the frustration of not knowing what to do. The father began having nightmares in which he attacked a doctor and shot him dead.

A plastic surgeon who knew of the Johns Hopkins program for helping hermaphroditic babies finally was called in as a consultant. He suggested the possibility of reassigning the baby as a girl. This was a new and frightening idea to the parents, and at first they shied away from it. Not long afterward, however, they happened to tune in on the last part of a television program about the work with transexuals at Johns Hopkins. On the screen was an adult male-to-female transexual who, they could see for themselves, looked and talked like a normal, attractive woman. After that they worked their way to the decision to reassign their son as a girl. They began using a girl's name, letting the child's hair grow, and choosing noncommittal clothes for this twin. A short time later, when the twins were seventeen months old, they made the trip to Johns Hopkins. They needed reassurance that the program they had undertaken was the right thing for the child, and they wanted the necessary treatment from a hospital that was far enough from home to minimize the risk that gossip would leak back to their community.

The professional resources of the Johns Hopkins Hospital and specialty clinics were promptly mobilized to assess the possible alternatives. The first thing to consider was the child's gender identity. From conception to the age of fifteen months, every force had consistently steered this child toward differentiation of a male gender identity, except that, from the age of seven months, there had been no penis to confirm the other sex determinants. However, since the child had only just begun to talk when the parents had decided on reassignment, there was an excellent chance that gender identity would not by then have differentiated very far in the male direction. That was encouraging, but there was also the question of the parents' expectations. For fifteen months, this child had been their son; could they make the difficult adjustment of accepting the same child as their daughter? It was a vital consideration, for any lingering doubts whatsoever in their minds would weaken the child's identification as a girl and woman.

The medical psychologist described the alternatives to the parents, using nontechnical words, diagrams, and photographs of children who had been reassigned. On the one hand, he explained, if the child grew up as a boy, a plastic surgeon could graft skin from the child's belly to fashion a penis. Female-to-male transexuals had found, however, that after this kind of operation the tissues of the artificial penis often break down, allowing leakage during urination, and that the artificial urethral canal is not very good at resisting the inward advance of infection, which increases the danger of urinary and bladder infections. Another problem is that, since a skin graft penis has no touch or pain feelings, continuous care must be exercised to make sure that it does not become ulcerated by rubbing against clothing, or being bruised or squeezed. The most serious drawback, however, is that it has no sexual feeling and cannot erect. As a man, this child's testicles could generate the sperm to sire his own children, but it would be difficult to ejaculate them into the vagina, since he would have to use an artificial penis support for sexual intercourse and would not experience the normal frictional sensations that produce orgasm.

On the other hand, if the parents stood by their decision to reassign the child as a girl, surgeons could remove the testicles and construct feminine external genitals immediately. When she was eleven or twelve years old, she could be given the female hormones that would normally feminize her body for the rest of her life. Later a vaginal canal could be surgically constructed so that her genitals would be adequate for sexual intercourse and for sexual pleasure, including orgasm. She could become as good a mother as any other woman, but only by adoption.

The medical psychologist stressed that there would be no turning back once gender identity had differentiated. The child was still young enough so that whichever assignment was made, erotic interest would almost certainly direct itself toward the opposite sex later on, but the time for reaching a final decision was already short. He explained that whichever way they decided, it was essential that they decide wholeheartedly; the child would need all their support in differentiating a gender identity, and any lingering doubts in their minds would undermine that support.

Though not highly educated, the twins' parents are intelligent and exceptionally sensible people. They quickly grasped the risk of delay and of mental reservations, however well concealed, about the child's sex. With the alternatives thus spelled out, they reconfirmed their decision on sex reassignment: The child would be a girl. They had reached the conclusion of an agonizing decision in favor of castration. The girl's subsequent history proves how well all three of them succeeded in adjusting to that decision.

. . .

At the age of twenty-one months, the little girl was brought back to Johns Hopkins for the first stage of surgical feminization, removal of testicles and feminization of external genitals. When her body reaches adult size, she can decide when to schedule construction of the vaginal canal. If she waits until shortly before she is ready to begin her sex life, sexual intercourse will help to keep the canal elastic and unconstricted. Meanwhile, there's nothing about her genital appearance to make her feel self-conscious, even if she gets into the bathtub with her twin brother.

The twins and their parents come back to Johns Hopkins once a year for general psychological counseling and a checkup. Although the girl had been the dominant twin in infancy, by the time the children were four years old there was no mistaking which twin was the girl and which the boy. At five, the little girl already preferred dresses to pants, enjoyed wearing her hair ribbons, bracelets and frilly blouses, and loved being her daddy's little sweetheart. Throughout childhood, her stubbornness and the abundant physical energy she shares with her twin brother and expends freely have made her a tomboyish girl, but nonetheless a girl. Her dominance behavior has expressed itself in fussing over her brother, according to their parents, "like a mother hen," while he, in turn, takes up for his sister if he thinks anyone is threatening her. Their mother reported that dolls and a doll carriage headed her Christmas list when she was five and that, quite unlike her brother, the girl was neat and dainty, experimented happily with styles for her long hair, and often tried to help in the kitchen.

Although this girl is not yet a woman, her record to date offers convincing evidence that the gender identity gate is open at birth for a normal child no less than for one born with unfinished sex organs or one who was prenatally over- or underexposed to androgen, and that it stays open at least for something over a year after birth. . . .

Source: John Money and Patricia Tucker, *Sexual Signatures: On Being a Man or a Woman* (Boston: Little, Brown, 1975) pp. 91–95, 97–98.

UNIT 4 *Social Institutions*

Every society must meet certain basic social needs if it is to survive and to offer a satisfying life to its members. In each society, therefore, people create social institutions to meet these needs.

As we noted in our discussions in Chapter 4 ("Society"), an institution is a fairly stable cluster of norms, values, statuses, and roles, all of them centered around some social need. The family, for example, is an institution built around the needs to regulate sexual activity and to provide care and protection for the young. The educational institution focuses on the need to give young people formal training in the skills that they will require later in life. The economic institution centers on the social need for an orderly way of producing and distributing goods and services. Within these broad social institutions there are, of course, many smaller units: for example, high schools within the educational institution, churches within the wider religious institution.

The study of social institutions is important because they are a central part of social structure, and there is an intimate relationship between a society's institutional framework and the private experience of its members. In this unit we shall focus on several of the most important institutions in modern society: the family, education, religion, science, the economic order, and the political order. As you will see, social institutions are currently in a state of considerable flux as they are subjected to new demands and constant social change.

CHAPTER **14**   *The Family*

The family is the most basic and ancient of all institutions, and it remains the fundamental social unit in every society. Yet there are many people today who predict—some with despair and some with enthusiasm—the doom of the family system as we know it. The family, it is contended, is breaking down, the victim of moral decay or irresistible social forces. A mass of evidence is cited to support this view: a soaring divorce rate, an increase in illegitimacy, the changing role of women, the spread of sexual permissiveness, and the many new experimental alternatives to traditional marriage (Casler, 1974; Bell, 1977; Lasch, 1977; Reiss and Hoffman, 1979). But are these fears valid? In this chapter we shall begin with a sociological analysis of the institution, and then apply the insights of the discipline to the plight of the modern family. (To review the features of institutions in general, you can refer back to the discussion in Chapter 4, "Society.")

What exactly is a family? Our ideas on the subject may tend to be very ethnocentric, for they are often based on the middle-class ideal family, so relentlessly portrayed in TV commercials, that consists of a husband, a wife, and their dependent children. This particular family pattern, however, is far from typical. It is, in fact, a relatively recent development in human history. A more accurate conception of the family must take account of the many different family forms that have existed or still exist both in America and in other cultures.

The first characteristic of the family is that it consists of a group of people who are in some way related to one another. Second, its members live together for long periods. Third, the adults in the group assume responsibility for any offspring. And fourth, the members of the family form an economic unit—often for producing goods and services (as when all members share agricultural tasks) and always for consuming goods and services (such as food or housing). We may say, then, that *the family is a relatively permanent group of people related by ancestry, marriage, or adoption, who live together and form an economic unit and whose adult members assume responsibility for the young.* If this definition seems a little cumbersome, it is only because it has to include such a great variety of family forms.

Marriage and Kinship

Every human society institutionalizes some family system, for the family is a social arrangement that arises from biological imperatives unique to our species. Unlike the females of other species, the human female is sexually accessible throughout virtually the entire year. The fact that sexual relations are not restricted to a brief breeding season encourages mates to form stable, long-lasting bonds. In other species, moreover, the offspring are generally able to fend for themselves quite soon after being born or hatched. The human infant, however, is helpless and in need of constant care and protection for several years after birth. This period of dependency is far longer, in both relative and absolute terms, than that found in any other animal. The fact that women bear and suckle infants restricts their activity during this period, making them at least tempo-

rarily dependent on the protection and economic support of males. In the past, every society has also found it convenient (or at least the men in every society have found it so) to assign responsibility for child-rearing to women, leaving the men to concentrate on such activities as hunting, heavy agriculture, or fighting. The result has been a universal pattern in which men and women establish permanent bonds that maximize the efficiency of their child-rearing and economic activity: hence, the family.

Most of us spend most of our lives in two families: the family of *orientation,* into which we are born, and the family of *procreation,* which we later create ourselves. In every society a family is expected to be formed through marriage, a socially approved sexual union of some permanence between two or more people. This union is usually inaugurated through a socially approved ceremony, such as a wedding by a religious official, a registration of the union by a judge or other government servant, or even, in some societies, by an informal agreement between the parties or their parents. The offspring of married parents are considered *legitimate,* because society can allocate the social roles of mother and father to specific persons who are then responsible for the care and protection of the young. Children born into a family that has not been formed through marriage may be considered *illegitimate,* because although their mother is known, there may be nobody to take on the social role of father.

The family is a unit within a much wider social network of relatives, or kin. *Kinship* refers to a network of

Figure 14.1 The family, embedded in a wider network of relatives, or kin, is the fundamental social unit in all societies. In modern societies, close kin rarely live together, although they may assemble for ceremonial occasions such as funerals or weddings.

people related by common ancestry, adoption, or marriage. In many traditional societies, kinship is an important, or even the most important, basis of social organization, but in modern societies the family tends to become isolated from all but the closest kin. Many of us do not even know the names of our second cousins or similarly distant relatives. Frequently, even close kin gather only for a few ceremonial occasions such as Thanksgiving or funerals.

A kinship network is a highly complicated affair, as you will know if you have ever tried to construct your own family tree. Your closest, or primary, relatives—mother, father, brother, sister, spouse, daughter, and son—give a total of 7 possible types. Your secondary relatives—the primary relatives of your primary relatives, excluding your own primary relatives—provide 33 additional types, ranging from mothers-in-law to nephews. If you further include tertiary relatives—the primary relatives of your secondary relatives, excluding your own secondary relatives—you have 151 more types, giving a grand total of 191. Since many of these positions can be occupied by several people, the number of primary, secondary, and tertiary relatives can run to several hundred. A kinship network of this size is more than people can deal with, socially or even conceptually, so every society finds a way of arbitrarily excluding some categories of relatives from its conception of kin. The most common way of doing this in traditional societies, odd as it may seem to us, is simply to acknowledge as kin only the relatives on either the father's or the mother's side of the family. In North America we consider the relatives of both father and mother as kin, and generally solve the problem of numbers by regarding nearly all tertiary and many secondary relatives as too distant to be considered real kinfolk.

The Family: A Functionalist View

Although the family institution arose from our characteristics as a species, we are not merely biological animals; we are social animals as well. A full understanding of the universality of the family must take into account the *functions* that the institution performs for the maintenance of the entire social order, as well as for the survival of individuals. The family has several basic social functions in all societies (Murdock, 1949; Parsons and Bales, 1955).

Regulation of Sexual Behavior

No society allows people to mate at random, and no society regards sexual behavior purely as a matter of private choice. The marriage and family system provides a means of regulating sexual behavior by specifying who may mate with whom and under what circumstances they may do so.

Replacement of Members

A society cannot survive unless it has a system for replacing its members from generation to generation. The family provides a stable, institutionalized means through which this replacement can take place, with specific individuals occupying the social roles of mother and father and assuming defined responsibilities.

Socialization

Newborn infants do not become fully human until they are socialized, and the primary context for this socialization is the family. Because the child is theirs, the parents normally take particular care to monitor his or her behavior and to pass on the language, values, norms, and beliefs of the culture. Although in modern society many of these socialization functions have been taken over by other institutions—such as the schools, the churches, or the media—the family remains the earliest and most significant agency of socialization.

Care and Protection

Infants need warmth, food, shelter, and affection. The family provides an intimate atmosphere and an economic unit in which these needs can be provided. The adult family members, too, provide one another with material and emotional support that cannot be readily obtained outside the family context. The productive members can take care of those who, for reasons of age or other incapacity, cannot care for themselves.

Social Placement

Legitimate birth into a family gives the individual a stable place in society. We inherit from our family of orientation not only material goods but also our social status. We belong to the same racial or ethnic group and usually to the same religion and social class that our parents belong to. Our family background is the most significant single determinant of our status in society.

All these functions are necessary. As many critics have suggested, however, the family is not the only conceivable means through which they could be fulfilled. Yet the family fulfills them so effectively that it takes primary responsibility for them in every human culture.

The Family: A Conflict View

While conflict theorists do not dispute that the family has important social functions, they believe that the functionalist analysis does not tell the whole story. In particular, they note that the family is the principal institution in which male dominance of females is expressed.

Karl Marx's cowriter, Friedrich Engels (1942, originally published 1884), argued that marriage represents "the first class antagonism which appears in history . . . in which the well-being and development of the one group are attained by the misery and repression of the other." The relationship between the spouses in marriage, he claimed, provided the model on which later forms of oppression were based, especially that between capitalist and worker. This view has strongly influenced radical feminists, particularly around

Figure 14.2

"Just remember: Your mother was a Van Puyster and your father was a rat."

Copyright Wm. Hamilton

the turn of the century, when women were campaigning for the right to vote, and in the 1960s, when a later generation launched a new movement for liberation in all aspects of social and economic life.

There is certainly some truth to this argument, for in every family system known to us, husbands have had greater authority than their wives in all significant matters. In many societies, in fact, women have been treated for practical and legal purposes as the property of their husbands (or, if unmarried, of their fathers). This principle was embodied in the law of ancient Rome and has persisted in various forms in Western culture to this day. Until the 1960s, for example, married women in some parts of the United States were considered legally incompetent to make contracts or obtain credit without their husband's written consent, in much the same way that minors cannot exercise these privileges without the approval of a parent or guardian. Other traces of the old traditions are to be found in our contemporary wedding ceremony: in the standard form of vows, the bride solemnly promises to "obey" the groom, and it is her father who "gives her away" to her new husband, as though some piece of property were being transferred. (We can see the implications of this procedure more clearly if we imagine its opposite—the mother of the groom giving him away to the bride, and he then vowing to obey his wife for the rest of his life.)

Nonetheless, there is a serious difficulty with this view of the family, for it confuses the specific practices of various societies with the more general concept of the family as an institution. The fact that women have been subordinate in all family systems in the past does not necessarily mean that there is something inherently wrong with the whole idea, for it is entirely possible that utterly different family forms might emerge in the future. In some of the advanced industrial societies, in fact, there is already a strong trend toward equality between the spouses.

Tension over sex roles is only one aspect of conflict in the family. Another is violence among family members. As Steinmetz and Straus (1974) observe, "it would be hard to find a group or an institution in American society in which violence is more of an everyday occurrence than it is within the family." Although one of its functions is to provide care and protection for its members, the modern family is, according to the sociological research of the past decade, afflicted with a remarkable amount of violence between spouses, among siblings, and between parents and children. About a fifth of all murders in the United States are committed by a relative of the victim—in half of the cases, by the spouse. The police detest "disturbance calls"—usually family fights—because of the vicious and dangerous nature of so many of these conflicts; indeed, more police are killed intervening in these disputes than in almost any other type of situation they face. Each year about 7.5 million couples go through a violent episode in which one spouse tries to cause the other serious pain or injury. Wives assault their husbands as often as husbands assault their wives, and spouses are equally likely to kill each other. Although wives are rarely a match for their husbands in a fistfight, they are more likely to use lethal weapons (notably kitchen knives). In most nonfatal physical violence between the spouses, however, wives are very much the victims, and there is now growing awareness that wife-beating is a widespread and very serious problem. Each year, too, about 2.3 million children wield a gun or knife against a brother or sister, and parents kick, punch, or bite as many as 1.7 million children, batter 750,000 more, and attack 46,000 with knives or guns. Child abuse—involving such acts as burning children with cigarettes, locking them up in closets, tying them up for hours or days, or breaking their bones—is far more common than is generally realized, and probably causes many of the 2 million runaways that happen each year (Gil, 1970; Steinmetz and Straus, 1974; Gelles, 1974; Helfer and Kempe, 1978; Nagi, 1978; Straus et al., 1979).

One source of this violence may lie in the dynamics of the family as an intimate environment: close relationships are likely to involve more conflict than less intimate ones, since there are more occasions for tension to arise and more likelihood that deep emotions will be provoked (Skolnick, 1978). Another source may lie outside the family, in the frustrations that people experience as they go about their lives. Violence is frequently a response to frustration. If the person affected cannot strike back at the source of the problem—perhaps the arrogance of an employer, perhaps the lack of a job—the aggression may be readily redirected at family members. Perhaps most important, violence between husband and wife takes place in a general social context that has traditionally emphasized male dominance and even aggression on the one hand, and female subservience on the other. Wife-beating may be seen as an extreme outcome of the socially structured interaction between the sexes, in which women tend to be regarded not just as people, but also as objects of possession. In any event, the extent of violence in groups whose members are supposed to love and care for one another is not easily explained by functionalist theory, and suggests that the modern family may sometimes be under greater pressures than it can easily bear.

Family Patterns

Each society views its own patterns of marriage, family, and kinship as self-evidently right and proper, and usually as God-given as well. Much of the current concern about the fate of the modern family stems from this kind of ethnocentrism. If we assume that there is only one "right" family form, then naturally any change will be interpreted as heralding the doom of the whole institution. New family patterns that deviate from the "typical" form are frequently regarded as inherently immoral or undesirable rather than as potential alternatives in their own right. It is important to recognize, therefore, that there is an immense range in marriage, family, and kinship patterns; that each of these patterns is, at least in its own context, perfectly viable; and above all, that the family, like any other social institution, must inevitably change through time.

A Cross-Cultural Perspective

The family patterns of other cultures challenge many of our assumptions about the nature of marriage, family, and kinship (Murdock, 1949; Ford and Beach, 1955; Stephens, 1963; Fox, 1965; Murstein, 1974).

Incest Rules

There is one universal norm in all family patterns: people may not mate with anyone they choose. In every society there is an *incest taboo* that prohibits sexual intercourse between certain relatives. As we saw in Chapter 9 ("Sexuality and Society"), the revulsion felt against incest by people everywhere is not in any sense "instinctive"; like any other social norm, it is learned in the socialization process. This fact becomes fully apparent when we realize that different societies extend the incest taboo to quite different sets of relatives.

The taboo is almost universally applied to relations between parent and child and between brother and sister, the exceptions being in the royal households of the ancient Egyptian, Hawaiian, and Incan societies and among a few isolated African tribes. Beyond this, the boundaries of the taboo vary considerably from one culture to another. In the United States, all fifty states prohibit marriage between a person and his or her parent, grandparent, uncle or aunt, brother or sister, and niece or nephew; an additional twenty-nine states regard marriage between first cousins as incestuous, but the remainder do not. Many societies, however, do not make any distinction between *siblings* (brothers and sisters) and cousins. In these societies there are usually no separate words for "brother" and "cousin": they are regarded as the same kind of relative, and the incest taboo is therefore extended to first, second, third, and even more distant cousins as well. (Several American Indian tribes, such as the Shoshone, followed this pattern.) Other societies consider it incestuous to marry one's mother's sister's, or father's brother's, children, but may expect—or even require—that one should marry one's mother's brother's, or father's sister's, children. Biologically, of course, each type of cousin is equally close; but social norms define one union as revolting, the other as desirable. A few societies actually extend the taboo to social as well as sexual behavior. Among the Nama Hottentots, a brother and sister could not be alone together or even speak to one another, and a Crow husband could not talk to or even look at his mother-in-law.

The origin of the incest taboo is not, as is often assumed, the fear of mental or physical degeneration that may result from inbreeding. Such degeneration is by no means inevitable; inbreeding can sometimes reinforce desirable as well as undesirable traits. Morever, any ill effects of inbreeding might take place too slowly and erratically to be observable within the life span of a generation or two, so it is unlikely that peoples in simple, preindustrial societies would have linked cause and effect in such cases. The incest taboo, it seems, arose for three main reasons. First, it prevents rivalries and hostilities within the family. If incest were permitted, a father, for example, might be both the lover and disciplinarian of his daughter, and his daughter might be the rival of his wife. Second, the taboo prevents role confusions within the family. Without it, the offspring of a father-daughter union, for example, might be simulta-

neously the son and grandson of his own father. The family might be so dislocated that it could barely survive. Third, the incest taboo ensures that offspring marry into other kinship networks, thus creating the wider social and economic alliances that families would need to survive hardships ranging from famines to feuds.

Other Variations

One respect in which societies vary is that some are very specific about whom people may or should marry as well as whom they may not. Among some Arab peoples, a man has an absolute right to marry his father's brother's daughter, and he may demand a substantial gift from her family if he chooses not to do so. In several societies, a widow is automatically expected to marry her brother-in-law. Among some Australian aborigines, a man may marry only a woman in a specific group within a particular subsection of the opposite half of his tribe.

In advanced industrial societies it is generally assumed that marriage is founded on romantic love between the partners and that the choice of a mate should be left to the individual. But this concept of romantic love is entirely unknown in many societies and is considered laughable or tragic in many others. In most traditional societies, marriage is regarded as a practical economic arrangement or a matter of family alliances, not a love match. The marriage is accordingly negotiated by the parents of the partners, often with little or no consideration of their children's wishes. If love is a feature of these marriages at all, it is expected to be a result and not a cause of the union. The economic aspect of these marriages is especially apparent in those societies in which an intending groom must pay a bride-price to his prospective father-in-law. This practice is especially widespread in sub-Saharan Africa, where nearly all of the tribes expect a groom to exchange cattle for the bride.

Another norm that is usually taken for granted in the Western world is that the biological father should also play the social role of father, but in many societies this role is allocated instead to the mother's eldest brother. In these cases the biological father may have no social or economic responsibility for his children, although he is married to their mother. However, he may have to take responsibility for the children of his sisters. An extreme example of this practice existed in the nineteenth century among the Nayar of southern India. Before puberty, Nayar sisters were simultaneously married to the same man. But after three days the partners were divorced; the husband received gifts from the girls' family and then had nothing more to do with them. The women could then receive an unlimited number of lovers, and their eldest brother became responsible for any offspring (Gough, 1959).

In all Western nations, the law insists that a man have only one wife, and a woman only one husband, at a time, but this ideal is held by a minority of the societies of the world. In a survey of evidence from 238 societies, George Murdock (1949) found that only 43 insisted on restriction to one mate at a time. In 4 of the remaining societies a woman was permitted to have more than one husband, and in all the rest a man was allowed to have more than one wife, a ratio that reflects yet again the superior power and privileges of the male partner in the family institution. (Most of the societies in Murdock's sample were small-scale, preindustrial ones; the bulk of the world's population, of course, lives in larger, more industrialized societies in which it is normal to have only one spouse at a time.)

Another traditional Western assumption has been that people should not have premarital or extramarital sexual experience, a value still very strongly held by many people in industrial societies. In cross-cultural terms, however, this belief is something of an exotic curiosity. After a survey of the evidence from a sample of some 250 societies, Murdock concluded: "It seems unlikely that a general prohibition of sexual relations outside marriage occurs in as many as five percent of the peoples of the earth." Most societies accept premarital sexual experimentation with indifference or little disapproval. As Bronislaw Malinowski (1922) pointed out in his study of the Trobriand Islanders of the western Pacific, this practice can be functional, for it allows the partners to test their compatibility before they marry.

Children born of these nonmarital unions do not necessarily present a problem. They are legitimated either through their mother's subsequent marriage (not necessarily to the biological father) or through the taking of the social role of father by the mother's brother or father. In a few societies, such as the Mentawei of Indonesia, a woman must give birth before she can marry, for she is expected to prove her fertility to potential husbands. In most societies, the idea of virgin marriage is ludicrous; historically the concept has been largely restricted to the Middle East and to those cultures whose religions derive from that area—Judaism, Christianity, and Islam. Many societies also allow extramarital sex, although the privilege is far more often granted to the husband than to the wife. The traditional Eskimos were one of several peoples that practiced spouse-sharing under certain circumstances. As a good host, the Eskimo husband would automatically offer his wife to a male guest for the night, and both husband and wife might be deeply offended if the offer were refused.

Figure 14.3 The ideal that a husband should have several wives is still widely held in many parts of the world, and historically has been the favored marriage form of most societies. This picture shows a man in Turkey with several of his wives and their children. In most traditional societies, a man's prestige is linked to the number of his wives, and a large family is often an economic asset.

Americans generally assume that married partners should be adults of much the same age, although certain exceptions are made for an older man and a younger woman. Some societies offer strikingly contrasting patterns. The Kadara of Nigeria marry infants to one another. The Chuckchee of Siberia, believing that parental care is the best way of cementing the marriage bond, allow adult women to marry males of only two or three years of age; the new wives then look after the boys until they are old enough to assume their husbandly duties. And among the Tiwi of Australia, adult males marry females even before they are conceived. (See the reading "Courtship and Marriage Among the Tiwi" at the end of this chapter.)

Many of these practices may appear very peculiar to us. But we must recognize that our own practices would appear no less quaint and bizarre to other peoples and that our existing family system cannot necessarily be taken for granted as the only sensible or "right" one.

The Analysis of Family Patterns

How can we impose some conceptual order on such a wide range of family patterns? Sociologists find it possible to analyze all family types in terms of six basic dimensions.

Marriage Form

A marriage may be either *monogamous,* involving one man and one woman, or *polygamous,* involving a spouse of one sex and two or more spouses of the opposite sex. If the husband has more than one wife, the marriage form is called *polygyny;* if the wife has more than one husband, it is called *polyandry.* Although most societies favor polygyny rather than monogamy, most men in the world have only one wife—partly because the societies that insist on monogamy contain the bulk of the world's population, and partly because there are not enough women to permit widespread polygyny even in societies that favor it. Polyandry occurs only under exceptional conditions. The Toda of India, for example, practice female infanticide, so they have a large surplus of males.

Preferred Partners

Some groups expect or require members to marry outside the group, a pattern called *exogamy.* The Aranda of Australia, for example, divide their entire society into two

sections, and individuals may marry only someone from the opposite section. Exogamy is useful in building alliances between different groups. Other groups expect or require their members to marry within the group, a pattern called *endogamy.* Religious, racial, and ethnic groups generally practice endogamy, either because of prejudice or lack of contact between them and other groups, or as a means of maintaining their group solidarity. Many groups, such as American blacks and Jews, are primarily endogamous but accept some exogamous marriages.

Family Form

All family systems can be roughly categorized into one of two types. In the *extended family,* more than two generations of a kinship line live together, either in the same home or in adjacent dwellings. The head of the entire family is usually the eldest male, and all adults share some responsibility for child-rearing and other tasks. The extended family, found in most traditional, preindustrial societies, can be very large; it may contain several adult offspring of the head of the family, together with all their spouses and children. In the *nuclear family,* which is the dominant pat-

Figure 14.4

"First we were an extended family, then we were a nuclear family, and now we're divorced."

Drawing by Wm. Hamilton; © 1975
The New Yorker Magazine

tern in virtually all modern industrialized societies, the family group consists only of the parents and any dependent children they may have, and it lives apart from other relatives.

Residence Pattern

A newly married couple may be expected to live in an extended family with the father of the husband, the *patrilocal* pattern. Or they may be expected to live with the family of the wife, the *matrilocal* pattern. Increasingly commonly, they may establish a nuclear family in a new place of residence of their own, the *neolocal* pattern. Neolocal residence is the usual practice in modern industrialized societies.

Authority Relationships

Patterns of authority between husband and wife are always affected by the personalities of the spouses, but they generally follow the norms of the surrounding society. In nearly all societies the prevailing pattern is a *patriarchal* one in which the husband has the final say in family matters. There is no true *matriarchal* system in which women have final authority, although several societies give the wife greater influence than the husband in some domestic areas. Some matriarchal families are found in many societies, however, although never as the norm. They are matriarchal usually by default, through the death or desertion of the husband. A third and newly emerging pattern is that of the *egalitarian* family. In this pattern, which is becoming increasingly common in the modern world, husband and wife have a more or less equal say in family matters.

Descent and Inheritance

Descent may be traced, and property passed on, in one of three basic ways. Under the *patrilineal* system, descent and inheritance pass through the male side of the family. The mother's relatives are not considered kin, and females do not inherit property rights. Under the *matrilineal* system, the reverse is the case; the father's relatives are not regarded as kin, and property passes only through the female line. Under the *bilateral* system—more familiar to us but practiced by less than half the peoples of the world—descent and inheritance are traced through both sides of the family. The relatives of both parents are considered kin, and property may pass to both males and females.

The Transformation of the Family

Over the past two centuries or so, there has been a major, world-wide change in family patterns, involving the general collapse of the ancient extended family system and its replacement by the new nuclear system. In all industrialized countries, the small, isolated nuclear family is rapidly becoming, or has already become, the norm, and in the developing countries the extended family is facing disintegration as industrialization advances. As a result, neolocal residence has rapidly replaced patrilocal or matrilocal residence; the ideal of polygamy has steadily given way to the ideal of monogamy; patriarchal families have become more egalitarian; kinship is almost everywhere less important in social life; and people have come to see marriage more in terms of personal goals and less as an economic arrangement or kinship alliance.

This transformation is, of course, a general trend, not a hard and fast rule. Except among some Indian tribes, the extended family was never dominant in the United States or Canada, even in the days when they were agricultural societies. The nuclear family was fairly common in preindustrial Europe, and some extended families are still to be found in even the most advanced industrial societies. In some parts of the world, the emergence of the nuclear family preceded and probably facilitated industrialization; in some, the two processes took place more or less simultaneously; in others, industrialization seems to have provoked the later collapse of the extended family (Laslett, 1971, 1977; Laslett and Wall, 1972; Shorter, 1975; Stone, 1977). Nevertheless, the overall pattern is unmistakable: in industrialized societies, traditional family forms have given way to others that are better suited to the changed conditions of social and economic life.

The extended family is highly functional in a traditional, preindustrial society. It usually serves as a self-contained productive unit in which tasks can be divided among the members to ensure the optimum economic cooperation in agriculture, hunting, craft work, or other means of subsistence. Because every able-bodied member is an economic asset, large families are highly desirable. The extended family also provides many social and personal advantages to its members. If one of them is ill, others may take his or her place; if a family member dies, the surviving members are close at hand to give emotional support to the

Figure 14.5 The small nuclear family of parents and dependent children has become the dominant form in the modern world. The traditional extended family, in which many relatives live together, is no longer functional in a rapidly changing society.

bereaved. Old people usually have an honored and respected role in the extended family and spend their last years in the close company and care of the social group that matters to them the most.

In the urban environment typical of modern industrial societies, however, the extended family becomes dysfunctional. William Goode (1963) points out that there are a number of reasons why industrialization makes the nuclear family the more functional and therefore the dominant form in the modern world.

1. Life in an industrial society requires geographic mobility—workers must go to where the jobs and promotions are. They cannot do so if kinship obligations tie them to a particular area and prevent prolonged separation from relatives.

2. An industrial society offers a wide range of economic opportunities and with it the chance for people to change their social statuses. Socially mobile people have education, interests, and life experiences different from those whose status is traditional and static. The bonds of common interest between the relatives—who in the extended family would all live much the same lives—are therefore loosened and even shattered.

3. In an urban environment, formal, nonkin organizations and institutions—corporations, schools, hospitals, governments, welfare agencies, day-care centers, and media—assume many of the functions that were once the prerogative of the family. As the extended family has less to offer, people seek a new foundation for married life—close companionship with a single spouse and a deepened appreciation of their children as individuals rather than as productive assets.

4. Industrialism emphasizes personal achievement, not the circumstances of one's birth, as the route to success. This emphasis reverses the traditional pattern and makes kinship less significant as a determinant of social status. Individual goals become more important than kinship obligations, and people expect personal freedom in their choice of mate and place of residence.

5. In a modern society, children become an economic liability rather than an asset. The parents get no financial benefits from the vast expense of clothing, feeding, and educating their offspring: almost as soon as the young are

able to earn a living, they leave home and prepare to found their own separate families. People therefore find it convenient to restrict the size of their households, preferring to live in independent units away from other relatives.

Yet although the nuclear family is functional in modern society, it suffers from a number of dysfunctions as well—and this is the key to understanding many of its present difficulties. The family has been stripped of many of its former functions, but it has had new burdens imposed on it. In the extended family, the individual could turn for support to an array of relatives. Today the married partners can turn only to each other, and sometimes demand more from one another than either can provide. If members of an extended family were for some reason unable to play their roles, other members could take them over. In the nuclear family, on the other hand, the death, prolonged illness, or unemployment of a breadwinner can throw the entire family into severe crisis. In the extended family, people rarely had expectations of romantic love with their spouses; marriage was a practical, common-sense affair. In the nuclear family, far higher expectations exist, and if they are not fulfilled—and often they cannot be—discontent and unhappiness may result. The old had a meaningful role in the extended family, but they may have no role in the nuclear family. In our society an elderly person who loses a spouse may have to live alone or in an old-age home. In such a situation feelings of isolation, loneliness, and loss of personal worth are all too common.

Marriage and Family in America

"Love and marriage," an old popular song tells us, "go together like a horse and carriage." A compelling assumption in American society is that everyone will fall in love, will marry, will have children, and will have an emotionally satisfying lifetime relationship with the chosen partner. It is probably true that most of us fall in love at some point; it is certainly true that nearly all of us marry and have children; but it is likely that a great many of us—perhaps the majority—find that married life falls below our expectations. To find out what can go wrong and why, we must look in more detail at American family patterns and at romantic love, courtship, marriage, and marital breakdown and divorce.

The American Family

How does the "typical" American family fit into the family patterns we outlined earlier? First, it is *monogamous:* we may marry only one person at a time. Second, it is generally *endogamous:* most people marry within their own racial, ethnic, religious, and class group. Third, the system is *nuclear,* although occasionally a grandparent or other relative may live with the family group. Fourth, it is *neolocal,* with newlyweds almost always establishing a home of their own away from their families of orientation. Fifth, it is increasingly *egalitarian;* there are still strong patriarchal tendencies, but wives are becoming much more assertive than they were even a decade ago. Sixth, the American family is *bilateral.* Relatives of both husband and wife are regarded as kin, and property generally passes to both sons and daughters. There is one strong patrilineal element, however: both wife and children usually take the last name of the husband.

There have always been exceptions to this ideal pattern in the United States. For example, the Mormons openly practiced polygamy until 1896, when their acceptance of monogamy was made a condition for the admission of their home territory of Utah to the Union. A number of communes in the nineteenth century advocated and practiced free love, and similar communes exist today, many of them dating from the sixties and early seventies, when this life-style enjoyed popularity among young members of the "hippie" counterculture. Before the Civil War, slaves were not allowed to marry, but they were encouraged to mate in order to increase their number. There remain many ethnic and social-class differences among families in the United States, as is true elsewhere in the world. For example, lower-class families are more likely to be matriarchal by default (through the absence of the father) and to retain stronger ties with other kin than middle- and upper-class families (Gans, 1962b; Mindel and Habenstein, 1978; Schneider and Smith, 1978).

The most marked divergence from the ideal pattern may be among black Americans. In a controversial report prepared for the federal government, Daniel Moynihan (1965) argued that a major source of the problems faced by

Arrival of a new batch of lambs for the Mormon fold at Salt Lake City, Utah—the Deacons, Elders, Saints, and Prophets of the "New Dispensation" selecting additions to their family.

Figure 14.6 There have always been exceptions to the general American pattern of the monogamous nuclear family. The Mormons institutionalized polygamy, a practice that scandalized many other Americans. This anti-Mormon propaganda cartoon was published in 1880.

the black community was an unstable family structure. Moynihan pointed out that in 23 percent of all black homes the father was absent, that 24 percent of black births were illegitimate, and that 36 percent of black children were living in broken homes. A matriarchal family system, Moynihan argued, was the main obstacle to racial equality. This view has been heavily criticized. Viewed another way, Moynihan's data indicated that the overwhelming majority of blacks did have a stable family environment: 77 percent of the families had a father present, 76 percent of the children were legitimate, and 64 percent of the children were living with both parents—leaving the many social disadvantages suffered by this majority still to be explained. Moynihan's thesis seems to be a classic case of unintentionally blaming the victim for a fault that lies elsewhere, in this case in the institutionalized prejudice and discrimination of American society. It is true that fatherless families are found disproportionately in the black community, and that female-headed black families suffer exceptionally high rates of poverty; but it is equally clear that most black families conform to the pattern of the wider society (Willie, 1976).

Romantic Love

Romantic love is a culture trait found primarily in industrialized societies. Elsewhere in the world, pragmatic considerations rather than flights of fancy are often used to make a choice of partner, and romantic love is seen as an unfortunate inconvenience that gets in the way of the ordinary, rational process of mate selection. Traces of this attitude persist in the American upper classes, where daughters are expected to marry "well"—that is, to a male who is eligible by reason of family background and earning potential. Most Americans, however, see romantic love as essential for a successful marriage, and tend to look askance at anyone who marries for a more practical reason in which love plays no part.

The phenomenon of romantic love occurs when two young people meet and find one another personally and physically attractive. They become mutually absorbed, start to behave in what appears to be a flighty, even irrational manner, decide that they are right for one another, and may then enter a marriage whose success is expected to be guaranteed by their enduring love (Greenfield, 1965;

Reiss, 1971). Behavior of this kind is portrayed and warmly endorsed throughout American popular culture, by books, magazines, comics, records, popular songs, movies, and TV.

Romantic love is a noble ideal, and it can certainly provide a basis for the spouses to "live happily ever after." But a marriage can equally well be founded on much more practical considerations—as indeed they have been in most societies throughout most of history. Why is romantic love of such importance in the modern world? The reason seems to be that it has the following basic functions in maintaining the institution of the nuclear family (Goode, 1959):

1. Romantic love helps the young partners to loosen their bonds with their family of orientation, a step that is essential if a new neolocal nuclear family is to be created. Their total absorption in one another facilitates a transfer of commitment from existing family and kin to a new family of procreation, something that would be unlikely to happen under the extended family system.

2. Romantic love provides the couple with emotional support in the difficulties that they face in establishing a new life on their own. This love would not be so necessary in an extended family, where the relatives are able to confront problems cooperatively. In an extended family, in fact, romantic love might even be dysfunctional, for it could distract the couple from their wider obligations to other kin.

3. Romantic love serves as a bait to lure people into marriage. Whereas in the extended family system of traditional societies, it is automatically assumed that people will marry, in the modern world, people have considerable choice over whether or not they will get married. A contract to form a lifelong commitment to another person is not necessarily a very tempting proposition, however: to some, the prospect may look more like a noose than like a bed of roses. Without feelings of romantic love, many people might have no incentive to marry.

To most of us, particularly to those who are in love, romantic love seems to be the most natural thing in the world, but sociological analysis shows that it is a purely cultural product, arising in certain societies for specific reasons. In a different time or in a different society, you might never fall in love, nor would you expect to.

Figure 14.7 Romantic love, captured in this idealistic painting by the artist Pierre Auguste Cot, is a culture trait found primarily in the industrial societies of the world. Although Americans take romantic love for granted, it is unknown in many other societies, where far more practical considerations determine who will marry whom.

Courtship and Marriage

A courtship system is essentially a marriage market. (The metaphor of the "market" may seem a little unromantic, but, in fact, the participants do attempt to "sell" their assets—physical appearance, personal charms, talents and interests, and career prospects.) In the matter of mate selection, different courtship systems vary according to how much choice they permit the individual. The United States probably allows more freedom of choice than any other society. A parent who attempts to interfere in the dating habits or marriage plans of a son or daughter is considered meddlesome and is more likely to alienate than persuade the young lover.

In our predominantly urban and anonymous society, young people—often with access to automobiles—have an exceptional degree of privacy in their courting. The practice of dating enables them to find out about one another, to improve their own interpersonal skills in the market, to engage in sexual experimentation if they so wish, and finally to select a marriage partner.

Who marries whom, then? In general, the American mate-selection process is *homogamous:* individuals marry others much like themselves (Winch, 1958; Burgess and Wallin, 1973; Udry, 1974; Carter and Glick, 1976). Among the social characteristics that seem to attract people to one another are the following:

Similar age. Married partners tend to be of roughly the same age. Husbands are usually older than their wives, but this difference in age has been gradually declining throughout the century, from about 4 years in 1900 to about 2.5 years today.

Social class. Most people marry within their own social class. The reasons are obvious: we tend to live in class-segregated neighborhoods, to meet mostly people of the same class, and to share class-specific tastes and interests. Interclass marriages are relatively more common, however, among college students.

Religion. Most marriages are between people sharing the same religious faith, although Protestant interdenominational marriages are fairly common. Religious bodies generally oppose interfaith marriages, on the grounds that they may lead to personal conflicts, disagreements over the faith in which children should be raised, and an undermining of belief in a particular doctrine. Many people change their religion to that of their partner before marriage.

Education. Husbands and wives generally have a similar educational level, and some degree of intellectual parity seems to be demanded by marital partners. The college campus is, of course, a marriage market in its own right, and college-educated people are especially likely to marry people of similar educational achievement.

Racial and ethnic background. Members of racial and ethnic groups are more likely to marry within their own group than outside it. In particular, interracial marriages

Figure 14.8 Young people in the United States have exceptional freedom to pursue courtship in privacy and to make their own choice of marital partners. In many other societies courtship is closely supervised by the parents of the young people, but such intervention would be regarded as meddlesome by most young Americans.

are extremely rare. Until the sixties, several states had laws prohibiting interracial marriages, and such marriages still attract some social disapproval. Interracial marriages between blacks and whites are particularly unusual; in the majority of these cases, the husband is black and the wife white.

Physical characteristics. People tend to marry partners who are physically similar to themselves in height, weight, and even in hair color, state of health, and basal metabolism.

Cupid's arrow, then, does not strike at random. Despite extensive research by psychologists, there is little certainty about the personality characteristics that attract partners to one another (Berscheid and Walster, 1978). But the social characteristics of marriage partners are much easier to establish, and all research findings point in the same direction: we tend to choose as mates people who have social characteristics similar to our own.

Marital Breakdown

The divorce rate in the United States is believed to be the highest in the world, and statistics on the subject are often quoted as conclusive evidence of the decay of the family. But these statistics can be misleading, for they may be distorted by other factors that exaggerate or conceal the extent of marital breakdown.

Acually, there are three different methods of calculating the divorce rate. All three, however, yield a roughly similar picture of a rate that is high and increasing (Glick, 1979; Hacker, 1979).

1. *Extrapolation of patterns.* Data on existing trends in divorce can be extrapolated into the future to show what the fate of new marriages is likely to be. This evidence indicates that about 40 percent of the marriages currently entered into will end in divorce, the average duration of these ill-fated marriages being 6.6 years.

2. *Divorces per 1000 population.* The number of divorces in a given year can be expressed as a rate for every 1000 members of the population. In 1915, the rate was 1 per 1000; in 1940, 2 per 1000; in 1970, 3.5 per 1000; and in 1979, 5.3 per 1000.

3. *Ratio of marriages to divorces.* The number of marriages and divorces in a given year can be compared as a ratio. In 1920 there was about one divorce for every seven marriages; in 1940, one for every six; in 1960, one for every four, in 1970, one for every three; and in 1979, one for every two—approximately 1.2 million divorces and 2.3 million marriages.

The third of these methods can be particularly deceptive to a careless or untrained reader, for it can seem to suggest that divorce is now half as common as marriage. But the statistics are distorted by the fact that the population that is eligible for divorce is a huge one, containing everybody who is married, while the population eligible for marriage is comparatively small, consisting primarily of unmarried people between the ages of eighteen and thirty: not surprisingly, therefore, the ratio seems high in any given year. No matter which method is used, however, it is important to recognize that divorce statistics tell us only about the rate at which marriages are being formally dissolved—not about the rate at which they are breaking down. A rise in the divorce rate does not necessarily mean that more marriages are souring; it may merely mean that fewer people are willing to remain in an unhappy union. Also, the factors that influence the decision to marry or to divorce vary over time. The divorce rate, for example, may be pushed up by new laws that make divorces easier to get, or by better employment opportunities for women. The marriage rate, on the other hand, may be influenced by such factors as the proportion of the population aged eighteen to thirty at a given time, or by current social attitudes toward the desirability of marriage rather than some alternative, such as living together. Moreover, statistics on divorce do not tell the whole story. Many people have separated from their partners without bothering to go through the process of divorce, and an unknown number of marriages are merely "empty shells," in which the unloving partners stay together out of mere habit, because of religious scruples, or "for the sake of the children."

Divorce constitutes official social recognition that a marriage has failed, and it can be a traumatic experience for all concerned. Until a few years ago, most states granted a divorce only if the "guilt" of one partner could be proved. Ugly and acrimonious court cases resulted, with one spouse accusing the other of desertion, cruelty, adultery, or failure

MARRIAGE AND DIVORCE RATES: 1940 TO 1979

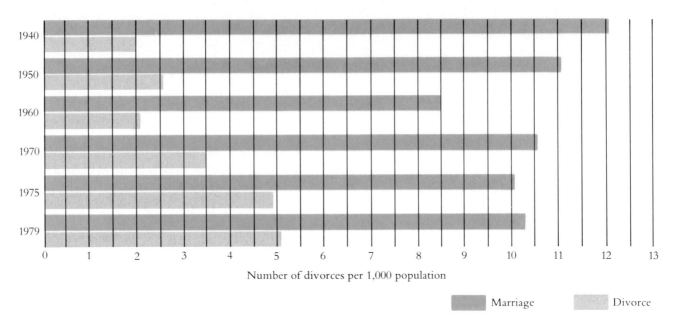

Number of divorces per 1,000 population

Marriage   Divorce

Source. U.S. Bureau of the Census, 1980.

Figure 14.9 In 1940 Americans married at a rate of 12.1 per 1000 people. The rate of divorce per 1000 population was a mere 2.0. As this chart indicates, the rate of divorce has steadily increased over the last three decades, and the rate of marriage has fluctuated and decreased only slightly. By the end of the past decade, the rate of divorce was one-half the marriage rate.

to provide economic support, but the actual grounds on which the divorce was granted often had little relationship to the real reasons for the marital breakdown. Most states now offer a "no fault" divorce on grounds of simple incompatibility, but there is still room for fierce resentment over alimony payments and the custody of offspring. Children are present in over 70 percent of the families that break up through divorce: more than a million children are involved every year.

The children inevitably suffer through the divorce of their parents, although many people believe that it may be even more emotionally disturbing for them to remain in a home where the marriage is deeply unhappy. The ex-wife, may face severe economic problems, especially if she has to raise young children. Some 37 percent of the American families in which the father is absent live below the poverty line; mothers who have to stay at home to take care of their children may have to become long-term welfare recipients. Only a quarter of divorced mothers receive child-support payments, partly because almost half of the former husbands ignore court orders and default on their obligations. Emotionally, both divorcing parties may be in for a difficult time. American social life is tailored to the needs of couples, and divorced partners may experience great loneliness and isolation. Divorce ruptures one's personal universe; it is no coincidence that men are much more likely to be fired from their jobs after divorce, nor that the death rate for divorced people is significantly higher than that for married people, at all age levels (Goode, 1956; Plateris, 1970; R. Weiss, 1975).

Who gets divorced? The social characteristics of divorce-prone partners have been well established. Divorces are especially common among urban couples, among those who marry very young, among those who marry after only short acquaintance, and among those whose relatives and friends disapprove of the marriage. In general, the people who are most likely to get divorced are those who, statistically, would be considered the least likely to marry. And the greater the wife's ability to support herself, the more likely she is to leave an unhappy marriage. Partners who have been married before are more likely to become involved in subsequent divorce. Most divorces take place within the first few years of marriage; the longer a marriage lasts, the less likely it is to end in divorce (Goode, 1956, 1976; Udry, 1974; Weiss, 1975; Carter and Glick, 1976).

Causes of Marital Breakdown

There are many causes for the collapse of marriages, but the following seem to be the main ones.

Stress on the Nuclear Family

As we have seen, the nuclear family is highly vulnerable if the breadwinner is for any reason unwilling or unable to meet economic obligations. This is especially true in the United States; in most other advanced industrial societies the state offers much more support to the family in the form of family allowances, preferential housing, child-care programs, free childhood medical and dental care, and free college education. In addition, the spouses in a nuclear

family have a very strong mutual dependency, especially after the children have left home, and may make heavy demands on one another for emotional support. The failure of one partner to meet the expectations of the other jeopardizes the marriage in a way that would hardly be possible under the extended family system.

The Fading of Romantic Love

Americans are thoroughly socialized into the expectation that romantic love will make their marriage happy ever after. But the heady joys of romantic love are usually short-lived, and the excitement of the earlier relationship is lessened or even lost in the daily routines of job and housework, diapers and dishwashing, mortgages and bills.

Figure 14.10 Americans are socialized to regard romantic love as the basis of marriage. When a marriage settles down into the ordinary routines of housework and job, romantic love may fade, and many Americans interpret this as a sign that their marriage is failing.

This does not mean that the partners no longer love one another; it is just that their love is likely to be of a different kind. It can be mature, companionable, and deeply fulfilling—but Americans are not socialized to recognize or appreciate this change. Believing that romantic love is the only possible basis for a successful marriage, many people lose faith in their marriages and may start looking for romance elsewhere.

The Changing Role of Women

In the past, the role of the wife in an American marriage was assumed to be that of housekeeper, child-rearer, and nurturant supporter of a husband who is active in the world beyond the home. More and more American women are rejecting this role, and in doing so are challenging the established structure of the nuclear family. Women are no longer confined to the home for much of their lives through pregnancy and the care of infants. The average family now has only 2.3 children, and the average woman now has her last child at the age of only twenty-six. Traditional family norms make little provision for the woman who wants an independent career, and even less for the family in which the wife earns more than the husband and becomes the primary breadwinner. The growing economic independence of women makes it much easier for them to divorce their mates, and it challenges the role relationship on which the nuclear family has been based (Kanter, 1978; Rubin, 1979).

Sexual Permissiveness

The development and widespread availability of contraceptives have separated two quite different functions of sexual relations—procreation and recreation. In the days when intercourse was likely to lead to pregnancy, it made sense for sexual intercourse to be restricted to marital partners, for our society makes little provision for the proper care of illegitimate children. But if the prospect of pregnancy is removed, many of the inhibitions against the use of sex for recreation disappear also. The nuclear family is founded on an assumption of monogamous fidelity, but increasing sexual permissiveness encourages many people to look outside their marriages for sexual satisfaction or, if they are unmarried, to enjoy sexual experience before marriage. The great majority of American men have engaged in premarital and/or extramarital intercourse, as have over half of American women. This experience gives the partners a standard by which to measure the performance of their spouses—an opportunity that the partners in a traditional virgin marriage did not have—and the spouses may be found wanting. Changing sexual norms inevitably threaten a family system based on the assumption that the partners will have an exclusive and mutually gratifying sexual relationship.

The Future of the Family

The American family is changing. The alterations that it is undergoing cannot be halted by laws or sermons, for they are the inevitable products of much more encompassing social and economic changes. But what will become of the family? We can gain some insights into its future by examining current trends in the institution, and by looking at some of the alternatives that already exist, if only in experimental form.

Current Trends

The changes in the family are perhaps even more extensive than is generally realized. Consider, for example, the familiar stereotype of the family consisting of a husband who works and a wife who stays home to care for their two dependent children. Such a family is not the norm, nor anything like it: it comprises less than 8 percent of the households in the United States.

One reason for the demise of that family is the sharp increase in the number of women in the work force. In 1940, only 27.4 percent of adult women worked; today, over 50 percent do, and most of these have children under the age of eighteen. The two-paycheck, dual-career marriage is now typical, and the increased economic power of wives is undermining the remaining patriarchal elements in the family system. It is still the case, of course, that most husbands earn more than their wives and that the husband's career is considered the more important of the two (if the husband is transferred or promoted to a job elsewhere in the country, the wife is expected to give up her career to accompany him, but the reverse expectation rarely applies). In the long run, however, American marriages will become more fully egalitarian as the incomes of the spouses become more equal (Rappoport and Rappoport, 1976; Hall and Hall, 1979; Bird, 1979).

Another significant change is the growing tendency of young people to postpone marriage. The average age of first marriage is now 24.0 for men and 21.5 for women, meaning that today's newlyweds are on average 1.5 years older than their counterparts in 1960. In that year, 28 percent of the women aged 20 to 24 had never married; two decades later, over 45 percent had stayed single. In addition, the number of people overall who live alone is rising at an astonishing rate: in 1979, one of every five households in the nation consisted of just one person, an increase of over 40 percent since 1970. Such statistics remind us how far we have come from the extended family household of time past (Glick, 1979).

Families are also getting smaller. The average family formed around the turn of the century included four children; that formed in the 1930s had three; and those formed today expect to have, on average, only two. After declining fairly consistently throughout the century, the American birth rate now seems to have stabilized at one of the lowest levels in the world. Partly because of this factor and partly because life expectancy has been steadily increasing for several generations, the average couple who remain married now spend about fourteen more years together in a childless home than their great-grandparents did (Glick, 1979).

A trend that is causing much alarm is the increase in illegitimate births, especially among teen-age girls. The illegitimacy rate rose very rapidly between World War II and the early 1970s: in 1940, the rate was 7.1 births per thousand women of childbearing age, but by 1970 it had risen to 25.7 per thousand. Then the rate dropped noticeably in 1971, when legal abortions became widely available, but it has now started to rise once more. One reason is that unmarried women are becoming more sexually active: by age nineteen, two-thirds of them have had intercourse, mostly premarital; and only about one-fourth of this group regularly practices birth control. The second reason is that fewer women are willing to enter "shotgun" marriages (although a quarter of all brides are either pregnant or already mothers by the time they reach the altar), and more of them are deciding to have and keep their babies rather than undergo abortions. One in every four women gets pregnant before the age of nineteen, and 80 percent of these pregnancies are premarital. By the end of the 1970s

about 14 percent of all births were illegitimate (Westoff, 1976; Zelnick et al., 1979).

A final trend of great significance is the increase in the number of one-parent families, particularly those headed by women. In 1979 almost one in every five American families was maintained by one parent, an increase of nearly 80 percent since the start of the decade. In some 17 percent of all families only the mother was present; in 2 percent of families, the father was the only parent. Indeed, during the decade of the 1970s, only one type of family showed a decline in absolute numbers: the household containing a married couple and their children.

Alternative Patterns

Several alternatives to the established nuclear pattern already exist. The following seem to be the most common (de Lora and de Lora, 1975; Stinnet and Birdsong, 1978; Murstein, 1978).

Serial Monogamy

A growing number of people marry more than once. In fact, the great majority of divorced partners marry someone else within a few years of divorcing. Now that divorces are easier to get and provoke less social disapproval than ever before, many people embark on a career of "serial" marriages. Indeed, the more often people have been divorced, the more likely it is that their subsequent marriage will end in the same way. Jessie Bernard (1973) suggests that serial marriage makes having several spouses more common in America than polygamy does in other societies. Serial monogamy allows the partners to maintain a commitment to marriage, if not to one spouse.

Communes

There have been many experiments in the United States aimed at establishing communal groups whose members may share both sexual relations and the task of raising children. There is great variation in the norms that operate within these communes. A few insist on free love, but in most of them the adults tend to pair off with one another, at least for periods of a few weeks or months. The limited evidence available suggests that "group marriages" are highly unstable (Ellis, 1970; Constantine, 1978), and despite the range of family systems in other cultures, an-

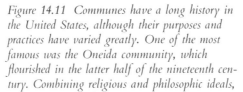

Figure 14.11 Communes have a long history in the United States, although their purposes and practices have varied greatly. One of the most famous was the Oneida community, which flourished in the latter half of the nineteenth century. Combining religious and philosophic ideals, *the members tried to set up an alternative community in which, at least in theory, all adults were married to one another and were parents to the group's children. Modern communes display a similar variety, although "free love" is probably not a typical feature.*

thropologists have never found a society that has institutionalized such a system. Communes with rather more restrictive sexual patterns have persisted for years and even decades, however. Although the appeal of communes seems to be rather limited, there is little doubt that they do represent an alternative family system (Melville, 1972; Muncy, 1974).

Exchange of Partners

"Swinging," or the mutually-agreed-to exchange of partners for the purposes of periodic extramarital sex, has become a popular pastime in some restricted sections of American society. The practice seems to appeal to people who wish to maintain their marriage but are dissatisfied with the sexual exclusiveness of their relationship. Research on "swinging" indicates that the participants are primarily middle class, middle-aged, and rather conservative in other matters, ranging from politics to tastes in furnishing. An elaborate communications network exists for "swingers," based on advertisements in a number of specialized magazines. It has been estimated that hundreds of thousands of Americans participate in the activity (Bartell, 1974; Denfield and Gordon, 1974; Murstein, 1978a).

"Open" Marriage

Some spouses want to make many of the mutual commitments implied by marriage, but are unwilling to accept certain of the obligations that marriage traditionally im-

poses. Their response is the "open" marriage—essentially, one in which the partners agree to certain flexible arrangements, sometimes including the right of each to have extramarital sexual relationships. In some cases the spouses draw up a formal contract specifying what the various rights and responsibilities of the partners are to be—a self-consciously "do-it-yourself" approach to the problem of how to modify existing family patterns to meet the needs of changing life-styles (O'Neil and O'Neil, 1973; Knapp and Whitehurst, 1978).

Cohabitation

Cohabitation, or "living together," is an increasingly common type of domestic and sexual arrangement, particularly among young people. Although it might have caused a minor neighborhood scandal a few decades ago, cohabitation is now likely to be viewed with tolerance or indifference in most urban communities. The number of unmarried people of opposite sex sharing a household doubled between 1970 and 1977 and now comprises over 2 million adults, three-quarters of them under forty-five years of age. Cohabitation is particularly popular among college students; surveys have shown that about a quarter of undergraduates have tried this arrangement, and that under suitable conditions the great majority of college students would be willing to live together with someone of the opposite sex. Cohabitation has some similarities with marriage in that the partners have considerable affection for, and commitment to, one another, and their sexual relationship is usually an exclusive one. For whatever reason, however, they are wary of making the formal commitment of marriage. Nonetheless, cohabitation serves in many cases as a "trial marriage," in which the partners explicitly decide to test their compatibility before taking the plunge into married life. Since 1977, courts in several states have ruled that an agreement by unmarried partners to share their property is valid; if the arrangement breaks up, one partner can sue the other for part of the property and even for maintenance ("palimony") in much the same way as a divorced person can. Although cohabitation accounts for little more than 2 percent of couples sharing a household in the United States, it will unquestionably become a more common alternative in the future (Arafat and Yorburg, 1973; Clayton and Voss, 1977; Bower and Christopherson, 1977; Macklin, 1978; Glick, 1979).

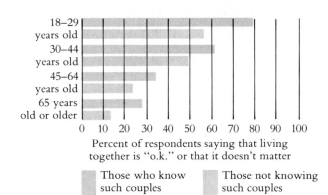

ACCEPTANCE OF UNMARRIED COUPLES LIVING TOGETHER

Percent of respondents saying that living together is "o.k." or that it doesn't matter

Those who know such couples   Those not knowing such couples

Source: The New York Times, November 28, 1977.

Figure 14.12 Americans are becoming increasingly tolerant of cohabitation, particularly if they have personal knowledge of couples who practice this life-style.

Single-Parent Families

The single-parent family is now emerging as the most common alternative to the traditional nuclear unit. As we have already noted, the main reason for this trend is the increased rate of divorce. Another factor is the increased willingness of unmarried women to keep their illegitimate children; as recently as the mid-1960s, for example, nearly two-thirds of illegitimate white babies were given away for adoption; by 1980, more than 90 percent were being kept by their mothers. The single-parent family is becoming so common that nearly half of all children born today will spend a significant portion of their lives before the age of eighteen as part of one. It should be noted, however, that the single-parent family is usually a temporary form, in that most of the parents involved either marry or remarry during the period in which they are raising their children (R. Weiss, 1979; Glick, 1979).

Figure 14.13

"We understand, Mummy. Daddy still likes you and all that, but he likes Mrs. Wilkie better."

Copyright Wm. Hamilton

Gay-Parent Families

Most homosexual men and women form stable, long-lasting relationships with a person of the same sex at some time in their lives. Changing attitudes have made these unions far more socially acceptable than in the past, and indeed some churches are now performing weddings for gay couples, although these marriages have no legal force. A more significant change, perhaps, is the willingness of many courts to grant custody of children to a gay parent—usually the mother. In some cases, families with two gay adults are created, usually when a divorced lesbian mother forms a relationship with another woman. For several years, more-

over, social welfare agencies in New York and other large cities have been placing orphaned or runaway gay teenage boys—who are unwelcome in heterosexual foster homes—in the custody of gay males, usually couples. One interesting possibility, incidentally, is suggested by the rapid advances in the availability and technology of artificial insemination: if they so choose, lesbian women may be able to become mothers without having had any heterosexual relationships at all (Frank, 1974; Tanner, 1978; Bell and Weinberg, 1978).

Remaining Single

We have already seen that a growing number of people are living alone. This increase is particularly noticeable among those under the age of thirty-five: between 1970 and 1977 the number of these young adults occupying a household alone increased by a staggering 134 percent. Although most of these people will eventually marry, it does seem likely that there will be an increase in the proportion of the population remaining single throughout life, from about 4 percent today to perhaps 8 percent or more by the end of the century. For those who do not want children and do not see marriage as a prerequisite for sexual experience, married life may seem to offer few advantages, and in fact most young people who live alone cite freedom and independence as the main reasons for their choice. It is important to recognize that remaining single is not necessarily a matter of never having found the "right" partner; for many people, it is a deliberate decision about personal life-style (M. Adam, 1976; P. Stein, 1976, Libby, 1978).

The existence of patterns such as these does not mean, however, that the nuclear family is about to disappear. Some 96 percent of all Americans get married at some point in their lives, and even the divorced are still deeply committed to marriage—their marriage rate at all ages is higher than that for single or widowed persons. What is more likely is that the United States, a pluralist society with an extraordinary range of subcultures and a strong emphasis on individualism and freedom of choice, will increasingly tolerate a variety of alternative marriage and family styles. No other society has ever endorsed more than one family form at a time, but no other society has been both as heterogeneous and as rapidly changing. The family in the

PROBABILITIES OF MARRIAGE AND REMARRIAGE

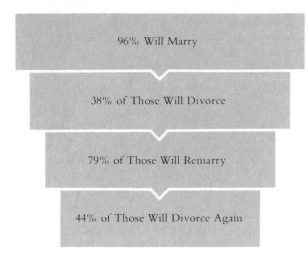

96% Will Marry

38% of Those Will Divorce

79% of Those Will Remarry

44% of Those Will Divorce Again

Source: Bureau of the Census.

Figure 14.14 Marriage remains extremely popular in American society: as this chart shows, nearly everyone gets married, and even the divorced are likely to try the experience again—and again.

sense that we defined it earlier—a relatively permanent group of related people, living together, forming an economic unit, and sharing responsibility for offspring—is here to stay as a permanent feature of human society. Of the 77.3 million households in America in 1979, three-quarters contained families of one kind or another. The most popular form of the family for the foreseeable future is the nuclear family. Whatever its disadvantages, it seems to be the most functional and satisfying family form in the modern world. As the social and economic factors that affect all institutions continue to change, the nuclear family will doubtless respond with internal structural changes, but it seems destined to remain the preferred and dominant system in all industrial societies.

Summary

1. The family is the most basic of all social institutions. It consists of a relatively permanent group whose members are related by ancestry, marriage, or adoption, who live together and form an economic unit, and whose adult members assume responsibility for the young. The family is expected to be formed through a marriage which legitimates any offspring. The family is part of a wider network of relatives, or kin.

2. The family is universal partly because it is highly functional. The main functions of the family are the regulation of sexual behavior, the replacement of members, socialization, care and protection, and social placement.

3. Conflict theorists emphasize that the family is the main institution in which male dominance of females is expressed, and they argue that the extraordinary degree of violence in the family is a symptom of its underlying tension.

4. Family patterns vary widely from one society to another; even the incest taboo takes different forms in different cultures.

5. Family patterns can be analyzed in terms of their variation along six basic dimensions: marriage form, preferred partners, family form, residence pattern, authority relationships, and descent and inheritance.

6. Industrialism and urbanization have been accompanied by a world-wide transformation of the family; the extended family is dysfunctional in the modern environment and is giving way to the nuclear form. The nuclear family, however, experiences distinctive problems resulting from the extensive reliance that the husband and wife have on one another.

7. The American family is monogamous, endogamous, nuclear, neolocal, increasingly egalitarian, and bilateral, although there are some class and racial variations on this pattern. Americans place high emphasis on romantic love, which is functional for a nuclear family system.

8. American marriage tends to be homogamous: people generally marry others with similar social characteristics.

9. The American divorce rate is very high; the partners most likely to get divorced are those whose social charac-

teristics differ markedly. The main causes of divorce are stress on the nuclear family, the fading of romantic love after marriage, the changing role of women, and certain effects of sexual permissiveness.

10. Current trends in the American family include an increase in the number of working wives; a growing tendency for marriage to be postponed and for people to live alone; the decrease in family size; the high illegitimacy rate and tendency for unwed pregnant women to have and keep their children; and the increase in the number of one-parent families, particularly those maintained by women.

11. There are a number of existing alternatives to traditional marriage and family arrangements, such as serial monogamy, communes, exchange of partners, "open" marriage, cohabitation, single-parent families, gay-parent families, and remaining single. The great majority of Americans continue to marry, however, and although a range of alternative marriage and family styles are likely to be tolerated, the nuclear family seems to be here to stay.

Important Terms

family (350)	extended family (356)
marriage (350)	nuclear family (356)
legitimate (350)	patrilocal (357)
illegitimate (350)	matrilocal (357)
kinship (350)	neolocal (357)
incest taboo (353)	patriarchal (357)
sibling (354)	matriarchal (357)
monogamy (356)	egalitarian (357)
polygamy (356)	patrilineal (357)
polygyny (356)	matrilineal (357)
polyandry (356)	bilateral (357)
exogamy (356)	homogamy (362)
endogamy (356)	

Suggested Readings

BANE, MARY J. *Here to Stay.* New York: Basic Books, 1976.

The author analyzes sociological data on the American family, and cogently argues that the institution is not declining but, rather, is changing.

BERNARD, JESSIE. *The Future of Marriage.* New York: Bantam, 1973.

A lively discussion of current and future changes in marriage and the family.

GORDON, MICHAEL. *The American Family: Past, Present, and Future.* New York: Random House, 1978.

An excellent sociological discussion of the American family, viewed in both an historical and a contemporary perspective.

LASCH, CHRISTOPHER. *Haven in a Heartless World: The Family Besieged.* New York: Basic Books, 1977.

A controversial book in which the author attributes many problems of modern society to the breakdown of the family.

MURSTEIN, BERNARD I. (ed.). *Exploring Intimate Lifestyles.* New York: Springer, 1978.

An interesting collection of articles on various emerging alternatives to the traditional family system.

SKOLNICK, ARLENE. *The Intimate Environment: Exploring Marriage and the Family.* 2nd. ed. Boston: Little, Brown, 1978.

A careful analysis of some of the problems facing the contemporary family, with an analysis of changes that are taking place in sexual behavior, marriage patterns, and child-rearing.

SPIRO, MELFORD. *Children of the Kibbutz.* Cambridge, Mass.: Harvard University Press, 1958.

A study of the Israeli kibbutz, or commune, with special attention to the process and consequences of child-rearing in this unusual setting.

STRAUSS, MURRAY A., et al. *Behind Closed Doors: A Survey of Family Violence in America.* Garden City, N.Y.: Doubleday, 1979.

The book presents evidence of widespread violence in American families, ranging from wife-beating to child abuse, and suggests some possible causes and solutions.

Reading

Courtship and Marriage Among the Tiwi *Cherry and Charles Lindholm*

The Tiwi are a hunting and gathering people living on an island off the Australian coast. This account of their norms of sexual behavior, courtship, and marriage points to the extraordinary contrast between our own family norms and those of preindustrial peoples.

Moving quickly between the trees, the women lead the young girl away from the bush camp, where they have been staying in isolation during her first menstruation, and wend their way to another camp in a small clearing. . . .

Soon the women and the girl reach the second campsite and emerge from the bush. The men are waiting. The girl at once lies down on the ground, feigning sleep. Her father, a dignified man in his fifties, steps forward and places an intricately carved ceremonial spear between her legs. He then hands the spear to another man, who embraces it as though it were a woman and addresses it as "wife." This man, only a few years younger than her father, has become by this ritual the girl's son-in-law, the legal husband of all her future daughters!

This unique rite, which combines a puberty ceremony with a marriage contract for the pubescent girl's as-yet-unborn daughters (there is no other marriage ceremony), is enacted by the Tiwi people of Melville Island, which lies 25 miles off the northern coast of Australia. The Tiwi, when discovered by Westerners in 1636, had perhaps the world's most rudimentary technology, even simpler than that of their kinsmen, the Australian aborigines. Their only tool was a stone hand ax, their only weapons, wooden spears and throwing sticks. They had no

agriculture, no pottery, no homes except temporary brush shelters, no clothing aside from women's bark aprons, no domesticated animal but the dog. Separated from Australia by a dangerous strait, the Tiwi have pursued their own separate evolution since they came or were blown here, perhaps from Southeast Asia, at least 17,000 years ago.

Until very recently, the Tiwi lived as hunters and gatherers in a region of relative plenty. Originally, they were divided into nine bands of 100 to 300 persons, each controlling a part of the 2,240 square miles of Melville Island. But although people identify with their territorial band, the main unit of cooperation and daily activity is the household. This is the group that lives together, forages together and shares food. The larger households may consist of an elder man with his wives, children and various relatives, perhaps 25 people in all. Women dig yams with their sticks and collect the plentiful nuts of palm trees. Together with the young men, they forage for oysters, cockles, eggs, snails, and hunt bandicoots, lizards, tree rats and carpet snakes. By custom, the men hunt the creatures of the sea and air, such as geese and crocodiles. The work of women and young men provides by far the largest part of the food supply, and the elder men, who have many wives—the record, 29—as well as daughters and sons-in-law, can live in leisure on what they provide. Thus, as many as 50 people may camp together. But a small household need not live within such a camp to survive, and even a man alone can easily forage enough to provide for himself. None need fear starvation on Melville.

Within [their] . . . simple and almost arcadian setting, an amazingly complex family system has developed, which unites matrilineal descent (tracing the lineage through the mother only) with cross-generational marriage, and which revolves around one very straightforward premise: All the women, regardless of age, must be married. Because of this fundamental rule, the newly menstruating girl is introduced to her son-in-law. His presence is guarantee of his intentions, and he henceforth becomes a constant presence in his mother-in-law's camp, where his duty is to provide her with food and support. In return, all her daughters are pledged to him as future wives. The relationship between the two is lifelong, but should he fail in his duties, he may be stripped of his rights.

The new mother-in-law was, of course, also married before she was born, as her mother went through the same puberty-betrothal rites. The young girl's husband, an elderly man, is at her menstrual ceremony. He now pursues his wife, catches her and sits her down beneath a tree. He and his brothers hurl spears at the tree, which represents her, perhaps in imitation of the sexual act that will lead to her impregnation. The brothers, by participating in this rite, stake their claim over the girl should her husband die.

The ritual ends and the girl returns to the main camp. In the flickering firelight, she contemplates the sleeping form of her husband on the opposite side of the campfire. They will sleep apart in this way and have no sexual relations until after her fourth menstrual period; at that time, she will no longer be regarded as a girl but as a young woman. She remembers the night, two years before, when her father took her to her husband's campfire and informed her that this man was her husband and she would sleep there from now on. She was not afraid. Her three older sisters were also his wives and had been sleeping with him for some time. They had told her that he was a kind and gentle old man. According to custom, her husband had deflowered her with his finger and then, gradually and patiently, had initiated her into sex; it had been a whole year before they had actual intercourse. The girl believes that the sexual activity with her husband is the sole cause of her present transformation from girlhood to womanhood; her menstruation and the development of her breasts and bodily hair are all the result of sexual intercourse with this man. "He grew me up," she thinks with gratitude.

Her fourth period ends and she officially becomes a young woman. One stage of her life is over. Now she is held totally responsible for her own actions. She is no longer a pupil, neither economically nor sexually, and is expected to contribute as an adult to the camp's food supplies and take an active part on ceremonial occasions. Her position within the household, however, is not one of much prestige; she has as yet produced no children. Her husband's senior wife, who is old enough to be her mother and who in fact fulfills the role of mother-teacher to the younger wives, runs the household with a practiced expertise, organizing the gathering of food, delegating jobs and generally supervising all domestic activities, including the rearing of the children. The children themselves make no distinction between their actual mothers and their mothers' co-wives, calling every woman "mother." If one woman has too little milk to feed her infant, another woman (often a sister co-wife) will also feed the child.

After some time, the young woman realizes that she is pregnant. While the birth of a child would bring her respect and improve her status, it would restrict, if not render quite impossible, her one completely independent and autonomous activity: extramarital affairs. Although the senior wife has been keeping a watchful eye over her in order to prevent adulterous liaisons, her sister co-wives have been helping her to arrange secret rendezvous in the bush while she is supposedly engaged in foraging. She and her young lover have been careful not to be seen walking together in the bush, and he has taken the precaution of stepping in her footprints when following her to their meeting place. In this way, their relationship has been conducted with the decorum necessary to avoid public attention and her husband's anger.

Reluctant to interrupt her love life just yet, she decides to abort the pregnancy and preserve her freedom. This she does by drinking the milk of the milkwood tree and hitting her stomach with a stick. In the course of time, she again becomes pregnant but this time does not consider abortion. She has been meeting her lover too frequently. The husband has become suspicious. He has given the younger wife a mild beating and formally complained to her family, who have warned her to mend her ways.

And so the young woman enters motherhood. The actual paternity of the infant does not concern her because, although she knows that sexual intercourse must take place for a child to be born, she also knows that her pregnancy could not have occurred without her husband first seeing the child in a dream. Her husband had dreamed the child some time before. Then of course, it was still a spirit-child, living in the spirit world of the as-yet-unborn and seeking its father in the world of the living. The child had found the father in the father's dream and was thus able to cross from the spirit world into this one.

Because she has produced a child, the young mother is regarded as an equal among the other women in the camp. She may now express her opinions and give advice. Moreover, she has given birth to a girl and thus gained esteem in the eyes of both her husband and son-in-law. The latter is pleased because his mother-in-law has fulfilled her part of the contract made at her puberty ceremony and has provided him with a wife. Her husband is glad because when his daughter reaches puberty he will have the right to make the marriage contract between her unborn daughters and the man of his choice. The young mother herself is also happy, because now she has begun to gain status within the community and can look forward to her power increasing as she produces more children.

Her future will include a succession of husbands, since there is a wide age gap between men and their young wives. These new marriages of the young widow with other husbands brings to the fore the basic concern of Tiwi society: the prestige and honor gained through the control of women's marriages. The central issue in Tiwi marriages is not sex but the establishment of a man's authority over his wives and the regulation of the marriages of their daughters and daughters' daughters. At each successive marriage, various individuals dispute about their rights to the girl; the girl's "father" (the man married to her mother) negotiates with her brothers over whom she should be given to; her dead husband's brothers enter in as well, demanding she be given to them. Each seeks advantage for his own prestige. A man who is able to control the marriages of many women will, in turn, be rewarded with many wives from the grateful recipients, for women are not given without a promise of a return. He will then begin accumulating wives and will become a great man, a man of renown. The woman, too, as she becomes older and more respected, acquires some voice in her marriages; no woman can be married to someone she dislikes.

In their efforts to gain wives and indebted in-laws, the Tiwi exemplify a phenomenon that is characteristic of people at this level of development: the use of marriage exchange as a tool for gaining prestige, leadership and political authority. The Tiwi produce no surplus; have no essential manufacture; no scarce resources occur naturally. The products of the island are available to all and everyone is capable of utilizing them. There is nothing an ambitious Tiwi can try to monopolize except women. In nature, the number of men is approximately equal to the number of women, but the institution of marriage means that an artificial scarcity of women can be created. . . .

Two factors operate in this process by which women seem to become poker chips in male games of prestige. The first is age. The second is individual ability to manipulate the marriage exchange.

The Tiwi, like many other people with simple technologies, view age and authority as equivalent. Among men, the increment in status that comes with age is indicated concretely by their control over an increasing number of women. A man will be at least in his mid thirties before the girl he has been promised becomes old enough to live with him. Until then, affairs with older men's wives satisfy his sexual needs. But after the first wife arrives more wives will follow, since a man's contract with his mother-in-law calls for marriage to all of her daughters, and one man may have contracts with several mothers-in-law.

In general, the younger men acquiesce to the system because they hope to gain by it eventually. They, too, will become elders and control wives. However, young men do not remain chaste nor are young wives satisfied with the attentions of their husbands, especially if the husband is very old and has many wives. As long as illicit sexual liasons are kept secret, they do not threaten the power structure of the Tiwi society, and most women manage a number of affairs during their lives. Nevertheless, elder men are leery of strong romantic relationships between a young wife and her lover, for such a relationship may evolve into an elopement, an act that is the most reprehensible in Tiwi culture.

It is a political rebellion that unites all the elder men, who are ordinarily rivals, against the young lovers. The pair will be pursued and captured, and the young man subjected to an ordeal. He is forced to face his elderly accuser, who has painted himself white to signify his anger, within a circle of other Tiwi, male and female. The old man, chewing his beard in fury, recites a detailed list of the wrongdoer's sins, particularly harping on his ingratitude. Finally, he begins throwing spears at the young man, who, after some dodging, should allow himself to be hit so that blood flows. Some young men are defiant and throw the spears back. This may be the transgressor's death warrant, for the other elders will then join in the spear-throwing, perhaps killing him. The other young men do not interfere. Their desire to break the rules of the gerontocracy is offset by their desire to retain the system, which promises them respect, power and many wives in old age.

Source: Cherry Lindholm and Charles Lindholm, "Mating Power Among the Tiwi," *Science Digest* (Sept./Oct. 1980), pp. 79–83, 114.

CHAPTER 15 *Education*

The word "school" comes from an ancient Greek word meaning "leisure." The link between the two words may not seem obvious today, but in preindustrial societies schooling had little practical use and was undertaken only by those with the time and money to pursue the cultivation of the mind for its own sake. The rest of the population began their working lives at adolescence or even earlier. Most people acquired all the knowledge and skills they needed through ordinary, everyday contacts with parents and other kin.

With the rise of industrialism, however, mass schooling became a necessity. Knowledge expanded rapidly, the pace of social change increased, and many new economic roles were created. In a modern industrial society, people need to acquire specialized knowledge and skills if they are to fill their roles competently. Their education, therefore, cannot be left to chance. It requires attendance at specialized formal organizations such as elementary schools, high schools, and colleges. In all industrial societies, education is a central social institution.

In its broadest sense, "education" is almost synonymous with "socialization," since both involve the passing on of culture from one person or group to another. The distinguishing feature of education in modern industrial societies, however, is that it has become an institutionalized, formal activity. These societies deliberately organize the educational experience, make it compulsory for people in certain age groups, train specialists to act as educators, and provide locations and equipment for the teaching and learning process. For our present purposes, then, *education is the systematic, formalized transmission of knowledge, skills, and values.*

In terms of the number of people involved, education is the largest single industry in the United States. If we include students, teachers, and administrators and other staff, almost one American in three currently participates in the institution—a figure without parallel anywhere else in the world. There are several reasons for this remarkable emphasis on education. First, a large number of skilled and literate people is essential to the survival of such a highly industrialized society. Second, educational credentials, such as high school diplomas and college degrees, have become a valuable resource in the competition for good jobs and high incomes. Third, Americans have historically had a deep faith in the virtues of mass education, even if it means educating millions of people to levels far above those demanded by most jobs in the economy. We tend to regard education as a cure-all for a variety of social ills, and it is no accident that in recent years the schools have been used in controversial attempts to bring about social and racial equalities. As we shall see, the results have been somewhat disappointing, largely because of a failure to make a realistic sociological assessment of the schools' potential for bringing about social reform.

Characteristics of American Education

American education has several characteristics not found in the same combination in any other society. Many of the virtues and problems of our educational system stem from this unique blend of features.

Commitment to Mass Education

It is taken for granted in America that everyone has a basic right to at least some formal education and that the state should therefore provide free elementary and high school education for the masses. Schooling for every child was pioneered by the United States, and by the time of the Civil War most states were offering free education to white residents. This development took place long before similar systems were introduced in Europe. European countries were much less inclined to regard mass education as a virtue in itself; instead, they have always tended to tailor their educational planning to their economic needs.

The expansion of mass education in the United States in the course of this century has been unequaled anywhere. In 1900, about 7 percent of Americans in the appropriate age group were graduated from high school; by 1920 this figure had risen to 17 percent; by 1940, to 50 percent; and it stands today at over 80 percent. More than two-thirds of the present American population has a high school diploma, and the adult population has a median of 12.4 years of education. The proportion of high school graduates attending college has also risen steeply, from 4 percent in 1900 to 16 percent in 1940 to about 40 percent by the beginning of the 1980s. By comparison, in Canada less than 20 percent of the people between the ages of eighteen and twenty-one are in college. In Western Europe opportunities for advanced education are even more scarce: only about 20 percent of the sixteen- and seventeen-year-olds are still in school, and only about 10 percent of all children proceed to college. The less developed nations of the world present an even greater contrast. Although they try to provide all children with a few years of elementary education, only a small minority obtain secondary education, and a person's chances of attending a college are minimal. More than half of the world's population can neither read nor write, and the absolute number of illiterates is actually increasing (see Figure 15.1).

This extension of educational opportunities in America has not been without its price, for mass education on this scale inevitably means some lowering of academic standards. Other industrialized countries, such as Great Britain and France, have generally insisted on high standards, even though this meant denying educational opportunities to the less academically able. Until the late sixties, for example, British schoolchildren were required to take a tough examination at the age of eleven, and on the basis of the results, were sent to one of two quite different kinds of schools. The "secondary modern" schools, to which the vast majority of children went, offered vocational training and only a basic academic curriculum; most of these children left school at the age of fifteen or sixteen. The "grammar" schools, attended by a small minority of children, had very high academic standards, emphasized such subjects as Latin and ancient Greek, and prepared their students for the university. (This system has now been abolished, and British secondary schools increasingly resemble those of America.)

ILLITERACY RATES

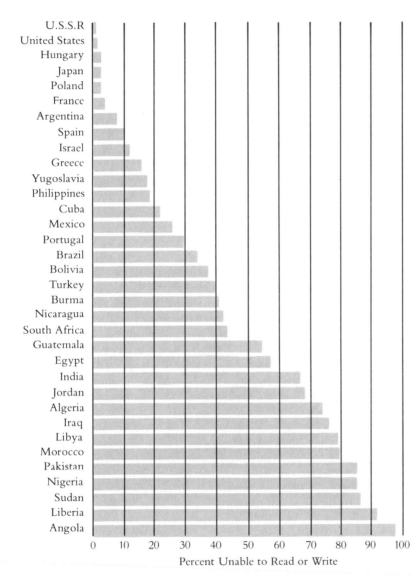

U.S.S.R
United States
Hungary
Japan
Poland
France
Argentina
Spain
Israel
Greece
Yugoslavia
Philippines
Cuba
Mexico
Portugal
Brazil
Bolivia
Turkey
Burma
Nicaragua
South Africa
Guatemala
Egypt
India
Jordan
Algeria
Iraq
Libya
Morocco
Pakistan
Nigeria
Sudan
Liberia
Angola

0   10   20   30   40   50   60   70   80   90   100
Percent Unable to Read or Write

Source: Bureau of the Census, *Statistical Abstract of the United States, 1979*
(Washington, D.C.: U.S. Government Printing Office, 1979),
pp. 891–892.

Figure 15.1 As this figure shows, many countries have very high illiteracy rates. At present, more than half of the world's population can neither read nor write. The absolute number of illiterate people is actually increasing, primarily because educational facilities in the developing nations cannot keep pace with their population growth.

Figure 15.2 Like most children in the less developed nations of the world, these elementary school pupils in Mali have little chance of attending high school. Compulsory secondary education is found only in the industrialized nations of the world, where teen-agers are not needed in the labor force and where there are sufficient resources to maintain an extensive educational system.

Formal education in America is not merely freely available: it is actually compulsory. There are still many societies where this is not the case, or where schooling is compulsory for only the first few grades. American parents are legally obliged to send their children to school, although they may choose between public and private (including religious) education—choices that are not offered in many other countries. Education in the United States is financed by taxing everyone, including people without children and people whose children attend private schools. The implication is that public education benefits the entire society, not merely those who happen to receive it. Every child is thus entitled to at least twelve years of schooling at public expense, and we even expect some skilled professionals to spend twenty years or more in school—a period equal to half the life expectancy in some of the less developed countries of the world.

Utilitarian Emphasis

Our commitment to mass education arises partly from our historic belief not only that education is valuable and desirable in itself but also that it can serve a variety of social goals. At the founding of the Republic, Thomas Jefferson argued that the schools should be used to ensure the success of democracy. If the voters were merely an ignorant rabble, Jefferson believed, the American experiment was probably doomed.

Since the nineteenth century, there has been a growing belief that the schools can be used for a wide range of utilitarian purposes, including the solving of social problems that were once considered a more appropriate concern for the family or the church. Education was first used as a tool for social engineering in attempts to "Americanize" immigrants and to "civilize" Indian children. Since then we have continued to lay new burdens on the schools. In the sixties the "war on poverty" placed great emphasis on education, in the belief that the culture of the poor, not their lack of money, was the source of their problem. If drug addiction spreads, we immediately start drug-education programs. When the teen-age pregnancy rate soars, the schools are expected to reduce it through effective sex education, and when young drivers cause too many accidents, we rely on the schools to teach them to drive safely.

There is little evidence that these and similar programs have had much effect and a good deal of evidence that they have not, but our faith in education as a cure-all persists anyway. Other societies, of course, have used the schools to change attitudes and behavior—the outstanding examples are probably Nazi Germany and modern China—but they have done so in conjunction with sweeping changes in other social institutions at the same time. The faith that the schools *alone* can bring about social change is distinctively American. As sociologists of education are increasingly pointing out, there seems to be very little empirical justification for this faith, and it may be that we have cherished expectations of the institution that it cannot fulfill alone (Hurn, 1978).

Community Control

Most other countries regard education as a national enterprise, and many have uniform national curriculums, teacher salaries, funding policies, and examinations. Not long ago it was said, a little cynically, that the minister of education in France could state exactly which book every child at a given grade was using during a particular hour of any schoolday. In the United States, however, the schools are regarded as the concern of the community they serve, and most decisions—ranging from the hiring of teachers to the selection or even banning of school library books—are in the hands of a local school board elected by the voters of the community. At present the individual states provide about 40 percent of the funding for the schools, the federal government provides about 10 percent, and the remainder comes from local school districts—most of it derived from property taxes.

Compared with control from a distant national government, community control has many obvious advantages, and it is a tradition that is highly valued and zealously guarded. But it is also one that results in schools in wealthy neighborhoods being far more lavishly funded than schools in poorer areas. When taxable property per pupil is measured, some school districts have as much as ten thousand times the potential income of others (Reischauer et al., 1973). Thus, in one recent year, a district in South Dakota was spending $175 per pupil, while a district in Wyoming was spending $14,554. The average class size in Tennessee was over 23 pupils, while in Vermont it was

PUBLIC SCHOOL EXPENDITURES AND
PERSONAL INCOME, 1978, BY STATES

State	Average per Pupil		Per Capita Personal Income	
	Total	Rank	Total	Rank
United States	$1,739	—	$7,810	—
Alabama	1,281	44	6,247	47
Alaska	3,341	1	10,851	1
Arizona	1,436	34	7,374	30
Arkansas	1,193	48	6,183	49
California	1,674	20	8,850	5
Colorado	1,649	21	8,001	15
Connecticut	1,914	16	8,914	4
Delaware	2,138	4	8,604	8
District of Columbia	2,368	—	10,022	—
Florida	1,594	22	7,505	27
Georgia	1,189	49	6,700	37
Hawaii	1,963	12	8,380	11
Idaho	1,206	47	6,813	36
Illinois	2,058	8	8,745	7
Indiana	1,449	33	7,696	23
Iowa	2,002	10	7,873	17
Kansas	1,682	19	8,001	15
Kentucky	1,294	43	6,615	40
Louisiana	1,481	30	6,640	38
Maine	1,522	28	6,333	46
Maryland	2,100	6	8,306	12
Massachusetts	2,137	5	8,063	14
Michigan	1,975	11	8,442	10
Minnesota	1,962	13	7,847	18
Mississippi	1,220	45	5,736	50
Missouri	1,425	35	7,342	31
Montana	1,906	17	7,051	33
Nebraska	1,526	26	7,391	29
Nevada	1,526	26	9,032	3
New Hampshire	1,366	38	7,277	32
New Jersey	2,333	3	8,818	6
New Mexico	1,476	31	6,505	43
New York	2,527	2	8,267	13
North Carolina	1,343	41	6,607	41
North Dakota	1,518	29	7,478	28
Ohio	1,581	23	7,812	20
Oklahoma	1,461	32	6,951	34
Oregon	1,929	15	7,839	19
Pennsylvania	2,079	7	7,733	21
Rhode Island	1,810	18	7,526	26
South Carolina	1,340	42	6,242	48
South Dakota	1,385	36	6,841	35
Tennessee	1,209	46	6,489	44
Texas	1,352	40	7,697	22
Utah	1,363	39	6,622	39
Vermont	1,550	25	6,541	42
Virginia	1,560	24	7,624	24
Washington	1,951	14	8,450	9
West Virginia	1,374	37	6,456	45
Wisconsin	(NA)	—	7,597	25
Wyoming	2,007	9	9,096	2

Source: U.S. Bureau of the Census, *Statistical Abstract of the United States, 1979* (Washington, D.C.: U.S. Government Printing Office), p. 157.

Figure 15.3 There is a great variation in the per student expenditure on public schools from one state to another. These variations are closely related to the per capita income in each state. The physical quality of the school environment is therefore dependent on the relative wealth of the state concerned.

nearer 16. As Figure 15.3 shows, expenditures per pupil vary widely from state to state. Community control has the drawback, then, that the quality of a child's educational experience may depend on the neighborhood in which he or she happens to live.

Education: The Functionalist Perspective

The functionalist perspective explains the central importance of the schools by emphasizing the part they play in maintaining the social order as a whole. Several distinct functions of education can be identified.

Cultural Transmission

If society is to survive, its culture must be handed down from one generation to the next. The schools are used to provide young people with the knowledge, skills, and values that a complex modern society considers especially important. Thus we learn about our history, geography, and language. We learn how to read, write, and manipulate numbers. We learn about patriotism, the virtues of our political system, and our culture's norms of behavior and morality. This function of education is an essentially conservative one, for the schools are transmitting the culture of the past, or, at best, the present. In a traditional society, this conservatism may not matter much, because culture changes very slowly. In a modern society, however, teachers of the older generation may find it impossible to equip students to face a future that can never be fully anticipated.

Figure 15.4 Soviet children's pageants under portraits of Lenin immediately suggest "indoctrination" to an American audience. But is the American practice of pledging allegiance to the flag (often beneath portraits of national heroes) really any different?

In their transmission of cultural values, too, schools in all societies engage, deliberately or otherwise, in indoctrination. We are well aware of this practice in certain other societies whose values are different from ours, but tend to overlook it in our own because the values we are taught seem so "natural" to us. But if a schoolteacher deals with controversial values—if, for example, he or she tries to present the life and thought of Karl Marx in a favorable light, or discusses sexual practices that are accepted in other societies but considered highly deviant in our own—a community furor is likely to result.

Social Integration

Modern societies frequently contain many different ethnic, racial, religious, or other subcultures. Education can help to integrate the young members of these minorities into a common culture, encouraging the development of a relatively homogeneous society with shared values. In the United States the schools have always been considered an important factor in the "melting pot" process. Children of immigrants may arrive in the first grade unable to speak more than a few words of English, but they emerge from school, at least in theory, able to take their place in the mainstream of American life. This social integration function is particularly important in many of the less developed nations. The borders of these countries were often established by European colonial powers without any regard to tribal, linguistic, or ethnic barriers. Consequently, some new nations contain literally hundreds of different language groups that lack a common cultural tradition and often have a history of mutual hostility. These countries explicitly use the schools to generate a common sense of national loyalty among the young.

Personal Development

The schools teach a variety of facts and skills, most of which are expected to be of some practical use to the students later in their lives. They also provide the students with the opportunity to acquire something more subtle, but at least as important: the habits of thought, the broader perspectives, that are the mark of an educated person. In both the formal curriculum and in informal interaction with peers and teachers, students learn a great deal about themselves and about the world that surrounds them. Some of this learning is relevant to their future occupational roles, but much of it is more valuable for personal emotional, social, and intellectual development. To take but one example, level of education has a strong impact on attitudes and opinions. A "don't know" response to questions in national opinion polls is consistently linked to low educational attainment, irrespective of the subject of the poll. The higher one's level of education, the more likely one is to reject prejudice and intolerant thinking. Each additional year of college appears to make a student more democratic in outlook and more tolerant toward civil liberties issues (Feldman and Newcomb, 1969; Nunn et al., 1978; Hyman and Wright, 1979).

Screening and Selection

Education is an important avenue to occupational and financial success in industrial societies because the schools screen and select students for different kinds of jobs. The more desirable a job, the larger the number of people who would like to have it, and an important function of the schools is to limit access to various occupations by granting the necessary diplomas, degrees, or other credentials to some students but not to others. From the elementary years onward, the schools constantly test students and evaluate their achievements, channeling some toward technical vocations, some toward academic subjects, and some straight into the job market. The credentials that people possess at the end of their education have a strong influence on their life chances.

Innovation

Educational institutions do not merely transmit existing knowledge; they add to the cultural heritage by developing new knowledge and skills as well. This function arises partly because the experience of education stimulates intellectual curiosity and critical thought, and partly because college and university teachers are usually expected to conduct research that will increase scientific knowledge. A good deal of research now takes place outside the schools—in government, industry, and specialized research institutes—but the college professor has a double role as teacher and researcher. This role can generate tensions; in fact,

Figure 15.5 The schools screen and select students for their later occupational roles. Examinations and grading serve to distinguish the academically able from the less able, and those who fail to meet the required standards are gradually eased out of the educational system and into the work force.

many professors complain that they face the choice of neglecting either their research or their students. Colleges and universities remain primarily responsible for *basic* research, which is concerned with establishing new knowledge. *Applied* research, which tries to find practical uses for knowledge, is increasingly pursued outside the college context.

Latent Functions

The functions discussed so far are of the type that sociologists call *manifest*—that is, they are recognized and intended. But education also has functions of a *latent* type, functions that are not generally recognized and were never intended (Merton, 1968). For example, schools serve as "babysitting" agencies. They free parents from child-rearing tasks and permit them to work outside the home. Colleges and even high schools serve as a "marriage market," by giving young people of fairly similar background a chance to interact with one another in a way that would not be possible if their social orbits were restricted to the home and workplace. By isolating the young from the rest of society, the schools also have the latent function of permitting distinctive youth cultures to form. In the sixties and early seventies, for example, many college students adopted political and social norms that were often radically at odds with those of the wider society, and the college campus became a focus of unrest. The schools may also serve the latent function of keeping adolescents—who are not expected to have full-time jobs—occupied and out of trouble. In addition to their formal curricula, the schools also teach habits of punctuality, docility, and obedience to authority, a latent function that has a useful payoff when young people move on to offices and factories. One further latent function of education in the United States, which we shall discuss in more detail below, is that of perpetuating the class and racial inequalities of our society.

Education: The Conflict Perspective

A functionalist analysis of education gives a useful understanding of the role this institution has in society. But the analysis does not tell the whole story, for it tends to ignore the fact that education can become deeply involved in social conflict. The conflict perspective, on the other hand, focuses on the ways different social groups use education as a means of getting or keeping power, wealth, and prestige.

The "Credential Society"

The United States has been described as a "credential society"—one in which overwhelming importance is attached to educational qualifications of various kinds (Collins, 1979). During this century, and particularly since World War II, the proportion of the population with high school diplomas, bachelor's and master's degrees, and even doctorates has increased at an astonishing pace. Why has this happened? The functionalist answer would be that education has expanded in response to economic growth: that new and more challenging jobs have demanded higher levels of skill, and that the schools have helped to keep the social system in balance by producing the necessary trained workers.

Until recently this common-sense explanation was almost unquestioned. The evidence, however, gives it surprisingly little support. Some new jobs that require advanced knowledge and skills have of course appeared (like that of the atomic physicist). But the content of most jobs has not changed in the course of this century. The level of skills required of file clerks, typists, cashiers, assembly-line workers, lawyers, teachers, receptionists, sales representatives, or bus drivers is generally little different than it was decades ago. Yet the same kinds of jobs now demand more advanced qualifications. In fact, upgrading of this nature accounts for most of the increased educational requirements for jobs during this century. Only about 15 percent of the increase results from the appearance of new, high-skill jobs (Berg, 1970; Freeman, 1976; Collins, 1971b, 1979).

Why do employers demand ever higher educational credentials from their workers? There seem to be two reasons. First, they use formal qualifications to make their task of screening and selecting job applicants easier; and when there is an oversupply of job candidates with the necessary credentials, employers simply increase the required qualifications. Second, employers share the widespread belief that better-educated workers are more productive than those who are less educated. Yet numerous studies have shown that, contrary to popular opinion, there is little or no relationship between educational achievement and job performance or productivity. For example, good grades in a graduate school of medicine or education are poor predictors of whether someone will become a good doctor or teacher (Gintis, 1971; Collins, 1979). The skills required to get an A grade in a college course on anatomy or educational philosophy are not the same as the skills needed to deal with a medical emergency or an unruly junior high school class. The schools and colleges teach very little (other than basic literacy and numeracy) that is directly relevant to the world of work. Most people pick up the necessary skills on the job, not in the classroom, and the characteristics that make for a successful career (such as initiative, leadership, drive, negotiating ability, willingness to take risks, and persuasiveness) are not even taught in the schools. It seems that the schools produce graduates with any number of educational credentials but with few specifically job-related skills; in fact, nearly half of the country's college graduates work in fields they consider unrelated to their major subjects (Solomon et al., 1977).

Education and Social Mobility

On the whole, a higher credential means higher earnings—simply because the value the job market places on it makes it a major asset in the competition for the best jobs. If you turn back to Figure 10.4 on page 241, where the prestige rankings of various occupations are listed, you will notice that the most prestigious jobs tend to be those that are known not only to yield the highest incomes but also to require the longest education. In their landmark study of *social mobility* (movement from one status to another) in the United States, Peter Blau and Otis Duncan (1967) found that the most important factor affecting whether a son achieved a higher status than his father's was the amount of education the son attained. A high level of education is a scarce and valued resource, for which people compete vigorously. According to conflict theorists, the remarkable expansion of American education in recent decades has less to do with the demands of the economy than with competition for power, wealth, and prestige. In their view, the pressure for ever-increasing credentials comes from two main sources: the professions, which insist on high membership qualifications as a means of protecting their own interests, and the consumers of education who want credentials for their own advantage.

Figure 15.6

"First of all, I'd like to say I really feel I got my thirty-two thousand dollars' worth."

Drawing by Lorenz; © 1978
The New Yorker Magazine, Inc.

A *profession* is an occupation requiring extensive, systematic knowledge of or training in an art or science. Professionals try to maintain a clear distinction between themselves and lay persons, typically by the use of some form of licensing or certification, which is usually awarded only after a long socialization process involving a college degree or other advanced credential. A major purpose of this requirement is to limit entrance into the profession, thereby increasing its prestige, autonomy, and earning power. As hundreds of occupations have become professionalized—first those of the physician and the lawyer, then of the engineer and the accountant, and now those of the police officer, the social worker, and the real estate broker—the demands on the schools for more and higher credentials have increased (Bledstein, 1976; Larson, 1977). (Professions are discussed in more detail in Chapter 18, "The Economic Order.")

The consumers of education, too, are well aware that education is the key to social mobility. When the Gallup poll asked Americans in 1972 why they wanted their children to become educated, the most frequent response was "To get a better job"; only 15 percent felt that education was "To stimulate their minds." Four years later, the poll found that 80 percent of the adult population wanted to see high schools "put more emphasis on careers." And a 1979 survey of college freshmen by the American Council on Education found that nearly two-thirds cite "being very well-off financially" as a "very important goal" of their college education. In recent years Americans have flocked to colleges in such numbers that—as you are no doubt keenly aware—there is now a glut of college graduates on the job market. The competition for credentials, combined with a slowdown in economic growth, has left American society with more graduates than there are "college level" jobs to be filled. As a result, many of today's college students and graduates will have to work at a lower level of skill and income than they had anticipated. By the mid-seventies, in fact, nearly half of the employed college graduates were "underutilized" in this way (Berg et al., 1978). It is not possible to predict precisely how many graduates will be affected by unemployment or underemployment in the next few years, since such an estimate involves guesswork about the future of the economy; but it seems likely that by the mid-eighties a third of all college graduates will be in jobs that would normally not require a degree (Froomkin, 1976; Wiegner, 1978).

In the light of these depressing statistics, is a college degree really worth the effort and expense? Caroline Bird (1975) suggested that, on average, a student who went directly to work after high school and put the equivalent of college tuition fees in a savings account would, by the time of retirement, have earned over half a million dollars more than a college graduate. Other analysts strongly dispute this view, and maintain that a college degree will yield as much as a 30 percent annual return on tuition costs, particularly if the economy improves in the decades ahead (Mincer, 1974; Witmer, 1976). In addition, a college degree offers many benefits, even if it does not lead automatically to a "college-level" job. A graduate has an advantage over nongraduates in the competition for the pleasanter, better-paid, and more prestigious of the remaining jobs. And a college education offers people an opportunity to grow and be challenged in a variety of ways that cannot be measured in dollars and cents (Hyman et al., 1975; Bowen, 1977; Drew, 1978). In fact, young Americans show continuing enthusiasm for college degrees. Most high school graduates with college plans are responding to economic uncertainty, not by abandoning their education, but by switching from such subjects as English and history to engineering or business administration—fields that supposedly offer more potential for social mobility.

Inside the School

Every school is a miniature social system, with its own statuses and roles, subcultures, values and traditions, and rituals and ceremonies. Each school, classroom, and clique is an interacting social unit. The study of what actually goes on inside the school has been an important focus of sociological research (P. Jackson, 1968; Boocock, 1978).

The Formal Structure of the School

Perhaps the most obvious feature of the school is that it is a formal, *bureaucratic* organization (Roberts, 1970). The school is no longer housed in a single room and staffed by a schoolmarm who teaches all pupils and all subjects; the educational process has been rationalized in the interests of efficiency. Pupils are grouped according to age, subject, and, in many schools, according to ability; teachers are specialists, with some of them, such as department heads, having formal authority over others; and an administrative staff supervises the entire operation. Procedures are kept as uniform as possible so that the school can be run in an orderly and predictable way.

A result of this bureaucratization is that the school atmosphere is necessarily repressive to some extent. Pupils

Figure 15.7 The traditional schoolhouse, here portrayed by the American artist Winslow Homer, has long since yielded to the large modern school with its specialized staff, its rules and regulations, and its formal administrative hierarchy. In these respects, as in virtually all others, changes in the schools have reflected changes in the society they serve.

may be obliged to remain silent, to line up and march on command, to sit still for hours, to be punctual, and even to request permission to use the toilet. In elementary schools and high schools, the degree of regimentation is greater than any that the students, except those who later enter the military or the prisons, will encounter again in their lifetime. The college atmosphere is much more permissive, but no student who has been through the veritable circus of form-filling known as "registration" can doubt the basically bureaucratic nature of college organization.

To be efficient a bureaucracy must fit individuals to its own administrative needs, rather than fit its procedures to the needs of individuals. As a result, the elementary schools and high schools tend to emphasize conformity and obedience, and they have difficulty dealing with spontaneity, energy, excitement, and individual creativity. Although the schools pay lip service to the ideal of encouraging students to think critically, they are generally authoritarian; although they preach the value of democratic participation, they are reluctant to practice it in the classroom. Controversial topics are apt to be avoided, and school textbooks, still usually portraying "nice" and "typical" middle-class white Americans, are as notable for what they fail to teach as for what they do teach (Silberman, 1971). The emphasis on obedience and conformity has been held responsible by many educators for the widespread apathy of students, particulary in high schools (for example, Holt, 1964, 1972; Goodman, 1970; Friedenberg, 1969; Farber, 1970).

Like all formal organizations, the school contains many informal groups. Peer groups and cliques, for example, are of great importance in the culture of a school or college and may exert far more influence over the behavior and attitudes of individual students than do the efforts of the teachers, counselors, or administrators. In particular, students who are not academically gifted or interested in schoolwork may find alternative sources of gratification among their peers. Status within the peer group may thus compensate for academic failure (J. S. Coleman, 1961).

Competitiveness

Like our economic system, the educational system prizes competition. The use of grading encourages students to compete with one another for academic achievement, and the losers are gradually eliminated from the system altogether and sent into the work force. In many other cultures, this kind of competitive behavior is unknown or considered antisocial. In China, for example, members of a class are expected to help one another, but in our schools,

Figure 15.8 A characteristic feature of American education is competitiveness. From the earliest school years, children are taught to compete against one another. This emphasis on competition helps to socialize the children for the competitiveness they will encounter later in almost every aspect of American life.

mutual assistance may be regarded as cheating. Jules Henry (1963) points to this cultural contrast between ourselves and other peoples:

> Boris had trouble reducing "$^{12}/_{16}$" to the lowest terms, and could only get as far as "$^6/_8$." The teacher asked him quietly if that was as far as he could reduce it. She suggested he "think." Much heaving up and down and waving of hands by the other children, all frantic to correct him. Boris pretty unhappy, probably mentally paralyzed. The teacher, quiet, patient, ignores the others and concentrates with looks and voice on Boris. . . . After a minute or two, she becomes more urgent, but there is no response from Boris. She then turns to the class and says, "Well, who can tell Boris what the number is?" A forest of hands appears, and the teacher calls Peggy. Peggy says that four may be divided into the numerator and the denominator. Thus Boris's failure has made it possible for Peggy to succeed; his depression is the price of her exhilaration; his misery the occasion of her rejoicing. This is the standard condition of the American elementary school. . . . So often somebody's success has been bought at the cost of our failure. To a Zuni, Hopi, or Dakota Indian, Peggy's performance would seem cruel beyond belief, for competition, the wringing of success from somebody else's failure, is a form of torture foreign to those noncompetitive redskins.

Competition within the school is, in fact, an essential part of the American socialization process. By being taught to compete with others for rewards, the children are, in effect, being prepared for economic roles in a capitalist society (Bowles and Gintis, 1976).

The competition for good grades can become so intense that it may actually begin to defeat the academic goals of education. As Ronald Dore (1976) points out, "Not all schooling is educational. Much of it is mere qualification-earning . . . ritualistic, tedious, suffused with anxiety and boredom, destructive of curiosity and imagination; in short, anti-educational." In studies of student culture at the college level, Howard Becker and his associates found that students concentrated more on strategies to get good grades than on acquiring the knowledge the grades supposedly represent. For example, students are more likely to take a "soft" course that offers an assured credit, but little else, rather than take an intellectually stimulating seminar that offers no credit at all. They often seek out "easy" teachers rather than those known to be tough graders. They tend to avoid reading that seems irrelevant to their tests, and they

pump professors for hints about upcoming exams. Some enterprising students try to bluff and flatter their professors in the hope that this will improve their grades. Sororities and fraternities often maintain files of old tests and term papers for the use of their members, and in some cases students resort to various methods of cheating in order to "make the grade" (Hughes et al., 1962; Becker et al., 1968).

Declining Academic Standards

If we were to judge by grades alone, we would have to conclude that academic achievement in American schools is soaring: today's students get at least 25 percent more As and Bs than the students of fifteen years ago did. Unfortunately, however, they know far less. Scores on Standard Achievement Tests and other measures show a steady decline in student abilities since the mid-sixties. A 1979 study by the National Assessment of Educational Progress found that a third of the nation's thirteen-year-olds and a quarter of the seventeen-year-olds cannot correctly multiply 671 by 402, and less than half of those between the ages of thirteen and seventeen can reckon the area of a square when the length of only one side is given. Standards of reading and writing continue to sag, and to compensate for this trend many textbooks are now written at two grade levels below the grade for which they are intended. High schools have been sued by pupils who found, after graduating, that they were insufficiently literate to complete a job application form, and most of the nation's colleges now offer courses in remedial English and math to their incoming freshmen.

The increase in the number of A and B grades awarded to students is easily explained: parents and pupils have applied irresistible pressure on the schools to produce ever better results, and "grade inflation" has followed. But why are academic standards declining? The question has been much debated, and several potential culprits have been identified.

1. Modern child-rearing practices are comparatively permissive, and this, some people believe, may have left the young without the self-discipline necessary for academic success.

2. The traditional family structure is breaking down

under the impact of such factors as easy divorces and a high rate of illegitimacy. Many young people therefore lack the stable home background that would otherwise complement the efforts of the schools.

3. Television has immense influence on the young: the average child spends far more time in front of a TV set than in school. Television encourages a passive orientation: viewers expect to be entertained, and can switch channels as soon as unwelcome demands are made on their powers of concentration. Many teachers feel that TV has sharply reduced the average pupil's attention span.

4. Conflicting demands have been placed on the school system, ranging from teaching about drugs and sex to correcting past social injustices, and these new functions may interfere with the school's traditional tasks.

5. The quality of teaching is poor in many schools. The average high school teacher earns less than the average plumber, and the profession does not attract the most able people. High school graduates who intend to go into teaching score far lower on SAT measures than the average college-bound student—34 points below on verbal tests, and 43 points below on math.

6. Authority is breaking down in many urban schools, and teachers are often less concerned with teaching than with merely maintaining some semblance of order. Over 100,000 teachers are assaulted by their pupils each year, and disciplinary problems undermine the educational effort in many classrooms.

7. New and inadequately tested teaching fads have disrupted the learning process. The introduction of the much-vaunted "new math," for example, has been followed by a sharp decline in math skills. The "open classroom," with its various "learning centers," easily degenerates into a chaotic shambles. And trendy, elective curriculums may have left many students short on fundamentals.

The cause of the decline in student abilities probably lies in some combination of these factors. However, the public appears to have fixed on the relatively permissive environment of the schools since the mid-sixties as the reason for the fall in academic standards. It now seems that the pendulum is swinging back in the direction of a more subject-

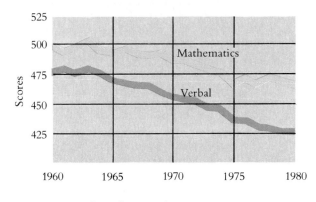

AVERAGE SCHOLASTIC APTITUDE TEST SCORES

Source: The College Board, 1980.

Figure 15.9 Since the mid-1960s, scores on Standard Achievement Tests in both verbal and mathematical skills have been declining. At the same time, however, the proportion of students who get A and B grades has been increasing. The result has been "grade inflation."

centered than child-centered education—a "back to basics" movement that would place renewed emphasis on the traditional curriculum (Ravitch, 1978, Postman, 1979).

The Self-Fulfilling Prophecy

The result of academic competition—the success or failure of individual students—becomes part of an official record: individuals become labeled as bright or dull and are treated accordingly. This differential treatment is most obvious in the tracking system, which segregates students in the belief that they will learn better if they are grouped with others of similar ability. This assumption is widely held, but the evidence for its validity is doubtful at best. One analysis of research on the question reported that some forty-one separate studies had found favorable results from tracking, but seventy-seven other studies had found either mixed or unfavorable results (National Education Association, 1968).

The labeling of students as "bright" or "dull" can have important effects on their later academic careers. Teachers' expectations and attitudes are influenced by these labels, and so are the self-concepts of the students themselves. The process of labeling may involve a *self-fulfilling prophecy*. Believing that certain children will fail, the school treats them as failures, with the result that they do fail. Some important experiments by the psychologist Robert Rosenthal suggest the possible effects of this kind of labeling. In one experiment, Rosenthal (1966) divided a number of rats at random into two groups and told his introductory psychology students that one group contained fast learners and the other slow learners. He then asked the students to perform various experiments with the rats to determine their learning ability. The students reported that the "fast learners" were indeed much more "intelligent" than the "slow learners." The reasons for this finding are not entirely clear. Perhaps the students gave the "fast learners" the benefit of the doubt in ambiguous situations; perhaps they treated them more gently and made the rats more confident. In any case, there is no doubt that the students' expectations influenced their assessments of the rats' behavior.

Rosenthal (1969) next tried a similar experiment in an elementary school. He told the teachers that he had developed a new test to identify children whose learning abilities were likely to spurt ahead during the coming school year. The children were duly tested and the teachers were given a list of "spurters" with instructions to watch their progress without revealing their expectations to the children or the children's parents in any way. In actual fact, the test was a fake, and Rosenthal had merely chosen the names of the "spurters" at random. The only characteristic that distinguished these children from their classmates, then, was the teachers' expectation that their work would improve. A year later, Rosenthal found that the "spurters," particularly in the early grades, had made significantly greater academic gains than a control group of "nonspurters." He concluded that the teachers had changed their attitudes toward the children in subtle ways that had influenced the pupils' progress. Rosenthal's findings remain controversial, however, as later attempts to replicate his experiment have produced varying results. His findings have been supported by some studies but not by others, suggesting that more research is needed to discover the precise conditions, if any,

under which the self-fulfilling prophecy operates (Rist, 1970; Gephart, 1970; Barber et al., 1969; Leacock, 1969; Rubovits and Maehr, 1971, 1973; Brophy and Good, 1970; Ritchie, 1977).

Grading, tracking, and counseling all gradually eliminate from the educational system those students who are not considered bright enough to benefit from further schooling. Unlike other educational systems, such as the British one discussed earlier, ours does not abruptly separate the academic sheep from the goats. Instead, we use a more subtle process of "cooling out" unwanted students (Clark, 1960; London, 1978). Students thus learn slowly that the social prizes a good education brings are restricted to the few, and that hard work is not enough to ensure success. Since the vast majority of the students who are "cooled out" are from the lower social classes, the educational system helps to legitimate social inequality by making academic failure seem the result of individual inadequacies alone. The idea is that everyone is supposed to have the same chance but that only some are able to make use of it.

Social Inequality and the Schools

A crucial insight of the conflict perspective is that people do not have equal opportunity to achieve educational success. In practice, their chances are strongly influenced by the social class of the family into which they were born. Social stratification distributes educational opportunities as unequally as it distributes wealth, power, and prestige. By reinforcing the advantages that some people already have over others as a result of an accident of birth, the schools preserve the social inequalities that already exist (Rist, 1973; Squires, 1979; Persell, 1979).

Class, Race, and Education

It is obvious that educational achievement is related to income, but it is not always so obvious that social class affects educational attainment. The fact is, however, that the average higher-status child stays in school longer and achieves better results while there than the average lower-status child. The superior educational achievement of the upper-status person is then translated into further social and economic advantages.

EDUCATIONAL ATTAINMENT BY GROUP
(PERCENT OF PERSONS 25 YEARS AND OVER)

		White	Black	Hispanic
High school	1972	36.4	24.9	n.a.*
graduate	1976	66.1	43.8	39.3
	1979	70.0	49.0	42.0
Some college	1972	24.0	11.6	n.a.*
	1976	28.8	15.6	14.5
	1979	32.0	19.0	16.0
Four or more	1972	12.6	5.1	n.a.*
years of college	1976	15.4	6.6	6.1
	1979	17.0	8.0	7.0

Source: Bureau of Labor Statistics; Bureau of the Census.   * not available

Figure 15.10 The percentage of those completing high school, and of those attending college, is far greater among whites than among blacks or Hispanics, although the gap has been narrowing in recent years.

There is no shortage of evidence on the different achievements of children from different social classes. In a major study, William Sewell (1971) followed the fortunes of some randomly selected high school pupils for fourteen years. He divided his sample into four groups on the basis of their socioeconomic status and found that those in the highest group were four times more likely to attend college, six times more likely to graduate, and nine times more likely to receive graduate or professional training than those in the lowest-status group. In general, white lower-class children receive about 1.5 fewer years of high school education than their middle-class counterparts. Intelligence is not the only or even the main determinant of who goes to college and finally gets a degree. In fact, a high school graduate of high intelligence but low social status is no more likely to attend college than a graduate with low intelligence but high social status. Less than 10 percent of students with high incomes and high abilities fail to enter college, whereas a quarter of low-income students with comparable abilities do not continue their education beyond high school (Jencks, 1972). Because race and class overlap to a great extent, minority groups also have a lower average educational achievement than whites (see Figure 15.10).

What, then, are the specific factors related to social class that can account for these discrepancies? It seems there are several.

Costs of Education

To keep a child in high school and especially to put a student through college is an expensive undertaking, particularly when indirect costs, such as the loss of the student's potential earnings, are taken into account. The more wealthy a family is, the more able it is to bear these costs.

Family Expectations

If the family expects that a child will remain in high school and attend college, the expectation will influence the motivation of the student. Middle- and upper-class families are inclined to take it for granted that their children will do well academically; lower-class families are much less likely to make the same assumption.

Cultural Background

Middle- and upper-class children are socialized in a way that maximizes their learning potential. Compared with lower-class children, for example, they grow up in smaller families, live in homes that are more likely to be stocked with books, are more likely to be given educational toys, are more encouraged to defer immediate gratification in favor of long-term goals, and are more exposed to the values needed for educational success.

Childhood Nutrition

Children raised in impoverished surroundings face serious physical obstacles to educational success. There is mounting evidence that chronic malnutrition in the prenatal period and infancy can permanently impair intellectual development, while malnutrition in older children can depress their levels of energy and powers of concentration (Levitsky, 1979). Malnutrition is not a problem restricted to distant underdeveloped nations; it is surprisingly common in the United States, especially in impoverished rural areas.

Language Problems

Schools teach pupils in "standard," middle-class American English. Some students from minority groups—particularly Hispanic-Americans—enter school scarcely able to speak any English. They inevitably suffer an initial setback, from which they may never recover. Black English and lower-class white English also differ in important respects from "standard" American English, and the pupils may be penalized for language that appears "ungrammatical." Moreover, they may actually fail to understand much of what the teacher says to them (Bernstein, 1971). (In fact, these variants of English are not in any sense "ungrammatical." They have a perfectly regular system of grammatical rules and are simply dialects of the language, just as valid as those of the Australians, the Irish, the queen of England, or, for that matter, middle-class Americans. The "correct" grammar and pronunciation of any language is merely the dialect of the upper classes in the society where it is spoken.)

Teacher Attitudes

Most teachers have middle-class values and attitudes and may become biased against students who fail to display them. Teachers tend to appreciate students who are punctual, clean, "moral," neat, hard-working, obedient, and ambitious. Pupils who do not behave according to middle-class norms risk being considered "bad" students, regardless of their intelligence and ability.

Labeling

As we have seen, once a child is labeled a dull student, a self-fulfilling prophecy may follow. Lower-ability children are often put in slower tracks, or ability groups, and counseled to make "realistic" career choices. If these children internalize the self-concept that the school offers, their academic motivation may be undermined. There is also evidence that the quality of counseling in school is directly related to the social class of the pupil, irrespective of individual talent (Cicourel and Kitsuse, 1963), and that class and race strongly affect the high school track to which a student is assigned, regardless of IQ or earlier achievement (Schafer et al., 1967).

Peer-Group Influence

Peer groups in schools and colleges strongly influence the academic motivation and career plans of their members. These peer groups are usually composed of people of similar social background. Especially in high school, the importance of college plans to individual students is closely linked to the aspirations of their friends (Campbell and Alexander, 1964; Krauss, 1964). In working-class peer groups, the norm may be to enter the work force at high school graduation or even before (S. M. Miller, 1964).

Class, Race, and Intelligence

Educational achievement is highly correlated with intelligence as measured on *IQ* (intelligence quotient) tests. Again, however, it seems that class, not measured intelligence, is the critical factor influencing achievement, for IQ scores are strongly influenced by social-class background. Lower-class whites score less well on IQ tests than middle- and upper-class whites, as do members of disadvantaged minority groups. Blacks, for example, score on the average ten to fifteen points below whites on these tests. However, individual members of both races are found at every point on the entire ability range, and middle-class Northern blacks generally do better than lower-class Southern whites. The issue of race and intelligence became highly controversial when the psychologist Arthur Jensen (1969, 1979) implied that the differences in IQ between blacks and whites could be partially explained by hereditary factors—a view that has been refuted by scientists from several disciplines.

To evaluate this issue we must look at both "intelligence" and at IQ tests. Exactly what "intelligence" is, nobody knows. Psychologists have been trying to define the concept throughout this century without much success. It is generally agreed, however, that intelligence is a combination of two factors: an innate, *inherited* element that sets a limit on a person's intellectual potential, and a learned, *environmental* element that determines how far that potential will be fulfilled. Since there is no such thing as a person who has not been exposed to socialization in some environment, there is no way to measure either the innate or the learned component alone. Both are inextricably mixed in any individual.

An IQ test measures "intelligence" by comparing the subject's performance on a number of specific tasks with the performance of the rest of his or her age group. The IQ test is misnamed, however, for it is not really a test of "intelligence" at all, whatever intelligence may be. It is actually a test of academic aptitude in a very limited range of fields, primarily in linguistic, spatial, symbolic, and mathematical knowledge and reasoning. The tests ignore many other intellectual capacities that are not directly relevant to the school curriculum—such as creativity (for example, literary imagination, art appreciation, or the ability to compose music), or social skills (for example, persuasiveness, wit, or the ability to be "street-wise").

Because IQ tests use language and assume basic information on the part of the person being tested, they are *culture-bound.* That is, they require a familiarity with knowledge and assumptions more likely to be shared by one group than by another. Children reared in a culture or subculture other than that of the white middle-class America assumed by the tests are consequently at a disadvantage. The fact that a child who has never seen or heard of an eggplant cannot select it as the "odd one out" in a series of fruits does not mean that the child is unintelligent. An American child would not do well on a test that required the subject to select the poisonous insect from a series of four scorpions, but a child reared in the Sahara desert would have little difficulty in getting the answer right. What is often tested in IQ tests, then, is not "intelligence" but rather culturally acquired knowledge, which is a very different thing. The middle-class child has greater access to the kind of knowledge, experience, and skills demanded by these tests.

There is also strong evidence that blacks find the testing situation itself more stressful than whites and that this stress affects their performance. If blacks are tested by a black tester, they do better than if tested by one who is white. If they are told that their results will be compared with those

of other blacks, they do better than if told their results will be compared with those of whites. The average difference in IQ scores between these situations of greater and less stress is about eight points, meaning that this single factor alone can explain more than half the difference found between the average scores of blacks and whites. For these reasons, very few social scientists accept Jensen's argument. Racial and social-class differences in IQ test results are adequately explained by cultural factors. The problem is, however, that IQ tests are widely used as a basis for labeling and tracking students, providing yet another opportunity for the self-fulfilling prophecy of academic success or failure to occur.

Figure 15.11 Intelligence is the outcome of an interaction between heredity and environment. Genetic makeup provides the individual's basic potential, but how that potential is fulfilled depends on the person's learning experiences.

A "Culture Bound" Intelligence Test

These test items were constructed by a black psychologist. The tone is humorous, but the underlying intention is more serious; to show how a person's performance on an IQ test is influenced by cultural knowledge. If you are white, you may find yourself unable to answer a single question.

1. Who did "Stagger Lee" kill?
(A) His mother, (B) Frankie, (C) Johnny, (D) His girl-friend, (E) Billy.

2. A "gas head" is a person who has a . . .
(A) Fast-moving car, (B) Stable of "lace," (C) "Process," (D) Habit of stealing cars, (E) Long jail record for arson.

3. If a man is called a "blood," then he is a . . .
(A) Fighter, (B) Mexican-American, (C) Negro, (D) Hungry hemophile, (E) Redman or Indian.

4. If you throw the dice and 7 is showing on the top, what is facing down?
(A) Seven, (B) Snake Eyes, (C) Boxcars, (D) Little Joes, (E) 11.

5. Cheap chitlings (not the kind you purchase at a frozen-food counter) will taste rubbery unless they are cooked long enough. How soon can you quit cooking them to eat and enjoy them?
(A) 45 minutes, (B) 2 hours, (C) 24 hours, (D) 1 week (on a low flame), (E) 1 hour.

6. "Down home" (the South) today, for the average "soul brother" who is picking cotton (in season) from sunup until sundown, what is the average earning (take home) for one full day?
(A) $.75, (B) $1.65, (C) $3.50, (D) $5, (E) $12.

7. A "handkerchief head" is . . .
(A) A cool cat, (B) A porter, (C) An Uncle Tom, (D) A hoddi, (E) A preacher.

8. "Jet" is . . .
(A) An East Oakland motorcycle club, (B) One of the gangs in "West Side Story," (C) A news and gossip magazine, (D) A way of life for the very rich.

9. "And Jesus said, 'Walk together, children . . .' "
(A) "Don't get weary. There's a great camp meeting," (B) "For we shall overcome," (C) "For the family that walks together talks together," (D) "By your patience you will win your souls" (Luke 21:19), (E) "Mind the things that are above, not the things that are on earth" (Col. 3:3).

10. If a pimp is up tight with a woman who gets state aid, what does he mean when he talks about "Mother's Day"?
(A) Second Sunday in May, (B) Third Sunday in June, (C) First of every month, (D) None of these, (E) First and fifteenth of every month.

11. Jazz pianist Ahmad Jamal took an Arabic name after becoming really famous. Previously he had some fame with what he called his "slave name." What was his name?
(A) Willie Lee Jackson, (B) LeRoi Jones, (C) Wilbur McDougal, (D) Fritz Jones, (E) Andy Johnson.

12. What is Willie Mae's last name?
(A) Schwartz, (B) Matsuda, (C) Gomez, (D) Turner, (E) O'Flaherty.

13. What are the "Dixie hummingbirds"?
(A) A part of the KKK, (B) A swamp disease, (C) A modern gospel group, (D) A Mississippi paramilitary group, (E) Deacons.

14. "Bo Diddley" is a . . .
(A) Game for children, (B) Down home cheap wine, (C) Down home singer, (D) New dance, (E) Mojo call.

15. "Hully Gully" came from . . .
(A) East Oakland, (B) Fillmore, (C) Watts, (D) Harlem, (E) Motor City.

16. Which word is most out of place here?
(A) Slib, (B) Blood, (C) Gray, (D) Spook, (E) Black.

The Answers

1.(E) 3.(C) 5.(C) 7.(C) 9.(A) 11.(D) 13.(C) 15.(C)
2.(C) 4.(A) 6.(D) 8.(C) 10.(E) 12.(D) 14.(C) 16.(C)

Source: New York Times, July 2, 1968.

Equality of Educational Opportunity

In a situation of equal educational opportunity, we would expect that a random member of any given social class or racial group would have the same probability of entering college that a random member of any other group would have. Accidental factors such as sex, race, or class would not affect educational achievement. A major thrust of recent American domestic policy has been to equalize educational opportunity, particularly between white and minority-group children. The ultimate goal of this policy has been to provide minority-group members with the educational channels to social mobility they have been denied in the past.

In 1954, the U.S. Supreme Court ruled that segregated schools were inherently unequal and ordered school systems to desegregate. But progress was painfully slow. Twenty years later, nearly 50 percent of black schoolchildren were attending schools that were over 90 percent black, and almost 80 percent of white children were attending schools that were over 90 percent white. Surprisingly, school desegregation has generally been more readily accomplished in the South than elsewhere, even though most states outside the South have never had segregated schools by law. The problem in the North and West has proved much more difficult because school segregation there is caused mainly by segregated residential patterns. Black migrants from the South moved to these regions in large numbers after World War II and settled primarily in inner-city ghettos. Around the same time the suburbs began to expand rapidly, and whites deserted the city centers. The predominantly black and predominantly white neighborhoods that resulted have now spawned a series of segregated local school systems.

This pattern was tolerated until the civil rights movement and the racial disturbances of the sixties finally provoked the federal government into action. The elimination of social inequality between the races became a pressing national concern—and, true to form, Americans looked to the schools to do the job.

The Coleman Report

The Civil Rights Act of 1964 called for an investigation into racial inequalities in educational opportunities, and a

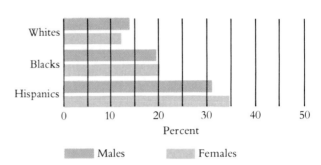

HIGH SCHOOL DROPOUT RATES

Source: U.S. Department of Education, Census Bureau, and the College Board, 1980.

Figure 15.12 As this chart suggests, pupils do not, in practice, have equality of educational opportunity: the likelihood of dropping out of high school is affected by such factors as race, sex, and ethnicity. This means that the average white male, for example, has a greater chance of finishing school than the average Hispanic female.

team of sociologists led by James Coleman was asked to conduct a major study on the subject. The researchers gathered data from nearly 4000 schools and surveyed some 570,000 students and 60,000 teachers. There was a general expectation that the study would find important differences in the quality of education offered to whites and blacks. Coleman himself predicted that the differences would be "striking" (Hodgson, 1973).

The popular assumption was soon challenged. Coleman (1966) did find a major gap in the achievement of black and white students: 84 percent of blacks performed below the median level of whites. But to his astonishment, he found relatively little difference between predominantly black and predominantly white schools in virtually every factor he analyzed, including expenditure per pupil, age of buildings, library facilities, laboratory facilities, number of books, class size, and measurable teacher characteristics. In fact, most of the variation in pupil achievement was not between one school or another but between pupils within the same schools. The facilities a school had at its disposal and the amount of money spent per pupil did not have any significant effect on pupil performance. The cause-and-effect relationship between input of resources and output of achievement, so long taken for granted, hardly existed.

What, then, accounted for the differences in black and white academic achievement? Coleman's crucial finding was that achievement in all schools is principally related, not to the characteristics of the schools, but to the social-class background of the pupils themselves. He concluded:

> Schools bring little influence to bear on a child's achievement that is independent of his background and general social context. ... This very lack of independent effect means that the inequalities imposed on children by their home, neighborhood, and peer evaluation are carried along to become the inequalities with which they confront adult life at the end of school.

Black students, it seemed, were underachieving mainly because they came from predominantly lower-class homes. White students were doing better because they came from predominantly middle-class homes, where they were better prepared and motivated for the academic demands of school life. Coleman also found some evidence to show that when blacks attended desegregated schools, their performance improved, presumably because these schools had a more "middle-class" atmosphere. White pupils' achievement in desegregated schools was unaffected by the presence of blacks.

Coleman's findings had a profound impact on educational policy. Many members of minority groups, it was widely held, suffered from *cultural deprivation,* or deficiencies in home, family, and neighborhood background that left them ill equipped to compete in the larger culture. They therefore needed *compensatory education*—programs designed to teach them the knowledge and skills that would make up for their supposed cultural deprivation. Some of these programs have been successful, but most have proved disappointing, perhaps because they were not sufficiently intensive or prolonged. The idea that minority groups are "culturally deprived" has also come in for strong criticism in more recent years. This notion may simply be a case of white, middle-class ethnocentrism toward subcultures whose characteristics are assumed to be inferior simply because they are different.

Busing and School Integration

The Coleman report also provided a strong incentive for the busing of pupils from one neighborhood to another to correct racial imbalances within school systems. The Supreme Court has reasoned that if it is unconstitutional to segregate schoolchildren, it must be constitutional to ensure that they are desegregated. But while the courts have been prepared to order busing within school districts, they have been reluctant to order it between central cities and the surrounding suburbs; for this reason, many metropolitan-area schools remain as segregated as before. Even where busing does take place, it is usually "one-way"—that is, minority students are bused to white schools, but whites rarely are bused to schools with a nonwhite majority (Schaefer, 1979).

The great majority of school systems that have been desegregated through busing have gone through the process with little difficulty. In some areas, however, strong resentment and even outright violence have resulted, and busing has become a highly controversial issue. Opinion polls throughout the seventies showed that a large majority of the public favors school integration, but that an even larger majority opposes busing, the only practicable way to achieve that goal. Although much of this opposition stems from outright racism, it is clear that there are other reasons for questioning the merits of busing. First, many people—nonwhite as well as white—resent interference in local community control over education and feel that their sense of neighborhood identity is violated by busing. Second, busing, particularly where it is imposed on reluctant communities, may yield few if any benefits for the minority children concerned. A case study by Ray Rist (1978), for example, found that one school system concentrated less on integrating minority children than on making them "invisible"; their presence was merely the token, not the substance, of integration. And contrary to Coleman's expectations, school desegregation has generally failed to have much effect on minority children's achievement, probably because it has so often taken place in an atmosphere of hostility, resentment, or indifference (St. John, 1975; Gerard and Miller, 1975; Rist, 1979). Third, there is some evidence that busing may actually be counterproductive. Coleman himself has now become a strong opponent of busing because he believes that it is hastening the "white

Figure 15.13 In most American communities, the busing of children to ensure racial balance in the classroom has passed without incident. In some cases, however, the white community has reacted with hostility and even violence. These photographs show two contrasting responses: in Boston, police escorts were necessary for the buses bringing black children to white schools; in Cleveland, members of both the black and the white community worked together to make busing successful.

flight" from the central cities to the suburbs and is thus making integration even more difficult to achieve (Coleman et al., 1975). Some sociologists support this interpretation (for example, Giles, 1978), but others claim that the white exodus is merely part of a long-term suburbanization process that would have occurred in any case (Pettigrew and Green, 1976; Rossell, 1976). But whatever the cause, the fact is that most big-city schools are now more segregated than they have ever been: there are simply not enough white children to integrate them.

A 1979 Harris poll reported that 85 percent of whites and 43 percent of blacks oppose busing for racial integration. Yet nearly half the whites felt that black children would do better in integrated schools, and more than half were convinced that within five years "most black and white children will be going to school together." Complaints about the actual experience of desegregation through busing were so few and mild that the pollsters commented: "Rarely has there been a case where so many have been opposed to an idea which appears not to work badly at all when put into practice."

Can Education Create Equality?

Faith in the view that social inequality can be reduced by equalizing educational opportunity was further shaken when Christopher Jencks (1972) published his controversial book *Inequality*. After a careful analysis of the available data, Jencks came to the conclusion that changing the schools would have hardly any effect on social inequality. Economic inequality is certainly related to educational achievement—but it is not caused by it. The source of the inequality lies beyond the schools, which merely reflect the situation in the wider society. Americans, Jencks charges, have a "recurrent fantasy" that schools can solve their problems: they are guilty of "muddleheaded ideas about the various causes and cures of poverty and inequality."

Providing equality of opportunity cannot ensure social and economic equality, because people are differently equipped to take advantage of opportunities. It is like giving everyone an equal chance to run in a footrace, even though some are lead-footed, lame, or have never trained for an athletic event. The "equal" chance merely ensures that those who are already better equipped are able to maintain their advantage. Jencks suggests that a fairer conception of equality would involve equality of social and economic results, which would require a major redistribution of the nation's wealth. But this is not a conception to which, as a people, Americans have very much inclination. Americans prefer to see life as a race to be won by the "fittest"—and our present educational system reflects these values.

The findings of Coleman and of Jencks have noticeably dampened enthusiasm for using the schools to bring about social change. Their work echoes that of Emile Durkheim, who made the first systematic sociological analysis of education around the turn of the century. The schools, Durkheim pointed out, are primarily concerned with transmitting the culture of the past and perhaps of the present. They are shaped by existing forces in society and therefore cannot be a significant instrument of social change in themselves.

The schools will change as other institutions change, and if change is to be brought about, policymakers must focus on other areas of society, particularly the political and economic institutions. The schools will then change, faithfully reinforcing the social and cultural changes that have taken place in the wider society.

Summary

1. Education is the systematic, formalized transmission of knowledge, skills, and values. Mass education is a recent historical development, made necessary by industrialization.

2. American education has a unique combination of characteristics: commitment to elementary and high school education for all, a utilitarian emphasis on education, and a strong tradition of community control.

3. Education has several important social functions: cultural transmission, social integration, personal development, screening and selection, innovation, and a number of latent functions.

4. A conflict perspective emphasizes that educational credentials are a valuable resource in the competition for jobs. Level of education is closely correlated with social mobility, but educational achievement is in turn influenced by social background. The schools thus reinforce existing inequalities.

5. American schools are organized as formal, bureaucratic structures. They place great emphasis on competition for such rewards as grades. In recent years, academic standards have declined markedly. By treating pupils differently according to their supposed abilities, teachers may cause a self-fulfilling prophecy under which pupils perform according to the school's expectations.

6. There are discrepancies in the average educational achievement of people from different social classes and races. Class and race distinctions overlap, and the racial differences are the product of class differences. Several specific factors account for these class differences: costs of education, family expectations, cultural background, childhood nutrition, language problems, teacher attitudes, labeling of students, and peer-group influence.

7. Measured intelligence is also to some extent correlated with the class and race of the individual. Racial differences in IQ are not inherited; higher-status blacks, for example, have higher average IQ scores than lower-status whites. IQ tests are an unsatisfactory way of measuring intelligence, because they are culture-bound and tend to test learned knowledge, not innate ability.

8. Attempts have been made to equalize educational opportunity in the belief that this will lead to greater social equality. The Coleman report, however, found that the quality of school facilities hardly affects student performance; student achievement is primarily determined by class background. Minority students may do better in desegregated schools, however, because these schools have a more middle-class atmosphere. Partly for this reason, controversial measures such as busing have been used to integrate the schools. Jencks argues that the schools cannot be used to change society because they merely reflect existing political and economic arrangements: only when these arrangements are changed will the schools change in consequence.

Important Terms

education (377)	IQ (393)
manifest function (383)	culture-bound (393)
latent function (383)	cultural deprivation (396)
social mobility (385)	compensatory education
profession (385)	(396)
bureaucracy (386)	
self-fulfilling prophecy (390)	

Suggested Readings

COLLINS, RANDALL. *The Credential Society: An Historical Sociology of Education and Stratification.* New York: Academic Press, 1979.

A carefully documented conflict analysis of the expansion of American education.

HURN, CHRISTOPHER J. *The Limits and Possibilities of Schooling.* Boston: Allyn and Bacon, 1978.

A useful introduction to the sociology of education, with a realistic assessment of the schools' potential to change society.

ILLICH, IVAN. *Deschooling Society.* New York: Harper and Row, 1971.

A thought-provoking argument for abandoning formal schooling, which, the author claims, turns education into a commodity and stifles personal development and activity.

JENCKS, CHRISTOPHER, et al. *Inequality.* New York: Basic Books, 1972.

A devastating critique of the American "myth" that the schools can be used to bring about social equality. Jencks includes some provocative suggestions for how this equality could actually be created.

LOEHLIN, JOHN C., et al. *Race Differences in Intelligence.* San Francisco: Freeman, 1975.

A clear discussion of race (and class) differences in IQ. The authors reject the view that these differences are genetically determined and present formidable evidence to support their conclusion.

LONDON, HOWARD B. *The Culture of a Community College.* New York: Praeger, 1978.

An interesting study of community college students' attitudes toward their educational experience.

LORTIE, DAN C. *Schoolteacher: A Sociological Study.* Chicago: University of Chicago Press, 1975.

A sociological analysis of the teacher's role and problems.

ROSENTHAL, ROBERT, AND LENORE JACOBSON. *Pygmalion in the Classroom.* New York: Holt, Rinehart and Winston, 1968.

An account of Rosenthal's experiments of the self-fulfilling prophecy in education.

SILBERMAN, CHARLES E. *Crisis in the Classroom.* New York: Random House, 1970.

A lively and trenchant criticism of American educational practices.

CHAPTER **16**   *Religion*

Some form of religion has existed in every society that we know of. Religious beliefs and practices are very ancient, predating the emergence of modern *Homo sapiens*. Even the primitive Neanderthals, it seems, had some concept of a supernatural realm that lay beyond everyday reality. Among the fossilized remains of these cave dwellers, anthropologists have found artifacts buried with the dead, presumably as tokens to be taken along on the journey to the afterlife.

Although religion is a universal social institution, it takes a multitude of forms. Believers may worship gods, ancestors, or totems; they may practice solitary meditation, frenzied rituals, or solemn prayer. The great variety of religious behavior and belief makes "religion" very difficult to define. Sociologists have offered hundreds of definitions in the past, but many of their attempts have been biased by ethnocentric Judeo-Christian ideas about religion. These ideas are based on a number of central beliefs: that there exists one supreme being or God; that God created the universe and all life and takes a continuing interest in the creation; that there is a life hereafter; and that one's moral behavior in this life influences one's fate in the next. In cross-cultural terms, however, this particular combination of beliefs is unusual. Many religions do not recognize a supreme being, and a number do not believe in gods at all. Several religions ignore questions about the origins of the universe and life, leaving these problems to be dealt with instead by nonreligious myth. Many religions assume that the gods take little or no interest in human affairs. Some have almost nothing to say about life after death, and many—perhaps most—do not link one's earthly morality with one's fate beyond the grave. Obviously, religion cannot be defined simply in Judeo-Christian terms. What, then, are its essential features?

Figure 16.1 All religions recognize the sacred, a realm of experience so awesome that it cannot be approached except through special procedures, or rituals. These photographs show three such rituals. In the first, Asian Buddhists engage in silent contemplation in a temple. In the second, Greek Orthodox clergy lead a procession during religious festivities on the island of Corfu. In the third, members of an Indian sect are seen covered with blood after cutting and piercing their own flesh as a way of confirming their faith and devotion. Rituals of some kind exist in every religion.

A good starting point is the work of Emile Durkheim, one of the first sociologists to study religion. Durkheim pointed out that a single feature is common to all religions, a distinction and opposition between the sacred and the profane. The *sacred* is anything that inspires awe, reverence, and deep respect. It has extraordinary, supernatural, and often dangerous qualities and can usually be approached only through some *ritual*—a formal, stylized procedure, such as prayer, incantation, or ceremonial cleansing. Anything can be regarded as sacred: a god, a rock, the moon, a king, a tree, or a symbol such as a cross. The *profane,* on the other hand, is anything that is regarded as part of the ordinary rather than of the supernatural world; as such, it may have the power to weaken, soil, or corrupt. Of course, the profane, too, may be embodied by a rock, the moon, a king, a tree, or a symbol: something becomes sacred or profane only when it is socially defined as such by a community of believers.

We can say, then, that *religion is a system of communally held beliefs and practices that are oriented toward some sacred, supernatural realm.* Without this combination of elements there can be no religion. (An individual's private beliefs about the supernatural are not "religion" if they are not institutionalized and shared by a community.)

The Sociological Approach to Religion

Mr. Thwackum, a character in Henry Fielding's novel *Tom Jones,* declares: "When I mention religion, I mean the Christian religion; and not only the Christian religion, but the Protestant religion; and not only the Protestant religion, but the Church of England." Most people are like Mr. Thwackum: when they mention religion, they have their own in mind.

Whatever our religious beliefs may be, we usually learn them from other people through socialization into a particular faith (or through resocialization, if we convert from one faith to another). The religious convictions that anyone holds are thus influenced by the historical and social context in which that person happens to live. Someone born in ancient Rome would probably have believed that Jupiter is father of the Gods; at any rate, he or she would certainly not have been a Jehovah's Witness or a Hindu. Similarly, if your parents are Catholic, you are probably Catholic; if they are Mormon, you too are probably a Mormon. We are not the passive prisoners of our upbringing, of course, but even people who decide to convert from one religion to another must almost inevitably select their new faith from the unique range of options that their particular society happens to offer.

The fact that a religious doctrine is culturally learned does not tell us anything about whether it is "true" or not: it might be the case, for example, that the learning process is inspired by some divine plan or purpose. What this cultural variety does mean, however, is that there are a large number of religions, many of whose members are convinced that theirs is the one true faith and that all others are misguided, superstitious, or ungodly. Where does this leave sociologists who study religion? Can and should they make judgments in these matters?

The answer is that sociology cannot be concerned with the truth or falsity of any religion: like other empirical sciences, such as economics or chemistry, sociology is simply not competent to investigate the supernatural or to play umpire between competing faiths. Individual sociologists may be personally committed to a religious viewpoint—as indeed many of the leading contemporary sociologists of religion are (Berger, 1969; Bellah, 1970; Greeley, 1972; B. Johnson, 1977). But sociological research is necessarily directed at the social rather than the theological aspects of religion. Regardless of whether or not God exists, religion, like any other institution, has social characteristics that can be studied by the methods of social science.

Sociologists of religion focus on such issues as the relationship between society and religion. The sociologist can show, for example, that all religions reflect the cultural concerns of the societies in which they arise: war-prone societies tend to have gods of war; agricultural societies, gods of fertility. Strongly patriarchal societies, such as those of the Middle East, tend to have masculine gods (it was within this context that both Islam and Christianity derived the concept of God as "He" rather than "She"). Societies that accord much greater power and prestige to men likewise tend to have religions dominated by male officials; it is therefore not surprising that priests, rabbis, and other clergy have been exclusively male in the past, or that this situation is gradually changing as sex roles in general become more flexible. Another example is that most Western Christians, being white, tend to think of both God and Jesus as white. The idea of a black God is almost unimaginable to them, and portraits of Jesus frequently present him as a blond Caucasian rather than as the person of Semitic features he no doubt was. In many African churches, on the other hand, statues and portraits of Jesus show him with dark, Negroid features.

Types of Religion

Sociologists who study religion have tried to bring some conceptual order to their field by classifying different religions into a series of basic types. One useful classification is that of Reece McGee (1975), who divides religions into four main categories according to their central belief: religions of simple supernaturalism, animism, theism, and abstract ideals. These are merely artificial categories, of course, and not all religions will fit neatly into this classification.

Simple supernaturalism. This type of religion is fairly common in very simple preindustrial societies. Believers do not recognize gods or spirits, but they assume that supernatural forces influence human events for better or worse. The Melanesian Islanders of the South Pacific, for example, believe in *mana,* a diffuse, impersonal force that may exist in both people and natural objects. A person does not necessarily have mana but can sometimes gain it by performing the appropriate rituals. Mana can be good or bad, perhaps causing arrows to fly straight or to miss their target. Some forms of simple supernaturalism still linger in the Western world: for example, the gambler's belief in "luck" or a soldier's reliance on a protective charm such as a rabbit's foot.

Animism. This kind of religion recognizes active, animate spirits operating in the world. These spirits may be found both in people and in otherwise inanimate natural phenomena such as rivers, mountains, and the weather. The spirits are personified: they are assumed, like people, to have motives and emotions. The spirits of animistic religion may be benevolent or evil, or they may even be indifferent to human beings, but they are not gods, for they are not worshiped. People must take account of these spirits, however, and may try to influence them by the use of *magic,* or rituals that harness supernatural power for human ends. Animistic religions have been particularly common among the tribes of Africa and the Americas. In these communities

there is typically a part-time specialist in the use of religious rituals, the shaman or "witch doctor." Some animism persists in the Western world in such occult forms as spiritualism and black magic.

Theism. Religions of this kind center on a belief in gods. A god is presumed to be powerful, to have at least some interest in human affairs, and to be worthy of worship. In societies with theistic religions there are often part-time or full-time religious officials, such as priests, who preside over religious ceremonies and interpret the wishes of the god or gods. In cross-cultural terms the most common form of theism is *polytheism,* a belief in a number of gods. There is usually a "high god," often the "father" of the other gods and somewhat more powerful than they are. The lesser gods generally have specific spheres of influence, such as war, earthquakes, athletics, rain, and so on. A second form of theism is *monotheism,* the belief in a single supreme being. Although there are only three monotheistic religions in the modern world—Judaism, Christianity, and Islam—they have the greatest number of adherents. Actually, none of these three closely related faiths is purely

Figure 16.2 Only three of the thousands of religions in the world have developed monotheistic beliefs: Judaism, Islam, and Christianity. The latter two have such a large number of adherents, however, that a majority of the world's population believes in a single god. Michaelangelo's portrayal of the creation of Adam suggests a typical feature of monotheistic religion, the assumption that an all-powerful god created the universe and takes a continuing interest in what he has created.

ESTIMATED MEMBERSHIP OF THE PRINCIPAL RELIGIONS OF THE WORLD

Religions	North America	South America	Europe	Asia	Africa	Oceania	World
Total Christian	235,109,500	177,266,000	342,630,400	95,987,240	129,717,000	18,063,500	998,773,640
Roman Catholic	132,489,000	165,640,000	176,087,300	55,077,000	47,224,500	4,395,500	580,913,300
Eastern Orthodox	4,763,000	517,000	57,035,600	2,428,000	14,306,000	414,000	79,463,600
Protestant	97,857,500	11,109,000	109,507,500	38,482,240	68,186,500	13,254,000	338,396,740
Jewish	6,155,340	635,800	4,061,620	3,212,860	176,400	76,000	14,318,020
Muslim	371,200	251,500	14,145,000	427,266,000	145,214,700	87,000	587,335,400
Zoroastrian	250	2,100	7,000	254,000	650	.....	264,000
Shinto	60,000	92,000	.....	57,003,000	200	.....	57,155,200
Taoist	16,000	10,000	.....	31,261,000	.....	.....	31,287,000
Confucian	97,100	70,150	.....	157,887,500	1,500	80,300	158,136,550
Buddhist	171,250	192,300	192,000	254,241,000	14,000	30,000	254,840,550
Hindu	88,500	849,300	350,000	473,073,000	1,079,800	499,000	475,939,600
Totals	242,069,140	179,369,150	361,386,020	1,500,185,600	276,204,250	18,835,800	2,578,049,960
Population	365,314,000	242,560,000	749,373,000	2,460,380,000	447,905,000	23,035,000	4,288,567,000

Source: Encyclopaedia Britannica Book of the Year, 1980.

Figure 16.3 The major religions of the world have achieved their success largely because they offer a satisfying theodicy, or explanation for eternal human problems such as suffering, death, and the meaning of life.

monotheistic. Different versions of Christianity, for example, still contain a number of semidivine lesser figures who in practice are sometimes prayed to or even worshiped, such as angels, saints, and the Virgin Mary. Some versions regard God as a trinity of the Father, Son, and Holy Ghost, while others accord Jesus a more independent status as a being who is simultaneously human and divine. All three religions place such great emphasis on one supreme being, however, that for most purposes they can be considered monotheistic.

Abstract ideals. This type of religion, which is found predominantly in Asia, centers not on the worship of a god but rather on ways of thinking and behaving. The goal is to reach an elevated state of consciousness, and in this way to fulfill one's human potential to the utmost. The best known of the religions that focus on abstract ideals is Buddhism, which is concerned not with worship but with the attempt to become "at one with the universe" through many years of meditation. Some Western belief systems,

such as humanism, bear many similarities to religions of abstract ideals, but they are not truly religious, for they lack the ritual and the orientation toward the sacred and supernatural that characterize religions. Since the mid-1960s there has been growing interest among Western youth in Eastern religions of abstract ideals.

Most religions do not try to win converts, and their adherents are usually indifferent toward the religions of others. Several of the major world religions shown in Figure 16.3, however, have tried to win converts at some point in their history. A common feature of these world religions is that they have a convincing *theodicy*, an emotionally satisfying explanation for such great problems of earthly existence as human origins, suffering, and death (Berger, 1967, 1969). We are born, live a brief span of years, often suffer, and then die. This universal sequence can easily seem purposeless, but a theodicy tries to give it meaning by explaining or justifying the presence of evil and misfortune in the world.

Theodicies can explain human problems in many ways. The Hindu doctrine of reincarnation deals with suffering and evil by extending the life span indefinitely. One's present existence becomes merely a tiny link in an endless chain, in which death and misery seem only temporary and insignificant. The mysticism of Buddhism or Taoism offers the believer salvation at a spiritual level, where earthly cares become unimportant. Christian theodicy holds out the hope of eternal salvation in heaven in recompense for ordeals on earth. In the Calvinist version, worldly woes are the fault of sinful humans, not of God; God's purposes are unfathomable, and He thus cannot be criticized for human misfortune. The Zoroastrian theodicy sees the universe as a battleground between the evenly balanced forces of good and evil. It is the duty of humans to throw their weight on the side of good; and it is their failure to do so that accounts for their misfortunes. In Shintoism, which focuses on ancestor worship, one's misfortunes and death are made more tolerable by the knowledge that one's life will be remembered and celebrated by one's descendants forever (Berger, 1969).

Religion: A Functionalist Analysis

Our discussion of theodicies implies that religion has some function in social life; and, in fact, the functionalist perspective offers many insights into the role of religion in society.

The Work of Durkheim

Emile Durkheim, one of the earliest functionalist theorists, was the first sociologist to apply the perspective to religion in a systematic way. His study *The Elementary Forms of Religious Life* was first published in 1912 and has since become a classic. Many of Durkheim's contemporaries regarded religion as hardly worthy of consideration. They saw it as nothing more than a primitive relic from a superstitious past and generally expected that it would disappear in the more sophisticated modern world. But Durkheim was impressed by the fact that religion is universal in human society, and he wondered why this should be so. His answer was that religion has a vital function in maintaining the social system as a whole.

Durkheim reasoned that if he could understand the social significance of the most simple form of religion, he would have the key to understanding the functions of all religion. He therefore focused on what he believed was the most simple religion in existence, the totemism of Australian aborigines. The *totem* is usually some commonplace object, such as an animal or a plant, around which each aborigine clan is organized and from which it takes its name. The totem is regarded as sacred and is frequently the center of various taboos (for instance, members of a given clan are usually forbidden to eat their particular totem). The totem, then, is both a religious symbol and also the symbol of the society itself. From this fact Durkheim concluded that when people worship religion, they are really worshiping nothing more than their own society: "divinity is merely society transformed and symbolically conceived."

What happens in the evolution of totemism, Durkheim argued, is that the clan gathers for periodic meetings. This crowd situation creates emotional excitement of a kind the members would never feel alone. The participants do not recognize that their fervor comes from society; rather, they assume it has a supernatural origin: "Men know well that they are acted upon, but they do not know by whom." They pick on some nearby item, such as a plant or animal, and make this the symbol of both their clan gathering (or society) and their experience of ecstasy (or religion). Their shared religious belief arises from the society and, in turn, it helps to hold the society together.

The solidarity of the community is further enhanced by religious rituals, which bring people together, reaffirm group values, and help to transmit the cultural heritage from one generation to the next. Various rituals also serve to maintain taboos and prohibitions and to comfort people in moments of distress, especially at the time of death. Shared religious beliefs and the rituals that go with them are so important, Durkheim argued, that every society needs a religion, or at least some belief system that serves the same functions. The cause of much of the social disorder in modern societies, he contended, is that "the old gods are growing old or are already dead, and others are not yet born." In other words, people no longer believe deeply in religion, but they have found no satisfying substitute. Lacking commitment to a shared belief system, they tend to pursue their private interests without regard for their fellows.

The Functions of Religion

Much of Durkheim's work on religion was purely speculative. His account of the origins of religion, for example, would not be accepted by most modern sociologists. The real value of his analysis is his recognition of the vital social functions that religion plays in society. Modern sociologists have elaborated on Durkheim's ideas, and several of these social functions have been identified.

1. *Social solidarity.* Religion functions as a form of social "cement." It unites the believers by regularly bringing them together to enact various rituals, and by providing them with the shared values and beliefs that bind them into a community.

2. *Provision of meaning.* Religion provides a theodicy that gives meaningful answers to ultimate and eternal questions about existence. It offers explanations of human predicaments and gives purpose to a universe that might otherwise seem meaningless.

3. *Social control.* The more important values and norms of a society—for example, those relating to human life, sexual behavior, and property—tend to be incorporated not only in law but also in religious doctrine. The teachings found in such sacred scriptures as the Bible and the Koran would have far less force if they were regarded as the work of ordinary mortals. By powerfully reinforcing crucial values and norms, religion helps to maintain social control over individual behavior.

4. *Social change.* Religion can sometimes inspire or facilitate social change. Religious values provide moral standards against which existing social arrangements can be measured, and perhaps found wanting. The civil rights and antiwar movements of the 1960s, for example, derived much of their impetus from religious teachings about brotherhood and peace. New religious movements are particularly likely to be critical of the social order and to encourage their adherents to criticize or challenge it.

5. *Psychological support.* Religion provides individuals with emotional support in the uncertainty of the world. For example, it helps people during major events of the life cycle. Although puberty rites are no longer practiced in the United States (the nearest equivalent is the Jewish bar mitzvah), birth, marriage, and death are almost always marked by religious rituals such as baptisms, weddings, and funerals.

Figure 16.4 Religion is almost always an element in the rituals that mark the major points of the life cycle, as these pictures suggest. Seen here are a Greek Orthodox baptism, a Jewish wedding, and a funeral pyre in Indonesia.

Figure 16.5 Modern communist movements have many similarities with traditional religious movements, and often serve many of the same functions—such as uniting a community through shared rituals and beliefs or providing a sense of purpose in life. Like traditional religions, they also have their "sacred" texts, their martyrs, and their saints. The veneration that communist movements have for their founders, such as Marx and Lenin, is also similar to the veneration that religious movements have for their prophets. This picture shows May Day celebrations in Moscow's Red Square.

Functional Equivalents of Religion

As Durkheim emphasized, a society requires some shared set of beliefs. Although religion may meet this need, other belief systems may be *functional equivalents;* that is, they may serve the same function. Many such belief systems have been proposed, including psychotherapy, science, humanism, fascism, and communism. Some sociologists believe that these and other belief systems fulfill the functions of religion so well that they can actually be regarded as "religions."

It is true that some of these belief systems have features similar to those of traditional Western religion. Consider the case of modern communism. It has its founding prophet, Karl Marx. It has sacred texts, the works of Marx,

Engels, or, in different versions, Mao or Trotsky. It has its saints among those who were martyred in the cause of socialist revolution, such as Che Guevara, and it has its shrines, such as the tomb of Lenin in Moscow's Red Square. Like traditional religion, communism claims to have access to ultimate truth, and regards all alternative views as false. Similarly, it attempts to explain suffering in the world, and it offers a vision of a better life based on a moral command—"from each according to his ability, to each according to his needs." Like some religions, it has a missionary zeal to convert the world to its principles. The experience of conversion to communism can be similar to conversion to a new religion; the novelist Arthur Koestler, for example, describes his own conversion (which he later recanted) in these terms:

Something had clicked in my brain which shook me like a mental explosion. To say that one had "seen the light" is a poor description of the mental rapture which only the convert knows (regardless of what faith he has been converted to). The new light seems to pour from all directions across the skull; the whole universe falls into pattern like the stray pieces of a jigsaw puzzle assembled by magic at one stroke. There is now an answer to every question, doubts and conflicts are a matter of the tortured past—a past already remote, when one had lived in dismal ignorance in the tasteless, colorless world of those who *don't know.* [Quoted in Crossman, 1952]

The essential difference between such belief systems and religion is, of course, that though the former serve some of the same functions as religion, they are not oriented toward the supernatural, a distinction that should not be disregarded.

Religion: A Conflict Analysis

Although religion may often be functional for society, it can also be deeply implicated in social conflict. A full understanding of the role of religion in society must take account of this fact.

The Work of Marx

The conflict approach to religion derives largely from the writings of Karl Marx, who saw religion as a form of false consciousness and as a tool of the powerful in the struggles between competing social classes.

To Marx, belief in religion was a profound form of human alienation. By *alienation* Marx meant the process through which people lose their control over the social world they have created, with the result that they find themselves "alien" in a hostile social environment. Thus, people create systems of government, law, marriage, feudalism, industrialism, or slavery, then lose their sense of social authorship of these products, taking them for granted as though they were part of an unchanging natural order. Nowhere is this process more poignant than in the field of religion: people create gods, lose their awareness that they have done so, and then worship or fear the very gods they created. For this reason, declared Marx, "the criticism of religion is the premise of all criticism." In other words, if

one can critically understand religion, one can develop a similar understanding of all social institutions.

Moreover, Marx claimed, the *dominant* religion in any society is always the religion of its economically and politically dominant class, and it always provides a justification for existing inequalities and injustices. The dominant religion legitimates the interests of the ruling class and offers "pie in the sky" to the oppressed, thus ensuring that they are satisfied with their lot. Marx proclaimed passionately:

> Man makes religion, religion does not make man.... Religious suffering is at the same time an expression of real suffering and a protest against real suffering. Religion is the sigh of the oppressed creature, the sentiment of a heartless world, and the soul of soulless conditions. It is the opium of the people.
>
> The abolition of religion, as the illusory happiness of men, is a demand for their real happiness. The call to abandon their illusions about their condition is a call to abandon a condition that requires illusions.... The immediate task is to unmask human alienation.... Thus the criticism of heaven transforms itself into the criticism of earth, the criticism of religion into the criticism of law, and the criticism of theology into the criticism of politics. [1964b, originally published 1848]

Marx argued that in simple societies that have no class divisions, religion is simply a matter of superstition. In all other societies, he insisted, the dominant religion supports the status quo and diverts the attention of the oppressed from their real problems.

Religion and Social Conflict

There is no shortage of historical evidence to support Marx's view that the dominant religion in any society legitimates the interests of the ruling class. In fact, it is difficult to find a contrary example.

The most striking instances of religious legitimation of political authority occurred in those ancient societies in which the rulers were believed to be divine, or at least descended from gods. The pharaohs of ancient Egypt, for example, were regarded by their subjects as sacred—which made rebellion against them virtually unthinkable. Somewhat more subtle, though just as effective, were the religious ideologies that upheld the Indian caste system or the late European feudal system. As we saw in Chapter 10 ("Social Stratification"), Hindu doctrine threatens Indians who try to change their caste status with reincarnation as a member of a lower caste, or even as an animal. Similarly, the feudal system drew legitimacy from the notion of the "divine right" of kings to rule as God's representatives on earth, and to delegate some of that sacred authority to the nobility.

A further example is provided by European colonialism. In the nineteenth century, countries such as Britain, France, and Germany seized vast territories in Africa, Asia, the South Pacific, and elsewhere. The motives for this colonial invasion of foreign lands were military, political, and economic, but European churches justified colonialism on religious grounds—the conversion of the heathen. Missionaries established themselves among the "primitive" peoples of the colonies in the belief that it was "the white man's burden" to introduce them to Christian civilization. The missionaries were undoubtedly sincere. Nevertheless, the effect of their efforts was often to shatter traditional tribal structure and customs (such as polygamy) and to introduce Western values of hard work and deferred gratification, thereby helping to transform these independent peoples into a work force for the colonists. The conversion of the colonized peoples to Christianity also made it easier for the Europeans to control them: those who believe that the meek shall inherit the earth are not likely to overthrow their rulers. As Friedrich Engels caustically remarked, religion tends to make the masses "submissive to the behests of the masters it had pleased God to place over them."

In the United States, too, the dominant religious organizations have generally legitimated the status quo. This tendency can readily be seen in their attitudes toward slavery and racial inequality. Although a few minor religious organizations vigorously denounced slavery from the outset, all the major religious groups in the South supported it. Indeed, as Kenneth Stampp (1956) notes, they taught that slavery accorded with the will of God:

> Through religious instruction the [slaves] learned that slavery had a divine sanction, that insolence was as much an offense against God as against the temporal master. They received the biblical command that servants should obey the masters, and they heard of the punishments awaiting the disobedient slave in the hereafter.

When the nation divided on the issue, the churches did likewise: around the time of the Civil War several of them (including the Methodists, Baptists, and Presbyterians) split into opposing sides. After the war, the churches in the South generally supported racial segregation, while those in the North were mostly silent on the issue. But as the attitudes of political authorities continued to change over the years, so did those of the churches: by the 1950s, when the Supreme Court and federal government set themselves irrevocably against racial discrimination, almost all the churches declared themselves in favor of civil rights. Even today, however, religion remains one of the most segregated of all American institutions: most congregations are virtually all white or all nonwhite, and some religious organizations draw almost their whole membership from one race only. Throughout the entire history of American race relations, the major churches have tended to mirror rather than challenge the social realities of the time.

Religion in the United States has often proved to be a conservative force on other matters of political controversy, and this has been particularly true of some Protestant bodies. During the social turmoil of the 1960s, Rodney Stark and his associates (1971) found that more than a third of a sample of Protestant ministers in California had never commented in their sermons on the major political and moral issue of the day, the Vietnam war. The more literally the clergymen claimed to interpret the Bible, the less likely they were to preach about social problems. More recently, some fundamentalist clergy have tried to intervene directly in the political process, notably through such conservative groups as the "Moral Majority," which actively supports some candidates for public office and opposes others.

The role of religion in social conflict is not limited to the legitimation of the existing order. Religion is often present, too, in conflicts between societies or between groups of different faiths within a society. A nation at war invariably assumes that its gods are on its side—even when, as in the case of the two world wars of this century, several of the warring nations worship the same deity. Wars fought on ostensibly religious grounds are often marked by extreme bloodiness and fanaticism, but religious differences are not necessarily the *causes* of the wars, even though the participants themselves may think they are. The Crusades, for example, appear at first sight to have been a purely religious conflict between Christians and Muslims. A closer analysis suggests an additional reason, however: the European nobility launched the Crusades partly to gain control of the

Figure 16.6 The medieval witch craze took the lives of some 500,000 people in Europe between the fifteenth and seventeenth centuries. Once a woman was accused of witchcraft, she was doomed: she would be tortured until she either died or confessed; and if she confessed, she was executed.

trade routes to the East and partly to divert widespread unrest among their peasantry. Similarly, the continuing conflict in Northern Ireland seems on the surface to be simply one between Protestants and Catholics, but its roots lie much deeper. For historical reasons, the members of the middle and upper classes are mainly Protestant and pro-British, whereas the Catholics are mainly of the working class and favor secession from Britain. Religious differences may thus serve as a justification for, rather than being a cause of, conflict (S. Beach, 1977).

Let's look at two situations in which religious turmoil masks an underlying social conflict: the medieval witch craze and millenarian movements.

The Medieval Witch Craze

A belief in witchcraft appears in almost all societies, but the reaction to supposed witchcraft in Europe between the fifteenth and seventeenth centuries is without parallel.

Basing their action on the biblical text "Thou shalt not suffer a witch to live" (Exodus 22:18), the Protestant and Catholic clergy burned perhaps as many as 500,000 people to death during this period (M. Harris, 1974).

Although the Church had discouraged belief in witchcraft for several centuries before this period, the official attitude changed early in the fifteenth century, when it became heretical to deny the existence of witches. It was widely believed that thousands of people, mostly old women, had made a pact with the devil. The historian Hugh Trevor-Roper (1967) outlines some of the myths that were accepted at the time:

> Every night these ill-advised ladies were anointing themselves with "devil's grease," made out of the fat of murdered infants, and thus lubricated, were slipping through cracks and keyholes and up chimneys, mounting on broomsticks or spindles or airborne goats, and flying off . . . to a diabolical rendezvous, the Witches' sabbat. . . . They all joined to worship the Devil and danced around him to the sound of macabre music made

with curious instruments—horse's skulls, oak logs, human bones, etc. They kissed him in homage, under the tail if he were a goat, on the lips if he were a toad. After which, at a word of command from him, they threw themselves into promiscuous sexual orgies and settled down to a feast.... In Savoy, roast or boiled children; in Spain, exhumed corpses, preferably of kinsfolk; in Alsace, fricassees of bats.... In the intervals between these acts of public devotion, the old ladies ...occupied themselves by suckling familiar spirits in the form of weasels, moles, bats, toads, or other convenient creatures.

"Witches" were held accountable for many other deeds, such as causing hailstorms, crop failures, and sickness. Once suspects were formally accused of witchcraft, there was usually no way out: they were tortured on the rack, often with red-hot irons, until they confessed or died; and if they confessed, they were burned alive. Moreover, the supposed witches were forced to give the names of some of their supposed accomplices—who were tortured in turn until even more supposed witches were named. The number of witches naturally multiplied rapidly, and the hysteria about witchcraft grew accordingly. The judges and clergy benefited from the witch craze: they enjoyed the gratitude of the people and even billed the families of the deceased for the cost of the firewood and the celebratory banquets they held after each burning. For two centuries Europe lived in dread of witches, until more enlightened and rational thought finally gained ascendance on the Continent.

How can we explain the witch craze? Again, the conflict perspective is helpful. Two historical factors seem to have played a part. The conflict between Catholicism and Protestantism reached its height during the witch craze, and both churches used the accusation of witchcraft as a means of social control over heretics and potential heretics. Equally important, Europe was in a state of deep economic, political, and social unrest at the time. As Marvin Harris (1974) suggests, the fear of witchcraft served to divert the attention of the wretched peasantry away from the real source of their problems:

> The principal result of the witch-hunt system (aside from charred bodies) was that the poor came to believe that they were being victimized by witches and devils instead of princes and popes. Did your roof leak, your cow abort, your oats wither, your wine go sour, your head ache, your baby die? ... Did ... prices soar, wages fall, jobs grow scarce? It was the work of witches.... Against the people's phantom enemies, Church and state mounted a bold campaign.... The practical significance of the witch mania therefore was that it shifted responsibility for the crisis of late medieval society from both Church and state to imaginary demons in human form.... It demobilized the poor and the dispossessed, increased their social distance, filled them with mutual suspicions, pitted neighbor against neighbor, heightened everyone's insecurity, made everyone feel helpless and dependent on the governing class.

Millenarian Movements

A *millenarian movement* is one that prophesies a cataclysmic upheaval within the immediate future, such as a radical change in the social order, a return to some golden age of the past, or even the end of the world. (The word comes from "millennium," the prophesied thousand-year reign of Christ.)

Millenarian movements have been recorded in all parts of the world, but they are found mainly in simple, preindustrial societies that have been colonized by Europeans. A millenarian prophecy often contains a modified version of Judeo-Christian beliefs. The colonized people, for example, may equate themselves with the Israelites in search of the promised land, and the colonizers with the Egyptian oppressors. All the movements, however, have one theme in common: a reversal of the social order, in which those who accept the prophecy will be triumphant over their enemies (who are usually their rulers).

A typical millenarian movement arose among the Plains Indians of the United States at the time of their desperate defense of their lands and cultures against the invading settlers. This movement was the Ghost Dance cult, which erupted in the 1870s and again in the 1890s. Various prophets foretold that if the appropriate dances and rituals were performed, dead ancestors would arise from the grave, the tribes would be immune to the invaders' bullets, the whites would be driven back to the ocean, the vanishing buffalo would return in vast numbers, and the old way of life would be restored. Belief in the Ghost Dance cult was destroyed by the slaughter of the Indians at the Battle of Wounded Knee (Mooney, 1965).

Figure 16.7 The Ghost Dance cult arose among the Plains Indians after they had been defeated in battle several times. Military attempts to restore their lost lands and shattered culture had failed, and they turned instead to a religious means. Millenarian movements of this kind have frequently occurred in colonial situations.

Another millenarian movement arose among the Xhosa, a tribe of nomadic pastoralists in southern Africa. In the middle of the past century they came into competition with Dutch settlers, themselves nomadic pastoralists, who were penetrating the continent from the south. The two groups fought several bloody wars, which the Dutch settlers won as a result of their superior military technology. A prophet arose among the Xhosa, claiming that if the people slaughtered all their cattle and destroyed all their stores of food, the sun would rise blood-red the following day. Cattle, grain, and guns would emerge from the ground, the dead ancestors would return, and the whites would be driven back to the ocean from which they had come. The Xhosa accepted the prophecy, destroyed their cattle and food, and waited on the hilltops for the blood-red dawn. At least twenty thousand starved to death.

How can we explain these extraordinary forms of religious behavior? The conflict perspective is useful here, for it directs attention to the fact that all millenarian movements are, in effect, "religions of the oppressed" (Lanternari, 1963; B. Wilson, 1973). Before adopting the new religion, the members have felt a sense of injustice or deprivation. The religion offers compensation—not as "pie-in-the-sky" in the hereafter, but here on earth, and soon. The recruits are people whose traditional norms and values are no longer relevant to their new plight. In their confusion or desperation they will grasp at any hope, and the millenarian movement provides a sense of purpose once more. An important feature of these religions is that they often serve as the forerunner to militant political movements (Cohn, 1962; Worsley, 1968). The millenarian movement provides the basis for group unity and collective organization, which in turn makes political action possible.

Religious movements, then, are often a source of social change. Although a society's dominant religion almost always supports the status quo, less privileged groups may be inspired by their own religions (or more radical versions of the dominant religion) to challenge the existing order. For example, the conversion of colonial peoples to Christianity may at first have led them to accept foreign rule, but their newly acquired Christian values later encouraged them to reject it. Many of the leaders of colonial nationalist movements were educated in mission schools, where they were taught Christian ideals of brotherhood and equality—

Figure 16.8 An interesting form of millenarian movement is the "cargo cult" of Melanesia. When the Melanesians of the South Pacific were colonized by Europeans, they were deeply impressed by the quantity and variety of goods that arrived as cargo into their country. Prophets declared that the cargo was being manufactured and sent to the Melanesians by their own ancestors, but was being intercepted by the colonists. Millenarian movements arose, typically prophesying that if all crops and food were destroyed and if harbors (and later, airstrips) were built, cargo would miraculously appear. In a few cases the prophecies were confirmed: when the Melanesians had destroyed their food stocks, the colonial administration was obliged to ship in fresh supplies to prevent mass starvation —an event that gave added impetus to the movements. Cargo cults persist in Melanesia today.

and took them seriously. Religious values have played an important part in many other social movements. Thus, although most American churches at first endorsed slavery and were slow to support civil rights, there were always some religious organizations—ranging from the Quakers to the Black Muslims—who worked consistently for change. When they finally endorsed the antislavery and civil rights movements, the major religious organizations lent immense practical and moral force to the campaigns. The essential point is that change is rarely sparked by the dominant religious bodies, for these are too closely linked with the establishment; it is far more likely to come from newer religious movements at the fringes of society. One such movement was early Calvinism, whose "Protestant ethic" diverged markedly from the traditional values of European society.

Religion and Social Change: The "Protestant Ethic"

The role of religion (or any other belief system) in social change is an important topic in sociology. There is a long-standing controversy over whether ideas and beliefs can change culture and society, or whether, instead, our cul-tural and social experience determines the content of our beliefs.

Karl Marx was one of the first social theorists to address this question. He argued that all human culture can be divided into two basic categories: real, or *material*, culture (especially the economy) and ideal, or *nonmaterial*, culture (such as ideas, law, philosophy, and religion). The material culture, he asserted, is paramount. The economic base of a society influences the character of its belief systems, and these ideas merely justify the existing economic arrangements in general and the class system in particular. Religion thus reflects but does not change society.

Max Weber partially disagreed with this view. He accepted that Marx's approach was useful and might be correct in many instances, but he maintained that under certain circumstances religious or other ideas could influence social change. Weber was fascinated by the growth of modern capitalism, which was rapidly transforming the European and American societies of his time. But why had capitalism first developed in Europe rather than in, say, China or India? Weber undertook a massive study of the major world religions and the societies in which they are found, and concluded that the answer lay in the emergence in Europe of a specific type of religious belief—Protestant puritanism, especially Calvinism.

Modern capitalism, Weber pointed out, is unlike traditional commercial activity. Formerly, pirates or merchants earned money in a haphazard way, spent it at once in luxurious living, and placed a higher value on consuming wealth than on earning it. The spirit of modern capitalism is quite different: it emphasizes the methodical accumulation of wealth through rational, calculated procedures, such as accounting and long-range planning. Hard work and making money are highly valued for their own sake. To spend money on idle luxury is considered disreputable; instead, the capital must be reinvested to earn yet more capital.

Weber argued that this new approach arose out of the "Protestant ethic" of regular, conscientious work and deferred gratification. The early Calvinists believed that God had predestined them to salvation in heaven or damnation in hell since the beginning of time. There was nothing they could do to change their fates, and only a small minority were among the elect who would go to heaven. The duty of believers was to abstain from pleasure and to work for the glory of God. But because of their great psychological anxiety about their ultimate destiny, the Calvinists looked for "signs" that they were among the elect—and were pleased to take worldly success as just such a sign. The more successful people were at work, the more likely it seemed that they were to be among the elect—and since profits could not be spent on pleasure, they had to be reinvested. Thus, argued Weber, modern capitalism was born. Ironically, the very people who rejected material comforts unwittingly created industrial capitalism, the foundation of modern affluence. By a further irony, industrialism in turn encouraged the rational-scientific world view, in which traditional religion has little place. Modern capitalists, although they are no longer Puritans, have retained traces of the "Protestant ethic" of diligent work, thrift, and deferred gratification (Weber, 1958a, originally published 1904).

Other religions, Weber argued, did not provide the same incentive for this kind of social and economic change. Catholicism stresses rewards in heaven and encourages its followers to be satisfied with their lot on earth. Hinduism threatens a lower form of life after reincarnation to anyone who tries to attain a higher caste status. Buddhism stresses mysticism, far removed from earthly goals. Taoism requires the believer to withdraw from worldly temptations. Confucianism emphasizes a static social structure as a part of the

Figure 16.9 John Calvin, whose religious doctrines gave rise to Puritanism. Max Weber tried to establish a link between the "Protestant ethic" and the development of capitalism. He argued that because these early Puritans felt they had to work hard for the glory of God and could not spend their income on luxurious living, they simply reinvested their capital, and thus created the new economic system. Other religions, Weber argued, lacked the concern for hard work in this world that characterized Puritan Protestantism.

natural order. Although Islam is an activist religion, it lacks the emphasis on thrift and hard work. All these religions served to discourage the growth of capitalism (Weber, 1951, 1952, 1958b, 1963).

Weber's thesis is often misunderstood and misrepresented, even in college textbooks. Its intent was neither to disprove Marx's view that society usually shapes belief systems, rather than vice versa, nor to prove that the "Protestant ethic" was the "cause" of capitalism. Weber merely wanted to show Protestantism as an important influence on the development of capitalism—an idea he offered only as a tentative hypothesis.

It is certainly possible that Weber's analysis of capitalism was wrong. For one thing, capitalism did not arise in some Calvinist societies, and it sometimes emerged in non-Calvinist ones. Scotland, for example, which was Calvinist, failed to develop early capitalism; and England, which was not Calvinist, was the birthplace of the Industrial Revolution. Certainly there is no way of proving that the "salvation panic" of the Calvinists led them to become capitalists. They may have done so for other reasons, such as the fact that they were more likely than Catholics to live in urban areas, or that their religion encouraged hard work, or even that they were not so wedded to tradition as were Catholics of the time. Weber's hypothesis is one of the most provocative in all sociology, but its subject is so vast and complex that his argument is probably unverifiable. Weber simply bit off more than he or anyone else could chew.

Most Western sociologists probably accept Weber's hypothesis as being at least plausible, and they generally agree that religion or other belief systems can influence society. The material and nonmaterial components of culture are best seen as parts of an interacting system, each influencing the other in different ways at different times.

Types of Religious Organization

The "Protestant ethic" arose in a religious movement that had broken away from a larger and more established body, the Catholic Church. The Catholic Church, in turn, had originated centuries earlier as an offshoot of Judaism. These are but two examples of a constant process by which new and different religious organizations are formed.

Religious organizations can be conveniently divided into one of four basic types: the ecclesia, the denomination, the sect, and the cult (Weber, 1963; Niebuhr, 1929; Troeltsch, 1931; Johnstone, 1975). The distinctions are important because participation in one of these types of organization correlates with specific types of belief and practice.

The *ecclesia* is a religious organization that claims the membership of everyone in a society or even in several societies. A powerful, bureaucratized organization with a hierarchy of full-time officials, it gives complete support to the state authorities and expects the same from them in turn. People who are born into a society with such an "official" religion become members almost automatically. The Roman Catholic Church was such an organization for centuries until Protestantism began to compete with it in several countries. Strictly speaking, there is probably no true ecclesia in the modern world, but there are several religious organizations that approximate one—the Anglican Church in England, the Catholic Church in Spain, the Lutheran Church in Sweden, and Islam in Saudi Arabia and Iran.

The *denomination* (or "church") is one of two or more religious organizations that claim the allegiance of a substantial part of the population. The denomination does not demand official support from the state and may even be at odds with it on occasion. Like the ecclesia, it has a formal, bureaucratic structure, with trained clergy and other officials. The denomination is well established and "respectable," drawing its members primarily from the middle and upper classes. Many of them are born into the faith, but the denomination accepts as a member almost anyone who wants to join. Although they may compete for recruits, denominations are generally tolerant of one another. In the United States the Catholic Church, various large Protestant churches such as the Methodist and Episcopalian, and mainstream Judaism are examples of this type of organization.

The *sect* is a less formally organized body, often one that has split off from a denomination. Its members are generally recruited by conversion, with membership restricted to those who can pass tests of their faith and who give continuing proof of their commitment. The sect is less socially "respectable" than the denomination, and its members are usually of relatively low socioeconomic status. Intolerant of other religious organizations, it is dogmatic and fundamentalist, believing in a literal interpretation of the Scriptures. The sect also tends to be indifferent or even hostile to political authority, which it often regards as too worldly and corrupt. Usually it has no trained clergy, and rituals of worship emphasize emotion, spontaneity, and extensive participation by the congregation. Most sects tend to be short-lived, but some gradually become denominations—always with an accompanying loss of fervor and gain in social respectability. Contemporary sects include the Jehovah's Witnesses, the Assembly of God, Jews for Jesus, and a variety of Pentecostal, evangelical, and similar movements.

The *cult* is the most loosely organized and the most temporary of all forms of religious organization. It has few

CHARACTERISTICS OF SECTS AND CHURCHES

Characteristic	Sect	Denomination (Church)
Size	Smaller	Larger
Relationship with other religious groups	Rejects—feels that the sect alone has the "truth."	Accepts other denominations—willing to work with them.
Wealth (church property, buildings, salary of clergy, income of members)	Limited.	Extensive.
Religious services	Emotional emphasis; informal; extensive congregational participation.	Intellectual emphasis; formal; limited congregational participation.
Clergy	Little if any professional training; frequently part-time.	Professionally trained; full-time.
Doctrines	Literal interpretation of Scriptures; emphasis upon other-worldly rewards.	Liberal interpretations of Scriptures; emphasis on rewards in this world.
Membership requirements	Accepts only those who have continuing emotional commitment; most members are converts.	Accepts almost anyone who wishes to join; many members born into the organization.
Relationship with secular world	"At war" with the secular world which is defined as "evil."	Generally endorses prevailing culture and social arrangements.
Social class of members	Mainly lower class.	Mainly middle class.

Source: Adapted from Glenn M. Vernon, *Sociology of Religion* (New York: McGraw-Hill, 1962), p. 174.

Figure 16.10 The two most important forms of religious organization in the United States are the church (denomination) and the sect. As a general rule, the church is more "respectable" than the sect; its members have higher social status; it interprets Scriptures more liberally; and it is more inclined to make compromises with secular society.

coherent doctrines and imposes minimal demands on believers: like the denomination but unlike the sect, the cult is open to almost anyone who wishes to participate. There is little demand for moral purity; instead, the cult centers around the personal benefits and experiences that it offers its members. Modern examples of the cult might include such loosely structured groups as believers in astrology, transcendental meditation, or spiritualism. (The popular media sometimes use the work "cult" to refer to supposedly exotic new religious organizations, such as the "Jesus Freaks" or "Moonies," but in sociological terms most of these groups are more accurately described as sects.)

Since the ecclesia and the cult play a relatively unimportant role in most modern societies, sociologists usually focus on denominations and sects, often using the more colloquial word "church" to refer to the denominations. Although there is immense variety within each category, the overall differences between the two types of organization seem more significant. The membership, rituals, and beliefs of churches and sects are not static, however: they are in constant flux, and this process is a vital element in religious change. Sects are continually formed as groups break off from churches in search of moral purity that the parent body seems to have lost. Most of these new sects wither and die; a few retain the intensity of conviction that first inspired them; and some survive only to grow steadily less committed to the the faith—occasionally, in fact, to become churches from which new sects break off.

Why is it that sects, if they survive at all, tend to become more staid and respectable over time? Richard Niebuhr (1929) suggested two main reasons. First, the generation that founded the sect will eventually die off, leaving it in the hands of a new generation consisting largely of people who were born into the organization. Almost inevitably, these people will have less emotional commitment to the sect's doctrines than those who converted to it. The second reason is that the destiny of a sect is closely linked to the changing social and economic circumstances of its members. Sects generally draw their initial members from the ranks of those who, perhaps because of poverty, persecution, or displacement from their traditional community, are unable to "make it" in the wider society. Indeed, therein lies part of the appeal of the sect: its theodicy teaches that the values and material goals of the rest of society are not worth striving for anyway, and implies that despite their disadvantages the members are morally superior to non-members. Over time, however, a large part of the sect's membership may become upwardly mobile, and its con-

gregations may grow to value their new affluence and respectability more highly than their pristine doctrines. The Methodists, for example, started out as a sect of the poor, and their spontaneous, unrestrained rituals scandalized the established church they had left. Today the Methodists are among the most affluent, restrained, and respectable of all Protestant denominations. Similarly, the Mormons were once an oppressed sect, persecuted in state after state until they settled in the area that became Utah. But as the Mormons became more successful in conventional economic and political activities, they abandoned some earlier fundamentalist teachings (notably that permitting polygamy, which they had to give up in order to gain statehood for Utah) (O'Dea, 1957). The status of the organization now seems to be transitional between that of a sect and a denomination. The Seventh-Day Adventists, too, began as a millenarian sect prophesying the end of the world on a specific date. That day having come and gone, they are presently developing from a sect into a church, with an increasingly middle-class membership and a trained clergy.

Religion in the United States

Many of the founding fathers of the United States were suspicious of organized religion. In the Europe from which the early settlers had recently emigrated, the church had great political influence and was closely associated with the

Figure 16.11 These two pictures illustrate characteristic differences between the church and the sect. The first photograph shows a denominational ritual, in which God's blessings are sought for the success of a fox hunt. The second shows an adult being baptized as a member of fundamentalist sect. It is almost inconceivable that the people in the first picture would submit to such a baptism, or that those in the second picture would consider a fox hunt an appropriate focus of God's concerns.

state. The influence of organized religion was generally conservative, and the church was seen by many radicals of the time as a buttress of the monarchy and its absolute rule. In the two hundred years since then, however, religion has come to be one of the most highly regarded of American institutions, and one of the least politically controversial.

Some Characteristics

Americans consider themselves a deeply religious people, and religion plays an important role in American life. This role is different in many respects from that of religion in other societies, however, for the American institution has several distinctive characteristics.

1. The United States has no official, "established" religion. The constitution specifically separates church from state, and there is no formal or legal assumption that one particular faith is more "true" than any other. The state rarely intervenes in religious matters, and religious organizations generally avoid political controversy. There are exceptions, of course, when both state and church claim jurisdiction over the same area (such as the issues of abortion and school prayers).

2. Although freedom of religion is an important value in America, there is an implicit assumption that Americans should be religious—not necessarily attending church or synagogue, but believing in God and expressing at least lip service to religious principles. For this reason, a professed atheist would be at a distinct disadvantage as a candidate for public office; similarly, school principals might jeopardize their position by being openly irreligious.

3. In most societies there are only a handful of significant religious organizations. In Canada, for example, 90 percent of the population is Christian; half of them are Catholic and half are Protestant, and three-quarters of the Protestants belong to two denominations, the Anglican Church and the United Church of Canada. The United States, in contrast, displays great religious pluralism. Although the country is also about 90 percent Christian, the largest denomination, the Catholic Church, has only about 27 percent of total church allegiance. Some 60 percent of Americans are Protestant, but they are fragmented into so many denominations and sects that none of them can claim even a tenth of the total religiously affiliated population. Although about two dozen organizations account for the preferences of almost the entire religious population, there are, by one recent count, 1187 distinct denominations, sects, and cults, a fact that suggests that the United States may be the most religiously diverse society in history (Melton, 1979).

4. Americans are generally tolerant of religious diversity, particularly within the Christian churches. Officials of different religions avoid public debates over potentially controversial theological issues. Sects and cults do not receive quite the same tolerance, but except in rare cases their right to exist and propagate their beliefs is scarcely questioned.

5. Religion in the United States is not merely a set of beliefs and rituals. It can also be a source of personal and group identity. The most obvious example is the American Jewish community, an ethnic group held together by its common religion (Sklare, 1971, 1974). Catholicism, too, is one of the most important features distinguishing ethnic groups such as the Poles from other Americans (Greeley, 1977). These groups make considerable use of church schools, a practice that enhances ethnic identification among younger members who might otherwise be assimilated more readily into the American mainstream. Churches are also an important institution in the black community, where they are a significant source of group solidarity and identity.

Correlates of Religious Affiliation

Membership in a particular church or sect has a number of important correlates. Whether religious affiliation actually causes any of these relationships is difficult to judge, because so many other factors (such as ethnic-group membership) may complicate the picture.

One of the clearest correlations is that between socio-economic status and religious affiliation. Jews earn higher incomes than gentiles, and Catholics—perhaps surprisingly, in view of their reputation as a heavily blue-collar community—earn more than any Protestant group. Direct Catholic-Protestant comparisons can be misleading, however, for they obscure differences within the faiths: Spanish-speaking Catholics, for example, have particularly low incomes, and the income range between the wealthier and the poorer Protestant organizations is very wide (Greeley, 1977). There is a distinct hierarchy of income and prestige among the Protestant denominations: the Episcopalians lead the field, followed by the Congregationalists, Presbyterians, Methodists, Lutherans, and Baptists. There is some evidence that upwardly mobile people, particularly in small communities, tend to switch from one denomination to another as their social status rises (Lauer, 1975; Nelsen, 1976; Newport, 1979).

Jews, who have a long tradition of respect for learning, are the best educated of the religious groups and play a disproportionate role in the nation's intellectual life. Among Protestant denominations, educational level varies along much the same lines as income. Catholics' educational achievements, which once lagged behind those of Protestants, are now at the national average. Catholics are underrepresented in the nation's better colleges and faculties, however. Jews are virtually excluded from positions of corporate leadership except in the retail trade, and there is evidence that Catholics suffer much the same kind of discrimination: the upper levels of foundations, corporations, politics, the media, and the arts are dominated by white, Anglo-Saxon Protestants (Greeley, 1977).

Religious affiliation also correlates with political-party preference. A 1978 National Opinion Research Center (NORC) survey found that 52 percent of Protestants are Democrats and 36 percent Republicans; of Catholics, 65 percent are Democrats and 21 percent Republicans; and of Jews, 78 percent are Democrats and only 11 percent Republicans. The Protestant preference for the Democratic party appears in a different light if broken into its racial components: 80 percent of black Protestants are Democrats, while white Protestants are almost evenly divided between the parties. Black Americans no doubt prefer the Democratic party because it has the better record on civil liberties and social welfare issues. The Catholic preference for the Democratic party is a traditional one, dating back to the times when impoverished Catholic immigrants traded their votes for jobs and other benefits from the Democratic "machines" in major Eastern cities. The heavy Jewish support for the Democratic party is probably linked to a long-standing Jewish concern for civil libertarian issues. (The religious affiliation of individual candidates can also be a factor at the polls, it seems. When John Kennedy, a Catholic, ran for president in 1960, he drew unusually high Catholic support but lost many Protestant voters who were normally Democrats; when Jimmy Carter, a "born-again" Southern Baptist, ran for president in 1976, many Protestant Republicans and Catholic Democrats switched their allegiance.)

Attitudes toward social issues also correlate with religious affiliation: Jews are generally the most liberal, followed by Catholics and then Protestants. For example, a 1978 NORC survey found that 49 percent of Protestants opposed premarital sex, compared with 42 percent of Catholics and 20 percent of Jews. The same survey found that 87 percent of Jews would oppose the removal of a hypothetical atheist book from a public library, compared with 65 percent of Catholics and 56 percent of Protestants. The relatively conservative Protestant ranking on many such issues is heavily weighted by the fundamentalist sects; the denominations are markedly more liberal.

There is also evidence that intensity of religious commitment correlates with racial prejudice. For example, Charles Glock and Rodney Stark (1966) found that people who attend church frequently and who believe in orthodox religious doctrine are politically more conservative and more prejudiced than people who are less religious on these criteria. A majority of churchgoers were found to be prejudiced against minority groups, including Jews. Half of the churchgoing Christians in the United States, in fact, still blamed the Jews for the crucifixion of Jesus, even though this view has no basis in either Christian doctrine or historical fact. On the same page of a questionnaire on which

RELIGIOUS BELIEFS OF PEOPLE BELONGING TO DIFFERENT CHRISTIAN CHURCHES AND SECTS (IN PERCENT)

Congre-gational	Metho-dist	Episco-palian	Disciples of Christ	Presby-terian	American Lutheran	American Baptist	Missouri Lutheran	Southern Baptist	Sects	Total Protestant	Roman Catholic
I know God really exists and I have no doubts about it.											
41	60	63	76	75	73	78	81	99	96	71	81
Jesus is the Divine Son of God and I have no doubts about it.											
40	54	59	74	72	74	76	93	99	97	69	86
Jesus was born of a virgin. Percentage who said "completely true."											
21	34	39	62	57	66	69	92	99	96	57	81
Miracles actually happened just as the Bible says they did.											
28	37	41	62	58	69	62	89	92	92	57	74
There is life beyond death. Percentage who answered "completely true."											
36	49	53	64	69	70	72	84	97	94	65	75
The Devil actually exists. Percentage who answered "completely true."											
6	13	17	18	31	49	49	77	92	90	38	66

Source: Charles Y. Glock and Rodney Stark, *American Piety: The Nature of Religious Commitment* (Berkeley: University of California Press, 1968), Chap. 2.

Figure 16.12 The extent to which Christians accept some basic doctrines of their religion varies sharply from one denomination or sect to another; sect members are much more likely to accept the truth of the doctrines.

the overwhelming majority of respondents had declared their commitment to Christian brotherhood, more than 40 percent said they would move their homes if several black families came to live in their neighborhoods, and nearly a third said they did not want blacks in their churches. This evidence does not mean, of course, that religious affiliation is necessarily a *cause* of these attitudes; many other explanations are possible. It may be that conservative people are more attracted by organized religion than liberals are, or even that conservatives are more likely to live in the suburban and rural areas where church attendance is expected by local customs and norms.

The actual content of religious belief also varies from one denomination or sect to another, as suggested by another study by Glock and Stark (1968), which found sharp differences in the extent of belief in basic Christian doctrines. For example, only 21 percent of Congregationalists, compared with 96 percent of members of various sects, believed that Jesus was born of a virgin (see Figure 16.12).

Civil Religion in the United States

In an average week, about 40 percent of the American population attends a church service. This attendance rate is by far the highest in the advanced industrial societies of the world; in Britain, by comparison, weekly attendance is only 15 percent. Does this mean that Americans are a very religious people?

Over the years, opinion polls have consistently shown that almost all Americans espouse some religious faith. In 1975, when the Gallup poll surveyed sixty nations, it found that in professed religious commitment, the United States ranks behind only one other country—India. Only a minority of Europeans, for example, believe in life after death: the percentage ranges from 46 percent in Italy to a mere 35 percent in Scandinavia; and in Japan only 18 percent profess this belief. In contrast, nearly 71 percent of Americans say they believe in life after death. An annual Gallup poll also asks Americans whether they believe in "God or a universal spirit," and every year the question gets an overwhelmingly affirmative answer: the percentage saying "yes" fluctuates between 94 and 96 percent. The evidence seems to indicate that Americans are a remarkably religious people.

But are they? Most sociologists think not. Attendance at church or even a declaration of belief in God is not necessarily good evidence for religious commitment, unless we know why people attend church, what kind of god they believe in, and what effect, if any, their attendance has on their behavior. Drawing on Durkheim's idea that religion is simply the celebration of the social, Will Herberg (1960) argues that the United States is "at once the most secular and the most religious of societies" and suggests that, apart from a few sects, the churches of America really worship "the American way of life." Most Americans tend to use religion primarily for social rather than religious purposes, finding in their church a source of community and in its beliefs a justification for the American values of good neighborliness, self-help, individualism, hard work, and anticommunism. Being a good American involves being religious; President Eisenhower once commented that it did not matter which religion a person believed in, as long as he or she had one.

Robert Bellah (1970) has suggested that the United States really has a "civil religion," in which religious elements are used to sanctify and celebrate its way of life. The Pledge of Allegiance declares that the country is one nation "under God." Its coins declare, "In God we trust." Americans often seem to believe that their social order and historical mission are specifically sanctioned by God. John F. Kennedy captured this idea in his inaugural address:

> With a good conscience our only sure reward, with history the final judge of our deeds, let us go forth to lead the land we love, asking His blessing and His help, but knowing that here on earth God's work must truly be our own.

Political leaders must always pay at least lip service to religious belief; in fact, every presidential inaugural except one (Washington's second) makes mention of God—but only rhetorically, at the beginning or end of the speech. Religion is an element in oaths of office, party conventions, courtroom procedures, and indeed nearly all formal public occasions. Even the Boy Scouts give a "God and country" award, a phrase that implies, to say the least, a compatibility of interest between the two. Many of the nation's

secular symbols also have a sacred quality—the flag, the eagle, the Constitution, the Bill of Rights, "America the Beautiful," "The Star-Spangled Banner," Washington, Jefferson, and Lincoln. This civil religion is not Catholic, Protestant, Jewish, or allied to any other faith; it is sufficiently broad and nonspecific to be acceptable to anyone.

Although there is, no doubt, much validity to this analysis, it fails to take account of the many organizations that are, in fact, specifically or even exclusively religious in their orientation; that are hostile or at best indifferent toward the state; and that have as their driving force their members' deeply felt experience of faith, or even ecstasy. And as we shall see, these are the religious organizations that are currently gaining ground.

Current Trends

The institution of religion in modern America is anything but static: change is apparent everywhere. John Wilson (1978) asserts that "one inescapable conclusion to be drawn from the studies of the contemporary transformations of religion is that traditional religious forms are disappearing, and new forms are emerging." Although there is disagreement about the ultimate fate of traditional religion and the future viability of new forms, sociologists are agreed that the period since the early 1960s has been one of unusual religious innovation (Needleman, 1970; Ellwood, 1973; Zaretsky and Leone, 1974; Glock and Bellah, 1976; B. Wilson, 1976; Wuthnow, 1976, 1978; Robbins et al., 1978; Robbins and Anthony, 1980). Three distinct trends can be discerned: the decline of established religion, the fundamentalist revival, and the emergence of new religions.

The Decline of Established Religion

For several years now, there has been evidence of a significant decline in commitment to the Roman Catholic Church, to the established Protestant denominations, and to mainstream Judaism.

The Catholic Church has perhaps suffered the most in this respect, and the main reason seems to have been the 1968 papal encyclical banning artificial birth control. Opinion polls show that the majority of American Catholics disregard the ban, and in rejecting the church's authority on this issue, they have come to question it on many others. By the early 1970s, 78 percent of married

Catholic women in the childbearing years were using contraceptive devices, and 83 percent of all Catholics favored their use (Bumpass and Westoff, 1973; Greeley, 1977). Other signs of rebellion are legion: a 1978 Roper poll found that, church teachings to the contrary, Catholics are more tolerant of interfaith marriages, and are more likely to enter them, than are Protestants and Jews; moreover, Catholics have a higher divorce rate than either of the other two groups. More than half of the nation's Catholics, surprisingly enough, agree that "there is no reason why a man and a woman shouldn't live together without being married if they choose to do so," and nearly half reject the doctrine that popes derive their authority in a direct line from Jesus. The most spectacular sign of change, however, has been the drop in average weekly attendance at mass—from a high of 72 percent in 1954 to only 52 percent in 1978.

The decline of established Protestant denominations is likewise reflected in lay participation: their membership has either leveled off or shrunk. Martin Marty (1970) has commented that American Protestantism has a "two-party" system, consisting of the modernists and the fundamentalists. The modernists are liberal in their politics, intellectual in their religious commitment, and nonliteral in their interpretation of the Bible, parts of which they regard as myth. The fundamentalists are politically conservative, emotionally committed to their religion, and regard the Bible as the literal word of God. Although both modernists and fundamentalists are to be found in many denominations and sects, the established denominations are essentially modernist in outlook, whereas the sects are basically fundamentalist. To a great extent, the modernists' loss of adherents has been the fundamentalists' gain. Average weekly church attendance among Protestants has remained fairly constant since 1954, never falling below 37 percent and never rising above 44 percent; in 1979 it was 40 percent. But this general trend obscures a significant shift in patterns of lay participation: the denominations' attendance has dropped noticeably, while that of the sects has increased sharply.

Judaism has also been under unusual internal pressure. Although older sects, such as the Hassidic Jews, have continued to insist on rigorous orthodoxy, new movements among the young (most notably the Jews for Jesus sect) have proposed heretical modifications of traditional doc-

16.13 *Like any other social institution, religion is subject to social change. In recent years women have challenged the dominant position of men in all other institutions, and it is not surprising that they are now demanding an equal role with men in religion. Until recently, virtually all the religious organizations in America restricted such roles as priest, rabbi, or minister to men, and most still continue to deny women access to these roles.*

trine. Partly because Jewish doctrine does not place as much emphasis on formal worship as Christian doctrine does, Jewish attendance at synagogue is far lower than church attendance of Catholics or Protestants: only 17 percent go to synagogue more than once a month. More significant, however, is an increasing trend toward interfaith marriages. In 1960, less than 5 percent of Jews married non-Jews; by the mid-1970s, more than a third of their marriages involved a partner of a different faith. It must be expected that in many cases the children of these unions will be raised outside the Jewish religion. For a religious group that recruits almost entirely by birth and does not encourage conversion, this trend is an ominous one.

The Fundamentalist Revival

Fundamentalist religious organizations have grown rapidly in recent years, with the most marked increases in membership occurring among the Seventh-Day Adventists, the Southern Baptist Convention, and the Mormons. Many of these new members are young people, apparently disillusioned with the formalism and doctrinal liberalism of the established denominations. As Dean Kelley (1972) suggests, much of the appeal of fundamentalist sects is their very strictness and exclusivity: they provide a theodicy that gives definite answers in a bewildering world, and they offer a firm sense of belonging. Along with this revival has come an increased political activism, sponsored directly or indirectly by fundamentalist organizations. Unlike the modernist churches, which support state initiatives in such areas as civil rights and antipoverty programs, the fundamentalist groups are hostile to many current social changes, which they regard as morally wicked. For this reason, many of them have been active in campaigns against legalized abortion, women's liberation, gay rights, and many other issues. The activities of the "Moral Majority" and similar groups are credited with helping to defeat several liberal senators in the 1980 elections.

Related to the fundamentalist revival is Pentecostalism, the supposed infusion of the Holy Spirit into religious rituals and personal experiences. Typically, Pentecostalism takes the form of such practices as speaking in tongues, frequent gesticulating, uttering prophecies, and faith healing. The Protestant denominations are generally wary of Pentecostalism: several of them, in fact, went through a Pentecostal phase generations ago when they were still

Figure 16.14 The "charismatic" movement has won a large number of adherents among both Protestants and Catholics. The movement, which is reluctantly tolerated by church hierarchies, aims at an ecstatic, emotional renewal of faith.

sects, and they are now apt to regard this type of religious expression as somewhat vulgar. Some denominations tolerate Pentecostal services in certain congregations, but others do not; as a result, a variety of new Holiness and other Pentecostal sects have sprung up. The Catholic Church, though equally uneasy about Pentecostalism, can find no doctrinal grounds for opposing the practice, so allows it as a "charismatic renewal" of faith. By permitting Pentecostal masses—which are held at different times from regular services, and have been attended by several million Catholics—the church has thus far headed off a sectarian split on the issue. Pentecostalism clearly meets some worshipers' need for an immediate, spontaneous, and emotional experience of faith—an experience that many of the established denominations no longer offer (Harrison, 1974; Laurentin, 1977).

The Emergence of New Religions

An astonishing variety of new sects and cults has appeared in the United States since the 1960s, some with beliefs and names—ranging from the Divine Light Mission to the Church of the Psychedelic Venus—that seem alien or exotic to most Americans. Many of these organizations have vanished almost as rapidly as they emerged; some linger on as local, one-congregation groups with only a handful of members; but a few have flourished, sometimes attracting publicity that is out of all proportion to their size.

Typical of these new sects is the Children of God, one of the few organized groups (other than numerous small communes) to crystallize out of the "Jesus Freak" movement that emerged from the "hippie" counterculture of the 1960s. The original Jesus Freaks were predominantly white and middle-class. Disillusioned by the materialism and rationalism of the older generation and of the society as a whole, they had turned to radical politics or, more commonly, to psychedelic drugs, only to find that neither offered the solutions they were looking for. Finally, they embraced a version of Christianity that was fundamentalist, Pentecostal, and millenarian. The Children of God sect retains many of these early characteristics. Its several thousand members, mostly middle-class whites in their teens or early twenties, are attracted by the sect's emphasis on the experiential rather than the intellectual aspects of religion. They frequently compare their personal experi-ences of Jesus and of drugs ("It's such a rush," or "I'm high on Jesus"); conversely, they have little interest in abstract theology, reducing doctrine to the simple dogmas "Jesus saves" and "The end of the world is coming." What distinguishes this sect from more conventional fundamentalist or Pentecostal groups is its insistence that members must surrender all their possessions to the organization; that they must isolate themselves from the rest of the world (except when performing such necessary tasks as "street work," the conversion of outsiders); and that the leader of the sect, Moses David, is a prophet inspired by God. According to David, the Bible is God's word for yesterday; the new scriptures he issues at regular intervals are God's word for today, and the Children of God are the select few chosen to receive it (Fox and Adams, 1972; Peterson and Mauss, 1973; Balswick, 1974; Davis and Richardson, 1976; Stoner and Parke, 1977; Richardson et al., 1979).

One of the most visible of the new religions is the Hare Krishna movement, whose members, clad in saffron robes and often with heads shaved, may be seen dancing, chanting, and begging in such public places as urban streets and airports. The movement centers around a Hindu sect, the International Society for Krishna Consciousness, which was imported from India in 1965. Its leader, or guru, is worshiped—not as a god, but as a living representative of the deity. The sect requires that its members associate only with other devotees and that they practice an ascetic, celibate life-style. Science, rationality, education, aggression,

Figure 16.15 Religious sects such as the Hare Krishna movement, have attracted numbers of youthful adherents in recent years. Although Americans are generally tolerant of religious diversity, these religious movements lack the "respectability" of the more established churches and therefore attract a certain amount of hostility.

and competition are all negatively valued. The sect offers its members a complete personal transformation, based on the adoption of both new beliefs and new body imagery such as hairstyles and clothing. Although this religion rejects many core American values, its recruits come from the American mainstream: they are mainly middle-class white Americans in their early twenties, many of them college dropouts. The religion has been considerably modified for its American participants, however. In original Indian doctrine, the achievement of Krishna consciousness requires many years of study and contemplation. In the American version, some Krishna consciousness can be achieved merely by performing the appropriate rituals, particularly chanting—an innovation which, though unorthodox, recognizes the American concern with technical means and immediate results (Judah, 1974; Daner, 1976; Cox, 1977).

Another new religion is the Unification Church, founded by Sun Myung Moon, a Korean industrialist. When the sect was imported to the United States in the early 1960s, it was a millenarian movement predicting the end of the world in 1967. As is usual in such cases, the prophecy was not fulfilled. (A failed prediction does not necessarily mean a failed sect, however: the Jehovah's Witnesses have awaited the apocalypse on five specific dates since 1914, during which time their membership has grown from a few thousand to more than 2 million people in 210 countries.) Moon responded to the failure of his prophecy by developing a much more elaborate doctrine, containing elements of anticommunism, Eastern religions, and fundamentalist Christianity: in essence, he claims that the Koreans are the Chosen People; that a transformation of the world will occur within the foreseeable future; and that he himself is Lord of the Second Advent—a successor to Jesus, who failed in his mission. The sect claims over 40,000 members in the United States, although the actual number is probably much lower. Most members are middle-class whites in their late teens or early twenties, often with some college education, and they frequently join the sect at a time of personal crisis or loneliness. Members are expected to give all their property to the sect, to associate only with one another, and to spend much of their time collecting money for the organization. According to Moon's "divine principle" of "heavenly deception," they may mislead the public when asking for donations—for example, by claiming that they represent some charity. It is often charged that Moon has amassed a considerable financial empire, whose assets range from real estate to fishing fleets, and that he enjoys an affluent life-style that contrasts markedly with the virtual poverty of the sect's ordinary members—although the same criticism could be leveled at the hierarchy of more established religious organizations as well (Lofland, 1966, 1977; Robbins et al., 1976; Edwards, 1979; Galanter et al., 1979; Bromley and Shupe, 1979).

Many of the new religions have severely strained the American tolerance for diversity of belief. One reason for the hostility toward some of the sects and cults, no doubt, is simply their apparently alien character: to Americans who share the dominant religious tradition, the doctrines of the new groups often seem implausible, if not bizarre, and their public activities are an irritant. Another reason is the strong suspicion that such movements as the Unification Church and Scientology are not really religions at all, but rather fraudulent commercial enterprises whose objective is to enrich their founders at the expense of their gullible (and psychologically vulnerable) members. Another source of

Figure 16.16

"*I know just how you feel. We have two punks and a Moonie.*"

Copyright Wm. Hamilton

hostility is the belief that some new religions recruit by "brainwashing" potential converts. It is certainly true that many new sects discourage members' contacts with outsiders and particularly with parents and former associates, that they maintain a barrage of religious indoctrination within their communities, and that they generally treat new recruits as children, depriving them of any opportunity to make independent decisions (the Children of God even call new members "babes"). Some parents, deeply concerned at the defection of their sons or daughters to sects, have hired professional "deprogrammers" who kidnap the converts and submit them to intense psychological and even physical pressure to reject their new faith. The whole issue raises serious questions about religious freedom and civil liberties (Patrick, 1976; Enroth, 1977; Richardson, 1978; Delgado, 1980; Levine, 1980; Anthony et al., 1980).

Evaluation

What are we to make of all these changes in American religion? Why are they taking place, and what might be their long-term significance? As sociologists have pointed out, the current trends are not as novel or unprecedented as they might seem. Some shift in allegiance from established denominations to fundamentalist sects is nothing new; indeed, the United States has seen no less than four "Great Awakenings" of revivalism: in the periods 1725–1750, 1800–1835, 1875–1914, and—under the leadership of Billy Graham—from the end of World War II until the late 1950s. The emergence of new sects and cults is nothing new, either: the United States was the birthplace of such religious organizations as the Jehovah's Witnesses, the Mormons, the Seventh-Day Adventists, the Spiritualists, and the Christian Scientists, to name only a few of the more successful groups. Nor is hostility toward and harassment of new religions unprecedented in the American experience: Quakers, Mennonites, Hutterites, Mormons, Christian Scientists, and others have all been subjected to attempts at suppression, ranging from subtle discrimination to violence, arson, and murder (J. Wilson, 1978).

As we might expect, the religious changes that have taken place since the 1960s appear to be related to the social changes of the same period. The 1960s were a time of unusual social, political, and cultural turmoil. Many traditional American values—especially those centered on mate-

rialism, success, achievement, deferred gratification, rationality, science, or competition—were widely questioned for the first time. To the extent that existing religious organizations failed to take account of these changes, the formation of new groups was stimulated. What is new about American religion, then, is its growing pluralism and the sense of options this has engendered in many individuals.

Indeed, as Martin Marty (1976) points out, many Americans use religion as a means of establishing and asserting their identities. Increasingly, therefore, they are apt to pick and choose among religious organizations, rather like consumers looking for the particular product that best suits their own needs. Thus, those who seek a mystical transcendence may join one group; those who want a strict, unambiguous doctrine that relieves them of the responsibility for making decisions will choose another. There are obvious parallels between this use of religion to satisfy individual needs and the use of "self-help" therapies (such as bioenergetics, transactional analysis, gestalt training, *est* training, primal-scream therapy, or transcendental meditation) for similar purposes. In fact, some new sects and cults, such as Scientology and the Synanon group, originated as lay therapies and self-improvement organizations (Schur, 1976; Wallis, 1977). It is also interesting to note that some of the new sects do not appeal, as older sects did, to the economically deprived: rather, they cater to the psychologically deprived, particularly middle-class youth in search of a meaning they cannot find elsewhere. Only time will tell whether any of the new religions grow into the churches of the future—or whether, like such bygone sects as the Diggers, the Shakers, and the Levellers, they totally disappear.

Secularization: Fact or Myth?

As industrialization has advanced in countries around the world, the apparent tendency has been for the societies concerned to become more secular, or worldly, in their institutions, values, and beliefs. *Secularization* is the process by which religion loses its influence in society. The questions then arise, How far has secularization proceeded? What are its causes? and What is the future, if any, of religion?

While there is general (though not unanimous) agreement among sociologists that the world is becoming secularized, there is little consensus on how the process can be measured. Among the factors that have been studied are trends in the amount of money spent on new religious buildings, the decrease in the prestige of the clergy, the proportion of marriages that take place in a secular rather than a religious setting, the number of religious books published annually, and the ratio of religious to secular paintings displayed in public galleries. These measures generally suggest a trend toward secularization, but it is not a uniform one and proceeds by fits and starts (Cox, 1965; B. Wilson, 1966; Greeley, 1972; Martin, 1969; Glasner, 1977).

More useful, perhaps, are opinion-poll data on people's beliefs in God, life after death, and specific religious teachings. In the 1975 international Gallup survey cited earlier, the pollsters found a "collapse" of religious belief in all the advanced industrial societies they studied, with the excep-

PERCENTAGE ATTENDING CHURCH IN THE UNITED STATES DURING AVERAGE WEEK

Year	%	Year	%
1955	49	1968	43
1956	46	1969	42
1957	47	1970	42
1958	49	1971	40
1959	47	1972	40
1960	47	1973	40
1961	47	1974	40
1962	46	1975	40
1963	46	1976	42
1964	45	1977	41
1965	44	1978	41
1966	44	1979	40
1967	45	1980	40

Source: Gallup polls

Figure 16.17 The percentage of Americans who attend church during an average week has been declining fairly steadily for the past two decades, with attendance figures dropping most rapidly among Catholics. Major Protestant denominations have also lost participants, but this trend has been offset by increased participation in fundamentalist Protestant sects. American church attendance is still significantly higher, however, than attendance in any other advanced industrial society.

tions of Canada, where there was a noticeable but smaller decline in faith, and the United States, where belief continued at a remarkably high level. Also useful are data on membership of religious organizations and on attendance at worship. These measures have their limitations, however. For example, figures for church or sect membership are often unreliable because some organizations count as a member everyone who has been baptized; some count everyone who has affirmed membership as an adult; and some include the entire group that they feel ought to belong. Even when attendance statistics are reliable, they are not necessarily a good indication of how "religious" people actually are. One can attend worship for many reasons, ranging from habit to piety to a desire for social status. The evidence from most industrial societies points to a decline, though an uneven one, in both membership of religious organizations and in attendance at services. This trend appears in both the United States and Canada, but to a significantly lesser degree than in any other advanced industrial society. In the United States, for example, 68 percent of the population were members of (rather than merely believers in) a particular faith in 1976, down from 77 percent forty years previously. Average weekly church attendance in the United States has declined somewhat over the past two decades, but has leveled off at around 40 percent (see Figure 16.17). Canadian attendance has typically been two or three percentage points lower.

The most obvious form of secularization, however, occurs on such a large and diffuse scale that it is difficult to measure. This trend is nevertheless an unmistakable one: the extent to which traditional religion becomes a separate and distinct institution with a limited role in society. The principal cause of this secularization lies in the complexity of the modern urbanized, industrialized world. In small-scale, simple societies, religion extends to every aspect of experience. It suffuses all social institutions—law, family, art, politics, economic activity. Everyday routines, such as eating, hunting, or caring for the sick, are surrounded with religious ritual. Most people have much the same kind of daily tasks and experiences, and they share readily in a common, unchallenged belief system. In a complex modern society, however, many new, specialized institutions arise. Hospitals take care of the sick; welfare agencies aid the poor; police and courts handle deviant behavior; schools transmit knowledge; science explains the universe; economic institutions organize the production and distribution of goods; government oversees society. Traditional religion eventually becomes a separate and distinct institution with a limited field of influence, and may even find itself in competition with other institutions, such as science or government. At the same time people play highly specific occupational roles and follow different life-styles, and their varying experiences lead them to view the world in different ways. For the first time, they have a measure of choice about what they will believe, and many opt for different interpretations of reality. Religion, once vital to every area of experience, may appear to have little relevance to many aspects of daily life. Religious commitment, if it exists at all, tends to become part-time rather than total (Luckmann, 1967).

This analysis raises an intriguing question. If advanced industrialization inevitably erodes traditional religious institutions, then why is it that the only exceptions to the trend are the United States, the most industrialized society in the world, and Canada, a highly industrialized society with many cultural similarities to the United States? Clearly, we should expect the exact opposite to be the case. A plausible answer, suggested by Peter Berger (1969), is that whereas the churches in Western Europe and elsewhere have generally adhered to their traditional ways, and as a result have been pushed to the margins of their secular societies, the churches in North America have remained nearer the center of society by becoming secularized themselves. More concerned with self-preservation than with their original mission, they have modified their doctrines and rituals in an attempt to become more "relevant" to the modern world. In effect, they participate in the secularized civil religion; only the sects, which uphold traditional doctrines, have become marginal to the society.

Of course, the fact that industrialization has generally led to secularization in the past does not mean that this must necessarily always be so in the future. Particularly in times of uncertainty and rapid social change, people may look to religious values to stabilize and revitalize their culture (Linton, 1943; Wallace, 1956). The current fundamentalist revival in the United States is undoubtedly a reaction to the moral uncertainties caused by the social and economic changes of the 1960s and 1970s. In the same way, a fundamentalist upsurge is now sweeping much of the Islamic world as a sudden deluge of oil money thrusts Iran,

Figure 16.18 Many American churches have tried to counter the charge that they are irrelevant by becoming more deeply involved in secular activities, ranging from youth clubs to political activism. Critics of this tendency protest that the churches risk loosing sight of their traditional religious role in society.

Saudi Arabia, and other traditionalist societies headlong into modernization and social change (Said, 1979). It may even be the case, in fact, that the need for religion will eventually reassert itself most powerfully in precisely those societies that become the most industrialized, rationalized, and materialistic.

What then, is the future of religion? It is important to distinguish carefully between secularization as it affects traditional, established religious forms, and secularization as it affects other orientations toward the sacred and supernatural. There is much evidence that traditional religion is being eroded; this in itself is hardly surprising, because social change must inevitably modify all institutions over time. There is virtually no evidence, however, that popular belief in some supernatural, transcendent reality is disappearing, in North America or indeed anywhere else. According to Gallup polls in 1976 and 1978, for example, three-quarters of the American population know their astrological "sign," and 29 percent believe their lives are governed by the stars. In acknowledgment of widespread superstition, airlines have no row 13, and high-rise buildings have no thirteenth floor. Millions believe in one or more of such practices as fortunetelling, palmistry, numerology, hexing, tarot-card reading, and seances with the dead. Indeed, a quarter of the population claims to have seen a ghost at some time or another. All these beliefs and practices run directly contrary to the teachings of the established churches, yet they thrive in North America and other advanced industrial societies (Martin, 1967, 1969; Greeley, 1975; Moore, 1977; Wuthnow, 1978). And new cults and sects appear in unprecedented profusion.

For many years it was widely felt that as science progressively provided rational explanations for the mysteries of the universe, religion would have less and less of a role to play and would eventually disappear, unmasked as nothing more than superstition. No serious thinker accepts that view today. There are still gaps in our understanding that science can never fill. On the ultimately important questions—of the meaning and purpose of life and the nature of morality—science is utterly silent and, by its very nature, always will be. We can probably anticipate a continuing decline in allegiance to traditional religions, for they will have to compete with an increasing number of other belief systems that many people will find at least as rationally or emotionally satisfying. But this does not mean that there will be no place for a belief in the sacred and the supernatural. Few citizens of modern societies would utterly deny the possibility of some supernatural, transcendental realm that lies beyond the boundaries of ordinary experience, and in this fundamental sense religion is probably here to stay.

Summary

1. Religion is a system of communally held beliefs and practices that are oriented toward some sacred, supernatural realm. According to Durkheim, all religions distinguish between the sacred and the profane.

2. The sociological approach focuses on the social rather than the theological aspects of religion, and traces the interrelationships between religion and society.

3. Religions can be conveniently classified into four main types: simple supernaturalism, animism, theism, and abstract ideals. The major world religions have convincing explanations of the human predicament.

4. Durkheim analyzed the totemism of Australian aborigines from a functionalist perspective and concluded that religious belief and ritual function to enhance social solidarity. The most important functions of religion are those of maintaining social solidarity; providing meaningful answers to ultimate questions; reinforcing social control; promoting social change; and offering psychological support to individuals in crisis. Some secular belief systems, such as communism, may serve as functional equivalents of religion in certain respects.

5. Marx analyzed religion from a conflict perspective. He saw religious belief as a form of alienation and argued that the dominant religion tends to support the status quo in any society. Religion does play this role in many societies and is often an element in social conflict, as such examples as the medieval witch craze and millenarian movements suggest. Religion can, however, sometimes be a source of radical change.

6. According to Weber's "Protestant ethic" thesis, modern capitalism arose partly as a result of the Puritan tendency to work hard and reinvest money rather than spend it. His theory allows a greater role for ideas in social change than Marx's theory does. Marx saw ideas as reflecting rather than causing change.

7. There are four main types of religious organization: the ecclesia, the denomination ("church"), the sect, and the cult. There is a dynamic relationship between church and sect, and this is a source of religious change.

8. Distinctive features of American religion include the following: there is no "official" religion; citizens are expected to pay at least lip service to religious faith; there is considerable religious pluralism; religious diversity is tolerated, except in a few cases; religion can be a source of personal or group identity. Membership in various religious organizations correlates with, but does not necessarily cause, differences in socioeconomic status, education, political preference, attitudes toward social issues, prejudice, and religious beliefs.

9. Current trends in American religion include the decline

of established religion, a fundamentalist revival, and the emergence of new religions. These developments are related to social changes that have made Americans more inclined to choose a faith that meets individualistic needs.

10. Secularization can be measured in various ways; the general conclusion is that the influence of traditional religious forms is undermined by industrialization and the complex, heterogeneous societies that it creates. Various other beliefs in the sacred or supernatural abound, however, and new religions proliferate. A fully secularized society is unlikely: some forms of religion persist because they address vital issues that other belief systems ignore.

Important Terms

sacred (402)

ritual (402)

profane (402)

religion (402)

simple
  supernaturalism (403)

animism (404)

magic (404)

theism (404)

polytheism (404)

monotheism (404)

abstract ideals (405)

theodicy (405)

totem (406)

functional
  equivalent (408)

alienation (409)

millenarian
  movement (412)

ecclesia (416)

denomination (416)

sect (416)

cult (416)

secularization (427)

Suggested Readings

BERGER, PETER L. *A Rumor of Angels: Modern Society and the Rediscovery of the Supernatural.* New York: Doubleday, 1969.

Thoughtfully and elegantly written, this book argues that there is still a place for religion in the modern world and that a sociological approach to religion can be combined with religious faith.

GLOCK, CHARLES Y. *Religion in Sociological Perspective: Essays in the Empirical Study of Religion.* Belmont, Calif.: Wadsworth, 1973.

An excellent collection of articles by modern sociologists of religion. The selection gives a good overview of research in the field.

GREELEY, ANDREW M. *The American Catholic: A Social Portrait.* New York: Basic Books, 1977.

An important study of Catholics in the United States. Based on survey data, the study disproves many popular myths about Catholic attitudes and other social characteristics.

JOHNSTONE, RONALD L. *Religion and Society in Interaction: The Sociology of Religion.* Englewood Cliffs, N.J.: Prentice-Hall, 1975.

A short and readable introduction to the sociology of religion, recommended for the student who wants an accessible overview of the field.

MARTY, MARTIN E. *A Nation of Behavers.* Chicago: University of Chicago Press, 1976.

A provocative book, in which the author argues that American religious groups are distinguished more by what they do than by what they supposedly believe: people therefore often use religion to establish their identities and social location.

ROBBINS, THOMAS, and DICK ANTHONY (eds.). *In Gods We Trust: New Patterns of Religious Pluralism in America.* New Brunswick, N.J.: Transaction Books, 1980.

A broad-ranging collection of articles dealing with the current religious ferment in America.

WILSON, JOHN. *Religion in American Society: The Effective Presence.* Englewood Cliffs, N.J.: Prentice-Hall, 1978.

A detailed and up-to-date sociology of American religion. Wilson utilizes both conflict and functionalist perspectives and emphasizes religious changes.

WORSLEY, PETER. *The Trumpet Shall Sound.* London: McGibbon & Kee, 1957.

A fascinating study of the "cargo cult" millenarian movements of Melanesia; the book has become a classic in the sociology of religion.

ZARETSKY, IRVING I., and MARK P. LEONE (eds.). *Religious Movements in Contemporary America.* Princeton, N.J.: Princeton University Press, 1974.

A wide-ranging and informative collection of articles dealing with new sects, cults, and other movements in modern American religion. The book provides an excellent sampling of sociological work in the field.

Reading

Evil Eyes and Religious Choices *Barbara Hargrove*

There has been strong criticism of some of the methods allegedly employed by certain religious sects. In this reading, Barbara Hargrove considers whether these criticisms are justified.

There are charges that young people who are recruited to such groups as Sun Myung Moon's Unification Church, Hare Krishna, or the Children of God have undergone a total change of personality. They have rejected their families and their families' values, cut off ties with former friends, given up cherished career patterns and hobbies. They are said to show evidence of psychosis, of schizophrenia, of loss of creativity. They are described as exhibiting robot-like behavior or having a typical glassy-eyed "thousand-mile stare." They no longer engage in rational discussion, it is said, but keep using the jargon and advancing the ideology of the group. . . .

It is assumed that this behavior is the product of a deliberate, sinister, and highly sophisticated plot to take over the minds and souls of young people and turn them into "robots." This is done, supposedly, through forced isolation, deprivation of food, sleep, and other essentials, psychological persuasion of the most coercive kind, and other forcible measures which sometimes assume mythological proportions in the conversation of parents and former members who have gone through the deprogramming which is the reversal of that process. All evidence points to the fact that the deprogramming cause has become at least as much a social movement as the groups it seeks to oppose.

One obvious question to ask is whether these young converts are simply that—converts—to a religious group which is labeled deviant by the society, or at least by that portion of the society from which they have come. There is little doubt that most of the groups originally accused of brainwashing fall into the deviant category, though there is also evidence that the charges are spreading to less deviant ones. For example, a number of conservative Christian groups have been so challenged, and similar charges were raised by parents of several students at the University of Kansas who converted to Roman Catholicism and entered a monastic order in France after a humanities course about such orders in medieval society. In the long run, no religious group is likely to be considered normative if it demands total commitment in the form of withdrawal from ordinary career patterns or familiar social networks.

This is not only true now, but can be found throughout history. A glance through any history of the church will turn up large numbers of people, many of them young, who caused their families great anguish by taking seriously the biblical injunction, "He who loves father or mother more than me is not worthy of me . . . and he who does not take up his cross and follow me is not worthy of me."
. . .

The convert is a person who shifts [his or her] overall organizing framework of meaning from one pattern to another which is significantly different. It is a little like comparing a relief map of a country to a political map, where seeing the area organized into mountain ranges, river valleys, and the like, is likely to call forth a considerably different response from that to a map showing states, counties, and cities. The territory is the same, but its meaning seems altered.

Usually people learn the basic features of their reality "map" in the family, and find it reinforced, if expanded, in the later socialization of such institutions as school and church. Definitions that are significantly different from those widely shared in the society may result in difficulty in the economic and political realm as well as in these more formative institutions. So the turning of a person to a different "map" for his or her authority as a guide to meaning can be seen as an indication of failure by parents or school or church—a badge of shame to them.

At the same time, there are reasons for negative feelings toward family and old friends on the part of the convert. As Peter Berger put it in *The Sacred Canopy*, "the individual who wishes to convert, and (more importantly) to 'stay converted,' must engineer his social life in accordance with this purpose. Thus he must dissociate himself from those individuals or groups . . . of his past religious reality, and associate himself all the more intensively and (if possible) exclusively with those who serve to maintain his new one."

The convert's new frame of reference relies not only on the direct response of other members of the group he or she has joined, but also on certain authorities they share—sacred writings, leaders of the movement, and the like. Part of the changed behavior seen in a convert derives from this choice of new bases of authority and legitimation, from which new lines of reasoning will arise. It is much more comfortable to be among people for whom such approaches seem rational and right, to be with people who share the same categories and authorities. Often, even if the new way of looking at the world does not necessarily call for changed behavior or appearance, people may adopt certain characteristic styles of action or address in order to identify one another as fellow-believers, to know who it is one may expect to share common assumptions, to talk with without defensiveness, to give mutual aid in what has been defined as a common struggle.

To others who do not share their frame of reference—and of course this includes the families and friends with whom the former worldview was shared—such a change in accepted categories of meaning and sources of authority seems a clear loss of rationality. The convert will no longer "listen to reason." Their attention is fixed elsewhere, so that they may seem a thousand miles away, regardless of whether their eyes actually have a "thousand-mile stare." New styles of response, new priorities concerning ideal personality types, may well lead to the appearance of an abrupt change in personality patterns. . . . All this, of course, is completely unfathomable to those who assume that the old self still exists in the familiar body of their child or friend.

Harvey Cox has suggested that in all societies where new religious movements have attracted young people, their parents and others in the "establishment" will develop some "evil eye" theory, insisting that their children have been bewitched. (One is reminded of the tale of the Pied Piper of Hamelin.) Brainwashing, in this case, may be seen as the evil eye theory appropriate to a modern scientific culture. This kind of definition of conversion also fits our common tendency to define any deviance as illness. Conversion in this instance is simply a case of induced mental illness. . . . There is in this "evil eye" theory no more place for rational decision making or personal freedom of choice than could be found in the old theories of witchcraft, sorcery, and possession. In a society which aspires toward values of individual autonomy, why should we find such a theory so widely applied to recruitment to religions which are considered deviant? Perhaps we have forgotten other explanations which might have carried with them more satisfactory methods of dealing with the situation.

A failure to recognize the importance of religion in the society leads to overlooking those human needs which are most often served by religious involvement. In particular, a secular society which prides itself on being objectively rational in the scientific mode may offer little challenge or hope to the young person who longs to be fully involved in activity which is of value, even at personal risk or danger. Objective rationality has a hard time satisfying those who would be heroes, who spurn the pragmatic tests of self-interest. Many of the groups in question have the particular appeal of calling converts to become saviors of the world, however they define the salvation they would offer.

Time and time again, converts give as their reason for joining the fact that here they had found a group of people who cared about one another, and who cared for them as persons. The other questions, those of doctrine or public consequence, were never even considered until group reinforcement had already made the doctrine seem reasonable and the consequences right. At this point, the assumption that people can be brainwashed has essentially become a self-fulfilling prophecy. Without any basis on which to ask questions of the group, they join it out of felt needs, out of hungers which have not been satisfied in their lives outside the group, and then submit themselves willingly to its influence.

An evil eye definition of conversion has both its source and its consequences in the willingness by members of the dominant society to avoid dealing with those weaknesses of the society that create needs which are met by new religious groups. Bewitchment or brainwashing must be the fault of the deceiver, not of those whose children are deceived nor of the society from which they come. No critical examination of other possible causes is thought necessary. And so no remedial action is required other than the exorcism of the evil influence.

Why are young people so impressed by a group of people who show genuine love and concern? Have they never met such responses elsewhere? Why is it so attractive to be recruited to save the world? In what ways have recruits come to understand that it is so in need of saving? . . . These are the kinds of questions which conversions elicit, and which definitions like brainwashing allow us to ignore.

Source: Barbara Hargrove, "Evil Eyes and Religious Choices," *Society* (May-June 1980).

CHAPTER **17**   *Science*

Science, although unknown to many societies in the past, has become a central institution in the life of all modern industrial societies. A society such as our own depends for its very existence on advanced scientific knowledge and its technological applications—aircraft and antibiotics, telecommunications and assembly lines, skyscrapers and synthetic fabrics, computers and automobiles. Nor is it just our material existence that depends on science and technology. Our view of the world has been radically changed over the past century by scientific thought in such various fields as biology, physics, astronomy, psychology, medicine, and sociology. If you try to imagine what our society will be like in the years or generations ahead, your ideas are likely to be based on the assumption that science and technology will continue, for better or worse, to transform our way of life.

The terms "science" and "technology" are often used as synonyms in ordinary speech. But although the two happen to be closely linked in industrial society, they are distinct phenomena. *Science refers to the logical, systematic methods by which knowledge of nature is obtained, and to the actual knowledge accumulated by these methods.* On the other hand, *technology* refers to the practical applications of knowledge about nature. The goals of science and technology are not the same. Science is concerned with the pursuit of knowledge about nature; technology is concerned with putting that knowledge to some use.

Every society has at least a simple technology, even if it is limited to such techniques as making bows and arrows, fire, or canoes. All primitive peoples have some body of practical knowledge on which their technology is based. But this kind of knowledge is not science. It is derived from earlier trial-and-error experience, not from an understanding of the abstract principles involved. The cave

435

dweller may know how to light a fire but does not know why it burns, or why some substances burn whereas others do not.

Science, unlike technology, has appeared only rarely in human societies in the past. Scientific knowledge requires a logical, systematic understanding of the principles that underlie natural events. A scientific understanding of the world is necessary, however, for an advanced technology. Automobiles or atomic reactors cannot be built without precise knowledge of the relevant scientific principles. The close link between science and technology that we take for granted today is a relatively recent development. Yet it has launched the process of industrialization and modernization that is radically changing the way of life of people all over the world.

Paradoxically, the study of science has always been a rather neglected area of sociology. Despite increased interest in the topic in recent years, it still remains a marginal one to most sociologists. One reason for this neglect has probably been the great prestige that science has enjoyed from the time of the Industrial Revolution until World War II. Throughout this period, people generally agreed that scientific advance was the route to human happiness. Science was not seen as problematic, and most sociologists took it for granted or ignored it. Faith in science began to falter when the atomic bomb was dropped on Hiroshima near the end of World War II, for the explosion brought the abrupt realization that scientific knowledge could now be used to destroy life on earth. The prestige of science, though still high, has since been further eroded (Etzioni and Nunn, 1974; Ravetz, 1977). Many of our most urgent global problems are the unforeseen results of scientific advance and technological innovation. The ecological crisis, for example, is widely seen as the outcome of the uncontrolled application of scientific knowledge to industrial technology. The world-wide population explosion, too, is partly a result of the introduction of new medical technologies to developing countries; we may watch the harrowing consequences on our TV sets over the next few decades as millions of people die from the effects of starvation.

Recent opinion polls show that public attitudes toward science now seem to be growing more ambiguous, even though they remain basically favorable. We still acknowledge the extraordinary benefits we derive from science. Ideas of "getting back to nature" have a certain romantic

appeal only until we consider the prospect of toothache without painkillers or homes without electricity. But many people are becoming less enthusiastic about headlong scientific and technological advance, and sociologists are now studying science and technology more critically than ever before.

The Institutionalization of Science

Science has emerged only relatively recently as a major social institution (Ben-David, 1971). How and why did this development take place?

The Historical Background

A few ancient peoples, such as the Arabs, the Greeks, and the Mayans, accumulated a considerable amount of scientific knowledge, particularly in the fields of mathematics and astronomy. They had hardly any specialized scientific roles, however, and they made little effort to link science to technology. The Greeks had a particularly elaborate science, which, had they applied it to technology, might have speeded up the modernization process by many centuries. Why did they fail to do so? The reason seems to lie in the values and social structure of ancient Greek society. The Greeks rigidly differentiated between slaves, who were responsible for work, and citizens, who ideally refrained from such lowly activity and instead pursued intellectual pleasures. To the Greeks, science was simply an aspect of philosophy, and they sought knowledge about the natural world much more as a value in itself than for practical purposes (Farrington, 1949). The Romans were less interested than the Greeks in abstract ideas, and although Greek scientific knowledge was available to them, they based most of their own technology on rule-of-thumb methods rather than scientific principles. With the fall of the Roman Empire, scientific advance came to a halt for almost a thousand years, largely because scientific inquiry was discouraged by the medieval Church.

The rebirth of learning in the sixteenth and seventeenth centuries marked the beginning of modern science, although there were still no specialized scientific roles. In England, where much of this scientific innovation took place, science was practiced mainly by gentlemen of lei-

Figure 17.1 The earliest forms of systematic science were astronomy and mathematics, which were practiced many centuries ago by a few peoples in Asia, Africa, the Middle East, Europe, and Central and South America. These ancient peoples made some practical use of their scientific knowledge in a few limited areas of immediate concern to their societies, such as agriculture, architecture, and navigation. For the most part, however, they pursued science for its own sake and failed to link science to technology.

Figure 17.2 Until the twentieth century, science was practiced primarily by gentlemen equipped with intellectual curiosity and private wealth. The activity was not very highly valued by society, for its practical purposes were not widely recognized. Few scientists were full-time professionals; the field was dominated by what we would today regard as gifted amateurs. Note that these scientists of the mid-nineteenth century are wearing the formal clothes of the upper class even at work in the laboratory.

sure. The handful of scientists in this period can still be counted and named, and nearly all of them made significant scientific discoveries. The problems they dealt with were very often the problems that faced their society and economy: the bulk of their research was in fields relevant to warfare, navigation, or industry (Merton, 1970).

Almost until the beginning of the present century, science remained a respectable leisure activity whose usefulness was not socially recognized. Universities were gradually admitting science to the curriculum, but they continued to concentrate on more prestigious traditional subjects such as classical languages and philosophy. Specialized scientific roles existed mainly in the universities, and scientific research was largely confined to the ivory tower of the academic world.

The Modern Institution

In the course of this century, however, the relationship between science and technology has become fully recognized and exploited. The "little science" of the previous centuries has now become "big science," deeply involved in big organizations, big money, and big politics. The number of scientists in the world has grown so rapidly that in the early sixties, Derek Price (1963) calculated that over 90 percent of all scientists who had ever lived were alive at that time. Nearly 100,000 scientific journals are currently published, and more than 2 million individual scientific papers appear each year.

Largely because American society relies so heavily on advanced technology, science has rapidly emerged—particularly since World War II—as one of our dominant social institutions. The number of scientific roles in the United States has expanded enormously. There are now more than 2.7 million scientists and engineers in the United States, of whom 566,000 are engaged in full-time research (Bureau of the Census, 1980). These research scientists rarely work in their own private laboratories. Nearly all of them are employed by large formal organizations: industry is the largest single employer, followed by educational institutions and government. The scientist in a university or college still has considerable freedom to choose the area of research, provided some organization or interest can be persuaded to fund it. In industry and government, however, the scientist's specific tasks are usually set by the organization in accordance with its own goals.

A technological society such as the United States supports science and scientists because it expects a payoff. The federal government provides just over half of the funds for scientific research, and most of the rest is supplied by industry. More concerned with useful technologies than with the pursuit of knowledge for its own sake, these sponsors tend to allocate funds to *applied research,* which aims at finding technological uses for scientific knowledge, rather than to *basic research,* which aims mainly at increasing the sum of knowledge. In the "little science" of previous centuries, most scientific resources were devoted to basic research; in the modern United States, however, only 12.5 percent of all research funds are spent on work of this kind (Bureau of the Census, 1980). The determination of how money should be allocated, be it for cancer research or space technology, is the outcome of a political process and has little to do with what scientists themselves regard as the most pressing social or scientific priorities.

The rapid rate of increase in scientific knowledge—about 90 percent of which has been determined within living memory—has had important effects on the scientific community. Science is no longer a field for the gifted amateur. Scientists must spend many years in training and can rarely expect to make a significant contribution until they have mastered a relatively specialized subsection of some field. Scientific disciplines have become more and more specialized, and even within these specialties the scientist may find it difficult to keep up with the literature that reports new advances in the field. To handle this problem, scientists form social organizations of various kinds. These organizations may be either large formal bodies, such as the American Association for the Advancement of Science, or small, informal, "invisible colleges" containing a network of scientists in the same field who share information with one another. Such organizations enable individual scientists to stay abreast of developments, to find answers to specific questions, to sense new trends, and to obtain critical responses to their own work (Price, 1963; Crane, 1972; Griffith and Mullins, 1972).

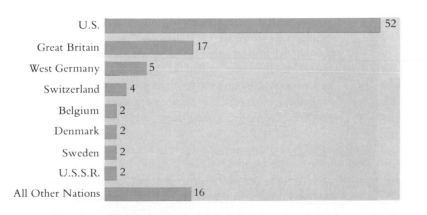

NUMBER OF NOBEL PRIZE WINNERS BY NATIONALITY, 1971–1980

U.S.	52
Great Britain	17
West Germany	5
Switzerland	4
Belgium	2
Denmark	2
Sweden	2
U.S.S.R.	2
All Other Nations	16

Figure 17.3 The United States has won a remarkably high proportion of Nobel prizes. The main reason for this performance appears to be the extensive support that government, industry, and educational institutions give to research. In countries such as the Soviet Union, the government is the only source of research funds, and the atmosphere of academic freedom so vital to research is lacking.

The Norms of Science

The scientific community has developed a set of *norms* that are expected to govern the professional behavior of its individual members. According to Robert Merton (1942), four principal norms constitute the "moral imperatives" of science: universalism, communalism, disinterestedness, and organized skepticism. Like other functionalists, Merton emphasizes consensus rather than conflict, and claims that these norms reflect widely shared values of scientists.

Universalism emphasizes the universal nature of the scientific enterprise and its findings. The particular charac-

Figure 17.4 Albert Einstein was perhaps the greatest scientist of the century, but his work was scorned in Nazi Germany because he was Jewish and was highly critical of Hitler. In taking this attitude, the Nazis violated the "moral imperatives" of science. Widespread attitudes of this kind would severely hinder scientific progress.

teristics of individual scientists—such as their race, class, or national origin—are irrelevant. Research findings must be evaluated purely in terms of their scientific worth.

Communalism is the principle that scientific knowledge should not be the personal property of the discoverer. It should be made available instead to the entire scientific community. All science rests on a shared heritage of past discoveries, and no individual can claim property rights over the outcome of research. A few scientists may be fortunate enough to have their discoveries named after them (Boyle's law, the Salk vaccine, Einstein's theory of relativity, Darwin's theory of evolution), but the discoveries are common property. (Technology, in contrast, can become private or corporate property through the use of patents.)

Disinterestedness is the requirement that scientists should be free from self-interest in their professional roles. Of course, scientists may legitimately hope that their work will be recognized and praised by the scientific community. But this recognition should be sufficient reward, and the scientist's main aim should be to contribute to the sum of scientific knowledge. In other careers—in business, say, or politics—it is almost expected that people will distort the facts to serve their own ends, but in the scientific community the dishonest manipulation of data or any other fraudulent practice is not tolerated.

Organized skepticism refers to the expectation that scientists will suspend judgment until all the facts are at hand. No theory, however ancient and respected or new and revolutionary, can be accepted uncritically. There are no sacred areas in science that should not be critically investigated, even if political or religious dogma forbids it. The skepticism of the scientific community is "organized" in the sense that it is built into the scientific method itself and is binding on all members of the community.

Although Merton (1973) recognizes that these norms, like any others, are sometimes violated, there is growing evidence that he may have placed too much emphasis on the impersonal, self-critical, open-minded traits of the scientific community. Many studies more influenced by conflict theory (Mitroff, 1974a, 1974b; Edge and Mulkay, 1976) have shown that scientists frequently violate all four norms. For example, they often violate the norm of universalism, preferring to judge research on the basis of such personal criteria as the reputation of the researcher. They violate the norm of communalism by secretly guarding their research in progress for fear that other scientists will "steal" their work and thus get credit for it. Scientists sometimes violate the norm of disinterestedness; not too surprisingly, they may be as greedy and ambitious as anyone else. The norm of organized skepticism is perhaps the most frequently violated of all. Like the rest of us, scientists have their private values and prejudices, and they may be passionately committed to particular viewpoints or theories.

In his study of forty-two leading scientists who took part in the Apollo moon-research project, Ian Mitroff (1974b) found that every one of them "thought the notion of the objective, emotionally disinterested scientist naive." One scientist commented:

> The uninvolved, unemotional scientist is just as much a fiction as the mad scientist who will destroy the world for knowledge. Most of the scientists I know have theories and are looking for data to support them; they're not sorting impersonally through the data looking for a theory to fit the data. . . .
>
> You don't consciously falsify evidence in science but you put less priority on a piece of data that goes against you. No reputable scientist does this consciously but you do it subconsciously.

In fact, the scientists felt that impassioned commitment would further, rather than hinder, the cause of scientific innovation. One of them remarked:

> I can't recall any scientist I've ever known who has made a fundamental contribution who was impartial to his discoveries or to his ideas. You not only don't discover anything by being impartial but you don't even test it by being impartial. The severest test of an idea occurs when you've done everything in your power to make the best possible case for it and it still doesn't hold water. Nowhere in all this are you impartial.

And another commented:

> You can't understand science in terms of the simple-minded articles that appear in the journals. Science is an intensely personal enterprise. Every scientific idea needs a personal representative who will defend and nourish that idea so that it doesn't suffer a premature death.

It seems that there are two sets of norms in the scientific community: the idealized norms that specify how scientists ought to behave, and the "counternorms" that describe

Figure 17.5

"*We go to Stockholm, we accept our prize, and then I never want to see your ugly mug again!*"

Drawing by Wm. Hamilton; © 1972
The New Yorker Magazine, Inc.

how many of them are tempted to behave in practice. Their actual behavior probably tends to be a compromise outcome, whose content depends on the individual scientist and the particular circumstances. The scientific community, however, uses the idealized norms as an ideology to justify its own interests to outsiders (especially to providers of research funds), and the public image of the scientist is certainly more influenced by the idealized norms than the less publicized counternorms (Mulkay, 1976).

The Social Process of Innovation

The object of scientific inquiry is *innovation*, the discovery of new knowledge. This innovation does not take place at random, for science is not just the creation of a few curious individuals performing whatever experiments happen to capture their fancy. As a social institution, science is subject to the influence of social forces, both within and beyond the scientific community—forces that strongly affect both the rate and the direction of scientific innovation.

Paradigms in Science

The social process of innovation is the subject of one of the most influential books in the philosophy and sociology of science, Thomas Kuhn's *The Structure of Scientific Revolutions* (1962). Kuhn is concerned with two aspects of the process of innovation: the steady innovation of what he calls *"normal" science,* in which knowledge is gradually increased, and the radical innovation of a *scientific "revolution,"* in which scientists come to look at their subject matter in an entirely different way, or even to establish a new discipline. Most scientific advance is of the "normal" kind, but occasionally—as when Copernican astronomy replaced the old earth-centered view of the universe, or when Einstein's physics replaced the Newtonian model—a scientific revolution takes place.

Kuhn starts with the assertion that science, contrary to popular belief, does not develop merely by a simple accumulation of individual discoveries and inventions. What often happens is that a community of scientists in a particular discipline develops a shared set of concepts, methods, and assumptions about their subject matter. Kuhn calls such a set of beliefs a *paradigm.* These paradigms determine what is regarded as a problem, a solution, a discovery, or an appropriate research method. The work of the scientist is, in effect, an attempt to fit nature into the conceptual box provided by the current paradigm. Physicists committed to the Newtonian paradigm, for example, interpreted physical phenomena in one way; physicists committed to the Einsteinian paradigm interpret them in another way. The training of a scientist is essentially an introduction to the prevailing paradigm. Textbooks, for example, generally do not present a variety of ways of looking at the same phenomenon. They teach the existing assumptions, usually presenting them as accepted truth even though most of them may appear as ludicrous to future generations as pre-Copernican astronomy does to us in the twentieth century.

The paradigm, however, is necessary for "normal" scientific innovation. Nature is much too vast and complex for haphazard, random investigations to be very successful. The paradigm defines the problems that must be solved and the means that should be used to solve them, and it focuses the attention of an entire scientific community upon them. If a science has no paradigm, little progress will be made. Such was the case, for example, with the investigation of electricity until Benjamin Franklin supplied a set of assumptions that were generally acceptable and fruitful. Research guided by a paradigm produces a rapid accumulation of knowledge and permits the advance of "normal" science.

Why, then, do scientific "revolutions" come about? The reason is that research under a particular paradigm will continually generate new problems, some of which can be solved under the paradigm and some of which cannot. Problems that cannot be fitted to the existing paradigm are called *anomalies.* At first anomalies may be shelved and ignored, or the paradigm may be modified to take account of them. In the end, however, so many anomalies may emerge that the existing paradigm becomes a mere patchwork, incapable of containing or explaining them. At this point the discipline concerned is in a *crisis* situation, and scientists begin to cast around for some entirely new paradigm that will yield better results. When it is found, a scientific revolution takes place. Many scientists resist the change, but if the new paradigm makes more sense of reality, it will finally triumph. In this way the Copernican view of the universe finally replaced the centuries-old Ptolemaic system, an unwieldy one that had the sun revolving around the earth, which was held to be the center of the universe. Endless efforts had been made to modify the Ptolemaic system to account for new astronomical discoveries, but in the end the system simply did not "work," and there was general recognition that a new one was needed. In the same way, Einstein's view of the universe provided answers to anomalies that Newton's view could not explain. Now Einstein's system is generating serious anomalies that are leading to continual modifications of his paradigm.

Science is not a matter of a steady accumulation of knowledge. Theories are proposed, used, and abandoned, and the existing knowledge at any period is only provisional, never final and irrefutable. One philosopher of science, Karl Popper (1959), takes the view that it is never possible to prove anything in science with absolute finality, since there is always the possibility that an exception will be found to every scientific "law." All we can do is disprove hypotheses. Our scientific knowledge consists entirely of theories that are not yet disproved, although one day they might be.

The way a scientist interprets reality depends on the assumptions of the scientific community at the time, which are in turn influenced by other social forces. Between 1690 and 1769, for example, the planet Uranus was observed on at least seventeen different occasions, but because existing beliefs, influenced by religious doctrine, discounted the possibility of an extra planet, it was classified as a star. When the astronomer William Herschel observed the planet on successive days in 1769, he noticed that it moved. Clearly, it could not be a star, so Herschel assumed that it was a comet—the only other legitimate assumption permitted by the existing paradigm. Only when the "comet" failed to behave like one did Herschel finally conclude that Uranus must be a planet—and once the possibility of other planets was recognized, astronomers looked for and found them. What we see in the world depends not just on what we look at. It also depends on what our previous training has taught us to find (Kuhn, 1962).

Competition in Science

Another important factor in the social process of innovation is competition among scientists. Fame and honor go to the scientist who arrives first at a discovery. The scientist who gets there second by independent work is ignored, no matter how meritorious his or her work. The socialization of scientists emphasizes the importance of doing original research. Ph.D. dissertations, for example, are expected to make a new contribution to the field, not merely to replicate work that has already been done. (Partly for this reason, many research studies in sociology and other sciences have never been independently verified. Researchers get no acclaim for following in the footsteps of others, so they prefer to break new ground.)

Professional recognition is of great importance to the scientist. In the United States this recognition is closely tied to career prospects in higher education. The scientist must "publish or perish" because tenure and promotion usually depend on a continuing output of journal articles and scholarly books. The American scientific community is highly stratified, with the greatest honors going to a very small number of scientists. Social mobility in the scientific community correlates strongly with the volume of an individual's publications. The more original work a scientist publishes, the more honors—in the form of prizes, awards,

Figure 17.6

"I see by the current issue of 'Lab News,' Ridgeway, that you've been working for the last twenty years on the same problem I've been working on for the last twenty years."

Drawing by Opie; © 1976
The New Yorker Magazine, Inc.

honorary degrees, promotion, or citation by others in their own publications—he or she receives. The higher a scientist rises in the prestige hierarchy, the easier it becomes to publish and to get funds for further research (Merton, 1973; Cole and Cole, 1973; Allison and Stewart, 1974; Zuckerman, 1977; Gaston, 1978).

The exchange of new information in return for professional recognition is thus an important process in the scientific community. The phenomenon is familiar to sociologists and anthropologists in another guise, gift-giving. In every human society, if a gift is offered and accepted, the act of acceptance increases the prestige of the giver. Research publications are in effect a gift (they are even called "contributions") from the researcher to the scientific community. If the gift is accepted—that is, if the research is published—the enhanced prestige of the researcher is publicly acknowledged (Hagstrom, 1965). However, the gift can be accepted only if it is original. For this reason there are often intense *priority disputes* in science, arguments about who made a particular discovery first. The fear of being "scooped," or anticipated, by another researcher is so great that in some disciplines there are special publications consisting entirely of announcements by scientists that they are completing research on a particular topic and intend to publish specific findings in due course. The authors thus hope to claim priority over other researchers who might publish fuller results in the interim. One study found that more than 60 percent of scientists had been anticipated by others at least once in their careers, 17 percent had been anticipated more than twice, and about a third were worried about being anticipated in their present research (Hagstrom, 1974).

The desire for recognition may be dysfunctional in that it encourages secrecy, but it has several functional effects as well. First, it encourages scientists to make their findings known as soon as possible. For example, Darwin developed the theory of evolution for seventeen years before he published it; he was finally spurred to write his book, in the space of a few months, only by the realization that he was about to be "scooped" by Alfred Russel Wallace. Second, competition reduces a wasteful duplication of effort, for scientists are motivated to tackle only those problems that others are not working on. Scientific effort is thus efficiently allocated among the various problems that exist. Third, competition encourages scientists to explore new specialties or even to found new disciplines in existing areas of ignorance, where their chances of making significant contributions are greatest. Many new disciplines were created by applying paradigms from one field to an entirely new field. Sociology, for example, was originally conceived as "social physics," in the novel belief that "laws" analogous to those of nature could be applied to human society. Similarly, molecular biology was created primarily by nuclear physicists who deserted their own field in order to apply its paradigm to the science of living organisms (Hagstrom, 1965, 1974; Polanyi, 1951).

Resistance to Innovation

A major new scientific discovery or theory often causes an intellectual scandal. Indeed, resistance to radical innovation has been the norm rather than the exception in the scientific community (Kuhn, 1962). Galileo's colleagues refused to look through his telescope to see the moons of Jupiter. Giordano Bruno was burned at the stake for proclaiming

Figure 17.7 Galileo on trial by the medieval Church. His offense was to support the theory that the earth moves around the sun, and not vice versa. Galileo was forced to recant his view on pain of death, but legend has it that he muttered under his breath, "Yet it still moves."

that the earth revolved around the sun. Pasteur's germ theory was ignored by the surgeons of his time, who could have saved countless lives by washing their hands and instruments before operating on patients. Harvey's theory of the circulation of the blood was greeted with howls of laughter when he delivered a paper on the subject to other physicians. Freud was shouted down by his outraged colleagues when he outlined his theory of childhood sexuality. The discoveries of modern physics, such as gravitation, relativity, wave theory, and quantum theory, were vigorously resisted by many scientists for years after they were first announced. An attempt by a contemporary biologist, Edward Wilson, to launch *sociobiology*—a scientific discipline that attempts to use biological principles to explain the behavior of all social animals, including that of human beings—has been bitterly opposed by scientists in several fields. Why are so many scientists so reluctant to accept scientific innovation? An examination of a case study will throw some light on the problem.

Case Study: The Theory of Evolution

In 1650, James Ussher, an Irish prelate and scholar, determined on the basis of the available "evidence" (all of which he found in the Old Testament) that God created Adam and Eve "on 23 October 4004 BC, at nine o'clock in the morning." This calculation won wide acceptance and was part of popular religious belief for more than 200 years. Few people in western Europe doubted that the world was more than about 6000 years old.

The first challenge to this dogma came from geologists, who wondered whether what they saw in rock formations could have been the product of a few thousand years of history. The layers of sand, gravel, clay, limestone, and other minerals, many of them containing fossils of extinct animals, could be explained only in terms of natural processes extending over millions of years. The first geologist to present this view systematically was James Hutton. His work, published in 1785, was scorned. Theologians and scientists alike took the view that the extinct creatures had either been killed in Noah's flood, or else had never existed—the fossils had been created by God as part of the rocks in which they were found. Yet the geological evidence mounted, and it could not be contained within the existing belief that the world was a mere 6000 years old. By

1830, opinions had changed sufficiently to allow Sir Charles Lyell's *Principles of Geology,* a book declaring that the earth was millions of years old, to be warmly received by the scientific, if not the theological, community. The stage was set for a new interpretation of the fossilized and the living evidence about life on earth.

Darwin's Theory

In 1859 Charles Darwin published his sensational work *On the Origin of Species,* in which he argued that life forms had been continually evolving over thousands or millions of years. The inescapable conclusion was that living species could not have been created in their present form. Yet the intellectual climate of the time was such that Darwin did not dare to deal with the evolution of the human species in his book. He commented privately, "I think I shall avoid the whole subject, as so surrounded by prejudices, though I fully admit it is the highest and most interesting problem." In only one passage in his book did he refer obliquely to human evolution, merely commenting that "light will be thrown on the origin of man and his history." The implication of Darwin's theory, however, was only too clear: the various primate species, including *Homo sapiens,* had evolved from common ancestors.

The conflict between science and religion, which had been proceeding unabated since Copernicus and Galileo challenged the medieval view of the universe, reached perhaps its final climax in a famous debate at Oxford University in 1860. The disputants were Bishop Wilberforce, who still accepted Ussher's calculation of the date of Creation, and T. H. Huxley, a scientist who supported Darwin. At a critical moment in the debate, the bishop turned to Huxley and asked him whether he was related to an ape on his mother's or his father's side. Huxley instantly replied that if he had to choose for an ancestor between an ape and someone who could discuss a serious question only with ridicule rather than logic, he "would not hesitate for a moment to prefer the ape." In the "inextinguishable laughter" that followed, the bishop sat down, his speech unfinished. In the succeeding years public opinion swung rapidly to the side of the evolutionists, and since that period, organized religion has generally recognized that because scientific and religious questions are directed at different aspects of experience, the two may coexist without friction.

Figure 17.8 A caricature of Charles Darwin, showing him emerging from the jungle. Although Darwin suffered a torrent of abuse when his theory was first published, it fitted the facts that other theories could not explain and was quickly accepted by scientists as a result.

Piltdown Man

At around the time of the publication of Darwin's book, the first fossil of a Neanderthal human was discovered. All that was needed to prove Darwin's theory was the "missing link," an intermediate form between the "brutish" Neanderthal and modern *Homo sapiens*. In 1912 it seemed that this evolutionary link had been discovered in England in the form of Piltdown man, whose fossil head contained a noble human brow with a cruder, apelike jaw. The fossil fitted perfectly with existing conceptions, and its discovery caused immense excitement. Some 500 essays were written about the creature, and the site of the discovery was designated a national monument. In fact, however, the head was the work of an unknown forger and consisted of a relatively modern human skull and the jaw of an orangutan. Several tests available to scientists at the time would have proved that the specimen was a fraud—the jaw was bone, not stone, and was thus not even a fossil, and the teeth had been filed down to alter their shape. Yet nobody examined the find carefully enough to discover the forgery. A few scientists were suspicious about Piltdown man and published critical articles, but they were almost universally ignored or even ridiculed. Not until 1953, forty years later, did scientists take the trouble to reexamine the original specimen, which was immediately pronounced a forgery.

Why did scientists finally begin to doubt that Piltdown man was genuine? The main reason was the discovery of other hominid fossils of different species that also appeared to be intermediate between *Homo sapiens* and some apelike ancestor. Several of these hominids, particularly the species *Australopithecus*, fitted the specifications of the "missing link" far more neatly than Piltdown man, which increasingly appeared to be an anomaly in the emerging picture of human evolution (Millar, 1974).

Analysis

These instances of resistance to innovation point again to the importance of paradigms in science. When the geological and fossil evidence contradicted the accepted paradigm of the seventeenth, eighteenth, and early nineteenth centuries—a paradigm supposedly based on the Genesis story of Creation—the facts were either ignored or reinterpreted to fit the paradigm. But the anomalies mounted, and the paradigm began to collapse. Theories such as those of Lyell in geology and Darwin in biology began to win wide acceptance, for they provided a better explanation of the evidence. Yet once the scientific revolution had taken place, resistance to further innovation set in once more: Piltdown man fitted the new paradigm perfectly. Only after four more decades of research that pointed overwhelmingly to the anomalous position of Piltdown man did scientists finally make the investigations that uncovered one of the most preposterous frauds in scientific history.

In most of the period covered by the case study, the "moral imperatives" of science—the four norms outlined by Merton—were widely suspended. What many scientists actually did, as some still do when confronted with radical innovation, was to use the existing paradigm as a norm, rejecting as unacceptable any new theories or discoveries that deviated from or undermined it (Mulkay, 1972). Scientists may be reluctant to give up ideas that have proved useful in the past, particularly when their reputations and research funds are tied to their work under the existing paradigm.

The case study also reveals the influence of wider social forces on the scientific community. In the seventeenth and eighteenth centuries, scientists were blinded to the facts by the popular religious dogma of the time. By the late nineteenth and twentieth centuries, this religious world view was no longer uncritically accepted, and there was growing faith that science could unlock the mysteries of nature. New theories quickly gained acceptance. But when it seemed that the problem of human evolution had been solved, scientists were reluctant to admit fresh evidence that would upset their tidy theories—or worse, make them look foolish in the eyes of the public.

The case study raises one further question about the influence of social factors on scientific innovation. The time lag between an innovation and its final acceptance was far greater in the past than it is today. Copernicus's view of the universe was not generally accepted for a century after his death. The principle of the eyeglass was known in 1286, but Galen's theory of sight, which ruled out the artificial correction of vision, was taught in medical schools until 1700. It took centuries for scientists to accept the evidence of the earth's age, but it took only decades before most of them accepted the evidence for the evolution of the species. Fossil finds during the 1960s and the 1970s have upset previous theories of our evolutionary origins, but scientists have modified their paradigm to take account of these discoveries within months rather than years. Why is scientific innovation now so much more readily accepted?

Kingsley Davis (1949) suggests that four factors make a society more or less willing to accept innovation. The first is the society's *attitude toward change*. Western society is no longer suspicious of change; we believe in "progress" and acknowledge the role of scientific innovation in bringing about that progress. The second factor is the *institutionalization* of science. When science becomes a central rather than a marginal activity and when scientists are socially rewarded for new discoveries, innovation takes place much faster. The third factor is *specialization*. Life is short and intellect is limited. If scientists are amateurs in several fields, they are less likely to make discoveries than highly specialized practitioners who are intimately acquainted with a particular field. The fourth factor is the *methods of communication* available to a society. If new ideas can be conveniently stored and quickly transmitted, information becomes more accessible and can more readily be put to use. All four factors operate to make American society exceptionally well adapted to accept rather than to resist innovation.

The Social Control of Science and Technology

Science and technology are not simply the work of isolated individuals: the selection of research problems and the rate and direction of innovation are strongly influenced by social forces. It is no accident, for example, that so much applied research in the United States focuses on the development of military and commercial products. It follows that science and technology cannot be regarded as somehow independent of society. Like any other cultural products, they are created and controlled by countless individual men and women. The difficulty is that this control is haphazard. We have created a complex institution to ensure the development of science and technology, but we have created few means of monitoring and controlling their effects—despite the impact these effects can have on the social order.

The lack of systematic social control over scientific and technological innovation presents three main problems:

PUBLIC ATTITUDES TOWARD SCIENCE

Do you agree or don't you agree that scientific research and technological development . . .	Agree	Disagree	Not Sure
are necessary to keep the country prosperous?	92%	4%	4%
are the only way we can clean up air and water pollution?	69	20	11
are the main factors in increasing productivity?	69	16	15
make people want to acquire more possessions rather than enjoying nonmaterial experiences?	65	22	13
are the real basis of our military strength?	64	21	15
will eventually mean a four-day workweek?	62	21	17
make everything bigger and more impersonal?	56	30	14
tend to overproduce products, and this is wasteful?	52	36	12
are a way to make the rich get richer and the poor poorer?	48	37	15
make the country prosperous enough to take care of the needs of the poor?	46	38	16
are the only way we can create enough jobs for people who need them?	44	42	14
lead to far too much use of scarce raw materials and natural resources?	42	38	20
eventually lead to the loss of jobs?	39	44	17
cause air and water pollution to get worse?	33	51	16

Source: Harris poll, 1978.

Figure 17.9 Opinion polls show some decline in public confidence that science can solve many human problems. Although science is still viewed favorably in most respects, there do seem to be ambiguous feelings about the direction in which scientific advance is leading us.

1. A relatively haphazard scientific and technological advance may have many unforeseen social effects, particularly in terms of the quality of the environment. Consider, for example, the growing list of chemicals and food additives that may contribute to human cancers; the increasing atmospheric pollution that some scientists think may lead to climatic changes which could cause a new ice age; the mounting health problem caused by chemical wastes that have been improperly disposed of; and the ominous threat of major accidents in nuclear power plants.

2. Unless society ensures that innovations in science and technology take place in accordance with defined social goals, there may be distortion in the priorities given to research efforts in different fields. Critics argue that under the existing arrangements, scarce and valuable resources may be devoted to producing such trivia as self-heating shaving cream, when they might otherwise be devoted to more socially desirable ends, such as medical research or energy conservation.

3. A highly technological society poses a possible threat to democracy. Public participation in the decision-making process may become difficult because the relevant facts about many important issues—such as the wisdom of building nuclear breeder reactors—may be beyond the comprehension of both voters and their elected representatives. Several writers (for example, Galbraith, 1967; Lakoff, 1977) have warned of the dangers of *technocracy*, or rule by experts. In modern corporations and government

departments the real decisions are often made behind the scenes by experts whose specialized knowledge and recommendations are relied upon by those who are officially responsible for the decisions.

Any attempt to apply a more systematic form of social control over science and technology would probably run into severe problems. One such problem involves a conflict of values. The object of science is the pursuit of knowledge, and ideally this activity should take place in an atmosphere of complete intellectual freedom. There are enough unhappy examples in the past of nonscientists attempting to dictate to scientists what they should and should not investigate for us to be wary of doing the same. Should we impose restrictions on research, and if so, what restrictions? A similar conflict of values might arise if society attempted to shift priorities in applied research from the manufacture of trivial commercial products to other social goals. Radical changes in these priorities would inevitably interfere with the workings of the capitalist system that most Americans value so highly.

Another problem involves the moral responsibility for decisions about research that may have far-reaching consequences. The development of the hydrogen bomb is but one example of many in which technical and moral issues are not easily separated in practice. At present, scientists usually cannot and do not control the uses to which their work is put, although there are signs that many scientists are now very disturbed about this situation. Ought the responsibility for decisions about new research and technology rest with scientists themselves, or with government, or with some new control agency such as a "science court" with full legal powers to restrict certain research? The question is a vital one, for scientific and technological advance in the years ahead may change our material and social environment in ways that many people might consider undesirable.

Some of the scientific research currently in progress illustrates the significance of this problem. Scientists are now working on techniques that may make it possible for parents to determine the sex of their children. If a marketable product eventually emerges, commercial interests may

Figure 17.10 Modern science and technology have given us the power to destroy life on the planet. Unfortunately, one of the most recognizable symbols of the twentieth century is the familiar mushroom cloud of an atomic explosion. Nothing points more dramatically to the need for effective social controls over the direction of scientific innovation and the uses to which this knowledge is put.

Technology: Servant or Master?

Since technological change forces social changes upon us, this has had the effect of abdicating all control over our social environment to a kind of whimsical deity. While we think of ourselves as a people of change and progress, masters of our environment and our fate, we are no more entitled to this designation than the most superstitious savage, for our relation to change is entirely passive. We poke our noses out the door each day and wonder breathlessly what new disruptions technology has in store for us. We talk of technology as the servant of man, but it is a servant that now dominates the household, too powerful to fire, upon whom everyone is helplessly dependent. We tiptoe about and speculate upon his mood. What will be the effects of such-and-such an invention? How will it change our daily lives? We never ask, do we *want* this, is it worth it? (We did not ask ourselves, for example, if the trivial conveniences offered by the automobile could really offset the calamitous disruption and depersonalization of our lives that it brought about.) We simply say "You can't stop progress" and shuffle back inside.

We pride ourselves on being a "democracy" but we are in fact slaves. We submit to an absolute ruler whose edicts and whims we never question. We watch him carefully, hang on his every word; for technology is a harsh and capricious king, demanding prompt and absolute obedience.... We have passively surrendered to every degradation, every atrocity, every enslavement that our technological ingenuity has brought about. We laugh at the old lady who holds off the highway bulldozers with a shotgun, but we laugh because we are Uncle Toms. We try to outdo each other in singing the praises of the oppressor, although in fact the value of technology in terms of human satisfaction remains at best undemonstrated. For when evaluating its effects we always adopt the basic assumptions and perspective of technology itself, and never examine it in terms of the totality of human experience. We say this or that invention is valuable because it generates other inventions—because it is a means to some other means—not because it achieves an ultimate human end. We play down the "side effects" that so often become the main effects and completely negate any alleged benefits. The advantages of *all* technological "progress" will after all be totally outweighed the moment nuclear war breaks out (an event which, given the inadequacy of precautions and the number of fanatical fingers close to the trigger, is only a matter of time unless radical changes are made).

Source: Philip Slater, *The Pursuit of Loneliness: American Culture at the Breaking Point* (Boston: Beacon, 1970), pp. 44–45.

encourage widespread sex selection of children. This may sound like a socially useful technology until we consider one factor. Opinion polls in the United States and elsewhere have indicated that a large majority of parents would prefer to have boys rather than girls (Williamson, 1976). The result of sex selection might be a society in which males heavily outnumber females, with important effects on population structure, family patterns, and sexual norms. Do we want this kind of situation, and should the decision be left to commercial interests?

Another controversial field of research involves the rearrangement of living molecules, in particular the DNA molecule that determines the hereditary characteristics of all living things. This research can have many uses, ranging from the control of insect pests to the treatment of cancers. The danger exists, however, that new and harmful strains of viruses and bacteria can be created in the course of this research. Human beings would have no natural immunity to these strains. The escape of such new life forms into circulation could lead to catastrophic, world-wide epidemics. Scientists have been quick to recognize this danger and have themselves set up strict guidelines and safety procedures for DNA research. Some scientists, however, believe that even these safeguards are inadequate and have called for a total ban on this kind of research.

The awesome problems posed by science and technology are an example of the "culture lag" problem discussed earlier. Science and technology have developed far faster than have social mechanisms to control them. A century ago, science was marginal to society and technology was relatively undeveloped. Today they offer the prospect of social upheaval and even the destruction of human life—or the potential for unprecedented social benefits and new levels of civilized existence. An urgent social challenge in the future will be to ensure that science and technology develop exclusively in the second direction.

Summary

1. Science has become an important institution in modern society, largely because it has been linked to technology. An industrial society depends heavily on scientific knowledge and its technological applications, although there are signs of concern about the potential effects of headlong scientific and technological advance.

2. Science emerged only recently as a major institution. Until the Industrial Revolution there were few specialized scientific roles, but since that time science has enjoyed extensive social support.

3. Merton claimed that the scientific community works under four basic norms: universalism, communalism, disinterestedness, and organized skepticism. More recent evidence shows that these norms tend to be violated at times.

4. Innovation in science is not a random matter; it is influenced by social forces. Scientists work under paradigms, or sets of assumptions about the discipline. Normal scientific advance takes place under the paradigm until serious anomalies are generated; at this point, a scientific revolution may take place. Competition among scientists, often expressed in priority disputes, encourages them to make original contributions and to explore new areas.

5. Scientists sometimes resist innovation, as a case study of the theory of evolution reveals. Scientists may be reluctant to give up ideas that have proved useful in the past, although this conservative tendency is less noticeable in contemporary industrial societies.

6. The lack of adequate social control of science and technology presents several problems, for innovation may have undesirable social consequences that were not anticipated. The development of suitable methods of control poses a major challenge for the future.

Important Terms

science (435)	"normal" science (442)
technology (435)	scientific "revolution" (442)
applied research (439)	paradigm (442)
basic research (439)	anomaly (442)
norms of science (440)	priority dispute (444)
innovation (441)	technocracy (448)

Suggested Readings

BARNES, J. A. *Who Should Know What?* New York: Cambridge University Press, 1980.

An examination of the ethical obligations faced by social scientists when they collect and publish information.

EVANS, CHRISTOPHER. *The Micro Millennium.* New York: Viking, 1979.

A fascinating account of how advances in computer technology may change social life in the future.

GASTON, JERRY (ed.). *Sociology of Science.* San Francisco: Jossey-Bass, 1978.

A useful collection of recent articles on this rapidly growing field.

KUHN, THOMAS S. *The Structure of Scientific Revolutions.* Chicago: University of Chicago Press, 1962.

A highly influential book. Kuhn outlines his concept of the scientific paradigm and shows the role of paradigms in both "normal" and "revolutionary" scientific innovation.

MERTON, ROBERT K. *Sociology of Science: Theoretical and Empirical Investigations.* Norman W. Storer (ed.). Chicago: University of Chicago Press, 1973.

An important collection of articles on the sociology of science by Robert Merton, the leading sociologist in the field.

MILLAR, RONALD. *The Piltdown Man.* New York: St. Martin's Press, 1974.

A readable account of the famous Piltdown man hoax. Millar includes extensive historical background on the resistance to evolutionary theory.

MULKAY, MICHAEL J. *The Social Process of Innovation.* New York: Macmillan, 1972.

A short discussion of the social processes that influence the rate and direction of scientific innovation, with special emphasis on the phenomenon of resistance to new scientific theories.

WATSON, JAMES D. *The Double Helix: A Personal Account of the Discovery of the Structure of DNA.* New York: Atheneum, 1968.

A candid and lively book about scientific innovation by a scientist who, as a twenty-three-year-old American graduate student, saw and seized the chance to share a Nobel prize.

ZUCKERMAN, HARRIET. *Scientific Elite: Nobel Laureates in the United States.* New York: Free Press, 1977.

An interesting study of Nobel prize winners and the scientific community from which they emerge. The book also offers useful insights into the process and methods of sociological research.

CHAPTER **18**   *The Economic Order*

The human animal needs food and shelter in order to survive: these are basic necessities. Beyond these requirements, people in all societies feel that they have "needs" for certain other goods and services as well—in one society, perhaps, for bows and arrows and the attention of a witch doctor; in another society, for a color TV set and the skills of an auto mechanic. Whether they are biological or social, human needs can usually be satisfied only by human effort. Most goods and services are scarce. People must work to produce them and must find some way of distributing them among the various members of the society. This activity, basic to our species, is the substance of economic life. *The economic order is the institutionalized system for producing and distributing goods and services.*

Economic activity is important not only because it sustains life. Throughout this book we have noted the central importance of economic production for human culture and social structure as well. The principal means of production that a society uses—hunting and gathering, horticulture, pastoralism, agriculture, or industrialism—strongly influences the size and complexity of the society and the character of its cultural and social life. Changes in the means of economic production are therefore inevitably accompanied by sweeping changes elsewhere in society. We have also noted, in the work of Karl Marx and others, the close link between economic and political issues, particularly in the area of social inequality. Goods and services are rarely equally distributed in a society, because the more powerful groups are able to secure a disproportionate supply for themselves and to control the political process by which inequalities are maintained. And we must also recognize the importance of economic activity in personal life. Work makes up a major part of our waking lives, and our occu-

Figure 18.1 Unlike preindustrial societies, a modern industrial society like the United States has a very complex division of labor with many thousands of job specialties. The economies of industrialized societies are highly diversified, and it is both more efficient and more convenient if people specialize in particular occupations.

pations usually define our social status. Work is therefore a significant source of personal and social identity: in fact, one of the first questions we ask a person we have just met is "What do you do?" The answer to that single question enables us to predict, with a good deal of accuracy, a person's social class, income, level of education, type of residential neighborhood, and various other social traits.

In this chapter we shall be focusing on one of the most basic of all human activities, with implications that extend into many areas of individual and social life. We shall not examine the actual mechanics of the economy in detail; that is primarily the task of economists. We shall concentrate instead on the social basis and consequences of economic activity.

The Division of Labor

Every human society, however large or small, establishes some *division of labor* among its members: people are expected to specialize, at least to some extent, in particular economic activities. This division of labor occurs in all societies because it is highly *functional*. By assigning particular people to do specific jobs, it ensures that they will become expert in their work. The division of labor thus enhances the efficiency of economic life. However, it may have other far-reaching effects as well.

Increased Specialization

There has been a general historical trend toward increased specialization in economic activities, a trend that has gone furthest in modern industrial societies.

In small-scale hunting and gathering societies there is little division of labor except on grounds of age and sex. The very young and very old are not expected to do the same work as other members of the community, and men and women always have some specific tasks assigned to them. Otherwise, most people in these societies participate in much the same kinds of activities, and there are very few full-time, specialized occupational roles. In the more advanced horticultural and pastoral societies, and especially in agricultural societies, there is a much greater division of labor. These societies can produce an economic surplus, an achievement that has two main results. First, some people are freed from basic subsistence activities and can specialize in other roles—perhaps as artists, traders, or soldiers. Second, powerful groups are able to gain control of the surplus wealth and to live largely from the work of others. In agricultural societies, the division of labor becomes based on class distinctions as well as on individual differences.

This more elaborate division of labor persists in industrial societies, although class differences typically become less extreme in the more advanced societies of this type, thanks to the growth of a large new middle class. But industrialism breeds an entirely new form of division of labor: the high degree of specialization found in factories, offices, and other formal organizations, in which each individual contributes only a minute part to the final product. In the most simple preindustrial society, the number of specialized occupational roles—if any exist at all—can probably be counted on the fingers of one hand. In 1850, in the early stages of industrialism in the United States, the census recorded a grand total of 323 occupations. In the contemporary United States, according to the U.S. Department of Labor, there are over 20,000 job specialties. This calculation, incidentally, refers only to legitimate occupations. It excludes such jobs as dope pusher, pimp, pickpocket, counterfeiter, and con artist, all of which, of course, include many further subspecialties. In its *Dictionary of Occupational Titles* the Department of Labor (1977) lists such highly specialized occupations as blintze roller, alligator farmer, oxtail washer, cherry-bomb finisher, corset stringer, earmuff assembler, gherkin pickler, and chicken sexer.

The assembly line of the modern factory has come to epitomize the division of labor in modern industry. This is particularly true in the auto industry, where a worker may tighten identical bolts hundreds of times an hour, day after day and month after month. The potential consequences of this kind of work were suggested as long ago as 1776, when Adam Smith published his classic work, *The Wealth of Nations:*

The man whose whole life is spent in performing a few simple operations . . . has no occasion to exert his understanding or to exercise his invention. . . . He naturally loses, therefore, the habit of such exertion, and generally becomes as stupid and ignorant as it is possible for a human creature to become.

A more restrained comment was made by Alexis de Tocqueville, a French observer of early industrial development in the United States:

What can be expected of a man who has spent twenty years of his life in making heads for pins? And to what can that mighty human intelligence which has so often stirred the world be applied in him . . . ? When a workman has spent a considerable proportion of his existence in this manner, his thoughts are forever set upon the object of his daily toil. . . . The workman becomes more weak, more narrow-minded, and more dependent. The art advances, the artisan recedes. [1954, originally published 1835]

Such a situation is obviously of great sociological and personal significance, a topic to which we shall return when we come to consider the relationship between work and alienation.

Anomie and the Division of Labor

In his important work *The Division of Labor in Society* (1893), the French sociologist Emile Durkheim tried to determine the social effects of the division of labor in modern societies. A major theme in nearly all Durkheim's writings is the idea that a society is held together by its members' sharing of similar norms and values. The nature of this social solidarity, according to Durkheim, depends on the extent of the division of labor, because the more diversified people's work is, the more different their norms and values become.

Traditional societies, Durkheim argued, are held together by what he called *mechanical solidarity*. Because these societies are small and because everyone does much the same work, the members are all socialized in the same pattern, share the same experiences, and hold common values. These values, which are mainly religious in nature, form a "collective consciousness" for the community, a set of norms, beliefs, and assumptions shared by one and all. There is little individuality, and the society consists basically of a collection of kinship groups, all with similar characteristics.

Modern societies, on the other hand, are held together by what Durkheim called *organic solidarity,* a much looser bond. Because these societies are large and their members play a variety of economic roles, people have quite different experiences, hold different values, and socialize their children in many varying patterns. They have fewer beliefs in common, and religion shrinks in importance. The collective consciousness has much less binding power on the community, and people no longer unquestioningly accept the assumptions it contains. People think of themselves as individuals first and as members of a kinship or wider social group second. The society thus consists of a series of interconnected individuals, each with different characteristics. The basis for social solidarity is no longer the *similarity* of the members but rather their *differences*. Because they are now interdependent, they must rely on one another if their society is to function effectively.

The essential problem in modern society, Durkheim argued, is that the division of labor, by emphasizing differences among people, inevitably makes them more aware of themselves as individuals. In turn, these feelings of individualism undermine loyalty to the community and its shared values, sentiments, and beliefs. The result is *anomie*—a state of normlessness in both the society and the individual. As social norms become confused or break down, people feel ever more detached from their fellows. Having little commitment to shared norms, they lack social guidelines for personal conduct and are inclined to pursue their private desires without regard for the interests of society as a whole. Social control of individual behavior becomes ineffective, and the society is threatened with disorganization or even disintegration as a result.

Durkheim was probably correct in his view that the division of labor and the resulting growth of individualism would break down shared commitment to social norms, and it seems plausible that there is widespread anomie in modern societies. Yet these societies do retain at least a broad consensus on norms and values, as we can readily see when we contrast one society with another—say, the United States with China. Although this consensus seems much weaker than that in preindustrial societies, it is probably still strong enough to guide most individual behavior and to avert the social breakdown that Durkheim feared. Durkheim's analysis remains valuable, however, for his acute insights into the far-ranging effects that the division of labor has on social and personal life.

Figure 18.2 *In a traditional, preindustrial community, such as this village in the Sudan, there is hardly any division of labor except on the grounds of age and sex. People wear similar clothes, reside in similar dwellings, share similar ideas, and live much the same lives. Such a society, Durkheim argued, is held together by "mechanical solidarity," or the basic similarity of its members. A diversified modern industrial society, in contrast, is held together by "organic solidarity," or the dissimilarity of people who have to depend on one another's specialized skills.*

The Sociology of Occupations

Sociologists who study economic life are especially interested in the changes that industrialization causes in the occupational structure of a society. Their interest focuses primarily on two patterns that accompany the industrialization process in all societies: first, the changing nature and content of occupations; second, the tendency for occupations that were once poorly esteemed to become professionalized. Let's examine each of these patterns.

Primary, Secondary, and Tertiary Sectors

Work in an industrial society takes place in any one of three main sectors, with the proportion of the labor force in any one sector depending on the society's level of industrial development. *Primary industry* involves the gathering and extracting of undeveloped natural resources—for example, mining, fishing, forestry, and agriculture. *Secondary industry* involves turning the raw materials produced by primary industry into manufactured goods—for example, automobiles, furniture, canned foods. *Tertiary industry* involves service activities—for example, medicine, banking, teaching, laundering, automobile maintenance.

In the early stages of industrialism most workers are employed in primary industry, tapping the natural resources on which later industrial development can build. In the later stages, secondary industry becomes the dominant sector as more and more economic activity is devoted to producing manufactured goods. In the most advanced stages of industrialism, tertiary industry becomes dominant, with the bulk of the work force employed in service occupations. In the 1950s the United States became the first country in the world to have more than half of its labor force engaged in tertiary industry. White-collar workers are now the largest single occupational category; the blue-collar category is shrinking rapidly; and farm workers, who represented nearly 40 percent of the labor force at the turn

Figure 18.3   There are three main sectors of work in an industrial society. Workers in primary industry are involved in extracting raw materials, such as agricultural products, from the environment. Workers in secondary industry transform raw materials, such as cotton, into manufactured objects, such as twine. Workers in tertiary industry supply services, such as that of the physician, to other members of society. As an industrial society becomes more advanced, the proportion of workers in secondary and, later, in tertiary industry grows larger.

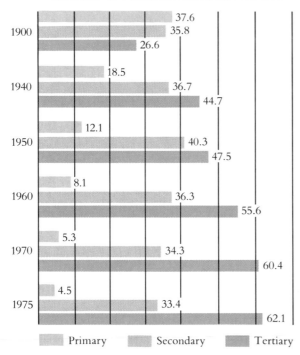

DISTRIBUTION OF PRIMARY, SECONDARY, AND
TERTIARY OCCUPATIONAL GROUPS AS
PERCENT OF TOTAL LABOR FORCE 1900–1975

Year	Primary	Secondary	Tertiary
1900	37.6	35.8	26.6
1940	18.5	36.7	44.7
1950	12.1	40.3	47.5
1960	8.1	36.3	55.6
1970	5.3	34.3	60.4
1975	4.5	33.4	62.1

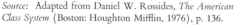
Primary   Secondary   Tertiary

Source: Adapted from Daniel W. Rossides, *The American Class System* (Boston: Houghton Mifflin, 1976), p. 136.

Figure 18.4   The proportion of American workers engaged in primary industry has dropped sharply since the turn of the century; the proportion in secondary industry is now shrinking, and the proportion in tertiary industry is rising rapidly.

of the century, now comprise less than 5 percent of all workers. The immense productivity of industrialism has created unprecedented wealth and with it a demand for a variety of new services, while advances in industrial technology have freed many workers from the hard manual labor that was more typical of the earlier stages of industrialism. As a result, more and more people are acquiring professional, technical, or managerial skills, and the American occupational structure is now radically unlike that found in less economically developed societies.

Professionalization

As we noted in Chapter 15 ("Education"), a *profession* is an occupation requiring extensive, systematic knowledge of, or training in, an art or science. Professions are generally the most highly paid and prestigious of occupations, and professionals perform many of society's most important roles—such as those, for example, in teaching, scientific research, law, medicine, and technology (Parsons, 1954).

Professions are distinguished from other occupations by several characteristics. First, the skill of professionals is based on systematic, theoretical knowledge, not merely on training in particular techniques. Second, professionals have considerable autonomy over their work. Their clients are presumed to be incompetent to make judgments about the problems with which the profession is concerned: you can

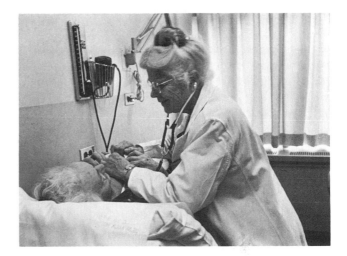

give instructions to your hairdresser or tailor but cannot advise a doctor or lawyer on matters of medicine or law. Third, professionals form associations that regulate their profession's internal affairs and represent its interests to outside bodies. Fourth, admission to a profession is carefully controlled by the existing members. Anyone can claim to be a salesperson or a carpenter, but someone who claims to be a surgeon or a professor without having the necessary credentials is an imposter. Becoming a professional involves taking an examination, receiving a licence, and acquiring a title, and this process is usually regulated by the professional association concerned. Fifth, professions have a code of ethics that all their members are expected to adhere to; the penalty for a breach of this code may be expulsion from the profession (Greenwood, 1962). Most occupations have some of these characteristics to some degree, but only professions place such great emphasis on all of them (Etzioni, 1969).

It is common for nonprofessionals to try to "professionalize" their occupations in the hope of achieving greater prestige and income. This transformation generally follows a typical sequence. The first step is the creation of a professional association, one of whose first tasks is to establish the qualifications for membership. The second step is to change the name of the occupation, perhaps from "plumber" to "sanitary engineer," so that public identification with the old, low-status occupation is broken. The third step is to

establish a code of ethics, which serves to raise the esteem in which the occupation is held and provides a means of keeping out "undesirable" members. The fourth step is to persuade political authorities to require all members of the occupation to have formal certification and to ensure that training facilities fall, as far as possible, under the control of the professional association (Wilensky, 1964; W. Moore, 1970; Larson, 1977). The rationale for this crucial step is that certificates or other credentials are necessary to maintain sound professional standards, but requiring high qualifications serves an additional purpose: it restricts entry to the profession, thus ensuring a strong demand for the services of its existing members. In fact, if too many people earn the necessary credentials, the qualifications for the job are simply raised again—which is a major reason why the same occupations demand ever higher levels of education over time (Bledstein, 1976). Attempts to professionalize jobs in the primary and secondary sectors of industry generally meet with only limited success. These jobs usually do not involve sophisticated training, are often regarded by the public as "hard" or even "dirty" work that virtually anyone could do, and continue to have relatively low prestige despite efforts at professionalization. In the "cleaner" white-collar jobs of the tertiary sector, however, professionalization tends to be more successful, and the number of jobs with professional or at least semiprofessional status is expanding rapidly.

Work and Alienation

Whether we see it as a source of fulfillment and satisfaction or as a source of boredom and indignity, whether we view it as enjoyable in itself or simply as a means of making a living, work is a central part of our lives. We derive our social status primarily from our work and from the income that it produces. In American society, the person who is poorly paid or habitually out of work is apt to be dismissed as "worthless," whereas the holder of a respected, well-paid job is honored. Work helps to define the social roles of both sexes. The husband who is a breadwinner generally finds his masculinity and responsibility as a husband and father reaffirmed, while the wife's sense of identity may be influenced by whether she has an independent career or is "only a housewife." Retired people often feel a shattering loss of identity and purpose when they stop working, for work integrates people into society, offering a place in the world and a sense of being useful and needed (Berger, 1964). Given the importance of work in social life, it is small wonder that signs of worker alienation have attracted a great deal of attention.

The Concept of Alienation

The word "alienation" has come into popular usage as a catch-all term for a variety of psychological ills, so we must define its sociological meaning closely. Essentially, *alienation* refers to the sense of powerlessness, isolation, and meaninglessness experienced by human beings when they are confronted with social institutions and conditions that they cannot control and consider oppressive (Seeman, 1959).

The concept of alienation was introduced to modern sociology by Karl Marx. In his view, alienation occurs when people lose the recognition that society and social institutions are constructed by human beings and can therefore be changed by them. The social world thus confronts people as an uncontrollable, hostile thing, leaving them "alien" in the very environment that they have created. Marx applied this idea to many social institutions, such as law, government, religion, and the economy. In the religious sphere, for example, people create religions, lose the sense that religions are socially created, and helplessly allow their lives to be dominated by the very institution they have constructed. So it is with the economic order.

People establish economic systems, feel powerless to change these systems when they become oppressed by them, and thus become the victims of their own institutions.

Marx believed that the capacity for labor is one of the most distinctive human characteristics. All other species, he argued, are merely objects in the world; human beings alone are subjects, because they consciously act on and create the world, shaping their lives, cultures, and personalities in the process. In modern societies, however, people have become alienated from their work, and thus from nature, from other human beings, and from themselves.

An important source of this alienation, in Marx's view, is the extreme division of labor in modern societies. Each worker has a specific, restricted, and limiting role that makes it impossible to apply the full human capacities of the hands, the mind, and the emotions to work. The worker has diminished responsibility, does not own the tools with which the work is done, does not own the final product, does not have the right to make decisions—and is therefore reduced to a minute part of a process, a mere cog in a machine. Work becomes an enforced activity, not a creative and satisfying one. This situation is aggravated in capitalist economies, in which the profit produced by the labor of the worker goes to someone else. Marx's summary of the nature of alienation at work, written well over a century ago, seems as relevant today as it was then:

> What, then, constitutes the alienation of labor? First, the fact that labor is *external* to the worker, i.e., it does not belong to his essential being; that in his work, therefore, he does not affirm himself but denies himself, does not feel content but unhappy, does not develop freely his physical and mental energy but mortifies his body and ruins his mind. The worker therefore only feels himself outside his work, and in his work feels outside himself. He is at home when he is not working, and when he is working he is not at home. His labor is therefore not voluntary, but coerced; it is *forced labor*. It is therefore not the satisfaction of a need; it is merely a *means* to satisfy needs external to it. Its alien character emerges clearly in the fact that as soon as no physical or other compulsion exists, labor is shunned like the plague. External labor, labor in which man alienates himself, is a labor of self-sacrifice. Lastly, the external character of labor for the worker appears in the fact that it is not his own, but someone else's, that it does not belong to him, that he belongs, not to himself, but to another. [1964a, originally published 1844]

Work on the Auto Assembly Line

"Is it true," an auto worker asked wistfully, "that you get to do fifteen different jobs on a Cadillac?" "I heard," said another, "that with Volvos you follow one car all the way down the line."

Such are the yearnings of young auto workers at the Vega plant in Lordstown, Ohio. Their average age is twenty-four, and they work on the fastest auto assembly line in the world. Their jobs are so subdivided that few workers can feel they are making a car.

The assembly line carries 101 cars past each worker every hour. Most GM lines run under sixty. At 101 cars an hour, a worker has thirty-six seconds to perform his assigned snaps, knocks, twists, or squirts on each car. The line was running at this speed in October when a new management group, General Motors Assembly Division (GMAD or Gee-Mad), took over the plant. Within four months they fired 500 to 800 [out of 7000 assembly line] workers. Their jobs were divided among the remaining workers, adding a few more snaps, knocks, twists, or squirts to each man's task. The job had been boring and unbearable before. When it remained boring and became a bit more unbearable there was a 97 percent vote to strike. More amazing— 85 percent went down to the union hall to vote. . . .

Hanging around the parking lot between shifts, I learned immediately that to these young workers, "It's not the money."

"It pays good," said one, "but it's driving me crazy."

"I don't want more money," said another. "None of us do."

"I do," said his friend. "So I can quit quicker."

"It's the job," everyone said. But they found it hard to describe the job itself.

"My father worked in auto for thirty-five years," said a cleancut lad, "and he never talked about the job. What's there to say? A car comes, I weld it. A car comes, I weld it. A car comes, I weld it. One hundred and one times an hour."

I asked a young wife, "What does your husband tell you about his work?"

"He doesn't say what he does. Only if something happened like, 'My hair caught on fire,' or, 'Something fell in my face.'"

"There's a lot of variety in the paint shop," said a dapper twenty-two-year-old up from West Virginia. "You clip on the color hose, bleed out the old color, and squirt. Clip, bleed, squirt, think; clip, bleed, squirt, yawn; clip, bleed, squirt, scratch your nose. Only now the Gee-Mads have taken away the time to scratch your nose." . . .

I asked about diversions. "What do you do to keep from going crazy?"

"I have fantasies. You know what I keep imagining? I see a car coming down. It's red. So I know it's gonna have a black seat, black dash, black interiors. But I keep thinking what if somebody up there sends down the wrong color interiors—like orange, and me putting in yellow cushions, bright yellow!"

"There's always water fights, paint fights, or laugh, talk, tell jokes. Anything so you don't feel like a machine."

But everyone had the same hope: "You're always waiting for the line to break down." . . .

Source: Barbara Garson, "Luddites in Lordstown," in Rosabeth Moss Kanter and Barry A. Stein (eds.), *Life in Organizations* (New York: Basic Books, 1979).

Worker Alienation in the United States

In 1973, the U.S. Department of Health, Education, and Welfare issued a report, *Work in America,* that captured the public attention as few government reports ever do. The report focused on alienation in the American work force, and its account of the "blue-collar blues" and "white-collar woes" was instantly recognizable to millions of people. Alienation, the report found, is a common, growing, and serious problem in American economic life:

Significant numbers of American workers are dissatisfied with the quality of their working lives. Dull, repetitive, seemingly meaningless tasks, offering little challenge or autonomy, are causing discontent among workers at all occupational levels. . . . Many workers . . . feel locked in, their mobility blocked, the opportunity to grow lacking in their jobs, challenge missing from their tasks. Young workers appear to be as committed to the institution of work as their elders have been, but many are rebelling against the anachronistic authoritarianism of the workplace.

Figure 18.5 Assembly-line work is usually considered one of the most alienating forms of labor. It demands little imagination or commitment from the worker, who is reduced to a mere element in the manufacturing process, a "cog in the machine."

The University of Michigan's Institute for Social Research conducted national surveys of worker satisfaction in 1969, 1973, and 1977 (Staines and Quinn, 1979). The results showed that although most workers are fairly satisfied with their jobs, there has been a significant increase in dissatisfaction since 1973—particularly among college graduates. Indeed, the extent of worker dissatisfaction varies significantly from job to job and from one social group to another. In terms of income, the most dissatisfied workers are those who earn the least. In technical, managerial, and professional occupations, people are apt to be more satisfied than in manufacturing, service, and wholesale occupations. Differences in income provide only a partial explanation for this difference between job categories, however. Low-income workers have much less control over their working environment than do professional and other high-income workers, a factor that also influences worker satisfaction (Kohn, 1976).

The most dissatisfied group are black workers, probably because they are concentrated in low-paying, dead-end occupations: 37 percent express negative attitudes toward their jobs. The second most dissatisfied group are workers under thirty with some college education, among whom about one in four is dissatisfied. Their dissatisfaction may be partly related to the disillusion they experience in the regimented world of work after the relative freedom of the college environment, and partly to the fact that many of them have been unable to get the kinds of jobs that they had expected their education would secure for them. The third most dissatisfied group are females under thirty, who seem especially likely to resent the lingering sex-based division of labor that restricts so many women to low-paying, uninteresting jobs and denies them the opportunities available to similarly qualified men. In general, younger workers are more dissatisfied than older workers—probably because the young expect their jobs to be interesting and fulfilling, whereas older workers have lower expectations.

Asking people whether they are satisfied with their jobs is one way of detecting worker alienation. Another way is to ask them if they would choose the same job over again. The answers to this question, the *Work in America* report found, suggest an even higher level of alienation: only 43 percent of white-collar workers and only 24 percent of blue-collar workers indicated they would choose the same occupation again. Interestingly, the report also found that worker satisfaction is the best predictor of life expectancy—better even than such standard measures as a rating by an examining physician or the extent of tobacco use.

"Human Relations" in Industry

Employers are now keenly interested in redesigning work as a means of reducing alienation, improving labor-management relations, and stepping up production, and they are calling on industrial sociologists to help them. Indeed, many of the attempts to humanize the workplace over the past few decades have been based on insights gained from sociological research into industrial relations. Earlier in the century, the worker in industry was regarded as little more than another machine. "Efficiency experts" ignored the worker's psychological and social characteristics and concentrated instead on the physical aspects of the job to be done. The chief advocate of this approach was Frederick Winslow Taylor, an engineer who fathered "time and motion" studies of work and recommended "scientific management." Taylor believed that maximum efficiency would be achieved if the worker were strictly disciplined and if every physical movement at work were carefully planned in advance down to the tiniest detail.

This view was shattered by the research conducted during the thirties by Elton Mayo and his associates at the Hawthorne plant of the Western Electric company. In their most famous experiment, the researchers systematically altered the working conditions of a group of employees to find out how the changes would influence productivity. First, they changed the method of payment from hourly wages to group piecework. Production went up. Then they introduced brief rest periods. Production rose again. Next they served refreshments twice a day, and production rose once more. The researchers tried new experiments, introducing additional breaks in the working day, or letting workers go home early. With each change, production rose. Finally, the researchers returned the group to their original working conditions—and production rose to even greater heights! What was happening? The answer—a sociological commonplace now but a revolutionary finding then—is that the workers had formed a close-knit primary group. Flattered by the attention that they were receiving and the variety that was introduced into their working lives, they had established their own norms for productivity and were trying to please the researchers by working harder (Roethlisberger and Dickson, 1939; Mayo, 1966). Sociologists are now fully aware of the influence of peer-group norms on worker productivity. It is not so much wages or even working conditions that seem to directly affect output; it is the consensus of the workers regarding what a reasonable output should be. Individual workers who exceed the output are considered "rate-busters" and are informally pressured into conforming to group norms.

Mayo's findings led to a new "human relations" approach in industry that emphasizes the concerns of the worker. The growth of labor unions, whose formation was vigorously resisted until the thirties in a series of particularly bloody conflicts, has also given workers considerable influence over their working conditions. The environment of the contemporary office or factory is infinitely more congenial than it was even a few decades ago. Why, then, has worker alienation come to the fore as a serious social problem?

One reason is that organizations have grown very much larger, leaving people in an ever more impersonal work situation in which their contributions seem meaningless. Another reason is that changes in the organization of work have not kept pace with workers' rising expectations. Better educated than their predecessors and enjoying a comparatively affluent leisure life, modern workers see a stark contrast between the conditions within and beyond the place of work. Conditions that would have been tolerated by an earlier generation are considered oppressive today.

Employers are beginning to recognize this situation, and we can expect many innovative attempts to improve the human aspects of working conditions in the future. These will include giving workers more responsibility, encouraging group decision making, rotating jobs so that workers do not spend months or years at the same task, modifying the minute division of labor on the assembly line, sharing profits with workers, and offering increased leisure time in return for increased productivity.

Unemployment

Although some groups in the United States have always faced high rates of unemployment, the period since the Great Depression has been, until recently, one of almost continuous economic expansion. Since the mid-1970s, however, a series of recessions has created a serious problem of unemployment. In 1975, the unemployment rate soared to a postwar record of 9 percent, and it approached that level again in 1980, when over 8 million American workers found themselves without a job.

No society ever has completely full employment, in the sense that everybody able to work actually has a job. There is always a certain amount of unemployment, because even under the most favorable conditions, there will be potential workers who are ill for long periods, who are changing jobs, or who are looking for work after graduating from school.

For this reason, most countries consider that they have full employment if the unemployment rate is about 2 percent or less. In the United States a rather higher unemployment rate—around 4 percent of the work force—is regarded as tolerable, and there is real alarm only if the rate goes much above that level. In practice, official statistics probably underestimate the extent of unemployment, for the Bureau of Labor Statistics classifies people as unemployed only if they have actively looked for a job during the previous four weeks but have not worked at all in the previous week. The people who have simply given up looking for a job (about 1 million in 1980) and the people who have worked even a few hours at a temporary job in the previous week are therefore not counted as unemployed. And since the bureau bases its information on random telephone surveys, it also excludes migrant workers, drifters, and others who do not have a permanent home with a listed telephone number.

The loss of a job can have a devastating impact on the individual. The immediate effect, of course, is a sharp drop in income. Unemployment benefits typically offer less than half the individual's previous earnings, and many people are not even entitled to these benefits—for example, the self-employed, recent graduates who have not held a steady job in the previous year, and people who have been unemployed for a long period. (Most unemployment benefits last for only nine months, and none are payable after more than a year of unemployment.) The economic strain on the jobless is very severe, particularly for those who have young children or long-term commitments for expenses such as mortgages or college tuitions.

But the effects of unemployment are not merely financial; they are also social and psychological. As one out-of-work teacher put it:

> It's difficult when you strip away all the things that supposedly hold you together in terms of an identity. Your work, your money, whatever is power to you, whatever is responsibility, whatever means freedom and choice. I had to ask myself, "Who am I now? What will I do now?" [Maurer, 1979]

Figure 18.6 The depressed economic conditions of recent years have led to widespread unemployment. Millions of people have been thrown out of work, including many who took their job security for granted.

All too often, prolonged unemployment may thrust the individual into boredom, despair, ill-temper, apathy, and, perhaps, conflict with other family members or alcoholism. Even those who keep their jobs are affected by high rates of unemployment, for they begin to fear for their own future. Lacking the confidence that workers have in times of full employment, they negotiate less aggressively for improvements in pay or working conditions, for they and the employers know that if they do not like the job as it is, others will gladly take it. Unemployment is always accompanied, in fact, by underemployment—the situation in which people are working either for abnormally low wages or at jobs below their level of skill.

Why has unemployment become a problem in the United States in recent years? The answers are complex—so complex, in fact, that few economists can agree on them—but we can state some of the causes that are fairly clear.

First, however, we should distinguish between the general rate of unemployment in the society as a whole and the rate of unemployment among specific categories of the population, for they do not necessarily have the same origins. The general rate of unemployment is to some extent the result of various factors beyond the society's control—most notably, the rapid rise in the price of oil over the past decade. This increase in such a vital commodity has disrupted the international economy, generating inflation and stagnation in countries all over the world. All societies have been affected in varying degrees, but they have reacted in different ways. In the Soviet Union and other socialist societies, full employment is maintained at all costs, even if it means hiring redundant workers at low wages in unproductive government jobs. In Western Europe, unemployment rates have been kept relatively low, but only at the price of inflation rates that have exceeded 25 percent a year in some countries—a level far greater than would be tolerated in the United States. In Japan, where there is a strong mutual loyalty between employers and their workers, corporations have been willing to lose money rather than fire their employees. In the United States, however, both government and employers assume less responsibility for avoiding unemployment or for helping those who lose their jobs. Other factors specific to the United States have compounded the problem. In this highly technological society, for example, mechanization, automation, and computerization have thrown many unskilled workers out of their jobs. The labor market, too, has been dramatically altered by the rapid growth in the number of women seeking jobs, and by the large number of young adults in the postwar "baby boom" generation, who are now chasing whatever jobs remain.

Unemployment, however, is not spread uniformly throughout the nation: as Figure 18.7 indicates, specific categories of the population are disproportionately likely to be without jobs. As we might expect, these are the same categories that bear the brunt of discrimination in virtually every other aspect of social life: hence, the rate is higher for women than for men, higher for nonwhites than for whites, and higher for blue-collar (working-class) workers than for white-collar (middle- and upper-class) workers. The rate is higher, too, for teen-agers than for adults; and if the aged were not forced off the labor market by mandatory retirement, it would doubtless be very high for them also. Numerous other categories also face high rates of unemployment—people approaching retirement age, migrant and seasonal workers, and people living in places (particularly decaying inner cities and depressed rural regions) that have persistent pockets of unemployment because the residents lack skills and the communities lack industries. In all these cases, social rather than individual factors are primarily responsible for high rates of unemployment. Women, blacks, and Hispanics, for example, lack the qualifications or experience of white men as a result of past discrimination and unequal opportunity, and affirmative action and similar programs have so far had little impact on their employment prospects.

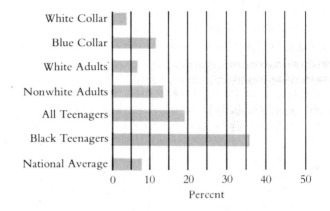

UNEMPLOYMENT RATES IN
SELECTED CATEGORIES

Source: Bureau of Labor Statistics, 1980.

Figure 18.7 As this chart shows, unemployment is not randomly distributed among the population: it is more likely to affect some categories of workers than others. In general, the categories that suffer high rates of unemployment are those that are also disadvantaged, or even discriminated against, in other areas of social life.

PROSPECTS IN SELECTED "COLLEGE-LEVEL" JOBS THROUGH THE 1980s.

Engineers	22.5	Dietitians	42.9	Designers	10.1
Aero-astronautic	20.7	Optometrists	25.9	Editors and reporters	25.7
Chemical	20.0	Pharmacists	17.0	Musicians and composers	34.6
Civil	22.8	Physicians, M.D., osteopaths	34.2	Painters and sculptors	6.5
Electrical	21.5	Podiatrists	53.1	Photographers	15.1
Industrial	26.0	Registered nurses	45.3	Public relations specialists	24.4
Mechanical	19.0	Therapists	39.9	Radio and television announcers	24.1
Metallurgical	29.0	Veterinarians	34.5	Other Professional, Technical	19.1
Mining	58.3	Clinical laboratory technologists	21.6	Accountants	25.0
Petroleum	37.7	Dental hygienists	85.7	Architects	59.2
Sales	−5.9	Technicians (except health)	30.5	Archivists and curators	15.4
Life and Physical Scientists	24.7	Airplane pilots	38.7	Clergy	5.4
Agricultural	32.0	Air-traffic controllers	22.1	Religious, except clergy	25.0
Atmospheric, space	12.0	Flight engineers	28.9	Foresters, conservationists	16.3
Biological	27.2	Radio operators	27.8	Judges	8.7
Chemists	23.5	Computer Specialists	30.8	Lawyers	23.2
Geologists	41.3	Computer programmers	29.6	Librarians	8.6
Marine	21.1	Computer systems analysts	37.6	Operations, systems research	14.7
Physicists and Astronomers	6.0	Other computer specialists	6.1	Personnel, labor relations	12.4
Mathematical Specialists	28.1	Social Scientists	36.1	Research workers	6.6
Actuaries	32.2	Economists	38.8	Recreation workers	26.4
Mathematicians	8.7	Political scientists	65.4	Social workers	18.9
Statisticians	35.2	Psychologists	34.6	Vocation, education counselors	9.3
Science Technicians	28.3	Sociologists	59.1	Buyers, Sales, Loan Managers	43.2
Agricultural, biological		Urban and regional planners	29.4	Bank, financial managers	51.5
(except health)	24.2	Teachers	−3.7	Credit managers	14.3
Chemical	25.4	Adult-education teachers	12.8	Buyers, wholesale, retail	19.6
Drafters	32.8	College and university	−14.3	Purchasing agents, buyers	44.3
Electrical, electronic	29.2	Elementary school	16.6	Sales manager, retail trade	54.0
Industrial engineering	29.3	Preschool, kindergarten	18.7	Other sales managers	37.4
Mathematical	58.3	Secondary school	−26.5	Administrators, Inspectors	18.7
Mechanical engineering	31.8	Entertainers and Other Artists	16.9	Health administrators	53.7
Surveyors	17.9	Actors	34.3	Officials, administrators, public	10.0
Engineering, science	26.6	Athletes and kindred workers	8.1	Postmasters, mail supervisors	31.6
Medical Workers	40.4	Authors	15.2	College administrators	6.6
Chiropractors	17.2	Dancers	37.5	School administrators	3.6
Dentists	30.0				

The New York Times National Recruitment Survey/October 12, 1980

Figure 18.8 This table shows expected trends in employment in selected "college-level" jobs during the present decade. The expected percentage in- *crease in the number of jobs is given opposite each occupation; where a minus sign appears (as in the case of schoolteachers), a decrease is anticipated.*

One category of the population that suffers less from unemployment than from underemployment is that of recent college graduates, many of whom find themselves working as cab drivers, tour guides, or supermarket checkout clerks—jobs demanding far less skill than these degree-holders offer, and paying far less money than they feel entitled to. This unhappy situation is the result of several factors. One, of course, is the general slowdown in economic growth. Until the end of the sixties, college graduates were in great demand, and the schools produced as many as possible. But when the economic downturn began, the colleges continued to turn out graduates in record numbers for a market that was shrinking. By the mid-1970s the number of college graduates was double that in the mid-1960s, but the number of "college-level" jobs (that is, positions in the technical, managerial, professional, and administrative fields) had increased by only a third. This discrepancy still persists: the educational and economic institutions are badly out of balance, for the one is supplying more personnel and skills than the other can absorb. In time the balance will be restored (either by the colleges' reducing their output, or by the economy's increasing its demand for graduates, or by some combination of both), but until then, a substantial proportion of recent graduates will inevitably be underemployed. Moreover, an improvement in the economy will not necessarily brighten the picture in the way one might expect, for today's graduates are following on the heels of the "baby boom" generation that is already crowding the job market and will be in fierce competition for promotions for the next few decades. In 1975 there were 39 million workers in the prime age bracket of twenty-five to forty-four, the period that employers regard as offering the greatest potential for the development of ambitions and skills. But by 1990 there will be 60.5 million people in this bracket, elbowing and jostling one another in a dense labor market. It will require a significant economic expansion during the year ahead for the labor market to absorb this entire generation at their appropriate level of skills, and still leave enough opportunity for the new graduates who follow them. This is not to imply that there will be a grave shortage of new, "graduate-level" jobs: as Figure 18.8 shows, many of these occupations will expand markedly in the 1980s. But the competition for the best of these jobs is likely to be intense.

Capitalism and Socialism

There are two basic economic systems through which an industrial society can produce and distribute goods and services: capitalism and socialism. In the former the means of production and distribution are privately owned; in the latter they are publicly owned. There are strong ideological differences between countries adopting either strategy, and as a result, the differences between these systems have tended to be overemphasized. In fact, however, there is little basis for the common view that capitalism and socialism represent "either/or" alternatives. In practice the American economy, generally regarded as a model of capitalism, has many socialistic features. It is, for example, subject to extensive government regulation and efforts to redistribute wealth. Similarly, the Soviet economy, generally regarded as a model of socialism, has many capitalistic features. Among other things, there are great differences in individual income, and there is an increasing reliance on financial "incentives" for workers.

It would also be grossly inaccurate to regard either all capitalist or all socialist societies as being fundamentally identical. In practice there is great variety in these two kinds of economy, ranging from the most capitalist societies, such as the United States and Canada, through intermediate societies, such as Britain, Sweden, and Yugoslavia, to the most socialist societies, such as Albania and China. The terms "capitalist" and "socialist" represent *ideal types*—abstract concepts that are approximated to a greater or lesser extent by existing societies. Before we consider these types in detail, we must examine the concept of property, for the ownership of property is the chief bone of contention between the advocates of each type of economic system.

The Concept of Property

In everyday speech we think of "property" as referring to objects. Strictly speaking, however, *property* refers not to an object but to the *rights* that the owner of the object has in relation to others who are not owners of the object. Property is established in a society through social norms, often expressed in law, that define the conditions under which people may own objects. Property rights are backed by the state and enforced through its legal institutions. We can own private property in the United States, for example, only because the law allows us to. Property not only confers rights on the owner; it may impose responsibilities and limitations as well. No society permits unrestricted rights over property. If you own land in a residential area, you may not build a factory or a pig farm on it.

Property exists because resources are scarce; if they were all as unlimited and inexhaustible as the air, nobody would think to claim ownership. Ownership of property may take one of three forms:

1. *Communal ownership* exists when property belongs to the community as a whole and may be used by any member of the community. Communal ownership of land is frequently found in small preindustrial societies (it was the traditional form, for example, among most American Indian tribes).

2. *Private ownership* exists when property belongs to specific individuals. Private property is recognized in all societies. In some it may be restricted to a few household possessions; in others it may include assets worth millions of dollars.

3. *Public ownership* exists when property belongs to the state or some other recognized political authority that claims the property on behalf of the people as a whole. A good deal of property in industrial societies (such as highways and schools) is publicly owned.

Ownership does not merely create a relationship between the owner and the object; it also creates a relationship between the owner and nonowners. Those who own the means of producing and distributing goods and services—means such as land, factories, and capital funds—are potentially in a position of power over those who do not. The debate between the advocates of capitalism and socialism hinges on this question. Advocates of capitalism contend that the interests of all are served best if there is a minimum of public ownership of the means of production and distribution. Advocates of socialism argue that private ownership leads to exploitation and inequality, which can be avoided if the means of production and distribution are publicly owned. The issue is so important that it has divided the major industrial societies of the modern world into two opposing, armed camps.

Capitalism

In its ideal form, *capitalism* contains two essential ingredients: the deliberate pursuit of *personal profit* as the goal of economic activity, and *free competition* among both the buyers and the sellers of goods and services. As Max Weber remarked, the outstanding characteristic of capitalism is production "for the pursuit of profit, and ever renewed

Figure 18.9 John D. Rockefeller was one of the most successful capitalists of all time, and, not too surprisingly, was an enthusiastic advocate of the system. Rockefeller was disturbed, however, by his public image as a hard and greedy man, so every year, on his birthday, he would encourage some young boy to become a capitalist by giving him a nickel. In his later years, Rockefeller increased his annual largesse to a dime.

profit." There is nothing unusual about people seeking their own self-interest, but the distinguishing feature of capitalism is that it defines this activity as normal, morally acceptable, and socially desirable. Competition, however, is also regarded as necessary if the capitalist system is to work effectively. As John D. Rockefeller put it, competition "is not an evil tendency in business. It is merely a working out of a law of nature and a law of God" (quoted in Hofstadter, 1955).

Why is the pursuit of profit and an atmosphere of unrestricted competition so necessary for capitalism? The reason, Adam Smith argued in 1776, is that under these conditions the forces of supply and demand will ensure the production of the best possible products at the lowest possible price. The profit motive will provide the incentive for individual capitalists to produce the goods and services the public wants. Competition among capitalists will give the public the opportunity to compare the quality and prices of goods, so that producers who are inefficient or who charge excessive prices will be put out of business. The "invisible hand" of market forces thus ensures the greatest good for the entire society. Efficient producers are rewarded with profits, and consumers get quality products at competitive prices. For the system to work, however, there should ideally be a minimum of government interference in economic life. If the government attempts to regulate the supply of, or demand for, goods, the forces of the market will be upset, producers will lose their incentive to produce, and prices will be artificially distorted. The government should therefore adopt a policy of *laissez faire,* meaning "leave it alone."

In practice, this pure form of capitalism has never existed, although it was perhaps approximated in the early phases of industrial development. Particularly since the Great Depression, when the capitalist system seemed in danger of total collapse, it has been generally accepted that there must be some government regulation of the economy. The U.S. government now finds it necessary to supervise many details of economic activity. It sets minimum prices for some commodities and puts ceilings on the prices of others. It intervenes in international trade and concerns itself with the balance of payments with other countries. It protects some natural resources and encourages the exploitation of others. It lays down minimum wage standards,

Figure 18.10

Wm Hamilton

"Let's face it, Tom. It's not just the money, it's what the money can buy—more money, for instance."

Copyright Wm. Hamilton

provides for unemployment benefits, and sometimes supervises labor-management relations. It regulates the level of production and consumption through its budget and its tax policy. The growth of *monopolies,* single firms that dominate an industry, and of *oligopolies,* groups of a few firms that dominate an industry, has sometimes eliminated competition and made it possible for these firms to fix prices. For this reason, the government has the authority to prevent the concentration of economic power. Another respect in which the United States departs from the capitalist ideal type is that private ownership of competing firms by individual capitalists is now largely a thing of the past, for the American economy has come to be dominated by giant corporations owned by many thousands of shareholders. (Corporate ownership of property is still considered private ownership, however, because a corporation is, for most legal purposes, a person.)

Modern American capitalism is thus unlike the classical model in many respects. Nevertheless, our ideology still legitimates free competition and the pursuit of private profit, and our government is consequently reluctant to restrict either. Above all, Americans believe that their social and economic interests are best served if the means of production and distribution are privately owned, and they strongly resist any attempt to establish public ownership over them. It is this feature that makes the United States the most capitalistic society in the world.

Socialism

Socialism rests on entirely different assumptions. The pursuit of private profit is regarded as fundamentally immoral, because one person's profit is another person's loss. Under capitalism, it is argued, workers are paid less than the value of what they produce, and the surplus wealth is seized as profit by the owners. In addition, competition among different firms producing similar products is a waste of resources. Thus, the ultimate result of capitalism is social inequality and social conflict.

Socialism, on the other hand, proposes that production should be designed to serve social goals, and whether it is profitable or not is of secondary importance. Since private owners exploit both workers and consumers and will not produce unprofitable goods or services, whatever the social need for them, it is necessary for the means of production to be taken into public ownership and run in the best interests of society as a whole. Similarly, the means of distribution of wealth must be publicly owned to ensure that goods and services flow to those who need them rather than only to those who can afford them. The aims of a socialist economy, then, are the efficient production of needed goods and services and the achievement of social equality by preventing the accumulation of private wealth. To this end, the government must regulate the economy in accordance with long-term national plans, and it must not hesitate to establish artificial price levels or to run important industries at a loss if necessary.

The economy of modern socialist societies, such as the Soviet Union, conforms in some respects to this classic model. The means of production and distribution—land, machines, factories, capital funds, banks, retail outlets, and so on—are publicly owned. Speculative investment and the

Figure 18.11 Under socialism, the government regulates the economy in accordance with social goals, particularly that of economic equality among the people. These Chinese are living in an apartment supplied by the state to factory workers, at a rental equivalent to about 5 percent of wages. The apartment may seem inadequate by American standards, but compared to housing standards before the Chinese Revolution it is a tremendous improvement. Critics argue, however, that this system discourages individual initiative.

pursuit of private profit are not only considered undesirable; they are crimes of theft punishable in certain instances with the death penalty. The economy is closely regulated in accordance with national economic plans that are designed to meet specified social goals—even if this means depriving people of inessentials, such as the latest in fashionable clothing, in favor of investment in heavy industry that will generate more wealth in the long run. People are permitted private ownership of personal goods, such as household furniture and automobiles, but may not own property that produces wealth. In the Soviet Union and all other socialist societies, however, there are marked differences in income between ordinary workers and those in managerial and other executive positions, and the distribution of wealth is thus often very unequal. Several socialist societies are also experimenting with "incentive payments" to encourage higher production among workers—a practice not very different from offering them greater "profit" for working harder.

Democratic Socialism

A compromise between the capitalist and socialist models is that of *democratic socialism,* which is practiced by nearly all the countries of Western Europe. Under this system, the state takes ownership of only strategic industries and services, such as railways, airlines, mines, banks, radio, TV, telephone systems, medical services, colleges, and important manufacturing enterprises such as chemicals and steel. Private ownership of other means of production is permitted, even encouraged, but the economy is closely regulated in accordance with national priorities. Very high tax rates are used to prevent excessive profits or an undue concentration of wealth. A measure of social equality is ensured through extensive welfare services. In Great Britain, for example, college education and medical services are available free of charge, and about a third of the population lives in heavily subsidized public housing.

Communism

A fourth alternative, which is hypothetical at this point and seems likely to remain so, is *communism.* The socialist societies of Eastern Europe and Asia are usually but incorrectly described as "communist" in the United States, but they never describe themselves in this way. Although these countries are ruled by communist parties, they believe that they are still at the stage of socialism, a preparatory step before a truly communist society is achieved. Since no communist society has ever existed, and since the writings of Marx and other advocates of communism are somewhat vague in their vision of one, it is not entirely clear what a communist society would look like. In general, however, it would have some of the characteristics implied in the previously described communal ownership pattern that is currently found only in primitive societies. The role of the state would shrink; there would be an abundance of goods and services; people would no longer regard property as "private"; and wealth and power would be shared in harmony by the community as a whole. Under socialism, people are paid according to their work, but under communism individuals would contribute according to their abilities and receive according to their needs. The history of human alienation and strife would be over, and each person would be able to fulfill his or her human potential to the full. The major problem with such a society is that nobody seems to know quite how to arrive there. It has become increasingly evident over the past few decades that the socialist countries of the world are "stuck" in the socialist stage and have virtually no idea of how to get beyond it.

It is important to recognize that when Marx advocated communism, it was the concept of communism we have just outlined that he had in mind, not the Soviet version of socialism. Much of the antagonism to Marxist thought in the United States stems from a confusion between Marx's ideas and contemporary Soviet practice. On the basis of his writings, however, it seems highly unlikely that Marx would have regarded modern Soviet society with much enthusiasm.

Corporate Capitalism in the United States

The modern American economy, as we have seen, is no longer based on the competitive efforts of innumerable private capitalists. It is now dominated by large *corporations,* formal, commercial organizations that have widely dispersed ownership and that may exert enormous political and economic power.

THE LARGEST INDUSTRIAL COMPANIES IN THE WORLD (RANKED BY SALES)

Figure 18.12 The economies of Western nations, and of much of the rest of the world, are dominated by a handful of giant corporations. The bulk of these corporations are U.S.-owned.

Company	Headquarters	Sales ($000)	Net Income ($000)
Exxon	New York	79,106,471	4,295,243
General Motors	Detroit	66,311,200	2,892,700
Royal Dutch/Shell Group	The Hague/London	59,416,560	6,474,283
Mobil	New York	44,720,908	2,007,158
Ford Motor	Dearborn, Mich.	43,513,700	1,169,300
British Petroleum	London	38,713,496	3,439,582
Texaco	Harrison, N.Y.	38,350,370	1,759,069
Standard Oil of California	San Francisco	29,947,554	1,784,694
Gulf Oil	Pittsburgh	23,910,000	1,322,000
International Business Machines	Armonk, N.Y.	22,862,776	3,011,259
General Electric	Fairfield, Conn.	22,460,600	1,408,800
Unilever	London/Rotterdam	21,748,583	920,320
ENI	Rome	18,984,960	89,040
Standard Oil (Ind.)	Chicago	18,610,347	1,506,618
Fiat	Turin (Italy)	18,300,000	N.A.
Française des Pétroles	Paris	17,305,220	1,137,282
Peugeot-Citroën	Paris	17,270,104	254,318
International Telephone & Tel.	New York	17,197,423	380,685
Volkswagenwerk	Wolfsburg (Germany)	16,765,683	371,534
Philips' Gloeilampenfabrieken	Eindhoven (Netherlands)	16,576,123	308,701
Atlantic Richfield	Los Angeles	16,233,959	1,165,894
Renault	Paris	16,117,376	241,520
Siemens	Munich	15,069,575	361,938
Daimler-Benz	Stuttgart	14,942,324	347,794
Hoechst	Frankfurt	14,785,464	141,684
Shell Oil	Houston	14,431,211	1,125,561
Bayer	Leverkusen (Germany)	14,196,027	239,376
BASF	Ludwigshafen on Rhine	14,138,872	338,040
Petróleos de Venezuela	Caracas	14,115,899	2,907,291
Toyota Motor	Toyota City (Japan)	14,012,345	510,290
Thyssen	Duisburg (Germany)	13,636,918	87,262
Elf Aquitaine	Paris	13,385,876	1,310,132
Nestlé	Vevey (Switzerland)	13,016,940	490,865
U.S. Steel	Pittsburgh	12,929,100	(293,000)
Nissan Motor	Yokohama (Japan)	12,652,060	331,206
Conoco	Stamford, Conn.	12,647,998	815,360
Hitachi	Tokyo	12,632,844	484,190
Nippon Steel	Tokyo	12,595,259	243,562
E.I. du Pont de Nemours	Wilmington, Del.	12,571,800	938,900
Chrysler	Highland Park, Mich.	12,001,900	(1,097,300)
Mitsubishi Heavy Industries	Tokyo	11,959,912	111,616
Imperial Chemical Industries	London	11,391,003	880,638
Tenneco	Houston	11,209,000	571,000

Source: Fortune (August 11, 1980), p. 204.

Corporations and the American Economy

The corporation is a relatively new social invention that first achieved prominence in the late nineteenth century. Corporations have no single owner. They are owned by thousands or even hundreds of thousands of stockholders, and some of these stockholders are other corporations. In fact, most corporate stock in the United States is actually owned by corporate investors. In theory, the stockholders control the corporation by electing a board of directors and by voting on company policies at annual stockholders' meetings. In practice, however, the widely dispersed stockholders cannot effectively control corporate activities, and they merely rubber-stamp decisions that have already been made for them. The boards of directors are essentially self-perpetuating bodies whose recommendations, including nominations for new board members, are approved by stockholders as a matter of course. The day-to-day running of the corporation is in the hands of the management, which not only supervises company operations but also makes most of the major policy decisions, which in turn are usually approved by the board. The most important effect of this situation is that it tends to separate *ownership* of the firm from *control* of the firm. Those who control the corporation—the managers and to a lesser extent the directors—are for most purposes responsible to nobody but themselves. As long as they continue to maximize profits, the stockholders generally remain content.

The size and economic power of the major corporations is immense. The top 100 corporations—less than 0.01 percent of all corporations in the United States—own more than half of the manufacturing assets in the country. The top 0.5 percent account for 75 percent of assets, and the top 1 percent for 81 percent of assets (Means, 1970; Galbraith, 1973). Of the nearly 14,000 banks in the United States, the largest 10 hold over a quarter of all bank assets and deposits, while 10 of the 18,000 insurance companies hold almost 60 percent of all insurance company assets (Anderson, 1974). According to a 1978 report by the Senate Subcommittee on Reports, Accounting, and Finances, fewer than two dozen corporations—most of them banks—own enough stock to control 122 of the nation's largest corporations, which in turn represent over 40 percent of the value of all stock in the United States. Some of the largest corporations, such as

Exxon and General Motors, have budgets that are larger than those of every country in the world other than the United States and the Soviet Union.

The domination of the American economy by large corporations has several important consequences. One of them, explored more fully in Chapter 19 ("The Political Order"), is that these corporations are able to apply political leverage on national policy, winning favors for themselves, influencing the country's tax structure, and successfully blocking efforts to prevent the growth of oligopolies in particular industries. Corporate capitalism, according to the economist John Kenneth Galbraith (1971), has become so large and complex and invests so much time and capital in its enterprises that it can no longer afford the hazards of free competition; the stakes are too high. As a result, government and corporations cooperate informally in running what is in effect a planned economy, with minimal competition among the major enterprises.

At the highest levels of corporate industry there is very little of the competition considered so essential in the classic model of capitalism. Corporations compete not with the quality or price of their products but rather through their advertising. This tendency, which is apparent, for example, in the automobile, banking, and airline industries, involves an extraordinary waste of resources on the production of basically similar goods and services and on extensive advertising designed to make them appear different. In fact, a 1978 survey by the International Advertising Association found that the United States accounts for more advertising expenditures than the rest of the world put together—some 57 percent of the total. Americans are literally bombarded with ads, receiving, on the average, a minimum of 560 advertising messages each day from such sources as TV, radio, newspapers, and billboards (Toffler, 1970). This advertising, much of it devoted not only to making otherwise indistinguishable products seem distinctive but also to creating artificial demands for otherwise unwanted products, represents a diversion of more than $35 billion each year from more socially useful goals.

Large oligopolies are often able to use advertising to influence public tastes and preferences. The auto industry, to cite an obvious example, has persuaded Americans that the appearance, though not necessarily the quality and performance, of cars should change every year. Under the

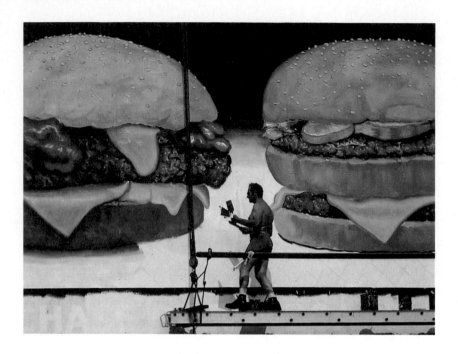

Figure 18.13 A characteristic feature of all capitalist societies is extensive commercial advertising. Although some advertising offers useful information to consumers, much of it is devoted to creating artificial demands for various products. Without such advertising, demand for many goods or services might shrink to insignificance, and entire industries could face economic ruin.

Figure 18.14

"Safety? Of course we're committed to safety—we're committed to safety and any other damn thing that sells cars."

Copyright Wm. Hamilton

policy of "planned obsolescence," American cars are deliberately designed to last only a few years. It is technically feasible to build cars that would last far longer than they do at present, but social values have been so manipulated by auto-industry advertising that possession of a car more than a few years old is almost a social stigma. A former chairman of General Motors explained that "planned obsolescence, in my view, is another word for progress," but the word also represents huge corporate profits, spectacular waste of scarce mineral resources, and an increased price tag on every car sold to the American public. The auto industry also managed, at least until the eighties, to persuade Americans to buy large, gas-greedy cars, despite ample evidence that world oil reserves were being rapidly depleted and that sharp price increases were therefore unavoidable. The American auto industry has since become a victim of its own short-sightedness, but the irresponsible manipulation of public tastes and diversion of scarce resources is perhaps inevitable in any society that makes private profit the main goal of economic activity.

Figure 18.15 Many American multinational corporations have become important factors on the world political and economic scene. In a number of instances, these corporations have greater financial resources than the countries in which they operate, and decisions by corporate executives in the United States can have a profound impact on nations thousands of miles away. Critics charge that the economies of many Third World countries are increasingly organized to serve the needs of foreign countries rather than their own. For example, diverse crops are grown in lesser amounts for local consumption, and single crops (such as coffee) in large amounts for export. The wealth produced in these countries by the activities of the multinationals is shared between the local elite and the corporations themselves, leaving the masses of the people poorer and hungrier than before.

One further feature of corporate capitalism in the United States merits consideration: what Galbraith (1966) has termed the contrast between "private affluence" and "public squalor." The American public has learned to prefer to spend its money on the consumption of goods and services provided by private enterprise rather than on taxes for goods and services provided by public authorities. The United States therefore has a generally affluent private life in the midst of generally squalid public facilities such as mass-transit systems and urban schools. This ordering of priorities would seem peculiar to many other societies, but it is taken for granted in the United States, where people have learned to value highly the particular life-style that corporate capitalism has made possible.

Multinational Corporations

In the past, corporations concentrated their efforts in a single industry. Today they diversify into a host of industries by buying controlling shares in other corporations.

Most of the largest corporations have now become multinational in scale by establishing industries abroad or taking over existing foreign corporations. For example, the International Telephone and Telegraph company (ITT), which has diversified into hundreds of industries entirely unrelated to telephones and telegraphs, now employs over 400,000 workers in sixty-eight countries. Exxon operates in nearly one hundred countries, and its fleet of tankers constitutes a navy as big as Great Britain's. Many multinational corporations are wealthier than some of the countries in which they operate. The corporations already account for more than a quarter of total world economic production, a share that will rise to over one-half by the end of the century. Three hundred of the largest five hundred multinationals are owned by one country, the United States. American corporate industry abroad is now the third largest economy in the world, after the United States and the Soviet Union (Jacoby, 1970; Segal, 1973; Barnet and Muller, 1974; Said and Simmons, 1975).

Subject to the authority of no one nation, having a

largely fictional responsibility to their far-flung shareholders, dedicated to the pursuit of profit, and run by a tiny elite of managers and directors, these corporations are posing problems on a global scale. Decisions taken by a small group of people in the United States can mean prosperity or unemployment in nations thousands of miles away, and they can also mean direct political interference in other societies. In the investigations that followed President Nixon's resignation over the Watergate affair, it became clear that American armaments, aircraft, and oil companies, among others, had not hesitated to bribe government officials elsewhere in the world in order to win contracts or influence the policies of foreign governments. ITT secretly requested the Nixon administration to overthrow the government of Chile, offering up to $1 million to the federal government as a contribution toward the expenses involved. Exxon paid nearly $60 million to government officials in fifteen countries, including $27 million to several Italian political parties. Lockheed distributed nearly $200 million in bribes and other payoffs in a number of countries, and the resulting scandals implicated the prince of the Netherlands, the prime minister of Japan, military leaders in Colombia, and cabinet members in Italy. More than 500 American corporations, most of them multinational, have admitted making illegal or "questionable" payments.

Of course, the multinationals may have some positive role to play: they encourage economic development in the poorer countries of the world by importing the necessary skills, technology, and capital. But their motives are purely commercial: to exploit cheap labor and resources, to develop new markets, and to extract profits from the countries where they operate. And their commercial intentions may yield political results, for their patterns of investment and other activity can affect issues of intervention and nonintervention, war and peace. Increasingly, multinational corporations are joining nation-states as the main actors in international relations. Already more influential than many countries, the large multinationals are developing world-wide interests and the "foreign policies" that go with these interests. These huge corporations have evolved much more quickly than have any means to apply social control over them. They now represent a disturbing concentration of unscrutinized political and economic power that may have immense, long-term social impact (Said and Simmons, 1975; Ball, 1975; Vernon, 1977).

Summary

1. The economic order is the institutionalized system for distributing goods and services. Economic activity is important because it sustains life, because a society's main means of economic production influences culture and social structure, because economic and political issues are very closely linked, and because an individual's work is a major source of personal identity and social status.

2. Every society establishes a division of labor among its members. There has been a general trend toward increased specialization, which has gone furthest in modern industrial societies. Durkheim distinguished between societies integrated by mechanical solidarity and those integrated by organic solidarity; the latter are more prone to anomie.

3. One important concern of the sociology of occupations is the changing proportion of workers in primary, secondary, and tertiary industry. A second concern is the growth of professions and the process by which jobs are professionalized.

4. Alienation refers to the sense of powerlessness and meaninglessness experienced by people confronted with social institutions that they consider oppressive and cannot control. Karl Marx linked alienation to the extreme division of labor, which reduces the worker's autonomy and individual contribution almost to insignificance. Worker alienation has become recognized as a growing problem in the United States, although an attempt has been made to combat the problem through a "human relations" approach to industry.

5. Capitalism and socialism represent two basic ways in which goods can be produced and distributed. Both concepts represent ideal types and are approximated in varying degrees by different societies. The two systems differ primarily over whether economic resources should be privately or publicly owned. Democratic socialism represents a compromise between the two, while communism is a hypothetical advance on socialism.

6. The American economy is dominated by large corporations whose power and influence have important implications for the economy and society. Many corporations have now become multinational in scope and influence, and they represent a disturbing concentration of economic—and therefore political—power.

Important Terms

economic order (453)

division of labor (454)

mechanical
  solidarity (456)

organic solidarity (456)

anomie (456)

primary industry (457)

secondary industry (457)

tertiary industry (457)

profession (458)

alienation (460)

ideal type (467)

property (467)

communal
  ownership (468)

private ownership (468)

public ownership (468)

capitalism (468)

laissez faire (469)

monopoly (469)

oligopoly (469)

socialism (470)

democratic
  socialism (471)

communism (471)

corporation (471)

Suggested Readings

MARX, KARL. *Selected Writings in Sociology and Social Philosophy.* Tom Bottomore and Maximilian Rubel (eds.). Baltimore, Md.: Penguin, 1964.

A selection of excerpts from Marx's major works. The selections include Marx's writings on the concept of alienation and his impassioned denunciations of alienated labor.

NADER, RALPH, et al. *Taming the Giant Corporation.* New York: W. W. Norton, 1976.

A critical study of large modern corporations. Nader and his associates suggest some ways to make these organizations more socially responsible.

RITZER, GEORGE. *Working: Conflict and Change.* 2nd ed. Englewood Cliffs, N.J.: Prentice-Hall, 1977.

A good sociological overview of work in modern America.

SMELSER, NEIL J. *The Sociology of Economic Life.* 2nd ed. Englewood Cliffs, N.J.: Prentice-Hall, 1976.

A succinct treatment of the relationship between economy and society.

TERKEL, STUDS. *Working.* New York: Random House, 1974.

A fascinating collection of tape-recorded interviews with workers across the United States. The book, which became a best seller, has great human interest as well as sociological significance.

VERNON, RAYMOND. *Storm over the Multinationals: The Real Issues.* Cambridge, Mass.: Harvard University Press, 1977.

A useful discussion of multinational corporations, with a full analysis of their advantages and disadvantages for other nations.

Work in America: Report of a Special Task Force to the Secretary of Health, Education, and Welfare. Cambridge, Mass.: MIT Press, 1973.

Written in clear, nontechnical language, this government report recounts the "white-collar woes" and "blue-collar blues" of alienated American workers.

CHAPTER 19   *The Political Order*

Over 2000 years ago the philosopher Aristotle observed that we are political animals. We are indeed, and necessarily so, for politics is an inevitable consequence of social living. In every society some valued resources are scarce, and politics is essentially the process of deciding "who gets what, when, and how" (Lasswell, 1936). The character of political institutions and behavior varies a great deal from one society or group to another, but the political process itself is universal.

The political order is the institutionalized system through which some individuals and groups acquire and exercise power over others. This chapter will focus primarily on the political process at the highest level of power in modern society, the state. Max Weber (1946), who laid the foundations of modern political sociology, defined the *state* as the institution that successfully claims a monopoly on the right to use force within a given territory. Of course, the state may choose to delegate some of its powers to other agencies, such as local authorities, the police, or the military. In the final analysis, however, the state can override all other agencies and is thus the central and most vital component of the political order. The "state," incidentally, is not quite the same thing as the "government." The state is an impersonal social institution, whereas the government is the collection of individuals who happen to be directing the power of the state at any given moment.

Power

Politics is about power—about who gets it, how it is obtained, how it is applied, and to what purposes it is put. Max Weber defined *power* as the ability to control the behavior of others, even in the absence of their consent. Put another way, power is the capacity to participate effectively in a decision-making process. Those who for one reason or another cannot affect the process are therefore powerless. Power may be exercised blatantly or subtly, legally or illegally, justly or unjustly. It may derive from many sources, such as wealth, status, prestige, numbers, or organizational efficiency. Its ultimate basis, however, is the ability to compel obedience, if necessary through the threat or use of force.

The exercise of power may be either legitimate or illegitimate. Power is considered *legitimate* only if people generally recognize that those who apply it have the right to do so—perhaps because they are elected government officials, perhaps because they are an aristocracy whose commands are never questioned, perhaps because they are believed to be inspired by God. Weber used the term *authority* to refer to legitimate power. Power is considered *illegitimate,* on the other hand, if people believe that those who apply it do not have the right to do so—perhaps because they are acting illegally, perhaps because they hold no public office, perhaps because they are newly successful revolutionaries who have not yet entrenched their regime. Weber called illegitimate power *coercion.*

A simple example will illustrate this distinction more fully. If a judge rules that you must pay a fine, you will probably obey: if you do not, the judge has the power to make you suffer other negative consequences. If an armed mugger in the street demands your money, you will likewise probably hand it over: the mugger also has the power to make you suffer negative consequences if you refuse. But you regard the judge's demand as legitimate. It rests on judicial authority, and you recognize that the judge has the *right* to fine you even if you disagree with and resent the decision. You do not accept, however, that the mugger has any *right* whatever to take your money. You pay up simply because you are being coerced.

Power based on authority is usually unquestioningly accepted by those to whom it is applied, for obedience to it has become a social norm. Power based on coercion, on the other hand, tends to be unstable, because people obey only out of fear and will disobey at the first opportunity. For this reason every political system must be regarded as legitimate by its participants if it is to survive. Most people must consider it desirable, workable, and better than any

alternatives. If the bulk of the citizens in any society no longer consider their political system legitimate, it is doomed, for its power can then rest only on coercion, which will fail in the long run. The French, Russian, American, and Iranian revolutions, for example, were preceded by an erosion of the legitimacy of the existing systems. The authority of the respective monarchies was questioned and their power, based increasingly on coercion rather than on unquestioning loyalty, inevitably crumbled.

Types of Authority

Max Weber distinguished three basic types of legitimate authority: traditional authority, legal-rational authority, and charismatic authority. Each type is legitimate because it rests on the implicit or explicit consent of the governed. A person who can successfully claim one of these types of authority is regarded as having the right to compel obedience, at least within socially specified limits.

Traditional Authority

In a political system based on *traditional authority,* power is legitimated by ancient custom. The authority of the ruler is generally founded on unwritten laws and has an almost sacred quality. Chieftainships and monarchies have always relied on traditional authority, and historically it has been the most common source of the legitimation of power.

People obey traditional authority because "it has always been that way": the right of the king to rule is not open to question. Claim to traditional authority is usually based on birthright, with the status of ruler generally passing to the eldest son of the incumbent. In some cases the power of the ruler over the subjects seems virtually unlimited, but in practice there are always informal social norms setting the boundaries within which power can be exercised. If a ruler exceeds these limits, as many Roman emperors did, people may regard such use of power as illegitimate and coercive, and may even try to depose the ruler. However, they are likely to remain loyal to the system of traditional authority, recognizing the close kin of the overthrown ruler as having the strongest claim to the succession. But when a society begins to modernize, support for systems based on traditional authority wanes, and some people look for a more rational alternative.

Figure 19.1 The power of hereditary rulers, such as kings, queens, emperors, chieftains, and shahs, is legitimated by traditional authority: people tend to obey because "it has always been that way," and it generally does not occur to them that the situation could or should be changed. As a result of the disappearance of hereditary rule in most of the modern world, traditional authority is now rarely the basis for a ruler's legitimacy. This portrait shows one of the most powerful monarchs of history, Queen Elizabeth I of England.

Legal-Rational Authority

In a system based on *legal-rational authority,* power is legitimated by explicit rules and procedures that define the rights and obligations of the rulers. The rules and procedures are typically found in a written constitution and set of laws that, at least in theory, have been socially agreed upon. This form of authority is characteristic of the political systems of most modern societies.

Legal-rational authority stresses a "government of laws, not of people." The power of an official in a country such as the United States, Canada, or the Soviet Union derives from the office the person holds, not from personal characteristics such as birthright. Officials can exercise power only within legally defined limits that have been formally set in advance. Americans thus acknowledge the right of a president or even of a minor bureaucrat to exercise power, provided that person does not exceed the specific boundaries of authority that attach to his or her respective office. When President Nixon did overstep these boundaries, his acts were considered illegitimate—an abuse of power—and he was forced to resign. A similar or worse fate would doubtless await a modern Soviet leader who used power in ways considered illegitimate in that country.

Figure 19.2 The power of the rulers of most modern societies is legitimated by legal-rational authority. Their power derives from the office they hold, not from personal characteristics such as ancestry. Holders of public office, like these members of the United States Congress, may exercise power only within the limits defined by the laws and the Constitution.

Figure 19.3 The power of certain leaders is legitimated by charismatic authority. Other people attribute exceptional and sometimes even supernatural qualities to such leaders, and this charisma alone makes their authority seem legitimate to their followers. Charismatic leaders may, of course, enjoy legitimacy from some other source as well, but this is not relevant to their charismatic appeal. Churchill, Castro, Eva Perón, Martin Luther King, Jr., John Kennedy, and Mao are typical examples of charismatic leaders.

Charismatic Authority

In a system based on *charismatic authority*, power is legitimated by the exceptional or even supernatural character that people attribute to particular political, religious, or military leaders. Weber called this extraordinary quality *charisma*. Typical charismatic leaders include such figures as Jesus, Joan of Arc, Hitler, Gandhi, Napoleon, Mao, Castro, Julius Caesar, Alexander the Great, Churchill, and the Ayatollah Khomeini. The charismatic leader is seen as a person of destiny who is inspired by unusual vision, by lofty principles, or even by God. The charisma of these leaders is itself sufficient to make their authority seem legitimate to their followers. Whether they can also lay claim to traditional or legal-rational authority is of little relevance to their popular appeal.

Charisma is a spontaneous, irrational phenomenon that often poses a threat to systems based on traditional or legal-rational authority. Revolutions are commonly led by charismatic figures who win personal allegiance and are regarded as the symbol of radical changes to come. Yet charismatic authority is inherently unstable. It has no rules or traditions to guide conduct, and because it rests on the unique characteristics of a particular individual, it is undermined if the leader fails or dies. Successful revolutions led by charismatic figures such as Mao, Castro, or Khomeini almost always face a problem of succession, for those who take over are unlikely to have the qualities of their

predecessor. For this reason, systems based on charismatic authority are usually short-lived. Many of them collapse. Others are either slowly *routinized* into legal-rational systems based on bureaucratic rules and procedures, or—more commonly in the past than today—into traditional systems in which power passes to the descendants of the original leader.

Each of these forms of authority represents an *ideal type.* In other words, each is an abstraction that is only approximated to a greater or lesser extent by any actual political system. In practice, political systems and political leaders may derive their authority from more than one source. The power of the American presidency, for example, is legitimated primarily by legal-rational authority, but the office has existed for so long that it now seems to have traditional authority as well. Richard Nixon demonstrated this fact in the closing months of his presidency. Nixon lacked personal charisma and his legal-rational authority was being eroded by allegations that he had committed serious crimes during his election and his tenure of the presidency. Yet he was able to stave off his fate for some time by appealing to traditional loyalties to the office of the presidency—a confusion of the office and its temporary occupant more appropriate for a traditional monarchy. John Kennedy, a highly charismatic personality, may be said to have enjoyed legitimacy from all three sources of authority—charismatic, legal-rational, and traditional.

The State

We have noted that the state has a monopoly of the legitimate use of force within a given territory. That territory comprises a nation, which, conversely, may be defined as a geographically distinct collectivity of people ruled by a state. The nation-state, however, is a relatively recent historical development. The anthropologist George Murdock (1949) tells us that

> for 99 percent of the [time] that man has inhabited this earth, he lived, thrived, and developed without any true government whatsoever, and as late as 100 years ago half the peoples of the world—not half the population but half the tribes or nations—still ordered their lives exclusively through informal controls without the benefit of political institutions.

The nation-state emerged in Europe only a few centuries ago, spread later to the Americas, and arose in most parts of Africa and Asia only in the course of this century. Before that time the state, if it existed at all, was a very rudimentary affair. Rulers certainly laid claim to authority over large areas, but there was little sense of nationhood, and the rulers could rarely achieve a successful monopoly of authority. Often, in fact, their authority was confined to an urban area and its rural hinterland; the combined territory formed a city-state. Even the early empires, such as that of Rome, were, in effect, alliances between city-states and small kingdoms, each claiming authority over its own citizens and only grudgingly recognizing the center of power.

The emergence of the state as a separate institution is closely linked to the level of cultural evolution of a society, and in particular to its means of subsistence (Fried, 1967; Service, 1971, 1975; Lenski and Lenski, 1978). As noted in Chapter 4 ("Society"), formal political institutions are absent in hunting and gathering societies. Each community is independent, and decisions are made by group consensus. In pastoral and horticultural societies, where populations are larger and there may be a food surplus, some individuals become more powerful and wealthy than others. They pass their status on to their descendants, and patterns of chieftainship emerge. In agricultural societies a very large food surplus is possible, and this can be converted into wealth and power. Entire categories of the population become wealthier than others, and social classes appear for the first time. In these societies—which may contain millions of people—a central political authority is needed to maintain social order and organize social life. The state thus emerges as a distinct social institution, with power typically concentrated in the hands of a monarch or emperor. The power of the ruler is legitimated by traditional authority, and an elaborate court bureaucracy and full-time military organization are established.

In industrial societies the nature of the state changes radically. The unprecedented wealth produced by industrialism permits the emergence of a large middle class. Rising levels of aspiration, combined with mass education, produce a more politically sophisticated population. Arbitrary rule is no longer acceptable, and traditional authority is replaced by legal-rational authority as the basis of the state's legitimacy. The responsibilities of the state expand enormously because it is explicitly concerned with improving social conditions. The state assumes responsibilities in areas as diverse as welfare, education, medicine, public transport, scientific research, and economic planning. State expenditures rise dramatically: the U.S. government, for example, had an annual budget of about $4.3 million at the end of the eighteenth century, compared with about $650 billion in 1980. The size of the government bureaucracy shows a corresponding increase. A century and a half ago the federal government employed 5000 people; today it employs nearly 3 million, and the total of all federal, state, and local government employees exceeds 15 million people. (As Figure 19.5 shows, most of the growth in government bureaucracy has been at the local rather than federal level.) The state thus becomes a central social institution.

Figure 19.4 The state does not exist in the simplest of preindustrial societies. Among these Middle Eastern pastoralists, for example, all decisions are made through group consensus, and the power of the headman is very limited. The state is present only in societies that are stratified into classes or castes.

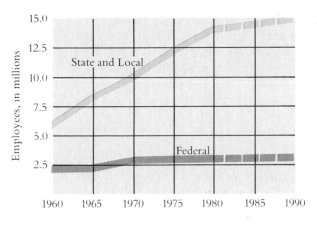

FEDERAL AND LOCAL GOVERNMENT
EMPLOYEES, 1960–1990

Source: Bureau of Labor Statistics.

Figure 19.5 Government bureaucracies have grown very large in the United States, as this graph suggests. The number of federal government employees, however, has remained fairly steady for some time, while that of local and state governments has risen sharply. These are ironic facts in view of the widespread belief that the size of the federal bureaucracy is a major social problem that could be relieved if only more of its functions were delegated to local and state authorities.

The Functionalist Approach

From the functionalist perspective, the emergence of the state and its dominant position in modern societies can be explained in terms of the *functions* that it serves in the maintenance of the social system as a whole. Four major functions of the state can be identified.

Enforcement of Norms

In small, traditional communities, norms are usually unwritten and are generally enforced by spontaneous community action. In a highly complex and rapidly changing modern society such a system would be unworkable. The state accordingly takes the responsibility for codifying important norms in the form of laws. It also tries to ensure that these norms are obeyed by applying formal negative sanctions to offenders. Laws are used to define and suppress certain forms of deviance; these are the criminal laws. Laws are also used to define and protect the rights of individuals and groups; these are the civil laws.

Arbitration of Conflict

The state provides an institutionalized process for deciding "who gets what, when, and how." Conflict over the allocation of scarce resources and over national goals must be kept within manageable limits, or society might become a jungle in which different groups pursue their own interests without restraint. The state acts as arbitrator, or umpire, between conflicting interests, establishing means for resolving disputes and determining policies.

Planning and Direction

A complex modern society requires coordinated and systematic planning and direction. The economy must be closely monitored and attempts made to prevent unemployment or inflation. The output of trained workers must be geared to the demands of industry and commerce. Research funds must be allocated in accordance with national priorities. The effects of pollution on the environment must be gauged and if necessary counteracted. Highways must be put where people need them. Welfare must be distributed to the poor, and pensions to the aged. The decisions involved in these and countless other actions must be based on knowledge derived from reliable data, which have to be systematically collected and analyzed. To a greater or lesser degree the decisions must be centralized if uniform and coherent policies are to emerge.

Relations with Other Societies

The state is responsible for political, economic, and military relations with other societies. It forms alliances with friendly states and participates in international organizations. It forms trading agreements with other societies and attempts to protect its country's foreign investments. It engages in acts of diplomacy and, if necessary, defense or aggression against other states. None of these functions could be met without a high degree of centralized control and authority. If the state is to be effective in its relations with other states, it must have the capacity to be taken seriously.

Figure 19.6 An important function of the state is the enforcement of norms. In small, traditional societies social control can be applied effectively through informal community reactions. A large modern society, on the other hand, requires a formal system of social control, including laws, policing, and judicial processes.

A single theme underlies all four functions: the preservation of social order. This view of the role of the state is an ancient one, long predating modern sociological theory. It was perhaps best presented by the conservative English philosopher Thomas Hobbes (1588–1679), who argued for a strong state with unchallenged legitimacy. Hobbes claimed that in the "state of nature" that supposedly existed before the establishment of political authority, life was "solitary, poor, nasty, brutish, and short." There was no justice or injustice, right or wrong, good or bad, since there was no authority to define, establish, and maintain order. Despairing of the situation, people made a "social contract"

to form the state. This contract could never be broken, because no matter how oppressive the state might be, it would always be preferable to the earlier chaos.

Hobbes's analysis was implicitly functional and explicitly conservative. His central notion, although now less philosophically and romantically expressed, is still widely accepted in the United States and elsewhere: the main duty of the state is to preserve law and order.

The Conflict Approach

An alternative view of the state is that it emerged and exists largely to safeguard the interests of the privileged. In other words, the state protects the "haves" in their conflict with the "have-nots."

This view was systematically presented by the French philosopher Jean Jacques Rousseau (1712–1778), whose writings provided much of the inspiration for the French Revolution. Rousseau rejected Hobbes's view that people in the original "state of nature" were brutal and self-seeking. Instead, he saw them as "noble savages," free, happy, and peaceful. The establishment of the state was the source of their problems, not the solution of them: "Man is born free, yet everywhere he is in chains."

How, then, did the state arise? The answer, claimed Rousseau (1950, originally published 1762), lay in the creation of private property:

> The first man who, having enclosed a piece of ground, bethought himself of saying, "This is mine," and found people simple enough to believe him, was the real founder of civil society. From how many crimes, wars, and murders, from how many horrors and misfortunes might not anyone have saved mankind, by pulling up the stake, or filling up the ditch, and crying to his fellows: "Beware of listening to this imposter; you are undone if you once forget that the fruits of the earth belong to us all, and the earth itself to nobody!"

Once private property had been established, the people of the "state of nature" took to fighting among themselves, and eventually agreed on a "social contract" to form the state so that order could be achieved once more. But the state did not apply impartial justice; it merely protected the interests of the wealthy. The state "bound new fetters to the poor, and gave new powers to the rich ... and, for the advantage of a few ambitious individuals, subjected all mankind to perpetual labor, slavery, and wretchedness."

Since the "state of nature" was preferable to unjust rule by central authority, Rousseau recommended that the state be overthrown and that a new social contract be made—one that gave power to the people, not the state.

The most influential modern conflict theory of the state is of course that of Karl Marx, as put forward in the *Communist Manifesto* (1848) and elsewhere. Marx's analysis draws on Rousseau's insights but is a much more sophisticated one. The key to his analysis is the idea that the nature of economic production in a particular society influences the character of its culture and social structure. In every society those who control the means of economic production (such as slaves, land, or capital) are the ruling class. All except the most primitive societies, Marx claimed, are divided into two or more classes, one of which dominates and exploits the others. The ruling class always uses social institutions, particularly the state, to maintain its privileged position. For this reason, social institutions always serve to maintain the status quo, not to change it. The state itself is simply the "executive committee" of the ruling class, protecting that class's interests and allowing it to enjoy the surplus wealth produced by the workers.

Class conflict, Marx maintained, is the dynamic force in history:

> The history of all hitherto existing societies is the history of class struggle. . . . Freedman and slave, patrician and plebeian, lord and serf, guildmaster and journeyman, in a word, oppressor and oppressed, stood in constant opposition to one another, carried on an uninterrupted, now hidden, now open fight, a fight that each time ended, either in a revolutionary reconstruction of society at large, or the common ruin of the contending parties. [Marx and Engels, 1970, originally published 1848]

Marx traced a series of stages through which human society evolves, according to the means of production that is dominant at each stage. The first is *primitive communism,* in which there is no private property and therefore no classes. The second is *slavery,* in which one class owns and exploits the members of another. The third is *feudalism,* in which a class of aristocratic landowners exploits the mass of peasants. The fourth is *capitalism,* in which the owners of wealth exploit the mass of industrial workers. Each of these systems is more economically productive than its predecessor, but the tensions of class conflict lead to a revolution that ushers in the next stage. The fifth stage, *socialism,*

Figure 19.7

"*When my distinguished colleague refers to the will of the 'people,' does he mean his 'people' or my 'people'?*"

Drawing by Richter; © 1976
The New Yorker Magazine, Inc.

occurs when the industrial workers have finally revolted. They establish a temporary "dictatorship of the proletariat" to prevent attempts by reactionaries to return to the old system and to guide social change toward the final stage. This is the stage of *communism,* in which property is communally owned and in which, Marx believed, people would enjoy true freedom and the fulfillment of their human potential for the first time in history.

If the state exists primarily to safeguard the interests of the ruling class, then what happens to the state in the classless communist society? Marx's collaborator, Engels, declared optimistically that it would just "wither away." Modern scholarship indicates that the ideas of Marx and Engels were not nearly as similar as has always been assumed in the past, and it is very doubtful if Marx took such a naive view. Yet Marx's own conception of the state in a classless society is not very clear. He merely commented, rather mysteriously, that "the government of people will be replaced by the administration of things," and that "free-dom consists in converting the state from an organ su-perimposed on society into one completely subordinate to it."

The idea that the role of the state will be significantly reduced in a classless society is perhaps the weakest element in Marx's analysis. In countries that are currently at the stage of socialism, such as the Soviet Union and China, the state clearly has more power than it does in capitalist societies. Nor does it seem that socialist societies have any idea of how to achieve the abolition of the state, even if that remains their goal.

Evaluation

Marx was undoubtedly correct in his view that a *major* function of the state is to protect the interests of the ruling class. As we have noted, the state comes into existence only when classes emerge in society. The historical evidence confirms that the ruling classes in all societies have without exception been the economically dominant classes as well. The sociological evidence confirms that institutions and other cultural arrangements generally tend to support the status quo, and therefore to support the interests of the class that benefits from it.

Marx failed to recognize, however, that the role of the state is not *only* an oppressive one. As our functional anal-ysis shows, the state has several functions that are not necessarily related to class conflict. These functions would have to be fulfilled by a strong central authority in any modern society, class-based or classless. In fact, a socialist or communist society must regulate the lives of its citizens much more closely than a capitalist society has to, because it supervises not only the production of wealth but also its distribution. For this reason, the power of the state is likely to increase in a socialist society, and even more so in a communist society.

The functionalist and conflict approaches, then, each give us only a partial view of social reality. The function-alist approach shows the need for the institution of the state, while the conflict approach reveals the role that the state plays in competition among different social classes and in maintaining social inequality. Taken together, the two perspectives give us a better understanding of the modern state.

Democracy

Democracy comes from a Greek word meaning "rule of the people," and this is no doubt what Lincoln had in mind when he defined democracy as "government of the people, by the people, and for the people." In practice, no such system has ever existed. Pure democracy would mean that every citizen would have the right to participate in every decision, a situation that would lead to complete chaos and would leave little time for all kinds of other activities. This ideal form of democracy has been approximated only in very small communities, such as the ancient Greek city-states and early New England towns. Even in these cases, however, certain people were denied the right of participa-tion—non-property-holders and women in New England, and both women and slaves in Greece.

In practice, the societies we consider democratic are those that explicitly recognize that the powers of govern-ment derive from the consent of the governed. These soci-eties have institutionalized procedures for choosing period-ically among contenders for public office. They have a *representative democracy;* that is, the voters elect representa-tives who are responsible for making political decisions. A characteristic of all democracies is that the right of the individual to choose among alternatives is held in high regard, and this right presupposes civil liberties such as freedom of speech and assembly.

Representative democracy is historically recent, rare, and fragile. It is found almost exclusively in a handful of Western European countries and in the countries that they colonized and implanted with their own traditions. In most instances, these transplants were short-lived. Many societies, notably several newly independent African na-tions and the socialist countries of Eastern Europe, retain the trappings of representative democracy in that they do hold periodic elections. The outcome of these elections is a foregone conclusion, however, because there is only one party and thus no choice among alternatives. The practice of one-party "democracy" is defended on the grounds that the party already "knows" what the people want, or that party strife would be socially divisive. In the absence of free elections, there is obviously no way of finding out whether this diagnosis is correct. The suspicion must linger that a party that is reluctant to face a free election is afraid it might lose.

Figure 19.8 Nazi Germany was a dictatorship in which the state assumed totalitarian powers. The Nazis demanded absolute conformity to their racial and other political beliefs and recognized no limits to the power of the state. This picture shows members of the Hitler Youth parading past the dictator (on the balcony at left).

Democracy is one of several possible forms of government. Most societies in the past have been governed by *autocracy*, the rule of a single individual, who usually holds the hereditary status of emperor, king, or chief. Apart from a few isolated *dictatorships*—nonhereditary rule by a single individual who cannot be removed from office by legal means—autocracy is very rare in the modern world. The most common form of nondemocratic rule is *oligarchy*, or rule by a few. The socialist societies of Eastern Europe and Asia are regarded in the West as oligarchies because in practice they are ruled by a bureaucratic elite. A few Latin American countries are still ruled by oligarchies consisting of a handful of extremely wealthy families. In both Latin America and Africa a new form of oligarchy, the *junta*, or rule by military officers who have achieved a coup, is increasingly common. In some nondemocratic states, the government assumes *totalitarian* powers. A totalitarian government recognizes no limits to its authority and is willing to regulate any aspect of social life. The outstanding historical example of the totalitarian state is undoubtedly Nazi Germany, but the governments of many other societies, particularly those ruled by communists and those ruled by right-wing juntas, have strong totalitarian tendencies.

Prerequisites for Democracy

Why is democratic government so rare and why has it been successfully established almost exclusively in societies of a certain type, namely, advanced industrial countries? It seems that democracy can thrive only when most of several basic conditions have been met.

Advanced Economic Development

Seymour Martin Lipset (1959c) surveyed data from forty-eight societies and found a strong correlation between the level of economic development and the presence of democratic institutions. The reasons for this relationship are complex, but two basic factors seem to be particularly important. First, an advanced economy always contains an urbanized, literate, and sophisticated population that expects and demands some participation in the political process. Second, societies with advanced economies tend to be politically stable. This stability probably derives from the presence of a large middle class that has a stake in the society and is reluctant to support political upheavals of any kind. Lacking the very large oppressed classes found in agricultural or early industrial societies, these countries can afford to offer their citizens political alternatives without fearing that society would be torn apart in any resulting conflict. In societies with a large lower class—such as most of the nations of Africa, Latin America, and Asia—there is likely to be strong opposition from the ruling class to the extension of democratic rights.

Restraints on Government Power

Democracy is best served if there are institutional checks on the power of the state. These restraints can be of many different kinds: laws limiting the exercise of power, constitutional arrangements for the impeachment of officials, free criticism by the press and other media, or simply informal norms so powerful that they cannot be violated. These norms, which specify the "rules of the game," are easily overlooked, but they are a vital part of any democratic system.

An excellent example of the force of informal norms is provided by Great Britain, which is unique among modern societies in having no written constitution. Like the United States, the country has two legislative chambers. The House of Commons is elected by popular vote, and the majority party forms the national government. The House of Lords, which has to approve legislation passed in the House of Commons, is not elected. Its members are mostly hereditary aristocrats who generally support the right-wing Conservative party. When the left-wing Labour party has a majority in the House of Commons and forms a government, the House of Lords could easily reject all its legislation. But in practice it very rarely attempts to do so. The House of Lords informally recognizes the superior legitimacy of the popularly elected House of Commons, and its Conservative members abstain from voting in sufficiently large numbers to allow the small minority of Labour lords to become a majority. When the Conservatives control the House of Commons, the Conservative lords present themselves for voting and ensure the passage of government legislation.

Absence of Major Cleavages

Democracy is most likely to survive in a society in which there is a general consensus on basic values and a widespread commitment to existing political institutions. A clear-cut political cleavage, or split, tends to divide society into militant camps that are unwilling to make the compromises necessary for democracy to work. The greater the potential or actual conflict in a society, the more pressures are put on the government to become "strong" in order to contain them. In societies marked by extreme disunity—such as Lebanon with its religious divisions, South Africa with its racial divisions, or Bolivia with its economic divisions—democratic institutions are generally either unstable or absent.

Tolerance of Dissent

A tolerance of criticism and of dissenting opinions is fundamental to democracy. Governing parties must resist the temptation to equate their own policies with the national good, or they will tend to regard opposition as disloyal or even treasonable. President Johnson and more particularly President Nixon were inclined to regard opposition to their military policies in Southeast Asia as outright subversion, and both abused such agencies as the CIA, the FBI, and the Pentagon in an attempt to suppress dissent. One result was that dissenting groups, feeling blocked from the normal political process, turned to other avenues of protest that greatly sharpened internal conflict in the United States.

Another danger to democracy is that of the "tyranny of the majority." In some cases the democratic process may work in such a way that a small minority—blacks in the United States, for example—is a permanent loser. For groups in this position, democracy might as well not exist, and it is important that government should recognize the grievances of minorities that have little political clout. If the losers in the political process do not accept the legitimacy of the process under which they have lost, they may resort to more radical tactics outside the institutional framework.

Access to Information

A democracy requires its citizens to make informed choices. If citizens are denied access to the information they need to make these choices, or if they are given false or misleading information, the democratic process may become a sham. It is therefore important that the media not be censored, that citizens have the right of free speech, and that public officials tell the truth.

The practice of some recent presidents of concealing information from, or lying to, Congress and the public is clearly contrary to democratic values. When President Johnson was running for reelection in 1964, he campaigned against an air war in Vietnam even though he had already made a decision to launch such a war. When President Nixon took office, he promised "to tell the people the hard truth" and to provide "an open administration." Nixon then proceeded to bomb Cambodia for fourteen months while denying that he was doing so, and he secretly sent troops into Laos in violation of specific prohibitions voted by Congress and signed by himself. If neither the voters nor their representatives are aware of the policies their government is pursuing, democratic participation is clearly impossible.

Diffusion of Power

If power is diffuse and no one group can obtain a monopoly over it, the prospects for democracy are enhanced. One way of diffusing power is to distribute it among various branches of government. The U.S. Constitution separates the powers of the executive, legislative, and judicial branches, and they often provide an effective check on one another. The abuses of executive power in the Watergate affair, for example, were investigated and halted by the other two branches. Another way of diffusing power is to distribute it to regional and local governments. Power may also be spread beyond government into other institutions and organizations. The existence of separate centers of power in labor unions, corporations, churches, and elsewhere provides a system of checks and balances and ensures that each group must take account of the others.

Liberty and Equality

The socialist societies of Eastern Europe and Asia claim to be democratic and dedicated to human freedom, although their political systems have few of the features that we have identified as prerequisites for democracy, as we understand the term in the West. Yet the leaders of these societies are not being cynical. They, and no doubt many of their citizens, believe that they live in democracies and that their people are free. Conversely, they also believe that our societies are undemocratic and unfree. How can this be?

The source of the difficulty lies in the way "freedom" is defined. In our society we are primarily concerned with freedom "of": freedom of speech, freedom of assembly, freedom of the press, freedom of the individual to make a fortune. In their societies they are primarily concerned with freedom "from": freedom from want, freedom from hunger, freedom from unemployment, freedom from exploitation by people who want to make a fortune. Put another way, we interpret freedom as meaning "liberty"; they interpret it as meaning "equality."

Liberty and equality are uneasy bedfellows. In general, the more you have of one, the less you will have of the other. Your liberty to be richer than anyone else violates other people's right to be your equal; other people's right to be your equal violates your liberty to earn more than anyone else. The United States has chosen to emphasize personal liberty, an emphasis that can lead only to social inequality. Socialist societies have stressed equality, an emphasis that can lead only to infringements of personal liberty. Most Western European countries have chosen a middle way, that of "democratic socialism"; they attempt to balance the demands of liberty and equality more evenly. There is no way to *prove* that any one of these solutions is more desirable, moral, or "right" than any other. The question is a matter of philosophic preference.

Most people, of course, do not rationally consider the various alternatives. They simply accept the system they have been socialized to believe in. Extensive research on political socialization has shown that people take the legitimacy of their particular political system for granted very early in life, and usually adopt the political views of their parents. By the time they are in elementary school, children take an overwhelmingly favorable view of their country's system (Greenstein, 1965; Hyman, 1969; Jaros, 1974; Jennings and Niemi, 1974; Renshon, 1977).

The American Political Process

After several years of high school civics and history classes, you are already familiar with the formal elements of the American political system, such as the electoral process, the role of the presidency, and the way legislation is passed. In this chapter, therefore, we shall focus on the more informal but no less vital processes of party politics and interest-group lobbying. These processes are "unofficial"—that is, they are not included in any formal diagram of how the system "works." But they are very important.

Political Parties

Political parties are collectivities of people organized for the specific purpose of gaining legitimate control of government. Parties are a vital element in a democracy. They link the voter to government; they define policy alternatives; they transmit public opinion from the level of the citizen to the level of the leadership; they mobilize grass-roots political participation; and they recruit and offer candidates for public office.

Political parties in America are virtually unique among democracies. In other countries, parties are usually closely tied to either the working class or to the middle and upper classes (Lipset, 1959a). They have very specific programs, which are contained in policy documents issued before elections, and their differences over policy are usually clear-cut and significant. Every member of a party is expected to support every aspect of the party's program in public, and failure to do so can lead to expulsion from the party. Each party applies strict discipline over its legislators, requiring them to be present for voting and instructing them on how to vote. People may become candidates for a party nomination only if they are approved by the party organization. There are no primary elections, and candidates are selected behind closed doors by a small group of party activists. The electorate generally votes for the party, not the individual, because voters are oriented toward policies, not personalities. A politician who is expelled from a party for deviations from its official line has little chance of being reelected, because there is little or no advantage in being an incumbent.

American parties are different in several respects. Although there is a strong tendency for the lower and working classes to vote Democratic and the upper middle and upper classes to vote Republican, both parties have a wide base of support and rarely introduce class issues into their campaigns. Each party has a liberal and a conservative wing, and it is quite possible for voters to be faced with a choice between a liberal Republican and a conservative

Figure 19.9 American political parties are essentially loose coalitions, more interested in gaining control of government than in very specific programs. The parties meet at the national level only once every four years for the purpose of selecting a presidential candidate. In general, they choose a candidate who will appeal to the political center; in the few instances when a party has chosen a candidate whom the public perceives as very left- or right-wing, he has been heavily defeated.

Democrat. The parties try to avoid very specific or controversial policy proposals, and their platforms usually consist of vague generalities that are intended to appeal to the political center. There is no expectation that candidates will support every detail of the party platform and no means of disciplining them if they do not. Both parties have weak national organizations. In effect, they are federations of state and local parties that meet together only once every four years to select a presidential candidate. Any member of a party can seek its nomination for any local, state, or national office, and in states where there are primary elections an individual can win the nomination even in the face of opposition from party officials. Americans are willing to vote for the individual, not the party; so an incumbent who is well known therefore has a strong advantage in an election.

American parties are essentially loose coalitions, less concerned with ideology and coherent programs than with winning office. Both the Democratic and Republican parties accept the main structural features of American society, including its class system and capitalist economy, and both aim at winning the middle ground in politics. If either party nominates a candidate for national office who veers too far to the left or the right, it invites a landslide defeat, such as those that befell Barry Goldwater in 1964 and George McGovern in 1972.

Interest Groups

The party systems of other democracies ensure great predictability of legislative voting because most legislators toe the party line and are not so subject to external influence. In contrast, the loose nature of American parties and their lack of internal discipline require that a new coalition of congressional votes be assembled on each new issue. This feature encourages activities by interest groups to affect the outcome of various votes. An *interest group* is an organization or group of people that attempts to influence political decisions that might affect its members. These groups may be small or large, temporary or permanent, secretive or open, but they all try to gain access to and sway those who have power. In general, the larger and better funded the group is, the more influence it has.

Interest groups use a variety of tactics. They may collect petitions, take court action, bribe officials, advertise in the media, donate money to election campaigns, pledge the votes of their members to certain candidates, organize a flood of letters to legislators on particular issues, or seek direct contact with members of Congress and the executive branch of government. The tactic of directly persuading decision makers is called *lobbying*. Many large interest groups—including over 500 corporations—maintain highly paid, full-time professional lobbyists in Washington. There are believed to be about 15,000 of these lobbyists—the Ford Motor Company alone has a full-time Washington lobby of 40 people—and they meet regularly with legislators and government officials.

Well-organized and well-funded interest groups are often very successful in their efforts, most of which take place without any public knowledge. The extremely complicated tax laws of the United States contain a great many provisions and exemptions designed to benefit special interests, and these are almost always the result of behind-the-scenes lobbying. Interest groups also apply pressure on the making of both domestic and foreign policy. For example, the American Medical Association (AMA), which represents many of the country's physicians, has prevented the introduction of a national health-insurance program through a series of vigorous efforts, including campaign contributions to opponents of legislators who favored the program. And as mentioned in Chapter 18 ("The Economic Order"), the International Telephone and Telegraph Corporation (ITT) persuaded the Nixon administration to try to bring about a coup in Chile, where ITT feared for the safety of its investments (Sampson, 1973).

The principal resource of these powerful interest groups is money. Political campaigns can be very costly: in the 1978 Senate elections, for example, the candidates of the two major parties spent an average of over $900,000 each. Candidates who outspent their opponents won 28 of 33 contested seats; these victors laid out an average of $1.2 million to gain election. The bulk of this money came from Political Action Committees (PACs)—organizations established by interest groups for the purpose of raising and distributing campaign funds. In the 1978 election, 1500 PACs funneled some $54 million into House and Senate campaigns. A notable contributor was the oil industry, long recognized as one of the most influential lobbies in the country: it gave $1.3 million to 34 senators—an average of over $40,000 each—and, in addition, contributed $1.1 million to candidates for the House. In the same year, the AMA contributed more than $1.6 million to members of Congress. Between 1976 and 1978, 50 members of the House received over $12,000 each from the AMA; of these, 48 voted against a proposal, strongly opposed by the AMA, to hold down hospital costs. In 1980, two-thirds of the members of both House and Senate had received campaign funds from this organization. Another highly effective interest group is the National Rifle Association (NRA), whose lobbying efforts have killed fourteen different gun-control bills since the late sixties, despite opinion polls that consistently show a large majority of the people in favor of such legislation. In 1978 the NRA gave over half a million dollars to 21 senators and 142 members of Congress. (In addition to PAC donations, there may also be further, illegal contributions: the Watergate-related scandals revealed over 500 U.S. corporations making bribes of one kind or another to public officials in the United States and abroad.) It can be safely assumed that the various interest groups expect and obtain some payoff in return for their generosity; one does not shower members of Congress with money, year after year, for no reason (Green and Newfield, 1980; Jacobson, 1980).

Political sociologists are divided over whether the activities of interest groups are beneficial or harmful to democracy. On the one hand, these groups, frequently operating in secrecy, are often able to win favors that might not be in the public interest. The ordinary voter's influence is thus reduced. What chance, for example, do unorganized individuals have of bringing about change in the nation's tax structure when they are competing with the efforts of wealthy and highly organized groups to keep it the way it is? On the other hand, the existence of a number of interest groups, many of them with conflicting goals, may prevent the development of a monopoly of power and influence. Furthermore, the interest group provides an effective means for otherwise powerless citizens to gain political influence. A mass of unorganized citizens concerned about civil rights or ecology, for example, has little means of exerting influence. If they form an interest group, they have a potentially far greater access to the decision-making process.

American political culture thus encourages an informal, behind-the-scenes interaction among parties, elected officials, and private interest groups. An understanding of this process gives a much fuller picture of our political life than an analysis of formal institutions and processes alone. But where does power really lie? Who makes the decisions?

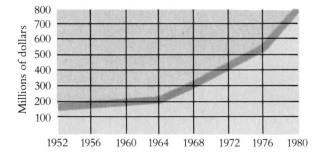

ELECTION CAMPAIGN EXPENDITURES,
1952–1980

Source: Citizen's Research Foundation, 1980.

Figure 19.10 The costs of running election campaigns have escalated dramatically in recent years, as this graph shows: in the 1980 elections, candidates for local, state, and national office spent over $800 million. Most of this money comes from contributions from PACs and other sources—a situation that can easily result in undue influence by private contributors on the way public representatives vote.

Who Rules?

In a democracy, power is theoretically vested in the people, who periodically delegate it to their representatives. The difficulty is, of course, that power may pass to the representatives themselves and to those individuals and interests who have privileged access to the decision-making process. The growth of mass political parties in the late nineteenth and early twentieth centuries appeared at first to promise an end to the ancient pattern of rule by a small elite. Yet disillusion set in early when it seemed that even in these new, theoretically democratic parties, power was concentrated in the hands of the leadership.

Three important social scientists of this period addressed the problem, and they all came to similar conclusions. Robert Michels (1911) argued that in any organization, concentration of power was essential to efficiency (see Chapter 7, "Social Groups"). Vilfredo Pareto (1935) pointed out that elites are present in all societies, communities, and organizations. Some people have greater skill, determination, ambition, intelligence, or manipulative ability than others, and they tend to dominate the group. Pareto saw no reason why political life should be any different. He believed it is important, however, that political systems be "open," permitting new rulers to replace old ones in a continual "circulation of elites." Gaetano Mosca (1939) insisted that every society contains a class that rules and a class that is ruled; the ruling class is always a minority. This situation, he argued, will always be found in any society.

Do these principles apply to the United States? Is there a "ruling class," and do the ordinary voters have much influence over the political decisions that affect their lives? Let's look first at two important theories on the subject, and then at some empirical evidence.

The Power-Elite Thesis

In his book *The Power Elite*, C. Wright Mills (1956) argues that the United States is dominated by a small, informal elite of powerful and influential individuals. This "power elite" is not a conspiracy; the members have usually not even sought the extraordinary power that they enjoy. Rather, they exercise this power because they happen to hold important positions in the three sets of great organi-

Figure 19.11

"Let's not split hairs, Senator. We both know that big government and private enterprise worship at the same church."

Drawing by Stan Hunt; © 1978
The New Yorker Magazine, Inc.

zations that, over the course of this century, have come to dominate American society: government bureaucracy, large corporations, and the military.

> The power elite is composed of men whose positions enable them to transcend the ordinary environments of ordinary men and women; they are in a position to make decisions having major consequences.... They are in command of the major hierarchies and organizations of modern society. They rule the big organizations. They run the machinery of state and claim its prerogatives. They direct the military establishment. They occupy the strategic command posts of the social structure, in which are centered the effective means of the power and the wealth and the celebrity which they enjoy.

Our advanced capitalist system, Mills argues, requires highly coordinated, long-range decision making among government, corporations, and the military, which is by far the biggest single spender and consumer in the United States. The leading officials of these organizations are therefore in constant contact with one another, and they often make informal decisions of great social and political importance. The power elite is composed of men of very similar social background. They are mostly born in America of American parents; they are from urban areas; they are predominantly Protestant; and a great number of them have attended Ivy League colleges. Except for the politicians, most of them are from the East. The members of the power elite know one another personally and share very similar attitudes, values, and interests. They sit together on corporation boards and government commissions, and thus form an "interlocking directorate" that coordinates activities and policies.

Mills argues that there are three distinct levels of power and influence in the United States. At the highest level is the power elite, which operates informally and invisibly and makes all the most important decisions in domestic and especially foreign policy. The middle level consists of the legislative branch of government, the various interest groups, and local opinion leaders. Decisions at this level, made mostly through lobbying and the legislative process, are usually of secondary importance. At the third and lowest level is the mass of powerless, unorganized citizens, who have little direct influence on decisions that may affect their lives and, in fact, are often unaware that the decisions are even being made.

The Pluralist Thesis

Some sociologists reject Mills's argument, mainly on the grounds that they do not believe power is as concentrated as Mills suggests. These sociologists offer a more pluralistic model of the American power structure. They stress the diversity rather than the similarity of the many organizations and groups that exercise power and influence.

TWO PORTRAITS OF THE AMERICAN POWER STRUCTURE

Power Structure	Mills—Power Elite	Riesman—Pluralism
Levels	Unified power elite. Diversified and balanced plurality of interest groups. Mass of unorganized people have no power over elite.	No dominant power elite. Diversified and balanced plurality of interest groups. Mass of unorganized people have some power over interest groups.
Operation	One group determines all major policies. Manipulation of people at the bottom by group at the top.	Who determines policy depends on the issue. Competition among organized groups.
Basis	Coincidence of interests among major institutions (economic, military, governmental).	Diversity of interests among major organized groups.
Consequences	Enhancement of interests of corporations, armed forces, and executive branch of government. Decline of true democracy.	No one group or class is favored significantly over others. Decline of effective leadership.

Source: Adapted from William Kornhauser, "Power Elite or Veto Groups?" in Seymour Martin Lipset and Leo Lowenthal (eds.), *Culture and Social Character* (New York: Free Press, 1961).

Figure 19.12 This table compares some features of the "power elite" and "pluralist" interpretations of the American power structure. Mills's model emphasizes the concentration of power in the hands of a few people who use it to further their own interests; Riesman's model implies that power is more diversified and that many more groups benefit as a result.

David Riesman (1961) acknowledges that power is unequally distributed in American society but denies that there is any coordinated power elite. The decision makers, he suggests, are not nearly as unified as Mills contends. The conflicting interests of the various groups at the upper levels of power ensure that no one group is able to maintain a monopoly of the decision-making process. Riesman argues that there are two levels of power in the United States. The upper level consists of what he calls *veto groups*, strong interest groups that try to protect themselves by blocking any of the other groups' proposals that might encroach on their own interests. Power is not highly centralized. Instead, shifting coalitions emerge depending on the issue at stake, and in the long run no one group is favored over the others. At the second level is the unorganized public, which Riesman believes is not so much dominated by the veto groups as sought by them as an ally in their campaigns. Those who seek power must therefore take account of public opinion if they are to be successful. In Riesman's view there is no coordinated elite that dominates society in its own interests.

Empirical Studies

Both of these analyses have won a good deal of support from sociologists. Their validity is difficult to evaluate, however, because they deal with a largely invisible and informal process that cannot easily be studied. But research in some areas can throw light on the problem. Important studies have been made on the backgrounds of the country's political, industrial, and military elite; of the extent of popular participation in the political process; of local community politics; and of the "military-industrial complex."

The "Governing Class"

In a systematic attempt to discover whether the United States has a "governing class" of the kind described by Mills, G. William Domhoff (1967, 1971) tried to find out who the members of the American upper class were. His criteria for membership in this class included being listed in the exclusive *Social Register,* having gone to a select private school, having millionaire status, and belonging to prestigious men's clubs in large cities.

Domhoff found that this uppermost social class consisted of not more than 0.5 percent of the population. The members were not only extremely wealthy. A disproportionate number of them held high-level positions in important social organizations. These included corporations, banks, insurance companies, the diplomatic service, the CIA, charitable foundations, the military, the mass media, the National Security Council, the Council on Foreign Relations, government departments, and the boards of trustees of universities and colleges. Moreover, these people were closely knit through intermarriage, attendance at the same schools and universities, membership in the same clubs, and service on boards of important governmental and economic organizations. Other studies of the nation's economic elite have generally confirmed this picture (Kolko, 1962; Lundberg, 1968; Mintz and Cohen, 1973; Blume et al., 1974; Allen, 1974; Dye, 1974; G. Moore, 1979; Useem, 1978, 1979; Domhoff, 1980).

This group clearly bears many similarities to the "power elite" described by Mills, and Domhoff concluded that it constitutes the governing class of the United States. The evidence seems convincing, but the case is not proved. The members of this elite may not necessarily work for their own advantage; there may be severe disagreements among them; and there may be many restraints on the power that they exercise. The fact that the elite exists seems beyond dispute, but how much power it has and how it uses it remains debatable.

Political Participation

To what extent are people at the other end of the power structure—the ordinary voters—actively involved in the political process? Research has shown that political participation is closely correlated with social class. The lower a person's social status, the less likely that person is to register as a voter, to vote, to belong to a political organization, or to attempt to influence the views of others (Verba and Nie, 1972; Alford and Friedland, 1975; Wolfinger and Rosenstone, 1980).

The turnout of voters in American elections is strikingly low compared with that in most other democracies. Only about 60 percent of the electorate vote in national elections, compared with about 85 percent in Great Britain and nearly 90 percent in such countries as Denmark, Italy, and

West Germany. Furthermore, about a quarter of Americans who are eligible to vote do not bother to register. Moreover, the percentage of registered voters who actually take the trouble to vote is steadily declining, even for widely publicized and hotly contested presidential elections. The trend over the past two decades is a clear and ominous one: 62.8 percent of registered voters cast a ballot in 1960; 61.9 percent in 1964; 60.9 percent in 1968; 55.5 percent in 1972; 54.4 percent in 1976; and 52.3 percent in 1980. Since so many voting-age Americans either did not register or did not vote, Ronald Reagan's "landslide" victory in 1980 was based on the support of less than a third of the potential electorate. Voter turnout in years when there is no presidential contest is even lower, and has been declining steadily since 1962. In the off-year elections of 1978, only 34 percent of eligible voters went to the polls. The remainder—nearly 100 million Americans aged eighteen or over—stayed home.

The fact that the young and people of lower social status are less likely to vote is open to varying interpretations. It is possible, for example, that they are quite happy with the

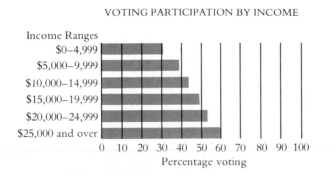

VOTING PARTICIPATION BY INCOME

Income Ranges

$0–4,999

$5,000–9,999

$10,000–14,999

$15,000–19,999

$20,000–24,999

$25,000 and over

0   10 20 30 40 50 60 70 80 90 100

Percentage voting

Source: U.S. Bureau of the Census.

Figure 19.13   The likelihood of voting correlates strongly with the income of the voter. This fact seems to indicate a pervasive apathy among poorer voters toward the political system.

system, have no fear that either party will alter it much, and therefore see no real need to vote. It is more plausible, however, that, perceiving no relationship between voting and political influence, they do not bother to vote. Surveys of nonvoters lend support to this view; a high proportion cite feelings of political alienation as the reason for their apathy (Ladd, 1978; Hadley, 1978).

Community Politics

The relatively small scale of towns and cities makes it comparatively easy to analyze their political processes. A number of studies have done this, sometimes in the hope that patterns of power and influence in communities will provide insights into those of the wider society.

The general finding of these studies has been that power is exercised by small elites, although the nature of the elites varies from one community to another. In the late nineteenth and early twentieth centuries, for example, large cities such as New York, Philadelphia, Boston, and San Francisco were ruled by the party "machine," the local organization of the dominant party. These machines, headed by a party "boss," effectively traded votes for jobs and other benefits. The base of the machine's power was the lower class, in most cases containing large numbers of new immigrants. Except in Chicago, where the Democratic party machine of the "boss," the late mayor Richard Daley, persisted into the seventies, this system is largely a thing of the past.

Studies made over the past few decades have reported different patterns. In his study of Atlanta, Georgia, Floyd Hunter (1953) found that most decisions were made by an economic elite consisting mainly of corporation executives and bankers. These men communicated informally, shared a similar point of view on major community issues, and determined local policies. Ordinary members of the community were not aware that this elite existed, and they regarded their elected public officials as their real leaders. Hunter found, however, that the elected leaders were not the actual decision makers; they carried out decisions made by others who had the ability to influence them. In a study of New Haven, Connecticut, Robert Dahl (1961) found the community power structure was much less centralized than in Atlanta, with a far wider participation in decision making. The upper class, Dahl found, had withdrawn from the community political arena by moving to the suburbs. The lower class was also excluded from decision making, since it had no effective means of asserting influence. The actual power structure was a shifting coalition of public officials and private individuals, with different people participating in decisions on different issues. Men and women from the middle and upper middle class appeared to have the greatest influence but took part only in decisions affecting their own particular interests. Other community studies reveal no consistent pattern other than that decisions are made by small elites in every case (Walton, 1966). Who these elites are, how much influence they have, and to what extent they are unified are questions that seem to depend on the characteristics of the community itself.

The Military-Industrial Complex

The term *military-industrial complex* was first used by President Dwight Eisenhower in his farewell address to the American people. Eisenhower warned that

> the conjunction of an immense military establishment and a large arms industry is new to the American experience. The total influence . . . economic, political, even spiritual . . . is felt in every statehouse, every office of the Federal government. . . . We must not fail to recognize its grave implications. Our toil, resources, and livelihood are all involved; so is the very structure of our society. In the councils of government we must guard against the unwarranted influence, whether sought or unsought, by the military-industrial complex. The potential for a disastrous rise of misplaced power exists and will persist. [Quoted in Melman, 1970]

The military-industrial complex is an informal system of mutual influence between the Pentagon, which buys armaments, and major U.S. corporations, which sell them. The Pentagon relies heavily on the small number of giant corporations that have the technological expertise to supply sophisticated weaponry. The corporations, in turn, are dependent on the Pentagon, because manufacturing goods for the military is much more profitable than competitive commercial production. Less than 10 percent of Pentagon contracts are open for competitive bidding, and the Pentagon allows corporations to make very large profits and to incur vast "cost overruns" on the original estimated prices of products. The F-111 aircraft, for example, was originally ordered at a price of $2.4 million each; the plane finally saw

service at a price in excess of $13 million apiece. The CH-53A helicopter, planned to cost under $2 million, as of 1980 cost over $10 million. A rescue submarine ordered at a price of $3 million eventually sold at $125 million. In recent years, in fact, the price of thirty-eight of our major weapons systems jumped by an average of nearly 50 percent between the time they were ordered and the time they were delivered. Contracts that do not involve competitive bidding and permit huge cost overruns naturally appeal to corporations, and they have flocked to gain a piece of the action: the Pentagon signs agreements with over 20,000 prime contractors and more than 100,000 smaller contractors. About two dozen major corporations, however, hold more than 50 percent of the prime contracts.

Inefficiency in the manufacture of American military equipment is now legendary. The B-70 aircraft, developed at a cost of over $1.5 billion, was such a disaster that only two of the planes were ever built. One promptly crashed and the other is now in a museum. The Sheridan tank, which cost $1 billion to develop, is a lumbering monster that will never see a battle. A new atomic submarine launched in California immediately sank to the bottom of the ocean; the salvage costs alone were estimated at $35 million. The nuclear ANP aircraft was abandoned after more than $511 million had been invested to develop it. The Seamaster aircraft was scrapped after an investment of $330 million; the Navaho missile, after an investment of nearly $680 million; and the Dyna-soar missile, after an investment of $405 million (Sherrill, 1970; Melman, 1970). The F-111 aircraft proved virtually unflyable and unfit for military combat: the planes in the first contingent sent to Vietnam either crashed or were readily shot down, sometimes by rifle fire. The Pentagon canceled its original contract for the F-111 but paid the manufacturer, General Dynamics, compensation of $215.5 million. (The Pentagon now intends to modify the plane at a cost of $6 billion.) Why does the Pentagon tolerate these inefficiencies? Because it is a captive customer of the major corporations. If they should collapse into bankruptcy through loss of Pentagon contracts and overrun handouts, the Pentagon would be left without a weapons supply. In any event, the sums involved are a drop in the bucket to the Pentagon, which since World War II has spent well over $1 trillion— that is, 1,000,000 times $1,000,000—on defense.

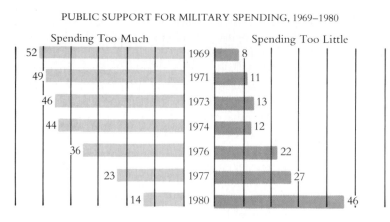

PUBLIC SUPPORT FOR MILITARY SPENDING, 1969–1980

Spending Too Much		Spending Too Little
52	1969	8
49	1971	11
46	1973	13
44	1974	12
36	1976	22
23	1977	27
14	1980	46

Source: Gallup Poll; The New York Times–CBS News Poll, June 16, 1980.

Figure 19.14 Public opinion has swung in favor of increased military expenditure in recent years, largely because of suspicion about the motives of the Soviet Union. Soviet military expenditures have increased steadily for several years, and the United States seemed powerless to prevent Soviet intervention in Afghanistan and pressure on Poland in 1980. It is likely that the two superpowers will become involved in a renewed arms race during the 1980s.

The Pentagon has immense importance in the U.S. economy. It is the largest single formal organization in world history. It is housed in the world's largest office building. It is the world's largest home builder. It finances half of all federal government research. It owns more property than any one single organization in the world, controls an area of land equal to the size of New York State, and has assets worth over $200 billion. One in every nine jobs in the United States is dependent on the military establishment, and over a third of federal civilian employees work for the Pentagon. Defense money flows into more than three-fourths of the nation's congressional districts, and some 350 American communities have at least one defense plant or factory. The Pentagon spends over $190 million a year on propaganda, and without any authorization from Congress has kept confidential files on one out of every eight Americans (Melman, 1970; McDonald, 1970; Kaufman, 1970; Sherrill, 1970; Anderson and Gibson, 1978).

Because large corporations such as Lockheed and General Dynamics derive most of their income from defense contracts, they constantly lobby the Pentagon and Congress to spend ever larger sums on defense. Most of the corporations have permanent lobbyists in Washington, and many try to maintain their links with the Pentagon by hiring ex-military officers: it is estimated that at least 5000 ex-

officers are in the defense industry (M. Edwards, 1975). Many of these men presumably retained influence with their former colleagues. Military officials who are responsible for negotiating contracts and who may hope for a corporate appointment when they retire are also, to say the least, put in a compromising situation. The Pentagon itself employs the largest professional lobby in Washington—one lobbyist for every two members of Congress. These lobbyists urge Congress to increase defense expenditures and to take care of the interests of prime contractors. When Lockheed found itself on the brink of bankruptcy in 1971, for example, Congress bailed the company out with a loan of $250 million—an act more typical of a socialist society than one priding itself on free enterprise. The Pentagon worked furiously to win the loan for Lockheed, a company that employed 210 ex-military officers at the time. It is also worth noting that more than half of the company directors of the major defense contractors are members of the tight-knit "governing class" identified by Domhoff.

Mills argued that "military capitalism" is at the heart of the power elite, a view that seems highly plausible. In 1980 the Pentagon's budget was $122 billion; by 1985 it is expected to exceed $178 billion. The Pentagon plans such costly new projects as the cruise missile ($9 billion), the F/A-18 warplane ($25 billion), the Trident submarine ($28 billion), and the MX missile system (at $33 billion, the most expensive construction project in history). The soaring level of defense expenditure, at a time when the United States has long had the capacity to destroy life on the planet several times over, is partly, of course, a response to the perceived threat of Soviet military and political ambitions. But the size of the defense budget can be fully explained only in terms of continuing corporate pressure for profits from weapons production. As Ernest Fitzgerald (1973) sourly comments, "the Pentagon and its supporting cast of contractors unite to pick the public pocket."

What, then, is the nature of the American power structure: a "power elite" or a series of competing "veto groups"? We still lack the detailed information we need to give a definitive answer to this question, but on the basis of the available evidence it seems that both views are too simplistic. It is likely that decision making in foreign policy is controlled by a very small elite but that domestic issues are determined by shifting coalitions of elites. There are probably a number of power elites in American society that are united on some issues but in disagreement on others (Kornhauser, 1966; Rose, 1967). What does seem clear, however, is that most important political decisions are made behind the scenes by a very small and privileged part of the population. This elite consists primarily, though not exclusively, of officials in the executive branch of the federal government and at the head of the great industrial and financial corporations.

Revolutions

Most political change is *evolutionary*: it grows out of existing conditions. Under some circumstances, however, *revolutionary* change takes place, involving the overthrow of existing institutions and the radical reconstruction of the social and political order.

The philosophic justification for revolution in modern times can be traced back to yet another of the "social contract" theorists, John Locke (1632–1704). Like Hobbes and Rousseau, Locke argued that political authority had been created by a social contract made in the original "state of nature." But Locke held that people in the "state of nature" were free and that they had created government for the sole purpose of guaranteeing their freedom. If a government violated this trust, the contract was broken, and the people had the right to rebel in order to restore their freedom. The leaders of the American Revolution were deeply influenced by Locke's writings, and the Declaration of Independence echoes his theory in its specific justification of a people's right to revolt:

> We hold these truths to be self-evident, that all men are created equal, that they are endowed by their Creator with certain inalienable rights, that among these are life, liberty, and the pursuit of happiness. That to secure these rights, governments are instituted among men, deriving their just powers from the consent of the governed.... That whenever any form of government becomes destructive of these ends it is the right of the people to alter or abolish it and to institute new government, laying its foundations on such principles and organizing its powers in such form as to them shall seem most likely to effect their safety and happiness.

Unlike a *coup d'etat*, which involves a restricted use of force to replace one set of leaders with another (usually consisting of military officers), a revolution generally involves mass violence. Sociologists have long been interested in the conditions that give rise to such a situation, and several factors have been identified (Brinton, 1960; B. Moore, 1966, 1979; Gurr, 1970; Davies, 1962, 1971; Skocpol, 1979). If all the following conditions are present, a revolution is a distinct possibility, although not a certainty. Each situation has its own unique characteristics that may affect the chances for revolution.

1. Alternative channels to change must be blocked, and significant groups in society must feel that they have no access to power. Revolutions are more likely if the rulers refuse to accept change or keep the pace of change too slow, while suppressing efforts by other groups to bring about change.

2. There must be a widespread awareness that valued resources, such as wealth and power, are unfairly distributed. Unless a large part of the population feels a continuing sense of grievance, a revolution is unlikely.

3. People must be aware that there are alternatives to the existing system and must feel that they are entitled to benefits that have been denied them in the past. To be poor or oppressed is not in itself sufficient grounds for revolution.

REVOLUTION

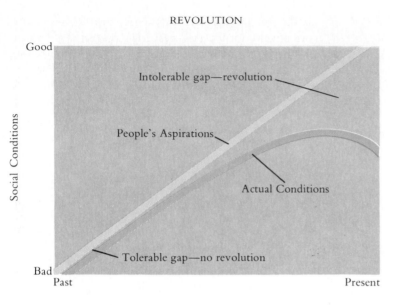

Figure 19.15 Social unrest is likely when people's aspirations run ahead of improvements in their actual conditions. Oppressive conditions in themselves will not cause a revolution unless people have come to expect better conditions.

Source: Adapted from James C. Davies, "Toward a Theory of Revolution," *American Sociological Review*, 27 (1962), p.7.

If it were, most of the world would be in revolt at this moment, since well over half the global population is impoverished and is denied democratic rights. Revolutions occur only in the context of *rising expectations*: people who have accepted the situation in the past must sense that it is their right to have something better in the future. Paradoxically, revolutions are sometimes sparked by minor concessions from the rulers, for these improvements encourage the oppressed people to believe that things might improve still further in the future. If their rising aspirations are not met, they may revolt.

4. Existing political institutions must usually be weak or even on the verge of breakdown. The ruling elite in prerevolutionary situations is often divided. The system is failing to "work," and the legitimacy of the form of government is being eroded, so that the system is maintained by coercion. In many revolutionary situations the government is so weak that prolonged or widespread bloodshed is not needed to bring it down: it frequently collapses at the first push.

5. A breakdown of the state's military apparatus must occur, with the result that the armed forces cannot or will not repress the uprising; frequently, in fact, members of the military change sides and join the rebels. The military is often in a demoralized condition before the revolution breaks out—perhaps because it has been defeated in war, or perhaps because it senses public resentment at its role in maintaining the despised rulers in office. If the military falters, the regime may fall.

Revolutions are almost always led not by members of the oppressed class but rather by well-educated members of the middle class. A revolution does not need the support of the majority of the people; it is sufficient if those who support the government are in a minority and most other people are apathetic. Revolutions are usually followed by periods of great uncertainty as the new regime attempts to establish its own legitimacy. There are often power struggles within the revolutionary movement once the revolution has taken place. The indiscriminate guillotining that

Figure 19.16 *Revolutions are frequently followed by the execution of members of the ruling class. This practice is largely motivated, of course, by hatred and revenge, but the revolutionaries have an additional reason for their action. By eliminating leading members of the old ruling class, the new rulers destroy any further claims that the previous regime might have to legitimacy, and thus make it easier to establish their own authority. When the communists took control of Russia after the 1917 revolution, for example, they murdered the entire royal family in a brutal but calculated act that removed any possibility of a return to the czarist system. These illustrations show the post-revolutionary executions of Louis XIV of France, the Emperor Maximillian of Mexico, and Iranian opponents of the country's revolutionary rulers.*

followed the French Revolution is a particularly gory example of this trend, but it conforms to a widespread pattern. The final victors are usually the most disciplined and even ruthless of the revolutionaries, which is one reason why communists are often able to benefit from revolutions fought largely by liberals and noncommunist radicals.

Revolutions tend to be followed by the creation of non-democratic and even totalitarian political institutions, largely because the new regime has not achieved full legitimacy and fears challenges to its authority, but these controls are likely to be gradually lessened once the political order becomes stable.

Summary

1. The political order is the institutionalized system through which some people acquire and exercise power over others. The highest level of power is that of the state, the institution that claims a monopoly on the legitimate use of force within a given territory.

2. Power is the ability to compel obedience, even in the absence of consent by those who obey. Power may be regarded as legitimate (authority) or illegitimate (coercion). There are three basic types of authority: traditional, legal-rational, and charismatic.

3. The emergence of the state is linked to the level of evolution of a society; it appears first in agricultural societies and becomes a dominant institution in industrial societies. The functionalist perspective emphasizes the functions of the state in maintaining social order: enforcing norms; arbitrating conflict; planning and giving direction; and regulating relationships with other societies. The conflict perspective emphasizes the role of the state in maintaining the status quo and thus protecting the interests of the dominant class. These approaches are not necessarily incompatible.

4. Democracy is rare and exists only as representative democracy. The prerequisites for democracy are advanced economic development; restraints on government power; absence of major cleavages; tolerance of dissent; free access to information; and diffusion of power. Liberty and equality are to some extent incompatible: capitalist societies emphasize liberty; socialist societies, equality.

5. The American political process involves an important interaction between interest groups and parties. American parties are loose coalitions, and legislative votes are often unpredictable. Powerful interest groups may therefore lobby successfully for their own advantage.

6. Mills argued that the United States is ruled by a power elite. Riesman argued that important decisions are made through the interplay of veto groups. Studies of the governing class, of political participation, of community politics, and of the military-industrial complex all indicate that important decisions are made by powerful interests.

7. Revolutions may occur under certain conditions: when avenues to change are blocked; when there is a widespread sense of grievance; when expectations are rising but not being met; and when the legitimacy of existing institutions is crumbling.

Important Terms

political order (479)
state (479)
power (479)
legitimate power (480)
authority (480)
illegitimate power (480)
coercion (480)
traditional authority (480)
legal-rational authority (481)
charismatic authority (482)
ideal type (483)
class conflict (487)
democracy (488)
representative democracy (488)
oligarchy (489)
totalitarian (489)
political party (492)
interest group (493)
lobbying (493)
power elite (495)
veto groups (497)
military-industrial complex (499)
revolution (501)
coup d'etat (501)
rising expectations (502)

Suggested Readings

DAHL, ROBERT. *Who Governs?* New Haven, Conn.: Yale University Press, 1961.

A classic study of community politics. Dahl traces the patterns of political influence in New Haven, Connecticut, showing how different interest groups dominate the decision-making process on different issues.

DOMHOFF, G. WILLIAM. *Who Rules America?* Englewood Cliffs, N.J.: Prentice-Hall, 1967.

An important study of the American "governing class," the close-knit group who, Domhoff contends, are able to translate their economic resources into immense political influence in the United States.

EPSTEIN, LEON B. *Political Parties in Western Democracies.* 2nd ed. New Brunswick, N.J.: Transaction Books, 1979.

An excellent comparative study of political parties, focusing mainly on those of the United States and Great Britain.

GASTIL, RAYMOND D. *Freedom in the World: Political Rights and Civil Liberties.* New Brunswick, N.J.: Transaction Books, 1980.

A useful, country-by-country survey of freedom and civil liberties around the world.

MELMAN, SEYMOUR. *Pentagon Capitalism.* New York: McGraw-Hill, 1970.

A fascinating study of the Pentagon, its use of public money, and its relationships with the major corporate weapons suppliers.

MILLS, C. WRIGHT. *The Power Elite*. New York: Oxford University Press, 1956.

This is the book that first raised the issue of "who rules" in the United States. Mills argues forcefully that American political life is dominated by a "power elite" drawn from the executive branch of government, the military, and major corporations.

MOORE, BARRINGTON. *Social Origins of Dictatorship and Democracy*. Boston: Beacon Press, 1966.

An important and interesting analysis of the way societies achieve either democratic or dictatorial governments.

ORUM, ANTHONY M. *Introduction to Political Sociology*. Englewood Cliffs, N.J.: Prentice-Hall, 1978.

An excellent overview of theory and research in political sociology. The book is recommended for a general introduction to the field.

SAMPSON, ANTHONY. *The Sovereign State of ITT*. Greenwich, Conn.: Fawcett Books, 1973.

A highly readable account of the political activities and influence of one of America's largest corporations, the International Telephone and Telegraph Corporation. Sampson details the various domestic and international intrigues of the organization.

UNIT 5 *Social Change in the Modern World*

Everything changes, and human societies are no exception. Yet throughout the greater part of the history of our species, social change has been relatively slow. Most people lived much the same lives as their parents and grandparents before them, and they expected that their children and grandchildren would lead similar lives as well. Today this is no longer true. The modern industrial world is in a state of constant and rapid social change, and we take it for granted that social and technological innovations will continue to transform our lives in the years that lie ahead.

The chapters in this unit deal with some of the issues involved in this process of change. The first chapter confronts some of the most pressing problems of the modern world—health, rapid population growth, and environmental destruction—and shows how the dynamic interplay among them may threaten the human future. The second chapter deals with urbanization and the nature of urban life, a crucial topic in a world that has become heavily urbanized only in the course of the present century. The third chapter in the unit discusses collective behavior and social movements—those concerted acts of large numbers of people that often provoke social change. The final chapter takes up the more general problem of explaining and directing social change, a problem that sociologists have grappled with since the founding of the discipline.

CHAPTER 20   *Population and Health*

Every night the sun sets on an additional 250,000 human beings. Some 50,000 years ago the human population was so small that there was an average of 200 square miles of the earth's surface for each individual. If population growth were to continue at its present rate, there would be 100 people for every square yard of the earth's surface within 900 years. Obviously, such an absurd situation could never occur: one way or another, population growth will stop long before that point is reached.

The human population already stands at over 4.5 billion, and at current growth rates that number will double within forty-one years. Yet about a quarter of the existing inhabitants of the earth are undernourished or malnourished, and they are dying from the effects of starvation at the rate of more than 10 million every year. There can be little question that unchecked population growth is the most critical social problem in the modern world, with potential consequences in terms of sheer human misery that are almost unimaginable.

In the modern, industrialized world, we often feel insulated from nature and confident that our technology can give us mastery over the natural environment. We forget all too easily that human beings are animals, ultimately as dependent on the environment for their health and survival as any other species. No natural environment can withstand an infinite increase in the animal or plant populations that it supports. It is doubtful if the planet can continue to provide the food and other raw materials that huge human populations require, or if the health of these populations can tolerate the pollution caused by ever-expanding industrial production.

Population growth, health, and environmental problems are thus closely linked. For analytic purposes we shall look first at the dynamics of population growth, then at health, and finally at the human relationship to the environment, but throughout our discussion we shall bear in mind the close connection among all three.

The Study of Population

No human population is ever completely stable. Some populations grow and others decline. The size of some populations changes rapidly, while that of others changes much more slowly. Some populations have a high proportion of young people, others, of old people. Most populations contain more females than males, particularly in the oldest generation, but the exact ratio of the sexes varies over time and from place to place. These and other population characteristics are the result of processes that can be scientifically analyzed.

The Science of Demography

Demography is the study of the size, composition, distribution, and changes in human populations. In the United States this science is usually regarded as a subdiscipline of sociology, for the reason that population dynamics are strongly affected by social factors. If a society places restrictions on abortion or the use of contraceptives, the number of births will tend to increase. If a society places taboos on premarital intercourse or on marital intercourse for some time after childbirth, the number of births will tend to decline. Social values that encourage large families exert pressure for population increase. Values that encourage women to pursue independent careers tend to depress population growth, as does a social belief that too many children are an economic burden. Standards of public health and the availability of medical services obviously affect the length of the average life in any given society.

Demography thus consists of more than simply extending lines on graphs. The science must take full account of all factors, social, cultural, and environmental, that may affect population trends. Since these factors cannot always be accurately forecast, demographic projections into the distant future are necessarily inexact. Nor is unpredictability the only problem that demographers have to face. Many of the statistics that they have to work with are merely estimates, which in many cases are unreliable. A number of developing nations do not have an efficient and regular population census, and demographic statistics from many of these countries are based to some extent on guesswork. The United States has an elaborate population census every ten years, but the Bureau of the Census believes that about 5 million people—vagrants, illegal immigrants, illiterates, and others—were omitted from its 1970 census, and at least 7 million from the 1980 census. In fact, the 1980 census provoked a series of lawsuits from a number of city governments, all charging an undercount of their residents.

Despite these limitations, however, demographers can use current data to give reasonably accurate projections for the relatively short term—say, the next quarter-century or so. They can also offer long-range projections, but these will hold good only under specified hypothetical conditions.

The Dynamics of Demographic Change

Population growth or decline in a given society is affected by three factors: the birth rate, the death rate, and the rate of migration into or out of the society.

Birth Rate

The crude *birth rate* in a given population is usually expressed as the number of births per year per thousand members of the population. In Bangladesh, for example, the birth rate is high, 40 per thousand; in the United States it is low, 15.8 per thousand. This statistical measure is called the "crude" rate because it does not give us specific information about the births. It does not tell us, for example, about the birth ratio of male to female, black to white, middle class to lower class, or any other categories. For each such category a separate statistical measure, the specific birth rate, can be constructed.

The birth rate tells us about the *fertility* of the women in a given society: in other words, it tells us how many children the average woman is bearing. Fertility must be distinguished from *fecundity,* or the potential number of children that could be born to a woman of childbearing age. The fecundity of a physically normal woman during this period is about twenty to twenty-five children. In

Figure 20.1 The fertility of women (the actual number of children they bear) rarely approaches their fecundity (the number they are theoretically capable of bearing). Although some women, like the mother of this late-nineteenth-century Wisconsin family, may approach the fecundity level of twenty to twenty-five children, in practice very few women do so.

practice the actual fertility of women in any society does not even approach this level of fecundity, because cultural, social, economic, and health factors prevent such prolific breeding.

Death Rate

The crude *death rate* in a given population is usually expressed as the number of deaths per year per thousand members of the population. In Bangladesh the death rate is high, 20 per thousand, while in the United States it is comparatively low, 8.7 per thousand. Again, it is possible to construct specific death rates for particular categories in the population. The infant death rate for American racial minorities, for example, is 21.1 per thousand, while that for whites is 12.0 per thousand.

The death rate in any society is related to the average *life expectancy* of its members at birth, that is, the number of years that the average newborn can be expected to live. In the United States, life expectancy has increased from about forty years at the turn of the century to nearly seventy-four years today, largely as a result of a decline in the infant mortality rate. Life expectancy must be distinguished from *life span*, the maximum length of life possible in a particular species. Although human life expectancy in most societies has increased markedly during this century, the life span has increased little, if at all, and very few people live be-

yond a hundred. We have been unable to extend the life span because we have been unable to combat the diseases of old age—cancer and degenerative conditions of the heart, lungs, kidneys, and other organs—as easily as the infectious diseases of childhood.

Migration Rate

The crude *migration rate* in a given population is usually expressed as the number of immigrants (people entering the population) or emigrants (people leaving the population) per year per thousand members of the population. Again, specific rates can be constructed for particular categories of immigrants and emigrants.

Migration rates obviously do not affect the increase or decrease in global population, but they may be an important factor in specific societies. The United States is a case in point: in recent years, immigration has accounted for more than half of the society's annual growth rate. Immigration to North America in the late nineteenth and early twentieth centuries was part of the most massive migration in history, in which some 75 million Europeans left their continent and settled in North and South America, parts of Africa, and Australasia. Migration is the product of two interacting factors. The first is *push,* which refers to the conditions that encourage people to emigrate (such as the potato famine in Ireland). The second factor is *pull,* which refers to the conditions that encourage them to immigrate to a particular place (such as the promise of a new and better life in the United States).

Growth Rate

Changes in population size are measured by the *growth rate,* which represents the number of births minus the number of deaths and is usually expressed as an annual percentage. (In most countries, migration is now a negligible factor in population growth, and for this reason migration statistics are often omitted from growth-rate calculations.) The average world growth rate at the moment is about 1.7 percent. The United States now has a relatively low growth rate of 0.7 percent, and a few areas in Europe, such as both East and West Germany, actually have negative growth rates, meaning that their populations are shrinking. The industrialized countries of the world generally have low growth rates of less than 1 percent, but the developing nations typically have rates well above 2 percent. Some, such as Kenya and Nicaragua, have rates above 3 percent.

Expressed in percentage terms, these differences seem small. But their long-term impact is staggering. The reason is that population growth is *exponential:* the increase each year is based not on the original figure but on the total for the preceding year. A population of 10,000 with a growth rate of 3 percent will thus increase in ten years not by 30 percent, to 13,000, but by about 34 percent, to 13,439. A very useful concept in analyzing the effects of exponential growth is *doubling time,* the period it takes for a population to double its numbers. A population growing at 1 percent will double itself in 70 years; a population growing at 2 percent will double itself in 35 years; and a population growing at 3 percent will double itself in 23 years. Thus the population of Great Britain, currently growing at around 0.1 percent each year, would take about 1155 years to double if present rates were maintained, but the population of Mexico, growing at 3.1 percent each year, would double within 22 years.

The history of world population growth gives some idea of the dizzying speed of exponential growth. In 8000 B.C. the total human population was probably about 5 million people. By A.D. 1 it had risen to about 250 million. A thousand years later it had increased to around 300 million, and by 1650 to half a billion. By the end of the next two

WORLD POPULATION GROWTH IN HISTORY

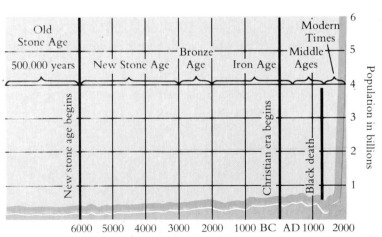

Figure 20.2 This graph gives some idea of the implications of exponential population growth. Clearly, growth at this rate will have to come to a drastic halt, either through a decline in the birth rate, an increase in the death rate, or both.

Source: Population Reference Bureau, "How Many People Have Ever Lived on Earth?" *The Population Bulletin*, 18 (February 1962), p. 5

The Dangers of Exponential Growth

Common as it is, exponential growth can yield surprising results—results that have fascinated mankind for centuries. There is an old Persian legend about a clever courtier who presented a beautiful chessboard to his king and requested that the king give him in return 1 grain of rice for the first square on the board, 2 grains for the second square, 4 grains for the third, and so forth. The king readily agreed and ordered rice to be brought from his stores. The fourth square of the chessboard required 8 grains, the tenth square 512 grains, the fifteenth required 16,384, and the twenty-first square gave the courtier more than a million grains of rice. By the fortieth square a million million rice grains had to be brought from the storerooms. The king's entire rice supply was exhausted long before he reached the sixty-fourth square. Exponential increase is deceptive because it generates immense numbers very quickly.

A French riddle for children illustrates another aspect of exponential growth—the apparent suddenness with which it approaches a fixed limit. Suppose you own a pond on which a water lily is growing. The lily plant doubles in size each day. If the lily were allowed to grow unchecked, it would completely cover the pond in thirty days, choking off the other forms of life in the water. For a long time the lily plant seems small, and so you decide not to worry about cutting it back until it covers half the pond. On what day will that be? On the twenty-ninth day, of course. You have one day to save your pond.

Source: Donnella H. Meadows et al., *The Limits to Growth* (A Potomac Associates book published by Universe Books, N.Y., 1972).

centuries, it had doubled to a billion; eighty years later, in 1930, it had doubled again, to 2 billion. The most recent doubling to 4 billion was completed in fifty years, by 1980, and the next doubling, if the present growth rate continues, will take forty-one years. About one out of every twenty persons who have ever inhabited this planet is alive today, and by the year 2000 the world will contain well over twice as many people as when most readers of this book were born.

Obviously, population cannot continue to increase at this rate. The process can be halted only by a sharp decrease in the birth rate, by a sharp increase in the death rate, or by some combination of the two. If each set of parents reproduced only enough children to replace themselves (about 2.1 children per family, to allow for those who died young or for other reasons did not reproduce themselves), we would ultimately have *zero population growth* (ZPG), a situation in which population size would remain stable.

Age Structure

A stable world population is a long way off, however. Even if every set of parents in the world had only 2.1 children from this moment on, world population would continue to increase for many years. The reason is that the children who have already been born would still have to grow up and reproduce themselves. The *age structure* of a population—the relative proportions of different age categories it contains—is therefore an important element in predicting demographic trends.

In most developed societies roughly one-fourth of the population are under the age of fifteen. In Sweden, for example, the figure is 21 percent; in Hungary, 21 percent; in Canada, 26 percent; and in the United States, 22 percent. But in the developing nations the proportion of people under fifteen is very much larger. In Brazil, it is 41 percent; in Kenya, 50 percent; in Algeria, 47 percent. These countries consequently have a vast potential for future population growth, regardless of whether their birth rates decline in the next few years. Indeed, even if parents the world over reproduced only enough children to replace themselves from now on, population would still soar to around 7 billion before it stabilized. But there appears to be little prospect of any drastic decline in global birth rates—a fact that makes the alternative "solution," a sharp increase in the death rate through famine, disease, and war, all the more probable.

Let's look at the population problem in more detail, first in the world as a whole, and then in the United States.

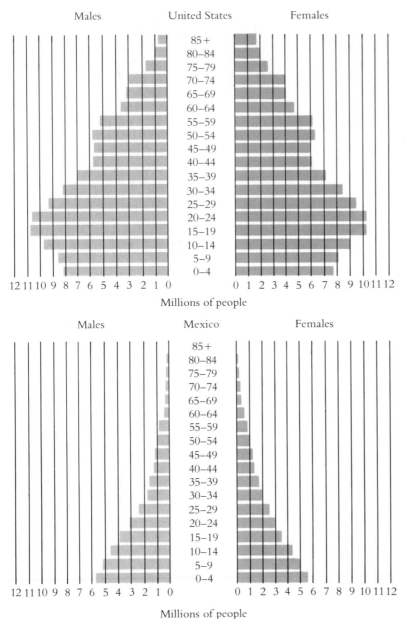

AGE STRUCTURES OF THE UNITED STATES AND MEXICO

Figure 20.3 The age structure of a population tells us a great deal about its demographic future. The proportion of the population under fifteen is very much smaller in the United States than it is in Mexico. Mexico therefore has a far greater potential for population increase as the younger members of society grow up and reproduce themselves.

Source: *Scientific American,* 243 (September 1980), p. 196.

The World Population Problem

Birth rates were always very high in preindustrial societies. In most of these societies large families were highly valued. Each new member was an economic asset in groups that had to hunt or tend animals or wrest their living from the soil, and the high infant death rate encouraged people to raise large numbers of children in the hope that some of them would survive into adulthood. In the early stages of the Industrial Revolution in England, however, this traditional value was seriously questioned for the first time.

The Malthusian Trap

In 1798, an English parson, Thomas Malthus, published a book entitled *Essay on the Principles of Population,* a work that aroused strong antagonism from his contemporaries. Malthus lived in an age of great optimism, dominated by the idea of the "perfectibility of man." According to this notion, a new golden age of abundance and bliss would be achieved in the future through the marvels of industrial technology. Malthus set out to shatter this idea through a very simple argument, based on his observation that the European population was growing rapidly at the time.

The natural tendency of population growth, Malthus pointed out, is to increase exponentially. But food supply depends on a fixed amount of land, so increases in agricultural production can be made only in a simple, additive fashion by bringing new land under cultivation. Inevitably, therefore, population tends to outrun the means of subsistence. At this point certain factors intervene to keep population within the limits set by food supply—those factors being "war, pestilence, and famine." Human beings, Malthus argued, were destined forever to press against the limits of the food supply. Misery, hunger, and poverty were the inevitable fate of the majority of the human species.

This argument was not a popular one. Malthus became known as the "gloomy parson," and one contemporary critic called his theory "that black and terrible demon that is always ready to stifle the hopes of humanity" (quoted in Heilbroner, 1967). Malthus himself offered little hope. The only suggestions he made were the abolition of poor relief and state support of poor children—in order to cut the growth rate of the lower classes—and "moral restraint" on the part of the rest of the population. But Malthus did not

Figure 20.4 Thomas Malthus, who in 1798 pointed out that the human population cannot increase indefinitely in a world of limited resources.

foresee the technical improvements that were later achieved in agriculture, making possible a vastly increased yield from a fixed amount of land; nor did he foresee the decline in birth rates that took place in the industrialized nations in the nineteenth and twentieth centuries. Both Europe and the United States grew in affluence and even in numbers, and it seemed for a while that Malthus had been wrong. Since then, however, an unprecedented population explosion has occurred in the poorer nations of the world, and we have come to recognize that the affluence of the wealthier nations has largely depended on their exploitation of the limited resources of the developing countries. The underlying logic of Malthus's argument is difficult to refute: population cannot increase indefinitely in a world that has finite resources. We find ourselves in the Malthusian trap once more.

In demographic terms, the countries of the world fall into two main categories: the developed nations, such as the United States, which have relatively low birth and growth rates, and the developing nations, such as Nigeria, with relatively high birth and growth rates. Between these two

Figure 20.5 Mechanized agriculture, the use of chemical fertilizers, and the introduction of new high-yield grains have all greatly increased food production in the modern world, and particularly in the United States, where the average farmer produces more than twice the yield of the average Soviet farmer. Nevertheless, even though American food exports to the rest of the world have doubled since 1970, global population may soon outstrip the world's food supply.

lies a third group of countries with intermediate birth and growth rates; these are mostly the smaller and more industrialized of the developing nations, such as South Korea. Rapid population growth is therefore primarily a problem of the poorest nations of the world: in Asia, life expectancy is fifty-eight years and the per capita gross national product is $760; in Africa, life expectancy is forty-nine years and the per capita gross national product is $530. In Europe and North America, by contrast, life expectancy is nearly seventy-four years, while the per capita gross national product is $5650 in Europe and $9650 in North America.

Much of the world's poverty results from the unequal distribution of its resources, but even if all the food in the world were distributed at the dietary level that we take for granted in the United States, it would feed only one-third of the current world population. Moreover, the gap between the rich and the poor nations is steadily widening and is likely to continue to do so. If we project future demographic trends in the developing nations, the picture becomes bleaker still. Kenya, growing at a rate of 3.9 percent a year, with a per capita gross national product of $320, will double its population in 20 years. Mexico, with a 1980 population of 68.2 million people, and a per capita gross national product of $1290, would have more than 2 billion people in 100 years if present growth rates were to continue—a population half as large as the entire present world population.

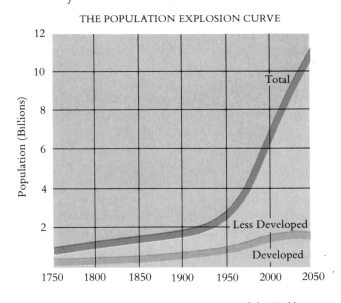

THE POPULATION EXPLOSION CURVE

Source: Nathan Keyfitz, "World Resources and the World Middle Class," *Scientific American*, 235 (July 1976), p. 29.

Figure 20.6 As this graph shows, most of the population growth until the year 2050 will take place in the less developed countries. The already wide gap between the per capita incomes of the developed and less developed societies is expected to grow even greater—and ironically, the poorer countries' population growth is a major reason for their poverty.

The Causes of Rapid Population Growth

Why is population increasing at such a speed in the developing nations? The main reason is the change in the ratio of births to deaths. The death rate in these societies has been sharply reduced by the introduction, however haphazard, of modern standards of sanitation, nutrition, and medicine, but the birth rate has remained extremely high. In the early industrial societies these innovations in public health occurred in a slow process extending over many decades, and there was time for cultural values about family size to adjust to the changed material conditions. In the newly developing nations, however, vaccinations, sewage systems, pesticides, and new dietary practices have been introduced with dramatic suddenness, causing a sharp drop in death rates while the birth rates remain at or near their previous levels. (Algeria, for example, has a birth rate of 48 and a death rate of 13; Mexico, a birth rate of 37 and a death rate of 6.) As a result, the overall rate of population increase in the developing countries is about 2 percent—a rate sufficient to double their populations no less than ten times in 116 years.

A complicating factor is that the developing nations, unlike the early industrial societies, are facing rapid population growth at a time when they already have very large populations. The high rate of growth, operating on this large population base, therefore produces a much greater increase in absolute numbers of people than the comparable population expansions that took place in Europe and North America in earlier years.

Given this sharp decline in death rates and an already existing population strain, why have birth rates remained high in the developing nations? The reason is that unlike technological innovations, such as modern medical techniques, which have an obvious utility and tend to be rapidly accepted into a society, changes in cultural values tend to be accepted only slowly. In many traditional societies a man's virility is gauged by the number of children he fathers, and most traditional societies emphasize the domestic role of the wife as mother and child-rearer. These cultural patterns are not easily changed. A large family was always an asset in a rural economy in the past, and people in a tradition-bound society may have difficulty appreciating that this situation has changed within the course of

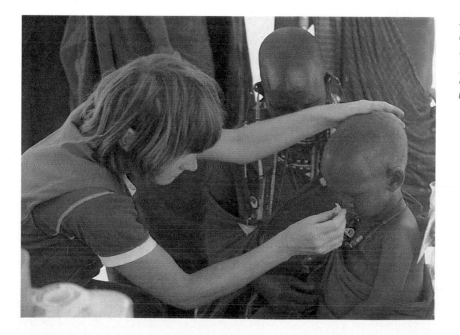

Figure 20.7 The main reason for the rapid population growth rate in the less developed countries is the decline in their death rates, particularly among young children. Modern medical techniques have helped to dramatically reduce the death rate in these societies, but the birth rate remains very high.

Figure 20.8 Many traditional, preindustrial societies still consider a large family an economic asset. In these societies the family is the main unit of production, and each additional child represents another potential worker in the fields.

a few decades. Even today a large family may serve important functions for parents in developing societies. In countries that lack a system of social security, children provide the only guarantee that one will be looked after in old age.

Many religions, too, emphasize some version of the Judeo-Christian injunction to "be fruitful and multiply." An old Arab proverb declares that "to have many children is to be blessed by Allah," and Islamic religion in several

countries is opposed to birth control. The Catholic Church, which is particularly influential in South America—where very high birth rates and grinding poverty are prevalent almost everywhere—has always opposed the use of contraceptives. To complicate matters further, many peoples regard high birth rates as essential for their economic or political strength. Argentina banned the use of contraceptives in 1974 as part of a planned campaign to double its population as soon as possible, in the supposed interests of economic development. In 1980 Chile launched a campaign for "a significant increase in population," in order to ensure "national security." In the wretchedly poor country of Bangladesh, once described by Henry Kissinger as "an international basket case," the first minister of family planning was the father of eighteen children. He was opposed to birth control in principle, and his first act was to curtail family-planning programs. Bangladesh, he felt, can be politically secure only if it has as many people as its neighbor, China—whose population represents over a fifth of humanity. Similar arguments about the political desirability of a population increase are heard all over the world—for example, among some Israelis, some white South Africans, and some black Americans. Throughout history, in short, large families and growing nations have been considered a fundamentally good thing. This value has deeply pervaded culture and institutional arrangements, and it is not easily or rapidly changed.

The Theory of Demographic Transition

There is a glimmer of hope in this otherwise bleak picture. We have noted that the early industrial societies faced a rapid population increase as their living standards rose and their death rates fell. We noted also that their growth rates tended to level off afterward as a result of a fall in the birth rates. This historical sequence has led some demographers to ask whether the same process might occur in other countries as they also industrialize. The theory of *demographic transition* holds that the growth rate of a population tends to stabilize once a certain level of economic development is achieved, primarily because people in urban, industrialized societies prefer small families and voluntarily limit the number of their children. In these modern societies children are not an economic asset at all; to feed and educate them places a considerable burden on the parents but yields no economic rewards. According to demographic-transition theory, people generally tend to have as many children as they believe they can support. The problem in the developing societies, then, is that people's attitudes have not yet caught up with their rapidly changing circumstances.

The demographic transition appears to proceed through three basic stages:

Stage one is the situation found in all traditional societies. There is a very high birth rate and a very high death rate, especially among infants. As a result, population numbers remain fairly stable.

Stage two is the situation found in all developing societies in the early stages of industrialism. The birth rate remains high but the death rate drops sharply as a result of improved living standards and medical care. As a result, population grows very rapidly.

Stage three is the situation found in advanced industrial societies. The birth rate drops as large families come to be seen as a liability, and the death rate remains low. As a result, the population growth rate gradually declines toward zero and remains fairly stable.

This transition is now almost complete in Europe, North America, and Japan. Encouragingly, some of the smaller and more economically advanced developing nations—such as Tunisia, Taiwan, Cuba, and Costa Rica—are showing signs of a steady decline in birth rates, suggesting that they are in transition between stages two and three. The remaining developing nations, however, are in stage two—and it is these countries that have some of the largest populations in the world and so make the greatest contribution to global population growth. But in time—if the demographic-transition theory is correct—they should show signs of a declining birth rate.

How valid is this theory? First, we must recognize that it is merely a hypothesis. The fact that some societies have followed a pattern of demographic transition does not mean that every society will do so. It is possible that specific factors operating in a particular society could speed the transition—or delay it, or even "freeze" it at a particular point. The Japanese demographic transition, for example,

THE DEMOGRAPHIC TRANSITION

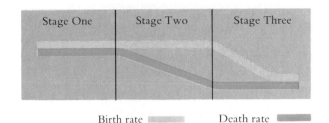

Figure 20.9 *According to demographic-transition theory, the high population growth rate in the less developed countries should be only a temporary phenomenon. Before industrialization, these societies have similar birth and death rates, and population remains constant (stage one). As these societies industrialize, the death rate drops, but the birth rate remains constant, leading to a population increase (stage two). But with further industrialization, the birth rate should drop to much the same level as the death rate (stage three). This has been the pattern in the existing industrialized societies, but there can be no certainty that this pattern will be repeated elsewhere.*

did not follow the historical pattern of Western societies, but was influenced instead by unique factors in Japanese culture and society. The Japanese government started a deliberate policy of population limitation after World War II, relying on abortion as a primary means of birth control. The result was the most spectacular drop in birth rates ever recorded—from 34 per thousand to 14 per thousand in the ten years between 1947 and 1957. Half of the conceptions in Japan during this time were terminated by abortions. But this particular transition was possible only because Japan, unlike many other developing societies, already had a strong central government that had traditionally enjoyed the loyalty of the entire nation and because the Japanese, unlike many other peoples, did not regard abortion as basically immoral. If these factors had not operated, it is doubtful whether Japan could have achieved the transition in the time that it did (Taeuber, 1960).

Figure 20.10

*"Excuse me, sir. I am prepared to make you
a rather attractive offer for your square."*

Drawing by Weber; © 1971
The New Yorker Magazine, Inc.

The second problem with demographic-transition the-ory is that it assumes that an economic "threshold" must be reached before the transition will take place. Dudley Kirk (1971) points out that there is generally a close connection between a decline in birth rates and the level of socioeco-nomic development, with per capita income and education level as important factors. If this view is correct, we cannot expect a transition in the developing nations until they are more economically advanced. Yet the poorest and most populous nations are precisely those that find economic advancement most difficult. The reasons lie in the vicious cycle of poverty and overpopulation.

A country with a rapidly growing population has a disproportionate number of young people, as we have seen. As a result, the work force contains a relatively small part of the population. If, as is the case in most developing nations, 40 to 50 percent of the population is under fifteen, and if a further substantial portion is diseased, disabled, or aged, then the work force must put much or most of its efforts into feeding the unproductive members of society.

Per capita income is therefore very low, and living stand-ards and educational levels are consequently depressed. Moreover, capital cannot be accumulated in the quantities necessary to spur economic development. In a society with a stable population, about 3 to 5 percent of national income would have to be invested to create a 1 percent increase in per capita income. In a society with a 3 percent population growth rate, the investment would have to be very much greater—often more than developing countries can afford. As a result, whatever economic advances these countries make may be literally eaten up by their increasing popula-tions and used to accommodate more people rather than improve the health and welfare of the existing population. A country whose population doubles in twenty or thirty years has to double its national income in that period—a staggering task—merely to maintain the same level of sub-sistence.

To complicate matters still further, the planet may not even have the resources to support huge human populations at anything remotely resembling the standard of living of the advanced industrial societies. To bring everyone up to our economic level would require, for example, that we extract 75 times as much iron, 100 times as much copper, 200 times as much lead, 75 times as much zinc, and 250 times as much tin as we now do every year (Ehrlich and Ehrlich, 1972). Yet there is evidence that, even at present rates of extraction, known supplies of several of these min-erals may be exhausted around the end of this century (Meadows et al., 1972). Nor is it easy to see how the environment could tolerate the amount of pollution in-volved in a world consisting entirely of heavily populated and fully industrialized societies. It is possible that some of the developing societies will never reach the level of socio-economic development that has historically been necessary before a demographic transition occurred.

Population in the United States

The United States is the world's wealthiest nation, fully capable of supporting its population at a very high standard of living. Does the society have a population problem? To answer the question, we must first look at its demographic characteristics.

American Demographic Characteristics

The current population of the United States exceeds 226 million. Females outnumber males by about 5.5 million, or about 2.5 percent, and the population is overwhelmingly white. Blacks represent about 11.7 percent of the population. This proportion has held fairly steady for about twenty years and represents a marked decrease from the early nineteenth century, when nearly a fifth of the population was black. The exact size of the other large minority, the Hispanics, is not known (many fail to complete census forms because of language problems or because they are illegal aliens), but this group probably represents about 6 percent of the population. The median age of the population, about 30 years, is relatively high, both in comparison with most other countries and with the nation's historical past. Population tends to be concentrated in the coastal and Great Lakes areas, and the nation is becoming increasingly urbanized; nearly 73 percent of Americans now live in metropolitan areas. There is a continuing population shift from large cities to suburbs and small towns, from low-income to high-income areas, and from the Northeast to the "sun belt" states of the South and Southwest.

The birth rate is low and reflects a consistent trend of declining fertility over the past 150 years. In 1820, the birth rate was 55 per thousand, but this level dropped steadily until it hit a low of 17 per thousand during the Great Depression of the thirties. The years after World War II saw a "baby boom," resulting from a backlog of delayed marriages and a greatly improved economic climate, and the birth rate rose again to around 25 per thousand in the late fifties. Then it declined once more, from 23.7 in 1960 to a record low of 14.8 in 1970, but rose slightly to 15.8 by the end of the decade. The baby boom was not anticipated by demographers, and neither was the "birth dearth" of the seventies. The large number of children born in the postwar years created a "bulge" in the age structure of the population, and the baby-boom generation is now of marriageable age. The result should be an "echo effect" as this large generation reproduces itself, but there are few signs that this is taking place. The reasons are not clear, but the low birth rate seems to be the result of several factors—the economic recession, the desire of young women to have a career outside the home, the tendency of many young adults to postpone marriage, a growing unwillingness to raise large families, improved birth-control techniques, and easier access to abortions.

At present, the average American woman is bearing 1.9 children, somewhat less than the 2.1 figure required for zero population growth. Demographers expect the rate to increase slightly, however, as the economic climate improves and as young adults who have delayed marriage begin to raise families. Census Bureau surveys indicate that young married women expect to have rather more than two children on average. Many of them, too, will have more children than they intend. In one study, Larry Bumpass and Charles Westoff (1970) found that a fifth of all births to American women were unwanted at the time of conception. The birth rate varies considerably between different segments of the population. It is higher for blacks than for whites, higher for the working class than for the middle class, and higher for Catholics than it is for Protestants or Jews.

The death rate in the United States is also low, at 8.7 per thousand, and life expectancy is extremely high at 73.8 years of age. Average life expectancy varies according to race and sex: 78.3 years for white females, 74.5 years for nonwhite females, 70.6 years for white males, and only 65.5 years for nonwhite males (Bureau of the Census, 1980). About 11 percent of the population is sixty-five and over, and this proportion will increase markedly as the baby-boom generation grows older in the years ahead. The death rate will therefore increase noticeably as this generation reaches its seventieth decade.

Does the United States Have a Population Problem?

An affluent society with a low birth and growth rate may not at first sight appear to have a population problem. But the national Commission on Population Growth and the American Future (1972) reported that population growth threatens severe problems for American society—and for the rest of the world—and recommended a national policy of zero population growth.

The commission pointed out that even if reproduction stabilizes now at replacement levels, the population will continue to increase for many years as the existing younger

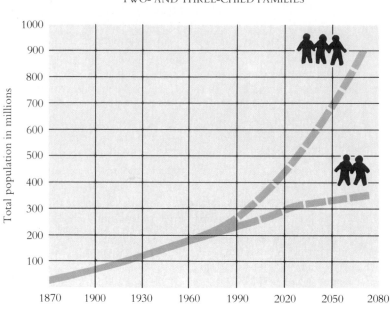

U.S. POPULATION PROJECTIONS:
TWO- AND THREE-CHILD FAMILIES

Source: Report of the Commission on Population Growth and the American
Future, *Population and the American Future* (Washington, D.C.: U.S. Government
Printing Office, 1972), p. 23.

*Figure 20.11 The difference in size between two-
and three-child families may not seem very significant, but the long-term impact would be enormous. These projections were made by a presidential commission, which strongly recommended the
limitation of family size in the United States.*

generation enters the childbearing period. If the average American family has only two children, population will rise to 307 million by the year 2020, and if the average family has three children, it will rise to 477 million. Even the lower rate of increase would have enormous consequences. Cities would become more crowded, and more rural land would have to be converted to urban or industrial use. New demands would be made on already strained energy resources. Pollution of land, sea, rivers, and air would increase—the more so if we expect this larger population to enjoy a higher standard of living than it does at present. Immense sums would have to be spent on duplicating existing facilities, such as schools and hospitals, rather than on improving these facilities and raising living standards. Fresh sources of food, lumber, minerals, and

other raw materials—including water, which is already in short supply in many parts of the United States—would have to be found. As demands for these dwindling resources multiplied, prices would skyrocket. The commission looked for economic advantages in population increase but found none. Instead, it reported, the quality of life would suffer and a number of serious social problems would be created.

We also have to take into account the global impact of American population growth. In international terms, a new American child is something of a disaster, for he or she presents a greater threat to the ecology of the planet than fifty Asian babies. With less than 6 percent of the world's population, we use more than a third of the earth's energy and material resources and generate almost half of its pollution. We already use, for example, a third of the world's tin, half of its newsprint and rubber, a fourth of its steel, and a fifth of its cotton, and we rely on foreign sources for twenty-two of seventy-four minerals considered essential in industrial societies. Adding another 50 million Americans to the population—which we shall probably do by the year 2000—would be the equivalent, in ecological terms, of adding another 2 billion or so Asians to the world. Our population growth cannot be considered in isolation from the rest of the world, for the various nations are increasingly interdependent. We rely on them for raw materials; if those materials are exhausted, or if other peoples need to use them to support their own growing populations, we suffer. Other peoples rely on us, as one of the few countries that periodically produces an agricultural surplus, for their food. If we need that food for our own expanding population, they starve.

For these reasons the commission strongly recommended a series of measures designed to reduce population growth. The most crucial recommendations were probably the most controversial. These included the removal of formal and informal restrictions against sterilization, the provision of readily available abortion facilities, thorough sex education in the schools, and the removal of restrictions on the distribution of contraceptive information and devices to the public, including minors. President Nixon rejected these recommendations as "immoral."

What Can Be Done?

It is obvious that unless population growth is rapidly halted, the world faces a disaster whose toll in human lives and human misery is barely conceivable. What steps can be taken to avoid this fate? There are four basic strategies that can be used: family planning, incentives, economic reform, and outright coercion.

Family Planning

This strategy involves couples' use of contraception to limit the number of their offspring. Nearly all the nations of Asia and many countries in other parts of the world are already committed to population limitation through family planning. But no society has yet managed to achieve a signifi-

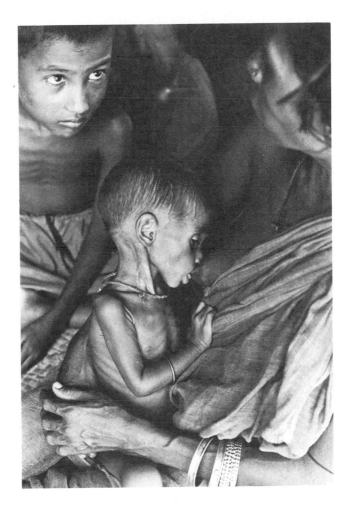

Figure 20.12 Scenes such as this are likely to become more, rather than less, common in the decades ahead. If population growth continues at anything like its present pace, undernourishment or even outright starvation will be the fate of most people on earth.

cant drop in its birth rate through this means alone. The main reason is that family planning, by definition, permits parents to determine how large their family is to be, and the parents' notion of the ideal family size may not accord with the needs of society.

The experience of India, the first country to introduce a policy of population limitation, is instructive. At its present growth rates, India could have a population of well over 1 billion by the year 2000, which it could not possibly hope to feed, let alone clothe, house, and educate. Even today, 98 percent of the Indian population has an inadequate diet. The Indian birth rate has declined from 52.4 at the beginning of the century to about 34 today, but the death rate has declined even faster, from 46.8 to 15, resulting in a huge population increase. India started an official family-planning program in 1952, and by the mid-seventies devoted 1 percent of its budget to family planning. This was the largest percentage of a national budget that any nation had ever applied to population limitation, yet it represented less than eight cents a year for each person in the country. An immediate problem, then, was that information about, and facilities for, contraception and sterilization simply did not reach millions of Indians. The Indian government next attempted far sterner measures, including threats to the jobs of government employees who had more than two children and an aggressive program to encourage (and sometimes force) men to be sterilized. Largely in response to these policies, Indian voters threw their government out of office in 1977. Subsequent governments have soft-pedaled the family-planning issue. Westerners are often guilty of the "technological fallacy," the belief that merely applying technology to a problem will solve it. But people have to be persuaded to make use of contraceptive technology, and they will not do so if the technology runs counter to their values. Although millions of Indians have been sterilized or have accepted contraceptives, it seems that many of them, perhaps the majority, have done so only *after* they have produced what they believe is a sufficiently large family.

Incentives

This strategy includes various methods of encouraging people to limit the number of their children. Several countries have experimented with the use of gifts or cash rewards to people who accept sterilization or contraceptive devices. Another proposal is to give tax exemptions to people with only a few children, instead of the current practice of giving exemptions to parents of large families. This proposal has the disadvantage, however, that the children of large but poor families would suffer greater hardships. Kingsley Davis (1967, 1976b) has argued that basic changes must be engineered in social values and attitudes to encourage smaller families. Once social norms oppose prolific reproduction, he points out, most people will conform. Women, for example, might be offered more satisfying and appealing careers outside the home. Advantages in taxation, housing, and recreation might be given to single rather than to married people. The schools' responsibility for socializing children might be increased, thus diminishing the parents' responsibility and hence the "ego-identity which plays such a strong role in parental motivation." Such steps might limit the birth rate, but no government has yet attempted these or similar social changes with that intention in mind, and none seems likely to.

Economic Reforms

The demographic transition, as we have seen, is closely linked to economic progress: the better off people are, the more inclined they become to limit the size of their families. Most of the less developed nations do not have the means to achieve the rapid economic growth necessary to raise standards of living to the appropriate level, and it seems that only massive investment by the advanced industrialized societies would provide them with the capital they need. Since this investment is unlikely to be forthcoming to any significant degree, most demographers have been pessimistic about the prospects for a demographic transition in the larger and poorer nations.

More recently, however, some demographers have begun to wonder whether a different kind of economic reform would achieve a lowered growth rate. Although the birth rates of most of the developing nations have not dropped appreciably, some of them, like Costa Rica, Singapore, and China, have achieved a marked decline. The Chinese transition is a highly impressive one; although exact data are not available, it seems that the growth rate has been reduced from a typically high level a few years ago to a current low of around 1.5. Part of the reduction is the result of policies that encourage delayed marriage and abstinence from premarital sex. But many demographers now believe that the crucial factor is the reasonably fair distribution of the society's resources. In other words, if people are allowed to enjoy such basics of life as food, shelter, clothing, health care, education (especially for women), and a sense that things will get better in the future, then they tend to voluntarily limit the size of their families. The family-planning efforts of many other developing nations fail, it seems, because the resources of these societies are unfairly shared: typically, a tiny elite enjoys a disproportionate share (and its birth rate drops), but the mass of the people remain in hopeless poverty (and maintain high birth rates). If this analysis is correct, then policies that focus on a sharing of resources, rather than exclusively on economic development that may benefit only a minority, may be the best way to reduce global population growth (Rich, 1973; Hernandez, 1974; Ehrlich and Ehrlich, 1979; Alba, 1980).

Coercion

This strategy would be the least popular but the most effective means of limiting population. The state would simply determine how many children each set of parents might have and would then proceed, by any of a variety of methods, to enforce its policies. One method might be to issue child licenses to each woman, entitling her to have as many children as a zero population growth permits (Boulding, 1964). Another might be to administer a chemical inhibitor on fertility to the entire population, perhaps by adding it periodically to the water supply in order to regulate births (Ketchel, 1968). Another method, less subtle still, might be to automatically sterilize each couple after the birth of their second child.

These are not very amiable suggestions, and they involve the intrusion of the power of the state into some of the most sacred areas of private life. Yet we have long recognized that individuals do not have absolute rights: their personal liberties are often restricted for the good of society. We cannot fire guns where we choose, or discriminate against anyone we choose, or throw our garbage where we choose, or employ child labor if we choose. Our right to swing our fists ends where someone else's nose begins. In due course we may be forced to consider whether our freedom to bring children into the world is subject to the same principle. Coercion must necessarily be a last resort, undertaken with the most extreme reluctance, but in the end it may prove the lesser of the evils confronting us.

Figure 20.13 In most developing societies, a small minority of the population enjoys the bulk of the society's wealth and has a low birth rate, while the rest of the population lives in poverty and has a high birth rate—a tendency starkly illustrated by this photograph of homeless Indians sleeping on the sidewalk in front of a luxury apartment building. Some demographers believe that a more equal sharing of resources would encourage a general decline of birth rates.

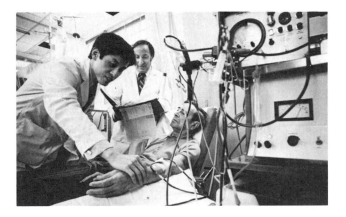

Figure 20.14 The kind of treatment that people receive for their ailments is very much dependent on the culture or subculture they happen to belong to. Among the San of the Kalahari desert and among some American fundamentalists, spiritual healing through a "laying on of hands" is considered appropriate; but most people in industrialized societies are likely to seek a cure through doctors and hospitals.

Health and Society

As our discussion of population dynamics has made apparent, health and sickness are much more than personal or physiological issues. Social factors profoundly affect not only our life expectancy but also our chances of becoming ill, the kind of diseases we are likely to get, the type and quality of the treatment we receive, and our chances for a successful recovery. For example, until recently a common illness among the horticultural Fore people of New Guinea was kuru, a fatal viral infection of the brain. This disease was transmitted by an unusual cultural practice of this tribe: as a mark of respect to their dead kinfolk, they ate them. Now that cannibalism is no longer practiced by the Fore, the disease has virtually died out. But although the culture of the Fore made them susceptible to kuru, it also exempted them from some of the illnesses that are specific to industrialized societies, such as the lethal diseases of the lungs that occur among coal miners or asbestos workers. In a similar way, the social and medical response to an ill person is culturally variable: in one society, sorcery might be considered the cause of the problem, and the attempted cure might consist of charms supplied by a witch doctor; in another, the identical ailment may be attributed to a malignant growth of cells, and may be treated with x-rays, hospitalization, surgery, and a battery of medications.

Social influences on health and sickness are most clearly revealed in the different patterns of disease and mortality in preindustrial and industrial societies. The most common causes of death in preindustrial societies are acute infections, nutritional disorders, and parasites; and the highest mortality rates are among young children, who succumb to such diseases as diptheria, polio, typhoid, and protein deficiency. In industrial societies, on the other hand, the most common causes of death are chronic, noninfectious ailments; and the highest mortality rates are among the aged, who die of such diseases as cancer, strokes, heart disease, and emphysema.

Each society therefore has typical patterns of health and illness that are closely linked to its cultural practices. The United States, for example, has the highest rate of heart disease in the world, a problem that arises in part from a general lack of exercise and a diet rich in animal fats. Americans have by far the highest homicide rate in the industrialized world, partly because the society tolerates a high level of aggression in males (who commit most murders) and partly because, unlike other modern societies, it allows very easy access to handguns (which are used in most killings). In a world where hunger is the permanent lot of a quarter of the species, Americans have the highest rate of obesity, a direct result of a sedentary way of life combined with a starchy, fatty, sugary diet. Stress-related diseases, such as ulcers and hypertension, are also extremely common, and their prevalence is probably linked to the fast, competitive pace of urban life. The death rate from accidents—the third leading cause of death after heart disease and cancer—is remarkably high, largely because of the carnage caused by automobile accidents. Respiratory ailments, particularly lung cancer and emphysema, are becoming more common, primarily as a result of cigarette smoking and atmospheric pollution. The death rate from drug overdoses is also relatively high, largely because the indiscriminate prescription of barbiturates by many physicians makes these drugs widely available.

Patterns of health and disease vary not only from one society to another but also from group to group within a society. *Epidemiology*—the study of the distribution of diseases within a population—is a major concern of medical sociology, and decades of research in this area have shown that the differences in the incidence of sickness and mortality among various segments of society are striking. We

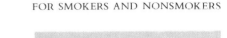

RATIO OF DEATH RATES BY CAUSE
FOR SMOKERS AND NONSMOKERS

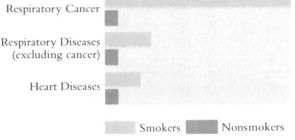

Source: State Mutual Life Assurance Company.

Figure 20.15 Although such illicit drugs as marijuana, heroin, and LSD attract the most adverse public comment, the main killer drugs in the United States are alcohol and tobacco. As this chart shows, cigarette smokers run a much greater risk of death from certain causes than nonsmokers do.

have already noted, for example, that women live longer than men, that whites live longer than nonwhites, and that the old are more likely to suffer from chronic diseases than are the young, who are more likely to contract acute infections. Another highly significant epidemiological finding is that the higher people's socioeconomic status, the healthier they tend to be and the longer they are likely to live. Nearly all health problems—ranging from mental disorders to cancer—are more prevalent in the lower social classes than in the higher ones. There seem to be several reasons for this tendency: as a general rule, people of higher social status enjoy better nutrition, are more able to interpret their symptoms and so seek earlier treatment, and have access to superior medical care (Twaddle and Hessler, 1977; Totness, 1980).

The Medical Institution

All societies have a structured response to sickness among their members. In each society there is some form of *sick role*—a pattern of behavior expected of a person who is ill

(Parsons, 1951). In a sense, the sick person is a social deviant: he or she fails to conform to approved norms of healthful behavior and therefore no longer fulfills normal role obligations. But unlike other deviants, the sick person is not stigmatized or punished—provided he or she seeks help and tries to get better. The sick person's cooperation in the treatment process indicates to others that he or she is not merely lazy or malingering, and thus allows them to tolerate the abandonment of normal roles. The exact content of the sick role, of course, varies somewhat from culture to culture and even from one subculture to another—Italian-Americans, for example, are far more expressive about aches and pains than Polish-Americans, who are more stoical—but in all cases the individual is expected to announce the symptoms, to hope for some measure of sympathy from others, and to be grateful for whatever assistance they offer.

Every society also has experts in the diagnosis and treatment of ailments. Whether their healing powers are real or imaginary, these healers always have very high social status, for they are believed to have access to vital knowledge that the ordinary person lacks—knowledge that can mean the difference between health and sickness, life and death. In the most simple, preindustrial societies, the healer is typically also the priest, shaman, or witch doctor. Such a person is believed to have direct contact with gods or spirits and to be able to divine the cause of a disease (which is often thought to be sorcery) and its cure (which may involve magic and perhaps herbal or other folk remedies, some of which may actually be effective).

In modern industrial societies the general trend toward an increasingly refined division of labor has divided the role of shaman into several specialties. The religious role has become a separate one, usually unrelated to medicine; the dispensing of potions, balms, pills, and other remedies is now left mainly to pharmacists; a good deal of routine care has become the province of nurses and other personnel; and the role of healer, or physician, has been divided into that of general practitioner and an array of specialists, ranging from gynecologists to brain surgeons. This cluster of interrelated roles and statuses, together with various norms and values about sickness and treatment, now constitutes an increasingly important (and costly) institution in the social structure of all modern nations.

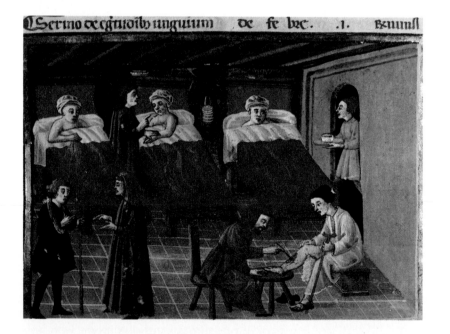

Figure 20.16 All societies have some form of "sick role," the pattern of behavior expected of someone who is ill. As this painting of a hospital in late medieval Italy suggests, the role usually involves surrender of control over the treatment of the illness to socially recognized experts in healing.

The social status of physicians in the Western world has been rising fairly steadily since the seventeenth century. Before that time, the medical profession was, on the whole, a serious social menace. Medical knowledge was largely based on ignorance, dogma, and superstition, and many of the most favored treatments—such as the copious blood-letting of patients, often with filthy scalpels—were more likely to kill than cure. In fact, the roles of surgeon and barber were often played by the same person, for the skills involved were considered fairly similar. From the late seventeenth century onward, however, physicians became steadily more scientific in their approach to medicine and health, and by the nineteenth century they were making systematic use of the experimental method. Medicine became a science, and physicians became professionals. As we noted in Chapter 18 ("The Economic Order"), a *profession* is an occupation requiring extensive, systematic training in an art or science. Professionals are able, among other things, to restrict access to their occupation, to command relatively high fees for their work, to enjoy considerable autonomy and independence in their professional lives, and to establish professional associations that regulate the affairs of the profession and its members. As a result of the successful professionalization of their field, physicians now have the highest public prestige rating of any occupation, and earn higher annual salaries than any other professionals.

Until World War II most American physicians were solo practitioners, serving as family doctors, treating patients in their offices, and making house calls. Hospitals, meanwhile, essentially provided a hotel service for the sick, together with some assistance and facilities unavailable in the doctor's office. Today, medicine is practiced primarily in large urban hospitals: many people no longer have a family doctor, and instead go for treatment of even relatively minor ailments to the so-called emergency rooms of hospitals. There are several reasons for this revolutionary trend in health care. One is the high degree of specialization that medical science has achieved: treatment of diseases now often requires the collaboration of physicians from several subfields of the discipline. Another is that a great deal of modern medical equipment is so expensive that only large hospitals can afford to buy and use it. A third reason is that most patients no longer pay their doctors directly: third parties, such as Medicaid, Medicare, and private in-

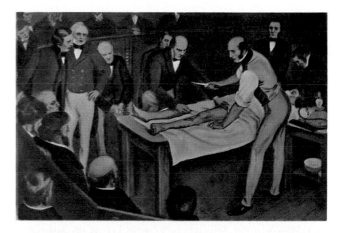

Figure 20.17 Particularly during the course of this century, the medical profession has come to rely ever more heavily on science and technology. The surgeons of a century ago would have very little understanding of the tools and techniques used by their counterparts today.

surance plans, pay the bills, but they do so only if treatment takes place in a hospital. Finally, the emphasis in modern American medicine is on, not the treatment of ordinary aches and pains, but rather on advanced research into diseases that may yield dramatic cures. American medicine has relatively little interest in the maintenance of health or the prevention of illness; the overwhelming focus is on already-existing disease and new methods for curing it. This research is best performed in a university-based teaching hospital, where the necessary grants, patients, colleagues, equipment, and assistance are available.

Problems of Health Care in America

American health care presents two basic problems: it costs too much—both in relation to other nations and in relation to people's incomes—and for many people, it is difficult to get. The price of the nation's health-care bill has soared from about $3.8 billion in 1940 to nearly $245 billion in 1980 (see Figure 20.18), and continues to rise rapidly. About 23 million Americans are not covered by health insurance of any kind, and even those who are covered find that their insurance rarely pays for all medical expenses, particularly those of a very long illness. Serious illness can

wipe out the savings and undermine the living standards of most families, and, indeed, half the bankruptcies every year are precipitated by medical bills. Moreover, physicians and health services are unevenly distributed: affluent suburban areas have an oversupply of doctors; poorer urban areas and many rural areas have a marked undersupply. And whereas the affluent can buy the immediate services of personal physicians, the poor may have to attend municipal clinics and hospitals, waiting for hours on end to be seen, and often being treated by different physicians, or even medical students, on every visit.

The basic problem, it seems, lies in a unique aspect of health care in the United States: it is a service that is run primarily for profit, meaning that people must buy the skills of doctors and the drugs of pharmacists in the same way that they might buy the skills of auto mechanics or the goods of a grocer. Every other modern industrial society runs its health service on the assumption that the type and quality of treatment a sick person receives should be determined by the person's illness, not the person's income. Typically, other nations have some system of national health insurance that makes medical facilities available free, or at a nominal charge, to whoever needs them. In most Western European countries, for example, a sick person can stay for months in the hospital, receive the services of

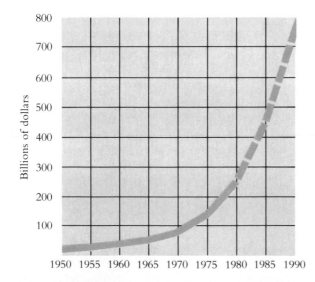

RISING HEALTH CARE COSTS, 1950–1990

Figure 20.18 A major problem of the American health-care system is the extraordinary rise in medical costs. Almost one out of every ten dollars spent in the modern United States goes on health-related items or services.

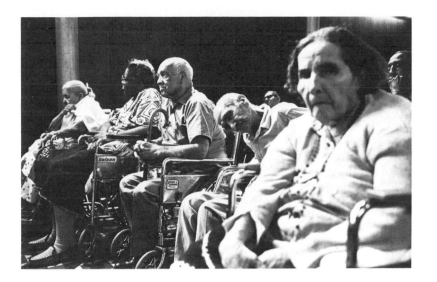

Figure 20.19 One of the most tragic aspects of the American health-care system is the state of nursing homes, many of which are simply places for warehousing the elderly. Most nursing homes are run for financial gain, and their substantial profits are often achieved by keeping the costs of patient care to a minimum. Although a few homes have achieved excellent reputations, congressional and law-enforcement investigations of the industry have uncovered numerous scandals, including the involvement of organized crime in this lucrative field.

doctors and surgeons, be treated with the most sophisticated equipment, and pay little or nothing. But in the United States, the health-service industry is one of the largest and most profitable enterprises in the entire economy, and the combined lobbying efforts of the physicians, drug companies, private hospitals, and nursing-home operators have managed to keep it that way by preventing the introduction of so-called socialized medicine. Many epidemiological features of the American population, such as the great difference in infant mortality rates between the rich and the poor or between white and black, can be fully understood only in these terms.

Population, Health, and the Environment

Every animal or plant species is the product of a lengthy process of evolution that makes the organism uniquely adapted to the environment that supports it. Each species is able to remain healthy and to survive only by exploiting that environment, and if for one reason or another it can no longer do so, it becomes extinct. The ultimate extinction of organisms is the rule rather than the exception in the biological world; it is calculated that over 99.9 percent of all species that have ever lived met this fate.

The Science of Ecology

Ecology is the science of the relationship between living organisms and their environments. The discipline emerged as a natural science in the late nineteenth century and is still primarily the domain of biologists and zoologists. In the twentieth century, however, social scientists have systematically applied ecological principles to the study of human societies and populations. Anthropologists have found the ecological approach a useful means of analyzing cultural arrangements. As we saw in Chapter 4 ("Society"), the subsistence strategy that a society uses to exploit its environment—hunting and gathering, pastoralism, horticulture, agriculture, or industrialism—has important effects on social structure and culture. In particular, the subsistence strategy strongly affects the potential size of a population. If all societies still relied on hunting and gathering for their subsistence, world population would have leveled off at around 10 million people. But the industrial mode of production, which is always linked to advanced medical and other technologies, permits a small part of the population to feed the rest and thus makes high population growth rates possible. If this method for exploiting the environment were for any reason to become difficult or impossible, social disorganization, starvation, disease, and a population collapse would follow.

Sociologists have also been deeply interested in *human ecology*, the interrelationship between human groups and their natural environment. Researchers working in this field have studied both the geographic distribution of the entire species over the planet and the spatial distribution of local populations. We know, for example, that although our species is highly adaptable and can even alter hostile environments (including the surface of the moon) to meet its needs, about 50 to 75 percent of the earth's land area nevertheless remains inhospitable to us. In fact, world population is so unevenly distributed that about half the people of the world live on 5 percent of the land area (Hauser, 1969). Some of the most promising work in the human ecology of local populations was conducted at the University of Chicago in the thirties and forties and is discussed in Chapter 21 ("Urbanization and Urban Life"). More recently, however, an awareness of the "ecological crisis" has led social and natural scientists from several disciplines to focus on the complex interrelationship among industrialism, human health, population growth, and the global environment.

The problem posed by large-scale industrialism is two-fold. First, it generates pollution of the natural environment, threatening or destroying life in a chain reaction that can run from the tiniest microorganism to human beings. Second, it depletes natural resources such as wood, oil, and minerals, many of which are in short supply and cannot be replaced. The industrial mode of production has made possible high living standards for a minority of the world's population, but at the cost of increasing despoilation and exploitation of the environment. Industrialism has also encouraged a huge increase in human population, and the populous developing nations understandably want to raise their living standards as well. The question that arises is whether a world population that will double in forty-one years, and thus produce twice as many people to consume and pollute, can be supported by the environment.

The Elements of Ecology

Life on earth exists only in the biosphere, a thin film of soil, air, and water at or near the surface of the planet. Within this biosphere all living organisms exist in a delicate balance with one another and with the environmental resources that support them. A fundamental ecological concept is the *ecosystem*, a self-sustaining community of organisms within its natural environment. An ecosystem may be as small as a drop of pond water or as large as the biosphere itself, but the same principle of mutual interdependence always applies. Energy and inorganic (nonliving) matter are both essential for life. The energy is derived directly or indirectly from the sun, and the inorganic matter from the soil and the air. Green plants convert the sun's energy and the inorganic nutrients into organic, living matter. The plants are eaten by animals, many of which are consumed in turn by other animals in highly complex food chains. Finally, insects, bacteria, fungi, and other decomposers break down the dead bodies of plants and animals, releasing the nutrients back into the ecosystem and completing the cycle.

We may think nothing of the bacteria in the soil, but if we destroy them, we destroy ourselves, for all life depends on these lowly creatures. We poison insects at our peril, for insects are an element in a food chain that may ultimately concentrate the poison in the bodies of animals, including ourselves, for whom it was never intended. In preindustrial societies people treat nature with respect, considering themselves a part of, rather than set apart from, the natural world; this attitude was typical, for example, among the Indian tribes of North America in precolonial times. In industrial society our attitude is different. We consider ourselves the lords of creation and see nature primarily as a resource for exploitation. As our "needs" increase, our capacity for exploitation expands. We do not see our ravaging of the environment as "ravaging" at all; it is "progress" or "development." We are so used to exploiting natural resources and dumping our waste products into the environment that we forget that resources are limited and exhaustible and that pollution can disrupt the ecological balance on which our health and survival depend.

Pollution

The atmosphere of most American cities is heavily polluted. The average resident of New York City, for example, inhales the equivalent in toxic materials of thirty-eight cigarettes a day; pollution cuts out up to 40 percent of Chicago's sunlight; Los Angeles is often shrouded in a petrochemical smog. Automobiles, municipal incinerators,

Figure 20.20 Although the industrial mode of production has produced unprecedented wealth, it has often disrupted the natural environment in unforeseen ways. Atmospheric pollution, for example, has become a serious public health hazard in many areas, and it may have effects on the global climate that are not yet fully understood.

utility companies, and industrial plants dump more than 200 million tons of waste into the atmosphere every day, almost a ton a day for each American. Air pollution on this scale unquestionably affects public health and is probably directly implicated in the rapidly rising rates for lung diseases—the fastest growing cause of death in the nation.

Another serious source of pollution arises from the widespread agricultural use of pesticides and herbicides which, as we have noted, are transmitted and concentrated through the food chain until they turn up, sometimes years later, in the bodies of other organisms. The breastmilk of American women contains up to ten times more of the insecticide DDT than is permitted in dairy milk for human consumption. DDT is an extremely stable chemical that does not break down for decades after it is used, and the United States alone has released more than 1 billion pounds of the substance into the environment. Every morsel of food that we eat, even the so-called organic food favored by health enthusiasts, is tainted with pesticides and insecticides. These chemicals are found even in polar bears, thousands of miles from the source of the pollution. The combined effects of habitat destruction and pesticide pollution have exterminated many species and currently threaten the survival of 280 mammal, 350 bird, and 20,000 plant species (Goldsmith et al., 1972).

Serious though the spread of pesticides and herbicides may be, it is only a minor aspect of the problem of chemical pollution. In the United States alone, scientists create at least 1000 new chemical compounds every year. The great majority of these substances do not exist in nature, so we have evolved no natural defenses against any harmful effects they might have. Nearly 50,000 synthetic chemicals are now on the market, where they are used—often to our great benefit—in such fields as medicine, food processing, and manufacturing. But about 35,000 of these chemicals are classified by the Environmental Protection Agency as either definitely or potentially harmful to human health. Most of these substances have not been fully tested for their possible effects on human beings; and many of those that initially seem innocuous may have dangerous long-term consequences. Scientists believe that the great majority of cancers are environmentally caused and they have established links between exposure to some substances and the later appearance of the diseases (for example, vinyl chloride with liver cancer, asbestos with lung cancer, benzene with leukemia). In many cases the disease does not show up for fifteen or twenty years after the exposure. It is highly likely that Americans are being exposed today to supposedly safe new chemicals that will prove, decades hence, to have lethal consequences (S. Epstein, 1978; M. Brown, 1980).

Figure 20.21 The introduction of new, synthetic chemicals to the global ecosystem, usually for agricultural or industrial purposes, may pose serious long-term dangers to the human population. The potential effects of such chemicals on human beings are imperfectly understood, and may not be known until people have been exposed to these substances for decades.

Unhappily, a great deal of long-term chemical damage has already been done, because a significant part of the nation's supply of ground water (on which more than half the population depends for domestic use) is threatened with contamination. Ground water, lying anywhere from a few feet to half a mile below the earth's surface, accumulates and moves very slowly, and once contaminated, it is virtually impossible to clean. In 1980 the Environmental Protection Agency located 180,000 dumping grounds and "lagoons" of industrial wastes—many of them long since abandoned, many of them containing toxic chemicals, and most of them lacking any lining that might prevent poisons from leaching through to the ground water and thence, years later, into the drinking water of distant communities. (In 1980, for example, hundreds of families in Love Canal, New York, had to be evacuated from their homes because seepage from a disused dumping ground was suspected of causing a high rate of cancers, birth defects, and other illnesses.) The contamination of ground water may prove a much greater threat to health than the more immediately obvious pollution of surface water, because lakes and rivers are to some extent self-purifying.

Another potential threat to health and life is the presence of seventy-eight nuclear power plants. A "meltdown" and explosion at any one of them would release radioactive fallout hundreds of times greater than that of the atomic bomb dropped on Hiroshima. Although there are constant assurances from the nuclear industry that these reactors are entirely safe, opinion polls show growing public opposition to them, despite our heavy dependence on the energy they supply. There appear to be good grounds for this public concern. In 1978, the reactors logged 2835 "reportable occurrences"—incidents that violate rules of the Nuclear Regulatory Commission or threaten public safety—and every single reactor had at least one "unscheduled shutdown." In 1979 there were over 2300 such incidents, including an "unscheduled shutdown" at Three Mile Island, Pennsylvania, where a crippled and leaking reactor came close to a meltdown, forcing more than 200,000 people to flee their homes. The disposal of nuclear waste—some of which is radioactive for up to 300,000 years—is a further problem of appalling potential, with no satisfactory solution in sight.

The impact of pollution on global weather patterns could also have a drastic effect on population and society all over the world. Pollutants such as industrial emissions, the trails of jet aircraft, dust from mechanized agriculture, and excess carbon dioxide from the burning of fuels and wastes, threaten to alter the earth's atmosphere and temperature. If the global temperature rises by as little as another four or five degrees, the polar icecaps will begin to melt, raising sea levels by as much as 300 feet and flooding coastal areas all over the world. If it drops by a few degrees, the world will be plunged into a new ice age that would envelope the

Northern Hemisphere, burying cities such as Chicago under ice three miles deep. At present, fortunately for us, our atmospheric pollutants have contrary effects. Some, such as carbon dioxide, prevent heat radiating back into space and thus keep the planet warmer. Others, such as dust from agriculture, block out the sun's rays and thus keep it cooler. We have stumbled on this happy balance by accident, however, and there is no reason to suppose that it will be maintained indefinitely (Hobbs, et al., 1974; Bryson, 1974; MacDonald et al., 1979).

Resource Depletion

The shortage of resources—raw materials and energy—is also a growing problem for industrial societies. The United States alone consumes a third of the world's energy, more than 60 percent of the natural gas, more than 40 percent of the aluminum and coal, one third of the petroleum, platinum, and copper, and about a quarter of the gold, iron, lead, silver, and zinc. If current patterns of exploitation are continued, many of these resources will be exhausted very soon. The known reserves of iron and chromium may be gone in less than a hundred years, of nickel in about fifty years, of aluminum in about thirty years, and of copper, lead, tin, and zinc in twenty years or less. It is possible, although by no means certain, that synthetic substitutes for some of these materials might be invented. New resources of these minerals will also no doubt be found, although the rate of discovery of new deposits has been dropping rapidly in recent years. Low-grade resources that are not economically worthwhile to exploit at present might be used, but the price of these commodities would then soar.

Like much of our pollution, a good deal of resource depletion is unnecessary and results from irresponsibility and greed. But the problem cannot be reduced to a simple conflict between the "bad guys" who ravage the environment and the "good guys" who are committed to its preservation. All of us are presumably in favor of conserving resources and protecting the environment, yet all of us are guilty of practices that worsen the problem. Collectively, these practices may threaten our health as individuals and our future as a population, but changing them could prove very costly and very inconvenient, and might involve hard and uncomfortable choices.

Given the interrelationship among health, population, and the environment, can industrial growth continue? One major research effort attempted to answer this question, and the response—a very controversial one—was negative. A research team at the Massachusetts Institute of Technology used a computer model to project current trends of population increase, industrial output, food production, resource depletion, and pollution well into the next century. The report, entitled *The Limits to Growth* (Meadows et al., 1972), concluded that industrial society faces an inevitable and disastrous collapse within a hundred years, and possibly a good deal sooner, unless both population growth and industrial growth are brought to an immediate halt.

The MIT team devised various scenarios for the future, but the result of each was the same: collapse. If current trends continue unchanged, a shortage of raw materials will destroy the industrial base of society and produce a sharp rise in the death rate through famine. If huge new resources are discovered and developed, industrialism will advance more rapidly than ever, but the resulting pollution would ravage public health, overwhelm the environment, destroy the agricultural base, and cause a devastation of population. If technology succeeds in controlling pollution, population will soar and will outstrip the capacity of the land to produce food. And so on. No matter how the factors were varied, all growth projections ended in mass starvation, the exhaustion of resources, intolerable pollution, or some combination of the three. The only solution, the MIT team concluded, is for world population to be stabilized and for industrial growth to be halted. (This and other future scenarios are discussed in Chapter 23 ("Modernization and Social Change.")

These gloomy forecasts have attracted a great deal of criticism. Predicting the future is a risky matter at the best of times, and to project highly complex trends for many decades into the future, when one cannot be aware of subsequent factors that might affect them, is not a very reliable way of making forecasts. If data on agricultural production a century ago had been used to project trends into the 1980s, they would have pointed to global mass starvation at this moment. But the "green revolution" (the introduction of new hybrid species of high-yield grain) and highly mechanized agricultural techniques have greatly increased food production in a way that could not have been anticipated. In 1850, New York City was faced with a "horse crisis." The number of horses was increasing exponentially and the streets were piled with horse dung. A simple projection would have indicated that the streets of New York would by now be piled with dung to a height of fourteen stories, but this prediction could not take account of several intervening factors, most notably the replacement of horses by automobiles.

Yet although the precise calculations of the MIT team are open to criticism, their underlying logic is difficult to dispute. Nobody denies that the planet has a finite amount of resources or that it can tolerate only a limited amount of pollution. If world population continues to grow rapidly, if industrialism spreads around the world, and if pollution and resource depletion continue at an increasing rate—and all these things are happening—where is human society headed? The most optimistic answer to these questions would be that, one way or another, sweeping social changes await us.

Summary

1. Rapid population growth in a context of limited resources is probably the most serious social problem in the modern world.

2. Demography is the study of population composition and change. The principal factors involved in demographic change are the birth rate, the death rate, and the migration rate. Population growth rate, which takes place exponentially, is also influenced by the age structure of the population concerned.

3. Malthus pointed out that population tends to grow faster than the food supply. This problem has been averted in the past by new technologies and decreased birth rates in advanced industrial societies, but it has now become an acute one in less developed societies.

4. The main reason for rapid population growth is the fact that death rates have declined while birth rates have remained high. Moreover, the highest growth rates are in countries that already have large populations. Cultural values have always emphasized the desirability of large families, and these values have been slow to change.

5. The theory of demographic transition holds that birth rates will decline once developing societies become more industrialized. Specific factors in some societies, however, may inhibit or even prevent the transition. In particular, the poorest nations may have great difficulty in reaching an adequate level of industrialization.

6. The American birth and death rates are both relatively low, although the birth rate may increase slightly through an "echo effect" from the post-World War II "baby boom."

7. The United States has a population problem. Further U.S. population increases will tax natural resources and will place a disproportionate burden on other societies.

8. There are four possible strategies for reducing birth rates: family planning, the use of incentives, economic reform, and coercion.

9. Health is a social as well as a personal and physical matter: social factors affect patterns of disease, treatment, and mortality. These patterns vary greatly, both cross-culturally and within given societies. Epidemiological studies reveal different patterns among various categories of the American population.

10. All societies have a structured response to illness: in particular, there is a sick role and a healer role. In America, physicians form a powerful and prestigious profession, and medical treatment increasingly takes place in hospitals.

11. Two major problems of the American health-care system are its high costs to consumers and the unequal distribution of doctors and health-care facilities. Unlike all other modern industrial societies, the United States treats health care as a commercial enterprise rather than as a social service.

12. Ecology is the science of the relationship of organisms to their environments. Human ecology applies ecological principles to human populations. All organisms exist in ecosystems that are delicate and easily disrupted.

13. Pollution and resource depletion may have drastic effects on health and population dynamics in industrial societies. The MIT *Limits to Growth* study predicted ultimate population and economic collapse if current trends continue, although these findings have been strongly criticized. The underlying logic of the report's arguments, however, is difficult to refute.

Important Terms

demography (510)

birth rate (510)

fertility (510)

fecundity (510)

death rate (511)

life expectancy (511)

life span (511)

migration rate (511)

push (511)

pull (511)

growth rate (512)

exponential growth (512)

doubling time (512)

zero population growth (513)

age structure (513)

demographic transition (518)

family planning (523)

epidemiology (527)

sick role (527)

profession (529)

ecology (531)

human ecology (532)

ecosystem (532)

Suggested Readings

BROWN, MICHAEL. *Laying Waste*. New York: Pantheon, 1980.

An interesting and relevant account of the poisoning of the American environment by synthetic chemicals.

EHRLICH, PAUL R., et al. *Ecoscience: Population, Resources, Environment*. San Francisco: Freeman, 1977.

An excellent introduction to the science of ecology, by authors who emphasize the interrelationships among population growth, pollution, and resource depletion.

EPSTEIN, SAMUEL S. *The Politics of Cancer*. San Francisco: Sierra Club Books, 1978.

A powerful and controversial argument that modern industry has irresponsibly introduced a variety of cancer-causing substances into the environment.

KRAUSE, ELLIOT A. *Power and Illness: The Political Sociology of Health and Medical Care*. New York: Elsevier, 1977.

An important critique of the American health-care system, written from a conflict perspective.

MATRASS, JUDAH. *Introduction to Population: A Sociological Approach*. Englewood Cliffs, N.J.: Prentice-Hall, 1977.

A useful text that provides a general introduction to population dynamics.

PRESIDENTIAL COMMISSION ON WORLD HUNGER. *Overcoming World Hunger: The Challenge Ahead*. Washington, D.C.: U.S. Government Printing Office, 1980.

A clear and stark summary of the extent of hunger in the world and of the prospects for feeding the growing global population now and in the future.

TWADDLE, ANDREW C., and RICHARD M. HESSLER. *A Sociology of Health*. St. Louis: Mosby, 1977.

An excellent overview of the medical institution and the relationship between health, disease, and society.

U.S. BUREAU OF THE CENSUS. *Statistical Abstract of the United States*. Washington, D.C.: U.S. Government Printing Office.

An annual Census Bureau publication, containing up-to-date information on the American population and a remarkable variety of aspects of American life.

WRONG, DENNIS H. *Population and Society*. 3rd ed. New York: Random House, 1976.

A short and clear introduction to demography.

CHAPTER **21** *Urbanization and Urban Life*

Urbanization is one of the most significant trends in the modern world. The human animal has inhabited the planet for over 2 million years, yet our ancestors lived in small primary groups for all but five or six thousand years of that time. The growth of large cities that contain the bulk of a society's population is thus a very recent development, yet it is occurring all over the world at an astonishing speed. Our new, highly urbanized social environment offers challenges and opportunities that are without precedent in the history of the species.

A city is a permanent concentration of relatively large numbers of people who do not produce their own food. Large-scale urbanization has occurred only in the course of the past century. Until 1850 not more than 5 percent of the global population was urbanized, and no society had more than half of its members living in cities. In 1850 only one city, London, had more than 1 million inhabitants. Yet today all the industrialized societies of the world are heavily urbanized, and over 150 cities contain more than 1 million people. If present trends continue, there will be more than 500 cities with over 1 million inhabitants by the end of the century—60 of them containing over 5 million people, and 6 of them with populations of over 20 million. By then, more than half the world's people will live in cities (Salas, 1980).

The United States is a prime example of this trend. You probably live in an urban area: most Americans do. Yet the first U.S. census in 1790 recorded only twenty-four urban places, of which only two had populations of more than 25,000. In 1820 nearly 80 percent of the American people still lived on farms. But by 1920 half the population lived in urban areas; by 1950, 65 percent; and by 1980 the proportion had risen to over 73 percent. Two out of every three

Americans now reside in urban areas of at least 1 million people, and more than half of the population lives on 1 percent of the nation's land mass.

Urbanization has radically changed traditional patterns of social life and the nature of human communities. A *community* is a social group with a common territorial base and a shared sense of common interests and "belonging." The differences between a community of a few hundred people and one of several millions are so great that some sociologists doubt whether a large city can be usefully described as a "community" at all. An important task of sociology has been to analyze the nature of urban life and the differences between it and the life of traditional communities.

The study of cities is significant not only because of the impact that urban life has on city residents. Urbanization also implies that the culture and values of the city become dominant in the entire society, reaching through economic, political, and media networks into the most remote rural villages. And the study of cities is important for an additional reason: the city is the locus of nearly all the social problems that beset modern societies. In the United States the problems of the inner cities have become so severe, in fact, that many people doubt whether they can survive as livable environments at all.

The Urbanization Process

Why did it take so long for cities to develop, and why has urbanization spread so rapidly during the past century? The answer lies in the very nature of the city as a dense concentration of people who do not produce their own food. The emergence of cities depended initially on the development of agricultural techniques that were sufficiently advanced to permit a food surplus. Only when farmers could produce more food than they needed to sustain themselves was it possible for large numbers of people to abandon agriculture and to engage instead in other specialized roles, such as those of merchant or craft worker. These roles, unlike that of the farmer, require minimal land area and are more conveniently performed in a concentrated human population. Thus the city was born. But the subsequent growth and spread of cities was hampered for centuries by inadequate means of transporting and storing food. The larger the concentration of people in a city, the more food they require and the greater the distance it must be transported. Large-scale urbanization had to await the Industrial Revolution, which led to highly developed facilities for road, rail, sea, and air transport and advanced technologies for storage by such means as canning, refrigeration, and the use of chemical preservatives.

Figure 21.1 Throughout most of human history, communities were rarely much larger than this one in the Niger Republic. The initial growth of the city became possible only after the invention of agriculture, and the emergence of the huge modern city had to await the invention of industrialism.

Figure 21.2 The preindustrial city, such as this one in Morocco, differs radically from the city in modern industrial societies. It is very much smaller—we would call it a town, not a city—and its social organization is based on kinship networks. There is no "downtown," because commercial operations are spread throughout the city.

The Preindustrial City

The first urban settlements appeared between five and six thousand years ago in the Middle East and in Asia, on the fertile banks of the Nile, Tigris, Euphrates, Indus, and Yellow rivers. In later centuries techniques for domesticating animals and plants were either invented in, or diffused to, other parts of the world, and urban settlements began to appear elsewhere in Asia and the Middle East, in Europe, in Central and South America, and in North and West Africa.

By modern standards, the earliest of these settlements were so small that we would hardly consider them cities at all. The biblical city of Ur occupied only about 220 acres, and even Babylon, one of the largest of these ancient settlements, covered a mere 3.2 square miles (Mumford, 1961). The small scale of the ancient cities resulted from several factors. The rudimentary agricultural techniques still in use could not produce a very large surplus; on average, it took about seventy-five farmers to support one city inhabitant. Facilities for communication and transport were primitive. Roads hardly existed (the wheel was unknown in many early settlements) and food usually had to be laboriously carried by human beings or animals from farming areas to the cities. In the first few centuries A.D.,

Rome became the largest of all the preindustrial cities, but its population never numbered more than a few hundred thousand people. The major urban settlements that developed after the collapse of the Roman Empire were also not very populous. These medieval cities had poor sanitation and a total lack of sewage facilities; as a result, they suffered periodic epidemics and plagues, which sometimes wiped out more than half their population in a matter of weeks. The most notorious epidemic, the "Black Death," killed at least a quarter of the population of Europe as it spread across the continent between the years 1348 and 1350. Even in later centuries, urban development took place slowly until the spread of international trade led to the growth of new cities, such as Venice and Genoa, at the commercial centers of the world.

Small as all these preindustrial cities were, they revolutionized human social organization. The relatively large market offered by the urban population encouraged occupational specialization and an increasingly refined division of labor. The cities became a crossroads for trade, communication, and ideas, and the center of learning and innovation. Economic and political institutions became more complex. The city-state, in which an urban settlement dominated its hinterland, became the typical political unit and the source of legal and military authority.

The preindustrial city differed from the modern industrial city in features other than size. As Gideon Sjoberg (1960) points out, kinship networks were the basis of social organization within these cities. Class or caste systems were generally very rigid, and there was little social mobility. With rare exceptions, such as some of the ancient Greek city-states, governments were monarchies or oligarchies. There was usually no separate commercial district; the equivalent of "downtown" was the political and religious center of the community. Traders and artisans worked at home, using their houses as shops, and people following particular trades or crafts often lived and worked in distinct parts of the city. The city itself was commonly divided into "quarters" for various occupational, religious, or other social groups. In many cases the quarters were walled off from one another and their inhabitants locked into their own districts at night. In medieval Europe, for example, Jews were confined to "ghetto" areas of the city. Traces of ancient quarters can still be found in many North African towns today.

The Industrial City

As we have seen, it is no accident that the rapid growth and spread of cities coincided with the advance of the Industrial Revolution. The huge modern city must rest on an industrial base. It relies for its existence on the high productivity of mechanized agriculture, on sophisticated communications, transport, and storage facilities, and on the variety of specialized, nonagricultural jobs that industrialism creates. In 1790 only 5 percent of the American population lived in cities; today less than 5 percent work on farms. So advanced are our agricultural techniques that this relatively tiny labor force not only abundantly fulfills the food requirements of the remaining 95 percent of the population but also produces a food surplus available for export to other nations.

There are notable differences between the typical cities of advanced industrial societies and those of less developed societies that have only recently embarked on the modernization process. As we saw in Chapter 20 ("Population

Figure 21.3 A large modern city like Toronto requires an industrial base: its citizens work mostly in offices and factories, and the large, densely settled population must rely on food imported from elsewhere.

and Health"), social changes in less developed societies have resulted in a spectacular population increase, often beyond the capacity of the agricultural base to support it. Displaced rural migrants flock to the cities in search of work, only to find that there is none. Industrial development has not yet created enough jobs, and the migrants cannot be absorbed. Many cities in these countries consequently have a large homeless and unemployed population, and are surrounded by settlements of impoverished squatters.

Cities in the more advanced industrial societies rarely face this problem and continue to absorb rural migrants who have come to the urban area in search of better jobs. The larger cities in these societies generally have a fairly similar form. The urban area contains a *central city,* often inhabited by a small number of the very wealthy and a large number of the very poor. The central city is typically surrounded by *suburbs,* primarily residential areas that have grown up around the city as the urban population has expanded. This combined area is called a *metropolis,* and it forms an economic and geographic unity. In several advanced industrial societies, metropolitan areas have expanded to such an extent that they have merged with adjacent metropolises. The result is a *megalopolis,* a virtually unbroken urban tract consisting of two or more central cities and their surrounding suburbs. If current trends persist, most inhabitants of industrial societies will eventually live in sprawling megalopolises containing many millions of people and stretching in some instances for hundreds of miles—a far cry from our ancestral communities of a handful of cave dwellers.

The Nature of Urban Life

What are the defining characteristics of urban life, and in what ways does the urban community differ from the small rural community? A good deal of sociological effort over the past century has gone into attempting to answer this question. Some sociologists have taken a pessimistic and dismal view of urban life, claiming that it imposes severe strains on human relationships. Others have delighted in the many advantages and diverse opportunities that urban living is supposed to offer.

Figure 21.4 In many parts of the world, cities are surrounded by squatter settlements. These settlements, like this one in southern Africa, are occupied by people who have left agricultural work in the countryside in search of better jobs. All too often, however, the city, already greatly overpopulated, has no jobs to offer.

Figure 21.5 These contrasting paintings suggest the differences between small-scale, traditional communities and the large-scale urban environment of today. The first picture, Peasant Dance, *by Pieter Brueghel the elder, was painted about 1567. The work captures the features of what Tönnies called the* Gemeinschaft—*its intimacy of interpersonal relationships and sense of community solidarity. The second picture,* The Subway, *was painted in 1950 by George Tooker. This work reflects some of the features of the* Gesellschaft—*its anonymity and lack of shared commitment. But while there is some truth in both of these portraits, the features of each are exaggerated. It is unlikely that the peasant community was always so sociable, and the modern city is hardly so impersonal.*

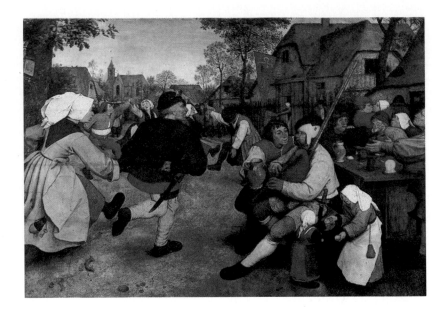

Gemeinschaft and Gesellschaft

Ferdinand Tönnies (1855–1936) was one of the first sociologists to examine the differences between urban and rural communities. His analysis, first published in Germany in 1887, has become a sociological classic and remains influential. Tönnies made a distinction between two forms of social grouping: the *Gemeinschaft* and the *Gesellschaft,* which in Chapter 4 ("Society") we roughly translated as "community" and "association."

The *Gemeinschaft* is a small community in which most people know each other. Interpersonal relationships are close, people are oriented toward the interests and activities of the group as a whole, and they have a strong feeling of unity. People share the same values, and social control over any deviance is exercised through informal means, such as gossip and personal persuasion. Kinship ties are strong, and social life centers on the family.

The *Gesellschaft,* on the other hand, contains a large population in which most people are strangers to one another. Relationships are impersonal and are often based on the functional need that people have for one another rather than on any emotional commitment. People are oriented toward personal rather than group goals, and they do not

necessarily hold the same values. Social control cannot be effectively applied by informal methods, so laws and formal sanctions have to be used to ensure social order. Tradition and custom no longer have a strong influence on individual behavior, and kinship ceases to be the most important basis of social organization. In short, urbanization implies that the community with strong interpersonal bonds is replaced by an association of individuals, most of whose relationships are temporary and impersonal.

The Chicago School

Tönnies's work influenced sociologists at the University of Chicago in the 1920s and 1930s. These sociologists, notably Robert Park, Louis Wirth, and Ernest Burgess, were especially interested in the problems of the city, and their work laid the foundations for modern urban sociology.

The classic statement of the Chicago School's position is contained in the essay "Urbanism as a Way of Life," published by Wirth in 1938. In it, Wirth drew not only on the work of Tönnies but also on that of another German sociologist, Georg Simmel (1858–1918). Simmel had pointed out that residents of modern cities receive a constant barrage of stimuli and impressions. If they took every

person they met seriously, or responded to each new situation with excitement and surprise, social life would be almost impossible. The high population density in cities, Simmel argued, forces people to take an offhand, matter-of-fact attitude toward their environment and to treat most people impersonally. Elaborating on this theme, Wirth emphasized three distinctive features of the city: its *size,* its *population density,* and its *social diversity.* These three features combine to produce a style of life that is much more anonymous than that found in small communities. Individuals become almost insignificant in the city, and cannot know more than a tiny proportion of their fellows. Urban residents no doubt are acquainted with far more people than villagers are, but they know these people in a more superficial and transitory way. The inhabitants of the city interact with one another largely in terms of highly specific roles—for example, as street vendor, banker, grocer, or mail carrier—and not as whole persons. Relationships are generally based not on affection and trust but on rational self-interest. The roles that the city resident plays in relation to others are usually a means to pursuing or maintaining economic advantages. "The clock and the traffic signal," Wirth remarked, "are symbolic of the basis of our social order in the urban world." The city, in his view, consists of a large number of people who are essentially alone in the midst of the crowd: though physically very close to one another, they are socially very distant.

Wirth pointed out that cities have more diverse populations than small communities. Urban areas therefore tend to become segregated along class, racial, or ethnic lines as people of similar background congregate together. Moreover, the division of labor in the city is far more elaborate than that in a small community. This specialization of jobs and services leads to the development of areas that have specific functions and characteristics, such as Hollywood, Beverly Hills, Wall Street, Broadway, the Tenderloin, or Beacon Hill. Confronted with this range of life-styles and personalities, the city resident becomes more tolerant of diversity and deviance than someone living in a small rural community. Urban residents are therefore more *relativistic:* that is, they are less likely to take their own viewpoints for granted and more likely to see the validity of other viewpoints and life-styles. Paradoxically, however, it is sometimes difficult to maintain a sense of individuality in the anonymous mass environment of the city. Urban services and facilities must be uniform in the interests of efficiency, and as a result they cannot take individual differences into account.

Figure 21.6   Although an earlier generation of sociologists was inclined to emphasize the impersonality of life in the city, modern researchers have found that many urban areas (particularly "ethnic villages") display strong community solidarity and richly varied social relationships.

Urbanism: A Reassessment

The work of the Chicago School tended to be rather pessimistic about urban life. In this respect it conformed to a long tradition of antiurban bias that has existed in American life from the time of Jefferson to the present day. Other peoples, from the Greeks and Romans to contemporary Europeans, have unstintingly praised the city as the center of intellectual and cultural life. (Even such words as "civilized" and "urbane" derive from Latin words referring to the city.) Americans, on the other hand, have always tended to consider urban life somewhat distasteful, and have felt that the good life is essentially one of neighborliness in a small, intimate community. The work of the Chicago School may have been distorted by this traditional view, as well as two other factors: most of its members had small-town origins themselves, and they did almost all their research in the Chicago central city at a time when it was in a state of severe social disorganization. Several sociologists have argued that Wirth's analysis contains unconscious biases and is in need of reassessment (for example, Greer, 1962; Stein, 1964; Wilensky, 1966; Faris, 1967; Sennet, 1970).

One such reevaluation has been provided by Herbert Gans (1962a, 1962b, 1968). He suggests that although Wirth's analysis may still have some relevance to the central cities, it does not apply to the outlying metropolitan areas. Even within the central city, Gans finds thriving communities. Some of them are restricted to specific neighborhoods and often take the form of "urban villages." In these communities, which are primarily ethnic neighborhoods, kinship ties remain very strong, and there is a genuine sense of community loyalty and shared values. Other communities consist of scattered individuals whose shared interests and pursuits give them a sense of common identity that transcends their physical distance. Urban artists, writers, or intellectuals, for example, may form a community without actually living in the same area of the city. Other research in Chicago by Gerald Suttles (1970) has shown that strong feelings of community solidarity exist in slum neighborhoods. Suttles found that residents were often acutely aware of the boundaries of their communities and strongly identified with their own neighborhoods.

A fair reassessment of the nature of urban life must take account of both its drawbacks and its advantages. There is little doubt that urban life involves more impersonality and possibly more isolation than life in a traditional rural community. Urban life separates people from the web of close community relationships, and it subjects them to the irritations of bureaucratic social organization. It cuts them off from the beauty of the natural environment and exposes them to too many people, too much noise, and too much pollution. It immerses them in social problems such as poverty, racial conflict, drug addiction, and crime.

But rural life is not all wine and roses. The traditional community lacks many of the comforts and amenities of the city. Large urban populations can support a cultural life of a richness and diversity never found in a small community. The city allows occupational specialization and thus far greater opportunities for fulfilling talents. Its anonymity is something for which many people are grateful. The close relationships of the small community can too often mean that everyone pries into everyone else's affairs. Nonconformists thrive in the more tolerant atmosphere of the city, where behavior that might scandalize a traditional community is ignored or may even be accepted. The city provides a more cosmopolitan outlook, in contrast to the relatively narrow, conservative, and provincial outlook of the small community. Urban living thus offers a much greater opportunity for intellectual and personal freedom.

Urban Ecology

An important contribution of the Chicago School was its emphasis on an *ecological approach* to urban analysis.

The Ecological Approach

Ecology, a natural science concerned with the relationship of living organisms to their environment, has been usefully adapted to the study of patterns of urban development and land use. Cities do not dot the earth randomly, nor do they grow in random fashion. They develop as the result of a complex interplay of environmental and social factors.

Several factors in the natural environment determine the location of cities. Large cities, for example, are generally not found in inhospitable zones—jungles, deserts, polar regions, or at very high altitudes. Most major cities developed from villages and towns that grew up along shorelines or navigable rivers or, more recently, railroads. These settlements became centers of trade and communication and thus had the potential to develop into cities. The growth pattern of an urban settlement is also influenced by factors in the natural environment. For example, mountains must be skirted, lakes and marshes must be avoided if they cannot be drained, and housing and industry must be placed conveniently near water and raw materials.

Social factors also influence the appearance and development of cities. For instance, a city may be established as a result of a political decision: Brazil created the new capital of Brasilia in the midst of the jungle in order to stimulate the economic development of the country's interior; Great Britain has built several entirely new towns to relieve population pressure on existing cities. Political decisions may also mark a city for destruction: Carthage, for example, was razed by the ancient Romans, and Dresden was leveled by American bombs in World War II. Prevailing ideas about architecture and the desirability of town planning also influence urban growth patterns. The grid pattern of Manhattan, since copied by many American cities, is the product of a planning decision made in 1811. The actual use to which land is put often depends on economic factors, because owners tend to devote their land to whatever use gives them the greatest gain. Land on a hillside, with a commanding view of a valley below, is of more value for upper-class residential property than for factories, which are more conveniently situated on flat land near major transport arteries.

The location of particular social groups is also influenced by ecological factors. Certain kinds of land use, such as parking lots and junkyards, quickly generate urban blight in the surrounding area, even if there was little decay there to begin with. The intrusion of such forms of land use, or the arrival of a group considered "undesirable" by existing residents, frequently results in a mass departure of the original inhabitants. The exodus is not an immediate one, however. The first intrusions may pass unnoticed, but at a certain stage, the "tipping point," older residents seem to agree that the character of the neighborhood is irreversibly changed and that they should leave if possible. The location of the neighborhoods of different groups is thus related to such factors as their relative incomes, which determine where they can afford to live, and to their feelings of group solidarity or prejudice against outsiders.

Social inventions such as the automobile and mass transit systems also influence urban patterns. If workers have to walk to their factories every day, their homes must be near the workplace, but if they can drive to work, they can easily live fifteen miles away. If large numbers of the urban labor force move away from the city center, services and facilities will tend to follow them, perhaps leaving a vacuum that is filled by deterioration.

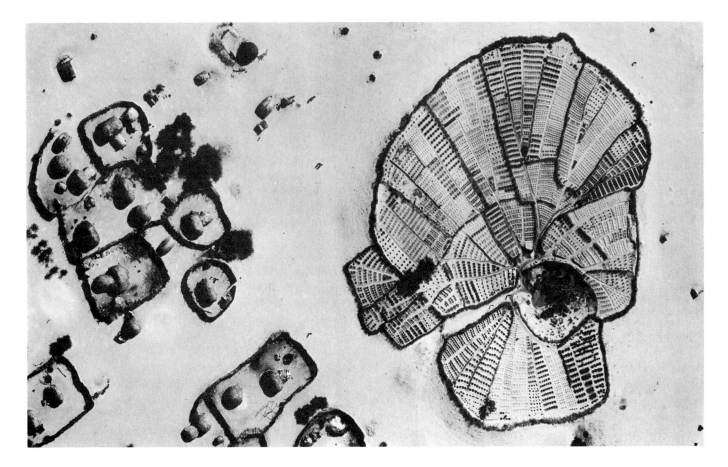

Figure 21.7 The ecological approach to urban analysis focuses on the social and environmental factors that influence the physical arrangements of human settlements. In this photograph of a small community in the Sahara desert, you will notice that the houses (left) are set some distance away from the oasis (right). The reason for this arrangement is that the gardens on which these people depend for food must be situated as closely as possible to the water source, so that the labor of carrying water to the plants is minimized. The factors that affect the physical layout of a large modern city are not so easily determined, but the same ecological principles apply.

Patterns of Urban Growth

Several theorists have offered specific models that help to explain the distribution patterns of people and facilities within the physical space of a modern city. Three theories have attracted special attention: the concentric-zone theory, the sector theory, and the multiple-nuclei theory. Each of these theories is represented diagrammatically in Figure 21.8.

The Concentric-Zone Theory

Using the large city of Chicago as their principal source of evidence, Robert Park, Ernest Burgess, and R. D. McKenzie (1925) suggested that a modern city typically consists of a series of concentric zones. These zones radiate out from the downtown center, and each successive zone contains a different type of land use. The first zone is the *central business district,* containing retail stores, banks, hotels, theaters, business and professional offices, railroad and bus stations, and city government buildings. The second zone is the *zone in transition.* The transition is caused by the steady encroachment of business and industry into what were once residential neighborhoods, often containing the homes of the wealthy. This process is the classic pattern of slum growth. Wealthy families leave their old homes near the city center under competition for space from the central business district. The residences are then converted to apartment dwellings, rooming houses, and marginal business establishments such as restaurants. These zones generally deteriorate into shabbiness and readily become ghettos for minority groups or the center of the urban vice trade. The third zone is the *zone of working people's homes,* consisting of aging, relatively inexpensive family residences and apartments. The homes are superior to those in the zone of transition, however, and are often filled with people who have escaped from the second zone. The fourth zone is the *residential zone,* inhabited mainly by small-business operators and professionals. Land use here is less intensive than in the more central zones. There are a large number of single-family residences, and the proportion of homes that are owned rather than rented is quite high. The final zone is the *commuters' zone,* consisting of small towns from which the affluent travel to their work in the city. The neighborhoods in the commuters' zone are beyond the city limits, but most of their inhabitants work in the urban area.

This model is, of course, merely an ideal type that stresses the relationship between social status and distance from the city center. Many factors, such as environmental obstacles or determined resistance by residents of one zone to invaders from the next, may influence the actual pattern of development.

The Sector Theory

Homer Hoyt (1939) proposed the sector theory of urban development as a better model for the growth of American cities since the appearance of the automobile. Hoyt recognized that cities grow outward from the center, but he saw growth as taking place largely in "sectors" of land use—wedge-shaped areas that extend from the center to the periphery, rather like slices cut from a pie. As the city

THREE MODELS OF THE INTERNAL STRUCTURE OF CITIES

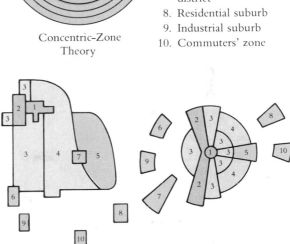

1. Central business district
2. Wholesale light manufacturing
3. Low-class residential
4. Middle-class residential
5. High-class residential
6. Heavy manufacturing
7. Outlying business district
8. Residential suburb
9. Industrial suburb
10. Commuters' zone

Concentric-Zone Theory

Multiple-Nuclei Theory   Sector Theory

Source: Adapted from Chauncy D. Harris and Edward L. Ullman, "The Nature of Cities," *Annals of the American Academy of Political and Social Science,* 242 (November 1945).

Figure 21.8 This diagram shows the three theories that have been proposed to describe typical patterns of development in modern cities: the concentric-zone theory, the sector theory, and the multiple-nuclei theory. The figure shows the total number of categories (zones, sectors, and nuclei, ten in all) presented in all three theories, and places them simultaneously within each of the three models.

expands, both low- and high-rent areas move outward, but the area in which they originated may keep its character and is not necessarily abandoned. Nor do upper-class residential areas encircle the city entirely. They tend to cluster at certain points on the boundary, usually on the outer edge of high-rent sectors. Industrial areas, too, do not necessarily form a concentric zone. They may also take a wedge-shaped form because they spread outward along river valleys, watercourses, and railroad lines. Hoyt's theory, too, is merely an ideal type, one that may provide a better model for at least some cities than the concentric-zone theory. It does not represent a universal pattern, and specific exceptions to it have been found—for example, in the case of Boston's Beacon Hill, a midtown upper-class residential area that has retained its character for several generations (Firey, 1947).

The Multiple-Nuclei Theory

This theory, proposed by C. D. Harris and Edward Ullman (1945), places less emphasis on the downtown business area. Instead, it suggests that a city has a series of nuclei, each of which is the center of a specialized area. In addition to the business district, for example, there may be "bright lights" areas, light- or heavy-manufacturing areas, or government administrative centers. Each of these nuclei influences the character and development of the surrounding district. The nuclei develop for several reasons. Some activities require specialized facilities—for example, the commercial area needs easy public access, and the port area needs a waterfront. Some activities benefit from being concentrated in one district—for example, retail outlets draw more customers, and financial and business institutions benefit from easy communication. Certain activities, such as industrial manufacturing and entertainments, cannot be reconciled in the same area and therefore tend to be segregated. Like the other models, the multiple-nuclei theory fits some cities better than others. It seems most applicable to those cities that have developed since the arrival of the automobile and therefore have more decentralization of facilities.

Each of the theories provides a way of analyzing urban development patterns—no easy task when the cities are constantly changing and when new developments are being superimposed on older patterns. We have to remember, too, that these models are derived from American data and may not apply to cities in other countries. In societies in the early stages of industrialization, for example, the most prestigious residences are usually at the center of the city, not in the suburbs. The city center is usually focused on religious and political institutions rather than on business. Commercial activity is scattered throughout the city, not concentrated away from private residences.

The American City and Its Problems

Most Americans live in urban areas, but this does not mean that they live in the central cities. In fact, slightly more Americans reside in the suburbs of metropolitan areas than the central cities themselves, and many others live in urban areas with relatively small populations. The Bureau of the Census regards any locality with more than 2500 inhabitants as an urban area, and it deliberately ignores the boundaries of cities and suburbs in its analysis of urban data. The bureau recognizes that the political boundaries are less important than the social, economic, and communications network that integrates various urban communities into one unit, and it analyzes large-scale urban settlements through the concept of a *Standard Metropolitan Statistical Area* (SMSA). An SMSA is any area that contains a city (or a combination of a city and its surrounding suburbs) that has a total population of 50,000 or more. At present the bureau recognizes 279 SMSAs, and these urban areas contain about 73 percent of the American population.

The bureau also takes account of the megalopolis, which it calls a *Standard Consolidated Area* (SCA), and it recognizes a total of thirteen areas that have developed or will shortly develop into continuous urban sprawls of this kind. The outstanding megalopolis at present is the chain of hundreds of cities and suburbs on the eastern seaboard from Massachusetts to Virginia—a tract that runs through ten states and contains over 40 million people. Other important megalopolises are currently developing in California (San Francisco–Los Angeles–San Diego), Florida (Jacksonville-Tampa-Miami), Texas (Dallas-San Antonio-Houston), and the Great Lakes area (Chicago-Pittsburgh). (See Figure 21.9)

URBAN REGIONS: YEAR 2000

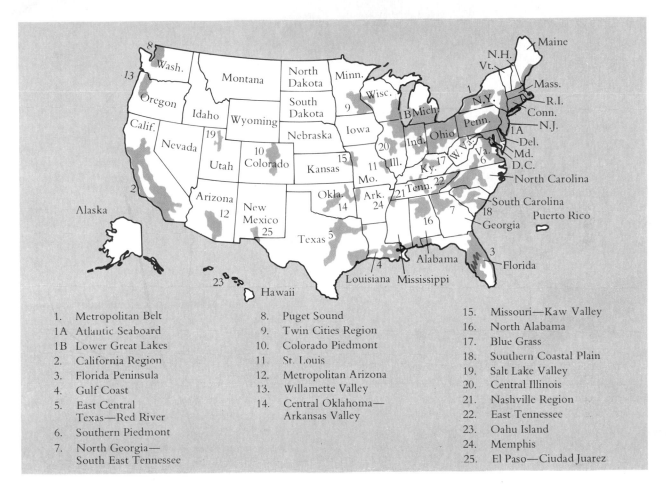

1.	Metropolitan Belt	8.	Puget Sound	15.	Missouri—Kaw Valley
1A	Atlantic Seaboard	9.	Twin Cities Region	16.	North Alabama
1B	Lower Great Lakes	10.	Colorado Piedmont	17.	Blue Grass
2.	California Region	11.	St. Louis	18.	Southern Coastal Plain
3.	Florida Peninsula	12.	Metropolitan Arizona	19.	Salt Lake Valley
4.	Gulf Coast	13.	Willamette Valley	20.	Central Illinois
5.	East Central	14.	Central Oklahoma—	21.	Nashville Region
	Texas—Red River		Arkansas Valley	22.	East Tennessee
6.	Southern Piedmont			23.	Oahu Island
7.	North Georgia—			24.	Memphis
	South East Tennessee			25.	El Paso—Ciudad Juarez

Source: Presidential Commission on Population Growth and the American Future, *Population Growth and the American Future* (Washington, D.C.: U.S. Government Printing Office, 1972).

Figure 21.9 By the year 2000, many regions of the country will contain unbroken urban tracts, or megalopolises, some of them stretching for hundreds of miles and containing tens of millions of people.

Figure 21.10 Suburban living has often been scorned and satirized, yet is has a very strong appeal for many Americans—including, obviously, the millions who have fled the central cities over the last few decades.

The Suburbs

One of the most outstanding features of urbanization in the United States is the rapid growth of the suburbs—a development that is largely responsible for the current plight of the central cities. In 1920, some 17 percent of the American people lived in the suburbs; in 1930, 19 percent; in 1940, 20 percent; in 1950, 24 percent. The rate of suburban growth during that period was steady but slow. In the ensuing years, however, the drift to the suburbs became a mass flight: 33 percent of the population lived in the suburbs in 1960 and 37 percent in 1970. Almost within a single generation, more Americans had come to live in the suburbs than in the central cities or rural areas.

Several factors made the movement to the suburbs possible. One was the construction of federally subsidized highways, which made it easier for workers to commute to the city. Another was the shortage of central-city housing. Land was exhausted in the older cities, and a construction industry that had mastered techniques for mass home building began to exploit the outlying areas. The postwar boom in the American economy made home ownership available to millions of Americans for the first time, and they were aided by ample mortgages from the Veterans Administration and the Federal Housing Authority. Suburban living, too, seemed highly attractive. It offered an ideal compromise between urban and rural life: one could be close enough to the city to enjoy its amenities but far away enough to avoid its inconveniences.

Life in the suburbs has been the object of a great deal of scorn and satire. It is often thought that the suburbs are dull, homogeneous middle-class bastions, in which the residents are obsessed with the neatness of their lawns and "keeping up with the Joneses." There may be some truth in this picture, but it is probably exaggerated. Suburban residents in general are doubtless more politically conservative, more morally conventional, and more oriented toward family life and the local community than city residents. But the suburbs—many of which are now predominantly working-class or include a high proportion of residents from diverse racial and ethnic backgrounds—appear to be much more heterogeneous and less unlike some central-city neighborhoods than popular beliefs allow (B. Berger, 1961; Gans, 1967; Clark and Sterlieb, 1979). The character of many suburbs, in fact, is changing rapidly. A large and rapidly growing proportion of suburbanites now work in their own suburbs, or in other suburbs nearby. Factories, superhighways, and office complexes are sprouting up, and many of the symptoms generally associated with urban decay are appearing. In fact, there has even been an exodus of some of the wealthier residents to suburbs still farther afield.

The Central Cities

The Greek philosopher Aristotle once described the city as "a common life to a noble end." That is hardly the kind of description we would apply to central cities in America today, especially those of the older metropolises. The word "city" is more likely to conjure forth images of decaying housing, rundown schools, high rates of crime and drug addiction, racial segregation and tension, overburdened welfare rolls, and deteriorating public services. Why are so many social problems concentrated in the central cities of metropolitan areas?

An underlying factor is the growth of the suburbs, which has largely removed the middle class and its local tax money from the central cities. These cities have therefore had to rely for their income on a population that consists disproportionately of poor people, making it generally impossible to compensate for the shrinkage of revenue by raising taxes. The poorer city residents simply cannot afford to pay higher taxes. In addition, higher taxes are likely to act as a further incentive to wealthier residents and businesses to move to the suburbs, where property taxes are frequently lower. To make matters worse, the central city has comparatively more ancient buildings, a far higher crime rate, older public facilities and schools, and a greater proportion of unemployed residents. As a result, it must spend much more money per capita on fire and police protection, building maintenance, transport systems, schools, and welfare if it is to offer services comparable to those of the suburbs. Central-city residents not only pay more than many suburban residents in local taxes; they also get less for their money.

Under these circumstances it is hardly surprising that the urban environment has continued to deteriorate and that the suburbs have continued to expand. As the suburbs have expanded, commerce and industry have deserted the central cities to take advantage of this new source of customers and labor. New York City alone has lost more than 700,000 jobs since 1970—enough to support about 1.5 million people, or a city the size of San Diego. And because racial and class divisions tend to overlap, the suburbs have been and remain primarily white, while the cities are becoming steadily more black. Almost three-fourths of black Americans now live in metropolitan areas, and of these, 80 percent live in the central cities, mostly in ghettos. Metropolitan residential patterns have thus created a state of segregation almost as effective as that once imposed in the South by law. This segregation, some of whose effects are considered in Chapter 15 ("Education"), is proving nearly impossible to eliminate. Unlike most other forms of segregation, which involve overt acts by some people against others, this kind cannot be abolished virtually overnight through legislation.

As a whole, the residents of the central cities are rather more heterogeneous than those of the suburbs. The city contains a variety of racial and ethnic groups, and despite the loss of much of its middle class, it has a greater social-class heterogeneity than most individual suburbs. Herbert Gans (1962a) distinguishes five basic categories of central-city residents. The *cosmopolites* are those who choose to live in the city because of its unrivaled cultural facilities—artists, students, writers, intellectuals, and professional people. The *unmarried or childless* are mostly young adults who come to the city to be close to job opportunities. They rent apartments until they get married, and then tend to move to the suburbs, where they buy homes and raise their families. The *ethnic villagers* are ethnic groups who retain their traditional ways of life in their own neighborhoods, which, though they may be physically deteriorating, are socially highly structured. The ethnic villagers have a strong sense of community and tend to limit their contact with the rest of the metropolitan area. The *deprived* are the very poor, the handicapped, and the nonwhite population, who are concentrated in the most undesirable residential areas. The *trapped* are those who would like to leave the central city but cannot. This category consists of people who are downwardly mobile or chronically unemployed, people who are very old or living on small fixed incomes, and people whose neighborhood is being invaded by other ethnic or racial groups but who cannot afford to get out.

City Planning

City planning is not new; the Romans, the Egyptians, and other people practiced it more than 2000 years ago. The object of city planning varies, however, from time to time and place to place. The intention may be to encourage growth or to restrict it, to develop land for building purposes or to preserve it for parks, to make urban life more efficient or to make it more beautiful.

Figure 21.11

"It's called grass; it's softer to walk on than concrete."

The goals of city planning in the United States have often been vague and inconsistent. Many plans, when finally adopted, are more the outcome of a political conflict between competing interest groups than of reasoned and objective analysis. Any city plan involves clashes of interests and values. Do we construct a new highway from the suburb to the city center in the interests of the suburbanites, or do we refuse to build it in the interests of the central-city working-class residents through whose neighborhoods the highway will run? Do we want our downtown area to be neat, clean, and quiet, or would we prefer a more hectic and colorful scene, complete with street vendors and rows of small stores?

For many years attempts have been made to solve some of the problems of the central cities through *urban renewal*—in other words, through demolishing "undesirable"

areas and replacing them with something else. Two difficulties arise: determining what is "undesirable" and determining what the "something else" should be. In Boston, for example, urban renewal involved the demolition of an "undesirable" residential neighborhood that also happened to be an Italian "ethnic village." Herbert Gans (1962b) found that this renewal program was deeply resented by the residents, some of whom grieved for years at the destruction of their community.

In many cities lower-class residential areas have been demolished only to be replaced by more profitable forms of construction: luxury apartments and high-rise office buildings. Urban renewal programs have destroyed more than ten times as many low-income housing units as they have replaced. The result has often been an increased demand for low-income housing that leads to even higher rents for the poor. There is also a concern that many of the "renewed" urban centers are uninteresting and arid places to live in or even to walk about in. Jane Jacobs (1961), one critic of many urban renewal programs, writes contemptuously of "cultural centers that are unable to support a good bookstore . . . civic centers that are avoided by everyone but bums . . . promenades that go from no place to nowhere and have no promenaders." Planners have been slow to recognize that we cannot tear down neighborhoods and displace their residents without providing alternative accommodations for them; and they frequently seem unaware that new construction projects must blend harmoniously with the living city.

One major obstacle to urban reform and effective metropolitan planning is the fragmentation of metropolitan governments. The problems of the metropolis—highways, mass transit, pollution, school segregation, police protection, public utilities—are regional. The city and the suburbs are politically separate but interdependent in all other respects. The suburbs are viable only because a large number of their residents are able to work in the central cities. Moreover, suburban residents rely on many city services that they do not support through their taxes. Yet some metropolitan regions have dozens of different local authorities, each jealously guarding its own domain in the name of the American tradition of "community control." Los Angeles, for example, has a small central city, a county of nine other cities, and sixty-seven smaller self-governing communities.

A rational solution to many problems would be to recognize that the political boundaries between cities and suburbs are outdated. Each of the existing communities could retain some measure of local autonomy while being integrated into a single metropolitan unit with a common tax base. This is precisely the solution, in fact, that has been adopted by the Canadians for the Toronto metropolitan area and by the British for the Greater London area. There are a few examples of this kind of arrangement in the United States, such as the metropolitan government of the seven counties surrounding the Twin Cities of Minneapolis and St. Paul. A rather different solution has been arrived at in Texas, allowing cities of over 100,000 population to unilaterally annex unincorporated suburbs within five miles of their borders. Houston, for example, has escaped some of the problems of other cities by simply including adjacent suburbs within its boundaries, whether the suburban residents liked it or not; as a result, the city has 50 percent more territory than it did fifteen years ago, and it retains a healthy tax base. There is little sign, however, that these examples will be widely adopted in the United States. The suburbanites, who have more political muscle than the central-city residents, usually believe that they have everything to gain by preserving their distance from the troubled central cities.

Current Trends

There are a number of significant trends in the current urban scene, some of them representing a continuation of existing conditions, while others are an abrupt departure from them.

Urban Finances

Many of the older central cities are in a state of financial crisis and some, including even New York, have been on the brink of bankruptcy. The main reason is the loss of people and jobs: during the 1970s population declined in eighteen of the nation's largest twenty-five cities. A second reason is that the unfavorable economic climate of the past few years has made citizens resistant to high local taxes and has led to cutbacks in federal aid to cities. The older cities are desperately in need of funds—not for ambitious new projects but merely to maintain or replace decaying facilities. Boston, for example, loses 80 million gallons of water a day—half the city's supply—because of leaks in its ancient system of pipes. The streets of New York have over 100,000 potholes of various sizes and shapes, with new holes appearing more quickly than the city can afford to repair the old ones. San Francisco has dozens of sewage overflows each year because the same pipes must handle both sewage and storm water (Herbers, 1978). Private funds for urban improvement are also in short supply, thanks in part to the refusal of many banks to lend mortgage money for the purchase or improvement of housing in inner-city areas. This practice is known as "redlining" (from the bankers' alleged habit of drawing red lines on a map around those areas they do not want to invest in). A 1978 National Training and Information Center study of mortgage activity in eight major cities found that many inner-city neighborhoods were virtually without loans for home purchase or improvement. The lack of both public and private financing is likely to accelerate the process of central-city deterioration.

Suburban Change

We have already noted that the suburbs are changing as many of the familiar urban problems reappear in a suburban setting. But other changes may be in the offing, for the suburbs were originally designed for a life-style that has been radically altered by the social changes of recent years. In the period of suburban expansion immediately after World War II, the "traditional" American family—a father who worked, a mother who was a housewife, and two or three children—was still common. Today less than 8 percent of American families fit that description, and the suburbs are simply not designed for the convenience of the more than 90 percent of families remaining—for people who do not need large, single-family houses, or who cannot afford two cars to get to and from two jobs in distant areas. By the end of the 1980s, 45 percent of American households will be headed by a single person—never married, divorced, or widowed—for whom a single-family home may be inappropriate. In addition, a prerequisite for suburban living has always been the private automobile and a plentiful supply of cheap gasoline; the rising costs of both and periodic shortages of fuel must inevitably lessen the appeal of driving to the shopping center, and nearly everywhere else, let alone commuting daily from home to job. Precisely how the suburbs will change in response to these new conditions is not yet clear, but it seems certain that the suburban life-style will conform even less to the popular stereotype in the future than it already does now (Kowinski, 1980).

Sunbelt Growth

A major demographic shift is taking place in the United States as growing numbers of people migrate from the older cities of the Northeast and Midwest to the "sunbelt" cities of the South and Southwest. States such as Arizona, Texas, Colorado, Nevada, and Florida exert a dual appeal to "snowbelt" residents: they have a more favorable climate and offer better economic opportunities. While most large American cities lost population during the 1970s, "sunbelt" cities such as Houston, San Diego, San Antonio, Phoenix, San Jose, and Jacksonville all grew larger. The long-term consequences of this migration may be immense, for it signifies the slow demise of the old New York–Chicago axis of economic power and influence and the emergence of a new axis centered on Houston and Los Angeles and based on new, high-technology industries such as aerospace development or microchip production. Political power will inevitably follow this demographic and economic shift, and, indeed, the snowbelt has already lost several congressional seats to the sunbelt states (Perry and Watkins, 1978).

Rural Growth

Gallup polls since the mid-1960s have consistently shown that a majority of the population considers a small town or rural area to be the ideal place to live. A growing number of people are now acting on that opinion and are moving to such areas as southern New Hampshire, central Illinois, or the Ozark Mountains. Between 1970 and 1980 the population of nonmetropolitan areas grew 40 percent faster than that of metropolitan areas, leaving the former with a net gain of 3 million people. Most of these migrants are better educated and younger than those who remain behind; although their new environment offers less in earnings, they apparently consider its other features adequate compensation. This voluntary reversal of the general trend toward increasing urbanization appears to be historically unprecedented, in the United States or indeed anywhere else. (Some societies, such as China and the Soviet Union, have tried to slow urbanization by restricting migration from rural areas; others, like Cambodia and South Africa, have tried for political reasons to reverse urbanization by deporting city residents to the countryside; but in all these cases, urbanization has been checked only by the deliberate use of state power.) Whether this reverse migration will remain a relatively small-scale trend or heralds another significant demographic shift remains to be seen (Herbers, 1980).

Condominium Ownership

Home ownership is part of the American dream, and, in fact, the United States is one of the very few countries in which a majority of families do own their homes. (In most other Western nations, in contrast, house prices are far higher than in the United States and incomes are significantly lower, so a much smaller proportion of the population can afford to buy a home.) During the seventies, however, the average price of a new single-family home doubled to over $70,000, a figure beyond the means of most American families. For many Americans, then, home ownership is likely to take a different form: that of the condominium, a multiple-unit structure of which each tenant owns only a part. Condominiums typically take the form of either apartment buildings or densely built "townhouses," but in each case the effect is the same: to provide cheaper accommodations by reducing the costs of land and construction. This form of home ownership, virtually unknown a few years ago, represented about 5 percent of the housing stock by the end of the seventies and is becoming the norm so rapidly that by the turn of the century most American families are expected to live in condominiums of one kind or another.

Rent Controls

In communities all over the United States there is controversy about rent controls, which impose legal limits on the amount by which rents can be increased. These controls are understandably very popular among renters, and are particularly common in states where rent-control proposals can be placed on the ballot by voter initiatives. One reason these proposals are controversial is, of course, that they antagonize the landlords and their allies in the real estate industry. Another reason, however, is that rent controls could well become counterproductive and hurt the very people they were meant to help. If landlords and property developers feel they cannot get sufficient profit from apartment buildings, they will tend to convert existing buildings to condominiums and to produce new buildings for sale rather than for rent. In time, the stock of rental accommodation will be reduced, making it more scarce and increasing the pressure for higher rents. In extreme situations, landlords may simply "milk" older buildings; that is, they may extract whatever rent they can but reinvest none of it in building maintenance. This practice seems to have been especially prevalent in New York City, where landlords, unable to run some of their apartment houses profitably, simply let them go to ruin until they were abandoned. In many cases these buildings, insured for large sums, were then deliberately set on fire: in the South Bronx, an astonishing 30,000 buildings were burned in the ten years from 1967 to 1977, during which time a once respectable community was turned into an urban wasteland.

"Recycling" Buildings

Another fairly recent but increasingly common trend is that of "recycling" older buildings, or putting them to new uses. In the past, Americans paid little attention to the country's architectural heritage: when a building had served its purposes, the tendency was to tear it down and replace it. But changing economic conditions have made Americans look anew at some older buildings, and they have found in them a charm, a human scale, and a solidity of construction that are often absent from more modern structures. One form of recycling is "gentrification," in which middle-class people ("gentry") buy and renovate older buildings in central-city neighborhoods, turning rooming houses, warehouses, abandoned firehouses, and the like into single-family homes. Gentrification has radically altered formerly decaying neighborhoods such as Park Slope in Brooklyn, SoHo in Manhattan, Queen's Village in Philadelphia, and Adams-Morgan in Washington, D.C. In some cases, however, the process has displaced poorer residents who cannot afford to live in the upgraded neighborhoods. A second form of recycling is the renovation, through public funds, of deteriorating or abandoned central-city facilities, such as old markets. Twenty years ago these areas would have been targeted for "urban renewal," to be demolished and replaced by featureless highrise buildings. Instead, careful recycling has produced such immensely successful projects as Ghirardelli Square in San Francisco, the rehabilitated Skid Row in Sacramento, and Faneuil Hall in Boston—lively and colorful market areas that attract millions of visitors every year. Unlike so many

Figure 21.12 The South Bronx, with its acres of abandoned houses and apartments, has come to symbolize urban decay in America.

Figure 21.13 Boston's Faneuil Hall–Quincy Market area is an outstandingly successful renovation of a complex of abandoned buildings. Such "recycling" of older buildings is likely to become more common than the older strategy of "urban renewal," which all too often involved the destruction of neighborhood character and the construction, at huge expense, of featureless boxes of steel and concrete.

other urban-planning episodes, these renovations have not neglected the human element in the process that either brings a great city to life or else makes it an arid and sterile environment.

Summary

1. A city is a permanent concentration of fairly large numbers of people who do not produce their own food. Urbanization is one of the most significant trends in the modern world. It has radically altered the nature of human communities. Cities are also the primary locus of most modern social problems.

2. Urbanization requires the development of agricultural techniques and means of transporting and storing food. Preindustrial cities remained small, but industrialization has encouraged the growth of large cities. Industrial cities typically contain a central city and suburbs, which together form a metropolis. When metropolises merge, they form a megalopolis.

3. Tönnies's distinction between the small, intimate *Gemeinschaft* and the large, impersonal *Gesellschaft* has influenced theories of urbanism, particularly those of the

Chicago School. Wirth emphasized the size, population density, and social diversity of cities, which led to urban anonymity, heterogeneity, and relativism. Reassessments by later writers suggest that intimate communities do, in fact, exist in large cities.

4. The ecological approach attempts to explain the appearance and growth of cities in terms of influences from both the social and natural environment. Three main models of urban growth have been proposed: the concentric-zone theory, the sector theory, and the multiple-nuclei theory.

5. The United States is a highly urbanized society. Suburbs have expanded rapidly and now contain more people than central cities do. The central cities are in a state of crisis, largely as a result of the flight of middle-class residents and their local tax money to the suburbs. The population remaining in the central cities is relatively heterogeneous but also disproportionately poor.

6. City planning has focused recently on urban renewal, but many programs have been criticized for disrupting communities or penalizing the poor. A major obstacle to urban reform is the political boundaries between cities and suburbs. A rational solution would be to integrate all metropolitan communities for local tax purposes.

7. Current trends affecting urbanism include a financial crisis for many older cities; changes in the nature of suburban life; the growth of "sunbelt" cities; a new migration from metropolitan to nonmetropolitan areas; the spread of condominium ownership; increased pressures for rent controls; and the recycling of older buildings.

Important Terms

city (539)	concentric-zone theory (548)
community (540)	sector theory (549)
preindustrial city (541)	multiple-nuclei theory (550)
industrial city (542)	
central city (543)	Standard Metropolitan Statistical Area (SMSA) (550)
suburb (543)	
metropolis (543)	Standard Consolidated Area (SCA) (550)
megalopolis (543)	
Gemeinschaft (544)	urban renewal (554)
Gesellschaft (544)	
ecological approach (547)	

Suggested Readings

ABRAHAMSON, MARK. *Urban Sociology*. 2nd ed. Englewood Cliffs, N.J.: Prentice-Hall, 1980.

A succinct introduction to the field of urban sociology; the book is recommended for a good overview of the subject.

BANFIELD, EDWARD. *The Unheavenly City Revisited*. Boston: Little, Brown, 1974.

A controversial book about the problems of modern American cities, which, the author asserts, are much more healthy than most critics allow.

FEAGIN, JOE R. (ed.). *The Urban Scene: Myths and Realities*. 2nd ed. New York: Random House, 1979.

A useful selection of articles covering various aspects of contemporary urban life.

GANS, HERBERT J. *The Urban Villagers*. New York: Free Press, 1962.

An account of the tight-knit communities that are found in American cities. It focuses on a case study of the destruction through urban renewal of an Italian neighborhood in Boston.

JACOBS, JANE. *The Death and Life of Great American Cities*. New York: Random House, 1961.

A critical assessment of some urban renewal programs in American cities. Jacobs makes a number of suggestions for more constructive urban planning.

KARP, DAVID A. et al. *Being Urban*. Lexington, Mass.: Heath, 1976.

An interactionist analysis of urbanism, focusing on the meanings that city life has for urban residents.

MUMFORD, LEWIS. *The City in History*. New York: Harcourt Brace Jovanovich, 1961.

A rich and fascinating account of the rise and role of cities in history by one of the foremost experts in the field.

SALE, KIRKPATRICK. *Human Scale*. New York: Cloward, McCann, and Geoghegan, 1980.

An interesting discussion of urban planning by a writer who advocates small-scale developments as a means of countering urban impersonality.

VIDICH, ARTHUR, and JOSEPH BENSMAN. *Small Town in Mass Society*. Princeton, N.J.: Princeton University Press, 1958.

A report of a research study on a small town, showing how the community held a misconceived idea of its own autonomy and freedom from the influence of urban America.

CHAPTER **22** *Collective Behavior and Social Movements*

Most social behavior follows a regular and patterned course. People play their roles and interact with one another according to the norms that define the behavior expected in various situations. Consider social behavior in your own sociology lecture class. People arrive more or less on time, they seat themselves in an orderly way, they listen and take notes, they ask questions at appropriate points, and they leave when the lecture is over. There are an infinite number of other things that a group of students could do in a room, but in practice everyone behaves in a fairly predictable fashion.

But suppose that a fire suddenly breaks out in the room. Immediately, the norms that prevailed a few moments before are suspended, and social behavior becomes unstructured and unpredictable. It is even possible, although certainly not inevitable, that a panic will result. If this happens, cooperative behavior will break down. There will be a disorderly rush to the exits, even though this response will actually reduce everyone's chance of escape. It is also possible that there will be little panic, particularly if leaders emerge to supervise an orderly exit. But whether the crowd panics or not, its behavior is no longer guided by everyday norms.

Sociologists use the term "collective behavior" to refer to group behavior that is apparently not guided by the usual norms of conduct. Often, in fact, it seems that the people concerned are actually improvising new norms on the spot. We can say, then, that *collective behavior refers to relatively spontaneous and unstructured ways of thinking, feeling, and acting on the part of large numbers of people.* The concept includes a wide range of social behavior, much of it unusual or even bizarre: a crowd in panic, a lynch mob, a craze, fad, or fashion, rumors, riots, mass hysteria, and the ebb and

Figure 22.1 Collective behavior involves relatively unstructured social activity: the usual norms that govern conduct either break down or are ambiguous and confusing, and people are uncertain of what to do. This photograph shows some of these features: notice, for example, how the "body language" of members of the crowd reveals their uncertainty. Not all collective behavior is quite so dramatic, but the same basic principles apply.

flow of public opinion. We need only consider social action in a much more structured setting—say, in a formal organization such as a government bureaucracy—to appreciate the contrast between the more routine activities of human groups and these episodes of collective behavior.

There is another form of social behavior that can also disturb the established patterns of social life—sometimes in more profound and lasting ways. This is the behavior of people in social movements, such as those for women's liberation or against nuclear power. *A social movement consists of a large number of people who have joined together to bring about or to resist some social or cultural change.* Formerly, many sociologists regarded social movements as yet another type of collective behavior. Several of the early researchers of social movements were hostile to the movements' efforts to change society, and it was all too easy for them to dismiss these campaigns as examples of irrational collective behavior: they implied that if there was nothing much wrong with the status quo, then there must be something wrong with the people who challenged it. Today, however, most sociologists see social movements as an essentially separate phenomenon. It is true, of course, that some

movements—like the "hippie" counterculture of the sixties—seem to fit the definition of collective behavior. Such movements are loosely structured, their norms are flexible, they have few statuses and roles, and their goals are vague. But sociologists are now aware, in many cases through personal experience of the civil rights, antiwar, or women's liberation movements, that some social movements are highly structured, may endure for years, do hold clearly defined goals, and have well-established statuses, roles, and norms. For the analytic purposes of this chapter we shall regard collective behavior and social movements as distinct forms of social action, while still recognizing that there are sometimes similarities between them.

A Theory of Collective Behavior

The study of collective behavior is hindered by several problems. To begin with, the behavior is so unstructured that it may be difficult to find underlying regularities or to generalize from one specific incident to others. In addition, collective behavior often occurs as a spontaneous outburst.

It cannot easily be created or reproduced for the convenience of the sociologist, who may have to rely instead on the recollections (often contradictory and inaccurate) of untrained observers who were there at the time. A third problem is that the concept of "collective behavior" is something of a grab bag, for it includes an extraordinary range of phenomena, from fashions to riots, that seem to have little in common. All these difficulties present a formidable challenge to sociologists who try to find a general explanation for the behavior.

Smelser's Theory

One of the most influential attempts at a comprehensive theory of collective behavior is that of Neil Smelser (1962). Smelser argues that collective behavior is essentially an attempt by people to alter their environment when they are under stressful conditions of uncertainty, threat, or strain. The form that their collective behavior actually takes de-

Figure 22.2 Social movements are of particular sociological interest because they often play an important role in social change. The French Revolution, for example, inspired democratic reforms in France and many other countries. Although social movements appear on the surface to be very similar to some forms of collective behavior, they are often more organized, and enduring.

pends largely on how they define the situation that is bothering them. If they do not understand their situation, for example, they are likely to respond through, say, a rumor or a riot. The more elaborate their definition of their situation, the more structured their collective reaction is likely to be.

Smelser identifies six basic conditions that, taken together, provide "necessary and sufficient" grounds for collective behavior to occur. In other words, collective behavior will not take place unless these six conditions are present, and if all six are present, some form of collective behavior is inevitable:

1. *Structural conduciveness.* This term refers to the surrounding conditions that make a particular form of collective behavior possible in the first place. The Great Depression, for example, was preceded by a financial panic in which people dumped their stocks and withdrew their money from banks, causing stock values to drop and banks to collapse. This panic was possible only because the United States had a stock market, on which stock could be bought and sold in a short space of time, and a banking system in which banks never had enough ready cash to repay all their depositors. These features of the economy provided the structural conditions that facilitated the financial panic, which was a classic example of collective behavior.

2. *Structural strains.* Any social condition that places a strain on people—poverty, conflict, discrimination, uncertainty about the future—encourages them to make a collective effort to relieve the problem. Prison riots, for instance, are examples of collective behavior that arises in response to a structural strain imposed by the confining and often brutalizing nature of prison life.

3. *Generalized belief.* Structural conduciveness and structural strains are not in themselves sufficient to provoke collective behavior. People must also develop some general belief about their situation—by identifying the problem, forming their opinions about it, and defining appropriate responses. The members of racist lynch mobs in the United States, for example, had developed a generalized belief, or ideology, about the subordinate status of blacks and about appropriate methods for maintaining the status quo. This ideology identified the supposed nature and causes of any racial problem and was used to justify the collective action of lynching.

4. *Precipitating factors.* Collective behavior does not "just happen." If the preceding conditions are present, a single incident, often exaggerated by rumor, may be sufficient to trigger collective behavior. The precipitating factor serves to confirm the suspicion and uneasiness that already exist. In all the ghetto riots that have been studied, for example, a specific incident—usually involving a conflict between local residents and the police—precipitated the outbreak of violence. In many cases the violence was fanned by exaggerated rumors concerning the incident.

5. *Mobilization for action.* Even when the precipitating incident has taken place, collective behavior will not occur unless the people involved become organized for action. This organization can be of the most rudimentary and unstructured form. Mere physical closeness in a milling crowd creates social interaction and some group cohesion. If leaders emerge and encourage the others to act, collective behavior will probably follow. When police raided a gay bar in Greenwich Village in New York in 1969, some of the patrons strenuously resisted arrest. Their example mobilized other patrons and sympathetic onlookers, and a serious riot followed. (The national publicity from this event greatly stimulated the growth of a new social movement for gay liberation.)

6. *Mechanisms of social control.* Even if the preceding conditions have been met, the success or failure of social-control mechanisms will determine whether collective behavior will take place. These mechanisms include such social responses as police behavior, media treatment, and the reactions of other individuals and groups. The social-control mechanisms may be so strong that collective behavior is suppressed; or they may be too weak to prevent the behavior; or they may be counterproductive and may actually magnify the behavior. In the campus disturbances of the sixties and early seventies, for example, various college administrations used different control tactics, ranging from negotiating with the protesters to having them arrested by the police. Such responses served in some cases to prevent or deflect collective action and in other cases to provoke it.

Smelser's theory may provide a useful means of analyzing collective behavior. Fads, fashions, and crazes, for example, can be interpreted as a response to conditions of boredom; panics, as a response to conditions of threat; or

riots, as a response to conditions of strain and resentment. The usefulness of Smelser's approach is vividly demonstrated in its application to the following specific example of collective behavior.

An Illustration: The Peoples Temple Mass Suicide

The Peoples Temple was a religious sect founded in Indianapolis in 1956 by Jim Jones, a preacher and community activist. In the mid-sixties he relocated the headquarters of the sect to California, where membership increased to several thousand. Most of the members were poor and most were black, and it seems they were attracted by the sect's combination of fundamentalist Christianity and an activist philosophy that offered a refuge from, and a challenge to, hypocrisy, racism, and evil. Jones himself was a fairly respected member of the wider community; he served on the San Francisco human rights commission and often worked closely with local politicians. In 1974 he leased land from the government of the South American country of Guyana, and cleared a 900-acre site in the jungle in order to set up a utopian community, far from the pressures of the secular world. In due course, over a thousand members of the sect emigrated to the new community, which their leader egotistically named Jonestown. There is nothing particularly unusual about this step: American religious groups, from the Amish to the Mormons, have tried to separate themselves from a hostile society by heading off into the wilderness to found a new community based on their own principles. But what later happened in the jungle was one of the most extraordinary and tragic episodes of collective behavior in American history (Kilduff and Javers, 1978; C. Krause et al., 1978; Lifton, 1979).

In the isolated jungle environment, the members increasingly came to rely on and even to adulate their leader. At the same time, Jones's personality, apparently already unstable, began to deteriorate; in particular, he was subject to bouts of paranoid suspicion and delusions of grandeur. Rumors began to circulate in the United States about conditions in the settlement: that Jones sexually abused the members, that sadistic beatings were used to maintain discipline; that armed guards prevented people from leaving of their own free will. In 1978 California congressman Leo Ryan visited the community in order to find out whether some of his constituents were in fact being kept virtual prisoners there. Soon after his arrival, Peoples Temple members shot and killed Ryan, three accompanying news reporters, and one defector from the sect. Jones, convinced by now that American or Guyanese authorities would destroy his community, decided that death would be preferable—not just for himself, but for the entire sect. He summoned his followers and—taking care to tape-record the proceedings for posterity—he told them that life was no longer worth living, that they should "die with dignity" in a "revolutionary suicide protesting the conditions of an inhumane world." A large vat of Kool-Aid spiked with cyanide was prepared. The children in the community were the first to die; mothers watched as nurses squirted the poison into the mouths of infants. The adults followed; a few struggled and were forced to swallow the mixture, but most drank it voluntarily. At the end more than 900 Americans, including Jones, lay dead, their bodies piled two and even three deep around the main compound. This bizarre episode cannot be satisfactorily explained in the simplistic terms of pop psychology (for example, that Jones had a magnetic personality and had brainwashed his followers); we need to examine the entire social context of the events in order to comprehend them. Smelser's theory provides a useful framework to achieve such an understanding, for each of his six preconditions were met at Jonestown.

1. *Structural conduciveness.* If someone like Jim Jones appeared in your sociology class and suggested that everyone immediately commit revolutionary suicide, he would probably be ignored, laughed at, or ejected; the structural conduciveness that might make his appeal effective would be absent. In Jonestown, however, things were different: a close-knit group of highly disciplined people were isolated from the outside world and almost idolized their leader, a man who had brought meaning and hope to their lives. These conditions made an episode of collective behavior possible in the first place.

2. *Structural strain.* The members of the community were under great strain. They had come to Jonestown because it offered an escape from the secular world; now investigators from the United States government had arrived in the community, and, according to Jones, they intended to destroy it. Jonestown, in fact, had become a "total institution" like a prison or mental hospital, in which the inhabitants had lost the power to make meaningful decisions over their lives.

Figure 22.3 The 1978 mass suicide of American members of the Peoples Temple sect was one of the most remarkable episodes of collective behavior in the nation's history. The actions of the people concerned can be fully understood only in terms of their social context at the time.

3. *Generalized belief.* Jones's own paranoid suspicions about the motives of outsiders had come to be shared by virtually all the members of the community: they felt that they were threatened by the Guyanese and American governments, by defectors, even by self-doubt. Jones, in fact, had made a habit of playing on the guilt feelings of the members by making them write letters of confession if they seemed to deviate from the ideological beliefs of the group as a whole.

4. *Precipitating factors.* The precipitating factor in this case was the murder of a congressman and of representatives of the mass media. It is not clear whether these acts were committed on Jones's specific instructions, but they made it certain that full-scale investigations and prosecutions would follow and that the community's days would be numbered.

5. *Mobilization for action.* The mobilization of the members for action came when Jones summoned them to a meeting and, using all the sources of authority at his command, urged them to kill themselves. There had even been some preparatory mobilization for this event; on previous occasions, Jones had called the members together and ordered them to prove their faith by drinking from a poisoned vat—telling them only afterward that the drink was harmless.

6. *Mechanisms of social control.* In this situation, all the mechanisms of social control favored the suicidal outcome. The social control that might have existed if the event had occurred elsewhere—in San Francisco, say—was entirely absent: there were no officials or even neighbors who might apply pressure on the group or on individuals within it to behave differently. Within the community, the mechanisms of social control encouraged the mass suicide: the leader demanded it, peer-group pressure supported it, and armed guards enforced it.

Rumors

A *rumor* is information that is transmitted informally from anonymous sources. The spreading of a rumor is itself a form of collective behavior, and rumors are in turn an important element in virtually all other kinds of collective behavior.

Rumor Characteristics

A rumor may be true, false, or a combination of truth and falsehood. Its origin is usually difficult to check, and it is transmitted outside the formal communications system of press, TV, government announcements, and the like. Rumors are especially likely to arise in situations where people are deprived of information or where they do not trust the official information they are given. A rumor thus is a substitute for hard news: people want information, and rumor fills their need if reliable information is lacking (Rosnow and Fine, 1976).

One insight into the importance of rumor in a tense, strained situation came in the aftermath of serious riots that took place in Detroit in 1967, when a newspaper strike eliminated an important source of "official" information. A rumor-control center was established in the city, and within less than a month it had received some 10,000 calls from people wanting confirmation of rumors they had heard, including reports of concentration camps for blacks and incidents of interracial violence and even castration (Rosenthal, 1971). In a strained situation (particularly in a milling, excitable crowd in which it is difficult to check or evaluate rumors) stories such as these can easily provoke violent outbursts.

The way rumors are passed on has been quite thoroughly studied through the use of controlled experiments and analyses of actual cases. Experiments have usually been sophisticated versions of the children's game of "pass it on." People are given a story and asked to spread it to others, and then various versions of the rumor are compared. Gordon Allport and Leo Postman (1947) showed that what happens to the rumor depends on its content, on the number of people involved in the chain of transmission, and on their attitudes toward the rumor. Some rumors change little, but others, especially those that excite emotions, may be severely distorted. In general, part of the content drops out and the remainder is organized around some dominant theme. The ultimate form of the rumor is often influenced by the special interests of the people involved, because they tend to reshape and pass on those parts of the rumor that fit their preconceptions about the subject matter.

Ralph Turner (1964) and Tamotsu Shibutani (1966) have pointed out that a rumor should not be regarded simply as the transmission and possible distortion of information. It also represents a collective attempt to gain information and understanding about some area of ignorance. As Shibutani notes, this attempt is "collective" in that many people contribute to the spread of a rumor, and they can play many different roles in doing so. Some take the role of "messenger" by relaying the rumor. Some take the role of "interpreter" by placing it in context and speculating on its implications. Others may be "skeptics" who urge caution and express doubt. Some become "protagonists," forcefully arguing in favor of one interpretation rather than another. Others play the role of "decision makers" and try to initiate action on the basis of the rumor. Most people become an "audience" and are mere spectators in the process. A rumor can thus be seen as a form of communication in which people pool their resources to construct a meaningful interpretation of an ambiguous situation. In doing so they may sometimes improve the accuracy of the rumor rather than distort the truth.

The Death of Paul McCartney

A classic example of rumor as a form of collective behavior occurred in 1969 when a Detroit disk jockey referred in passing to a fictional story about the death of a Beatle, Paul McCartney. Within a few days a rumor of McCartney's demise had spread to at least three continents, with knowledge of its origin completely lost. McCartney, it was believed, had died in an auto accident some years previously, but his record company had replaced him with a look-alike and persuaded the remaining Beatles to hush up the event in the interests of future album sales. But the Beatles, faithful to their fans, had inserted various clues about McCartney's death in their records in order to let others in on the secret.

In the weeks following, thousands of people ransacked Beatles albums in search of these alleged clues. They amassed a great deal of evidence to "prove" the rumor, much of which was printed in the underground press. After

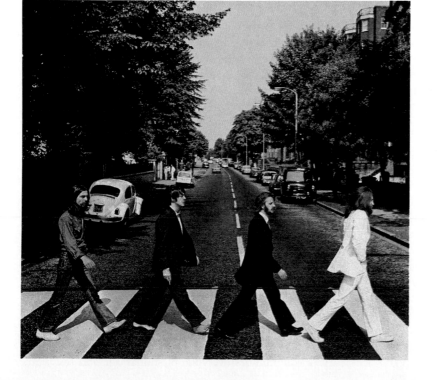

Figure 22.4 In their search for evidence to confirm the death of Paul McCartney, Beatles fans looked for and found hidden meanings on album covers. On the Abbey Road *cover, the Beatles appeared to be walking in funeral procession. John Lennon was in white (the priest), Ringo Starr was in a black suit (the undertaker), McCartney was barefooted, out of step, and had his eyes closed (the corpse), and George Harrison was in working clothes (the gravedigger). To clinch matters, a car in the background had the registration number 28IF, meaning—what else?—that McCartney would be twenty-eight if he were still alive.*

playing records in the normal way and discovering many lyrics supposedly referring to the death, ingenious investigators began to play them backward, and found even more startling evidence. On the track "Revolution No. 9," for example, a ghostly voice was heard intoning "Turn me on, dead man." On the front cover of the *Sergeant Pepper* album, a hand was spotted above McCartney's head—a symbol of death, it was alleged, in ancient Greek or perhaps Indian mythology—while McCartney himself wore an armband reading "OPD," presumably short for "Officially Pronounced Dead." On the back cover of the album, moreover, all the Beatles were facing outward—except McCartney, who had his back turned to the camera. And in the *Magical Mystery Tour* album photograph, McCartney was found to be wearing, significantly, a black carnation, in contrast to the red blossoms sported by the other Beatles.

In a final spurt of enthusiasm, investigators held up Beatles album covers to mirrors, hoping to find some message in the reverse image. They did not go unrewarded: the word "Beatles" on the reversed cover of *Magical Mystery Tour,* if viewed with an appropriate squint, yielded a telephone number. A fresh rumor spread that calls to this number, allegedly in London, would be answered with a full account of McCartney's death. For a period of several days the owner of the number, a British journalist, received hundreds of calls—most of them from the United States and most of them collect—from determined Beatles fans. When repeated denials by record-company officials failed to have much impact on the rumor, Paul McCartney finally squashed it himself, while admitting, "If I were dead, I'd be the last to know about it."

To understand the spread of this irrational rumor we must consider the social role of the Beatles and their relationship to the youth culture of the time. The Beatles were by far the most popular and influential rock group. They had pioneered or spread a number of innovative trends, not only in music but also in fashions (notably long hair for males) and in fads (such as dabbling in Eastern religion and using psychedelic drugs as a route to new consciousness). They had greatly influenced the development of the sixties youth culture, and as the public reaction to the assassination of John Lennon in 1980 reaffirmed, they were cult heroes for whom millions of people felt strong emotions. For this reason, *any* rumor about the Beatles was likely to spread; there was an eager audience for news about all their doings, however trivial. But why should this particular rumor have been so widely believed? Part of the reason was that there was already anxiety about the Beatles. Rumors were circulating—this time correct—that the group was about to break up. The rumor of McCartney's death was made more plausible by the fact that the Beatles had not appeared together in public for several years, so it would have been at least possible for a fake McCartney to have been substituted in their more recent records and photographs. The rock audience was accustomed to analyzing rock lyrics for hidden significance—if only because the meaning of many lyrics had to be disguised if they were to be allowed on the air—and the surrealistic images of many Beatles songs lent themselves to whatever interpretation people chose to put on them. Moreover, several leading rock stars had died in the eighteen months preceding the McCartney rumor, providing an atmosphere in which the story seemed more credible. Conflict between the generations was particularly acute at the time, and many young people were highly distrustful of the establishment, including the media and record-company officials who tried to discount the rumor. Finally, there was growing disillusion in the "counterculture," which was failing to change society to any significant extent and appeared to be disintegrating from within. It is not surprising that this anxiety and disillusion were projected through rumor onto the most prominent symbol of the youth movement, the Beatles.

Fashions and Fads

Fashions and fads are two closely related forms of collective behavior. Both tend to arise fairly spontaneously and to be relatively short-lived, although they may occasionally become more permanently incorporated into a culture.

Fashions

Fashions are the currently accepted styles of appearance and behavior. The fact that some style is called a "fashion" implies a social recognition that it is temporary and will eventually be replaced by a new style. In small-scale, traditional communities, fashions are virtually unknown. In these communities everyone of similar age and sex wears much the same clothing and behaves in much the same way, and there is little change in styles from year to year or even from generation to generation. In modern societies, however, fashions may change very rapidly indeed: automobile bodies assume new contours every year, and women's hemlines rise and fall with the passage of the seasons.

One reason for the emphasis on fashion in modern societies is that these societies are oriented toward the future rather than the past; novelty is considered desirable rather than threatening. A second reason, closely related, is that powerful commercial interests encourage changes in fashions because they profit from the demand for new styles. A further reason is that in a competitive, status-conscious society, fashion is used to indicate one's social characteristics to others. People may wish to appear attractive, distinctive, or affluent, and a new fashion enables them to do so—for a while at least. (Conversely, the drab, baggy uniform of tunics and pants worn by virtually every citizen of modern China reflects the noncompetitive, self-consciously "classless" nature of that society.)

Not all fashions are deliberately imposed on the population, however, and people may resist new fashions, even in the face of massive advertising campaigns designed to influence public taste. The greatest flop in auto-industry history was the Ford Edsel, mass-produced in the fifties but almost unanimously scorned by American consumers, who considered it monstrously ugly. Fashions can arise at any level of society, not merely in the upper social strata, and can then spread outward from their point of origin. Blue jeans, for example, are the traditional clothes of the working class, but they recently became acceptable "designer" items for youthful members of the middle and upper classes. A new fashion is generally more likely to be accepted if it does not differ too much from existing fashions. If you consider consecutive changes in automobile styles, for example, you will find few, if any, abrupt changes in appearance. Each new fashion is essentially a modification of its predecessor.

Fads

A *fad* is a temporary form of conduct that is followed enthusiastically by large numbers of people. Fads differ from fashions not only in that they are typically even more temporary but also in that they are usually mildly scorned by the majority of the population. Those who participate in a fad are labeled as faddists; they are believed to follow a fad simply because it has "caught on," not because it has any intrinsic value. Those who are "in fashion," on the other hand, are more positively regarded, for their behavior is appropriate for as long as the fashion lasts.

Some notable fads in recent decades have been the hula hoop, "streaking," roller-disco, jogging (at least for many of those involved), and the use of particular catch phrases (such as the various "outs" of recent years: far out, drop out, spaced out, bummed out, psyched out, tuned out, blissed out, grossed out, downed out, and luded out). A fad often provides a means of asserting personal identity. It is a way of showing that one is worth noticing, that one is a little different from everyone else (Klapp, 1969). For this reason, fads tend to appeal primarily to young people, who often have less stable identities than their elders. When a fad becomes so widespread that it no longer offers a distinctive identity to its adherents, it tends to be regarded as something of a bore and is usually abandoned.

Figure 22.5

"Hi guys, Floyd Otis—a Pisces into domestic wines, martial arts, and the primal scream."

Copyright Wm. Hamilton

Some fads win popularity because they offer the promise—frequently illusory—of personal advantage to their adherents. Of the hundreds of different forms of psychotherapy that are available in the United States, ranging from "orgonomy" to "psychodrama," many have the characteristics of fads. Grandiose claims are made for some new therapeutic technique, such as "primal scream" therapy; people flock to participate; disillusion sets in; and finally the fad is abandoned by all but a few zealots (Schur,

Figure 22.6 A short-lived but popular fad of the 1950s, much practiced by college students, was telephone-booth cramming. Fads tend to appeal mostly to young people, who are often anxious to assert their personal identity by being a little "different." Once the fad becomes too commonplace, of course, it quickly loses its appeal.

1976; Rosen, 1977). A similar form of fad is the financial craze, which involves widespread and reckless investment in dubious ventures, ranging from a gold rush to speculation in marginal real estate. One of the most extraordinary of these crazes was the tulip mania that occurred in Holland in 1634. The Dutch suddenly developed a passion for tulips, which rose rapidly in value. People at every level of society invested in the flowers and their bulbs, and many speculators made vast fortunes. Hoping to get rich quick, many people sold their homes and land to invest even more money in tulips, which at the height of the craze were worth their weight in gold. But suddenly, a rumor spread that the price of tulips was about to fall. Tulip owners desperately tried to sell their bulbs and blooms, but there were no buyers. The price of the flowers fell to well below its normal level, and thousands of speculators were ruined. But even today, the Dutch are internationally famous for the quality of their tulips—an indication of how a brief episode of collective behavior can leave lingering social effects.

Panics

A *panic* is a form of collective behavior in which a group of people, faced with an immediate threat, react in an uncoordinated and irrational way. Their behavior is uncoordinated in the sense that cooperative social relationships break down. It is irrational in the sense that people's actions are not appropriate for the goals they wish to achieve.

The progress of a panic follows a fairly typical course. A sudden crisis occurs; people experience intense fear; normal social expectations are disrupted; each individual tries desperately to escape from the source of danger; mutual cooperation breaks down; and the situation becomes even more threatening as a result. Panics are especially likely to occur in unusual conditions in which everyday norms have little relevance, such as fires, floods, shipwrecks, earthquakes, or military invasions. Some kind of response is necessary in these situations, but there are few, if any, social norms that specify an appropriate reaction. Thus, when a passenger aircraft makes a crash landing, people may attempt to flee before fire breaks out and causes an explosion, but they only succeed in hampering themselves and others by creating bottlenecks at the exits. Awareness of the bottlenecks may

Figure 22.7 The stock-market collapse of 1929 was a classic example of a financial panic. Fearing that the price of stocks would fall, investors rushed to sell their holdings, thus forcing the price down even lower. As the panic spread, huge fortunes were wiped out in hours or even minutes, and thousands of investors were ruined.

lead to increased panic, with people fighting and trampling one another in the effort to escape. Despite intensive training of airline personnel in emergency evacuation procedures, a high proportion of passenger fatalities are caused by a panic that prevents people from escaping in time.

The most dramatic panics are those that occur in situations of extreme emergency, but not all panics are quite so frantic or short-lived. A different form of this collective behavior is the financial panic, which is typically provoked by rumors that the price of stocks will fall or that a bank will be unable to repay its depositors. The classic example, of course, occurred at the outset of the Great Depression in 1929: as in other forms of panic, the individuals involved tried to protect their own interests, and in so doing they worsened the situation for themselves and everyone else. By trying to sell their stocks as quickly as possible, people ensured that the price of stocks did fall; by demanding their money back from banks, they ensured that the banks actually did collapse. The stock market came perilously close

to another crash in 1980, when rumors that Texas billionaire Bunker Hunt was unable to cover a billion-dollar call on his silver speculations sent shock waves through Wall Street. As one broker on the trading floor of the New York stock exchange commented, "I've never seen anything like it. You heard the noise go from a dull, controlled level to a sudden, explosive roar—and then there was panic." Within ninety minutes, the Dow Jones average of major industrial stocks had plunged to its lowest level in five years, ruining many thousands of speculators in the process.

Mass Hysteria

Mass hysteria is a form of collective behavior involving widespread and contagious anxiety, usually caused by some unfounded belief. In extreme cases mass hysteria can result in panic, particularly if the source of the anxiety is believed to be sufficiently close or threatening. The medieval witch hunts discussed in Chapter 16 ("Religion") are an example of mass hysteria, created in this instance by the illusory belief that many of the problems of late medieval society were caused by witches. McCarthyism, the secular witch hunt that aimed at finding communists in influential positions in American society in the 1950s, also had many of the characteristics of mass hysteria.

Let us look briefly at three instances of mass hysteria that have been closely studied by sociologists.

The Martian Invasion of Earth

In 1938 a radio dramatization of H. G. Wells's novel about an invasion from Mars, *The War of the Worlds,* was broadcast in the New York area. The result was mass hysteria and even outright panic, involving perhaps as many as 1 million of the 6 million people who heard the broadcast.

Although an announcer made the fictional nature of the program clear at the outset, many people tuned in late and did not realize that they were listening to a play. The dramatization itself started innocently enough, with what purported to be a music concert. The music was interrupted with an announcement of strange atmospheric disturbances, followed by an interview with an expert who assured listeners that this could not possibly be the start of a

Martian invasion. The music continued, only to be interrupted again by an eye-witness account of a strange meteorite that had landed near New York:

> Just a minute! Something's happening! Ladies and gentlemen, this is terrific! . . . The thing must be hollow! . . . Good heavens, something's wriggling out. . . . There, I can see the thing's body. It's large as a bear and glistens like wet leather. But that face. It . . . it's indescribable. I can hardly force myself to keep looking at it. The eyes are black and gleam like a serpent. The mouth is V-shaped with saliva dripping from its rimless lips that seem to quiver and pulsate. The crowd falls back. . . . What's that? There's a jet of flame . . . and it leaps right at the advancing men. . . . Good Lord, they're turning to flame! [quoted in Cantril, 1940]

This "on-the-spot" transmission ended abruptly, and various "experts," "public officials," and "scientists" then took turns at commenting on the invasion. The listeners were eventually told:

> Ladies and gentlemen, I have a grave announcement to make. Incredible as it may seem, both the observations of science and the evidence of our eyes lead to the inescapable assumption that those strange beings who landed in the Jersey farmlands tonight are the vanguard of an invading army from the planet Mars. The battle which took place tonight at Govers Mill has ended in one of the most startling defeats ever suffered by an army in modern times; seven thousand men armed with rifles and machine guns pitted against a single fighting machine of the invaders from Mars. One hundred and twenty known survivors.

A very large number of people accepted this broadcast as fact, not fiction. Some of them hid in cellars. Others bundled their children into their cars and drove as fast as they could from the scene of the supposed invasion. Others telephoned their relatives to give them the terrible news and to say farewell. Others simply prayed and waited for the inevitable end. Crowds gathered excitedly in public places, and fresh rumors about the invasion were generated.

Why did such an improbable tale of invasion from outer space have such a devastating effect? One reason was undoubtedly the skill of the dramatists, who used an unusual and imaginative form of presentation. The use of the "bulletin" format, with comments from supposed scientific experts and public officials, gave a certain credibility to the events. Equally important, however, was the fact that in this pretelevision age people relied heavily on the radio for up-to-the-minute news, much of which at this time dealt with the growing tensions in a Europe that stood on the brink of World War II. Listeners were glued to their radio sets as never before, had learned to expect interruptions of their scheduled programs, and anticipated that these interruptions might deal with conflict and warfare (Cantril, 1940). In addition, knowledge of other planets was far less extensive than it is today. Observations of Mars had led some astronomers to the mistaken conclusion that its surface was criss-crossed by "canals," presumably constructed by highly intelligent Martians. Belief in the possibility of advanced life forms on Mars was quite widespread among the public.

The Phantom Anesthetist of Mattoon

In early September 1944, a woman in Mattoon, Illinois, told the police that she and her daughter had been the victims of an unseen intruder who had sprayed them with sweet-smelling gas, which had temporarily paralyzed them and made them feel ill. The local newspaper made the event its page-one story, under the headline "Anesthetic Prowler on the Loose." The day after the report appeared, three similar attacks were alleged to have taken place. Because of a holiday period, these accounts were not printed in the press for two days, and no attacks took place during this time. When the reports were finally printed, the number of attacks rose sharply for nearly a week, with as many as seven incidents being reported in a single evening. In all, the phantom anesthetist claimed twenty-seven victims.

Police efforts to trap the maniac were unsuccessful. Although some people claimed to have seen him fleetingly, or even to have heard him pumping his spray gun, the combined efforts of local police, state police, and bands of armed citizens who patrolled the streets were entirely fruitless. The police were so efficiently organized that they were able to arrive at the scene of a complaint, according to the police chief, "even before the phone was back on the hook," but they found nothing. Scientific experts could find no chemical traces of the gas, knew of no gas that could cause the reported effects, and strongly doubted if a gas of this kind—so potent, yet so quick to disappear without trace—could even exist. Doubts started to set in: Was there really an anesthetist on the loose, or were people imagining the attacks? Newspapers began to print articles and interviews on the subject of mass hysteria—and the attacks stopped abruptly, never to be repeated. Medical, scientific, psychological, and police conclusions all pointed in the same direction. There never had been a phantom anesthetist in Mattoon.

How can we account for this episode of mass hysteria? In a careful study of the incident, Donald M. Johnson (1945) found that nearly all the victims were women whose average educational and economic levels were significantly lower than the average for Mattoon as a whole. Three-fourths of the victims, in fact, had not gone beyond elementary school. The husbands of several of the women were away in the army, a fact that presumably left them feeling isolated and vulnerable. In more than half of the cases for which Johnson could obtain information, there were symptoms of psychological stress: the victims spoke of having "always been nervous," of needing "doctoring for nerves," and of how they "never slept much." In short, the victims of the phantom anesthetist were precisely those whom Smelser's theory predicts might become involved in an unstructured outburst of collective behavior such as mass hysteria—people with a sense of unhappiness or discontent and no clear idea of the cause.

Why did the outbreak of mass hysteria spread in the way that it did? Johnson (1945) concluded:

> [The first victim] had a mild hysterical attack, an event which is not at all uncommon, which is, on the contrary, familiar to most physicians. The crucial point is that her interpretation of her symptoms was rather dramatic ... with the result that an exciting uncritical story of the case appeared in the evening newspaper. As the news spread, other people reported similar symptoms, more exciting stories were written, and so the affair snowballed.
>
> But such acute outbursts are necessarily self-limiting. The bizarre details which captured the public imagination at the beginning of the episode became rather ridiculous when studied more leisurely. The drama of the story lost tang with time and the absurdities showed through.

One interesting result of the more critical public attitude was that police calls in Mattoon reached a new low for several days after the attacks ceased. The citizens, it seems, were reluctant to risk making fools of themselves, and routine complaints about prowlers and similar incidents dropped off sharply.

The Seattle Windshield-Pitting Epidemic

In late March 1954, Seattle newspapers carried occasional reports of damage to automobile windshields in a city eighty miles to the north—damage that the police suspected was caused by vandals. On the morning of April 14, newspapers reported windshield damage in a town only sixty-five miles away, and later that day similar cases were reported only forty-five miles from the city limits. On the same evening, the mysterious windshield-pitting agent struck Seattle itself: between April 14 and April 15, over 15,000 people called the Seattle police department to complain about damage to their windshields.

The windshield damage usually consisted of small pitting marks, rarely larger than bubbles about the size of a thumbnail. Many people tried to protect their windshields by covering them with cardboard or by garaging their cars, but even these tactics did not guarantee immunity. Clearly, vandals could not be responsible. The most suspected culprit was the H-bomb, which had recently been tested in the Pacific. On the evening of April 15, the mayor of Seattle dramatically announced that the pitting was "no longer a police matter" and called on the state governor and the president of the United States for help. Yet the epidemic ended almost as soon as it had started. Newspapers suggested on April 16 that mass hysteria, not radioactive fallout, was the cause of the problem. On that day the police received only forty-six complaints; on April 17, only ten; and thereafter, none at all. The epidemic was over almost as soon as it had begun.

Careful scientific analysis of the pitted windshields revealed that the amount of pitting increased with the age and mileage of the car in question, and that there was no evidence of pitting that could not be explained by ordinary road damage. What had happened was that the residents of Seattle, for the first time, had started to look *at* their windshields instead of *through* them.

In a study of the epidemic, Nahum Medalia and Otto Larsen (1958) found that for two months before the episode, Seattle newspapers had been printing reports about H-bomb tests and fallout, "hinting darkly at doom and disaster." The epidemic, they suggest, may have served to relieve the tensions that had been built up, if only by focusing these diffuse anxieties on a very narrow area of experience, automobile windshields.

Crowds

A *crowd* is a temporary collection of people in close physical proximity. The social structure of a crowd is very simple, rarely consisting of more than a distinction between leaders and others, but crowds are always more than just aggregates of individuals. Physical closeness leads to social interaction, even if the members of the crowd actually try to avoid interpersonal contact. The mere awareness of the presence of others leads to a subtle but rich interchange of impressions, based on the establishment or avoidance of eye contact, facial expressions, gestures, postures, and even styles of clothing.

Crowd Characteristics

Crowds vary greatly in character and behavior. A crowd of one type—say, a crowd of football spectators—can be quickly transformed into a crowd of a quite different type, such as a rampaging mob. Most crowds, however, have certain characteristics in common:

1. *Suggestibility.* People in a crowd tend to be more suggestible than usual. They are more likely to go along with the opinions, feelings, and actions of the rest of the crowd.

2. *Anonymity.* The individual feels relatively insignificant and unrecognized in a crowd. The crowd often appears to act as a whole, and its individual members are not and do not feel readily identifiable.

3. *Spontaneity.* Members of a crowd tend to behave in a more spontaneous manner than they would on their own. They do not reflect on their actions as much as usual and are more likely to let their behavior be guided by their emotions.

4. *Invulnerability.* Because members of crowds feel anonymous, they are inclined to feel that they cannot be personally "got at." They may behave in ways that would be less likely if they felt social-control mechanisms could be applied to them as individuals.

Types of Crowds

Herbert Blumer (1951) distinguishes four basic types of crowds:

Casual crowds are the most loosely structured of all crowds and consist of a collection of individuals, such as an ordinary crowd in a street, who have little or no purpose in common. The individual members have little emotional involvement in the crowd and can easily detach themselves

from it. Their physical closeness implies some social interaction, however, and a precipitating incident—such as a traffic accident or attempted suicide leap from a nearby building—can produce greater structure and more social cohesion.

Conventional crowds are deliberately planned and relatively structured; they are "conventional" in the sense that their behavior follows established social norms or conventions. An audience in a theater, for example, is a conventional crowd, although circumstances such as an emergency can disrupt the crowd's conventional behavior.

Expressive crowds are usually organized to permit the personal gratification of their members, an activity that is viewed as an end in itself. A college dance, a religious revival meeting, and a rock festival are all examples of expressive crowds.

Acting crowds, as the term implies, are crowds in action—mobbing, rioting, or engaging in other extreme forms of behavior. The acting crowd is the least common but sometimes the most socially significant of the four basic crowd types. To take an outstanding historical example, the French Revolution, whose impact spread far beyond the borders of France, was precipitated by a mob assault on the notorious Paris prison, the Bastille.

Figure 22.8 There are four basic types of crowd: a conventional crowd—its behavior is largely governed by social norms and conventions and is therefore relatively predictable; a casual crowd—a very temporary and loosely structured gathering; an expressive crowd—the members are primarily concerned with expressing their own feelings and interests; an acting crowd—the members are not content merely to observe events; they take concerted action.

Theories of Crowd Behavior

Crowd behavior, particularly the apparently irrational and often destructive behavior of acting crowds, has always fascinated sociologists. How can this unusual phenomenon, so unlike everyday group behavior, be explained? Smelser's theory offers us a general explanation, but other theorists have looked for specific factors in the crowd situation that might give us a better understanding of this form of collective behavior. Two main theories have been proposed.

The "Contagion" Theory

Some theorists have regarded crowd behavior, especially that of the acting crowd, as the product of a group *"contagion"* in which individuals lose much of their self-identity and even self-control. The earliest systematic version of the theory was proposed in 1895 by a French writer, Gustave Le Bon. He argued that a "collective mind" emerges in crowd situations, with the conscious personality of the individual members almost disappearing.

Le Bon believed that the members of a crowd are dominated by a single impulse and act almost identically. People are less capable of rational thought once they are caught up in the frenzy of the crowd, and the "collective mind" is, in effect, merely the lowest common denominator of the emotions of the members. Le Bon was an aristocrat, and like most members of upper classes everywhere, he thoroughly disliked crowds drawn from the ranks of ordinary citizens. The reason, of course, was that a dissatisfied crowd readily becomes a militant mob, which is why governments facing popular unrest often go to great lengths to ban all public gatherings, even of as few as three people. Le Bon was firmly convinced that a person in a crowd "descends several rungs in the ladder of civilization. Isolated, he may be a cultivated individual; in a crowd, he is a barbarian; that is, a creature acting by instinct."

We know today that the idea of a "collective mind" is a fallacy. The behavior of a crowd is the sum of the behavior of its individual members, and there is no crowd "mind" with an independent existence. We are also more sensitive to the antidemocratic bias in Le Bon's work. Yet other parts of his theory remain influential, and many social scientists have attempted to analyze the way individual personality seems to become merged into and influenced by the crowd.

There is no doubt that members of crowds are subject to a certain amount of contagion from others. They are more suggestible, and they feel a strong sense of social integration into the group, with a corresponding loss of personal identity. People in crowds look to others for cues, narrow their field of emotional and intellectual focus, and behave in less critical and reflecting ways. This is particularly true if the crowd is closely packed. For this reason, religious and political speakers whose audience is scattered about a room often ask those present to move to the front and fill any vacant seats. Crowd contagion can also be manipulated by "planting" supporters in the room with instructions to applaud at prearranged points: once a few people start clapping (or laughing or even coughing), others usually do so as well.

The "Emergent-Norms" Theory

One important criticism of the "contagion" theory is that it tends to regard crowd behavior as a unique phenomenon, lying beyond the normal boundaries of social scientific investigation. Some sociologists, notably Ralph Turner (1964), have argued strongly that crowd behavior can be analyzed in terms of ordinary social and psychological processes and that "contagion" is not, in itself, an adequate explanation.

Turner challenges the assumption that all members of crowds tend to behave in almost identical ways. In fact, he argues, there are considerable differences in the motives, attitudes, and actions of crowd members. Some of those present may be impulsive participants, others passive supporters, others passers-by who have become onlookers, others opportunistic individuals who are seeking their own gratification from the crowd situation. The unanimity of crowds is often an illusion. Even in the midst of a riot, people may have varying motives and intentions and may behave in markedly different ways (Turner, 1964; Turner and Killian, 1972).

The *"emergent-norms"* approach is an attempt to incorporate crowd behavior into the framework of existing sociological theory. What actually happens in a crowd, Turner argues, is that new norms emerge in the course of social interaction. These norms define appropriate behavior in the crowd situation and arise from the visible actions of a few people. In the ambiguous situation that exists in the crowd, these few activists are able to define the norms—

whether they are norms regarding applause, violence, or anything else—for most of the other members. Many of the others do not agree with the direction that is being taken, but out of fear of ridicule, coercion, or even personal injury, they refrain from offering opposition. As a result, casual observers may believe that the crowd is unanimous. Crowd behavior is thus explicable in the same terms as other social behavior: that is, it is influenced by the prevailing social norms. The only difference is that the crowd itself improvises the norms on the spot and then starts to enforce them, informally, on its members.

Mobs

One important form of the acting crowd is the mob. A *mob* is an emotionally aroused crowd bent on violent action. Mobs usually have leaders, are single-minded in their aggressive intent, and impose strong conformity on their members. The mob has immediate and limited objectives and is a particularly temporary and unstable form of collective behavior.

One example of mob behavior, common in American history but extremely rare elsewhere, is the lynch mob. Lynching is part of an American vigilante tradition, in which self-appointed groups of citizens, in order to serve their own version of law and order, kill people whom they define as criminal or undesirable. Lynching is thus a curious combination of moral self-righteousness and brutal sadism. The practice has historically taken place primarily in the West and the South. Until the turn of the century the victims were both white and nonwhite, but during this century they have been increasingly and overwhelmingly black. During the Reconstruction period after the Civil War, "nigger hunts" were organized in which whole groups of freed slaves were rounded up and murdered: in the decade 1889–1899, some 1,875 lynchings were reported, and many more doubtless went unrecorded (Cantril, 1963). Between 1900 and 1950, well over 3000 people were lynched in the United States, less than 200 of them white. Contrary to popular belief, lynching of blacks was not usually associated with charges of sexual offenses against white women. Rape or attempted rape was allegedly involved in only one-fourth of the cases. Other blacks were hanged, shot, mutilated, and burned to death for such offenses as "trying to act like a white man," "making

boastful remarks," "insisting on voting," "giving poor entertainment," "being too prosperous," and "riding in a train with white passengers" (Raper, 1933).

Virtually all the lynchings recorded in this century have been the result of mob action, often by the Ku Klux Klan and almost always with little or no opposition from law-enforcement agencies. Local social norms, in fact, appeared to allow police and prison officials to give only token resistance to lynching attempts, and even this resistance was tolerated only because it would safeguard the officials in the event of a subsequent inquiry. Participants in lynch mobs have typically been whites of very low social status, and their acts may be interpreted as a venting of their frustrations onto a defenseless scapegoat group. Support for this view is provided by the fact that between 1882 and 1930 there was a significant relationship between the price of cotton in Southern states and the frequency of lynchings. Poor whites suffered intense frustrations in economic bad times; unable to strike at their social superiors, the white landowning class, they turned their aggression on the blacks (Raper, 1933). The lynch mob now seems to have faded from the American scene.

Riots

A second important form of acting-crowd behavior is the *riot,* a violent and destructive collective outburst. Rioting crowds differ from mobs in that their behavior is less structured, purposive, and unified; it may even involve a number of different groups in different locations engaging in similar but not necessarily identical behavior. Whereas the mob usually has some specific target—lynching a victim, attacking a police vehicle, burning down a foreign embassy—a riot involves much more generalized behavior with few specific objectives other than the creation of disorder.

The most recent outbreak of rioting in the United States was the series of ghetto riots that shook cities in Florida and other Southern states at the start of the present decade, although these were minor compared to the ghetto riots that occurred in Northern cities in the sixties. The riot has a long history in the United States, and many previous outbreaks were much more bloody than those of recent decades. Extensive antidraft riots took place in New York in 1863 when working-class whites protested attempts to

Figure 22.9 Riots were fairly frequent in urban America during the latter half of the nineteenth century and the early twentieth century. Although some of these outbursts were race riots, most of them, such as the Haymarket riot in Chicago in 1888, were sparked by industrial unrest.

draft them into the Civil War. Labor history in the United States was marked by bitter conflict and riots until the 1930s. Serious race riots took place in many cities earlier in this century, notably in Chicago in 1919 and Detroit in 1943. These race riots were quite unlike the ghetto riots of the sixties. They were initiated by white mobs who engaged mainly in acts of violence against individual blacks.

The ghetto riots of the 1960s, in contrast to those of the 1940s and 1980, were primarily directed not against persons but against property. Although the police and national guard who attempted to suppress the riots were mostly white, these disturbances were not "race" riots as such; there was little interracial conflict between ordinary citizens. The riots of the 1960s were essentially *protest* riots, the outcome of frustration and resentment at a society that promised equality but did not deliver it. The worst of the riots took place in 1967 and caused so much concern that a National Commission on Civil Disorders (the Kerner Commission) was appointed to investigate them. Smelser's theory of collective behavior fits the commission's findings remarkably well.

The commission reported that riots occurred in more than twenty cities in 1967. In every instance there had been

a reservoir of growing discontent, and a single precipitating factor, usually involving white police, had sparked the riot. Efforts at social control had often aggravated the situation, leading to fresh and more extensive outbursts, and exaggerated rumors had often heightened tension on the part of both rioters and police. The underlying cause of the riots, the commission found, was the institutionalized racism of American society.

In Smelser's terms, then, the *structural conduciveness* was the existence of depressed black ghettos in urban areas. The *structural strain* was the discrepancy between American ideals of equality and the reality of institutionalized racism. The *generalized belief* was the blacks' recognition that discrimination was the source of their problem and that decades of peaceful protest had brought little change. The *precipitating factors* were isolated incidents of tension or conflict, and rumors about these incidents. The *mobilization for action* took place when some individuals began an outright attack on police or property, setting an example for others. The *mechanisms of social control* were the reactions of police and other elements, including ghetto residents who urged rioters to "cool it." These mechanisms generally failed to prevent the outburst of collective behavior.

Publics and Public Opinion

Most of the forms of collective behavior we have considered so far involve a certain amount of direct contact and even contagion among the participants. The study of publics and public opinion presents a somewhat different picture, however, because the participants are much more dispersed and much more inclined to make individual decisions.

Publics

A *public* is a substantial number of people with a shared interest in some issue on which there are differing opinions. We sometimes speak loosely of the whole population as "the public," but this conception is really a fiction. In practice, there are as many publics as there are issues, and there is no issue for which the entire population is a public, simply because many people are ignorant of, or uninterested in, any specific issue. The Gallup poll, for example, has found that it is very rare for more than 80 percent of the American population to be aware of a particular issue, and the percentage is often very much lower. The public for a single issue—such as abortion, a political scandal, fluoridation of water, or protection of the environment—expands or contracts as more people gain or lose interest in the topic.

The activities of a public are more rational than those of a crowd. Some members of a public may think and feel alike, but they are individuals making personal decisions and so are less susceptible to contagion and suggestibility. Some of the interaction within a public takes place on a face-to-face basis among friends, associates, and family members, but much of it occurs indirectly through the mass media. A public does not act together (although some of its members may join in collective behavior or social movements), but it does form opinions on the issue around which it is focused.

Public Opinion

Public opinion is the sum of the decisions of the members of a public on a particular issue. Because people may constantly change their views, opinion on many issues is often in a state of flux. An assessment of public opinion is therefore valid only for the time and place in which it was made.

In a society such as America, considerable importance is placed on public opinion. The United States is a democratic society in which elected officials must pay some attention to the opinions of their electorates, and it is a capitalist society in which commercial interests must take account of consumer opinions about various goods and services. A great deal of effort consequently goes into finding out what the public thinks about particular issues—and into influencing or changing these opinions. Billions of dollars are spent annually on public-opinion polls and market surveys and on media campaigns to build favorable public images of candidates, policies, corporations, and products. These campaigns are forms of *propaganda*—information or viewpoints that are presented with the deliberate intention of persuading the audience to adopt a particular opinion. Propaganda may be true or false, but its objective is always the same: to influence public opinion toward a specific conclusion.

Public opinion arises in an informal way, making it difficult to study. We do know, however, that people are not the passive victims of advertisers and other media

Figure 22.10

"And what is your opinion of yourself?"

Drawing by Dana Fradon; © 1977
The New Yorker Magazine, Inc.

Propaganda Techniques

Propagandists can use several very simple methods to persuade their audiences. All these techniques have one element in common: they make an appeal to the values and attitudes of the audience. The next time you watch advertisements on television, you might try to identify the particular techniques being used.

1. *Glittering generalities* is a technique of surrounding a product, candidate, or policy with rather meaningless words that evoke a favorable response. Politicians, for example, become lyrical about "freedom," "democracy," "the individual," or "a better future," and have successfully campaigned on such slogans as "New Frontier," "Great Society," or even "Law and Order."

2. *Name-calling* is a method used in negative propaganda: it attempts to attach an unfavorable label to something that the propagandist opposes. Opponents of plans for a national health insurance program, for example, have successfully branded these plans as "socialized medicine." This phrase conjures up images of socialism, a concept to which the American public reacts very unfavorably.

3. *Transfer* is a method of winning approval for something by associating it with something else that is known to be viewed favorably. The most obvious example is the practice of associating commercial products with attractive female models, however irrelevant the link between the two may be.

4. *Testimonial* is the technique of using famous or respected people to make public statements favoring or opposing something. Commercial advertisers, for example, commonly use sports heroes, movie stars, or even retired astronauts to recommend their products on television and in magazines.

5. *Plain folks* is the method of identifying the propagandist's ideas or product with "ordinary" people. Political and commercial advertisers often use interviews with what appear to be ordinary citizens (they are generally actors) praising a product, policy, or candidate in what seem to be down-to-earth, common-sense terms.

6. *Card stacking* is an argument in which the facts (or falsehoods) are arranged in such a way that only one conclusion seems to be logically possible. This method is commonly used in commercial advertisements that compare one brand to another.

7. *Bandwagon* is a method that tries to build support for a particular viewpoint or product by creating the impression that "everyone is doing it." The implication is that the audience is being "left out" of a popular trend and should "get with it."

Source: Adapted from Alfred McClung Lee and Elizabeth Bryant Lee, *The Fine Art of Propaganda* (New York: Octagon, 1971).

persuaders. Opinions are not formed in a vacuum; they are made in the context of existing cultural and personal preconceptions. Moreover, people do not necessarily get their opinions directly from media sources. Information and viewpoints are sifted through other people, particularly family, friends, and workmates. For example, we are more likely to be influenced to see a movie by a friend who recommends it to us than by a newspaper advertisement. A public is also influenced by prominent members of the community who act as *opinion leaders.* These people usually have higher social status than the public they influence, and they are more interested in the subject at issue. They spend greater time studying the controversy, form definite opinions about it, and interpret the issue for others. Labor union officials, for example, are likely to have a strong influence over union members' opinions on economic and labor issues, and this influence may extend to other areas as well. Contagion may also play a role in the formation of public opinion through what is known as the "bandwagon" effect. If it appears that opinion is swinging rapidly in one direction, many people—particularly those who were previously undecided or who had no very strong commitment to the other side—tend to change their viewpoints. This is why commercial advertisers often stress an "everybody is doing it" theme and why candidates in presidential primaries are so eager to do well in the early stages of their campaigns.

Public opinion can now be measured by opinion polls with a high degree of accuracy. A properly chosen sample of as few as 3000 voters can be used to predict the outcome of a national election, usually to within less than 2 percentage points of the final result. The problems of constructing, using, and interpreting opinion polls have already been discussed in Chapter 2 ("Doing Sociology: The Methods of Research"), and will not be repeated here. It should be noted, however, that opinion polls can themselves be an important influence on public opinion. Publication of poll findings gives people the opportunity to compare their opinions with others, and any strong trend in the findings may have an impact on individual suggestibility. Some political scientists are disturbed at the possibility that preelection publication of polls on how people intend to vote may influence the way some people actually do vote, even to the extent of altering the results of elections. If it appears from poll findings that candidate A is significantly ahead of candidate B, undecided voters may

join a bandwagon in favor of candidate A, and other voters, particularly the disheartened supporters of candidate B, may choose not to vote at all in the belief that doing so will make little difference to the result.

A Theory of Social Movements

The tendency for people to join together and to seek or resist change through social movements is as old as history: the biblical exodus from Egypt, for example, was one such social movement, as were the periodic revolutionary movements that slaves and subject peoples mounted against the ancient Romans. In most preindustrial societies, however, social movements are apt to take the form of religious cults or sects—such as the cargo cults and other millenarian movements discussed in Chapter 16 ("Religion")—perhaps because preindustrial people interpret their misfortunes in religious rather than social, political, or economic terms. In modern industrial societies, however, and particularly in those that have democratic systems and so permit dissent, social movements are a recurrent and permanent feature of life. In these heterogeneous societies, there are always groups or interests anxious to influence the course of events, and their activities are part of the ongoing political process through which decisions about the future are made.

Figure 22.11 Social movements often play an important role in the formation of public opinion. The movements draw attention to controversial social issues and provoke debate about these subjects. Social change often emerges from the ensuing clash of interests and opinions.

Social movements are important precisely because they deliberately intervene in history. Their members are not content to be the passive playthings of social forces: instead, they try to affect the social order through direct action. Many of these movements, of course, have little or no impact, but others have brought about lasting and profound social and cultural changes. Our lives today would be utterly different had it not been for the efforts of the diverse social movements that were responsible for, say, the American Revolution, the abolition of slavery, the introduction of compulsory schooling, the extension of the vote to women, or the legalization of birth-control devices. A major concern of sociologists has therefore been to find out what causes social movements to arise in the first place.

Psychological Theories

Early writers on the subject, notably Gustave Le Bon (1895), tended to focus on the psychological characteristics of those who took part in social movements. As we have already seen, these theorists were typically hostile to social movements, which they regarded as simply one more form of irrational collective behavior. From this viewpoint, those who challenge the status quo are, almost by definition, unbalanced, and social movements are little more than long-lasting mobs. This tradition persisted until the 1960s, although the psychological explanations became much more subtle. Essentially, the various writers who took this approach suggested that social movements attract people who have a personality defect of some kind and that membership in the movements meets their psychological needs by making them feel important or useful (Cantril, 1942; Hoffer, 1951; Toch, 1965; Feuer, 1969). But there are obvious problems with this approach. First, if social movements exist purely to deal with psychological discontent, why should people join one movement rather than another—say, the Ku Klux Klan rather than the civil rights movement? Second, why should some movements (such as that for women's liberation) be largely successful, while others (such as the movement to make Sunday sport illegal) make little or no headway? Third, might it not be possible that the sources of social movements lie not in psychological conditions, but, rather, in social ones; that is, is it not possible that something is "wrong" with society, not with the people who try to change it?

Strain Theories

Largely in response to these criticisms, several sociologists began to develop a new approach to the issue. According to this view, which became popular in the 1960s, the main factor behind the emergence of social movements is some form of social "strain." Smelser's theory of collective behavior is one such strain theory, and, in fact, Smelser originally intended that it should be applicable to social movements as well as to such phenomena as riots and panics. As applied to the ecology movement, for example, this theory would hold that the strain caused by the existence of pollution in a society supposedly committed to the preservation of health and of the environment led to a new social movement aimed at resolving that strain. Other sociologists propose a somewhat different but related argument: that people's feelings of *deprivation* are the source of social movements. This deprivation can be absolute (when people totally lack some social reward or rewards) or relative (when people have a lesser share of these rewards than other groups to whom they compare themselves). According to these sociologists, grievances caused by deprivation encourage those affected to launch a social movement that would improve their situation (Davies, 1962, 1971; Aberle, 1966; Klapp, 1969; Gurr, 1971).

This approach has the virtue of locating the source of social movements more firmly in social rather than psychological conditions. But it also runs into a serious problem. There is, surely, a certain amount of strain in all societies at some time or another, and virtually everyone feels deprived (either absolutely, or relative to other people) in some respects. Yet these conditions of strain or deprivation do not automatically lead to social movements. American blacks, for example, were subject to strain and deprivation long before the civil rights movement, as were women before the women's movement, gays before the gay liberation movement, and so on. Why did these movements arise when they did, rather than earlier—or later? Theories of strain do not really answer this question, still less make it possible to predict when a social movement will arise. Indeed, some social movements have occurred at times when virtually nobody, including sociologists, foresaw that they would. The student movement of the 1960s, for example, suddenly disrupted campuses across the nation at a time when scholars and editorial writers were deploring student apathy; the women's movement was so unexpected that its main problem, in its early years, was to convince most women (let alone men) that women were, in fact, subject to any strain or deprivation at all. There is a dangerous circularity in strain theories: How do we know there was strain? Because a social movement arose. Why did the social movement arise? Because there was strain. Clearly, theories focusing on strain or deprivation are inadequate in important respects.

Resource-Mobilization Theory

A more recent approach, associated particularly with the work of John McCarthy and Mayer Zald, overcomes many of these difficulties. This theory emphasizes *resource mobilization,* the way in which a social movement organizes and makes use of whatever resources are available to it. Dissatisfaction may well exist in society—whether because of psychological frustration, social strain, feelings of deprivation, or for any other reason—but a social movement will not emerge until people organize and take action by using the resources at their command. These resources may be of many kinds—for example, access to a duplicating machine, the services of professional organizers, contacts with the media, links with other social movements, the presence of sympathizers who are willing to devote time and money to the cause, or even the ability to tap millions of dollars of campaign funds from individuals and groups that favor the movement's goals. The focus of sociological attention, therefore, should be on how and why people actually do mobilize their resources and launch a movement (McCarthy and Zald, 1977; Zald and McCarthy, 1979; Oberschall, 1973; J. Wilson, 1973; Gamson, 1975).

McCarthy and Zald place particular emphasis on the role of outsiders in getting a social movement launched. These outsiders may be amateurs who sympathize with the group concerned, or they may even be professionals whose job it is to organize people into movements of one sort or another. In either case, the outsiders help to mobilize the group's resources and thus to bring the social movement into being—or, if it already exists, to inject new dynamism into it. For example, white liberal Northerners, often college students, played a crucial role in the early days of the civil rights movement; their efforts in the South, particularly in organizing sit-ins at segregated facilities and in

Figure 22.12 The resource-mobilization theory emphasizes that the existence of grievances is not sufficient to launch a social movement. Chicano migrant workers in the American Southwest have been exploited for generations, but they have formed a social movement to protest these conditions only within the past two decades. As the theory suggests, a social movement requires talented leaders, such as Cesar Chavez, who are able to mobilize whatever resources are available (such as the workers' capacity to strike, or the willingness of others to boycott produce picked by underpaid laborers).

encouraging blacks to register as voters, lent great impetus to the movement. Another example is provided by the senior citizens' campaign for Medicaid. Elderly people are disproportionately likely to be both sick and poor, so it seems probable that they experienced strain and deprivation as a result of the high costs of medical care. Yet there was virtually no pressure from the aged for a program like Medicare until after legislation to create such a program was introduced into Congress. At that point, the American Medical Association, the physicians' interest group, claimed that there was no evidence that senior citizens even wanted

Medicaid. Only then did the labor movement, in the form of the AFL-CIO, begin to organize senior citizens. It sent professionals to work with associations and other groups of the elderly and to mobilize whatever resources the aged could command. The result was a powerful senior citizens' lobby for Medicaid, which Congress soon approved. A similar process can be seen at the international level. In nearly all the developing nations of the Third World, the bulk of the population lives in poverty under the rule of antidemocratic regimes. Yet this situation of strain and deprivation is generally insufficient to provoke a major social movement for revolution. The Soviet Union is well aware of this fact, and has consistently attempted, often through the use of Cuban or East German "advisers," to mobilize popular resentment into revolutionary movements and to ensure the subsequent success of those movements.

Social-Movement Characteristics

Although there is extraordinary diversity in the goals, tactics, membership, size, and fate of social movements, they do display certain recurrent features.

Levels of Activity

Social movements, unlike forms of collective behavior, are fairly well structured and may last for many years. Their members are not scattered, randomly-acting individuals, nor are they restricted to a single community; rather, the movements involve the coordinated venture of a large number of people who are consciously acting to bring about or prevent change. Their activities, however, can take place at three different levels:

General social movements take the form of broad but relatively unorganized currents in history. Examples are liberalism, abolitionism, or anticolonialism—movements that spanned nations and generations.

Specific social movements are smaller and more organized collectivities that coalesce out of a general social movement. For example, the general social movement against inequality and discrimination has in the past few decades produced such specific social movements as those promoting the interests of, among others, blacks, Indians, Chicanos, gays,

and women. Specific movements within a general movement often learn from one another's experiences and expertise, and sometimes may pool their resources for certain purposes.

Social-movement organizations are complex, formal organizations with hierarchical authority structures, including constitutions, officials, rules and regulations, and the like. Specific social movements usually include several social-movement organizations: for example, the ecology movement includes the Sierra Club and Friends of the Earth; the social movement of the aged includes the Grey Panthers and the National Association of Retired Persons. The general trend in modern societies, in keeping with their overall tendency toward rationalization and bureaucratization, is for social movements to become highly organized and professionalized at an early stage of their existence (McCarthy and Zald, 1973). In fact, a movement may become so highly structured that it really ceases to be a social movement any longer, and simply becomes a formal organization representing the interests of its particular constituents.

Types of Social Movements

All social movements have an *ideology*, or set of beliefs, that justifies the social arrangements that the movement desires. The ideology of every movement provides a diagnosis of what is wrong, an explanation of how the problem came about and why it persists, a prescription for how to correct the situation, and a scenario of how matters would get worse if the movement were to fail. Although the leaders of social movements may have very specific ideas about the nature of the ideology, ordinary members or sympathizers often have only a vague conception of its content.

Social movements can be classified into different types, largely according to the kind of ideology they hold and the implications that it has for their activities.

Regressive movements are those that aim to "put the clock back." Their members view certain social changes with suspicion and distaste, and try to reverse the current trends. The "Moral Majority" is an example of a regressive movement, in this case one that resists the trends toward permissiveness and greater civil liberties that have taken place in the course of this century.

Figure 22.13 Of all types of social movements, the ones that can have the greatest social impact are revolutionary movements. The revolutionaries in America and in Iran (here shown toppling equestrian statues of, respectively, George III and the shah) radically altered the history and culture of their societies.

Reform movements are basically satisfied with the existing social order but believe certain reforms are necessary, usually in specific areas of society. The antinuclear movement, the ecology movement, and the consumer movement are all examples of this type of social movement.

Revolutionary movements are deeply dissatisfied with the social order and work to reorganize the entire society in accordance with their own ideological blueprint. A successful revolutionary movement, such as those that gave birth to the United States, the Soviet Union, and the People's Republic of China, can launch sweeping social and historical change.

Utopian movements envision a radically changed and blissful life, either on a large scale at some time in the future or on a smaller scale in the present. The utopian ideal and the means of achieving it are often vague, but many utopian movements have quite specific programs for social change. The "counterculture" of the sixties and several contemporary religious sects and cults are examples of utopian movements.

Tactics of Social Movements

All social movements must use tactics of some sort to further their goals. One purpose of these tactics is to retain and enhance the loyalty of the members and to increase their number. A social movement usually contains a small, central "core" of leaders and other devotees; beyond that, there is a wider circle of members and participants who play a greater or lesser part in the movement's activities; and further beyond that, there is a general constituency of potential supporters who are vaguely sympathetic to the movement's objectives. The tactics of the movement should therefore aim at mobilizing this entire reservoir of support. A second purpose of the tactics is to persuade those who are not sympathetic to the movement's goals (and this probably includes the political authorities) to change their attitudes. If those with political power do not respond to the movement's demands, then the movement may adopt disruptive tactics aimed at forcing change.

The actual tactics that are adopted depend in some measure on what type of movement is involved: a reform movement is far less likely than a revolutionary one to use bombing, kidnapping, or assassination, for it is concerned to retain the good will of those in positions of power, and its

leaders and members are likely to have strong moral objections to the use of violence. A second important influence on tactics is the degree to which the movement has become institutionalized. A movement that already has access to the power structure, such as the National Association for the Advancement of Colored People, is more likely to work through private lobbying than through spectacular public demonstrations. Movements that have little access to power, however, are more likely to create "news events," for they soon learn that they will otherwise be ignored. For that reason, members of the early anti-Vietnam-war movement publicly burned their draft cards; members of the early antinuclear movement occupied the construction site of a new reactor in Seabrook, New Hampshire; members of the "Yippie" movement—the political wing of the hippies—scattered dollar bills from the gallery of the New York Stock Exchange, sending stock-brokers to their knees in a frantic (and symbolic) scramble for money. Such events are quickly seized on by the mass media, which obligingly give free publicity to the movement involved and thus help to increase public awareness of its ideology.

Sometimes, too, social movements turn to outright violence as a means of achieving their goals. The Palestinian

Figure 22.14 Social movements that have little or no access to the power structure—such as the Youth International Party ("Yippies")—are inclined to stage "newsworthy" events in order to get publicity for their cause. By publicly running "Nobody" for president, the Yippies attracted more attention to their views than they might have if, say, they had merely issued a statement claiming that the electoral process is a sham.

Liberation Movement, for example, achieved international notoriety, and attracted world-wide attention to its previously ignored grievances, through its aircraft hijackings and assassinations, and especially through its brutal murder of athletes at the 1976 Munich Olympics. In general, social movements turn to violence only when other channels are blocked or ineffective, or when those in positions of power use violence to repress the movements. Unhappily, it seems that violence can often be a successful tactic and therefore, from the point of view of those who espouse it, a rational one. William Gamson (1975) studied several hundred groups that had challenged the American power structure between 1800 and 1945. These movements, which ranged from the American Birth Control League to the Communist Labor Party, used a variety of tactics, but the 25 percent or so that tried deliberate violence to persons or property were, on the whole, more successful than the majority that did not.

Social Movements and Social Problems

Social movements play a vital part in the process by which a social problem is brought to public attention. Some undesirable conditions can exist for years or even centuries before they are recognized as social problems. Slavery, poverty, and pollution were all generally regarded as either unimportant or inevitable until social movements drew these conditions to public attention, mobilized public opinion, and campaigned for change.

The degree of success of a social movement determines not only to what extent a social problem is resolved but also what happens to the movement itself. Several sociologists have pointed out that the interplay of social problems and social movements produces a "life cycle," or "natural history," that often ends in either the disappearance of the movement, or in its institutionalization—that is, its attainment of a permanent place in the established order, usually as a formal, bureaucratic organization with close links to the power structure of the society. Malcolm Spector and John I. Kitsuse (1973, 1977), for example, outline a fairly typical life cycle of four stages through which a social movement may pass—assuming that it exists long enough to complete the entire cycle.

THE LIFE CYCLE OF SOCIAL MOVEMENTS AND SOCIAL PROBLEMS

STAGE I: Agitation

Some people perceive a gap between social ideals and social reality. They form a new movement and try to arouse public concern about this social condition.

STAGE II: Legitimation and Cooptation

The movement is successful at winning public support and thus becomes "respectable"; it is coopted by government and other agencies.

STAGE III: Bureaucratization and Reaction

The movement becomes primarily concerned with its own day-to-day administrative problems; it is criticized for losing sight of the problem it was supposed to solve.

STAGE IV: Reemergence of the Movement

Awareness of the problem is rekindled, coupled with dissatisfaction over existing attempts to solve it. The original movement regroups, or new social movements begin to agitate for change.

22.15 Social movements typically go through a "life cycle" of birth, growth, decay, and perhaps rebirth, as shown in this chart. Of course, the process depicted here is merely a model; some individual movements may depart from it to a greater or lesser extent.

1. *Agitation.* In this stage, members of the new movement try to stir up public opinion in favor of their viewpoint. In most cases, these efforts are unsuccessful, and the would-be movement simply withers away. The reasons for this early failure can be many. The claims the members make on behalf of their cause may be false or outrageously exaggerated—or may seem so to most people. Or the movement may be composed of people too powerless and lacking in resources to have much public impact. Or the members may use counterproductive tactics that merely antagonize rather than persuade the public. Or the movement may collide with another movement or movements that have far greater resources, and it may be overwhelmed in the resulting competition for public support.

2. *Legitimation and co-optation.* If it survives the first phase, a movement may enter a stage in which its objectives gain widespread support and the movement itself becomes respectable. At this point, government or other authorities recognize that the movement's claims are valid and they attempt to co-opt, or absorb, its leaders and policies. Leaders who were once dismissed as cranks may now find that the increasing success of the movement has made them celebrities; they are sought after by the media and consulted by government agencies. Once the civil rights movement became a national force, for example, federal and state authorities that had earlier ignored or even tried to suppress the movement began, instead, to invite civil rights leaders to participate in the commissions and agencies responsible for future policy in the area. Similarly, corporations that once had all-male boards of directors as a matter of course are now appointing women directors, if only in token numbers; corporations whose boards once consisted solely of representatives of management and shareholders are now including labor union officials. The principal effect of legitimation and co-optation is that the social movement loses much of its initiative; control of the handling of the problem passes to established governmental or other organizations.

3. *Bureaucratization and reaction.* In the third stage the organizations that deal with social problems become steadily more bureaucratized, whether they have been incorporated into government or not. As we noted in Chapter 7 ("Social Groups"), a characteristic feature of large formal organizations, such as government agencies, is that they tend to become more engrossed in day-to-day administrative tasks than in the long-term challenge of confronting the problems they were originally set up to solve. Failure to deal effectively with these problems rarely leads to the abolition of the agency responsible, however: indeed, the organization is likely to prosper, for it demands a larger budget and still more officials on the grounds that its existing resources are inadequate to achieve solutions. Inevitably, a public reaction sets in, and the organization focuses more on the growing complaints about its failure to solve the problems than on actually solving them. Government agencies such as the Bureau of Indian Affairs and the Department of Energy, for example, are widely perceived by, respectively, Indians and conservationists as part of the problem, not the solution.

4. *Reemergence of the movement.* In the fourth stage, discontent accumulates to such an extent that the movement reemerges, although this time it campaigns not only against the social conditions in question but also against the relevant policies, programs, and organizations that have become institutionalized in the name of changing those conditions. Sometimes members of the original movement may regroup and renew their campaigns, but often new movements emerge, led and supported by people who were previously uninvolved but who now see themselves as victims of bureaucratic incompetence and insensitivity. Thus the cycle begins again. But the process has not been entirely unfruitful; although dissatisfaction may persist, it is likely that some progress will have been made. Social problems are rarely, if ever, solved through single, dramatic strokes of policy. Rather, they are ameliorated, or made better, through a series of piecemeal approaches that gradually eliminate most of the conditions that gave rise to the problem.

The process of routinization by which groups that were once elements in a social movement become formal organizations with bureaucratic structures is well exemplified by the history of the American labor movement. In the late nineteenth century, American workers were deeply resentful of their low pay, poor working conditions, and lack of

Figure 22.16

"Would a study shut them up?"

Figure 22.17 This picture of child laborers was taken in the United States early in the twentieth century. It gives some idea of the social conditions that the early labor movement crusaded against. Like many social movements, however, the labor movement became more conservative as its original goals were achieved, and many large unions are now defenders of the status quo rather than radical critics of it.

the right to form unions. Workers joined together to take collective action, and the labor movement was born. Labor unions emerged, and after many years of tension and violence, they won official recognition from Congress and employers. Many unions grew and prospered, secured many gains for their members, became vast formal organizations, and are now part of the very establishment that the early labor movement set out to attack. The Teamsters' Union, to cite one of the more notorious examples, has a president who enjoys an annual salary of $156,250, an unlimited expense account, and a private jet for his personal use. The union has been accused, among many other charges, of betraying its members' interests, of corruptly using their pension funds almost as a bank for organized crime, and of using the same methods to enforce conformity among its members and potential members that capitalists once used to break strikes and bring resentful workers into line (Brill, 1978; Moldea, 1978). This unhappy result is by no means typical, however; most movements never achieve anything like the success of the American labor movement; they are rarely linked to the established power structure to the same degree; and few lose much of their early idealism to the same extent.

Summary

1. Collective behavior refers to relatively spontaneous and unstructured action by large numbers of people. Social movements are more structured, and attempt to bring about or resist change. Collective behavior and social movements are an important ingredient in social change.

2. Smelser's theory holds that collective behavior can and will take place if six factors are present: structural conduciveness, structural strains, generalized belief, precipitating factors, mobilization for action, and the influence of mechanisms for social control. The Peoples Temple mass suicide illustrates the theory.

3. The content of rumors tends to be shortened and reshaped during the process of transmission. Rumors may be seen as a collective attempt to define an ambiguous situation. The "death" of Paul McCartney provides an example of rumor.

4. Fashions are found primarily in modern industrial societies, where they are promoted by commercial interests and used to signal individual status. Fads are short-lived and often provide a means of asserting personal identity.

5. Panics involve irrational and uncoordinated behavior in the face of threat. Some occur in temporary situations of extreme emergency (such as fires), others in more diffuse situations of threat (such as stock-market collapses).

6. Mass hysteria involves contagious anxiety, usually caused by an unfounded belief. Examples are the "Martian invasion" of earth, the phantom anesthetist of Mattoon, and the Seattle windshield-pitting epidemic.

7. Crowd characteristics include suggestibility, anonymity, spontaneity, and invulnerability. Crowds may be classified as casual crowds, conventional crowds, expressive crowds, or acting crowds, The contagion theory holds that crowd members lose personal identity in crowd situations and are easily influenced by others; the emergent-norms theory holds that crowd behavior involves a collective improvisation of new norms.

8. Mobs are acting crowds bent on violence; the lynch mob is an example. Riots are destructive collective outbursts but involve less purposive, unified, and structured behavior than that of mobs. Smelser's theory can be usefully applied to the ghetto riots of the sixties.

9. Publics involve numbers of people with opinions on a controversial issue. Their behavior is more individualistic than those of other forms of collective behavior. Public opinion may be influenced to some extent by advertising and propaganda. Public opinion can be measured by opinion polls, and poll findings may influence public opinion.

10. Social movements are a recurrent aspect of social life, and their activities may achieve changes of great historical significance. Their emergence has been explained as the result of members' psychological needs, as the result of social strain, and, more recently, as the result of resource mobilization—people's organization of whatever resources are available in order to achieve their goals.

11. There are three main levels of social-movement activity: general movements, specific movements, and social-movement organizations. All movements have an ideology that justifies the social arrangements they desire. Depending on the nature of their goals, movements may be regressive, reformist, revolutionary, or utopian. They may also resort to a variety of tactics, including violence.

12. Social movements bring social problems to public attention and thus bring about social change. The "life cycle" of social movements is often closely interlinked with the social problems they address.

Important Terms

collective behavior (561)	expressive crowd (575)
social movement (562)	acting crowd (575)
structural conduciveness (563)	contagion theory (576)
structural strains (563)	emergent-norms theory (576)
generalized belief (563)	mob (577)
precipitating factors (564)	riot (577)
mobilization for action (564)	public (579)
mechanisms of social control (564)	public opinion (579)
rumor (566)	propaganda (579)
fashion (568)	opinion leaders (580)
fad (569)	resource mobilization (583)
panic (570)	regressive movements (584)
mass hysteria (571)	reform movements (585)
crowd (574)	revolutionary movements (585)
casual crowd (574)	utopian movements (585)
conventional crowd (575)	

Suggested Readings

EVANS, ROBERT (ed). *Social Movements.* 2nd ed. Chicago: Rand McNally, 1973.

A useful collection of articles on social movements, including both theoretical material and actual case studies.

FREEMAN, JO. *The Politics of Women's Liberation.* New York: MacKay, 1975.

An excellent history of the women's movement, written by a participant.

GENEVIE, LOUIS (ed.). *Collective Behavior and Social Movements.* Ithaca, Ill.: Peacock, 1978.

A good selection of sociological writing on various aspects of collective behavior and social movements; the book is recommended for an overview of the field.

MAUSS, ARMAND L., and JULIE CAMILE WOLFE (eds.). *This Land of Promises: The Rise and Fall of Social Problems in America.* Philadelphia: Lippincott, 1977.

An interesting series of articles focusing on the relationship between social movements and social problems.

ROSNOW, RALPH L., and GARY ALAN FINE. *Rumor and Gossip.* New York: Elsevier, 1976.

A readable study of rumor and its relationship to some other forms of collective behavior.

SMELSER, NEIL J. *Theory of Collective Behavior.* New York: Free Press, 1962.

A highly influential analysis of various forms of collective behavior. Smelser interprets collective behavior as an attempt by people to alter their social environment.

TURNER, RALPH H., and LEWIS M. KILLIAN. *Collective Behavior.* 2nd ed. Englewood Cliffs, N.J.: Prentice-Hall, 1972.

A comprehensive treatment of collective behavior. The book includes readings, case studies, and theoretical analysis of a wide range of collective phenomena.

WORSLEY, PETER. *The Trumpet Shall Sound.* London: MacGibbon & Kee, 1957.

An interesting descriptive and analytical account of the various "cargo-cult" movements in the South Pacific. Worsley's account throws light on other, less exotic social movements nearer home.

ZALD, MAYER N., and JOHN D. MCCARTHY (eds.). *The Dynamics of Social Movements.* Cambridge, Mass.: Winthrop, 1979.

An important collection of articles representative of the new resource-mobilization approach to social movements.

CHAPTER **23**   *Social Change and Modernization*

"Everything changes," observed the ancient Greek philosopher Heraclitus. It was he who pointed out that a man cannot step twice into the same river—for he is not quite the same man, nor is it quite the same river. This principle applies to every phenomenon known to us, from the behavior of subatomic particles to the expansion of the universe, from the growth and decay of living organisms to changes in individual personality. Societies, as we are only too well aware in the modern world, also change. We have pointed to these changes throughout this book, placing particular emphasis on the transformation that accompanies the shift from preindustrial to industrial society. Yet, although social change is a central concern of sociology, the question of how, why, and in what ways societies change remains one of the most intriguing and difficult problems in the discipline.

Social change is the alteration in patterns of culture, social structure, and social behavior over time. No society can successfully prevent change, not even those that try to do so, although some societies are more resistant to change than others. But the rate, nature, and direction of change differ greatly from one society to another. In the past 200 years, the United States has changed from a predominantly agricultural society into a highly urbanized and industrialized one. In the same period, the society of the BaMbuti pygmies of the Central African forests has changed hardly at all. Why? And why in all but the most inhospitable parts of the world do we find the ruins of great civilizations? What caused them to flourish, and what caused them to collapse? Why did civilization arise in India long before it appeared in Europe? Why did industrialism arise in Europe rather than in India? Does social change take place in a random, haphazard manner, or are recurrent patterns to be found in all societies? Are all human societies moving toward similar social forms and a common destiny, or will they differ in the future as much as they have in the past?

These are important questions, and they are as old as sociology itself. The man who first coined the term "sociology," Auguste Comte, believed that the new science could lay bare the processes of social change and thus make it possible to plan the human future in a rational way. Almost without exception, the most distinguished sociologists of the nineteenth and twentieth centuries have grappled with the problem of social change. But it must be confessed that sociology has, so far, failed to fully meet the challenge. Many theories have been offered, but none has won general acceptance. As Wilbert Moore (1960) comments: "The mention of 'theory of social change' will make most social scientists appear defensive, furtive, guilt-ridden, or frightened."

Why does the study of social change present such problems? There are two basic reasons. One is that to understand social change, or *dynamics,* we must first understand social order and stability, or *statics.* In other words, we cannot know precisely why or how societies change until we know precisely why and how they form relatively stable units in the first place. We know that societies—despite the astonishing variety of different individuals and groups they may contain—tend to "hang together," or to be integrated. But we still have no generally accepted theory of why this should be so—of why a society should not simply disintegrate into its component parts. Again, many theories have been proposed—such as the functional need people have for one another, the political authority of the state, the inborn sociability of our species, or the existence of shared values that "glue" a society together. None of these theories, however, seems to offer a really comprehensive explanation of social order.

The second reason for the difficulty of developing a general theory is that social change involves many complex and varied factors. If any sample of pure water is heated to 100 degrees centigrade at sea level, it will boil. We can identify heat as the cause of the change, and we can predict that the same thing will happen in all similar circumstances in the future. Changes in human societies are not so easily anticipated. Each society is unique, and any changes that take place are likely to result from a complex of interacting factors—environmental, technological, personal, cultural, political, religious, economic, and so on. To discover the cause or causes of change is therefore very difficult indeed—especially since we cannot "rerun" history or conduct lab-

Figure 23.1 The tempo of social change in a given society is usually reflected in that society's art. Ancient Egypt, for example, was a fairly static society, and over a period of several centuries, all Egyptian painting followed an almost identical style: in particular, people were always portrayed in profile, with no attempt at depth or perspective. In modern industrial societies, in contrast, artistic styles, like social styles, change very rapidly, and many different styles compete for public attention. Modern art also reflects the diversity, values, and preoccupations of the societies in which it is found. (The principle that the nature and concerns of art reflect those of the society in which it arises is a basic insight of the sociology of art. If you look at the various paintings that are reproduced earlier in this book, you will see this principle clearly revealed.)

oratory experiments in large-scale social change to test our theories. And because each society is unique, we must be hesitant about using the experiences of one society as the basis for confident predictions about changes in another.

These problems are not impossible to overcome; they are merely difficult. In principle, we should be able to understand social change. It is a basic assumption of science that all events have causes. If this were not so, the social and physical world would be unintelligible to us. Sociology is still an infant science, dealing with a highly complicated subject, but we already have a good, if partial and tentative, understanding of the processes of social change. In this chapter we shall consider three major topics: first, some specific factors that can cause social changes; second, some general theories of social change; and third, the foremost example of social change in the modern world, namely, modernization. Finally, we shall assess the prospects for predicting social change in the future, particularly as it concerns "postindustrial" societies.

Some Sources of Change

Sociologists have identified a number of specific factors that, in their interaction with other factors, may generate changes in all societies. The precise nature and direction of the changes, however, depend very much on the unique conditions of the place and time in which they occur.

Figure 23.2 An apparently minor innovation can have far-reaching and complex effects, many of which were unintended and unforeseen. For example, cars were at first used by a small leisure class for the ostentatious display of wealth, but when Henry Ford used mass production to make them available to ordinary American families, pervasive social changes followed.

The automobile industry has become the largest manufacturing enterprise in the United States. The assembly line, first developed in the auto industry, has been duplicated in thousands of other industries. Huge multinational corporations have emerged to produce millions of cars each year. America's greed for gasoline has helped to make oil a critical factor in international politics and economics. A national system of roads and highways has been created at huge expense, linking communities and facilitating travel in a way that the railroad could never have achieved. Elaborate traffic laws have become necessary, and tens of thousands of Americans are killed in road accidents every year. Cities have become congested with traffic, and urban settlement patterns have been drastically changed by the development of new suburbs, whose residents can commute by car to work in cities. Leisure and dating patterns have changed. Air pollution from auto exhausts has become a major problem. Few of these changes were anticipated and few of them were desired, but all can be traced directly or indirectly to the advent of the private automobile.

Figure 23.3 Although environmental changes are usually too slow to have a noticeable effect on human societies, there are certain exceptions. An obvious case is the eruption of a volcano, such as Mount St. Helen's. If this volcano continues to erupt on a large scale, it will make human settlement and agriculture in the surrounding area impossible to sustain.

The Physical Environment

As we saw in Chapter 3 ("Culture"), the physical environment has a strong influence on the culture and social structure of a society. People living in the arctic tundra must obviously evolve social forms different from those of people living in arid deserts or on tropical islands. The Australian aborigines inhabit a continent that had no indigenous animals suitable for domestication and virtually no indigenous plants suitable for systematic cultivation. It is hardly surprising, therefore, that they remained hunters and gatherers and did not become a pastoral, horticultural, or agricultural society. Even in the most advanced industrial societies, which are able to make significant changes in the natural surroundings, the environment still sets limits. For example, the finite capacity of the environment to tolerate pollution may restrict future industrial growth.

The physical environment, then, may influence the character of a society and its culture, and it may set limits on some forms of social change. But this is not the same as *causing* change. Social change that is directly caused by environmental factors is in fact quite rare, although it does occur. Around 1500 B.C., for example, a volcanic eruption

in the Aegean Sea created a massive tidal wave that destroyed the highly developed Minoan civilization on the island of Crete—a catastrophe, incidentally, that probably gave rise to the legend of Atlantis, a civilization that allegedly sank beneath the sea. Other environmental phenomena such as severe earthquakes, floods, or droughts may cause changes in population structure or may even provoke migrations, but major environmental changes usually take place too slowly to have much impact on social life. Many such changes, in fact, are actually caused by human action: much of the desert of North Africa and the land erosion of the Andes was caused by human interference in the ecology of these regions.

Most environmental influences on social change occur through an interaction between social and environmental forces. Societies that have been located at geographic crossroads—such as those at the land bridge between Europe, Asia, and Africa—have always been centers of social change. Societies that have been geographically isolated have tended to change less. It is no accident that the most "primitive" peoples of the world have lived in geographic isolation from other societies, separated from them by oceans, deserts, mountain ranges, or jungle.

Population

Any significant increase or decrease in population size or growth rates may affect or even disrupt social life. A population that grows too large puts impossible demands on resources. The result, as it has so often been in history, may be mass migration, usually resulting in cultural diffusion and sometimes in wars as the migrants invade other territories. Or the result may be social disorganization and conflict over scarce resources within the society itself. A population that grows too slowly or even declines in numbers faces the danger of extinction. The latter problem is not one that most societies have to face today, but the former—overpopulation—is probably the most pressing social problem in the contemporary world. If global population continues to increase at anything like its current rate, demands for food and other natural resources will become insupportable. Far-reaching social changes will follow, including an abrupt population decline as the death rate soars as a result of malnutrition, disease, and, quite probably, even wars.

The size of a population also has a strong influence on social relationships. In small, thinly settled populations, most relationships are primary: people know one another on an informal, face-to-face basis. In larger and more densely settled populations, social life changes markedly. Secondary relationships multiply, new agencies of social control emerge, new institutions appear, and formal organizations replace many informal groups. Population growth thus has important effects throughout social life.

Changes in the demographic structure of a population also cause social changes. The post–World War II "baby boom" gave the United States a disproportionate number of young people, which made a massive expansion of educational facilities necessary in the fifties and sixties. Today, members of that generation are flooding the market for jobs, housing, and other resources. And as the "baby-boom" generation ages, the United States will become "top heavy" with old people, resulting in still further social changes. Medical science will focus increasingly on the problems of the aged, and geriatrics will become a growth area in medicine. New provision will have to be made for the elderly, probably through an extension of old-age homes and similar facilities. Younger workers will find that an increasing part of what they earn goes in taxes to support the growing ranks of the retired. Existing schools will stand empty or be converted to other uses, and funeral homes will enjoy an unprecedented boom.

Ideas

What role do ideas, particularly belief systems, or *ideologies*, play in social change? This question is one of the oldest and most controversial in sociology. Karl Marx, who first raised the problem, argued strongly that social conditions shape people's ideologies, not the other way around. In his view, it is not the ideology of socialism that makes workers resent the oppression of capitalism; it is the oppression of capitalism that makes workers embrace the ideology of socialism. Similarly, Marx saw the ideology of capitalism as nothing more than an attempt to justify the capitalist class's exploitation of the workers. Capitalism itself had been created not by an ideology but by the social forces that had overthrown feudalism in favor of this new system.

As we noted in Chapter 16 ("Religion"), Max Weber contested this view. He argued that the "Protestant ethic" of hard work and deferred gratification had spurred the development of the capitalist system. The failure of other non-Western societies to develop capitalism, he believed, was partly due to their lack of a similar ideology. Weber thus gave ideas a much greater role in causing social change than did Marx. Durkheim took a broadly similar view. He accepted that ideas derive from social conditions but believed that they might then become independent "social facts" that could act back on society and cause social change.

There can be no question that ideologies arise from social conditions and that people generally tend to accept belief systems that they perceive (rightly or wrongly) as serving their own interests. In this sense Marx was correct. But it seems that Weber and Durkheim were equally correct in their view that ideas can also influence the course of events: they can become "detached," as it were, from the social conditions in which they originally arose and can then have an independent effect on social action. For example, the ban on artificial birth control by the Catholic Church and other Christian groups stems ultimately from the stern morality of the ancient Israelites. The Israelites were a small tribe, subject to a high infant-mortality rate and surrounded by enemies, so they placed great value on

Figure 23.4 This nineteenth-century painting of the United States's "manifest destiny"—to expand across the North American continent—captures a popular and influential idea of the time. But did the idea of a manifest destiny actually help cause the expansion—or did it merely justify an expansion that was actually caused by more mundane factors, such as population pressure and economic ambition? Some theorists have held that ideas merely reflect social and economic conditions; others, that ideas can actually affect the course of social and economic change.

large families. This value was transmitted to Christianity, and disapproval of artificial birth control eventually became part of the official doctrine of several churches, even though the origins of the value had been forgotten. The belief that birth control is somehow immoral is inappropriate, however, in developing nations where resources are limited and population is rocketing. Failure to introduce effective birth-control methods will inevitably lead to major social changes in these countries, including changes caused by mass poverty and even mass starvation.

Ideas, often expressed in slogans, have been an important ingredient in many social changes. The cry for "liberty, equality, fraternity" in the French Revolution influenced political events in that country and in many others. The concept of "the brotherhood of man" was used by those who wished to abolish slavery in the United States and elsewhere. Appeals to the ideal of "democracy" and "civil rights" helped swing American public opinion in favor of extending the vote to women and to blacks. Yet none of these ideas existed in a vacuum; they were influential only in the context of other social forces.

Ideas are a particularly important element in social

change in countries that are oriented to change as a way of life. The reason is that we try to shape the future in terms of our concepts of what it should be like. Our ideas determine what we regard as needs, and we take social action to bring about the changes necessary to meet those needs.

"Events"

The term "events" is used by the sociologist Robert Nisbet (1969, 1970) to refer to random, unpredictable happenings that affect the course of social change. An assassin's bullet ended the Kennedy presidency, initiating the presidency of Lyndon Johnson and making possible his policies in Southeast Asia and elsewhere. An alert night watchman noticed that a burglary was in process at the Watergate building in Washington, and set in motion a series of investigations that led to the downfall of Richard Nixon and to the presidency of Gerald Ford. Crucial battles have been lost by the mistake of a general, or abandoned because of superstitious fear of a solar eclipse.

Although a few sociologists (for example, McIver, 1942) have tried to deal with this random ingredient in social change, most have been reluctant to do so for the reason that "events" of this kind seem to fall beyond the scope of scientific analysis. As Nisbet points out, however, the actual event need not always be the decisive factor in social change. The system as a whole may sometimes be "ripe" for change, and the event may merely "trigger" it. Corruption and deceit in American politics is a problem of long standing. Sooner or later someone was likely to get caught, and that someone happened to be Richard Nixon. The United States has its share of psychopaths and lacks a responsible system of gun control; sooner or later someone was likely to assassinate a president. Attempts were made in recent decades on the lives of Presidents Roosevelt, Truman, Kennedy, and Ford; the president who became a fatal victim was John Kennedy. To at least some extent, then, "events" can be explained in terms of existing social conditions. Nevertheless, the often random nature of "events" does pose a very difficult problem to any general theory of social change. Imagine, for example, the effect of nuclear war between the major powers as a result of human or electronic error.

Cultural Innovation

Changes in a society's culture tend to involve social changes as well. As we noted in Chapter 3 ("Culture"), there are three distinct sources of cultural innovation: discovery, invention, and diffusion.

Discovery

A *discovery* is the perception of an aspect of reality that already exists: the principle of the lever, a new continent, the composition of the atmosphere, or the circulation of the blood. A new discovery, if shared within the society, becomes an addition to the society's culture and store of knowledge. It becomes a source of social change, however, only when it is put to use. Europeans knew of other continents for centuries, but it was only when they colonized parts of these territories that social change resulted, in both the colonies and the countries that colonized them. The ancient Greeks discovered the principle of steam power; in fact, a steam engine was built as a toy in Alexandria around 100 A.D. But the principle was not put to serious use, and thus did not generate social change, for nearly 1700 years after it was discovered.

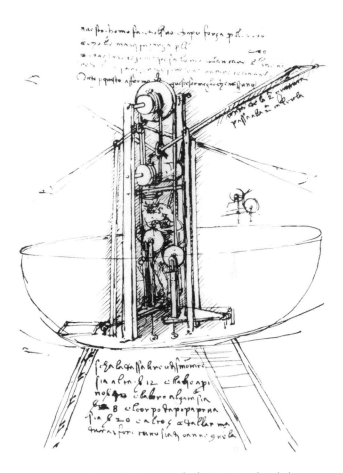

Figure 23.5 Leonardo da Vinci produced this sketch of a helicopter (powered by human muscle) in the fifteenth century. Many of Leonardo's designs for new machines were workable in principle and were centuries ahead of their time. But the machines could not be constructed, for his society lacked the technological knowledge to build and power them. Rapid technological innovation is possible only in a society that already has a large store of knowledge to draw on, for all inventions are based on previous knowledge.

SIMULTANEOUS DISCOVERIES AND INVENTIONS

Discovery of the planet Neptune	By Adams (1845)
	Leverrier (1845)
Discovery of oxygen	By Scheele (1774)
	Priestley (1774)
Logarithms	By Napier-Briggs (1614)
	Burgi (1620)
Photography	By Daguerre–Niepe (1839)
	Talbot (1839)
Kinetic theory of gases	By Clausius (1850)
	Rankine (1850)
Discovery of sunspots	By Galileo (1611)
	Fabricius (1611)
	Scheiner (1611)
	Harriott (1611)
Laws of heredity	By Mendel (1865)
	DeVries (1900)
	Correns (1900)
	Tschermak (1900)

Source: William F. Ogburn, *Social Change* (New York: Viking, 1922), pp. 90–122.

Figure 23.6 These are some of the 150 discoveries and inventions that William Ogburn found had been made almost simultaneously. In most cases the inventors were unaware of one another's work. They all lived in similar cultures, however, and so had access to the same store of cultural knowledge. Once sufficient knowledge has accumulated in a particular field, new inventions become almost inevitable.

Invention

An *invention* is the combination or new use of existing knowledge to produce something that did not exist before. Inventions may be either material (can openers, cigarettes, spacecraft) or social (corporations, slavery, democratic institutions). All inventions are based on previous knowledge, discoveries, and inventions. For this reason, the nature and rate of inventions in a particular society depend on its existing store of knowledge. The cave dweller has little knowledge to work with, and merely to produce a bow and arrow is a considerable intellectual achievement. We are no cleverer than our "primitive" ancestors; we simply have more knowledge to build on. As Ralph Linton (1936) remarked, "If Einstein had been born into a primitive tribe which was unable to count beyond three, lifelong application to mathematics probably would not have carried him beyond the development of a decimal system based on fingers and toes." Inventions occur exponentially: the more inventions that exist in a culture, the more rapidly further inventions can be made. To take a simple example: 3 elements can theoretically be combined into 6 new combinations, 4 into 24, 5 into 125, and so on. Given a sufficient cultural store of knowledge, new inventions become almost inevitable. Ogburn (1950) listed 150 inventions that were made almost simultaneously by different scientists living in the same or similar cultures (see Figure 23.6). This fact helps to explain why the modernization process took so much longer in those societies that had to make the necessary discoveries and inventions than it did in those societies that merely had to adopt them from others.

Diffusion

The process of *diffusion* involves the spread of cultural elements—both material artifacts and ideas—from one society to another. George Murdock (1934) has estimated that about 90 percent of the contents of every culture have been acquired from other societies, and some social scientists (for example, Kroeber, 1937) see diffusion as the main source of cultural and social change. The most outstanding contemporary social change, modernization, represents the diffusion of industrialism from the advanced to the less developed societies. Each culture accepts elements from other cultures selectively, however. Material artifacts that prove useful are more readily accepted than new norms, values, or beliefs. Innovations must also be compatible with the culture of the society into which they diffuse. For these reasons, white settlers in America accepted the Indians' tobacco but not their religion.

Human Action

One obvious source of social change is human action, which may bring about social changes whether they are intended and foreseen or not. Two types of human action are particularly important: the acts of powerful leaders and other individuals, and the social movements and collective behaviors of large numbers of people.

Figure 23.7 Diffusion is the process by which cultural elements spread from one society to another. Mexico has a long tradition of public mural painting, a cultural trait that has diffused to the United States as a result of Chicano migration. But, as always happens in situations of cultural diffusion, the trait has been modified in its new environment. The murals of Los Angeles and other cities with large Chicano populations are less relevant to Mexico than to life in the urban barrios of the United States.

The precise influence of individuals on the course of history and social change is very difficult to judge. Take the case of Julius Caesar. As a general in the army of the Roman republic, he made the historic decision to cross the river Rubicon, march on Rome, and overthrow the republican form of government, replacing it with a dictatorship. His act led directly to an imperial form of government, and the empire passed from him through his adopted son Augustus to tyrants such as Nero and Caligula. If Caesar had not taken that step, the Roman republic might have survived; Augustus, Nero, Caligula, and the rest would not have become emperors; and the entire history of the Western world would have taken a different course. Or would it? We cannot know. We cannot conduct an experiment in which we remove Caesar from the scene and wait to see what happens.

Historians and biographers have often taken what is sometimes called the "great man" theory of history and social change. Sociologists have generally rejected this approach, taking the view that history makes individuals rather than that individuals make history. Sociologists see the personality and ambitions of leaders, like those of anyone else, as being strongly influenced by the culture in which the particular figures were born and socialized. From the sociological perspective, the social changes that individuals appear to have created are better seen as the product of deeper social forces. Caesar could destroy the Roman republic only because it was already on its last legs; fifty years earlier his act would have been impossible and even unthinkable. If he had not acted when he did, others might have done so instead, and later events might have followed a broadly similar course. Nor can World War II be attributed simply to the personality and ambitions of Adolf Hitler. Hitler certainly influenced the course of events, but if there had not been severe social, ethnic, and economic strains in Germany at the time, he might never have come to power or have had the opportunity to put his policies into effect. If a person of the same personality and ideas were to appear in a different society or a different time—say, in modern Canada—his impact on history would extend no further than the local prison or mental hospital.

The role of collective action in social change poses less difficulty. Collective behavior (such as fads, fashions, and riots), and social movements (such as those that aim to bring about reforms or even revolutions), represent an

Figure 23.8 One of the most important sources of social change is human action, particularly the concerted action by radical movements such as Mao's communist revolution, which created modern China. These movements actively intervene in the course of history, attempting to influence the direction of change.

attempt by people to change their social environment (Smelser, 1962; Zald and McCarthy, 1979). Large-scale movements—for women's liberation, civil rights, national independence, religious conversion, and so on—are a vital source of social change. So, too, are the actions of other social agencies and institutions, particularly governments that determine policies in the deliberate attempt to change society.

Technology

Technology—the practical applications of scientific or other knowledge—is a major source of social change. We have only to look around us to see how our way of life and social behavior are influenced by various technologies, ranging from kitchen gadgets to automobiles.

Most technological innovations are based on existing scientific knowledge and technology. The more advanced a society is in this respect, therefore, the faster the pace of technological change is likely to be. And the more rapid the technological change, the more rapid is the social change that it generates.

A mere sixty-six years elapsed between the first faltering flight of the Wright brothers and the landing of the first astronauts on the moon. The rate of technological change in modern industrial societies has no historical precedent. Throughout most of history, people lived in a world little different from that of their parents, and they expected their children and grandchildren to live much the same lives as they did. Traditional societies assume an almost unchanging social world and are typically very suspicious of change. In the modern world, however, we accept change as the norm. We look for novelty, we are oriented to the future rather than the past, and we expect constant improvements in our material environment. Alvin Toffler (1970) has argued that we are living in a permanent state of "future shock." The future, he contends, continually intrudes into the stability of the present. Ours is a "throwaway" society in which change takes place faster than we can adjust to it.

The pace of technological change has implications for every area of society. Medical advances have lengthened life expectancy and slashed the death rate, radically altering population structure. Innovations in industrial technology displace thousands of workers and render recently manufactured machinery obsolete within a few years. Cultural activities are transformed through such innovations as radio, television, and phonograph records. People require long years of training and education if they are to function effectively in a highly technological society, and increasingly they need reeducation later in life if they are to keep up with advances in knowledge and techniques. The socialization process, which in simple societies consists almost entirely of passing the culture of one generation on to the next, becomes both more complex and more inadequate, for the knowledge of one generation grows obsolete in some respects even before it can be transmitted to the young; and the young, for their part, cannot be fully socialized for a future that cannot be anticipated with any certainty. The influence of technology on society seems so powerful that some sociologists have supported the theory of *technological determinism*—the view that the technology available to a society is an important determinant of its culture, social structure, and even of its history. There is a strong element of technological determinism in the work of Karl Marx, who called attention to the way technologies of economic production affect the social order. Several American social scientists, notably Thorstein Veblen (1922) and William Ogburn (1950), have also argued that specific historical developments and culture traits are the direct result of particular technologies.

Within limits, this view has considerable validity. It is obvious, for example, that the technology that a society uses to produce energy sets certain limits on its way of life. A society that relies on the muscle power of its own members is under severe restrictions. People must spend much of their time producing food, and must live in small, isolated groups. A society that uses the power of animals has far more options. It can develop agriculture, and with it a larger population in a smaller area, an economic surplus, specialized nonproductive roles for some of its members, and a system of social stratification. A society that uses machines driven by natural forces—wind, water, steam, electricity, nuclear fusion—has vastly greater potential for internal complexity and for supporting a population of many millions (Davis, 1948; Lenski, 1966; White, 1959).

When specific social and historical events are explained in terms of technological determinism, however, the case is much harder to prove. William Ogburn attempted to trace links of this kind. He argued, for example, that the invention of the cotton gin in 1793 encouraged the use of slavery in the United States. The cotton gin greatly increased the productivity and thus the profits of the textile industry, and many more slaves were needed to work on the new cotton plantations that sprang into being. Like Karl Marx, Ogburn divided human culture into material and nonmaterial elements. He acknowledged that a change could initially take place in either element but argued that changes usually occur in the material culture first. People accept new tools much more readily than they accept new ideas,

Figure 23.9 The rate of technological change in modern societies is without precedent. This glider, piloted by Orville Wright, was considered something of a marvel in 1908; the space craft that brought this astronaut to the moon is already obsolete. The reason for the rapid pace of technological innovation is that each innovation builds on previous ones. The greater the accumulation of technology, therefore, the faster the rate of innovation is likely to be.

Figure 23.10 A single technological innovation can have far-reaching effects. Until the invention of gunpowder, castles and battlements provided an adequate defense against military opponents, for battering rams could rarely force an entry. The invention of gunpowder made possible the use of cannon, which could blast a hole in the stoutest gate or wall. The hitherto impregnable castles became almost useless; few were built thereafter, and new patterns of warfare emerged instead.

values, or norms, but these technological innovations inevitably lead to changes in the nonmaterial culture. As a result, there is always a *culture lag* as the nonmaterial aspects attempt to "catch up" with changes in the material parts of culture. Ogburn argued that this culture lag is a continuing source of social disorganization and social problems.

This argument is persuasive, as you will appreciate if you consider the social impact of such innovations as gunpowder, the compass, the printing press, the automobile, the elevator (which makes skyscrapers practical), or the jet engine. But the theory has its limitations. Technological change, such as the introduction of the cotton gin, always occurs in the context of other influences. It is very difficult, if not impossible, to prove that the technological factor was the main cause of social change. Moreover, the precise effect of technological innovation depends on the culture into which it is introduced. Technology and other elements in society are best seen as parts of an interacting system.

Evaluation

This list of specific factors in social change is formidable, but by no means exhaustive. Can any one factor, then, be paramount, or are some factors perhaps more frequently involved in change than others?

There are no simple answers to such questions, for social change is too complex to permit them. The essential point is that change is never the product of any one factor. As Parsons (1966) reminds us:

> No claim that social change is determined by economic interests, ideas, personalities of particular individuals, geographic conditions, and so on, is acceptable. All such single-factor theories belong to the kindergarten stage of a social science's development. Any single factor is always interdependent with several others.

Existing conditions determine which changes will be accepted, which will be rejected, and which will be adopted in modified form. The highly conservative rulers of Tibet were able to keep the wheel out of their mountain kingdom for almost a thousand years. Sub-Saharan African peoples, to whom cattle are a form of wealth, have refused to practice "rational" stock-rearing methods that would give them fewer but healthier cattle. Islam is being accepted more readily than Christianity in many parts of Africa, largely because it is not seen as a "white" religion and because it permits polygyny, which most African peoples practice. A remarkably broad range of changes is acceptable in the United States because it is a change-oriented culture with a commitment to science, technology, and the pursuit of a better society.

Theories of Social Change

A number of general theories of social change have been proposed, not only by sociologists but also by historians and anthropologists, for their respective disciplines all have a common interest in the subject. The various theories may be grouped conveniently into four main categories: evolutionary, cyclical, functional, and conflict theories. The study of these theories, incidentally, gives us an interesting insight into the sociology of knowledge and belief. Each type of theory won acceptance because it fitted so well with popular assumptions that prevailed at the time.

Evolutionary Theories

Evolutionary theories are based on the assumption that societies gradually develop from simple beginnings into ever more complex forms. This assumption rests on both anthropological and historical evidence. We know from the cross-cultural data that there have been and still are many small-scale, simple societies, such as those of hunters and gatherers, horticulturalists, and pastoralists. We know from the historical data that many small, simple societies have grown steadily larger, and some of them have been transformed into the huge industrial societies of the modern world. But how is this evidence to be interpreted?

The Early Theorists: Unilinear Evolution

Early sociologists, beginning with Auguste Comte, believed that human societies evolve in a *unilinear* way—that is, in "one line" of development that recurs in every society. These thinkers also made an assumption that was unusual at the time, although it is familiar to us today: that social "change" meant "progress" toward something better. They saw change as positive and beneficial, because the evolutionary process implied that societies would necessarily reach new and higher levels of civilization.

The middle and late nineteenth century was an era of colonial expansion, in which soldiers, missionaries, merchants, and adventurers from European countries penetrated distant lands whose peoples had been almost unknown to the rest of the world. The new science of anthropology arose, dedicated to the study of the exotic, "primitive" peoples whose cultures were described in letters and books by the early colonists. However, few of the early anthropologists did any actual field work among the peoples they studied. Anthropology was mainly an "armchair" discipline that relied on the reports—often inaccurate and sometimes irresponsibly imaginative—of untrained observers in faraway places. Working primarily from this kind of information, a number of early anthropologists claimed that all societies passed through a number of stages, beginning in primitive origins and climaxing in Western civilization. Lewis Henry Morgan, for example, believed that there are three basic stages in the process: savagery, barbarism, and civilization.

This evolutionary view of social change drew much of its impetus from Charles Darwin's *On the Origin of Species*, published in 1859. Darwin had shown that all life forms had evolved from distant origins and that the general direction of biological evolution was toward greater com-

Figure 23.11 Evolutionary theories of social change won widespread support in Europe because they made Western civilization seem a "higher" form than that of other peoples—and so justified the European colonists' exploitation of the labor and resources of distant lands. This photograph shows a nineteenth-century colonial official on an outpost in the Atlantic.

plexity. Other writers immediately applied this theory to human society. The cultures of different societies around the world, they argued, offered glimpses of what culture must have been like at different stages of the evolutionary process; the most primitive cultures and peoples were the closest to the original state of the human species, while the cultures and peoples of Western societies were the most advanced.

Herbert Spencer's sociology even applied Darwin's principle of "the survival of the fittest" to human societies. He claimed that Western "races," classes, or societies had survived and evolved to "higher" levels than non-Western ones because they were better adapted to face the conditions of life. This view, known as *social Darwinism,* won extraordinarily wide acceptance in the late nineteenth century. It survived in both Europe and the United States until World War I, and was used to justify the dominance of whites over nonwhites, of the rich over the poor, and of the powerful over the weak.

Evaluation

It is easy to see why these early evolutionary doctrines were readily accepted. The discovery of so many "primitive" peoples posed a difficult question: Why were some societies more "advanced" than others? Evolutionary theory provided not only an answer but also a flattering and convenient justification for colonial rule over "lesser peoples." There was little conception of cultural relativity at the time. People judged other cultures purely in terms of their own culture's standards and, not surprisingly, found them inferior. The ethnocentric belief that all human societies were evolving in a unilinear way toward one crowning achievement—Western civilization—provided an ideology that legitimized the political and economic interests of the colonizers. The enforced spread of Western culture was conveniently thought of as "the white man's burden"—the thankless but noble task of bringing "higher" forms of civilization to "inferior" peoples.

One problem with evolutionary theories of this unilinear type is that they described but did not explain social change. They offered no account of how or why societies should evolve toward the Western pattern. A second and fatal problem is that they were based on faulty interpretations of the data. Armchair theorists grouped vastly different cultures into misleading categories so that they

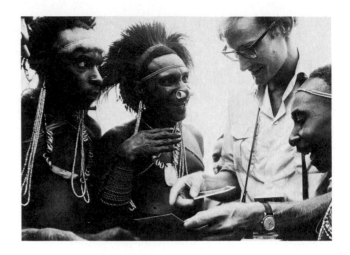

Figure 23.12 *The evolutionary theorists of the nineteenth century assumed that all societies evolve in the same unilinear manner through a series of "stages," culminating in Western civilization. As the ethnographic evidence from preindustrial societies mounted, however, it became clear that no such sequence of stages exists. The "primitive" people in the southwestern Pacific, for example, are being introduced directly to Western culture, thereby skipping the various "stages" that, according to this evolutionary theory, they should pass through.*

would fit into whatever "stages" they thought they had found. The trends in Western history were ethnocentrically equated with "progress," largely because only one aspect of change—technological and economic development—was emphasized. Other peoples might regard Western cultures as technologically developed yet morally backward, but the evolutionary theorists never considered this more relativistic view. In later years, however, the ethnographic data gathered firsthand from traditional societies soon showed that they did not follow the same step-by-step evolutionary sequence. They developed in different ways, often by borrowing ideas and innovations from other societies. The San ("Bushmen") of the Kalahari and the aborigines of Australia, for example, are among the most supposedly "primitive" peoples in the world. Yet they are being introduced directly to industrial society, and are thus skipping the "stages" that, according to evolutionary theory, they should first pass through. By the 1920s, unilinear evolutionary theory in sociology and anthropology was dead as the dodo.

A Modern View: Multilinear Evolution

More recently, however, anthropologists have again developed an interest in social and cultural evolution. But this time they see the process as a *tendency*, not a universal "law," and they do not press the analogy between societies and living organisms. They point out, however, that societies generally tend to move from small-scale, simple forms of social structure and culture to large-scale, complex forms. Modern anthropologists (for example, Steward, 1956) agree that this evolutionary process is *multilinear*. In other words, it can take place in many different ways, and change does not necessarily follow exactly the same direction in every society. Unlike earlier theorists, modern anthropologists no longer believe that "change" necessarily means "progress." They do not assume that greater social complexity produces greater human happiness. This view, much more tentative than that of the early evolutionists, is now finding its way into the mainstream of anthropological and sociological thought (for example, Lenski, 1966; Lenski and Lenski, 1978; Fried, 1967; Parsons, 1966; Service, 1971).

Cyclical Theories

It was largely the senseless slaughter of World War I and the growing signs of social and economic disorganization in the industrial societies early in this century that led many people to wonder whether social "change" really meant social "progress" after all. In the aftermath of these events new theories of social change were proposed—theories that focused instead on the cyclical nature of change as displayed in the rise and fall of civilizations. The assumption that Western civilization was the crowning achievement of history seemed much less certain, and there even arose the question, Might not this civilization be destined, like all its predecessors, to extinction? And if so, what forces were responsible for these cycles of change?

Spengler: The Destiny of Civilizations

In 1918, a German schoolteacher, Oswald Spengler, published *The Decline of the West*. His sweeping, poetic account of the rise and fall of civilizations won wide readership and acclaim. The fate of civilizations, Spengler declared, was a matter of "destiny." Each civilization is like a biological organism and has a similar life cycle: birth, maturity, old age, and death. All creative activity takes place in the early stages of the cycle; as the civilization matures, it loses its original inspiration, becomes more materialistic, and de-

Figure 23.13 Cyclical theories of social change focus on the rise and fall of civilizations, attempting to discover and account for these patterns of growth and decay. This picture shows the ancient Inca city of Machu Pichu in Peru. Located on an isolated 8000-foot-high mountaintop in the Andes, it was deserted by its inhabitants several centuries ago, for reasons that are not known. The city remained "lost" until it was discovered in 1911.

clines. Spengler concluded that Western societies were entering a period of decay—as evidenced by wars, conflict, and social breakdown—that heralded their doom (Spengler, 1926; originally published 1918, 1922). Spengler's theory is out of fashion today. Although no sociologist would be so foolish as to reject the possibility that Western civilization and the societies that share it might ultimately be doomed, "destiny" is hardly an adequate explanation of social change.

Toynbee: Challenge and Response

A somewhat more promising theory was offered by Arnold Toynbee, a British historian with considerable sociological insight. His multivolume work *A Study of History* (1946) draws on material from twenty-one civilizations. The key concepts in his theory are those of "challenge" and "response." Every society faces challenges—at first, challenges posed by the environment; later, challenges from internal and external enemies. The nature of the society's responses determines its fate. The achievements of a civilization consist of its successful responses to major challenges; if it cannot mount effective responses, it dies. Toynbee's work is more optimistic than Spengler's: history, he argues, is a series of cycles of decay and growth, but each new civilization is able to borrow from other cultures and to learn from their mistakes. It is therefore possible for each new cycle to offer higher levels of achievement. Unlike Spengler's cycles, Toynbee's build upon one another—rather like a circular staircase. His arguments, however, are not very persuasive. He never fully explains why only some societies are able to successfully meet the challenges they encounter, or why a society should overcome one challenge but succumb to another. Few sociologists—or historians, for that matter—believe that the complexity of human history and social change can be explained through Toynbee's theory.

Evaluation

Cyclical theories of social change may at first seem attractive because they deal with an observed historical fact: all civilizations of the past have risen and fallen. But this does not mean that historical and social change is necessarily cyclical. The fact that the sun has risen and set every day in recorded history gives us good reason to suppose that it will do so again tomorrow. Changes in human societies, however, are not subject to such inexorable "laws"—or if they

Figure 23.14

*"Once upon a time, long, long ago,
way before everything got screwed up . . ."*

Copyright Wm. Hamilton

are, the cyclical theorists have failed to discover them. To say that cyclical changes are caused by a tendency for change to occur in cycles explains nothing: it is like explaining the movement of an automobile in terms of its "automotive tendency." These theories also place too much emphasis on mysterious forces such as "destiny" and too little emphasis on human action. If, as is conceivable, a human society were to develop both the knowledge and the means necessary to control and direct social change, what would become of these supposedly inevitable cycles?

Functionalist Theories

Functionalist theories of social change start with the advantage that they deal with social statics before dealing with social dynamics. In the opinion of some critics, however, their very emphasis on social order and stability has prevented them from giving an adequate theory of social change (for example, Mills, 1959; Dahrendorf, 1958).

The functionalist perspective was first systematically applied by Emile Durkheim, who examined several aspects of society by asking what function they play in maintaining the social order as a whole. Religion, he found, has the function of providing a common set of values that enhance the solidarity of the believers; the schools have the function

Figure 23.15 In a small-scale, preindustrial society, such as that of the Hoti Indians of Central America, institutions are undifferentiated: for example, the family institution is responsible for education, economic production, and many aspects of religious ceremony, political decision making, warfare, and so on. According to functionalist theory, social change consists largely of the process by which these functions are differentiated into several interrelated institutions as a society becomes more complex. It is assumed, however, that in all societies the various parts of the social system are more or less in balance, and that changes occur mainly to correct any imbalances that develop.

of passing culture from one generation to the next. The American sociologist Talcott Parsons, drawing on the work of Durkheim and other early European sociologists—not including Marx—tried to develop a general theory of social order based on the functionalist perspective.

Parsons's Theory of Social Order

Parsons's writings are wordy, abstract, and make singularly difficult reading. The basic idea of his early work, however, is not very complex. In brief, Parsons (1937, 1951) argued that a society consists of interdependent parts, each of which helps to maintain the stability of the entire system. Cultural patterns, particularly shared norms and values, hold the society together. Because these patterns are inherently conservative, they also serve to resist radical changes. Society is able to absorb disruptive forces because it is constantly straining for *equilibrium,* or balance.

The focus of Parsons's early writings was thus on social statistics, not social dynamics. In his major work, *The Social System* (1951), Parsons devoted only one chapter to social change, which he saw as something that must be "introduced into the system." His approach thus failed to account for change: How could disruptions, even revolutions, occur in this stable, self-regulating system? Moreover, changes tended to be regarded as dysfunctions, as unwelcome irritants that disturbed the smooth functioning of society.

Throughout the forties and fifties, Parsons's work dominated American sociology. American society was enjoying a period of relative cohesion and stability, and Parsons's emphasis on society as a balanced system that integrated small yet necessary changes was in tune with the times. But the major social conflict in the United States in the late fifties and throughout the sixties raised many doubts about Parsons's assumptions. C. Wright Mills and other sociologists (for example, Lockwood, 1956) questioned whether a theory of equilibrium and stability is relevant to societies that are in a state of constant change and social conflict. In his later writings, Parsons (1961, 1966) confronted this problem and attempted to include social change in his functionalist model.

Parsons's Theory of Social Change

Parsons came to see change not as something that disturbs the social equilibrium but as something that alters it, with the result that a qualitatively new equilibrium results. He acknowledges that changes may arise from two sources. They may come either from outside the society, through contact with other societies, or they may come from inside the society, through adjustments that must be made to resolve strains within the system.

Figure 23.16 According to Marx, conflict between classes is a major source of social change. An oppressed class will inevitably revolt against its rulers, and, if successful, will usher in a new social order. This photograph shows a clash between police and rioting workers in Petrograd at the start of the Russian Revolution in 1917.

Parsons also adopts what amounts to an evolutionary view of the changes that take place as a society becomes progressively more complex. Two processes, he argues, are at work. In simple societies, institutions are undifferentiated: that is, a single institution serves many different functions. The family, for example, is responsible for reproduction, education, economic production, and socialization. As a society becomes more complex, a process of *differentiation* takes place. Various institutions, such as schools and corporations, emerge and take over the functions that were previously undifferentiated. But the new institutions must be linked together once more, this time by the process of *integration*. New norms, for example, must evolve to govern the relationship between the school and the home, and "bridging institutions," such as law courts, must resolve conflicts between other components of the system.

Evaluation

Parsons's work is an ambitious attempt to explain both social statics and social dynamics, although his focus is still overwhelmingly on the former. His theory remains limited, however, in that it does not presume to cover all possible forms of social change. It deals only with the institutional changes that take place as a society modernizes. Other functionalists have nevertheless accepted that tensions may cause social changes of many types, even in the most harmonious social system. Robert Merton (1968), for example, writes of the "strain, tension, contradiction, and discrepancy between the component parts of social structure" that may provoke social change. In so doing, however, he is borrowing concepts from conflict theories of change. As we shall see, a blend of conflict and functionalist ideas can prove fruitful.

Conflict Theories

Karl Marx declared that "violence is the midwife of history." In a similar vein, Mao wrote that "change comes from the barrel of a gun." The conflict theory of change, of which Marx is the most prominent and eloquent exponent, holds that change is caused by tensions between competing interests in society.

Marx: Change Through Class Conflict

"All history," Marx and Engels wrote in *The Communist Manifesto* (1848), "is the history of class conflict." As we have noted earlier, Marx believed that the character of social and cultural forms is influenced by the economic base of society—specifically, by the mode of production that is used and by the relationships that exist between those who own the means of production and those who work for them. History is the story of conflict between the exploiting and the exploited classes. This conflict repeats itself again and again until capitalism is overthrown by the workers and a socialist state is created. Socialism is the forerunner of the ultimate social form, communism. Marx's theories have been dealt with in several previous chapters and need not be elaborated here. The essential point is that Marx and other conflict theorists after him see society as fundamentally dynamic, not static. They regard conflict as a normal, not an abnormal, process, and they believe that the existing conditions in any society contain the seeds of future social changes.

Other Conflicts as Sources of Change

Later Marxist writers kept Marx's emphasis on class conflict as the source of social change, but other conflict theorists, although influenced by Marx, have focused on conflict between groups other than social classes. An early German sociologist, Georg Simmel (1904, 1955), claimed that conflict binds people together in interaction: although hate and envy may drive them apart, they cannot enter into conflict without interacting with their opponents. Moreover, conflict encourages people of similar interests to bind together to achieve their objectives. In this way, Simmel argued, continuous conflict keeps a society dynamic and changing. Ralf Dahrendorf (1958) regards the view that "all history is the history of class conflict" as an "unjustifiable oversimplification." He points to conflicts be-

Figure 23.17 Many conflict theorists emphasize a variety of tensions and competition as a major source of nonrevolutionary social change. Thus conflict between capitalists and workers in the United States has led to many changes in industrial organization and working conditions. This engraving shows an 1892 battle between workers and agents hired by the employers.

tween racial groups, between nations, between political parties, and between religious groups as examples involving units other than social classes. All these conflicts, he believes, can lead to social changes.

Evaluation

Tension and disputes over values and scarce resources is clearly a cause of social change. Conflict theory does not account for all forms of social change, but it does give us a means of analyzing some of the most significant events in history and contemporary society. It can be applied, for example, to the overthrow of feudalism and its replacement by capitalist industrialism, or to the civil rights movement in the United States and continuing changes in patterns of race relations. Yet it is not a comprehensive theory of social change. Conflict theory cannot, for example, tell us why technology is having such a dramatic effect on the rate of social change in the United States. It cannot tell us why forms of family organization are changing. Above all, it cannot tell us much about the future direction of social change. Even hard-line Marxists have been unable to predict successfully the countries, or the periods, in which socialist revolutions will occur, although they are able to provide plausible explanations of similar changes in the past. But a fully satisfactory theory must do more than explain history. It must also give us sufficient understanding of social dynamics for us to be able to predict, at least in broad outline, the future implications of present trends.

A Synthesis

Some of the theories that attempt to explain social change are clearly unsatisfactory, and no single theory seems able to account for all social change. Where, then, does our survey leave us?

Cyclical theories of change seem unacceptable. They are too speculative, too subjective, and they give no explanation of how or why change takes place. *Unilinear evolutionary* theories are also unacceptable, for they are based on faulty data about other cultures. *Multilinear evolutionary* theory, however, may prove more useful. It seems to fit the facts: societies generally tend to evolve from the small and simple to the large and complex. They do so in different ways, but a change in the mode of production is always involved, usually culminating in industrialism. The theory also helps explain why these changes take place. The more elaborate a culture becomes, the greater the probability of new invention and discovery. And the more efficient the mode of production becomes, the greater use a society is able to make of its environment. It is able to produce a steadily greater economic surplus, which permits population growth, urbanization, and modernization. But the theory is not fully satisfactory, for it explains only one

dimension of social change—the evolution of societies from simple to complex, from preindustrial to industrial. It tells us nothing, for example, about wars, revolutions, migrations, and other important forms of change.

Functionalist and *conflict* theories seem at first sight to be at odds with one another, and indeed the debate between advocates of each view has become quite heated at times. If we look at the basic assumptions of each approach, the contrast seems quite glaring.

1. Functionalist theory holds that every society is relatively stable; conflict theory holds that every society is in a process of continuous change.

2. Functionalist theory holds that every society is well integrated; conflict theory holds that every society experiences continuous conflict and tension.

3. Functionalist theory holds that every element in society contributes to its functioning; conflict theory holds that every element in society contributes to its change.

4. Functionalist theory holds that every society is bound together by the common values of its members; conflict theory holds that every society is bound together by the coercion of some of its members by others.

As Ralf Dahrendorf (1958) points out, however, both parts of all the above statements are true, although they may seem contradictory. The reason for the paradox lies in the contradictory nature of society itself. Societies *are* stable, enduring systems, but they *do* experience conflict and continuous change. The functionalist and conflict approaches are merely focusing on different aspects of social reality: one mainly on statics, one mainly on dynamics.

There seems to be no logical reason why the two theories cannot be integrated to a considerable extent (Smelser, 1967; Gouldner, 1970; Van den Berghe, 1963). As we have noted, Merton has introduced the concepts of "strain" and "tension" from conflict theory into functionalist theory. In a similar vein, Lewis Coser (1956) has written about the "functions" of conflict in society. Conflict, Coser points out, can be functional for the social system because it prevents stagnation and generates necessary changes.

Evolutionary theory, in its multilinear form, is compatible with either functionalist or conflict theory. If we take an evolutionary perspective on social change and combine it with functionalist or conflict theory—or, where appropriate, with both—we have the best general theory of social change. It remains an imperfect theory, admittedly, but it provides a rich understanding of many forms of social change.

Modernization

Modernization is the process of economic and social change that is brought about by the introduction of the industrial mode of production into a preindustrial society. The process is now sweeping the globe as the less developed nations of the world follow the patterns established by the more advanced industrial societies. Modernization represents one of the most significant social changes in history, for it has implications for nearly every other area of social life—a testimony to the powerful influence of the economic order on other aspects of society.

The Modernization Process

Until a few centuries ago, the human population of the world consisted of a large number of relatively localized and isolated societies, most of whose members lived at a subsistence level in economies based on hunting, gathering, horticulture, pastoralism, or agriculture. The Industrial Revolution ushered in an entirely new type of society, one that produced unprecedented wealth but also undermined or destroyed traditional forms of social organization and created new ones in their place. The modernization process in the early industrial societies of Europe took several generations. In these countries culture and social structure were able to adapt relatively slowly, although not necessarily very easily, to the social changes involved.

In the less developed parts of the world, however, change has come much more rapidly and with many more dislocating effects. Some of the previously undeveloped societies were thrust into the modernization process whether their inhabitants wished it or not. The early industrial

Figure 23.18 Nearly all the less developed nations of the world are attempting to modernize, even though they lack many of the resources necessary to achieve this goal rapidly and effectively. These Chinese workers are building a massive irrigation project, but are doing so without the industrial machinery that Westerners would consider essential for the project. Every year more than 100 million Chinese take part in public-works projects of this kind.

powers needed cheap labor and raw materials for their industries and markets for their products, and they used their far-flung colonies to fuel their own economic development. More recently, particularly since dozens of former colonial nations achieved their independence after World War II, undeveloped countries have embarked on crash programs of modernization.

These countries are hoping to achieve in the space of a few years the material advantages that the older industrial nations have taken nearly two centuries to gain. The result has often been a tug-of-war between the forces of modernization and the sentiments of tradition, with serious social disorganization as the result. The responses to disorganization have taken many different forms: military coups by army officers determined to impose social order; millenarian religious movements prophesying a return to a golden age of the past or the advent of a new golden age in the future; revolutions aimed at reconstructing society in accordance with a coherent program for social change; or nationalism as a new ideology to unite the people for the challenge of modernization. Iran provides a case in point: a sudden influx of oil wealth, combined with an autocratic shah's attempt to transform a backward nation into an industrial and military power, provoked a violent revolution, a return to more fundamentalist religious principles, a new feeling of Iranian nationalism, and continuing political disagreement between traditionalists and those favoring renewed modernization. But whatever the drawbacks of modernization, there are few societies in the world today that are not openly committed to the process.

The Social Effects of Modernization

The modernization process affects virtually every area of society. We have already encountered many of its effects throughout this book, but by reviewing them in one place we can gain a better picture of their interrelatedness and their scale. In brief, modernization has the following characteristic effects.

Culture

Culture is no longer maintained and enacted primarily in the small rural community. It becomes a widely shared mass culture, spread not only within the society but from society to society by the mass media and through travel.

Within mass cultures, however, a variety of new subcultures appear, so that large modernized societies are more heterogeneous in their values and outlook than are small traditional societies.

Personal Values

Personal values and attitudes alter markedly. People are more change-oriented. They look to the future rather than to the past; they are less fatalistic and have more faith in the human capacity to dominate and transform the environment. Perhaps most important, they develop a strong sense of individualism, with a corresponding loss of loyalty to a community.

Social Groups

The small, primary group—particularly the kinship network—is no longer able to meet most social or individual needs. For many purposes it is replaced by anonymous secondary groups. Most social institutions become bureaucratized, and large formal organizations, such as industrial corporations or government departments, multiply throughout the society, and become new centers of power and influence.

Social Stratification

In the early stages of industrialization there is a yawning gap between the incomes of the privileged few and the masses. In the more advanced industrial societies, however, the growing wealth of the society tends to be more equally shared. Rigid forms of stratification based on ascribed characteristics, such as race or caste, tend to dissolve. The rate of social mobility increases, and social status is increasingly achieved by personal effort rather than ascribed on arbitrary grounds.

Social Inequalities

The nature and degree of other forms of social inequality also change. In the early stages of industrialization, women tend to stay home and therefore have low status relative to men; in the later stages, their growing participation in the work force brings them greater equality. Modernization profoundly affects the status of the elderly: they lose the powerful and privileged position they had in preindustrial societies, and find themselves with few useful roles to play. Power shifts to the middle-aged, and youthfulness becomes more highly valued, in many respects, than maturity. Because large modern societies often include conquered or immigrant minorities, they frequently face problems of racial and ethnic inequalities.

The Family

The extended family system, found in nearly all traditional societies, is shattered. The family is no longer a unit of production, and the extended family becomes dysfunctional in a society requiring geographic and social mobility among its members. The monogamous nuclear family takes its place, and traditional kinship ties are loosened or broken.

Education

Formal organizations, the schools, take over many of the family's earlier socialization functions. Education is extended to the masses, not just to the privileged few, because an industrial work force must be skilled and literate. Universities, colleges, and research institutes multiply, serving both to transmit and to create specialized knowledge.

Religion

A single traditional religion is no longer the central element in a society's belief system. Cults, sects, and denominations multiply, and increasing numbers of people interpret the world through secular rather than religious principles. The process of secularization leaves religion as a marginal social institution.

Science

Science emerges for the first time as a major social institution, largely because industrialization relies on the technological applications of scientific knowledge. Technical efficiency becomes a value—an end, not simply a means—and people look to technology for the solutions to their problems, including the many unexpected problems that technology creates.

Economics

Economic activity is based on industrial production, which produces unprecedented wealth. The division of labor becomes highly specialized, and increasing numbers of people work in "white collar" rather than "blue collar" jobs. Alienation becomes a persistent feature of the workplace.

Figure 23.19 A typical feature of the modernization process is the discrepancy that exists in developing nations between people's traditional obligations and the new world that industrialization is creating around them. For example, many Muslim nations are experiencing tension between the conservative force of their religion and the innovations thrust upon them by their new oil wealth.

Economies become oriented toward socialist or capitalist systems of production and distribution. In capitalist societies, national and even multinational corporations become new centers of economic power and political influence.

Politics

A strong, centralized state emerges if none existed previously, and it regulates more and more areas of social and economic life. The long-term trend in the advanced industrialized societies has been toward greater formal democracy, but the newer modernizing societies are almost without exception ruled by new elites who cannot be removed from office by popular vote.

Population and Health

Death rates decline sharply as modern medical facilities are extended to the population. In the older industrial countries, birth rates have slowly declined as well, but in the developing nations, social norms have not yet adjusted to the decline in death rates, and large families are still highly valued. The result has been a population explosion unprecedented in human history.

Ecology

Pollution, rarely a problem in preindustrial societies, becomes a serious by-product of modernization; and as more societies grow more industrialized, pollution destroys or endangers thousands of other life forms. Depletion of scarce nonrenewable resources is a further grave problem associated with modernization.

Urbanization

Cities grow rapidly, largely because industries are concentrated in urban areas and people are attracted by job opportunities. In all highly industrialized countries a majority of the population now lives in urban areas, and urbanization is currently taking place even faster in some developing nations than it has in the older industrial countries.

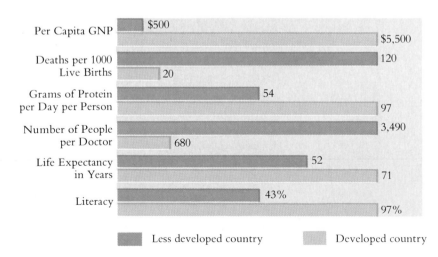

THE DEVELOPMENT GAP

	Less developed country	Developed country
Per Capita GNP	$500	$5,500
Deaths per 1000 Live Births	120	20
Grams of Protein per Day per Person	54	97
Number of People per Doctor	3,490	680
Life Expectancy in Years	52	71
Literacy	43%	97%

Source: Report of the Presidential Commission on World Hunger, Overcoming World Hunger: The Challenge Ahead (June 1980), p. 4.

Figure 23.20 As this chart shows, there is a yawning gap between the standards of living in the developing countries of the Third World and those of developed industrial societies. Moreover, the gap is steadily widening. The inequalities between the developed and less developed nations will become one of the most critical problems of the future.

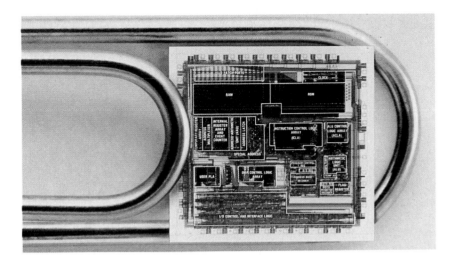

Figure 23.21 This micro chip, smaller than a paper clip, contains more information than could be stored in hundreds of filing cabinets. Chips of this kind can be put to an astonishing variety of uses, and in the next few years will be present in many familiar appliances and machines, ranging from telephones to automobiles.

The scale, significance, and consequences of these changes are immense—so much so that their implications are still difficult to grasp fully. As we noted in Chapter 4 ("Society"), the transition from a preindustrial to an industrial mode of production marks the most radical break in the course of sociocultural evolution. This transformation was precisely what the major figures of sociology in the nineteenth century were trying to understand, and sociologists grapple with the problem to this day.

A Postindustrial Society?

To what extent does our present understanding of social change permit us to predict the future? We are able to do so within limits, particularly for those societies that have not yet reached our level of industrial development. The United States, Canada, and other advanced industrial societies such as the Soviet Union provide the mirrors in which developing societies can see the outlines of their own futures, and sociological analysis enables us to predict the general lines that social change in these countries will follow. But when we look to our own future, we have no example to guide us. We can, however, make fairly confident predictions about specific areas of society. We can anticipate the likely effect of population growth and we can project the future trends in urbanization, for example. But

when it comes to predicting the overall form of our society in the future, we are somewhat in the dark.

Nevertheless, there is no shortage of attempts to predict this future. Christopher Evans (1979) has written about the "micro millennium"—a society in which life is transformed by the conveniences made available through a revolution in computer technology. Alvin Toffler (1970) has written about a society in a permanent state of "future shock," where technological and social change takes place much faster than people's ability to adjust to it. William Ophuls (1977) describes a "scarcity society," in which depletion of resources leads to a lower standard of living and a strong, authoritarian state that regulates conflict among groups struggling for their piece of the diminishing pie. Fred Hirsch (1976) explains how a future society will have to recognize that there are limits to growth, and will have to develop a "steady-state," no-growth economy.

Sociologists have been particularly interested in the view that industrial society is soon to be modified or even replaced by a social order based primarily on a new, highly technological form of production. There is no consensus on what this new social order should be called, but among the terms that have been proposed are "technetronic," "postmodern," "superindustrial," and "postindustrial." The term *postindustrial* seems to have won the greatest popularity, and that is the term we shall use here (Touraine, 1971; Bell, 1973).

Some Effects of Nuclear Attack

Many predictions have been made about the future of industrial, or even postindustrial, society, yet all these forecasts could be made irrelevant by nuclear warfare, which—whether launched deliberately or accidently—is surely the greatest threat to the human future. At present, five countries have nuclear weapons (the United States, the Soviet Union, Britain, France, and China), and several others are believed to be currently developing them (including Israel, Iraq, India, Pakistan, and South Africa). By the end of the century, dozens of smaller nations—many of them on hostile terms with one another—may have nuclear bombs. The following is a summary of some of the medical effects of nuclear attack.

Recent talk by public figures about winning or even surviving a nuclear war reflects a widespread failure to appreciate the facts. Any nuclear war would inevitably cause death, disease and suffering of epidemic proportions for which effective medical intervention on any realistic scale would be impossible. This recognition leads to the same conclusion that public-health specialists have reached for such contemporary epidemics as those of lung cancer and heart disease: Prevention is essential for effective control.

What can be said about the kinds of epidemics that would result from the use of nuclear weapons? The effects of a hypothetical nuclear attack on a major U.S. city were described in articles last year in the *Scientific American,* and in 1962 in the *New England Journal of Medicine.* They were based on studies prepared by the Joint Congressional Committee on Atomic Energy and the Atomic Energy Commission, which is now part of the Department of Energy.

The city's hypothetical disaster begins with a 20-megaton bomb—equivalent to 20 million tons of TNT, 1,000 times the power of the Hiroshima bomb—exploding at ground level in a downtown area and excavating a crater a half-mile in diameter. Even the most heavily reinforced concrete structures will not survive within a four-mile radius—which encompasses most of the hospitals and medical personnel in the area. As far as 15 miles from the blast, all frame buildings would be damaged beyond repair.

The detonation of the bomb would release so much thermal energy that, up to 40 miles away, retinal burns incurred by looking at the fireball would cause blindness. More than 20 miles from the center, the firestorm—fueled by ignited houses, foliage, and oil and gasoline storage tanks—would increase the already catastrophic damage caused by the blast.

Among the 3.5 million people in the city and surrounding area, the blast and firestorm would cause 2.2 million fatalities; survivors would be badly burned, blinded and otherwise seriously wounded. Many would be disoriented. The need would be great for medical care, food, water, shelter and clothing, but all would be gravely inadequate.

These are the short-term effects. The problems of radiation sickness—including intractable nausea, vomiting and diarrhea, bleeding, hair loss, severe infection and often death—would grow in the period ahead.

In the aftermath of a nuclear attack on the U.S. city in question, what are the prospects for medical care? Using as a base a figure of 6,560 physicians in the area at the time of attack, the 1962 study projects that almost 5,000 would be killed immediately or fatally injured, and that only 900 would be in a condition to render post-attack medical care. The ratio of injured persons to physicians thus would exceed 1,700 to 1. If a physician spent an average of only 15 minutes with each injured person and worked 16 hours each day, the studies project, it would take 16 to 26 days for each casualty to be seen once.

Thus, it is unrealistic to seriously suggest medical response to the overwhelming health problems that would follow a nuclear attack. Medical measures would be woefully ineffective in dealing with the burden of cancer and genetic defects afflicting survivors and future generations. Radioactivity would make the blast area uninhabitable for months. Most of the area's water supply, sanitation resources and transportation and industrial capacity would be destroyed.

At present, more than 50,000 nuclear weapons are deployed and ready. Many dwarf in destructive power the bomb used against Hiroshima. Sufficient nuclear bombs exist outside the United States to subject every major U.S. city repeatedly to the kind of destruction described above.

One might ask the purpose of detailing such almost unthinkable conditions. But, actually, the conditions are not unthinkable; rather, they are infrequently thought about, much less discussed. Among the painful results of the silence are the continuing proliferation of nuclear weapons and the failures to reject nuclear war as a "viable option" in the management of world problems.

Source: Howard H. Hiatt, "The Medical Facts of Nuclear Attack," *International Herald Tribune,* August 9–10, 1980.

Figure 23.22 Predicting the future is no easy task, for prophets are always bound by the assumptions of their own time and place, even though they may be unaware of the fact. This drawing, nearly a hundred years old, shows one Frenchman's view of what the twentieth century would be like. He extended his own assumptions—about fashions of dress, the use of cast iron in manufacturing, and architecture, for example—into the future, but with results that are wildly inaccurate. How might the versions of the future portrayed in such contemporary efforts as the "Star Wars" movies, or even in the prophecies of sociologists, look a hundred years from now?

The trend to a postindustrial society is said to be based on two main factors. The first is the change in the occupational structure of advanced industrial societies. More and more workers are employed in tertiary industry, providing services for other members of society rather than extracting raw materials or manufacturing goods. Work in this sector of the economy is becoming more professionalized and is generally regarded as more pleasant and less alienating than work in the primary and secondary sectors.

The second factor is technological development, which is making traditional methods of work outmoded, primarily through advances in electronic engineering. A single computer, for example, can take over the work of virtually the entire accounting department of a large firm. In industry, the assembly line is often replaced by automated production. *Automation* is a system in which machines themselves, often guided by computers, monitor and control the manufacturing process. The worker no longer labors on an assembly line, but instead becomes a technician, periodically checking the information provided by machines to ensure that everything is functioning correctly. Work becomes cleaner, lighter, and often requires more skills and greater responsibilities. For this reason workers in automated industries appear less alienated than workers in more traditional industries (Blauner, 1964). Automation also requires fewer workers, although whether this results in unemployment or in increased leisure time for the same number of workers depends on prevailing corporate and national policies.

These trends, it is argued, herald a society in which there will be greatly increased leisure time, a heavy reliance on people with skill and knowledge, a central role for technological innovation, and an emphasis on personal development and fulfillment through education and consumption rather than on constant and arduous work.

All this sounds most promising, but it neglects one crucial factor. A postindustrial society would still require a substantial industrial base and a constant supply of oil and other raw materials, and there is no reason to suppose that its industries would stop polluting the environment. As we noted in Chapter 20 ("Population and Health"), one research team developed a computer model that projected current trends of population increase, resource depletion, food production, pollution, and industrial output well into the next century (Meadows et al., 1972). The computer predicted an inevitable collapse of industrial society within a hundred years, and possibly a good deal sooner—unless population growth and industrial growth are brought to an immediate halt. Although this was a highly controversial finding based on questionable methods, its general conclusion is representative of a number of predictions about the future of industrial society. These pessimistic predictions all note—correctly—that the size of the global population and the rate of industrial output are rapidly increasing, and that they are doing so in a world that has limited and diminishing resources. This combination of facts does not encourage optimism about the long-term future of industrialism. Whether the new level of postindustrial civilization can be safely achieved or whether industrial societies will prove to be "self-extinguishing" remains to be seen. Certainly, the answer to the question will have the profoundest implications for social life as we know it—and that answer may be apparent well within the lifetimes of most readers of this book.

We cannot yet know whether there will be a "micro millenium," a "scarcity society," an ecological collapse, a "postindustrial society," or any of the other future scenarios that are envisioned for us. All these are very different predictions, for the reason that each writer focuses on one or a few aspects of change in the modern world and projects this trend, largely through guesswork, into the future. Lacking any general theory of social change, these and other "futurologists" cannot provide a systematic and persuasive picture of the future. Until an adequate theory of social change is produced, such a picture will continue to elude us. The task of producing that theory remains no less a challenge today than it did when the new discipline of sociology was born.

Summary

1. Social change is the alteration in patterns of culture, social structure, and social behavior over time. The process is universal but occurs at different rates and in different ways. Social change is often difficult to analyze because we lack a full understanding of social statics and because changes usually have very complex origins.

2. Some specific sources of change are the following: the physical environment, which limits changes in population size or composition but rarely causes change; ideas, which in interaction with other factors can generate change; "events," or apparently random occurrences, that provoke change; cultural innovation, which takes the forms of discovery, invention, and diffusion; human action, in the sense that individuals, groups, and agencies such as governments can influence social change; and technology, which generates changes in society and culture, often causing a culture lag. Change is never the result of one specific factor; several factors always operate together.

3. Evolutionary theories hold that societies evolve from simple to complex forms. Early ethnocentric theorists believed that the process is unilinear and culminates in Western civilization; many modern social scientists believe that evolution is multilinear. They also refuse to equate "change" with "progress."

4. Cyclical theories hold that change recurs in cycles over time. Spengler believed societies have life cycles and that their fate is a matter of "destiny." Toynbee believed that societies advance or decline according to their "responses" to "challenges."

5. Functionalist theories focus mainly on social statics. Parsons, however, sees change as a process by which the social equilibrium is altered so that a new equilibrium results. This process takes place through differentiation and integration.

6. Conflict theorists, influenced by Marx, see conflict as intrinsic to society and as the main source of social change. The theory explains some change but has not given very accurate predictions in the past.

7. Cyclical theories are too speculative and are not explanatory. Unilinear evolutionary theories were based on faulty data. Multilinear evolutionary theories seem useful but explain only one dimension of change. Functionalist and conflict theories seem to contradict one another but actually focus on different aspects of the same reality. Multilinear, functionalist, and conflict theories may sometimes be combined to explain many forms of social change.

8. Modernization is the process of social change that results from the introduction of industrialism into a preindustrial society. It causes sweeping changes in society.

9. Different writers have projected very different futures for industrial society. A widespread view is that we shall achieve a postindustrial society, marked by increased leisure and affluence, but it is not clear how such societies would overcome global problems of resource depletion, pollution, and overpopulation.

Important Terms

social change (593)	social Darwinism (606)
dynamics (594)	multilinear evolution (607)
statics (594)	
ideology (597)	equilibrium (609)
discovery (599)	differentiation (610)
invention (600)	integration (610)
diffusion (600)	modernization (613)
technological determinant (603)	postindustrial society (617)
unilinear evolution (605)	automation (619)

Suggested Readings

BELL, DANIEL. *The Coming of Postindustrial Society.* New York: Basic Books, 1973.

A leading prophet of the "postindustrial society" explains why and how we are entering that stage and outlines the characteristics of this new social form.

EVANS, CHRISTOPHER. *The Micro Millenium.* New York: Viking, 1979.

An interesting account of what life might be like if the micro-chip revolution in computer technology transforms many aspects of social life.

ETZIONI, AMITAI, and EVA ETZIONI-HALEVY. *Social Change.* New York: Basic Books, 1973.

An important collection of articles on various aspects of social change. The book includes excerpts from the writings of several classical and modern theorists on the subject.

GOULDNER, ALVIN. *The Coming Crisis of Western Sociology.* New York: Avon, 1970.

An important book on sociological theory. Gouldner argues strongly that aspects of conflict and functionalist theory can and should be combined to produce a better understanding of social processes.

LAUER, ROBERT H. (ed.). *Perspectives on Social Change.* 2nd ed. Boston: Allyn and Bacon, 1977.

A useful survey of theory and research on the phenomenon of social and cultural change.

MEAD, MARGARET. *Culture and Commitment.* New York: Doubleday, 1970.

An anthropologist examines the effect of rapid technological change on modern societies, placing particular emphasis on the cleavage that change can create between the generations.

NISBET, ROBERT. *History of the Idea of Progress.* New York: Basic Books, 1979.

An elegantly written account of the Western idea that change implies progress toward something better.

OGBURN, WILLIAM F. *Social Change.* New York: Viking, 1950.

A classic work in the field. Ogburn presents his concept of "culture lag" and discusses the social disorganization that technological changes can create.

PASCARELLA, PERRY. *Technology: Fire in a Dark World.* New York: Van Nostrand Reinhold, 1979.

An interesting defense of the virtues of technology and technological advance in the modern world.

Techniques of Library Research

The library, besides housing the works of novelists, poets, biographers, and playwrights, is also a storehouse of scientific knowledge. Every library is systematically organized so that this knowledge can be easily located and retrieved, and the purpose of this appendix is to acquaint you with some of the ways you can "plug into" the sociological information that the library contains.

Your method of tracking down information will depend very much on the exact kind of information you are looking for. The following categories cover most situations.

If you are looking for general information on a particular subject:

A useful place to start might be a general encyclopedia such as the *Britannica* or the *Americana;* or you can try the seventeen-volume *International Encyclopaedia of the Social Sciences*, which contains general reviews written by experts in various fields. Every encyclopedia contains instructions on how to use it, and at the end of each article you will find additional references that you can use for follow-up.

You can also consult the *Reader's Guide to Periodical Literature*, which covers such nontechnical sources as *Time, Newsweek,* and the *New Republic*. The index will direct you to articles that have been published on the subject you are interested in. You should be wary, though, of these non-scholarly sources. They often give a useful introduction to some issue, but they usually lack the objectivity and precision of good sociology. A very useful guide to more scientific articles is the *Social Sciences Index*, which will direct you to more reliable sources in sociology and related fields.

For specifically sociological information, you can start with *Sociological Abstracts*, which arranges all sociological books, articles, and papers presented to professional meetings, according to subject area. The publication includes a brief summary of the content of each item, together with the names of the authors and the source of the material. Similar abstracts are available in related areas, such as *Psychological Abstracts, Crime and Delinquency Abstracts, Education Abstracts,* and *Poverty and Human Resources Abstracts.* There is also a *Dissertation Abstracts,* covering unpublished doctoral dissertations.

You may also wish to refer to major journals covering various aspects of the discipline. Four highly regarded journals that print articles of general sociological interest are the *American Journal of Sociology,* the *American Sociological Review, Social Forces,* and the *British Journal of Sociology.* There are also a number of journals on specific areas, such as *Sociology of Education, Journal of Health and Social Behavior, Social Problems, Public Opinion Quarterly, Issues in Criminology, Journal of Marriage and the Family,* and *Journal of Abnormal and Social Psychology.*

If you are looking for a specific book or article but don't know the name of the author:

Many libraries have a separate card catalog that lists books by title; if your library has such a catalog, you can easily trace a book without knowing its author's name. An alternative method is to refer to *Books in Print,* a two-volume annual publication. One volume lists all books in print alphabetically by author; the other volume lists them alphabetically by title. If you are looking for an article but do not know the name of the author, you can look through the articles listed under the relevant subject heading in the *Reader's Guide to Periodical Literature, The Social Sciences Index,* or *Sociological Abstracts.*

If you want information about specific events:

A good place to look is in newspaper files. Certain newspapers are known as "journals of record"—in other words, they not only cover "newsworthy" events but also try to preserve a record of significant social events, and print lengthy extracts from government reports and similar material. The two outstanding journals of record in the English-speaking world are the *New York Times* and the London *Times.* Both maintain an index of all names and events that have appeared in their columns, and this index will direct you to any article they have published on the subject you are interested in.

If you want information about particular people:

One obvious source is the newspaper files just mentioned (obituaries in newspapers are a particularly useful source of information about people who are dead). Information can also be obtained from such volumes as *Who's Who, Who Was Who, Current Biography,* or *American Men and Women of Science.* The latter is in two volumes, one covering the physical and biological sciences and the other covering the behavioral sciences and humanities.

If you want statistical information:

The best place to start is usually *Statistical Abstracts,* an annual publication that contains information about virtually every aspect of American life on which statistics are kept. The *Census Report,* published every ten years, gives many details about the characteristics of the American population. You might also consult *Statistical Sources: A Subject Guide to Data on Industrial, Business, Social, Educational, Financial, and Other Topics for the U.S. and Internationally.* This useful volume will direct you to other sources of information that you may not know about: if you are looking for information on crime trends, for example, it will direct you to such sources as the annual *Uniform Crime Reports* of the FBI.

You will always find that sources generate more sources, because each reference will lead you to several more. Unless you want a broad overview of a topic, then, it is best to have very specific information in mind, or you might be overwhelmed by the richness of the data waiting for you! Above all, remember that when you are in any difficulty, you should not hesitate to *ask the librarian.* Some people are reluctant to "bother" the librarian, or feel that he or she may not know about the specific information that is sought. But the librarian is a professional trained in library science, and has an intimate knowledge of the general methods for locating information and of the specific resources of your library. The librarian will be glad to help, so if you are unable to find what you are looking for, just ask.

Glossary

Absolute deprivation The lack of the basic necessities of life.

Account In social interaction, an excuse or justification for inappropriate behavior that has taken place.

Achieved status A social status that an individual achieves at least partly through personal effort or failings, such as that of college graduate or prison convict.

Agency of socialization An institution or other structured situation in which socialization takes place, such as the family, the school, the peer group, or the mass media.

Age structure Refers to the relative proportions of different age categories in a population.

Aggregate A collection of people who happen to be in the same place at the same time (passengers on a bus, for example).

Agricultural society A society whose primary subsistence strategy is the cultivation of crops through the use of plows and draft animals.

Alienation The sense of powerlessness, isolation, and meaninglessness experienced by people when they are confronted with social institutions and conditions that they believe they cannot control and consider oppressive.

Aligning actions Strategies used by social actors to smooth the course of interaction when their behavior is potentially disruptive.

Anomaly In the sociology of science, a problem that cannot be explained in terms of the existing paradigm.

Anomie The confused condition that exists in both individuals and society when social norms are conflicting, weak, or absent.

Anthropology A social science that focuses primarily on the cultures of small-scale, preindustrial societies and on the physical evolution of the human species.

Anticipatory socialization Socialization that is directed toward learning future roles.

Applied research Research aimed at finding technological applications for scientific knowledge.

Ascribed status A social status assigned to the individual by society on arbitrary grounds over which the individual has little or no control, such as age, race, or sex.

Association A large secondary group, usually taking the form of a formal organization.

Authoritarian personality A set of distinctive personality traits, including conformity, intolerance, and insecurity, alleged to be typical of many prejudiced people.

Authority Power that is regarded as legitimate by those over whom it is exercised (in contrast to coercion).

Autocracy Rule by a single individual.

Automation A system in which machines themselves monitor and control a manufacturing process.

Basic research Research aimed at increasing the sum of knowledge (in contrast to applied research, which is aimed at finding technological applications for knowledge).

Behaviorism A theory of learning that focuses on actual behavior, which is believed to be the result of conditioning through rewards and punishments.

Bias The tendency, often unconscious, to interpret facts in ways that are influenced by subjective values and attitudes.

Bilateral system A family system in which descent and inheritance are reckoned through both the male and female lines.

Birth rate A statistical measure, usually expressed as the number of births per year per thousand members of a given population.

Bureaucracy A hierarchical authority structure that operates under explicit rules and procedures; bureaucracies are found in all formal organizations.

Bystander apathy The tendency of witnesses to take no action when confronted by an emergency affecting others.

Capitalism A class-based political and economic system in which most wealth is privately owned and may be reinvested to produce profit for those who own it.

Case study A detailed record of an event, group, or social process.

Caste system A system of social stratification in which status is ascribed at birth and in which there is virtually no social mobility or intermarriage between the strata.

Category A number of people who may never have met one another but who share similar characteristics, such as age, race, or sex.

Charisma An exceptional personal, or even supernatural, quality that people attribute to particular individuals.

Charismatic authority Authority that is legitimated by the unusual, exceptional, or even supernatural qualities that people attribute to those who exercise it.

City A permanent concentration of relatively large numbers of people who do not produce their own food.

Class A group of people of roughly equivalent status in an unequal society.

Class conflict The struggle between social classes, primarily between the class that owns the means of economic production and the class or classes that do not.

Class consciousness A social class's shared, objective awareness of the common situation and interests of its members.

Class system A system of social stratification in which categories of the population are ranked primarily according to economic status but in which there is some measure of achieved status and social mobility.

Closed system A system of social stratification in which virtually no social mobility is possible.

Coercion Power that is perceived as illegitimate by those over whom it is exercised (in contrast to authority).

Cognitive Refers to intellectual capacities such as perception, reasoning, and memory.

Collective behavior Relatively spontaneous and unstructured ways of thinking, feeling, and acting on the part of a large number of people.

Collective consciousness A set of norms, values, and assumptions shared by a community or society.

Communism A political and economic system in which, ideally, wealth and power are shared equally by the community as a whole because of the common ownership of the means of production and distribution.

Community A social group with a common territorial base and a shared sense of common interests and "belonging."

Concentric-zone theory A theory that cities typically consist of a series of zones radiating out from a downtown center, with each successive zone containing a different type of land use.

Concrete operational stage A stage of cognitive development in which thinking is tied to the physical world and is insufficiently developed to deal with abstract or hypothetical concepts.

Conditioning A process of learning through the association of acts with their consequences.

Conflict perspective A theoretical perspective of society that emphasizes conflict as a permanent feature of social life, an important influence on social structure and culture, and a significant source of social change.

Conformity Adherence to social norms.

Control group A group of subjects in an experiment who are not exposed to the independent variable introduced by the researcher but whose experience is the same in all other respects to that of the experimental group, which is exposed to the variable.

Controls Statistical or experimental methods that serve to exclude the possibility that external factors might influence a relationship that a researcher is studying.

Correlation A regular, recurrent association between variables, generally expressed in statistical terms.

Counterculture A subculture that is fundamentally at odds with the dominant culture.

Coup d'etat A restricted use of force to replace one set of leaders with another, usually military officers.

Crime An act that has been formally prohibited by political authority, usually through the enactment of a law.

Crimes without victims Crimes such as gambling, prostitution, or illicit drug use that have no direct victim, except possibly the offender.

Crowd A temporary collection of people in close physical proximity.

Cult A loosely organized religious or other social movement that tends to lack coherent doctrines and to impose minimal demands on its members.

Cultural anthropology The scientific study of the cultures of other peoples, particularly in small-scale, preindustrial societies.

Cultural integration A situation in which the various elements in a culture complement one another, or "fit together."

Cultural relativism The recognition that one culture or subculture cannot be arbitrarily judged by the standards of another.

Cultural universals Practices that are found in every culture.

Culture All the shared products of human society, comprising its total way of life. Culture includes material products (houses, cities, etc.) and nonmaterial products (religions, languages, etc.).

Culture lag The time discrepancy between the introduction of a change in material culture and the adaptation of nonmaterial culture to the change.

Culture of poverty A distinctive culture said to exist among the poor in industrialized societies.

Cyclical theories Theories holding that social change tends to recur in cycles over time.

Death rate A statistical measure, usually expressed as the number of deaths per year per thousand members of a given population.

De facto discrimination Discrimination that is entrenched in social customs and institutions.

De jure discrimination Discrimination that is entrenched in law.

Democracy A system of government in which citizens have the right to participate in the decision-making process and in which the rulers acknowledge that their power derives from the consent of the governed.

Democratic socialism A political and economic system that aims at creating a high degree of social equality while preserving the freedom of the individual.

Demographic-transition theory A theory that maintains that the growth rate of a population tends to decrease and stabilize once a certain level of economic development has been achieved.

Demography The scientific study of the size, composition, distribution, and changes in human populations.

Denomination One of two or more well-established religious organizations that claim the allegiance of a substantial part of a population.

Dependent variable A variable that is changed or influenced by the effect of another variable, termed the independent variable.

Detached observation A case-study method in which the researcher remains aloof from the process involved, often with the result that the subjects do not know they are being studied.

Developmental approach An approach to the psychology of learning that emphasizes the individual's internal interpretations of the world and regards learning as a process of continual development through different stages.

Developmental socialization Socialization that builds on already acquired skills and knowledge.

Deviance Behavior or characteristics that violate significant social norms and expectations and are negatively valued by large numbers of people in consequence.

Deviant career Permanent and habitual deviance among people who regard themselves, and are regarded by others, as deviant.

Differential association Refers to a theory that explains deviant behavior in terms of cultural transmission through regular and intensive association with existing deviants.

Differentiation In social theory, the tendency for societies to treat their members differently on such grounds as age, sex, or race. In Parsonian theory, the process by which new institutions emerge to assume functions that were previously undifferentiated within a single institution.

Diffusion The spread of cultural elements from one culture to another.

Disclaimer In social interaction, an excuse or justification for inappropriate behavior that is about to take place.

Discovery The perception of an aspect of reality that already exists.

Discrimination Action against other people on the grounds of their group membership, particularly the refusal to grant such people opportunities that would be granted to similarly qualified members of one's own group.

Division of labor The specialization by particular individuals or categories of individuals in particular economic activities.

Double standard Refers to social norms that tolerate male promiscuity while demanding female chastity.

Doubling time The period it takes for a population to double its numbers.

Dramaturgical approach A term used by Erving Goffman to describe his method of analysis of social interaction, which he studies as though the participants were actors in a theater.

Drive A basic inborn urge, arising either spontaneously or in response to a stimulus from the environment, and temporarily disappearing when it has been satisfied.

Dyad A group consisting of two people.

Dynamics Refers to the phenomenon of social change.

Dysfunction A consequence of some element in a social system that disrupts the equilibrium of the system or the functioning of another element within the system.

Ecclesia A well-established religious organization that claims the allegiance of everyone in a society or in several societies.

Ecological approach An analytic approach that studies social phenomena in the context of the total environment.

Ecology The science of the relationship between living organisms and their environments.

Economic determinism The theory that the economic base of society determines the general character of social structure and culture.

Economic order The institutionalized system for producing and distributing goods and services.

Ecosystem A self-sustaining community of organisms within its natural environment.

Education The systematic, formalized transmission of knowledge, skills, and values.

Egalitarian family A family in which the husband and wife have equal authority in family matters.

Ego In Freudian theory, the conscious, rational part of the self.

Endogamy A marriage pattern in which individuals marry within their own social group.

Epidemiology The study of the distribution of diseases within a population.

Equilibrium In functionalist theory, the overall balance that exists among the various elements in a social system.

Ethnic group A large number of people who, as a result of their shared cultural traits and high level of mutual interaction, come to regard themselves, and to be regarded, as a cultural unity.

Ethnocentrism The tendency to judge other cultures or subcultures by the standards of one's own.

Ethnography A study of the way of life of a human group, usually a small-scale, preindustrial society.

Ethnomethodology The study of how people construct and share their definitions of reality in their everyday interactions.

Evolution In biology and physical anthropology, the process by which organisms adapt their physical forms and behavioral patterns to the demands and opportunities of the environment. In sociology and cultural anthropology, the process by which societies become more complex, usually as a result of more efficient technologies for exploiting the environment.

Exogamy A marriage pattern in which individuals marry outside their own social group.

Experimental group A group of subjects in an experiment who are exposed to the independent variable introduced by the researcher, in contrast to the control group, which is not subjected to this variable but whose experience is the same in all other respects.

Extended family A family in which two or more generations of the same kinship line live together.

Externalization The process through which people create cultural products, such as social institutions, which then become "external" to the producers.

Fad A temporary form of conduct that is followed enthusiastically by large numbers of people.

False consciousness A subjective understanding of one's situation that does not accord with the objective facts of that situation.

Family A relatively permanent group of people related by ancestry, marriage, or adoption, who live together and form an economic unit, and whose adult members assume responsibility for the young.

Family of orientation The family into which one is born.

Family of procreation The family that we create for ourselves, as opposed to the family of orientation into which we are born.

Fashion A currently accepted style of appearance or behavior.

Fecundity The biological potential for bearing a number of children, in contrast to fertility, the actual number of births.

Fertility Refers to the actual number of births to the average woman of childbearing age in a given society, in contrast to fecundity, the potential number of births.

Feudalism A relatively closed system of social stratification in which a land-owning class exploits the mass of peasants and in which the rights and responsibilities of the classes are specified by tradition.

Folk society A term used by Robert Redfield to distinguish small, traditional societies from "urban" or large, modern societies.

Folkways The ordinary usages and conventions of everyday life; conformity to such norms is expected, but violations are not regarded as immoral.

Formal operational stage A stage of cognitive development at which intelligence is sufficiently developed to deal with abstract, hypothetical, and formal thought.

Formal organization A large social group that is deliberately and rationally designed to achieve specific objectives.

Formal sanction A social reward or punishment that is applied in an organized and patterned way (such as a graduation ceremony or an execution).

Function Any consequence that a given component in a social system has, either for the system as a whole or for some other component within it. A function is usually assumed to contribute to the overall stability of the system.

Functionalist perspective A theoretical perspective on society that emphasizes the functional interrelations of the various elements in a social system, and the contributions that these elements make toward social order.

Functional prerequisite An important social requirement that must be fulfilled if society is to function effectively.

Gemeinschaft A term used by Ferdinand Tönnies to describe a small community characterized by intimate, face-to-face contact, strong feelings of group loyalty, and a commitment to tradition.

Gender Refers to social conceptions about what personality traits and behavior are appropriate for members of each sex.

Generalization A statement about the recurrent relationships among particular variables.

Generalized other An internalized conception of the expectations of society as a whole.

Genocide The extermination of an entire population.

Gesellschaft A term used by Ferdinand Tönnies to describe a society marked by impersonal contacts, an emphasis on individualism rather than group loyalty, and a lack of commitment to traditional values.

Group A collection of people interacting together in an orderly way on the basis of shared expectations about each other's behavior.

Growth rate A statistical measure reflecting changes in population size; it represents the number of births minus the number of deaths and is usually expressed as an annual percentage.

Hawthorne effect The contamination of an experiment by changes in the subjects' behavior resulting from their assumptions about what the researcher is trying to prove.

Heterosexuality Sexual acts or feelings directed toward members of the opposite sex.

Homogamy Marriage between people with similar social characteristics.

Homo sapiens The modern human species (literally "man, the wise").

Homosexuality Sexual acts or feelings directed toward members of the same sex.

Horizontal mobility A change from one social status to another that is roughly equivalent.

Horticultural society A society relying for its subsistence primarily on the hoe cultivation of domesticated plants.

Human ecology The study of the interrelationship between human groups and their total environment.

Hunting and gathering society A society relying for its subsistence on such food as its members are able to hunt and gather; there is no domestication of plants and animals.

Hypothesis A tentative statement that predicts a relationship between variables.

Id In Freudian theory, the reservoir of drives present in the individual at birth and throughout life.

Ideal culture Culture as it is expressed in the values and norms that people claim to believe in, rather than as expressed in their actual practices.

Ideal type An abstract description, constructed by the sociologist from observations of a number of real cases in order to reveal their essential features.

Ideology A set of beliefs that justifies the interests (or supposed interests) of those who hold it; the dominant ideology in any society legitimates the existing social order.

Illegitimate birth Birth to unmarried parents.

Incest Socially forbidden sexual intercourse with close relatives.

Incest taboo A powerful social prohibition on sexual intercourse with specific categories of kinfolk.

Independent variable A variable that causes a change or variation in another variable, termed the dependent variable.

Industrial society A society relying for its subsistence primarily on mechanized production.

Informal sanction A social reward or punishment that is applied through the spontaneous reactions of other people (such as a pat on the back or a gesture of disapproval).

Ingroup The group to which an individual belongs and feels loyalty, as opposed to any outgroup to which the individual does not belong.

Innovation In the sociology of science, the discovery of new scientific knowledge. In the sociology of deviance, a form of deviant behavior that occurs when people accept socially approved goals but resort to socially disapproved means of achieving them.

Instinct A complex pattern of behavior that is genetically determined and appears in all normal members of a species under identical conditions.

Institution A stable cluster of values, norms, statuses, roles, and expectations that develop around a basic need of a society.

Institutionalized discrimination Discrimination, often subtle and informal, that deeply pervades social customs and institutions.

Integration In social theory, the tendency for the various elements in culture and society to be interlinked and interdependent. In Parsonian theory, the process by which newly differentiated institutions are linked together once more. In the sociology of race and ethnic relations, the free and unrestricted association of members of different groups.

Interactionist perspective A theoretical perspective on society that focuses on the micro order and emphasizes the social interaction among individuals.

Interest group An organization or group of people that attempts to influence political decisions that might affect its members.

Intergenerational mobility A change in the social status of family members from one generation to the next.

Internalization The socialization process through which people absorb cultural knowledge, making it part of their "internal" consciousness and personality.

Intragenerational mobility A change in status during the course of an individual's career.

Invention The combination or new use of existing knowledge to produce something that did not exist before.

IQ (Intelligence Quotient) test A test that measures certain aspects of "intelligence" (that is, academic aptitude in a very limited range of fields) by comparing the performance of a subject with the rest of that subject's age group.

Kinship A network of people related by common ancestry, adoption, or marriage.

Labeling theory A theory that explains deviant behavior in terms of a process through which some people successfully apply the label of "deviant" to others.

Laissez faire A policy of not regulating the economy (literally, "leave it alone").

Latent functions The unrecognized and unintended consequences of some element in a social system.

Law A rule that is formally enacted by a political authority and is backed by the power of the state.

Learning A change in an individual's thought, emotion, or behavior that results from previous experience.

Legal-rational authority Authority that is legitimated by explicit rules and procedures that define the rights and obligations of those who exercise it.

Legitimacy In political sociology, the term refers to a generally held belief that a particular political system is a valid and justified one.

Legitimate birth Birth to parents who are married.

Life chances Probabilities of benefiting from the opportunities that a society offers.

Life cycle The biological and social sequence of birth, childhood, maturity, old age, and death.

Life expectancy The average number of years that a newborn person in a given population can expect to live.

Life span The maximum length of life possible in a given species.

Linguistic relativity Refers to the fact that different languages dissect and organize reality in somewhat different ways, so that speakers of a particular language interpret the world through the unique forms that their language supplies.

Lobbying The practice of directly trying to persuade decision makers to adopt policies that favor one's own interests.

Looking-glass self The reflection of the self that is provided by the reactions of others to one's behavior.

Macro order The large-scale structures and processes of society.

Magic Rituals that attempt to harness supernatural powers for human ends.

Manifest functions The obvious and intended consequences of some element in a social system.

Marriage A socially approved sexual union of some permanence between two or more individuals.

Mass hysteria A form of collective behavior involving widespread and contagious anxiety, usually caused by an unfounded belief.

Mass media Forms of communication, such as television and newspapers, that reach a large audience without any personal contact between the senders and receivers of the messages.

Master status The most socially significant of an individual's various statuses (usually an occupational status).

Material culture The artifacts or physical objects created by human beings.

Matriarchal family One in which the wife has superior authority in family matters.

Matrilineal system A family system in which descent and inheritance are reckoned through the female side of the family.

Matrilocal residence pattern A family system in which a married couple is expected to live with the family of the wife.

Mechanical solidarity A form of social cohesion found primarily in small-scale preindustrial societies and based on the basic similarity of the members.

Megalopolis A virtually unbroken urban tract consisting of two or more metropolises.

Methodology A system of rules, principles, and procedures that guides scientific investigation.

Metropolis An urban area including a city and its surrounding suburbs.

Micro order The small-scale processes that constitute the ongoing life of a society.

Migration rate A statistical measure, usually expressed as the number of immigrants or emigrants per thousand members of a given population.

Military-industrial complex An informal system of mutual contact and influence between high officials in the Pentagon and major U.S. corporations.

Millenarian movement A religious movement that prophesies a cataclysm within the immediate future.

Minority group A group of people who, because of their physical or cultural characteristics, are differentiated from others in their society and treated unequally.

Mob An emotionally aroused crowd bent on violent action.

Modernization The process of economic and social transformation brought about by the introduction of industrialism into a society.

Monogamy A marriage form in which a person may not marry more than one other person at a time.

Monopoly In economic sociology, a single firm that dominates an industry.

Mores Powerful norms that are regarded as morally significant; violations are considered a serious matter.

Multilinear evolution Refers to a theory that sociocultural evolution may take different forms and directions in different societies.

Multiple-nuclei theory A theory that modern cities are typically organized around a number of specialized areas, each of which influences the character and development of the surrounding neighborhood.

Negative sanction A social punishment for disapproved behavior.

Neolocal residence pattern A family system in which a married couple establishes a new place of residence away from the families of the husband and the wife.

Nonmaterial culture Refers to social products that do not have a physical existence, such as language, customs, or religions.

Nonverbal communication Meaningful interaction between people that takes place through the use of symbols other than language.

Norm A shared rule or guideline that prescribes the appropriate behavior for people in a given situation.

Normal science A term used to describe a process of scientific innovation in which knowledge is steadily increased.

Nuclear family A family consisting of husband, wife, and their dependent children.

Objectivation The process by which cultural products are seen as having an existence and reality independent of those who produced them.

Objectivity Strictly speaking, a mode of interpreting reality in such a way that personal, subjective judgments are eliminated. In practice, objectivity refers to thought sufficiently disciplined to minimize distortions caused by personal bias.

Oligarchy Rule by a few people.

Oligopoly A situation that exists when a few firms dominate an industry.

Open system A system of social stratification in which social mobility is widely available.

Operational definition The particular definition of a concept to be used in the course of research.

Organic solidarity A form of social cohesion found primarily in large industrial societies and based on the differences among the members, which make them interdependent.

Outgroup A group to which an individual does not belong, as opposed to the ingroup to which the individual belongs and feels loyalty.

Panic A form of collective behavior in which a group of people, faced with an immediate threat, react in a fearful, uncoordinated, and irrational way.

Paradigm A set of concepts, methods, and assumptions shared by a community of scientists and guiding research in their discipline.

Participant observation A case-study method in which the researcher takes part in the activities of the people who are being studied.

Particular other An internalized concept of the expectations of specific other people.

Pastoral society A society relying for its subsistence primarily on domesticated herd animals.

Patriarchal family One in which the husband has superior authority in family matters.

Patrilineal system A family system in which both descent and inheritance are reckoned through the male line of the family.

Patrilocal residence pattern A family system in which a married couple is expected to live with the family of the husband.

Peer group Companions and associates of equivalent social status and usually of similar age.

Personality The fairly stable patterns of thought, feeling, and action that are typical of an individual.

Pluralism In political sociology, the diffusion of power among various groups and interests. In the sociology of race and ethnic relations, a situation in which different groups live in mutual respect while maintaining their own identities.

Political order The institutionalized system through which some individuals and groups acquire and exercise power over others.

Political party A collectivity of people organized for the specific purpose of gaining legitimate control of government.

Polyandry A marriage form in which a wife may have more than one husband at the same time.

Polygamy A marriage form in which a person of one sex may be married to two or more persons of the opposite sex at the same time.

Polygyny A marriage form in which a husband may have more than one wife at the same time.

Population In demography, the total collectivity of individuals in a designated social unit, usually a society. In survey research, the total category of persons on which the survey is based and from which any sample is drawn.

Positive sanction A social reward for approved behavior.

Postindustrial society An advanced form of society said to be currently emerging and to be based on sophisticated technology and increased leisure time.

Power The ability to control the behavior of others, even in the absence of their consent.

Power elite A small network of powerful and influential individuals who are alleged to make the most important political decisions in American society.

Preindustrial society A society that does not rely for its subsistence on mechanized production but concentrates instead on hunting and gathering, pastoralism, horticulture, or agriculture.

Prejudice A "prejudged" negative attitude, often directed at individuals because they are members of a negatively valued group.

Preoperational stage A stage of cognitive development in which intelligence is insufficiently developed to perform basic logical operations.

Prestige The respect enjoyed by individuals or groups as a result of their social status.

Primary deviance Deviant behavior that is temporary, trivial, or concealed, and thus is not regarded as deviant by the actor or by significant other people.

Primary group A group consisting of a small number of people who interact in direct, intimate, and personal ways.

Primary industry Economic activity devoted to the gathering and extracting of undeveloped natural resources.

Primary socialization The basic socialization that takes place in the early years of life.

Priority dispute A dispute about which scientist made a particular discovery first.

Profane In the sociology of religion, anything that is not sacred.

Profession An occupation requiring some knowledge of, and training in, an art or science.

Projection Attributing to others characteristics that one is unwilling to recognize in oneself.

Propaganda Information or viewpoints designed to persuade an audience to adopt a particular opinion.

Property The rights that an owner of an object has in relation to others who are not owners of the object.

Prostitution The relatively indiscriminate exchange of sexual favors for economic gain.

Public A substantial number of people with a shared interest in some issue on which there are differing opinions.

Public opinion The sum of the decisions of the members of a public on a particular issue.

Race A large number of people who, for social or geographical reasons, have interbred over a long period of time and who as a result share visible physical characteristics and regard themselves, and are regarded by others, as a biological unity.

Racism The domination and exploitation by one group of another group that is seen as different and inferior.

Random sample A sample of individuals drawn from a larger population in such a way that every member of the population has an equal chance of being selected.

Rationalization The process by which traditional, spontaneous methods of social organization are replaced by abstract, explicit, carefully calculated rules and procedures.

Real culture Culture as it is expressed in people's actual practices rather than in what they claim to believe in.

Rebellion In the sociology of deviance, a form of deviance that occurs when people reject both approved social goals and means and substitute new, disapproved goals and means instead; in political sociology, an uprising against authority.

Reference group A group to which people refer when making evaluations of themselves and their behavior.

Relative deprivation The inability to maintain the standards of living customary in a society. More generally, the sense, derived from comparison with other people, that one lacks the resources or rewards that are usual in the society.

Religion A system of communally held beliefs and practices that are oriented toward some sacred, supernatural realm.

Replication The process of repeating a research study to verify its findings.

Representative democracy A form of government in which people appoint representatives who are responsible for making decisions on their behalf.

Research design The actual plan for the collection and analysis of data in a given research project.

Resocialization Socialization that constitutes a sharp break with past experience and involves the internalization of radically different norms and values.

Resource mobilization The way in which a social movement organizes and makes use of whatever resources happen to be available.

Respondent A person actually surveyed in the course of survey research.

Retreatism In the sociology of deviance, a form of deviance that occurs when people reject both socially approved goals and the socially approved means of achieving them.

Reverse socialization Socialization that is transmitted from the younger generation to their elders.

Revolution The overthrow of existing political and sometimes other institutions and the radical reconstruction of the political order.

Riot A violent and destructive collective outburst.

Rising expectations A situation in which people who have accepted existing conditions in the past feel that it is their right to enjoy better conditions in the future.

Ritual An established form of procedure, particularly in religious ceremonies.

Ritualism In the sociology of deviance, a form of deviance that occurs when people abandon social goals but compulsively enact the approved means of achieving them.

Role The part a person occupying a particular status plays in society.

Role conflict A situation in which a person plays two or more roles whose requirements are difficult to reconcile.

Role expectation The generally accepted social norms that define how a particular role ought to be played.

Role performance The actual behavior of a person playing a particular role.

Role set A cluster of roles attached to a particular status.

Role strain A situation in which conflicting demands are built into the same role, or in which a person for some other reason cannot meet role expectations.

Role taking Taking, or pretending to take, the roles of other people, and thus seeing the world from their perspective.

Routinization The process by which a relatively informal, spontaneous social group or movement is transformed into a formal, rationalized, bureaucratized one.

Rumor Information that is transmitted informally from anonymous sources.

Sacred That which inspires awe, reverence, and deep respect.

Sample A small number of individuals drawn from a larger population.

Sanction A social reward or punishment for approved or disapproved behavior.

Scapegoating The placing of the blame for one's troubles on an individual or group incapable of offering resistance.

Science The logical, systematic methods by which reliable, empirical knowledge of nature is obtained, and the actual body of knowledge accumulated by these methods.

Scientific revolution A process of scientific innovation which involves a radical change in the way scientists conceptualize their subject matter.

Secondary deviance Deviant behavior that is regular or habitual and is regarded as deviant by both the actor and significant other people.

Secondary group A group consisting of a number of people who have few if any emotional ties with one another and who come together for a specific, practical purpose.

Secondary industry Economic activity devoted to the manufacture of goods from raw materials.

Sect A marginal religious organization that tends to be dogmatic and fundamentalist and to recruit its members by conversion.

Sector theory A theory that modern cities typically grow outward from a center in wedge-shaped sectors, with each sector containing a different type of land use.

Secularization The process by which traditional religious beliefs and institutions lose their influence in society.

Self An individual's conscious experience of a distinct, personal identity that is separate from all other people and things.

Self-fulfilling prophecy A prediction about some personal or social behavior that influences the actual behavior, so that the prophecy is confirmed by the result that it has caused.

Sensorimotor stage A stage of cognitive development in which intelligence is expressed only in terms of sensory and physical contact with the environment.

Sex (male and female) Refers to the division of the human species into the biological categories of male and female.

Sexism An ideology or belief system that legitimizes sexual inequalities by assuming that these inequalities are based on inborn characteristics.

Sex role The learned patterns of behavior expected of the sexes in any society.

Sibling One's brother or sister.

Sick role The pattern of behavior expected of a person who is ill.

Small group A group that contains sufficiently few members for the participants to relate to one another as individuals.

Social change The alteration in patterns of social structure, social institutions, and social behavior over time.

Social construction of reality The process by which definitions of reality are socially created, objectified, internalized, and then taken for granted.

Social control The mechanisms and processes by which a society ensures that its members generally behave in expected and approved ways.

Social Darwinism A theory that different societies and social groups are better fitted for survival than others, and consequently become more advanced or dominant.

Social inequality A situation in which people have different access to social rewards because of their personal or group characteristics.

Social interaction The process by which people act toward or respond to other people.

Socialism A political and economic system in which, ideally, classes are eliminated and production is for social benefit rather than private profit; the means of economic production are publicly owned but private ownership of consumer items is permitted.

Socialization The process of social interaction through which people acquire personality and learn the way of life of their society.

Social-learning theory A theory of learning that relies on behaviorist principles but recognizes that some learning is incidental or the result of imitation, even though no obvious rewards or punishments are present.

Social mobility Movement from one status to another in a stratified society.

Social movement A large number of people who have joined together to bring about or resist some social or cultural change.

Social psychology The scientific study of the influence of social context on human personality and behavior.

Social sciences A related group of disciplines that study various aspects of human behavior.

Social stratification The structured inequality of entire categories of people, who have different access to social rewards as a result of their statuses in the social hierarchy.

Social structure The organized relationship among the basic components of a social system.

Society A group of interacting individuals sharing the same territory and participating in a common culture.

Sociobiology A scientific discipline that attempts to use biological principles to explain the behavior of all social animals, including human beings.

Sociocultural evolution The tendency of societies to evolve from simple to complex forms as their subsistence strategies become more efficient.

Socioeconomic status (SES) A measure of social status that takes into account a complex of factors, such as educational background, place of residence, and income.

Sociology The scientific study of human society and social behavior.

Sport Competitive physical activity guided by established rules.

Spurious A term used to refer to a correlation between variables that is purely coincidental, not causal.

Standard Consolidated Area (SCA) The Bureau of the Census's term for an unbroken urban tract involving two or more SMSAs.

Standard Metropolitan Statistical Area (SMSA) The Bureau of the Census's term for any area that contains a city (or a city and its surrounding suburbs) with a total population of 50,000 or more.

State The institution that successfully claims a monopoly of the legitimate use of force within a given territory.

Statics Refers to the phenomenon of social order and stability.

Status A socially defined position in society.

Stereotype A rigid mental image that summarizes whatever is believed to be typical of a group or category.

Stigma A mark of social disgrace that sets aside those who are considered deviant from those who consider themselves "normal."

Stratified random sample A sample obtained by dividing a population into various categories and then drawing a random sample from each category.

Subculture A group that shares in the overall culture of a society but also has its own distinctive values, norms, and lifestyle.

Subjectivity The tendency to see the world from a viewpoint that derives from the observer's own opinions, attitudes, and experiences.

Superego In Freudian theory, the internalized moral authority of society within the self; the superego is roughly equivalent to conscience.

Surplus wealth Wealth over and above that necessary to meet the basic needs of its producers.

Symbol Anything that can meaningfully represent something else, such as a word, a gesture, or a flag.

Symbolic interaction The interaction between people that takes place through symbols, such as signs, gestures, and language.

Taboo A powerful social belief that a particular act is utterly loathsome and disgusting.

Technocracy Rule by technical experts.

Technological determinism The theory that the technology available to a society is an important determinant of its social structure and even its history.

Technology The practical applications of knowledge about nature.

Tertiary industry Economic activity devoted to the provision of services rather than the extraction of raw materials or the manufacture of goods.

Theodicy An emotionally satisfying religious explanation for the great problems of human existence, such as suffering, death, and the meaning of life.

Theoretical perspective A broad, generalized assumption or set of assumptions about society and social behavior that provides an overall orientation for the examination of specific problems.

Theory A statement that organizes a set of concepts in a meaningful way by explaining the relationship between them.

Total institution A place of residence where the inmates are confined for an entire period of their lives, are cut off from the rest of society, and are under the almost absolute control of the administrative authorities.

Totalitarian Refers to a government that recognizes no limits to its authority.

Totem A commonplace object, such as an animal or plant, whose symbolic representation is the focus of some religions.

Traditional authority Authority legitimated by ancient custom.

Triad A group consisting of three people.

Unilinear evolution Refers to a theory that sociocultural evolution follows the same course in all societies.

Value conflict Basic disagreement between groups over goals, ideals, policies, or other expressions of values.

Value freedom Refers to the position that sociologists can and should exclude personal judgments and biases from their work.

Value judgment A personal, subjective opinion based on the values of the observer.

Values Socially shared ideas about what is good, right, and desirable.

Variable A characteristic that can vary from one person, group, or context to another (such as age, race, intelligence, and violent behavior).

Verstehen Subjective interpretation of a social actor's behavior and intentions.

Vertical mobility A change to a higher or lower social status than the individual had initially.

Veto groups Strong interest groups that try to protect their interests by blocking proposals of other groups that might encroach on those interests.

White-collar crime Crimes committed by "respectable" persons of high status, frequently in the course of their occupations.

Zero population growth (ZPG) A situation in which population size remains stable over time.

References

ABERLE, DAVID. 1966. *The Peyote Religion Among the Navaho.* Chicago: Aldine.

ACUÑA, RODOLFO. 1980. *Occupied America: A History of Chicanos.* New York: Harper & Row.

ADAM, BARRY B. 1978. *The Survival of Domination: Inferiorization and Everyday Life.* New York: Elsevier.

ADAM, HERIBERT. 1972. *Modernizing Racial Domination: The Dynamics of South African Politics.* Berkeley: University of California Press.

ADAM, MARGARET. 1976. *Single Blessedness: Observations on the Single Status in Married Society.* New York: Basic Books.

ADAMS, ROBERT L., and ROBERT J. FOX. 1972. "Mainlining Jesus: The new trip." *Society,* 9:4, 50–56.

ADORNO, THEODORE W., et al. 1950. *The Authoritarian Personality.* New York: Norton.

AKERS, RONALD L. 1977. *Deviant Behavior: A Social Learning Approach.* 2nd ed. Belmont, Calif.: Wadsworth.

———, et al. 1979. "Social learning and deviant behavior: A specific test of a general theory." *American Sociological Review,* 44 (August), pp. 635–655.

ALBA, FRANCISCO. 1980. *The Population of Mexico.* New Brunswick, N.J.: Transaction Books.

ALBERT, ETHEL M. 1963. "Women of Burundi: A study of social values," in Denise Paulme (ed.), *Women of Tropical Africa.* Berkeley, Calif.: University of California Press.

ALFORD, ROBERT, and ROGER FRIEDLAND. 1975. "Political participation," in Alex Inkeles et al. (eds.), *Annual Review of Sociology.* Palo Alto, Calif.: Annual Reviews.

ALLEN, MICHAEL PATRICK. 1974. "The structure of interorganizational elite cooptation: Interlocking corporate directors." *American Sociological Review,* 39, pp. 393–406.

ALLISON, PAUL D., and JOHN A. STEWART. 1974. "Productivity differences among scientists: Evidence for cumulative advantage." *American Sociological Review,* 39, pp. 596–606.

ALLPORT, GORDON W., and LEO J. POSTMAN. 1947. *The Psychology of Rumor.* New York: Holt, Rinehart and Winston.

AMIR, MENACHEM. 1971. *Patterns of Forcible Rape.* Chicago: University of Chicago Press.

ANATOVSKY, AARON. 1974. "Class and the chance for life," in Lee Rainwater (ed.), *Inequality and Justice.* Chicago: Aldine.

ANDERSON, CHARLES H. 1974. *The Political Economy of Social Class.* Englewood Cliffs, N.J.: Prentice-Hall.

———, and JEFFRY R. GIBSON. 1978. *Toward a New Sociology.* 3rd ed. Homewood, Ill.: Dorsey Press.

ANTHONY, DICK, et al. 1980. "Legitimating repression." *Society,* 17:3, 39–42.

APA Monitor. 1974. "Homosexuality dropped as mental disorder," 5 (February), pp. 1, 9.

ARAFAT, IBITHAJ, and BETTY YORBURG. 1973. "On living together without marriage." *Journal of Sex Research,* 9, pp. 97–106.

ARGYLE, MICHAEL. 1969. *Social Interaction.* London: Methuen.

ARIES, PHILLIPE. 1962. *Centuries of Childhood: A Social History of Family Life.* New York: Knopf.

ARMER, J. MICHAEL. 1968. "Inter-society and intra-society correlations of occupational prestige." *American Journal of Sociology,* 74, pp. 28–63.

ASCH, SOLOMON. 1955. "Opinions and social pressure." *Scientific American,* 193, pp. 31–35.

ATCHLEY, ROBERT. 1977. *The Social Forces in Later Life: An Introduction to Social Gerontology.* 2nd ed. Belmont, Calif.: Wadsworth.

———. 1980. *The Social Forces in Later Life: An introduction to Social Gerontology.* 3rd ed. Belmont, Calif.: Wadsworth.

ATHANASIOU, ROBERT, et al. 1972. "Sex." *Psychology Today,* 4, pp. 39–52.

AUCHINCLOSS, KENNETH. 1970. "The ravaged environment." *Newsweek,* 26, pp. 30–32.

AXTHELM, PETE. 1970. *The City Game: Basketball in New York.* New York: Harper & Row.

BAHR, HOWARD M., et al. (eds.). 1972. *Native Americans Today: Sociological Perspectives.* New York: Harper & Row.

BALES, ROBERT F. 1950. *Interaction Process Analysis: A Method for the Study of Small Groups.* Cambridge, Mass.: Addison-Wesley.

———. 1953. "The equilibrium problem in small groups," in Talcott Parsons et al. (eds.), *Working Papers in the Theory of Action.* Glencoe. Ill.: Free Press.

———. 1970. *Personality and Interpersonal Behavior.* New York: Holt, Rinehart and Winston.

———, and FRED L. STRODTBECK. 1951. "Phases in group problem solving." *Journal of Abnormal and Social Psychology,* 46, pp. 485–495.

BALL, DONALD W. 1968. "Toward a sociology of telephones and telephoners," in Marcello Truzzi (ed.), *Sociology and Everyday Life.* Englewood Cliffs, N.J.: Prentice-Hall.

———, and JOHN W. LOY. 1975. *Sport and Social Order.* Reading, Mass.: Addison-Wesley.

BALL, GEORGE W. (ed.). 1975. *Global Companies: The Political Economy of World Business.* Englewood Cliffs, N.J.: Prentice-Hall.

BALSWICK, JACK O. 1974. "The Jesus People movement: A generational interpretation." *Journal of Social Issues,* 30, pp. 23–42.

———, and CHARLES W. PEEK. 1971: "The inexpressive male: A tragedy of American society." *Family Life Coordinator,* 20, pp. 363–368.

BANDURA, ALBERT. 1977. *Social Learning Theory.* Englewood Cliffs, N.J.: Prentice-Hall.

———, and RICHARD H. WALTERS. 1963. *Social Learning and Personality Development.* New York: Holt, Rinehart and Winston.

BANE, MARY JO. 1976. *Here to Stay: American Families in the Twentieth Century.* New York: Basic Books.

BARASH, DAVID P. 1977. *Sociobiology and Behavior.* New York: Elsevier.

BARBER, THEODORE, et al. 1969. "Five attempts to replicate the experimenter bias effect." *Journal of Consulting and Clinical Psychology,* 3, pp. 1–6.

BARBOUR, IAN G. 1980. *Technology, Environment, and Human Values.* New York: Praeger.

BARNET, RICHARD, and RONALD MULLER. 1974. *Global Reach: Power and the Multinational Corporations.* New York: Simon and Schuster.

BARNETT, H. G. 1953. *Innovation: The Basis of Cultural Change.* New York: McGraw-Hill.

BARRY, HERBERT, et al. 1957. "A cross-cultural survey of some sex differences in socialization." *Journal of Abnormal and Social Psychology,* 55, pp. 327–332.

BARTELL, GILBERT. 1974. "Group sex among the middle Americans," in James R. Smith and Lynn G. Smith (eds.), *Beyond Monogamy.* Baltimore, Md.: Johns Hopkins University Press.

BEACH, FRANK A. (ed.). 1965. *Sex and Behavior.* New York: Wiley.

——— (ed.). 1977. *Human Sexuality in Four Perspectives.* Baltimore, Md.: Johns Hopkins University Press.

BEACH, STEPHEN W. 1977. "Religion and political change in Northern Ireland." *Sociological Analysis,* 38:1, 37–48.

BECKER, HOWARD S. 1953. "Becoming a marijuana user." *American Journal of Sociology,* 59 (November), pp. 235–242.

——— (ed.). 1963a. *The Other Side.* New York: Free Press.

———. 1963b. *Outsiders: Studies in the Sociology of Deviance.* New York: Free Press.

———, et al. 1968. *Making the Grade: The Academic Side of College Life.* New York: Wiley.

BELL, ALAN P., and MARTIN S. WEINBERG. 1978. *Homosexualities: A*

Study of Diversity Among Men and Women. New York: Simon and Schuster.

BELL, CAROLYN SHAW. 1977. "Let's get rid of families." *Newsweek*, May 8, p. 19.

BELL, DANIEL. 1973. *The Coming of Postindustrial Society*. New York: Basic Books.

BELL, DERRICK A. 1973. "Racism in American courts." *California New Law Review*, 61, pp. 165–203.

BELL, ROBERT R. 1964. "Some factors related to the sexual satisfaction of the college-educated wife." *Family Life Coordinator*, 13, pp. 43–47.

BELLAH, ROBERT N. 1970. *Beyond Belief*. New York: Harper & Row.

BEM, SANDRA, and DARYL BEM. 1970. "We're all nonconscious sexists." *Psychology Today*, 4, p. 22.

BENAGH, JIM. 1976. *Making It to #1: How College Football and Basketball Teams Get There*. New York: Dodd, Mead.

BEN-DAVID, JOSEPH. 1971. *The Scientist's Role in Society*. Englewood Cliffs, N.J.: Prentice-Hall.

BENEDICT, RUTH. 1961. *Patterns of Culture*. Boston: Houghton Mifflin.

BENJAMIN, HARRY, and R. E. L. MASTERS. 1964. *Prostitution and Morality*. New York: Julian Press.

BENNET, EDWARD M., and LARRY R. COHEN. 1959. "Men and women: Personality patterns and contrasts." *Genetic Psychology Monographs*, 59, pp. 101–155.

BENNETT, JOHN W. 1976. *The Ecological Transition: Cultural Anthropology and Human Adaptation*. New York: Pergamon.

BENNIS, WARREN G. 1966. *Changing Organizations*. New York: McGraw-Hill.

———(ed.). 1970. *American Bureaucracy*. Chicago: Transaction Books.

BENSON, J. KENNETH. 1973. "The analysis of bureaucratic-professional conflict: Functional versus dialectic approaches." *Sociological Quarterly*, vol. 14.

BERELSON, BERNARD, and GARY G. STEINER. 1964. *Human Behavior: An Inventory of Scientific Findings*. New York: Harcourt, Brace, and World.

BERG, IVAR. 1970. *Education and Jobs: The Great Training Robbery*. New York: Praeger.

———, et al. 1978. *Managers and Work Reform: A Limited Engagement*. New York: Free Press.

BERGER, BENNET M. 1961. "The myth of suburbia." *Journal of Social Issues*, 17, pp. 38–49.

BERGER, PETER L. 1963. *Invitation to Sociology: A Humanistic Perspective*. New York: Doubleday.

———. 1964. "Some general observations on the problem of work," in Peter L. Berger (ed.), *The Human Shape of Work*. New York: Macmillan.

———. 1967. *The Sacred Canopy: Elements of a Sociological Theory of Religion*. New York: Doubleday.

———. 1969. *A Rumor of Angels: Modern Society and the Rediscovery of the Supernatural*. New York: Doubleday.

———, and THOMAS LUCKMANN. 1963. *The Social Construction of Reality*. New York: Doubleday.

BERK, RICHARD A., et al. 1980. "Poverty and crime: Some experimental evidence from ex-offenders." *American Sociological Review*, 45:5, 766–786.

BERLE, A. A., and G. C. MEANS. 1933. *The Modern Corporation and Private Property*. New York: Macmillan.

BERLIN, BRENT, and PAUL KAY. 1969. *Basic Color Terms: Their Universality and Evolution*. Berkeley, Calif.: University of California Press.

BERNARD, JESSIE. 1956. *Remarriage: A Study of Marriage*. New York: Dryden.

BERNARD, L. L. 1924. *Instinct*. New York: Holt, Rinehart and Winston.

BERNSTEIN, BASIL, 1971. *Class, Codes, and Control*. London: Routledge & Kegan Paul.

BERREMAN, GERALD D. 1973. *Caste in the Modern World*. Morristown, N.J.: General Learning Press.

BERRY, R. STEPHEN. 1970. "The chemistry and cost: Perspectives on polluted air—1970." *Bulletin of the Atomic Scientists*, 26, pp. 2, 34–41.

BERSCHEID, ELLEN, and ELAINE WALSTER. 1978. *Interpersonal Attraction*. 2nd ed. Reading, Mass.: Addison-Wesley.

BETTELHEIM, BRUNO. 1959. "Feral children and autistic children." *American Journal of Sociology*, 64, pp. 455–467.

BETTS, JOHN R. 1974. *America's Sporting Heritage 1850–1950*. Reading, Mass.: Addison-Wesley.

BIBBY, REGINALD W. 1979. "Religion and modernity: The Canadian case." *Journal for the Scientific Study of Religion*, 18:1, 1–17.

BIEBER, IRVING, et al. 1962. *Homosexuality: A Psychoanalytic Study*. New York: Basic Books.

BIRD, CAROLINE. 1975. *The Case Against College*. New York: McKay.

———. 1979. *The Two-Paycheck Marriage*. New York. Rawson Wade.

BIRDWHISTELL, RAY L. 1970. *Kinesics and Context*. Philadelphia: Pennsylvania University Press.

BIRENBAUM, ARNOLD, and EDWARD SAGARIN. 1973. "The deviant actor maintains his right to be present: The case of the nondrinker," in Arnold Birenbaum and Edward Sagarin (eds.), *People in Places: The Sociology of the Familiar*. New York: Praeger.

BLANKENSHIP, RALPH (ed.). 1977. *Colleagues in Organization: The Social Construction of Professional Work*. New York: Wiley.

BLAU, PETER M. 1963. *The Dynamics of Bureaucracy*. Rev. ed. Chicago: University of Chicago Press.

_____. 1964. *Exchange and Power in Social Life*. New York: Wiley.

_____, and W. RICHARD SCOTT. 1962. *Formal Organizations*. San Francisco: Chandler.

_____, and OTIS DUDLEY DUNCAN. 1967. *The American Occupational Structure*. New York: Wiley.

_____, and MARSHALL W. MEYER. 1971. *Bureaucracy in Modern Society*. 2nd ed. New York: Random House.

BLAUNER, ROBERT. 1964. *Alienation and Freedom*. Chicago: University of Chicago Press.

_____. 1972. *Racial Oppression in America*. New York: Harper & Row.

BLEDSTEIN, BURTON J. 1976. *The Culture of Professionalism: The Middle Class and the Development of Higher Education in America*. New York: Norton.

BLISHEN, BERNARD R., and H. A. McROBERTS. 1976. "A revised socioeconomic index for occupations in Canada." *Canadian Review of Sociology and Anthropology*, 13, pp. 71–79.

BLUMBERG, ABRAHAM S. 1967. *Criminal Justice*. Chicago: Quadrangle.

BLUME, MARSHALL E., et al. 1974. "Stock ownership in the United States: Characteristics and trends." *Survey of Current Business* (U.S. Department of Commerce), 54, pp. 16–40.

BLUMER, HERBERT. 1951. "Collective behavior," in Alfred McLung Lee (ed.), *New Outline of the Principles of Sociology*. New York: Barnes & Noble.

_____. 1962. "Society as symbolic interaction," in Arnold Rose (ed.), *Human Behavior and Social Processes: An Interactionist Approach*. Boston: Houghton Mifflin.

_____. 1969. *Symbolic Interactionism: Perspective and Method*. Englewood Cliffs, N.J.: Prentice-Hall.

_____. 1974. "Social movements," in R. Serge Denisoff (ed.), *The Sociology of Dissent*. New York: Harcourt Brace Jovanovich.

BLUMSTEIN, PHILIP, and PEPPER SCHWARTZ. 1974. "The acquisition of sexual identity: The bisexual case." Paper presented at the Annual Meetings of the American Sociological Association, August 25–29, Montreal, Canada.

BOOCOCK, SARANE SPENCE. 1978. "The social organization of the classroom." *Annual Review of Sociology*. Palo Alto, Calif.: Annual Reviews Inc.

_____. 1980. *Sociology of Education*. Boston: Houghton Mifflin.

BOSWELL, JAMES. 1980. *Christianity, Homosexuality, and Social Tolerance*. Chicago: University of Chicago Press.

BOTT, ELIZABETH. 1971. *Family and Social Network*. New York: Free Press.

BOULDING, KENNETH E. 1964. *The Meaning of the Twentieth Century: The Great Transition*. New York: Harper & Row.

_____. 1978. *Ecodynamics: A New Theory of Societal Evolution*. Beverly Hills, Calif.: Sage.

BOWEN, HOWARD R. 1977. *Investment in Learning: The Individual and the Social Value of American Higher Education*. San Francisco: Jossey-Bass.

BOWER, DONALD W., and VICTOR A. CHRISTOPHERSON. 1977. "University student cohabitation: A regional comparison of selected attitudes and behavior." *Journal of Marriage and the Family*, 39:3, 447–452.

BOWLBY, JOHN. 1969. *Attachment and Loss*. Vol. 1. New York: Basic Books.

BOWLES, SAMUEL, and HERBERT GINTIS. 1976. *Schooling in Capitalist America*. New York: Basic Books.

BRANDSATTER, HERMAN, et al. 1978. *Dynamics of Group Decisions*. Beverly Hills, Calif.: Sage.

BRIGGS, VERNON M., et al. 1977. *The Chicano Worker*. Austin: Texas University Press.

BRIM, ORVILLE G., et al. (eds.). 1970. *The Dying Patient*. New York: Russell Sage Foundation.

BRINTON, CRANE. 1960. *The Anatomy of Revolution*. New York: Random House.

BROMLEY, DAVID, and ANSON D. SHUPE. 1979. *"Moonies" in America: Cult, Church, and Crusade*. Beverly Hills, Calif.: Sage.

BRONFENBRENNER, URIE. 1970. *Two Worlds of Childhood*. New York: Russell Sage Foundation.

BROPHY, J. E., and T. L. GOOD. 1970. "Teachers' communication of differential expectations for children's classroom performance: Some behavioral data." *Journal of Educational Psychology*, 61, p. 356.

BROWER, JONATHAN R. 1972. "The racial basis of the division of labor among players in the National Football League as a function of stereotypes." Paper presented at the annual meetings of the Pacific Sociological Association, Portland.

_____. 1973. "The quota system: The white gatekeepers' regulation of professional football's black community." Paper presented at the annual meetings of the American Sociological Association, New York.

BROWN, ROGER. 1965. *Social Psychology*. New York: Free Press.

BROWNMILLER, SUSAN. 1975. *Against Our Will: Men, Women, and Rape*. New York: Simon and Schuster.

BRUCE-BIGGS, B. (ed.). 1979. *The New Class?* New Brunswick, N.J.: Transaction Books.

BRYANT, JAMES H. 1965. "Apprenticeships in prostitution." *Social Problems*, 12 (Winter), pp. 278–297.

BUCKLEY, W. 1958. "Social stratification and the functional theory of social differentiation." *American Sociological Review*, 23, pp. 369–375.

BUCKNER, H. T. 1970. "The transvestic career path." *Psychiatry*, 33, pp. 381–389.

BULLOUGH, VERN L. 1976. *Sexual Variance in Society and History.* New York: Wiley.

BUMPASS, LARRY, and CHARLES WESTOFF. 1970. "Unwanted births and U.S. population control." *Family Planning Perspectives,* 2, pp. 9–11.

BUREAU OF THE CENSUS. 1978a. "Characteristics of the population below the poverty level: 1976." *Current Population Reports,* Series P-60, no. 115, Washington, D.C.: U.S. Government Printing Office.

BUREAU OF THE CENSUS. 1978b. "Marital status and living arrangements: March 1978." *Current Population Reports,* Series P-20, no. 338, Washington, D.C.: U.S. Government Printing Office.

BUREAU OF THE CENSUS. 1978c. *Statistical Abstract of the United States, 1978.* Washington, D.C.: U.S. Government Printing Office.

BUREAU OF THE CENSUS. 1980. *Statistical Abstract of the United States, 1980.* Washington, D.C.: U.S. Government Printing Office.

BURGESS, ERNEST W., and PAUL WALLIN. 1973. *Engagement and Marriage.* Philadelphia: Lippincott.

BURGESS, ROBERT L., and RONALD L. AKERS. 1966. "A differential association-reinforcement theory of criminal behavior." *Social Problems,* 14, pp. 128–147.

BURGOON, JUDEE K., and STEPHEN B. JONES. 1976. "Toward a theory of personal space expectations and their violations." *Human Communication Research,* 2, pp. 131–146.

BURNETTE, ROBERT. 1971. *The Tortured Americans.* Englewood Cliffs, N.J.: Prentice-Hall.

BURNHAM, JAMES. 1941. *The Managerial Revolution.* New York: John Day.

BURRIDGE, KENELM O. L. 1957. "Disputing in Tangu." *American Anthropologist,* 59, pp. 763–780.

CAMPBELL, ERNEST Q., and C. NORMAN ALEXANDER. 1964. "Peer influences on adolescent educational aspirations and attainment." *American Sociological Review,* 29, pp. 58–75.

CANTRIL, HADLEY. 1940. *The Invasion from Mars.* Princeton, N.J.: Princeton University Press.

———. 1941. *The Psychology of Social Movements.* New York: Wiley.

———. 1963. *The Psychology of Social Movements.* New York: Wiley.

CAPLAN, ARTHUR L. (ed.). 1978. *The Sociobiology Debate.* New York: Harper & Row.

CARDEN, MAREN LOCKWOOD. 1975. *The New Feminist Movement.* Beverly Hills, Calif.: Sage.

CARTER, HUGH, and PAUL C. GLICK. 1976. *Marriage and Divorce: A Social and Economic Study.* Cambridge, Mass.: Harvard University Press.

CASLER, LAWRENCE. 1974. *Is Marriage Necessary?* New York: Human Sciences Press.

CENTERS, RICHARD. 1949. *The Psychology of Social Class.* Princeton, N.J.: Princeton University Press.

———, et al. 1971. "Conjugal power structure: A reexamination." *American Sociological Review,* 36, pp. 264–277.

CHAFETZ, JANET S. (ed.). 1978. *Masculine/Feminine or Human?* 2nd ed. Itasca, Ill.: Peacock.

CHAGNON, NAPOLEON A. 1967. "Yanamamö social organization and warfare," in Morton Fried et al. (eds.), *War: The Anthropology of Armed Conflict and Aggression.* New York: Doubleday.

———. 1977 *Yanamamö: The Fierce People.* 2nd ed. New York: Holt, Rinehart and Winston.

CHAMBLISS, WILLIAM J. 1973. "The Saints and the Roughnecks." *Society,* 11, pp. 24–31.

———, and MILTON MANKOFF (eds.). 1976. *Whose Law? What Order?* New York: Wiley.

CHAPMAN, JANE ROBERTS, and MARGARET GATES (eds.). 1978. *The Victimization of Women.* Beverly Hills, Calif.: Sage.

CHAPPELL, DUNCAN, et al. (eds.). 1977. *Rape: The Victim and the Offender.* New York: Columbia University Press.

CHEEK, WILLIAM F. 1970. *Black Resistance Before the Civil War.* Beverly Hills, Calif.: Glencoe Press.

CHINOY, ELY. 1955. *The Automobile Worker and the American Dream.* New York: Doubleday.

CHIRICOS, THEODORE G., and GORDON P. WALDO. 1975. "Socioeconomic status and criminal sentencing: An empirical assessment of a conflict proposition." *American Sociological Review,* 40, pp. 753–772.

CHOMSKY, NOAM. 1957. *Syntactic Structures.* The Hague: Mouton.

———. 1968. *Language and Mind.* New York: Harcourt Brace Jovanovich.

———. 1971. "The case against B. F. Skinner." *The New York Review of Books,* 17, pp. 18–24.

CHURCH, FRANK. 1973. Will they usher in a new world order?" *Center Magazine,* 6, pp. 15–18.

CICOUREL, AARON. 1974. *Cognitive Sociology.* New York: Free Press.

———, and JOHN I. KITSUSE. 1963. *The Educational Decision-Makers.* Indianapolis: Bobbs-Merrill.

CLAIBORN, W. L. 1969. "Expectancy effects in the classroom: A failure to replicate." *Journal of Educational Psychology,* 60, p. 377.

CLARK, BURTON R. 1960. "The 'cooling-out' function in higher education." *American Journal of Sociology,* 65, pp. 569–576.

———. 1962. *Educating the Expert Society.* San Francisco: Chandler.

CLARK, KENNETH. 1965. *Dark Ghetto.* New York: Harper & Row.

CLAUSEN, JOHN A., et. al. 1968. "Perspectives on child socialization," in John A. Clausen (ed.), *Socialization and Society*. Boston: Little, Brown.

CLAYTON, RICHARD R., and HARWIN L. VOSS. 1977. "Shacking up: Cohabitation in the 1970s." *Journal of Marriage and the Family*, 39:2, 273–283.

CLEMENT, WALLACE. 1975. *The Canadian Corporate Elite: An Analysis of Economic Power*. Toronto: McClelland and Stewart.

CLOWARD, RICHARD A., and LLOYD E. OHLIN. 1960. *Delinquency and Opportunity: A Theory of Delinquent Gangs*. New York: Free Press.

COAKLEY, JAY J. 1978. *Sport in Society: Issues and Controversies*. St. Louis: Mosby.

COHEN, ALBERT K. 1955. *Delinquent Boys: The Culture of the Gang*. New York: Free Press.

———. 1959. "The study of social disorganization and deviant behavior," in Robert K. Merton et al. (eds.), *Sociology Today: Problems and Prospects*. New York: Basic Books.

———. 1966. *Deviance and Control*. Englewood Cliffs, N.J.: Prentice-Hall.

———, and HAROLD M. HODGES, JR. 1963. "Characteristics of the lower-blue-collar classes." *Social Policy*, pp. 61–67.

COHEN, YEHUDI A. (ed.). 1974. *Man in Adaptation: The Cultural Present*. 2nd ed. Chicago: Aldine.

COHN, NORMAN. 1962. *The Pursuit of the Millennium*. New York: Oxford University Press.

COLE, STEPHEN, and JONATHAN COLE. 1977. *Social Stratification in Science*. Chicago: University of Chicago Press.

COLEMAN, JAMES C. 1976. *Abnormal Psychology and Modern Life*. 5th ed. Glenview, Ill.: Scott, Foresman.

COLEMAN, JAMES S. 1961. *The Adolescent Society*. New York: Doubleday.

———, et al. 1966. *Equality of Educational Opportunity*. Washington, D.C.: U.S. Government Printing Office.

———, et al. 1975. *Trends in School Desegregation, 1968–1973*. Washington, D.C.: Urban Institute.

COLEMAN, RICHARD P., and BERNICE L. NEUGARTEN. 1971. *Social Status in the City*. San Francisco: Jossey-Bass.

COLLINS, RANDALL. 1971a. "A conflict theory of sexual stratification." *Social Problems*, 19, pp. 3–12.

———. 1971b. "Functional and conflict theories of educational stratification." *American Sociological Review*, 36:6, 1002–1019.

———. 1974. *Conflict Sociology: Toward an Explanatory Science*. New York: Academic Press.

———. 1979. *The Credential Society*. New York: Academic Press.

COMMISSION ON POPULATION GROWTH AND THE AMERICAN FUTURE. 1972. *Population and the American Future: The Report of the Commission on Population Growth and the American Future*. Washington, D.C.: U.S. Government Printing Office.

COMMONER, BARRY. 1971. *The Closing Circle*. New York: Knopf.

COMSTOCK, GEORGE, et al. 1978. *Television and Human Behavior*. New York: Columbia University Press.

———. 1980. *Television in America*. Beverly Hills, Calif.: Sage.

CONCKLIN, JOHN E. (ed.). 1973. *The Crime Establishment*. Englewood Cliffs, N.J.: Prentice-Hall.

Congressional Quarterly. 1971. "White collar crime: Huge economic and moral drain," 29, pp. 1047–1049.

CONDRY, JOHN, and SANDRA CONDRY. 1976. "Sex differences: A study of the eye of the beholder." *Child Development*, 47, pp. 812–819.

CONNOR, WALTER D. 1979. *Hierarchy and Change in Eastern Europe and the U.S.S.R.* New York: Columbia University Press.

CONSTANTINE, LARRY L. 1978. "Multilateral relations revisited: Group marriage in extended perspective," in Bernard I. Murstein (ed.), *Exploring Intimate Life Styles*. New York: Springer.

CONSTANTINE, LARRY L., and JOAN M. CONSTANTINE. 1974. *Group Marriage*. New York: Macmillan.

COOK, M. 1970. "Experiments on orientation and proxemics." *Human Relations*, 23, pp. 61–76.

COOLEY, CHARLES HORTON. 1902. *Human Nature and the Social Order*. New York: Scribner's.

COOPER, A. J. 1969. "A clinical study of 'coital anxiety' in male potency disorders." *Journal of Psychometric Research*, 13, pp. 143–147.

COSER, LEWIS A. 1956. *The Functions of Social Conflict*. Glencoe, Ill.: Free Press.

———. 1962. "Some functions of deviant behavior and normative flexibility." *American Journal of Sociology*, 68, pp. 172–179.

COWAN, EDWARD. 1980. "Americans are believed to cheat the government out of at least $18 billion in income taxes for 79." *New York Times*, April 13, p. 28.

COX, HARVEY. 1965. *The Secular City*. New York: Macmillan.

———. 1977. *Turning East: The Promise and Peril of the New Orientalism*. New York: Simon and Schuster.

CRANE, DIANA. 1969. "Social structure in a group of scientists: A test of the 'invisible colleges' hypothesis." *American Sociological Review*, 34, pp. 335–351.

———. 1972. *Invisibile Colleges*. Chicago: University of Chicago Press.

CRESSEY, DONALD R. 1969. *Theft of the Nation: The Structure and Operations of Organized Crime in America*. New York: Harper & Row.

CROSSMAN, RICHARD (ed.). 1952. *The God That Failed*. New York: Bantam.

CUMMING, ELAINE, and WILLIAM E. HENRY. 1961. *Growing Old: The Process of Disengagement*. New York: Basic Books.

CUTRIGHT, PHILLIP. 1967. "Inequality: A cross-national analysis." *American Sociological Review*, 32, pp. 562–578.

DADZIE, K.K.S. 1980. "Economic Development." *Scientific American*, 243:3, 59–65.

DAHL, ROBERT. 1961. *Who Governs?* New Haven, Conn.: Yale University Press.

DAHRENDORF, RALF. 1958. "Toward a theory of social conflict." *The Journal of Conflict Resolution*, 11, pp. 170–183.

D'ANDRADE, ROY G. 1966. "Sex differences and cultural institutions," in Eleanor E. Maccoby (ed.), *The Development of Sex Differences*. Palo Alto, Calif.: Stanford University Press.

DANER, FRANCINE. 1976. *The American Children of Krsna: A Study of the Hare Krsna Movement*. New York: Holt, Rinehart & Winston.

DANK, BARRY M. 1971. "Coming out in the gay world." *Psychiatry*, 34 (May), pp. 180–197.

DARLEY, JOHN M., and BIBB LATANÉ. 1968. "Bystander intervention in emergencies: Diffusion of responsibility." *Journal of Personality and Social Psychology*, 8, pp. 377–383.

DAVIDSON, TERRY. 1978. *Conjugal Crime: Understanding and Changing the Wifebeating Pattern*. New York: Hawthorne.

DAVIES, JAMES C. 1962. "Toward a theory of revolution." *American Sociological Review*, 27, pp. 5–18.

————— (ed.). 1971. *When Men Revolt—and Why*. New York: Free Press.

DAVIS, ALAN J. 1968. "Sexual assaults in the Philadelphia prison system." *Transaction*, 6, pp. 28–35.

DAVIS, FRED. 1961. "Deviance disavowal: The management of strained interaction by the visibly handicapped." *Social Problems*, 9, pp. 120–132.

DAVIS, JAMES H. 1969. *Group Performance*. Reading, Mass.: Addison-Wesley.

DAVIS, KINGSLEY. 1932. "The sociology of prostitution." *American Sociological Review*, 2, pp. 744–755.

—————. 1940. "Extreme social isolation of a child." *American Journal of Sociology*, 45, pp. 554–564.

—————. 1947. "Final note on a case of extreme isolation." *American Journal of Sociology*, 50, pp. 432–437.

—————. 1948. *Human Society*. New York: Macmillan.

—————. 1967. "Population policy: Will current programs succeed?" *Science*, 158, pp. 730–739.

—————. 1976a. "Sexual behavior," in Robert K. Merton and Robert Nisbet (eds.), *Contemporary Social Problems*. 3rd ed. New York: Harcourt Brace Jovanovich.

—————. 1976b. "The world's population crisis," in Robert K. Merton and Robert Nisbet (eds.), *Contemporary Social Problems*. 3rd ed. New York: Harcourt Brace Jovanovich.

—————, and WILBERT E. MOORE. 1945. "Some principles of stratification." *American Sociological Review*, 10, pp. 242–249.

DAVIS, NANETTE J. 1971. "The prostitute: Developing a deviant identity," in James M. Henslin (ed.), *Studies in the Sociology of Sex*. New York: Appleton-Century-Crofts.

DAVIS, REX, and JAMES T. RICHARDSON. 1976. "The organization and functioning of the Children of God." *Sociological Analysis*, 37, pp. 349–448.

DAVIS, SHELTON. 1977. *Victims of the Miracle: Development and the Indians of Brazil*. New York: Columbia University Press.

DAY, ROBERT A., and JOANNE V. DAY. 1977. "A review of the current state of negotiated order theory: An appreciation and a critique." *Sociological Quarterly*, Winter, p. 18.

DELGADO, RICHARD. 1980. "Limits to proselytizing." *Society*, 17:3, 25–33.

DELORA, JACK R., and JOANN S. DELORA. 1975. *Intimate Life Styles: Marriage and Its Alternatives*. 2nd ed. Pacific Palisades, Calif.: Goodyear.

DELPH, EDWARD WILLIAM. 1978. *The Silent Community*. Berkeley, Calif.: Sage.

DE MAUSE, LLOYD (ed.). 1974. *The History of Childhood*. New York: The Psychohistory Press.

DENFIELD, DUANE, and MICHAEL GORDON. 1974. "The sociology of mate swapping: Or the family that swings together clings together," in James R. Smith and Lynn G. Smith (eds.), *Beyond Monogamy*. Baltimore, Md.: Johns Hopkins Press.

DENITCH, BOGDAN. 1979. *Legitimation of Regimes: International Frameworks for Analysis*. Berkeley, Calif.: Sage.

DENLINGER, KENNETH, and LEONARD SHAPIRO. 1975. *Athletes for Sale*. New York: Crowell.

DENNIS, WAYNE. 1960. "Causes of retardation among institutionalized children: Iran." *Journal of Genetic Psychology*, 96, pp. 47–59.

—————, and PERGROUHI NAJARIAN. 1957. "Infant development under environmental handicap." *Psychological Monographs*, 71, pp. 1–3.

DENTLER, ROBERT A., and LAWRENCE J. MONROE. 1961. "Social correlates of early adolescent theft." *American Sociological Review*, 26, pp. 733–743.

DENTON, JOHN A. 1978. *Medical Sociology*. Boston: Houghton Mifflin.

DEPARTMENT OF HEALTH, EDUCATION, AND WELFARE. 1972. *Welfare: Myths vs. Facts*. Washington, D.C.: U.S. Government Printing Office.

DEPARTMENT OF LABOR. 1977. *Dictionary of Occupational Titles*. Washington, D.C.: U.S. Government Printing Office.

DE TOCQUEVILLE, ALEXIS. 1954, originally published 1835. *Democracy in America II*. Phillips Bradley (ed.). New York: Random House.

DEUTSCHER, IRWIN. 1973. *What We Say, What We Do: Sentiments and Acts*. Glenview, Ill.: Scott, Foresman.

DIAMOND, MILTON. 1965. "A critical evaluation of the ontogeny of human sexual behavior." *Quarterly Review of Biology*, 40, pp. 147–173.

—————. 1977. "Human sexual development: Biological foundations for social development," in Frank A. Beach (ed.), *Human Sexuality in Four Perspectives.* Baltimore, Md.: Johns Hopkins University Press.

DINNERSTEIN, LEONARD, et al. 1979. *Natives and Strangers: Ethnic Groups and the Building of America.* New York: Oxford University Press.

DJILAS, MILOVAN. 1957. *The New Class: An Analysis of the Communist System.* New York: Praeger.

DOBSON, RICHARD B. 1977. "Mobility and stratification in the Soviet Union." *Annual Review of Sociology.* Palo Alto, Calif.: Annual Reviews.

DOLESCHAL, EUGENE, and NORAH KLAPMUTS. 1973. *Toward a New Criminology.* Hackensack, N.J.: National Council on Crime and Delinquency.

DOMHOFF, G. WILLIAM. 1967. *Who Rules America?* Englewood Cliffs, N.J.: Prentice-Hall.

———. 1970. *The Higher Circles.* New York: Random House.

———. 1978. *Who Really Rules?* New Brunswick, N.J.: Transaction Books.

——— (ed.). 1980. *Power Structure Research.* Beverly Hills, Calif.: Sage.

DORE, RONALD. 1976. *The Diploma Disease: Education, Qualification, and Development.* London: Allen and Unwin.

DOUNTON, JAMES V. 1979. *Sacred Journeys: The Conversion of Young Americans to Divine Light Mission.* New York: Columbia University Press.

DREITZEL, HANS P. 1970. *Recent Sociology No. 2: Patterns of Communicative Behavior.* New York: Macmillan.

DREW, DAVID E. (ed.). 1978. *Competency, Careers, and College: New Directions for Education and Work.* San Francisco: Jossey-Bass.

DUBERMAN, MARTIN. 1974. "The bisexual debate." *New Times,* 2, pp. 34–41.

DURKHEIM, EMILE. 1954, originally published 1912. *The Elementary Forms of Religious Life.* Joseph W. Swain (trans.). Glencoe, Ill.: Free Press.

———. 1964a, originally published 1893. *The Division of Labor in Society.* George Simpson (trans.). Glencoe, Ill.: Free Press.

———. 1964b, originally published 1897. *Suicide.* Glencoe, Ill.: Free Press.

DURSO, JOSEPH. 1975. *The Sports Factory: An Investigation into College Sports.* New York: Quadrangle.

DUVERGER, MAURICE. 1954. *Political Parties.* New York: Wiley.

DYE, THOMAS R. 1976. *Who's Running America?* Englewood Cliffs, N.J.: Prentice-Hall.

Economic Report of the President, 1974. Washington, D.C.: U.S. Government Printing Office.

EDGE, D. O., and MICHAEL MULKAY. 1976. *Astronomy Transformed.* New York: Wiley Interscience.

EDWARDS, CHRISTOPHER. 1979. *Crazy for God.* Englewood Cliffs,

N.J.: Prentice-Hall.

EDWARDS, HARRY. 1969. *The Revolt of the Black Athlete.* New York: Free Press.

———. 1973. *Sociology of Sport.* Homewood, Ill.: Dorsey.

EHRBAR, A. F. 1980. "How to save Social Security." *Fortune,* August 25, pp. 34–39.

EHRLICH, PAUL R. 1970. *The Population Explosion: Facts and Fiction.* Palo Alto, Calif.: Zero Population Growth.

———, and ANNE H. EHRLICH. 1972. *Population/Resources/Environment: Issues in Human Ecology.* San Francisco: W.H. Freeman.

———, and ANNE H. EHRLICH. 1979. "What happened to the population bomb?" *Human Nature,* 2:1, 88–92.

———, et al. 1977. *Ecoscience: Population, Resources, Environment.* San Francisco: W.H. Freeman.

EITZEN, D. STANLEY. 1976. "Sport and social status in American public secondary education." *Review of Sport and Leisure,* 1 (Fall), pp. 139–155.

———, and NORMAN R. YETMAN. 1977. "Immune from racism?" *Civil Rights Digest,* 9 (Winter), pp. 2–13.

———, and GEORGE H. SAGE. 1978. *Sociology of American Sport.* Dubuque, Iowa: William C. Brown.

EKMAN, PAUL, et al. 1972. *Emotion in the Human Face.* New York: Pergamon.

ELIAS, NORBERT. 1978. *What Is Sociology?* New York: Columbia University Press.

ELKINS, STANLEY M. 1963. *Slavery: A Problem in American Institutional and Intellectual Life.* New York: Grosset & Dunlap.

ELLING, RAY H. 1980. *Cross-National Study of Health Systems.* New Brunswick, N.J.: Transaction Books.

ELLIS, ALBERT. 1970. "Group marriage: A possible alternative?" in Herbert A. Otto (ed.), *The Family in Search of a Future.* New York: Appleton-Century-Crofts.

ELLUL, JACQUES. 1964. *The Technological Society.* New York: Knopf.

ELLWOOD, ROBERT S. 1973. *Religious and Spiritual Groups in Modern America.* Englewood Cliffs, N.J.: Prentice-Hall.

EMPEY, LAMAR T., and MAYNARD ERICKSON. 1966. "Hidden delinquency and social status." *Social Forces,* 44, pp. 546–554.

ENGELS, FRIEDRICH. 1942. *The Origin of the Family, Private Property, and the State.* New York: International Publishing.

ENROTH, RONALD E. 1977. *Youth, Brainwashing, and Extremist Cults.* Grand Rapids, Mich.: Zondervan.

ERICKSON, MAYNARD L. 1971. "The group context of delinquent behavior." *Social Problems,* 19, pp. 114–129.

———. 1973. "Group violations, socioeconomic status and official delinquency." *Social Forces,* 52, pp. 41–52.

ERIKSON, ERIK H. 1964. *Childhood and Society.* New York: Norton.

ERIKSON, KAI T. 1966. *Wayward Puritans: A Study in the Sociology of Deviance.* New York: Wiley.

ETTMORE, E. M. 1980. *Lesbians, Women, and Society*. London: Routledge and Kegan Paul.

ETZIONI, AMITAI. 1964. *Modern Organizations*. Englewood Cliffs, N.J.: Prentice-Hall.

———— (ed.). 1969. *The Semi-Professions and Their Organization*. New York: Free Press.

————. 1975. *A Comparative Analysis of Complex Organizations*. Revised and enlarged ed. Glencoe, Ill.: Free Press.

————, and CLYDE NUNN. 1974. "The public appreciation of science in contemporary America." *Daedalus*, 103, pp. 191-205.

EVANS, CHRISTOPHER. 1979. *The Mico Millennium*. New York: Viking.

EVANS, LAURA J. 1978. "Sexual harassment: Women's hidden occupational hazard," in Jane R. Chapman and Margaret Gates (eds.), *The Victimization of Women*. Beverly Hills, Calif.: Sage.

EVANS-PRITCHARD, E. E. 1970. "Sexual inversion among the Azande." *American Anthropologist*, 72, pp. 1428-1433.

FALKMAN, PETER, and DONALD P. IRISH. 1974. "Socialization—resocialization—reverse socialization: Analysis and societal significance." Paper presented to the Midwest Sociological Society annual meeting, Omaha, Nebraska, April 5.

FARBER, JERRY. 1970. *The Student as Nigger*. New York: Simon and Schuster.

FARIS, ROBERT E. L. 1967. *Chicago Sociology, 1920-1932*. San Francisco: Chandler.

FARLEY, LIN. 1978. *Sexual Shakedown: The Sexual Harassment of Women on the Job*. New York: McGraw-Hill.

FARRINGTON, BANJAMIN. 1949. *Greek Science, II*. London: Penguin.

FAST, JULIUS. 1970. *Body Language*. New York: Evans.

FEAGIN, JOE R. 1975. *Subordinating the Poor: Welfare and American Beliefs*. Englewood Cliffs, N.J.: Prentice-Hall.

————. 1978. *Race and Ethnic Relations*. Englewood Cliffs, N.J.: Prentice-Hall.

FELDMAN, KENNETH A., and THEODORE NEWCOMB. 1969. *The Impact of College upon Students*. San Francisco: Jossey-Bass.

FELIPE, N., and R. SOMMER. 1966. "Invasions of personal space." *Social Problems*, 14, pp. 206-214.

FESTINGER, et al. 1956. *When Prophecy Fails*. New York: Harper & Row.

FEUER, LEWIS S. 1969. *Conflict of Generations*. New York: Basic Books.

FIEDLER, FRED. 1969. "Style or circumstance: The leadership enigma." *Psychology Today*, 2, pp. 38-43.

FIREY, WALTER. 1947. *Land Use in Central Boston*. Cambridge, Mass.: Harvard University Press.

FISCHER, DAVID HACKETT. 1978. *Growing Old in America*. New York: Oxford University Press.

FITZGERALD, ERNEST. 1973. "The Pentagon as the enemy of capitalism." *World*, 2, pp. 18-21.

FOLGER, J. K. 1972. "The job market for college graduates." *Journal of Higher Education*, 43, pp. 203-222.

FONER, ANNE. 1980. "The sociology of age stratification: A review of some recent publications." *Contemporary Sociology* 9:6, 771-779.

FORD, CLELLAN S., and FRANK A. BEACH. 1951. *Patterns of Sexual Behavior*. New York: Harper & Row.

FOX, ROBIN. 1967. *Kinship and Marriage*. London: Pelican.

FOX, THOMAS G., and S. M. MILLER. 1965. "Inter-country variations: Occupational stratification and mobility." *Studies in Comparative International Development*, 1, pp. 3-10.

————, and S. M. MILLER. 1966. "Economic, political, and social determinants of mobility: An international cross-sectional analysis." *Acta Sociologica*, 9:1-2, 76-93.

FRANK, LUCINDA. 1974. "Homosexuals as foster parents." *New York Times*, May 7, pp. 47, 55.

FREEDMAN, DANIEL G. 1979. *Human Sociobiology: A Holistic Approach*. New York: Free Press.

FREEDMAN, MARCIA, and IVAR BERG. 1978. "Investments in education: Public policies and private risks," in David E. Drew (ed.), *Competency, Careers, and College*. San Francisco: Jossey-Bass.

FREEMAN, JO. 1975. *The Politics of Women's Liberation*. New York: McKay.

FREEMAN, RICHARD. 1976. *The Overeducated American*. New York: Academic Press.

FRIED, MARC. 1975. "Social differences in mental health," in John Kosa and Irving Kenneth Zola (eds.), *Poverty and Health*. Cambridge, Mass.: Harvard University Press.

FRIED, MORTON. 1967. *The Evolution of Political Society*. New York: Random House.

FRIEDENBERG, EDGAR. 1969. "What do schools do?" *This Magazine Is About Schools*, 3, pp. 24-37.

FRIEDL, ERNESTINE. 1975. *Women and Men: An Anthropologist's View*. New York: Holt, Rinehart and Winston.

FRIEDMAN, RICHARD C., et al. (eds.). 1974. *Sex Differences in Behavior*. New York: Wiley.

FRIEDSON, ELLIOT. 1980. *Doctoring Together: A Study of Professional Social Control*. Chicago: University of Chicago Press.

FROOMKIN, JOSEPH. 1976. *Supply and Demand for Persons with Post-secondary Education*. Washington, D.C.: Joseph Froomkin Inc.

FUCHS, VICTOR. 1974. *Who Shall Live? Health, Economics, and Social Choice*. New York: Basic Books.

GAGER, NANCY, and KATHLEEN SCHURR. 1976. *Sexual Assault*. New York: Grosset and Dunlap.

GAGNON, JOHN, and WILLIAM SIMON (eds.). 1967. *Sexual Deviance.* Chicago: Aldine.

———, and WILLIAM SIMON. 1973. *Sexual Conduct: The Social Sources of Human Sexuality.* Chicago: Aldine.

GALBRAITH, JOHN KENNETH. 1966. *The Affluent Society.* Boston: Beacon.

———. 1967. *The New Industrial State.* New York: Signet.

———. 1971. *The New Industrial State.* 2nd ed. Boston: Houghton Mifflin.

———. 1973. *Economics and the Public Purpose.* Boston: Houghton Mifflin.

GALLMAN, ROBERT E. 1969. "Trends in size distribution in wealth in the nineteenth century: Some speculation," in Lee Soltow (ed.), *Six Papers on the Size Distribution of Wealth and Income.* New York: Columbia University Press.

GAMSON, WILLIAM. 1968. *Power and Discontent.* Homewood, Ill.: Dorsey.

———. 1975. *The Strategy of Social Protest.* Homewood, Ill.: Dorsey.

GANS, HERBERT J. 1962a. "Urbanism and suburbanism as ways of life," in Arnold M. Rose (ed.), *Human Behavior and Social Processes.* Boston: Houghton Mifflin.

———. 1962b. *The Urban Villagers.* New York: Free Press.

———. 1967. *The Levittowners: Way of Life and Politics in a New Suburban Community.* New York: Pantheon.

——— (ed.). 1968. *People and Plans: Essays on Urban Problems and Solutions.* New York: Basic Books.

———. 1973. *More Equality.* New York: Pantheon.

GARFINKEL, HAROLD. 1956. "Conditions of successful degradation ceremonies," *American Journal of Sociology,* 61, pp. 420–424.

———. 1964. "Studies of the routine grounds of everyday activities." *Social Problems,* 11, pp. 225–250.

———. 1967. *Studies in Ethnomethodology.* Englewood Cliffs, N.J.: Prentice-Hall.

———. 1970. "The ethnomethodological paradigm," in Hans Peter Dreitzel (ed.), *Recent Sociology No. 2: Patterns of Communicative Behavior.* New York: Macmillan.

GARVEY, CATHERINE. 1977. *Play.* Cambridge, Mass.: Harvard University Press.

GASTON, JERRY. 1978. *The Reward System in British and American Science.* New York: Wiley.

GATHORNE-HARDY, JONATHAN. 1978. *The Old School Tie: The Phenomenon of the English Public School.* New York: Viking.

GEERTZ, CLIFFORD. 1968. "The impact of the concept of culture on the concept of man," in Yehudi A. Cohen (ed.), *Man and Adaptation: The Cultural Present.* Chicago: Aldine.

GEIS, GILBERT, and ROBERT F. MEIER (eds.). 1977. *White Collar Crime.* New York: Free Press.

GELANTER, MARK, et al. 1979. "The Moonies: A psychological study of conversion membership in a contemporary religious sect." *American Journal of Psychiatry,* 136, pp. 165–170.

GELLES, RICHARD. 1979. *Family Violence.* Beverly Hills, Calif.: Sage.

GEPHART, WILLIAM J. 1970. "Will the real Pygmalion please stand up?" *American Educational Research Journal,* 7, pp. 473–474.

GERARD, HAROLD B., and NORMAN MILLER. 1976. *School Desegregation: A Long-Term Study.* New York: Plenum.

GERBER, E. R., et al. 1974. *The American Woman in Sport.* Reading, Mass.: Addison-Wesley.

GESELL, ARNOLD. 1940. *The First Five Years of Life: A Guide to the Study of the Preschool Child.* New York: Harper & Row.

GIL, DAVID. 1970. *Violence Against Children: Physical Child Abuse in the United States.* Cambridge, Mass.: Harvard University Press.

GILES, MICHAEL W. 1978. "White enrollment stability and school desegregation: A two-level analysis." *American Sociological Review,* 43, pp. 848–864.

GINTIS, HERBERT. 1971. "Education and the characteristics of worker productivity." *American Economic Review,* 61, pp. 266–279.

GLASER, BARNEY G., and ANSELM L. STRAUSS. 1965. *Awareness of Dying.* Chicago: Aldine.

———, and ANSELM L. STRAUSS. 1968. *Time for Dying.* Chicago: Aldine.

GLASNER, PETER E. 1977. *The Sociology of Secularization.* London: Routledge and Kegan Paul.

GLENN, NORVAL D. 1974. "Income inequality in the United States," in Joseph Lepreato and Lionel S. Lewis (eds.), *Social Stratification.* New York: Harper & Row.

GLICK, PAUL C. 1979. "The Future of the American Family." *Current Population Reports, Bureau of the Census,* Special Studies, Series P-23, No. 78. Washington, D.C.: U.S. Government Printing Office.

GLOCK, CHARLES Y., and RODNEY STARK. 1965. *Religion and Society in Tension.* Chicago: Rand McNally.

———, and RODNEY STARK. 1966. *Christian Beliefs and Anti-Semitism.* New York: Harper & Row.

———, and RODNEY STARK. 1968. *American Piety: The Nature of Religious Commitment.* Berkeley, Calif.: University of California Press.

———, and ROBERT N. BELLAH (eds.). 1976. *The New Religious Consciousness.* Berkeley, Calif.: University of California Press.

GLUECK, SHELDON, and ELEANOR GLUECK. 1956. *Physique and Delinquency.* New York: Harper & Row.

GOFFMAN, ERVING. 1959. *The Presentation of the Self in Everyday Life.* New York: Doubleday.

———. 1961. *Asylums: Essays on the Social Situation of Mental Patients and Other Inmates.* Chicago: Aldine.

———. 1963a. *Behavior in Public Places.* New York: Free Press.

_____. 1963b. *Stigma: Notes on the Management of Spoiled Identity.* Englewood Cliffs, N.J.: Prentice-Hall.

_____. 1966. *Encounters.* Indianapolis: Bobbs-Merrill.

_____. 1967. *Interaction Ritual: Essays on Face-to-Face Behavior.* New York: Doubleday.

_____. 1969. *Strategic Interaction.* Philadelphia: University of Pennsylvania Press.

_____. 1971. *Relations in Public.* New York: Basic Books.

_____. 1974. *Frame Analysis: An Essay on the Organization of Experience.* New York: Harper & Row.

_____. 1976. *Gender Advertisements.* New York: Harper & Row.

GOLD, MARTIN. 1970. *Delinquent Behavior in an American City.* Belmont, Calif.: Brooks/Cole.

GOLDBERG, PHILIP. 1968. "Are women prejudiced against women?" *Trans-Action,* 5, pp. 28–30.

GOLDFARB, WILLIAM. 1945. "Psychological privation in infancy and subsequent adjustment." *American Journal of Orthopsychiatry,* 15, pp. 247–253.

GOLDSMITH, EDWARD, et al. 1972. "Blueprint for survival." *The Ecologist,* 2, pp. 2–6.

GOODE, WILLIAM J. 1956. *The Family.* Englewood Cliffs, N.J.: Prentice-Hall.

_____. 1959. "The theoretical importance of love," *American Sociological Review,* 24, pp. 38–47.

_____. 1963. *World Revolution and Family Patterns.* New York: Free Press.

_____. 1965. *After Divorce.* New York: Free Press.

GOODMAN, PAUL. 1970. "High school is too much." *Psychology Today,* 4, pp. 25–34.

GORDON, MICHAEL. 1978. *The American Family: Past, Present, and Future.* New York: Random House.

GORDON, MILTON M. 1961. "Assimilation in America: Theory and reality." *Daedalus,* 90, pp. 363–365.

_____. 1978. *Human Nature, Class, and Ethnicity.* New York: Oxford University Press.

GORING, CHARLES. 1913. *The English Convict.* London: His Majesty's Stationery Office.

GORTMAKER, STEVEN L. 1979. "Poverty and infant mortality in the United States." *American Sociological Review,* 44, pp. 280–292.

GOUGH, KATHLEEN E. 1959. "The Nayars and the definition of marriage." *Journal of the Royal Anthropological Institute,* 89, pp. 23–24.

GOULDNER, ALVIN W. 1970. *The Coming Crisis of Western Sociology.* New York: Avon.

_____. 1979. *The Future of Intellectuals and the Rise of the New Class.* New York: Seabury Press.

_____, and TIMOTHY SPREHE. 1965. "Sociologists look at themselves." *Transaction,* 2, pp. 42–44.

GOVE, WALTER R. (ed.). 1975. *The Labeling of Deviance.* New York: Wiley.

_____. (ed.). 1980. *The Labeling of Deviance: Evaluating a Perspective.* Beverly Hills, Calif.: Sage.

GRAHAM, HUGH DAVIS, and TED ROBERT GURR. 1969. *Violence in America: Historical Perspectives.* New York: Bantam.

GREELEY, ANDREW M. 1972. *The Denominational Society.* Glenview, Ill.: Scott, Foresman.

_____. 1974. *Ethnicity in the United States.* New York: Wiley.

_____. 1975. *The Sociology of the Paranormal: A Reconnaissance.* Beverly Hills, Calif.: Sage.

_____. 1976. *Ethnicity, Domination, and Inequality.* Beverly Hills, Calif.: Sage.

_____. 1977. *The American Catholic: A Social Portrait.* New York: Basic Books.

GREEN, BETTY R., and DONALD P. IRISH (eds.). 1971. *Death Education: Preparation for Living.* Cambridge, Mass.: Schenkman.

GREEN, MARK J. 1972. "The high cost of monopoly." *The Progressive,* pp. 15–19.

_____, and JACK NEWFIELD. 1980. "Who owns Congress?" *The Village Voice,* April 21, pp. 1, 16–22.

GREEN, RICHARD, and JOHN MONEY. 1969. *Transsexualism and Sex Reassignment.* Baltimore, Md.: Johns Hopkins University Press.

GREENFIELD, SIDNEY M. 1965. "Love and marriage in modern America: A functional analysis." *The Sociological Quarterly,* 6, pp. 361–377.

GREENSTEIN, FRED I. 1965. *Children and Politics.* New Haven, Conn.: Yale University Press.

GREENWALD, HAROLD. 1958. *The Call Girl.* New York: Ballantine.

_____. 1970. *The Affluent Prostitute: A Social and Psychological Study.* New York: Walker.

GREENWOOD, E. 1962. "Attributes of a profession," in S. Nosow and W. H. Form (eds.), *Man, Work and Society.* New York: Basic Books.

GREER, SCOTT A. 1962. *The Emerging City: Myth and Reality.* New York: Free Press.

GREGORY, MICHAEL S., et al. (eds.). 1978. *Sociobiology and Human Nature: An Interdisciplinary Critique and Defense.* San Francisco: Jossey-Bass.

GRIFFIN, L. J., and K. A. ALEXANDER. 1978. "Schooling and socioeconomic attainments: High school and college influences." *American Journal of Sociology,* 84, pp. 319–347.

GRIFFITH, BELVER C., and NICHOLAS C. MULLINS. 1972. "Coherent social groups in scientific change." *Science,* 177, pp. 959–964.

GRONBJERG, KIRSTEN, et al. 1978. *Poverty and Social Change.* Chicago: University of Chicago Press.

GROSS, NEAL. 1953. "Social class identification in the urban community." *American Sociological Review,* 18, pp. 398–404.

GRUNEAU, RICHARD S. "Sport, social differentiation, and social inequality," in Donald W. Ball and John W. Loy (eds.), *Sport and Social Order*. Reading, Mass.: Addison-Wesley.

GURR, TED. 1970. *Why Men Rebel*. Princeton, N.J.: Princeton University Press.

GUSFIELD, JOSEPH R. 1969. *Symbolic Crusade*. Urbana, Ill.: University of Illinois Press.

HAAN, NORMA, and D. DAY. 1974. "A longitudinal study of sameness in personality development: Adolescence to later adulthood." *International Journal of Aging and Human Development*, 5, pp. 11–39.

HACKER, ANDREW. 1979. "Divorce à la mode." *New York Review of Books*, May 3, pp. 23–25.

HACKER, HELEN. 1951. "Women as a minority group." *Social Forces*, 30, pp. 60–69.

HADDEN, JEFFREY K. 1969. *The Gathering Storm in the Churches*. Garden City, N.Y.: Doubleday.

HADLEY, ARTHUR T. 1978. *The Empty Polling Booth*. Englewood Cliffs, N.J.: Prentice-Hall.

HAGAN, JOHN, et al. 1980. "The differential sentencing of white-collar offenders in ten federal district courts." *American Sociological Review*, 45, pp. 802–820.

HAGSTROM, WILLIAM O. 1965. *The Scientific Community*. New York: Basic Books.

_____. 1974. "Competition in science." *American Sociological Review*, 39, pp. 1–18.

HALL, EDWARD T. 1959. *The Silent Language*. New York: Doubleday.

_____. 1966. *The Hidden Dimension*. New York: Doubleday.

_____, and MILDRED R. HALL. 1976. "The sounds of silence," in Jeffrey E. Nash and James P. Spradley (eds.), *Sociology: A Descriptive Approach*. Chicago: Rand McNally.

HALL, FRANCINE, and DOUGLAS T. HALL. 1979. *The Two-Career Couple*. Reading, Mass.: Addison-Wesley.

HALL, PETER M., and JOHN P. HEWITT. 1970. "The quasi-theory of communication and the management of dissent." *Social Problems*, 18, pp. 17–27.

HALL, RICHARD H. (ed.). 1972a. *The Formal Organization*. New York: Basic Books.

_____. 1972b. *Organizations: Structure and Process*. Englewood Cliffs, N.J.: Prentice-Hall.

HARDESTY, DONALD L. 1977. *Ecological Anthropology*. New York: Wiley.

HARE, A. PAUL. 1976 *Handbook of Small Group Research*. 2nd ed. New York: Free Press.

_____, et al. (eds.). 1965. *Small Groups: Studies in Social Interaction*. New York: Knopf.

HARLOW, HARRY F. 1958. "The nature of love." *American Psychologist*, 13, pp. 673–685.

_____. 1965. "The affectional systems," in Allan Schrier et al. (eds.), *Behavior of Nonhuman Primates: Modern Research Trends*. New York: Academic Press.

_____, and MARGARET K. HARLOW. 1962. "Social deprivation in monkeys." *Scientific American*, 207, November, pp. 137–147.

_____, and R. R. ZIMMERMAN. 1959. "Affectional responses in the infant monkey." *Science*, 130, pp. 421–423.

HARRIS, C. D., and EDWARD L. ULLMAN. 1945. "The nature of cities." *The Annals of the American Academy of Political and Social Science*, 242, pp. 7–17.

HARRIS, MARVIN. 1974. *Cows, Pigs, Wars, and Witches: The Riddles of Culture*. New York: Random House.

_____. 1975. *Culture, People, and Nature: An Introduction to General Anthropology*. 2nd ed. New York: Crowell.

_____. 1977. *Cannibals and Kings: The Origins of Cultures*. New York: Random House.

_____. 1979. *Cultural Materialism: The Struggle for a Science of Culture*. New York: Random House.

HARRISON, MICHAEL. 1974. "Sources of recruitment to Catholic Pentecostalism." *Journal for the Scientific Study of Religion*, 13, pp. 49–64.

HARRY, JOSEPH, and WILLIAM B. DE VALL. 1978. *The Social Organization of Gay Males*. New York: Praeger.

HARTLEY, EUGENE. 1946. *Problems in Prejudice*. New York: King's Crown Press.

HARTLEY, RUTH E. 1970. "American core culture: Changes and continuities," in Georgene H. Seward and Robert C. Williamson (eds.), *Sex Roles in a Changing Society*. New York: Random House.

HAUSER, PHILIP M. (ed.). 1969. *The Population Dilemma*. 2nd ed. Englewood Cliffs, N.J.: Prentice-Hall.

HAUSER, ROBERT M., and DAVID L. FEATHERMAN. 1978. *Opportunity and Change*. New York: Academic Press.

HEILBRONER, ROBERT. 1967. *The Worldly Philosophers*. 3rd ed. New York: Simon and Schuster.

HELFER, RAY E., and C. HENRY KEMPE (eds.). 1978. *The Battered Child*. Berkeley, Calif.: University of California Press.

HENRY, JULES. 1963. *Culture Against Man*. New York: Random House.

HENSLIN, JAMES M. 1968. "Trust and the cab driver," in Marcello Truzzi (ed.), *Sociology and Everyday Life*. Englewood Cliffs, N.J.: Prentice-Hall.

_____. 1975. *Introducing Sociology*. New York: Free Press.

_____, and MAE A. BRIGGS. 1971. "Dramaturgical desexualization: The sociology of the vaginal examination," in James M. Heslin (ed.), *Studies in the Sociology of Sex*. New York: Appleton-Century-Crofts.

HERBERG, WILL. 1960. *Protestant, Catholic, Jew*. New York: Doubleday.

HERBERS, JOHN. 1978. "Beneath the streets, old cities crumble and decay." *New York Times,* April 9, pp. 1, 47.

HERNANDEZ, CARROL A., et al. (eds.). 1976. *Chicanos: Social and Psychological Perspectives.* 2nd ed. St. Louis: Mosby.

HERNANDEZ, JOSE. 1974. *People, Power, and Policy: A New View on Population.* Palo Alto, Calif.: National Press Books.

HESS, RUTH B. (ed.). 1980. *Growing Old in America.* New Brunswick, N.J.: Transaction Books.

HEUSSENSTAMM, FRANCES K. 1971. "Bumper stickers and cops." *Transaction,* 8, pp. 32–33.

HEWITT, JOHN P., and RANDALL STOKES. 1975. "Disclaimers." *American Sociological Review,* 40, pp. 1–11.

HEYL, BARBARA S. 1977. *The Madame as Entrepreneur: The Political Economy of a House of Prostitution.* New Brunswick, N.J.: Transaction Books.

HILBERMAN, ELAINE. 1976. *The Rape Victim.* New York: Basic Books.

HILL, JANE H. 1978. "Apes and language." *Annual Review of Anthropology.* Palo Alto, Calif.: Annual Reviews.

HILLIER, E. T. 1933. *Principles of Sociology.* New York: Harper & Row.

HINDELANG, MICHAEL J. 1971a. "Age, sex, and the versatility of delinquent involvements." *Social Problems,* 18, pp. 522–535.

———. 1971b. "The social versus solitary nature of delinquent involvement." *British Journal of Criminology,* 11, pp. 167–175.

———. 1978. "Race and involvement in common law personal crimes." *American Sociological Review,* 43, pp. 93–109.

———. et al. 1979. "Correlates of delinquency: The illusion of discrepancy between self-report and official measures." *American Sociological Review,* 44, pp. 995–1014.

HIRSCHI, TRAVIS. 1969. *Causes of Delinquency.* Berkeley, Calif.: University of California Press.

HITLER, ADOLF. 1948. *Mein Kampf.* Ralph Mannheim (trans.). Boston: Houghton Mifflin.

HOBBES, THOMAS. 1958, originally published 1598. *Leviathan.* New York: Liberal Arts Press.

HODGE, ROBERT W., and DONALD J. TREIMAN. 1968. "Class identification in the United States." *American Journal of Sociology,* 73, pp. 535–547.

HODGE, ROBERT W., et al. 1964. "Occupational prestige in the United States, 1925–1963." *American Journal of Sociology,* 70, pp. 286–302.

———, et. al. 1966. "A comparative study of occupational prestige," in R. Bendix and S. M. Lipset (eds.), *Class, Status, and Power.* 2nd ed. New York: Free Press.

HOEPNER, B. J. (ed.). 1974. *Women's Athletics: Coping with Controversy.* Washington, D.C.: American Association for Health, Physical Education, and Recreation.

HOFFER, ERIC. 1951. *The True Believer.* New York: Holt, Rinehart and Winston.

HOFSTADTER, RICHARD. 1955. *Social Darwinism in American Thought.* Boston: Beacon.

HOLLANDER, EDWIN P. 1964. *Leaders, Groups, and Influence.* New York: Oxford University Press.

HOLLINGSHEAD, AUGUST B. 1949. *Elmstown's Youth.* New York: Wiley.

———, and FREDERICK REDLICH. 1958. *Social Class and Mental Disorder.* New York: Wiley.

HOLMSTROM, LINDA LYTLE, and ANN WOLBERT BURGESS. 1976. *The Victim of Rape: Institutional Reactions.* New York: Wiley.

HOLT, JOHN. 1964. *How Children Fail.* New York: Pitman.

———. 1972. "The little red prison." *Harper's,* 244, pp. 80–82.

HOMANS, GEORGE C. 1950. *The Human Group.* New York: Harcourt Brace Jovanovich.

———. 1974. *Social Behavior: Its Elementary Forms.* Rev. ed. New York: Harcourt Brace Jovanovich.

HOOKER, EVELYN. 1957. "The adjustment of the male overt homosexual." *Journal of Projective Techniques,* 21, pp. 18–31.

———. 1962. "The homosexual community," in *Proceedings of the XVI International Congress of Applied Psychology, Vol. 2, Personality Research.* Copenhagen: Munksgaard.

———. 1965. "An empirical study of some relations between sexual patterns and gender identity in male homosexuals," in ohn Money (ed.), *Sex Research—New Developments.* New York: Holt, Rinehart and Winston.

———. 1969. "Parental relations and male homosexuality in patient and nonpatient samples." *Journal of Consulting and Clinical Psychology,* 33, pp. 140–142.

HORNER, MATINA. 1968. "Sex differences in achievement motivation and performance in competitive and noncompetitive situations." Doctoral dissertation, University of Michigan.

———. 1969. "Fail: Bright women." *Psychology Today,* 3, p. 36ff.

———. 1972. "Toward an understanding of achievement: Related conflicts in women." *Journal of Social Issues,* 29, pp. 157–175.

HOROWITZ, IRVING LOUIS. 1967. *The Rise and Fall of Project Camelot.* Cambridge, Mass.: MIT Press.

HOUGH, JERRY F. 1977. *The Soviet Union and Social Science Theory.* Cambridge, Mass.: Harvard University Press.

HOWE, FLORENCE. 1971. "Sex role stereotypes start early." *Saturday Review,* 54, pp. 76–82.

HOYT, HOMER. 1939. *The Structure and Growth of Residential Neighborhoods in American Cities.* Washington, D.C.: Federal Housing Authority.

HUBER, JOAN, and WILLIAM FORM. 1973. *Income and Ideology.* New York: Free Press.

HUGHES, EVERETT C., et al. 1962. "Student culture and academic effort," in Nevitt Sanford (ed.), *The American College: A Psy-*

chological and Social Interpretation of Higher Learning. New York: Wiley.

HUMPHREYS, LAUD. 1970. *Tearoom Trade: Impersonal Sex in Public Places.* Chicago: Aldine.

_____. 1971. "New styles in homosexual manliness." *Transaction,* 8, pp. 38–46.

_____. 1972. *Out of the Closets: The Sociology of Homosexual Liberation.* Englewood Cliffs, N.J.: Prentice-Hall.

HUNT, MORTON. 1959. *The Natural History of Love.* New York: Knopf.

_____. 1974. *Sexual Behavior in the 1970's.* New York: Dell.

HUNTER, FLOYD. 1953. *Community Power Structure.* Chapel Hill, N.C.: University of North Carolina Press.

HUTTON, J. H. 1963. *Caste in India: Its Nature, Functions, and Origins.* 4th ed. London: Oxford University Press.

HYMAN, HERBERT H. 1969. *Political Socialization: A Study in the Psychology of Political Behavior.* New York: Free Press.

_____, and CHARLES R. WRIGHT. 1971. "Trends in voluntary associated memberships of American adults: Replication based on secondary analysis of national sample surveys." *American Sociological Review,* 23, pp. 191–206.

_____, and CHARLES R. WRIGHT. 1979. *Education's Lasting Influence on Values.* Chicago: University of Chicago Press.

_____, et al. 1975. *The Enduring Effects of Education.* Chicago: University of Chicago Press.

IANNI, FRANCES A. J., and ELIZABETH REUSS–IANNI (eds.). 1976. *The Crime Society.* New York: New American Library.

INKELES, ALEX. 1950. "Social stratification and mobility in the Soviet Union: 1940-1950." *American Sociological Review,* 15, pp. 465–479.

_____, and PETER H. ROSSI. 1956. "National comparisons of occupational prestige." *American Journal of Sociology,* 66, pp. 329–339.

_____, and DAVID H. SMITH. 1974. *Becoming Modern: Individual Change in Six Developing Countries.* Cambridge, Mass.: Harvard University Press.

JACKSON, DONALD. 1974. "Justice for none." *New Times,* 2, January 11, pp. 48–57.

JACKSON, ELTON F., and HARRY J. CROCKETT, JR. 1964. "Occupational mobility in the United States: A point estimate and a trend comparison." *American Sociological Review,* 24, pp. 5–15.

JACKSON, PHILIP. 1968. *Life in Classrooms.* New York: Holt, Rinehart and Winston.

JACOBS, JANE. 1961. *The Death and Life of Great American Cities.* New York: Random House.

_____. 1980. *The Question of Separatism: Quebec and the Struggle over Sovereignty.* New York: Random House.

JACOBSON, GARY C. 1980. *Money in Congressional Elections.* New Haven, Conn.: Yale University Press.

JACOBY, NEIL H. 1970. "The multinational corporation." *Center Magazine,* 3, pp. 37–55.

JANIS, IRVING L. 1972. *Victims of Groupthink.* Boston: Houghton Mifflin.

_____, and LEON MANN. 1977. *Decision Making: A Psychological Analysis of Conflict, Choice, and Commitment.* New York: Free Press.

JAROS, DEAN. 1974. *Socialization to Politics.* New York: Praeger.

JEFFERY, C. R. (ed.). 1979. *Biology and Crime.* Beverly Hills, Calif.: Sage.

JENCKS, CHRISTOPHER, et al. 1972. *Inequality: A Reassessment of the Effect of Family and Schooling in America.* New York: Basic Books.

_____, 1980. "Heredity, environment, and public policy reconsidered." *American Sociological Review,* 45, pp. 723–736.

_____, et al. 1979. *Who Gets Ahead? The Determinants of Economic Success in America.* New York: Basic Books.

JENNINGS, M. KENT, and RICHARD G. NIEMI. 1974. *The Political Character of Adolescence.* Princeton, N.J.: Princeton University Press.

JENSEN, ARTHUR. 1969. "How much can we boost IQ and scholastic achievement?" *Howard Educational Review,* 39, pp. 273–274.

_____. 1979. *Bias in Mental Testing.* New York: Free Press.

JOHNSON, BENTON. 1977. "Sociological theory and religious truth." *Sociological Analysis,* 38:4, 368–388.

JOHNSON, DONALD M. 1945. "The phantom anesthetist of Mattoon: A field study of mass hysteria." *Journal of Abnormal and Social Psychology,* 40, pp. 175–186.

JOHNSON, JOHN M., and JACK DOUGLAS (eds.). 1978. *Crime at the Top.* Philadelphia: Lippincott.

JOHNSON, NORRIS R., and DAVID P. MARPLE. 1973. "Racial discrimination in professional basketball." *Sociological Focus,* 6 (Fall), pp. 6–18.

JOHNSTONE, RONALD L. 1975. *Religion and Society in Interaction: The Sociology of Religion.* Englewood Cliffs, N.J.: Prentice-Hall.

JORGENSEN, JAMES. 1980. *The Graying of America.* New York: Dial Press.

JUDAH, J. STILLSON. 1974. *Hare Krishna and The Counterculture.* New York: Wiley.

JUSTICE, BLAIR, and RITA JUSTICE. 1979. *The Broken Taboo: Sex in the Family.* New York: Human Sciences.

KAHL, JOSEPH A. 1957. *The American Class Structure.* New York: Holt, Rinehart and Winston.

_____. 1961. *The American Class Structure.* 2nd ed. New York: Holt, Rinehart and Winston.

KALISH, RICHARD A. 1975. *Late Adulthood: Perspectives on Human Development*. Monterey, Calif.: Brooks/Cole.

KANTER, ROSABETH MOSS. 1973. *Communes: Creating and Managing the Collective Life*. New York: Harper & Row.

———. 1977. *Work and Family in the United States*. New York: Russell Sage Foundation.

———, and BARRY STEIN (eds.). 1979. *Life in Organizations*. New York: Basic Books.

KATCHER, ALLAN. 1955: "The discrimination of sex differences by young children." *Journal of Genetic Psychology*, 87 (September), pp. 131–143.

KATZ, MARLAINE L. 1972. "Female motive to avoid success: A psychological barrier or a response to deviance." Manuscript, School of Education, Stanford University, Palo Alto, Calif.

KAUFMAN, RICHARD F. 1970. *The War Profiteers*. Indianapolis: Bobbs-Merrill.

KAYSON, CARL. 1972. "The computer that printed W★O★L★F." *Foreign Affairs*, 50 (July), pp. 663–666.

KELLY, DEAN M. 1972. *Why the Conservative Churches Are Growing: A Study in the Sociology of Religion*. New York: Harper & Row.

KELLY, RAYMOND C. 1977. *Etoro Social Structure: A Study in Cultural Contradiction*. Ann Arbor: University of Michigan Press.

KEMPE, C. HENRY, and RAY E. HELFER (eds.). 1980. *The Battered Child*. 3rd ed. Chicago: University of Chicago Press.

KENISTON, KENNETH. 1970. "Youth: A new stage of life." *American Scholar*, 39 (Autumn), pp. 631–654.

KESSLER, RONALD C., and PAUL D. CLEARY. 1980. "Social class and psychological distress." *American Sociological Review*, 45, pp. 463–478.

KETCHEL, MELVIN M. 1968. "Fertility control agents as a possible solution to the world population problem." *Perspectives in Biology and Medicine*, 11, pp. 687–703.

KETT, JOSEPH F. 1979. *Rites of Passage*. New York: Basic Books.

KIEFER, CHRISTINE W. 1974. *Changing Cultures, Changing Lives: An Ethnographic Study of Three Generations of Japanese Americans*. San Francisco: Jossey–Bass.

KILDUFF, MARSHALL, and RON JAVERS. 1979. *The Suicide Cult*. New York: Bantam.

KINSEY, ALFRED C., et al. 1948. *Sexual Behavior in the Human Male*. Philadelphia: W. B. Saunders.

———, et al. 1953. *Sexual Behavior in the Human Female*. Philadelphia: W. B. Saunders.

KIRK, DUDLEY. 1971. "A new demographic transition," in Study Committee of the National Academy of Sciences, *Rapid Population Growth: Consequences and Policy Implications*. Baltimore: John Hopkins University Press.

KIRKHAM, GEORGE L. 1971. "Homosexuality in prison," in James M. Henslin (ed.), *Studies in the Sociology of Sex*. New York: Appleton-Century-Crofts.

KITANO, HARRY L. 1976. *Japanese Americans: The Evolution of a Subculture*. 2nd ed. Englewood Cliffs, N.J.: Prentice-Hall.

KLAPP, ORIN. 1969. *Collective Search for Identity*. New York: Holt, Rinehart and Winston.

KLEIN, RUDOLF. 1972. "Growth and its enemies." *Commentary*, 53, pp. 37–45.

KLEIN, VIOLA. 1975. *The Feminine Character: History of an Ideology*. Urbana, Ill.: University of Illinois Press.

KLUCKHOHN, CLYDE. 1948. "As an anthropologist views it," in Albert Deutch (ed.), *Sex Habits of American Men*. New York: Prentice-Hall.

———. 1962. "Universal categories of culture," in Sol Tax (ed.), *Anthropology Today: Selections*. Chicago: University of Chicago Press.

KNAPP, JACQUELYN J., and ROBERT N. WHITEHURST. 1978. "Sexually open marriages and relationships: Issues and prospects," in Bernard I. Murstein (ed.), *Exploring Intimate Life Styles*. New York: Springer.

KOGAN, N., and WALLACH, M. A. 1964. *Risk Taking: A Study in Cognition and Personality*. New York: Holt, Rinehart and Winston.

KOHLBERG, LAWRENCE. 1966. "A cognitive-developmental analysis of children's sex-role concepts and attitudes," in Eleanor E. Maccoby (ed.), *The Development of Sex Differences*. Palo Alto, Calif.: Stanford University Press.

———. 1969. "Stage and sequence: The cognitive-developmental approach to socialization," in David A. Goslin (ed.), *Handbook of Socialization Theory and Research*. Chicago: Rand McNally.

KOHN, MELVIN L. 1963. "Social class and parent-child relationships: An interpretation." *American Journal of Sociology*, 68, pp. 471–480.

———. 1971. "Bureaucratic man: A portrait and an interpretation." *American Sociological Review*, 36, pp. 461–474.

———. 1977. *Class and Conformity*. 2nd ed. Homewood, Ill.: Dorsey.

———. 1976. "Occupational structure and alienation," *American Journal of Sociology*, 82, pp. 111–130.

———. 1978. "The benefits of bureaucracy." *Human Nature*. August.

KOLKO, GABRIEL. 1962. *Wealth and Power in America: An Analysis of Social Class and Income Distribution*. New York: Praeger.

KOMAROVSKY, MIRRA. 1962. *Blue-Collar Marriage*. New York: Random House.

———. 1973. "Cultural contradictions and sex roles: The masculine case." *American Journal of Sociology*, 78, pp. 873–884.

KOMISAR, LUCY. 1971. "The image of woman in advertising," in Vivian Gornick and Barbara K. Moran (eds.), *Women in Sexist Society: Studies in Power and Powerlessness*. New York: Basic Books.

KORNHAUSER, WILLIAM. 1966. " 'Power elite' or 'veto groups'?" in Reinhard Bendix and Seymour Martin Lipset (eds.), *Class, Status, and Power*. 2nd ed. New York: Free Press.

KOSA, JOHN, and IRVING KENNETH ZOLA (eds.). 1975. *Poverty and Health: A Sociological Analysis*. Cambridge, Mass.: Harvard University Press.

KOTTAK, CONRAD PHILLIP. 1978. *Anthropology: Exploration of Human Diversity*. 2nd ed. New York: Random House.

KOTZ, DAVID M. 1979. *Bank Control of Large Corporations*. Berkeley, Calif.: University of California Press.

KOWINSKI, WILLIAM S. 1980. "Suburbia: End of the golden age." *New York Times Magazine*, March 16, pp. 16–19, 106–109.

KRAUSE, CHARLES A., et al. 1979. *Guyana Massacre*. New York: Berkeley.

KRAUSE, ELLIOT A. 1977. *Power and Illness: The Political Sociology of Health and Medical Care*. New York: Elsevier.

KRAUSS, IRVING. 1964. "Sources of educational aspirations among working class youth." *American Sociological Review*, 29, pp. 867–879.

KRICUS, RICHARD. 1976. *Pursuing the American Dream: White Ethnics and the New Populism*. Bloomington, Ind.: Indiana University Press.

KROEBER, A. L. 1937. "Diffusionism," in Edward Seligman and Alvin Johnson (eds.), *The Encyclopaedia of the Social Sciences*, Vol. III, pp. 139–142.

KUBLER-ROSS, ELISABETH. 1969. *On Death and Dying*. New York: Macmillan.

_____. 1972. "Facing up to death." *Today's Education*, 16, pp. 30–32.

_____. 1975. *Death: The Final Stage of Growth*. Englewood Cliffs, N.J.: Prentice-Hall.

KUHN, MANFORD, and THOMAS S. McPARTLAND. 1954. "An empirical investigation of self-attitudes." *American Sociological Review*, 19, pp. 68–76.

KUHN, THOMAS S. 1962. *The Structure of Scientific Revolutions*. Chicago: University of Chicago Press.

KUNEN, JAMES S. 1973. "The rebels of '70." *New York Times Magazine*, October 28, p. 22.

KUPER, LEO. (ed.). 1975. *Race, Science, and Society*. New York: Columbia University Press.

KUZNETS, SIMON. 1953. *Share of Upper Income Groups in Income and Savings*. New York: National Bureau of Economic Research.

LA BARRE, WESTON. 1954. *The Human Animal*. Chicago: University of Chicago Press.

LADD, EVERETT C. 1978. *Where Have All the Voters Gone? The Fracturing of America's Political Parties*. New York: Norton.

LAKOFF, SANFORD A. 1977. "Scientists, technologists, and political power," in Ina Spiegel–Rösing and Derek de Solla Price (eds.), *Science, Technology, and Society*. Beverly Hills, Calif.: Sage.

LAMPMAN, ROBERT. 1962. *The Share of the Top Wealth Holders in National Wealth*. Princeton, N.J.: Princeton University Press.

LANE, DAVID. 1976. *The Socialist Industrial State*. London: Allen and Unwin.

_____. 1978. *Politics and Society in the U.S.S.R.* New York: New York University Press.

LANE, HARLAN. 1976. *The Wild Boy of Aveyron*. Cambridge, Mass.: Harvard University Press.

LANER, MARY RIEGE. 1974. "Prostitution as an illegal vocation: A sociological overview," in Clifton D. Bryant (ed.), *Deviant Behavior*. Chicago: Rand McNally.

LANGTON, JOHN. 1979. "Darwinism and the behavioral theory of sociocultural evolution: An analysis." *American Journal of Sociology*, 85, pp. 288–309.

LANTERNARI, VITTORIO. 1963. *Religions of the Oppressed: A Study of Modern Messianic Cults*. New York: Knopf.

LAPIDUS, GAIL WARSHOFSKY. 1978. *Women in Soviet Society*. Berkeley, Calif.: University of California Press.

LAPIERE, RICHARD T. 1934. "Attitudes versus action." *Social Forces*, 13, pp. 230–237.

LARSON, MARGALI SARFATTI. 1977. *The Rise of Professionalism: A Sociological Analysis*. Berkeley: University of California Press.

LASCH, CHRISTOPHER. 1977. *Haven in a Heartless World: The Family Besieged*. New York: Basic Books.

LASLETT, PETER. 1971. *The World We Have Lost*. 2nd ed. New York: Scribner's.

_____. 1977. "Characteristics of the Western family considered over time." *Journal of Family History*, 2:2, 89–115.

_____, and RICHARD WALL (eds.). 1972. *Household and Family in Past Time*. Cambridge, Eng.: Cambridge University Press.

LASSWELL, HAROLD D. 1936. *Politics: Who Gets What, When, and How*. New York: McGraw-Hill.

LATANÉ, BIBB, and JOHN M. DARLEY. 1968. "Group inhibition of bystander intervention." *Journal of Personality and Social Psychology*, 8, pp. 377–383.

_____, and JOHN M. DARLEY. 1969. "Bystander apathy." *American Scientist*, 57, pp. 244–268.

_____, and JEAN A. RODIN. 1969. "A lady in distress: Inhibiting effects of friends and strangers on bystander intervention." *Journal of Experimental Social Psychology*, 5, pp. 189–202.

LAUER, ROBERT. 1975. "Occupational and religious mobility in a small city." *Sociological Quarterly*, 16, pp. 380–392.

LAURENTIN, R. 1977. *Catholic Pentecostalism.* Garden City, N.Y.: Doubleday.

LAZERWITZ, BERNARD, and MICHAEL HARRISON. 1979. "American Jewish denominations: A social and religious profile." *American Sociological Review,* 44, pp. 656–666.

LEACOCK, ELEANOR. 1969. *Teaching and Learning in City Schools.* New York: Basic Books.

LE BON, GUSTAVE. 1960, originally published 1895. *The Mind of the Crowd.* New York: Viking.

LEE, RICHARD B. 1968. "What hunters do for a living, or how to make out on scarce resources," in Richard B. Lee and Irvin DeVore (eds.), *Man the Hunter.* Chicago: Aldine.

———. 1979. *The !Kung San: Men, Women, and Work in a Foraging Society.* New York: Cambridge University Press.

LEHMAN, EDWARD W., and AMITAI ETZIONI (eds.). 1980. *Sociology of Complex Organizations.* 3rd ed. New York: Holt, Rinehart and Winston.

LEITER, KENNETH. 1980. *A Primer on Ethnomethodology.* New York: Oxford University Press.

LE MASTERS, E. E. 1975. *Blue Collar Aristocrats: Life Styles at a Working-Class Tavern.* Madison, Wisc.: University of Wisconsin Press.

LEMERT, EDWIN M. 1951. *Social Pathology.* New York: McGraw-Hill.

———. 1967. *Human Deviance, Social Problems, and Social Control.* Englewood Cliffs, N.J.: Prentice-Hall.

———. 1974. "Beyond Mead: The societal reaction to deviance." *Social Problems,* 21, pp. 457–468.

LENSKI, GERHARD. 1966. *Power and Privilege: A Theory of Social Stratification.* New York: McGraw-Hill.

———, and JEAN LENSKI. 1978. *Human Societies.* 3rd ed. New York: McGraw-Hill.

LEONARD, KAREN ISAKSEN. 1978. *Social History of an Indian Caste.* Berkeley, Calif.: University of California Press.

LEONARD, WILBERT M. 1980. *A Sociological Perspective of Sport.* Minneapolis: Burgess.

LERNER, M. J., and C. H. SIMMONS. 1966. "Observer's reaction to the 'innocent victim': Compassion or rejection?" *Journal of Personality and Social Psychology,* 4, pp. 203–210.

LEVINE, EDWARD M. 1980. "Deprogramming without tears." *Society,* 17:3, 34–38.

LEVINSON, DANIEL J. 1979. *The Seasons of a Man's Life.* New York: Ballinger.

LÉVI-STRAUSS, CLAUDE. 1966. *The Savage Mind.* Chicago: University of Chicago Press.

LEVITSKY, DAVID A. (ed.). 1979. *Malnutrition, Environment, and Behavior: New Perspectives.* Ithaca, N.Y.: Cornell University Press.

LEWIS, OSCAR. 1966. "The culture of poverty." *Scientific American,* 215, pp. 19–25.

———. 1968. *La Vida.* New York: Vintage.

LI, WEN L. 1976. "Chinese Americans: Expulsion from the Melting Pot," in Anthony C. Dworkin and Rosalind J. Dworkin (eds.), *The Minority Report.* New York: Praeger.

LIAZOS, ALEXANDER. 1972. "The poverty of the sociology of deviance: Nuts, sluts, and preverts." *Social Problems,* 20, pp. 103–120.

LIBBY, ROGER W. 1978. "Creative singlehood as a life style: Beyond marriage as a rite of passage," in Bernard I. Murstein (ed.), *Exploring Intimate Life Styles.* New York: Springer.

LIEBOW, ELLIOT. 1967. *Tally's Corner: A Study of Negro Streetcorner Men.* Boston: Little, Brown.

LIENHARDT, GODFREY. 1966. *Social Anthropology.* London: Oxford University Press.

LINDESMITH, ALFRED R., et al. 1975. *Social Psychology.* 4th ed. New York: Holt, Rinehart and Winston.

LINDSEY, ROBERT. 1979. "U.S. Hispanic populace growing faster than any other minority." *New York Times,* February 18, pp. 1, 16.

LINTON, RALPH. 1936. *The Study of Man.* New York: Appleton-Century-Crofts.

———. 1943. "Nativistic movements." *American Anthropologist* 45, pp. 230–240.

———. 1945. *The Cultural Background of Personality.* New York: Free Press.

LIPSET, SEYMOUR MARTIN. 1959a. "Democracy and working-class authoritarianism." *American Sociological Review,* 24, pp. 482–501.

———. 1959b. *Political Man.* New York: Doubleday.

———. 1959c. "Some social prerequisites for democracy: Economic development and political legitimacy." *American Political Science Review,* 53, pp. 74–86.

———. 1973. "Commentary: Social stratification research and Soviet scholarship," in Murray Yanovitch and Westley A. Fischer (trans. and eds.), *Social Stratification and Mobility in the USSR.* White Plains, N.Y.: International Arts and Sciences Press.

———, and REINHARD BENDIX. 1959. *Social Mobility in Industrial Society.* Berkeley, Calif.: University of California Press.

———, et al. 1956. *Union Democracy: The Inside Politics of the International Typographical Union.* Glencoe, Ill.: Free Press.

LIZOTTE, ALAN J. 1978. "Extra-legal factors in Chicago's criminal courts: Testing the conflict model of criminal justice." *Social Problems,* 25, pp. 564–580.

LOCKWOOD, DANIEL. 1979. *Prison Sexual Violence.* New York: Elsevier.

LOCKWOOD, DAVID. 1956. "Some notes on 'The Social System'." *British Journal of Sociology*, 7, p. 2.

LOFLAND, JOHN. 1966. *Doomsday Cult*. Englewood Cliffs, N.J.: Prentice–Hall.

_____. 1969. *Deviance and Identity*. Englewood Cliffs, N.J.: Prentice–Hall.

_____. 1977. *Doomsday Cult*. Enlarged ed. New York: Irvington.

LOMBROSO, CESARE. 1911. *Crime: Its Causes and Remedies*. Boston: Little, Boston.

LONDON, HOWARD B. 1978. *The Culture of a Community College*. New York: Praeger.

LOPEZ, ADALBERTO (ed.). 1980. *The Puerto Ricans*. Cambridge, Mass.: Schenkman.

LORTIE, DAN C. 1975. *School Teacher: A Sociological Study*. Chicago: University of Chicago Press.

LOWIE, ROBERT H. 1940. *Introduction to Cultural Anthropology*. New York: Holt, Rinehart and Winston.

LOY, JOHN W. 1969. "The study of sport and social mobility," in Gerald S. Kenyon (ed.), *Aspects of Contemporary Sport Sociology*. Chicago: Athletic Institute.

_____, and GERALD S. KENYON (eds.). 1969. *Sport, Culture, and Society*. New York: Macmillan.

_____, and JOSEPH F. MCELVOGUE. 1970. "Racial segregation in American sport." *International Review of Sport Sociology*, November, pp. 39–55.

_____, et al. 1978. *Sport and Social Systems*. Reading, Mass.: Addison–Wesley.

LUFT, HAROLD S. 1978. *Poverty and Health: Economic Causes and Consequences of Health Problems*. Cambridge, Mass.: Ballinger.

LUNDBERG, FERDINAND. 1968. *The Rich and the Super-Rich*. New York: Bantam.

LUSCHEN, GUNTHER. 1969. "Social stratification and social mobility among young sportsmen," in John W. Loy and Gerald S. Kenyon (eds.), *Sport, Culture, and Society*. New York: Macmillan.

_____. 1976. "Cheating in sports," in Daniel M. Landers (ed.), *Social Problems in Athletics*. Urbana, Ill.: University of Illinois Press.

LYMAN, STANFORD M. 1974. *Chinese Americans*. New York: Random House.

LYND, ROBERT S., and HELEN M. LYND. 1929. *Middletown: A Study in American Culture*. New York: Harcourt Brace.

MACCOBY, ELEANOR, and CAROL JACKLIN. 1974. *The Psychology of Sex Differences*. Palo Alto, Calif.: Stanford University Press.

MACDONALD, GORDON, et al. 1979. *The Long-Term Impact of Atmospheric Carbon Dioxide on Climate*. Washington, D.C.: U.S. Department of Energy.

MACKLIN, ELEANOR D. 1978. "Nonmarital heterosexual cohabitation." *Marriage and Family Review*, 1:2, pp. 1–12.

MALINOWSKI, BRONISLAW. 1922. *The Argonauts of the Western Pacific*. New York: Dutton.

_____. 1926. *Crime and Custom in Savage Society*. New York: Harcourt, Brace.

_____. 1948. *Magic, Science and Religion and Other Essays*. Glencoe, Ill.: Free Press.

MALSON, LUCIEN. 1972. *Wolf Children and the Problem of Human Nature*. New York: Monthly Review Press.

MANKOFF, MILTON. 1971. "Societal reaction and career deviance: A critical analysis." *Sociological Quarterly*, 12, pp. 204–218.

MARMOR, JUDD (ed.). *Homosexual Behavior: A Modern Reappraisal*. New York: Basic Books.

MARSHALL, VICTOR W. 1975. "Socialization for impending death in a retirement village." *American Journal of Sociology*, 80, pp. 1124–1144.

MARTIN, DAVID. 1967. *A Sociology of English Religion*. London: SCM Press.

_____. 1969. *The Religious and the Secular*. London: Routledge and Kegan Paul.

MARTIN, DEL, and PHYLIS LYON. 1972. *Lesbian Women*. New York: Bantam.

MARTIN, M. KAY, and BARBARA VOORHIES. 1975. *Female of the Species*. New York: Columbia University Press.

MARTY, MARTIN E. 1970. *The Righteous Empire*. New York: Dial Press.

_____. 1976. *A Nation of Behavers*. Chicago: University of Chicago Press.

MARX, GARY T. 1967. *Protest and Prejudice*. New York: Harper & Row.

MARX, KARL. 1964a. *Economic and Political Manuscripts of 1844*. New York: International Publishers.

_____. 1964b, originally published in 1848. *Selected Writings in Sociology and Social Philosophy*. T. B. Bottomore and Maximillian Rubel (eds.). Baltimore, Md.: Penguin.

_____. 1967, originally published 1843. *Critique of Hegel's Philosophy of Right*, in Lloyd D. Easton and Kurt Guddat (trans. and eds.), *Writings of the Young Marx on Philosophy and Society*. New York: Doubleday.

_____. 1967, originally published 1867–1895. *Das Capital*. New York: International Publishers.

_____. 1969, originally published 1852. "The eighteenth brumaire of Louis Napoleon," in *Karl Marx: Selected Works*. Vol. 1. Moscow: Progress Publishers.

_____, and FRIEDRICH ENGELS. 1970. *Selected Works*. Vol. 3. Moscow: Progress Publishers.

MASTERS, WILLIAM H., and VIRGINIA E. JOHNSON. 1970. *Human Sexual Inadequacy.* Boston: Little, Brown.

———, and VIRGINIA E. JOHNSON. 1975. *The Pleasure Bond: A New Look at Sexuality and Commitment.* Boston: Little, Brown.

———, and VIRGINIA E. JOHNSON. 1979. *Homosexuality in Perspective.* Boston: Little, Brown.

MATTHEWS, MERVYN. 1972. *Class and Society in Soviet Russia.* London: Allen Lane.

———. 1979. *Privilege in the Soviet Union: A Study of Elite Life-Styles Under Communism.* London: Allen and Unwin.

MATZA, DAVID. 1964. *Delinquency and Drift.* New York: Wiley.

MAUGH, THOMAS H. 1974. "Marijuana: The grass may no longer be greener." *Science,* 74, pp. 683–685.

MAURER, HARRY. 1979. *Not Working: An Oral History of the Unemployed.* New York: Holt, Rinehart and Winston.

MAYER, J. P. 1943. *Max Weber and German Politics.* London: Faber & Faber.

MAYO, ELTON. 1966. *Human Problems of an Industrial Civilization.* New York: Viking.

MCCANN, H. GILMAN. 1978. *Chemistry Transformed.* Norwood, N.J.: Ablex.

MCCARTHY, JOHN D., and MAYER N. ZALD. 1973. *The Trend of Social Movements in America: Professionalization and Resource Mobilization.* Morristown, N.J.: General Learning Press.

———, and MAYER N. ZALD. 1977. "Resource mobilization and social movements: A partial theory." *American Journal of Sociology,* 82:6, 1212–1241.

MCDONALD, DONALD. 1970. "Militarism in America." *Center Magazine,* 3, pp. 12–33.

MCGEE, REECE. 1975. *Points of Departure.* Hinsdale, Ill.: Dryden Press.

MCGRATH, JOSEPH E. 1978. "Small group research." *American Behavioral Scientist,* 21:5, pp. 651–671.

MCIVER, ROBERT M. 1942. *Social Causation.* New York: Ginn.

MCKEE, J., and A. SHERRIFFS. 1956. "The differential evaluation of males and females." *Journal of Personality,* 25, pp. 357–371.

MCLEAN, CHARLES. 1978. *The Wolf Children.* New York: Hill and Wang.

MEAD, GEORGE HERBERT. 1934. *Mind, Self, and Society: From the Standpoint of a Social Behaviorist.* Charles W. Morris (ed.). Chicago: University of Chicago Press.

MEAD, MARGARET. 1935. *Sex and Temperament in Three Primitive Societies.* New York: Dell.

———. 1970. *Culture and Commitment.* New York: Doubleday.

MEADOWS, DONNELLA H., et al. 1972. *The Limits to Growth.* New York: New American Library.

MEANS, GARDINER S. 1970. "Economic concentration," in Maurice Zeitlin (ed.), *American Society Inc.* Chicago: Markham.

MEARS, WALTER R. 1977. "Ending the welfare myths." *New York Post,* May 27, p. 36.

MEDALIA, NAHUM Z., and OTTO N. LARSEN. 1958. "Diffusion and belief in a collective delusion: The Seattle windshield pitting epidemic." *American Sociological Review,* 23, pp. 221–232.

MELMAN, SEYMOUR. 1970. *Pentagon Capitalism: The Political Economy of War.* New York: McGraw-Hill.

MELTON, J. GORDON. 1979. *Encyclopaedia of American Religions.* Gaithersburg, Md.: Consortium Books.

MELVILLE, KEITH. 1972. *Communes and the Counter Culture.* New York: Morrow.

MENDELSOHN, ROBERT, and SHIRLEY DOBIE. 1970. "Women's self-conception: A block to career development." Manuscript, La-Fayette Clinic, Department of Mental Health, Detroit, Michigan.

MERTON, ROBERT K. 1938. "Social structure and anomie." *American Sociological Review,* 3, pp. 672–682.

———. 1942. "Science and technology in a democratic order." *Journal of Legal and Political Science,* 1, pp. 115–126.

———. 1949. "Discrimination and the American creed," in Robert M. McIver (ed.), *Discrimination and National Welfare.* New York: Harper.

———. 1968. *Social Theory and Social Structure.* 2nd ed. New York: Free Press.

———. 1970, originally published 1938. *Science, Technology, and Society in Seventeenth Century England.* New York: Howard Fertig.

———. 1973. *Sociology of Science: Theoretical and Empirical Investigations.* Norman W. Storer (ed.). Chicago: University of Chicago Press.

MICHELS, ROBERT. 1967, originally published 1911. *Political Parties.* New York: Free Press.

MIDDLETON, RUSSELL. 1962. "Brother-sister and father-daughter marriage in ancient Egypt." *American Sociological Review,* 27, pp. 103–111.

MILGRAM, STANLEY. 1973. *Obedience to Authority: An Experimental View.* New York: Harper & Row.

MILLAR, RONALD. 1974. *The Piltdown Man.* New York: St. Martin's Press.

MILLER, HERMAN P. 1972. "Recent trends in family income," in Gerald W. Thielbar et al. (eds.), *Issues in Social Inequality.* Boston: Little, Brown.

MILLER, S. M. 1960. "Comparative social mobility." *Current Sociology,* 9, pp. 1–72.

———. 1964. "The outlook of working class youth," in Arthur P. Shostak and William Gomberg (eds.), *Blue-Collar World: Studies of the American Worker.* Englewood Cliffs, N.J.: Prentice-Hall.

MILLER, WALTER. 1958. "Lower class culture as a generating milieu of gang delinquency." *Journal of Sociological Issues,* 14, pp. 5–19.

MILLS, C. WRIGHT. 1956. *The Power Elite.* New York: Oxford University Press.

_____. 1959. *The Sociological Imagination.* New York: Oxford University Press.

MILLS, THEODORE. 1967. *The Sociology of Small Groups.* Englewood Cliffs, N.J.: Prentice-Hall.

MINCER, JACOB. 1974. *Schooling, Experience, and Earnings.* New York: Columbia University Press.

MINDEL, CHARLES H., and ROBERT W. HABENSTEIN. 1978. *Ethnic Families in America: Patterns and Variations.* New York: Elsevier.

MIRANDE, ALFREDO, and EVANGELICA ENRIQUES. 1979. *La Chicana.* Chicago: University of Chicago Press.

MITCHELL, JACK N. 1978. *Social Exchange, Dramaturgy, and Ethnomethodology.* New York: Elsevier.

MITFORD, JESSICA. 1973. *Kind and Usual Punishment.* New York: Knopf.

MITROFF, IAN I. 1974a. *The Subjective Side of Science.* Amsterdam: Elsevier.

_____. 1974b. "Norms and counter-norms in a select group of the Apollo moon scientists: A case study in the ambivalence of scientists." *American Sociological Review,* 39, pp. 579–595.

MONEY, JOHN, and ANKE A. EHRHARDT. 1972. *Man and Woman, Boy and Girl.* Baltimore, Md.: Johns Hopkins University Press.

MONTAGU, ASHLEY (ed.). 1975. *Race and IQ.* New York: Oxford University Press.

_____. (ed.). 1978. *Learning Non-Aggression: The Experience of Non-Literate Societies.* New York: Oxford University Press.

_____. (ed.). 1980. *Sociobiology Examined.* New York: Oxford University Press.

MOONEY, JAMES. 1965. *The Ghost-Dance Religion and Sioux Outbreak of 1890.* Chicago: University of Chicago Press.

MOORE, BARRINGTON. 1966. *Social Origins and Dictatorship and Democracy.* Boston: Beacon.

_____. 1979. *Injustice: The Social Bases of Obedience and Revolt.* New York: Pantheon.

MOORE, GWEN. 1979. "The structure of a national elite network." *American Sociological Review,* 44, pp. 673–692.

MOORE, JOHN W., and HARRY PACHON. 1976. *Mexican Americans.* 2nd ed. Englewood Cliffs, N.J.: Prentice-Hall.

MOORE, R. LAURENCE. 1977. *In Search of White Crows: Spiritualism, Parapsychology, and American Culture.* New York: Oxford University Press.

MOORE, WILBERT E. 1960. "A reconsideration of theories of social change." *American Sociological Review,* 25, pp. 810–818.

_____. 1970. *The Professions.* Beverly Hills, Calif.: Sage.

_____. 1979. *World Modernization.* New York: Elsevier.

MORRIS, DESMOND. 1977. *Manwatching: A Field Guide to Human Behavior.* New York: Abrams.

_____, et al. 1979. *Gestures.* New York: Stein and Day.

MOSCA, GAETANO. 1939. *The Ruling Class.* New York: McGraw-Hill.

MOSSE, GEORGE L. 1978. *Toward the Final Solution: A History of European Racism.* New York: Howard Fertig.

MOUNIN, GEORGES. 1976. "Chimpanzees, language, and communication." *Current Anthropology.* 17, pp. 1–22.

MOYNIHAN, DANIEL PATRICK. 1965. *The Negro Family: The Case for National Action.* Washington, D.C.: Office of Policy Planning and Research, U.S. Department of Labor.

MULKAY, MICHAEL, J. 1972. *The Social Process of Innovation: A Study in the Sociology of Science.* New York: Macmillan.

_____. 1976. "Norms and ideology in science." *Social Science Information,* 15, pp. 637–656.

MUMFORD, LEWIS. 1961. *The City in History.* New York: Harcourt Brace Jovanovitch.

MUNCY, RAYMOND LEE. 1974. *Sex and Marriage in Utopian Communities.* Baltimore, Md.: Penguin.

MURDOCK, GEORGE P. 1934. *Our Primitive Contemporaries.* New York: Macmillan.

_____. 1935. "Comparative data on the division of labor by sex." *Social Forces,* 15, pp. 551–553.

_____. 1945. "The common denominator of cultures," in Ralph Linton (ed.), *The Science of Man and the World Crisis.* New York: Columbia University Press.

_____. 1949. *Social Structure.* New York: Macmillan.

_____. 1957. "World ethnographic sample." *American Anthropologist,* 54, pp. 664–687.

MURSTEIN, BERNARD I. 1974. *Love, Sex, and Marriage Through the Ages.* New York: Springer.

_____. 1978a. "Swinging," in Bernard I. Murstein (ed.), *Exploring Intimate Life Styles.* New York: Springer.

_____. (ed.). 1978b. *Exploring Intimate Life Styles.* New York: Springer.

MYRDAL, GUNNAR. 1944. *An American Dilemma.* New York: Harper & Row.

NAGI, SAAD Z. 1978. *Child Maltreatment in the United States.* New York: Columbia University Press.

NANCE, JOHN. 1975. *The Gentle Tasaday: A Stone Age People in the Philippine Rain Forest.* New York: Harcourt Brace Jovanovich.

NASH, MANNING. 1962. "Race and the ideology of race." *Current Anthropology,* 3, pp. 285–288.

NATIONAL ADVISORY COMMISSION ON CIVIL DISORDERS (KERNER

COMMISSION). 1968. *Report of National Advisory Commission on Civil Disorders.* New York: Bantam.

NATIONAL COMMISSION ON MARIJUANA AND DRUG ABUSE. 1973. *Marijuana: A Signal of Misunderstanding.* Washington, D.C.: U.S. Government Printing Office.

NATIONAL EDUCATION ASSOCIATION. 1968. *Ability Grouping: Research Summary 1968-se.* Washington, D.C.: NEA Research Division.

NAVASKY, VICTOR S. 1980. *Naming Names.* New York: Viking.

NEEDLEMAN, JACOB. 1970. *The New Religions.* Garden City, N.Y.: Doubleday.

NELSEN, HART. 1976. "Musical pews: Rural and urban modes of occupational and religious mobility." *Sociology and Social Research,* 60, pp. 279–289.

NEWCOMB, THEODORE. 1958. "Attitude development as a function of reference groups: The Bennington study," in Guy E. Swanson et al. (eds.), *Readings in Social Psychology.* New York: Holt, Rinehart and Winston.

NEWPORT, FRANK. 1979. "The religious switcher in the United States." *American Sociological Review,* 44, pp. 528–552.

NEWTON, ESTHER. 1972. *Mother Camp: Female Impersonation in America.* Englewood Cliffs, N.J.: Prentice-Hall.

NIEBUHR, RICHARD H. 1929. *The Social Sources of Denominationalism.* New York: Holt.

NISBET, ROBERT A. 1953. *The Quest for Community.* New York: Oxford University Press.

_____. 1969. *Social Change and History.* New York: Oxford University Press.

_____. 1970. *The Social Bond.* New York: Knopf.

NIXON, HOWARD L. 1976. *Sport and Social Organization.* Indianapolis: Bobbs-Merrill.

NIXON, RICHARD M. 1971. "Remarks of the President at the Republican Governors' Conference." Washington, D.C.: Office of the White House Press Secretary.

NOEL, DON. 1968. "The theory of the origin of ethnic stratification." *Social Problems,* 16, pp. 157–172.

_____ (ed.). 1972. *The Origins of American Slavery and Racism.* Columbus, Ohio: Merrill.

NORUM, G. A., et al. 1967. "Seating patterns and group tasks." *Psychology in the Schools,* 4, p. 3.

NOVAK, MICHAEL. 1971. "White ethnic." *Harper's,* 243, pp. 44–50.

NUNN, CLYDE Z., et al. 1978. *Tolerance for Nonconformity: A National Survey of Americans' Changing Commitment to Civil Liberties.* San Francisco: Jossey-Bass.

OAKLEY, ANN. 1974. *The Sociology of Housework.* New York: Pantheon.

OBERSCHALL, ANTHONY. 1973. *Social Conflict and Social Movements.* Englewood Cliffs, N.J.: Prentice-Hall.

O'DEA, THOMAS. 1957. *The Mormons.* Chicago: University of Chicago Press.

OELSNER, LESLIE. 1972. "Scales of justice." *New York Times News Service,* September.

OGBURN, WILLIAM F. 1950. *Social Change.* New York: Viking.

OLSEN, JACK. 1968. *The Black Athlete.* New York: Time-Life Books.

O'NEIL, NENA, and GEORGE O'NEIL. 1973. *Open Marriage.* New York: Avon.

OPHULS, WILLIAM. 1974. "The scarcity society." *Harper's,* 246, pp. 47–52.

ORNATI, OSCAR. 1966. *Poverty Amid Affluence.* New York: Twentieth Century Fund.

ORUM, ANTHONY. 1978. *Introduction to Political Sociology: The Social Anatomy of the Body Politic.* Englewood Cliffs, N.J.: Prentice-Hall.

ORWELL, G. 1949. *1984.* New York: New American Library.

OWEN, D. R. 1972. "The 47 XYY male: A review." *Psychological Bulletin,* 78, pp. 209–233.

PAINE, NATHANIEL. 1897. "Early American broadsides 1680–1800." *Proceedings, American Antiquarian Society.*

PALMORE, ERDMAN, and K. MANTON. 1974. "Modernization and the status of the aged: International correlations." *Journal of Gerontology,* 29, pp. 205–210.

PANKHURST, JERRY, and MICHAEL PAUL SACKS (eds.). 1980. *Contemporary Soviet Society.* New York: Praeger.

PARETO, VILFREDO. 1935. *Mind and Society.* New York: Harcourt Brace Jovanovitch.

PARK, ROBERT E., et al. 1925. *The City.* Chicago: University of Chicago Press.

PARKE, ROSS D. 1979. "The father of the child." *The Sciences,* 19, pp. 12–15.

PARKIN, FRANK. 1971. *Class Inequality and the Social Order.* London: McGibbon & Kee.

PARRILLO, VINCENT N. 1980. *Strangers to These Shores: Race and Ethnic Relations in the United States.* Boston: Houghton Mifflin.

PARSONS, TALCOTT. 1937. *The Structure of Social Action.* New York: McGraw-Hill.

_____. 1940. "An analytic approach to the theory of social stratification." *American Journal of Sociology,* 45, pp. 841–862.

_____. 1951. *The Social System.* Glencoe, Ill.: Free Press.

_____. 1954. "The professions and social structure," in Talcott Parsons (ed.), *Essays in Sociological Theory.* New York: Free Press.

_____. 1961. "Some considerations on the theory of social change." *Rural Sociology,* 26, pp. 219–239.

_____. 1966. *Societies: Evolutionary and Comparative Perspectives.* Englewood Cliffs, N.J.: Prentice-Hall.

————, et al. 1955. *Family, Socialization, and Interaction Process.* Glencoe, Ill.: Free Press.

PASCAL, ANTHONY M., and LEONARD A. RAPPING. 1970. *Racial Discrimination in Organized Baseball.* Santa Monica, Calif.: Rand Corporation.

PATRICK, TED. 1976. *Let Our Children Go.* New York: Ballantine.

PATTERSON, M. L., et al. 1971. "Compensatory reactions to spatial intrusion." *Sociometry,* 34, pp. 114–121.

PATTERSON, ORLANDO. 1977. *Ethnic Chauvinism: The Reactionary Impulse.* New York: Stein and Day.

PATTISON, E. MANSELL (ed.). 1979. *The Experience of Dying.* Englewood Cliffs, N.J.: Prentice-Hall.

PEDERSON, D. M. 1973. "Developmental trends in personal space." *Journal of Psychology,* 83, pp. 3–9.

PERROW, CHARLES, 1979. *Complex Organizations: A Critical Essay.* 2nd ed. Glenview, Ill.: Scott, Foresman.

PERRY, DAVID C., and ALFRED J. WATKINS (eds.). 1978. *The Rise of the Sunbelt Cities.* Beverly Hills, Calif.: Sage.

PERRY, STEWART E. 1978. *San Francisco Scavengers: Dirty Work and the Pride of Ownership.* Berkeley, Calif.: University of California Press.

PERSELL, CAROLINE H. *Education and Inequality.* New York: Basic Books.

PETERSON, DONALD W., and ARMAND L. MAUSS. 1973. "The cross and the commune: An interpretation of the Jesus People," in Charles Y. Glock (ed.), *Religion in Sociological Perspective.* Belmont, Calif.: Wadsworth.

PETTIGREW, THOMAS F., and ROBERT GREEN. 1976. "School desegregation in large cities: A critique of the Coleman 'white flight' thesis." *Harvard Educational Review,* 46, pp. 1–53.

PHELPS-BROWN, HENRY. 1977. *The Inequality of Pay.* Oxford, Eng.: Oxford University Press.

PHETERSON, GAIL I., et al. 1971. "Evaluation of the performance of women as a function of their sex, achievement, and personal history." *Journal of Personality and Social Psychology,* 19, pp. 114–118.

PHILLIPS, JOHN C. 1976. "Toward an explanation of racial variations in top level sports participation." *International Review of Sport Sociology,* November, pp. 39–55.

PIAGET, JEAN. 1950. *The Psychology of Intelligence.* London: Routledge & Kegan Paul.

————. 1954. *The Construction of Reality in the Child.* New York: Basic Books.

————, and BARBEL INHELDER. 1969. *The Psychology of the Child.* New York: Basic Books.

PILIAVAN, IRVIN, and SCOTT BRIAR. 1964. "Police encounters with juveniles." *American Journal of Sociology,* 70, pp. 206–214.

PINEO, PETER C., and JOHN PORTER. 1967. "Occupational prestige in Canada." *Canadian Review of Sociology and Anthropology,* 4,

pp. 24–40.

PIVEN, FRANCES FOX, and RICHARD A. CLOWARD. 1977. *Poor Peoples' Movements: Why They Succeed, How They Fail.* New York: Pantheon.

PLUMMER, KENNETH. 1975. *Sexual Stigma.* London: Routledge & Kegan Paul.

POGREBIN, LETTY C. 1980. *Growing Up Free.* New York: McGraw-Hill.

POLANYI, MICHAEL. 1951. *The Logic of Liberty.* London: Routledge & Kegan Paul.

POLSKY, NED. 1964. *Hustlers, Beats, and Others.* Chicago: Aldine.

POMEROY, WARDELL B. 1965. "Some aspects of prostitution." *Journal of Sex Research,* 1, pp. 177–187.

————. 1972. *Dr. Kinsey and the Institute for Sex Research.* New York: Harper & Row.

PONSE, BARBARA. 1978. *Identities in the Lesbian World: The Social Construction of Self.* Westport, Conn.: Greenwood Press.

POPPER, KARL R. 1959. *The Logic of Scientific Discovery.* New York: Basic Books.

PORTER, JOHN. 1968. "The future of upward mobility." *American Sociological Review,* 33, pp. 5–19.

PORTER, JOHN. 1965. *The Vertical Mosaic: An Analysis of Social Class and Power in Canada.* Toronto: University of Toronto Press.

POSTMAN, NEIL. 1979. *Teaching as a Conserving Activity.* New York: Delacorte Press.

POWERS, THOMAS. 1971. "Learning to die." *Harper's,* 242, pp. 72–80.

PRATT, HENRY J. 1976. *The Gray Lobby.* Chicago: University of Chicago Press.

PRESIDENT'S COMMISSION ON LAW ENFORCEMENT AND THE ADMINISTRATION OF JUSTICE. 1967. *The Challenge of Crime in a Free Society.* Washington, D.C.: U.S. Government Printing Office.

PRESIDENT'S COMMISSION ON OBSCENITY AND PORNOGRAPHY. 1970. *Report of the President's Commission on Obscenity and Pornography.* New York: Bantam.

PRICE, DEREK J. DE SOLLA. 1963. *Big Science, Little Science.* New York: Columbia University Press.

PROVENCE, S., and LIPTON, R. C. 1962. *Infants in Institutions.* New York: International Universities Press.

PSATHAS, GEORGE (ed.). 1979. *Everyday Language: Studies in Ethnomethodology.* New York: Lovington.

QUANDAGNO, JILL S. 1979. "Paradigms in evolutionary theory: The sociobiological method of natural selection." *American Sociological Review,* 44, pp. 100–109.

RADCLIFFE-BROWN, A. R. 1935. "On the concept of functionalism in the social sciences." *American Anthropologist,* 37, pp. 394–402.

———. 1952. *Structure and Function in Primitive Society*. Glencoe, Ill.: Free Press.

RAINWATER, LEE. 1964. "Marital satisfaction in four cultures of poverty." *Journal of Marriage and the Family*, 26, pp. 457–466.

———. 1966. "Some aspects of lower class sexual behavior." *Journal of Social Issues*, 22, pp. 96–108.

———. 1974. *What Money Buys: Inequality and the Social Meanings of Income*. New York: Basic Books.

———, et al. 1959. *Working Man's Wife*. Chicago: Oceana Publications.

RAPER, ARTHUR. 1933. *The Tragedy of Lynching*. Chapel Hill, N.C.: University of North Carolina Press.

RAPPOPORT, RHONA, and ROBERT RAPPOPORT. 1976. *Dual Career Families Re-examined*. New York: Harper & Row.

RAVETZ, JEROME R. 1977. "Criticisms of science," in Ina Spiegel-Rosing and Derek de Solla Price, *Science, Technology, and Society*. Beverly Hills, Calif.: Sage.

RAVITCH, DIANNE. 1978. *The Revisionists Revised: A Critique of the Radical Attack on the Schools*. New York: Basic Books.

READ, KENNETH. 1965. *The High Valley*. New York: Scribner's.

REDFIELD, ROBERT. 1941. *The Folk Culture of Yucatan*. Chicago: University of Chicago Press.

———. 1953. *The Primitive World and Its Transformation*. Ithaca, N.Y.: Cornell University Press.

REIMAN, JEFFREY H. 1979. *The Rich Get Richer and the Poor Get Prison*. New York: Wiley.

REISS, ALBERT J., JR. 1961. "The social integration of peers and queers." *Social Problems*, 9, pp. 102–120.

———, et al. 1961. *Occupation and Social Status*. New York: Free Press.

REISS, DAVID, and HOWARD HOFFMAN. 1979. *The American Family: Dying or Developing?* New York: Plenum

RENSHON, STANLEY ALLEN (ed.). 1977. *Handbook of Political Socialization: Theory and Research*. New York: Free Press.

RICH, WILLIAM. 1973. *Smaller Families Through Social and Economic Progress*. Washington, D.C.: Overseas Development Council.

RICHARDSON, JAMES T., et al. 1979. *Organized Miracles*. New Brunswick, N.J.: Transaction Books.

———. (ed.). 1978. *Conversion Careers: In and Out of the New Religions*. Beverly Hills, Calif.: Sage.

RIESMAN, DAVID. 1961. *The Lonely Crowd*. New Haven, Conn.: Yale University Press.

RILEY, MATILDA W. 1971. "Social gerontology and the age stratification of society." *Gerontologist*, 11, pp. 79–87.

———, et al. 1972. *Aging and Society. Volume 3. A Sociology of Age Stratification*. New York: Russell Sage Foundation.

RIST, RAY C. 1970. "Student social class and teacher expectations: The self-fulfilling prophecy in ghetto education." *Harvard Educational Review*, 40, pp. 411–451.

———. 1973. *The Urban School: A Factory for Failure*. New York: Doubleday.

———. 1978. *The Invisible Children: School Integration in American Society*. Cambridge, Mass.: Harvard University Press.

——— (ed.). 1979. *Desegregated Schools: Appraisals of an American Experiment*. New York: Academic Press.

RITCHIE, JOHN W. 1977. "The magic feather: Education and the power of positive thinking." *Teachers College Record*, 78:4, 477–486.

ROBBINS, THOMAS, et al. 1976. "The last civil religion: Reverend Moon and the Unification Church." *Sociological Analysis*, 37, pp. 111–125.

———, et al. 1978. "Theory and research on today's 'new religions.'" *Sociological Analysis*, 39, pp. 95–122.

———, and Dick Anthony (eds.). 1979. *In Gods We Trust: New Patterns of Religious Pluralism in America*. New Brunswick, N.J.: Transaction Books.

ROBERTS, JOAN L. 1970. *Scene of the Battle: Group Behavior in Urban Classrooms*. New York: Doubleday.

ROBERTSON, IAN. 1976. "Social stratification," in David E. Hunter and Phillip Whitten (eds.), *The Study of Anthropology*. New York: Harper & Row.

———. 1978. "Education in South Africa," in Ian Robertson and Phillip Whitten (eds.), *Race and Politics in South Africa*. New Brunswick, N.J.: Transaction Books.

———. 1980. *Social Problems*. 2nd ed. New York: Random House.

ROETHLISBERGER, FRITZ J., and WILLIAM J. DICKSON. 1939. *Management and the Worker*. Cambridge, Mass.: Harvard University Press.

ROSE, ARNOLD M. 1967. *The Power Structure*. New York: Oxford University Press.

ROSE, PETER I. 1980. *They and We: Racial and Ethnic Relations in the United States*. 3rd ed. New York: Random House.

ROSEN, R. D. 1977. *Psychobabble: Fast Talk and Quick Cure in the Era of Feeling*. New York: Atheneum.

ROSENBERG, EDWIN. 1978. "Sport as work: Characteristics and career patterns." Paper presented to the meetings of the Pacific Sociology Association, Spokane.

ROSENBLATT, AARON. 1967. "Negroes in baseball: The failure of success." *Transaction*, 4, pp. 51–53.

ROSENFIELD, JEFFREY P. 1978. *The Legacy of Aging: A Sociology of Inheritance and Disinheritance*. Norwood, N.J.: Ablex.

ROSENGRANT, T. 1973. "The relationship of race and sex on proxemic behavior and source credibility." Paper presented at the International Communication Association Convention, Montreal, April.

ROSENTHAL, D. 1970. *Genetic Theory and Abnormal Behavior*. New York: McGraw-Hill.

ROSENTHAL, M. 1971. "Where rumor raged." *Transaction*, 8, pp. 34–43.

ROSENTHAL, ROBERT. 1966. *Experimenter Effects in Behavioral Research*. New York: Appleton-Century-Crofts.

_____, and LENORE JACOBSON. 1968. *Pygmalion in the Classroom: Teacher Expectation and Pupils' Intellectual Development*. New York: Holt, Rinehart and Winston.

ROSETT, ARTHUR, and DONALD R. CRESSEY. 1976. *Justice by Consent*. Philadelphia: Lippincott.

ROSNOW, RALPH L., and GARY ALAN FINE. 1976. *Rumor and Gossip*. New York: Elsevier.

ROSS, H. LAWRENCE. 1965. "Uptown and downtown: A study of middle class residential areas." *American Sociological Review*, 30, pp. 255–259.

ROSS, JAMES B., and MARY M. McLAUGHLIN (eds.). 1949. *The Portable Medieval Reader*. New York: Viking.

ROSSELL, CHRISTINE. 1976. "School desegregation and white flight." *Political Science Quarterly*, 90, pp. 675–698.

ROSSIDES, DANIEL W. 1976. *The American Class System*. Boston: Houghton Mifflin.

ROSZAK, THEODORE. 1969. *The Making of a Counter-Culture: Reflections on the Technocratic Society and Its Youthful Opposition*. New York: Doubleday.

ROTHMAN, SHEILA M. 1978. *Woman's Proper Place: A History of Changing Ideals and Practices, 1870 to the Present*. New York: Basic Books.

ROTHSCHILD-WHITT, JOYCE. 1979. "The collectivist organization: An alternative to rational-bureaucratic models." *American Sociological Review*, 44, pp. 509–527.

ROUSSEAU, JEAN JACQUES. 1950, originally published 1762. *The Social Contract*. New York: Dutton.

RUBIN, LILLIAN. 1976. *Worlds of Pain: Life in the Working Class Family*. New York: Basic Books.

_____. 1979. *Women of a Certain Age*. New York: Harper & Row.

RUBOVITS, P. C., and A. L. MAEHR. 1971. "Pygmalion analyzed: Toward an explanation of the Rosenthal-Jacobson findings." *Journal of Personality and Social Psychology*, 19, pp. 197–203.

_____, and A. L. MAEHR. 1973. "Pygmalion black and white." *Journal of Personality and Social Psychology*, 25, pp. 210–218.

RUSSELL, DIANA E. H. 1975. *The Politics of Rape: The Victim's Perspective*. New York: Stein and Day.

RUSSELL, M. A. HAMILTON. 1971. "Cigarette smoking: Natural history of a dependence disorder." *British Journal of Medical Psychology*, 44, pp. 1–16.

RUTTER, MICHAEL. 1974. *The Qualities of Mothering: Maternal Deprivation Reassessed*. New York: Aronson.

RYAN, WILLIAM. 1976. *Blaming the Victim*. Rev. ed. New York: Vintage.

SAFILIOS-ROTHSCHILD, CONSTANTINE. 1974. *Woman and Social Policy*. Englewood Cliffs, N.J.: Prentice-Hall.

SAGARIN, EDWARD. 1973. "The good guys, the bad guys, and the gay guys." *Contemporary Sociology*, 2, pp. 3–13.

_____. 1975. *Deviants and Deviance*. New York: Praeger.

SAGE, GEORGE H. 1974. *Sport and American Society*. Reading, Mass.: Addison-Wesley.

SAHLINS, MARSHALL D. 1972. *Stone Age Economics*. Chicago: Aldine.

_____. 1976. *The Use and Abuse of Biology*. Ann Arbor: University of Michigan Press.

_____, and ELMAN R. SERVICE. 1960. *Evolution and Culture*. Ann Arbor: University of Michigan Press.

SAID, ABDUL A., and LUIZ R. SIMMONS. 1975. *The New Sovereigns: Multinational Corporations as World Powers*. Englewood Cliffs, N.J.: Prentice-Hall.

SAID, EDWARD. 1979. *Orientalism*. New York: Pantheon.

SALAS, RAFAEL M. 1980. *Annual Report of the Executive Director, United Nations Fund for Population Activities*. New York: United Nations.

SALINS, PETER D. 1980. *The Ecology of Housing Destruction*. New York: New York University Press.

SAMPSON, ANTHONY. 1973. *The Sovereign State of ITT*. Greenwich, Conn.: Fawcett.

SAPIR, EDWARD. 1929. "The status of linguistics as a science." *Language*, 5, pp. 207–214.

SCHAEFER, RICHARD T. 1979. *Racial and Ethnic Relations*. Boston: Little, Brown.

SCHEFF, THOMAS J. 1966. *Being Mentally Ill: A Sociological Theory*. Chicago: Aldine.

SCHLEGEL, ALICE (ed.). 1977. *Sexual Stratification: A Cross-Cultural View*. New York: Columbia University Press.

SCHNEIDER, DAVID M., and RAYMOND T. SMITH. 1978. *Class Differences in American Kinship*. Ann Arbor: University of Michigan Press.

SCHULTZ, TERRI. 1980. "The untaxed millions." *New York Times Magazine*, March 16, pp. 42–60.

SCHUR, EDWIN M. 1965. *Crimes Without Victims—Deviant Behavior and Public Policy*. Englewood Cliffs, N.J.: Prentice-Hall.

_____. 1976. *The Awareness Trap: Self Absorption Instead of Social Change*. New York: Quadrangle.

SCHUTZ, ALFRED. 1962. *Collected Papers, I: The Problem of Social Reality*. The Hague: Martinus Nijhoff.

SCOTT, MARVIN B., and STANFORD M. LYMAN. 1968. "Accounts." *American Sociological Review*, 33, pp. 46–62.

_____. 1971. *Labeling Deviant Behavior: Its Sociological Implications*. New York: Harper & Row.

SEARS, ROBERT R., et al. 1957. *Patterns of Child Rearing*. Evanston, Ill.: Row, Peterson.

SEEMAN, MELVIN. 1959. "On the meaning of alienation." *American Sociological Review*, 24, pp. 783–789.

SEGAL, RONALD. 1973. "Everywhere at home, at home nowhere." *Center Magazine*, 6, pp. 8–14.

SELLIN, THORSTEN. 1938. *Culture Conflict and Crime.* New York: Social Science Research Council.

———. 1980. *The Penalty of Death.* Beverly Hills, Calif.: Sage.

SELZNICK, GERTRUDE JAEGER, and STEPHEN STEINBERG. 1969. *The Tenacity of Prejudice.* New York: Harper & Row.

SELZNICK, PHILIP. 1943. "An approach to a theory of bureaucracy." *American Sociological Review*, 8, pp. 47–54.

SENNET, RICHARD. 1970. *The Uses of Disorder.* New York: Knopf.

SERVICE, ELMAN R. 1971. *Primitive Social Organization: An Evolutionary Perspective.* New York: Random House.

———. 1975. *Origins of the State and Civilization: The Process of Cultural Evolution.* New York: Norton.

SEWELL, WILLIAM H. 1971. "Inequality of opportunity for higher education." *American Sociological Review*, 36, pp. 793–808.

———, and ROBERT M. HAUSER. 1975. *Education, Occupation, and Earnings.* New York: Academic Press.

SHATTUCK, ROGER. 1980. *The Forbidden Experiment.* New York: Farrar, Straus and Giroux.

SHAW, CLIFFORD R., and HENRY D. MCKAY. 1929. *Delinquency Areas.* Chicago: University of Chicago Press.

SHELDON, WILLIAM H. 1940. *The Varieties of Human Physique.* New York: Harper.

———, et al. 1949. *Varieties of Delinquent Youth.* New York: Harper & Row.

SHERIF, MUZAFER. 1956. "Experiments in group conflict." *Scientific American*, 195, pp. 54–58.

SHERRILL, ROBERT. 1970. "The war machine." *Playboy*, 17, pp. 134, 214–228.

SHIBUTANI, TAMOTSU. 1966. *Improvised News: A Sociological Study of Rumor.* Indianapolis: Bobbs–Merrill.

SHORT, JAMES F., and F. IVAN NYE. 1957. "Reported behavior as a criterion of delinquent behavior." *Social Problems*, 5, pp. 207–213.

SHORTER, EDWARD. 1975. *The Making of the Modern Family.* New York: Basic Books.

SHUPE, ANSON D., and DAVID G. BROMLEY. 1980. *The New Vigilantes: Deprogrammers, Anti-cultists and the New Religions.* Beverly Hills, Calif.: Sage.

SILBERMAN, CHARLES E. 1970. "Murder in the classroom: How the public schools kill dreams and mutilate minds." *The Atlantic*, 225, pp. 82–94.

———. 1971. *Crisis in the Classroom: The Remaking of American Education.* New York: Random House.

———. 1978. *Criminal Violence, Criminal Justice.* New York: Random House.

SILLS, DAVID L. 1957. *The Volunteers.* Glencoe, Ill.: Free Press.

SIMMEL, GEORG. 1904. "The sociology of conflict," Albion Small (transl.). *American Journal of Sociology*, 9, p. 490 ff.

———. 1955. *Conflict and the Web of Group Affiliations.* Kurt Wolff (transl.). Glencoe, Ill.: Free Press.

SIMMONS, JACK L. 1969. *Deviants.* Berkeley, Calif.: Glendessary Press.

SIMPSON, GEORGE E., and J. MILTON YINGER. 1972. *Racial and Cultural Minorities: An Analysis of Prejudice and Discrimination.* 4th ed. New York: Harper & Row.

SINGH, J. A. L., and ROBERT M. ZINGG. 1942. *Wolf Children and Feral Man.* New York: Harper & Row.

SINGH, VIJAI P. 1976. *Caste, Clan, and Democracy: Changes in a Stratification System.* Cambridge, Mass.: Schenkman.

SJOBERG, GIDEON. 1960. *The Preindustrial City.* New York: Free Press.

SKINNER, B. F. 1971. *Beyond Freedom and Dignity.* New York: Knopf.

SKLARE, MARSHALL. 1971. *America's Jews.* New York: Random House.

——— (ed.). 1974. *The Jew in American Society.* New York: Behrman House.

SKOCPOL, THEDA. 1979. *States and Social Revolutions.* New York: Cambridge University Press.

SKOLNICK, ARLENE. 1978. *The Intimate Environment: Exploring Marriage and Family.* 2nd ed. Boston: Little, Brown.

SKOLNICK, JEROME H. 1969. *The Politics of Protest.* New York: Simon and Schuster.

SKULLY, GERALD W. 1974. "Discrimination: The case of baseball," in Roger G. Noll (ed.), *Government and the Sports Business.* Washington, D.C.: Brookings Institution.

SLATER, PHILIP E. 1955. "Role differentiation in small groups," in A. Paul Hare et al. (eds.), *Small Groups: Studies in Social Interaction.* New York: Knopf.

———. 1970. *The Pursuit of Loneliness: American Culture at the Breaking Point.* Boston: Beacon.

SMELSER, NEIL J. 1962. *Theory of Collective Behavior.* New York: Free Press.

———. 1967. *Sociology: An Introduction.* New York: Wiley.

———. 1973. "Toward a theory of modernization," in Amitai Etzioni and Eva Etzioni–Halevy (eds.), *Social Change: Sources, Patterns, and Consequences.* New York: Basic Books.

SMITH, ADAM. 1910. *The Wealth of Nations.* London: Dent.

SMITH, JAMES R., and LYNN G. SMITH (eds.). 1974. *Beyond Monogamy: Recent Studies of Sexual Alternatives in Marriage.* Baltimore: Johns Hopkins University Press.

SMITH, LILLIAN. 1949. *Killers of the Dream.* New York: Norton.

SOLMON, LEWIS C., et al. 1977. *College as a Training Ground for Jobs.* New York: Praeger.

SOMMER, R. 1965. "Further studies of small group ecology." *Sociometry*, 28, pp. 337–348.

SORENSEN, ROBERT. 1973. *Adolescent Sexuality in Contemporary America*. Cleveland: World.

SOROKIN, PITIRIM A. 1927. *Social Mobility*. New York: Harper.

———. 1937. *Social and Cultural Dynamics*. New York: American Books.

———. 1941. *The Crisis of Our Age*. New York: E. P. Dutton.

SPECTOR, MALCOLM, and JOHN I. KITSUSE. 1973. "Social problems: A re-formulation." *Social Problems*, 21, pp. 145–159.

———, and JOHN I. KITSUSE. 1977. *Constructing Social Problems*. Menlo Park, Calif.: Cummings.

SPENGLER, OSWALD. 1962, originally published 1918, 1922. *The Decline of the West*. New York: Knopf.

SPITZ, RENÉ A. 1945. "Hospitalism: An inquiry into the genesis of psychiatric conditions in early childhood," in Anna Freud et al. (eds.), *The Psychoanalytic Study of the Child*. New York: International Universities Press.

SQUIRES, GREGORY D. 1979. *Education, Jobs, and the U.S. Class Structure*. New Brunswick, N.J.: Transaction Books.

SRINIVAS, M. N. 1966. *Social Change in Modern India*. Berkeley, Calif.: University of California Press.

SROLE, LEO, et al. 1962. *Mental Health in the Metropolis*. New York: McGraw-Hill.

ST. JOHN, NANCY H. 1975. *School Desegregation: Outcomes for Children*. New York: Wiley.

STAINES, GRAHAM L., and ROBERT P. QUINN. 1979. "American workers evaluate the quality of their jobs." *Monthly Labor Review*, January, pp. 2–12.

STAMPP, KENNETH. 1956. *The Peculiar Institution*. New York: Knopf.

STARK, RODNEY, and CHARLES Y. GLOCK. 1965. "The new denominationalism." *Review of Religious Research*, 7, pp. 8–17.

———, et al. 1971. *Wayward Shepherds: Prejudice and the Protestant Clergy*. New York: Harper & Row.

———, and WILLIAM SIMS BAINBRIDGE. 1980. "Networks of faith: Interpersonal bonds and recruitment to cults and sects." *American Journal of Sociology*, 85:6, 1376–1395.

STEIN, HOWARD F., and ROBERT F. HILL. 1977. *The Ethnic Imperative*. University Park, Pa.: University of Pennsylvania Press.

STEIN, LEONARD T. 1977. "Male and Female: The doctor-nurse game," in James P. Spradley and David W. McCurdy (eds.), *Conformity and Conflict*. 3rd ed. Boston: Little, Brown.

STEIN, MAURICE R. 1964. *The Eclipse of Community: An Interpretation of American Studies*. New York: Harper & Row.

STEIN, PETER. 1976. *Single*. Englewood Cliffs, N.J.: Prentice-Hall.

STEINER, STAN. 1974. *The Islands: The Worlds of the Puerto Ricans*. New York: Harper & Row.

STEINMETZ, SUSANNE K., and MURRAY S. STRAUS. 1974. *Violence in the Family*. New York: Dodd, Mead.

STEPHENS, WILLIAM N. 1963. *The Family in Cross Cultural Perspective*. New York: Holt, Rinehart and Winston.

STERN, PHILIP M. 1973. *The Rape of the Taxpayer*. New York: Random House.

STEWARD, JULIAN H. 1955. *Theory of Culture Change*. Urbana, Ill.: University of Illinois Press.

STINNET, NICK, and CRAIG WAYNE BIRDSONG. 1978. *The Family and Alternate Life Styles*. Chicago: Nelson Hall.

STOCKTON, WILLIAM. 1978. "Going home: The Puerto Ricans' new migration." *New York Times*, May 12, pp. 20–22, 88–93.

STODDARD, ALWIN R. 1974. *Mexican Americans*. 2nd ed. New York: Random House.

STOGDILL, RALPH M. 1974. *Handbook of Leadership: A Survey of Theory and Research*. New York: Free Press.

STOKES, RANDALL, and JOHN P. HEWITT. 1976. "Aligning actions." *American Sociological Review*, 41, pp. 838–849.

STONE, LAWRENCE. 1977. *The Family, Sex, and Marriage in England, 1500–1800*. New York: Harper & Row.

STONER, CARROLL, and JOANNE PARKE. 1977. *All God's Children*. Radnor, Pa.: Chilton.

STONER, J. A. F. 1961. "A comparison of individual and group decisions involving risk." Unpublished master's thesis, Massachusetts Institute of Technology.

STORER, NORMAN W. (ed.). 1973. *Sociology of Science: Theoretical and Empirical Investigations*. Chicago: University of Chicago Press.

STOUFFER, SAMUEL A. 1955. *Communism, Conformity, and Civil Liberties*. New York: Doubleday.

STRAUS, MURRAY A., et al. 1979. *Behind Closed Doors: A Study of Family Violence in America*. Garden City, N.Y.: Doubleday.

STRAUSS, ANSELM. 1978. *Negotiations: Varieties, Contexts, Processes, and Social Order*. San Francisco: Jossey-Bass.

———(ed.). 1979. *Where Medicine Fails*. 3rd ed. New Brunswick, N.J.: Transaction Books.

SUDNOW, DAVID. 1972. *Studies in Social Interaction*. New York: Free Press.

SUMNER, WILLIAM GRAHAM. 1906. *Folkways*. Boston: Ginn

SUTHERLAND, EDWIN H. 1939. *Principles of Criminology*. Philadelphia: Lippincott.

———. 1940. "White collar criminality." *American Sociological Review*, 5, pp. 1–12.

SUTTLES, GERALD. 1970. *The Social Order of the Slum*. Chicago: University of Chicago Press.

SWANSON, GUY E. 1960. *The Birth of the Gods*. Ann Arbor: University of Michigan Press.

SYMONDS, CAROLYN. 1971. "Sexual mate swapping: Violation of norms and reconciliation of guilt," in James M. Henslin (ed.), *Studies in the Sociology of Sex*. New York: Appleton-Century-Crofts.

TAEUBER, IRENE B. 1960. "Japan's demographic transition reexamined." *Population Studies*. 14, pp. 28–39.

TAKOOSHIAN, HAROLD, and HERZEL BODINGER. 1979. "Street crime in 18 American cities: A national field experiment." Paper presented at the annual meeting of the American Sociological Association, Boston, August.

TALAMINI, JOHN T., and CHARLES H. PAGE (eds.). 1973. *Sport and Society: An Anthology*. Boston: Little, Brown.

TANNER, DONNA M. 1978. *The Lesbian Couple*. Lexington, Mass.: Heath.

TAYLOR, GORDON RATTRAY. 1970. *Sex in History*. New York: Vanguard.

TAYLOR, IAN, et al. 1973. *The New Criminology*. London: Routledge & Kegan Paul.

THOMPSON, N. L., et al. 1971. "Personal adjustment of male and female homosexuals and heterosexuals." *Journal of Abnormal Psychology*, 78, pp. 237–240.

THOMPSON, SPENCER K. 1975. "Gender labels and early sex-role development." *Child Development*, 46, pp. 339–347.

THOMPSON, VICTOR. 1961. *Modern Organizations*. New York: Knopf.

TITTLE, CHARLES R., et al. 1978. "The myth of social class and criminality: An empirical assessment of the empirical evidence." *American Sociological Review*, 43, pp. 643–656.

TOCH, HANS. 1965. *The Social Psychology of Social Movements*. Indianapolis: Bobbs-Merrill.

TOFFLER, ALVIN., 1970. *Future Shock*. New York: Random House.

TÖNNIES, FERDINAND. 1957, originally published in 1887. *Community and Society*. East Lansing, Mich.: Michigan State University Press.

TOURAINE, ALAN. 1971. *The Post-Industrial Society*. New York: Random House.

TOURNEY, G., et al. 1975. "Hormonal relationships in homosexual men." *American Journal of Psychiatry*, 132, pp. 288–290.

TOWNSEND, PETER. 1979. *Poverty in the United Kingdom*. Berkeley, Calif.: University of California Press.

TOYNBEE, ARNOLD. 1946. *A Study of History*. New York: Oxford University Press.

TREIMAN, DONALD J. 1977. *Occupational Prestige in Comparative Perspective*. New York: Academic Press.

———, and K. TERRELL. 1972. "The role of education in status attainment: A comparison of the United States and Britain." Paper delivered at the annual meeting of American Sociological Association, September, New Orleans.

TREVOR-ROPER, H. R. 1967. *Religion, Reformation and Social Change*. London: Macmillan.

TROELTSCH, ERNST. 1931. *The Social Teachings of the Christian Churches*. New York: Macmillan.

TRUZZI, MARCELLO. 1968. "Lilliputians in Gulliver's land: The social role of the dwarf," in Marcello Truzzi (ed.), *Sociology and Everyday Life*. Englewood Cliffs, N.J.: Prentice-Hall.

TUCHMAN, GAYLE, et al. (eds.). 1978. *Hearth and Home: Images of Women in the Mass Media*. New York: Oxford University Press.

TUMIN, MELVIN M. 1953. "Some principles of stratification: A critical analysis." *American Sociological Review*, 18, pp. 378–394.

———. 1955. "Rewards and task orientations." *American Sociological Review*, 20, pp. 419–423.

———. 1963. "On inequality." *American Sociological Review*, 28, pp. 19–26.

TURNER, RALPH H. 1962. "Role taking: Process versus conformity," in Arnold Rose (ed.), *Human Behavior and Social Processes: An Interactionist Approach*. Boston: Houghton Mifflin.

———. 1964. "Collective behavior," in Robert E. L. Fatis (ed.), *Handbook of Modern Sociology*. Chicago: Rand McNally.

———, and LEWIS M. KILLIAN. 1972. *Collective Behavior*. 2nd ed. Englewood Cliffs, N.J.: Prentice-Hall.

TUSSING, A. DALE. 1974. "The dual welfare system." *Society*, 11, pp. 50–57.

TWADDLE, ANDREW C. 1979. *Sickness Behavior and the Sick Role*. Cambridge, Mass.: Schenkman.

UDRY, J. RICHARD. 1974. *The Social Context of Marriage*. Philadelphia: Lippincott.

UNDERWOOD, JOHN. 1980. "Student athletes: The sham, the shame." *Sports Illustrated*, 52:21, May, pp. 36–73.

UNGER, RHODA K. 1980. *Female and Male: Sex and Gender*. Harper & Row.

U'REN, MARJORIE B. 1971. "The image of women in textbooks," in Vivian Gornick and Barbara K. Moran (eds.), *Women in Sexist Society: Studies in Power and Powerlessness*. New York: Basic Books.

USEEM, MICHAEL. 1978. "The inner group of the American capitalist class." *Social Problems*, 25, pp. 225–240.

———. 1979. "The social organization of the American business elite and participation of corporation directors in the governance of American institutions." *American Sociological Review*, 44, pp. 553–572.

VAN BAAL, J. 1966. *Dema: Description and Analysis of Manind–anim Culture (South New Guinea)*. The Hague: M. Nijhoff.

VAN DEN BERGHE, PIERRE L. 1963. "Dialectic and functionalism: Toward a theoretic synthesis." *American Sociological Review*, 28, pp. 695–705.

———. 1978. *Man in Society: A Biosocial View*. 2nd ed. New York: Elsevier.

VANDER ZANDEN, JAMES W. 1972. *American Minority Relations: The Sociology of Racial and Ethnic Groups*. 3rd ed. New York: Ronald.

VAYDA, ANDREW P. (ed.). 1969. *Environment and Cultural Behavior*. Garden City, N.Y.: Natural History Press.

VEBLEN, THORSTEIN. 1922. *The Instinct of Workmanship*. New

York: Huebsch.

VERBA, SIDNEY, and NORMAN H. NIE. 1972. *Participation in America.* New York: Harper & Row.

VERNON, RAYMOND. 1977. *Storm over the Multinationals.* Cambridge, Mass.: Harvard University Press.

VIDAL, FEDERICO S. 1976. "Mutayr: A tribe of Saudi Arabian pastoral nomads," in David E. Hunter and Phillip Whitten (eds.), *The Study of Anthropology.* New York: Harper & Row.

VLADECK, BRUCE C. 1980. *Unloving Care: The Nursing Home Tragedy.* New York: Basic Books.

VOSS, HARWIN L. 1966. "Socio-economic status and reported delinquent behavior." *Social Problems,* 13, pp. 314–324.

WAGENHEIM, KALL. 1975. *Puerto Rico: A Profile.* 2nd ed. New York: Praeger.

WAGLEY, CHARLES, and MARVIN HARRIS. 1964. *Minorities in the New World.* New York: Columbia University Press.

WALKER, MARCIA, and STANLEY BRODSKY. 1976. *Sexual Assault: The Victim and the Rapist.* Lexington, Mass.: Lexington Books.

WALLACE, ANTHONY F. C. 1956. "Revitalization movements." *American Anthropologist,* 58, pp. 264–281.

WALLERSTEIN, JAMES S., and CLEMENT J. WYLE. 1947. "Our law-abiding law breakers." *Federal Probation,* 25, pp. 107–112.

WALLIS, ROY (ed.). 1975. *Sectarianism.* New York: Wiley.

———. 1977. *The Road to Total Freedom: A Sociological Analysis of Scientology.* New York: Columbia University Press.

WALTERS, JAMES, and NICK STINNETT. 1971. "Parent-child relationships: A decade review of research." *Journal of Marriage and the Family,* 33, pp. 70–111.

WALTON, JOHN. 1966. "Substance and artifact: The current status of research on community power structure." *American Journal of Sociology,* 71, pp. 430–438.

WARNER, W. LLOYD, and PAUL S. LUNT. 1941. *The Social Life of a Modern Community.* New Haven: Yale University Press.

———, et al. 1949. *Social Class in America.* New York: Harper.

WARREN, CAROL A. B. 1974. *Identity and Community in the Gay World.* New York: Wiley.

WATSON, J. B. 1924. *Behavior.* New York: Norton.

WATSON, PETER J., and MARTHA MEDNICK. 1970. "Race, social class, and the motive to avoid success in women." *Journal of Cross-Cultural Psychology,* 1, pp. 284–291.

WEBER, MAX. 1922. *Economy and Society.* Ephraim Fischoff et al. (transl.), 1968. New York: Bedminster Press.

———. 1946. *From Max Weber: Essays in Sociology.* H. H. Gerth and C. Wright Mills (trans./eds.). New York: Oxford University Press.

———. 1951. *The Religion of China.* New York: Free Press.

———. 1952. *Ancient Judaism.* New York: Free Press.

———. 1958a. *The Protestant Ethic and the Spirit of Capitalism.* New York: Scribner's.

———. 1958b. *The Religion of India.* New York: Free Press.

———. 1963. *The Sociology of Religion.* Boston: Beacon Press.

WEINBERG, MARTIN S. 1965. "Sexual modesty, social meanings, and the nudist camp." *Social Problems,* 12, pp. 311–318.

———, and COLIN J. WILLIAMS. 1974. *Male Homosexuals: Their Problems and Adjustments.* New York: Oxford University Press.

WEINREB, LLOYD L. 1977. *Denial of Justice: Criminal Process in the United States.* New York: Free Press.

WEISS, ROBERT S. 1975. *Marital Separation.* New York: Basic Books.

———. 1979. *Going It Alone: The Family Life and Social Situation of the Single Parent.* New York: Basic Books.

WEITZ, SHIRLEY. 1977. *Sex Roles: Biological, Psychological, and Social Foundations.* New York: Oxford University Press

——— (ed.). 1979. *Nonverbal Communication.* New York: Oxford University Press.

WEITZMAN, LENORE J., et al. 1972. "Sex role socialization in picture books for preschool children." *American Journal of Sociology,* 77, pp. 1125–1149.

WESTHUES, KENNETH. 1972. *Society's Shadow: Studies in the Sociology of Countercultures.* Toronto: McGraw–Hill Ryerson.

WHITE, LESLIE A. 1959. *The Evolution of Culture.* New York: McGraw–Hill.

———. 1969. *The Science of Culture.* New York: Farrar, Straus & Giroux.

WHITE, RALPH K., and RONALD O. LIPPITT. 1960. *Autocracy and Democracy.* New York: Harper & Row.

WHYTE, WILLIAM F. 1943. *Street-Corner Society: The Social Structure of an Italian Slum.* Chicago: University of Chicago Press.

WHYTE, WILLIAM H. 1956. *The Organization Man.* New York: Simon and Schuster.

WIEGNER, KATHLEEN. 1978. "Can't somebody turn the damned thing off?" *Forbes,* August 7, pp. 47–53.

WIESNER, JEROME B. 1973. "Technology is for mankind." *Technology Review,* May, pp. 10–13.

WILENSKY, H. L. 1964. "The professionalization of everyone?" *American Journal of Sociology,* 70, pp. 137–158.

———. 1966. "A second look at the traditional view of urbanism," in R. Warren (ed.), *Perspectives on the Urban Community.* Chicago: Rand McNally.

———. 1978. "The political economy of income distribution: Issues in the analysis of government approaches to the reduction of inequality," in J. Milton Yinger and Stephen J. Cutler (eds.), *Major Social Issues: A Multidisciplinary View.* New York: Free Press.

WILES, P. J. D. 1976. *Distribution of Income: East and West.* New York: Elsevier.

WILLIAMS, FREDERICK, et al. 1981. *Children, Television, and Sex-Role Stereotyping.* New York: Praeger.

WILLIAMS, JAY R., and MARTIN GOLD. 1972. "From delinquent

behavior to official delinquency." *Social Problems,* 20, pp. 209–229.

WILLIAMS, ROBIN M., JR. 1964. *Strangers Next Door.* Englewood Cliffs, N.J.: Prentice-Hall.

———. 1970. *American Society: A Sociological Interpretation.* 3rd ed. New York: Knopf.

WILLIE, CHARLES V. 1976. *A New Look at Black Families.* Bayside, N.Y.: General Hall.

WILSON, JAMES Q. 1975. "Lock 'em up." *New York Times Magazine,* March 9, pp. 11, 44–48.

WILSON, JOHN. 1973. *Introduction to Social Movements.* New York: Basic Books.

WILSON, ROBERT A., and BILL HOSOKAWA. 1980. *East to America: A History of the Japanese in the United States.* New York: Morrow.

WILSON, WILLIAM J. 1973. *Power, Racism, and Privilege.* New York: Free Press.

———. 1978. *The Declining Significance of Race: Blacks and Changing American Institutions.* Chicago: University of Chicago Press.

WINCH, ROBERT F. 1958. *Mate Selection.* New York: Harper.

WINICK, CHARLES, and PAUL M. KINSIE. 1971. *The Lively Commerce: Prostitution in the United States.* Chicago: Aldine.

WIRTH, LOUIS. 1931. "Culture conflict and misconduct." *Social Forces,* 9, pp. 484–492.

———. 1938. "Urbanism as a way of life." *American Journal of Sociology,* 44, pp. 8–20.

———. 1945. "The problem of minority groups," in Ralph Linton (ed.), *The Science of Man in the World Crisis.* New York: Columbia University Press.

WISE, DAVID. 1973. *The Politics of Lying.* New York: Random House.

WOLF, DEBORAH GOLEMAN. 1979. *The Lesbian Community.* Berkeley, Calif.: University of California Press.

WOLFINGER, RAYMOND E., and STEVEN J. ROSENSTONE. 1980. *Who Votes?* New Haven: Yale University Press.

WOMACK, JOHN, JR. 1972. "The Chicanos." *The New York Review of Books,* August 31, pp. 12–18.

WORSLEY, PETER. 1957. *The Trumpet Shall Sound.* London: MacGibbon & Kee.

WRONG, DENNIS H. 1959. "The functional theory of stratification: Some neglected considerations." *American Sociological Review,* 24, pp. 772–782.

———. 1961. "The oversocialized conception of man in modern sociology." *American Sociological Review,* 26, pp. 183–193.

WYRICK, W. 1974. "Biophysical perspectives," in E. Gerber et al. (eds.). *The American Woman in Sport.* Reading, Mass.: Addison-Wesley.

WYSOR, BETTY. 1974. *The Lesbian Myth.* New York: Random House.

YANOWITCH, MURRAY. 1977. *Social and Economic Inequality in the Soviet Union.* White Plains, N.Y.: M. E. Sharpe.

YARROW, L. J. 1963. "Research in dimensions of early maternal care." *Merrill-Palmer Quarterly,* 9, pp. 101–114.

YINGER, MILTON M. 1960. "Contraculture and subculture." *American Sociological Review,* 25, pp. 625–635.

———. 1977. "Countercultures and social change." *American Sociological Review,* 42, pp. 833–853.

YORBURG, BETTY. 1974. *Sexual Identity: Sex Roles and Social Change.* New York: Wiley.

YOUNG, JOCK. 1971. *The Drugtakers.* London: Paladin.

ZALD, MAYER N., and MICHAEL A. BERGER. 1978. "Social movements in organizations: Coups d'etat, insurgency, and mass movements." *American Journal of Sociology,* 83, pp. 823–861.

———, and JOHN D. McCARTHY (eds.). 1979. *The Dynamics of Social Movements.* Cambridge, Mass.: Winthrop.

ZANDER, ALVIN. 1979. "The psychology of group processes." *Annual Review of Psychology.* Palo Alto, Calif.: Annual Reviews, Inc.

ZANGWILL, ISRAEL. 1933. *The Melting Pot.* New York: Macmillan.

ZARETSKY, IRVING I., and MARK P. LEONE. 1974. *Religious Movements in Contemporary America.* Princeton, N.J.: Princeton University Press.

ZELNICK, MELVIN, and JOHN F. KANTNER. 1977. "Sexual and contraceptive experience of young unmarried women in the United States, 1976 and 1971." *Family Planning Perspectives,* 9:55.

———. 1978. "First pregnancies in women aged 15–19: 1976 and 1971." *Family Planning Perspectives,* 10:11.

———, et al. 1979. "Probabilities of intercourse and conception among U.S. teenage women, 1971 and 1976." *Family Planning Perspectives,* 11:3.

ZIMBARDO, PHILIP G. 1969. "The human choice: Individuation, reason, and order vs. deindividuation, impulse, and chaos." *Nebraska Symposium on Motivation,* 17, pp. 237–307.

ZINKIN, TAYA. 1962. *Caste Today.* London: Oxford University Press.

ZUCKERMAN, HARRIET. 1977. *Scientific Elite: Nobel Laureates in the United States.* New York: Free Press.

ZURCHER, LOUIS A. 1970. "The 'friendly' poker game: A study of an ephemeral role." *Social Forces,* 49, pp. 173–186.

Acknowledgments

UNIT OPENERS

1. *Mit gelber Jacke,* August Macke, 1913. Watercolor. Ulmer Museum, Ulm.

2. *The Man with the Axe,* Paul Gauguin, 1891. From the Collection of Mr. and Mrs. Alexander Lewyt.

3. *Willis Avenue Bridge,* Ben Shahn, 1940. Tempera on paper over composition board, 23″ × 31-3/8″. Collection, The Museum of Modern Art, New York, Gift of Lincoln Kirstein.

4. *Sunday Afternoon,* Fernando Botero, 1972. From the Collection of Joachim Jean Aberbach, New York.

5. *Preparedness,* Roy Lichtenstein, 1968. Collection, The Solomon R. Guggenheim Museum, New York. Photo: Robert E. Mates.

CHAPTER 1
1.0 Wally McNamee, Woodfin Camp
1.1 Burt Glinn, Magnum
1.2 *top left,* Leonard Freed, Magnum; *top right,* John Moss, Photo Researchers; *bottom,* Marc Riboud, Magnum
1.3–1.5 The Bettmann Archive
1.6 Brown Brothers
1.7 The Bettmann Archive
1.8 and 1.9 The Granger Collection
1.10 and 1.11 American Sociological Association
1.12 Ben Martin, TIME Magazine © Time, Inc.
1.13 Joe Munroe, Photo Researchers
1.14 Jim Anderson, Black Star
1.15 Guy Gillette, Photo Researchers
1.16 *top,* Thomas D. W. Friedmann, Photo Researchers; *bottom,* John Henry Sullivan, Jr., Photo Researchers

CHAPTER 2
2.0 Paul Fusco, Magnum
2.1 The Bettmann Archive
2.2 Syndication International
2.3 The Granger Collection
2.4 United Press International

2.6 Owen Franken, Sygma
2.7 Howard Petrick, Nancy Palmer Photo Agency
2.8 *both,* United Press International
2.10 Olivier Rebbot, Woodfin Camp

CHAPTER 3
3.0 June Lundborg
3.1 George Holton, Photo Researchers
3.2 *from left to right,* Ylla, Photo Researchers; A. W. Ambler, Photo Researchers; Toni Angermayer, Photo Researchers
3.3 Flip Schulke, Black Star
3.4 John Launois, Black Star
3.5 Carl Frank, Photo Researchers
3.6 *top,* C. C. Bonnington, Woodfin Camp; *bottom,* Malcolm S. Kirk, Peter Arnold
3.7 Paolo Koch, Photo Researchers
3.8 *left,* Claus Meyer, Black Star; *right,* Eve Arnold, Magnum
3.9 Joseph Martin, Scala/Editorial Photocolor Archives
3.11 Marc and Evelyne Bernheim, Woodfin Camp

CHAPTER 4
4.0 Ray Ellis, Photo Researchers
4.1 Sipa/Frillet, Black Star
4.3 Ed Lettau, Photo Researchers
4.5 Stan Pantovic, Photo Researchers
4.8 *both,* United Press International
4.9 David Moore, Black Star
4.10 Roland and Sabrina Michaud, Woodfin Camp
4.11 Loren McIntyre, Woodfin Camp
4.12 Mathias Oppersdorff
4.13 Kenneth Murray, Nancy Palmer Photo Agency
4.14 *left,* Raimondo Borea; *right,* Malcolm Kirk, Peter Arnold

CHAPTER 5
5.0 Kryn Taconis, Magnum
5.1 *from left to right,* Olivier Rebbot, Woodfin Camp; Georg Gerster, Photo Researchers; John Launois, Black Star
5.2 Erika Stone, Peter Arnold
5.3 University of Wisconsin Primate Laboratory
5.4 Jan Lukas, Photo Researchers
5.5 George Roos, Peter Arnold
5.6 Richard Hutchings, Photo Researchers
5.7 Burk Uzzle, Magnum
5.9 *The James Family,* 1751, Arthur Devis, The Granger Collection
5.10 Fritz Goro, LIFE Magazine © 1955 Time, Inc.
5.11 B. D. Vidibar, Photo Researchers

CHAPTER 6
6.0 Courtesy of VISTA, Alabama, Brown
6.3 Jan Lukas, Photo Researchers
6.4 Abagail Heyman, Magnum
6.6 *top,* Serge de Sazo, Photo Researchers; *bottom,* United Press International

6.7 *top,* Jeffrey Jay Foxx, Woodfin Camp; *bottom,* Bill Stanton, Magnum
6.8 Ken Heyman
6.9 *top,* R. Rowan, Photo Researchers; *bottom,* Larry Mulvehill, Photo Researchers
6.10 Andrew Sacks, Editorial Photocolor Archives
6.11 Charles Gatewood
6.12 *all,* Michael Abramson
6.13 John Moss, Photo Researchers

CHAPTER 7
7.0 Ernest Baxter, Black Star
7.1 Beryl Goldberg
7.2 Larry Mulvehill, Photo Researchers
7.3 *top left,* Larry Mulvehill, Photo Researchers; *top right,* Leonard Freed, Magnum; *bottom,* Jim Amos, Photo Researchers
7.5 James H. Karales, Peter Arnold
7.8 The Metropolitan Museum of Art, George A. Hearn Fund, 1956
7.9 Robert Isear, DPI
7.10 Dan Brinzac, Peter Arnold
7.13 Timothy Eagen

CHAPTER 8
8.0 Michael Evans, Nancy Palmer Photo Agency
8.1 *left,* Courtesy of Tattoo Art Museum, San Francisco, photo courtesy of Charles Gatewood; *right,* Jehangir Gazdar, Woodfin Camp
8.2 *left,* The Bettmann Archive; *right,* United Press International
8.5 Ken Heyman
8.6 Virginia Hamilton
8.7 Jim Anderson, Woodfin Camp
8.9 George Gardner
8.13 *top,* Snark International/Editorial Photocolor Archives; *bottom,* Bruce Anspach, Editorial Photocolor Archives
8.14 The Bettmann Archive

CHAPTER 9
9.0 Joel Gordon
9.1 Jeffrey Jay Foxx, Woodfin Camp
9.2 *from bottom left to far right,* Loren McIntyre, Woodfin Camp; Thomas Höpker, Woodfin Camp; Georg Gerster, Photo Researchers; Jacques Jangoux, Peter Arnold; Malcolm S. Kirk, Peter Arnold; Jacques Jangoux, Peter Arnold; United Press International
9.4 and 9.5 Scala/Editorial Photocolor Archives
9.6 Ron Sieg
9.7 The Bettmann Archive
9.8 Andrew Lawson
9.9 Beryl Goldberg
9.11 Joel Gordon
9.12 Scala/Editorial Photocolor Archives
9.14 Leif Skoogfors, Woodfin Camp

CHAPTER 10
10.0 Fred Lyon, Photo Researchers
10.1 *left,* Erika Stone; *right,* Ken Heyman

10.2 Bruce Roberts, Photo Researchers
10.3 Scala/Editorial Photocolor Archives
10.5 Judith Aronson
10.6 Inge Morath, Magnum
10.7 Lebeck, Stern/Black Star
10.8 United Press International
10.10 George Holton, Photo Researchers

CHAPTER 11

11.0 Jan Lukas, Editorial Photocolor Archives
11.6 Richard Pipes, Nancy Palmer Photo Agency
11.7 *left,* Joan Menschenfreund; *right,* Andy Levin, Black Star
11.8 *left,* Joel Gordon; *right,* James Sempepos
11.10 *left,* Kenneth Murray, Nancy Palmer Photo Agency; *right,* Martine Franck, Woodfin Camp
11.11 *top,* Marcia Keegan, Peter Arnold; *bottom,* James Romeo, Photo Researchers

CHAPTER 12

12.0 Charles Moore, Black Star
12.1 *from left to right,* Hubertos Kanos, Photo Researchers; Paolo Koch, Photo Researchers; John Veltri, Photo Researchers; Chester Higgins, Photo Researchers; Yorum Lehmann, Peter Arnold; R. B. Hott, Photo Researchers; Paolo Koch, Photo Researchers; A. Topping, Photo Researchers
12.2 Brown Brothers
12.3 J. P. Laffont, Sygma
12.4 United Press International
12.5 J. P. Laffont, Sygma
12.6 Michele Bogre, Sygma
12.7 The Bettmann Archive
12.8 *top,* Owen Franken, Sygma; *bottom left,* Baughman, Sygma; *bottom right,* Norris McNamara, Nancy Palmer Photo Agency
12.9 The Bettmann Archive
12.11 *from top left to bottom right,* The Bettmann Archive; Danny Lyon, Magnum; Leonard Freed, Magnum; Bruce Davidson, Magnum; Stephen Shames, Black Star; United Press International
12.12 Thomas Nebbia, Woodfin Camp
12.13 John Veltri, Photo Researchers
12.14 *left,* Montana Historical Society, Helena; *right,* Dan Budnik, Woodfin Camp
12.15 Hansel Meith, LIFE Magazine © Time, Inc.
12.16 Bettye Lane, Photo Researchers
12.17 The Bettmann Archive

CHAPTER 13

13.0 Sepp Seitz, Woodfin Camp
13.1 *left,* The Bettmann Archive; *right,* Sudhir Vaikkatil, Peter Arnold
13.2 Universitätsbibliothek, Heidelberg
13.4 *both,* Jacques Jangoux, Peter Arnold
13.9 Michael Uffer, Photo Researchers
13.11 Tom Hollyman, Photo Researchers
13.12 *top,* Suzanne Szasz, Photo Researchers; *bottom,* Charles Harbutt, Magnum

13.14 Beryl Goldberg
13.15 Bernard Pierre Wolff, Photo Researchers
13.16 Sepp Seitz, Woodfin Camp
13.18 B. D. Vidibar, Photo Researchers
13.19 Roger Appleton, Photo Researchers
13.20 *left,* Tor Eigeland, Black Star; *right,* Paul Fusco, Magnum

CHAPTER 14

14.0 Joel Gordon
14.1 Lester Sloan, Woodfin Camp
14.3 Ergun Cagatay, Liaison Photo Agency
14.5 Timothy Eagon, Woodfin Camp
14.6 Culver Pictures
14.7 The Metropolitan Museum of Art, Bequest of Catherine Lorillard Wolfe, 1887
14.8 Bill Stanton, Magnum
14.10 Charles Gatewood
14.11 *left,* The Bettmann Archive; *right,* Adam Woolfitt, Woodfin Camp

CHAPTER 15

15.0 Inger McCabe, Photo Researchers
15.2 Victor Engelbert, Photo Researchers
15.4 *top,* M. Monestier, Sygma; *bottom,* Susan Johns, Photo Researchers
15.5 Stephen Collins, Photo Researchers
15.7 The Bettmann Archive
15.8 Ken Heyman
15.11 Thom O'Connor, Black Star
15.12 *left,* Lee Lockwood, Black Star; *right,* Faverty, Liaison Photo Agency

CHAPTER 16

16.0 Mathias Oppersdorff
16.1 *top left,* Marc Bernheim, Woodfin Camp; *top right,* James H. Karales, Peter Arnold; *bottom,* Jehangir Gazdar, Woodfin Camp
16.2 Scala/Editorial Photocolor Archives
16.4 *from left to right,* James H. Karales, Peter Arnold; Yoram Kahana, Peter Arnold; Jack Field, Photo Researchers
16.5 Tass from Sovfoto
16.6 and 16.7 The Bettmann Archive
16.8 Victor Engelbert, Photo Researchers
16.9 The New York Public Library
16.11 *left,* Vinnie Fish, Photo Researchers; *right,* Dan Guravich, Photo Researchers
16.13 Paul Conklin, Monkmeyer Press Photo Service
16.14 Robert Davis, Black Star
16.15 Dick Hanley, Photo Researchers
16.18 Don Rutledge, Black Star

CHAPTER 17

17.0 Dale Wittner, TIME Magazine
17.1 *top,* The Bettmann Archive; *bottom,* The Granger Collection
17.2 The New York Public Library

17.4 Philippe Halsman, Magnum
17.7 The Bettmann Archive
17.8 The New York Public Library
17.10 Lookout Mountain Air Force Station, photo courtesy of Department of Energy

CHAPTER 18
18.0 Georg Gerster, Photo Researchers
18.1 *from bottom left to far right,* Tom Tracy, Black Star; EPA/Documerica; Robert Isear, DPI; J. Alex Langley, DPI; Joan Menschenfreund; Ken Kay, DPI
18.2 George Rodger, Magnum
18.3 *from left to right,* Georg Gerster, Photo Researchers; Ken Heyman; Raimondo Borea
18.5 Ken Heyman
18.6 Charles Gatewood
18.9 *New York Daily News* photo
18.11 Paolo Koch, Photo Researchers
18.13 Charles Gatewood
18.15 Ken Heyman

CHAPTER 19
19.0 Dennis Brack, Black Star
19.1 The Bettmann Archive
19.2 Paul Conklin, Monkmeyer Press Photo Service
19.3 *from bottom left to far right,* Marc Riboud, Magnum; United Press International; United Press International; Gerhard Gscheidle, Peter Arnold; Henriques, Magnum; J.A.F./Paris, Magnum
19.4 Tony Howarth, Woodfin Camp
19.6 Ted Cowell, Black Star
19.8 United Press International
19.9 Shelly Katz, Black Star
19.16 *top, both,* The Bettmann Archive; *bottom,* United Press International

CHAPTER 20
20.0 Henri Cartier-Bresson, Magnum
20.1 Brown Brothers
20.4 The Bettmann Archive
20.5 John Zoiner, Peter Arnold
20.7 Yoram Kahana, Peter Arnold
20.8 Burt Glinn, Magnum
20.12 Harmit Singh, Photo Researchers
20.13 Nik Wheeler, Sygma
20.14 *top left,* Irven DeVore, Anthro-Photo; *top right,* Beryl Goldberg; *bottom,* Joel Gordon
20.16 Scala/Editorial Photocolor Archives
20.17 *top,* The Bettmann Archive; *bottom,* Jim Pozarik, Liaison Photo Agency
20.19 Sepp Seitz, Woodfin Camp
20.20 EPA/Documerica
20.21 Joe Munroe, Photo Researchers

CHAPTER 21
21.0 Bonnie Geller, Peter Arnold
21.1 Georg Gerster, Photo Researchers

21.2 Bruno Barbey, Magnum
21.3 Adele Hodge, Black Star
21.4 Abbas, Liaison Photo Agency
21.5 *left,* The Granger Collection; *right,* Collection of the Whitney Museum of American Art: Juliana Force Purchase, Egg tempera on composition board, 18 × 36 inches
21.6 Jacqueline Gill, Editorial Photocolor Archives
21.7 Georg Gerster, Photo Researchers
21.10 Robert A. Isaacs, Photo Researchers
21.12 Dan Porges, Peter Arnold
21.13 June Lundborg

CHAPTER 22
22.0 Gerhard Gscheidle, Peter Arnold
22.1 Klaus D. Francke, Peter Arnold
22.2 The Bettmann Archive
22.3 Frank Johnston, Woodfin Camp
22.4 E.M.I. Recording, Capitol Records, Inc.
22.6 Joe Munroe, Photo Researchers
22.7 Brown Brothers
22.8 *from left to right,* Ken Heyman; Raimondo Borea; Homer Sykes, Woodfin Camp; Charles Harbutt, Magnum
22.9 The Granger Collection
22.11 *top left,* Dennis Brack, Black Star; *top right,* M. C. Hugh, Sygma; *bottom,* Timothy Eagen, Woodfin Camp
22.12 United Press International
22.13 *left,* The Bettmann Archive; *right,* P. Chauvel, Sygma
22.14 Eve Arnold, Magnum
22.17 The Bettmann Archive

CHAPTER 23
23.0 Elliott Erwitt, Magnum
23.1 V-Dia/Editorial Photocolor Archives
23.2 *left,* United Press International; *right,* John Bryson, Photo Researchers
23.3 John T. Barr, Liaison Photo Agency
23.4 Library of Congress
23.5 The Bettmann Archive
23.7 Lester Sloan, Woodfin Camp
23.8 The Bettmann Archive
23.9 *top,* The Bettmann Archive; *bottom,* NASA
23.10 The Bettmann Archive
23.11 Gernsheim Collection, Humanities Research Center, The University of Texas at Austin
23.12 Barbara Kirk, Peter Arnold
23.13 Beryl Goldberg
23.15 Jacques Jangoux, Peter Arnold
23.16 Tass from Sovfoto
23.17 The Bettmann Archive
23.18 Eastfoto
23.19 Marc Riboud, Magnum
23.21 Courtesy of Bell Laboratories
23.22 The Bettmann Archive

Index